Table of Contents

Preface

The MySQL database management system has gained a large following in recent years. This has been true especially in the Linux and open source communities, but MySQL has an increasing foothold in the commercial sector as well. MySQL is well liked for several reasons: it's fast, and it's easy to set up, use, and administer. MySQL runs under many varieties of Unix and Windows, and MySQL-based programs can be written in many languages. Historically, MySQL has been especially popular for constructing database-backed web sites that involve dynamic content generation. Moreover, with the introduction of features in MySQL 5.0 such as views, triggers, and stored procedures and functions, the penetration of MySQL into other areas of application development is on the upswing.

With MySQL's popularity comes the need to address the questions posed by its users about how to solve specific problems. That is the purpose of *MySQL Cookbook*. It's designed to serve as a handy resource to which you can turn when you need quick solutions or techniques for attacking particular types of questions that come up when you use MySQL. Naturally, because it's a cookbook, it contains recipes: straightforward instructions you can follow rather than develop your own code from scratch. It's written using a problem-and-solution format designed to be extremely practical and to make the contents easy to read and assimilate. It contains many short sections, each describing how to write a query, apply a technique, or develop a script to solve a problem of limited and specific scope. This book doesn't attempt to develop full-fledged, complex applications. Instead, it's intended to assist you in developing such applications yourself by helping you get past problems that have you stumped.

For example, a common question is, "How can I deal with quotes and special characters in data values when I'm writing queries?" That's not difficult, but figuring out how to do it is frustrating when you're not sure where to start. This book demonstrates what to do; it shows you where to begin and how to proceed from there. This knowledge will serve you repeatedly, because after you see what's involved, you'll be able to apply the technique to any kind of data, such as text, images, sound or video clips, news articles, compressed files, or PDF documents. Another common question is, "Can I access data from multiple tables at the same time?" The answer is "Yes," and it's easy to do because it's just a matter of knowing the proper SQL syntax. But it's not always clear how until you see examples, which this book gives you. Other things that you'll learn from this book include:

- How to use SQL to select, sort, and summarize rows.
- How to find matches or mismatches between rows in two tables.
- How to perform a transaction.
- How to determine intervals between dates or times, including age calculations.
- How to identify or remove duplicate rows.
- How to store images into MySQL and retrieve them for display in web pages.
- How to get LOAD DATA to read your datafiles properly or find which values in the file are invalid.
- How to use *strict* mode to prevent entry of bad data into your database.
- How to copy a table or a database to another server.
- How to generate sequence numbers to use as unique row identifiers.
- How to write stored procedures and functions.
- How to use a view as a "virtual table."
- How to set up triggers that activate to perform specific data-handling operations when you insert or update table rows.
- How to create database events that execute according to a schedule.

One part of knowing how to use MySQL is understanding how to communicate with the server—that is, how to use SQL, the language through which queries are formulated. Therefore, one major emphasis of this book is on using SQL to formulate queries that answer particular kinds of questions. One helpful tool for learning and using SQL is the *mysql* client program that is included in MySQL distributions. By using this client interactively, you can send SQL statements to the server and see the results. This is extremely useful because it provides a direct interface to SQL. The *mysql* client is so useful, in fact, that the entire first chapter is devoted to it.

But the ability to issue SQL queries alone is not enough. Information extracted from a database often needs to be processed further or presented in a particular way to be useful. What if you have queries with complex interrelationships, such as when you need to use the results of one query as the basis for others? Or what if you need to generate a specialized report with very specific formatting requirements? These problems bring us to the other major emphasis of the book—how to write programs that interact with the MySQL server through an application programming interface (API). When you know how to use MySQL from within the context of a programming language, you gain the ability to exploit MySQL's capabilities in the following ways:

- You can remember the result from a query and use it at a later time.
- You have full access to the expressive power of a general-purpose programming language. This enables you to make decisions based on success or failure of a query,

or on the content of the rows that are returned, and then tailor the actions taken accordingly.

- You can format and display query results however you like. If you're writing a command-line script, you can generate plain text. If it's a web-based script, you can generate an HTML table. If it's an application that extracts information for transfer to some other system, you might generate a datafile expressed in XML.

When you combine SQL with a general purpose programming language, you have an extremely flexible framework for issuing queries and processing their results. Programming languages increase your capabilities by giving you a great deal of additional power to perform complex database operations. This doesn't mean this book is complicated, though. It keeps things simple, showing how to construct small building blocks by using techniques that are easy to understand and easily mastered.

I'll leave it to you to combine these techniques in your own programs, which you can do to produce arbitrarily complex applications. After all, the genetic code is based on only four nucleic acids, but these basic elements have been combined to produce the astonishing array of biological life we see all around us. Similarly, there are only 12 notes in the scale, but in the hands of skilled composers, they can be interwoven to produce a rich and endless variety of music. In the same way, when you take a set of simple recipes, add your imagination, and apply them to the database programming problems you want to solve, you can produce applications that perhaps are not works of art, but are certainly useful and will help you and others be more productive.

Who This Book Is For

This book should be useful for anybody who uses MySQL, ranging from individuals who want to use a database for personal projects such as a blog or Wiki, to professional database and web developers. The book should also appeal to people who do not now use MySQL, but would like to. For example, it should be useful if you want to learn about databases but realize that a "big" database system such as Oracle isn't the best choice as a learning tool.

If you're relatively new to MySQL, you'll probably find lots of ways to use it here that you hadn't thought of. If you're more experienced, you'll probably be familiar with many of the problems addressed here, but you may not have had to solve them before and should find the book a great timesaver; take advantage of the recipes given in the book, and use them in your own programs rather than figuring out how to write the code from scratch.

The book also can be useful for people who aren't even using MySQL. You might suppose that because this is a MySQL cookbook and not a PostgreSQL cookbook or an InterBase cookbook that it won't apply to database systems other than MySQL. To some extent that's true, because some of the SQL constructs are MySQL-specific. But many of the queries use standard SQL that is portable to many other database engines, so you should be able to use them with little or no modification. In addition, several programming language interfaces provide database-independent access methods; you use them the same way regardless of which type of database server you connect to.

The material ranges from introductory to advanced, so if a recipe describes techniques that seem obvious to you, skip it. Or if you find that you don't understand a recipe, it may be best to set it aside for a while and come back to it later, perhaps after reading some of the preceding recipes.

More advanced readers may wonder on occasion why, in a book on MySQL, I sometimes provide explanatory material on certain basic topics that are not directly MySQL-related, such as how to set environment variables. I decided to do this based on my experience in helping people who are just getting started with MySQL. One thing that makes MySQL attractive is that it is easy to use, which makes it a popular choice for people without extensive background in databases. However, many of these same people also tend to be thwarted by simple impediments to more effective use of MySQL, as evidenced by the common question, "How can I avoid having to type the full pathname of *mysql* each time I invoke it?" Experienced readers will recognize immediately that this is simply a matter of setting the PATH environment variable to include the directory where *mysql* is installed. But other readers will not, particularly Windows users who are used to dealing only with a graphical interface and, more recently, Mac OS X users who find their familiar user interface now augmented by the powerful but sometimes mysterious command line provided by the Terminal application. If that describes you, I hope that you'll find these more elementary sections helpful for knocking down barriers that keep you from using MySQL more easily. If you're a more advanced user, just skip over such sections.

What's in This Book

It's very likely when you use this book that you'll have an application in mind you're trying to develop but are not sure how to implement certain pieces of it. In this case, you'll already know what type of problem you want to solve, so you should search the table of contents or the index looking for a recipe that shows how to do what you want. Ideally, the recipe will be just what you had in mind. Failing that, you should be able to find a recipe for a similar problem that you can adapt to suit the issue at hand. I try to explain the principles involved in developing each technique so that you'll be able to modify it to fit the particular requirements of your own applications.

Another way to approach this book is to just read through it with no specific problem in mind. This can help you because it will give you a broader understanding of the things MySQL can do, so I recommend that you page through the book occasionally. It's a more effective tool if you have a general familiarity with it and know the kinds of problems it addresses.

As you get into later chapters, you'll sometimes find recipes that assume a knowledge of topics covered in earlier chapters. This also applies within a chapter, where later sections often use techniques discussed earlier in the chapter. If you jump into a chapter and find a recipe that uses a technique with which you're not familiar, check the table of contents or the index to find where the technique is covered. You should find that it's been explained earlier. For example, if you find that a recipe sorts a query result using an ORDER BY clause that you don't understand, turn to Chapter 7, which discusses various sorting methods and explains how they work.

The following paragraphs summarize each chapter to give you an overview of the book's contents.

Chapter 1, *Using the mysql Client Program*, describes how to use the standard MySQL command-line client. *mysql* is often the first or primary interface to MySQL that people use, and it's important to know how to exploit its capabilities. This program enables you to issue queries and see their results interactively, so it's good for quick experimentation. You can also use it in batch mode to execute canned SQL scripts or send its output into other programs. In addition, the chapter discusses other ways to use *mysql*, such as how to number output lines or make long lines more readable, how to generate various output formats, and how to log *mysql* sessions.

Chapter 2, *Writing MySQL-Based Programs*, demonstrates the basic elements of MySQL programming: how to connect to the server, issue queries, retrieve the results, and handle errors. It also discusses how to handle special characters and NULL values in queries, how to write library files to encapsulate code for commonly used operations, and describes various ways to gather the parameters needed for making connections to the server.

Chapter 3, *Selecting Data from Tables*, covers several aspects of the SELECT statement, which is the primary vehicle for retrieving data from the MySQL server: specifying which columns and rows you want to retrieve, performing comparisons, dealing with NULL values, and selecting one section of a query result. Later chapters cover some of these topics in more detail, but this chapter provides an overview of the concepts on which they depend. You should read it if you need some introductory background on row selection or you don't yet know a lot about SQL.

Chapter 4, *Table Management*, covers table cloning, copying results into other tables, using temporary tables, and checking or changing a table's storage engine.

Chapter 5, *Working with Strings*, describes how to deal with string data. It covers character sets and collations, string comparisons, dealing with case-sensitivity issues, pattern matching, breaking apart and combining strings, and performing FULLTEXT searches.

Chapter 6, *Working with Dates and Times*, shows how to work with temporal data. It describes MySQL's date format and how to display date values in other formats. It also covers how to use MySQL's special TIMESTAMP data type, how to set the time zone, conversion between different temporal units, how to perform date arithmetic to compute intervals or generate one date from another, and leap-year calculations.

Chapter 7, *Sorting Query Results*, describes how to put the rows of a query result in the order you want. This includes specifying the sort direction, dealing with NULL values, accounting for string case sensitivity, and sorting by dates or partial column values. It also provides examples that show how to sort special kinds of values, such as domain names, IP numbers, and ENUM values.

Chapter 8, *Generating Summaries*, shows techniques that are useful for assessing the general characteristics of a set of data, such as how many values it contains or what its minimum, maximum, or average values are.

Chapter 9, *Obtaining and Using Metadata*, discusses how to get information *about* the data that a query returns, such as the number of rows or columns in the result, or the name and type of each column. It also shows how to ask MySQL what databases and tables are available or find out about the structure of a table and its columns.

Chapter 10, *Importing and Exporting Data*, describes how to transfer information between MySQL and other programs. This includes how to convert files from one format to another, extract or rearrange columns in datafiles, check and validate data, rewrite values such as dates that often come in a variety of formats, and how to figure out which data values cause problems when you load them into MySQL with LOAD DATA.

Chapter 11, *Generating and Using Sequences*, discusses AUTO_INCREMENT columns, MySQL's mechanism for producing sequence numbers. It shows how to generate new sequence values or determine the most recent value, how to resequence a column, how to begin a sequence at a given value, and how to set up a table so that it can maintain multiple sequences at once. It also shows how to use AUTO_INCREMENT values to maintain a master-detail relationship between tables, including some of the pitfalls to avoid.

Chapter 12, *Using Multiple Tables*, shows how to perform joins, which are operations that combine rows in one table with those from another. It demonstrates how to compare tables to find matches or mismatches, produce master-detail lists and summaries, enumerate many-to-many relationships, and update or delete rows in one table based on the contents of another.

Chapter 13, *Statistical Techniques*, illustrates how to produce descriptive statistics, frequency distributions, regressions, and correlations. It also covers how to randomize a set of rows or pick a row at random from the set.

Chapter 14, *Handling Duplicates*, discusses how to identify, count, and remove duplicate rows—and how to prevent them from occurring in the first place.

Chapter 15, *Performing Transactions*, shows how to handle multiple SQL statements that must execute together as a unit. It discusses how to control MySQL's auto-commit mode, and how to commit or roll back transactions, and demonstrates some workarounds you can use for non-transactional storage engines.

Chapter 16, *Using Stored Routines, Triggers, and Events*, describes how to write stored functions and procedures that are stored on the server side, triggers that activate when tables are modified, and events that execute on a scheduled basis.

Chapter 17, *Introduction to MySQL on the Web*, gets you set up to write web-based MySQL scripts. Web programming enables you to generate dynamic pages from database content or collect information for storage in your database. The chapter discusses how to configure Apache to run Perl, Ruby, PHP, and Python scripts, and how to configure Tomcat to run Java scripts written using JSP notation. It also provides an overview of the Java Standard Tag Library (JSTL) that is used heavily for JSP pages in the following chapters.

Chapter 18, *Incorporating Query Results in Web Pages*, shows how to use the results of queries to produce various types of HTML structures, such as paragraphs, lists, tables, hyperlinks, and navigation indexes. It also describes how to store images into MySQL, and retrieve and display them later, and how to send a downloadable result set to a browser. The chapter also includes a section that demonstrates how to use a template package to generate web pages.

Chapter 19, *Processing Web Input with MySQL*, discusses how to obtain input from users over the Web and use it to create new database rows or as the basis for performing searches. It deals heavily with form processing, including how to construct form elements, such as radio buttons, pop-up menus, or checkboxes, based on information contained in your database.

Chapter 20, *Using MySQL-Based Web Session Management*, describes how to write web applications that remember information across multiple requests, using MySQL for backing store. This is useful when you want to collect information in stages, or when you need to make decisions based on what the user has done earlier.

Appendix A, *Obtaining MySQL Software*, indicates where to get the source code for the examples shown in this book, and where to get the software you need to use MySQL and write your own database programs.

Appendix B, *Executing Commands from the Command Line*, provides background on executing commands at the command prompt and how to set environment variables such as PATH.

Appendix C, *JSP and Tomcat Primer*, provides a general overview of JSP and installation instructions for the Tomcat web server. Read this if you need to install Tomcat or are not familiar with it, or if you're never written pages using JSP notation.

Appendix D, *References*, lists sources of information that provide additional information about topics covered in this book. It also lists some books that provide introductory background for the programming languages used here.

MySQL APIs Used in This Book

MySQL programming interfaces exist for many languages, including C, C++, Eiffel, Java, Pascal, Perl, PHP, Python, Ruby, Smalltalk, and Tcl. Given this fact, writing a MySQL cookbook presents an author with something of a challenge. Clearly, the book should provide recipes for doing many interesting and useful things with MySQL, but which API or APIs should the book use? Showing an implementation of every recipe in every language would result either in covering very few recipes or in a very, very large book! It would also result in a lot of redundancy when implementations in different languages bear a strong resemblance to each other. On the other hand, it's worthwhile taking advantage of multiple languages, because one language often will be more suitable than another for solving a particular type of problem.

To resolve this dilemma, I've picked a small number of APIs from among those that are available and used them to write the recipes in this book. This limits its scope to a manageable number of APIs while allowing some latitude to choose from among them:

- The Perl and Ruby DBI modules
- PHP, using the PEAR DB module
- Python, using the DB-API module
- Java, using the JDBC interface

Why these languages? Perl and PHP were easy to pick. Perl is arguably the most widely used language on the Web, and it became so based on certain strengths such as its text-processing capabilities. In particular, it's very popular for writing MySQL programs. PHP also is widely deployed. One of PHP's strengths is the ease with which you can use it to access databases, making it a natural choice for MySQL scripting. Python and Java are perhaps not as popular as Perl or PHP for MySQL programming, but each has significant numbers of followers. In the Java community in particular, MySQL has a strong following among developers who use JavaServer Pages (JSP) technology to build database-backed web applications. Ruby was not covered in the first edition, but I have included it for the second because Ruby is much more popular now and it has an easy to use database-access module modeled after the Perl module.

I believe these languages taken together reflect pretty well the majority of the existing user base of MySQL programmers. If you prefer some language not shown here, you can still use this book, but be sure to pay careful attention to Chapter 2, to familiarize yourself with the book's primary APIs. Knowing how to perform database operations with the programming interfaces used here will help you understand the recipes in later chapters so that you can translate them for other languages.

Conventions Used in This Book

The following font conventions are used throughout the book:

Constant width
> Used for program listings, as well as within paragraphs to refer to program elements such as variable or function names, databases, data types, environment variables, statements, and keywords.

Constant width bold

Used to indicate text that you type when running commands.

Constant width italic

Used to indicate variable input; you should substitute a value of your own choosing.

Italic

Used for URLs, hostnames, names of directories and files, Unix commands and options, programs, and occasionally for emphasis.

This icon indicates a tip, suggestion, or general note.

This icon indicates a warning or caution.

Commands often are shown with a prompt to illustrate the context in which they are used. Commands that you issue from the command line are shown with a % prompt:

```
% chmod 600 my.cnf
```

That prompt is one that Unix users are used to seeing, but it doesn't necessarily signify that a command will work only under Unix. Unless indicated otherwise, commands shown with a % prompt generally should work under Windows, too.

If you should run a command under Unix as the **root** user, the prompt is # instead:

```
# perl -MCPAN -e shell
```

Commands that are specific only to Windows use the C:\> prompt:

```
C:\> "C:\Program Files\MySQL\MySQL Server 5.0\bin\mysql"
```

SQL statements that are issued from within the *mysql* client program are shown with a mysql> prompt and terminated with a semicolon:

```
mysql> SELECT * FROM my_table;
```

For examples that show a query result as you would see it when using *mysql*, I sometimes truncate the output, using an ellipsis (...) to indicate that the result consists of more rows than are shown. The following query produces many rows of output, of which those in the middle have been omitted:

```
mysql> SELECT name, abbrev FROM states ORDER BY name;
+-----------------+--------+
| name            | abbrev |
+-----------------+--------+
| Alabama         | AL     |
```

```
| Alaska         | AK    |
| Arizona        | AZ    |
...
| West Virginia  | WV    |
| Wisconsin      | WI    |
| Wyoming        | WY    |
+----------------+-------+
```

Examples that show only the syntax for SQL statements do not include the mysql>
prompt, but they do include semicolons as necessary to make it clearer where statements end. For example, this is a single statement:

```
CREATE TABLE t1 (i INT)
SELECT * FROM t2;
```

But this example represents two statements:

```
CREATE TABLE t1 (i INT);
SELECT * FROM t2;
```

The semicolon is a notational convenience used within *mysql* as a statement terminator.
But it is not part of SQL itself, so when you issue SQL statements from within programs
that you write (for example, using Perl or Java), you should not include terminating
semicolons.

The MySQL Cookbook Companion Web Site

MySQL Cookbook has a companion web site that you can visit to obtain the source
code and sample data for examples developed throughout this book:

> *http://www.kitebird.com/mysql-cookbook/*

The sample data and errata are also available at the O'Reilly web site listed in the "How
to Contact Us" section.

The main software distribution is named **recipes**, and you'll find many references to it
throughout the book. You can use the distribution to save a lot of typing. For example,
when you see a CREATE TABLE statement in the book that describes what a database table
looks like, you'll usually find an SQL batch file in the *tables* directory of the **recipes**
distribution that you can use to create the table instead of entering the definition manually. Change location into the *tables* directory, and then execute the following
command, where *filename* is the name of the file containing the CREATE TABLE statement:

```
% mysql cookbook < filename
```

If you need to specify MySQL username or password options, put them before the
database name.

For more information about the **recipes** distribution, see Appendix A.

The Kitebird site also makes some of the examples from the book available online so
that you can try them from your browser.

Version and Platform Notes

Development of the code in this book took place under MySQL 5.0 and 5.1. Because new features are added to MySQL on a regular basis, some examples will not work under older versions. For example, MySQL 5.0 introduces views, triggers, and stored procedures and functions, and the INFORMATION_SCHEMA metadata database. MySQL 5.1 introduces events.

On occasion, I point out workarounds that you can use in MySQL 4.1 to compensate for the lack of a 5.0 feature. For example, the INFORMATION_SCHEMA database is used extensively for getting information about table structure, but does not exist prior to MySQL 5.0. Sometimes this information can be obtained by using statements such as SHOW COLUMNS, and that's what recipes in the first edition used. These recipes are still available from the Kitebird site as part of the recipes distribution for the first edition. If you have an older version of MySQL, you may find it worthwhile to obtain a copy of the older distribution.

The versions of the database API modules that were current as of this writing are Perl DBI 1.52, DBD::mysql 3.0, Ruby DBI 0.1.1, PEAR DB 1.7.6, MySQLdb 1.2.0, and MySQL Connector/J 3.1. Perl DBI requires Perl 5.6 or higher, although it's slated to require Perl 5.8 or higher beginning with DBI 1.51. Ruby DBI requires Ruby 1.8.0 or higher. Most PHP scripts shown here will run under either PHP 4.1 or PHP 5 (I recommend PHP 5). MySQLdb requires Python 2.3.4 or higher. MySQL Connector/J requires Java SDK 1.2 or higher (1.4 or higher is recommended).

I do not assume that you are using Unix, although that is my own preferred development platform. (In this book, "Unix" also refers to Unix-like systems such as Linux and Mac OS X.) Most of the material here should be applicable both to Unix and Windows. The operating systems I used most to develop the recipes in this book were Mac OS X, Gentoo Linux, and Windows XP. If you use Windows, I assume that you're using a relatively recent version such as Windows 2000 or XP. Some features discussed in this book are not supported on older non-NT-based versions such as Windows Me or 98.

I do assume that MySQL is installed already and available for you to use. I also assume that if you plan to write your own MySQL-based programs, you're reasonably familiar with the language you'll use. If you need to install software, see Appendix A. If you require background material on the programming languages used here, see Appendix D.

Upgrade Note for First Edition Readers

If you have the first edition of *MySQL Cookbook*, be warned that the PHP library files in the second edition have the same names as in the first edition, but are incompatible with them. If you are using any PHP scripts that depend on the first edition library files, they will break if you install the second edition library files on top of them. To prevent this from happening, use the following procedure:

1. Change location into the directory where you installed the first edition library files and make a copy of each one:

```
% cp Cookbook.php Cookbook1.php
% cp Cookbook_Utils.php Cookbook_Utils1.php
% cp Cookbook_Webutils.php Cookbook_Webutils1.php
% cp Cookbook_Session.php Cookbook_Session1.php
```

2. Find all PHP scripts that include the first edition library files, and change them to include the *1.php files instead. For example, a script that includes Cookbook_Utils.php should be changed to include Cookbook_Utils1.php. (Some of the library files themselves include other library files, so you'll also need to edit the *1.php files.)

3. Test the modified scripts to make sure that they work correctly with the *1.php files.

Now you can install the second edition library files on top of the first edition files that have the same names. PHP scripts from the second edition will use these new library files, and old scripts should continue to work correctly.

Additional Resources

Any language that attracts a following can benefit from the efforts of its user community because people who use the language produce code that they make available to others. Perl in particular is served by an extensive support network designed to provide external modules that are not distributed with Perl itself. This is called the Comprehensive Perl Archive Network (CPAN), a mechanism for organizing and distributing Perl code and documentation. CPAN contains modules that enable database access, web programming, and XML processing, to name a few of direct relevance to this cookbook. External support exists for the other languages as well: Ruby has the Ruby Application Archive, PHP has the PEAR archive, and Python has a module archive called the Vaults of Parnassus. For Java, a good starting point is Sun's Java site. The following table shows sites that you can visit to find more information.

API language	Where to find external support
Perl	http://cpan.perl.org/
Ruby	http://raa.ruby-lang.org/
PHP	http://pear.php.net/
Python	http://www.python.org/
Java	http://java.sun.com/

Using Code Examples

This book is here to help you get your job done. In general, you may use the code in this book in your programs and documentation. You do not need to contact us for permission unless you're reproducing a significant portion of the code. For example, writing a program that uses several chunks of code from this book does not require permission. Selling or distributing a CD-ROM of examples from O'Reilly books does require permission. Answering a question by citing this book and quoting example code does not require permission. Incorporating a significant amount of example code from this book into your product's documentation does require permission.

We appreciate, but do not require, attribution. An attribution usually includes the title, author, publisher, and ISBN. For example: "*MySQL Cookbook*, Second Edition, by Paul DuBois. Copyright 2007 O'Reilly Media, Inc., 978-0-596-52708-2."

If you feel your use of code examples falls outside fair use or the permission given above, feel free to contact us at *permissions@oreilly.com*.

Safari® Enabled

 When you see a Safari® Enabled icon on the cover of your favorite technology book, that means the book is available online through the O'Reilly Network Safari Bookshelf.

Safari offers a solution that's better than e-books. It's a virtual library that lets you easily search thousands of top tech books, cut and paste code samples, download chapters, and find quick answers when you need the most accurate, current information. Try it for free at *http://safari.oreilly.com*.

How to Contact Us

Please address comments and questions concerning this book to the publisher:

> O'Reilly Media, Inc.
> 1005 Gravenstein Highway North
> Sebastopol, CA 95472
> 800-998-9938 (in the United States or Canada)
> 707-829-0515 (international or local)
> 707-829-0104 (fax)

We have a web page for this book, where we list errata, examples, and any additional information. You can access this page at:

> *http://www.oreilly.com/catalog/mysqlckbk2*

To comment or ask technical questions about this book, send email to:

> *bookquestions@oreilly.com*

For more information about our books, conferences, Resource Centers, and the O'Reilly Network, see our web site at:

> *http://www.oreilly.com*

Acknowledgments

Second Edition

Thanks to my technical reviewer, Richard Sonnen, who spotted a number of problems and made many suggestions to improve the book. Andy Oram prodded me to begin the second edition and served as its initial editor. When other duties called him away, Brian Jepson took over. My thanks to both for providing editorial oversight and direction. Adam Witwer directed the production process. Mary Anne Mayo copyedited the text, and Sada Preisch proofread it. Joe Wizda wrote the index.

Thanks to my wife Karen, who again provided valuable support during the process of producing this new edition.

First Edition

I'd like to thank my technical reviewers, Tim Allwine, David Lane, Hugh Williams, and Justin Zobel. They made several helpful suggestions and corrections with regard to both organizational structure and technical accuracy. Several members of MySQL AB were gracious enough to add their comments: In particular, principal MySQL developer Monty Widenius combed the text and spotted many problems. Arjen Lentz, Jani Tolonen, Sergei Golubchik, and Zak Greant reviewed sections of the manuscript as well. Andy Dustman, author of the Python MySQLdb module, and Mark Matthews, author of MM.MySQL and MySQL Connector/J, also provided feedback. My thanks to all for improving the manuscript; any errors remaining are my own.

Laurie Petrycki, executive editor, conceived the idea for the book and provided valuable overall editorial guidance and cattle-prodding. Lenny Muellner, tools expert, assisted in the conversion of the manuscript from my original format into something printable. David Chu acted as editorial assistant. Ellie Volckhausen designed the cover, which I am happy to see is reptilian in nature. Linley Dolby served as the production editor and proofreader, and Colleen Gorman, Darren Kelly, Jeffrey Holcomb, Brian Sawyer, and Claire Cloutier provided quality control.

Some authors are able to compose text productively while sitting at a keyboard, but I write better while sitting far from a computer—preferably with a cup of coffee. That being so, I'd like to acknowledge my debt to the Sow's Ear coffee shop in Verona for providing pleasant surroundings in which to spend many hours scribbling on paper.

My wife Karen provided considerable support and understanding in what turned out to be a much longer endeavor than anticipated. Her encouragement is much appreciated, and her patience something to marvel at.

## CHAPTER 1

Using the mysql Client Program

1.0 Introduction

The MySQL database system uses a client-server architecture that centers around the server, *mysqld*. The server is the program that actually manipulates databases. Client programs don't do that directly. Instead, they communicate your intent to the server by means of statements written in Structured Query Language (SQL). Client programs are installed locally on the machine from which you want to access MySQL, but the server can be installed anywhere, as long as clients can connect to it. MySQL is an inherently networked database system, so clients can communicate with a server that is running locally on your machine or one that is running somewhere else, perhaps on a machine on the other side of the planet. Clients can be written for many different purposes, but each interacts with the server by connecting to it, sending SQL statements to it to have database operations performed, and receiving the statement results from it.

One such client is the *mysql* program that is included in MySQL distributions. When used interactively, *mysql* prompts you for a statement, sends it to the MySQL server for execution, and then displays the results. This capability makes *mysql* useful in its own right, but it's also a valuable tool to help you with your MySQL programming activities. It's often convenient to be able to quickly review the structure of a table that you're accessing from within a script, to try a statement before using it in a program to make sure that it produces the right kind of output, and so forth. *mysql* is just right for these jobs. *mysql* also can be used noninteractively; for example, to read statements from a file or from other programs. This enables you to use *mysql* from within scripts or *cron* jobs or in conjunction with other applications.

This chapter describes *mysql*'s capabilities so that you can use it more effectively:

- Starting and stopping *mysql*
- Specifying connection parameters and using option files
- Setting your PATH variable so that your command interpreter can find *mysql* (and other MySQL programs)

- Issuing SQL statements interactively and using batch files
- Canceling and editing statements
- Controlling *mysql* output format

To use the examples shown in this book, you'll need a MySQL user account and a database to work with. The first two sections of the chapter describe how to use *mysql* to set these up. For demonstration purposes, the examples assume that you'll use MySQL as follows:

- The MySQL server is running on the local host
- Your MySQL username and password are `cbuser` and `cbpass`
- Your database is named `cookbook`

For your own experimentation, you can violate any of these assumptions. Your server need not be running locally, and you need not use the username, password, or database name that are used in this book. Naturally, if you use different default values on your system, you'll need to change the examples accordingly.

Even if you do not use `cookbook` as the name of your database, I recommend that you create a database to be dedicated specifically to trying the examples shown here, rather than trying them with a database that you're using currently for other purposes. Otherwise, the names of your existing tables may conflict with those used in the examples, and you'll have to make modifications to the examples that are unnecessary when you use a separate database.

If you have another favorite client program to use for issuing queries, some of the concepts covered in this chapter may not apply. For example, you might prefer the graphical MySQL Query Browser program, which provides a point-and-click interface to MySQL databases. In this case, some of the principles will be different, such as the way that you terminate SQL statements. In *mysql*, you terminate statements with semicolon (;) characters, whereas in MySQL Query Browser there is an Execute button for terminating statements. Another popular interface is phpMyAdmin, which enables you to access MySQL through your web browser.

Scripts that create the tables used in this chapter can be found in the *tables* directory of the `recipes` distribution. Other scripts are located in the *mysql* directory. For information about obtaining the `recipes` distribution, see Appendix A.

1.1 Setting Up a MySQL User Account

Problem

You need to create an account to use for connecting to the MySQL server running on a given host.

Solution

Use the GRANT statement to set up the MySQL user account. Then use the account's name and password to make connections to the server.

Discussion

Connecting to a MySQL server requires a username and password. You can also specify the name of the host on which the server is running. If you don't specify connection parameters explicitly, *mysql* assumes default values. For example, if you specify no hostname, *mysql* typically assumes that the server is running on the local host.

If someone else has set you up with an account, just use that account to create and use databases. If not, the following example shows how to use the *mysql* program to connect to the server and issue a GRANT statement that sets up a user account with privileges for accessing a database named **cookbook**. In the commands shown, the % represents the prompt displayed by your shell or command interpreter, and mysql> is the prompt displayed by *mysql*. Text that you type is shown in bold. Nonbold text (including the prompts) is program output; you do not type it. The arguments to *mysql* include -h localhost to connect to the MySQL server running on the local host, -p to tell *mysql* to prompt for a password, and -u root to connect as the MySQL root user.

```
% mysql -h localhost -p -u root
Enter password: ******
mysql> GRANT ALL ON cookbook.* TO 'cbuser'@'localhost' IDENTIFIED BY 'cbpass';
Query OK, 0 rows affected (0.09 sec)
mysql> QUIT
Bye
```

If you get a message indicating that *mysql* cannot be found or that it is a bad command when you enter the *mysql* command shown on the first line, see Recipe 1.7. Otherwise, when *mysql* prints the password prompt, enter the MySQL root password where you see the ******. (If the MySQL root user has no password, just press the Enter (or Return) key at the password prompt.) Then issue a GRANT statement like the one shown.

To grant the **cbuser** account access to a database other than **cookbook**, substitute the database name where you see **cookbook** in the GRANT statement. To grant access for the **cookbook** database to an existing account, substitute that account for 'cbuser'@'localhost'. However, in this case, omit the IDENTIFIED BY 'cbpass' part of the statement because otherwise you'll change the existing account's current password.

The hostname part of 'cbuser'@'localhost' indicates the host *from which* you'll be connecting to the MySQL server when you want to access the **cookbook** database. To set up an account that will connect to a server running on the local host, use localhost, as shown. If you plan to make connections to the server from another host, substitute that host in the GRANT statement. For example, if you'll be connecting to the server from a host named *xyz.com*, the GRANT statement should look like this:

```
mysql> GRANT ALL ON cookbook.* TO 'cbuser'@'xyz.com' IDENTIFIED BY 'cbpass';
```

It may have occurred to you that there's a bit of a paradox involved in the procedure just described. That is, to set up a cbuser account that can make connections to the MySQL server, you must connect to the server first so that you can issue the GRANT statement. I'm assuming that you can already connect as the MySQL root user, because GRANT can be used only by a user such as root that has the administrative privileges needed to set up other user accounts. If you can't connect to the server as root, ask your MySQL administrator to set up the cbuser account for you.

After the cbuser account has been set up, verify that you can use it to connect to the MySQL server. From the host that was named in the GRANT statement, run the following command to do this (the host named after -h should be the host that is running the MySQL server):

```
% mysql -h localhost -p -u cbuser
Enter password: cbpass
```

Now you can proceed to create the cookbook database and tables within it, as described in Recipe 1.2. (To make it easier to start *mysql* without specifying connection parameters each time, you can put them in an option file. See Recipe 1.4.)

MySQL Accounts and Login Accounts

MySQL accounts are different from login accounts for your operating system. For example, the MySQL root user and the Unix root user are separate and have nothing to do with each other, even though the username is the same in each case. This means they are very likely to have different passwords. It also means you cannot create new MySQL accounts by creating login accounts for your operating system; use the GRANT statement instead.

1.2 Creating a Database and a Sample Table

Problem

You want to create a database and set up tables within it.

Solution

Use a CREATE DATABASE statement to create the database, a CREATE TABLE statement for each table that you want to use, and INSERT statements to add rows to the tables.

Discussion

The GRANT statement shown in Recipe 1.1 sets up privileges for accessing the cookbook database but does not create the database. You need to create it explicitly before you can use it. This section shows how to do that, and also how to create a table and load it with some sample data that can be used for examples in the following sections.

Connect to the MySQL server as shown at the end of Recipe 1.1. After you've connected successfully, create the database:

```
mysql> CREATE DATABASE cookbook;
```

Now you have a database, so you can create tables in it. First, select cookbook as the default database:

```
mysql> USE cookbook;
```

Then issue the following statements to create a simple table and populate it with a few rows:[*]

```
mysql> CREATE TABLE limbs (thing VARCHAR(20), legs INT, arms INT);
mysql> INSERT INTO limbs (thing,legs,arms) VALUES('human',2,2);
mysql> INSERT INTO limbs (thing,legs,arms) VALUES('insect',6,0);
mysql> INSERT INTO limbs (thing,legs,arms) VALUES('squid',0,10);
mysql> INSERT INTO limbs (thing,legs,arms) VALUES('octopus',0,8);
mysql> INSERT INTO limbs (thing,legs,arms) VALUES('fish',0,0);
mysql> INSERT INTO limbs (thing,legs,arms) VALUES('centipede',100,0);
mysql> INSERT INTO limbs (thing,legs,arms) VALUES('table',4,0);
mysql> INSERT INTO limbs (thing,legs,arms) VALUES('armchair',4,2);
mysql> INSERT INTO limbs (thing,legs,arms) VALUES('phonograph',0,1);
mysql> INSERT INTO limbs (thing,legs,arms) VALUES('tripod',3,0);
mysql> INSERT INTO limbs (thing,legs,arms) VALUES('Peg Leg Pete',1,2);
mysql> INSERT INTO limbs (thing,legs,arms) VALUES('space alien',NULL,NULL);
```

The table is named limbs and contains three columns to record the number of legs and arms possessed by various life forms and objects. The physiology of the alien in the last row is such that the proper values for the arms and legs column cannot be determined; NULL indicates "unknown value."

Verify that the rows were inserted properly into the table by issuing a SELECT statement:

```
mysql> SELECT * FROM limbs;
+--------------+------+------+
| thing        | legs | arms |
+--------------+------+------+
| human        |    2 |    2 |
| insect       |    6 |    0 |
| squid        |    0 |   10 |
| octopus      |    0 |    8 |
| fish         |    0 |    0 |
| centipede    |  100 |    0 |
| table        |    4 |    0 |
| armchair     |    4 |    2 |
| phonograph   |    0 |    1 |
| tripod       |    3 |    0 |
| Peg Leg Pete |    1 |    2 |
| space alien  | NULL | NULL |
+--------------+------+------+
```

---

[*] If you don't want to enter the complete text of the INSERT statements (and I don't blame you), skip ahead to Recipe 1.10 for a shortcut. If you don't want to type in *any* of the statements, skip ahead to Recipe 1.12.

At this point, you're all set up with a database and a table. For general instructions on issuing SQL statements, see Recipe 1.8.

 Statements in this book are shown with SQL keywords such as SELECT or INSERT in uppercase for distinctiveness. However, that's just a typographical convention. You can enter keywords in any lettercase.

1.3 Starting and Stopping mysql

Problem

You want to start and stop the *mysql* program.

Solution

Invoke *mysql* from your command prompt to start it, specifying any connection parameters that may be necessary. To leave *mysql*, use a QUIT statement.

Discussion

To start the *mysql* program, try just typing its name at your command-line prompt. If *mysql* starts up correctly, you'll see a short message, followed by a mysql> prompt that indicates the program is ready to accept statements. To illustrate, here's what the welcome message looks like (to save space, I won't show it in any further examples):

```
% mysql
Welcome to the MySQL monitor.  Commands end with ; or \g.
Your MySQL connection id is 18427 to server version: 5.0.27-log

Type 'help;' or '\h' for help. Type '\c' to clear the buffer.

mysql>
```

If you invoke *mysql* and you get an error message that it cannot be found or is an invalid command, that means your command interpreter doesn't know where *mysql* is installed. See Recipe 1.7 for instructions on setting the PATH environment variable that your command interpreter uses to find commands.

If *mysql* tries to start but exits immediately with an "access denied" message, you need to specify connection parameters. The most commonly needed parameters are the host to connect to (the host that runs the MySQL server), your MySQL username, and a password. For example:

```
% mysql -h localhost -p -u cbuser
Enter password: cbpass
```

If you don't have a MySQL username and password, you must obtain permission to use the MySQL server, as described earlier in Recipe 1.1.

The way you specify connection parameters for *mysql* also applies to other MySQL programs such as *mysqldump* and *mysqladmin*. For example, to generate a dump file named *cookbook.sql* that contains a backup of the tables in the cookbook database, execute *mysqldump* like this:

```
% mysqldump -h localhost -p -u cbuser cookbook > cookbook.sql
Enter password: cbpass
```

Some operations require an administrative MySQL account. The *mysqladmin* program can perform operations that are available only to the MySQL root account, so you need to invoke it as follows:

```
% mysqladmin -p -u root shutdown
Enter password:          ← enter MySQL root account password here
```

In general, I'll show commands for MySQL programs in examples with no connection parameter options. I assume that you'll supply any parameters that you need, either on the command line or in an option file (Recipe 1.4) so that you don't have to type them each time you invoke *mysql*, *mysqldump*, and so forth.

The syntax and default values for the connection parameter options are shown in the following table. These options have both a single-dash short form and a double-dash long form.

Parameter type	Option syntax forms	Default value
Hostname	-h *hostname* --host=*hostname*	localhost
Username	-u *username* --user=*username*	Your login name
Password	-p --password	None

If the value that you use for an option is the same as its default value, you can omit the option. However, as the table indicates, there is no default password. To supply one, use a -p or --password option, and then enter your password when *mysql* prompts you for it:

```
% mysql -p
Enter password:          ← enter your password here
```

If you like, you can specify the password directly on the command line by using -p*password* (note that there is no space after the -p) or --password=*password*. I don't recommend doing this on a multiple-user machine, because the password may be visible to other users who are running tools, such as *ps*, that report process information.

To terminate a *mysql* session, issue a QUIT command:

```
mysql> QUIT
```

You can also terminate the session by issuing an EXIT command or (under Unix) by typing Ctrl-D.

The Meaning of localhost in MySQL

One of the parameters you specify when connecting to a MySQL server is the host on which the server is running. Most programs treat the hostname *localhost* and the IP address 127.0.0.1 as synonyms for "the local host." Under Unix, MySQL programs behave differently: by convention, they treat the hostname *localhost* specially and attempt to connect to the local server using a Unix domain socket file. To force a TCP/IP connection to the local server, use the IP address 127.0.0.1 rather than the hostname *localhost*. Alternatively, specify a --protocol=tcp option to force use of TCP/IP for connecting.

The default port number is 3306 for TCP/IP connections. The pathname for the Unix domain socket varies, although it's often */tmp/mysql.sock*. To specify the socket file pathname explicitly, use a -S *file_name* or --socket=*file_name* option.

1.4 Specifying Connection Parameters Using Option Files

Problem

You don't want to type connection parameters on the command line every time you invoke *mysql* or other MySQL programs.

Solution

Put the parameters in an option file.

Discussion

To avoid entering connection parameters manually, put them in an option file for *mysql* to read automatically. Under Unix, your personal option file is named *.my.cnf* in your home directory. There are also site-wide option files that administrators can use to specify parameters that apply globally to all users. You can use */etc/my.cnf* or the *my.cnf* file in the MySQL installation directory. Under Windows, the option files you can use are the *my.ini* file in your MySQL installation directory (for example, *C:\Program Files\MySQL\MySQL Server 5.0*), *my.ini* in your Windows directory (this is something like *C:\WINDOWS* or *C:\WINNT*), or the *C:\my.cnf* file.

Windows Explorer might hide filename extensions when it displays files, so a file named *my.ini* or *my.cnf* may appear to be named just *my*. Your version of Windows may allow you to disable extension-hiding. Alternatively, issue a DIR command in a console window to see complete filenames.

The following example illustrates the format used to write MySQL option files:

```
# general client program connection options
[client]
host     = localhost
user     = cbuser
password = cbpass

# options specific to the mysql program
[mysql]
skip-auto-rehash
pager="/usr/bin/less -E" # specify pager for interactive mode
```

This format has the following general characteristics:

- Lines are written in groups (or sections). The first line of a group specifies the group name within square brackets, and the remaining lines specify options associated with the group. The example file just shown has a [client] group and a [mysql] group. Within a group, write option lines in *name=value* format, where *name* corresponds to an option name (without leading dashes) and *value* is the option's value. If an option doesn't take any value (such as for the skip-auto-rehash option), list the name by itself with no trailing *=value* part.

- In option files, only the long form of an option is allowed. This is in contrast to command lines, where options often can be specified using a short form or a long form. For example, on the command line, the hostname can be given using either -h *hostname* or --host=*hostname*. In an option file, only host=*hostname* is allowed.

- In option files, spaces are allowed around the = that separates an option name and value. This contrasts with command lines, where no spaces around = are allowed.

- If an option value contains spaces or other special characters, you can quote it using single or double quotes. The pager option illustrates this.

- If you don't need some particular parameter, just leave out the corresponding line. For example, if you normally connect to the default host (localhost), you don't need any host line. On Unix, if your MySQL username is the same as your operating system login name, you can omit the user line.

- It's common to use an option file to specify options for connection parameters (such as host, user, and password). However, the file can list options that have other purposes. The pager option shown for the [mysql] group specifies the paging program that *mysql* should use for displaying output in interactive mode. It has nothing to do with how the program connects to the server.

- The usual option group for specifying client connection parameters is [client]. This group actually is used by all the standard MySQL clients. By listing an option in this group, you make it easier to invoke not just *mysql*, but also other programs such as *mysqldump* and *mysqladmin*. Just make sure that any option you put in this group is understood by *all* client programs. For example, if you put *mysql*-specific options such as skip-auto-rehash or pager in the [client] group, that will result in "unknown option" errors for all other programs that use the [client] group, and they won't run properly.

- You can define multiple groups in an option file. A common convention is for a program to look for parameters in the [client] group and in the group named for the program itself. This provides a convenient way to list general client parameters that you want all client programs to use, but you can still specify options that apply only to a particular program. The preceding sample option file illustrates this convention for the *mysql* program, which gets general connection parameters from the [client] group and also picks up the skip-auto-rehash and pager options from the [mysql] group.

- If a parameter appears multiple times in an option file, the last value found takes precedence. Normally, you should list any program-specific groups following the [client] group so that if there is any overlap in the options set by the two groups, the more general options will be overridden by the program-specific values.

- Lines beginning with # or ; characters are ignored as comments. Blank lines are ignored, too. # can be used to write comments at the end of option lines, as shown for the pager option.

- Option files must be plain-text files. If you create an option file with a word processor that uses some nontext format by default, be sure to save the file explicitly as text. Windows users especially should take note of this.

- Options that specify file or directory pathnames should be written using / as the pathname separator character, even under Windows, which uses \ as the pathname separator. Alternatively, write \ by doubling it as \\ (this is necessary because \ is the MySQL escape character in strings).

If you want to find out which options the *mysql* program will read from option files, use this command:

```
% mysql --print-defaults
```

You can also use the *my_print_defaults* utility, which takes as arguments the names of the option file groups that it should read. For example, *mysql* looks in both the [client] and [mysql] groups for options, so you can check which values it will read from option files by using this command:

```
% my_print_defaults client mysql
```

1.5 Protecting Option Files from Other Users

Problem

Your MySQL username and password are stored in your option file, and you don't want other users to be able to read that file.

Solution

Set the file's mode to make it accessible only by you.

Discussion

On a multiple-user operating system such as Unix, you should protect your option file to prevent other users from reading it and finding out how to connect to MySQL using your account. Use *chmod* to make the file private by setting its mode to enable access only by yourself. Either of the following commands do this:

```
% chmod 600 .my.cnf
% chmod go-rwx .my.cnf
```

On Windows, you can use Windows Explorer to set file permissions.

1.6 Mixing Command-Line and Option File Parameters

Problem

You'd rather not store your MySQL password in an option file, but you don't want to enter your username and server host manually.

Solution

Put the username and host in the option file, but not the password. Instead, specify the password interactively when you invoke the *mysql* program. *mysql* looks both in the option file and on the command line for connection parameters. If an option is specified in both places, the one on the command line takes precedence.

Discussion

mysql first reads your option file to see what connection parameters are listed there, and then checks the command line for additional parameters. This means you can specify some options one way, and some the other way. For example, you can list your username and hostname in an option file, but use a password option on the command line:

```
% mysql -p
Enter password:        ← enter your password here
```

Command-line parameters take precedence over parameters found in your option file, so if for some reason you need to override an option file parameter, just specify it on the command line. For example, you might list your regular MySQL username and password in the option file for general-purpose use. If you need to connect on occasion as the MySQL root user, specify the user and password options on the command line to override the option file values:

```
% mysql -p -u root
Enter password:        ← enter MySQL root account password here
```

To explicitly specify "no password" when there is a nonempty password in the option file, use -p on the command line, and then press Enter when *mysql* prompts you for the password:

```
% mysql -p
Enter password:        ← press Enter here
```

1.7 What to Do if mysql Cannot Be Found

Problem

When you invoke *mysql* from the command line, your command interpreter can't find it.

Solution

Add the directory where *mysql* is installed to your PATH setting. You'll then be able to run *mysql* from any directory easily.

Discussion

If your shell or command interpreter can't find *mysql* when you invoke it, you'll see some sort of error message. It might look like this under Unix:

```
% mysql
mysql: Command not found.
```

Or like this under Windows:

```
C:\> mysql
Bad command or invalid filename
```

One way to tell your command interpreter where to find *mysql* is to type its full pathname each time you run it. The command might look like this under Unix:

```
% /usr/local/mysql/bin/mysql
```

Or like this under Windows:

```
C:\> "C:\Program Files\MySQL\MySQL Server 5.0\bin\mysql"
```

Typing long pathnames gets tiresome pretty quickly. You can avoid the need to do so by changing location into the directory where *mysql* is installed before you run it. However, I recommend that you *not* do that. If you do, you'll be tempted to put all your datafiles and SQL batch files in the same directory as *mysql*, thus unnecessarily cluttering up what should be a location intended only for programs.

A better solution is to make sure that the directory where *mysql* is installed is included in the value of the PATH environment variable that lists pathnames of directories where the command interpreter looks for commands. You can then invoke *mysql* from any directory by entering just its name, and your command interpreter will be able to find it. This eliminates a lot of unnecessary pathname typing.

An additional significant benefit is that because you can easily run *mysql* from anywhere, you won't need to put your datafiles in the directory where *mysql* is located. When you don't have to run *mysql* from a particular location, you're free to organize your files in a way that makes sense to you, not in a way imposed by some artificial necessity. For example, you can create a directory under your home directory for each database you have and put the work files associated with a given database in the appropriate directory.

For instructions on setting your PATH variable, see Appendix B.

I've pointed out the importance of the PATH search path variable here because I have seen many questions from people who aren't aware of the existence of such a thing, and who consequently try to do all their MySQL-related work in the *bin* directory where *mysql* is installed. This seems particularly common among Windows users.

On Windows, another way to avoid typing the pathname or changing into the *mysql* directory is to create a shortcut and place it in a more convenient location such as the desktop. This makes it easy to start *mysql* just by opening the shortcut. To specify command options or the startup directory, edit the shortcut's properties. If you don't always invoke *mysql* with the same options, it might be useful to create one shortcut for each set of options you need. For example, create one shortcut to connect as an ordinary user for general work and another to connect as the MySQL root user for administrative purposes.

1.8 Issuing SQL Statements

Problem

You've started *mysql*, and now you want to send SQL statements to the MySQL server to be executed.

Solution

Just type them in, but be sure to let *mysql* know where each one ends.

Discussion

When you invoke *mysql*, it displays a mysql> prompt to tell you that it's ready for input. To issue a SQL statement at the mysql> prompt, type it in, add a semicolon (;) at the end to signify the end of the statement, and press Enter. An explicit statement terminator is necessary; *mysql* doesn't interpret Enter as a terminator because you can enter a statement using multiple input lines. The semicolon is the most common terminator, but you can also use \g ("go") as a synonym for the semicolon. Thus, the following examples are equivalent ways of issuing the same statement, even though they are entered differently and terminated differently:

```
mysql> SELECT NOW();
+---------------------+
| NOW()               |
+---------------------+
| 2005-11-15 16:18:10 |
+---------------------+
mysql> SELECT
    -> NOW()\g
+---------------------+
| NOW()               |
+---------------------+
| 2005-11-15 16:18:18 |
+---------------------+
```

Notice that for the second statement the prompt changes from `mysql>` to `->` on the second input line. *mysql* changes the prompt this way to let you know that it's still waiting to see the statement terminator.

Be sure to understand that neither the `;` character nor the `\g` sequence that serve as statement terminators are part of the statement itself. They're conventions used by the *mysql* program, which recognizes these terminators and strips them from the input before sending the statement to the MySQL server. It's important to remember this when you write your own programs that send statements to the server (as we'll begin to do in the next chapter). In such programs, you don't include any terminator characters; the end of the statement string itself signifies the end of the statement. In fact, adding a terminator may well cause the statement to fail with an error.

See Also

mysql also can read statements from a file or from another program. See Recipes 1.12 and 1.13.

1.9 Canceling a Partially Entered Statement

Problem

You start to enter a statement, and then decide not to issue it after all.

Solution

Cancel the statement using your line-kill character or the `\c` sequence.

Discussion

If you change your mind about issuing a statement that you're entering, cancel it. If the statement is on a single line, backspace over it or use your line-kill character to erase the entire line. (The particular line-kill character to use depends on your terminal setup; for me, and most Unix/Linux users, the character is Ctrl-U; Windows users should press Esc.)

If you've entered a statement over multiple lines, the line-kill character erases only the last line. To cancel the statement completely, enter \c, and press Enter. This returns you to the mysql> prompt:

```
mysql> SELECT *
    -> FROM limbs
    -> ORDER BY\c
mysql>
```

Sometimes \c appears to do nothing (that is, the mysql> prompt does not reappear), which leads to the sense that you're "trapped" in a statement and can't escape. If \c is ineffective, the cause usually is that you began typing a quoted string and haven't yet entered the matching end quote that terminates the string. Let *mysql*'s prompt help you figure out what to do here:

- If the prompt has changed from mysql> to ">, That means *mysql* is looking for a terminating double quote. If the prompt is '> or `> instead, *mysql* is looking for a terminating single quote or backtick. Type the appropriate matching quote to end the string, and then type \c followed by Enter.

- If the prompt is /*>, you're in the middle of typing a C-style /* ... */ comment. End the comment by typing */, and then type \c followed by Enter.

1.10 Repeating and Editing SQL Statements

Problem

The statement you just entered contains an error, and you want to fix it without typing the whole thing again. Or you want to repeat an earlier statement without retyping it.

Solution

Use *mysql*'s built-in input-line editing capabilities.

Discussion

If you issue a long statement only to find that it contains a syntax error, what should you do? Type in the entire corrected statement from scratch? No need: *mysql* maintains a statement history and supports input-line editing. This enables you to recall statements so that you can modify and reissue them easily.

There are many, many editing functions, but most people tend to use a small set of commands for the majority of their editing. A basic set of useful commands is shown in the following table. Typically, you use Up Arrow to recall the previous line, Left Arrow and Right Arrow to move around within the line, and Backspace or Delete to erase characters. To add new characters to the line, just move the cursor to the appropriate spot, and type them in. When you're done editing, press Enter to issue the statement (the cursor need not be at the end of the line when you do this).

Editing key	Effect of key
Up Arrow	Scroll up through statement history
Down Arrow	Scroll down through statement history
Left Arrow	Move left within line
Right Arrow	Move right within line
Ctrl-A	Move to beginning of line
Ctrl-E	Move to end of line
Backspace	Delete previous character
Ctrl-D	Delete character under cursor

On Windows, the arrow key and Backspace editing functions are available as described in the table, Home and End take the place of Ctrl-A and Ctrl-E, and pressing F7 gives you a menu of recent commands.

Input-line editing is useful for more than just fixing mistakes. You can use it to try variant forms of a statement without retyping the entire thing each time. It's also handy for entering a series of similar statements. For example, if you want to use the statement history to issue the series of INSERT statements shown earlier in Recipe 1.2 to create the limbs table, first enter the initial INSERT statement. Then, to issue each successive statement, press the Up Arrow key to recall the previous statement with the cursor at the end, backspace back through the column values to erase them, enter the new values, and press Enter.

The input-line editing capabilities in *mysql* are based on the GNU Readline library. You can read its documentation to find out more about the many editing functions that are available. Readline documentation is part of the *bash* manual, which is available online at *http://www.gnu.org/manual/*.

1.11 Using Auto-Completion for Database and Table Names

Problem

You wish there was a way to type database and table names more quickly.

Solution

There is: use *mysql*'s name auto-completion facility.

Discussion

Normally, when you use *mysql* interactively, it reads the list of database names and the names of the tables and columns in your default (current) database when it starts up. *mysql* remembers this information to provide name-completion capabilities that are useful for entering statements with fewer keystrokes:

1. Type in a partial database, table, or column name, and then hit the Tab key.
2. If the partial name is unique, *mysql* completes it for you. Otherwise, you can hit Tab again to see the possible matches.
3. Enter additional characters, and hit Tab again once to complete it or twice to see the new set of matches.

mysql's name auto-completion capability is based on the table names in the default database, and thus is not available within a *mysql* session until you select a database, either on the command line or with a USE statement.

Auto-completion enables you to cut down the amount of typing you do. However, if you don't use this feature, reading name-completion information from the MySQL server may be counterproductive because it can cause *mysql* to start more slowly when you have a lot of tables in your database. To tell *mysql* not to read this information so that it starts up more quickly, specify the -A (or --skip-auto-rehash) option on the *mysql* command line. Alternatively, put a skip-auto-rehash line in the [mysql] group of your MySQL option file:

```
[mysql]
skip-auto-rehash
```

To force *mysql* to read name completion information even if it was invoked in no-completion mode, issue a REHASH or \# command at the mysql> prompt.

1.12 Telling mysql to Read Statements from a File

Problem

You want *mysql* to read statements stored in a file so that you don't have to enter them manually.

Solution

Redirect *mysql*'s input, or use the SOURCE command.

Discussion

By default, the *mysql* program reads input interactively from the terminal, but you can feed it statements in batch mode using other input sources such as a file, another program, or the command arguments. You can also use copy and paste as a source of statement input. This section discusses how to read statements from a file. The next few sections discuss how to take input from other sources.

To create an SQL script for *mysql* to execute in batch mode, put your statements in a text file. Then invoke *mysql*, and redirect its input to read from that file:

```
% mysql cookbook < filename
```

Statements that are read from an input file substitute for what you'd normally type in by hand, so they must be terminated with semicolons (or \g), just as if you were entering them manually. One difference between interactive and batch modes is the default output style. For interactive mode, the default is tabular (boxed) format. For batch mode, the default is to delimit column values with tabs. However, you can select whichever output style you want using the appropriate command option. See Recipe 1.18.

Batch mode is convenient when you need to issue a given set of statements on multiple occasions because you need not enter them manually each time. For example, batch mode makes it easy to set up *cron* jobs that run with no user intervention. SQL scripts also are useful for distributing statements to other people. That is, in fact, how SQL examples from this book are distributed. Many of the examples shown here can be run using script files that are available in the accompanying **recipes** source distribution. (See Appendix A.) You can feed these files to *mysql* in batch mode to avoid typing statements yourself. For example, when a recipe shows a **CREATE TABLE** statement that describes what a particular table looks like, you'll usually find an SQL batch file in the **recipes** distribution that can be used to create (and perhaps load data into) the table. Recall that Recipe 1.2 showed the statements for creating and populating the **limbs** table. Those statements were shown as you would enter them manually, but the **recipes** distribution includes a *limbs.sql* file that contains statements to do the same thing. The file looks like this:

```
DROP TABLE IF EXISTS limbs;
CREATE TABLE limbs
(
  thing VARCHAR(20),   # what the thing is
  legs  INT,           # number of legs it has
  arms  INT            # number of arms it has
);

INSERT INTO limbs (thing,legs,arms) VALUES('human',2,2);
INSERT INTO limbs (thing,legs,arms) VALUES('insect',6,0);
INSERT INTO limbs (thing,legs,arms) VALUES('squid',0,10);
INSERT INTO limbs (thing,legs,arms) VALUES('octopus',0,8);
INSERT INTO limbs (thing,legs,arms) VALUES('fish',0,0);
INSERT INTO limbs (thing,legs,arms) VALUES('centipede',100,0);
```

```
INSERT INTO limbs (thing,legs,arms) VALUES('table',4,0);
INSERT INTO limbs (thing,legs,arms) VALUES('armchair',4,2);
INSERT INTO limbs (thing,legs,arms) VALUES('phonograph',0,1);
INSERT INTO limbs (thing,legs,arms) VALUES('tripod',3,0);
INSERT INTO limbs (thing,legs,arms) VALUES('Peg Leg Pete',1,2);
INSERT INTO limbs (thing,legs,arms) VALUES('space alien',NULL,NULL);
```

To execute the statements in this SQL script file in batch mode, change location into
the *tables* directory of the recipes distribution that contains the table-creation scripts,
and then run this command:

```
% mysql cookbook < limbs.sql
```

You'll note that the script contains a statement to drop the table if it exists before
creating the table anew and loading it with data. That enables you to experiment with
the table without worrying about changing its contents because you can restore the
table to its baseline state any time by running the script again.

The command just shown illustrates how to specify an input file for *mysql* on the command line. Alternatively, you can read a file of SQL statements from within a *mysql*
session using a SOURCE *filename* command (or \. *filename*, which is synonymous).
Suppose that the SQL script file *test.sql* contains the following statements:

```
SELECT NOW();
SELECT COUNT(*) FROM limbs;
```

You can execute that file from within *mysql* as follows:

```
mysql> SOURCE test.sql;
+---------------------+
| NOW()               |
+---------------------+
| 2006-07-04 10:35:08 |
+---------------------+
1 row in set (0.00 sec)
+----------+
| COUNT(*) |
+----------+
|       12 |
+----------+
1 row in set (0.01 sec)
```

SQL scripts can themselves include SOURCE or \. commands to include other scripts.
This gives you additional flexibility but also raises the danger that it's possible to create
a source loop. Normally, you should take care to avoid such loops. If you're feeling
mischievous and want to create a loop deliberately to find out how deep *mysql* can nest
input files, here's how to do it. First, issue the following two statements manually to
create a counter table to keep track of the source file depth and initialize the nesting
level to zero:

```
mysql> CREATE TABLE counter (depth INT);
mysql> INSERT INTO counter SET depth = 0;
```

Then create a script file *loop.sql* that contains the following lines (be sure each line ends with a semicolon):

```
UPDATE counter SET depth = depth + 1;
SELECT depth FROM counter;
SOURCE loop.sql;
```

Finally, invoke *mysql*, and issue a SOURCE command to read the script file:

```
% mysql cookbook
mysql> SOURCE loop.sql;
```

The first two statements in *loop.sql* increment the nesting counter and display the current depth value. In the third statement, *loop.sql* sources itself, thus creating an input loop. You'll see the output whiz by, with the counter display incrementing each time through the loop. Eventually *mysql* will run out of file descriptors and stop with an error:

```
ERROR:
Failed to open file 'loop.sql', error: 24
```

What is error 24? Find out by using MySQL's *perror* (print error) utility:

```
% perror 24
OS error code 24:   Too many open files
```

In other words, you have hit the limit imposed by the operating system on the number of open files you can have.

1.13 Telling mysql to Read Statements from Other Programs

Problem

You want to shove the output from another program into *mysql*.

Solution

Use a pipe.

Discussion

Recipe 1.12 used the following command to show how *mysql* can read SQL statements from a file:

```
% mysql cookbook < limbs.sql
```

mysql can also read a pipe, which means that it can receive output from other programs as its input. As a trivial example, the preceding command is equivalent to this one:

```
% cat limbs.sql | mysql cookbook
```

Before you tell me that I've qualified for this week's "useless use of *cat* award," [†] allow me to observe that you can substitute other commands for *cat*. The point is that *any* command that produces output consisting of semicolon-terminated SQL statements can be used as an input source for *mysql*. This can be useful in many ways. For example, the *mysqldump* utility generates database backups by writing a set of SQL statements that recreate the database. To process *mysqldump* output, feed it to *mysql*. This means you can use the combination of *mysqldump* and *mysql* to copy a database over the network to another MySQL server:

```
% mysqldump cookbook | mysql -h some.other.host.com cookbook
```

Program-generated SQL also can be useful when you need to populate a table with test data but don't want to write the INSERT statements by hand. Instead, write a short program that generates the statements, and then send its output to *mysql* using a pipe:

```
% generate-test-data | mysql cookbook
```

See Also

Chapter 10 discusses *mysqldump* further.

1.14 Entering an SQL One-Liner

Problem

You want to specify a statement to be executed directly on the *mysql* command line.

Solution

mysql can read a statement from its argument list.

Discussion

To execute a statement directly from the command line, specify it using the -e (or --execute) option. For example, to find out how many rows are in the limbs table, run this command:

```
% mysql -e "SELECT COUNT(*) FROM limbs" cookbook
+----------+
| COUNT(*) |
+----------+
|       12 |
+----------+
```

To execute multiple statements this way, separate them with semicolons:

[†] Under Windows, the equivalent would be the "useless use of *type* award":

```
C:\> type limbs.sql | mysql cookbook
```

```
% mysql -e "SELECT COUNT(*) FROM limbs;SELECT NOW()" cookbook
+----------+
| COUNT(*) |
+----------+
|       12 |
+----------+
+---------------------+
| NOW()               |
+---------------------+
| 2006-07-04 10:42:22 |
+---------------------+
```

By default, results generated by statements that are specified with -e are displayed in tabular format if output goes to the terminal, and in tab-delimited format otherwise. To learn what these different formats are, see Recipe 1.17. To choose a particular format, see Recipe 1.18.

1.15 Using Copy and Paste as a mysql Input Source

Problem

You want to take advantage of your graphical user interface (GUI) to make *mysql* easier to use.

Solution

Use copy and paste to supply *mysql* with statements to execute. In this way, you can take advantage of your GUI's capabilities to augment the terminal interface presented by *mysql*.

Discussion

Copy and paste is useful in a windowing environment that enables you to run multiple programs at once and transfer information between them. If you have a document containing statements open in a window, you can just copy the statements from there and paste them into the window in which you're running *mysql*. This is equivalent to typing the statements yourself, but often quicker. For statements that you issue frequently, keeping them visible in a separate window can be a good way to make sure they're always at your fingertips.

1.16 Preventing Query Output from Scrolling off the Screen

Problem

Query output zooms off the top of your screen before you can see it.

Solution

Tell *mysql* to display output a page at a time, or run *mysql* in a window that allows scrollback.

Discussion

If a statement produces many lines of output, normally the lines just scroll right off the top of the screen. To prevent this, tell *mysql* to present output a page at a time by specifying the `--pager` option.‡ `--pager=program` tells *mysql* to use a specific program as your pager:

```
% mysql --pager=/usr/bin/less
```

`--pager` by itself (with no option value) tells *mysql* to use your default pager, as specified in your PAGER environment variable:

```
% mysql --pager
```

If your PAGER variable isn't set, you must either define it or use the first form of the command to specify a pager program explicitly. To define PAGER, use the instructions given in Appendix B for setting environment variables.

Within a *mysql* session, you can turn paging on or off using `\P` or `\n`, respectively. `\P` without an argument enables paging using the program specified in your PAGER variable. `\P` with an argument enables paging using the argument as the name of the paging program:

```
mysql> \P
PAGER set to /bin/more
mysql> \P /usr/bin/less
PAGER set to /usr/bin/less
mysql> \n
PAGER set to stdout
```

Another way to deal with long result sets is to use a terminal program that allows you to scroll back through previous output. Programs such as *xterm* for the X Window System, Terminal for Mac OS X, or the console window for Windows allow you to set the number of output lines saved in the scrollback buffer. Under Windows, you can set up a console window that allows scrollback by using the following procedure:

1. Locate the Console item in the Control Panel or *cmd.exe* in the following directory: *WINDOWS\system32*.

2. Create a shortcut to the item by right-clicking on it and dragging the mouse to where you want to place the shortcut (on the desktop, for example).

3. Right-click on the shortcut, and select the Properties item from the menu that appears.

---

‡ The `--pager` option is not available under Windows.

4. Select the Layout tab in the resulting Properties window.

5. Set the screen buffer height to the number of lines you want to save, and click the OK button.

Now you can launch the shortcut to get a scrollable console window that allows output produced by commands in that window to be retrieved using the scrollbar.

1.17 Sending Query Output to a File or to a Program

Problem

You want *mysql* output to go somewhere other than your screen.

Solution

Redirect *mysql*'s output, or use a pipe.

Discussion

mysql chooses its default output format according to whether you run it interactively or noninteractively. Under interactive use, *mysql* normally sends its output to the terminal and writes query results using tabular format:

```
mysql> SELECT * FROM limbs;
+--------------+------+------+
| thing        | legs | arms |
+--------------+------+------+
| human        |    2 |    2 |
| insect       |    6 |    0 |
| squid        |    0 |   10 |
| octopus      |    0 |    8 |
| fish         |    0 |    0 |
| centipede    |  100 |    0 |
| table        |    4 |    0 |
| armchair     |    4 |    2 |
| phonograph   |    0 |    1 |
| tripod       |    3 |    0 |
| Peg Leg Pete |    1 |    2 |
| space alien  | NULL | NULL |
+--------------+------+------+
12 rows in set (0.00 sec)
```

In noninteractive mode (that is, when either the input or output is redirected), *mysql* writes output in tab-delimited format:

```
% echo "SELECT * FROM limbs" | mysql cookbook
thing   legs    arms
human   2       2
insect  6       0
squid   0       10
octopus 0       8
```

```
fish      0        0
centipede          100      0
table    4         0
armchair           4        2
phonograph         0        1
tripod   3         0
Peg Leg Pete       1        2
space alien        NULL     NULL
```

However, in either context, you can select any of *mysql*'s output formats using the appropriate command option. This section describes how to send *mysql* output somewhere other than the terminal. The next several sections discuss the various *mysql* output formats and how to select them explicitly according to your needs when the default format isn't what you want.

To save output from *mysql* in a file, use your shell's standard redirection capability:

```
% mysql cookbook > outputfile
```

If you run *mysql* interactively with the output redirected, you won't be able to see what you're typing, so generally in this case you'll also take statement input from a file (or another program):

```
% mysql cookbook < inputfile > outputfile
```

You can also send statement output to another program. For example, if you want to mail query output to someone, you might do so like this:

```
% mysql cookbook < inputfile | mail paul
```

Note that because *mysql* runs noninteractively in that context, it produces tab-delimited output, which the mail recipient may find more difficult to read than tabular output. Recipe 1.18 shows how to fix this problem.

1.18 Selecting Tabular or Tab-Delimited Query Output Format

Problem

mysql produces tabular output when you want tab-delimited output, or vice versa.

Solution

Select the desired format explicitly with the appropriate command option.

Discussion

When you use *mysql* noninteractively (such as to read statements from a file or to send results into a pipe), it writes output in tab-delimited format by default. Sometimes it's desirable to produce tabular output instead. (These formats are described in Recipe 1.17.) For example, if you want to print or mail statement results, tab-delimited output doesn't look very nice. Use the -t (or --table) option to produce tabular output that is more readable:

```
% mysql -t cookbook < inputfile | lpr
% mysql -t cookbook < inputfile | mail paul
```

The inverse operation is to produce batch (tab-delimited) output in interactive mode. To do this, use -B or --batch.

1.19 Specifying Arbitrary Output Column Delimiters

Problem

You want *mysql* to produce statement output using a delimiter other than tabs.

Solution

mysql itself offers no capability for setting the output delimiter, but you can postprocess *mysql* output to reformat it.

Discussion

In noninteractive mode, *mysql* separates output columns by tabs and there is no option for specifying the output delimiter. Under some circumstances, it might be desirable to produce output that uses a different delimiter. Suppose that you want to create an output file for use by a program that expects values to be separated by colon characters (:) rather than tabs. Under Unix, you can convert tabs to arbitrary delimiters by using a utility such as *tr* or *sed*. For example, to change tabs to colons, any of the following commands would work (*TAB* indicates where you type a tab character):§

```
% mysql cookbook < inputfile | sed -e "s/TAB/:/g" > outputfile
% mysql cookbook < inputfile | tr "TAB" ":" > outputfile
% mysql cookbook < inputfile | tr "\011" ":" > outputfile
```

sed is more powerful than *tr* because it understands regular expressions and allows multiple substitutions. This is useful when you want to produce output in something like comma-separated values (CSV) format, which requires three substitutions:

1. Escape any quote characters that appear in the data by doubling them, so that when you use the resulting CSV file, they won't be interpreted as column delimiters.

2. Change the tabs to commas.

3. Surround column values with quotes.

sed allows all three substitutions to be performed in a single command:

---

§ The syntax for some versions of *tr* is different; consult your local documentation. Also, some shells use the tab character for special purposes such as filename completion. For such shells, type a literal tab into the command by preceding it with Ctrl-V.

```
% mysql cookbook < inputfile \
    | sed -e 's/"/""/g' -e 's/TAB/","/g' -e 's/^/"/' -e 's/$/"/' > outputfile
```

That's fairly cryptic, to say the least. You can achieve the same result with other languages that may be easier to read. Here's a short Perl script that does the same thing as the *sed* command (it converts tab-delimited input to CSV output), and includes comments to document how it works:

```perl
#!/usr/bin/perl -w
# csv.pl - convert tab-delimited input to comma-separated values output
while (<>)          # read next input line
{
  s/"/""/g;         # double any quotes within column values
  s/\t/","/g;       # put "," between column values
  s/^/"/;           # add " before the first value
  s/$/"/;           # add " after the last value
  print;            # print the result
}
```

If you name the script *csv.pl*, you can use it like this:

```
% mysql cookbook < inputfile  | csv.pl > outputfile
```

If you run the command under a version of Windows that doesn't know how to associate *.pl* files with Perl, it might be necessary to invoke Perl explicitly:

```
C:\> mysql cookbook < inputfile  | perl csv.pl > outputfile
```

tr and *sed* normally are unavailable under Windows. If you need a cross-platform solution, Perl may be more suitable because it runs under both Unix and Windows. (On Unix systems, Perl usually is preinstalled. On Windows, it is freely available for you to install.)

See Also

An even better way to produce CSV output is to use the Perl Text::CSV_XS module, which was designed for that purpose. This module is discussed in Chapter 10, where it's used to construct a general-purpose file reformatter.

1.20 Producing HTML or XML Output

Problem

You'd like to turn a query result into HTML or XML.

Solution

mysql can do that for you. Use mysql -H or mysql -X.

Discussion

mysql generates an HTML table from each query result set if you use the -H (or --html) option. This gives you a quick way to produce sample output for inclusion into a web page that shows what the result of a statement looks like. Here's an example that shows the difference between tabular format and HTML table output (a few line breaks have been added to the HTML output to make it easier to read):

```
% mysql -e "SELECT * FROM limbs WHERE legs=0" cookbook
+------------+------+------+
| thing      | legs | arms |
+------------+------+------+
| squid      |    0 |   10 |
| octopus    |    0 |    8 |
| fish       |    0 |    0 |
| phonograph |    0 |    1 |
+------------+------+------+
% mysql -H -e "SELECT * FROM limbs WHERE legs=0" cookbook
<TABLE BORDER=1>
<TR><TH>thing</TH><TH>legs</TH><TH>arms</TH></TR>
<TR><TD>squid</TD><TD>0</TD><TD>10</TD></TR>
<TR><TD>octopus</TD><TD>0</TD><TD>8</TD></TR>
<TR><TD>fish</TD><TD>0</TD><TD>0</TD></TR>
<TR><TD>phonograph</TD><TD>0</TD><TD>1</TD></TR>
</TABLE>
```

The first line of the table contains column headings. If you don't want a header row, see Recipe 1.21.

mysql creates an XML document from the result of a statement if you use the -X (or --xml) option:

```
% mysql -X -e "SELECT * FROM limbs WHERE legs=0" cookbook
<?xml version="1.0"?>

<resultset statement="select * from limbs where legs=0
">
  <row>
    <field name="thing">squid</field>
    <field name="legs">0</field>
    <field name="arms">10</field>
  </row>

  <row>
    <field name="thing">octopus</field>
    <field name="legs">0</field>
    <field name="arms">8</field>
  </row>

  <row>
    <field name="thing">fish</field>
    <field name="legs">0</field>
    <field name="arms">0</field>
  </row>
```

```
<row>
  <field name="thing">phonograph</field>
  <field name="legs">0</field>
  <field name="arms">1</field>
</row>
</resultset>
```

You can also write your own XML generator that directly processes query results into XML. See Recipe 10.39.

The -H, --html -X, and --xml options produce output only for statements that generate a result set. There is no output for statements such as INSERT or UPDATE.

See Also

For information on writing your own programs that generate HTML from query results, see Chapter 17.

1.21 Suppressing Column Headings in Query Output

Problem

You don't want to include column headings in query output.

Solution

Turn headings off with the appropriate command option. Normally, this is --skip-column-names, but you can also use -ss.

Discussion

Tab-delimited format is convenient for generating datafiles that you can import into other programs. However, the first row of output for each query lists the column headings by default, which may not always be what you want. Suppose that you have a program named *summarize* that produces various descriptive statistics for a column of numbers. If you're producing output from *mysql* to be used with this program, you wouldn't want the header row because it would throw off the results. That is, if you ran a command like this, the output would be inaccurate because *summarize* would count the column heading:

```
% mysql -e "SELECT arms FROM limbs" cookbook | summarize
```

To create output that contains only data values, suppress the column header row with the --skip-column-names option:

```
% mysql --skip-column-names -e "SELECT arms FROM limbs" cookbook | summarize
```

You can achieve the same effect as `--skip-column-names` by specifying the "silent" option (-s or `--silent`) twice:

```
% mysql -ss -e "SELECT arms FROM limbs" cookbook | summarize
```

1.22 Making Long Output Lines More Readable

Problem

You have a query that produces long output lines that wrap around and look messy on your screen.

Solution

Use vertical output format.

Discussion

Some statements generate output lines that are so long they take up more than one line on your terminal, which can make query results difficult to read. Here is an example that shows what excessively long query output lines might look like on your screen:

```
mysql> SHOW FULL COLUMNS FROM limbs;
+-------+-------------+-------------------+------+-----+---------+-------+-----
--------------------------+---------+
| Field | Type        | Collation         | Null | Key | Default | Extra | Priv
ileges                    | Comment |
+-------+-------------+-------------------+------+-----+---------+-------+-----
--------------------------+---------+
| thing | varchar(20) | latin1_swedish_ci | YES  |     | NULL    |       | sele
ct,insert,update,references |         |
| legs  | int(11)     | NULL              | YES  |     | NULL    |       | sele
ct,insert,update,references |         |
| arms  | int(11)     | NULL              | YES  |     | NULL    |       | sele
ct,insert,update,references |         |
+-------+-------------+-------------------+------+-----+---------+-------+-----
--------------------------+---------+
```

To avoid the problem, generate "vertical" output with each column value on a separate line. This is done by terminating a statement with `\G` rather than with a `;` character or with `\g`. Here's what the result from the preceding statement looks like when displayed using vertical format:

```
mysql> SHOW FULL COLUMNS FROM limbs\G
*************************** 1. row ***************************
    Field: thing
     Type: varchar(20)
Collation: latin1_swedish_ci
     Null: YES
      Key:
  Default: NULL
```

```
      Extra:
 Privileges: select,insert,update,references
    Comment:
*************************** 2. row ***************************
      Field: legs
       Type: int(11)
  Collation: NULL
       Null: YES
        Key:
    Default: NULL
      Extra:
 Privileges: select,insert,update,references
    Comment:
*************************** 3. row ***************************
      Field: arms
       Type: int(11)
  Collation: NULL
       Null: YES
        Key:
    Default: NULL
      Extra:
 Privileges: select,insert,update,references
    Comment:
```

To specify vertical output from the command line, use the -E (or --vertical) option when you invoke *mysql*. This affects all statements issued during the session, something that can be useful when using *mysql* to execute a script. (If you write the statements in the SQL script file using the usual semicolon terminator, you can select normal or vertical output from the command line by selective use of -E.)

1.23 Controlling mysql's Verbosity Level

Problem

You want *mysql* to produce more output. Or less.

Solution

Use the -v or -s options for more or less verbosity.

Discussion

When you run *mysql* noninteractively, not only does the default output format change, it becomes more terse. For example, *mysql* doesn't print row counts or indicate how long statements took to execute. To tell *mysql* to be more verbose, use -v or --verbose. These options can be specified multiple times for increasing verbosity. Try the following commands to see how the output differs:

```
% echo "SELECT NOW()" | mysql
% echo "SELECT NOW()" | mysql -v
```

```
% echo "SELECT NOW()" | mysql -vv
% echo "SELECT NOW()" | mysql -vvv
```

The counterparts of -v and --verbose are -s and --silent, which also can be used multiple times for increased effect.

1.24 Logging Interactive mysql Sessions

Problem

You want to keep a record of what you did in a *mysql* session.

Solution

Create a tee file.

Discussion

If you maintain a log of an interactive MySQL session, you can refer back to it later to see what you did and how. Under Unix, you can use the *script* program to save a log of a terminal session. This works for arbitrary commands, so it works for interactive *mysql* sessions, too. However, *script* also adds a carriage return to every line of the transcript, and it includes any backspacing and corrections you make as you're typing. A method of logging an interactive *mysql* session that doesn't add extra messy junk to the logfile (and that works under both Unix and Windows) is to start *mysql* with a --tee option that specifies the name of the file in which to record the session:‖

```
% mysql --tee=tmp.out cookbook
```

To control session logging from within *mysql*, use \T and \t to turn tee output on or off, respectively. This is useful if you want to record only certain parts of a session:

```
mysql> \T tmp.out
Logging to file 'tmp.out'
mysql> \t
Outfile disabled.
```

A tee file contains the statements that you enter as well as the output from those statements, so it's a convenient way to keep a complete record of them. It's useful, for example, when you want to print or mail a session or parts of it, or for capturing statement output to include as an example in a document. It's also a good way to try statements to make sure that you have the syntax correct before putting them in a script file; you can create the script from the tee file later by editing it to remove everything except those statements you want to keep.

‖ It's called a "tee" because it's similar to the Unix *tee* utility. On Unix, read the *tee* manual page for more background:

```
% man tee
```

mysql appends session output to the end of the tee file rather than overwriting it. If you want an existing file to contain only the contents of a single session, remove the file first before invoking *mysql*.

1.25 Creating mysql Scripts from Previously Executed Statements

Problem

You want to reuse statements that you issued during an earlier *mysql* session.

Solution

Use a tee file from the earlier session, or look in *mysql*'s statement history file.

Discussion

One way to create a batch file is to enter your statements into the file from scratch with a text editor and hope that you don't make any mistakes while typing them. But it's often easier to use statements that you've already verified as correct. How? First, try the statements "by hand" using *mysql* in interactive mode to make sure they work properly. Then extract the statements from a record of your session to create the batch file. Two sources of information are particularly useful for creating SQL scripts:

- You can record all or parts of a *mysql* session by using the `--tee` command option or the `\T` command from within *mysql*. (See Recipe 1.24.)
- Under Unix, a second option is to use your history file. *mysql* maintains a record of your statements, which it stores in the file *.mysql_history* in your home directory.

A tee file session log has more context because it contains statement input and output both, not just the text of the statements. This additional information can make it easier to locate the parts of the session you want. (Of course, you must also remove the extra stuff to create a batch file from the tee file.) Conversely, the history file is more concise. It contains only the statements you issue, so there are fewer extraneous lines to delete to obtain the statements you want. Choose whichever source of information best suits your needs.

1.26 Using User-Defined Variables in SQL Statements

Problem

You want to save a value produced by an expression so that you can refer to it in a subsequent statement.

Solution

Use a user-defined variable to store the value for later use.

Discussion

You can assign a value returned by a SELECT statement to a user-defined variable, and then refer to the variable later in your *mysql* session. This provides a way to save a result returned from one statement, and then refer to it later in other statements. The syntax for assigning a value to a user variable within a SELECT statement is @*var_name* := *value*, where *var_name* is the variable name, and *value* is a value that you're retrieving. The variable can be used in subsequent statements wherever an expression is allowed, such as in a WHERE clause or in an INSERT statement.

A common situation in which user variables come in handy is when you need to issue successive statements on multiple tables that are related by a common key value. Suppose that you have a customers table with a cust_id column that identifies each customer, and an orders table that also has a cust_id column to indicate which customer each order is associated with. If you have a customer name and you want to delete the customer record as well as all the customer's orders, you need to determine the proper cust_id value for that customer, and then delete rows from both the customers and orders tables that match the ID. One way to do this is to first save the ID value in a variable, and then refer to the variable in the DELETE statements:

```
mysql> SELECT @id := cust_id FROM customers WHERE cust_id='customer name';
mysql> DELETE FROM orders WHERE cust_id = @id;
mysql> DELETE FROM customers WHERE cust_id = @id;
```

The preceding SELECT statement assigns a column value to a variable, but variables also can be assigned values from arbitrary expressions. The following statement determines the highest sum of the arms and legs columns in the limbs table and assigns it to the @max_limbs variable:

```
mysql> SELECT @max_limbs := MAX(arms+legs) FROM limbs;
```

Another use for a variable is to save the result from LAST_INSERT_ID( ) after creating a new row in a table that has an AUTO_INCREMENT column:

```
mysql> SELECT @last_id := LAST_INSERT_ID();
```

LAST_INSERT_ID( ) returns the value of the new AUTO_INCREMENT value. By saving it in a variable, you can refer to the value several times in subsequent statements, even if you issue other statements that create their own AUTO_INCREMENT values and thus change the value returned by LAST_INSERT_ID( ). This technique is discussed further in Chapter 11.

User variables hold single values. If you assign a value to a variable using a statement that returns multiple rows, the value from the last row is used:

```
mysql> SELECT @name := thing FROM limbs WHERE legs = 0;
+----------------+
```

```
| @name := thing |
+----------------+
| squid          |
| octopus        |
| fish           |
| phonograph     |
+----------------+
mysql> SELECT @name;
+------------+
| @name      |
+------------+
| phonograph |
+------------+
```

If the statement returns no rows, no assignment takes place, and the variable retains its previous value. If the variable has not been used previously, that value is NULL:

```
mysql> SELECT @name2 := thing FROM limbs WHERE legs < 0;
Empty set (0.00 sec)
mysql> SELECT @name2;
+--------+
| @name2 |
+--------+
| NULL   |
+--------+
```

To set a variable explicitly to a particular value, use a SET statement. SET syntax can use either := or = to assign the value:

```
mysql> SET @sum = 4 + 7;
mysql> SELECT @sum;
+------+
| @sum |
+------+
|   11 |
+------+
```

SET also can be used to assign a SELECT result to a variable, provided that you write the SELECT as a subquery (that is, within parentheses), and it returns a single value. For example:

```
mysql> SET @max_limbs = (SELECT MAX(arms+legs) FROM limbs);
```

A given variable's value persists until you assign it another value or until the end of your *mysql* session, whichever comes first.

User variable names are not case-sensitive:

```
mysql> SET @x = 1, @X = 2; SELECT @x, @X;
+------+------+
| @x   | @X   |
+------+------+
| 2    | 2    |
+------+------+
```

Before MySQL 5.0, user variable names *are* case-sensitive.

User variables can appear only where expressions are allowed, not where constants or literal identifiers must be provided. Although it's tempting to attempt to use variables for such things as table names, it doesn't work. For example, you might try to generate a temporary table name using a variable as follows, but it won't work:

```
mysql> SET @tbl_name = CONCAT('tbl_',FLOOR(RAND()*1000000));
mysql> CREATE TABLE @tbl_name (int_col INT);
ERROR 1064: You have an error in your SQL syntax near '@tbl_name
(int_col INT)'
```

User variables are a MySQL-specific extension to standard SQL. They will not work with other database engines.

1.27 Numbering Query Output Lines

Problem

You'd like the lines of a query result nicely numbered.

Solution

Postprocess the output from *mysql* or use a user-defined variable.

Discussion

The --skip-column-names option for *mysql* can be useful in combination with cat -n when you want to number the output rows from a query under Unix:

```
% mysql --skip-column-names -e "SELECT thing, arms FROM limbs" cookbook | cat -n
     1   human     2
     2   insect    0
     3   squid     10
     4   octopus   8
     5   fish      0
     6   centipede         0
     7   table     0
     8   armchair          2
     9   phonograph        1
    10   tripod    0
    11   Peg Leg Pete      2
    12   NULL
```

Another option is to use a user variable. Expressions involving variables are evaluated for each row of a query result, a property that you can use to provide a column of row numbers in the output:

```
mysql> SET @n = 0;
mysql> SELECT @n := @n+1 AS rownum, thing, arms, legs FROM limbs;
+--------+--------------+------+------+
| rownum | thing        | arms | legs |
+--------+--------------+------+------+
|      1 | human        |    2 |    2 |
|      2 | insect       |    0 |    6 |
|      3 | squid        |   10 |    0 |
|      4 | octopus      |    8 |    0 |
|      5 | fish         |    0 |    0 |
|      6 | centipede    |    0 |  100 |
|      7 | table        |    0 |    4 |
|      8 | armchair     |    2 |    4 |
|      9 | phonograph   |    1 |    0 |
|     10 | tripod       |    0 |    3 |
|     11 | Peg Leg Pete |    2 |    1 |
|     12 | space alien  | NULL | NULL |
+--------+--------------+------+------+
```

1.28 Using mysql as a Calculator

Problem

You need a quick way to evaluate an expression.

Solution

Use *mysql* as a calculator. MySQL doesn't require every SELECT statement to refer to a table, so you can select the results of arbitrary expressions.

Discussion

SELECT statements typically refer to some table or tables from which you're retrieving rows. However, in MySQL, SELECT need not reference any table at all, which means that you can use the *mysql* program as a calculator for evaluating an expression:

```
mysql> SELECT (17 + 23) / SQRT(64);
+----------------------+
| (17 + 23) / SQRT(64) |
+----------------------+
|           5.00000000 |
+----------------------+
```

This is also useful for checking how a comparison works. For example, to determine whether a given string comparison is case-sensitive, try a statement such as the following:

```
mysql> SELECT 'ABC' = 'abc';
+---------------+
| 'ABC' = 'abc' |
+---------------+
|             1 |
+---------------+
```

The result of this comparison is 1 (meaning "true"; in general, nonzero values are true). Expressions that evaluate to false return zero:

```
mysql> SELECT 'ABC' = 'abcd';
+----------------+
| 'ABC' = 'abcd' |
+----------------+
|              0 |
+----------------+
```

User variables can store the results of intermediate calculations. The following statements use variables this way to compute the total cost of a hotel bill:

```
mysql> SET @daily_room_charge = 100.00;
mysql> SET @num_of_nights = 3;
mysql> SET @tax_percent = 8;
mysql> SET @total_room_charge = @daily_room_charge * @num_of_nights;
mysql> SET @tax = (@total_room_charge * @tax_percent) / 100;
mysql> SET @total = @total_room_charge + @tax;
mysql> SELECT @total;
+--------+
| @total |
+--------+
|    324 |
+--------+
```

1.29 Using mysql in Shell Scripts

Problem

You want to invoke *mysql* from within a shell script rather than use it interactively.

Solution

There's no rule against this. Just be sure to supply the appropriate arguments to the command.

Discussion

If you need to process query results within a program, you'll typically use a MySQL programming interface designed specifically for the language you're using (for example, in a Perl script, you use the DBI interface; see Recipe 2.1). But for simple, short, or quick-and-dirty tasks, it might be easier just to invoke *mysql* directly from within a shell script, possibly postprocessing the results with other commands. For example, an easy way to write a MySQL server status tester is to use a shell script that invokes *mysql*, as is demonstrated in this section. Shell scripts are also useful for prototyping programs that you intend to convert for use with a programming interface later.

For Unix shell scripting, I recommend that you stick to shells in the Bourne shell family, such as *sh*, *bash*, or *ksh*. (The *csh* and *tcsh* shells are more suited to interactive use than to scripting.) This section provides some examples showing how to write Unix scripts for */bin/sh*, and comments briefly on Windows scripting.

See Appendix B if you need instructions for running programs from your command interpreter or for making sure that your PATH environment variable is set properly to tell your command interpreter which directories to search for installed programs.

The scripts discussed here can be found in the *mysql* directory of the recipes distribution.

Writing shell scripts under Unix

Here is a shell script that reports the current uptime of the MySQL server. It runs a SHOW STATUS statement to get the value of the Uptime status variable that contains the server uptime in seconds:[#]

```
#!/bin/sh
# mysql_uptime.sh - report server uptime in seconds

mysql --skip-column-names -B -e "SHOW /*!50002 GLOBAL */ STATUS LIKE 'Uptime'"
```

The *mysql_uptime.sh* script runs *mysql* using --skip-column-names to suppress the column header line, -B to generate batch (tab-delimited) output, and -e to indicate the statement string to execute. The first line of the script that begins with #! is special. It indicates the pathname of the program that should be invoked to execute the rest of the script, */bin/sh* in this case. To use the script, create a file named *mysql_uptime.sh* that contains the preceding lines, make it executable with chmod +x, and run it. The resulting output looks like this:

```
% ./mysql_uptime.sh
Uptime  1260142
```

The command shown here begins with ./, indicating that the script is located in your current directory. If you move the script to a directory named in your PATH setting, you can invoke it from anywhere, but then you should omit the leading ./ when you run the script.

If you prefer a report that lists the time in days, hours, minutes, and seconds rather than just seconds, you can use the output from the *mysql* STATUS statement, which provides the following information:

```
mysql> STATUS;
Connection id:          12347
```

[#] For an explanation of the /*!50002 GLOBAL */ comment, see Recipe 9.12.

```
Current database:           cookbook
Current user:               cbuser@localhost
Current pager:              stdout
Using outfile:              ' '
Server version:             5.0.27-log
Protocol version:           10
Connection:                 Localhost via UNIX socket
Server characterset:        latin1
Db       characterset:      latin1
Client characterset:        latin1
Conn.    characterset:      latin1
UNIX socket:                /tmp/mysql.sock
Uptime:                     14 days 14 hours 2 min 46 sec
```

For uptime reporting, the only relevant part of that information is the line that begins with Uptime. It's a simple matter to write a script that sends a STATUS command to the server and filters the output with *grep* to extract the desired line:

```
#!/bin/sh
# mysql_uptime2.sh - report server uptime

mysql -e STATUS | grep "^Uptime"
```

The result looks like this:

```
% ./mysql_uptime2.sh
Uptime:                     14 days 14 hours 2 min 46 sec
```

The preceding two scripts specify the statement to be executed using the -e command option, but you can use other *mysql* input sources described earlier in the chapter, such as files and pipes. For example, the following *mysql_uptime3.sh* script is like *mysql_uptime2.sh* but provides input to *mysql* using a pipe:

```
#!/bin/sh
# mysql_uptime3.sh - report server uptime

echo STATUS | mysql | grep "^Uptime"
```

Some shells support the concept of a "here-document," which serves essentially the same purpose as file input to a command, except that no explicit filename is involved. (In other words, the document is located "right here" in the script, not stored in an external file.) To provide input to a command using a here-document, use the following syntax:

```
command <<MARKER
input line 1
input line 2
input line 3
...
MARKER
```

<<MARKER signals the beginning of the input and indicates the marker symbol to look for at the end of the input. The symbol that you use for MARKER is relatively arbitrary,

but should be some distinctive identifier that does not occur in the input given to the command.

Here-documents are a useful alternative to the -e option when you need to specify a lengthy statement or multiple statements as input. In such cases, when -e becomes awkward to use, a here-document is more convenient and easier to write. Suppose that you have a log table `log_tbl` that contains a column `date_added` to indicate when each row was added. A statement to report the number of rows that were added yesterday looks like this:

```
SELECT COUNT(*) As 'New log entries:'
FROM log_tbl
WHERE date_added = DATE_SUB(CURDATE(),INTERVAL 1 DAY);
```

That statement could be specified in a script using -e, but the command line would be difficult to read because the statement is so long. A here-document is a more suitable choice in this case because you can write the statement in more readable form:

```
#!/bin/sh
# new_log_entries.sh - count yesterday's log entries

mysql cookbook <<MYSQL_INPUT
SELECT COUNT(*) As 'New log entries:'
FROM log_tbl
WHERE date_added = DATE_SUB(CURDATE(),INTERVAL 1 DAY);
MYSQL_INPUT
```

When you use -e or here-documents, you can refer to shell variables within the statement input—although the following example demonstrates that it might be best to avoid the practice. Suppose that you have a simple script *count_rows.sh* for counting the rows of any table in the cookbook database:

```
#!/bin/sh
# count_rows.sh - count rows in cookbook database table

# require one argument on the command line
if [ $# -ne 1 ]; then
  echo "Usage: count_rows.sh tbl_name";
  exit 1;
fi

# use argument ($1) in the query string
mysql cookbook <<MYSQL_INPUT
SELECT COUNT(*) AS 'Rows in table:' FROM $1;
MYSQL_INPUT
```

The script uses the $# shell variable, which holds the command-line argument count, and $1, which holds the first argument after the script name. *count_rows.sh* makes sure that exactly one argument was provided, and then uses it as a table name in a row-counting statement. To run the script, invoke it with a table name argument:

```
% ./count_rows.sh limbs
Rows in table:
12
```

Variable substitution can be helpful for constructing statements, but you should use this capability with caution. If your script can be executed by other users on your system, someone can invoke it with malicious intent as follows:

```
% ./count_rows.sh "limbs;DROP TABLE limbs"
```

This is a simple form of "SQL injection" attack. After argument substitution, the resulting input to *mysql* looks like this:

```
SELECT COUNT(*) AS 'Rows in table:' FROM limbs;DROP TABLE limbs;
```

This input counts the table rows, and then destroys the table! For this reason, it may be prudent to limit use of variable substitution to your own private scripts. Alternatively, rewrite the script using an API that enables special characters such as ; to be dealt with and rendered harmless. Recipe 2.5 covers techniques for doing this.

Writing shell scripts under Windows

Under Windows, you can run *mysql* from within a batch file (a file with a *.bat* extension). Here is a Windows batch file, *mysql_uptime.bat*, that is similar to the *mysql_uptime.sh* Unix shell script shown earlier:

```
@ECHO OFF
REM mysql_uptime.bat - report server uptime in seconds

mysql --skip-column-names -B -e "SHOW /*!50002 GLOBAL */ STATUS LIKE 'Uptime'"
```

Batch files can be invoked without the *.bat* extension:

```
C:\> mysql_uptime
Uptime  9609
```

Windows scripting has some serious limitations, however. For example, here-documents are not supported, and command argument quoting capabilities are more limited. One way around these problems is to install a more reasonable working environment; see the sidebar "Finding the Windows Command Line Restrictive?"

Finding the Windows Command Line Restrictive?

If you're a Unix user who is comfortable with the shells and utilities that are part of the Unix command-line interface, you probably take for granted some of the commands used in this chapter, such as *grep*, *sed*, and *tr*. These tools are so commonly available on Unix systems that it can be a rude and painful shock to realize that they are nowhere to be found if at some point you find it necessary to work at the console prompt under Windows.

One way to make the Windows command-line environment more palatable is to install Cygnus tools for Windows (Cygwin) or Unix for Windows (UWIN). These packages include some of the more popular Unix shells as well as many of the utilities that Unix users have come to expect. Programming tools such as compilers are available with each package as well. The package distributions may be obtained at the following locations:

http://www.research.att.com/sw/tools/uwin/
http://www.cygwin.com/

These distributions can change the way you use this book under Windows, because they eliminate some of the exceptions where I qualify commands as available under Unix but not Windows. By installing Cygwin or UWIN, many of those distinctions become irrelevant.

## CHAPTER 2

Writing MySQL-Based Programs

2.0 Introduction

This chapter discusses how to write programs that use MySQL. It covers basic application programming interface (API) operations that are fundamental to the programming recipes developed in later chapters. These operations include connecting to the MySQL server, issuing statements, and retrieving the results.

MySQL-based client programs can be written using several languages. The languages covered in this book are Perl, Ruby, PHP, Python, and Java, for which we'll use the interfaces in the following table. Appendix A indicates where to get the software for each interface.

Language	Interface
Perl	Perl DBI
Ruby	Ruby DBI
PHP	PEAR DB
Python	DB-API
Java	JDBC

MySQL client APIs provide the following capabilities, each of which is covered in a section of this chapter:

Connecting to the MySQL server, selecting a database, and disconnecting from the server
> Every program that uses MySQL must first establish a connection to the server, and most programs also select a default database to use. In addition, well-behaved MySQL programs close the connection to the server when they're done with it.

Checking for errors
> Many people write MySQL programs that perform no error checking at all. Such programs are difficult to debug when things go wrong. Any database operation can fail and you should know how to find out when that occurs and why. That

knowledge enables you to take appropriate action such as terminating the program or informing the user of the problem.

Executing SQL statements and retrieving results

The whole point of connecting to a database server is to execute SQL statements. Each API provides at least one way to do this, as well as several methods for processing statements results.

Handling special characters and NULL values in statements

One way to write a statement that refers to specific data values is to embed the values directly in the statement string. However, some characters such as quotes and backslashes have special meaning, and you must take certain precautions when constructing statements containing them. The same is true for NULL values. If you do not handle these properly, your programs may generate SQL statements that are erroneous or that yield unexpected results. If you incorporate data from external sources into queries, you might become open to SQL injection attacks. Most APIs provide a way of writing statements that enables you to refer to data values symbolically. When you execute the statement, you supply the data values separately and the API places them into the statement string after properly encoding any special characters or NULL values.

Identifying NULL values in result sets

NULL values are special not only when you construct statements, but also in results returned from statements. Each API provides a convention for recognizing and dealing with them.

No matter which programming language you use, it's necessary to know how to perform each of the fundamental database API operations, so each operation is shown in all five languages. Seeing how each API handles a given operation should help you see the correspondences between APIs more easily and better understand the recipes shown in the following chapters, even if they're written in a language you don't use very much. (Later chapters usually illustrate recipe implementations using only one or two languages.)

It may seem overwhelming to see each recipe in several languages if you're interested only in one particular API. If so, I advise you to approach the recipes as follows: read just the introductory part that provides the general background, and then go directly to the section for the language in which you're interested. Skip the other languages. Should you develop an interest in writing programs in other languages later, you can always come back and read the other sections then.

This chapter also discusses the following topics, which are not directly part of MySQL APIs but can help you use them more easily:

Writing library files

As you write program after program, you may find that there are certain operations you carry out repeatedly. Library files provide a way to encapsulate the code for these operations so that you can perform them from multiple scripts without including all the code in each script. This reduces code duplication and makes your programs more portable. This section shows how to write a library file for each API that includes a routine for connecting to the server—one operation that every program that uses MySQL must perform. (Later chapters develop additional library routines for other operations.)

Additional techniques for obtaining connection parameters

An early section on establishing connections to the MySQL server relies on connection parameters hardwired into the code. However, there are several other ways to obtain parameters, ranging from storing them in a separate file to allowing the user to specify them at runtime.

To avoid manually typing in the example programs, you should obtain the `recipes` source distribution. (See Appendix A.) Then, when an example says something like "create a file named *xyz* that contains the following information ...," you can just use the corresponding file from the `recipes` distribution. The scripts for this chapter are located under the *api* directory, with the exception of the library files that can be found in the *lib* directory.

The primary table used for examples in this chapter is named `profile`. It first appears in Recipe 2.4, which you should know in case you skip around in the chapter and wonder where it came from. See also the section at the very end of the chapter about resetting the `profile` table to a known state for use in later chapters.

 The programs discussed here can be run from the command line. For instructions on invoking programs for each of the languages covered here, see Appendix B.

Assumptions

To use the material in this chapter most effectively, you should make sure that the following assumptions are satisfied:

- MySQL programming support must be installed for any language processors that you plan to use. If you need to install any of the APIs, see Appendix A.

- You should already have set up a MySQL user account for accessing the server and a database to use for trying statements. As described in Recipe 1.1, the examples in this book use a MySQL account that has a username and password of `cbuser` and `cbpass`, and we'll connect to a MySQL server running on the local host to access a database named `cookbook`. If you need to create the account or the database, see the instructions in that recipe.

- The discussion here assumes a certain basic understanding of the API languages. If a recipe uses language constructs with which you're not familiar, consult a good general text that covers that language. Appendix D lists some resources that may be helpful.

- Proper execution of some of the programs might require that you set certain environment variables. See Appendix B, for general information about setting environment variables, and Recipe 2.3 for details about environment variables that apply specifically to searching for library files.

MySQL Client API Architecture

One thing that all MySQL client programs have in common, no matter which language you use, is that they connect to the server using some kind of application programming interface that implements a communications protocol. This is true regardless of the program's purpose, whether it's a command-line utility, a job that runs automatically on a predetermined schedule, or a script that's used from a web server to make database content available over the Web. MySQL APIs provide a standard way for you, the application developer, to express database operations. Each API translates your instructions into something the MySQL server can understand.

The server itself speaks a low-level protocol that I call the *raw protocol*. This is the level at which direct communication takes place over the network between the server and its clients. A client establishes a connection to the port on which the server is listening and communicates with it by speaking the client-server protocol in its most basic terms. (Basically, the client fills in data structures and shoves them over the network.) It's not productive to attempt to communicate directly with the server at this level, nor to write programs that do so. The raw protocol is a binary communication stream that is efficient, but not particularly easy to use, a fact that usually deters developers from attempting to write programs that talk to the server this way. More convenient access to the MySQL server is available through a programming interface that is written at a level above that of the raw protocol. The interface handles the details of the raw protocol on behalf of your programs. It provides calls for operations such as connecting to the server, sending statements, retrieving the results of statements, and obtaining statement status information.

Most MySQL APIs do not implement the raw protocol directly. Instead, they are linked to and rely on the MySQL client library that is included with MySQL distributions. The client library is written in C and thus provides the basis of an interface for communicating with the server from within C programs. The majority of the standard clients in the MySQL distribution are written in C and use this API. You can use it in your own programs, too, and should consider doing so if you want the most efficient programs possible. However, most third-party application development is not done in C. Instead, the C API is most often used indirectly as an embedded library within other languages. This is how MySQL communication is implemented for Perl, Ruby, PHP, Python, and several other languages. The MySQL API for these higher-level languages is written as a "wrapper" around the C routines, which are linked to the language processor.

The benefit of this approach is that it allows a language processor to talk to the MySQL server on your behalf using the C routines while providing an interface in which you specify database operations more conveniently. For example, scripting languages such as Perl or Ruby typically make it easy to manipulate text without having to allocate string buffers or dispose of them when you're done with them the way you do in C. Higher-level languages let you concentrate more on what you're trying to do and less on the details that you must think about when you're writing directly in C.

This book doesn't cover the C API in any detail because we never use it directly; the programs developed in this book use higher-level interfaces that are built on top of the C API. However, if you'd like to write MySQL client programs in C, the following sources of information may be helpful:

- The *MySQL Reference Manual* contains a chapter that describes all the C API functions. You should also have a look at the source for the standard MySQL clients provided with the MySQL source distribution that are written in C. Source distributions and the manual both are available at the MySQL web site, *http:// dev.mysql.com/*, and you can obtain the manual in printed form from MySQL Press.

- The book *MySQL* by Paul DuBois (Sams) contains reference material for the C API, and also includes a chapter that provides detailed tutorial instructions for writing MySQL programs in C. The chapter is available online at *http://www.kitebird.com/ mysql-book/*. The source code for the sample programs discussed in the chapter is available from the same site for you to study and use. Those programs were deliberately written for instructional purposes, so you may find them easier to understand than the standard clients in the MySQL source distribution.

Java interfaces for MySQL do not use the C client library. They implement the raw protocol directly but map protocol operations onto the JDBC interface. You write your Java programs using standard JDBC calls, and JDBC passes your requests for database operations to the lower-level MySQL interface, which converts them to operations that communicate with the MySQL server using the raw protocol.

The MySQL programming interfaces used in this book share a common design principle: they all use a two-level architecture. The top level of this architecture provides database-independent methods that implement database access in a portable way that's the same no matter which database management system you're using, be it MySQL, PostgreSQL, Oracle, or whatever. The lower level consists of a set of drivers, each of which implements the details for a particular database system. The two-level architecture enables application programs to use an abstract interface that is not tied to the details involved with accessing any particular database server. This enhances portability of your programs because you just select a different lower-level driver to use a different type of database. That's the theory, at least. In practice, perfect portability can be somewhat elusive:

- The interface methods provided by the top level of the architecture are consistent regardless of the driver you use, but it's still possible to issue SQL statements that contain constructs supported only by a particular server. For MySQL, a good example is the SHOW statement that provides information about database and table structure. If you use SHOW with a non-MySQL server, an error is the likely result.

- Lower-level drivers often extend the abstract interface to make it more convenient to get at database-specific features. For example, the MySQL driver for Perl DBI makes the most recent AUTO_INCREMENT value available as an attribute of the database handle so that you can access it as `$dbh->{mysql_insertid}`. These features often make it easier to write a program initially, but at the same time make it less portable and require some rewriting should you port the program to use with another database system.

Despite these factors that compromise portability to some extent, the general portability characteristics of the two-level architecture provide significant benefits for MySQL developers.

Another thing that the APIs used in this book have in common is that they are object-oriented. Whether you write in Perl, Ruby, PHP, Python, or Java, the operation that connects to the MySQL server returns a value that enables you to process statements in an object-oriented manner. For example, when you connect to the database server, you get a database connection object that you use to further interact with the server. The interfaces also provide other objects, such as objects for statements, result sets, or metadata.

Now let's see how to use these programming interfaces to perform the most fundamental MySQL operations: connecting to and disconnecting from the server.

2.1 Connecting, Selecting a Database, and Disconnecting

Problem

You need to establish a connection to the server to access a database, and to shut down the connection when you're done.

Solution

Each API provides routines for connecting and disconnecting. The connection routines require that you provide parameters specifying the hostname that is running the MySQL server and the MySQL account that you want to use. You can also select a default database.

Discussion

The programs in this section show how to perform three fundamental operations that are common to the vast majority of MySQL programs:

Establishing a connection to the MySQL server
  Every program that uses MySQL does this, no matter which API you use. The details on specifying connection parameters vary between APIs, and some APIs provide more flexibility than others. However, there are many common elements.

For example, you must specify the host that is running the server, as well as the username and password for the MySQL account to use for accessing the server.

Selecting a database

Most MySQL programs select a default database.

Disconnecting from the server

Each API provides a way to close an open connection. It's best to close the connection as soon as you're done using the server so that it can free up any resources that are allocated to servicing the connection. Otherwise, if your program performs additional computations after accessing the server, the connection will be held open longer than necessary. It's also preferable to close the connection explicitly. If a program simply terminates without closing the connection, the MySQL server eventually notices, but shutting down the connection explicitly enables the server to perform an immediate orderly close on its end.

The example programs for each API in this section show how to connect to the server, select the **cookbook** database, and disconnect.

On occasion you might want to write a MySQL program that doesn't select a database. This could be the case if you plan to issue a statement that doesn't require a default database, such as `SHOW VARIABLES` or `SELECT VERSION( )`. Or perhaps you're writing an interactive program that connects to the server and enables the user to specify the database after the connection has been made. To cover such situations, the discussion for each API also indicates how to connect without selecting any default database.

Perl

To write MySQL scripts in Perl, you should have the DBI module installed, as well as the MySQL-specific driver module, DBD::mysql. Appendix A contains information on getting these modules if they're not already installed.

Here is a simple Perl script that connects to the **cookbook** database and then disconnects:

```perl
#!/usr/bin/perl
# connect.pl - connect to the MySQL server

use strict;
use warnings;
use DBI;

my $dsn = "DBI:mysql:host=localhost;database=cookbook";
my $dbh = DBI->connect ($dsn, "cbuser", "cbpass")
            or die "Cannot connect to server\n";
print "Connected\n";
$dbh->disconnect ();
print "Disconnected\n";
```

To try the script, create a file named *connect.pl* that contains the preceding code and run it from the command line. (Under Unix, you may need to change the path on the first line of the script if your Perl program is located somewhere other than */usr/bin/*

perl.) You should see the program print two lines of output indicating that it connected and disconnected successfully:

```
% connect.pl
Connected
Disconnected
```

If you need background on running Perl programs, see Appendix B.

The `use strict` line turns on strict variable checking and causes Perl to complain about any variables that are used without having been declared first. This is a sensible precaution because it helps find errors that might otherwise go undetected.

The `use warnings` line turns on warning mode so that Perl produces warnings for any questionable constructs. Our example script has no such constructs, but it's a good idea to get in the habit of enabling warnings to catch problems that occur during the script development process. `use warnings` is similar to specifying the Perl -w command-line option, but provides more control over which warnings you want to see. (Execute a `perldoc warnings` command for more information.)

The `use DBI` statement tells Perl that the program needs to load the DBI module. It's unnecessary to load the MySQL driver module (DBD::mysql) explicitly, because DBI does that itself when the script connects to the database server.

The next two lines establish the connection to MySQL by setting up a data source name (DSN) and calling the DBI `connect( )` method. The arguments to `connect( )` are the DSN, the MySQL username and password, and any connection attributes you want to specify. The DSN is required. The other arguments are optional, although usually it's necessary to supply a username and password.

The DSN specifies which database driver to use and other options indicating where to connect. For MySQL programs, the DSN has the format `DBI:mysql:options`. The second colon in the DSN is *not* optional, even if you specify no options.

The three DSN components have the following meanings:

- The first component is always `DBI`. It's not case-sensitive; `dbi` or `Dbi` would do just as well.

- The second component tells DBI which database driver to use. For MySQL, the name must be `mysql`, and it *is* case-sensitive. You can't use `MySQL`, `MYSQL`, or any other variation.

- The third component, if present, is a semicolon-separated list of *name=value* pairs that specify additional connection options. The order of any option pairs you provide doesn't matter. For our purposes here, the two most relevant options are `host` and `database`. They specify the hostname where the MySQL server is running and the default database you want to use.

Given this information, the DSN for connecting to the `cookbook` database on the local host *localhost* looks like this:

```
DBI:mysql:host=localhost;database=cookbook
```

If you leave out the host option, its default value is localhost. Thus, these two DSNs are equivalent:

```
DBI:mysql:host=localhost;database=cookbook
DBI:mysql:database=cookbook
```

If you omit the database option, the connect( ) operation selects no default database.

The second and third arguments of the connect( ) call are your MySQL username and password. You can also provide a fourth argument following the password to specify attributes that control DBI's behavior when errors occur. With no attributes, DBI by default prints error messages when errors occur but does not terminate your script. That's why *connect.pl* checks whether connect( ) returns undef to indicate failure:

```
my $dbh = DBI->connect ($dsn, "cbuser", "cbpass")
            or die "Cannot connect to server\n";
```

Other error-handling strategies are possible. For example, you can tell DBI to terminate the script automatically when an error occurs in a DBI call by disabling the PrintError attribute and enabling RaiseError instead. Then you don't have to check for errors yourself (although you also lose the ability to decide how your program will recover from errors):

```
my $dbh = DBI->connect ($dsn, $user_name, $password,
            {PrintError => 0, RaiseError => 1});
```

Recipe 2.2 discusses error handling further.

Another common attribute is AutoCommit, which sets the connection's auto-commit mode for transactions. In MySQL, this is enabled by default for new connections, but we'll set it from this point on to make the initial connection state explicit:

```
my $dbh = DBI->connect ($dsn, $user_name, $password,
            {PrintError => 0, RaiseError => 1, AutoCommit => 1});
```

As shown, the fourth argument to connect( ) is a reference to a hash of connection attribute name/value pairs. An alternative way of writing this code is as follows:

```
my %conn_attrs = (PrintError => 0, RaiseError => 1, AutoCommit => 1);
my $dbh = DBI->connect ($dsn, $user_name, $password, \%conn_attrs);
```

Use whichever style you prefer. The scripts in this book use the %conn_attr hash to make the connect( ) call simpler to read.

Assuming that connect( )succeeds, it returns a database handle that contains information about the state of the connection. (In DBI parlance, references to objects are called *handles*.) Later we'll see other handles such as statement handles, which are associated with particular statements. Perl DBI scripts in this book conventionally use $dbh and $sth to signify database and statement handles.

Additional connection parameters. For *localhost* connections, you can provide a mysql_socket option in the DSN to specify the path to the Unix domain socket:

```
my $dsn = "DBI:mysql:host=localhost;database=cookbook"
        . ";mysql_socket=/var/tmp/mysql.sock";
```

For non-*localhost* (TCP/IP) connections, you can provide a `port` option to specify the port number:

```
my $dsn = "DBI:mysql:host=mysql.example.com;database=cookbook"
        . ";port=3307";
```

Ruby

To write MySQL scripts in Ruby, you should have the DBI module installed, as well as the MySQL-specific driver module. Both are included in the Ruby DBI distribution. Appendix A contains information on getting Ruby DBI if it's not already installed.

Here is a simple Ruby script that connects to the cookbook database and then disconnects:

```
#!/usr/bin/ruby -w
# connect.rb - connect to the MySQL server

require "dbi"

begin
  dsn = "DBI:Mysql:host=localhost;database=cookbook"
  dbh = DBI.connect(dsn, "cbuser", "cbpass")
  puts "Connected"
rescue
  puts "Cannot connect to server"
  exit(1)
end
dbh.disconnect
puts "Disconnected"
```

To try the script, create a file named *connect.rb* that contains the preceding code. (Under Unix, you may need to change the path on the first line of the script if your Ruby program is located somewhere other than */usr/bin/ruby*.) You should see the program print two lines of output indicating that it connected and disconnected successfully:

```
% connect.rb
Connected
Disconnected
```

If you need background on running Ruby programs, see Appendix B.

The `-w` option turns on warning mode so that Ruby produces warnings for any questionable constructs. Our example script has no such constructs, but it's a good idea to get in the habit of using `-w` to catch problems that occur during the script development process.

The `require` statement tells Ruby that the program needs to load the DBI module. It's unnecessary to load the MySQL driver module explicitly, because DBI does that itself when the script connects to the database server.

The connection is established by passing a data source name and the MySQL username and password to the `connect( )` method. The DSN is required. The other arguments are optional, although usually it's necessary to supply a username and password.

The DSN specifies which database driver to use and other options that indicate where to connect. For MySQL programs, the DSN typically has one of these formats:

```
DBI:Mysql:db_name:host_name
DBI:Mysql:name=value;name=value ...
```

The DSN components have the following meanings:

- The first component is always `DBI` or `dbi`.
- The second component tells DBI which database driver to use. For MySQL, the name is `Mysql`.
- The third component, if present, is either a database name and hostname separated by a colon, or a semicolon-separated list of *name=value* pairs that specify additional connection options. The order of any option pairs you provide doesn't matter. For our purposes here, the two most relevant options are `host` and `database`. They specify the hostname of the server on which MySQL is running and the default database you want to use. As with Perl DBI, the second colon in the DSN is *not* optional, even if you specify no options.

Given this information, the DSN for connecting to the `cookbook` database on the local host *localhost* looks like this:

```
DBI:Mysql:host=localhost;database=cookbook
```

If you leave out the `host` option, its default value is `localhost`. Thus, these two DSNs are equivalent:

```
DBI:Mysql:host=localhost;database=cookbook
DBI:Mysql:database=cookbook
```

If you omit the `database` option, the `connect( )` operation selects no default database.

Assuming that `connect( )` succeeds, it returns a database handle that contains information about the state of the connection. Ruby DBI scripts in this book conventionally use `dbh` to signify a database handle.

If the `connect( )` method fails, there is no special return value to check for. Ruby programs raise exceptions when problems occur. To handle errors, put the statements that might fail inside a `begin` block, and use a `rescue` clause that contains the error-handling code. Exceptions that occur at the top level of a script (that is, outside of any `begin` block) are caught by the default exception handler, which prints a stack trace and exits.

Additional connection parameters. For *localhost* connections, you can provide a `socket` option in the DSN to specify the path to the Unix domain socket:

```
dsn = "DBI:Mysql:host=localhost;database=cookbook" +
        ";socket=/var/tmp/mysql.sock"
```

For non-*localhost* (TCP/IP) connections, you can provide a **port** option to specify the port number:

```
dsn = "DBI:Mysql:host=mysql.example.com;database=cookbook" +
      ";port=3307"
```

PHP

To write PHP scripts that use MySQL, your PHP interpreter must have MySQL support compiled in. If it doesn't, your scripts will be unable to connect to your MySQL server. Should that occur, check the instructions included with your PHP distribution to see how to enable MySQL support.

PHP actually has two extensions that enable the use of MySQL. The first, **mysql**, is the original MySQL extension. It provides a set of functions that have names beginning with **mysql_**. The second, **mysqli**, or "MySQL improved," provides functions with names that begin with **mysqli_**. For purposes of this book, you can use either extension, although I recommend **mysqli**.

In any case, PHP scripts in this book won't use either extension directly. Instead, they use the DB module from the PHP Extension and Add-on Repository (PEAR). The PEAR DB module provides an interface to whichever underlying MySQL extension that you decide to use. This means that in addition to whichever PHP MySQL extension you choose, it's also necessary to have PEAR installed. Appendix A contains information on getting PEAR if it's not already installed.

PHP scripts usually are written for use with a web server. I'll assume that if you're going to use PHP that way here, you can simply copy PHP scripts into your server's document tree, request them from your browser, and they will execute. For example, if you run Apache as the web server on the host *localhost* and you install a PHP script *myscript.php* at the top level of the Apache document tree, you should be able to access the script by requesting this URL:

```
http://localhost/myscript.php
```

This book uses the *.php* extension (suffix) for PHP script filenames, so your web server must be configured to recognize the *.php* extension. Otherwise, when you request a PHP script from your browser, the server will simply send the literal text of the script and that is what you'll see in your browser window. You don't want this to happen, particularly if the script contains the username and password that you use for connecting to MySQL. For information about configuring Apache for use with PHP, see Recipe 17.2.

PHP scripts often are written as a mixture of HTML and PHP code, with the PHP code embedded between the special `<?php` and `?>` tags. Here is a simple example:

```
<html>
<head><title>A simple page</title></head>
<body>
<p>
<?php
```

```
    print ("I am PHP code, hear me roar!\n");
  ?>
  </p>
  </body>
  </html>
```

PHP can be configured to recognize "short" tags as well, which are written as `<?` and `?>`. This book does not assume that you have short tags enabled, so none of the PHP scripts shown here use them.

Here is a simple PHP script that connects to the cookbook database and then disconnects:

```
<?php
# connect.php - connect to the MySQL server

require_once "DB.php";

$dsn = "mysqli://cbuser:cbpass@localhost/cookbook";
$conn =& DB::connect ($dsn);
if (PEAR::isError ($conn))
  die ("Cannot connect to server\n");
print ("Connected\n");
$conn->disconnect ();
print ("Disconnected\n");
?>
```

For brevity, when I show examples consisting entirely of PHP code, typically I'll omit the enclosing `<?php` and `?>` tags. (Thus, if you see no tags in a PHP example, assume that `<?php` and `?>` surround the entire block of code that is shown.) Examples that switch between HTML and PHP code do include the tags, to make it clear what is PHP code and what is not.

The `require_once` statement accesses the *DB.php* file that is required to use the PEAR DB module. `require_once` is just one of several PHP file-inclusion statements:

- `include` instructs PHP to read the named file. `require` is like `include` except that PHP reads the file even if the `require` occurs inside a control structure that never executes (such as an `if` block for which the condition is never `true`).

- `include_once` and `require_once` are like `include` and `require` except that if the file has already been read, its contents are not processed again. This is useful for avoiding multiple-declaration problems that can easily occur in situations where library files include other library files.

`$dsn` is the data source name that indicates how to connect to the database server. Its general syntax is as follows:

```
phptype://user_name:password@host_name/db_name
```

The *phptype* value is the PHP driver type. For MySQL, it should be either `mysql` or `mysqli` to indicate which MySQL extension to use. You can choose either one, as long as your PHP interpreter has the chosen extension compiled in.

The PEAR DB `connect( )` method uses the DSN to connect to MySQL. If the connection attempt succeeds, `connect( )` returns a connection object that can be used to access other MySQL-related methods. PHP scripts in this book conventionally use `$conn` to signify connection objects.

If the connection attempt fails, `connect( )` returns an error object. To determine whether the returned object represents an error, use the `PEAR::isError( )` method.

Note that the assignment of the `connect( )` result uses the `=&` operator and not the `=` operator. `=&` assigns a reference to the return value, whereas `=` creates a copy of the value. In this context, `=` would create another object that is not needed. (PHP scripts in this book generally use `=&` for assigning the result of connection attempts, but see Recipe 20.3 for one instance that uses `=` to make sure that the assigned connection object persists longer than the function call in which it occurs.)

The last part of the DSN shown in the preceding example is the database name. To connect without selecting a default database, just omit it from the end of the DSN:

```
$dsn = "mysqli://cbuser:cbpass@localhost";
$conn =& DB::connect ($dsn);
```

To try the *connect.php* script, copy it to your web server's document tree and request it using your browser. Alternatively, if you have a standalone version of the PHP interpreter that can be run from the command line, you can try the script without a web server or browser:

```
% php connect.php
Connected
Disconnected
```

If you need background on running PHP programs, see Appendix B.

As an alternative to specifying the DSN in string format, you can provide the connection parameters using an array:

```
$dsn = array
(
  "phptype"  => "mysqli",
  "username" => "cbuser",
  "password" => "cbpass",
  "hostspec" => "localhost",
  "database" => "cookbook"
);
$conn =& DB::connect ($dsn);
if (PEAR::isError ($conn))
  print ("Cannot connect to server\n");
```

To connect without selecting a default database using an array-format DSN, omit the `database` member from the array.

Additional connection parameters. To use a specific Unix domain socket file or TCP/IP port number, modify the parameters used at connect time. The following two examples use an array-format DSN to do this.

For *localhost* connections, you can specify a pathname for the Unix domain socket file by including a `socket` member in the DSN array:

```
$dsn = array
(
  "phptype"  => "mysqli",
  "username" => "cbuser",
  "password" => "cbpass",
  "hostspec" => "localhost",
  "socket"   => "/var/tmp/mysql.sock",
  "database" => "cookbook"
);
$conn =& DB::connect ($dsn);
if (PEAR::isError ($conn))
  print ("Cannot connect to server\n");
```

For non-*localhost* (TCP/IP) connections, you can specify the port number by including a `port` member in the DSN array:

```
$dsn = array
(
  "phptype"  => "mysqli",
  "username" => "cbuser",
  "password" => "cbpass",
  "hostspec" => "mysql.example.com",
  "port"     => 3307,
  "database" => "cookbook"
);
$conn =& DB::connect ($dsn);
if (PEAR::isError ($conn))
  print ("Cannot connect to server\n");
```

You can use the PHP initialization file (typically named *php.ini*) to specify a default hostname, username, password, socket path, or port number. For the `mysql` extension, set the values of the `mysql.default_host`, `mysql.default_user`, `mysql.default_pass word`, `mysql.default_socket`, or `mysql.default_port` configuration variables. For `mysqli`, the corresponding variable names begin with `mysqli` (and the password variable is `mysql_default_pw`). These variables affect PHP scripts globally: for scripts that do not specify those parameters, the defaults from *php.ini* are used.

Python

To write MySQL programs in Python, you need the MySQLdb module that provides MySQL connectivity for Python's DB-API interface. Appendix A, contains information on getting MySQLdb if it's not already installed.

To use the DB-API interface, import the database driver module that you want to use (which is MySQLdb for MySQL programs). Then create a database connection object by calling the driver's `connect( )` method. This object provides access to other DB-API methods, such as the `close( )` method that severs the connection to the database server. Here is a short Python program, *connect.py*, that illustrates these operations:

```
#!/usr/bin/python
# connect.py - connect to the MySQL server

import sys
import MySQLdb

try:
  conn = MySQLdb.connect (db = "cookbook",
                          host = "localhost",
                          user = "cbuser",
                          passwd = "cbpass")
  print "Connected"
except:
  print "Cannot connect to server"
  sys.exit (1)

conn.close ()
print "Disconnected"
```

To try the script, create a file named *connect.py* that contains the preceding code. (Under Unix, you may need to change the path on the first line of the script if your Python program is located somewhere other than */usr/bin/python*.) You should see the program print two lines of output indicating that it connected and disconnected successfully:

```
% connect.py
Connected
Disconnected
```

If you need background on running Python programs, see Appendix B.

The import lines give the script access to the sys module (needed for the sys.exit( ) method) and to the MySQLdb module. Then the script attempts to establish a connection to the MySQL server by calling connect( ) to obtain a connection object, conn. Python scripts in this book conventionally use conn to signify connection objects.

If the connect( ) method fails, there is no special return value to check for. Python programs raise exceptions when problems occur. To handle errors, put the statements that might fail inside a try statement and use an except clause that contains the error-handling code. Exceptions that occur at the top level of a script (that is, outside of any try statement) are caught by the default exception handler, which prints a stack trace and exits.

Because the connect( ) call uses named arguments, their order does not matter. If you omit the host argument from the connect( ) call, its default value is localhost. If you omit the db argument or pass a db value of "" (the empty string), the connect( ) operation selects no default database. If you pass a value of None, however, the call will fail.

Additional connection parameters. For *localhost* connections, you can provide a unix_socket parameter to specify the path to the Unix domain socket file:

```
conn = MySQLdb.connect (db = "cookbook",
                        host = "localhost",
                        unix_socket = "/var/tmp/mysql.sock",
```

```
                              user = "cbuser",
                              passwd = "cbpass")
```

For non-*localhost* (TCP/IP) connections, you can provide a `port` parameter to specify the port number:

```
conn = MySQLdb.connect (db = "cookbook",
                        host = "mysql.example.com",
                        port = 3307,
                        user = "cbuser",
                        passwd = "cbpass")
```

Java

Database programs in Java are written using the JDBC interface, together with a driver for the particular database engine you want to access. That is, the JDBC architecture provides a generic interface used in conjunction with a database-specific driver. Java is similar to Ruby and Python in that you don't test specific method calls for return values that indicate an error. Instead, you provide handlers to be called when exceptions are thrown.

Java programming requires a software development kit (SDK), and you will need to set your `JAVA_HOME` environment variable to the location where your SDK is installed. To write MySQL-based Java programs, you'll also need a MySQL-specific JDBC driver. Programs in this book use MySQL Connector/J, the driver provided by MySQL AB. Appendix A, has information on getting MySQL Connector/J if it's not already installed. Appendix B, has information about obtaining an SDK and setting `JAVA_HOME`.

The following Java program, *Connect.java*, illustrates how to connect to and disconnect from the MySQL server, and select `cookbook` as the default database:

```java
// Connect.java - connect to the MySQL server

import java.sql.*;

public class Connect
{
  public static void main (String[] args)
  {
    Connection conn = null;
    String url = "jdbc:mysql://localhost/cookbook";
    String userName = "cbuser";
    String password = "cbpass";

    try
    {
      Class.forName ("com.mysql.jdbc.Driver").newInstance ();
      conn = DriverManager.getConnection (url, userName, password);
      System.out.println ("Connected");
    }
    catch (Exception e)
    {
      System.err.println ("Cannot connect to server");
      System.exit (1);
```

```
      }
      if (conn != null)
      {
        try
        {
          conn.close ();
          System.out.println ("Disconnected");
        }
        catch (Exception e) { /* ignore close errors */ }
      }
    }
  }
```

The `import java.sql.*` statement references the classes and interfaces that provide access to the data types you use to manage different aspects of your interaction with the database server. These are required for all JDBC programs.

Connecting to the server is a two-step process. First, register the database driver with JDBC by calling `Class.forName( )`. The `Class.forName( )` method requires a driver name; for MySQL Connector/J, use `com.mysql.jdbc.Driver`. Then call `DriverManager.getConnection( )` to initiate the connection and obtain a `Connection` object that maintains information about the state of the connection. Java programs in this book conventionally use `conn` to signify connection objects.

`DriverManager.getConnection( )` takes three arguments: a URL that describes where to connect and the database to use, the MySQL username, and the password. The URL string has this format:

    jdbc:*driver*://*host_name*/*db_name*

This format follows the Java convention that the URL for connecting to a network resource begins with a *protocol designator*. For JDBC programs, the protocol is `jdbc`, and you'll also need a *subprotocol designator* that specifies the driver name (`mysql`, for MySQL programs). Many parts of the connection URL are optional, but the leading protocol and subprotocol designators are not. If you omit *host_name*, the default host value is `localhost`. If you omit the database name, the connect operation selects no default database. However, you should not omit any of the slashes in any case. For example, to connect to the local host without selecting a default database, the URL is:

    jdbc:mysql:///

To try the program, compile it and execute it. The `class` statement indicates the program's name, which in this case is `Connect`. The name of the file containing the program should match this name and include a *.java* extension, so the filename for the program is *Connect.java.*[*] Compile the program using *javac*:

    % **javac Connect.java**

If you prefer a different Java compiler, just substitute its name for *javac*.

---

[*] If you make a copy of *Connect.java* to use as the basis for a new program, you'll need to change the class name in the `class` statement to match the name of your new file.

The Java compiler generates compiled byte code to produce a class file named *Connect.class*. Use the *java* program to run the class file (specified without the *.class* extension):

```
% java Connect
Connected
Disconnected
```

You might need to set your CLASSPATH environment variable before the example program will compile and run. The value of CLASSPATH should include at least your current directory (.) and the path to the MySQL Connector/J JDBC driver. If you need background on running Java programs or setting CLASSPATH, see Appendix B.

Beware of Class.forName( )!

The example program *Connect.java* registers the JDBC driver like this:

```
Class.forName ("com.mysql.jdbc.Driver").newInstance ();
```

You're supposed to be able to register drivers without invoking newInstance( ), like so:

```
Class.forName ("com.mysql.jdbc.Driver");
```

However, that call doesn't work for some Java implementations, so be sure to use newInstance( ), or you may find yourself enacting the Java motto, "write once, debug everywhere."

Some JDBC drivers (MySQL Connector/J among them) allow you to specify the username and password as parameters at the end of the URL. In this case, you omit the second and third arguments of the getConnection( ) call. Using that URL style, the code that establishes the connection in the example program can be written like this:

```
// connect using username and password included in URL
Connection conn = null;
String url = "jdbc:mysql://localhost/cookbook?user=cbuser&password=cbpass";

try
{
  Class.forName ("com.mysql.jdbc.Driver").newInstance ();
  conn = DriverManager.getConnection (url);
  System.out.println ("Connected");
}
```

The character that separates the user and password parameters should be &, not ;.

Additional connection parameters. MySQL Connector/J does not support Unix domain socket file connections, so even connections for which the hostname is localhost are made via TCP/IP. You can specify an explicit port number by adding *:port_num* to the hostname in the connection URL:

```
String url = "jdbc:mysql://mysql.example.com:3307/cookbook";
```

2.2 Checking for Errors

Problem

Something went wrong with your program, and you don't know what.

Solution

Everyone has problems getting programs to work correctly. But if you don't anticipate difficulties by checking for errors, you make the job a lot harder. Add some error-checking code so that your programs can help you figure out what went wrong.

Discussion

After working through Recipe 2.1, you now know how to connect to the MySQL server. It's also a good idea to know how to check for errors and how to retrieve specific error information from the API, so that's what we'll cover next. You're probably anxious to see how to do more interesting things (such as issuing statements and getting back the results), but error checking is fundamentally important. Programs sometimes fail, especially during development, and if you don't know how to determine why failures occur, you'll be flying blind.

When errors occur, MySQL provides three values:

- A MySQL-specific error number
- A MySQL-specific descriptive text error message
- An SQLSTATE error code that is a five-character value defined according to the ANSI and ODBC standards

Various sections in this recipe in this section show how to access this information. Most of the later recipes in this book that display error information print only the MySQL-specific values, but the recipes here show how to access the SQLSTATE value as well, for those APIs that expose it.

The example programs demonstrate how to check for errors but will in fact execute without any problems if your MySQL account is set up properly. Thus, you may have to modify the examples slightly to force errors to occur so that the error-handling statements are triggered. That is easy to do. For example, you can change a connection-establishment call to supply a bad password.

A general debugging aid that is not specific to any API is to check the MySQL server's query log to see what statements the server actually is receiving. (This requires that you have query logging enabled and that you have access to the log.) The query log often will show you that a statement is malformed in a particular way and give you a clue that your program is not constructing the proper statement string. If you're running a script under a web server and it fails, check the web server's error log.

Don't Shoot Yourself in the Foot: Check for Errors

The principle that you should check for errors is not so obvious or widely appreciated as one might hope. Many messages posted on MySQL-related mailing lists are requests for help with programs that fail for reasons unknown to the people that wrote them. In a surprising number of cases, the reason these people are mystified by their programs is that they put in *no* error checking, and thus gave themselves no way to know that there was a problem or to find out what it was! You cannot help yourself this way. Plan for failure by checking for errors so that you can take appropriate action when they occur.

Perl

The DBI module provides two attributes that control what happens when DBI method invocations fail:

- `PrintError`, if enabled, causes DBI to print an error message using `warn( )`.
- `RaiseError`, if enabled, causes DBI to print an error message using `die( )`. This terminates your script.

By default, `PrintError` is enabled, and `RaiseError` is disabled, so a script continues executing after printing a message if an error occurs. Either or both attributes can be specified in the `connect( )` call. Setting an attribute to 1 or 0 enables or disables it, respectively. To specify either or both attributes, pass them in a hash reference as the fourth argument to the `connect( )` call.

The following code sets only the `AutoCommit` attribute and uses the default settings for the error-handling attributes. If the `connect( )` call fails, this results in a warning message, but the script continues to execute:

```
my %conn_attrs = (AutoCommit => 1);
my $dbh = DBI->connect ($dsn, "cbuser", "cbpass", \%conn_attrs);
```

However, because you really can't do much if the connection attempt fails, it's often prudent to exit instead after DBI prints a message:

```
my %conn_attrs = (AutoCommit => 1);
my $dbh = DBI->connect ($dsn, "cbuser", "cbpass", \%conn_attrs)
            or exit;
```

To print your own error messages, leave `RaiseError` disabled, and disable `PrintError` as well. Then test the results of DBI method calls yourself. When a method fails, the `$DBI::err`, `$DBI::errstr`, and `$DBI::state` variables contain the MySQL error number, a descriptive error string, and the SQLSTATE value, respectively:

```
my %conn_attrs = (PrintError => 0, AutoCommit => 1);
my $dbh = DBI->connect ($dsn, "cbuser", "cbpass", \%conn_attrs)
            or die "Connection error: "
                . "$DBI::errstr ($DBI::err/$DBI::state)\n";
```

If no error occurs, $DBI::err will be 0 or undef, $DBI::errstr will be the empty string or undef, and $DBI::state will be empty or 00000.

When you check for errors, access these variables immediately after invoking the DBI method that sets them. If you invoke another method before using them, their values will be reset.

The default settings (PrintError enabled, RaiseError disabled) are not so useful if you're printing your own messages. In this case, DBI prints a message automatically, and then your script prints its own message. This is at best redundant, and at worst confusing to the person using the script.

If you enable RaiseError, you can call DBI methods without checking for return values that indicate errors. If a method fails, DBI prints an error and terminates your script. If the method returns, you can assume it succeeded. This is the easiest approach for script writers: let DBI do all the error checking! However, if PrintError and RaiseError both are enabled, DBI may call warn( ) and die( ) in succession, resulting in error messages being printed twice. To avoid this problem, it's best to disable Print Error whenever you enable RaiseError. That's the approach generally used in this book, as illustrated here:

```
my %conn_attrs = (PrintError => 0, RaiseError => 1, AutoCommit => 1);
my $dbh = DBI->connect ($dsn, "cbuser", "cbpass", \%conn_attrs);
```

If you don't want the all-or-nothing behavior of enabling RaiseError for automatic error checking versus having to do all your own checking, you can adopt a mixed approach. Individual handles have PrintError and RaiseError attributes that can be enabled or disabled selectively. For example, you can enable RaiseError globally by turning it on when you call connect( ), and then disable it selectively on a per-handle basis. Suppose that you have a script that reads the username and password from the command-line arguments, and then loops while the user enters statements to be executed. In this case, you'd probably want DBI to die and print the error message automatically if the connection fails (there's not much you can do if the user doesn't provide a valid name and password). After connecting, on the other hand, you wouldn't want the script to exit just because the user enters a syntactically invalid statement. It would be better for the script to trap the error, print a message, and then loop to get the next statement. The following code shows how this can be done. The do( ) method used in the example executes a statement and returns undef to indicate an error:

```
my $user_name = shift (@ARGV);
my $password = shift (@ARGV);
my %conn_attrs = (PrintError => 0, RaiseError => 1, AutoCommit => 1);
my $dbh = DBI->connect ($dsn, $user_name, $password, \%conn_attrs);
$dbh->{RaiseError} = 0; # disable automatic termination on error
print "Enter queries to be executed, one per line; terminate with Control-D\n";
while (<>)                # read and execute queries
{
    $dbh->do ($_) or warn "Query failed: $DBI::errstr ($DBI::err)\en";
}
$dbh->{RaiseError} = 1; # re-enable automatic termination on error
```

If `RaiseError` is enabled, you can trap errors without terminating your program by executing code within an **eval** block. If an error occurs within the block, **eval** fails and returns a message in the $@ variable. Typically, you use **eval** something like this:

```
eval
{
  # statements that might fail go here...
};
if ($@)
{
  print "An error occurred: $@\n";
}
```

This technique is commonly used to implement transactions. For an example, see Recipe 15.4.

Using `RaiseError` in combination with **eval** differs from using `RaiseError` alone in the following ways:

- Errors terminate only the **eval** block, not the entire script.
- Any error terminates the **eval** block, whereas `RaiseError` applies only to DBI-related errors.

When you use **eval** with `RaiseError` enabled, be sure to disable `PrintError`. Otherwise, in some versions of DBI, an error may simply cause `warn( )` to be called without terminating the **eval** block as you expect.

In addition to using the error-handling attributes `PrintError` and `RaiseError`, you can get lots of useful information about your script's execution by turning on DBI's tracing mechanism. Invoke the **trace( )** method with an argument indicating the trace level. Levels 1 to 9 enable tracing with increasingly more verbose output, and level 0 disables tracing:

```
DBI->trace (1);      # enable tracing, minimal output
DBI->trace (3);      # elevate trace level
DBI->trace (0);      # disable tracing
```

Individual database and statement handles have **trace( )** methods, too. That means you can localize tracing to a single handle if you want.

Trace output normally goes to your terminal (or, in the case of a web script, to the web server's error log). You can write trace output to a specific file by providing a second argument indicating a filename:

```
DBI->trace (1, "/tmp/trace.out");
```

If the trace file already exists, trace output is appended to the end; the file's contents are not cleared first. Beware of turning on a file trace while developing a script, and then forgetting to disable the trace when you put the script into production. You'll eventually find to your chagrin that the trace file has become quite large. Or worse, a filesystem will fill up, and you'll have no idea why!

Ruby

Ruby signals errors by raising exceptions and Ruby programs handle errors by catching exceptions in a `rescue` clause of a `begin` block. Ruby DBI methods raise exceptions when they fail and provide error information by means of a `DBI::DatabaseError` object. To get the MySQL error number, error message, and SQLSTATE value, access the `err`, `errstr`, and `state` methods of this object. The following example shows how to trap exceptions and access error information in a DBI script:

```
begin
  dsn = "DBI:Mysql:host=localhost;database=cookbook"
  dbh = DBI.connect(dsn, "cbuser", "cbpass")
  puts "Connected"
rescue DBI::DatabaseError => e
  puts "Cannot connect to server"
  puts "Error code: #{e.err}"
  puts "Error message: #{e.errstr}"
  puts "Error SQLSTATE: #{e.state}"
  exit(1)
end
```

PHP

A PEAR DB method indicates success or failure by means of its return value. If the method fails, the return value is an error object. If the method succeeds, the return value is something else:

- The `connect()` method returns a connection object for interacting with the database server.

- The `query()` method for executing SQL statements returns a result set object for statements such as `SELECT` that return rows, or the `DB_OK` value for statements such as `INSERT`, `UPDATE`, or `DELETE` that modify rows.

To determine whether a method return value is an error object, pass it to the `PEAR::isError()` method, check the `PEAR::isError()` result, and take action accordingly. For example, the following code prints "Connected" if `connect()` succeeds and exits with a generic error message if not:

```
$dsn = "mysqli://cbuser:cbpass@localhost/cookbook";
$conn =& DB::connect ($dsn);
if (PEAR::isError ($conn))
  die ("Cannot connect to server\n");
print ("Connected\n");
```

To obtain more specific information when a PEAR DB method fails, use the methods provided by the error object:

- `getCode()` and `getMessage()` return an error number and message, respectively. These are standard values provided by PEAR that are not MySQL specific.

- `getUserInfo()` and `getDebugInfo()` return MySQL-specific information.

The following listing shows how each method displays the error information returned by PEAR DB when a connect error occurs:

```
$dsn = "mysqli://cbuser:cbpass@localhost/cookbook";
$conn =& DB::connect ($dsn);
if (PEAR::isError ($conn))
{
  print ("Cannot connect to server.\n");
  printf ("Error code: %d\n", $conn->getCode ());
  printf ("Error message: %s\n", $conn->getMessage ());
  printf ("Error debug info: %s\n", $conn->getDebugInfo ());
  printf ("Error user info: %s\n", $conn->getUserInfo ());
  exit (1);
}
```

Python

Python signals errors by raising exceptions, and Python programs handle errors by catching exceptions in the **except** clause of a **try** statement. To obtain MySQL-specific error information, name an exception class, and provide a variable to receive the information. Here's an example:

```
try:
  conn = MySQLdb.connect (db = "cookbook",
                          host = "localhost",
                          user = "cbuser",
                          passwd = "cbpass")
  print "Connected"
except MySQLdb.Error, e:
  print "Cannot connect to server"
  print "Error code:", e.args[0]
  print "Error message:", e.args[1]
  sys.exit (1)
```

If an exception occurs, the first and second elements of **e.args** are set to the error number and error message, respectively. (Note that the **Error** class is accessed through the MySQLdb driver module name.)

Java

Java programs handle errors by catching exceptions. If you simply want to do the minimum amount of work, print a stack trace to inform the user where the problem lies:

```
try
{
  /* ... some database operation ... */
}
catch (Exception e)
{
  e.printStackTrace ();
}
```

The stack trace shows the location of the problem but not necessarily what the problem is. It may not be all that meaningful except to you, the program's developer. To be more specific, you can print the error message and code associated with an exception:

- All Exception objects support the getMessage( ) method. JDBC methods may throw exceptions using SQLException objects; these are like Exception objects but also support getErrorCode( ) and getSQLState( ) methods. getErrorCode( ) and getMessage( ) return the MySQL-specific error number and message string. getSQLState( ) returns a string containing the SQLSTATE value.

- You can also get information about nonfatal warnings, which some methods generate using SQLWarning objects. SQLWarning is a subclass of SQLException, but warnings are accumulated in a list rather than thrown immediately, so they don't interrupt your program, and you can print them at your leisure.

The following example program, *Error.java*, demonstrates how to access error messages by printing all the error information it can get its hands on. It attempts to connect to the MySQL server and prints exception information if the attempt fails. Then it issues a statement and prints exception and warning information if the statement fails:

```
// Error.java - demonstrate MySQL error-handling

import java.sql.*;

public class Error
{
  public static void main (String[] args)
  {
    Connection conn = null;
    String url = "jdbc:mysql://localhost/cookbook";
    String userName = "cbuser";
    String password = "cbpass";

    try
    {
      Class.forName ("com.mysql.jdbc.Driver").newInstance ();
      conn = DriverManager.getConnection (url, userName, password);
      System.out.println ("Connected");
      tryQuery (conn);    // issue a query
    }
    catch (Exception e)
    {
      System.err.println ("Cannot connect to server");
      System.err.println (e);
      if (e instanceof SQLException)  // JDBC-specific exception?
      {
        // print general message, plus any database-specific message
        // (e must be cast from Exception to SQLException to
        // access the SQLException-specific methods)
        System.err.println ("SQLException: " + e.getMessage ());
        System.err.println ("SQLState: "
                            + ((SQLException) e).getSQLState ());
        System.err.println ("VendorCode: "
```

```
                          + ((SQLException) e).getErrorCode ());
      }
    }
    finally
    {
      if (conn != null)
      {
        try
        {
          conn.close ();
          System.out.println ("Disconnected");
        }
        catch (SQLException e)
        {
          // print general message, plus any database-specific message
          System.err.println ("SQLException: " + e.getMessage ());
          System.err.println ("SQLState: " + e.getSQLState ());
          System.err.println ("VendorCode: " + e.getErrorCode ());
        }
      }
    }
  }

  public static void tryQuery (Connection conn)
  {
    try
    {
      // issue a simple query
      Statement s = conn.createStatement ();
      s.execute ("USE cookbook");
      s.close ();

      // print any accumulated warnings
      SQLWarning w = conn.getWarnings ();
      while (w != null)
      {
        System.err.println ("SQLWarning: " + w.getMessage ());
        System.err.println ("SQLState: " + w.getSQLState ());
        System.err.println ("VendorCode: " + w.getErrorCode ());
        w = w.getNextWarning ();
      }
    }
    catch (SQLException e)
    {
      // print general message, plus any database-specific message
      System.err.println ("SQLException: " + e.getMessage ());
      System.err.println ("SQLState: " + e.getSQLState ());
      System.err.println ("VendorCode: " + e.getErrorCode ());
    }
  }
}
```

2.3 Writing Library Files

Problem

You notice that you're writing the same code to perform common operations in multiple programs.

Solution

Put routines to perform those operations in a library file, and have your programs access the library. Then write the code only once. You might need to set an environment variable so that your scripts can find the library.

Discussion

This section describes how to put code for common operations in library files. Encapsulation (or modularization) isn't really a "recipe" so much as a programming technique. Its principal benefit is that you don't have to repeat code in each program you write. Instead, you just call a routine that's in the library. For example, by putting the code for connecting to the **cookbook** database into a library routine, you need not write out all the parameters associated with making that connection. Simply invoke the routine from your program, and you're connected.

Connection establishment isn't the only operation you can encapsulate, of course. Later sections in this book develop other utility functions to be placed in library files. All such files, including those shown in this section, can be found under the *lib* directory of the **recipes** distribution. As you write your own programs, you'll probably identify several operations that you perform often and that are good candidates for inclusion in a library. The techniques demonstrated in this section will help you write your own library files.

Library files have other benefits besides making it easier to write programs. They can help portability. For example, if you write connection parameters directly into each program that connects to the MySQL server, you have to change all those programs if you move them to another machine that uses different parameters. If instead you write your programs to connect to the database by calling a library routine, you localize the changes that need to be made: it's necessary to modify only the affected library routine, not all the programs that use it.

Code encapsulation also can improve security in some ways. If you make a private library file readable only to yourself, only scripts run by you can execute routines in the file. Or suppose that you have some scripts located in your web server's document tree. A properly configured server will execute the scripts and send their output to remote clients. But if the server becomes misconfigured somehow, the result can be that your scripts are sent to clients as plain text, thus displaying your MySQL username and password. (And you'll probably realize it too late. Oops.) If the code for establishing a connection to the MySQL server is placed in a library file that's located outside the document tree, those parameters won't be exposed to clients.

 Be aware that if you install a library file to be readable by your web server, you don't have much security should you share the web server with other developers. Any of those developers can write a web script to read and display your library file because, by default, the script runs with the permissions of the web server and thus will have access to the library.

The examples of programs that follow demonstrate how to write, for each API, a library file that contains a routine for connecting to the **cookbook** database on the MySQL server. The calling program can use the error-checking techniques discussed in Recipe 2.2 to determine whether a connection attempt fails. The connection routine for each language except PHP returns a database handle or connection object when it succeeds or raises an exception if the connection cannot be established. The PHP routine returns an object that represents a connection or an error, because that is what the PEAR DB connection method does (it does not raise an exception).

Libraries are of no utility in themselves, so each one's use is illustrated by a short "test harness" program. You can use any of these harness programs as the basis for creating new programs of your own: make a copy of the file and add your own code between the connect and disconnect calls.

Library file writing involves not only the question of what to put in the file but also subsidiary issues such as where to install the file so it can be accessed by your programs, and (on multiuser systems such as Unix) how to set its access privileges so its contents aren't exposed to people who shouldn't see it.

Choosing a library file installation location

If you install a library file in a directory that a language processor searches by default, programs written in that language need do nothing special to access the library. However, if you install a library file in a directory that the language processor does not search by default, you'll have to tell your scripts how to find the library. There are two common ways to do this:

- Most languages provide a statement that can be used within a script to add directories to the language processor search path. This requires that you modify each script that needs the library.

- You can set an environment or configuration variable that changes the language processor search path. This approach requires that each user who uses scripts that require the library to set the appropriate variable. Alternatively, if the language processor has a configuration file, you might be able to set a parameter in the file that affects scripts globally for all users.

We'll use the second approach. For our API languages, the following table shows the relevant variables. In each case, the variable value is a directory or list of directories.

Language	Variable name	Variable type
Perl	PERL5LIB	Environment variable
Ruby	RUBYLIB	Environment variable
PHP	include_path	Configuration variable
Python	PYTHONPATH	Environment variable
Java	CLASSPATH	Environment variable

For general information on setting environment variables, see Appendix B. You can use those instructions to set environment variables to the values in the following discussion.

Suppose that you want to install library files in a directory that language processors do not search by default. For purposes of illustration, let's use */usr/local/lib/mcb* on Unix or *C:\lib\mcb* on Windows. (To put the files somewhere else, adjust the pathnames in the variable settings accordingly. For example, you might want to use a different directory, or you might want to put libraries for each language in separate directories.)

Under Unix, if you put Perl library files in the */usr/local/lib/mcb* directory, you can set the PERL5LIB environment variable. For a shell in the Bourne shell family (*sh*, *bash*, *ksh*), set the variable like this in the appropriate startup file:

```
export PERL5LIB=/usr/local/lib/mcb
```

 If you are using the original Bourne shell, sh, you may need to split this into two commands:

```
PERL5LIB=/usr/local/lib/mcb
export PERL5LIB
```

For a shell in the C shell family (*csh*, *tcsh*), set PERL5LIB like this in your *.login* file:

```
setenv PERL5LIB /usr/local/lib/mcb
```

Under Windows, if you put Perl library files in *C:\lib\mcb*, you can set PERL5LIB as follows:

```
PERL5LIB=C:\lib\mcb
```

In each case, the variable setting tells Perl to look in the specified directory for library files, in addition to whatever other directories it would search by default. If you set PERL5LIB to name multiple directories, the separator character between directory pathnames is colon (:) on Unix or semicolon (;) on Windows.

The other environment variables (RUBYLIB, PYTHONPATH, and CLASSPATH) are specified using the same syntax.

Setting these environment variables as just discussed should suffice for scripts that you run from the command line. But for scripts that are intended to be executed by a web server, you'll likely have to configure the server as well so that it can find the library files. See Recipe 17.2 for details on how to do this.

For PHP, the search path is defined by the value of the `include_path` variable in the *php.ini* PHP initialization file. On Unix, the file's pathname is likely to be */usr/lib/php.ini* or */usr/local/lib/php.ini*. Under Windows, the file is likely to be found in the Windows directory or under the main PHP installation directory. The value of `include_path` is defined with a line like this:

```
include_path = "value"
```

value is specified using the same syntax as for environment variables that name directories. That is, it's a list of directory names, with the names separated by colons on Unix or semicolons on Windows. For example, on Unix, if you want PHP to look for include files in the current directory and in */usr/local/lib/mcb*, set `include_path` like this:

```
include_path = ".:/usr/local/lib/mcb"
```

On Windows, to search the current directory and *C:\lib\mcb*, set `include_path` like this:

```
include_path = ".;C:\lib\mcb"
```

If you modify the *php.ini* file, and PHP is running as an Apache module, you'll need to restart Apache to make your changes take effect.

Setting library file access privileges

Questions about file ownership and access mode are issues about which you'll need to make decisions if you're using a multiple-user system such as Unix:

- If a library file is private and contains code to be used only by you, the file can be placed under your own account and made accessible only to you. Assuming that a library file *mylib* is already owned by you, you can make it private like this:

    ```
    % chmod 600 mylib
    ```

- If the library file is to be used only by your web server, you can install it in a server library directory and make the file owned by and accessible only to the server user ID. You may need to be `root` to do this. For example, if the web server runs as `wwwusr`, the following commands make the file private to that user:

    ```
    # chown wwwusr mylib
    # chmod 600 mylib
    ```

- If the library file is public, you can place it in a location that your programming language searches automatically when it looks for libraries. (Most language processors search for libraries in some default set of directories.) You may need to be root to install files in one of these directories. Then you can make the file world-readable:

```
# chmod 444 mylib
```

Now let's construct a library for each API. Each section here demonstrates how to write the library file itself and discusses how to use the library from within programs.

Perl

In Perl, library files are called modules, and typically have an extension of *.pm* ("Perl module"). Here's a sample module file, *Cookbook.pm*, that implements a module named Cookbook. (It's conventional for the basename of a Perl module file to be the same as the identifier on the package line in the file.)

```perl
package Cookbook;
# Cookbook.pm - library file with utility method for connecting to MySQL
# via Perl DBI module

use strict;
use warnings;
use DBI;

my $db_name = "cookbook";
my $host_name = "localhost";
my $user_name = "cbuser";
my $password = "cbpass";
my $port_num = undef;
my $socket_file = undef;

# Establish a connection to the cookbook database, returning a database
# handle.  Raise an exception if the connection cannot be established.

sub connect
{
my $dsn = "DBI:mysql:host=$host_name";
my %conn_attrs = (PrintError => 0, RaiseError => 1, AutoCommit => 1);

  $dsn .= ";database=$db_name" if defined $db_name;
  $dsn .= ";mysql_socket=$socket_file" if defined $socket_file;
  $dsn .= ";port=$port_num" if defined $port_num;

  return (DBI->connect ($dsn, $user_name, $password, \%conn_attrs));
}

1;  # return true
```

The module encapsulates the code for establishing a connection to the MySQL server into a connect( ) method, and the package identifier establishes a Cookbook namespace for the module, so you invoke the connect( ) method using the module name:

```perl
$dbh = Cookbook::connect ();
```

The final line of the module file is a statement that trivially evaluates to true. This is needed because Perl assumes that something is wrong with a module and exits after reading it if the module doesn't return a true value.

Perl locates library files by searching through the directories named in its @INC array. This array contains a default list of directories. To check the value of this variable on your system, invoke Perl as follows at the command line:

```
% perl -V
```

The last part of the output from the command shows the directories listed in the @INC array. If you install a library file in one of those directories, your scripts will find it automatically. If you install the module somewhere else, you need to tell your scripts where to find it by setting the PERL5LIB environment variable, as discussed earlier in the introduction to this recipe.

After installing the *Cookbook.pm* module, try it from a test harness script *harness.pl* written as follows:

```perl
#!/usr/bin/perl
# harness.pl - test harness for Cookbook.pm library

use strict;
use warnings;
use Cookbook;

my $dbh;
eval
{
  $dbh = Cookbook::connect ();
  print "Connected\n";
};
die "$@" if $@;
$dbh->disconnect ();
print "Disconnected\n";
```

harness.pl has no use DBI statement. It's not necessary because the *Cookbook.php* library file itself imports the DBI module, so any script that uses Cookbook also gains access to DBI.

If you don't want to bother catching connection errors explicitly, you can write the body of the script more simply. In this case, Perl will catch any connection exception and terminate the script after printing the error message generated by the connect( ) method:

```perl
my $dbh = Cookbook::connect ();
print "Connected\n";
$dbh->disconnect ();
print "Disconnected\n";
```

Ruby

The following Ruby library file, *Cookbook.rb*, defines a Cookbook class that implements a connect method:

```
# Cookbook.rb - library file with utility method for connecting to MySQL
# via Ruby DBI module

require "dbi"

# Establish a connection to the cookbook database, returning a database
# handle.  Raise an exception if the connection cannot be established.

class Cookbook
  @@host = "localhost"
  @@db_name = "cookbook"
  @@user_name = "cbuser"
  @@password = "cbpass"

  # class method for connecting to server to access
  # cookbook database; returns database handle object.

  def Cookbook.connect
    return DBI.connect("DBI:Mysql:host=#{@@host};database=#{@@db_name}",
                       @@user_name, @@password)
  end
end
```

The connect method is defined in the library as Cookbook.connect because Ruby class methods are defined as *class_name.method_name*.

Ruby locates library files by searching through the directories named in its $LOAD_PATH variable (also known as $:), which is an array that contains a default list of directories. To check the value of this variable on your system, use Ruby to execute this statement:

```
puts $LOAD_PATH
```

If you install a library file in one of those directories, your scripts will find it automatically. If you install the file somewhere else, you need to tell your scripts where to find it by setting the RUBYLIB environment variable, as discussed earlier in the introduction to this recipe.

After installing the *Cookbook.rb* library file, try it from a test harness script *harness.rb* written as follows:

```
#!/usr/bin/ruby -w
# harness.rb - test harness for Cookbook.rb library

require "Cookbook"

begin
  dbh = Cookbook.connect
  print "Connected\n"
rescue DBI::DatabaseError => e
```

```
      puts "Cannot connect to server"
      puts "Error code: #{e.err}"
      puts "Error message: #{e.errstr}"
      exit(1)
end
dbh.disconnect
print "Disconnected\n"
```

harness.rb has no **require** statement for the DBI module. It's not necessary, because the Cookbook module itself imports DBI, so any script that imports Cookbook also gains access to DBI.

If you just want a script to die if an error occurs without checking for an exception yourself, write the body of the script like this:

```
dbh = Cookbook.connect
print "Connected\n"
dbh.disconnect
print "Disconnected\n"
```

PHP

The contents of PHP library files are written like regular PHP scripts. You can write such a file, *Cookbook.php*, that implements a Cookbook class with a connect( ) method as follows:

```
<?php
# Cookbook.php - library file with utility method for connecting to MySQL
# via PEAR DB module

require_once "DB.php";

class Cookbook
{
  # Establish a connection to the cookbook database, returning a
  # connection object, or an error object if an error occurs.

  function connect ()
  {
    $dsn = array (
              "phptype"  => "mysqli",
              "username" => "cbuser",
              "password" => "cbpass",
              "hostspec" => "localhost",
              "database" => "cookbook"
           );
    return (DB::connect ($dsn));
  }

} # end Cookbook

?>
```

Although most PHP examples throughout this book don't show the <?php and ?> tags, I've shown them as part of *Cookbook.php* here to emphasize that library files must enclose all PHP code within those tags. The PHP interpreter doesn't make any assumptions about the contents of a library file when it begins parsing it because you might include a file that contains nothing but HTML. Therefore, you must use `<?php` and `?>` to specify explicitly which parts of the library file should be considered as PHP code rather than as HTML, just as you do in the main script.

PHP looks for libraries by searching the directories named in the value of the `include_path` variable in the PHP initialization file, as described earlier in the introduction to this recipe. Assuming that *Cookbook.php* is installed in one of those directories, you can access it from a test harness script *harness.php* written as follows:

```php
<?php
# harness.php - test harness for Cookbook.php library

require_once "Cookbook.php";

$conn =& Cookbook::connect ();
if (PEAR::isError ($conn))
  die ("Cannot connect to server: " . $conn->getMessage () . "\n");
print ("Connected\n");
$conn->disconnect ();
print ("Disconnected\n");

?>
```

harness.php has no statement to include *DB.php*. It's not necessary because the Cookbook module itself includes *DB.php*, which gives any script that includes *Cookbook.php* access to *DB.php*.

Where Should PHP Library Files Be Installed?

PHP scripts often are placed in the document tree of your web server, and clients can request them directly. For PHP library files, I recommend that you place them somewhere outside the document tree, especially if (like *Cookbook.php*) they contain usernames and passwords. This is particularly true if you use a different extension such as *.inc* for the names of include files. If you do that and install include files in the document tree, they might be requested directly by clients and be displayed as plain text, exposing their contents. To prevent that from happening, reconfigure Apache so that it treats files with the *.inc* extension as PHP code to be processed by the PHP interpreter rather than being displayed literally.

Python

Python libraries are written as modules and referenced from scripts using `import` or `from` statements. To create a method for connecting to MySQL, we can write a module file *Cookbook.py*:

```python
# Cookbook.py - library file with utility method for connecting to MySQL
# via MySQLdb module
```

```
import MySQLdb

host_name = "localhost"
db_name = "cookbook"
user_name = "cbuser"
password = "cbpass"

# Establish a connection to the cookbook database, returning a connection
# object.  Raise an exception if the connection cannot be established.

def connect ():
  return MySQLdb.connect (db = db_name,
                          host = host_name,
                          user = user_name,
                          passwd = password)
```

The filename basename determines the module name, so the module is called
Cookbook. Module methods are accessed through the module name; thus you would
invoke the connect( ) method of the Cookbook module like this:

```
conn = Cookbook.connect ();
```

The Python interpreter searches for modules in directories named in the sys.path variable. You can find out what the default value of sys.path is on your system by running
Python interactively and entering a couple of commands:

```
% python
>>> import sys
>>> sys.path
```

If you install *Cookbook.py* in one of the directories named by sys.path, your scripts will
find it with no special handling. If you install *Cookbook.py* somewhere else, you'll need
to set the PYTHONPATH environment variable, as discussed earlier in the introduction to
this recipe.

After installing the *Cookbook.py* library file, try it from a test harness script
harness.py written as follows:

```
#!/usr/bin/python
# harness.py - test harness for Cookbook.py library

import sys
import MySQLdb
import Cookbook

try:
  conn = Cookbook.connect ()
  print "Connected"
except MySQLdb.Error, e:
  print "Cannot connect to server"
  print "Error code:", e.args[0]
  print "Error message:", e.args[1]
  sys.exit (1)
```

```
conn.close ()
print "Disconnected"
```

 The *Cookbook.py* file imports the MySQLdb module, but a script that imports Cookbook does not thereby gain access to MySQLdb. If the script needs MySQLdb-specific information (such as MySQLdb.Error), the script must also import MySQLdb.

If you just want a script to die if an error occurs without checking for an exception yourself, write the body of the script like this:

```
conn = Cookbook.connect ()
print "Connected"
conn.close ()
print "Disconnected"
```

Java

Java library files are similar to Java programs in most ways:

- The class line in the source file indicates a class name.
- The file should have the same name as the class (with a *.java* extension).
- You compile the *.java* file to produce a *.class* file.

Java library files also differ from Java programs in some ways:

- Unlike regular program files, Java library files have no main( ) function.
- A library file should begin with a package identifier that specifies the location of the class within the Java namespace.

A common convention for Java package identifiers is to begin them with the reverse domain of the code author; this helps make identifiers unique and avoids conflict with classes written by other authors. Domain names proceed right to left from more general to more specific within the domain namespace, whereas the Java class namespace proceeds left to right from general to specific. Thus, to use a domain as the prefix for a package name within the Java class namespace, it's necessary to reverse it. In my case, the domain is *kitebird.com*, so if I write a library file and place it under mcb within my domain's namespace, the library begins with a package statement like this:

```
package com.kitebird.mcb;
```

Java packages developed for this book are placed within the com.kitebird.mcb namespace to ensure their uniqueness in the package namespace.

The following library file, *Cookbook.java*, defines a Cookbook class that implements a connect( ) method for connecting to the cookbook database. connect( ) returns a Connection object if it succeeds, and throws an exception otherwise. To help the caller deal with failures, the Cookbook class also defines getErrorMessage( ) and `printErrorMessage()` utility methods that return the error message as a string or print it to `System.err`.

```java
// Cookbook.java - library file with utility method for connecting to MySQL
// via MySQL Connector/J

package com.kitebird.mcb;

import java.sql.*;

public class Cookbook
{
  // Establish a connection to the cookbook database, returning
  // a connection object.  Throw an exception if the connection
  // cannot be established.

  public static Connection connect () throws Exception
  {
    String url = "jdbc:mysql://localhost/cookbook";
    String user = "cbuser";
    String password = "cbpass";

    Class.forName ("com.mysql.jdbc.Driver").newInstance ();
    return (DriverManager.getConnection (url, user, password));
  }

  // Return an error message as a string

  public static String getErrorMessage (Exception e)
  {
    StringBuffer s = new StringBuffer ();
    if (e instanceof SQLException)  // JDBC-specific exception?
    {
      // print general message, plus any database-specific message
      s.append ("Error message: " + e.getMessage () + "\n");
      s.append ("Error code: " + ((SQLException) e).getErrorCode () + "\n");
    }
    else
    {
      s.append (e + "\n");
    }
    return (s.toString ());
  }

  // Get the error message and print it to System.err

  public static void printErrorMessage (Exception e)
  {
    System.err.println (Cookbook.getErrorMessage (e));
  }
}
```

The routines within the class are declared using the **static** keyword, which makes them class methods rather than instance methods. That is done here because the class is used directly rather than creating an object from it and invoking the methods through the object.

To use the *Cookbook.java* file, compile it to produce *Cookbook.class*, and then install the class file in a directory that corresponds to the package identifier. This means that *Cookbook.class* should be installed in a directory named *com/kitebird/mcb* (or *com\kitebird\mcb* under Windows) that is located under some directory named in your CLASSPATH setting. For example, if CLASSPATH includes */usr/local/lib/mcb* under Unix, you can install *Cookbook.class* in the */usr/local/lib/mcb/com/kitebird/mcb* directory. (See the Java discussion in Recipe 2.1 for more information about the CLASSPATH variable.)

To use the Cookbook class from within a Java program, import it, and then invoke the Cookbook.connect( ) method. The following test harness program, *Harness.java*, shows how to do this:

```java
// Harness.java - test harness for Cookbook library class

import java.sql.*;
import com.kitebird.mcb.Cookbook;

public class Harness
{
  public static void main (String[] args)
  {
    Connection conn = null;
    try
    {
      conn = Cookbook.connect ();
      System.out.println ("Connected");
    }
    catch (Exception e)
    {
      Cookbook.printErrorMessage (e);
      System.exit (1);
    }
    finally
    {
      if (conn != null)
      {
        try
        {
          conn.close ();
          System.out.println ("Disconnected");
        }
        catch (Exception e)
        {
          String err = Cookbook.getErrorMessage (e);
          System.out.println (err);
        }
      }
    }
  }
}
```

Harness.java also shows how to use the error message utility methods from the Cookbook class when a MySQL-related exception occurs:

- `printErrorMessage( )` takes the exception object and uses it to print an error message to `System.err`.
- `getErrorMessage( )` returns the error message as a string. You can display the message yourself, write it to a logfile, or whatever.

2.4 Issuing Statements and Retrieving Results

Problem

You want your program to send an SQL statement to the MySQL server and retrieve whatever result it produces.

Solution

Some statements return only a status code; others return a result set (a set of rows). Some APIs provide different methods for issuing each type of statement. If so, use the method that's appropriate for the statement to be executed.

Discussion

There are two general categories of SQL statements that you can execute. Some statements retrieve information from the database; others make changes to that information. These two types of statements are handled differently. In addition, some APIs provide several different routines for issuing statements, which complicates matters further. Before we get to the examples demonstrating how to issue statements from within each API, I'll show the database table that the examples use, and then further discuss the two statement categories and outline a general strategy for processing statements in each category.

In Chapter 1, we created a table named `limbs` to try some sample statements. In this chapter, we'll use a different table named `profile`. It's based on the idea of a "buddy list," that is, the set of people we like to keep in touch with while we're online. To maintain a profile about each person, we can use the following table definition:

```
CREATE TABLE profile
(
  id    INT UNSIGNED NOT NULL AUTO_INCREMENT,
  name  CHAR(20) NOT NULL,
  birth DATE,
  color ENUM('blue','red','green','brown','black','white'),
  foods SET('lutefisk','burrito','curry','eggroll','fadge','pizza'),
  cats  INT,
  PRIMARY KEY (id)
);
```

The profile table indicates the things that are important to us about each buddy: name, age, favorite color, favorite foods, and number of cats—obviously one of those goofy tables that are used only for examples in a book![†] The table also includes an id column containing unique values so that we can distinguish rows from each other, even if two buddies have the same name. id and name are declared as NOT NULL because they're each required to have a value. The other columns are allowed to be NULL (and that is implicitly their default value) because we might not know the value to put into them for any given individual. That is, we'll use NULL to signify "unknown."

Notice that although we want to keep track of age, there is no age column in the table. Instead, there is a birth column of DATE type. That's because ages change, but birthdays don't. If we recorded age values, we'd have to keep updating them. Storing the birth date is better because it's stable, and we can use it to calculate age at any given moment. (Recipe 6.11 discusses age calculations.) color is an ENUM column; color values can be any one of the listed values. foods is a SET, which allows the value to be chosen as any combination of the individual set members. That way we can record multiple favorite foods for any buddy.

To create the table, use the *profile.sql* script in the *tables* directory of the recipes distribution. Change location into that directory, and then run the following command:

```
% mysql cookbook < profile.sql
```

Another way to create the table is to issue the CREATE TABLE statement manually from within the *mysql* program, but I recommend that you use the script because it also loads sample data into the table. That way you can experiment with the table, and then restore it if you change its contents by running the script again. (See the last recipe of this chapter on the importance of restoring the profile table.)

The initial contents of the profile table as loaded by the *profile.sql* script look like this:

```
mysql> SELECT * FROM profile;
+----+---------+------------+-------+-----------------------+------+
| id | name    | birth      | color | foods                 | cats |
+----+---------+------------+-------+-----------------------+------+
|  1 | Fred    | 1970-04-13 | black | lutefisk,fadge,pizza  |    0 |
|  2 | Mort    | 1969-09-30 | white | burrito,curry,eggroll |    3 |
|  3 | Brit    | 1957-12-01 | red   | burrito,curry,pizza   |    1 |
|  4 | Carl    | 1973-11-02 | red   | eggroll,pizza         |    4 |
|  5 | Sean    | 1963-07-04 | blue  | burrito,curry         |    5 |
|  6 | Alan    | 1965-02-14 | red   | curry,fadge           |    1 |
|  7 | Mara    | 1968-09-17 | green | lutefisk,fadge        |    1 |
|  8 | Shepard | 1975-09-02 | black | curry,pizza           |    2 |
|  9 | Dick    | 1952-08-20 | green | lutefisk,fadge        |    0 |
| 10 | Tony    | 1960-05-01 | white | burrito,pizza         |    0 |
+----+---------+------------+-------+-----------------------+------+
```

[†] Actually, it's not that goofy. The table uses several different data types for its columns, and these come in handy later for illustrating how to solve problems that pertain to specific data types.

Although most of the columns in the `profile` table allow `NULL` values, none of the rows in the sample dataset actually contain `NULL` yet. That is because `NULL` values complicate statement processing a bit and I don't want to deal with those complications until we get to Recipes 2.5 and 2.7.

SQL statement categories

SQL statements can be divided into two broad categories:

- Statements that do not return a result set (that is, a set of rows). Statements in this category include `INSERT`, `DELETE`, and `UPDATE`. As a general rule, statements of this type generally change the database in some way. There are some exceptions, such as `USE db_name`, which changes the default (current) database for your session without making any changes to the database itself. The example data-modifying statement used in this section is an `UPDATE`:

  ```
  UPDATE profile SET cats = cats+1 WHERE name = 'Fred'
  ```

  We'll cover how to issue this statement and determine the number of rows that it affects.

- Statements that return a result set, such as `SELECT`, `SHOW`, `EXPLAIN`, and `DESCRIBE`. I refer to such statements generically as `SELECT` statements, but you should understand that category to include any statement that returns rows. The example row-retrieval statement used in this section is a `SELECT`:

  ```
  SELECT id, name, cats FROM profile
  ```

  We'll cover how to issue this statement, fetch the rows in the result set, and determine the number of rows and columns in the result set. (If you need information such as the column names or data types, you must access the result set metadata. Recipe 9.2 shows how to do this.)

The first step in processing an SQL statement is to send it to the MySQL server for execution. Some APIs (those for Perl, Ruby, and Java, for example) recognize a distinction between the two categories of statements and provide separate calls for executing them. Other APIs (such as those for PHP and Python) have a single call that can be used for any statement. However, one thing all APIs have in common is that you don't use any special character to indicate the end of the statement. No terminator is necessary because the end of the statement string implicitly terminates the statement. This differs from the way that you issue statements in the *mysql* program, where you terminate statements using a semicolon (;) or \g. (It also differs from the way that I normally show the syntax for SQL statements in examples, because usually I include semicolons to make it clear where statements end.)

When you send a statement to the server, you should be prepared to handle errors if it did not execute successfully. *Do not neglect to do this!* If a statement fails and you proceed on the basis that it succeeded, your program won't work. For the most part, error-checking code is not shown in this section, but that is for brevity. The sample scripts in the `recipes` distribution from which the examples are taken do include error handling, based on the techniques illustrated in Recipe 2.2.

If a statement does execute without error, your next step depends on the type of statement you issued. If it's one that returns no result set, there's nothing else to do, unless you want to check how many rows were affected by the statement. If the statement does return a result set, you can fetch its rows, and then close the result set. If you are executing a statement in a context where you don't necessarily know whether it returns a result set, Recipe 9.3 discusses how to tell.

Perl

The Perl DBI module provides two basic approaches to SQL statement execution, depending on whether you expect to get back a result set. To issue a statement such as `INSERT` or `UPDATE` that returns no result set, use the database handle `do( )` method. It executes the statement and returns the number of rows affected by it, or `undef` if an error occurs. For example, if Fred gets a new cat, the following statement can be used to increment his `cats` count by one:

```
my $count = $dbh->do ("UPDATE profile SET cats = cats+1
                        WHERE name = 'Fred'");
if ($count)    # print row count if no error occurred
{
  $count += 0;
  print "Number of rows updated: $count\n";
}
```

If the statement executes successfully but affects no rows, `do( )` returns a special value, `"0E0"` (that is, the value zero in scientific notation, expressed as a string). `"0E0"` can be used for testing the execution status of a statement because it is true in Boolean contexts (unlike `undef`). For successful statements, it can also be used when counting how many rows were affected because it is treated as the number zero in numeric contexts. Of course, if you print that value as is, you'll print `"0E0"`, which might look kind of weird to people who use your program. The preceding example shows one way to make sure that doesn't happen: add zero to the value to explicitly coerce it to numeric form so that it displays as 0. You can also use `printf` with a `%d` format specifier to cause an implicit numeric conversion:

```
my $count = $dbh->do ("UPDATE profile SET cats = cats+1
                        WHERE name = 'Fred'");
if ($count)    # print row count if no error occurred
{
  printf "Number of rows updated: %d\n", $count;
}
```

If `RaiseError` is enabled, your script terminates automatically if a DBI-related error occurs, so you don't need to bother checking `$count` to see whether `do( )` failed. In that case, you can simplify the code somewhat:

```
my $count = $dbh->do ("UPDATE profile SET cats = cats+1
                        WHERE name = 'Fred'");
printf "Number of rows updated: %d\n", $count;
```

To process a statement such as SELECT that does return a result set, use a different approach that involves several steps:

1. Specify the statement to be executed by calling prepare( ) using the database handle. If prepare( ) is successful, it returns a statement handle to use with all subsequent operations on the statement. (If an error occurs, the script terminates if RaiseError is enabled; otherwise, prepare( ) returns undef.)

2. Call execute( ) to execute the statement and generate the result set.

3. Perform a loop to fetch the rows returned by the statement. DBI provides several methods that you can use in this loop; we cover them shortly.

4. If you don't fetch the entire result set, release resources associated with it by calling finish( ).

The following example illustrates these steps, using fetchrow_array( ) as the row-fetching method and assuming that RaiseError is enabled so that errors terminate the script:

```
my $sth = $dbh->prepare ("SELECT id, name, cats FROM profile");
$sth->execute ();
my $count = 0;
while (my @val = $sth->fetchrow_array ())
{
  print "id: $val[0], name: $val[1], cats: $val[2]\n";
  ++$count;
}
$sth->finish ();
print "Number of rows returned: $count\n";
```

The row-fetching loop just shown is followed by a call to finish( ), which closes the result set and tells the server that it can free any resources associated with it. You don't actually need to call finish( ) if you fetch every row in the set, because DBI notices when you've reached the last row and releases the set for you. The only time it's important to invoke finish( ) explicitly is when you don't fetch the entire result set. Thus, the example could have omitted the finish( ) call without ill effect.

The example illustrates that if you want to know how many rows a result set contains, you should count them yourself while you're fetching them. Do not use the DBI rows( ) method for this purpose; the DBI documentation discourages this practice. (The reason is that rows( ) is not necessarily reliable for SELECT statements—not because of some deficiency in DBI, but because of differences in the behavior of various database engines.)

DBI has several methods that fetch a row at a time. The one used in the previous example, fetchrow_array( ), returns an array containing the next row or an empty list when there are no more rows. Array elements are accessed as $val[0], $val[1], ..., and are present in the array in the same order they are named in the SELECT statement. The size of the array tells you how many columns the result set has.

The fetchrow_array( ) method is most useful for statements that explicitly name the columns to select. (If you retrieve columns with SELECT *, there are no guarantees about the positions of columns within the array.)

fetchrow_arrayref( ) is like fetchrow_array( ), except that it returns a reference to the array or undef when there are no more rows. Array elements are accessed as $ref->[0], $ref->[1], and so forth. As with fetchrow_array( ), the values are present in the order named in the statement:

```
my $sth = $dbh->prepare ("SELECT id, name, cats FROM profile");
$sth->execute ();
my $count = 0;
while (my $ref = $sth->fetchrow_arrayref ())
{
  print "id: $ref->[0], name: $ref->[1], cats: $ref->[2]\n";
  ++$count;
}
print "Number of rows returned: $count\n";
```

fetchrow_hashref( ) returns a reference to a hash structure, or undef when there are no more rows:

```
my $sth = $dbh->prepare ("SELECT id, name, cats FROM profile");
$sth->execute ();
my $count = 0;
while (my $ref = $sth->fetchrow_hashref ())
{
  print "id: $ref->{id}, name: $ref->{name}, cats: $ref->{cats}\n";
  ++$count;
}
print "Number of rows returned: $count\n";
```

To access the elements of the hash, use the names of the columns that are selected by the statement ($ref->{id}, $ref->{name}, and so forth). fetchrow_hashref( ) is particularly useful for SELECT * statements because you can access elements of rows without knowing anything about the order in which columns are returned. You just need to know their names. On the other hand, it's more expensive to set up a hash than an array, so fetchrow_hashref( ) is slower than fetchrow_array( ) or fetchrow_arrayref( ). It's also possible to "lose" row elements if they have the same name because column names must be unique. The following statement selects two values, but fetchrow_hashref( ) would return a hash structure containing a single element named id:

```
SELECT id, id FROM profile
```

To avoid this problem, you can use column aliases to ensure that like-named columns have distinct names in the result set. The following statement retrieves the same columns as the previous statement, but gives them the distinct names id and id2:

```
SELECT id, id AS id2 FROM profile
```

Admittedly, this statement is pretty silly. However, if you're retrieving columns from multiple tables, you can very easily run into the problem of having columns in the result set that have the same name. An example where this occurs may be seen in Recipe 12.16.

In addition to the methods for performing the statement execution process just described, DBI provides several high-level retrieval methods that issue a statement and return the result set in a single operation. All of these are database handle methods that create and dispose of the statement handle internally before returning the result set. Where the methods differ is the form in which they return the result. Some return the entire result set, others return a single row or column of the set, as summarized in the following table:

Method	Return value
selectrow_array( )	First row of result set as an array
selectrow_arrayref( )	First row of result set as a reference to an array
selectrow_hashref( )	First row of result set as a reference to a hash
selectcol_arrayref( )	First column of result set as a reference to an array
selectall_arrayref( )	Entire result set as a reference to an array of array references
selectall_hashref( )	Entire result set as a reference to a hash of hash references

Most of these methods return a reference. The exception is selectrow_array( ), which selects the first row of the result set and returns an array or a scalar, depending on how you call it. In array context, selectrow_array( ) returns the entire row as an array (or the empty list if no row was selected). This is useful for statements from which you expect to obtain only a single row:

```
my @val = $dbh->selectrow_array ("SELECT name, birth, foods FROM profile
                                  WHERE id = 3");
```

When selectrow_array( ) is called in array context, the return value can be used to determine the size of the result set. The column count is the number of elements in the array, and the row count is 1 or 0:

```
my $ncols = @val;
my $nrows = ($ncols ? 1 : 0);
```

You can also invoke selectrow_array( ) in scalar context, in which case it returns only the first column from the row. This is especially convenient for statements that return a single value:

```
my $buddy_count = $dbh->selectrow_array ("SELECT COUNT(*) FROM profile");
```

If a statement returns no result, selectrow_array( ) returns an empty array or undef, depending on whether you call it in array or scalar context.

selectrow_arrayref( ) and selectrow_hashref( ) select the first row of the result set and return a reference to it or undef if no row was selected. To access the column values, treat the reference the same way you treat the return value from `fetchrow_arrayref()` or `fetchrow_hashref()`. You can also use the reference to get the row and column counts:

```
my $ref = $dbh->selectrow_arrayref ($stmt);
my $ncols = (defined ($ref) ? @{$ref} : 0);
my $nrows = ($ncols ? 1 : 0);

my $ref = $dbh->selectrow_hashref ($stmt);
my $ncols = (defined ($ref) ? keys (%{$ref}) : 0);
my $nrows = ($ncols ? 1 : 0);
```

With `selectcol_arrayref()`, a reference to a single-column array is returned, representing the first column of the result set. Assuming a non-`undef` return value, elements of the array are accessed as `$ref->[i]` for the value from row i. The number of rows is the number of elements in the array, and the column count is 1 or 0:

```
my $ref = $dbh->selectcol_arrayref ($stmt);
my $nrows = (defined ($ref) ? @{$ref} : 0);
my $ncols = ($nrows ? 1 : 0);
```

`selectall_arrayref()` returns a reference to an array, where the array contains an element for each row of the result. Each of these elements is a reference to an array. To access row i of the result set, use `$ref->[i]` to get a reference to the row. Then treat the row reference the same way as a return value from `fetchrow_arrayref()` to access individual column values in the row. The result set row and column counts are available as follows:

```
my $ref = $dbh->selectall_arrayref ($stmt);
my $nrows = (defined ($ref) ? @{$ref} : 0);
my $ncols = ($nrows ? @{$ref->[0]} : 0);
```

`selectall_hashref()` is somewhat similar to `selectall_arrayref()` but returns a reference to a hash, each element of which is a hash reference to a row of the result. To call it, specify an argument that indicates which column to use for hash keys. For example, if you're retrieving rows from the `profile` table, the primary key is the `id` column:

```
my $ref = $dbh->selectall_hashref ("SELECT * FROM profile", "id");
```

Then access rows using the keys of the hash. For example, if one of the rows has a key column value of 12, the hash reference for the row is accessed as `$ref->{12}`. That row value is keyed on column names, which you can use to access individual column elements (for example, `$ref->{12}->{name}`). The result set row and column counts are available as follows:

```
my @keys = (defined ($ref) ? keys (%{$ref}) : ());
my $nrows = scalar (@keys);
my $ncols = ($nrows ? keys (%{$ref->{$keys[0]}}) : 0);
```

The various `selectall_XXX()` methods are useful when you need to process a result set more than once because Perl DBI provides no way to "rewind" a result set. By assigning the entire result set to a variable, you can iterate through its elements multiple times.

Take care when using the high-level methods if you have RaiseError disabled. In that case, a method's return value may not always enable you to distinguish an error from an empty result set. For example, if you call selectrow_array( ) in scalar context to retrieve a single value, an undef return value is particularly ambiguous because it may indicate any of three things: an error, an empty result set, or a result set consisting of a single NULL value. If you need to test for an error, you can check the value of $DBI::errstr, $DBI::err, or $DBI::state.

Ruby

As with Perl DBI, Ruby DBI provides two approaches to SQL statement execution. With either approach, if a statement-execution method fails with an error, it raises an exception.

For statements such as INSERT or UPDATE that return no result set, invoke the do database handle method. Its return value indicates the number of rows affected:

```
count = dbh.do("UPDATE profile SET cats = cats+1 WHERE name = 'Fred'")
puts "Number of rows updated: #{count}"
```

For statements such as SELECT that return a result set, invoke the execute database handle method. execute returns a statement handle to use for fetching the rows of the result set. The statement handle has several methods of its own that enable row fetching to be done in different ways. After you are done with the statement handle, invoke its finish method. (Unlike Perl DBI, where it is necessary to invoke finish only if you do not fetch the entire result set, in Ruby you should call finish for every statement handle that you create.) To determine the number of rows in the result set, count them as you fetch them.

The following example executes a SELECT statement and uses the statement handle's fetch method in a while loop:

```
count = 0
sth = dbh.execute("SELECT id, name, cats FROM profile")
while row = sth.fetch do
  printf "id: %s, name: %s, cats: %s\n", row[0], row[1], row[2]
  count += 1
end
sth.finish
puts "Number of rows returned: #{count}"
```

You can also use fetch as an iterator that returns each row in turn:

```
count = 0
sth = dbh.execute("SELECT id, name, cats FROM profile")
sth.fetch do |row|
  printf "id: %s, name: %s, cats: %s\n", row[0], row[1], row[2]
  count += 1
end
sth.finish
puts "Number of rows returned: #{count}"
```

In iterator context (such as just shown), the each method is a synonym for fetch.

The `fetch` method returns `DBI::Row` objects. As just shown, you can access column values within the row by position (beginning with 0). `DBI::Row` objects also provide access to columns by name:

```
sth.fetch do |row|
  printf "id: %s, name: %s, cats: %s\n",
          row["id"], row["name"], row["cats"]
end
```

To fetch all rows at once, use `fetch_all`, which returns an array of `DBI::Row` objects:

```
sth = dbh.execute("SELECT id, name, cats FROM profile")
rows = sth.fetch_all
sth.finish
rows.each do |row|
  printf "id: %s, name: %s, cats: %s\n",
          row["id"], row["name"], row["cats"]
end
```

`row.size` tells you the number of columns in the result set.

To fetch each row as a hash keyed on column names, use the `fetch_hash` method. It can be called in a loop or used as an iterator. The following example shows the iterator approach:

```
count = 0
sth = dbh.execute("SELECT id, name, cats FROM profile")
sth.fetch_hash do |row|
  printf "id: %s, name: %s, cats: %s\n",
          row["id"], row["name"], row["cats"]
  count += 1
end
sth.finish
puts "Number of rows returned: #{count}"
```

The preceding examples invoke `execute` to get a statement handle and then invoke `finish` when that handle is no longer needed. Another way to invoke `execute` is with a code block. In this case, it passes the statement handle to the block and invokes `finish` on that handle automatically. For example:

```
count = 0
dbh.execute("SELECT id, name, cats FROM profile") do |sth|
  sth.fetch do |row|
    printf "id: %s, name: %s, cats: %s\n", row[0], row[1], row[2]
    count += 1
  end
end
puts "Number of rows returned: #{count}"
```

Ruby DBI has some higher-level database handle methods for executing statements to produce result sets:

- `select_one` executes a query and returns the first row as an array (or `nil` if the result is empty):

  ```
  row = dbh.select_one("SELECT id, name, cats FROM profile WHERE id = 3")
  ```

- select_all executes a query and returns an array of DBI::Row objects, one per row of the result set. The array is empty if the result is empty:

```
rows = dbh.select_all( "SELECT id, name, cats FROM profile")
```

The select_all method is useful when you need to process a result set more than once because Ruby DBI provides no way to "rewind" a result set. By fetching the entire result set as an array of row objects, you can iterate through its elements multiple times. If you need to run through the rows only once, you can apply an iterator directly to select_all:

```
dbh.select_all("SELECT id, name, cats FROM profile").each do |row|
  printf "id: %s, name: %s, cats: %s\n",
         row["id"], row["name"], row["cats"]
end
```

PHP

In PHP, PEAR DB doesn't have separate methods for issuing statements that return result sets and those that do not. Instead, the query( ) method executes any kind of statement. query( ) takes a statement string argument and returns a result value that you can test with PEAR::isError( ) to determine whether the statement failed. If PEAR::isError( ) is true, it means that your statement was bad: it was syntactically invalid, you didn't have permission to access a table named in the statement, or some other problem prevented the statement from executing.

If the statement executed properly, what you do at that point depends on the type of statement. For statements such as INSERT or UPDATE that don't return rows, the statement has completed. If you want, you can call the connection object's affectedRows( ) method to find out how many rows were changed:

```
$result =& $conn->query ("UPDATE profile SET cats = cats+1
                          WHERE name = 'Fred'");
if (PEAR::isError ($result))
  die ("Oops, the statement failed");
printf ("Number of rows updated: %d\n", $conn->affectedRows ());
```

For statements such as SELECT that return a result set, the query( ) method returns a result set object. Generally, you use this object to call a row-fetching method in a loop, and then call its free( ) method to release the result set. Here's an example that shows how to issue a SELECT statement and use the result set object to fetch the rows:

```
$result =& $conn->query ("SELECT id, name, cats FROM profile");
if (PEAR::isError ($result))
  die ("Oops, the statement failed");
while ($row =& $result->fetchRow (DB_FETCHMODE_ORDERED))
  print ("id: $row[0], name: $row[1], cats: $row[2]\n");
printf ("Number of rows returned: %d\n", $result->numRows ());
$result->free ();
```

The example demonstrates several methods that result set objects have:

- To obtain the rows in the result set, execute a loop in which you invoke the fetchRow( ) method.
- To obtain a count of the number of rows in the result set, invoke numRows( ).
- When there are no more rows, invoke the free( ) method.

The fetchRow( ) method returns the next row of the result set or NULL when there are no more rows. fetchRow( ) takes an argument that indicates what type of value it should return. As shown in the preceding example, with an argument of DB_FETCHMODE_ORDERED, fetchRow( ) returns an array with elements that correspond to the columns selected by the statement and that are accessed using numeric subscripts. The size of the array indicates the number of columns in the result set.

With an argument of DB_FETCHMODE_ASSOC, fetchRow( ) returns an associative array containing values that are accessed by column name:

```
$result =& $conn->query ("SELECT id, name, cats FROM profile");
if (PEAR::isError ($result))
  die ("Oops, the statement failed");
while ($row =& $result->fetchRow (DB_FETCHMODE_ASSOC))
{
  printf ("id: %s, name: %s, cats: %s\n",
      $row["id"], $row["name"], $row["cats"]);
}
printf ("Number of rows returned: %d\n", $result->numRows ());
$result->free ();
```

With an argument of DB_FETCHMODE_OBJECT, fetchRow( ) returns an object having members that are accessed using the column names:

```
$result =& $conn->query ("SELECT id, name, cats FROM profile");
if (PEAR::isError ($result))
  die ("Oops, the statement failed");
while ($row =& $result->fetchRow (DB_FETCHMODE_OBJECT))
  print ("id: $row->id, name: $row->name, cats: $row->cats\n");
printf ("Number of rows returned: %d\n", $result->numRows ());
$result->free ();
```

If you invoke fetchRow( ) without an argument, it uses the default fetch mode. Normally, this is DB_FETCHMODE_ORDERED unless you have changed it by calling the setFetch Mode( ) connection object method. For example, to use DB_FETCHMODE_ASSOC as the default fetch mode for a connection, do this:

```
$conn->setFetchMode (DB_FETCHMODE_ASSOC);
```

Python

The Python DB-API interface does not have distinct calls for SQL statements that return a result set and those that do not. To process a statement in Python, use your database connection object to get a cursor object. Then use the cursor's execute( ) method to send the statement to the server. If the statement fails with an error, execute( ) raises an exception. Otherwise, if there is no result set, the statement is completed, and you can use the cursor's `rowcount` attribute to determine how many rows were changed:

```
cursor = conn.cursor ()
cursor.execute ("UPDATE profile SET cats = cats+1 WHERE name = 'Fred'")
print "Number of rows updated: %d" % cursor.rowcount
```

Note that `rowcount` is an attribute, not a method. Refer to it as `rowcount`, not `rowcount( )`, or an exception will be raised.

 The Python DB-API specification indicates that database connections should begin with auto-commit mode *disabled*, so MySQLdb disables auto-commit when it connects to the MySQL server. One implication is that if you use transactional tables, modifications to them will be rolled back when you close the connection unless you commit the changes first. Changes to nontransactional tables such as MyISAM tables are committed automatically, so this issue does not arise. For more information on auto-commit mode, see Chapter 15 (Recipe 15.7 in particular).

If the statement does return a result set, fetch its rows, and then close the set. DB-API provides a couple of methods for retrieving rows. `fetchone( )` returns the next row as a sequence (or `None` when there are no more rows):

```
cursor = conn.cursor ()
cursor.execute ("SELECT id, name, cats FROM profile")
while 1:
  row = cursor.fetchone ()
  if row == None:
    break
  print "id: %s, name: %s, cats: %s" % (row[0], row[1], row[2])
print "Number of rows returned: %d" % cursor.rowcount
cursor.close ()
```

As you can see from the preceding example, the `rowcount` attribute is useful for `SELECT` statements, too; it indicates the number of rows in the result set.

`len(row)` tells you the number of columns in the result set.

Another row-fetching method, `fetchall( )`, returns the entire result set as a sequence of row sequences. You can iterate through the sequence to access the rows:

```
cursor = conn.cursor ()
cursor.execute ("SELECT id, name, cats FROM profile")
rows = cursor.fetchall ()
for row in rows:
  print "id: %s, name: %s, cats: %s" % (row[0], row[1], row[2])
print "Number of rows returned: %d" % cursor.rowcount
cursor.close ()
```

DB-API doesn't provide any way to rewind a result set, so `fetchall( )` can be convenient when you need to iterate through the rows of the result set more than once or access individual values directly. For example, if `rows` holds the result set, you can access the value of the third column in the second row as `rows[1][2]` (indexes begin at 0, not 1).

To access row values by column name, specify the `DictCursor` cursor type when you create the cursor object. This causes rows to be returned as Python dictionary objects with named elements:

```
cursor = conn.cursor (MySQLdb.cursors.DictCursor)
cursor.execute ("SELECT id, name, cats FROM profile")
for row in cursor.fetchall ():
  print "id: %s, name: %s, cats: %s" % (row["id"], row["name"], row["cats"])
print "Number of rows returned: %d" % cursor.rowcount
cursor.close ()
```

The preceding example also demonstrates how to use `fetch_all( )` directly as an iterator.

Java

The JDBC interface provides specific object types for the various phases of SQL statement processing. Statements are issued in JDBC by using Java objects of one type. The results, if there are any, are returned as objects of another type.

To issue a statement, the first step is to get a `Statement` object by calling the `createStatement( )` method of your `Connection` object:

```
Statement s = conn.createStatement ();
```

Now use the `Statement` object to send the statement to the server. JDBC provides several methods for doing this. Choose the one that's appropriate for the type of statement you want to issue: `executeUpdate( )` for statements that don't return a result set, `executeQuery( )` for statements that do, and `execute( )` when you don't know. Each method raises an exception if the statement fails with an error.

The `executeUpdate( )` method sends a statement that generates no result set to the server and returns a count indicating the number of rows that were affected. When you're done with the statement object, close it. The following example illustrates this sequence of events:

```
Statement s = conn.createStatement ();
int count = s.executeUpdate (
            "UPDATE profile SET cats = cats+1 WHERE name = 'Fred'");
s.close ();   // close statement
System.out.println ("Number of rows updated: " + count);
```

For statements that return a result set, use `executeQuery( )`. Then get a result set object, and use it to retrieve the row values. When you're done, close the result set and statement objects:

```
Statement s = conn.createStatement ();
s.executeQuery ("SELECT id, name, cats FROM profile");
ResultSet rs = s.getResultSet ();
int count = 0;
```

```
while (rs.next ())  // loop through rows of result set
{
  int id = rs.getInt (1);    // extract columns 1, 2, and 3
  String name = rs.getString (2);
  int cats = rs.getInt (3);
  System.out.println ("id: " + id
                        + ", name: " + name
                        + ", cats: " + cats);
  ++count;
}
rs.close ();  // close result set
s.close ();   // close statement
System.out.println ("Number of rows returned: " + count);
```

The `ResultSet` object returned by the `getResultSet( )` method of your `Statement` object has a number of methods of its own, such as `next( )` to fetch rows and various `getXXX( )` methods that access columns of the current row. Initially, the result set is positioned just before the first row of the set. Call `next( )` to fetch each row in succession until it returns false, which means that there are no more rows. To determine the number of rows in a result set, count them yourself, as shown in the preceding example.

To access column values, use methods such as `getInt( )`, `getString( )`, `getFloat( )`, and `getDate( )`. To obtain the column value as a generic object, use `getObject( )`. The `getXXX( )` calls can be invoked with an argument that indicates either column position (beginning at 1, not 0) or column name. The previous example shows how to retrieve the `id`, `name`, and `cats` columns by position. To access columns by name instead, the row-fetching loop of that example can be rewritten as follows:

```
while (rs.next ())  // loop through rows of result set
{
  int id = rs.getInt ("id");
  String name = rs.getString ("name");
  int cats = rs.getInt ("cats");
  System.out.println ("id: " + id
                        + ", name: " + name
                        + ", cats: " + cats);
  ++count;
}
```

You can retrieve a given column value using any `getXXX( )` call that makes sense for the data type. For example, you can use `getString( )` to retrieve any column value as a string:

```
String id = rs.getString ("id");
String name = rs.getString ("name");
String cats = rs.getString ("cats");
System.out.println ("id: " + id
                      + ", name: " + name
                      + ", cats: " + cats);
```

Or you can use `getObject( )` to retrieve values as generic objects and convert the values as necessary. The following example uses `toString( )` to convert object values to printable form:

```
Object id = rs.getObject ("id");
Object name = rs.getObject ("name");
Object cats = rs.getObject ("cats");
System.out.println ("id: " + id.toString ()
                    + ", name: " + name.toString ()
                    + ", cats: " + cats.toString ());
```

To find out how many columns are in the result set, access the result set's metadata:

```
ResultSet rs = s.getResultSet ();
ResultSetMetaData md = rs.getMetaData (); // get result set metadata
int ncols = md.getColumnCount ();           // get column count from metadata
```

The third JDBC statement-execution method, execute( ), works for either type of statement. It's particularly useful when you receive a statement string from an external source and don't know whether it generates a result set. The return value from execute( ) indicates the statement type so that you can process it appropriately: if execute( ) returns true, there is a result set, otherwise not. Typically, you'd use it something like this, where stmtStr represents an arbitrary SQL statement:

```
Statement s = conn.createStatement ();
if (s.execute (stmtStr))
{
  // there is a result set
  ResultSet rs = s.getResultSet ();

  // ... process result set here ...

  rs.close ();  // close result set
}
else
{
  // there is no result set, just print the row count
  System.out.println ("Number of rows affected: " + s.getUpdateCount ());
}
s.close ();   // close statement
```

2.5 Handling Special Characters and NULL Values in Statements

Problem

You need to construct SQL statements that refer to data values containing special characters such as quotes or backslashes, or special values such as NULL. Or you are constructing statements using data obtained from external sources and want to avoid being subject to SQL injection attacks.

Solution

Use your API's placeholder mechanism or quoting function to make data safe for insertion.

Discussion

Up to this point in the chapter, our statements have used "safe" data values that require no special treatment. For example, we can easily construct the following SQL statements from within a program by putting the data values literally into the statement strings:

```
SELECT * FROM profile WHERE age > 40 AND color = 'green'

INSERT INTO profile (name,color) VALUES('Gary','blue')
```

However, some data values are not so easily handled and can cause problems if you are not careful. Statements might use values that contain special characters such as quotes, backslashes, binary data, or values that are NULL. The following discussion describes the difficulties caused by these types of values and the proper methods for handling them.

Suppose that you want to execute this INSERT statement:

```
INSERT INTO profile (name,birth,color,foods,cats)
VALUES('Alison','1973-01-12','blue','eggroll',4);
```

There's nothing unusual about that. But if you change the name column value to something like De'Mont that contains a single quote, the statement becomes syntactically invalid:

```
INSERT INTO profile (name,birth,color,foods,cats)
VALUES('De'Mont','1973-01-12','blue','eggroll',4);
```

The problem is that there is a single quote inside a single-quoted string. To make the statement legal, the quote could be escaped by preceding it either with a single quote or with a backslash:

```
INSERT INTO profile (name,birth,color,foods,cats)
VALUES('De''Mont','1973-01-12','blue','eggroll',4);

INSERT INTO profile (name,birth,color,foods,cats)
VALUES('De\'Mont','1973-01-12','blue','eggroll',4);
```

Alternatively, you could quote the name value itself within double quotes rather than within single quotes (assuming that the ANSI_QUOTES SQL mode is not enabled):

```
INSERT INTO profile (name,birth,color,foods,cats)
VALUES("De'Mont",'1973-01-12','blue','eggroll',4);
```

If you are writing a statement literally in your program, you can escape or quote the name value by hand because you know what the value is. But if a variable holds the name value, you don't necessarily know what the variable's value is. Worse yet, single quote isn't the only character you must be prepared to deal with; double quotes and backslashes cause problems, too. And if you want to store binary data such as images or sound clips in your database, a value might contain anything—not just quotes or backslashes, but other characters such as nulls (zero-valued bytes). The need to handle special characters properly is particularly acute in a web environment where statements are constructed using form input (for example, if you're searching for rows that match search terms entered by the remote user). You must be able to handle any kind of input in a general way, because you can't predict in advance what kind of information a user will supply. In fact, it is not uncommon for malicious users to enter garbage values containing problematic characters in a deliberate attempt to compromise the security of your server. That is a standard technique for finding insecure scripts that can be exploited.

The SQL NULL value is not a special character, but it too requires special treatment. In SQL, NULL indicates "no value." This can have several meanings depending on context, such as "unknown," "missing," "out of range," and so forth. Our statements thus far have not used NULL values, to avoid dealing with the complications that they introduce, but now it's time to address these issues. For example, if you don't know De'Mont's favorite color, you can set the color column to NULL—but not by writing the statement like this:

```
INSERT INTO profile (name,birth,color,foods,cats)
VALUES('De''Mont','1973-01-12','NULL','eggroll',4);
```

Instead, the NULL value should have no enclosing quotes:

```
INSERT INTO profile (name,birth,color,foods,cats)
VALUES('De''Mont','1973-01-12',NULL,'eggroll',4);
```

If you were writing the statement literally in your program, you'd simply write the word "NULL" without enclosing quotes. But if the color value comes from a variable, the proper action is not so obvious. You must know something about the variable's value to be able to determine whether to enclose it within quotes when you construct the statement.

There are two general means at your disposal for dealing with special characters such as quotes and backslashes, and with special values such as NULL:

- Use placeholders in the statement string to refer to data values symbolically, and then bind the data values to the placeholders when you execute the statement. Generally, this is the preferred method because the API itself will do all or most of the work for you of providing quotes around values as necessary, quoting or escaping special characters within the data value, and possibly interpreting a special value to map onto NULL without enclosing quotes.

- Use a quoting function (if your API provides one) for converting data values to a safe form that is suitable for use in statement strings.

This section shows how to use these techniques to handle special characters and NULL values for each API. One of the examples demonstrated here shows how to insert a profile table row that contains De'Mont for the name value and NULL for the color value. However, the principles shown here have general utility and handle any special characters, including those found in binary data. (See Chapter 18 for examples showing how to work with images, which are one kind of binary data.) Also, the principles are not limited to INSERT statements. They work for other kinds of statements as well, such as SELECT. One of the other examples shown here demonstrates how to execute a SELECT statement using placeholders.

Special characters come up in other contexts that are not covered here:

- The placeholder and quoting techniques described here are *only* for data values and not for identifiers such as database or table names. For discussion of the problem of quoting identifiers, refer to Recipe 2.6.
- This section covers the issue of getting special characters *into* your database. A related issue not covered here is the inverse operation of transforming special characters in values returned *from* your database for display in various contexts. For example, if you're generating HTML pages that include values taken from your database, you have to convert < and > characters in those values to the HTML entities < and > to make sure they display properly. Recipe 17.4 discusses that topic.

Using placeholders

Placeholders enable you to avoid writing data values literally into SQL statements. Using this approach, you write the statement using placeholders—special characters that indicate where the values go. One common placeholder character is ?. For APIs that use that character, the INSERT statement would be rewritten to use placeholders like this:

```
INSERT INTO profile (name,birth,color,foods,cats)
VALUES(?,?,?,?,?)
```

You then pass the statement string to the database and supply the data values separately. The values are bound to the placeholders to replace them, resulting in a statement that contains the data values.

One of the benefits of using placeholders is that parameter binding operations automatically handle escaping of characters such as quotes and backslashes. This can be especially useful if you're inserting binary data such as images into your database or using data values with unknown content such as input submitted by a remote user through a form on a web page. Also, there is usually some special value that you can bind to a placeholder to indicate that you want an SQL NULL value in the resulting statement.

A second benefit of placeholders is that you can "prepare" a statement in advance and then reuse it by binding different values to it each time it's executed. Some database interfaces have this capability, which allows some preparsing or even execution planning to be done prior to executing the statement. For a statement that is executed multiple times later, this reduces overhead because anything that can be done prior to execution need be done only once, not once per execution. Prepared statements thus encourage statement reuse. Statements become more generic because they contain placeholders rather than specific data values. If you're executing an operation over and over, you may be able to reuse a prepared statement and simply bind different data values to it each time you execute it. If so, you gain a performance benefit, at least for database systems that support query planning. For example, if a program issues a particular type of SELECT statement several times while it runs, such a database system can construct a plan for the statement and then reuse it each time, rather than rebuild the plan over and over. MySQL doesn't build query plans in advance, so you don't get any performance boost from using prepared statements. However, if you port a program to a database that does not use query plans and you've written your program to use prepared statements, you can get this advantage of prepared statements automatically. You don't have to convert from nonprepared statements to enjoy that benefit.

A third benefit is that code that uses placeholder-based statements can be easier to read, although that's somewhat subjective. As you read through this section, compare the statements used here with those from Recipe 2.4 that did not use placeholders to see which you prefer.

Generating a List of Placeholders

You cannot bind an array of data values to a single placeholder. Each value must be bound to a separate placeholder. If you want to use placeholders for a list of data values that may vary in number, you must construct a list of placeholder characters. For example, in Perl, the following statement creates a string consisting of *n* placeholder characters separated by commas:

```
$str = join (",", ("?") x n);
```

The x repetition operator, when applied to a list, produces *n* copies of the list, so the join( ) call joins these lists to produce a single string containing *n* comma-separated instances of the ? character. This is handy when you want to bind an array of data values to a list of placeholders in a statement string because the size of the array indicates how many placeholder characters are needed:

```
$str = join (",", ("?") x @values);
```

In Ruby, the * operator can be used to similar effect:

```
str = (["?"] * values.size).join(",")
```

Another Perl method of generating a list of placeholders that is perhaps less cryptic looks like this:

```
$str = "?" if @values;
for (my $i = 1; $i < @values; $i++)
{
  $str .= ",?";
}
```

This method's syntax is less Perl-specific and therefore easier to translate into other languages. For example, the equivalent method in Python looks like this:

```python
str = ""
if len (values) > 0:
  str = "?"
  for i in range (1, len (values)):
    str = str + ",?"
```

Using a quoting function

Some APIs provide a quoting function that takes a data value as its argument and returns a properly quoted and escaped value suitable for safe insertion into an SQL statement. This is less common than using placeholders, but it can be useful for constructing statements that you do not intend to execute immediately. However, you do need to have a connection open to the database server while you use such a quoting function because the proper quoting rules cannot be selected until the database driver is known. (Some database systems have different quoting rules from others.)

Perl

To use placeholders in Perl DBI scripts, put a ? in your SQL statement string at each location where you want to insert a data value, and then bind the values to the statement. You can bind values by passing them to do( ) or execute( ), or by calling a DBI method specifically intended for placeholder substitution.

With do( ), you can add the **profile** row for De'Mont by passing the statement string and the data values in the same call:

```perl
my $count = $dbh->do ("INSERT INTO profile (name,birth,color,foods,cats)
                VALUES(?,?,?,?,?)",
               undef,
               "De'Mont", "1973-01-12", undef, "eggroll", 4);
```

The arguments after the statement string should be **undef** followed by the data values, one value for each placeholder. (The **undef** argument that follows the statement string is a historical artifact, but it must be present.)

Alternatively, use **prepare( )** plus **execute( )**. Pass the statement string to **prepare( )** to get a statement handle, and then use that handle to pass the data values via **execute( )**:

```perl
my $sth = $dbh->prepare ("INSERT INTO profile (name,birth,color,foods,cats)
                VALUES(?,?,?,?,?)");
my $count = $sth->execute ("De'Mont", "1973-01-12", undef, "eggroll", 4);
```

If you need to issue the same statement over and over again, you can use **prepare( )** once and call **execute( )** each time you need to run the statement.

In either case, the resulting statement generated by DBI is as follows:

```
INSERT INTO profile (name,birth,color,foods,cats)
VALUES('De\'Mont','1973-01-12',NULL,'eggroll','4')
```

Note how DBI adds quotes around data values, even though there were none around the ? placeholder characters in the original statement string. (The placeholder mechanism adds quotes around numeric values, too, but that's okay because the MySQL server performs type conversion as necessary to convert strings to numbers.) Also note the DBI convention that when you bind undef to a placeholder, DBI puts a NULL into the statement and correctly refrains from adding enclosing quotes.

You can use these methods for other types of statements as well. For example, the following SELECT statement uses a placeholder to look for rows that have a cats value larger than 2:

```
my $sth = $dbh->prepare ("SELECT * FROM profile WHERE cats > ?");
$sth->execute (2);
while (my $ref = $sth->fetchrow_hashref ())
{
  print "id: $ref->{id}, name: $ref->{name}, cats: $ref->{cats}\n";
}
```

Another way to bind values to placeholders is to use the bind_param( ) call. It takes two arguments: a placeholder position and a value to bind to the placeholder at that position. (Placeholder positions begin with 1, not 0.) The preceding INSERT and SELECT examples can be rewritten to use bind_param( ) as follows:

```
my $sth = $dbh->prepare ("INSERT INTO profile (name,birth,color,foods,cats)
                          VALUES(?,?,?,?,?)");
$sth->bind_param (1, "De'Mont");
$sth->bind_param (2, "1973-01-12");
$sth->bind_param (3, undef);
$sth->bind_param (4, "eggroll");
$sth->bind_param (5, 4);
my $count = $sth->execute ();

my $sth = $dbh->prepare ("SELECT * FROM profile WHERE cats > ?");
$sth->bind_param (1, 2);
$sth->execute ();
while (my $ref = $sth->fetchrow_hashref ())
{
  print "id: $ref->{id}, name: $ref->{name}, cats: $ref->{cats}\n";
}
```

No matter which method you use for placeholders, don't put any quotes around the ? characters, not even for placeholders that represent strings. DBI adds quotes as necessary on its own. In fact, if you do put quotes around the placeholder character, DBI interprets it as the literal string constant "?", not as a placeholder.

The high-level retrieval methods such as selectrow_array( ) and selectall_arrayref( ) can be used with placeholders, too. Like the do( ) method, the arguments are the statement string and undef, followed by the data values to bind to the placeholders that occur in the statement string. Here's an example:

```
my $ref = $dbh->selectall_arrayref (
              "SELECT name, birth, foods FROM profile
```

```
                    WHERE id > ? AND color = ?",
                    undef, 3, "green");
```

Perl DBI also provides a quote( ) database handle method as an alternative to using placeholders. Here's how to use quote( ) to create a statement string that inserts a new row in the profile table:

```
my $stmt = sprintf ("INSERT INTO profile (name,birth,color,foods,cats)
                    VALUES(%s,%s,%s,%s,%s)",
                    $dbh->quote ("De'Mont"),
                    $dbh->quote ("1973-01-12"),
                    $dbh->quote (undef),
                    $dbh->quote ("eggroll"),
                    $dbh->quote (4));
my $count = $dbh->do ($stmt);
```

The statement string generated by this code is the same as when you use placeholders. The %s format specifiers are written without enclosing quotes because quote( ) provides them automatically as necessary: non-undef values are inserted with quotes, and undef values are inserted as NULL without quotes.

Ruby

Ruby DBI uses ? as the placeholder character in SQL statements and nil as the value to use for binding an SQL NULL value to a placeholder.

To use placeholders with do, pass the statement string followed by the data values to bind to the placeholders:

```
count = dbh.do("INSERT INTO profile (name,birth,color,foods,cats)
                VALUES(?,?,?,?,?)",
               "De'Mont", "1973-01-12", nil, "eggroll", 4)
```

Alternatively, pass the statement string to prepare to get a statement handle, and then use that handle to invoke execute with the data values:

```
sth = dbh.prepare("INSERT INTO profile (name,birth,color,foods,cats)
                    VALUES(?,?,?,?,?)")
count = sth.execute("De'Mont", "1973-01-12", nil, "eggroll", 4)
```

Regardless of how you construct the statement, DBI includes a properly escaped quote and a properly unquoted NULL value:

```
INSERT INTO profile (name,birth,color,foods,cats)
VALUES('De\'Mont','1973-01-12',NULL,'eggroll',4)
```

The approach that uses prepare plus execute is useful for a statement that is executed multiple times with different data values. For a statement to be executed just once, you can skip the prepare step. Pass the statement string to the database handle execute method, followed by the data values. The following example processes a SELECT statement this way:

```
sth = dbh.execute("SELECT * FROM profile WHERE cats > ?", 2)
sth.fetch do |row|
  printf "id: %s, name: %s, cats: %s\n", row["id"], row["name"], row["cats"]
```

```
end
sth.finish
```

The Ruby DBI placeholder mechanism provides quotes around data values as necessary when they are bound to the statement string, so do not put quotes around the ? characters in the string.

The Ruby DBI `quote( )` database handle method is an alternative to placeholders. The following example uses `quote( )` to produce the `INSERT` statement for De'Mont:

```
stmt = sprintf "INSERT INTO profile (name,birth,color,foods,cats)
                VALUES(%s,%s,%s,%s,%s)",
            dbh.quote("De'Mont"),
            dbh.quote("1973-01-12"),
            dbh.quote(nil),
            dbh.quote("eggroll"),
            dbh.quote(4)
count = dbh.do(stmt)
```

The statement string generated by this code is the same as when you use placeholders. The `%s` format specifiers are written without enclosing quotes because `quote( )` provides them automatically as necessary: non-`nil` values are inserted with quotes, and `nil` values are inserted as `NULL` without quotes.

PHP

The PEAR DB module allows placeholders to be used with the `query( )` method that executes SQL statements, or you can use `prepare( )` to prepare a statement, and `execute( )` to supply the data values and execute the prepared statement. PEAR DB uses ? as the placeholder marker in SQL statements and the PHP `NULL` as the value to use when binding an SQL `NULL` value to a placeholder.

With `query( )`, pass the statement string followed by an array that contains the data values to bind to the placeholders:

```
$result =& $conn->query ("INSERT INTO profile (name,birth,color,foods,cats)
                VALUES(?,?,?,?,?)",
                array ("De'Mont","1973-01-12",NULL,"eggroll",4));
if (PEAR::isError ($result))
  die ("Oops, the statement failed");
```

Alternatively, pass the statement string to `prepare( )` to get a statement object. Pass this object and the array of data values to `execute( )`:

```
$stmt =& $conn->prepare ("INSERT INTO profile (name,birth,color,foods,cats)
                VALUES(?,?,?,?,?)");
if (PEAR::isError ($stmt))
  die ("Oops, statement preparation failed");
$result =& $conn->execute ($stmt,
                array ("De'Mont","1973-01-12",NULL,"eggroll",4));
if (PEAR::isError ($result))
  die ("Oops, statement execution failed");
```

The statement constructed either way includes a properly escaped quote and a properly unquoted NULL value:

```
INSERT INTO profile (name,birth,color,foods,cats)
VALUES('De\'Mont','1973-01-12',NULL,'eggroll',4)
```

If there is only one placeholder, the array of data values has only a single member:

```
$result =& $conn->query ("SELECT * FROM profile WHERE cats > ?", array (2));
if (PEAR::isError ($result))
  die ("Oops, the statement failed");
while ($row =& $result->fetchRow (DB_FETCHMODE_ASSOC))
{
  printf ("id: %s, name: %s, cats: %s\n",
      $row["id"], $row["name"], $row["cats"]);
}
$result->free ();
```

In that case, you can specify the data value without using an array. The following two query( ) invocations are equivalent:

```
$result =& $conn->query ("SELECT * FROM profile WHERE cats > ?", array (2));
$result =& $conn->query ("SELECT * FROM profile WHERE cats > ?", 2)
```

The PEAR DB placeholder mechanism provides quotes around data values as necessary when they are bound to the statement string, so do not put quotes around the ? characters in the string.

The PEAR DB quoteSmart( ) method can be used instead of placeholders for quoting data values. The following example inserts the row for De'Mont after using quoteSmart( ) to construct the statement string:

```
$stmt = sprintf ("INSERT INTO profile (name,birth,color,foods,cats)
                  VALUES(%s,%s,%s,%s,%s)",
                  $conn->quoteSmart ("De'Mont"),
                  $conn->quoteSmart ("1973-01-12"),
                  $conn->quoteSmart (NULL),
                  $conn->quoteSmart ("eggroll"),
                  $conn->quoteSmart (4));
$result =& $conn->query ($stmt);
if (PEAR::isError ($result))
  die ("Oops, the statement failed");
```

PEAR DB also has an escapeSimple( ) quoting method, but it's inferior to quoteSmart( ). For example, it doesn't handle NULL values properly.

Python

Python's MySQLdb module implements placeholders using format specifiers in the SQL statement string. To use placeholders, invoke the execute( ) method with two arguments: a statement string containing format specifiers and a sequence containing the values to bind to the statement string. To add the profile table row for De'Mont, the code looks like this:

```
cursor = conn.cursor ()
cursor.execute ("""
                INSERT INTO profile (name,birth,color,foods,cats)
                VALUES(%s,%s,%s,%s,%s)
                """, ("De'Mont", "1973-01-12", None, "eggroll", 4))
```

Some of the Python DB-API driver modules support several format specifiers (such as %d for integers and %f for floating-point numbers). With MySQLdb, you should use a placeholder of %s to format all data values as strings. MySQL will perform type conversion as necessary. To place a literal % character into the statement, use %% in the statement string.

The parameter binding mechanism adds quotes around data values where necessary. DB-API treats None as logically equivalent to the SQL NULL value, so you can bind None to a placeholder to produce a NULL in the statement string. The statement that is sent to the server by the preceding execute( ) call looks like this:

```
INSERT INTO profile (name,birth,color,foods,cats)
VALUES('De\'Mont','1973-01-12',NULL,'eggroll',4)
```

If you have only a single value *val* to bind to a placeholder, you can write it as a sequence using the syntax (*val*,). The following SELECT statement demonstrates this:

```
cursor = conn.cursor ()
cursor.execute ("SELECT * FROM profile WHERE cats = %s", (2,))
for row in cursor.fetchall ():
  print row
cursor.close ()
```

Python's placeholder mechanism provides quotes around data values as necessary when they are bound to the statement string, so do not put quotes around the %s format specifiers in the string.

With MySQLdb, an alternative method of quoting data values is to use the literal( ) method. To produce the INSERT statement for De'Mont by using literal( ), do this:

```
cursor = conn.cursor ()
stmt = """
        INSERT INTO profile (name,birth,color,foods,cats)
        VALUES(%s,%s,%s,%s,%s)
        """ % \
        (conn.literal ("De'Mont"), \
        conn.literal ("1973-01-12"), \
        conn.literal (None), \
        conn.literal ("eggroll"), \
        conn.literal (4))
cursor.execute (stmt)
```

Java

JDBC provides support for placeholders if you use prepared statements. Recall that the process for issuing nonprepared statements in JDBC is to create a Statement object and then pass the statement string to one of the statement-issuing functions executeUpdate( ), executeQuery( ), or execute( ). To use a prepared statement instead, create a `PreparedStatement` object by passing a statement string containing `?` placeholder characters to your connection object's `prepareStatement( )` method. Then bind your data values to the statement using set*XXX*( ) methods. Finally, execute the statement by calling executeUpdate( ), executeQuery( ), or execute( ) with an empty argument list.

Here is an example that uses executeUpdate( ) to issue an `INSERT` statement that adds the `profile` table row for De'Mont:

```
PreparedStatement s;
int count;
s = conn.prepareStatement (
          "INSERT INTO profile (name,birth,color,foods,cats)"
          + " VALUES(?,?,?,?,?)");
s.setString (1, "De'Mont");          // bind values to placeholders
s.setString (2, "1973-01-12");
s.setNull (3, java.sql.Types.CHAR);
s.setString (4, "eggroll");
s.setInt (5, 4);
count = s.executeUpdate ();
s.close ();    // close statement
```

The set*XXX*( ) methods that bind data values to statements take two arguments: a placeholder position (beginning with 1, not 0) and the value to bind to the placeholder. Choose each value-binding call to match the data type of the column to which the value is bound: setString( ) to bind a string to the `name` column, setInt( ) to bind an integer to the `cats` column, and so forth. (Actually, I cheated a bit by using setString( ) to treat the date value for `birth` as a string.)

One difference between JDBC and the other APIs is that you don't specify a special value to bind a `NULL` to a placeholder by specifying some special value (such as undef in Perl or nil in Ruby). Instead, you invoke a special method setNull( ), in which the second argument indicates the type of the column (`java.sql.Types.CHAR` for a string, `java.sql.Types.INTEGER` for an integer, and so forth).

The set*XXX*( ) calls add quotes around data values if necessary, so do not put quotes around the `?` placeholder characters in the statement string.

For a statement that returns a result set, the preparation process is similar, but you execute the prepared statement with executeQuery( ) instead:

```
PreparedStatement s;
s = conn.prepareStatement ("SELECT * FROM profile WHERE cats > ?");
s.setInt (1, 2); // bind 2 to first placeholder
s.executeQuery ();
// ... process result set here ...
s.close ();      // close statement
```

2.6 Handling Special Characters in Identifiers

Problem

You need to construct SQL statements that refer to identifiers containing special characters.

Solution

Quote the identifiers so that they can be inserted safely into statement strings.

Discussion

Recipe 2.5 discusses how to handle special characters in data values by using placeholders or quoting methods. Special characters also can be present in identifiers such as database, table, and column names. For example, the table name some table contains a space, which is not allowed by default:

```
mysql> CREATE TABLE some table (i INT);
ERROR 1064 (42000): You have an error in your SQL syntax near 'table (i INT)'
```

Special characters are handled differently in identifiers than in data values. To make an identifier safe for insertion into an SQL statement, quote it by enclosing it within backticks:

```
mysql> CREATE TABLE `some table` (i INT);
Query OK, 0 rows affected (0.04 sec)
```

If a quoting character appears within the identifier itself, double it when quoting the identifier. For example, quote abc`def as `abc``def`.

In MySQL, backticks are always allowed for identifier quoting. If the ANSI_QUOTES SQL mode is enabled, the double-quote character also is legal for quoting identifiers. Thus, both of the following statements are equivalent with the ANSI_QUOTES SQL mode enabled:

```
CREATE TABLE `some table` (i INT);
CREATE TABLE "some table" (i INT);
```

If it's necessary to know which identifier quoting characters are allowable, issue a SELECT @@sql_mode statement to retrieve the SQL mode and check whether its value includes ANSI_QUOTES.

Be aware that although strings in MySQL normally can be quoted using either single-quote or double-quote characters ('abc', "abc"), that is not true when ANSI_QUOTES is enabled. In that case, MySQL interprets 'abc' as a string and "abc" as an identifier, so you must use only single quotes for strings.

Within a program, you can use an identifier-quoting routine if your API provides one, or write one yourself if it does not. Perl DBI has a quote_identifier( ) method that returns a properly quoted identifier. For an API that has no such method, you can quote an identifier by enclosing it within backticks and doubling any backticks that occur within the identifier. Here's a Ruby routine that does so:

```ruby
def quote_identifier(ident)
  return "`" + ident.gsub(/`/, "``") + "`"
end
```

If you're willing to assume that an identifier has no internal backticks, you can simply enclose it within backticks.

Portability note: If you write your own identifier-quoting routines, remember that other DBMSs may require different quoting conventions.

In some contexts, identifiers might be used as data values, and should be handled as such. If you select information from INFORMATION_SCHEMA, the metadata database, it's common to indicate which rows to return by specifying database object names in the WHERE clause. For example, this statement retrieves the column names for the profile table in the cookbook database:

```sql
SELECT COLUMN_NAME FROM INFORMATION_SCHEMA.COLUMNS
WHERE TABLE_SCHEMA = 'cookbook' AND TABLE_NAME = 'item';
```

The database and table names are used here as data values, not as identifiers. Were you to construct this statement within a program, you would parameterize them using placeholders, not identifier quoting. For example, you might do this in Ruby:

```ruby
names = dbh.select_all(
            "SELECT COLUMN_NAME FROM INFORMATION_SCHEMA.COLUMNS
             WHERE TABLE_SCHEMA = ? AND TABLE_NAME = ?",
            db_name, tbl_name)
```

2.7 Identifying NULL Values in Result Sets

Problem

A query result includes NULL values, but you're not sure how to tell where they are.

Solution

Your API probably has some special value that represents NULL by convention. You just have to know what it is and how to test for it.

Discussion

Recipe 2.5 described how to refer to NULL values when you send statements *to* the database server. In this section, we'll deal instead with the question of how to recognize and process NULL values that are returned *from* the database server. In general, this is a matter of knowing what special value the API maps NULL values onto, or what method to call. These values are shown in the following table:

Language	NULL-detection value or method
Perl DBI	undef value
Ruby DBI	nil value
PHP PEAR DB	A NULL or unset value
Python DB-API	None value
Java JDBC	wasNull( ) method

The following sections show a very simple application of NULL value detection. The examples retrieve a result set and print all values in it, mapping NULL values onto the printable string "NULL".

To make sure the profile table has a row that contains some NULL values, use *mysql* to issue the following INSERT statement, and then issue the SELECT statement to verify that the resulting row has the expected values:

```
mysql> INSERT INTO profile (name) VALUES('Juan');
mysql> SELECT * FROM profile WHERE name = 'Juan';
+----+------+-------+-------+-------+------+
| id | name | birth | color | foods | cats |
+----+------+-------+-------+-------+------+
| 11 | Juan | NULL  | NULL  | NULL  | NULL |
+----+------+-------+-------+-------+------+
```

The id column might contain a different number, but the other columns should appear as shown, with values of NULL.

Perl

Perl DBI represents NULL values using undef. It's easy to detect such values using the defined( ) function, and it's particularly important to do so if you enable warnings with the Perl -w option or by including a use warnings line in your script. Otherwise, accessing undef values causes Perl to issue the following complaint:

```
Use of uninitialized value
```

To avoid this warning, test column values that might be undef with defined( ) before using them. The following code selects a few columns from the profile column and prints "NULL" for any undefined values in each row. This makes NULL values explicit in the output without activating any warning messages:

```
my $sth = $dbh->prepare ("SELECT name, birth, foods FROM profile");
$sth->execute ();
while (my $ref = $sth->fetchrow_hashref ())
{
  printf "name: %s, birth: %s, foods: %s\n",
        defined ($ref->{name}) ? $ref->{name} : "NULL",
        defined ($ref->{birth}) ? $ref->{birth} : "NULL",
        defined ($ref->{foods}) ? $ref->{foods} : "NULL";
}
```

Unfortunately, all that testing of column values is ponderous and becomes worse the more columns there are. To avoid this, you can test and set undefined values in a loop prior to printing them. Then the amount of code you have to write to perform the tests is constant, not proportional to the number of columns to be tested. The loop also makes no reference to specific column names, so it can more easily be copied and pasted to other programs or used as the basis for a utility routine:

```
my $sth = $dbh->prepare ("SELECT name, birth, foods FROM profile");
$sth->execute ();
while (my $ref = $sth->fetchrow_hashref ())
{
  foreach my $key (keys (%{$ref}))
  {
    $ref->{$key} = "NULL" unless defined ($ref->{$key});
  }
  printf "name: %s, birth: %s, foods: %s\n",
         $ref->{name}, $ref->{birth}, $ref->{foods};
}
```

If you fetch rows into an array rather than into a hash, you can use map to convert any undef values:

```
my $sth = $dbh->prepare ("SELECT name, birth, foods FROM profile");
$sth->execute ();
while (my @val = $sth->fetchrow_array ())
{
  @val = map { defined ($_) ? $_ : "NULL" } @val;
  printf "name: %s, birth: %s, foods: %s\n",
         $val[0], $val[1], $val[2];
}
```

Ruby

Ruby DBI represents NULL values using nil, which can be identified by applying the nil? method to a value. The following example uses nil? to determine whether to print result set values as is or as the string "NULL" for NULL values:

```
dbh.execute("SELECT name, birth, foods FROM profile") do |sth|
  sth.fetch do |row|
    for i in 0...row.length
      row[i] = "NULL" if row[i].nil? # is the column value NULL?
    end
    printf "id: %s, name: %s, cats: %s\n", row[0], row[1], row[2]
  end
end
```

A shorter alternative to the for loop is the collect! method, which takes each array element in turn and replaces it with the value returned by the code block:

```
row.collect! { |val| val.nil? ? "NULL" : val }
```

PHP

PHP represents SQL NULL values in result sets as the PHP NULL value. To determine whether a value from a result set represents a NULL value, compare it to the PHP NULL value using the === triple equal operator:

```
if ($val === NULL)
{
  # $val is a NULL value
}
```

In PHP, the triple equal operator means "exactly equal to." The usual == equal to comparison operator is not suitable here. If you use ==, PHP considers the NULL value, the empty string, and 0 all equal to each other.

An alternative to using === to test for NULL values is to use isset( ):

```
if (!isset ($val))
{
  # $val is a NULL value
}
```

The following code uses the === operator to identify NULL values in a result set and print them as the string "NULL":

```
$result =& $conn->query ("SELECT name, birth, foods FROM profile");
if (PEAR::isError ($result))
    die ("Oops, the statement failed");
while ($row =& $result->fetchRow ())
{
  foreach ($row as $key => $value)
  {
    if ($row[$key] === NULL)
      $row[$key] = "NULL";
  }
  print ("name: $row[0], birth: $row[1], foods: $row[2]\n");
}
$result->free ();
```

Python

Python DB-API programs represent NULL in result sets using None. The following example shows how to detect NULL values:

```
cursor = conn.cursor ()
cursor.execute ("SELECT name, birth, foods FROM profile")
for row in cursor.fetchall ():
  row = list (row)  # convert nonmutable tuple to mutable list
  for i in range (0, len (row)):
    if row[i] == None:  # is the column value NULL?
      row[i] = "NULL"
  print "name: %s, birth: %s, foods: %s" % (row[0], row[1], row[2])
cursor.close ()
```

The inner loop checks for NULL column values by looking for None and converts them to the string "NULL". Note how the example converts row to a mutable object prior to the loop; `fetchall( )` returns rows as sequence values, which are nonmutable (read-only).

Java

For JDBC programs, if it's possible for a column in a result set to contain NULL values, it's best to check for them explicitly. The way to do this is to fetch the value and then invoke `wasNull( )`, which returns `true` if the column is NULL and `false` otherwise. For example:

```
Object obj = rs.getObject (index);
if (rs.wasNull ())
{ /* the value's a NULL */ }
```

The preceding example uses `getObject( )`, but the principle holds for other get*XXX*( ) calls as well.

Here's an example that prints each row of a result set as a comma-separated list of values, with "NULL" printed for each NULL value:

```
Statement s = conn.createStatement ();
s.executeQuery ("SELECT name, birth, foods FROM profile");
ResultSet rs = s.getResultSet ();
ResultSetMetaData md = rs.getMetaData ();
int ncols = md.getColumnCount ();
while (rs.next ())  // loop through rows of result set
{
  for (int i = 0; i < ncols; i++) // loop through columns
  {
    String val = rs.getString (i+1);
    if (i > 0)
      System.out.print (", ");
    if (rs.wasNull ())
      System.out.print ("NULL");
    else
      System.out.print (val);
  }
  System.out.println ();
}
rs.close (); // close result set
s.close ();   // close statement
```

2.8 Techniques for Obtaining Connection Parameters

Problem

You need to obtain connection parameters for a script so that it can connect to a MySQL server.

Solution

There are lots of ways to do this. Take your pick from the alternatives in the following section.

Discussion

Any program that connects to MySQL needs to specify connection parameters such as the username, password, and hostname. The recipes shown so far have put connection parameters directly into the code that attempts to establish the connection, but that is not the only way for your programs to obtain the parameters. This section briefly surveys some of the techniques you can use and then shows how to implement two of them.

Hardwire the parameters into the program

> The parameters can be given either in the main source file or in a library file that is used by the program. This technique is convenient because users need not enter the values themselves. The flip side is that it's not very flexible. To change the parameters, you must modify your program.

Ask for the parameters interactively

> In a command-line environment, you can ask the user a series of questions. In a web or GUI environment, this might be done by presenting a form or dialog. Either way, this gets to be tedious for people who use the application frequently, due to the need to enter the parameters each time.

Get the parameters from the command line

> This method can be used either for commands that you run interactively or that are run from within a script. Like the method of obtaining parameters interactively, this requires you to supply parameters each time you use MySQL and can be similarly tiresome. (A factor that significantly mitigates this burden is that many shells enable you to easily recall commands from your history list for re-execution.)

Get the parameters from the execution environment

> The most common way to use this method is to set the appropriate environment variables in one of your shell's startup files (such as .*profile* for *sh*, *bash*, *ksh*; or .*login* for *csh* or *tcsh*). Programs that you run during your login session then can get parameter values by examining their environment.

Get the parameters from a separate file

> With this method, you store information such as the username and password in a file that programs can read before connecting to the MySQL server. Reading parameters from a file that's separate from your program gives you the benefit of not having to enter them each time you use the program, while allowing you to avoid hardwiring the values into the program itself. This technique is especially convenient for interactive programs, because then you need not enter parameters each time you run the program. Also, storing the values in a file enables you to centralize parameters for use by multiple programs, and you can use the file access mode for

security purposes. For example, you can keep other users from reading the file by setting its mode to restrict access to yourself.

The MySQL client library itself supports an option file mechanism, although not all APIs provide access to it. For those that don't, workarounds may exist. (As an example, Java supports the use of properties files and supplies utility routines for reading them.)

Use a combination of methods

It's often useful to combine some of the preceding methods, to give users the flexibility of providing parameters different ways. For example, MySQL clients such as *mysql* and *mysqladmin* look for option files in several locations and read any that are present. They then check the command-line arguments for further parameters. This enables users to specify connection parameters in an option file or on the command line.

These methods of obtaining connection parameters do involve some security concerns. Here is a brief summary of the issues:

- Any method that stores connection parameters in a file may compromise your system's security unless the file is protected against access by unauthorized users. This is true whether parameters are stored in a source file, an option file, or a script that invokes a command and specifies the parameters on the command line. (Web scripts that can be read only by the web server don't qualify as secure if other users have administrative access to the server.)

- Parameters specified on the command line or in environment variables are not particularly secure. While a program is executing, its command-line arguments and environment may be visible to other users who run process status commands such as ps -e. In particular, storing the password in an environment variable perhaps is best limited to those situations in which you're the only user on the machine or you trust all other users.

The rest of this section shows how to process command-line arguments to get connection parameters and how to read parameters from option files.

Getting parameters from the command line

The usual MySQL convention for command-line arguments (that is, the convention followed by standard clients such as *mysql* and *mysqladmin*) is to allow parameters to be specified using either a short option or a long option. For example, the username cbuser can be specified either as -u cbuser (or -ucbuser) or --user=cbuser. In addition, for either of the password options (-p or --password), the password value may be omitted after the option name to indicate that the program should prompt for the password interactively.

The next set of example programs shows how to process command arguments to obtain the hostname, username, and password. The standard flags for these are -h or --host, -u or --user, and -p or --password. You can write your own code to iterate through the argument list, but in general, it's much easier to use existing option-processing modules written for that purpose.

To enable a script to use other options, such as `--port` or `--socket`, you can use the code shown but extend the option-specifier arrays to include additional options. You'll also need to modify the connection-establishment code slightly to use the option values if they are given.

For those APIs shown here (Perl, Ruby, Python), the programs presented use a `getopt( )`-style function. For Java, look under the *api* directory in the `recipes` distribution for sample code that is not shown here, as well as instructions for using it.

 Insofar as possible, the examples mimic the option-handling behavior of the standard MySQL clients. An exception is that option-processing libraries may not allow for making the password value optional, and they provide no way of prompting the user for a password interactively if a password option is specified without a password value. Consequently, the example scripts are written so that if you use -p or --password, you must provide the password value following the option.

Perl. Perl passes command-line arguments to scripts via the `@ARGV` array, which can be processed using the `GetOptions( )` function of the Getopt::Long module. The following program shows how to parse the command arguments for connection parameters.

```perl
#!/usr/bin/perl
# cmdline.pl - demonstrate command-line option parsing in Perl

use strict;
use warnings;
use DBI;

use Getopt::Long;
$Getopt::Long::ignorecase = 0; # options are case sensitive
$Getopt::Long::bundling = 1;   # allow short options to be bundled

# connection parameters - all missing (undef) by default
my $host_name;
my $password;
my $user_name;

GetOptions (
  # =s means a string value is required after the option
  "host|h=s"      => \$host_name,
  "password|p=s"  => \$password,
  "user|u=s"      => \$user_name
) or exit (1);  # no error message needed; GetOptions() prints its own

# any remaining nonoption arguments are left
# in @ARGV and can be processed here as necessary

# construct data source name
```

```
my $dsn = "DBI:mysql:database=cookbook";
$dsn .= ";host=$host_name" if defined ($host_name);

# connect to server
my %conn_attrs = (PrintError => 0, RaiseError => 1, AutoCommit => 1);
my $dbh = DBI->connect ($dsn, $user_name, $password, \%conn_attrs);
print "Connected\n";

$dbh->disconnect ();
print "Disconnected\n";
```

The arguments to GetOptions( ) are pairs of option specifiers and references to the script variables into which option values should be placed. An option specifier lists both the long and short forms of the option (without leading dashes), followed by =s if the option requires a following value. For example, "host|h=s" allows both --host and -h and indicates that a following string value is required. You need not pass the @ARGV array because GetOptions( ) uses it implicitly. When GetOptions( ) returns, @ARGV contains any remaining nonoption arguments.

Ruby. Ruby programs access command-line arguments via the ARGV array, which you can process with the GetoptLong.new( ) method. The following program uses this method to parse the command arguments for connection parameters:

```ruby
#!/usr/bin/ruby -w
# cmdline.rb - demonstrate command-line option parsing in Ruby

require "getoptlong"
require "dbi"

# connection parameters - all missing (nil) by default
host_name = nil
password = nil
user_name = nil

opts = GetoptLong.new(
  [ "--host",     "-h",  GetoptLong::REQUIRED_ARGUMENT ],
  [ "--password", "-p",  GetoptLong::REQUIRED_ARGUMENT ],
  [ "--user",     "-u",  GetoptLong::REQUIRED_ARGUMENT ]
)

# iterate through options, extracting whatever values are present;
# opt will be the long-format option, arg is its value
opts.each do |opt, arg|
  case opt
  when "--host"
    host_name = arg
  when "--password"
    password = arg
  when "--user"
    user_name = arg
  end
end

# any remaining nonoption arguments are left
```

```
# in ARGV and can be processed here as necessary

# construct data source name
dsn = "DBI:Mysql:database=cookbook"
dsn << ";host=#{host_name}" unless host_name.nil?

# connect to server
begin
  dbh = DBI.connect(dsn, user_name, password)
  puts "Connected"
rescue DBI::DatabaseError => e
  puts "Cannot connect to server"
  puts "Error code: #{e.err}"
  puts "Error message: #{e.errstr}"
  exit(1)
end

dbh.disconnect()
puts "Disconnected"
```

To process the ARGV array, use the GetoptLong.new( ) method, and pass information to it that indicates which options to recognize. Each argument to this method is an array of three values:

- The long option name.
- The short option name.
- A flag that indicates whether the option requires a value. The allowable flags are GetoptLong::NO_ARGUMENT (option takes no value), GetoptLong::REQUIRED_ARGU MENT (option requires a value), and GetoptLong::OPTIONAL_ARGUMENT (option value is optional). For the example program, all options require a value.

Python. Python passes command arguments to scripts as a list via the sys.argv variable. You can access this variable and process its contents by importing the sys and getopt modules. The following program illustrates how to get parameters from the command arguments and use them for establishing a connection to the server:

```
#!/usr/bin/python
# cmdline.py - demonstrate command-line option parsing in Python

import sys
import getopt
import MySQLdb

try:
  opts, args = getopt.getopt (sys.argv[1:],
                              "h:p:u:",
                              [ "host=", "password=", "user=" ])
except getopt.error, e:
  # for errors, print program name and text of error message
  print "%s: %s" % (sys.argv[0], e)
  sys.exit (1)

# default connection parameter values (all empty)
```

```
host_name = password = user_name = ""

# iterate through options, extracting whatever values are present
for opt, arg in opts:
  if opt in ("-h", "--host"):
    host_name = arg
  elif opt in ("-p", "--password"):
    password = arg
  elif opt in ("-u", "--user"):
    user_name = arg

# any remaining nonoption arguments are left in
# args and can be processed here as necessary

try:
  conn = MySQLdb.connect (db = "cookbook",
                          host = host_name,
                          user = user_name,
                          passwd = password)
  print "Connected"
except MySQLdb.Error, e:
  print "Cannot connect to server"
  print "Error:", e.args[1]
  print "Code:", e.args[0]
  sys.exit (1)

conn.close ()
print "Disconnected"
```

getopt( ) takes either two or three arguments:

- A list of command arguments to be processed. This should not include the program name, sys.argv[0], so use sys.argv[1:] to refer to the list of arguments that follow the program name.

- A string naming the short option letters. In *cmdline.py*, each of these is followed by a colon character (:) to indicate that the option requires a following value.

- An optional list of long option names. In *cmdline.py*, each name is followed by = to indicate that the option requires a following value.

getopt( ) returns two values. The first is a list of option/value pairs, and the second is a list of any remaining nonoption arguments following the last option. *cmdline.py* iterates through the option list to determine which options are present and what their values are. Note that although you do not specify leading dashes in the option names passed to getopt( ), the names returned from that function do include leading dashes.

Getting parameters from option files

If your API allows it, you can specify connection parameters in a MySQL option file and the API will read the parameters from the file for you. For APIs that do not support option files directly, you may be able to arrange to read other types of files in which parameters are stored or to write your own functions that read option files.

Recipe 1.4 describes the format of MySQL option files. I'll assume that you've read the discussion there and concentrate here on how to use option files from within programs. Under Unix, user-specific options are specified by convention in *~/.my.cnf* (that is, in the *.my.cnf* file in your home directory). However, the MySQL option file mechanism can look in several different files if they exist (no option file is *required* to exist). The standard search order is */etc/my.cnf*, the *my.cnf* file in the MySQL installation directory, and the *~/.my.cnf* file for the current user. Under Windows, the option files you can use are the *my.ini* file in your MySQL installation directory (for example, *C:\Program Files\MySQL\MySQL Server 5.0*), *my.ini* in your Windows directory (this is something like *C:\Windows* or *C:\WINNT*), or the *my.cnf* file.

If multiple option files exist and a given parameter is specified in several of them, the last value found takes precedence.

MySQL option files are not used by your own programs unless you tell them to do so:

- Perl, Ruby, and Python provide direct API support for reading option files; simply indicate that you want to use them at the time that you connect to the server. It's possible to specify that only a particular file should be read, or that the standard search order should be used to look for multiple option files.

- PHP and Java do not support option files. As a workaround for PHP, we'll write a simple option file parsing function. For Java, we'll adopt a different approach that uses properties files.

Although the conventional name under Unix for the user-specific option file is *.my.cnf* in the current user's home directory, there's no rule that your programs must use this particular file. You can name an option file anything you like and put it wherever you want. For example, you might set up a file named *mcb.cnf* and install it in the */usr/local/lib/mcb* directory for use by scripts that access the cookbook database. Under some circumstances, you might even want to create multiple option files. Then, from within any given script, you can select the file that's appropriate for the type of permissions the script needs. For example, you might have one option file, *mcb.cnf*, that lists parameters for a full-access MySQL account, and another file, *mcb-ro.cnf*, that lists connection parameters for an account that needs only read-only access to MySQL. Another possibility is to list multiple groups within the same option file and have your scripts select options from the appropriate group.

Perl. Perl DBI scripts can use option files. To take advantage of this, place the appropriate option specifiers in the third component of the data source name string:

- To specify an option group, use `mysql_read_default_group=`*groupname*. This tells MySQL to search the standard option files for options in the named group and in the `[client]` group. The *groupname* value should be written without the square brackets that are part of the line that begins the group. For example, if a group in an option file begins with a `[my_prog]` line, specify `my_prog` as the *groupname* value.

To search the standard files but look only in the [client] group, *groupname* should be client.

- To name a specific option file, use mysql_read_default_file=*filename* in the DSN. When you do this, MySQL looks only in that file and only for options in the [client] group.

- If you specify both an option file and an option group, MySQL reads only the named file, but looks for options both in the named group and in the [client] group.

The following example tells MySQL to use the standard option file search order to look for options in both the [cookbook] and [client] groups:

```
my %conn_attrs = (PrintError => 0, RaiseError => 1, AutoCommit => 1);
# basic DSN
my $dsn = "DBI:mysql:database=cookbook";
# look in standard option files; use [cookbook] and [client] groups
$dsn .= ";mysql_read_default_group=cookbook";
my $dbh = DBI->connect ($dsn, undef, undef, \%conn_attrs);
```

The next example explicitly names the option file located in $ENV{HOME}, the home directory of the user running the script. Thus, MySQL will look only in that file and will use options from the [client] group:

```
my %conn_attrs = (PrintError => 0, RaiseError => 1, AutoCommit => 1);
# basic DSN
my $dsn = "DBI:mysql:database=cookbook";
# look in user-specific option file owned by the current user
$dsn .= ";mysql_read_default_file=$ENV{HOME}/.my.cnf";
my $dbh = DBI->connect ($dsn, undef, undef, \%conn_attrs);
```

If you pass an empty value (undef or the empty string) for the username or password arguments of the connect( ) call, connect( ) uses whatever values are found in the option file or files. A nonempty username or password in the connect( ) call overrides any option file value. Similarly, a host named in the DSN overrides any option file value. You can use this behavior to enable DBI scripts to obtain connection parameters both from option files as well as from the command line as follows:

1. Create $host_name, $user_name, and $password variables and initialize them to undef. Then parse the command-line arguments to set the variables to non-undef values if the corresponding options are present on the command line. (The *cmdline.pl* Perl script shown earlier in this recipe for processing command-line arguments demonstrates how to do this.)

2. After parsing the command arguments, construct the DSN string, and call connect( ). Use mysql_read_default_group and mysql_read_default_file in the DSN to specify how you want option files to be used, and, if $host_name is not undef, add host=$host_name to the DSN. In addition, pass $user_name and $password as the username and password arguments to connect( ). These will be

undef by default; if they were set from the command-line arguments, they will have non-undef values that override any option file values.

If a script follows this procedure, parameters given by the user on the command line are passed to connect( ) and take precedence over the contents of option files.

Ruby. Ruby DBI scripts can access option files by using a mechanism analogous to that used for Perl DBI, and the following examples correspond exactly to those shown in the preceding Perl discussion.

This example use the standard option file search order to look for options in both the [cookbook] and [client] groups:

```
# basic DSN
dsn = "DBI:Mysql:database=cookbook"
# look in standard option files; use [cookbook] and [client] groups
dsn << ";mysql_read_default_group=cookbook"
dbh = DBI.connect(dsn, nil, nil)
```

The following example uses the *.my.cnf* file in the current user's home directory to obtain parameters from the [client] group:

```
# basic DSN
dsn = "DBI:Mysql:database=cookbook"
# look in user-specific option file owned by the current user
dsn << ";mysql_read_default_file=#{ENV['HOME']}/.my.cnf"
dbh = DBI.connect(dsn, nil, nil)
```

PHP. PHP has no native support for using MySQL option files. To work around that limitation, use a function that reads an option file, such as the read_mysql_option_file( ) function shown in the following listing. It takes as arguments the name of an option file and an option group name or an array containing group names. (Group names should be named without square brackets.) It then reads any options present in the file for the named group or groups. If no option group argument is given, the function looks by default in the [client] group. The return value is an array of option name/value pairs, or FALSE if an error occurs. It is not an error for the file not to exist. (Note that quoted option values and trailing #-style comments following option values are legal in MySQL option files, but this function does not handle those constructs.)

```
function read_mysql_option_file ($filename, $group_list = "client")
{
  if (is_string ($group_list))          # convert string to array
    $group_list = array ($group_list);
  if (!is_array ($group_list))          # hmm ... garbage argument?
    return (FALSE);
  $opt = array ();                      # option name/value array
  if (!@($fp = fopen ($filename, "r"))) # if file does not exist,
    return ($opt);                      # return an empty list
  $in_named_group = 0;  # set nonzero while processing a named group
  while ($s = fgets ($fp, 1024))
  {
    $s = trim ($s);
```

```
    if (ereg ("^[#;]", $s))              # skip comments
      continue;
    if (ereg ("^\[([^]]+)]", $s, $arg))  # option group line?
    {
      # check whether we're in one of the desired groups
      $in_named_group = 0;
      foreach ($group_list as $key => $group_name)
      {
        if ($arg[1] == $group_name)
        {
          $in_named_group = 1;    # we are in a desired group
          break;
        }
      }
      continue;
    }
    if (!$in_named_group)          # we're not in a desired
      continue;                    # group, skip the line
    if (ereg ("^([^ \t=]+)[ \t]*=[ \t]*(.*)", $s, $arg))
      $opt[$arg[1]] = $arg[2];     # name=value
    else if (ereg ("^([^ \t]+)", $s, $arg))
      $opt[$arg[1]] = "";          # name only
    # else line is malformed
  }
  return ($opt);
}
```

Here are a couple of examples showing how to use read_mysql_option_file( ). The first reads a user's option file to get the [client] group parameters and then uses them to connect to the server. The second reads the system-wide option file, */etc/my.cnf*, and prints the server startup parameters that are found there (that is, the parameters in the [mysqld] and [server] groups):

```
$opt = read_mysql_option_file ("/u/paul/.my.cnf");
$dsn = array
(
  "phptype"  => "mysqli",
  "username" => $opt["user"],
  "password" => $opt["password"],
  "hostspec" => $opt["host"],
  "database" => "cookbook"
);
$conn =& DB::connect ($dsn);
if (PEAR::isError ($conn))
  print ("Cannot connect to server\n");

$opt = read_mysql_option_file ("/etc/my.cnf", array ("mysqld", "server"));
foreach ($opt as $name => $value)
  print ("$name => $value\n");
```

Python. The MySQLdb module for DB-API provides direct support for using MySQL option files. Specify an option file or option group using read_default_file or read_default_group arguments to the connect( ) method. These two arguments act the same way as the mysql_read_default_file and mysql_read_default_group options for the Perl DBI connect( ) method (see the Perl discussion earlier in this section). To use the standard option file search order to look for options in both the [cookbook] and [client] groups, do something like this:

```
conn = MySQLdb.connect (db = "cookbook", read_default_group = "cookbook")
```

The following example shows how to use the *.my.cnf* file in the current user's home directory to obtain parameters from the [client] group:

```
option_file = os.environ["HOME"] + "/" + ".my.cnf"
conn = MySQLdb.connect (db = "cookbook", read_default_file = option_file)
```

You must import the os module to access os.environ.

Java. The MySQL Connector/J JDBC driver doesn't support option files. However, the Java class library provides support for reading properties files that contain lines in *name=value* format. This is somewhat similar to MySQL option file format, although there are some differences (for example, properties files do not allow [*groupname*] lines). Here is a simple properties file:

```
# this file lists parameters for connecting to the MySQL server
user=cbuser
password=cbpass
host=localhost
```

The following program, *ReadPropsFile.java*, shows one way to read a properties file named *Cookbook.properties* to obtain connection parameters. The file must be in some directory that is named in your CLASSPATH variable, or else you must specify it using a full pathname (the example shown here assumes that the file is in a CLASSPATH directory):

```java
import java.sql.*;
import java.util.*;    // need this for properties file support

public class ReadPropsFile
{
  public static void main (String[] args)
  {
    Connection conn = null;
    String url = null;
    String propsFile = "Cookbook.properties";
    Properties props = new Properties ();

    try
    {
      props.load (ReadPropsFile.class.getResourceAsStream (propsFile));
    }
    catch (Exception e)
    {
      System.err.println ("Cannot read properties file");
      System.exit (1);
    }
    try
    {
      // construct connection URL, encoding username
      // and password as parameters at the end
```

```
        url = "jdbc:mysql://"
              + props.getProperty ("host")
              + "/cookbook"
              + "?user=" + props.getProperty ("user")
              + "&password=" + props.getProperty ("password");
        Class.forName ("com.mysql.jdbc.Driver").newInstance ();
        conn = DriverManager.getConnection (url);
        System.out.println ("Connected");
      }
      catch (Exception e)
      {
        System.err.println ("Cannot connect to server");
      }
      finally
      {
        try
        {
          if (conn != null)
          {
            conn.close ();
            System.out.println ("Disconnected");
          }
        }
        catch (SQLException e) { /* ignore close errors */ }
      }
    }
  }
```

If you want getProperty( ) to return a particular default value when the named property
is not found, pass that value as a second argument. For example, to use 127.0.0.1 as
the default host value, call getProperty( ) like this:

```
        String hostName = props.getProperty ("host", "127.0.0.1");
```

The *Cookbook.java* library file developed earlier in the chapter (Recipe 2.3) includes
an extra library call in the version of the file that you'll find in the *lib* directory of the
recipes distribution: a propsConnect( ) routine that is based on the concepts discussed
here. To use it, set up the contents of the properties file, *Cookbook.properties*, and copy
the file to the same location where you installed *Cookbook.class*. You can then establish
a connection within a program by importing the Cookbook class and calling
Cookbook.propsConnect( ) rather than by calling Cookbook.connect( ).

2.9 Conclusion and Words of Advice

This chapter discusses the basic operations provided by each of our APIs for handling
various aspects of interaction with the MySQL server. These operations enable you to
write programs that issue any kind of statement and retrieve the results. Up to this
point, we've used simple statements because the focus is on the APIs rather than on
SQL. The next chapter focuses on SQL instead, to show how to ask the database server
more complex questions.

Before you proceed, it would be a good idea to reset the `profile` table used in this chapter to a known state. Several statements in later chapters use this table; by reinitializing it, you'll get the same results displayed in those chapters when you run the statements shown there. To reset the table, change location into the *tables* directory of the `recipes` distribution, and run the following commands:

```
% mysql cookbook < profile.sql
% mysql cookbook < profile2.sql
```

## CHAPTER 3

Selecting Data from Tables

3.0 Introduction

This chapter focuses on the SELECT statement, which retrieves database information. It shows how to use SELECT to tell MySQL what you want to see. You should find the chapter helpful if your SQL background is limited or if you want to find out about the MySQL-specific extensions to SELECT syntax.

There are so many ways to write SELECT statements that we'll look at only a few of them. Consult the *MySQL Reference Manual* or a general MySQL text for more information about SELECT syntax and the functions and operators that you can use to extract and manipulate data.

SELECT gives you control over several aspects of row retrieval:

- Which table to use
- Which columns and rows to retrieve from the table
- How to name the output columns
- How to sort the rows

Many useful queries are quite simple and don't specify all those things. For example, some forms of SELECT don't even name a table—a fact used earlier in Recipe 1.28, which discusses how to use *mysql* as a calculator. Other nontable-based queries are useful for purposes such as determining what version of the server you're running or the name of the default database:

```
mysql> SELECT VERSION(), DATABASE();
+------------+------------+
| VERSION()  | DATABASE() |
+------------+------------+
| 5.0.27-log | cookbook   |
+------------+------------+
```

To answer more involved questions, normally you'll need to pull information from one or more tables. Many of the examples in this chapter use a table named mail, which contains rows that track mail message traffic between users on a set of hosts. The `mail` table definition looks like this:

```
CREATE TABLE mail
(
    t        DATETIME,  # when message was sent
    srcuser CHAR(8),   # sender (source user and host)
    srchost CHAR(20),
    dstuser CHAR(8),   # recipient (destination user and host)
    dsthost CHAR(20),
    size    BIGINT,    # message size in bytes
    INDEX (t)
);
```

And its contents look like this:

```
+---------------------+---------+---------+---------+---------+---------+
| t                   | srcuser | srchost | dstuser | dsthost | size    |
+---------------------+---------+---------+---------+---------+---------+
| 2006-05-11 10:15:08 | barb    | saturn  | tricia  | mars    |   58274 |
| 2006-05-12 12:48:13 | tricia  | mars    | gene    | venus   |  194925 |
| 2006-05-12 15:02:49 | phil    | mars    | phil    | saturn  |    1048 |
| 2006-05-13 13:59:18 | barb    | saturn  | tricia  | venus   |     271 |
| 2006-05-14 09:31:37 | gene    | venus   | barb    | mars    |    2291 |
| 2006-05-14 11:52:17 | phil    | mars    | tricia  | saturn  |    5781 |
| 2006-05-14 14:42:21 | barb    | venus   | barb    | venus   |   98151 |
| 2006-05-14 17:03:01 | tricia  | saturn  | phil    | venus   | 2394482 |
| 2006-05-15 07:17:48 | gene    | mars    | gene    | saturn  |    3824 |
| 2006-05-15 08:50:57 | phil    | venus   | phil    | venus   |     978 |
| 2006-05-15 10:25:52 | gene    | mars    | tricia  | saturn  |  998532 |
| 2006-05-15 17:35:31 | gene    | saturn  | gene    | mars    |    3856 |
| 2006-05-16 09:00:28 | gene    | venus   | barb    | mars    |     613 |
| 2006-05-16 23:04:19 | phil    | venus   | barb    | venus   |   10294 |
| 2006-05-17 12:49:23 | phil    | mars    | tricia  | saturn  |     873 |
| 2006-05-19 22:21:51 | gene    | saturn  | gene    | venus   |   23992 |
+---------------------+---------+---------+---------+---------+---------+
```

To create and load the `mail` table, change location into the *tables* directory of the `recipes` distribution, and run this command:

```
% mysql cookbook < mail.sql
```

This chapter also uses other tables from time to time. Some of these were used in previous chapters, while others are new. For any table that you need to create, do so the same way as for the `mail` table, using the appropriate script in the *tables* directory. In addition, the text for many of the scripts and programs used in this chapter can be found in the *select* directory. The files in that directory enable you to try the examples more easily.

You can execute many of the statements shown here by running them from within the *mysql* program, which is discussed in Chapter 1. A few of the examples involve issuing statements from within the context of a programming language. See Chapter 2 for background on programming techniques.

3.1 Specifying Which Columns to Select

Problem

You want to display some or all of the columns from a table.

Solution

Use SELECT * as a shortcut that selects all columns. However, with SELECT *, you always get all columns, and you can't assume anything about the order in which they'll appear. To retrieve only some of the columns, or require that they appear in a certain order, either name the columns explicitly in the desired display order or retrieve them into a data structure that makes their order irrelevant.

Discussion

To indicate what kind of information you want to select from a table, name a column or a list of columns and the table to use. The easiest way to display columns from a table is to use SELECT * FROM *tbl_name*. The * specifier is a shortcut for naming all the columns in a table:

```
mysql> SELECT * FROM mail;
+---------------------+---------+---------+---------+---------+---------+
| t                   | srcuser | srchost | dstuser | dsthost | size    |
+---------------------+---------+---------+---------+---------+---------+
| 2006-05-11 10:15:08 | barb    | saturn  | tricia  | mars    |   58274 |
| 2006-05-12 12:48:13 | tricia  | mars    | gene    | venus   |  194925 |
| 2006-05-12 15:02:49 | phil    | mars    | phil    | saturn  |    1048 |
| 2006-05-13 13:59:18 | barb    | saturn  | tricia  | venus   |     271 |
...
```

Using * is easy, but you cannot specify the column display order. An advantage of naming columns explicitly is that you can display them in whatever order you want. Suppose that you want hostnames to appear before usernames, rather than after. To accomplish this, name the columns as follows:

```
mysql> SELECT t, srchost, srcuser, dsthost, dstuser, size FROM mail;
+---------------------+---------+---------+---------+---------+---------+
| t                   | srchost | srcuser | dsthost | dstuser | size    |
+---------------------+---------+---------+---------+---------+---------+
| 2006-05-11 10:15:08 | saturn  | barb    | mars    | tricia  |   58274 |
| 2006-05-12 12:48:13 | mars    | tricia  | venus   | gene    |  194925 |
| 2006-05-12 15:02:49 | mars    | phil    | saturn  | phil    |    1048 |
| 2006-05-13 13:59:18 | saturn  | barb    | venus   | tricia  |     271 |
...
```

Another advantage of naming the columns compared to using * is that you can name just those columns you want to see and omit those in which you have no interest:

```
mysql> SELECT t, srcuser, srchost, size FROM mail;
+---------------------+---------+---------+---------+
```

```
| t                   | srcuser | srchost | size   |
+---------------------+---------+---------+--------+
| 2006-05-11 10:15:08 | barb    | saturn  |  58274 |
| 2006-05-12 12:48:13 | tricia  | mars    | 194925 |
| 2006-05-12 15:02:49 | phil    | mars    |   1048 |
| 2006-05-13 13:59:18 | barb    | saturn  |    271 |
...
```

The preceding examples use the *mysql* program to illustrate the differences between using * versus a list of names to specify output columns when issuing SELECT statements. These differences also can be significant when issuing statements from within programs that you write yourself, depending on how you fetch result set rows. If you select output columns using *, the server returns them using the order in which they are listed in the table definition—an order that may change if you change the definition with ALTER TABLE. If you fetch rows into an array that is indexed by column number, this indeterminate output column order makes it impossible to know which column each array element corresponds to. By naming output columns explicitly, you can fetch rows into an array with confidence that the columns will appear in the array in the same order that you named them in the statement.

Alternatively, your API may allow you to fetch rows into a structure containing elements that are accessed by name. For example, in Perl or Ruby, you can use a hash; in PHP, you can use an associative array or an object. If you use this approach, you can issue a SELECT * query and then use column names to access structure members. In this case, there is effectively no difference between selecting columns with * or by naming them explicitly: being able to access values by name within your program makes their order within result set rows irrelevant. This fact makes it tempting to take the easy way out by using SELECT * for all your queries. Nevertheless, even if you're not actually going to use every column, it's more efficient to name specifically only the columns you want so that the server doesn't send you information that you're just going to ignore. (An example that explains in more detail why you might want to avoid retrieving certain columns is given in Recipe 9.8, in the section "Selecting All Except Certain Columns.")

3.2 Specifying Which Rows to Select

Problem

You want to see only those rows that match certain criteria.

Solution

To specify which rows to return, add a WHERE clause to identify the rows that you want to see, such as customers that live in a particular city or tasks that have a status of "finished."

Discussion

Unless you qualify or restrict a `SELECT` query in some way, it retrieves every row in your table, which in many cases is a lot more information than you really want to see. To be more precise about which rows to select, provide a `WHERE` clause that specifies one or more conditions that rows must match.

Conditions can perform tests for equality, inequality, or relative ordering. For some types of data, such as strings, you can use pattern matches. The following statements select columns from rows from the `mail` table containing `srchost` values that are exactly equal to the string `'venus'` or that begin with the letter `'s'`:

```
mysql> SELECT t, srcuser, srchost  FROM mail WHERE srchost = 'venus';
+---------------------+---------+---------+
| t                   | srcuser | srchost |
+---------------------+---------+---------+
| 2006-05-14 09:31:37 | gene    | venus   |
| 2006-05-14 14:42:21 | barb    | venus   |
| 2006-05-15 08:50:57 | phil    | venus   |
| 2006-05-16 09:00:28 | gene    | venus   |
| 2006-05-16 23:04:19 | phil    | venus   |
+---------------------+---------+---------+
mysql> SELECT t, srcuser, srchost FROM mail WHERE srchost LIKE 's%';
+---------------------+---------+---------+
| t                   | srcuser | srchost |
+---------------------+---------+---------+
| 2006-05-11 10:15:08 | barb    | saturn  |
| 2006-05-13 13:59:18 | barb    | saturn  |
| 2006-05-14 17:03:01 | tricia  | saturn  |
| 2006-05-15 17:35:31 | gene    | saturn  |
| 2006-05-19 22:21:51 | gene    | saturn  |
+---------------------+---------+---------+
```

The `LIKE` operator in the previous query performs a pattern match, where `%` acts as a wildcard that matches any string. Recipe 5.10 discusses pattern matching further.

A `WHERE` clause can test multiple conditions and different conditions can test different columns. The following statement finds messages sent by `barb` to `tricia`:

```
mysql> SELECT * FROM mail WHERE srcuser = 'barb' AND dstuser = 'tricia';
+---------------------+---------+---------+---------+---------+-------+
| t                   | srcuser | srchost | dstuser | dsthost | size  |
+---------------------+---------+---------+---------+---------+-------+
| 2006-05-11 10:15:08 | barb    | saturn  | tricia  | mars    | 58274 |
| 2006-05-13 13:59:18 | barb    | saturn  | tricia  | venus   |   271 |
+---------------------+---------+---------+---------+---------+-------+
```

3.3 Giving Better Names to Query Result Columns

Problem

You don't like the names of the columns in a query result.

Solution

Use column aliases to supply names of your own choosing.

Discussion

When you retrieve a result set, MySQL gives every output column a name. (That's how the *mysql* program gets the names that you see displayed as the initial row of column headers in result set output.) By default, MySQL assigns the column names specified in the CREATE TABLE or ALTER TABLE statement to output columns, but if these defaults are not suitable, you can use column aliases to specify your own names.

This section explains aliases and shows how to use them to assign column names in statements. If you're writing a program that needs to retrieve information about column names (that is, column metadata), see Recipe 9.2.

If an output column in a result set comes directly from a table, MySQL uses the table column name for the output column name. For example, the following statement selects three table columns, the names of which become the corresponding output column names:

```
mysql> SELECT t, srcuser, size FROM mail;
+---------------------+---------+--------+
| t                   | srcuser | size   |
+---------------------+---------+--------+
| 2006-05-11 10:15:08 | barb    |  58274 |
| 2006-05-12 12:48:13 | tricia  | 194925 |
| 2006-05-12 15:02:49 | phil    |   1048 |
| 2006-05-13 13:59:18 | barb    |    271 |
...
```

If you generate a column by evaluating an expression, the expression itself is the column name. This can produce rather long and unwieldy names in result sets, as illustrated by the following statement that uses an expression to reformat the t column of the mail table:

```
mysql> SELECT
    -> CONCAT(MONTHNAME(t),' ',DAYOFMONTH(t),', ',YEAR(t)),
    -> srcuser, size FROM mail;
+----------------------------------------------------+---------+--------+
| CONCAT(MONTHNAME(t),' ',DAYOFMONTH(t),', ',YEAR(t)) | srcuser | size   |
+----------------------------------------------------+---------+--------+
| May 11, 2006                                       | barb    |  58274 |
| May 12, 2006                                       | tricia  | 194925 |
| May 12, 2006                                       | phil    |   1048 |
| May 13, 2006                                       | barb    |    271 |
...
```

The query in the preceding example is specifically contrived to illustrate how awful-looking column names can be. The reason it's contrived is that you probably wouldn't really write the query that way; the same result can be produced more easily using the DATE_FORMAT( ) function. But even if you use DATE_FORMAT( ), the column header is still ugly:

```
mysql> SELECT
    -> DATE_FORMAT(t,'%M %e, %Y'),
    -> srcuser, size FROM mail;
+---------------------------+---------+--------+
| DATE_FORMAT(t,'%M %e, %Y') | srcuser | size   |
+---------------------------+---------+--------+
| May 11, 2006              | barb    |  58274 |
| May 12, 2006              | tricia  | 194925 |
| May 12, 2006              | phil    |   1048 |
| May 13, 2006              | barb    |    271 |
...
```

To give an output column a name of your own choosing, use an AS *name* clause to specify a column alias (the keyword AS is optional). The following statement retrieves the same result as the previous one, but renames the first column to date_sent:

```
mysql> SELECT
    -> DATE_FORMAT(t,'%M %e, %Y') AS date_sent,
    -> srcuser, size FROM mail;
+--------------+---------+--------+
| date_sent    | srcuser | size   |
+--------------+---------+--------+
| May 11, 2006 | barb    |  58274 |
| May 12, 2006 | tricia  | 194925 |
| May 12, 2006 | phil    |   1048 |
| May 13, 2006 | barb    |    271 |
...
```

The alias makes the column name more concise, easier to read, and more meaningful. If you want to use a descriptive phrase, an alias can consist of several words. Aliases can be fairly arbitrary, although they are subject to a few restrictions; for example, they must be quoted if they are SQL keywords, contain spaces or other special characters, or are entirely numeric. The following statement retrieves the same data values as the preceding one but uses phrases to name the output columns:

```
mysql> SELECT
    -> DATE_FORMAT(t,'%M %e, %Y') AS 'Date of message',
    -> srcuser AS 'Message sender', size AS 'Number of bytes' FROM mail;
+-----------------+----------------+-----------------+
| Date of message | Message sender | Number of bytes |
+-----------------+----------------+-----------------+
| May 11, 2006    | barb           |           58274 |
| May 12, 2006    | tricia         |          194925 |
| May 12, 2006    | phil           |            1048 |
| May 13, 2006    | barb           |             271 |
...
```

You can apply an alias to any output column, not just those that come from tables:

```
mysql> SELECT '1+1+1' AS 'The expression', 1+1+1 AS 'The result';
+----------------+------------+
| The expression | The result |
```

```
+-----------------+------------+
| 1+1+1           |          3 |
+-----------------+------------+
```

Here, the value of the first column is '1+1+1' (quoted so that it is treated as a string), and the value of the second column is 1+1+1 (without quotes so that MySQL treats it as an expression and evaluates it). The aliases are descriptive phrases that help to clarify the relationship between the two column values.

If you use a single-word alias, and MySQL complains about it, the word probably is reserved. Quoting the alias should make it legal:

```
mysql> SELECT 1 AS INTEGER;
You have an error in your SQL syntax near 'INTEGER' at line 1
mysql> SELECT 1 AS 'INTEGER';
+---------+
| INTEGER |
+---------+
|       1 |
+---------+
```

3.4 Using Column Aliases to Make Programs Easier to Write

Problem

You're trying to refer to a column by name from within a program, but the column is calculated from an expression. Consequently, its name is difficult to use.

Solution

Use an alias to give the column a simpler name.

Discussion

Recipe 3.3 shows how column aliases make query results more meaningful when you're issuing queries interactively. Aliases also are useful for programming purposes. If you're writing a program that fetches rows into an array and accesses them by numeric column indexes, the presence or absence of column aliases makes no difference because aliases don't change the positions of columns within the result set. However, aliases make a big difference if you're accessing output columns by name because aliases change those names. You can exploit this fact to give your program easier names to work with. For example, if your query displays reformatted message time values from the `mail` table using the expression `DATE_FORMAT(t,'%M %e, %Y')`, that expression is also the name you'd have to use when referring to the output column. That's not very convenient. If you use `AS date_sent` to give the column an alias, you can refer to it a lot more easily using the name `date_sent`. Here's an example that shows how a Perl DBI script might process such values. It retrieves rows into a hash and refers to column values by name:

```
$sth = $dbh->prepare ("SELECT srcuser,
                        DATE_FORMAT(t,'%M %e, %Y') AS date_sent
                        FROM mail");
$sth->execute ();
while (my $ref = $sth->fetchrow_hashref ())
{
  printf "user: %s, date sent: %s\n", $ref->{srcuser}, $ref->{date_sent};
}
```

In Java, you'd do something like this, where the argument to getString( ) names the
column containing the value that you want to access:

```
Statement s = conn.createStatement ();
s.executeQuery ("SELECT srcuser,"
                + " DATE_FORMAT(t,'%M %e, %Y') AS date_sent"
                + " FROM mail");
ResultSet rs = s.getResultSet ();
while (rs.next ())  // loop through rows of result set
{
  String name = rs.getString ("srcuser");
  String dateSent = rs.getString ("date_sent");
  System.out.println ("user: " + name + ", date sent: " + dateSent);
}
rs.close ();
s.close ();
```

In Ruby, rows can be fetched as objects in which columns are accessible by either
position or name. In PHP, the PEAR DB module enables you to retrieve rows as associative arrays or objects, both of which are data structures that contain named elements.
With Python, use a cursor class that causes rows to be returned as dictionaries containing key/value pairs where the keys are the column names.

See Also

Recipe 2.4 shows for each of our programming languages how to fetch rows into data
structures that enable you to access columns values by column name. Also, the *select*
directory of the recipes directory has examples that show how to do this for the mail
table.

3.5 Combining Columns to Construct Composite Values

Problem

You want to display values that are constructed from multiple table columns.

Solution

One way to do this is to use CONCAT( ). You can also give the column a nicer name by
using an alias.

Discussion

Column values can be combined to produce composite output values. For example, this expression concatenates `srcuser` and `srchost` values into email address format:

```
CONCAT(srcuser,'@',srchost)
```

Such expressions tend to produce ugly column names, but you can use column aliases to provide better ones. The following statement uses the aliases `sender` and `recipient` to name output columns that are constructed by combining usernames and hostnames into email addresses:

```
mysql> SELECT
    -> DATE_FORMAT(t,'%M %e, %Y') AS date_sent,
    -> CONCAT(srcuser,'@',srchost) AS sender,
    -> CONCAT(dstuser,'@',dsthost) AS recipient,
    -> size FROM mail;
+--------------+--------------+--------------+--------+
| date_sent    | sender       | recipient    | size   |
+--------------+--------------+--------------+--------+
| May 11, 2006 | barb@saturn  | tricia@mars  |  58274 |
| May 12, 2006 | tricia@mars  | gene@venus   | 194925 |
| May 12, 2006 | phil@mars    | phil@saturn  |   1048 |
| May 13, 2006 | barb@saturn  | tricia@venus |    271 |
...
```

3.6 WHERE Clauses and Column Aliases

Problem

You want to refer to a column alias in a `WHERE` clause.

Solution

Sorry, you cannot. But there is a workaround.

Discussion

You cannot refer to column aliases in a `WHERE` clause. Thus, the following statement is illegal:

```
mysql> SELECT t, srcuser, dstuser, size/1024 AS kilobytes
    -> FROM mail WHERE kilobytes > 500;
ERROR 1054 (42S22): Unknown column 'kilobytes' in 'where clause'
```

The error occurs because an alias names an *output* column, whereas a `WHERE` clause operates on *input* columns to determine which rows to select for output. To make the statement legal, replace the alias in the `WHERE` clause with the column or expression that the alias represents:

```
mysql> SELECT t, srcuser, dstuser, size/1024 AS kilobytes
    -> FROM mail WHERE size/1024 > 500;
```

```
+---------------------+---------+---------+-----------+
| t                   | srcuser | dstuser | kilobytes |
+---------------------+---------+---------+-----------+
| 2006-05-14 17:03:01 | tricia  | phil    | 2338.3613 |
| 2006-05-15 10:25:52 | gene    | tricia  | 975.1289  |
+---------------------+---------+---------+-----------+
```

3.7 Debugging Comparison Expressions

Problem

You're curious about how a comparison in a WHERE clause works. Or perhaps about why it doesn't seem to be working.

Solution

Display the result of the comparison to get more information about it. This is a useful diagnostic or debugging technique.

Discussion

Normally, you put comparison operations in the WHERE clause of a query and use them to determine which rows to display:

```
mysql> SELECT * FROM mail WHERE srcuser < 'c' AND size > 5000;
+---------------------+---------+---------+---------+---------+-------+
| t                   | srcuser | srchost | dstuser | dsthost | size  |
+---------------------+---------+---------+---------+---------+-------+
| 2006-05-11 10:15:08 | barb    | saturn  | tricia  | mars    | 58274 |
| 2006-05-14 14:42:21 | barb    | venus   | barb    | venus   | 98151 |
+---------------------+---------+---------+---------+---------+-------+
```

But sometimes it's desirable to see the result of the comparison itself (for example, if you're not sure that the comparison is working the way you expect it to). To do this, just remove the WHERE clause, and put the comparison expression in the output column list, perhaps also including the values that you're comparing:

```
mysql> SELECT srcuser, srcuser < 'c', size, size > 5000 FROM mail;
+---------+---------------+--------+-------------+
| srcuser | srcuser < 'c' | size   | size > 5000 |
+---------+---------------+--------+-------------+
| barb    |             1 |  58274 |           1 |
| tricia  |             0 | 194925 |           1 |
| phil    |             0 |   1048 |           0 |
| barb    |             1 |    271 |           0 |
...
```

In these results, 1 means true and 0 means false.

3.8 Removing Duplicate Rows

Problem

Output from a query contains duplicate rows. You want to eliminate them.

Solution

Use DISTINCT.

Discussion

Some queries produce results containing duplicate rows. For example, to see who sent mail, you could query the mail table like this:

```
mysql> SELECT srcuser FROM mail;
+---------+
| srcuser |
+---------+
| barb    |
| tricia  |
| phil    |
| barb    |
| gene    |
| phil    |
| barb    |
| tricia  |
| gene    |
| phil    |
| gene    |
| gene    |
| gene    |
| phil    |
| phil    |
| gene    |
+---------+
```

That result is heavily redundant. Adding DISTINCT to the query removes the duplicate rows, producing a set of unique values:

```
mysql> SELECT DISTINCT srcuser FROM mail;
+---------+
| srcuser |
+---------+
| barb    |
| tricia  |
| phil    |
| gene    |
+---------+
```

DISTINCT works with multiple-column output, too. The following query shows which dates are represented in the mail table:

```
mysql> SELECT DISTINCT YEAR(t), MONTH(t), DAYOFMONTH(t) FROM mail;
+---------+----------+---------------+
| YEAR(t) | MONTH(t) | DAYOFMONTH(t) |
+---------+----------+---------------+
|    2006 |        5 |            11 |
|    2006 |        5 |            12 |
|    2006 |        5 |            13 |
|    2006 |        5 |            14 |
|    2006 |        5 |            15 |
|    2006 |        5 |            16 |
|    2006 |        5 |            17 |
|    2006 |        5 |            19 |
+---------+----------+---------------+
```

To count the number of unique values in a column, use COUNT(DISTINCT):

```
mysql> SELECT COUNT(DISTINCT srcuser) FROM mail;
+-------------------------+
| COUNT(DISTINCT srcuser) |
+-------------------------+
|                       4 |
+-------------------------+
```

See Also

Chapter 8 revisits DISTINCT and COUNT(DISTINCT). Chapter 14 discusses duplicate removal in more detail.

3.9 Working with NULL Values

Problem

You're trying to compare column values to NULL, but it isn't working.

Solution

You have to use the proper comparison operators: IS NULL, IS NOT NULL, or <=>.

Discussion

Conditions that involve NULL are special. You cannot use comparisons of the form *value* = NULL or *value* != NULL to check whether *value* is NULL. Such comparisons always produce a result of NULL because it's impossible to tell whether they are true or false. Even NULL = NULL produces NULL because you can't determine whether one unknown value is the same as another unknown value.

To look for columns that are or are not NULL, use the IS NULL or IS NOT NULL operator. Suppose that a table taxpayer contains taxpayer names and ID numbers, where a NULL value in the id column indicates that the value is unknown:

```
mysql> SELECT * FROM taxpayer;
+---------+--------+
| name    | id     |
+---------+--------+
| bernina | 198-48 |
| bertha  | NULL   |
| ben     | NULL   |
| bill    | 475-83 |
+---------+--------+
```

You can see that = and != do not identify NULL values as follows:

```
mysql> SELECT * FROM taxpayer WHERE id = NULL;
Empty set (0.00 sec)
mysql> SELECT * FROM taxpayer WHERE id != NULL;
Empty set (0.01 sec)
```

To find rows where the id column is or is not NULL, write the statements like this instead:

```
mysql> SELECT * FROM taxpayer WHERE id IS NULL;
+--------+------+
| name   | id   |
+--------+------+
| bertha | NULL |
| ben    | NULL |
+--------+------+
mysql> SELECT * FROM taxpayer WHERE id IS NOT NULL;
+---------+--------+
| name    | id     |
+---------+--------+
| bernina | 198-48 |
| bill    | 475-83 |
+---------+--------+
```

You can also use <=> to compare values, which (unlike the = operator) is true even for two NULL values:

```
mysql> SELECT NULL = NULL, NULL <=> NULL;
+-------------+---------------+
| NULL = NULL | NULL <=> NULL |
+-------------+---------------+
|        NULL |             1 |
+-------------+---------------+
```

Sometimes it's useful to map NULL values onto some other distinctive value that has more meaning in the context of your application. If NULL id values in the taxpayer table mean "unknown," you can display that fact by using IF( ) to map NULL onto the string Unknown:

```
mysql> SELECT name, IF(id IS NULL,'Unknown', id) AS 'id' FROM taxpayer;
+---------+---------+
| name    | id      |
+---------+---------+
| bernina | 198-48  |
| bertha  | Unknown |
| ben     | Unknown |
```

```
| bill     | 475-83  |
+---------+---------+
```

This technique actually works for any kind of value, but it's especially useful with NULL values because NULL tends to be given a variety of meanings: unknown, missing, not yet determined, out of range, and so forth. You can choose the label that makes most sense in a given context.

The preceding query can be written more concisely using IFNULL( ), which tests its first argument and returns it if it's not NULL, or returns its second argument otherwise:

```
mysql> SELECT name, IFNULL(id,'Unknown') AS 'id' FROM taxpayer;
+---------+---------+
| name    | id      |
+---------+---------+
| bernina | 198-48  |
| bertha  | Unknown |
| ben     | Unknown |
| bill    | 475-83  |
+---------+---------+
```

In other words, these two tests are equivalent:

```
IF(expr1 IS NOT NULL,expr1,expr2)
IFNULL(expr1,expr2)
```

From a readability standpoint, IF( ) often is easier to understand than IFNULL( ). From a computational perspective, IFNULL( ) is more efficient because *expr1* need not be evaluated twice, as happens with IF( ).

See Also

NULL values also behave specially with respect to sorting and summary operations. See Recipes 7.14 and 8.8.

3.10 Writing Comparisons Involving NULL in Programs

Problem

You're writing a program that looks for rows containing a specific value, but it fails when the value is NULL.

Solution

Choose the proper comparison operator according to whether the comparison value is or is not NULL.

Discussion

The need to use different comparison operators for NULL values than for non-NULL values leads to a subtle danger when constructing statement strings within programs. If you have a value stored in a variable that might represent a NULL value, you must account for that if you use the value in comparisons. For example, in Perl, undef represents a NULL value, so to construct a statement that finds rows in the taxpayer table matching some arbitrary value in an $id variable, you cannot do this:

```
$sth = $dbh->prepare ("SELECT * FROM taxpayer WHERE id = ?");
$sth->execute ($id);
```

The statement fails when $id is undef because the resulting statement becomes:

```
SELECT * FROM taxpayer WHERE id = NULL
```

A comparison of id = NULL is never true, so that statement returns no rows. To take into account the possibility that $id may be undef, construct the statement using the appropriate comparison operator like this:

```
$operator = (defined ($id) ? "=" : "IS");
$sth = $dbh->prepare ("SELECT * FROM taxpayer WHERE id $operator ?");
$sth->execute ($id);
```

This results in statements as follows for $id values of undef (NULL) or 43 (not NULL):

```
SELECT * FROM taxpayer WHERE id IS NULL
SELECT * FROM taxpayer WHERE id = 43
```

For inequality tests, set $operator like this instead:

```
$operator = (defined ($id) ? "!=" : "IS NOT");
```

Another way to avoid all this trouble, if it's not necessary to allow a column to contain NULL values, is to declare it NOT NULL when you create the table. For example, the taxpayer table could have been defined like this to disallow NULL values in either of its columns:

```
# taxpayer2.sql

# taxpayer table, defined with NOT NULL columns

DROP TABLE IF EXISTS taxpayer;
CREATE TABLE taxpayer
(
  name  CHAR(20) NOT NULL,
  id    CHAR(20) NOT NULL
);
```

3.11 Sorting a Result Set

Problem

Your query results aren't sorted the way you want.

Solution

MySQL can't read your mind. Add an `ORDER BY` clause to tell it exactly how you want result rows sorted.

Discussion

When you select rows, the MySQL server is free to return them in any order, unless you instruct it otherwise by saying how to sort the result. There are lots of ways to use sorting techniques. Chapter 7 explores this topic in detail. Briefly, you sort a result set by adding an `ORDER BY` clause that names the column or columns that you want to use for sorting. The following statement sorts rows by size:

```
mysql> SELECT * FROM mail WHERE size > 100000 ORDER BY size;
+---------------------+---------+---------+---------+---------+---------+
| t                   | srcuser | srchost | dstuser | dsthost | size    |
+---------------------+---------+---------+---------+---------+---------+
| 2006-05-12 12:48:13 | tricia  | mars    | gene    | venus   |  194925 |
| 2006-05-15 10:25:52 | gene    | mars    | tricia  | saturn  |  998532 |
| 2006-05-14 17:03:01 | tricia  | saturn  | phil    | venus   | 2394482 |
+---------------------+---------+---------+---------+---------+---------+
```

This statement names multiple columns in the `ORDER BY` clause to sort rows by host, and then by user within each host:

```
mysql> SELECT * FROM mail WHERE dstuser = 'tricia'
    -> ORDER BY srchost, srcuser;
+---------------------+---------+---------+---------+---------+---------+
| t                   | srcuser | srchost | dstuser | dsthost | size    |
+---------------------+---------+---------+---------+---------+---------+
| 2006-05-15 10:25:52 | gene    | mars    | tricia  | saturn  |  998532 |
| 2006-05-14 11:52:17 | phil    | mars    | tricia  | saturn  |    5781 |
| 2006-05-17 12:49:23 | phil    | mars    | tricia  | saturn  |     873 |
| 2006-05-11 10:15:08 | barb    | saturn  | tricia  | mars    |   58274 |
| 2006-05-13 13:59:18 | barb    | saturn  | tricia  | venus   |     271 |
+---------------------+---------+---------+---------+---------+---------+
```

To sort a column in reverse (descending) order, add the keyword `DESC` after its name in the `ORDER BY` clause:

```
mysql> SELECT * FROM mail WHERE size > 50000 ORDER BY size DESC;
+---------------------+---------+---------+---------+---------+---------+
| t                   | srcuser | srchost | dstuser | dsthost | size    |
+---------------------+---------+---------+---------+---------+---------+
| 2006-05-14 17:03:01 | tricia  | saturn  | phil    | venus   | 2394482 |
| 2006-05-15 10:25:52 | gene    | mars    | tricia  | saturn  |  998532 |
| 2006-05-12 12:48:13 | tricia  | mars    | gene    | venus   |  194925 |
| 2006-05-14 14:42:21 | barb    | venus   | barb    | venus   |   98151 |
| 2006-05-11 10:15:08 | barb    | saturn  | tricia  | mars    |   58274 |
+---------------------+---------+---------+---------+---------+---------+
```

3.12 Using Views to Simplify Table Access

Problem

You often retrieve values that are calculated from expressions and you want a simpler way to refer to those values than writing the expressions each time you need them.

Solution

Use a view defined such that its columns perform the desired calculations.

Discussion

In Recipe 3.5, we retrieved several values from the `mail` table, using expressions to calculate most of them:

```
mysql> SELECT
    -> DATE_FORMAT(t,'%M %e, %Y') AS date_sent,
    -> CONCAT(srcuser,'@',srchost) AS sender,
    -> CONCAT(dstuser,'@',dsthost) AS recipient,
    -> size FROM mail;
+--------------+--------------+--------------+--------+
| date_sent    | sender       | recipient    | size   |
+--------------+--------------+--------------+--------+
| May 11, 2006 | barb@saturn  | tricia@mars  |  58274 |
| May 12, 2006 | tricia@mars  | gene@venus   | 194925 |
| May 12, 2006 | phil@mars    | phil@saturn  |   1048 |
| May 13, 2006 | barb@saturn  | tricia@venus |    271 |
...
```

One problem with such a statement is that if you have to issue it often, it's inconvenient to write the expressions repeatedly. You can make the statement results easier to access by using a view. A *view* is a virtual table that does not contain any data itself. Instead, it's defined as the `SELECT` statement that retrieves the data of interest. The following view, `mail_view`, is equivalent to the `SELECT` statement just shown:

```
mysql> CREATE VIEW mail_view AS
    -> SELECT
    -> DATE_FORMAT(t,'%M %e, %Y') AS date_sent,
    -> CONCAT(srcuser,'@',srchost) AS sender,
    -> CONCAT(dstuser,'@',dsthost) AS recipient,
    -> size FROM mail;
```

To access the view contents, refer to it like any other table. You can select some or all of its columns, add a `WHERE` clause to restrict which rows to retrieve, use `ORDER BY` to sort the rows, and so forth. For example:

```
mysql> SELECT date_sent, sender, size FROM mail_view
    -> WHERE size > 100000 ORDER BY size;
+--------------+--------------+--------+
| date_sent    | sender       | size   |
+--------------+--------------+--------+
```

```
| May 12, 2006 | tricia@mars   |  194925 |
| May 15, 2006 | gene@mars     |  998532 |
| May 14, 2006 | tricia@saturn | 2394482 |
+--------------+---------------+---------+
```

3.13 Selecting Data from More Than One Table

Problem

You need to retrieve data from more than one table.

Solution

Use a join or a subquery.

Discussion

The queries shown so far select data from a single table, but sometimes you need to retrieve information from multiple tables. Two types of queries that accomplish this are joins and subqueries. A *join* matches rows in one table with rows in another and enables you to retrieve output rows that contain columns from either or both tables. A *subquery* is one query nested within the other. The result is a query that performs a comparison between values selected by the "inner" query against values selected by the "outer" query.

In this section, I will show a couple of brief examples to illustrate the basic ideas. Other examples appear elsewhere: subqueries are used in various examples throughout the book (for example, Recipes 3.16 and 3.17). Chapter 12 discusses joins in detail, including some that select from more than two tables.

The following examples use the `profile` table that was introduced in Chapter 2; recall that it lists the people on your buddy list. Let's extend the scenario that uses that table a little bit to include another table named `profile_contact`. This second table contains information about how to contact people listed in the `profile` table via various instant messaging systems and is defined like this:

```
CREATE TABLE profile_contact
(
  profile_id   INT UNSIGNED NOT NULL, # ID from profile table
  service      CHAR(20) NOT NULL,      # messaging service name
  contact_name CHAR(25) NOT NULL,      # name to use for contacting person
  INDEX (profile_id)
);
```

The table associates each row with the proper `profile` row via the `profile_id` column. The `service` and `contact_name` columns name the messaging service and the name to use for contacting the given person via that service. For the examples, assume that the table contains these rows:

```
mysql> SELECT * FROM profile_contact ORDER BY profile_id, service;
+------------+---------+---------------+
| profile_id | service | contact_name  |
+------------+---------+---------------+
|          1 | AIM     | user1-aimid   |
|          1 | MSN     | user1-msnid   |
|          2 | AIM     | user2-aimid   |
|          2 | MSN     | user2-msnid   |
|          2 | Yahoo   | user2-yahooid |
|          4 | Yahoo   | user4-yahooid |
+------------+---------+---------------+
```

A question that requires combining information from both tables is, "For each person in the profile table, show me the messaging services I can use to get in touch, and the contact name to use for each service." To answer this question, use a join. Select from both tables and match rows by comparing the id column from the profile table with the profile_id column from the profile_contact table:

```
mysql> SELECT id, name, service, contact_name
    -> FROM profile INNER JOIN profile_contact ON id = profile_id;
+----+------+---------+---------------+
| id | name | service | contact_name  |
+----+------+---------+---------------+
|  1 | Fred | AIM     | user1-aimid   |
|  1 | Fred | MSN     | user1-msnid   |
|  2 | Mort | AIM     | user2-aimid   |
|  2 | Mort | MSN     | user2-msnid   |
|  2 | Mort | Yahoo   | user2-yahooid |
|  4 | Carl | Yahoo   | user4-yahooid |
+----+------+---------+---------------+
```

In the FROM clause, the query indicates the tables from which data should be selected, and the ON clause tells MySQL which columns to use when searching for matches between the two tables. In the resulting output, rows include the id and name columns from the profile table, and the service and contact_name columns from the profile_contact table.

Here's another question for which both tables are used to derive the answer: "List all the profile_contact records for Mort." To pull the proper rows from the profile_contact table, you need to know Mort's ID, which is stored in the profile table. To write the query without looking up Mort's ID yourself, use a subquery that, given his name, looks it up for you:

```
mysql> SELECT * FROM profile_contact
    -> WHERE profile_id = (SELECT id FROM profile WHERE name = 'Mort');
+------------+---------+---------------+
| profile_id | service | contact_name  |
+------------+---------+---------------+
|          2 | AIM     | user2-aimid   |
|          2 | MSN     | user2-msnid   |
|          2 | Yahoo   | user2-yahooid |
+------------+---------+---------------+
```

Here the subquery appears as a nested SELECT statement enclosed within parentheses.

3.14 Selecting Rows from the Beginning or End of a Result Set

Problem

You want to see only certain rows from a result set, such as the first one or the last five.

Solution

Use a LIMIT clause, perhaps in conjunction with an ORDER BY clause.

Discussion

MySQL supports a LIMIT clause that tells the server to return only part of a result set. LIMIT is a MySQL-specific extension to SQL that is extremely valuable when your result set contains more rows than you want to see at a time. It enables you to retrieve just the first part of a result set or an arbitrary section of the set. Typically, LIMIT is used for the following kinds of problems:

- Answering questions about first or last, largest or smallest, newest or oldest, least or more expensive, and so forth.

- Splitting a result set into sections so that you can process it one piece at a time. This technique is common in web applications for displaying a large search result across several pages. Showing the result in sections enables display of smaller pages that are easier to understand. See Recipe 3.15 for details on this.

The following examples use the profile table that was introduced in Chapter 2. Its contents look like this:

```
mysql> SELECT * FROM profile;
+----+---------+------------+-------+----------------------+------+
| id | name    | birth      | color | foods                | cats |
+----+---------+------------+-------+----------------------+------+
|  1 | Fred    | 1970-04-13 | black | lutefisk,fadge,pizza |    0 |
|  2 | Mort    | 1969-09-30 | white | burrito,curry,eggroll |   3 |
|  3 | Brit    | 1957-12-01 | red   | burrito,curry,pizza  |    1 |
|  4 | Carl    | 1973-11-02 | red   | eggroll,pizza        |    4 |
|  5 | Sean    | 1963-07-04 | blue  | burrito,curry        |    5 |
|  6 | Alan    | 1965-02-14 | red   | curry,fadge          |    1 |
|  7 | Mara    | 1968-09-17 | green | lutefisk,fadge       |    1 |
|  8 | Shepard | 1975-09-02 | black | curry,pizza          |    2 |
|  9 | Dick    | 1952-08-20 | green | lutefisk,fadge       |    0 |
| 10 | Tony    | 1960-05-01 | white | burrito,pizza        |    0 |
+----+---------+------------+-------+----------------------+------+
```

To select the first *n* rows of a query result, add LIMIT *n* to the end of your SELECT statement:

```
mysql> SELECT * FROM profile LIMIT 1;
+----+------+------------+-------+----------------------+------+
| id | name | birth      | color | foods                | cats |
```

```
+----+------+------------+-------+-----------------------+------+
|  1 | Fred | 1970-04-13 | black | lutefisk,fadge,pizza  |    0 |
+----+------+------------+-------+-----------------------+------+
mysql> SELECT * FROM profile LIMIT 5;
+----+------+------------+-------+-----------------------+------+
| id | name | birth      | color | foods                 | cats |
+----+------+------------+-------+-----------------------+------+
|  1 | Fred | 1970-04-13 | black | lutefisk,fadge,pizza  |    0 |
|  2 | Mort | 1969-09-30 | white | burrito,curry,eggroll |    3 |
|  3 | Brit | 1957-12-01 | red   | burrito,curry,pizza   |    1 |
|  4 | Carl | 1973-11-02 | red   | eggroll,pizza         |    4 |
|  5 | Sean | 1963-07-04 | blue  | burrito,curry         |    5 |
+----+------+------------+-------+-----------------------+------+
```

Note that LIMIT *n* really means "return at most *n* rows." If you specify LIMIT 10, and the result set has only 3 rows, the server returns 3 rows.

The rows in the preceding query results aren't sorted into any particular order, so they may not be very meaningful. A more common technique is to use ORDER BY to sort the result set. Then you can use LIMIT to find smallest and largest values. For example, to find the row with the minimum (earliest) birth date, sort by the birth column, and then add LIMIT 1 to retrieve the first row:

```
mysql> SELECT * FROM profile ORDER BY birth LIMIT 1;
+----+------+------------+-------+-----------------+------+
| id | name | birth      | color | foods           | cats |
+----+------+------------+-------+-----------------+------+
|  9 | Dick | 1952-08-20 | green | lutefisk,fadge  |    0 |
+----+------+------------+-------+-----------------+------+
```

This works because MySQL processes the ORDER BY clause to sort the rows first, and then applies LIMIT.

To obtain rows from the end of a result set, sort them in the opposite order. The statement that finds the row with the most recent birth date is similar to the previous one, except that you sort in descending order:

```
mysql> SELECT * FROM profile ORDER BY birth DESC LIMIT 1;
+----+---------+------------+-------+-------------+------+
| id | name    | birth      | color | foods       | cats |
+----+---------+------------+-------+-------------+------+
|  8 | Shepard | 1975-09-02 | black | curry,pizza |    2 |
+----+---------+------------+-------+-------------+------+
```

To find the earliest or latest birthday within the calendar year, sort by the month and day of the birth values:

```
mysql> SELECT name, DATE_FORMAT(birth,'%m-%d') AS birthday
    -> FROM profile ORDER BY birthday LIMIT 1;
+------+----------+
| name | birthday |
+------+----------+
| Alan | 02-14    |
+------+----------+
```

You can obtain the same information by running these statements without LIMIT and ignoring everything but the first row. The advantage of using LIMIT is that the server returns just the first row, and the extra rows don't travel over the network at all. This is much more efficient than retrieving an entire result set, only to discard all but one row.

See Also

Be aware that using LIMIT *n* to select the "*n* smallest" or "*n* largest" values may not yield quite the results you expect. See Recipe 3.16 for some discussion on framing LIMIT clauses appropriately for the questions that you are asking.

LIMIT is useful in combination with RAND( ) to make random selections from a set of items. See Chapter 13.

You can use LIMIT to restrict the effect of a DELETE or UPDATE statement to a subset of the rows that would otherwise be deleted or updated, respectively. This can be useful in conjunction with a WHERE clause. For example, if a table contains five instances of a row, you can select them in a DELETE statement with an appropriate WHERE clause, and then remove the duplicates by adding LIMIT 4 to the end of the statement. This leaves only one copy of the row. For more information about uses of LIMIT in duplicate row removal, see Recipe 14.4.

3.15 Selecting Rows from the Middle of a Result Set

Problem

You don't want the first or last rows of a result set. Instead, you want to pull a section of rows out of the middle of the set, such as rows 21 through 40.

Solution

That's still a job for LIMIT. But you need to tell it the starting position within the result set in addition to the number of rows you want.

Discussion

LIMIT *n* tells the server to return the first *n* rows of a result set. LIMIT also has a two-argument form that enables you to pick out any arbitrary section of rows from a result. The arguments indicate how many rows to skip and how many to return. This means that you can use LIMIT to do such things as skip two rows and return the next, thus answering questions such as "what is the *third*-smallest or *third*-largest value?" These are questions that MIN( ) or MAX( ) are not suited for, but are easy with LIMIT:

```
mysql> SELECT * FROM profile ORDER BY birth LIMIT 2,1;
+----+------+------------+-------+---------------+------+
```

```
| id | name | birth      | color | foods          | cats |
+----+------+------------+-------+----------------+------+
| 10 | Tony | 1960-05-01 | white | burrito,pizza  |    0 |
+----+------+------------+-------+----------------+------+
mysql> SELECT * FROM profile ORDER BY birth DESC LIMIT 2,1;
+----+------+------------+-------+-----------------------+------+
| id | name | birth      | color | foods                 | cats |
+----+------+------------+-------+-----------------------+------+
|  1 | Fred | 1970-04-13 | black | lutefisk,fadge,pizza  |    0 |
+----+------+------------+-------+-----------------------+------+
```

The two-argument form of LIMIT also makes it possible to partition a result set into smaller sections. For example, to retrieve 20 rows at a time from a result, issue the same SELECT statement repeatedly, but vary the LIMIT clauses like so:

retrieve first 20 rows
```
SELECT ... FROM ... ORDER BY ... LIMIT 0, 20;
```
skip 20 rows, retrieve next 20
```
SELECT ... FROM ... ORDER BY ... LIMIT 20, 20;
```
skip 40 rows, retrieve next 20
```
SELECT ... FROM ... ORDER BY ... LIMIT 40, 20;
```
etc.

Web developers often use LIMIT this way to split a large search result into smaller, more manageable pieces so that it can be presented over several pages. We'll discuss this technique further in Recipe 19.10.

To determine the number of rows in a result set so that you can determine how many sections there are, you can issue a COUNT( ) statement first. For example, to display profile table rows in name order, four at a time, you can find out how many there are with the following statement:

```
mysql> SELECT COUNT(*) FROM profile;
+----------+
| COUNT(*) |
+----------+
|       10 |
+----------+
```

That tells you that you'll have three sets of rows (although the last one will have fewer than four rows), which you can retrieve as follows:

```
SELECT * FROM profile ORDER BY name LIMIT 0, 4;
SELECT * FROM profile ORDER BY name LIMIT 4, 4;
SELECT * FROM profile ORDER BY name LIMIT 8, 4;
```

You can also fetch a part of a result set and find out in the same statement how big the result would have been without the LIMIT clause. For example, to fetch the first four rows from the profile table and then obtain the size of the full result, run these statements:

```
SELECT SQL_CALC_FOUND_ROWS * FROM profile ORDER BY name LIMIT 4;
SELECT FOUND_ROWS();
```

The keyword `SQL_CALC_FOUND_ROWS` in the first statement tells MySQL to calculate the size of the entire result set even though the statement requests that only part of it be returned. The row count is available by calling `FOUND_ROWS( )`. If that function returns a value greater than four, there are other rows yet to be retrieved.

3.16 Choosing Appropriate LIMIT Values

Problem

`LIMIT` doesn't seem to do what you want it to.

Solution

Be sure that you understand what question you're asking. It may be that `LIMIT` is exposing some interesting subtleties in your data that you have not considered.

Discussion

`LIMIT` *n* is useful in conjunction with `ORDER BY` for selecting smallest or largest values from a result set. But does that actually give you the rows with the *n* smallest or largest values? Not necessarily! It does if your rows contain unique values, but not if there are duplicates. You may find it necessary to run a preliminary query first to help you choose the proper `LIMIT` value.

To see why this is, consider the following dataset, which shows the American League pitchers who won 15 or more games during the 2001 baseball season (you can find this data in the *al_winner.sql* file in the *tables* directory of the `recipes` distribution):

```
mysql> SELECT name, wins FROM al_winner
    -> ORDER BY wins DESC, name;
+----------------+------+
| name           | wins |
+----------------+------+
| Mulder, Mark   |   21 |
| Clemens, Roger |   20 |
| Moyer, Jamie   |   20 |
| Garcia, Freddy |   18 |
| Hudson, Tim    |   18 |
| Abbott, Paul   |   17 |
| Mays, Joe      |   17 |
| Mussina, Mike  |   17 |
| Sabathia, C.C. |   17 |
| Zito, Barry    |   17 |
| Buehrle, Mark  |   16 |
| Milton, Eric   |   15 |
| Pettitte, Andy |   15 |
| Radke, Brad    |   15 |
| Sele, Aaron    |   15 |
+----------------+------+
```

If you want to know who won the most games, adding `LIMIT 1` to the preceding statement gives you the correct answer because the maximum value is 21, and there is only one pitcher with that value (Mark Mulder). But what if you want the four highest game winners? The proper statements depend on what you mean by that, which can have various interpretations:

- If you just want the first four rows, sort the rows, and add `LIMIT 4`:

```
mysql> SELECT name, wins FROM al_winner
    -> ORDER BY wins DESC, name
    -> LIMIT 4;
+----------------+------+
| name           | wins |
+----------------+------+
| Mulder, Mark   |   21 |
| Clemens, Roger |   20 |
| Moyer, Jamie   |   20 |
| Garcia, Freddy |   18 |
+----------------+------+
```

  That may not suit your purposes because `LIMIT` imposes a cutoff that occurs in the middle of a set of pitchers with the same number of wins (Tim Hudson also won 18 games).

- To avoid making a cutoff in the middle of a set of rows with the same value, select rows with values greater than or equal to the value in the fourth row. Find out what that value is with `LIMIT`, and then use it in the `WHERE` clause of a second query to select rows:

```
mysql> SELECT wins FROM al_winner
    -> ORDER BY wins DESC, name
    -> LIMIT 3, 1;
+------+
| wins |
+------+
|   18 |
+------+
mysql> SELECT name, wins FROM al_winner
    -> WHERE wins >= 18
    -> ORDER BY wins DESC, name;
+----------------+------+
| name           | wins |
+----------------+------+
| Mulder, Mark   |   21 |
| Clemens, Roger |   20 |
| Moyer, Jamie   |   20 |
| Garcia, Freddy |   18 |
| Hudson, Tim    |   18 |
+----------------+------+
```

  To select these results in a single statement, without having to substitute the cutoff value from one statement manually into the other, use the first statement as a subquery of the second:

```
mysql> SELECT name, wins FROM al_winner
    -> WHERE wins >=
    ->   (SELECT wins FROM al_winner
    ->    ORDER BY wins DESC, name
    ->    LIMIT 3, 1)
    -> ORDER BY wins DESC, name;
+----------------+------+
| name           | wins |
+----------------+------+
| Mulder, Mark   |   21 |
| Clemens, Roger |   20 |
| Moyer, Jamie   |   20 |
| Garcia, Freddy |   18 |
| Hudson, Tim    |   18 |
+----------------+------+
```

- If you want to know all the pitchers with the four largest wins values, another approach is needed. Determine the fourth-largest value with DISTINCT and LIMIT, and then use it to select rows:

```
mysql> SELECT DISTINCT wins FROM al_winner
    -> ORDER BY wins DESC, name
    -> LIMIT 3, 1;
+------+
| wins |
+------+
|   17 |
+------+
mysql> SELECT name, wins FROM al_winner
    -> WHERE wins >= 17
    -> ORDER BY wins DESC, name;
+----------------+------+
| name           | wins |
+----------------+------+
| Mulder, Mark   |   21 |
| Clemens, Roger |   20 |
| Moyer, Jamie   |   20 |
| Garcia, Freddy |   18 |
| Hudson, Tim    |   18 |
| Abbott, Paul   |   17 |
| Mays, Joe      |   17 |
| Mussina, Mike  |   17 |
| Sabathia, C.C. |   17 |
| Zito, Barry    |   17 |
+----------------+------+
```

As in the previous example, these statements can be combined into one by using a subquery:

```
mysql> SELECT name, wins FROM al_winner
    -> WHERE wins >=
    ->   (SELECT DISTINCT wins FROM al_winner
    ->    ORDER BY wins DESC, name
    ->    LIMIT 3, 1)
    -> ORDER BY wins DESC, name;
+----------------+------+
```

```
| name           | wins |
+----------------+------+
| Mulder, Mark   |   21 |
| Clemens, Roger |   20 |
| Moyer, Jamie   |   20 |
| Garcia, Freddy |   18 |
| Hudson, Tim    |   18 |
| Abbott, Paul   |   17 |
| Mays, Joe      |   17 |
| Mussina, Mike  |   17 |
| Sabathia, C.C. |   17 |
| Zito, Barry    |   17 |
+----------------+------+
```

For this dataset, each method yields a different result for "four highest." The moral is that the way you use LIMIT may require some thought about what you really want to know.

3.17 What to Do When LIMIT Requires the "Wrong" Sort Order

Problem

LIMIT usually works best in conjunction with an ORDER BY clause that sorts rows. But sometimes the sort order is the opposite of what you want for the final result.

Solution

Use LIMIT in a subquery to retrieve the rows you want, and then use the outer query to sort them into the proper order.

Discussion

If you want the last four rows of a result set, you can obtain them easily by sorting the set in reverse order and using LIMIT 4. For example, the following statement returns the names and birth dates for the four people in the profile table who were born most recently:

```
mysql> SELECT name, birth FROM profile ORDER BY birth DESC LIMIT 4;
+---------+------------+
| name    | birth      |
+---------+------------+
| Shepard | 1975-09-02 |
| Carl    | 1973-11-02 |
| Fred    | 1970-04-13 |
| Mort    | 1969-09-30 |
+---------+------------+
```

But that requires sorting the birth values in descending order to place them at the head of the result set. What if you want the output rows to appear in ascending order instead?

One way to solve this problem is to use two statements. First, use COUNT( ) to find out how many rows are in the table:

```
mysql> SELECT COUNT(*) FROM profile;
+----------+
| COUNT(*) |
+----------+
|       10 |
+----------+
```

Then, sort the values in ascending order and use the two-argument form of LIMIT to skip all but the last four rows:

```
mysql> SELECT name, birth FROM profile ORDER BY birth LIMIT 6, 4;
+---------+------------+
| name    | birth      |
+---------+------------+
| Mort    | 1969-09-30 |
| Fred    | 1970-04-13 |
| Carl    | 1973-11-02 |
| Shepard | 1975-09-02 |
+---------+------------+
```

That's somewhat unsatisfactory because it requires that you determine how many rows to skip. A more general approach is use LIMIT within a subquery to select the rows that you want, and then sort them in opposite order in the outer query:

```
mysql> SELECT * FROM
    -> (SELECT name, birth FROM profile ORDER BY birth DESC LIMIT 4) AS t
    -> ORDER BY birth;
+---------+------------+
| name    | birth      |
+---------+------------+
| Mort    | 1969-09-30 |
| Fred    | 1970-04-13 |
| Carl    | 1973-11-02 |
| Shepard | 1975-09-02 |
+---------+------------+
```

AS t is used here because any table referred to in the FROM clause must have a name.

3.18 Calculating LIMIT Values from Expressions

Problem

You want to use expressions to specify the arguments for LIMIT.

Solution

Sadly, you cannot. You can use only literal integers—unless you issue the statement from within a program, in which case you can evaluate the expressions yourself and insert the resulting values into the statement string.

Discussion

Arguments to `LIMIT` must be literal integers, not expressions. Statements such as the following are illegal:

```
SELECT * FROM profile LIMIT 5+5;
SELECT * FROM profile LIMIT @skip_count, @show_count;
```

The same "no expressions allowed" principle applies if you're using an expression to calculate a `LIMIT` value in a program that constructs a statement string. You must evaluate the expression first, and then place the resulting value in the statement. For example, if you produce a statement string in Perl or PHP as follows, an error will result when you attempt to execute the statement:

```
$str = "SELECT * FROM profile LIMIT $x + $y";
```

To avoid the problem, evaluate the expression first:

```
$z = $x + $y;
$str = "SELECT * FROM profile LIMIT $z";
```

Or do this (but don't omit the parentheses or the expression won't evaluate properly):

```
$str = "SELECT * FROM profile LIMIT " . ($x + $y);
```

If you're constructing a two-argument `LIMIT` clause, evaluate both expressions before placing them into the statement string.

## CHAPTER 4

Table Management

4.0 Introduction

This chapter covers topics that relate to creating and populating tables:

- Cloning a table
- Copying one table to another
- Using temporary tables
- Generating unique table names
- Determining what storage engine a table uses or converting a table to use a different storage engine

To create and load the `mail` table used for examples in this chapter, change location into the *tables* directory of the `recipes` distribution, and run this command:

```
% mysql cookbook < mail.sql
```

4.1 Cloning a Table

Problem

You need into create a table that has exactly the same structure as an existing table.

Solution

Use `CREATE TABLE ... LIKE` to clone the table structure. If it's also necessary to copy some or all of the rows from the original table to the new one, use `INSERT INTO ... SELECT`.

Discussion

When you need to create a new table that is just like an existing table, use this statement:

```
CREATE TABLE new_table LIKE original_table;
```

The structure of the new table will be exactly the same as that of the original table, with a few exceptions: CREATE TABLE ... LIKE does not copy foreign key definitions, and it doesn't copy any DATA DIRECTORY or INDEX DIRECTORY table options that the table might use.

The new table will be empty. If you also need to copy the rows from the original table to the new table, use an INSERT INTO ... SELECT statement:

```
INSERT INTO new_table SELECT * FROM original_table;
```

To copy only part of the table, add an appropriate WHERE clause that identifies which rows to copy. For example, these statements create a copy of the mail table named mail2 and populate it with the rows only for mail sent by barb:

```
mysql> CREATE TABLE mail2 LIKE mail;
mysql> INSERT INTO mail2 SELECT * FROM mail WHERE srcuser = 'barb';
mysql> SELECT * FROM mail2;
+---------------------+---------+---------+---------+---------+-------+
| t                   | srcuser | srchost | dstuser | dsthost | size  |
+---------------------+---------+---------+---------+---------+-------+
| 2006-05-11 10:15:08 | barb    | saturn  | tricia  | mars    | 58274 |
| 2006-05-13 13:59:18 | barb    | saturn  | tricia  | venus   |   271 |
| 2006-05-14 14:42:21 | barb    | venus   | barb    | venus   | 98151 |
+---------------------+---------+---------+---------+---------+-------+
```

For more information about INSERT ... SELECT, see Recipe 4.2.

4.2 Saving a Query Result in a Table

Problem

You want to save the result from a SELECT statement into a table rather than display it.

Solution

If the table already exists, just use INSERT INTO ... SELECT to retrieve rows into it. If the table does not exist yet, use CREATE TABLE ... SELECT to create it on the fly from the SELECT result.

Discussion

The MySQL server normally returns the result of a SELECT statement to the client that issued the statement. For example, when you issue a statement from within the *mysql* program, the server returns the result to *mysql*, which in turn displays it to you on the screen. It's also possible to save the results of a SELECT statement in a table, which is useful in a number of ways:

- You can easily create a complete or partial copy of a table. If you're developing an algorithm that modifies a table, it's safer to work with a copy of a table so that you need not worry about the consequences of mistakes. Also, if the original table is large, creating a partial copy can speed the development process because queries run against it will take less time.

- For a data-loading operation based on information that might be malformed, you can load new rows into a temporary table, perform some preliminary checks, and correct the rows as necessary. When you're satisfied that the new rows are okay, copy them from the temporary table into your main table.

- Some applications maintain a large repository table and a smaller working table into which rows are inserted on a regular basis, copying the working table rows to the repository periodically and clearing the working table.

- If you're performing a number of similar summary operations on a large table, it may be more efficient to select summary information once into a second table and use that for further analysis, rather than run expensive summary operations repeatedly on the original table.

This section shows how to retrieve a result set into a table. The table names `src_tbl` and `dst_tbl` in the examples refer to the source table from which rows are selected and the destination table into which they are stored, respectively.

If the destination table already exists, use INSERT ... SELECT to copy the result set into it. For example, if `dst_tbl` contains an integer column i and a string column s, the following statement copies rows from `src_tbl` into `dst_tbl`, assigning column val to i and column name to s:

```
INSERT INTO dst_tbl (i, s) SELECT val, name FROM src_tbl;
```

The number of columns to be inserted must match the number of selected columns, and the correspondence between sets of columns is established by position rather than name. In the special case that you want to copy all columns from one table to another, you can shorten the statement to this form:

```
INSERT INTO dst_tbl SELECT * FROM src_tbl;
```

To copy only certain rows, add a WHERE clause that selects those rows:

```
INSERT INTO dst_tbl SELECT * FROM src_tbl
WHERE val > 100 AND name LIKE 'A%';
```

The SELECT statement can produce values from expressions, too. For example, the following statement counts the number of times each name occurs in `src_tbl` and stores both the counts and the names in `dst_tbl`:

```
INSERT INTO dst_tbl (i, s) SELECT COUNT(*), name
FROM src_tbl GROUP BY name;
```

If the destination table does not exist, you can create it first with a CREATE TABLE statement, and then copy rows into it with INSERT ... SELECT. A second option is to use CREATE TABLE ... SELECT, which creates the destination table directly from the result of the SELECT. For example, to create dst_tbl and copy the entire contents of src_tbl into it, do this:

```
CREATE TABLE dst_tbl SELECT * FROM src_tbl;
```

MySQL creates the columns in dst_tbl based on the name, number, and type of the columns in src_tbl. Should you want to copy only certain rows, add an appropriate WHERE clause. To create an empty table, use a WHERE clause that is always false:

```
CREATE TABLE dst_tbl SELECT * FROM src_tbl WHERE 0;
```

To copy only some of the columns, name the ones you want in the SELECT part of the statement. For example, if src_tbl contains columns a, b, c, and d, you can copy just b and d like this:

```
CREATE TABLE dst_tbl SELECT b, d FROM src_tbl;
```

To create columns in a different order from that in which they appear in the source table, name them in the desired order. If the source table contains columns a, b, and c, but you want them to appear in the destination table in the order c, a, and b, do this:

```
CREATE TABLE dst_tbl SELECT c, a, b FROM src_tbl;
```

To create additional columns in the destination table besides those selected from the source table, provide appropriate column definitions in the CREATE TABLE part of the statement. The following statement creates id as an AUTO_INCREMENT column in dst_tbl and adds columns a, b, and c from src_tbl:

```
CREATE TABLE dst_tbl
(
  id INT NOT NULL AUTO_INCREMENT,
  PRIMARY KEY (id)
)
SELECT a, b, c FROM src_tbl;
```

The resulting table contains four columns in the order id, a, b, c. Defined columns are assigned their default values. This means that id, being an AUTO_INCREMENT column, will be assigned successive sequence numbers starting from one. (See Recipe 11.1.)

If you derive a column's values from an expression, it's prudent to provide an alias to give the column a name. Suppose that src_tbl contains invoice information listing items in each invoice. The following statement then generates a summary of each invoice named in the table, along with the total cost of its items. The second column includes an alias because the default name for an expression is the expression itself, which is a difficult name to work with later:

```
CREATE TABLE dst_tbl
SELECT inv_no, SUM(unit_cost*quantity) AS total_cost
FROM src_tbl
GROUP BY inv_no;
```

CREATE TABLE ... SELECT is extremely convenient, but it does have some limitations. These stem primarily from the fact that the information available from a result set is not as extensive as what you can specify in a CREATE TABLE statement. If you derive a table column from an expression, for example, MySQL has no idea whether the column should be indexed or what its default value is. If it's important to include this information in the destination table, use the following techniques:

- To make the destination table an *exact* copy of the source table, use the cloning technique described in Recipe 4.1.

- If you want indexes in the destination table, you can specify them explicitly. For example, if `src_tbl` has a `PRIMARY KEY` on the `id` column, and a multiple-column index on `state` and `city`, you can specify them for `dst_tbl` as well:

    ```
    CREATE TABLE dst_tbl (PRIMARY KEY (id), INDEX(state,city))
    SELECT * FROM src_tbl;
    ```

- Column attributes such as `AUTO_INCREMENT` and a column's default value are not copied to the destination table. To preserve these attributes, create the table, and then use `ALTER TABLE` to apply the appropriate modifications to the column definition. For example, if `src_tbl` has an `id` column that is not only a `PRIMARY KEY` but an `AUTO_INCREMENT` column, copy the table, and then modify it:

    ```
    CREATE TABLE dst_tbl (PRIMARY KEY (id)) SELECT * FROM src_tbl;
    ALTER TABLE dst_tbl MODIFY id INT UNSIGNED NOT NULL AUTO_INCREMENT;
    ```

4.3 Creating Temporary Tables

Problem

You need a table only for a short time, and then you want it to disappear automatically.

Solution

Create a `TEMPORARY` table, and let MySQL take care of removing it.

Discussion

Some operations require a table that exists only temporarily and that should disappear when it's no longer needed. You can of course issue a `DROP TABLE` statement explicitly to remove a table when you're done with it. Another option is to use `CREATE TEMPORARY TABLE`. This statement is just like `CREATE TABLE` except that it creates a transient table that disappears when your connection to the server closes, if you haven't already removed it yourself. This is extremely useful behavior because you need not remember to remove the table. MySQL drops it for you automatically. `TEMPORARY` can be used with the usual table-creation methods:

- Create the table from explicit column definitions:

    ```
    CREATE TEMPORARY TABLE tbl_name (...column definitions...);
    ```

- Create the table from an existing table:

```
CREATE TEMPORARY TABLE new_table LIKE original_table;
```

- Create the table on the fly from a result set:

```
CREATE TEMPORARY TABLE tbl_name SELECT ... ;
```

Temporary tables are connection-specific, so several clients each can create a temporary table having the same name without interfering with each other. This makes it easier to write applications that use transient tables, because you need not ensure that the tables have unique names for each client. (See Recipe 4.5 for further discussion of table-naming issues.)

Another property of temporary tables is that they can be created with the same name as a permanent table. In this case, the temporary table "hides" the permanent table for the duration of its existence, which can be useful for making a copy of a table that you can modify without affecting the original by mistake. The DELETE statement in the following set of statements removes rows from a temporary mail table, leaving the original permanent one unaffected:

```
mysql> CREATE TEMPORARY TABLE mail SELECT * FROM mail;
mysql> SELECT COUNT(*) FROM mail;
+----------+
| COUNT(*) |
+----------+
|       16 |
+----------+
mysql> DELETE FROM mail;
mysql> SELECT COUNT(*) FROM mail;
+----------+
| COUNT(*) |
+----------+
|        0 |
+----------+
mysql> DROP TABLE mail;
mysql> SELECT COUNT(*) FROM mail;
+----------+
| COUNT(*) |
+----------+
|       16 |
+----------+
```

Although temporary tables created with CREATE TEMPORARY TABLE have the preceding benefits, keep the following caveats in mind:

- To reuse the temporary table within a given session, you'll still need to drop it explicitly before recreating it. It's only the *last* use within a session that you need no explicit DROP TABLE for. (If you've already created a temporary table with a given name, attempting to create a second one with that name results in an error.)

- If you modify a temporary table that "hides" a permanent table with the same name, be sure to test for errors resulting from dropped connections if you're using a programming interface that has reconnect capability enabled. If a client program automatically reconnects after it detects a dropped connection, you'll be modifying the permanent table after the reconnect, not the temporary table.

- Some APIs support persistent connections or connection pools. Use of these prevents temporary tables from being dropped as you expect when your script ends because the connection remains open for reuse by other scripts. Your script has no control over when the connection closes. This means it can be prudent to issue the following statement prior to creating a temporary table, just in case it's still hanging around from the previous execution of the script:

```
DROP TEMPORARY TABLE IF EXISTS tbl_name
```

The TEMPORARY keyword is useful here if the temporary table has already been dropped. It prevents the statement from dropping any permanent table that happens to have the same name.

4.4 Checking or Changing a Table's Storage Engine

Problem

You need to check which storage engine a table uses so that you can determine what engine capabilities are applicable. Or you need to change a table's storage engine because you realize that another engine has capabilities that are more desirable for the way you use the table.

Solution

To determine a table's storage engine, you can use any of several statements. To change the table's engine, use ALTER TABLE with an ENGINE clause.

Discussion

MySQL supports several storage engines, each of which have differing characteristics. For example, the InnoDB and BDB engines support transactions, whereas MyISAM does not. If you need to know whether a table supports transactions, check which storage engine it uses. If you need to use the table in transactions but the table's engine does not support them, you can convert the table to use a transaction-capable engine.

To determine the current engine for a table, check INFORMATION_SCHEMA or use the SHOW TABLE STATUS or SHOW CREATE TABLE statement. For the mail table, obtain engine information as follows:

```
mysql> SELECT ENGINE FROM INFORMATION_SCHEMA.TABLES
    -> WHERE TABLE_SCHEMA = 'cookbook' AND TABLE_NAME = 'mail';
+--------+
| ENGINE |
+--------+
| MyISAM |
```

```
+--------+

mysql> SHOW TABLE STATUS LIKE 'mail'\G
*************************** 1. row ***************************
          Name: mail
        Engine: MyISAM
...

mysql> SHOW CREATE TABLE mail\G
*************************** 1. row ***************************
       Table: mail
Create Table: CREATE TABLE `mail` (
  `t` datetime DEFAULT NULL,
  `srcuser` char(8) DEFAULT NULL,
  `srchost` char(20) DEFAULT NULL,
  `dstuser` char(8) DEFAULT NULL,
  `dsthost` char(20) DEFAULT NULL,
  `size` bigint(20) DEFAULT NULL,
  KEY `t` (`t`)
) ENGINE=MyISAM DEFAULT CHARSET=latin1
```

To change the storage engine used for a table, use **ALTER TABLE** with an **ENGINE** specifier. For example, to convert the **mail** table to use the InnoDB storage engine, use this statement:

```
ALTER TABLE mail ENGINE = InnoDB;
```

Be aware that converting a large table to a different storage engine might take a long time and be expensive in terms of CPU and I/O activity.

See Also

To determine which storage engines are supported by your MySQL server, see Recipe 9.13.

4.5 Generating Unique Table Names

Problem

You need to create a table with a name that is guaranteed not to exist already.

Solution

If you can create a **TEMPORARY** table, it doesn't matter if the name exists already. Otherwise, try to generate a value that is unique to your client program and incorporate it into the table name.

Discussion

MySQL is a multiple-client database server, so if a given script that creates a transient table might be invoked by several clients simultaneously, you must take care to keep multiple invocations of the script from fighting over the same table name. If the script creates tables using CREATE TEMPORARY TABLE, there is no problem because different clients can create temporary tables having the same name without clashing.

If you do not want to use a TEMPORARY table, you should make sure that each invocation of the script creates a uniquely named table and that it drops that table when it is no longer needed. To accomplish this, incorporate into the name some value that is guaranteed to be unique per invocation. A timestamp won't work, because it's easily possible for two instances of a script to be invoked within the same second. A random number may be somewhat better. For example, in Java, you can use the java.util.Random( ) class to create a table name like this:

```
import java.util.Random;
import java.lang.Math;

Random rand = new Random ();
int n = rand.nextInt ();  // generate random number
n = Math.abs (n);         // take absolute value
String tblName = "tmp_tbl_" + n;
```

Unfortunately, random numbers only reduce the possibility of name clashes, they do not eliminate it. Process ID (PID) values are a better source of unique values. PIDs are reused over time, but never for two processes at the same time, so a given PID is guaranteed to be unique among the set of currently executing processes. You can use this fact to create unique table names as follows:

Perl:

```
my $tbl_name = "tmp_tbl_$$";
```

Ruby:

```
tbl_name = "tmp_tbl_" + Process.pid.to_s
```

PHP:

```
$tbl_name = "tmp_tbl_" . posix_getpid ();
```

Python:

```
import os
tbl_name = "tmp_tbl_%d" % os.getpid ()
```

Note that even if you create a table name using a value such as a PID that is guaranteed to be unique to a given script invocation, there may still be a chance that the table will already exist. This can happen if a previous invocation of the script with the same PID created a table with the same name, but crashed before removing the table. On the other hand, any such table cannot still be in use because it will have been created by a process that is no longer running. Under these circumstances, it's safe to remove the table if it does exist by issuing the following statement:

```
DROP TABLE IF EXISTS tbl_name
```

Then you can go ahead and create the new table.

Connection identifiers are another source of unique values. The MySQL server reuses these numbers over time, but no two simultaneous connections to the server have the same ID. To get your connection ID, execute this statement, and retrieve the result:

```
SELECT CONNECTION_ID();
```

Some MySQL APIs expose the connection ID directly without requiring any statement to be executed. For example, in Perl DBI, use the `mysql_thread_id` attribute of your database handle:

```
my $tbl_name = "tmp_tbl_" . $dbh->{mysql_thread_id};
```

In Ruby DBI, do this:

```
tbl_name = "tmp_tbl_" + dbh.func(:thread_id).to_s
```

## CHAPTER 5

Working with Strings

5.0 Introduction

Like most types of data, string values can be compared for equality or inequality or relative ordering. However, strings have some additional features to consider:

- A string can be binary or nonbinary. Binary strings are used for raw data such as images, music files, or encrypted values. Nonbinary strings are used for character data such as text and are associated with a character set and collation (sorting order).

- A character set determines which characters are legal in a string. Collations can be chosen according to whether you need comparisons to be case-sensitive or case-insensitive, or to use the rules of a particular language.

- Data types for binary strings are BINARY, VARBINARY, and BLOB. Data types for non-binary strings are CHAR, VARCHAR, and TEXT, each of which allows CHARACTER SET and COLLATE attributes. See Recipe 5.2 for information about choosing data types for string columns.

- You can convert a binary string to a nonbinary string and vice versa, or convert a nonbinary string from one character set or collation to another.

- You can use a string in its entirety or extract substrings from it. Strings can be combined with other strings.

- You can apply pattern-matching operations to strings.

- FULLTEXT searching is available for efficient queries on large collections of text.

This chapter discusses how to use all those features, so that you can store, retrieve, and manipulate strings according to whatever requirements your applications have.

Scripts to create the tables used in this chapter can be found in the *tables* directory of the recipes distribution.

5.1 String Properties

One property of a string is whether it is binary or nonbinary:

- A binary string is a sequence of bytes. It can contain any type of information, such as images, MP3 files, or compressed or encrypted data. A binary string is not associated with a character set, even if you store a value such as abc that looks like ordinary text. Binary strings are compared byte by byte using numeric byte values.

- A nonbinary string is a sequence of characters. It stores text that has a particular character set and collation. The character set defines which characters can be stored in the string. The collation defines the comparison and sorting properties of the characters.

A characteristic of nonbinary strings is that they have a character set. To see which character sets are available, use this statement:

```
mysql> SHOW CHARACTER SET;
+----------+-----------------------------+---------------------+--------+
| Charset  | Description                 | Default collation   | Maxlen |
+----------+-----------------------------+---------------------+--------+
| big5     | Big5 Traditional Chinese    | big5_chinese_ci     |      2 |
| dec8     | DEC West European           | dec8_swedish_ci     |      1 |
| cp850    | DOS West European           | cp850_general_ci    |      1 |
| hp8      | HP West European            | hp8_english_ci      |      1 |
| koi8r    | KOI8-R Relcom Russian       | koi8r_general_ci    |      1 |
| latin1   | cp1252 West European        | latin1_swedish_ci   |      1 |
| latin2   | ISO 8859-2 Central European | latin2_general_ci   |      1 |
...
| utf8     | UTF-8 Unicode               | utf8_general_ci     |      3 |
| ucs2     | UCS-2 Unicode               | ucs2_general_ci     |      2 |
...
```

The default character set in MySQL is latin1. If you need to store characters from several languages in a single column, consider using one of the Unicode character sets (utf8 or ucs2) because they can represent characters from multiple languages.

Some character sets contain only single-byte characters, whereas others allow multibyte characters. For some multibyte character sets, all characters have a fixed length. Others contain characters of varying lengths. For example, Unicode data can be stored using the ucs2 character set in which all characters take two bytes or the utf8 character set in which characters take from one to three bytes.

You can determine whether a given string contains multibyte characters using the LENGTH( ) and CHAR_LENGTH( ) functions, which return the length of a string in bytes and characters, respectively. If LENGTH( ) is greater than CHAR_LENGTH( ) for a given string, multibyte characters are present.

- For the ucs2 Unicode character set, all characters are encoded using two bytes, even if they might be single-byte characters in another character set such as latin1. Thus, every ucs2 string contains multibyte characters:

```
mysql> SET @s = CONVERT('abc' USING ucs2);
mysql> SELECT LENGTH(@s), CHAR_LENGTH(@s);
+------------+-----------------+
| LENGTH(@s) | CHAR_LENGTH(@s) |
+------------+-----------------+
|          6 |               3 |
+------------+-----------------+
```

- The utf8 Unicode character set has multibyte characters, but a given utf8 string might contain only single-byte characters, as in the following example:

```
mysql> SET @s = CONVERT('abc' USING utf8);
mysql> SELECT LENGTH(@s), CHAR_LENGTH(@s);
+------------+-----------------+
| LENGTH(@s) | CHAR_LENGTH(@s) |
+------------+-----------------+
|          3 |               3 |
+------------+-----------------+
```

Another characteristic of nonbinary strings is *collation*, which determines the sort order of characters in the character set. Use SHOW COLLATION to see which collations are available; add a LIKE clause to see the collations for a particular character set:

```
mysql> SHOW COLLATION LIKE 'latin1%';
+-------------------+---------+----+---------+----------+---------+
| Collation         | Charset | Id | Default | Compiled | Sortlen |
+-------------------+---------+----+---------+----------+---------+
| latin1_german1_ci | latin1  |  5 |         | Yes      |       1 |
| latin1_swedish_ci | latin1  |  8 | Yes     | Yes      |       1 |
| latin1_danish_ci  | latin1  | 15 |         | Yes      |       1 |
| latin1_german2_ci | latin1  | 31 |         | Yes      |       2 |
| latin1_bin        | latin1  | 47 |         | Yes      |       1 |
| latin1_general_ci | latin1  | 48 |         | Yes      |       1 |
| latin1_general_cs | latin1  | 49 |         | Yes      |       1 |
| latin1_spanish_ci | latin1  | 94 |         | Yes      |       1 |
+-------------------+---------+----+---------+----------+---------+
```

In contexts where no collation is indicated, the collation with Yes in the Default column is the default collation used for strings in the given character set. As shown, the default collation for latin1 is latin1_swedish_ci. (Default collations are also displayed by SHOW CHARACTER SET.)

A collation can be case-sensitive (a and A are different), case-insensitive (a and A are the same), or binary (two characters are the same or different based on whether their numeric values are equal). A collation name ending in ci, cs, or bin is case-insensitive, case-sensitive, or binary, respectively.

A binary collation provides a sort order for nonbinary strings that is something like the order for binary strings, in the sense that comparisons for binary strings and binary collations both use numeric values. However, there is a difference: binary string comparisons are always based on single-byte units, whereas a binary collation compares nonbinary strings using *character* numeric values; depending on the character set, some of these might be multibyte values.

The following example illustrates how collation affects sort order. Suppose that a table contains a `latin1` string column and has the following rows:

```
mysql> CREATE TABLE t (c CHAR(3) CHARACTER SET latin1);
mysql> INSERT INTO t (c) VALUES('AAA'),('bbb'),('aaa'),('BBB');
mysql> SELECT c FROM t;
+------+
| c    |
+------+
| AAA  |
| bbb  |
| aaa  |
| BBB  |
+------+
```

By applying the `COLLATE` operator to the column, you can choose which collation to use for sorting and thus affect the order of the result:

- A case-insensitive collation sorts a and A together, placing them before b and B. However, for a given letter, it does not necessarily order one lettercase before another, as shown by the following result:

```
mysql> SELECT c FROM t ORDER BY c COLLATE latin1_swedish_ci;
+------+
| c    |
+------+
| AAA  |
| aaa  |
| bbb  |
| BBB  |
+------+
```

- A case-sensitive collation puts A and a before B and b, and sorts uppercase before lowercase:

```
mysql> SELECT c FROM t ORDER BY c COLLATE latin1_general_cs;
+------+
| c    |
+------+
| AAA  |
| aaa  |
| BBB  |
| bbb  |
+------+
```

- A binary collation sorts characters using their numeric values. Assuming that uppercase letters have numeric values less than those of lowercase letters, a binary collation results in the following ordering:

```
mysql> SELECT c FROM t ORDER BY c COLLATE latin1_bin;
+------+
| c    |
+------+
| AAA  |
| BBB  |
| aaa  |
```

```
| bbb  |
+------+
```

Note that, because characters in different lettercases have different numeric values, a binary collation produces a case-sensitive ordering. However, the order is different than that for the case-sensitive collation.

You can choose a language-specific collation if you require that comparison and sorting operations use the sorting rules of a particular language. For example, if you store strings using the utf8 character set, the default collation (utf8_general_ci) treats ch and ll as two-character strings. If you need the traditional Spanish ordering that treats ch and ll as single characters that follow c and l, respectively, use the utf8_spanish2_ci collation. The two collations produce different results, as shown here:

```
mysql> CREATE TABLE t (c CHAR(2) CHARACTER SET utf8);
mysql> INSERT INTO t (c) VALUES('cg'),('ch'),('ci'),('lk'),('ll'),('lm');
mysql> SELECT c FROM t ORDER BY c COLLATE utf8_general_ci;
+------+
| c    |
+------+
| cg   |
| ch   |
| ci   |
| lk   |
| ll   |
| lm   |
+------+
mysql> SELECT c FROM t ORDER BY c COLLATE utf8_spanish2_ci;
+------+
| c    |
+------+
| cg   |
| ci   |
| ch   |
| lk   |
| lm   |
| ll   |
+------+
```

5.2 Choosing a String Data Type

Problem

You need to store string data but aren't sure which is the most appropriate data type.

Solution

Choose the data type according to the characteristics of the information to be stored and how you need to use it. Consider questions such as these:

- Are the strings binary or nonbinary?
- Does case sensitivity matter?
- What is the maximum string length?
- Do you want to store fixed- or variable-length values?
- Do you need to retain trailing spaces?
- Is there a fixed set of allowable values?

Discussion

MySQL provides several binary and nonbinary string data types. These types come in pairs as shown in the following table.

Binary data type	Nonbinary data type	Maximum length
BINARY	CHAR	255
VARBINARY	VARCHAR	65,535
TINYBLOB	TINYTEXT	255
BLOB	TEXT	65,535
MEDIUMBLOB	MEDIUMTEXT	16,777,215
LONGBLOB	LONGTEXT	4,294,967,295

For the binary data types, the maximum length is the number of bytes the string must be able to hold. For the nonbinary types, the maximum length is the number of characters the string must be able to hold (which for a string containing multibyte characters requires more than that many bytes).

For the BINARY and CHAR data types, MySQL stores column values using a fixed width. For example, values stored in a BINARY(10) or CHAR(10) column always take 10 bytes or 10 characters, respectively. Shorter values are padded to the required length as necessary when stored. For BINARY, the pad value is 0x00 (the zero-valued byte, also known as ASCII NUL). CHAR values are padded with spaces. Trailing pad bytes or characters are stripped from BINARY and CHAR values when they are retrieved.

For VARBINARY, VARCHAR, and the BLOB and TEXT types, MySQL stores values using only as much storage as required, up to the maximum column length. No padding is added or stripped when values are stored or retrieved.

If you want to preserve trailing pad values that are present in the original strings that are stored, use a data type for which no stripping occurs. For example, if you're storing character (nonbinary) strings that might end with spaces, and you want to preserve them, use VARCHAR or one of the TEXT data types. The following statements illustrate the difference in trailing-space handling for CHAR and VARCHAR columns:

```
mysql> CREATE TABLE t (c1 CHAR(10), c2 VARCHAR(10));
mysql> INSERT INTO t (c1,c2) VALUES('abc      ','abc      ');
```

```
mysql> SELECT c1, c2, CHAR_LENGTH(c1), CHAR_LENGTH(c2) FROM t;
+------+-----------+-----------------+-----------------+
| c1   | c2        | CHAR_LENGTH(c1) | CHAR_LENGTH(c2) |
+------+-----------+-----------------+-----------------+
| abc  | abc       |               3 |              10 |
+------+-----------+-----------------+-----------------+
```

Thus, if you store a string that contains trailing spaces into a CHAR column, you will find that they're gone when you retrieve the value. Similar padding and stripping occurs for BINARY columns, except that the pad value is 0x00.

 Prior to MySQL 5.0.3, VARCHAR and VARBINARY have a maximum length of 255. Also, stripping of trailing pad values for retrieved values applies to VARCHAR and VARBINARY columns, so you should use one of the TEXT or BLOB types if you want to retain trailing spaces or 0x00 bytes.

A table can include a mix of binary and nonbinary string columns, and its nonbinary columns can use different character sets and collations. When you declare a nonbinary string column, use the CHARACTER SET and COLLATE attributes if you require a particular character set and collation. For example, if you need to store utf8 (Unicode) and sjis (Japanese) strings, you might define a table with two columns like this:

```
CREATE TABLE mytbl
(
  utf8data VARCHAR(100) CHARACTER SET utf8 COLLATE utf8_danish_ci,
  sjisdata VARCHAR(100) CHARACTER SET sjis COLLATE sjis_japanese_ci
);
```

It is allowable to omit CHARACTER SET, COLLATE, or both from a column definition:

- If you specify CHARACTER SET and omit COLLATE, the default collation for the character set is used.
- If you specify COLLATE and omit CHARACTER SET, the character set implied by the collation name (the first part of the name) is used. For example, utf8_danish_ci and sjis_japanese_ci imply utf8 and sjis, respectively. (This means that the CHARACTER SET attributes could have been omitted from the preceding CREATE TABLE statement.)
- If you omit both CHARACTER SET and COLLATE, the column is assigned the table default character set and collation. (A table definition can include those attributes following the closing parenthesis at the end of the CREATE TABLE statement. If present, they apply to columns that have no explicit character set or collation of their own. If omitted, the table defaults are taken from the database defaults. The database defaults can be specified when you create the database with the CREATE DATABASE statement. The server defaults apply to the database if they are omitted.)

The server default character set and collation are latin1 and latin1_swedish_ci unless you start the server with the --character-set-server and --collation-server options to specify different values. This means that, by default, strings use the `latin1` character set and are not case-sensitive.

MySQL also supports `ENUM` and `SET` string types, which are used for data that has a fixed set of allowable values. You can use the `CHARACTER SET` and `COLLATE` attributes for these data types as well.

5.3 Setting the Client Connection Character Set Properly

Problem

You're executing SQL statements or producing query results that don't use the default character set.

Solution

Use `SET NAMES` or an equivalent method to set your connection to the proper character set.

Discussion

When you send information back and forth between your application and the server, you should tell MySQL what the appropriate character set is. For example, the default character set is `latin1`, but that may not always be the proper character set to use for connections to the server. If you're working with Greek data, trying to display it using `latin1` will result in gibberish on your screen. If you're using Unicode strings in the `utf8` character set, `latin1` might not be sufficient to represent all the characters that you might need.

To deal with this problem, configure your connection with the server to use the appropriate character set. There are various ways to do this:

- If your client program supports the `--default-character-set` option, you can use it to set the character set at program invocation time. *mysql* is one such program. Put the option in an option file so that it takes effect each time you connect to the server:

  ```
  [mysql]
  default-character-set=utf8
  ```

- Issue a `SET NAMES` statement after you connect:

  ```
  mysql> SET NAMES 'utf8';
  ```

  `SET NAMES` also allows the connection collation to be specified:

  ```
  mysql> SET NAMES 'utf8' COLLATE 'utf8_general_ci';
  ```

- Some programming interfaces provide their own method of setting the character set. MySQL Connector/J for Java clients is one such interface. It detects the character set used on the server side automatically when you connect, but you can specify a different set explicitly by using the `characterEncoding` property in the connection URL. The property value should be the Java-style character-set name. For example, to select `utf8`, you might use a connection URL like this:

```
jdbc:mysql://localhost/cookbook?characterEncoding=UTF-8
```

This is preferable to `SET NAMES` because MySQL Connector/J performs character set conversion on behalf of the application but is unaware of which character set applies if you use `SET NAMES`.

By the way, you should make sure that the character set used by your display device matches what you're using for MySQL. Otherwise, even with MySQL handling the data properly, it might display as garbage. Suppose that you're using the *mysql* program in a terminal window and that you configure MySQL to use `utf8` and store `utf8`-encoded Japanese data. If you set your terminal window to use `euc-jp` encoding, that is also Japanese, but its encoding for Japanese characters is different from `utf8`, so the data will not display as you expect.

 `ucs2` cannot be used as the connection character set.

5.4 Writing String Literals

Problem
You need to write literal strings in SQL statements.

Solution
Learn the syntax rules that govern string values.

Discussion
Strings can be written several ways:

- Enclose the text of the string within single or double quotes:

    ```
    'my string'
    "my string"
    ```

    Be aware that you cannot use double quotes for quoting strings when the `ANSI_QUOTES` SQL mode is enabled. With that mode enabled, the server interprets double quote as the quoting character for identifiers such as table or column names, and not for strings. (See Recipe 2.6.) For this reason, it's preferable to adopt the convention of always writing quoted strings using single quotes. That way, MySQL will interpret them as strings and not as identifiers regardless of the `ANSI_QUOTES` setting.

- Use hexadecimal notation. Each pair of hex digits produces one byte of the string. abcd can be written using any of these formats:

```
0x61626364
X'61626364'
x'61626364'
```

MySQL treats strings written using hex notation as binary strings. Not coincidentally, it's common for applications to use hex strings when constructing SQL statements that refer to binary values:

```
INSERT INTO t SET binary_col = 0xdeadbeef;
```

- To specify a character set for interpretation of a literal string, use an introducer consisting of a character set name preceded by an underscore:

```
_latin1 'abcd'
_ucs2 'abcd'
```

An introducer tells the server how to interpret the following string. For `_latin1 'abcd'`, the server produces a string consisting of four single-byte characters. For `_ucs2 'abcd'`, the server produces a string consisting of two two-byte characters because ucs2 is a double-byte character set.

To ensure that a string is a binary string or that a nonbinary string has a specific character set or collation, use the instructions for string conversion given in Recipe 5.6.

If you need to write a quoted string that includes a quote character and you put the quote into the string as is, a syntax error results:

```
mysql> SELECT 'I'm asleep';
ERROR 1064 (42000): You have an error in your SQL syntax near 'asleep''
```

There are several ways to deal with this:

- Enclose a string containing single quotes within double quotes (assuming that `ANSI_QUOTES` is disabled):

```
mysql> SELECT "I'm asleep";
+------------+
| I'm asleep |
+------------+
| I'm asleep |
+------------+
```

The converse also works; a string containing double quotes can be enclosed within single quotes:

```
mysql> SELECT 'He said, "Boo!"';
+----------------+
| He said, "Boo!" |
+----------------+
```

```
| He said, "Boo!" |
+-----------------+
```

- To include a quote character within a string that is quoted by the same kind of quote, either double the quote or precede it by a backslash. When MySQL reads the statement, it will strip off the extra quote or the backslash:

```
mysql> SELECT 'I''m asleep', 'I\'m wide awake';
+------------+----------------+
| I'm asleep | I'm wide awake |
+------------+----------------+
| I'm asleep | I'm wide awake |
+------------+----------------+
mysql> SELECT "He said, ""Boo!""", "And I said, \"Yikes!\"";
+----------------+---------------------+
| He said, "Boo!" | And I said, "Yikes!" |
+----------------+---------------------+
| He said, "Boo!" | And I said, "Yikes!" |
+----------------+---------------------+
```

A backslash turns off any special meaning of the following character. (It causes a temporary escape from normal string processing rules, so sequences such as \' and \" are called escape sequences.) This means that backslash itself is special. To write a literal backslash within a string, you must double it:

```
mysql> SELECT 'Install MySQL in C:\\mysql on Windows';
+--------------------------------------+
| Install MySQL in C:\mysql on Windows |
+--------------------------------------+
| Install MySQL in C:\mysql on Windows |
+--------------------------------------+
```

Other escape sequences recognized by MySQL are \b (backspace), \n (newline, also called linefeed), \r (carriage return), \t (tab), and \0 (ASCII NUL).

- Write the string as a hex value:

```
mysql> SELECT 0x49276D2061736C656570;
+------------------------+
| 0x49276D2061736C656570 |
+------------------------+
| I'm asleep             |
+------------------------+
```

See Also

If you are issuing SQL statements from within a program, you can refer to strings or binary values symbolically and let your programming interface take care of quoting: use the placeholder mechanism provided by the language's database-access API. See Recipe 2.5 for details. Alternatively, load binary values such as images from files using the LOAD_FILE( ) function; Recipe 18.6 shows an example.

5.5 Checking a String's Character Set or Collation

Problem

You want to know the character set or collation of a string.

Solution

Use the CHARSET( ) or COLLATION( ) function.

Discussion

If you create a table using the following definition, you know that values stored in the column will have a character set of utf8 and a collation of utf8_danish_ci:

```
CREATE TABLE t (c CHAR(10) CHARACTER SET utf8 COLLATE utf8_danish_ci);
```

But sometimes it's not so clear what character set or collation applies to a string. Server configuration affects literal strings and some string functions, and other string functions return values in a specific character set. Symptoms that you have the wrong character set or collation are that a collation-mismatch error occurs for a comparison operation, or a lettercase conversion doesn't work properly. This section shows how to check what character set or collation a string has. Recipe 5.6 shows how to convert strings to a different character set or collation.

To find out what character set or collation a string has, use the CHARSET( ) or COLLATION( ) function. For example, did you know that the USER( ) function returns a Unicode string?

```
mysql> SELECT USER(), CHARSET(USER()), COLLATION(USER());
+-----------------+-----------------+-------------------+
| USER()          | CHARSET(USER()) | COLLATION(USER()) |
+-----------------+-----------------+-------------------+
| cbuser@localhost | utf8           | utf8_general_ci   |
+-----------------+-----------------+-------------------+
```

String values that take their character set and collation from the current configuration may change properties if the configuration changes. This is true for literal strings:

```
mysql> SET NAMES 'latin1';
mysql> SELECT CHARSET('abc'), COLLATION('abc');
+----------------+-------------------+
| CHARSET('abc') | COLLATION('abc')  |
+----------------+-------------------+
| latin1         | latin1_swedish_ci |
+----------------+-------------------+
mysql> SET NAMES latin7 COLLATE 'latin7_bin';
mysql> SELECT CHARSET('abc'), COLLATION('abc');
+----------------+-------------------+
| CHARSET('abc') | COLLATION('abc')  |
+----------------+-------------------+
```

```
| latin7         | latin7_bin       |
+----------------+------------------+
```

For a binary string, the `CHARSET( )` or `COLLATION( )` functions return a value of `binary`, which means that the string is compared and sorted based on numeric byte values, not character collation values. Several functions return binary strings, such as `MD5( )` and `PASSWORD( )`:

```
mysql> SELECT CHARSET(MD5('a')), COLLATION(MD5('a'));
+-------------------+---------------------+
| CHARSET(MD5('a')) | COLLATION(MD5('a')) |
+-------------------+---------------------+
| binary            | binary              |
+-------------------+---------------------+
mysql> SELECT CHARSET(PASSWORD('a')), COLLATION(PASSWORD('a'));
+------------------------+--------------------------+
| CHARSET(PASSWORD('a')) | COLLATION(PASSWORD('a')) |
+------------------------+--------------------------+
| binary                 | binary                   |
+------------------------+--------------------------+
```

It can be useful to know that a function or string expression produces a binary string if you're trying to perform lettercase conversion on the result and it's not working. See Recipe 5.8 for details.

5.6 Changing a String's Character Set or Collation

Problem

You want to convert a string from one character set or collation to another.

Solution

Use the `CONVERT( )` function to convert a string to another character set. Use the `COLLATE` operator to convert a string to another collation.

Discussion

To convert a string from one character set to another, use the `CONVERT( )` function:

```
mysql> SET @s1 = 'my string';
mysql> SET @s2 = CONVERT(@s1 USING utf8);
mysql> SELECT CHARSET(@s1), CHARSET(@s2);
+--------------+--------------+
| CHARSET(@s1) | CHARSET(@s2) |
+--------------+--------------+
| latin1       | utf8         |
+--------------+--------------+
```

To change the collation of a string, use the `COLLATE` operator:

```
mysql> SET @s1 = 'my string';
mysql> SET @s2 = @s1 COLLATE latin1_spanish_ci;
mysql> SELECT COLLATION(@s1), COLLATION(@s2);
+------------------+------------------+
| COLLATION(@s1)   | COLLATION(@s2)   |
+------------------+------------------+
| latin1_swedish_ci | latin1_spanish_ci |
+------------------+------------------+
```

The new collation must be legal for the character set of the string. For example, you can use the `utf8_general_ci` collation with `utf8` strings, but not with `latin1` strings:

```
mysql> SELECT _latin1 'abc' COLLATE utf8_bin;
ERROR 1253 (42000): COLLATION 'utf8_bin' is not valid for
CHARACTER SET 'latin1'
```

To convert both the character set and collation of a string, use `CONVERT( )` to change the character set, and apply the `COLLATE` operator to the result:

```
mysql> SET @s1 = 'my string';
mysql> SET @s2 = CONVERT(@s1 USING utf8) COLLATE utf8_spanish_ci;
mysql> SELECT CHARSET(@s1), COLLATION(@s1), CHARSET(@s2), COLLATION(@s2);
+--------------+-------------------+--------------+-----------------+
| CHARSET(@s1) | COLLATION(@s1)    | CHARSET(@s2) | COLLATION(@s2)  |
+--------------+-------------------+--------------+-----------------+
| latin1       | latin1_swedish_ci | utf8         | utf8_spanish_ci |
+--------------+-------------------+--------------+-----------------+
```

The `CONVERT( )` function can also be used to convert binary strings to nonbinary strings and vice versa. To produce a binary string, use `binary`; any other character set name produces a nonbinary string:

```
mysql> SET @s1 = 'my string';
mysql> SET @s2 = CONVERT(@s1 USING binary);
mysql> SET @s3 = CONVERT(@s2 USING utf8);
mysql> SELECT CHARSET(@s1), CHARSET(@s2), CHARSET(@s3);
+--------------+--------------+--------------+
| CHARSET(@s1) | CHARSET(@s2) | CHARSET(@s3) |
+--------------+--------------+--------------+
| latin1       | binary       | utf8         |
+--------------+--------------+--------------+
```

Alternatively, you can produce binary strings using the `BINARY` operator, which is equivalent to `CONVERT(str USING binary)`:

```
mysql> SET @s1 = 'my string';
mysql> SET @s2 = BINARY @s2;
mysql> SELECT CHARSET(@s1), CHARSET(@s2);
+--------------+--------------+
| CHARSET(@s1) | CHARSET(@s2) |
+--------------+--------------+
| latin1       | binary       |
+--------------+--------------+
```

5.7 Converting the Lettercase of a String

Problem

You want to convert a string to uppercase or lowercase.

Solution

Use the UPPER( ) or LOWER( ) function. If they don't work, see Recipe 5.8.

Discussion

The UPPER( ) and LOWER( ) functions convert the lettercase of a string:

```
mysql> SELECT thing, UPPER(thing), LOWER(thing) FROM limbs;
+--------------+--------------+--------------+
| thing        | UPPER(thing) | LOWER(thing) |
+--------------+--------------+--------------+
| human        | HUMAN        | human        |
| insect       | INSECT       | insect       |
| squid        | SQUID        | squid        |
| octopus      | OCTOPUS      | octopus      |
| fish         | FISH         | fish         |
| centipede    | CENTIPEDE    | centipede    |
| table        | TABLE        | table        |
| armchair     | ARMCHAIR     | armchair     |
| phonograph   | PHONOGRAPH   | phonograph   |
| tripod       | TRIPOD       | tripod       |
| Peg Leg Pete | PEG LEG PETE | peg leg pete |
| space alien  | SPACE ALIEN  | space alien  |
+--------------+--------------+--------------+
```

To convert the lettercase of only part of a string, break it into pieces, convert the relevant piece, and put the pieces back together. Suppose that you want to convert only the initial character of a string to uppercase. The following expression accomplishes that:

```
CONCAT(UPPER(LEFT(str,1)),MID(str,2))
```

But it's ugly to write an expression like that each time you need it. For convenience, define a stored function:

```
mysql> CREATE FUNCTION initial_cap (s VARCHAR(255))
    -> RETURNS VARCHAR(255) DETERMINISTIC
    -> RETURN CONCAT(UPPER(LEFT(s,1)),MID(s,2));
```

You can then capitalize initial characters more easily like this:

```
mysql> SELECT thing, initial_cap(thing) FROM limbs;
+--------------+--------------------+
| thing        | initial_cap(thing) |
+--------------+--------------------+
| human        | Human              |
| insect       | Insect             |
| squid        | Squid              |
```

```
| octopus     | Octopus       |
| fish        | Fish          |
| centipede   | Centipede     |
| table       | Table         |
| armchair    | Armchair      |
| phonograph  | Phonograph    |
| tripod      | Tripod        |
| Peg Leg Pete | Peg Leg Pete |
| space alien | Space alien   |
+-------------+---------------+
```

For more information about writing stored functions, see Chapter 16.

5.8 Converting the Lettercase of a "Stubborn" String

Problem

You want to convert a string to uppercase or lowercase, but UPPER( ) and LOWER( ) don't work.

Solution

You're probably trying to convert a binary string. Convert it to a nonbinary string so that it has a character set and collation and becomes subject to case mapping.

Discussion

The usual way to convert a string to uppercase or lowercase is to use the UPPER( ) or LOWER( ) function:

```
mysql> SET @s = 'aBcD';
mysql> SELECT UPPER(@s), LOWER(@s);
+-----------+-----------+
| UPPER(@s) | LOWER(@s) |
+-----------+-----------+
| ABCD      | abcd      |
+-----------+-----------+
```

But sometimes you'll run across a string that is "stubborn" and resists lettercase conversion. This is common for columns that have a BINARY or BLOB data type:

```
mysql> CREATE TABLE t (b BLOB) SELECT 'aBcD' AS b;
mysql> SELECT b, UPPER(b), LOWER(b) FROM t;
+------+----------+----------+
| b    | UPPER(b) | LOWER(b) |
+------+----------+----------+
| aBcD | aBcD     | aBcD     |
+------+----------+----------+
```

The cause of the problem here is that the column is a binary string: it has no character set or collation and lettercase does not apply. Thus, UPPER( ) and LOWER( ) do nothing, which can be confusing. Compounding the confusion is that lettercase conversion of binary strings *used* to work in older versions of MySQL, but does so no longer. What's going on? Here is the history:

- Before MySQL 4.1, all strings, including binary strings, were interpreted with respect to the server's default character set. Consequently, the UPPER( ) and LOWER( ) functions performed case mapping even for binary strings:

```
mysql> SET @s = BINARY 'aBcD';
mysql> SELECT @s, LOWER(@s), UPPER(@s);
+------+-----------+-----------+
| @s   | LOWER(@s) | UPPER(@s) |
+------+-----------+-----------+
| aBcD | abcd      | ABCD      |
+------+-----------+-----------+
```

- In MySQL 4.1, character set handling was revised significantly, with one of the changes being that character set and collation applied only to nonbinary strings. From 4.1 up, a binary string is just a sequence of bytes, and lettercase has no meaning, even if you store what looks like text in the string. As a result, the LOWER( ) and UPPER( ) functions do nothing when applied to binary strings:

```
mysql> SET @s = BINARY 'aBcD';
mysql> SELECT @s, LOWER(@s), UPPER(@s);
+------+-----------+-----------+
| @s   | LOWER(@s) | UPPER(@s) |
+------+-----------+-----------+
| aBcD | aBcD      | aBcD      |
+------+-----------+-----------+
```

To map a binary string to a given lettercase, convert it to a nonbinary string, choosing a character set that contains an alphabet with uppercase and lowercase characters. The case-conversion functions then will work as you expect because the collation provides case mapping. The following example uses the BLOB column from earlier in this section, but the same principles apply to binary string literals and string expressions:

```
mysql> SELECT b,
    -> UPPER(CONVERT(b USING latin1)) AS upper,
    -> LOWER(CONVERT(b USING latin1)) AS lower
    -> FROM t;
+------+-------+-------+
| b    | upper | lower |
+------+-------+-------+
| aBcD | ABCD  | abcd  |
+------+-------+-------+
```

The same kind of case-conversion problem occurs with functions that return binary strings, which is typical for functions such as MD5( ) or COMPRESS( ) that perform encryption or compression.

If you're not sure whether a string expression is binary or nonbinary, use the CHARSET( ) function. The following example shows that VERSION( ) returns a nonbinary string, but MD5( ) returns a binary string:

```
mysql> SELECT CHARSET(VERSION()), CHARSET(MD5('some string'));
+--------------------+----------------------------+
| CHARSET(VERSION()) | CHARSET(MD5('some string')) |
+--------------------+----------------------------+
| utf8               | binary                     |
+--------------------+----------------------------+
```

That result indicates that the string produced by VERSION( ) can be case-mapped directly, but the string produced by MD5( ) must first be converted to a nonbinary string:

```
mysql> SELECT UPPER(VERSION());
+------------------+
| UPPER(VERSION()) |
+------------------+
| 5.1.12-BETA-LOG  |
+------------------+
mysql> SELECT UPPER(CONVERT(MD5('some string') USING latin1));
+-------------------------------------------------+
| UPPER(CONVERT(MD5('some string') USING latin1)) |
+-------------------------------------------------+
| 5AC749FBEEC93607FC28D666BE85E73A                |
+-------------------------------------------------+
```

5.9 Controlling Case Sensitivity in String Comparisons

Problem

You want to know whether strings are equal or unequal, or which one appears first in lexical order.

Solution

Use a comparison operator. But remember that strings have properties such as case sensitivity that you must take into account. For example, a string comparison might be case-sensitive when you don't want it to be, or vice versa.

Discussion

As for other data types, you can compare string values for equality, inequality, or relative ordering:

```
mysql> SELECT 'cat' = 'cat', 'cat' = 'dog';
+---------------+---------------+
| 'cat' = 'cat' | 'cat' = 'dog' |
+---------------+---------------+
|             1 |             0 |
+---------------+---------------+
mysql> SELECT 'cat' != 'cat', 'cat' != 'dog';
+----------------+----------------+
| 'cat' != 'cat' | 'cat' != 'dog' |
+----------------+----------------+
|              0 |              1 |
+----------------+----------------+
```

```
                +----------------+----------------+
mysql> SELECT 'cat' < 'awk', 'cat' < 'dog';
                +----------------+----------------+
                | 'cat' < 'awk' | 'cat' < 'dog' |
                +----------------+----------------+
                |              0 |              1 |
                +----------------+----------------+
mysql> SELECT 'cat' BETWEEN 'awk' AND 'egret';
                +--------------------------------+
                | 'cat' BETWEEN 'awk' AND 'egret' |
                +--------------------------------+
                |                              1 |
                +--------------------------------+
```

However, comparison and sorting properties of strings are subject to certain complications that don't apply to other types of data. For example, sometimes you need to make sure a string operation is case-sensitive that would not otherwise be, or vice versa. This section describes how to do that for ordinary comparisons. Recipe 5.12 covers case sensitivity in pattern-matching operations.

String comparison properties depend on whether the operands are binary or nonbinary strings:

- A binary string is a sequence of bytes and is compared using numeric byte values. Lettercase has no meaning. However, because letters in different cases have different byte values, comparisons of binary strings effectively are case-sensitive. (That is, a and A are unequal.) If you want to compare binary strings so that lettercase does not matter, convert them to nonbinary strings that have a case-insensitive collation.

- A nonbinary string is a sequence of characters and is compared in character units. (Depending on the character set, some characters might have multiple bytes.) The string has a character set that defines the legal characters and a collation that defines their sort order. The collation also determines whether to consider characters in different lettercases the same in comparisons. If the collation is case-sensitive, and you want a case-insensitive collation (or vice versa), convert the strings to use a collation with the desired case-comparison properties.

By default, strings have a character set of latin1 and a collation of latin1_swedish_ci. This results in case-insensitive string comparisons.

The following example shows how two binary strings that compare as unequal can be handled so that they are equal when compared as case-insensitive nonbinary strings:

```
mysql> SET @s1 = BINARY 'cat', @s2 = BINARY 'CAT';
mysql> SELECT @s1 = @s2;
+-----------+
| @s1 = @s2 |
+-----------+
|         0 |
+-----------+
mysql> SET @s1 = CONVERT(@s1 USING latin1) COLLATE latin1_swedish_ci;
```

```
mysql> SET @s2 = CONVERT(@s2 USING latin1) COLLATE latin1_swedish_ci;
mysql> SELECT @s1 = @s2;
+-----------+
| @s1 = @s2 |
+-----------+
|         1 |
+-----------+
```

In this case, because `latin1_swedish_ci` is the default collation for `latin1`, you can omit the `COLLATE` operator:

```
mysql> SET @s1 = CONVERT(@s1 USING latin1);
mysql> SET @s2 = CONVERT(@s2 USING latin1);
mysql> SELECT @s1 = @s2;
+-----------+
| @s1 = @s2 |
+-----------+
|         1 |
+-----------+
```

The next example shows how to compare two strings that are not case-sensitive (as demonstrated by the first `SELECT`) in case-sensitive fashion (as demonstrated by the second):

```
mysql> SET @s1 = _latin1 'cat', @s2 = _latin1 'CAT';
mysql> SELECT @s1 = @s2;
+-----------+
| @s1 = @s2 |
+-----------+
|         1 |
+-----------+
mysql> SELECT @s1 COLLATE latin1_general_cs = @s2 COLLATE latin1_general_cs
    ->   AS '@s1 = @s2';
+-----------+
| @s1 = @s2 |
+-----------+
|         0 |
+-----------+
```

If you compare a binary string with a nonbinary string, the comparison treats both operands as binary strings:

```
mysql> SELECT _latin1 'cat' = BINARY 'CAT';
+------------------------------+
| _latin1 'cat' = BINARY 'CAT' |
+------------------------------+
|                            0 |
+------------------------------+
```

Thus, if you want to compare two nonbinary strings as binary strings, apply the `BINARY` operator to either one when comparing them:

```
mysql> SET @s1 = _latin1 'cat', @s2 = _latin1 'CAT';
mysql> SELECT @s1 = @s2, BINARY @s1 = @s2, @s1 = BINARY @s2;
+-----------+------------------+------------------+
| @s1 = @s2 | BINARY @s1 = @s2 | @s1 = BINARY @s2 |
```

```
+----------+-----------------+-----------------+
|        1 |               0 |               0 |
+----------+-----------------+-----------------+
```

If you find that you've declared a column using a type that is not suitable for the kind of comparisons for which you typically use it, use `ALTER TABLE` to change the type. Suppose that you have a table in which you store news articles:

```
CREATE TABLE news
(
  id      INT UNSIGNED NOT NULL AUTO_INCREMENT,
  article BLOB,
  PRIMARY KEY (id)
);
```

Here the `article` column is declared as a `BLOB`, which is a binary string type. This means that if you store text in the column, comparisons are made without regard to character set. (In effect, they are case-sensitive.) If that's not what you want, you can convert the column to a nonbinary type that has a case-insensitive collation using `ALTER TABLE`:

```
ALTER TABLE news
  MODIFY article TEXT CHARACTER SET utf8 COLLATE utf8_general_ci;
```

5.10 Pattern Matching with SQL Patterns

Problem

You want to perform a pattern match rather than a literal comparison.

Solution

Use the `LIKE` operator and an SQL pattern, described in this section. Or use a regular-expression pattern match, described in Recipe 5.11.

Discussion

Patterns are strings that contain special characters. These are known as *metacharacters* because they stand for something other than themselves. MySQL provides two kinds of pattern matching. One is based on SQL patterns and the other on regular expressions. SQL patterns are more standard among different database systems, but regular expressions are more powerful. The two kinds of pattern match uses different operators and different sets of metacharacters. This section describes SQL patterns. Recipe 5.11 describes regular expressions.

The example here uses a table named `metal` that contains the following rows:

```
+----------+
| name     |
+----------+
| copper   |
```

```
| gold     |
| iron     |
| lead     |
| mercury  |
| platinum |
| silver   |
| tin      |
+----------+
```

SQL pattern matching uses the `LIKE` and `NOT LIKE` operators rather than = and != to perform matching against a pattern string. Patterns may contain two special metacharacters: `_` matches any single character, and `%` matches any sequence of characters, including the empty string. You can use these characters to create patterns that match a variety of values:

- Strings that begin with a particular substring:

  ```
  mysql> SELECT name FROM metal WHERE name LIKE 'co%';
  +--------+
  | name   |
  +--------+
  | copper |
  +--------+
  ```

- Strings that end with a particular substring:

  ```
  mysql> SELECT name FROM metal WHERE name LIKE '%er';
  +--------+
  | name   |
  +--------+
  | copper |
  | silver |
  +--------+
  ```

- Strings that contain a particular substring at any position:

  ```
  mysql> SELECT name FROM metal WHERE name LIKE '%er%';
  +---------+
  | name    |
  +---------+
  | copper  |
  | mercury |
  | silver  |
  +---------+
  ```

- Strings that contain a substring at a specific position (the pattern matches only if pp occurs at the third position of the name column):

  ```
  mysql> SELECT name FROM metal where name LIKE '__pp%';
  +--------+
  | name   |
  +--------+
  | copper |
  +--------+
  ```

An SQL pattern matches successfully only if it matches the entire comparison value. Of the following two pattern matches, only the second succeeds:

```
'abc' LIKE 'b'
'abc' LIKE '%b%'
```

To reverse the sense of a pattern match, use NOT LIKE. The following statement finds strings that contain no i characters:

```
mysql> SELECT name FROM metal WHERE name NOT LIKE '%i%';
+---------+
| name    |
+---------+
| copper  |
| gold    |
| lead    |
| mercury |
+---------+
```

SQL patterns do not match NULL values. This is true both for LIKE and for NOT LIKE:

```
mysql> SELECT NULL LIKE '%', NULL NOT LIKE '%';
+---------------+-------------------+
| NULL LIKE '%' | NULL NOT LIKE '%' |
+---------------+-------------------+
|          NULL |              NULL |
+---------------+-------------------+
```

Using Patterns with Nonstring Values

Unlike some other database systems, MySQL allows pattern matches to be applied to nonstring values such as numbers or dates, which can sometimes be useful. The following table shows some ways to test a DATE value d using function calls that extract date parts and using the equivalent pattern matches. The pairs of expressions are true for dates occurring in the year 1976, in the month of April, or on the first day of the month:

Function value test	Pattern match test
YEAR(d) = 1976	d LIKE '1976-%'
MONTH(d) = 4	d LIKE '%-04-%'
DAYOFMONTH(d) = 1	d LIKE '%-01'

In some cases, pattern matches are equivalent to substring comparisons. For example, using patterns to find strings at one end or the other of a string is like using LEFT( ) or RIGHT( ):

Pattern match	Substring comparison
str LIKE 'abc%'	LEFT(str,3) = 'abc'
str LIKE '%abc'	RIGHT(str,3) = 'abc'

If you're matching against a column that is indexed and you have a choice of using a pattern or an equivalent LEFT( ) expression, you'll likely find that the pattern match is faster. MySQL can use the index to narrow the search for a pattern that begins with a literal string. With LEFT( ), it cannot.

5.11 Pattern Matching with Regular Expressions

Problem

You want to data type perform a pattern match rather than a literal comparison.

Solution

Use the REGEXP operator and a regular expression pattern, described in this section. Or use an SQL pattern, described in Recipe 5.10.

Discussion

SQL patterns (see Recipe 5.10) are likely to be implemented by other database systems, so they're reasonably portable beyond MySQL. On the other hand, they're somewhat limited. For example, you can easily write an SQL pattern %abc% to find strings that contain abc, but you cannot write a single SQL pattern to identify strings that contain any of the characters a, b, or c. Nor can you match string content based on character types such as letters or digits. For such operations, MySQL supports another type of pattern matching operation based on regular expressions and the REGEXP operator (or NOT REGEXP to reverse the sense of the match). REGEXP matching uses the pattern elements shown in the following table.

Pattern	What the pattern matches
^	Beginning of string
$	End of string
.	Any single character
[. . .]	Any character listed between the square brackets
[^ . . .]	Any character not listed between the square brackets
p1|p2|p3	Alternation; matches any of the patterns p1, p2, or p3
*	Zero or more instances of preceding element
+	One or more instances of preceding element
{n}	n instances of preceding element
{m,n}	m through n instances of preceding element

You may already be familiar with these regular expression pattern characters, because many of them are the same as those used by *vi*, *grep*, *sed*, and other Unix utilities that support regular expressions. Most of them are used also in the regular expressions understood by programming languages. (Chapter 10 discusses the use of pattern matching in programs for data validation and transformation.)

Recipe 5.10 showed how to use SQL patterns to match substrings at the beginning or end of a string, or at an arbitrary or specific position within a string. You can do the same things with regular expressions:

- Strings that begin with a particular substring:

  ```
  mysql> SELECT name FROM metal WHERE name REGEXP '^co';
  +--------+
  | name   |
  +--------+
  | copper |
  +--------+
  ```

- Strings that end with a particular substring:

  ```
  mysql> SELECT name FROM metal WHERE name REGEXP 'er$';
  +--------+
  | name   |
  +--------+
  | copper |
  | silver |
  +--------+
  ```

- Strings that contain a particular substring at any position:

  ```
  mysql> SELECT name FROM metal WHERE name REGEXP 'er';
  +---------+
  | name    |
  +---------+
  | copper  |
  | mercury |
  | silver  |
  +---------+
  ```

- Strings that contain a particular substring at a specific position:

  ```
  mysql> SELECT name FROM metal WHERE name REGEXP '^..pp';
  +--------+
  | name   |
  +--------+
  | copper |
  +--------+
  ```

In addition, regular expressions have other capabilities and can perform kinds of matches that SQL patterns cannot. For example, regular expressions can contain character classes, which match any character in the class:

- To write a character class, use square brackets and list the characters you want the class to match inside the brackets. Thus, the pattern [abc] matches either a, b, or c.

- Classes may indicate ranges of characters by using a dash between the beginning and end of the range. [a-z] matches any letter, [0-9] matches digits, and [a-z0-9] matches letters or digits.
- To negate a character class ("match any character but these"), begin the list with a ^ character. For example, [^0-9] matches anything but digits.

MySQL's regular-expression capabilities also support POSIX character classes. These match specific character sets, as described in the following table.

POSIX class	What the class matches
[:alnum:]	Alphabetic and numeric characters
[:alpha:]	Alphabetic characters
[:blank:]	Whitespace (space or tab characters)
[:cntrl:]	Control characters
[:digit:]	Digits
[:graph:]	Graphic (nonblank) characters
[:lower:]	Lowercase alphabetic characters
[:print:]	Graphic or space characters
[:punct:]	Punctuation characters
[:space:]	Space, tab, newline, carriage return
[:upper:]	Uppercase alphabetic characters
[:xdigit:]	Hexadecimal digits (0-9, a-f, A-F)

POSIX classes are intended for use within character classes, so you use them within square brackets. The following expression matches values that contain any hexadecimal digit character:

```
mysql> SELECT name, name REGEXP '[[:xdigit:]]' FROM metal;
+----------+---------------------------+
| name     | name REGEXP '[[:xdigit:]]' |
+----------+---------------------------+
| copper   |                         1 |
| gold     |                         1 |
| iron     |                         0 |
| lead     |                         1 |
| mercury  |                         1 |
| platinum |                         1 |
| silver   |                         1 |
| tin      |                         0 |
+----------+---------------------------+
```

Regular expressions can contain alternations. The syntax looks like this:

```
alternative1|alternative2|...
```

An alternation is similar to a character class in the sense that it matches if any of the alternatives match. But unlike a character class, the alternatives are not limited to single characters. They can be multiple-character strings or even patterns. The following alternation matches strings that begin with a vowel or end with er:

```
mysql> SELECT name FROM metal WHERE name REGEXP '^[aeiou]|er$';
+--------+
| name   |
+--------+
| copper |
| iron   |
| silver |
+--------+
```

Parentheses can be used to group alternations. For example, if you want to match strings that consist entirely of digits or entirely of letters, you might try this pattern, using an alternation:

```
mysql> SELECT 'Om' REGEXP '^[[:digit:]]+|[[:alpha:]]+$';
+------------------------------------------+
| 'Om' REGEXP '^[[:digit:]]+|[[:alpha:]]+$' |
+------------------------------------------+
|                                        1 |
+------------------------------------------+
```

However, as the query result shows, the pattern doesn't work. That's because the ^ groups with the first alternative, and the $ groups with the second alternative. So the pattern actually matches strings that begin with one or more digits, or strings that end with one or more letters. If you group the alternatives within parentheses, the ^ and $ apply to both of them, and the pattern acts as you expect:

```
mysql> SELECT 'Om' REGEXP '^([[:digit:]]+|[[:alpha:]]+)$';
+--------------------------------------------+
| 'Om' REGEXP '^([[:digit:]]+|[[:alpha:]]+)$' |
+--------------------------------------------+
|                                          0 |
+--------------------------------------------+
```

Unlike SQL pattern matches, which are successful only if the pattern matches the entire comparison value, regular expressions are successful if the pattern matches anywhere within the value. The following two pattern matches are equivalent in the sense that each one succeeds only for strings that contain a b character, but the first is more efficient because the pattern is simpler:

```
'abc' REGEXP 'b'
'abc' REGEXP '^.*b.*$'
```

Regular expressions do not match NULL values. This is true both for REGEXP and for NOT REGEXP:

```
mysql> SELECT NULL REGEXP '.*', NULL NOT REGEXP '.*';
+------------------+----------------------+
| NULL REGEXP '.*' | NULL NOT REGEXP '.*' |
+------------------+----------------------+
```

```
|              NULL |                 NULL |
+-------------------+----------------------+
```

The fact that a regular expression matches a string if the pattern is found anywhere in the string means you must take care not to inadvertently specify a pattern that matches the empty string. If you do, it will match any non-NULL value. For example, the pattern a* matches any number of a characters, even none. If your goal is to match only strings containing nonempty sequences of a characters, use a+ instead. The + requires one or more instances of the preceding pattern element for a match.

As with SQL pattern matches performed using LIKE, regular expression matches performed with REGEXP sometimes are equivalent to substring comparisons. The ^ and $ metacharacters serve much the same purpose as LEFT( ) or RIGHT( ), at least if you're looking for literal strings:

Pattern match	Substring comparison
str REGEXP '^abc'	LEFT(*str*,3) = 'abc'
str REGEXP 'abc$'	RIGHT(*str*,3) = 'abc'

For nonliteral strings, it's typically not possible to construct an equivalent substring comparison. For example, to match strings that begin with any nonempty sequence of digits, you can use this pattern match:

    str REGEXP '^[0-9]+'

That is something that LEFT( ) cannot do (and neither can LIKE, for that matter).

 A limitation of regular expression (REGEXP) matching compared to SQL pattern (LIKE) matching is that REGEXP works only for single-byte character sets. It cannot be expected to work with multibyte character sets such as utf8 or sjis.

5.12 Controlling Case Sensitivity in Pattern Matching

Problem

A pattern match is case-sensitive when you don't want it to be, or vice versa.

Solution

Alter the case sensitivity of the strings.

Discussion

The case sensitivity of a pattern match operation is like that of a string comparison. That is, it depends on whether the operands are binary or nonbinary strings, and for nonbinary strings, it depends on their collation. See Recipe 5.9 for discussion of how these factors apply to comparisons.

The default character set and collation are latin1 and latin1_swedish_ci, so pattern match operations are not case-sensitive by default:

```
mysql> SELECT 'a' LIKE 'A', 'a' REGEXP 'A';
+--------------+----------------+
| 'a' LIKE 'A' | 'a' REGEXP 'A' |
+--------------+----------------+
|            1 |              1 |
+--------------+----------------+
```

Note that a REGEXP operation that is not case-sensitive can lead to some unintuitive results:

```
mysql> SELECT 'a' REGEXP '[[:lower:]]', 'a' REGEXP '[[:upper:]]';
+-------------------------+-------------------------+
| 'a' REGEXP '[[:lower:]]' | 'a' REGEXP '[[:upper:]]' |
+-------------------------+-------------------------+
|                       1 |                       1 |
+-------------------------+-------------------------+
```

Both expressions are true because [:lower:] and [:upper:] are equivalent when case sensitivity doesn't matter.

If a pattern match uses different case-sensitive behavior from what you want, control it the same way as for string comparisons: convert the strings to binary or nonbinary as necessary or change the collation of nonbinary strings.

To make a pattern match case-sensitive, use a case-sensitive collation for either operand. For example, with the latin1 character set, use a collation of latin1_general_cs:

```
mysql> SET @s = 'a' COLLATE latin1_general_cs;
mysql> SELECT @s LIKE 'A', @s REGEXP 'A';
+-------------+---------------+
| @s LIKE 'A' | @s REGEXP 'A' |
+-------------+---------------+
|           0 |             0 |
+-------------+---------------+
```

Use of a case-sensitive collation also has the effect of causing [:lower:] and [:upper:] in regular expressions to match only lowercase and uppercase characters, respectively. The second expression in the following statement yields a result that really is true only for uppercase letters:

```
mysql> SET @s = 'a', @s_cs = 'a' COLLATE latin1_general_cs;
mysql> SELECT @s REGEXP '[[:upper:]]', @s_cs REGEXP '[[:upper:]]';
+-------------------------+----------------------------+
| @s REGEXP '[[:upper:]]' | @s_cs REGEXP '[[:upper:]]' |
+-------------------------+----------------------------+
|                       1 |                          0 |
+-------------------------+----------------------------+
```

5.13 Breaking Apart or Combining Strings

Problem

You want to extract a piece of a string or combine strings to form a larger string.

Solution

To obtain a piece of a string, use a substring-extraction function. To combine strings, use CONCAT( ).

Discussion

Strings can be broken apart by using appropriate substring-extraction functions. For example, LEFT( ), MID( ), and RIGHT( ) extract substrings from the left, middle, or right part of a string:

```
mysql> SELECT name, LEFT(name,2), MID(name,3,1), RIGHT(name,3) FROM metal;
+----------+--------------+---------------+---------------+
| name     | LEFT(name,2) | MID(name,3,1) | RIGHT(name,3) |
+----------+--------------+---------------+---------------+
| copper   | co           | p             | per           |
| gold     | go           | l             | old           |
| iron     | ir           | o             | ron           |
| lead     | le           | a             | ead           |
| mercury  | me           | r             | ury           |
| platinum | pl           | a             | num           |
| silver   | si           | l             | ver           |
| tin      | ti           | n             | tin           |
+----------+--------------+---------------+---------------+
```

For LEFT( ) and RIGHT( ), the second argument indicates how many characters to return from the left or right end of the string. For MID( ), the second argument is the starting position of the substring you want (beginning from 1), and the third argument indicates how many characters to return.

The SUBSTRING( ) function takes a string and a starting position, returning everything to the right of the position. MID( ) acts the same way if you omit its third argument because MID( ) is actually a synonym for SUBSTRING( ):

```
mysql> SELECT name, SUBSTRING(name,4), MID(name,4) FROM metal;
+----------+-------------------+-------------+
| name     | SUBSTRING(name,4) | MID(name,4) |
+----------+-------------------+-------------+
| copper   | per               | per         |
| gold     | d                 | d           |
| iron     | n                 | n           |
| lead     | d                 | d           |
| mercury  | cury              | cury        |
| platinum | tinum             | tinum       |
| silver   | ver               | ver         |
```

```
| tin      |                   |             |
+----------+-------------------+-------------+
```

Use `SUBSTRING_INDEX(str,c,n)` to return everything to the right or left of a given character. It searches into a string *str* for the *n*-th occurrence of the character *c* and returns everything to its left. If *n* is negative, the search for *c* starts from the right and returns everything to the right of the character:

```
mysql> SELECT name,
    -> SUBSTRING_INDEX(name,'r',1),
    -> SUBSTRING_INDEX(name,'i',-1)
    -> FROM metal;
+----------+----------------------------+-----------------------------+
| name     | SUBSTRING_INDEX(name,'r',1) | SUBSTRING_INDEX(name,'i',-1) |
+----------+----------------------------+-----------------------------+
| copper   | coppe                      | copper                      |
| gold     | gold                       | gold                        |
| iron     | i                          | ron                         |
| lead     | lead                       | lead                        |
| mercury  | me                         | mercury                     |
| platinum | platinum                   | num                         |
| silver   | silve                      | lver                        |
| tin      | tin                        | n                           |
+----------+----------------------------+-----------------------------+
```

Note that if there is no *n*-th occurrence of the character, `SUBSTRING_INDEX( )` returns the entire string. `SUBSTRING_INDEX( )` is case-sensitive.

Substrings can be used for purposes other than display, such as to perform comparisons. The following statement finds metal names having a first letter that lies in the last half of the alphabet:

```
mysql> SELECT name from metal WHERE LEFT(name,1) >= 'n';
+----------+
| name     |
+----------+
| platinum |
| silver   |
| tin      |
+----------+
```

To combine strings rather than pull them apart, use the `CONCAT( )` function. It concatenates all its arguments and returns the result:

```
mysql> SELECT CONCAT('Hello, ',USER(),', welcome to MySQL!') AS greeting;
+---------------------------------------------+
| greeting                                    |
+---------------------------------------------+
| Hello, cbuser@localhost, welcome to MySQL!  |
+---------------------------------------------+
mysql> SELECT CONCAT(name,' ends in "d": ',IF(RIGHT(name,1)='d','YES','NO'))
    -> AS 'ends in "d"?'
    -> FROM metal;
+-------------------------+
| ends in "d"?            |
```

```
+-------------------------+
| copper ends in "d": NO  |
| gold ends in "d": YES   |
| iron ends in "d": NO    |
| lead ends in "d": YES   |
| mercury ends in "d": NO |
| platinum ends in "d": NO |
| silver ends in "d": NO  |
| tin ends in "d": NO     |
+-------------------------+
```

Concatenation can be useful for modifying column values "in place." For example, the following UPDATE statement adds a string to the end of each name value in the metal table:

```
mysql> UPDATE metal SET name = CONCAT(name,'ide');
mysql> SELECT name FROM metal;
+-------------+
| name        |
+-------------+
| copperide   |
| goldide     |
| ironide     |
| leadide     |
| mercuryide  |
| platinumide |
| silveride   |
| tinide      |
+-------------+
```

To undo the operation, strip off the last three characters (the CHAR_LENGTH( ) function returns the length of a string in characters):

```
mysql> UPDATE metal SET name = LEFT(name,CHAR_LENGTH(name)-3);
mysql> SELECT name FROM metal;
+----------+
| name     |
+----------+
| copper   |
| gold     |
| iron     |
| lead     |
| mercury  |
| platinum |
| silver   |
| tin      |
+----------+
```

The concept of modifying a column in place can be applied to ENUM or SET values as well, which usually can be treated as string values even though they are stored internally as numbers. For example, to concatenate a SET element to an existing SET column, use CONCAT( ) to add the new value to the existing value, preceded by a comma. But remember to account for the possibility that the existing value might be NULL. In that case, set the column value equal to the new element, without the leading comma:

```
UPDATE tbl_name
SET set_col = IF(set_col IS NULL,val,CONCAT(set_col,',',val));
```

5.14 Searching for Substrings

Problem

You want to know whether a given string occurs within another string.

Solution

Use LOCATE( ).

Discussion

The LOCATE( ) function takes two arguments representing the substring that you're looking for and the string in which to look for it. The return value is the position at which the substring occurs, or 0 if it's not present. An optional third argument may be given to indicate the position within the string at which to start looking.

```
mysql> SELECT name, LOCATE('in',name), LOCATE('in',name,3) FROM metal;
+----------+-------------------+---------------------+
| name     | LOCATE('in',name) | LOCATE('in',name,3) |
+----------+-------------------+---------------------+
| copper   |                 0 |                   0 |
| gold     |                 0 |                   0 |
| iron     |                 0 |                   0 |
| lead     |                 0 |                   0 |
| mercury  |                 0 |                   0 |
| platinum |                 5 |                   5 |
| silver   |                 0 |                   0 |
| tin      |                 2 |                   0 |
+----------+-------------------+---------------------+
```

LOCATE( ) uses the collation of its arguments to determine whether the search is case-sensitive. See Recipes 5.6 and 5.9 for information about changing the comparison properties of the arguments if you want to change the search behavior.

5.15 Using FULLTEXT Searches

Problem

You want to search through a lot of text.

Solution

Use a FULLTEXT index.

Discussion

You can use pattern matches to look through any number of rows, but as the amount of text goes up, the match operation can become quite slow. It's also common to look for the same text in several string columns, which with pattern matching tends to result in unwieldy queries:

```
SELECT * from tbl_name
WHERE col1 LIKE 'pat' OR col2 LIKE 'pat' OR col3 LIKE 'pat' ...
```

A useful alternative is FULLTEXT searching, which is designed for looking through large amounts of text and can search multiple columns simultaneously. To use this capability, add a FULLTEXT index to your table, and then use the MATCH operator to look for strings in the indexed column or columns. FULLTEXT indexing can be used with MyISAM tables for nonbinary string data types (CHAR, VARCHAR, or TEXT).

FULLTEXT searching is best illustrated with a reasonably good-sized body of text. If you don't have a sample dataset, several repositories of freely available electronic text are available on the Internet. For the examples here, the one I've chosen is the complete text of the King James Version of the Bible (KJV), which is relatively large and has the useful property of being nicely structured by book, chapter, and verse. Because of its size, this dataset is not included with the recipes distribution, but is available separately as the mcb-kjv distribution at the *MySQL Cookbook* web site (see Appendix A). The mcb-kvj distribution includes a file *kjv.txt* that contains the verse records. Some sample records look like this:

```
O   Genesis 1   1   1   In the beginning God created the heaven and the earth.
O   Exodus  2   20  13  Thou shalt not kill.
N   Luke    42  17  32  Remember Lot's wife.
```

Each record contains the following fields:

- Book section. This is either O or N, signifying the Old or New Testament.
- Book name and corresponding book number, from 1 to 66.
- Chapter and verse numbers.
- Text of the verse.

To import the records into MySQL, create a table named kjv that looks like this:

```
CREATE TABLE kjv
(
  bsect ENUM('O','N') NOT NULL,       # book section (testament)
  bname VARCHAR(20) NOT NULL,         # book name
  bnum  TINYINT UNSIGNED NOT NULL,    # book number
  cnum  TINYINT UNSIGNED NOT NULL,    # chapter number
  vnum  TINYINT UNSIGNED NOT NULL,    # verse number
  vtext TEXT NOT NULL                 # text of verse
) ENGINE = MyISAM;
```

Then load the *kjv.txt* file into the table using this statement:

```
mysql> LOAD DATA LOCAL INFILE 'kjv.txt' INTO TABLE kjv;
```

You'll notice that the kjv table contains columns both for book names (Genesis, Exodus, ...) and for book numbers (1, 2, ...). The names and numbers have a fixed correspondence, and one can be derived from the other—a redundancy that means the table is not in normal form. It's possible to eliminate the redundancy by storing just the book numbers (which take less space than the names), and then producing the names when necessary in query results by joining the numbers to a small mapping table that associates each book number with the corresponding name. But I want to avoid using joins at this point. Thus, the table includes book names so that search results can be interpreted more easily, and numbers so that the results can be sorted easily into book order.

After populating the table, prepare it for use in FULLTEXT searching by adding a FULLTEXT index. This can be done using an ALTER TABLE statement:

```
mysql> ALTER TABLE kjv ADD FULLTEXT (vtext);
```

It's possible to include the index definition in the initial CREATE TABLE statement, but it's generally faster to create a nonindexed table and then add the index with ALTER TABLE after populating the table than to load a large dataset into an indexed table.

To perform a search using the index, use MATCH( ) to name the indexed column and AGAINST( ) to specify what text to look for. For example, you might wonder, "How many times does the name Mizraim occur?" To answer that question, search the vtext column using this statement:

```
mysql> SELECT COUNT(*) from kjv WHERE MATCH(vtext) AGAINST('Mizraim');
+----------+
| COUNT(*) |
+----------+
|        4 |
+----------+
```

To find out what those verses are, select the columns you want to see (the example here uses \G so that the results better fit the page):

```
mysql> SELECT bname, cnum, vnum, vtext
    -> FROM kjv WHERE MATCH(vtext) AGAINST('Mizraim')\G
*************************** 1. row ***************************
bname: Genesis
 cnum: 10
 vnum: 6
vtext: And the sons of Ham; Cush, and Mizraim, and Phut, and Canaan.
*************************** 2. row ***************************
bname: Genesis
 cnum: 10
 vnum: 13
vtext: And Mizraim begat Ludim, and Anamim, and Lehabim, and Naphtuhim,
*************************** 3. row ***************************
bname: 1 Chronicles
 cnum: 1
 vnum: 8
vtext: The sons of Ham; Cush, and Mizraim, Put, and Canaan.
*************************** 4. row ***************************
```

```
    bname: 1 Chronicles
     cnum: 1
     vnum: 11
    vtext: And Mizraim begat Ludim, and Anamim, and Lehabim, and Naphtuhim,
```

The results come out in book, chapter, and verse number order in this particular instance, but that's actually just coincidence. By default, FULLTEXT searches compute a relevance ranking and use it for sorting. To make sure a search result is sorted the way you want, add an explicit ORDER BY clause:

```
SELECT bname, cnum, vnum, vtext
FROM kjv WHERE MATCH(vtext) AGAINST('search string')
ORDER BY bnum, cnum, vnum;
```

If you want to see the relevance ranking, repeat the MATCH( ) ... AGAINST( ) expression in the output column list.

You can include additional criteria to narrow the search further. The following queries perform progressively more specific searches to find out how often the name Abraham occurs in the entire KJV, the New Testament, the Book of Hebrews, and Chapter 11 of Hebrews:

```
mysql> SELECT COUNT(*) from kjv WHERE MATCH(vtext) AGAINST('Abraham');
+----------+
| COUNT(*) |
+----------+
|      216 |
+----------+
mysql> SELECT COUNT(*) from kjv
    -> WHERE MATCH(vtext) AGAINST('Abraham')
    -> AND bsect = 'N';
+----------+
| COUNT(*) |
+----------+
|       66 |
+----------+
mysql> SELECT COUNT(*) from kjv
    -> WHERE MATCH(vtext) AGAINST('Abraham')
    -> AND bname = 'Hebrews';
+----------+
| COUNT(*) |
+----------+
|       10 |
+----------+
mysql> SELECT COUNT(*) from kjv
    -> WHERE MATCH(vtext) AGAINST('Abraham')
    -> AND bname = 'Hebrews' AND cnum = 11;
+----------+
| COUNT(*) |
+----------+
|        2 |
+----------+
```

If you expect to use search criteria that include other non-FULLTEXT columns frequently, you can increase the performance of such queries by adding regular indexes to those columns. For example, to index the book, chapter, and verse number columns, do this:

```
mysql> ALTER TABLE kjv ADD INDEX (bnum), ADD INDEX (cnum), ADD INDEX (vnum);
```

Search strings in FULLTEXT queries can include more than just a single word, and you might suppose that adding additional words would make a search more specific. But in fact that widens it, because a FULLTEXT search returns rows that contain any of the words. In effect, the query performs an OR search for any of the words. This is illustrated by the following queries, which identify successively larger numbers of verses as additional search words are added:

```
mysql> SELECT COUNT(*) from kjv
    -> WHERE MATCH(vtext) AGAINST('Abraham');
+----------+
| COUNT(*) |
+----------+
|      216 |
+----------+
mysql> SELECT COUNT(*) from kjv
    -> WHERE MATCH(vtext) AGAINST('Abraham Sarah');
+----------+
| COUNT(*) |
+----------+
|      230 |
+----------+
mysql> SELECT COUNT(*) from kjv
    -> WHERE MATCH(vtext) AGAINST('Abraham Sarah Ishmael Isaac');
+----------+
| COUNT(*) |
+----------+
|      317 |
+----------+
```

To perform a search in which each word in the search string must be present, see Recipe 5.17.

If you want to use a FULLTEXT search that looks through multiple columns simultaneously, name them all when you construct the index:

```
ALTER TABLE tbl_name ADD FULLTEXT (col1, col2, col3);
```

To issue a search query that uses this index, name those same columns in the MATCH( ) list:

```
SELECT ... FROM tbl_name
WHERE MATCH(col1, col2, col3) AGAINST('search string');
```

You'll need one such FULLTEXT index for each distinct combination of columns that you want to search.

See Also

FULLTEXT indexes provide a quick-and-easy way to set up a basic search engine. One way to use this capability is to provide a web-based interface to the indexed text. This book's web site (see Appendix A) includes a simple web-based KJV search page that demonstrates this. You can use it as the basis for your own search engine that operates on a different repository of text.

5.16 Using a FULLTEXT Search with Short Words

Problem

FULLTEXT searches for short words return no rows.

Solution

Change the indexing engine's minimum word length parameter.

Discussion

In a text like the KJV, certain words have special significance, such as "God" and "sin." However, if you perform FULLTEXT searches on the kjv table for those words, you'll observe a curious phenomenon—both words appear to be missing from the text entirely:

```
mysql> SELECT COUNT(*) FROM kjv WHERE MATCH(vtext) AGAINST('God');
+----------+
| COUNT(*) |
+----------+
|        0 |
+----------+
mysql> SELECT COUNT(*) FROM kjv WHERE MATCH(vtext) AGAINST('sin');
+----------+
| COUNT(*) |
+----------+
|        0 |
+----------+
```

One property of the indexing engine is that it ignores words that are "too common" (that is, words that occur in more than half the rows). This eliminates words such as "the" or "and" from the index, but that's not what is going on here. You can verify that by counting the total number of rows, and by using SQL pattern matches to count the number of rows containing each word:[*]

```
mysql> SELECT COUNT(*) AS 'total verses',
    -> COUNT(IF(vtext LIKE '%God%',1,NULL)) AS 'verses containing "God"',
    -> COUNT(IF(vtext LIKE '%sin%',1,NULL)) AS 'verses containing "sin"'
```

---

[*] The use of COUNT( ) to produce multiple counts from the same set of values is described in Recipe 8.1.

```
    -> FROM kjv;
+--------------+-------------------------+-------------------------+
| total verses | verses containing "God" | verses containing "sin" |
+--------------+-------------------------+-------------------------+
|        31102 |                    4118 |                    1292 |
+--------------+-------------------------+-------------------------+
```

Neither word is present in more than half the verses, so sheer frequency of occurrence doesn't account for the failure of a FULLTEXT search to find them. What's really happening is that by default, the indexing engine doesn't include words less than four characters long. The minimum word length is a configurable parameter, which you can change by setting the ft_min_word_len server variable. For example, to tell the indexing engine to include words as short as three characters, add a line to the [mysqld] group of the /etc/my.cnf file (or whatever option file you put server settings in):

```
[mysqld]
ft_min_word_len=3
```

After making this change, restart the server. Next, rebuild the FULLTEXT index to take advantage of the new setting:[†]

```
mysql> REPAIR TABLE kjv QUICK;
```

Finally, try the new index to verify that it includes shorter words:

```
mysql> SELECT COUNT(*) FROM kjv WHERE MATCH(vtext) AGAINST('God');
+----------+
| COUNT(*) |
+----------+
|     3878 |
+----------+
mysql> SELECT COUNT(*) FROM kjv WHERE MATCH(vtext) AGAINST('sin');
+----------+
| COUNT(*) |
+----------+
|      389 |
+----------+
```

That's better!

But why do the MATCH( ) queries find 3,878 and 389 rows, whereas the earlier LIKE queries find 4,118 and 1,292 rows? That's because the LIKE patterns match substrings and the FULLTEXT search performed by MATCH( ) matches whole words.

5.17 Requiring or Excluding FULLTEXT Search Words

Problem

You want to specifically require or disallow words in a FULLTEXT search.

[†] If you change ft_min_word_len, you must also use REPAIR TABLE to rebuild the indexes for all other tables that have FULLTEXT indexes.

Solution

Use a Boolean mode search.

Discussion

Normally, FULLTEXT searches return rows that contain any of the words in the search string, even if some of them are missing. For example, the following statement finds rows that contain either of the names David or Goliath:

```
mysql> SELECT COUNT(*) FROM kjv
    -> WHERE MATCH(vtext) AGAINST('David Goliath');
+----------+
| COUNT(*) |
+----------+
|      934 |
+----------+
```

This behavior is undesirable if you want only rows that contain both words. One way to do this is to rewrite the statement to look for each word separately and join the conditions with AND:

```
mysql> SELECT COUNT(*) FROM kjv
    -> WHERE MATCH(vtext) AGAINST('David')
    -> AND MATCH(vtext) AGAINST('Goliath');
+----------+
| COUNT(*) |
+----------+
|        2 |
+----------+
```

Another way to require multiple words is with a Boolean mode search. To do this, precede each word in the search string by a + character and add IN BOOLEAN MODE after the string:

```
mysql> SELECT COUNT(*) FROM kjv
    -> WHERE MATCH(vtext) AGAINST('+David +Goliath' IN BOOLEAN MODE)
+----------+
| COUNT(*) |
+----------+
|        2 |
+----------+
```

Boolean mode searches also allow you to exclude words. Just precede any disallowed word by a - character. The following queries select kjv rows containing the name David but not Goliath, or vice versa:

```
mysql> SELECT COUNT(*) FROM kjv
    -> WHERE MATCH(vtext) AGAINST('+David -Goliath' IN BOOLEAN MODE)
+----------+
| COUNT(*) |
+----------+
|      928 |
+----------+
mysql> SELECT COUNT(*) FROM kjv
```

```
    -> WHERE MATCH(vtext) AGAINST('-David +Goliath' IN BOOLEAN MODE)
+----------+
| COUNT(*) |
+----------+
|        4 |
+----------+
```

Another useful special character in Boolean searches is *; when appended to a search word, it acts as a wildcard operator. The following statement finds rows containing not only `whirl`, but also words such as `whirls`, `whirleth`, and `whirlwind`:

```
mysql> SELECT COUNT(*) FROM kjv
    -> WHERE MATCH(vtext) AGAINST('whirl*' IN BOOLEAN MODE);
+----------+
| COUNT(*) |
+----------+
|       28 |
+----------+
```

For a complete list of Boolean FULLTEXT operators, see the *MySQL Reference Manual*.

5.18 Performing Phrase Searches with a FULLTEXT Index

Problem

You want to perform a FULLTEXT search for a phrase; that is, for words that occur adjacent to each other and in a specific order.

Solution

Use the FULLTEXT phrase-search capability.

Discussion

To find rows that contain a particular phrase, you can't use a simple FULLTEXT search:

```
mysql> SELECT COUNT(*) FROM kjv
    -> WHERE MATCH(vtext) AGAINST('still small voice');
+----------+
| COUNT(*) |
+----------+
|      548 |
+----------+
```

The query returns a result, but it's not the result you're looking for. A FULLTEXT search computes a relevance ranking based on the presence of each word individually, no matter where it occurs within the **vtext** column, and the ranking will be nonzero as long as any of the words are present. Consequently, this kind of statement tends to find too many rows.

FULLTEXT searching supports phrase searching in Boolean mode. To use it, place the phrase in double quotes within the search string:

```
mysql> SELECT COUNT(*) FROM kjv
    -> WHERE MATCH(vtext) AGAINST('"still small voice"' IN BOOLEAN MODE);
+----------+
| COUNT(*) |
+----------+
|        1 |
+----------+
```

A phrase match succeeds if a column contains the same words as in the phrase, in the order specified.

## CHAPTER 6

Working with Dates and Times

6.0 Introduction

MySQL has several data types for representing dates and times, and several functions for operating on them. MySQL stores dates and times in specific formats, and it's important to understand them to avoid surprising results when you manipulate temporal data. This chapter covers the following aspects of working with date and time values in MySQL:

Choosing a temporal data type
> MySQL provides several temporal data types to choose from when you create tables. By knowing their properties, you'll be able to choose them appropriately.

Displaying dates and times
> MySQL displays temporal values using specific formats by default, but you can produce other formats by using the appropriate functions.

Changing the client time zone
> The server interprets TIMESTAMP values in the client's current time zone rather than its own. Clients in different time zones should set their zone so that the server can properly interpret TIMESTAMP values for them.

Determining the current date or time
> MySQL provides functions that return the date and time, which is useful for applications that need to know these values or need to calculate other temporal values in relation to them.

Using TIMESTAMP values to track row modifications
> The TIMESTAMP data type has some special properties that make it convenient for recording row creation and modification times automatically.

Breaking dates or times into component values
> You can split date and time values when you need only a piece, such as the month part of a date or the hour part of a time.

Synthesizing dates and times from component values
> The complement of splitting apart temporal values is to create them from subparts.

Converting between dates or times and basic units

Some temporal calculations such as date arithmetic operations are more easily performed using the number of days or seconds represented by a date or time value than by using the value itself. MySQL makes it possible to perform several kinds of conversions between date and time values and more basic units such as days or seconds.

Date and time arithmetic

You can add or subtract temporal values to produce other temporal values or calculate intervals between values. Applications for date and time arithmetic include age determination, relative date computation, and date shifting.

Selecting data based on temporal constraints

The calculations discussed in the preceding sections to produce output values can also be used in WHERE clauses to specify how to select rows using temporal conditions.

This chapter covers several MySQL functions for operating on date and time values, but there are many others. To familiarize yourself with the full set, consult the *MySQL Reference Manual*. The variety of functions available to you means that it's often possible to perform a given temporal calculation more than one way. I sometimes illustrate alternative methods for achieving a given result, and many of the problems addressed in this chapter can be solved in other ways than are shown here. I invite you to experiment to find other solutions. You may find a method that's more efficient or that you find more readable.

Scripts that implement the recipes discussed in this chapter can be found in the *dates* directory of the `recipes` source distribution. The scripts that create the tables used here are located in the *tables* directory.

6.1 Choosing a Temporal Data Type

Problem

You need to store temporal data but aren't sure which is the most appropriate data type.

Solution

Choose the data type according to the characteristics of the information to be stored and how you need to use it. Consider questions such as these:

- Do you need times only, dates only, or combined date and time values?
- What range of values do you require?
- Do you want automatic initialization of the column to the current date and time?

Discussion

MySQL provides `DATE` and `TIME` data types for representing date and time values separately, and `DATETIME` and `TIMESTAMP` types for combined date-and-time values. These values have the following characteristics:

- `DATE` values are handled as strings in *CCYY-MM-DD* format, where *CC*, *YY*, *MM*, and *DD* represent the century, year within century, month, and day parts of the date. The supported range for `DATE` values is `1000-01-01` to `9999-12-31`.

- `TIME` values are represented as strings in *hh:mm:ss* format, where *hh*, *mm*, and *ss* are the hours, minutes, and seconds parts of the time. `TIME` values often can be thought of as time-of-day values, but MySQL actually treats them as elapsed time. Thus, they may be greater than `23:59:59` or even negative. (The actual range of a `TIME` column is `-838:59:59` to `838:59:59`.)

- `DATETIME` and `TIMESTAMP` values are represented as combined date-and-time strings in *CCYY-MM-DD hh:mm:ss* format. (Before MySQL 4.1, `TIMESTAMP` display format was *CCYYMMDDhhmmss* numeric format. Older applications that depend on this display format must be updated for MySQL 4.1 and up.)

In many respects, you can treat the `DATETIME` and `TIMESTAMP` data types similarly, but watch out for these differences:

— `DATETIME` has a supported range of `1000-01-01 00:00:00` to `9999-12-31 23:59:59`, whereas `TIMESTAMP` values are valid only from the year 1970 to approximately 2037.

— The `TIMESTAMP` type has special auto-initialization and auto-update properties that are discussed further in Recipe 6.5.

— When a client inserts a `TIMESTAMP` value, the server converts it from the time zone associated with the client connection to UTC and stores the UTC value. When the client retrieves a `TIMESTAMP` value, the server performs the reverse operation to convert the UTC value back to the client connection time zone. Clients that are in different time zones from the server can configure their connection so that this conversion is appropriate for their own time zone (Recipe 6.3).

Many of the examples in this chapter draw on the following tables, which contain columns representing `TIME`, `DATE`, `DATETIME`, and `TIMESTAMP` values. (The `time_val` table has two columns for use in time interval calculation examples.)

```
mysql> SELECT t1, t2 FROM time_val;
+----------+----------+
| t1       | t2       |
+----------+----------+
| 15:00:00 | 15:00:00 |
| 05:01:30 | 02:30:20 |
| 12:30:20 | 17:30:45 |
+----------+----------+
mysql> SELECT d FROM date_val;
+------------+
| d          |
```

```
+------------+
| 1864-02-28 |
| 1900-01-15 |
| 1987-03-05 |
| 1999-12-31 |
| 2000-06-04 |
+------------+
mysql> SELECT dt FROM datetime_val;
+---------------------+
| dt                  |
+---------------------+
| 1970-01-01 00:00:00 |
| 1987-03-05 12:30:15 |
| 1999-12-31 09:00:00 |
| 2000-06-04 15:45:30 |
+---------------------+
mysql> SELECT ts FROM timestamp_val;
+---------------------+
| ts                  |
+---------------------+
| 1970-01-01 00:00:00 |
| 1987-03-05 12:30:15 |
| 1999-12-31 09:00:00 |
| 2000-06-04 15:45:30 |
+---------------------+
```

It is a good idea to create the time_val, date_val, datetime_val, and timestamp_val tables right now before reading further. (Use the appropriate scripts in the *tables* directory of the recipes distribution.)

6.2 Changing MySQL's Date Format

Problem

You want to change the ISO format that MySQL uses for representing date values.

Solution

You can't. However, you can rewrite non-ISO input values into ISO format when storing dates, and you can rewrite ISO values to other formats for display by using the DATE_FORMAT( ) function.

Discussion

The *CCYY-MM-DD* format that MySQL uses for DATE values follows the ISO 8601 standard for representing dates. Because the year, month, and day parts have a fixed length and appear left to right in date strings, this format has the useful property that dates sort naturally into the proper temporal order. Chapters 7 and 8 discuss ordering and grouping techniques for date-based values.

ISO format, although common, is not used by all database systems, which can cause problems if you want to move data between different systems. Moreover, people commonly like to represent dates in other formats such as *MM/DD/YY* or *DD-MM-CCYY*. This too can be a source of trouble, due to mismatches between human expectations of what dates should look like and the way that MySQL actually represents them.

A question frequently asked by people who are new to MySQL is, "How do I tell MySQL to store dates in a specific format such as *MM/DD/CCYY*?" That's the wrong question. The right question is, "If I have a date in a specific format, how can I store it in MySQL's supported format, and vice versa?" MySQL always stores dates in ISO format, a fact that has implications both for data entry and for processing retrieved query results:

- For data-entry purposes, to store values that are not in ISO format, you normally must rewrite them first. If you don't want to rewrite your dates, you need to store them as strings (for example, in a CHAR column). But then you can't operate on them as dates.

  Chapter 10 covers the topic of date rewriting for data entry. That chapter also discusses checking dates to verify that they're valid. In some cases, if your values are close to ISO format, rewriting may not be necessary. For example, MySQL interprets the string values 87-1-7 and 1987-1-7 and the numbers 870107 and 19870107 as the date 1987-01-07 when they are loaded into a DATE column.

- For display purposes, you can rewrite dates to non-ISO formats by using the DATE_FORMAT( ) function. It provides a lot of flexibility for changing date values into other formats (see later in this section). You can also use functions such as YEAR( ) to extract parts of dates for display (Recipe 6.6). Additional discussion can be found in Chapter 10.

When you enter date values, one way to rewrite non-ISO dates is to use the STR_TO_DATE( ) function. STR_TO_DATE( ) takes a string representing a temporal value and a format string that specifies the "syntax" of the value. Within the formatting string, you use special sequences of the form %c, where c specifies which part of the date to expect. For example, %Y, %M, and %d signify the four-digit year, the month name, and the two-digit day of the month. To insert the value May 13, 2007 into a DATE column, you can do this:

```
mysql> INSERT INTO t (d) VALUES(STR_TO_DATE('May 13, 2007','%M %d, %Y'));
mysql> SELECT d FROM t;
+------------+
| d          |
+------------+
| 2007-05-13 |
+------------+
```

For date display, MySQL uses ISO format (*CCYY-MM-DD*) unless you tell it otherwise. If you want to display dates or times in a format other than what MySQL uses by default, use the DATE_FORMAT( ) or TIME_FORMAT( ) functions to rewrite them. If you require a more specialized format that those functions cannot provide, write a stored function.

To rewrite date values into other formats, use the DATE_FORMAT( ) function, which takes two arguments: A DATE, DATETIME, or TIMESTAMP value, and a string describing how to display the value. The format string uses the same kind of specifiers as STR_TO_DATE( ). The following statement shows the values in the date_val table, both as MySQL displays them by default and as reformatted with DATE_FORMAT( ):

```
mysql> SELECT d, DATE_FORMAT(d,'%M %d, %Y') FROM date_val;
+------------+----------------------------+
| d          | DATE_FORMAT(d,'%M %d, %Y') |
+------------+----------------------------+
| 1864-02-28 | February 28, 1864          |
| 1900-01-15 | January 15, 1900           |
| 1987-03-05 | March 05, 1987             |
| 1999-12-31 | December 31, 1999          |
| 2000-06-04 | June 04, 2000              |
+------------+----------------------------+
```

DATE_FORMAT( ) tends to produce rather long column headings, so it's often useful to provide an alias to make a heading more concise or meaningful:

```
mysql> SELECT d, DATE_FORMAT(d,'%M %d, %Y') AS date FROM date_val;
+------------+-------------------+
| d          | date              |
+------------+-------------------+
| 1864-02-28 | February 28, 1864 |
| 1900-01-15 | January 15, 1900  |
| 1987-03-05 | March 05, 1987    |
| 1999-12-31 | December 31, 1999 |
| 2000-06-04 | June 04, 2000     |
+------------+-------------------+
```

The *MySQL Reference Manual* provides a complete list of format sequences to use with DATE_FORMAT( ), TIME_FORMAT( ), and STR_TO_DATE( ). Some of the more commonly used ones are shown in the following table:

Sequence	Meaning
%Y	Four-digit year
%y	Two-digit year
%M	Complete month name
%b	Month name, initial three letters
%m	Two-digit month of year (01..12)
%c	Month of year (1..12)
%d	Two-digit day of month (01..31)
%e	Day of month (1..31)
%W	Weekday name (Sunday..Saturday)
%r	12-hour time with AM or PM suffix
%T	24-hour time

Sequence	Meaning
%H	Two-digit hour
%i	Two-digit minute
%s	Two-digit second
%%	Literal %

The time-related format sequences shown in the table are useful only when you pass DATE_FORMAT( ) a value that has both date and time parts (a DATETIME or TIMESTAMP). The following statement demonstrates how to display DATETIME values from the datetime_val table using formats that include the time of day:

```
mysql> SELECT dt,
    -> DATE_FORMAT(dt,'%c/%e/%y %r') AS format1,
    -> DATE_FORMAT(dt,'%M %e, %Y %T') AS format2
    -> FROM datetime_val;
+---------------------+---------------------+----------------------------+
| dt                  | format1             | format2                    |
+---------------------+---------------------+----------------------------+
| 1970-01-01 00:00:00 | 1/1/70 12:00:00 AM  | January 1, 1970 00:00:00   |
| 1987-03-05 12:30:15 | 3/5/87 12:30:15 PM  | March 5, 1987 12:30:15     |
| 1999-12-31 09:00:00 | 12/31/99 09:00:00 AM| December 31, 1999 09:00:00 |
| 2000-06-04 15:45:30 | 6/4/00 03:45:30 PM  | June 4, 2000 15:45:30      |
+---------------------+---------------------+----------------------------+
```

TIME_FORMAT( ) is similar to DATE_FORMAT( ), but it understands only time-related specifiers in the format string. TIME_FORMAT( ) works with TIME, DATETIME, or TIMESTAMP values.

```
mysql> SELECT dt,
    -> TIME_FORMAT(dt, '%r') AS '12-hour time',
    -> TIME_FORMAT(dt, '%T') AS '24-hour time'
    -> FROM datetime_val;
+---------------------+--------------+--------------+
| dt                  | 12-hour time | 24-hour time |
+---------------------+--------------+--------------+
| 1970-01-01 00:00:00 | 12:00:00 AM  | 00:00:00     |
| 1987-03-05 12:30:15 | 12:30:15 PM  | 12:30:15     |
| 1999-12-31 09:00:00 | 09:00:00 AM  | 09:00:00     |
| 2000-06-04 15:45:30 | 03:45:30 PM  | 15:45:30     |
+---------------------+--------------+--------------+
```

If DATE_FORMAT( ) or TIME_FORMAT( ) cannot produce the results that you want, perhaps you can write a stored function that does. Suppose that you want to convert 24-hour TIME values to 12-hour format but with a suffix of a.m. or p.m. rather than AM or PM. The following function accomplishes that task. It uses TIME_FORMAT( ) to do most of the work, and then strips off the suffix supplied by %r and replaces it with the desired suffix:

```
CREATE FUNCTION time_ampm (t TIME)
RETURNS VARCHAR(13) # mm:dd:ss {a.m.|p.m.} format
BEGIN
  DECLARE ampm CHAR(4);
  IF TIME_TO_SEC(t) < 12*60*60 THEN
```

```
    SET ampm = 'a.m.';
  ELSE
    SET ampm = 'p.m.';
  END IF;
  RETURN CONCAT(LEFT(TIME_FORMAT(t, '%r'),9),ampm);
END;
```

Use the function like this:

```
mysql> SELECT t1, time_ampm(t1) FROM time_val;
+----------+---------------+
| t1       | time_ampm(t1) |
+----------+---------------+
| 15:00:00 | 03:00:00 p.m. |
| 05:01:30 | 05:01:30 a.m. |
| 12:30:20 | 12:30:20 p.m. |
+----------+---------------+
```

For more information about writing stored functions, see Chapter 16.

6.3 Setting the Client Time Zone

Problem

You have a client that is in a different time zone from the server, so when it stores TIMESTAMP values, they don't have the correct UTC values.

Solution

Have the client specify its time zone when it connects to the server by setting the time_zone system variable.

Discussion

MySQL interprets TIMESTAMP values with respect to each client's time zone. When a client inserts a TIMESTAMP value, the server converts it from the time zone associated with the client connection to UTC and stores the UTC value. (Internally, the server stores a TIMESTAMP value as the number of seconds since 1970-01-01 00:00:00 UTC.) When the client retrieves a TIMESTAMP value, the server performs the reverse operation to convert the UTC value back to the client connection time zone.

The default connection time zone is the server's time zone. The server examines its operating environment when it starts to determine this setting. (To use a different value, start the server with the --default-time-zone option.) If all clients are in the same time zone as the server, nothing special need be done for the proper TIMESTAMP time zone conversion to occur. But if a client is running in a time zone different from the server and inserts TIMESTAMP values, the UTC values won't be correct.

Suppose that the server and client A are in the same time zone, and client A issues these statements:

```
mysql> CREATE TABLE t (ts TIMESTAMP);
mysql> INSERT INTO t (ts) VALUES('2006-06-01 12:30:00');
mysql> SELECT ts FROM t;
+---------------------+
| ts                  |
+---------------------+
| 2006-06-01 12:30:00 |
+---------------------+
```

Here, client A sees the same value that it stored. A different client B will also see the same value if it retrieves it, but if client B is in a different time zone, that value isn't correct for its zone. Conversely, if client B stores a value, that value when returned by client A won't be correct for the client A time zone.

To deal with this problem so that TIMESTAMP conversions happen for the correct time zone, a client can set its time zone explicitly. To specify the client time zone, set the session value of the time_zone system variable. Suppose that the server has a global time zone of six hours ahead of UTC. Each client is assigned that same value as its initial session time zone:

```
mysql> SELECT @@global.time_zone, @@session.time_zone;
+--------------------+---------------------+
| @@global.time_zone | @@session.time_zone |
+--------------------+---------------------+
| +06:00             | +06:00              |
+--------------------+---------------------+
```

Client B mentioned earlier will see the same TIMESTAMP value as client A when it connects:

```
mysql> SELECT ts FROM t;
+---------------------+
| ts                  |
+---------------------+
| 2006-06-01 12:30:00 |
+---------------------+
```

If client B is only four hours ahead of UTC, it can set its time zone after connecting like this:

```
mysql> SET SESSION time_zone = '+04:00';
mysql> SELECT @@global.time_zone, @@session.time_zone;
+--------------------+---------------------+
| @@global.time_zone | @@session.time_zone |
+--------------------+---------------------+
| +06:00             | +04:00              |
+--------------------+---------------------+
```

Then when client B retrieves the TIMESTAMP value, it will be properly adjusted for its own time zone:

```
mysql> SELECT ts FROM t;
+---------------------+
| ts                  |
+---------------------+
| 2006-06-01 10:30:00 |
+---------------------+
```

The client time zone also affects the values displayed from functions that return the current date and time (Recipe 6.4).

See Also

To convert individual date-and-time values from one time zone to another, use the CONVERT_TZ( ) function (Recipe 6.12).

6.4 Determining the Current Date or Time

Problem

What's today's date? What time is it?

Solution

Use the CURDATE( ), CURTIME( ) or NOW( ) functions to get values expressed with respect to the connection time zone. Use UTC_DATE( ), UTC_TIME( ), or UTC_TIMESTAMP( ) for values in UTC time.

Discussion

Some applications need to know the current date or time, such as those that write log records tagged with the current date and time. This kind of information is also useful for date calculations that are performed in relation to the current date, such as finding the first (or last) day of the month, or determining the date for Wednesday of next week.

The current date and time are available through three functions. CURDATE( ) and CURTIME( ) return the date and time separately, and NOW( ) returns them both as a date-and-time value:

```
mysql> SELECT CURDATE(), CURTIME(), NOW();
+------------+-----------+---------------------+
| CURDATE()  | CURTIME() | NOW()               |
+------------+-----------+---------------------+
| 2006-06-03 | 09:41:50  | 2006-06-03 09:41:50 |
+------------+-----------+---------------------+
```

CURRENT_DATE and CURRENT_TIME are synonyms for CURDATE( ) and CURTIME( ). CURRENT_TIMESTAMP is a synonym for NOW( ).

The preceding functions return values for the client's connection time zone (Recipe 6.3). For values in UTC time, use the UTC_DATE( ), UTC_TIME( ), or UTC_TIMESTAMP( ) functions instead.

To obtain subparts of these values (such as the current day of the month or current hour of the day), use the techniques discussed in Recipe 6.6.

6.5 Using TIMESTAMP to Track Row Modification Times

Problem

You want a row's creation time or last modification time to be recorded automatically.

Solution

Use the TIMESTAMP data type, which has auto-initialization and auto-update properties.

Discussion

MySQL supports a TIMESTAMP data type that stores date-and-time values. Earlier sections covered the range of values for TIMESTAMP (Recipe 6.1) and the conversion of TIMESTAMP values to and from UTC when they are stored and retrieved (Recipe 6.3). This section focuses on how TIMESTAMP columns enable you to track row creation and update times automatically:

- One TIMESTAMP column in a table can be treated as special in either or both of the following ways:

  — The column is automatically initialized to the current date and time when new rows are created. This means you need not specify its value at all in an INSERT statement; MySQL initializes it automatically to the row's creation time. (This also occurs if you set the column to NULL.)

  — The column is automatically updated to the current date and time when you change any other column in the row from its current value. The update happens only if you actually *change* a column value; setting a column to its current value doesn't update the TIMESTAMP.

    This auto-update property sometimes surprises people who don't realize that changing another column also updates the TIMESTAMP column. This will never surprise *you*, of course, because you're aware of it!

- There can be multiple TIMESTAMP columns in a table, but only one of them can have the special properties just described. Other TIMESTAMP columns have a default value of zero, not the current date and time. Also, their value does not change automatically when you modify other columns; to update them, you must change them yourself.

- A `TIMESTAMP` column can be updated to the current date and time at any time by setting it to `NULL`, unless it has specifically been defined to allow `NULL` values. This is true for any `TIMESTAMP` column, not just the first one.

The special properties that relate to row creation and modification make the `TIMESTAMP` data type particularly suited for certain kinds of problems, such as automatically recording the times at which table rows are inserted or updated. The following discussion shows how to take advantage of these properties.

The syntax for defining `TIMESTAMP` columns is covered in full in the *MySQL Reference Manual*. Here we cover only some simple cases. By default, if you specify no special handling for the first `TIMESTAMP` column in a table, it is equivalent to specifying that it should have both the auto-initialize and auto-update properties explicitly. You can see this as follows, where the `SHOW CREATE TABLE` statement displays the full `TIMESTAMP` definition that results from the `CREATE TABLE` statement:

```
mysql> CREATE TABLE t (ts TIMESTAMP);
mysql> SHOW CREATE TABLE t\G
*************************** 1. row ***************************
       Table: t
Create Table: CREATE TABLE `t` (
  `ts` timestamp NOT NULL
  DEFAULT CURRENT_TIMESTAMP
  ON UPDATE CURRENT_TIMESTAMP
) ENGINE=MyISAM DEFAULT CHARSET=latin1
```

If you explicitly specify only the `DEFAULT` or `ON UPDATE` attribute for the `TIMESTAMP` column, it has only that attribute and not the other one.

The `NOT NULL` shown in the column definition might seem a curious thing, given that you *can* insert `NULL` into the column, and no error occurs. What this means is that, although you can specify `NULL` as the value to be inserted, you cannot *store* `NULL` because MySQL stores the current date and time instead.

To create a table in which each row contains a value that indicates when the row was created or most recently updated, include a `TIMESTAMP` column. MySQL will set the column to the current date and time when you create a new row, and update the column whenever you update the value of another column in the row. Suppose that you create a table `tsdemo1` with a `TIMESTAMP` as one of its columns:

```
CREATE TABLE tsdemo1
(
  ts  TIMESTAMP,
  val INT
);
```

In this case, the `ts` column has both the auto-initialize and auto-update properties, for reasons just discussed. Insert a couple of rows into the table, and then select its contents. (Issue the `INSERT` statements a few seconds apart so that the timestamps differ.) The first `INSERT` statement shows that you can set `ts` to the current date and time by omitting it from the INSERT statement entirely; the second shows that you can do so by setting ts explicitly to NULL:

```
mysql> INSERT INTO tsdemo1 (val) VALUES(5);
mysql> INSERT INTO tsdemo1 (ts,val) VALUES(NULL,10);
mysql> SELECT * FROM tsdemo1;
+---------------------+------+
| ts                  | val  |
+---------------------+------+
| 2006-06-03 08:21:26 |    5 |
| 2006-06-03 08:21:31 |   10 |
+---------------------+------+
```

Now issue a statement that changes one row's val column, and check its effect on the table's contents:

```
mysql> UPDATE tsdemo1 SET val = 6 WHERE val = 5;
mysql> SELECT * FROM tsdemo1;
+---------------------+------+
| ts                  | val  |
+---------------------+------+
| 2006-06-03 08:21:52 |    6 |
| 2006-06-03 08:21:31 |   10 |
+---------------------+------+
```

The result shows that the TIMESTAMP column of the modified row was updated.

If you modify multiple rows, the TIMESTAMP value in each of them is updated:

```
mysql> UPDATE tsdemo1 SET val = val + 1;
mysql> SELECT * FROM tsdemo1;
+---------------------+------+
| ts                  | val  |
+---------------------+------+
| 2006-06-03 08:22:00 |    7 |
| 2006-06-03 08:22:00 |   11 |
+---------------------+------+
```

An UPDATE statement that doesn't actually change the value in the val column doesn't update the TIMESTAMP value. To see this, set every row's val column to its current value, and then review the contents of the table:

```
mysql> UPDATE tsdemo1 SET val = val;
mysql> SELECT * FROM tsdemo1;
+---------------------+------+
| ts                  | val  |
+---------------------+------+
| 2006-06-03 08:22:00 |    7 |
| 2006-06-03 08:22:00 |   11 |
+---------------------+------+
```

If you want the TIMESTAMP column to be set initially to the time at which a row is created, but to remain constant thereafter, define it to auto-initialize but not auto-update. To do this, the TIMESTAMP definition can be given as shown in the following table:

```
CREATE TABLE tsdemo2
(
  t_create TIMESTAMP DEFAULT CURRENT_TIMESTAMP,
  val      INT
);
```

Create the table, and then insert records into it with the TIMESTAMP column not specified (or specified as NULL) to initialize it to the current date and time:

```
mysql> INSERT INTO tsdemo2 (val) VALUES(5);
mysql> INSERT INTO tsdemo2 (t_create,val) VALUES(NULL,10);
mysql> SELECT * FROM tsdemo2;
+---------------------+------+
| t_create            | val  |
+---------------------+------+
| 2006-06-03 08:26:00 |    5 |
| 2006-06-03 08:26:05 |   10 |
+---------------------+------+
```

After inserting the records, change the **val** column, and then verify that the update leaves the **t_create** column unchanged (that is, set to the record-creation time):

```
mysql> UPDATE tsdemo2 SET val = val + 1;
mysql> SELECT * FROM tsdemo2;
+---------------------+------+
| t_create            | val  |
+---------------------+------+
| 2006-06-03 08:26:00 |    6 |
| 2006-06-03 08:26:05 |   11 |
+---------------------+------+
```

See Also

If you want to simulate the TIMESTAMP auto-initialization and auto-update properties for other temporal types, you can use triggers (Recipe 16.5).

6.6 Extracting Parts of Dates or Times

Problem

You want to obtain just a part of a date or a time.

Solution

You have several options:

- Invoke a function specifically intended for extracting part of a temporal value, such as MONTH( ) or MINUTE( ). This is usually the fastest method for component extraction if you need only a single component of a value.

- Use a formatting function such as `DATE_FORMAT( )` or `TIME_FORMAT( )` with a format string that includes a specifier for the part of the value you want to obtain.

- Treat a temporal value as a string and use a function such as `LEFT( )` or `MID( )` to extract substrings corresponding to the desired part of the value.

Discussion

The following discussion shows different ways to extract parts of temporal values.

Decomposing dates or times using component-extraction functions

MySQL includes many functions for extracting date or time parts from temporal values. For example, `DATE( )` or `TIME( )` extracts the date or time part of temporal values:

```
mysql> SELECT dt, DATE(dt), TIME(dt) FROM datetime_val;
+---------------------+------------+----------+
| dt                  | DATE(dt)   | TIME(dt) |
+---------------------+------------+----------+
| 1970-01-01 00:00:00 | 1970-01-01 | 00:00:00 |
| 1987-03-05 12:30:15 | 1987-03-05 | 12:30:15 |
| 1999-12-31 09:00:00 | 1999-12-31 | 09:00:00 |
| 2000-06-04 15:45:30 | 2000-06-04 | 15:45:30 |
+---------------------+------------+----------+
```

Some of the other component-extraction functions are shown in the following list; consult the *MySQL Reference Manual* for a complete list. The date-related functions work with `DATE`, `DATETIME`, or `TIMESTAMP` values. The time-related functions work with `TIME`, `DATETIME`, or `TIMESTAMP` values.

Function	Return value
YEAR( )	Year of date
MONTH( )	Month number (1..12)
MONTHNAME( )	Month name (January..December)
DAYOFMONTH( )	Day of month (1..31)
DAYNAME( )	Day of week (Sunday..Saturday)
DAYOFWEEK( )	Day of week (1..7 for Sunday..Saturday)
WEEKDAY( )	Day of week (0..6 for Monday..Sunday)
DAYOFYEAR( )	Day of year (1..366)
HOUR( )	Hour of time (0..23)
MINUTE( )	Minute of time (0..59)
SECOND( )	Second of time (0..59)

Here's an example:

```
mysql> SELECT dt,
    -> YEAR(dt), DAYOFMONTH(dt),
```

```
        -> HOUR(dt), SECOND(dt)
        -> FROM datetime_val;
+---------------------+----------+---------------+----------+-----------+
| dt                  | YEAR(dt) | DAYOFMONTH(dt)| HOUR(dt) | SECOND(dt)|
+---------------------+----------+---------------+----------+-----------+
| 1970-01-01 00:00:00 |     1970 |             1 |        0 |         0 |
| 1987-03-05 12:30:15 |     1987 |             5 |       12 |        15 |
| 1999-12-31 09:00:00 |     1999 |            31 |        9 |         0 |
| 2000-06-04 15:45:30 |     2000 |             4 |       15 |        30 |
+---------------------+----------+---------------+----------+-----------+
```

Functions such as YEAR( ) or DAYOFMONTH( ) extract values that have an obvious correspondence to a substring of the temporal value to which you apply them. Other date component-extraction functions provide access to values that have no such correspondence. One is the day-of-year value:

```
mysql> SELECT d, DAYOFYEAR(d) FROM date_val;
+------------+--------------+
| d          | DAYOFYEAR(d) |
+------------+--------------+
| 1864-02-28 |           59 |
| 1900-01-15 |           15 |
| 1987-03-05 |           64 |
| 1999-12-31 |          365 |
| 2000-06-04 |          156 |
+------------+--------------+
```

Another is the day of the week, which can be obtained either by name or by number:

- DAYNAME( ) returns the complete day name. There is no function for returning the three-character name abbreviation, but you can get it easily by passing the full name to LEFT( ):

```
mysql> SELECT d, DAYNAME(d), LEFT(DAYNAME(d),3) FROM date_val;
+------------+-----------+--------------------+
| d          | DAYNAME(d)| LEFT(DAYNAME(d),3) |
+------------+-----------+--------------------+
| 1864-02-28 | Sunday    | Sun                |
| 1900-01-15 | Monday    | Mon                |
| 1987-03-05 | Thursday  | Thu                |
| 1999-12-31 | Friday    | Fri                |
| 2000-06-04 | Sunday    | Sun                |
+------------+-----------+--------------------+
```

- To get the day of the week as a number, use DAYOFWEEK( ) or WEEKDAY( ), but pay attention to the range of values each function returns. DAYOFWEEK( ) returns values from 1 to 7, corresponding to Sunday through Saturday: WEEKDAY( ) returns values from 0 to 6, corresponding to Monday through Sunday.

```
mysql> SELECT d, DAYNAME(d), DAYOFWEEK(d), WEEKDAY(d) FROM date_val;
+------------+-----------+--------------+------------+
| d          | DAYNAME(d)| DAYOFWEEK(d) | WEEKDAY(d) |
+------------+-----------+--------------+------------+
| 1864-02-28 | Sunday    |            1 |          6 |
| 1900-01-15 | Monday    |            2 |          0 |
```

```
| 1987-03-05 | Thursday  |        5 |       3 |
| 1999-12-31 | Friday    |        6 |       4 |
| 2000-06-04 | Sunday    |        1 |       6 |
+------------+-----------+----------+---------+
```

EXTRACT( ) is another function for obtaining individual parts of temporal values:

```
mysql> SELECT dt,
    -> EXTRACT(DAY FROM dt),
    -> EXTRACT(HOUR FROM dt)
    -> FROM datetime_val;
+---------------------+----------------------+-----------------------+
| dt                  | EXTRACT(DAY FROM dt)  | EXTRACT(HOUR FROM dt)  |
+---------------------+----------------------+-----------------------+
| 1970-01-01 00:00:00 |                    1 |                     0 |
| 1987-03-05 12:30:15 |                    5 |                    12 |
| 1999-12-31 09:00:00 |                   31 |                     9 |
| 2000-06-04 15:45:30 |                    4 |                    15 |
+---------------------+----------------------+-----------------------+
```

The keyword indicating what to extract from the value should be a unit specifier such as YEAR, MONTH, DAY, HOUR, MINUTE, or SECOND. (Check the *MySQL Reference Manual* for the full list.) Note that each unit specifier is given in singular form, not plural.

Obtaining the Current Year, Month, Day, Hour, Minute, or Second

The extraction functions shown in this recipe can be applied to CURDATE( ) or NOW( ) to obtain the current year, month, day, or day of week:

```
mysql> SELECT CURDATE(), YEAR(CURDATE()) AS year,
    -> MONTH(CURDATE()) AS month, MONTHNAME(CURDATE()) AS monthname,
    -> DAYOFMONTH(CURDATE()) AS day, DAYNAME(CURDATE()) AS dayname;
+------------+------+-------+-----------+------+----------+
| CURDATE()  | year | month | monthname | day  | dayname  |
+------------+------+-------+-----------+------+----------+
| 2006-06-03 | 2006 |     6 | June      |    3 | Saturday |
+------------+------+-------+-----------+------+----------+
```

Similarly, to obtain the current hour, minute, or second, pass CURTIME( ) or NOW( ) to a time-component function:

```
mysql> SELECT NOW(), HOUR(NOW()) AS hour,
    -> MINUTE(NOW()) AS minute, SECOND(NOW()) AS second;
+---------------------+------+--------+--------+
| NOW()               | hour | minute | second |
+---------------------+------+--------+--------+
| 2006-06-03 09:45:32 |    9 |     45 |     32 |
+---------------------+------+--------+--------+
```

Decomposing dates or times using formatting functions

The DATE_FORMAT( ) and TIME_FORMAT( ) functions reformat date and time values. By specifying appropriate format strings, you can extract individual parts of temporal values:

```
mysql> SELECT dt,
    -> DATE_FORMAT(dt,'%Y') AS year,
    -> DATE_FORMAT(dt,'%d') AS day,
    -> TIME_FORMAT(dt,'%H') AS hour,
    -> TIME_FORMAT(dt,'%s') AS second
    -> FROM datetime_val;
+---------------------+------+------+------+--------+
| dt                  | year | day  | hour | second |
+---------------------+------+------+------+--------+
| 1970-01-01 00:00:00 | 1970 | 01   | 00   | 00     |
| 1987-03-05 12:30:15 | 1987 | 05   | 12   | 15     |
| 1999-12-31 09:00:00 | 1999 | 31   | 09   | 00     |
| 2000-06-04 15:45:30 | 2000 | 04   | 15   | 30     |
+---------------------+------+------+------+--------+
```

Formatting functions enable you to extract more than one part of a value. For example, to extract the entire date or time from DATETIME values, do this:

```
mysql> SELECT dt,
    -> DATE_FORMAT(dt,'%Y-%m-%d') AS 'date part',
    -> TIME_FORMAT(dt,'%T') AS 'time part'
    -> FROM datetime_val;
+---------------------+------------+-----------+
| dt                  | date part  | time part |
+---------------------+------------+-----------+
| 1970-01-01 00:00:00 | 1970-01-01 | 00:00:00  |
| 1987-03-05 12:30:15 | 1987-03-05 | 12:30:15  |
| 1999-12-31 09:00:00 | 1999-12-31 | 09:00:00  |
| 2000-06-04 15:45:30 | 2000-06-04 | 15:45:30  |
+---------------------+------------+-----------+
```

One advantage of using formatting functions is that you can display the extracted values in a different form from that in which they're present in the original values. If you want to present a date differently from CCYY-MM-DD format or present a time without the seconds part, that's easy to do:

```
mysql> SELECT ts,
    -> DATE_FORMAT(ts,'%M %e, %Y') AS 'descriptive date',
    -> TIME_FORMAT(ts,'%H:%i') AS 'hours/minutes'
    -> FROM timestamp_val;
+---------------------+-------------------+---------------+
| ts                  | descriptive date  | hours/minutes |
+---------------------+-------------------+---------------+
| 1970-01-01 00:00:00 | January 1, 1970   | 00:00         |
| 1987-03-05 12:30:15 | March 5, 1987     | 12:30         |
| 1999-12-31 09:00:00 | December 31, 1999 | 09:00         |
| 2000-06-04 15:45:30 | June 4, 2000      | 15:45         |
+---------------------+-------------------+---------------+
```

Decomposing dates or times using string functions

The discussion in this section thus far has shown how to extract components of temporal values using functions such as YEAR( ), MONTH( ), and DATE_FORMAT( ). If you pass a date or time value to a string function, MySQL treats it as a string, so string functions provide another way to decompose temporal values. This means that you can extract

---

pieces of temporal values by using functions such as LEFT( ) or MID( ) to pull out substrings:

```
mysql> SELECT dt,
    -> LEFT(dt,4) AS year,
    -> MID(dt,9,2) AS day,
    -> RIGHT(dt,2) AS second
    -> FROM datetime_val;
+---------------------+------+------+--------+
| dt                  | year | day  | second |
+---------------------+------+------+--------+
| 1970-01-01 00:00:00 | 1970 | 01   | 00     |
| 1987-03-05 12:30:15 | 1987 | 05   | 15     |
| 1999-12-31 09:00:00 | 1999 | 31   | 00     |
| 2000-06-04 15:45:30 | 2000 | 04   | 30     |
+---------------------+------+------+--------+
```

You can obtain the entire date or time part from DATETIME or TIMESTAMP values using string-extraction functions such as LEFT( ) or RIGHT( ):

```
mysql> SELECT dt,
    -> LEFT(dt,10) AS date,
    -> RIGHT(dt,8) AS time
    -> FROM datetime_val;
+---------------------+------------+----------+
| dt                  | date       | time     |
+---------------------+------------+----------+
| 1970-01-01 00:00:00 | 1970-01-01 | 00:00:00 |
| 1987-03-05 12:30:15 | 1987-03-05 | 12:30:15 |
| 1999-12-31 09:00:00 | 1999-12-31 | 09:00:00 |
| 2000-06-04 15:45:30 | 2000-06-04 | 15:45:30 |
+---------------------+------------+----------+
mysql> SELECT ts,
    -> LEFT(ts,10) AS date,
    -> RIGHT(ts,8) AS time
    -> FROM timestamp_val;
+---------------------+------------+----------+
| ts                  | date       | time     |
+---------------------+------------+----------+
| 1970-01-01 00:00:00 | 1970-01-01 | 00:00:00 |
| 1987-03-05 12:30:15 | 1987-03-05 | 12:30:15 |
| 1999-12-31 09:00:00 | 1999-12-31 | 09:00:00 |
| 2000-06-04 15:45:30 | 2000-06-04 | 15:45:30 |
+---------------------+------------+----------+
```

Decomposition of temporal values with string functions is subject to a couple of constraints that component extraction and reformatting functions are not bound by:

- To use a substring function such as LEFT( ), MID( ), or RIGHT( ), you must have fixed-length strings. Although MySQL interprets the value 1987-1-1 as 1987-01-01 if you insert it into a DATE column, using RIGHT('1987-1-1',2) to extract the day part will not work. For values that have variable-length substrings, you may be able to use SUBSTRING_INDEX( ) instead. Alternatively, if your values are close to ISO format, perhaps you can standardize them to ISO format using the techniques described in Recipe 6.18. This converts them to have fixed-length substrings before you attempt to extract subparts.

- String functions cannot be used to obtain values that don't correspond to substrings of a date value, such as the day of the week or the day of the year.

6.7 Synthesizing Dates or Times from Component Values

Problem

You want to produce a new date from a given date by replacing parts of its values. Or you have the parts of a date or time and want to combine them to produce a date or time value.

Solution

You have several options:

- Use MAKETIME( ) to construct a TIME value from hour, minute, and second parts.
- Use DATE_FORMAT( ) or TIME_FORMAT( ) to combine parts of the existing value with parts you want to replace.
- Pull out the parts that you need with component-extraction functions and recombine the parts with CONCAT( ).

Discussion

The reverse of splitting a date or time value into components is synthesizing a temporal value from its constituent parts. Techniques for date and time synthesis include using composition functions, formatting functions, and string concatenation.

The MAKETIME( ) function takes component hour, minute, and second values as arguments and combines them to produce a time:

```
mysql> SELECT MAKETIME(10,30,58), MAKETIME(-5,0,11);
+--------------------+-------------------+
| MAKETIME(10,30,58) | MAKETIME(-5,0,11) |
+--------------------+-------------------+
| 10:30:58           | -05:00:11         |
+--------------------+-------------------+
```

There is also a MAKEDATE( ) function, but its arguments are year and day-of-year values:

```
mysql> SELECT MAKEDATE(2007,60);
+-------------------+
| MAKEDATE(2007,60) |
+-------------------+
| 2007-03-01        |
+-------------------+
```

I don't find MAKEDATE( ) very useful because I'm much more likely to be working with year, month, and day values than year and day-of-year values.

Date synthesis often is performed by beginning with a given date, and then keeping parts that you want to use and replacing the rest. For example, to produce the first day of the month in which a date falls, use DATE_FORMAT( ) to extract the year and month parts from the date and combine them with a day value of 01:

```
mysql> SELECT d, DATE_FORMAT(d,'%Y-%m-01') FROM date_val;
+------------+---------------------------+
| d          | DATE_FORMAT(d,'%Y-%m-01') |
+------------+---------------------------+
| 1864-02-28 | 1864-02-01                |
| 1900-01-15 | 1900-01-01                |
| 1987-03-05 | 1987-03-01                |
| 1999-12-31 | 1999-12-01                |
| 2000-06-04 | 2000-06-01                |
+------------+---------------------------+
```

TIME_FORMAT( ) can be used in a similar way. The following example produces time values that have the seconds part set to 00:

```
mysql> SELECT t1, TIME_FORMAT(t1,'%H:%i:00') FROM time_val;
+----------+----------------------------+
| t1       | TIME_FORMAT(t1,'%H:%i:00') |
+----------+----------------------------+
| 15:00:00 | 15:00:00                   |
| 05:01:30 | 05:01:00                   |
| 12:30:20 | 12:30:00                   |
+----------+----------------------------+
```

Another way to construct temporal values is to use date-part extraction functions in conjunction with CONCAT( ). However, this method often is messier than the DATE_FORMAT( ) technique just discussed, and it sometimes yields slightly different results:

```
mysql> SELECT d,
    -> CONCAT(YEAR(d),'-',MONTH(d),'-01')
    -> FROM date_val;
+------------+------------------------------------+
| d          | CONCAT(YEAR(d),'-',MONTH(d),'-01') |
+------------+------------------------------------+
| 1864-02-28 | 1864-2-01                          |
| 1900-01-15 | 1900-1-01                          |
| 1987-03-05 | 1987-3-01                          |
| 1999-12-31 | 1999-12-01                         |
| 2000-06-04 | 2000-6-01                          |
+------------+------------------------------------+
```

Note that the month values in some of these dates have only a single digit. To ensure that the month has two digits—as required for ISO format—use LPAD( ) to add a leading zero as necessary:

```
mysql> SELECT d,
    -> CONCAT(YEAR(d),'-',LPAD(MONTH(d),2,'0'),'-01')
```

```
    -> FROM date_val;
+------------+-------------------------------------------------+
| d          | CONCAT(YEAR(d),'-',LPAD(MONTH(d),2,'0'),'-01') |
+------------+-------------------------------------------------+
| 1864-02-28 | 1864-02-01                                      |
| 1900-01-15 | 1900-01-01                                      |
| 1987-03-05 | 1987-03-01                                      |
| 1999-12-31 | 1999-12-01                                      |
| 2000-06-04 | 2000-06-01                                      |
+------------+-------------------------------------------------+
```

Recipe 6.18 shows other ways to solve the problem of producing ISO dates from not-quite-ISO dates.

TIME values can be produced from hours, minutes, and seconds values using methods analogous to those for creating DATE values. For example, to change a TIME value so that its seconds part is 00, extract the hour and minute parts, and then recombine them with CONCAT( ):

```
mysql> SELECT t1,
    -> CONCAT(LPAD(HOUR(t1),2,'0'),':',LPAD(MINUTE(t1),2,'0'),':00')
    ->    AS recombined
    -> FROM time_val;
+----------+------------+
| t1       | recombined |
+----------+------------+
| 15:00:00 | 15:00:00   |
| 05:01:30 | 05:01:00   |
| 12:30:20 | 12:30:00   |
+----------+------------+
```

To produce a combined date-and-time value from separate date and time values, simply concatenate them with a space in between:

```
mysql> SET @d = '2006-02-28';
mysql> SET @t = '13:10:05';
mysql> SELECT @d, @t, CONCAT(@d,' ',@t);
+------------+----------+---------------------+
| @d         | @t       | CONCAT(@d,' ',@t)   |
+------------+----------+---------------------+
| 2006-02-28 | 13:10:05 | 2006-02-28 13:10:05 |
+------------+----------+---------------------+
```

6.8 Converting Between Temporal Data Types and Basic Units

Problem

You have a function temporal value such as a time or date that you want to convert to basic units such as seconds or days. This is often useful or necessary for performing temporal arithmetic operations (Recipes 6.9 and 6.10).

Solution

The conversion method depends on the type of value to be converted:

- To convert between time values and seconds, use the `TIME_TO_SEC( )` and `SEC_TO_TIME( )` functions.
- To convert between date values and days, use the `TO_DAYS( )` and `FROM_DAYS( )` functions.
- To convert between date-and-time values and seconds, use the `UNIX_TIMESTAMP( )` and `FROM_UNIXTIME( )` functions.

Discussion

The following discussion shows how to convert several types of temporal values to basic units and vice versa.

Converting between times and seconds

`TIME` values are specialized representations of a simpler unit (seconds), so you can convert back and forth from one to the other using the `TIME_TO_SEC( )` and `SEC_TO_TIME( )` functions.

`TIME_TO_SEC( )` converts a `TIME` value to the equivalent number of seconds, and `SEC_TO_TIME( )` does the opposite. The following statement demonstrates a simple conversion in both directions:

```
mysql> SELECT t1,
    -> TIME_TO_SEC(t1) AS 'TIME to seconds',
    -> SEC_TO_TIME(TIME_TO_SEC(t1)) AS 'TIME to seconds to TIME'
    -> FROM time_val;
+----------+-----------------+-------------------------+
| t1       | TIME to seconds | TIME to seconds to TIME |
+----------+-----------------+-------------------------+
| 15:00:00 |           54000 | 15:00:00                |
| 05:01:30 |           18090 | 05:01:30                |
| 12:30:20 |           45020 | 12:30:20                |
+----------+-----------------+-------------------------+
```

To express time values as minutes, hours, or days, perform the appropriate divisions:

```
mysql> SELECT t1,
    -> TIME_TO_SEC(t1) AS 'seconds',
    -> TIME_TO_SEC(t1)/60 AS 'minutes',
    -> TIME_TO_SEC(t1)/(60*60) AS 'hours',
    -> TIME_TO_SEC(t1)/(24*60*60) AS 'days'
    -> FROM time_val;
+----------+---------+----------+---------+--------+
| t1       | seconds | minutes  | hours   | days   |
+----------+---------+----------+---------+--------+
| 15:00:00 |   54000 | 900.0000 | 15.0000 | 0.6250 |
| 05:01:30 |   18090 | 301.5000 |  5.0250 | 0.2094 |
| 12:30:20 |   45020 | 750.3333 | 12.5056 | 0.5211 |
+----------+---------+----------+---------+--------+
```

Use FLOOR( ) if you prefer integer values that have no fractional part:

```
mysql> SELECT t1,
    -> TIME_TO_SEC(t1) AS 'seconds',
    -> FLOOR(TIME_TO_SEC(t1)/60) AS 'minutes',
    -> FLOOR(TIME_TO_SEC(t1)/(60*60)) AS 'hours',
    -> FLOOR(TIME_TO_SEC(t1)/(24*60*60)) AS 'days'
    -> FROM time_val;
+----------+---------+---------+-------+------+
| t1       | seconds | minutes | hours | days |
+----------+---------+---------+-------+------+
| 15:00:00 |   54000 |     900 |    15 |    0 |
| 05:01:30 |   18090 |     301 |     5 |    0 |
| 12:30:20 |   45020 |     750 |    12 |    0 |
+----------+---------+---------+-------+------+
```

If you pass TIME_TO_SEC( ) a date-and-time value, it extracts the time part and discards the date. This provides yet another means of extracting times from DATETIME and TIMESTAMP values (in addition to those already discussed in Recipe 6.6):

```
mysql> SELECT dt,
    -> TIME_TO_SEC(dt) AS 'time part in seconds',
    -> SEC_TO_TIME(TIME_TO_SEC(dt)) AS 'time part as TIME'
    -> FROM datetime_val;
+---------------------+----------------------+-------------------+
| dt                  | time part in seconds | time part as TIME |
+---------------------+----------------------+-------------------+
| 1970-01-01 00:00:00 |                    0 | 00:00:00          |
| 1987-03-05 12:30:15 |                45015 | 12:30:15          |
| 1999-12-31 09:00:00 |                32400 | 09:00:00          |
| 2000-06-04 15:45:30 |                56730 | 15:45:30          |
+---------------------+----------------------+-------------------+
mysql> SELECT ts,
    -> TIME_TO_SEC(ts) AS 'time part in seconds',
    -> SEC_TO_TIME(TIME_TO_SEC(ts)) AS 'time part as TIME'
    -> FROM timestamp_val;
+---------------------+----------------------+-------------------+
| ts                  | time part in seconds | time part as TIME |
+---------------------+----------------------+-------------------+
| 1970-01-01 00:00:00 |                    0 | 00:00:00          |
| 1987-03-05 12:30:15 |                45015 | 12:30:15          |
| 1999-12-31 09:00:00 |                32400 | 09:00:00          |
| 2000-06-04 15:45:30 |                56730 | 15:45:30          |
+---------------------+----------------------+-------------------+
```

Converting between dates and days

If you have a date but want a value in days, or vice versa, use the TO_DAYS( ) and FROM_DAYS( ) functions. Date-and-time values also can be converted to days if you're willing to suffer loss of the time part.

TO_DAYS( ) converts a date to the corresponding number of days, and FROM_DAYS( ) does the opposite:

```
mysql> SELECT d,
    -> TO_DAYS(d) AS 'DATE to days',
    -> FROM_DAYS(TO_DAYS(d)) AS 'DATE to days to DATE'
    -> FROM date_val;
+------------+--------------+----------------------+
| d          | DATE to days | DATE to days to DATE |
+------------+--------------+----------------------+
| 1864-02-28 |       680870 | 1864-02-28           |
| 1900-01-15 |       693975 | 1900-01-15           |
| 1987-03-05 |       725800 | 1987-03-05           |
| 1999-12-31 |       730484 | 1999-12-31           |
| 2000-06-04 |       730640 | 2000-06-04           |
+------------+--------------+----------------------+
```

When using TO_DAYS( ), it's best to stick to the advice of the *MySQL Reference Manual* and avoid DATE values that occur before the beginning of the Gregorian calendar (1582). Changes in the lengths of calendar years and months prior to that date make it difficult to speak meaningfully of what the value of "day 0" might be. This differs from TIME_TO_SEC( ), where the correspondence between a TIME value and the resulting seconds value is obvious and has a meaningful reference point of 0 seconds.

If you pass TO_DAYS( ) a date-and-time value, it extracts the date part and discards the time. This provides another means of extracting dates from DATETIME and TIMESTAMP values (in addition to those already discussed in Recipe 6.6):

```
mysql> SELECT dt,
    -> TO_DAYS(dt) AS 'date part in days',
    -> FROM_DAYS(TO_DAYS(dt)) AS 'date part as DATE'
    -> FROM datetime_val;
+---------------------+-------------------+-------------------+
| dt                  | date part in days | date part as DATE |
+---------------------+-------------------+-------------------+
| 1970-01-01 00:00:00 |            719528 | 1970-01-01        |
| 1987-03-05 12:30:15 |            725800 | 1987-03-05        |
| 1999-12-31 09:00:00 |            730484 | 1999-12-31        |
| 2000-06-04 15:45:30 |            730640 | 2000-06-04        |
+---------------------+-------------------+-------------------+
mysql> SELECT ts,
    -> TO_DAYS(ts) AS 'date part in days',
    -> FROM_DAYS(TO_DAYS(ts)) AS 'date part as DATE'
    -> FROM timestamp_val;
+---------------------+-------------------+-------------------+
| ts                  | date part in days | date part as DATE |
+---------------------+-------------------+-------------------+
| 1970-01-01 00:00:00 |            719528 | 1970-01-01        |
| 1987-03-05 12:30:15 |            725800 | 1987-03-05        |
| 1999-12-31 09:00:00 |            730484 | 1999-12-31        |
| 2000-06-04 15:45:30 |            730640 | 2000-06-04        |
+---------------------+-------------------+-------------------+
```

Converting between date-and-time values and seconds

For DATETIME or TIMESTAMP values that lie within the range of the TIMESTAMP data type (from the beginning of 1970 through approximately 2037), the UNIX_TIMESTAMP( ) and

`FROM_UNIXTIME( )` functions convert to and from the number of seconds elapsed since the beginning of 1970. The conversion to seconds offers higher precision for date-and-time values than a conversion to days, at the cost of a more limited range of values for which the conversion may be performed (`TIME_TO_SEC( )` is unsuitable for this because it discards the date):

```
mysql> SELECT dt,
    -> UNIX_TIMESTAMP(dt) AS seconds,
    -> FROM_UNIXTIME(UNIX_TIMESTAMP(dt)) AS timestamp
    -> FROM datetime_val;
+---------------------+-----------+---------------------+
| dt                  | seconds   | timestamp           |
+---------------------+-----------+---------------------+
| 1970-01-01 00:00:00 |     21600 | 1970-01-01 00:00:00 |
| 1987-03-05 12:30:15 | 541967415 | 1987-03-05 12:30:15 |
| 1999-12-31 09:00:00 | 946652400 | 1999-12-31 09:00:00 |
| 2000-06-04 15:45:30 | 960151530 | 2000-06-04 15:45:30 |
+---------------------+-----------+---------------------+
```

The relationship between the "UNIX" in the function names and the fact that the applicable range of values begins with 1970 is that `1970-01-01 00:00:00` UTC marks the "Unix epoch." The epoch is time zero, or the reference point for measuring time in Unix systems. That being so, you may find it curious that the preceding example shows a `UNIX_TIMESTAMP( )` value of `21600` for the first value in the `datetime_val` table. What's going on? Why isn't it `0`? The apparent discrepancy is due to the fact that the MySQL server interprets the `UNIX_TIMESTAMP( )` argument as a value in the client's local time zone and converts it to UTC. My server is in the U.S. Central time zone, six hours (21600 seconds) west of UTC.

`UNIX_TIMESTAMP( )` can convert `DATE` values to seconds, too. It treats such values as having an implicit time-of-day part of `00:00:00`:

```
mysql> SELECT
    -> CURDATE(),
    -> UNIX_TIMESTAMP(CURDATE()),
    -> FROM_UNIXTIME(UNIX_TIMESTAMP(CURDATE()))\G
*************************** 1. row ***************************
                        CURDATE(): 2006-05-30
        UNIX_TIMESTAMP(CURDATE()): 1148965200
FROM_UNIXTIME(UNIX_TIMESTAMP(CURDATE())): 2006-05-30 00:00:00
```

6.9 Calculating the Interval Between Two Dates or Times

Problem

You want to know how long it is between two dates or times. That is, you want to know the interval between two temporal values.

Solution

To calculate an interval, either use one of the temporal-difference functions, or convert your values to basic units and take the difference. The allowable functions depend on the types of the values for which you want to know the interval.

Discussion

The following discussion shows several ways to perform interval calculations.

Calculating intervals with temporal-difference functions

To calculate an interval in days between two date values, use the `DATEDIFF( )` function:

```
mysql> SET @d1 = '2010-01-01', @d2 = '2009-12-01';
mysql> SELECT DATEDIFF(@d1,@d2) AS 'd1 - d2', DATEDIFF(@d2,@d1) AS 'd2 - d1';
+---------+---------+
| d1 - d2 | d2 - d1 |
+---------+---------+
|      31 |     -31 |
+---------+---------+
```

`DATEDIFF( )` also works with date-and-time values, but it ignores the time part. This makes it suitable for producing day intervals for `DATE`, `DATETIME`, or `TIMESTAMP` values.

To calculate an interval between `TIME` values as another `TIME` value, use the `TIMEDIFF( )` function:

```
mysql> SET @t1 = '12:00:00', @t2 = '16:30:00';
mysql> SELECT TIMEDIFF(@t1,@t2) AS 't1 - t2', TIMEDIFF(@t2,@t1) AS 't2 - t1';
+-----------+----------+
| t1 - t2   | t2 - t1  |
+-----------+----------+
| -04:30:00 | 04:30:00 |
+-----------+----------+
```

`TIMEDIFF( )` also works for date-and-time values. That it, it accepts either time or date-and-time values, but the types of the arguments must match.

A time interval expressed as a `TIME` value can be broken down into components using the techniques shown in Recipe 6.6. For example, to express a time interval in terms of its constituent hours, minutes, and seconds values, calculate time interval subparts in SQL using the `HOUR( )`, `MINUTE( )`, and `SECOND( )` functions. (Don't forget that if your intervals may be negative, you need to take that into account.) To determine the components of the interval between the `t1` and `t2` columns in the `time_val` table, the following SQL statement does the trick:

```
mysql> SELECT t1, t2,
    -> TIMEDIFF(t2,t1) AS 't2 - t1 as TIME',
    -> IF(TIMEDIFF(t2,t1) >= 0,'+','-') AS sign,
    -> HOUR(TIMEDIFF(t2,t1)) AS hour,
    -> MINUTE(TIMEDIFF(t2,t1)) AS minute,
    -> SECOND(TIMEDIFF(t2,t1)) AS second
    -> FROM time_val;
```

```
+----------+----------+-----------------+------+------+--------+--------+
| t1       | t2       | t2 - t1 as TIME | sign | hour | minute | second |
+----------+----------+-----------------+------+------+--------+--------+
| 15:00:00 | 15:00:00 | 00:00:00        | +    | 0    | 0      | 0      |
| 05:01:30 | 02:30:20 | -02:31:10       | -    | 2    | 31     | 10     |
| 12:30:20 | 17:30:45 | 05:00:25        | +    | 5    | 0      | 25     |
+----------+----------+-----------------+------+------+--------+--------+
```

If you're working with date or date-and-time values, the TIMESTAMPDIFF( ) function provides another way to calculate intervals, and it enables you to specify the units in which intervals should be expressed. It has this syntax:

```
TIMESTAMPDIFF(unit,val1,val2)
```

unit is the interval unit and val1 and val2 are the values between which to calculate the interval. With TIMESTAMPDIFF( ), you can express an interval many different ways:

```
mysql> SET @dt1 = '1900-01-01 00:00:00', @dt2 = '1910-01-01 00:00:00';
mysql> SELECT
    -> TIMESTAMPDIFF(MINUTE,@dt1,@dt2) AS minutes,
    -> TIMESTAMPDIFF(HOUR,@dt1,@dt2) AS hours,
    -> TIMESTAMPDIFF(DAY,@dt1,@dt2) AS days,
    -> TIMESTAMPDIFF(WEEK,@dt1,@dt2) AS weeks,
    -> TIMESTAMPDIFF(YEAR,@dt1,@dt2) AS years;
+---------+-------+------+-------+-------+
| minutes | hours | days | weeks | years |
+---------+-------+------+-------+-------+
| 5258880 | 87648 | 3652 |   521 |    10 |
+---------+-------+------+-------+-------+
```

The allowable unit specifiers are FRAC_SECOND, SECOND, MINUTE, HOUR, DAY, WEEK, MONTH, QUARTER, or YEAR. Note that each of these unit specifiers is given in singular form, not plural.

Be aware of these properties of TIMESTAMPDIFF( ):

- Its value is negative if the first temporal value is greater then the second, which is opposite the order of the arguments for DATEDIFF( ) and TIMEDIFF( ).

- Despite the TIMESTAMP in its name, the TIMESTAMPDIFF( ) function arguments are not limited to the range of the TIMESTAMP data type.

- TIMESTAMPDIFF( ) requires MySQL 5.0 or higher. For older versions of MySQL, use one of the other interval-calculation techniques described in this section.

Calculating intervals using basic units

Another strategy for calculating intervals is to work with basic units such as seconds or days using this strategy:

1. Convert the temporal values that you're working with to basic units.

2. Take the difference between the values to calculate the interval, also in basic units.

3. If you want the result as a temporal value, convert it from basic units to the appropriate type.

The conversion functions involved in implementing this strategy depend on the types of the values between which you're calculating the interval:

- To convert between time values and seconds, use `TIME_TO_SEC( )` and `SEC_TO_TIME( )`.
- To convert between date values and days, use `TO_DAYS( )` and `FROM_DAYS( )`.
- To convert between date-and-time values and seconds, use `UNIX_TIMESTAMP( )` and `FROM_UNIXTIME( )`.

For more information about those conversion functions (and limitations on their applicability), see the discussion in Recipe 6.8. The following material assumes familiarity with that discussion.

Time interval calculation using basic units

To calculate intervals in seconds between pairs of time values, convert them to seconds with `TIME_TO_SEC( )`, and then take the difference. To express the resulting interval as a `TIME` value, pass it to `SEC_TO_TIME( )`. The following statement calculates the intervals between the `t1` and `t2` columns of the `time_val` table, expressing each interval both in seconds and as a `TIME` value:

```
mysql> SELECT t1, t2,
    -> TIME_TO_SEC(t2) - TIME_TO_SEC(t1) AS 't2 - t1 (in seconds)',
    -> SEC_TO_TIME(TIME_TO_SEC(t2) - TIME_TO_SEC(t1)) AS 't2 - t1 (as TIME)'
    -> FROM time_val;
+----------+----------+----------------------+-------------------+
| t1       | t2       | t2 - t1 (in seconds) | t2 - t1 (as TIME) |
+----------+----------+----------------------+-------------------+
| 15:00:00 | 15:00:00 |                    0 | 00:00:00          |
| 05:01:30 | 02:30:20 |                -9070 | -02:31:10         |
| 12:30:20 | 17:30:45 |                18025 | 05:00:25          |
+----------+----------+----------------------+-------------------+
```

Date or date-and-time interval calculation using basic units

When you calculate an interval between dates by converting both dates to a common unit in relation to a given reference point and take the difference, the range of values that you're working with determines which conversions are available:

- `DATE`, `DATETIME`, or `TIMESTAMP` values dating back to `1970-01-01 00:00:00` UTC—the date of the Unix epoch—can be converted to seconds elapsed since the epoch. If both dates lie within that range, you can calculate intervals to an accuracy of one second.
- Older dates from the beginning of the Gregorian calendar (1582) on can be converted to day values and used to compute intervals in days.
- Dates that begin earlier than either of these reference points present more of a problem. In such cases, you may find that your programming language offers computations that are not available or are difficult to perform in SQL. If so, consider processing date values directly from within your API language. (For example, the

Date::Calc and Date::Manip modules are available from CPAN for use within Perl scripts.)

To calculate an interval in days between date or date-and-time values, convert them to days with TO_DAYS( ), and take the difference:

```
mysql> SELECT TO_DAYS('1884-01-01') - TO_DAYS('1883-06-05') AS days;
+------+
| days |
+------+
|  210 |
+------+
```

For an interval in weeks, do the same thing and divide the result by seven:

```
mysql> SELECT (TO_DAYS('1884-01-01') - TO_DAYS('1883-06-05')) / 7 AS weeks;
+---------+
| weeks   |
+---------+
| 30.0000 |
+---------+
```

You cannot convert days to months or years by simple division, because those units vary in length. For calculations to yield date intervals expressed in those units, use the TIMESTAMPDIFF( ) function discussed earlier in this section.

For date-and-time values occurring within the TIMESTAMP range of 1970 to 2037, you can determine intervals to a resolution in seconds using the UNIX_TIMESTAMP( ) function. For example, the number of seconds between dates that lie two weeks apart can be computed like this:

```
mysql> SET @dt1 = '1984-01-01 09:00:00';
mysql> SET @dt2 = @dt1 + INTERVAL 14 DAY;
mysql> SELECT UNIX_TIMESTAMP(@dt2) - UNIX_TIMESTAMP(@dt1) AS seconds;
+---------+
| seconds |
+---------+
| 1209600 |
+---------+
```

To convert the interval in seconds to other units, perform the appropriate arithmetic operation. Seconds are easily converted to minutes, hours, days, or weeks:

```
mysql> SET @interval = UNIX_TIMESTAMP(@dt2) - UNIX_TIMESTAMP(@dt1);
mysql> SELECT @interval AS seconds,
    -> @interval / 60 AS minutes,
    -> @interval / (60 * 60) AS hours,
    -> @interval / (24 * 60 * 60) AS days,
    -> @interval / (7 * 24 * 60 * 60) AS weeks;
+---------+------------+----------+---------+--------+
| seconds | minutes    | hours    | days    | weeks  |
+---------+------------+----------+---------+--------+
| 1209600 | 20160.0000 | 336.0000 | 14.0000 | 2.0000 |
+---------+------------+----------+---------+--------+
```

To produce integer values (no fractional part), use the `FLOOR( )` function, as shown in Recipe 6.8. This applies to several of the following examples as well.

For values that occur outside the `TIMESTAMP` range, you can use an interval calculation method that is more general (but messier):

- Take the difference in days between the date parts of the values and multiply by 24 × 60 × 60 to convert to seconds.
- Offset the result by the difference in seconds between the time parts of the values.

Here's an example, using two date-and-time values that lie a week apart:

```
mysql> SET @dt1 = '1800-02-14 07:30:00';
mysql> SET @dt2 = @dt1 + INTERVAL 7 DAY;
mysql> SET @interval =
    ->    ((TO_DAYS(@dt2) - TO_DAYS(@dt1)) * 24*60*60)
    ->    + TIME_TO_SEC(@dt2) - TIME_TO_SEC(@dt1);
mysql> SELECT @interval AS seconds, SEC_TO_TIME(@interval) AS TIME;
+---------+-----------+
| seconds | TIME      |
+---------+-----------+
| 604800  | 168:00:00 |
+---------+-----------+
```

Do You Want an Interval or a Span?

When you take a difference between dates (or times), consider whether you want an interval or a span. Taking a difference between dates gives you the interval from one date to the next. If you want to know the range spanned by the two dates, you must add a unit. For example, it's a three-day interval from 2002-01-01 to 2002-01-04, but together they span a range of four days. If you're not getting the results you expect from a difference-of-values calculation, consider whether you need to apply an "off-by-one" correction.

6.10 Adding Date or Time Values

Problem

You want to add temporal values. For example, you want to add a given number of seconds to a time or determine what the date will be three weeks from today.

Solution

To add date or time values, you have several options:

- Use one of the temporal-addition functions.
- Use the + INTERVAL or - INTERVAL operator.

- Convert the values to basic units, and take the sum.

The allowable functions or operators depend on the types of the values that you want to add.

Discussion

The following discussion shows several ways to add temporal values.

Adding temporal values using temporal-addition functions or operators

To add a time or date-and-time value and a time value, use the `ADDTIME( )` function:

```
mysql> SET @t1 = '12:00:00', @t2 = '15:30:00';
mysql> SELECT ADDTIME(@t1,@t2);
+------------------+
| ADDTIME(@t1,@t2) |
+------------------+
| 27:30:00         |
+------------------+
mysql> SET @dt = '1984-03-01 12:00:00', @t = '12:00:00';
mysql> SELECT ADDTIME(@dt,@t);
+---------------------+
| ADDTIME(@dt,@t)     |
+---------------------+
| 1984-03-02 00:00:00 |
+---------------------+
```

To add a date or date-and-time value and a time value, use the `TIMESTAMP( )` function:

```
mysql> SET @d = '1984-03-01', @t = '15:30:00';
mysql> SELECT TIMESTAMP(@d,@t);
+---------------------+
| TIMESTAMP(@d,@t)    |
+---------------------+
| 1984-03-01 15:30:00 |
+---------------------+
mysql> SET @dt = '1984-03-01 12:00:00', @t = '12:00:00';
mysql> SELECT TIMESTAMP(@dt,@t);
+---------------------+
| TIMESTAMP(@dt,@t)   |
+---------------------+
| 1984-03-02 00:00:00 |
+---------------------+
```

MySQL also provides the `DATE_ADD( )` and `DATE_SUB( )` functions for adding intervals to dates and subtracting intervals from dates. Each function takes a date (or date-and-time) value d and an interval, expressed using the following syntax:

```
DATE_ADD(d,INTERVAL val unit)
DATE_SUB(d,INTERVAL val unit)
```

The `+ INTERVAL` and `- INTERVAL` operators are similar:

```
d + INTERVAL val unit
d - INTERVAL val unit
```

unit is the interval unit and *val* is an expression indicating the number of units. Some of the common unit specifiers are SECOND, MINUTE, HOUR, DAY, MONTH, and YEAR. (Check the *MySQL Reference Manual* for the full list.) Note that each of these unit specifiers is given in singular form, not plural.

Using DATE_ADD( ) or DATE_SUB( ), you can perform date arithmetic operations such as the following:

- Determine the date three days from today:

```
mysql> SELECT CURDATE(), DATE_ADD(CURDATE(),INTERVAL 3 DAY);
+------------+------------------------------------+
| CURDATE()  | DATE_ADD(CURDATE(),INTERVAL 3 DAY) |
+------------+------------------------------------+
| 2006-05-22 | 2006-05-25                         |
+------------+------------------------------------+
```

- Find the date a week ago:

```
mysql> SELECT CURDATE(), DATE_SUB(CURDATE(),INTERVAL 7 DAY);
+------------+------------------------------------+
| CURDATE()  | DATE_SUB(CURDATE(),INTERVAL 7 DAY) |
+------------+------------------------------------+
| 2006-05-22 | 2006-05-15                         |
+------------+------------------------------------+
```

As of MySQL 5.0, you can use 1 WEEK instead of 7 DAY, but the result is a DATETIME value rather than a DATE value.

- For questions where you need to know both the date and the time, begin with a DATETIME or TIMESTAMP value. To answer the question, "What time will it be in 60 hours?", do this:

```
mysql> SELECT NOW(), DATE_ADD(NOW(),INTERVAL 60 HOUR);
+---------------------+----------------------------------+
| NOW()               | DATE_ADD(NOW(),INTERVAL 60 HOUR)  |
+---------------------+----------------------------------+
| 2006-02-04 09:28:10 | 2006-02-06 21:28:10              |
+---------------------+----------------------------------+
```

- Some interval specifiers have both date and time parts. The following adds 14.5 hours to the current date and time:

```
mysql> SELECT NOW(), DATE_ADD(NOW(),INTERVAL '14:30' HOUR_MINUTE);
+---------------------+----------------------------------------------+
| NOW()               | DATE_ADD(NOW(),INTERVAL '14:30' HOUR_MINUTE) |
+---------------------+----------------------------------------------+
| 2006-02-04 09:28:31 | 2006-02-04 23:58:31                          |
+---------------------+----------------------------------------------+
```

Similarly, adding 3 days and 4 hours produces this result:

```
mysql> SELECT NOW(), DATE_ADD(NOW(),INTERVAL '3 4' DAY_HOUR);
+---------------------+-----------------------------------------+
| NOW()               | DATE_ADD(NOW(),INTERVAL '3 4' DAY_HOUR) |
+---------------------+-----------------------------------------+
```

```
|  2006-02-04 09:28:38  |  2006-02-07 13:28:38              |
+---------------------+------------------------------------+
```

DATE_ADD( ) and DATE_SUB( ) are interchangeable because one is the same as the other with the sign of the interval value flipped. These two calls are equivalent for any date value d:

```
DATE_ADD(d,INTERVAL -3 MONTH)
DATE_SUB(d,INTERVAL 3 MONTH)
```

You can also use the + INTERVAL and - INTERVAL operators to perform date interval addition and subtraction:

```
mysql> SELECT CURDATE(), CURDATE() + INTERVAL 1 YEAR;
+------------+----------------------------+
| CURDATE()  | CURDATE() + INTERVAL 1 YEAR |
+------------+----------------------------+
| 2006-05-22 | 2007-05-22                 |
+------------+----------------------------+
mysql> SELECT NOW(), NOW() - INTERVAL '1 12' DAY_HOUR;
+---------------------+--------------------------------+
| NOW()               | NOW() - INTERVAL '1 12' DAY_HOUR |
+---------------------+--------------------------------+
| 2006-05-22 19:00:50 | 2006-05-21 07:00:50            |
+---------------------+--------------------------------+
```

An alternative function for adding intervals to date or date-and-time values is TIMESTAMPADD( ), available in MySQL 5.0 or higher. Its arguments are similar to those for DATE_ADD( ), and, in fact, the following equivalence holds:

```
TIMESTAMPADD(unit,interval,d) = DATE_ADD(d,INTERVAL interval unit)
```

Adding temporal values using basic units

Another way to add intervals to date or date-and-time values is to perform temporal "shifting" via functions that convert to and from basic units. For background information about the applicable functions, see Recipe 6.8.

Adding time values using basic units. Adding times with basic units is similar to calculating intervals between times, except that you compute a sum rather than a difference. To add an interval value in seconds to a TIME value, convert the TIME to seconds so that both values are represented in the same units, add the values together, and convert the result back to a TIME. For example, two hours is 7200 seconds ($2 \times 60 \times 60$), so the following statement adds two hours to each t1 value in the time_val table:

```
mysql> SELECT t1,
    -> SEC_TO_TIME(TIME_TO_SEC(t1) + 7200) AS 't1 plus 2 hours'
    -> FROM time_val;
+----------+-----------------+
| t1       | t1 plus 2 hours |
+----------+-----------------+
| 15:00:00 | 17:00:00        |
| 05:01:30 | 07:01:30        |
```

```
| 12:30:20 | 14:30:20        |
+----------+-----------------+
```

If the interval itself is expressed as a TIME, it too should be converted to seconds before adding the values together. The following example calculates the sum of the two TIME values in each row of the time_val table:

```
mysql> SELECT t1, t2,
    -> TIME_TO_SEC(t1) + TIME_TO_SEC(t2)
    ->   AS 't1 + t2 (in seconds)',
    -> SEC_TO_TIME(TIME_TO_SEC(t1) + TIME_TO_SEC(t2))
    ->   AS 't1 + t2 (as TIME)'
    -> FROM time_val;
+----------+----------+----------------------+-------------------+
| t1       | t2       | t1 + t2 (in seconds) | t1 + t2 (as TIME) |
+----------+----------+----------------------+-------------------+
| 15:00:00 | 15:00:00 |               108000 | 30:00:00          |
| 05:01:30 | 02:30:20 |                27110 | 07:31:50          |
| 12:30:20 | 17:30:45 |               108065 | 30:01:05          |
+----------+----------+----------------------+-------------------+
```

It's important to recognize that MySQL TIME values really represent elapsed time, not time of day, so they don't reset to 0 after reaching 24 hours. You can see this in the first and third output rows from the previous statement. To produce time-of-day values, enforce a 24-hour wraparound using a modulo operation before converting the seconds value back to a TIME value. The number of seconds in a day is $24 \times 60 \times 60$, or 86,400, so to convert any seconds value s to lie within a 24-hour range, use the MOD( ) function or the % modulo operator like this:

```
MOD(s,86400)
s % 86400
s MOD 86400
```

 The allowable range of a TIME column is -838:59:59 to 838:59:59 (that is, -3020399 to 3020399 seconds). However, the range of TIME *expressions* can be greater, so when you add times together, you can easily produce a result that lies outside this range and that cannot be stored as is into a TIME column.

The three expressions are equivalent. Applying the first of them to the time calculations from the preceding example produces the following result:

```
mysql> SELECT t1, t2,
    -> MOD(TIME_TO_SEC(t1) + TIME_TO_SEC(t2), 86400)
    ->   AS 't1 + t2 (in seconds)',
    -> SEC_TO_TIME(MOD(TIME_TO_SEC(t1) + TIME_TO_SEC(t2), 86400))
    ->   AS 't1 + t2 (as TIME)'
    -> FROM time_val;
+----------+----------+----------------------+-------------------+
| t1       | t2       | t1 + t2 (in seconds) | t1 + t2 (as TIME) |
+----------+----------+----------------------+-------------------+
| 15:00:00 | 15:00:00 |                21600 | 06:00:00          |
```

```
| 05:01:30 | 02:30:20 |          27110 | 07:31:50 |
| 12:30:20 | 17:30:45 |          21665 | 06:01:05 |
+----------+----------+------------------+----------+
```

Adding to date or date-and-time values using basic units. By converting date or date-and-time values to basic units, you can shift them to produce other dates. For example, to shift a date forward or backward a week (seven days), use TO_DAYS( ) and FROM_DAYS( ):

```
mysql> SET @d = '2006-01-01';
mysql> SELECT @d AS date,
    -> FROM_DAYS(TO_DAYS(@d) + 7) AS 'date + 1 week',
    -> FROM_DAYS(TO_DAYS(@d) - 7) AS 'date - 1 week';
+------------+---------------+---------------+
| date       | date + 1 week | date - 1 week |
+------------+---------------+---------------+
| 2006-01-01 | 2006-01-08    | 2005-12-25    |
+------------+---------------+---------------+
```

TO_DAYS( ) also can convert DATETIME or TIMESTAMP values to days, if you don't mind having it chop off the time part:

```
mysql> SET @dt = '2006-01-01 12:30:45';
mysql> SELECT @dt AS datetime,
    -> FROM_DAYS(TO_DAYS(@dt) + 7) AS 'datetime + 1 week',
    -> FROM_DAYS(TO_DAYS(@dt) - 7) AS 'datetime - 1 week';
+---------------------+-------------------+-------------------+
| datetime            | datetime + 1 week | datetime - 1 week |
+---------------------+-------------------+-------------------+
| 2006-01-01 12:30:45 | 2006-01-08        | 2005-12-25        |
+---------------------+-------------------+-------------------+
```

To preserve the time with DATETIME or TIMESTAMP values, use UNIX_TIMESTAMP( ) and FROM_UNIXTIME( ) instead. The following statement shifts a DATETIME value forward and backward by an hour (3,600 seconds):

```
mysql> SET @dt = '2006-01-01 09:00:00';
mysql> SELECT @dt AS datetime,
    -> FROM_UNIXTIME(UNIX_TIMESTAMP(@dt) + 3600) AS 'datetime + 1 hour',
    -> FROM_UNIXTIME(UNIX_TIMESTAMP(@dt) - 3600) AS 'datetime - 1 hour';
+---------------------+---------------------+---------------------+
| datetime            | datetime + 1 hour   | datetime - 1 hour   |
+---------------------+---------------------+---------------------+
| 2006-01-01 09:00:00 | 2006-01-01 10:00:00 | 2006-01-01 08:00:00 |
+---------------------+---------------------+---------------------+
```

The preceding technique requires that both your initial value and the resulting value lie in the allowable range for TIMESTAMP values (1970 to approximately 2037).

6.11 Calculating Ages

Problem

You want to know how old someone is.

Solution

This is a date-arithmetic problem. It amounts to computing the interval between dates, but with a twist. For an age in years, it's necessary to account for the relative placement of the start and end dates within the calendar year. For an age in months, it's also necessary to account for the placement of the months and the days within the month.

Discussion

Age determination is a type of date interval calculation, but you cannot simply compute a difference in days and divide by 365. That doesn't work because leap years throw off the calculation. (The interval from 1995-03-01 to 1996-02-29 spans 365 days, but is not a year in age terms.) Using 365.25 is slightly more accurate, but still not correct for all dates. Instead, it's necessary to determine the difference between dates in years and then adjust for the relative location of the dates within the calendar year. (Suppose that Gretchen Smith was born on April 14, 1942. To compute how old Gretchen is now, we must account for where the current date falls within the calendar year: She's one age up through April 13 of the year, and one year older from April 14 through the end of the year.) This section shows how to perform this kind of calculation to determine ages in units of years or months.

The easiest way to calculate ages is to use the `TIMESTAMPDIFF()` function because you can pass it a birth date, a current date, and the unit in which you want the age to be expressed:

```
TIMESTAMPDIFF(unit,birth,current)
```

`TIMESTAMPDIFF()` handles the calculations necessary to adjust for differing month and year lengths and relative positions of the dates within the calendar year. Suppose that we have a `sibling` table that lists the birth dates of Gretchen Smith and her brothers Wilbur and Franz:

```
+----------+------------+
| name     | birth      |
+----------+------------+
| Gretchen | 1942-04-14 |
| Wilbur   | 1946-11-28 |
| Franz    | 1953-03-05 |
+----------+------------+
```

Using `TIMESTAMPDIFF()`, we can answer questions such as these:

- How old are the Smith children today?

```
mysql> SELECT name, birth, CURDATE() AS today,
    -> TIMESTAMPDIFF(YEAR,birth,CURDATE()) AS 'age in years'
    -> FROM sibling;
+----------+------------+------------+--------------+
| name     | birth      | today      | age in years |
+----------+------------+------------+--------------+
| Gretchen | 1942-04-14 | 2006-05-30 |           64 |
| Wilbur   | 1946-11-28 | 2006-05-30 |           59 |
```

```
| Franz    | 1953-03-05 | 2006-05-30 |            53 |
+----------+------------+------------+---------------+
```

- How old were Gretchen and Wilbur when Franz was born?

```
mysql> SELECT name, birth, '1953-03-05' AS 'Franz'' birthday',
    -> TIMESTAMPDIFF(YEAR,birth,'1953-03-05') AS 'age in years'
    -> FROM sibling WHERE name != 'Franz';
+----------+------------+----------------+--------------+
| name     | birth      | Franz' birthday | age in years |
+----------+------------+----------------+--------------+
| Gretchen | 1942-04-14 | 1953-03-05     |           10 |
| Wilbur   | 1946-11-28 | 1953-03-05     |            6 |
+----------+------------+----------------+--------------+
```

The preceding queries produce ages in years, but you can request other interval units if you like. For example, the current ages of the Smith children in months can be calculated like this:

```
mysql> SELECT name, birth, CURDATE() AS today,
    -> TIMESTAMPDIFF(MONTH,birth,CURDATE()) AS 'age in months'
    -> FROM sibling;
+----------+------------+------------+---------------+
| name     | birth      | today      | age in months |
+----------+------------+------------+---------------+
| Gretchen | 1942-04-14 | 2006-05-30 |           769 |
| Wilbur   | 1946-11-28 | 2006-05-30 |           714 |
| Franz    | 1953-03-05 | 2006-05-30 |           638 |
+----------+------------+------------+---------------+
```

TIMESTAMPDIFF( ) requires MySQL 5.0 or higher. For older versions of MySQL, you can calculate ages without it, but as the following discussion shows, it's necessary to do more work.

In general, given a birth date birth, an age in years on a target date d can be computed by the following logic:

```
if (d occurs earlier in the year than birth)
   age = YEAR(d) - YEAR(birth) - 1
if (d occurs on or later in the year than birth)
   age = YEAR(d) - YEAR(birth)
```

For both cases, the difference-in-years part of the calculation is the same. What distinguishes them is the relative ordering of the dates within the calendar year. However, this ordering cannot be determined with DAYOFYEAR( ), because that only works if both dates fall during years with the same number of days. For dates in different years, different calendar days may have the same DAYOFYEAR( ) value, as the following statement illustrates:

```
mysql> SELECT DAYOFYEAR('1995-03-01'), DAYOFYEAR('1996-02-29');
+-------------------------+-------------------------+
| DAYOFYEAR('1995-03-01') | DAYOFYEAR('1996-02-29') |
+-------------------------+-------------------------+
|                      60 |                      60 |
+-------------------------+-------------------------+
```

The fact that ISO date strings compare naturally in the proper order comes to our rescue here—or more precisely, the fact that the rightmost five characters that represent the month and day also compare properly:

```
mysql> SELECT RIGHT('1995-03-01',5), RIGHT('1996-02-29',5);
+-----------------------+-----------------------+
| RIGHT('1995-03-01',5) | RIGHT('1996-02-29',5) |
+-----------------------+-----------------------+
| 03-01                 | 02-29                 |
+-----------------------+-----------------------+
mysql> SELECT IF('02-29' < '03-01','02-29','03-01') AS earliest;
+----------+
| earliest |
+----------+
| 02-29    |
+----------+
```

This means that you can perform the "earlier-in-year" test for two dates, d1 and d2, like this:

```
RIGHT(d2,5) < RIGHT(d1,5)
```

The expression evaluates to 1 or 0, depending on the result of the test, so the result of the < comparison can be used to perform an age-in-years calculation:

```
YEAR(d2) - YEAR(d1) - (RIGHT(d2,5) < RIGHT(d1,5))
```

If you want to make it more obvious what the comparison result evaluates to, wrap it in an IF( ) function that explicitly returns 1 or 0:

```
YEAR(d2) - YEAR(d1) - IF(RIGHT(d2,5) < RIGHT(d1,5),1,0)
```

The following statement demonstrates how this formula works to calculate an age as of the beginning of 1975 for someone born on 1965-03-01. It shows the unadjusted age difference in years, the adjustment value, and the final age:

```
mysql> SET @birth = '1965-03-01';
mysql> SET @target = '1975-01-01';
mysql> SELECT @birth, @target,
    -> YEAR(@target) - YEAR(@birth) AS 'difference',
    -> IF(RIGHT(@target,5) < RIGHT(@birth,5),1,0) AS 'adjustment',
    -> YEAR(@target) - YEAR(@birth)
    -> - IF(RIGHT(@target,5) < RIGHT(@birth,5),1,0)
    -> AS 'age';
+------------+------------+------------+------------+------+
| @birth     | @target    | difference | adjustment | age  |
+------------+------------+------------+------------+------+
| 1965-03-01 | 1975-01-01 |         10 |          1 |    9 |
+------------+------------+------------+------------+------+
```

Let's try the age-in-years formula with the sibling table. We can check the formula using the same questions that we answered earlier with TIMESTAMPDIFF( ). The formula produces answers for questions such as the following:

- How old are the Smith children today?

```
mysql> SELECT name, birth, CURDATE() AS today,
    -> YEAR(CURDATE()) - YEAR(birth)
    ->   - IF(RIGHT(CURDATE(),5) < RIGHT(birth,5),1,0)
    ->   AS 'age in years'
    -> FROM sibling;
+----------+------------+------------+--------------+
| name     | birth      | today      | age in years |
+----------+------------+------------+--------------+
| Gretchen | 1942-04-14 | 2006-05-30 |           64 |
| Wilbur   | 1946-11-28 | 2006-05-30 |           59 |
| Franz    | 1953-03-05 | 2006-05-30 |           53 |
+----------+------------+------------+--------------+
```

- How old were Gretchen and Wilbur when Franz was born?

```
mysql> SELECT name, birth, '1953-03-05' AS 'Franz'' birthday',
    -> YEAR('1953-03-05') - YEAR(birth)
    ->   - IF(RIGHT('1953-03-05',5) < RIGHT(birth,5),1,0)
    ->   AS 'age in years'
    -> FROM sibling WHERE name != 'Franz';
+----------+------------+-----------------+--------------+
| name     | birth      | Franz' birthday | age in years |
+----------+------------+-----------------+--------------+
| Gretchen | 1942-04-14 | 1953-03-05      |           10 |
| Wilbur   | 1946-11-28 | 1953-03-05      |            6 |
+----------+------------+-----------------+--------------+
```

When performing calculations of this nature, be sure to remember that for comparisons on the *MM-DD* part of date strings to yield correct results, you must use ISO values like 1987-07-01 and not close-to-ISO values like 1987-7-1. For example, the following comparison produces a result that is correct in lexical terms but incorrect in temporal terms:

```
mysql> SELECT RIGHT('1987-7-1',5) < RIGHT('1987-10-01',5);
+---------------------------------------------+
| RIGHT('1987-7-1',5) < RIGHT('1987-10-01',5) |
+---------------------------------------------+
|                                           0 |
+---------------------------------------------+
```

The absence of leading zeros in the month and day parts of the first date makes the substring-based comparison fail. If you need to canonize not-quite-ISO date values, see Recipe 6.18.

The formula for calculating ages in months is similar to that for ages in years, except that we multiply the years difference by 12, add the months difference, and adjust for the relative day-in-month values of the two dates. In this case, we need to use the month and day part of each date separately, so we may as well extract them directly using MONTH( ) and DAYOFMONTH( ) rather than performing a comparison on the *MM-DD* part of the date strings. The current ages of the Smith children in months thus can be calculated like this:

```
mysql> SELECT name, birth, CURDATE() AS today,
    -> (YEAR(CURDATE()) - YEAR(birth)) * 12
    -> + (MONTH(CURDATE()) - MONTH(birth))
```

```
    ->    - IF(DAYOFMONTH(CURDATE()) < DAYOFMONTH(birth),1,0)
    ->    AS 'age in months'
    -> FROM sibling;
+----------+------------+------------+---------------+
| name     | birth      | today      | age in months |
+----------+------------+------------+---------------+
| Gretchen | 1942-04-14 | 2006-05-30 |           769 |
| Wilbur   | 1946-11-28 | 2006-05-30 |           714 |
| Franz    | 1953-03-05 | 2006-05-30 |           638 |
+----------+------------+------------+---------------+
```

6.12 Shifting a Date-and-Time Value to a Different Time Zone

Problem

You have a date-and-time value, but need to know what it would be in a different time zone. For example, you're having a teleconference with people in different parts of the world and you need to tell them the meeting time in their local time zones.

Solution

Use the CONVERT_TZ( ) function.

Discussion

The CONVERT_TZ( ) function takes three arguments: a date-and-time value and two time zone indicators. The function interprets the date-and-time value as a value in the first time zone and produces a result consisting of the value shifted into the second time zone.

Suppose that I live in Chicago, Illinois in the U.S., and that I need to have a meeting with people in several other parts of the world. The following table shows the location of each meeting participant and the time zone name for each.

Location	Time zone name
Chicago, Illinois, U.S.	US/Central
Berlin, Germany	Europe/Berlin
London, United Kingdom	Europe/London
Edmonton, Alberta, Canada	America/Edmonton
Brisbane, Australia	Australia/Brisbane

If the meeting is to take place at 9 AM local time for me on November 23, 2006, what time will that be for the other participants? The following statement uses CONVERT_TZ( ) to calculate the local times for each time zone:

```
mysql> SET @dt = '2006-11-23 09:00:00';
mysql> SELECT @dt AS Chicago,
    -> CONVERT_TZ(@dt,'US/Central','Europe/Berlin') AS Berlin,
    -> CONVERT_TZ(@dt,'US/Central','Europe/London') AS London,
    -> CONVERT_TZ(@dt,'US/Central','America/Edmonton') AS Edmonton,
    -> CONVERT_TZ(@dt,'US/Central','Australia/Brisbane') AS Brisbane\G
*************************** 1. row ***************************
 Chicago: 2006-11-23 09:00:00
  Berlin: 2006-11-23 16:00:00
  London: 2006-11-23 15:00:00
Edmonton: 2006-11-23 08:00:00
Brisbane: 2006-11-24 01:00:00
```

Let's hope the Brisbane participant doesn't mind being up after midnight.

The preceding example uses time zone names, so it requires that you have the time zone tables in the `mysql` database initialized with support for named time zones. (See the *MySQL Reference Manual* for information about setting up the time zone tables.) If you can't use named time zones, you can specify the zones in terms of their numeric relationship to UTC. This can be a little trickier because you might need to account for daylight saving time. The corresponding statement with numeric time zones looks like this:

```
mysql> SELECT @dt AS Chicago,
    -> CONVERT_TZ(@dt,'-06:00','+01:00') AS Berlin,
    -> CONVERT_TZ(@dt,'-06:00','+00:00') AS London,
    -> CONVERT_TZ(@dt,'-06:00','-07:00') AS Edmonton,
    -> CONVERT_TZ(@dt,'-06:00','+10:00') AS Brisbane\G
*************************** 1. row ***************************
 Chicago: 2006-11-23 09:00:00
  Berlin: 2006-11-23 16:00:00
  London: 2006-11-23 15:00:00
Edmonton: 2006-11-23 08:00:00
Brisbane: 2006-11-24 01:00:00
```

6.13 Finding the First Day, Last Day, or Length of a Month

Problem

Given a date, you want to determine the date for the first or last day of the month in which the date occurs, or the first or last day for the month *n* months away. A related problem is to determine the number of days in a month.

Solution

To determine the date for the first day in a month, use *date shifting* (an application of date arithmetic). To determine the date for the last day, use the `LAST_DAY( )` function. To determine the number of days in a month, find the date for the last day and use it as the argument to `DAYOFMONTH( )`.

Discussion

Sometimes you have a reference date and want to reach a target date that doesn't have a fixed relationship to the reference date. For example, the first or last days of the current month aren't a fixed number of days from the current date.

To find the first day of the month for a given date, shift the date back by one fewer days than its DAYOFMONTH( ) value:

```
mysql> SELECT d, DATE_SUB(d,INTERVAL DAYOFMONTH(d)-1 DAY) AS '1st of month'
    -> FROM date_val;
+------------+--------------+
| d          | 1st of month |
+------------+--------------+
| 1864-02-28 | 1864-02-01   |
| 1900-01-15 | 1900-01-01   |
| 1987-03-05 | 1987-03-01   |
| 1999-12-31 | 1999-12-01   |
| 2000-06-04 | 2000-06-01   |
+------------+--------------+
```

In the general case, to find the first of the month for any month n months away from a given date, calculate the first of the month for the date, and then shift the result by n months:

```
DATE_ADD(DATE_SUB(d,INTERVAL DAYOFMONTH(d)-1 DAY),INTERVAL n MONTH)
```

For example, to find the first day of the previous and following months relative to a given date, n is -1 and 1:

```
mysql> SELECT d,
    -> DATE_ADD(DATE_SUB(d,INTERVAL DAYOFMONTH(d)-1 DAY),INTERVAL -1 MONTH)
    ->    AS '1st of previous month',
    -> DATE_ADD(DATE_SUB(d,INTERVAL DAYOFMONTH(d)-1 DAY),INTERVAL 1 MONTH)
    ->    AS '1st of following month'
    -> FROM date_val;
+------------+-----------------------+------------------------+
| d          | 1st of previous month | 1st of following month |
+------------+-----------------------+------------------------+
| 1864-02-28 | 1864-01-01            | 1864-03-01             |
| 1900-01-15 | 1899-12-01            | 1900-02-01             |
| 1987-03-05 | 1987-02-01            | 1987-04-01             |
| 1999-12-31 | 1999-11-01            | 2000-01-01             |
| 2000-06-04 | 2000-05-01            | 2000-07-01             |
+------------+-----------------------+------------------------+
```

It's easier to find the last day of the month for a given date because there is a function for it:

```
mysql> SELECT d, LAST_DAY(d) AS 'last of month'
    -> FROM date_val;
+------------+---------------+
| d          | last of month |
+------------+---------------+
| 1864-02-28 | 1864-02-29    |
| 1900-01-15 | 1900-01-31    |
```

```
| 1987-03-05 | 1987-03-31 |
| 1999-12-31 | 1999-12-31 |
| 2000-06-04 | 2000-06-30 |
+------------+------------+
```

For the general case, to find the last of the month for any month *n* months away from a given date, shift the date by that many months first and then pass it to LAST_DAY( ):

```
LAST_DAY(DATE_ADD(d,INTERVAL n MONTH))
```

For example, to find the last day of the previous and following months relative to a given date, *n* is -1 and 1:

```
mysql> SELECT d,
    -> LAST_DAY(DATE_ADD(d,INTERVAL -1 MONTH))
    ->   AS 'last of previous month',
    -> LAST_DAY(DATE_ADD(d,INTERVAL 1 MONTH))
    ->  AS 'last of following month'
    -> FROM date_val;
+------------+------------------------+------------------------+
| d          | last of previous month | last of following month |
+------------+------------------------+------------------------+
| 1864-02-28 | 1864-01-31             | 1864-03-31             |
| 1900-01-15 | 1899-12-31             | 1900-02-28             |
| 1987-03-05 | 1987-02-28             | 1987-04-30             |
| 1999-12-31 | 1999-11-30             | 2000-01-31             |
| 2000-06-04 | 2000-05-31             | 2000-07-31             |
+------------+------------------------+------------------------+
```

To find the length of a month in days, determine the date of its last day with LAST_DAY( ), and then use DAYOFMONTH( ) to extract the day-of-month component from the result:

```
mysql> SELECT d, DAYOFMONTH(LAST_DAY(d)) AS 'days in month' FROM date_val;
+------------+---------------+
| d          | days in month |
+------------+---------------+
| 1864-02-28 |            29 |
| 1900-01-15 |            31 |
| 1987-03-05 |            31 |
| 1999-12-31 |            31 |
| 2000-06-04 |            30 |
+------------+---------------+
```

See Also

Recipe 6.17 later in this chapter discusses how to calculate month lengths from within a program without using SQL. (The trick is that you must account for leap years.)

6.14 Calculating Dates by Substring Replacement

Problem

Given a date, you want to produce another date from it when you know that the two dates share some components in common.

Solution

Treat a date or time value as a string, and perform direct replacement on parts of the string.

Discussion

In some cases, you can use substring replacement to calculate dates without performing any date arithmetic. For example, you can use string operations to produce the first-of-month value for a given date by replacing the day component with 01. You can do this either with DATE_FORMAT( ) or with CONCAT( ):

```
mysql> SELECT d,
    -> DATE_FORMAT(d,'%Y-%m-01') AS method1,
    -> CONCAT(YEAR(d),'-',LPAD(MONTH(d),2,'0'),'-01') AS method2
    -> FROM date_val;
+------------+------------+------------+
| d          | method1    | method2    |
+------------+------------+------------+
| 1864-02-28 | 1864-02-01 | 1864-02-01 |
| 1900-01-15 | 1900-01-01 | 1900-01-01 |
| 1987-03-05 | 1987-03-01 | 1987-03-01 |
| 1999-12-31 | 1999-12-01 | 1999-12-01 |
| 2000-06-04 | 2000-06-01 | 2000-06-01 |
+------------+------------+------------+
```

The string replacement technique can also be used to produce dates with a specific position within the calendar year. For New Year's Day (January 1), replace the month and day with 01:

```
mysql> SELECT d,
    -> DATE_FORMAT(d,'%Y-01-01') AS method1,
    -> CONCAT(YEAR(d),'-01-01') AS method2
    -> FROM date_val;
+------------+------------+------------+
| d          | method1    | method2    |
+------------+------------+------------+
| 1864-02-28 | 1864-01-01 | 1864-01-01 |
| 1900-01-15 | 1900-01-01 | 1900-01-01 |
| 1987-03-05 | 1987-01-01 | 1987-01-01 |
| 1999-12-31 | 1999-01-01 | 1999-01-01 |
| 2000-06-04 | 2000-01-01 | 2000-01-01 |
+------------+------------+------------+
```

For Christmas, replace the month and day with 12 and 25:

```
mysql> SELECT d,
    -> DATE_FORMAT(d,'%Y-12-25') AS method1,
    -> CONCAT(YEAR(d),'-12-25') AS method2
    -> FROM date_val;
+------------+------------+------------+
| d          | method1    | method2    |
+------------+------------+------------+
| 1864-02-28 | 1864-12-25 | 1864-12-25 |
| 1900-01-15 | 1900-12-25 | 1900-12-25 |
| 1987-03-05 | 1987-12-25 | 1987-12-25 |
| 1999-12-31 | 1999-12-25 | 1999-12-25 |
| 2000-06-04 | 2000-12-25 | 2000-12-25 |
+------------+------------+------------+
```

To perform the same operation for Christmas in other years, combine string replacement with date shifting. The following statement shows two ways to determine the date for Christmas two years hence. The first method finds Christmas for this year, and then shifts it two years forward. The second shifts the current date forward two years, and then finds Christmas in the resulting year:

```
mysql> SELECT CURDATE(),
    -> DATE_ADD(DATE_FORMAT(CURDATE(),'%Y-12-25'),INTERVAL 2 YEAR)
    ->   AS method1,
    -> DATE_FORMAT(DATE_ADD(CURDATE(),INTERVAL 2 YEAR),'%Y-12-25')
    ->   AS method2;
+------------+------------+------------+
| CURDATE()  | method1    | method2    |
+------------+------------+------------+
| 2006-05-22 | 2008-12-25 | 2008-12-25 |
+------------+------------+------------+
```

6.15 Finding the Day of the Week for a Date

Problem

You want to know the day of the week on which a date falls.

Solution

Use the DAYNAME( ) function.

Discussion

To determine the name of the day of the week for a given date, use DAYNAME( ):

```
mysql> SELECT CURDATE(), DAYNAME(CURDATE());
+------------+--------------------+
| CURDATE()  | DAYNAME(CURDATE()) |
+------------+--------------------+
| 2006-05-22 | Monday             |
+------------+--------------------+
```

`DAYNAME( )` is often useful in conjunction with other date-related techniques. For example, to determine the day of the week for the first of the month, use the first-of-month expression from Recipe 6.13 as the argument to `DAYNAME( )`:

```
mysql> SET @d = CURDATE();
mysql> SET @first = DATE_SUB(@d,INTERVAL DAYOFMONTH(@d)-1 DAY);
mysql> SELECT @d AS 'starting date',
    -> @first AS '1st of month date',
    -> DAYNAME(@first) AS '1st of month day';
+---------------+-------------------+------------------+
| starting date | 1st of month date | 1st of month day |
+---------------+-------------------+------------------+
| 2006-05-22    | 2006-05-01        | Monday           |
+---------------+-------------------+------------------+
```

6.16 Finding Dates for Any Weekday of a Given Week

Problem

You want to compute the date of some weekday for the week in which a given date lies. For example, suppose that you want to know the date of the Tuesday that falls in the same week as 2006-07-09.

Solution

This is an application of date shifting. Figure out the number of days between the starting weekday of the given date and the desired day, and shift the date by that many days.

Discussion

This section and the next describe how to convert one date to another when the target date is specified in terms of days of the week. To solve such problems, you need to know day-of-week values. Suppose you begin with a target date of 2006-07-09. If you want to know what date it is on Tuesday of the week in which that date lies, the calculation depends on what weekday it is. If it's a Monday, you add a day to produce 2006-07-10, but if it's a Wednesday, you subtract a day to produce 2006-07-08.

MySQL provides two functions that are useful here. `DAYOFWEEK( )` treats Sunday as the first day of the week and returns 1 through 7 for Sunday through Saturday. `WEEKDAY( )` treats Monday as the first day of the week and returns 0 through 6 for Monday through Sunday. (The examples shown here use `DAYOFWEEK( )`.) Another kind of day-of-week operation involves determining the name of the day. `DAYNAME( )` can be used for that.

Calculations that determine one day of the week from another depend on the day you start from as well as the day you want to reach. I find it easiest to shift the reference date first to a known point relative to the beginning of the week, and then shift forward:

- Shift the reference date back by its DAYOFWEEK( ) value, which always produces the date for the Saturday preceding the week.
- Shift the Saturday date by one day to reach the Sunday date, by two days to reach the Monday date, and so forth.

In SQL, those operations can be expressed as follows for a date d, where *n* is 1 through 7 to produce the dates for Sunday through Saturday:

```
DATE_ADD(DATE_SUB(d,INTERVAL DAYOFWEEK(d) DAY),INTERVAL n DAY)
```

That expression splits the "shift back to Saturday" and "shift forward" phases into separate operations, but because the intervals for both DATE_SUB( ) and DATE_ADD( ) are in days, the expression can be simplified into a single DATE_ADD( ) call:

```
DATE_ADD(d,INTERVAL n-DAYOFWEEK(d) DAY)
```

If we apply this formula to the dates in our date_val table, using an *n* of 1 for Sunday and 7 for Saturday to find the first and last days of the week, we get this result:

```
mysql> SELECT d, DAYNAME(d) AS day,
    -> DATE_ADD(d,INTERVAL 1-DAYOFWEEK(d) DAY) AS Sunday,
    -> DATE_ADD(d,INTERVAL 7-DAYOFWEEK(d) DAY) AS Saturday
    -> FROM date_val;
+------------+----------+------------+------------+
| d          | day      | Sunday     | Saturday   |
+------------+----------+------------+------------+
| 1864-02-28 | Sunday   | 1864-02-28 | 1864-03-05 |
| 1900-01-15 | Monday   | 1900-01-14 | 1900-01-20 |
| 1987-03-05 | Thursday | 1987-03-01 | 1987-03-07 |
| 1999-12-31 | Friday   | 1999-12-26 | 2000-01-01 |
| 2000-06-04 | Sunday   | 2000-06-04 | 2000-06-10 |
+------------+----------+------------+------------+
```

If you want to know the date of some weekday in a week relative to that of the target date, modify the preceding procedure a bit. First, determine the date of the desired weekday in the target date. Then shift the result into the desired week.

Calculating the date for a day of the week in some other week is a problem that breaks down into a day-within-week shift (using the formula just given) plus a week shift. These operations can be done in either order because the amount of shift within the week is the same whether or not you shift the reference date into a different week first. For example, to calculate Wednesday of a week by the preceding formula, *n* is 4. To compute the date for Wednesday two weeks ago, you can perform the day-within-week shift first, like this:

```
mysql> SET @target =
    -> DATE_SUB(DATE_ADD(CURDATE(),INTERVAL 4-DAYOFWEEK(CURDATE()) DAY),
    -> INTERVAL 14 DAY);
mysql> SELECT CURDATE(), @target, DAYNAME(@target);
+------------+------------+------------------+
| CURDATE()  | @target    | DAYNAME(@target) |
+------------+------------+------------------+
```

```
| 2006-05-22 | 2006-05-10 | Wednesday        |
+------------+------------+------------------+
```

Or you can perform the week shift first:

```
mysql> SET @target =
    -> DATE_ADD(DATE_SUB(CURDATE(),INTERVAL 14 DAY),
    -> INTERVAL 4-DAYOFWEEK(CURDATE()) DAY);
mysql> SELECT CURDATE(), @target, DAYNAME(@target);
+------------+------------+------------------+
| CURDATE()  | @target    | DAYNAME(@target) |
+------------+------------+------------------+
| 2006-05-22 | 2006-05-10 | Wednesday        |
+------------+------------+------------------+
```

Some applications need to determine dates such as the *n*-th instance of particular weekdays. For example, if you administer a payroll where paydays are the second and fourth Thursdays of each month, you'd need to know what those dates are. One way to do this for any given month is to begin with the first-of-month date and shift it forward. It's easy enough to shift the date to the Thursday in that week; the trick is to figure out how many weeks forward to shift the result to reach the second and fourth Thursdays. If the first of the month occurs on any day from Sunday through Thursday, you shift forward one week to reach the second Thursday. If the first of the month occurs on Friday or later, you shift forward by two weeks. The fourth Thursday is of course two weeks after that.

The following Perl code implements this logic to find all paydays in the year 2007. It runs a loop that constructs the first-of-month date for the months of the year. For each month, it issues a statement that determines the dates of the second and fourth Thursdays:

```perl
my $year = 2007;
print "MM/CCYY   2nd Thursday   4th Thursday\n";
foreach my $month (1..12)
{
  my $first = sprintf ("%04d-%02d-01", $year, $month);
  my ($thu2, $thu4) = $dbh->selectrow_array (qq{
                SELECT
                  DATE_ADD(
                    DATE_ADD(?,INTERVAL 5-DAYOFWEEK(?) DAY),
                    INTERVAL IF(DAYOFWEEK(?) <= 5, 7, 14) DAY),
                  DATE_ADD(
                    DATE_ADD(?,INTERVAL 5-DAYOFWEEK(?) DAY),
                    INTERVAL IF(DAYOFWEEK(?) <= 5, 21, 28) DAY)
                }, undef, $first, $first, $first, $first, $first, $first);
  printf "%02d/%04d   %s     %s\n", $month, $year, $thu2, $thu4;
}
```

The output from the program looks like this:

```
MM/CCYY    2nd Thursday   4th Thursday
01/2007    2007-01-11     2007-01-25
02/2007    2007-02-08     2007-02-22
03/2007    2007-03-08     2007-03-22
```

```
04/2007    2007-04-12    2007-04-26
05/2007    2007-05-10    2007-05-24
06/2007    2007-06-14    2007-06-28
07/2007    2007-07-12    2007-07-26
08/2007    2007-08-09    2007-08-23
09/2007    2007-09-13    2007-09-27
10/2007    2007-10-11    2007-10-25
11/2007    2007-11-08    2007-11-22
12/2007    2007-12-13    2007-12-27
```

6.17 Performing Leap Year Calculations

Problem

You need to perform a date calculation that must account for leap years. For example, the length of a month or a year depends on knowing whether the date falls in a leap year.

Solution

Know how to test whether a year is a leap year, and factor the result into your calculation.

Discussion

Date calculations are complicated by the fact that months don't all have the same number of days, and an additional headache is that February has an extra day during leap years. This recipe shows how to determine whether any given date falls within a leap year and how to take leap years into account when determining the length of a year or month.

Determining whether a date occurs in a leap year

To determine whether a date d falls within a leap year, obtain the year component using YEAR( ) and test the result. The common rule-of-thumb test for leap years is "divisible by four," which you can test using the % modulo operator like this:

```
YEAR(d) % 4 = 0
```

However, that test is not technically correct. (For example, the year 1900 is divisible by four, but is *not* a leap year.) For a year to qualify as a leap year, it must satisfy both of the following constraints:

- The year must be divisible by four.
- The year cannot be divisible by 100, unless it is also divisible by 400.

The meaning of the second constraint is that turn-of-century years are not leap years, except every fourth century. In SQL, you can express these conditions as follows:

```
(YEAR(d) % 4 = 0) AND ((YEAR(d) % 100 != 0) OR (YEAR(d) % 400 = 0))
```

Running our `date_val` table through both the rule-of-thumb leap-year test and the complete test produces the following results:

```
mysql> SELECT
    -> d,
    -> YEAR(d) % 4 = 0
    ->   AS 'rule-of-thumb test',
    -> (YEAR(d) % 4 = 0) AND ((YEAR(d) % 100 != 0) OR (YEAR(d) % 400 = 0))
    ->   AS 'complete test'
    -> FROM date_val;
+------------+--------------------+---------------+
| d          | rule-of-thumb test | complete test |
+------------+--------------------+---------------+
| 1864-02-28 |                  1 |             1 |
| 1900-01-15 |                  1 |             0 |
| 1987-03-05 |                  0 |             0 |
| 1999-12-31 |                  0 |             0 |
| 2000-06-04 |                  1 |             1 |
+------------+--------------------+---------------+
```

As you can see, the two tests don't always produce the same result. In particular, the rule-of-thumb test fails for the year 1900; the complete test result is correct because it accounts for the turn-of-century constraint.

Note that because the complete leap-year test needs to check the century, it requires four-digit year values. Two-digit years are ambiguous with respect to the century, making it impossible to assess the turn-of-century constraint.

If you're working with date values within a program, you can perform leap-year tests with your API language rather than at the SQL level. Pull off the first four digits of the date string to get the year, and then test it. If the language performs automatic string-to-number conversion of the year value, this is easy. Otherwise, you must explicitly convert the year value to numeric form before testing it.

Perl, PHP:

```
$year = substr ($date, 0, 4);
$is_leap = ($year % 4 == 0) && ($year % 100 != 0 || $year % 400 == 0);
```

Ruby:

```
year = date[0..3].to_i
is_leap = (year.modulo(4) == 0) &&
          (year.modulo(100) != 0 || year.modulo(400) == 0)
```

Python:

```
year = int (date[0:4])
is_leap = (year % 4 == 0) and (year % 100 != 0 or year % 400 == 0)
```

Java:

```
int year = Integer.valueOf (date.substring (0, 4)).intValue ();
boolean is_leap = (year % 4 == 0) && (year % 100 != 0 || year % 400 == 0);
```

Using leap year tests for year-length calculations

Years are usually 365 days long, but leap years have an extra day. To determine the length of a year in which a date falls, you can use one of the leap year tests just shown to figure out whether to add a day:

```
$year = substr ($date, 0, 4);
$is_leap = ($year % 4 == 0) && ($year % 100 != 0 || $year % 400 == 0);
$days_in_year = ($is_leap ? 366 : 365);
```

To compute a year's length in SQL, compute the date of the last day of the year and pass it to DAYOFYEAR( ):

```
mysql> SET @d = '2006-04-13';
mysql> SELECT DAYOFYEAR(DATE_FORMAT(@d,'%Y-12-31'));
+--------------------------------------+
| DAYOFYEAR(DATE_FORMAT(@d,'%Y-12-31')) |
+--------------------------------------+
|                                  365 |
+--------------------------------------+
mysql> SET @d = '2008-04-13';
mysql> SELECT DAYOFYEAR(DATE_FORMAT(@d,'%Y-12-31'));
+--------------------------------------+
| DAYOFYEAR(DATE_FORMAT(@d,'%Y-12-31')) |
+--------------------------------------+
|                                  366 |
+--------------------------------------+
```

Using leap year tests for month-length calculations

In Recipe 6.13, we discussed how to determine the number of days in a month by using the LAST_DAY( ) function in SQL statements.

Within an API language, you can write a non-SQL-based function that, given an ISO-format date argument, returns the number of days in the month during which the date occurs. This is straightforward except for February, where the function must return 29 or 28 depending on whether the year is a leap year. Here's a Ruby version:

```
def days_in_month(date)
  year = date[0..3].to_i
  month = date[5..6].to_i    # month, 1-based
  days_in_month = [31, 28, 31, 30, 31, 30, 31, 31, 30, 31, 30, 31]
  days = days_in_month[month-1]
  is_leap = (year.modulo(4) == 0) &&
            (year.modulo(100) != 0 || year.modulo(400) == 0)

  # add a day for Feb of leap years
  days += 1 if month == 2 && is_leap
  return days
end
```

6.18 Canonizing Not-Quite-ISO Date Strings

Problem

A date is in a format that's close to but not exactly ISO format.

Solution

Canonize the date by passing it to a function that always returns an ISO-format date result.

Discussion

Earlier in the chapter (Recipe 6.7), we ran into the problem that synthesizing dates with CONCAT( ) may produce values that are not quite in ISO format. For example, the following statement produces first-of-month values in which the month part may have only a single digit:

```
mysql> SELECT d, CONCAT(YEAR(d),'-',MONTH(d),'-01') FROM date_val;
+------------+----------------------------------+
| d          | CONCAT(YEAR(d),'-',MONTH(d),'-01') |
+------------+----------------------------------+
| 1864-02-28 | 1864-2-01                        |
| 1900-01-15 | 1900-1-01                        |
| 1987-03-05 | 1987-3-01                        |
| 1999-12-31 | 1999-12-01                       |
| 2000-06-04 | 2000-6-01                        |
+------------+----------------------------------+
```

In that section, a technique using LPAD( ) was shown for making sure the month values have two digits:

```
mysql> SELECT d, CONCAT(YEAR(d),'-',LPAD(MONTH(d),2,'0'),'-01') FROM date_val;
+------------+-----------------------------------------------+
| d          | CONCAT(YEAR(d),'-',LPAD(MONTH(d),2,'0'),'-01') |
+------------+-----------------------------------------------+
| 1864-02-28 | 1864-02-01                                    |
| 1900-01-15 | 1900-01-01                                    |
| 1987-03-05 | 1987-03-01                                    |
| 1999-12-31 | 1999-12-01                                    |
| 2000-06-04 | 2000-06-01                                    |
+------------+-----------------------------------------------+
```

Another way to standardize a close-to-ISO date is to use it in an expression that produces an ISO date result. For a date d, any of the following expressions will do:

```
DATE_ADD(d,INTERVAL 0 DAY)
d + INTERVAL 0 DAY
FROM_DAYS(TO_DAYS(d))
STR_TO_DATE(d,'%Y-%m-%d')
```

For example, the non-ISO results from the `CONCAT( )` operation can be converted into ISO format several different ways as follows:

```
mysql> SELECT
    -> CONCAT(YEAR(d),'-',MONTH(d),'-01') AS 'non-ISO',
    -> DATE_ADD(CONCAT(YEAR(d),'-',MONTH(d),'-01'),INTERVAL 0 DAY) AS 'ISO 1',
    -> CONCAT(YEAR(d),'-',MONTH(d),'-01') + INTERVAL 0 DAY AS 'ISO 2',
    -> FROM_DAYS(TO_DAYS(CONCAT(YEAR(d),'-',MONTH(d),'-01'))) AS 'ISO 3',
    -> STR_TO_DATE(CONCAT(YEAR(d),'-',MONTH(d),'-01'),'%Y-%m-%d') AS 'ISO 4'
    -> FROM date_val;
+------------+------------+------------+------------+------------+
| non-ISO    | ISO 1      | ISO 2      | ISO 3      | ISO 4      |
+------------+------------+------------+------------+------------+
| 1864-2-01  | 1864-02-01 | 1864-02-01 | 1864-02-01 | 1864-02-01 |
| 1900-1-01  | 1900-01-01 | 1900-01-01 | 1900-01-01 | 1900-01-01 |
| 1987-3-01  | 1987-03-01 | 1987-03-01 | 1987-03-01 | 1987-03-01 |
| 1999-12-01 | 1999-12-01 | 1999-12-01 | 1999-12-01 | 1999-12-01 |
| 2000-6-01  | 2000-06-01 | 2000-06-01 | 2000-06-01 | 2000-06-01 |
+------------+------------+------------+------------+------------+
```

See Also

Chapter 10 discusses leap year calculations in the context of date validation.

6.19 Treating Dates or Times as Numbers

Problem

You want to treat a temporal string as a number.

Solution

Perform a string-to-number conversion.

Discussion

In many cases, it is possible in MySQL to treat date and time values as numbers. This can sometimes be useful if you want to perform an arithmetic operation on the value. To force conversion of a temporal value to numeric form, add zero or use it in a numeric context:

```
mysql> SELECT t1,
    -> t1+0 AS 't1 as number',
    -> FLOOR(t1) AS 't1 as number',
    -> FLOOR(t1/10000) AS 'hour part'
    -> FROM time_val;
+----------+--------------+--------------+-----------+
| t1       | t1 as number | t1 as number | hour part |
+----------+--------------+--------------+-----------+
| 15:00:00 |       150000 |       150000 |        15 |
| 05:01:30 |        50130 |        50130 |         5 |
```

```
| 12:30:20 |        123020 |        123020 |     12 |
+----------+---------------+---------------+--------+
```

The same kind of conversion can be performed for date or date-and-time values. For
DATETIME columns, the conversion results in a fractional part. Use FLOOR( ) if that is not
desired:

```
mysql> SELECT d, d+0 FROM date_val;
+------------+----------+
| d          | d+0      |
+------------+----------+
| 1864-02-28 | 18640228 |
| 1900-01-15 | 19000115 |
| 1987-03-05 | 19870305 |
| 1999-12-31 | 19991231 |
| 2000-06-04 | 20000604 |
+------------+----------+
mysql> SELECT dt, dt+0, FLOOR(dt+0) FROM datetime_val;
+---------------------+----------------------+-----------------+
| dt                  | dt+0                 | FLOOR(dt+0)     |
+---------------------+----------------------+-----------------+
| 1970-01-01 00:00:00 | 19700101000000.000000 | 19700101000000 |
| 1987-03-05 12:30:15 | 19870305123015.000000 | 19870305123015 |
| 1999-12-31 09:00:00 | 19991231090000.000000 | 19991231090000 |
| 2000-06-04 15:45:30 | 20000604154530.000000 | 20000604154530 |
+---------------------+----------------------+-----------------+
```

A value produced by adding zero is not the same as that produced by conversion into
basic units like seconds or days. The result is essentially what you get by removing all
the delimiters from the string representation of the original value. Also, conversion to
numeric form works only for values that MySQL interprets temporally. If you try converting a literal string to a number by adding zero, you'll just get the first component
of the value. This is a conversion that can result in a warning:

```
mysql> SELECT '1999-01-01'+0, '1999-01-01 12:30:45'+0, '12:30:45'+0;
+---------------+-------------------------+--------------+
| '1999-01-01'+0 | '1999-01-01 12:30:45'+0 | '12:30:45'+0 |
+---------------+-------------------------+--------------+
|          1999 |                    1999 |           12 |
+---------------+-------------------------+--------------+
1 row in set, 3 warnings (0.00 sec)

mysql> SHOW WARNINGS;
+---------+------+----------------------------------------------------------+
| Level   | Code | Message                                                  |
+---------+------+----------------------------------------------------------+
| Warning | 1292 | Truncated incorrect DOUBLE value: '1999-01-01'           |
| Warning | 1292 | Truncated incorrect DOUBLE value: '1999-01-01 12:30:45'  |
| Warning | 1292 | Truncated incorrect DOUBLE value: '12:30:45'             |
+---------+------+----------------------------------------------------------+
```

This same thing happens if you add zero to the result of functions such as
DATE_FORMAT( ) and TIME_FORMAT( ), or if you pull out parts of DATETIME or TIMESTAMP
values with LEFT( ) or RIGHT( ). In +0 context, the results of these functions are treated

as strings, not temporal types, and conversion to a number uses only the first component of a string value.

6.20 Forcing MySQL to Treat Strings as Temporal Values

Problem

You want a string to be interpreted temporally.

Solution

Use the string in a temporal context to give MySQL a hint about how to treat it.

Discussion

If you need to make MySQL treat a string as a date or time, use it in an expression that provides a temporal context without changing the value. For example, you can't add zero to a literal TIME-formatted string to effect a time-to-number conversion, but if you use TIME_TO_SEC( ) and SEC_TO_TIME( ), you can. The two columns of the following result demonstrate this:

```
mysql> SELECT '12:30:45'+0, SEC_TO_TIME(TIME_TO_SEC('12:30:45'))+0;
+-------------+----------------------------------------+
| '12:30:45'+0 | SEC_TO_TIME(TIME_TO_SEC('12:30:45'))+0 |
+-------------+----------------------------------------+
|          12 |                                 123045 |
+-------------+----------------------------------------+
```

In the second column, the conversion to and from seconds leaves the value unchanged but results in a context where MySQL treats the result as a TIME value. For date values, the procedure is similar, but uses TO_DAYS( ) and FROM_DAYS( ):

```
mysql> SELECT '1999-01-01'+0, FROM_DAYS(TO_DAYS('1999-01-01'))+0;
+---------------+------------------------------------+
| '1999-01-01'+0 | FROM_DAYS(TO_DAYS('1999-01-01'))+0 |
+---------------+------------------------------------+
|          1999 |                           19990101 |
+---------------+------------------------------------+
```

For date-and-time values, you can use DATE_ADD( ) to introduce a temporal context:

```
mysql> SELECT
    -> DATE_ADD('1999-01-01 12:30:45',INTERVAL 0 DAY)+0 AS 'numeric datetime';
+------------------+
| numeric datetime |
+------------------+
|   19990101123045 |
+------------------+
```

6.21 Selecting Rows Based on Their Temporal Characteristics

Problem

You want to select rows based on temporal constraints.

Solution

Use a date or time condition in the WHERE clause. This may be based on direct comparison of column values with known values. Or it may be necessary to apply a function to column values to convert them to a more appropriate form for testing, such as using MONTH( ) to test the month part of a date.

Discussion

Most of the preceding date-based techniques were illustrated by example statements that produce date or time values as output. You can use the same techniques in WHERE clauses to place date-based restrictions on the rows selected by a statement. For example, you can select rows by looking for values that occur before or after a given date, within a date range, or that match particular month or day values.

Comparing dates to one another

The following statements find rows from the date_val table that occur either before 1900 or during the 1900s:

```
mysql> SELECT d FROM date_val where d < '1900-01-01';
+------------+
| d          |
+------------+
| 1864-02-28 |
+------------+
mysql> SELECT d FROM date_val where d BETWEEN '1900-01-01' AND '1999-12-31';
+------------+
| d          |
+------------+
| 1900-01-15 |
| 1987-03-05 |
| 1999-12-31 |
+------------+
```

When you don't know the exact date you want for a WHERE clause, you can often calculate it using an expression. For example, to perform an "on this day in history" statement to search for rows in a table history to find events occurring exactly 50 years ago, do this:

```
SELECT * FROM history WHERE d = DATE_SUB(CURDATE(),INTERVAL 50 YEAR);
```

You see this kind of thing in newspapers that run columns showing what the news events were in times past. (In essence, the statement identifies those events that have reached their *n*-th anniversary.) If you want to retrieve events that occurred "on this day" for any year rather than "on this date" for a specific year, the statement is a bit different. In that case, you need to find rows that match the current calendar day, ignoring the year. That topic is discussed in "Comparing dates to calendar days" later in this recipe.

Calculated dates are useful for range testing as well. For example, to find dates that occur within the last seven years, use DATE_SUB( ) to calculate the cutoff date:

```
mysql> SELECT d FROM date_val WHERE d >= DATE_SUB(CURDATE(),INTERVAL 7 YEAR);
+------------+
| d          |
+------------+
| 1999-12-31 |
| 2000-06-04 |
+------------+
```

Note that the expression in the WHERE clause isolates the date column d on one side of the comparison operator. This is usually a good idea; if the column is indexed, placing it alone on one side of a comparison enables MySQL to process the statement more efficiently. To illustrate, the preceding WHERE clause can be written in a way that's logically equivalent but much less efficient for MySQL to execute:

```
... WHERE DATE_ADD(d,INTERVAL 7 YEAR) >= CURDATE();
```

Here, the d column is used within an expression. That means *every* row must be retrieved so that the expression can be evaluated and tested, which makes any index on the column useless.

Sometimes it's not so obvious how to rewrite a comparison to isolate a date column on one side. For example, the following WHERE clause uses only part of the date column in the comparisons:

```
...WHERE YEAR(d) >= 1987 AND YEAR(d) <= 1991;
```

To rewrite the first comparison, eliminate the YEAR( ) call, and replace its right side with a complete date:

```
...WHERE d >= '1987-01-01' AND YEAR(d) <= 1991;
```

Rewriting the second comparison is a little trickier. You can eliminate the YEAR( ) call on the left side, just as with the first expression, but you can't just add -01-01 to the year on the right side. That produces the following result, which is incorrect:

```
...WHERE d >= '1987-01-01' AND d <= '1991-01-01';
```

That fails because dates from 1991-01-02 to 1991-12-31 fail the test, but should pass. To rewrite the second comparison correctly, either of the following will do:

```
...WHERE d >= '1987-01-01' AND d <= '1991-12-31';
...WHERE d >= '1987-01-01' AND d < '1992-01-01';
```

Another use for calculated dates occurs frequently in applications that create rows that have a limited lifetime. Such applications must be able to determine which rows to delete when performing an expiration operation. You can approach this problem a couple of ways:

- Store a date in each row indicating when it was created. (Do this by making the column a TIMESTAMP or by setting it to NOW( ); see Recipe 6.5 for details.) To perform an expiration operation later, determine which rows have a creation date that is too old by comparing that date to the current date. For example, the statement to expire rows that were created more than *n* days ago might look like this:

```
DELETE FROM mytbl WHERE create_date < DATE_SUB(NOW(),INTERVAL n DAY);
```

- Store an explicit expiration date in each row by calculating the expiration date with DATE_ADD( ) when the row is created. For a row that should expire in *n* days, you can do this:

```
INSERT INTO mytbl (expire_date,...)
VALUES(DATE_ADD(NOW(),INTERVAL n DAY),...);
```

To perform the expiration operation in this case, compare the expiration dates to the current date to see which ones have been reached:

```
DELETE FROM mytbl WHERE expire_date < NOW();
```

Comparing times to one another

Comparisons involving times are similar to those involving dates. For example, to find times that occurred from 9 AM to 2 PM, use an expression like one of the following:

```
...WHERE t1 BETWEEN '09:00:00' AND '14:00:00';
...WHERE HOUR(t1) BETWEEN 9 AND 14;
```

For an indexed TIME column, the first method would be more efficient. The second method has the property that it works not only for TIME columns, but for DATETIME and TIMESTAMP columns as well.

Comparing dates to calendar days

To answer questions about particular days of the year, use calendar day testing. The following examples illustrate how to do this in the context of looking for birthdays:

- Who has a birthday today? This requires matching a particular calendar day, so you extract the month and day but ignore the year when performing comparisons:

```
...WHERE MONTH(d) = MONTH(CURDATE()) AND DAYOFMONTH(d) = DAYOFMONTH(CURDATE());
```

This kind of statement commonly is applied to biographical data to find lists of actors, politicians, musicians, and so forth, who were born on a particular day of the year.

It's tempting to use DAYOFYEAR( ) to solve "on this day" problems, because it results in simpler statements. But DAYOFYEAR( ) doesn't work properly for leap years. The presence of February 29 throws off the values for days from March through December.

- Who has a birthday this month? In this case, it's necessary to check only the month:

  ```
  ...WHERE MONTH(d) = MONTH(CURDATE());
  ```

- Who has a birthday next month? The trick here is that you can't just add one to the current month to get the month number that qualifying dates must match. That gives you 13 for dates in December. To make sure that you get 1 (January), use either of the following techniques:

  ```
  ...WHERE MONTH(d) = MONTH(DATE_ADD(CURDATE(),INTERVAL 1 MONTH));
  ...WHERE MONTH(d) = MOD(MONTH(CURDATE()),12)+1;
  ```

## CHAPTER 7

Sorting Query Results

7.0 Introduction

This chapter covers sorting, an operation that is extremely important for controlling how MySQL displays results from **SELECT** statements. Sorting is performed by adding an **ORDER BY** clause to a query. Without such a clause, MySQL is free to return rows in any order, so sorting helps bring order to disorder and makes query results easier to examine and understand. (Sorting is also performed implicitly when you use a **GROUP BY** clause, as discussed in Recipe 8.13.)

You can sort rows of a query result several ways:

- Using a single column, a combination of columns, or even parts of columns
- Using ascending or descending order
- Using the result of an expression
- Using case-sensitive or case-insensitive string comparisons
- Using temporal ordering

The `driver_log` table is used for several examples in this chapter; it contains columns for recording daily mileage logs for a set of truck drivers:

```
mysql> SELECT * FROM driver_log;
+--------+-------+------------+-------+
| rec_id | name  | trav_date  | miles |
+--------+-------+------------+-------+
|      1 | Ben   | 2006-08-30 |   152 |
|      2 | Suzi  | 2006-08-29 |   391 |
|      3 | Henry | 2006-08-29 |   300 |
|      4 | Henry | 2006-08-27 |    96 |
|      5 | Ben   | 2006-08-29 |   131 |
|      6 | Henry | 2006-08-26 |   115 |
|      7 | Suzi  | 2006-09-02 |   502 |
|      8 | Henry | 2006-09-01 |   197 |
|      9 | Ben   | 2006-09-02 |    79 |
|     10 | Henry | 2006-08-30 |   203 |
+--------+-------+------------+-------+
```

Many other examples use the `mail` table (used in earlier chapters):

```
mysql> SELECT * FROM mail;
+---------------------+---------+---------+---------+---------+---------+
| t                   | srcuser | srchost | dstuser | dsthost | size    |
+---------------------+---------+---------+---------+---------+---------+
| 2006-05-11 10:15:08 | barb    | saturn  | tricia  | mars    |   58274 |
| 2006-05-12 12:48:13 | tricia  | mars    | gene    | venus   |  194925 |
| 2006-05-12 15:02:49 | phil    | mars    | phil    | saturn  |    1048 |
| 2006-05-13 13:59:18 | barb    | saturn  | tricia  | venus   |     271 |
| 2006-05-14 09:31:37 | gene    | venus   | barb    | mars    |    2291 |
| 2006-05-14 11:52:17 | phil    | mars    | tricia  | saturn  |    5781 |
| 2006-05-14 14:42:21 | barb    | venus   | barb    | venus   |   98151 |
| 2006-05-14 17:03:01 | tricia  | saturn  | phil    | venus   | 2394482 |
| 2006-05-15 07:17:48 | gene    | mars    | gene    | saturn  |    3824 |
| 2006-05-15 08:50:57 | phil    | venus   | phil    | venus   |     978 |
| 2006-05-15 10:25:52 | gene    | mars    | tricia  | saturn  |  998532 |
| 2006-05-15 17:35:31 | gene    | saturn  | gene    | mars    |    3856 |
| 2006-05-16 09:00:28 | gene    | venus   | barb    | mars    |     613 |
| 2006-05-16 23:04:19 | phil    | venus   | barb    | venus   |   10294 |
| 2006-05-17 12:49:23 | phil    | mars    | tricia  | saturn  |     873 |
| 2006-05-19 22:21:51 | gene    | saturn  | gene    | venus   |   23992 |
+---------------------+---------+---------+---------+---------+---------+
```

Other tables are used occasionally as well. You can create most of them with scripts found in the *tables* directory of the `recipes` distribution.

7.1 Using ORDER BY to Sort Query Results

Problem

Output rows from a query don't come out in the order you want.

Solution

Add an ORDER BY clause to the query to sort the result rows.

Discussion

The contents of the `driver_log` and `mail` tables shown in the chapter introduction are disorganized and difficult to make any sense of. The exception is that the values in the id and t columns are in order, but that's just coincidental. Rows do tend to be returned from a table in the order they were originally inserted, but only until the table is subjected to delete and update operations. Rows inserted after that are likely to be returned in the middle of the result set somewhere. Many MySQL users notice this disturbance in row retrieval order, which leads them to ask, "How can I store rows in my table so they come out in a particular order when I retrieve them?" The answer to this question is, "That's the wrong question." Storing rows is the server's job, and you should let the server do it. Besides, even if you can specify storage order, how would that help you if you want to see results sorted in different orders at different times?

When you select rows, they're pulled out of the database and returned in whatever order the server happens to use. This order might change, even for statements that don't sort rows, depending on which index the server happens to use when it executes a statement, because the index can affect the retrieval order. Even if your rows appear to come out in the proper order naturally, a relational database makes no guarantee about the order in which it returns rows—unless you tell it how. To arrange the rows from a query result into a specific order, sort them by adding an ORDER BY clause to your SELECT statement. Without ORDER BY, you may find that the retrieval order changes when you modify the contents of your table. With an ORDER BY clause, MySQL will always sort rows the way you indicate.

ORDER BY has the following general characteristics:

- You can sort using a single column of values or multiple columns.
- You can sort any column in either ascending order (the default) or descending order.
- You can refer to sort columns by name or by using an alias.

This section shows some basic sorting techniques, such as how to name the sort columns and specify the sort direction. The following sections illustrate how to perform more complex sorts. Paradoxically, you can even use ORDER BY to *disorder* a result set, which is useful for randomizing the rows or (in conjunction with LIMIT) for picking a row at random from a result set. Those uses for ORDER BY are described in Chapter 13.

The following set of examples demonstrates how to sort on a single column or multiple columns and how to sort in ascending or descending order. The examples select the rows in the driver_log table but sort them in different orders so that you can compare the effect of the different ORDER BY clauses.

This query produces a single-column sort using the driver name:

```
mysql> SELECT * FROM driver_log ORDER BY name;
+--------+-------+------------+-------+
| rec_id | name  | trav_date  | miles |
+--------+-------+------------+-------+
|      1 | Ben   | 2006-08-30 |   152 |
|      9 | Ben   | 2006-09-02 |    79 |
|      5 | Ben   | 2006-08-29 |   131 |
|      8 | Henry | 2006-09-01 |   197 |
|      6 | Henry | 2006-08-26 |   115 |
|      4 | Henry | 2006-08-27 |    96 |
|      3 | Henry | 2006-08-29 |   300 |
|     10 | Henry | 2006-08-30 |   203 |
|      7 | Suzi  | 2006-09-02 |   502 |
|      2 | Suzi  | 2006-08-29 |   391 |
+--------+-------+------------+-------+
```

The default sort direction is ascending. You can make the direction for an ascending sort explicit by adding ASC after the sorted column's name:

```
SELECT * FROM driver_log ORDER BY name ASC;
```

The opposite (or reverse) of ascending order is descending order, specified by adding DESC after the sorted column's name:

```
mysql> SELECT * FROM driver_log ORDER BY name DESC;
+--------+-------+------------+-------+
| rec_id | name  | trav_date  | miles |
+--------+-------+------------+-------+
|      2 | Suzi  | 2006-08-29 |   391 |
|      7 | Suzi  | 2006-09-02 |   502 |
|     10 | Henry | 2006-08-30 |   203 |
|      8 | Henry | 2006-09-01 |   197 |
|      6 | Henry | 2006-08-26 |   115 |
|      4 | Henry | 2006-08-27 |    96 |
|      3 | Henry | 2006-08-29 |   300 |
|      5 | Ben   | 2006-08-29 |   131 |
|      9 | Ben   | 2006-09-02 |    79 |
|      1 | Ben   | 2006-08-30 |   152 |
+--------+-------+------------+-------+
```

If you closely examine the output from the queries just shown, you'll notice that although the rows are sorted by name, the rows for any given name aren't in any special order. (The trav_date values aren't in date order for Henry or Ben, for example.) That's because MySQL doesn't sort something unless you tell it to:

- The overall order of rows returned by a query is indeterminate unless you specify an ORDER BY clause.

- Within a group of rows that sort together based on the values in a given column, the order of values in other columns also is indeterminate unless you name them in the ORDER BY clause.

To more fully control output order, specify a multiple-column sort by listing each column to use for sorting, separated by commas. The following query sorts in ascending order by name and by trav_date within the rows for each name:

```
mysql> SELECT * FROM driver_log ORDER BY name, trav_date;
+--------+-------+------------+-------+
| rec_id | name  | trav_date  | miles |
+--------+-------+------------+-------+
|      5 | Ben   | 2006-08-29 |   131 |
|      1 | Ben   | 2006-08-30 |   152 |
|      9 | Ben   | 2006-09-02 |    79 |
|      6 | Henry | 2006-08-26 |   115 |
|      4 | Henry | 2006-08-27 |    96 |
|      3 | Henry | 2006-08-29 |   300 |
|     10 | Henry | 2006-08-30 |   203 |
|      8 | Henry | 2006-09-01 |   197 |
|      2 | Suzi  | 2006-08-29 |   391 |
|      7 | Suzi  | 2006-09-02 |   502 |
+--------+-------+------------+-------+
```

Multiple-column sorts can be descending as well, but DESC must be specified after each column name to perform a fully descending sort:

```
mysql> SELECT * FROM driver_log ORDER BY name DESC, trav_date DESC;
+--------+-------+------------+-------+
| rec_id | name  | trav_date  | miles |
+--------+-------+------------+-------+
|      7 | Suzi  | 2006-09-02 |   502 |
|      2 | Suzi  | 2006-08-29 |   391 |
|      8 | Henry | 2006-09-01 |   197 |
|     10 | Henry | 2006-08-30 |   203 |
|      3 | Henry | 2006-08-29 |   300 |
|      4 | Henry | 2006-08-27 |    96 |
|      6 | Henry | 2006-08-26 |   115 |
|      9 | Ben   | 2006-09-02 |    79 |
|      1 | Ben   | 2006-08-30 |   152 |
|      5 | Ben   | 2006-08-29 |   131 |
+--------+-------+------------+-------+
```

Multiple-column ORDER BY clauses can perform mixed-order sorting where some columns are sorted in ascending order and others in descending order. The following query sorts by name in descending order and then by trav_date in ascending order for each name:

```
mysql> SELECT * FROM driver_log ORDER BY name DESC, trav_date;
+--------+-------+------------+-------+
| rec_id | name  | trav_date  | miles |
+--------+-------+------------+-------+
|      2 | Suzi  | 2006-08-29 |   391 |
|      7 | Suzi  | 2006-09-02 |   502 |
|      6 | Henry | 2006-08-26 |   115 |
|      4 | Henry | 2006-08-27 |    96 |
|      3 | Henry | 2006-08-29 |   300 |
|     10 | Henry | 2006-08-30 |   203 |
|      8 | Henry | 2006-09-01 |   197 |
|      5 | Ben   | 2006-08-29 |   131 |
|      1 | Ben   | 2006-08-30 |   152 |
|      9 | Ben   | 2006-09-02 |    79 |
+--------+-------+------------+-------+
```

The ORDER BY clauses in the queries shown thus far refer to the sorted columns by name. You can also name the columns by using aliases. That is, if an output column has an alias, you can refer to the alias in the ORDER BY clause:

```
mysql> SELECT name, trav_date, miles AS distance FROM driver_log
    -> ORDER BY distance;
+-------+------------+----------+
| name  | trav_date  | distance |
+-------+------------+----------+
| Ben   | 2006-09-02 |       79 |
| Henry | 2006-08-27 |       96 |
| Henry | 2006-08-26 |      115 |
| Ben   | 2006-08-29 |      131 |
| Ben   | 2006-08-30 |      152 |
| Henry | 2006-09-01 |      197 |
```

```
| Henry  | 2006-08-30 |       203 |
| Henry  | 2006-08-29 |       300 |
| Suzi   | 2006-08-29 |       391 |
| Suzi   | 2006-09-02 |       502 |
+--------+------------+-----------+
```

Columns specified by aliases can be sorted in either ascending or descending order, just like named columns:

```
mysql> SELECT name, trav_date, miles AS distance FROM driver_log
    -> ORDER BY distance DESC;
+--------+------------+----------+
| name   | trav_date  | distance |
+--------+------------+----------+
| Suzi   | 2006-09-02 |      502 |
| Suzi   | 2006-08-29 |      391 |
| Henry  | 2006-08-29 |      300 |
| Henry  | 2006-08-30 |      203 |
| Henry  | 2006-09-01 |      197 |
| Ben    | 2006-08-30 |      152 |
| Ben    | 2006-08-29 |      131 |
| Henry  | 2006-08-26 |      115 |
| Henry  | 2006-08-27 |       96 |
| Ben    | 2006-09-02 |       79 |
+--------+------------+----------+
```

Should You Sort Query Results Yourself?

If you're issuing a SELECT statement from within one of your own programs, you can retrieve an unsorted result set into a data structure, and then sort the data structure using your programming language. But why reinvent the wheel? The MySQL server is built to sort efficiently, and you may as well let it do its job.

A possible exception to this principle occurs when you need to sort a set of rows several different ways. In this case, rather than issuing several queries that differ only in the ORDER BY clause, it might be faster to retrieve the rows once, and re-sort them as necessary within your program. The attractiveness of this strategy generally diminishes if your result sets are very large and sorting them will use lots of memory and processing time.

7.2 Using Expressions for Sorting

Problem

You want to sort a query result based on values calculated from a column, rather than using the values actually stored in the column.

Solution

Put the expression that calculates the values in the ORDER BY clause.

Discussion

One of the columns in the `mail` table shows how large each mail message is, in bytes:

```
mysql> SELECT * FROM mail;
+---------------------+---------+---------+---------+---------+---------+
| t                   | srcuser | srchost | dstuser | dsthost | size    |
+---------------------+---------+---------+---------+---------+---------+
| 2006-05-11 10:15:08 | barb    | saturn  | tricia  | mars    |   58274 |
| 2006-05-12 12:48:13 | tricia  | mars    | gene    | venus   |  194925 |
| 2006-05-12 15:02:49 | phil    | mars    | phil    | saturn  |    1048 |
| 2006-05-13 13:59:18 | barb    | saturn  | tricia  | venus   |     271 |
...
```

Suppose that you want to retrieve rows for "big" mail messages (defined as those larger than 50,000 bytes), but you want them to be displayed and sorted by sizes in terms of kilobytes, not bytes. In this case, the values to sort are calculated by an expression:

```
FLOOR((size+1023)/1024)
```

Wondering about the `+1023` in the `FLOOR( )` expression? That's there so that `size` values group to the nearest upper boundary of the 1024-byte categories. Without it, the values group by lower boundaries (for example, a 2047-byte message would be reported as having a size of 1 kilobyte rather than 2). This technique is discussed in more detail in Recipe 8.12.

There are two ways to use an expression for sorting query results. First, you can put the expression directly in the `ORDER BY` clause:

```
mysql> SELECT t, srcuser, FLOOR((size+1023)/1024)
    -> FROM mail WHERE size > 50000
    -> ORDER BY FLOOR((size+1023)/1024);
+---------------------+---------+-------------------------+
| t                   | srcuser | FLOOR((size+1023)/1024) |
+---------------------+---------+-------------------------+
| 2006-05-11 10:15:08 | barb    |                      57 |
| 2006-05-14 14:42:21 | barb    |                      96 |
| 2006-05-12 12:48:13 | tricia  |                     191 |
| 2006-05-15 10:25:52 | gene    |                     976 |
| 2006-05-14 17:03:01 | tricia  |                    2339 |
+---------------------+---------+-------------------------+
```

Second, if you are sorting by an expression named in the output column list, you can give it an alias and refer to the alias in the `ORDER BY` clause:

```
mysql> SELECT t, srcuser, FLOOR((size+1023)/1024) AS kilobytes
    -> FROM mail WHERE size > 50000
    -> ORDER BY kilobytes;
+---------------------+---------+-----------+
| t                   | srcuser | kilobytes |
+---------------------+---------+-----------+
| 2006-05-11 10:15:08 | barb    |        57 |
| 2006-05-14 14:42:21 | barb    |        96 |
| 2006-05-12 12:48:13 | tricia  |       191 |
| 2006-05-15 10:25:52 | gene    |       976 |
```

```
| 2006-05-14 17:03:01 | tricia  |      2339 |
+---------------------+---------+-----------+
```

Although you can write the ORDER BY clause either way, there are at least two reasons you might prefer to use the alias method:

- It's easier to write the alias in the ORDER BY clause than to repeat the (rather cumbersome) expression—and if you change one, you'll need to change the other.
- The alias may be useful for display purposes, to provide a more meaningful column label. Note how the third column heading for the second of the two preceding queries is more meaningful.

7.3 Displaying One Set of Values While Sorting by Another

Problem

You want to sort a result set using values that you're not selecting.

Solution

That's not a problem. You can use columns in the ORDER BY clause that don't appear in the output column list.

Discussion

ORDER BY is not limited to sorting only those columns named in the output column list. It can sort using values that are "hidden" (that is, not displayed in the query output). This technique is commonly used when you have values that can be represented different ways and you want to display one type of value but sort by another. For example, you may want to display mail message sizes not in terms of bytes, but as strings such as 103K for 103 kilobytes. You can convert a byte count to that kind of value using this expression:

```
CONCAT(FLOOR((size+1023)/1024),'K')
```

However, such values are strings, so they sort lexically, not numerically. If you use them for sorting, a value such as 96K sorts after 2339K, even though it represents a smaller number:

```
mysql> SELECT t, srcuser,
    -> CONCAT(FLOOR((size+1023)/1024),'K') AS size_in_K
    -> FROM mail WHERE size > 50000
    -> ORDER BY size_in_K;
+---------------------+---------+-----------+
| t                   | srcuser | size_in_K |
+---------------------+---------+-----------+
| 2006-05-12 12:48:13 | tricia  | 191K      |
| 2006-05-14 17:03:01 | tricia  | 2339K     |
| 2006-05-11 10:15:08 | barb    | 57K       |
```

```
| 2006-05-14 14:42:21 | barb   | 96K    |
| 2006-05-15 10:25:52 | gene   | 976K   |
+---------------------+--------+--------+
```

To achieve the desired output order, display the string, but use the actual numeric size for sorting:

```
mysql> SELECT t, srcuser,
    -> CONCAT(FLOOR((size+1023)/1024),'K') AS size_in_K
    -> FROM mail WHERE size > 50000
    -> ORDER BY size;
+---------------------+---------+-----------+
| t                   | srcuser | size_in_K |
+---------------------+---------+-----------+
| 2006-05-11 10:15:08 | barb    | 57K       |
| 2006-05-14 14:42:21 | barb    | 96K       |
| 2006-05-12 12:48:13 | tricia  | 191K      |
| 2006-05-15 10:25:52 | gene    | 976K      |
| 2006-05-14 17:03:01 | tricia  | 2339K     |
+---------------------+---------+-----------+
```

Displaying values as strings but sorting them as numbers also can bail you out of some otherwise difficult situations. Members of sports teams typically are assigned a jersey number, which normally you might think should be stored using a numeric column. Not so fast! Some players like to have a jersey number of zero (0), and some like double-zero (00). If a team happens to have players with both numbers, you cannot represent them using a numeric column, because both values will be treated as the same number. The way out of the problem is to store jersey numbers as strings:

```
CREATE TABLE roster
(
  name        CHAR(30),    # player name
  jersey_num  CHAR(3)      # jersey number
);
```

Then the jersey numbers will display the same way you enter them, and 0 and 00 will be treated as distinct values. Unfortunately, although representing numbers as strings solves the problem of distinguishing 0 and 00, it introduces a different problem. Suppose that a team has the following players:

```
mysql> SELECT name, jersey_num FROM roster;
+-----------+------------+
| name      | jersey_num |
+-----------+------------+
| Lynne     | 29         |
| Ella      | 0          |
| Elizabeth | 100        |
| Nancy     | 00         |
| Jean      | 8          |
| Sherry    | 47         |
+-----------+------------+
```

The problem occurs when you try to sort the team members by jersey number. If those numbers are stored as strings, they'll sort lexically, and lexical order often differs from numeric order. That's certainly true for the team in question:

```
mysql> SELECT name, jersey_num FROM roster ORDER BY jersey_num;
+-----------+------------+
| name      | jersey_num |
+-----------+------------+
| Ella      | 0          |
| Nancy     | 00         |
| Elizabeth | 100        |
| Lynne     | 29         |
| Sherry    | 47         |
| Jean      | 8          |
+-----------+------------+
```

The values 100 and 8 are out of place. But that's easily solved. Display the string values, but use the numeric values for sorting. To accomplish this, add zero to the jersey_num values to force a string-to-number conversion:

```
mysql> SELECT name, jersey_num FROM roster ORDER BY jersey_num+0;
+-----------+------------+
| name      | jersey_num |
+-----------+------------+
| Ella      | 0          |
| Nancy     | 00         |
| Jean      | 8          |
| Lynne     | 29         |
| Sherry    | 47         |
| Elizabeth | 100        |
+-----------+------------+
```

The technique of displaying one value but sorting by another is also useful when you want to display composite values that are formed from multiple columns but that don't sort the way you want. For example, the mail table lists message senders using separate srcuser and srchost values. If you want to display message senders from the mail table as email addresses in srcuser@srchost format with the username first, you can construct those values using the following expression:

```
CONCAT(srcuser,'@',srchost)
```

However, those values are no good for sorting if you want to treat the hostname as more significant than the username. Instead, sort the results using the underlying column values rather than the displayed composite values:

```
mysql> SELECT t, CONCAT(srcuser,'@',srchost) AS sender, size
    -> FROM mail WHERE size > 50000
    -> ORDER BY srchost, srcuser;
+---------------------+-------------+--------+
| t                   | sender      | size   |
+---------------------+-------------+--------+
| 2006-05-15 10:25:52 | gene@mars   | 998532 |
| 2006-05-12 12:48:13 | tricia@mars | 194925 |
| 2006-05-11 10:15:08 | barb@saturn |  58274 |
```

```
| 2006-05-14 17:03:01 | tricia@saturn | 2394482 |
| 2006-05-14 14:42:21 | barb@venus    |   98151 |
+---------------------+---------------+---------+
```

The same idea commonly is applied to sorting people's names. Suppose that you have a table names that contains last and first names. To display rows sorted by last name first, the query is straightforward when the columns are displayed separately:

```
mysql> SELECT last_name, first_name FROM name
    -> ORDER BY last_name, first_name;
+-----------+------------+
| last_name | first_name |
+-----------+------------+
| Blue      | Vida       |
| Brown     | Kevin      |
| Gray      | Pete       |
| White     | Devon      |
| White     | Rondell    |
+-----------+------------+
```

If instead you want to display each name as a single string composed of the first name, a space, and the last name, you can begin the query like this:

```
SELECT CONCAT(first_name,' ',last_name) AS full_name FROM name ...
```

But then how do you sort the names so they come out in the last name order? The answer is to display the composite names, but refer to the constituent values in the ORDER BY clause:

```
mysql> SELECT CONCAT(first_name,' ',last_name) AS full_name
    -> FROM name
    -> ORDER BY last_name, first_name;
+---------------+
| full_name     |
+---------------+
| Vida Blue     |
| Kevin Brown   |
| Pete Gray     |
| Devon White   |
| Rondell White |
+---------------+
```

7.4 Controlling Case Sensitivity of String Sorts

Problem

String sorting operations are case-sensitive when you don't want them to be, or vice versa.

Solution

Alter the comparison characteristics of the sorted values.

Discussion

Chapter 5 discusses how string comparison properties depend on whether the strings are binary or nonbinary:

- Binary strings are sequences of bytes. They are compared byte by byte using numeric byte values. Character set and lettercase have no meaning for comparisons.
- Nonbinary strings are sequences of characters. They have a character set and collation and are compared character by character using the order defined by the collation.

These properties apply to string sorting as well, because sorting is based on comparison. To alter the sorting properties of a string column, you must alter its comparison properties. (For a summary of which string data types are binary and nonbinary, see Recipe 5.2.)

The examples in this section use a table that has case-insensitive and case-sensitive nonbinary columns, and a binary column:

```
CREATE TABLE str_val
(
  ci_str   CHAR(3) CHARACTER SET latin1 COLLATE latin1_swedish_ci,
  cs_str   CHAR(3) CHARACTER SET latin1 COLLATE latin1_general_cs,
  bin_str  BINARY(3)
);
```

Suppose that the table has the following contents:

```
+--------+--------+---------+
| ci_str | cs_str | bin_str |
+--------+--------+---------+
| AAA    | AAA    | AAA     |
| aaa    | aaa    | aaa     |
| bbb    | bbb    | bbb     |
| BBB    | BBB    | BBB     |
+--------+--------+---------+
```

Each column contains the same values, but the natural sort orders for the column data types produce three different results:

- The case-insensitive collation sorts a and A together, placing them before b and B. However, for a given letter, it does not necessarily order one lettercase before another, as shown by the following result:

```
mysql> SELECT ci_str FROM str_val ORDER BY ci_str;
+--------+
| ci_str |
+--------+
| AAA    |
| aaa    |
| bbb    |
| BBB    |
+--------+
```

- The case-sensitive collation puts A and a before B and b, and sorts uppercase before lowercase:

```
mysql> SELECT cs_str FROM str_val ORDER BY cs_str;
+--------+
| cs_str |
+--------+
| AAA    |
| aaa    |
| BBB    |
| bbb    |
+--------+
```

- The binary strings sort numerically. Assuming that uppercase letters have numeric values less than those of lowercase letters, a binary sort results in the following ordering:

```
mysql> SELECT bin_str FROM str_val ORDER BY bin_str;
+---------+
| bin_str |
+---------+
| AAA     |
| BBB     |
| aaa     |
| bbb     |
+---------+
```

You get the same result for a nonbinary string column that has a binary collation, as long as the column contains single-byte characters (for example, CHAR(3) CHARACTER SET latin1 COLLATE latin1_bin). For multibyte characters, a binary collation still produces a numeric sort, but the character values use multibyte numbers.

To alter the sorting properties of each column, use the techniques described in Recipe 5.9 for controlling how string comparisons work:

- To sort case-insensitive strings in case-sensitive fashion, order the sorted values using a case-sensitive collation:

```
mysql> SELECT ci_str FROM str_val
    -> ORDER BY ci_str COLLATE latin1_general_cs;
+--------+
| ci_str |
+--------+
| AAA    |
| aaa    |
| BBB    |
| bbb    |
+--------+
```

- To sort case-sensitive strings in case-insensitive fashion, order the sorted values using a case-insensitive collation:

```
mysql> SELECT cs_str FROM str_val
    -> ORDER BY cs_str COLLATE latin1_swedish_ci;
```

```
+--------+
| cs_str |
+--------+
| AAA    |
| aaa    |
| bbb    |
| BBB    |
+--------+
```

Another possibility is to sort using values that have all been converted to the same lettercase, which makes lettercase irrelevant:

```
mysql> SELECT cs_str FROM str_val
    -> ORDER BY UPPER(cs_str);
+--------+
| cs_str |
+--------+
| AAA    |
| aaa    |
| bbb    |
| BBB    |
+--------+
```

- Binary strings sort using numeric byte values, so there is no concept of lettercase involved. However, because letters in different cases have different byte values, comparisons of binary strings effectively are case-sensitive. (That is, a and A are unequal.) To sort binary strings using a case-insensitive ordering, convert them to nonbinary strings and apply an appropriate collation. For example, to perform a case-insensitive sort, use a statement like this:

```
mysql> SELECT bin_str FROM str_val
    -> ORDER BY CONVERT(bin_str USING latin1) COLLATE latin1_swedish_ci;
+---------+
| bin_str |
+---------+
| AAA     |
| aaa     |
| bbb     |
| BBB     |
+---------+
```

If the default collation is case-insensitive (as is true for latin1), you can omit the COLLATE clause.

7.5 Date-Based Sorting

Problem

You want to sort rows in temporal order.

Solution

Sort using a date or time data type. If some parts of the values are irrelevant for the sort that you want to accomplish, ignore them.

Discussion

Many database tables include date or time information and it's very often necessary to sort results in temporal order. MySQL knows how to sort temporal data types, so there's no special trick to ordering values in DATE, DATETIME, TIME, or TIMESTAMP columns. Let's begin with a table that contains values for each of those types:

```
mysql> SELECT * FROM temporal_val;
+------------+---------------------+----------+---------------------+
| d          | dt                  | t        | ts                  |
+------------+---------------------+----------+---------------------+
| 1970-01-01 | 1884-01-01 12:00:00 | 13:00:00 | 1980-01-01 02:00:00 |
| 1999-01-01 | 1860-01-01 12:00:00 | 19:00:00 | 2021-01-01 03:00:00 |
| 1981-01-01 | 1871-01-01 12:00:00 | 03:00:00 | 1975-01-01 04:00:00 |
| 1964-01-01 | 1899-01-01 12:00:00 | 01:00:00 | 1985-01-01 05:00:00 |
+------------+---------------------+----------+---------------------+
```

Using an ORDER BY clause with any of these columns sorts the values into the appropriate order:

```
mysql> SELECT * FROM temporal_val ORDER BY d;
+------------+---------------------+----------+---------------------+
| d          | dt                  | t        | ts                  |
+------------+---------------------+----------+---------------------+
| 1964-01-01 | 1899-01-01 12:00:00 | 01:00:00 | 1985-01-01 05:00:00 |
| 1970-01-01 | 1884-01-01 12:00:00 | 13:00:00 | 1980-01-01 02:00:00 |
| 1981-01-01 | 1871-01-01 12:00:00 | 03:00:00 | 1975-01-01 04:00:00 |
| 1999-01-01 | 1860-01-01 12:00:00 | 19:00:00 | 2021-01-01 03:00:00 |
+------------+---------------------+----------+---------------------+
mysql> SELECT * FROM temporal_val ORDER BY dt;
+------------+---------------------+----------+---------------------+
| d          | dt                  | t        | ts                  |
+------------+---------------------+----------+---------------------+
| 1999-01-01 | 1860-01-01 12:00:00 | 19:00:00 | 2021-01-01 03:00:00 |
| 1981-01-01 | 1871-01-01 12:00:00 | 03:00:00 | 1975-01-01 04:00:00 |
| 1970-01-01 | 1884-01-01 12:00:00 | 13:00:00 | 1980-01-01 02:00:00 |
| 1964-01-01 | 1899-01-01 12:00:00 | 01:00:00 | 1985-01-01 05:00:00 |
+------------+---------------------+----------+---------------------+
mysql> SELECT * FROM temporal_val ORDER BY t;
+------------+---------------------+----------+---------------------+
| d          | dt                  | t        | ts                  |
+------------+---------------------+----------+---------------------+
| 1964-01-01 | 1899-01-01 12:00:00 | 01:00:00 | 1985-01-01 05:00:00 |
| 1981-01-01 | 1871-01-01 12:00:00 | 03:00:00 | 1975-01-01 04:00:00 |
| 1970-01-01 | 1884-01-01 12:00:00 | 13:00:00 | 1980-01-01 02:00:00 |
| 1999-01-01 | 1860-01-01 12:00:00 | 19:00:00 | 2021-01-01 03:00:00 |
+------------+---------------------+----------+---------------------+
mysql> SELECT * FROM temporal_val ORDER BY ts;
+------------+---------------------+----------+---------------------+
| d          | dt                  | t        | ts                  |
```

```
+------------+---------------------+----------+---------------------+
| 1981-01-01 | 1871-01-01 12:00:00 | 03:00:00 | 1975-01-01 04:00:00 |
| 1970-01-01 | 1884-01-01 12:00:00 | 13:00:00 | 1980-01-01 02:00:00 |
| 1964-01-01 | 1899-01-01 12:00:00 | 01:00:00 | 1985-01-01 05:00:00 |
| 1999-01-01 | 1860-01-01 12:00:00 | 19:00:00 | 2021-01-01 03:00:00 |
+------------+---------------------+----------+---------------------+
```

Sometimes a temporal sort uses only part of a date or time column. In that case, use an expression that extracts the part or parts you need and sort the result using the expression. Some examples of this are given in the next few recipes.

7.6 Sorting by Calendar Day

Problem

You want to sort by day of the calendar year.

Solution

Sort using the month and day of date values, ignoring the year.

Discussion

Sorting in calendar order differs from sorting by date. You need to ignore the year part of the dates and sort using only the month and day to order rows in terms of where they fall during the calendar year. Suppose that you have an **event** table that looks like this when values are ordered by actual date of occurrence:

```
mysql> SELECT date, description FROM event ORDER BY date;
+------------+------------------------------------+
| date       | description                        |
+------------+------------------------------------+
| 1215-06-15 | Signing of the Magna Carta         |
| 1732-02-22 | George Washington's birthday       |
| 1776-07-14 | Bastille Day                       |
| 1789-07-04 | US Independence Day                |
| 1809-02-12 | Abraham Lincoln's birthday         |
| 1919-06-28 | Signing of the Treaty of Versailles|
| 1944-06-06 | D-Day at Normandy Beaches          |
| 1957-10-04 | Sputnik launch date                |
| 1958-01-31 | Explorer 1 launch date             |
| 1989-11-09 | Opening of the Berlin Wall         |
+------------+------------------------------------+
```

To put these items in calendar order, sort them by month, and then by day within month:

```
mysql> SELECT date, description FROM event
    -> ORDER BY MONTH(date), DAYOFMONTH(date);
+------------+------------------------------------+
| date       | description                        |
```

```
+------------+-----------------------------------+
| 1958-01-31 | Explorer 1 launch date            |
| 1809-02-12 | Abraham Lincoln's birthday        |
| 1732-02-22 | George Washington's birthday      |
| 1944-06-06 | D-Day at Normandy Beaches         |
| 1215-06-15 | Signing of the Magna Carta        |
| 1919-06-28 | Signing of the Treaty of Versailles |
| 1789-07-04 | US Independence Day               |
| 1776-07-14 | Bastille Day                      |
| 1957-10-04 | Sputnik launch date               |
| 1989-11-09 | Opening of the Berlin Wall        |
+------------+-----------------------------------+
```

MySQL also has a DAYOFYEAR( ) function that you might suspect would be useful for calendar day sorting:

```
mysql> SELECT date, description FROM event ORDER BY DAYOFYEAR(date);
+------------+-----------------------------------+
| date       | description                       |
+------------+-----------------------------------+
| 1958-01-31 | Explorer 1 launch date            |
| 1809-02-12 | Abraham Lincoln's birthday        |
| 1732-02-22 | George Washington's birthday      |
| 1944-06-06 | D-Day at Normandy Beaches         |
| 1215-06-15 | Signing of the Magna Carta        |
| 1919-06-28 | Signing of the Treaty of Versailles |
| 1789-07-04 | US Independence Day               |
| 1776-07-14 | Bastille Day                      |
| 1957-10-04 | Sputnik launch date               |
| 1989-11-09 | Opening of the Berlin Wall        |
+------------+-----------------------------------+
```

That appears to work, but only because the table doesn't have rows in it that expose a problem with using DAYOFYEAR( ) for sorting: it can generate the same value for different calendar days. For example, February 29 of leap years and March 1 of nonleap years have the same day-of-year value:

```
mysql> SELECT DAYOFYEAR('1996-02-29'), DAYOFYEAR('1997-03-01');
+-------------------------+-------------------------+
| DAYOFYEAR('1996-02-29') | DAYOFYEAR('1997-03-01') |
+-------------------------+-------------------------+
|                      60 |                      60 |
+-------------------------+-------------------------+
```

This property means that DAYOFYEAR( ) won't necessarily produce correct results for calendar sorting. It can group dates that actually occur on different calendar days.

If a table represents dates using separate year, month, and day columns, calendar sorting requires no date-part extraction. Just sort the relevant columns directly. For large datasets, sorting using separate date-part columns can be much faster than sorts based on extracting pieces of DATE values. There's no overhead for part extraction, but more important, you can index the date-part columns separately—something not possible with a DATE column. The principle here is that you should design the table to make it easy to extract or sort by the values that you expect to use a lot.

7.7 Sorting by Day of Week

Problem

You want to sort rows in day-of-week order.

Solution

Use DAYOFWEEK( ) to convert a date column to its numeric day-of-week value.

Discussion

Day-of-week sorting is similar to calendar-day sorting, except that you use different functions to get at the relevant ordering values.

You can get the day of the week using DAYNAME( ), but that produces strings that sort lexically rather than in day-of-week order (Sunday, Monday, Tuesday, and so forth). Here the technique of displaying one value but sorting by another is useful (see Recipe 7.3). Display day names using DAYNAME( ), but sort in day-of-week order using DAYOFWEEK( ), which returns numeric values from 1 to 7 for Sunday through Saturday:

```
mysql> SELECT DAYNAME(date) AS day, date, description
    -> FROM event
    -> ORDER BY DAYOFWEEK(date);
+----------+------------+------------------------------------+
| day      | date       | description                        |
+----------+------------+------------------------------------+
| Sunday   | 1809-02-12 | Abraham Lincoln's birthday         |
| Sunday   | 1776-07-14 | Bastille Day                       |
| Monday   | 1215-06-15 | Signing of the Magna Carta         |
| Tuesday  | 1944-06-06 | D-Day at Normandy Beaches          |
| Thursday | 1989-11-09 | Opening of the Berlin Wall         |
| Friday   | 1732-02-22 | George Washington's birthday       |
| Friday   | 1958-01-31 | Explorer 1 launch date             |
| Friday   | 1957-10-04 | Sputnik launch date                |
| Saturday | 1919-06-28 | Signing of the Treaty of Versailles|
| Saturday | 1789-07-04 | US Independence Day                |
+----------+------------+------------------------------------+
```

If you want to sort rows in day-of-week order but treat Monday as the first day of the week and Sunday as the last, you can use a the MOD( ) function to map Monday to 0, Tuesday to 1, ..., Sunday to 6:

```
mysql> SELECT DAYNAME(date), date, description
    -> FROM event
    -> ORDER BY MOD(DAYOFWEEK(date)+5, 7);
+---------------+------------+------------------------------------+
| DAYNAME(date) | date       | description                        |
+---------------+------------+------------------------------------+
| Monday        | 1215-06-15 | Signing of the Magna Carta         |
| Tuesday       | 1944-06-06 | D-Day at Normandy Beaches          |
| Thursday      | 1989-11-09 | Opening of the Berlin Wall         |
```

```
| Friday    | 1732-02-22 | George Washington's birthday      |
| Friday    | 1957-10-04 | Sputnik launch date               |
| Friday    | 1958-01-31 | Explorer 1 launch date            |
| Saturday  | 1789-07-04 | US Independence Day               |
| Saturday  | 1919-06-28 | Signing of the Treaty of Versailles |
| Sunday    | 1776-07-14 | Bastille Day                      |
| Sunday    | 1809-02-12 | Abraham Lincoln's birthday        |
+-----------+------------+-----------------------------------+
```

The following table shows the DAYOFWEEK( ) expressions to use for putting any day of the week first in the sort order:

Day to list first	DAYOFWEEK( ) expression
Sunday	DAYOFWEEK(date)
Monday	MOD(DAYOFWEEK(date)+5, 7)
Tuesday	MOD(DAYOFWEEK(date)+4, 7)
Wednesday	MOD(DAYOFWEEK(date)+3, 7)
Thursday	MOD(DAYOFWEEK(date)+2, 7)
Friday	MOD(DAYOFWEEK(date)+1, 7)
Saturday	MOD(DAYOFWEEK(date)+0, 7)

Another function that you can use for day-of-week sorting is WEEKDAY( ), although it returns a different set of values (0 for Monday through 6 for Sunday).

7.8 Sorting by Time of Day

Problem

You want to sort rows in time-of-day order.

Solution

Pull out the hour, minute, and second from the column that contains the time, and use them for sorting.

Discussion

Time-of-day sorting can be done different ways, depending on your column type. If the values are stored in a TIME column named timecol, just sort them directly using ORDER BY timecol. To put DATETIME or TIMESTAMP values in time-of-day order, extract the time parts and sort them. For example, the mail table contains DATETIME values, which can be sorted by time of day like this:

```
mysql> SELECT * FROM mail ORDER BY HOUR(t), MINUTE(t), SECOND(t);
+---------------------+---------+---------+---------+---------+---------+
| t                   | srcuser | srchost | dstuser | dsthost | size    |
```

```
+---------------------+---------+---------+---------+---------+---------+
| 2006-05-15 07:17:48 | gene    | mars    | gene    | saturn  |    3824 |
| 2006-05-15 08:50:57 | phil    | venus   | phil    | venus   |     978 |
| 2006-05-16 09:00:28 | gene    | venus   | barb    | mars    |     613 |
| 2006-05-14 09:31:37 | gene    | venus   | barb    | mars    |    2291 |
| 2006-05-11 10:15:08 | barb    | saturn  | tricia  | mars    |   58274 |
| 2006-05-15 10:25:52 | gene    | mars    | tricia  | saturn  |  998532 |
| 2006-05-14 11:52:17 | phil    | mars    | tricia  | saturn  |    5781 |
| 2006-05-12 12:48:13 | tricia  | mars    | gene    | venus   |  194925 |
...
```

You can also use TIME_TO_SEC( ), which strips off the date part and returns the time part as the corresponding number of seconds:

```
mysql> SELECT * FROM mail ORDER BY TIME_TO_SEC(t);
+---------------------+---------+---------+---------+---------+---------+
| t                   | srcuser | srchost | dstuser | dsthost | size    |
+---------------------+---------+---------+---------+---------+---------+
| 2006-05-15 07:17:48 | gene    | mars    | gene    | saturn  |    3824 |
| 2006-05-15 08:50:57 | phil    | venus   | phil    | venus   |     978 |
| 2006-05-16 09:00:28 | gene    | venus   | barb    | mars    |     613 |
| 2006-05-14 09:31:37 | gene    | venus   | barb    | mars    |    2291 |
| 2006-05-11 10:15:08 | barb    | saturn  | tricia  | mars    |   58274 |
| 2006-05-15 10:25:52 | gene    | mars    | tricia  | saturn  |  998532 |
| 2006-05-14 11:52:17 | phil    | mars    | tricia  | saturn  |    5781 |
| 2006-05-12 12:48:13 | tricia  | mars    | gene    | venus   |  194925 |
...
```

7.9 Sorting Using Substrings of Column Values

Problem

You want to sort a set of values using one or more substrings of each value.

Solution

Extract the hunks you want and sort them separately.

Discussion

This is a specific application of sorting by expression value (see Recipe 7.2). If you want to sort rows using just a particular portion of a column's values, extract the substring you need and use it in the ORDER BY clause. This is easiest if the substrings are at a fixed position and length within the column. For substrings of variable position or length, you may still be able to use them for sorting if there is some reliable way to identify them. The next several recipes show how to use substring extraction to produce specialized sort orders.

7.10 Sorting by Fixed-Length Substrings

Problem

You want to sort using parts of a column that occur at a given position within the column.

Solution

Pull out the parts you need with LEFT( ), MID( ), or RIGHT( ), and sort them.

Discussion

Suppose that you have a housewares table that acts as a catalog for houseware furnishings, and that items are identified by 10-character ID values consisting of three subparts: a three-character category abbreviation (such as DIN for "dining room" or KIT for "kitchen"), a five-digit serial number, and a two-character country code indicating where the part is manufactured:

```
mysql> SELECT * FROM housewares;
+------------+------------------+
| id         | description      |
+------------+------------------+
| DIN40672US | dining table     |
| KIT00372UK | garbage disposal |
| KIT01729JP | microwave oven   |
| BED00038SG | bedside lamp     |
| BTH00485US | shower stall     |
| BTH00415JP | lavatory         |
+------------+------------------+
```

This is not necessarily a good way to store complex ID values, and later we'll consider how to represent them using separate columns (see Recipe 11.11). But for now, assume that the values must be stored as just shown.

If you want to sort rows from this table based on the id values, just use the entire column value:

```
mysql> SELECT * FROM housewares ORDER BY id;
+------------+------------------+
| id         | description      |
+------------+------------------+
| BED00038SG | bedside lamp     |
| BTH00415JP | lavatory         |
| BTH00485US | shower stall     |
| DIN40672US | dining table     |
| KIT00372UK | garbage disposal |
| KIT01729JP | microwave oven   |
+------------+------------------+
```

But you might also have a need to sort on any of the three subparts (for example, to sort by country of manufacture). For that kind of operation, it's helpful to use functions that pull out pieces of a column, such as `LEFT( )`, `MID( )`, and `RIGHT( )`. These functions can be used to break apart the id values into their three components:

```
mysql> SELECT id,
    -> LEFT(id,3) AS category,
    -> MID(id,4,5) AS serial,
    -> RIGHT(id,2) AS country
    -> FROM housewares;
+------------+----------+--------+---------+
| id         | category | serial | country |
+------------+----------+--------+---------+
| DIN40672US | DIN      | 40672  | US      |
| KIT00372UK | KIT      | 00372  | UK      |
| KIT01729JP | KIT      | 01729  | JP      |
| BED00038SG | BED      | 00038  | SG      |
| BTH00485US | BTH      | 00485  | US      |
| BTH00415JP | BTH      | 00415  | JP      |
+------------+----------+--------+---------+
```

Any of those fixed-length substrings of the id values can be used for sorting, either alone or in combination. To sort by product category, extract the category value and use it in the ORDER BY clause:

```
mysql> SELECT * FROM housewares ORDER BY LEFT(id,3);
+------------+------------------+
| id         | description      |
+------------+------------------+
| BED00038SG | bedside lamp     |
| BTH00485US | shower stall     |
| BTH00415JP | lavatory         |
| DIN40672US | dining table     |
| KIT00372UK | garbage disposal |
| KIT01729JP | microwave oven   |
+------------+------------------+
```

To sort rows by product serial number, use `MID( )` to extract the middle five characters from the id values, beginning with the fourth:

```
mysql> SELECT * FROM housewares ORDER BY MID(id,4,5);
+------------+------------------+
| id         | description      |
+------------+------------------+
| BED00038SG | bedside lamp     |
| KIT00372UK | garbage disposal |
| BTH00415JP | lavatory         |
| BTH00485US | shower stall     |
| KIT01729JP | microwave oven   |
| DIN40672US | dining table     |
+------------+------------------+
```

This appears to be a numeric sort, but it's actually a string sort, because `MID( )` returns strings. It just so happens that the lexical and numeric sort order are the same in this case because the "numbers" have leading zeros to make them all the same length.

To sort by country code, use the rightmost two characters of the `id` values:

```
mysql> SELECT * FROM housewares ORDER BY RIGHT(id,2);
+------------+------------------+
| id         | description      |
+------------+------------------+
| KIT01729JP | microwave oven   |
| BTH00415JP | lavatory         |
| BED00038SG | bedside lamp     |
| KIT00372UK | garbage disposal |
| DIN40672US | dining table     |
| BTH00485US | shower stall     |
+------------+------------------+
```

You can also sort using combinations of substrings. For example, to sort by country code and serial number, the query looks like this:

```
mysql> SELECT * FROM housewares ORDER BY RIGHT(id,2), MID(id,4,5);
+------------+------------------+
| id         | description      |
+------------+------------------+
| BTH00415JP | lavatory         |
| KIT01729JP | microwave oven   |
| BED00038SG | bedside lamp     |
| KIT00372UK | garbage disposal |
| BTH00485US | shower stall     |
| DIN40672US | dining table     |
+------------+------------------+
```

7.11 Sorting by Variable-Length Substrings

Problem

You want to sort using parts of a column that do *not* occur at a given position within the column.

Solution

Figure out some way to identify the parts you need so that you can extract them. Otherwise, you're out of luck.

Discussion

If the substrings that you want to use for sorting vary in length, you need a reliable means of extracting just the part of the column values that you want. To see how this works, create a `housewares2` table that is like the `housewares` table used in Recipe 7.14, except that it has no leading zeros in the serial number part of the `id` values:

```
mysql> SELECT * FROM housewares2;
+------------+------------------+
| id         | description      |
+------------+------------------+
```

```
| DIN40672US | dining table    |
| KIT372UK   | garbage disposal |
| KIT1729JP  | microwave oven  |
| BED38SG    | bedside lamp    |
| BTH485US   | shower stall    |
| BTH415JP   | lavatory        |
+------------+------------------+
```

The category and country parts of the `id` values can be extracted and sorted using
`LEFT()` and `RIGHT()`, just as for the `housewares` table. But now the numeric segments of
the values have different lengths and cannot be extracted and sorted using a simple
`MID()` call. Instead, use `SUBSTRING()` to skip over the first three characters. Then, of the
remainder beginning with the fourth character (the first digit), take everything but the
rightmost two columns. One way to do this is as follows:

```
mysql> SELECT id, LEFT(SUBSTRING(id,4),CHAR_LENGTH(SUBSTRING(id,4)-2))
    -> FROM housewares2;
+------------+----------------------------------------------------+
| id         | LEFT(SUBSTRING(id,4),CHAR_LENGTH(SUBSTRING(id,4)-2)) |
+------------+----------------------------------------------------+
| DIN40672US | 40672                                              |
| KIT372UK   | 372                                                |
| KIT1729JP  | 1729                                               |
| BED38SG    | 38                                                 |
| BTH485US   | 485                                                |
| BTH415JP   | 415                                                |
+------------+----------------------------------------------------+
```

But that's more complex than necessary. The `SUBSTRING()` function takes an optional
third argument specifying a desired result length, and we know that the length of the
middle part is equal to the length of the string minus five (three for the characters at
the beginning and two for the characters at the end). The following query demonstrates
how to get the numeric middle part by beginning with the ID, and then stripping off
the rightmost suffix:

```
mysql> SELECT id, SUBSTRING(id,4), SUBSTRING(id,4,CHAR_LENGTH(id)-5)
    -> FROM housewares2;
+------------+-----------------+-----------------------------------+
| id         | SUBSTRING(id,4) | SUBSTRING(id,4,CHAR_LENGTH(id)-5) |
+------------+-----------------+-----------------------------------+
| DIN40672US | 40672US         | 40672                             |
| KIT372UK   | 372UK           | 372                               |
| KIT1729JP  | 1729JP          | 1729                              |
| BED38SG    | 38SG            | 38                                |
| BTH485US   | 485US           | 485                               |
| BTH415JP   | 415JP           | 415                               |
+------------+-----------------+-----------------------------------+
```

Unfortunately, although the final expression correctly extracts the numeric part from
the IDs, the resulting values are strings. Consequently, they sort lexically rather than
numerically:

```
mysql> SELECT * FROM housewares2
    -> ORDER BY SUBSTRING(id,4,CHAR_LENGTH(id)-5);
```

```
+------------+------------------+
| id         | description      |
+------------+------------------+
| KIT1729JP  | microwave oven   |
| KIT372UK   | garbage disposal |
| BED38SG    | bedside lamp     |
| DIN40672US | dining table     |
| BTH415JP   | lavatory         |
| BTH485US   | shower stall     |
+------------+------------------+
```

How to deal with that? One way is to add zero, which tells MySQL to perform a string-to-number conversion that results in a numeric sort of the serial number values:

```
mysql> SELECT * FROM housewares2
    -> ORDER BY SUBSTRING(id,4,CHAR_LENGTH(id)-5)+0;
+------------+------------------+
| id         | description      |
+------------+------------------+
| BED38SG    | bedside lamp     |
| KIT372UK   | garbage disposal |
| BTH415JP   | lavatory         |
| BTH485US   | shower stall     |
| KIT1729JP  | microwave oven   |
| DIN40672US | dining table     |
+------------+------------------+
```

But in this particular case, a simpler solution is possible. It's not necessary to calculate the length of the numeric part of the string, because the string-to-number conversion operation strips off trailing nonnumeric suffixes and provides the values needed to sort on the variable-length serial number portion of the id values. That means the third argument to SUBSTRING( ) actually isn't needed:

```
mysql> SELECT * FROM housewares2
    -> ORDER BY SUBSTRING(id,4)+0;
+------------+------------------+
| id         | description      |
+------------+------------------+
| BED38SG    | bedside lamp     |
| KIT372UK   | garbage disposal |
| BTH415JP   | lavatory         |
| BTH485US   | shower stall     |
| KIT1729JP  | microwave oven   |
| DIN40672US | dining table     |
+------------+------------------+
```

In the preceding example, the ability to extract variable-length substrings is based on the different kinds of characters in the middle of the ID values, compared to the characters on the ends (that is, digits versus nondigits). In other cases, you may be able to use delimiter characters to pull apart column values. For the next examples, assume a housewares3 table with id values that look like this:

```
mysql> SELECT * FROM housewares3;
+----------------+------------------+
| id             | description      |
```

```
+---------------+-------------------+
| 13-478-92-2   | dining table      |
| 873-48-649-63 | garbage disposal  |
| 8-4-2-1       | microwave oven    |
| 97-681-37-66  | bedside lamp      |
| 27-48-534-2   | shower stall      |
| 5764-56-89-72 | lavatory          |
+---------------+-------------------+
```

To extract segments from these values, use SUBSTRING_INDEX(str,c,n). It searches a string str for the n-th occurrence of a given character c and returns everything to the left of that character. For example, the following call returns 13-478:

```
SUBSTRING_INDEX('13-478-92-2','-',2)
```

If n is negative, the search for c proceeds from the right and returns the rightmost string. This call returns 478-92-2:

```
SUBSTRING_INDEX('13-478-92-2','-',-3)
```

By combining SUBSTRING_INDEX( ) calls with positive and negative indexes, it's possible to extract successive pieces from each id value. One way is to extract the first n segments of the value, and then pull off the rightmost one. By varying n from 1 to 4, we get the successive segments from left to right:

```
SUBSTRING_INDEX(SUBSTRING_INDEX(id,'-',1),'-',-1)
SUBSTRING_INDEX(SUBSTRING_INDEX(id,'-',2),'-',-1)
SUBSTRING_INDEX(SUBSTRING_INDEX(id,'-',3),'-',-1)
SUBSTRING_INDEX(SUBSTRING_INDEX(id,'-',4),'-',-1)
```

The first of those expressions can be optimized, because the inner SUBSTRING_INDEX( ) call returns a single-segment string and is sufficient by itself to return the leftmost id segment:

```
SUBSTRING_INDEX(id,'-',1)
```

Another way to obtain substrings is to extract the rightmost n segments of the value, and then pull off the first one. Here we vary n from −4 to −1:

```
SUBSTRING_INDEX(SUBSTRING_INDEX(id,'-',-4),'-',1)
SUBSTRING_INDEX(SUBSTRING_INDEX(id,'-',-3),'-',1)
SUBSTRING_INDEX(SUBSTRING_INDEX(id,'-',-2),'-',1)
SUBSTRING_INDEX(SUBSTRING_INDEX(id,'-',-1),'-',1)
```

Again, an optimization is possible. For the fourth expression, the inner SUBSTRING_INDEX( ) call is sufficient to return the final substring:

```
SUBSTRING_INDEX(id,'-',-1)
```

These expressions can be difficult to read and understand, and you probably should try experimenting with a few of them to see how they work. Here is an example that shows how to get the second and fourth segments from the id values:

```
mysql> SELECT
    -> id,
    -> SUBSTRING_INDEX(SUBSTRING_INDEX(id,'-',2),'-',-1) AS segment2,
```

```
        -> SUBSTRING_INDEX(SUBSTRING_INDEX(id,'-',4),'-',-1) AS segment4
        -> FROM housewares3;
+---------------+----------+----------+
| id            | segment2 | segment4 |
+---------------+----------+----------+
| 13-478-92-2   | 478      | 2        |
| 873-48-649-63 | 48       | 63       |
| 8-4-2-1       | 4        | 1        |
| 97-681-37-66  | 681      | 66       |
| 27-48-534-2   | 48       | 2        |
| 5764-56-89-72 | 56       | 72       |
+---------------+----------+----------+
```

To use the substrings for sorting, use the appropriate expressions in the ORDER BY clause. (Remember to force a string-to-number conversion by adding zero if you want the sort to be numeric rather than lexical.) The following two queries order the results based on the second id segment. The first sorts lexically, the second numerically:

```
mysql> SELECT * FROM housewares3
    -> ORDER BY SUBSTRING_INDEX(SUBSTRING_INDEX(id,'-',2),'-',-1);
+---------------+------------------+
| id            | description      |
+---------------+------------------+
| 8-4-2-1       | microwave oven   |
| 13-478-92-2   | dining table     |
| 873-48-649-63 | garbage disposal |
| 27-48-534-2   | shower stall     |
| 5764-56-89-72 | lavatory         |
| 97-681-37-66  | bedside lamp     |
+---------------+------------------+
mysql> SELECT * FROM housewares3
    -> ORDER BY SUBSTRING_INDEX(SUBSTRING_INDEX(id,'-',2),'-',-1)+0;
+---------------+------------------+
| id            | description      |
+---------------+------------------+
| 8-4-2-1       | microwave oven   |
| 873-48-649-63 | garbage disposal |
| 27-48-534-2   | shower stall     |
| 5764-56-89-72 | lavatory         |
| 13-478-92-2   | dining table     |
| 97-681-37-66  | bedside lamp     |
+---------------+------------------+
```

The substring-extraction expressions here are messy, but at least the column values to which we're applying the expressions have a consistent number of segments. To sort values that have varying numbers of segments, the job can be more difficult. The next section shows an example illustrating why that is.

7.12 Sorting Hostnames in Domain Order

Problem

You want to sort hostnames in domain order, with the rightmost parts of the names more significant than the leftmost parts.

Solution

Break apart the names, and sort the pieces from right to left.

Discussion

Hostnames are strings and therefore their natural sort order is lexical. However, it's often desirable to sort hostnames in domain order, where the rightmost segments of the hostname values are more significant than the leftmost segments. Suppose that you have a table hostname that contains the following names:

```
mysql> SELECT name FROM hostname ORDER BY name;
+--------------------+
| name               |
+--------------------+
| cvs.php.net        |
| dbi.perl.org       |
| jakarta.apache.org |
| lists.mysql.com    |
| mysql.com          |
| www.kitebird.com   |
+--------------------+
```

The preceding query demonstrates the natural lexical sort order of the name values. That differs from domain order, as shown by the following table.

Lexical order	Domain order
cvs.php.net	www.kitebird.com
dbi.perl.org	mysql.com
jakarta.apache.org	lists.mysql.com
lists.mysql.com	cvs.php.net
mysql.com	jakarta.apache.org
www.kitebird.com	dbi.perl.org

Producing domain-ordered output is a substring-sorting problem, where it's necessary to extract each segment of the names so they can be sorted in right-to-left fashion. There is also an additional complication if your values contain different numbers of segments, as our example hostnames do. (Most of them have three segments, but mysql.com has only two.)

To extract the pieces of the hostnames, begin by using `SUBSTRING_INDEX( )` in a manner similar to that described previously in Recipe 7.11. The hostname values have a maximum of three segments, from which the pieces can be extracted left to right like this:

```
SUBSTRING_INDEX(SUBSTRING_INDEX(name,'.',-3),'.',1)
SUBSTRING_INDEX(SUBSTRING_INDEX(name,'.',-2),'.',1)
SUBSTRING_INDEX(name,'.',-1)
```

These expressions work properly as long as all the hostnames have three components. But if a name has fewer than three, you don't get the correct result, as the following query demonstrates:

```
mysql> SELECT name,
    -> SUBSTRING_INDEX(SUBSTRING_INDEX(name,'.',-3),'.',1) AS leftmost,
    -> SUBSTRING_INDEX(SUBSTRING_INDEX(name,'.',-2),'.',1) AS middle,
    -> SUBSTRING_INDEX(name,'.',-1) AS rightmost
    -> FROM hostname;
+--------------------+----------+----------+-----------+
| name               | leftmost | middle   | rightmost |
+--------------------+----------+----------+-----------+
| cvs.php.net        | cvs      | php      | net       |
| dbi.perl.org       | dbi      | perl     | org       |
| lists.mysql.com    | lists    | mysql    | com       |
| mysql.com          | mysql    | mysql    | com       |
| jakarta.apache.org | jakarta  | apache   | org       |
| www.kitebird.com   | www      | kitebird | com       |
+--------------------+----------+----------+-----------+
```

Notice the output for the `mysql.com` row; it has `mysql` for the value of the `leftmost` column, where it should have an empty string. The segment-extraction expressions work by pulling off the rightmost *n* segments, and then returning the leftmost segment of the result. The source of the problem for `mysql.com` is that if there aren't *n* segments, the expression simply returns the leftmost segment of however many there are. To fix this problem, add a sufficient number of periods at the beginning of the hostname values to guarantee that they have the requisite number of segments:

```
mysql> SELECT name,
    -> SUBSTRING_INDEX(SUBSTRING_INDEX(CONCAT('..',name),'.',-3),'.',1)
    -> AS leftmost,
    -> SUBSTRING_INDEX(SUBSTRING_INDEX(CONCAT('.',name),'.',-2),'.',1)
    -> AS middle,
    -> SUBSTRING_INDEX(name,'.',-1) AS rightmost
    -> FROM hostname;
+--------------------+----------+----------+-----------+
| name               | leftmost | middle   | rightmost |
+--------------------+----------+----------+-----------+
| cvs.php.net        | cvs      | php      | net       |
| dbi.perl.org       | dbi      | perl     | org       |
| lists.mysql.com    | lists    | mysql    | com       |
| mysql.com          |          | mysql    | com       |
| jakarta.apache.org | jakarta  | apache   | org       |
| www.kitebird.com   | www      | kitebird | com       |
+--------------------+----------+----------+-----------+
```

That's pretty ugly. But these expressions do serve to extract the substrings that are needed for sorting hostname values correctly in right-to-left fashion:

```
mysql> SELECT name FROM hostname
    -> ORDER BY
    -> SUBSTRING_INDEX(name,'.',-1),
    -> SUBSTRING_INDEX(SUBSTRING_INDEX(CONCAT('.',name),'.',-2),'.',1),
    -> SUBSTRING_INDEX(SUBSTRING_INDEX(CONCAT('..',name),'.',-3),'.',1);
+--------------------+
| name               |
+--------------------+
| www.kitebird.com   |
| mysql.com          |
| lists.mysql.com    |
| cvs.php.net        |
| jakarta.apache.org |
| dbi.perl.org       |
+--------------------+
```

If you had hostnames with a maximum of four segments rather than three, you'd need to add to the `ORDER BY` clause another `SUBSTRING_INDEX( )` expression that adds three dots at the beginning of the hostname values.

7.13 Sorting Dotted-Quad IP Values in Numeric Order

Problem

You want to sort strings that represent IP numbers in numeric order.

Solution

Break apart the strings, and sort the pieces numerically. Or just use `INET_ATON( )`.

Discussion

If a table contains IP numbers represented as strings in dotted-quad notation (`111.122.133.144`), they'll sort lexically rather than numerically. To produce a numeric ordering instead, you can sort them as four-part values with each part sorted numerically. Or, to be more efficient, you can represent the IP numbers as 32-bit unsigned integers, which take less space and can be ordered by a simple numeric sort. This section shows both methods.

To sort string-valued dotted-quad IP numbers, use a technique similar to that for sorting hostnames, but with the following differences:

- Dotted quads always have four segments, so there's no need to add dots to the value before extracting substrings.

- Dotted quads sort left to right, so the order of the substrings used in the ORDER BY clause is opposite to that used for hostname sorting.

- The segments of dotted-quad values are numbers, so add zero to each substring to tell MySQL to use a numeric sort rather than a lexical one.

Suppose that you have a `hostip` table with a string-valued `ip` column containing IP numbers:

```
mysql> SELECT ip FROM hostip ORDER BY ip;
+-----------------+
| ip              |
+-----------------+
| 127.0.0.1       |
| 192.168.0.10    |
| 192.168.0.2     |
| 192.168.1.10    |
| 192.168.1.2     |
| 21.0.0.1        |
| 255.255.255.255 |
+-----------------+
```

The preceding query produces output sorted in lexical order. To sort the `ip` values numerically, you can extract each segment and add zero to convert it to a number using an ORDER BY clause like this:

```
mysql> SELECT ip FROM hostip
    -> ORDER BY
    -> SUBSTRING_INDEX(ip,'.',1)+0,
    -> SUBSTRING_INDEX(SUBSTRING_INDEX(ip,'.',-3),'.',1)+0,
    -> SUBSTRING_INDEX(SUBSTRING_INDEX(ip,'.',-2),'.',1)+0,
    -> SUBSTRING_INDEX(ip,'.',-1)+0;
+-----------------+
| ip              |
+-----------------+
| 21.0.0.1        |
| 127.0.0.1       |
| 192.168.0.2     |
| 192.168.0.10    |
| 192.168.1.2     |
| 192.168.1.10    |
| 255.255.255.255 |
+-----------------+
```

However, although that ORDER BY produces a correct result, it involves a lot of messing around. A simpler solution is possible: use the INET_ATON( ) function to convert network addresses in string form directly to their underlying numeric values and sort those numbers:

```
mysql> SELECT ip FROM hostip ORDER BY INET_ATON(ip);
+-----------------+
| ip              |
+-----------------+
| 21.0.0.1        |
| 127.0.0.1       |
```

```
| 192.168.0.2     |
| 192.168.0.10    |
| 192.168.1.2     |
| 192.168.1.10    |
| 255.255.255.255 |
+-----------------+
```

If you're tempted to sort by simply adding zero to the `ip` value and using `ORDER BY` on the result, consider the values that kind of string-to-number conversion actually produces:

```
mysql> SELECT ip, ip+0 FROM hostip;
+-----------------+---------+
| ip              | ip+0    |
+-----------------+---------+
| 127.0.0.1       |     127 |
| 192.168.0.2     | 192.168 |
| 192.168.0.10    | 192.168 |
| 192.168.1.2     | 192.168 |
| 192.168.1.10    | 192.168 |
| 255.255.255.255 | 255.255 |
| 21.0.0.1        |      21 |
+-----------------+---------+
```

The conversion retains only as much of each value as can be interpreted as a valid number. The remainder would be unavailable for sorting purposes, even though it's necessary to produce a correct ordering.

Use of `INET_ATON( )` in the `ORDER BY` clause is more efficient than six `SUBSTRING_INDEX( )` calls. Moreover, if you're willing to consider storing IP addresses as numbers rather than as strings, you avoid having to perform any conversion at all when sorting. You gain an additional benefit as well because if you index the column, the query optimizer may be able to use the index for certain queries. Numeric IP addresses have 32 bits, so you can use an `INT UNSIGNED` column to store them. For cases when you need to display those values in dotted-quad notation, convert them with the `INET_NTOA( )` function.

7.14 Floating Values to the Head or Tail of the Sort Order

Problem

You want a column to sort the way it normally does, except for a few values that you want at the beginning or end of the sort order. For example, suppose that you want to sort a list in lexical order except for certain high-priority values that should appear first no matter where they fall in the normal sort order.

Solution

Add another sort column to the ORDER BY clause that places those few values where you want them. The remaining sort columns will have their usual effect for the other values.

Discussion

If you want to sort a result set normally *except* that you want particular values first, create an additional sort column that is 0 for those values and 1 for everything else. This allows you to float the values to the head of the sort order. To put the values at the tail instead, use the additional column to map the values to 1 and all other values to 0.

For example, when a sorted column contains NULL values, MySQL puts them all together in the sort order (at the beginning for an ascending sort, at the end for a descending sort). It may seem a bit odd that NULL values are grouped, given that (as the following query shows) they are not considered equal in comparisons:

```
mysql> SELECT NULL = NULL;
+-------------+
| NULL = NULL |
+-------------+
|        NULL |
+-------------+
```

On the other hand, NULL values conceptually do seem more similar to each other than to non-NULL values, and there's no good way to distinguish one NULL from another, anyway. Normally, NULL values form a group at the beginning of the sort order (or at the end, if you specify DESC). If you want NULL values at a specific end of the sort order, you can force them to be placed where you want. Suppose that you have a table t with the following contents:

```
mysql> SELECT val FROM t;
+------+
| val  |
+------+
|    3 |
|  100 |
| NULL |
| NULL |
|    9 |
+------+
```

Normally, sorting puts the NULL values at the beginning for an ascending sort:

```
mysql> SELECT val FROM t ORDER BY val;
+------+
| val  |
+------+
| NULL |
| NULL |
|    3 |
|    9 |
```

```
| 100 |
+------+
```

To put them at the end instead, introduce an extra ORDER BY column that maps NULL values to a higher value than non-NULL values:

```
mysql> SELECT val FROM t ORDER BY IF(val IS NULL,1,0), val;
+------+
| val  |
+------+
|    3 |
|    9 |
|  100 |
| NULL |
| NULL |
+------+
```

The IF( ) expression creates a new column for the sort that is used as the primary sort value.

For descending sorts, NULL values group at the end. To put them at the beginning instead, use the same technique, but reverse the second and third arguments of the IF( ) function to map NULL values to a lower value than non-NULL values:

```
IF(val IS NULL,0,1)
```

The same technique is useful for floating values other than NULL values to either end of the sort order. Suppose that you want to sort mail table messages in sender/recipient order, but you want to put messages for a particular sender first. In the real world, the most interesting sender might be postmaster or root. Those names don't appear in the table, so let's use phil as the name of interest instead:

```
mysql> SELECT t, srcuser, dstuser, size
    -> FROM mail
    -> ORDER BY IF(srcuser='phil',0,1), srcuser, dstuser;
+---------------------+---------+---------+---------+
| t                   | srcuser | dstuser | size    |
+---------------------+---------+---------+---------+
| 2006-05-16 23:04:19 | phil    | barb    |   10294 |
| 2006-05-12 15:02:49 | phil    | phil    |    1048 |
| 2006-05-15 08:50:57 | phil    | phil    |     978 |
| 2006-05-14 11:52:17 | phil    | tricia  |    5781 |
| 2006-05-17 12:49:23 | phil    | tricia  |     873 |
| 2006-05-14 14:42:21 | barb    | barb    |   98151 |
| 2006-05-11 10:15:08 | barb    | tricia  |   58274 |
| 2006-05-13 13:59:18 | barb    | tricia  |     271 |
| 2006-05-14 09:31:37 | gene    | barb    |    2291 |
| 2006-05-16 09:00:28 | gene    | barb    |     613 |
| 2006-05-15 17:35:31 | gene    | gene    |    3856 |
| 2006-05-15 07:17:48 | gene    | gene    |    3824 |
| 2006-05-19 22:21:51 | gene    | gene    |   23992 |
| 2006-05-15 10:25:52 | gene    | tricia  |  998532 |
| 2006-05-12 12:48:13 | tricia  | gene    |  194925 |
| 2006-05-14 17:03:01 | tricia  | phil    | 2394482 |
+---------------------+---------+---------+---------+
```

The value of the extra sort column is 0 for rows in which the srcuser value is phil, and 1 for all other rows. By making that the most significant sort column, rows for messages sent by phil float to the top of the output. (To sink them to the bottom instead, either sort the column in reverse order using DESC, or reverse the order of the second and third arguments of the IF( ) function.)

You can also use this technique for particular conditions, not just specific values. To put first those rows where people sent messages to themselves, do this:

```
mysql> SELECT t, srcuser, dstuser, size
    -> FROM mail
    -> ORDER BY IF(srcuser=dstuser,0,1), srcuser, dstuser;
+---------------------+---------+---------+---------+
| t                   | srcuser | dstuser | size    |
+---------------------+---------+---------+---------+
| 2006-05-14 14:42:21 | barb    | barb    |   98151 |
| 2006-05-19 22:21:51 | gene    | gene    |   23992 |
| 2006-05-15 17:35:31 | gene    | gene    |    3856 |
| 2006-05-15 07:17:48 | gene    | gene    |    3824 |
| 2006-05-12 15:02:49 | phil    | phil    |    1048 |
| 2006-05-15 08:50:57 | phil    | phil    |     978 |
| 2006-05-11 10:15:08 | barb    | tricia  |   58274 |
| 2006-05-13 13:59:18 | barb    | tricia  |     271 |
| 2006-05-16 09:00:28 | gene    | barb    |     613 |
| 2006-05-14 09:31:37 | gene    | barb    |    2291 |
| 2006-05-15 10:25:52 | gene    | tricia  |  998532 |
| 2006-05-16 23:04:19 | phil    | barb    |   10294 |
| 2006-05-14 11:52:17 | phil    | tricia  |    5781 |
| 2006-05-17 12:49:23 | phil    | tricia  |     873 |
| 2006-05-12 12:48:13 | tricia  | gene    |  194925 |
| 2006-05-14 17:03:01 | tricia  | phil    | 2394482 |
+---------------------+---------+---------+---------+
```

If you have a pretty good idea about the contents of your table, you can sometimes eliminate the extra sort column. For example, srcuser is never NULL in the mail table, so the previous query can be rewritten as follows to use one less column in the ORDER BY clause (this relies on the property that NULL values sort ahead of all non-NULL values):

```
mysql> SELECT t, srcuser, dstuser, size
    -> FROM mail
    -> ORDER BY IF(srcuser=dstuser,NULL,srcuser), dstuser;
+---------------------+---------+---------+---------+
| t                   | srcuser | dstuser | size    |
+---------------------+---------+---------+---------+
| 2006-05-14 14:42:21 | barb    | barb    |   98151 |
| 2006-05-19 22:21:51 | gene    | gene    |   23992 |
| 2006-05-15 17:35:31 | gene    | gene    |    3856 |
| 2006-05-15 07:17:48 | gene    | gene    |    3824 |
| 2006-05-12 15:02:49 | phil    | phil    |    1048 |
| 2006-05-15 08:50:57 | phil    | phil    |     978 |
| 2006-05-11 10:15:08 | barb    | tricia  |   58274 |
| 2006-05-13 13:59:18 | barb    | tricia  |     271 |
| 2006-05-16 09:00:28 | gene    | barb    |     613 |
| 2006-05-14 09:31:37 | gene    | barb    |    2291 |
```

```
| 2006-05-15 10:25:52 | gene   | tricia | 998532  |
| 2006-05-16 23:04:19 | phil   | barb   | 10294   |
| 2006-05-14 11:52:17 | phil   | tricia | 5781    |
| 2006-05-17 12:49:23 | phil   | tricia | 873     |
| 2006-05-12 12:48:13 | tricia | gene   | 194925  |
| 2006-05-14 17:03:01 | tricia | phil   | 2394482 |
+---------------------+--------+--------+---------+
```

See Also

The technique of introducing additional sort columns is useful with UNION queries that produce the union of multiple SELECT statements. You can cause the SELECT results to appear one after the other and sort the rows within each individual SELECT. See Recipe 12.12 for details.

7.15 Sorting in User-Defined Orders

Problem

You want to define a nonstandard sort order for the values in a column.

Solution

Use FIELD( ) to map column values to a sequence that places the values in the desired order.

Discussion

Recipe 7.14 showed how to make a specific group of rows go to the head of the sort order. If you want to impose a specific order on *all* values in a column, use the FIELD( ) function to map them to a list of numeric values and use the numbers for sorting. FIELD( ) compares its first argument to the following arguments and returns a number indicating which one of them it matches. The following FIELD( ) call compares *value* to *str1*, *str2*, *str3*, and *str4*, and returns 1, 2, 3, or 4, depending on which one of them *value* is equal to:

```
FIELD(value,str1,str2,str3,str4)
```

The number of comparison values need not be four; FIELD( ) takes a variable-length argument list. If *value* is NULL or none of the values match, FIELD( ) returns 0.

FIELD( ) can be used to sort an arbitrary set of values into any order you please. For example, to display driver_log rows for Henry, Suzi, and Ben, in that order, do this:

```
mysql> SELECT * FROM driver_log
    -> ORDER BY FIELD(name,'Henry','Suzi','Ben');
+--------+-------+------------+-------+
| rec_id | name  | trav_date  | miles |
+--------+-------+------------+-------+
```

```
|      10 | Henry  | 2006-08-30  |    203 |
|       8 | Henry  | 2006-09-01  |    197 |
|       6 | Henry  | 2006-08-26  |    115 |
|       4 | Henry  | 2006-08-27  |     96 |
|       3 | Henry  | 2006-08-29  |    300 |
|       7 | Suzi   | 2006-09-02  |    502 |
|       2 | Suzi   | 2006-08-29  |    391 |
|       5 | Ben    | 2006-08-29  |    131 |
|       9 | Ben    | 2006-09-02  |     79 |
|       1 | Ben    | 2006-08-30  |    152 |
+--------+-------+------------+-------+
```

You can use FIELD( ) with column substrings, too. To sort items from the housewares table by country of manufacture using the order US, UK, JP, SG, do this:

```
mysql> SELECT id, description FROM housewares
    -> ORDER BY FIELD(RIGHT(id,2),'US','UK','JP','SG');
+------------+------------------+
| id         | description      |
+------------+------------------+
| DIN40672US | dining table     |
| BTH00485US | shower stall     |
| KIT00372UK | garbage disposal |
| KIT01729JP | microwave oven   |
| BTH00415JP | lavatory         |
| BED00038SG | bedside lamp     |
+------------+------------------+
```

More generally, FIELD( ) can be used to sort any kind of category-based values into a specific order when the categories don't sort naturally into that order.

7.16 Sorting ENUM Values

Problem

ENUM values don't sort like other string columns.

Solution

Learn how they work, and exploit those properties to your own advantage.

Discussion

ENUM is considered a string data type, but ENUM values actually are stored numerically with values ordered the same way they are listed in the table definition. These numeric values affect how enumerations are sorted, which can be very useful. Suppose that you have a table named weekday containing an enumeration column day that has weekday names as its members:

```
CREATE TABLE weekday
(
```

```
    day ENUM('Sunday','Monday','Tuesday','Wednesday',
             'Thursday','Friday','Saturday')
);
```

Internally, MySQL defines the enumeration values Sunday through Saturday in that definition to have numeric values from 1 to 7. To see this for yourself, create the table using the definition just shown, and then insert into it a row for each day of the week. However, to make the insertion order differ from sorted order (so that you can see the effect of sorting), add the days in random order:

```
mysql> INSERT INTO weekday (day) VALUES('Monday'),('Friday'),
    -> ('Tuesday'), ('Sunday'), ('Thursday'), ('Saturday'), ('Wednesday');
```

Then select the values, both as strings and as the internal numeric value (the latter are obtained by using +0 to effect a string-to-number conversion):

```
mysql> SELECT day, day+0 FROM weekday;
+-----------+-------+
| day       | day+0 |
+-----------+-------+
| Monday    |     2 |
| Friday    |     6 |
| Tuesday   |     3 |
| Sunday    |     1 |
| Thursday  |     5 |
| Saturday  |     7 |
| Wednesday |     4 |
+-----------+-------+
```

Notice that because the query includes no ORDER BY clause, the rows are returned in unsorted order. If you add an ORDER BY day clause, it becomes apparent that MySQL uses the internal numeric values for sorting:

```
mysql> SELECT day, day+0 FROM weekday ORDER BY day;
+-----------+-------+
| day       | day+0 |
+-----------+-------+
| Sunday    |     1 |
| Monday    |     2 |
| Tuesday   |     3 |
| Wednesday |     4 |
| Thursday  |     5 |
| Friday    |     6 |
| Saturday  |     7 |
+-----------+-------+
```

What about occasions when you do want to sort ENUM values in lexical order? Force them to be treated as strings for sorting using the CAST( ) function:

```
mysql> SELECT day, day+0 FROM weekday ORDER BY CAST(day AS CHAR);
+-----------+-------+
| day       | day+0 |
+-----------+-------+
| Friday    |     6 |
| Monday    |     2 |
```

```
| Saturday  |   7 |
| Sunday    |   1 |
| Thursday  |   5 |
| Tuesday   |   3 |
| Wednesday |   4 |
+-----------+-----+
```

If you always (or nearly always) sort a nonenumeration column in a specific nonlexical order, consider changing the data type to ENUM, with its values listed in the desired sort order. To see how this works, create a color table containing a string column, and populate it with some sample rows:

```
mysql> CREATE TABLE color (name CHAR(10));
mysql> INSERT INTO color (name) VALUES ('blue'),('green'),
    -> ('indigo'),('orange'),('red'),('violet'),('yellow');
```

Sorting by the name column at this point produces lexical order because the column contains CHAR values:

```
mysql> SELECT name FROM color ORDER BY name;
+--------+
| name   |
+--------+
| blue   |
| green  |
| indigo |
| orange |
| red    |
| violet |
| yellow |
+--------+
```

Now suppose that you want to sort the column by the order in which colors occur in the rainbow. (This order is given by the name "Roy G. Biv," where successive letters of that name indicate the first letter of the corresponding color name.) One way to produce a rainbow sort is to use FIELD( ):

```
mysql> SELECT name FROM color
    -> ORDER BY
    -> FIELD(name,'red','orange','yellow','green','blue','indigo','violet');
+--------+
| name   |
+--------+
| red    |
| orange |
| yellow |
| green  |
| blue   |
| indigo |
| violet |
+--------+
```

To accomplish the same end without FIELD( ), use ALTER TABLE to convert the name column to an ENUM that lists the colors in the desired sort order:

```
mysql> ALTER TABLE color
    -> MODIFY name
    -> ENUM('red','orange','yellow','green','blue','indigo','violet');
```

After converting the table, sorting on the name column produces rainbow sorting naturally with no special treatment:

```
mysql> SELECT name FROM color ORDER BY name;
+--------+
| name   |
+--------+
| red    |
| orange |
| yellow |
| green  |
| blue   |
| indigo |
| violet |
+--------+
```

## CHAPTER 8

Generating Summaries

8.0 Introduction

Database systems are useful for storing and retrieving records, but they can also summarize your data in more concise forms. Summaries are useful when you want the overall picture rather than the details. They're also typically more readily understood than a long list of records. Summary techniques enable you to answer questions such as "How many?" or "What is the total?" or "What is the range of values?" If you're running a business, you may want to know how many customers you have in each state, or how much sales volume you're generating each month. You could determine the per-state count by producing a list of customer records and counting them yourself, but that makes no sense when MySQL can count them for you. Similarly, to determine sales volume by month, a list of raw order information records is not especially useful if you have to add up the order amounts yourself. Let MySQL do it.

The examples just mentioned illustrate two common summary types. The first (the number of customer records per state) is a counting summary. The content of each record is important only for purposes of placing it into the proper group or category for counting. Such summaries are essentially histograms, where you sort items into a set of bins and count the number of items in each bin. The second example (sales volume per month) is an instance of a summary that's based on the contents of records —sales totals are computed from sales values in individual order records.

Yet another kind of summary produces neither counts nor sums, but simply a list of unique values. This is useful if you don't care how many instances of each value are present, but only *which* values are present. If you want to know the states in which you have customers, you want a list of the distinct state names contained in the records, not a list consisting of the state value from every record. Sometimes it's even useful to apply one summary technique to the result of another summary. For example, to determine how many states your customers live in, generate a list of unique customer states, and then count them.

The type of summaries that you generate may depend on the kind of data you're working with. A counting summary can be generated from any kind of values, whether they be numbers, strings, or dates. For summaries that involve sums or averages, only numeric values can be used. You can count instances of customer state names to produce a demographic analysis of your customer base, but you cannot add or average state names—that doesn't make sense.

Summary operations in MySQL involve the following SQL constructs:

- To compute a summary value from a set of individual values, use one of the functions known as *aggregate functions*. These are so called because they operate on aggregates (groups) of values. Aggregate functions include COUNT( ), which counts rows or values in a query result; MIN( ) and MAX( ), which find smallest and largest values; and SUM( ) and AVG( ), which produce sums and means of values. These functions can be used to compute a value for the entire result set, or with a GROUP BY clause to group the rows into subsets and obtain an aggregate value for each one.

- To obtain a list of unique values, use SELECT DISTINCT rather than SELECT.

- To count how many distinct values there are, use COUNT(DISTINCT) rather than COUNT( ).

The recipes in this chapter first illustrate basic summary techniques, and then show how to perform more complex summary operations. You'll find additional examples of summary methods in later chapters, particularly those that cover joins and statistical operations. (See Chapters 12 and 13.)

Summary queries sometimes involve complex expressions. For summaries that you execute often, keep in mind that views can make queries easier to use. Recipe 3.12 demonstrates the basic technique of creating a view. Recipe 8.1 shows how it applies to summary simplification, and you'll see easily how it can be used in later sections of the chapter as well.

The primary tables used for examples in this chapter are the driver_log and mail tables. These were also used heavily in Chapter 7, so they should look familiar. A third table used recurrently throughout the chapter is states, which has rows containing a few columns of information for each of the United States:

```
mysql> SELECT * FROM states ORDER BY name;
+----------------+--------+------------+----------+
| name           | abbrev | statehood  | pop      |
+----------------+--------+------------+----------+
| Alabama        | AL     | 1819-12-14 |  4530182 |
| Alaska         | AK     | 1959-01-03 |   655435 |
| Arizona        | AZ     | 1912-02-14 |  5743834 |
| Arkansas       | AR     | 1836-06-15 |  2752629 |
| California     | CA     | 1850-09-09 | 35893799 |
| Colorado       | CO     | 1876-08-01 |  4601403 |
| Connecticut    | CT     | 1788-01-09 |  3503604 |
...
```

The name and abbrev columns list the full state name and the corresponding abbreviation. The statehood column indicates the day on which the state entered the Union. pop is the state population as of July, 2004, as reported by the U.S. Census Bureau.

This chapter uses other tables occasionally as well. You can create most of them with the scripts found in the *tables* directory of the recipes distribution. Recipe 5.15 describes the kjv table.

8.1 Summarizing with COUNT( )

Problem

You want to count the number of rows in a table, the number of rows that match certain conditions, or the number of times that particular values occur.

Solution

Use the COUNT( ) function.

Discussion

To count the number of rows in an entire table or that match particular conditions, use the COUNT( ) function. For example, to display the contents of the rows in a table, you can use a SELECT * statement, but to count them instead, use SELECT COUNT(*). Without a WHERE clause, the statement counts all the rows in the table, such as in the following statement that shows how many rows the driver_log table contains:

```
mysql> SELECT COUNT(*) FROM driver_log;
+----------+
| COUNT(*) |
+----------+
|       10 |
+----------+
```

If you don't know how many U.S. states there are, this statement tells you:

```
mysql> SELECT COUNT(*) FROM states;
+----------+
| COUNT(*) |
+----------+
|       50 |
+----------+
```

COUNT(*) with no WHERE clause is very quick for MyISAM tables. However, for BDB or InnoDB tables, you may want to avoid it because the statement requires a full table scan, which can be slow for large tables. If an approximate row count is all you require, a workaround that avoids a full scan for those storage engines is to extract the TABLE_ROWS value from the INFORMATION_SCHEMA database:

```
mysql> SELECT TABLE_ROWS FROM INFORMATION_SCHEMA.TABLES
    -> WHERE TABLE_SCHEMA = 'cookbook' AND TABLE_NAME = 'states';
+------------+
| TABLE_ROWS |
+------------+
|         50 |
+------------+
```

Before MySQL 5.0, INFORMATION_SCHEMA is unavailable. Instead, use SHOW TABLE STATUS and extract the value of the Rows column.

To count only the number of rows that match certain conditions, include an appropriate WHERE clause in a SELECT COUNT(*) statement. The conditions can be chosen to make COUNT(*) useful for answering many kinds of questions:

- How many times did drivers travel more than 200 miles in a day?

```
mysql> SELECT COUNT(*) FROM driver_log WHERE miles > 200;
+----------+
| COUNT(*) |
+----------+
|        4 |
+----------+
```

- How many days did Suzi drive?

```
mysql> SELECT COUNT(*) FROM driver_log WHERE name = 'Suzi';
+----------+
| COUNT(*) |
+----------+
|        2 |
+----------+
```

- How many states did the United States consist of at the beginning of the 20th century?

```
mysql> SELECT COUNT(*) FROM states WHERE statehood < '1900-01-01';
+----------+
| COUNT(*) |
+----------+
|       45 |
+----------+
```

- How many of those states joined the Union in the 19th century?

```
mysql> SELECT COUNT(*) FROM states
    -> WHERE statehood BETWEEN '1800-01-01' AND '1899-12-31';
+----------+
| COUNT(*) |
+----------+
|       29 |
+----------+
```

The COUNT( ) function actually has two forms. The form we've been using, COUNT(*), counts rows. The other form, COUNT(expr), takes a column name or expression argument and counts the number of non-NULL values. The following statement shows how to produce both a row count for a table and a count of the number of non-NULL values in one of its columns:

```
SELECT COUNT(*), COUNT(mycol) FROM mytbl;
```

The fact that COUNT(*expr*) doesn't count NULL values is useful for producing multiple counts from the same set of rows. To count the number of Saturday and Sunday trips in the driver_log table with a single statement, do this:

```
mysql> SELECT
    -> COUNT(IF(DAYOFWEEK(trav_date)=7,1,NULL)) AS 'Saturday trips',
    -> COUNT(IF(DAYOFWEEK(trav_date)=1,1,NULL)) AS 'Sunday trips'
    -> FROM driver_log;
+----------------+--------------+
| Saturday trips | Sunday trips |
+----------------+--------------+
|              3 |            1 |
+----------------+--------------+
```

Or to count weekend versus weekday trips, do this:

```
mysql> SELECT
    -> COUNT(IF(DAYOFWEEK(trav_date) IN (1,7),1,NULL)) AS 'weekend trips',
    -> COUNT(IF(DAYOFWEEK(trav_date) IN (1,7),NULL,1)) AS 'weekday trips'
    -> FROM driver_log;
+---------------+---------------+
| weekend trips | weekday trips |
+---------------+---------------+
|             4 |             6 |
+---------------+---------------+
```

The IF( ) expressions determine, for each column value, whether it should be counted. If so, the expression evaluates to 1 and COUNT( ) counts it. If not, the expression evaluates to NULL and COUNT( ) ignores it. The effect is to count the number of values that satisfy the condition given as the first argument to IF( ).

Create a View to Simplify Using a Summary

If you need a given summary often, a view might be useful so that you need not type the summarizing expressions repeatedly. For example, the following view implements the weekend versus weekday trip summary:

```
mysql> CREATE VIEW trip_summary_view AS
    -> SELECT
    -> COUNT(IF(DAYOFWEEK(trav_date) IN (1,7),1,NULL)) AS weekend_trips,
    -> COUNT(IF(DAYOFWEEK(trav_date) IN (1,7),NULL,1)) AS weekday_trips
    -> FROM driver_log;
```

Selecting from this view is much easier than selecting directly from the underlying table:

```
mysql> SELECT * FROM trip_summary_view;
+---------------+---------------+
| weekend_trips | weekday_trips |
+---------------+---------------+
```

```
|             4 |             6 |
+---------------+---------------+
```

See Also

Recipe 8.8 further discusses the difference between COUNT(*) and COUNT(expr).

8.2 Summarizing with MIN( ) and MAX( )

Problem

You need to determine the smallest or largest of a set of values.

Solution

Use MIN( ) to find the smallest value, MAX( ) to find the largest.

Discussion

Finding smallest or largest values is somewhat akin to sorting, except that instead of producing an entire set of sorted values, you select only a single value at one end or the other of the sorted range. This kind of operation applies to questions about smallest, largest, oldest, newest, most expensive, least expensive, and so forth. One way to find such values is to use the MIN( ) and MAX( ) functions. (Another way to address these questions is to use LIMIT; see the discussions in Recipes 3.14 and 3.16.)

Because MIN( ) and MAX( ) determine the extreme values in a set, they're useful for characterizing ranges:

- What date range is represented by the rows in the mail table? What are the smallest and largest messages sent?

  ```
  mysql> SELECT
      -> MIN(t) AS earliest, MAX(t) AS latest,
      -> MIN(size) AS smallest, MAX(size) AS largest
      -> FROM mail;
  +---------------------+---------------------+----------+---------+
  | earliest            | latest              | smallest | largest |
  +---------------------+---------------------+----------+---------+
  | 2006-05-11 10:15:08 | 2006-05-19 22:21:51 |      271 | 2394482 |
  +---------------------+---------------------+----------+---------+
  ```

- What are the shortest and longest trips in the driver_log table?

  ```
  mysql> SELECT MIN(miles) AS shortest, MAX(miles) AS longest
      -> FROM driver_log;
  +----------+---------+
  | shortest | longest |
  +----------+---------+
  ```

```
|        79 |      502 |
+-----------+----------+
```

- What are the lowest and highest U.S. state populations?

```
mysql> SELECT MIN(pop) AS 'fewest people', MAX(pop) AS 'most people'
    -> FROM states;
+---------------+--------------+
| fewest people | most people  |
+---------------+--------------+
|        506529 |     35893799 |
+---------------+--------------+
```

- What are the first and last state names, lexically speaking?

```
mysql> SELECT MIN(name), MAX(name) FROM states;
+-----------+-----------+
| MIN(name) | MAX(name) |
+-----------+-----------+
| Alabama   | Wyoming   |
+-----------+-----------+
```

MIN( ) and MAX( ) need not be applied directly to column values. They also work with expressions or values that are derived from column values. For example, to find the lengths of the shortest and longest state names, do this:

```
mysql> SELECT
    -> MIN(CHAR_LENGTH(name)) AS shortest,
    -> MAX(CHAR_LENGTH(name)) AS longest
    -> FROM states;
+----------+---------+
| shortest | longest |
+----------+---------+
|        4 |      14 |
+----------+---------+
```

8.3 Summarizing with SUM( ) and AVG( )

Problem

You need to add a set of numbers or find their average.

Solution

Use the SUM( ) or AVG( ) functions.

Discussion

SUM( ) and AVG( ) produce the total and average (mean) of a set of values:

- What is the total amount of mail traffic and the average size of each message?

```
mysql> SELECT
    -> SUM(size) AS 'total traffic',
```

```
        -> AVG(size) AS 'average message size'
        -> FROM mail;
+---------------+----------------------+
| total traffic | average message size |
+---------------+----------------------+
|       3798185 |          237386.5625 |
+---------------+----------------------+
```

- How many miles did the drivers in the `driver_log` table travel? What was the average number of miles traveled per day?

```
mysql> SELECT
    -> SUM(miles) AS 'total miles',
    -> AVG(miles) AS 'average miles/day'
    -> FROM driver_log;
+-------------+-------------------+
| total miles | average miles/day |
+-------------+-------------------+
|        2166 |          216.6000 |
+-------------+-------------------+
```

- What is the total population of the United States?

```
mysql> SELECT SUM(pop) FROM states;
+-----------+
| SUM(pop)  |
+-----------+
| 293101881 |
+-----------+
```

The value represents the population reported for July 2004. The figure shown here differs from the U.S. population reported by the U.S. Census Bureau, because the states table doesn't contain a count for Washington, D.C.

SUM( ) and AVG( ) are strictly numeric functions, so they can't be used with strings or temporal values. On the other hand, sometimes you can convert nonnumeric values to useful numeric forms. Suppose that a table stores TIME values that represent elapsed time:

```
mysql> SELECT t1 FROM time_val;
+----------+
| t1       |
+----------+
| 15:00:00 |
| 05:01:30 |
| 12:30:20 |
+----------+
```

To compute the total elapsed time, use TIME_TO_SEC( ) to convert the values to seconds before summing them. The resulting sum also will be in seconds; pass it to SEC_TO_TIME( ) to convert the sum back to TIME format:

```
mysql> SELECT SUM(TIME_TO_SEC(t1)) AS 'total seconds',
    -> SEC_TO_TIME(SUM(TIME_TO_SEC(t1))) AS 'total time'
    -> FROM time_val;
+---------------+------------+
```

```
| total seconds | total time |
+---------------+------------+
|        117110 | 32:31:50   |
+---------------+------------+
```

See Also

The SUM( ) and AVG( ) functions are especially useful in applications that compute statistics. They're explored further in Chapter 13 along with STD( ), a related function that calculates standard deviations.

8.4 Using DISTINCT to Eliminate Duplicates

Problem

You want to know which values are present in a set of values, without displaying duplicate values multiple times. Or you want to know how many distinct values there are.

Solution

Use DISTINCT to select unique values or COUNT(DISTINCT) to count them.

Discussion

One summary operation that doesn't use aggregate functions is to determine which values or rows are contained in a dataset by eliminating duplicates. Do this with DISTINCT (or DISTINCTROW, which is synonymous). DISTINCT is useful for boiling down a query result, and often is combined with ORDER BY to place the values in more meaningful order. For example, to determine the names of the drivers listed in the driver_log table, use the following statement:

```
mysql> SELECT DISTINCT name FROM driver_log ORDER BY name;
+-------+
| name  |
+-------+
| Ben   |
| Henry |
| Suzi  |
+-------+
```

A statement without DISTINCT produces the same names, but is not nearly as easy to understand, even with a small dataset:

```
mysql> SELECT name FROM driver_log;
+-------+
| name  |
+-------+
| Ben   |
| Suzi  |
| Henry |
```

```
| Henry |
| Ben   |
| Henry |
| Suzi  |
| Henry |
| Ben   |
| Henry |
+-------+
```

To determine how many different drivers there are, use COUNT(DISTINCT):

```
mysql> SELECT COUNT(DISTINCT name) FROM driver_log;
+----------------------+
| COUNT(DISTINCT name) |
+----------------------+
|                    3 |
+----------------------+
```

COUNT(DISTINCT) ignores NULL values. Should you wish to count NULL as one of the values in the set if it's present, use one of the following expressions:

```
COUNT(DISTINCT val) + IF(COUNT(IF(val IS NULL,1,NULL))=0,0,1)
COUNT(DISTINCT val) + IF(SUM(ISNULL(val))=0,0,1)
COUNT(DISTINCT val) + (SUM(ISNULL(val))!=0)
```

DISTINCT queries often are useful in conjunction with aggregate functions to obtain a more complete characterization of your data. Suppose that you have a customer table that contains a state column indicating the state where customers are located. Applying COUNT(*) to the customer table indicates how many customers you have, using DISTINCT on the state values in the table tells you the number of states in which you have customers, and COUNT(DISTINCT) on the state values tells you how many states your customer base represents.

When used with multiple columns, DISTINCT shows the different combinations of values in the columns and COUNT(DISTINCT) counts the number of combinations. The following statements show the different sender/recipient pairs in the mail table and how many such pairs there are:

```
mysql> SELECT DISTINCT srcuser, dstuser FROM mail
    -> ORDER BY srcuser, dstuser;
+---------+---------+
| srcuser | dstuser |
+---------+---------+
| barb    | barb    |
| barb    | tricia  |
| gene    | barb    |
| gene    | gene    |
| gene    | tricia  |
| phil    | barb    |
| phil    | phil    |
| phil    | tricia  |
| tricia  | gene    |
| tricia  | phil    |
+---------+---------+
mysql> SELECT COUNT(DISTINCT srcuser, dstuser) FROM mail;
```

```
+----------------------------------+
| COUNT(DISTINCT srcuser, dstuser) |
+----------------------------------+
|                               10 |
+----------------------------------+
```

DISTINCT works with expressions, too, not just column values. To determine the number of hours of the day during which messages in the mail are sent, count the distinct HOUR( ) values:

```
mysql> SELECT COUNT(DISTINCT HOUR(t)) FROM mail;
+------------------------+
| COUNT(DISTINCT HOUR(t)) |
+------------------------+
|                     12 |
+------------------------+
```

To find out which hours those were, list them:

```
mysql> SELECT DISTINCT HOUR(t) AS hour FROM mail ORDER BY hour;
+------+
| hour |
+------+
|    7 |
|    8 |
|    9 |
|   10 |
|   11 |
|   12 |
|   13 |
|   14 |
|   15 |
|   17 |
|   22 |
|   23 |
+------+
```

Note that this statement doesn't tell you how many messages were sent each hour. That's covered in Recipe 8.15.

8.5 Finding Values Associated with Minimum and Maximum Values

Problem

You want to know the values for other columns in the row that contains a minimum or maximum value.

Solution

Use two statements and a user-defined variable. Or use a subquery. Or use a join.

Discussion

MIN( ) and MAX( ) find the endpoints of a range of values, but sometimes when finding a minimum or maximum value, you're also interested in other values from the row in which the value occurs. For example, you can find the largest state population like this:

```
mysql> SELECT MAX(pop) FROM states;
+----------+
| MAX(pop) |
+----------+
| 35893799 |
+----------+
```

But that doesn't show you which state has this population. The obvious attempt at getting that information looks like this:

```
mysql> SELECT MAX(pop), name FROM states WHERE pop = MAX(pop);
ERROR 1111 (HY000): Invalid use of group function
```

Probably everyone tries something like that sooner or later, but it doesn't work. Aggregate functions such as MIN( ) and MAX( ) cannot be used in WHERE clauses, which require expressions that apply to individual rows. The intent of the statement is to determine which row has the maximum population value, and then display the associated state name. The problem is that while you and I know perfectly well what we mean by writing such a thing, it makes no sense at all to MySQL. The statement fails because MySQL uses the WHERE clause to determine which rows to select, but it knows the value of an aggregate function only *after* selecting the rows from which the function's value is determined! So, in a sense, the statement is self-contradictory. You can solve this problem by saving the maximum population value in a user-defined variable and then comparing rows to the variable value:

```
mysql> SET @max = (SELECT MAX(pop) FROM states);
mysql> SELECT pop AS 'highest population', name FROM states WHERE pop = @max;
+--------------------+------------+
| highest population | name       |
+--------------------+------------+
|           35893799 | California |
+--------------------+------------+
```

For a single-statement solution, use a subquery in the WHERE clause that returns the maximum population value:

```
mysql> SELECT pop AS 'highest population', name FROM states
    -> WHERE pop = (SELECT MAX(pop) FROM states);
+--------------------+------------+
| highest population | name       |
+--------------------+------------+
|           35893799 | California |
+--------------------+------------+
```

This technique also works even if the minimum or maximum value itself isn't actually contained in the row, but is only derived from it. If you want to know the length of the shortest verse in the King James Version, that's easy to find:

```
mysql> SELECT MIN(CHAR_LENGTH(vtext)) FROM kjv;
+-------------------------+
| MIN(CHAR_LENGTH(vtext)) |
+-------------------------+
|                      11 |
+-------------------------+
```

If you want to know, "What verse is that?" do this instead:

```
mysql> SELECT bname, cnum, vnum, vtext FROM kjv
    -> WHERE CHAR_LENGTH(vtext) = (SELECT MIN(CHAR_LENGTH(vtext)) FROM kjv);
+-------+------+------+-------------+
| bname | cnum | vnum | vtext       |
+-------+------+------+-------------+
| John  |   11 |   35 | Jesus wept. |
+-------+------+------+-------------+
```

Yet another way to select other columns from rows containing a minimum or maximum value is to use a join. Select the value into another table, and then join it to the original table to select the row that matches the value. To find the row for the state with the highest population, use a join like this:

```
mysql> CREATE TABLE t SELECT MAX(pop) as maxpop FROM states;
mysql> SELECT states.* FROM states INNER JOIN t ON states.pop = t.maxpop;
+------------+--------+------------+----------+
| name       | abbrev | statehood  | pop      |
+------------+--------+------------+----------+
| California | CA     | 1850-09-09 | 35893799 |
+------------+--------+------------+----------+
```

See Also

For more information about joins, see Chapter 12, in particular, Recipe 12.6, which further discusses the problem of finding rows that contain groupwise minimum or maximum values.

8.6 Controlling String Case Sensitivity for MIN( ) and MAX( )

Problem

MIN( ) and MAX( ) select strings in case-sensitive fashion when you don't want them to, or vice versa.

Solution

Alter the comparison characteristics of the strings.

Discussion

Chapter 5 discusses how string comparison properties depend on whether the strings are binary or nonbinary:

- Binary strings are sequences of bytes. They are compared byte by byte using numeric byte values. Character set and lettercase have no meaning for comparisons.

- Nonbinary strings are sequences of characters. They have a character set and collation and are compared character by character using the order defined by the collation.

These properties also apply when you use a string column as the argument to the `MIN()` or `MAX()` functions because they are based on comparison. To alter how these functions work with a string column, you must alter the column's comparison properties. Recipe 5.9 discusses how to control these properties, and Recipe 7.4 shows how they apply to string sorts. The same principles apply to finding minimum and maximum string values, so I'll just summarize here, and you can read Recipe 7.4 for additional details.

- To compare case-insensitive strings in case-sensitive fashion, order the values using a case-sensitive collation:

    ```
    SELECT
    MIN(str_col COLLATE latin1_general_cs) AS min,
    MAX(str_col COLLATE latin1_general_cs) AS max
    FROM tbl;
    ```

- To compare case-sensitive strings in case-insensitive fashion, order the values using a case-insensitive collation:

    ```
    SELECT
    MIN(str_col COLLATE latin1_swedish_ci) AS min,
    MAX(str_col COLLATE latin1_swedish_ci) AS max
    FROM tbl;
    ```

    Another possibility is to compare values that have all been converted to the same lettercase, which makes lettercase irrelevant. However, that also changes the retrieved values:

    ```
    SELECT
    MIN(UPPER(str_col)) AS min,
    MAX(UPPER(str_col)) AS max
    FROM tbl;
    ```

- Binary strings compare using numeric byte values, so there is no concept of lettercase involved. However, because letters in different cases have different byte values, comparisons of binary strings effectively are case-sensitive (that is, a and A are unequal). To compare binary strings using a case-insensitive ordering, convert them to nonbinary strings, and apply an appropriate collation:

    ```
    SELECT
    MIN(CONVERT(str_col USING latin1) COLLATE latin1_swedish_ci) AS min,
    MAX(CONVERT(str_col USING latin1) COLLATE latin1_swedish_ci) AS max
    FROM tbl;
    ```

    If the default collation is case-insensitive (as is true for `latin1`), you can omit the `COLLATE` clause.

8.7 Dividing a Summary into Subgroups

Problem

You want to calculate a summary for each subgroup of a set of rows, not an overall summary value.

Solution

Use a `GROUP BY` clause to arrange rows into groups.

Discussion

The summary statements shown so far calculate summary values over all rows in the result set. For example, the following statement determines the number of records in the `mail` table, and thus the total number of mail messages that have been sent:

```
mysql> SELECT COUNT(*) FROM mail;
+----------+
| COUNT(*) |
+----------+
|       16 |
+----------+
```

Sometimes it's desirable to break a set of rows into subgroups and summarize each group. Do this by using aggregate functions in conjunction with a `GROUP BY` clause. To determine the number of messages per sender, group the rows by sender name, count how many times each name occurs, and display the names with the counts:

```
mysql> SELECT srcuser, COUNT(*) FROM mail
    -> GROUP BY srcuser;
+---------+----------+
| srcuser | COUNT(*) |
+---------+----------+
| barb    |        3 |
| gene    |        6 |
| phil    |        5 |
| tricia  |        2 |
+---------+----------+
```

That query summarizes the same column that is used for grouping (`srcuser`), but that's not always necessary. Suppose that you want a quick characterization of the `mail` table, showing for each sender listed in it the total amount of traffic sent (in bytes) and the average number of bytes per message. In this case, you still use the `srcuser` column to place the rows in groups, but the summary functions operate on the `size` values:

```
mysql> SELECT srcuser,
    -> SUM(size) AS 'total bytes',
    -> AVG(size) AS 'bytes per message'
    -> FROM mail GROUP BY srcuser;
+---------+-------------+-------------------+
```

```
| srcuser | total bytes | bytes per message |
+---------+-------------+-------------------+
| barb    |      156696 |         52232.0000 |
| gene    |     1033108 |        172184.6667 |
| phil    |       18974 |          3794.8000 |
| tricia  |     2589407 |       1294703.5000 |
+---------+-------------+-------------------+
```

Use as many grouping columns as necessary to achieve as fine-grained a summary as you require. The earlier query that shows the number of messages per sender is a coarse summary. To be more specific and find out how many messages each sender sent from each host, use two grouping columns. This produces a result with nested groups (groups within groups):

```
mysql> SELECT srcuser, srchost, COUNT(srcuser) FROM mail
    -> GROUP BY srcuser, srchost;
+---------+---------+----------------+
| srcuser | srchost | COUNT(srcuser) |
+---------+---------+----------------+
| barb    | saturn  |              2 |
| barb    | venus   |              1 |
| gene    | mars    |              2 |
| gene    | saturn  |              2 |
| gene    | venus   |              2 |
| phil    | mars    |              3 |
| phil    | venus   |              2 |
| tricia  | mars    |              1 |
| tricia  | saturn  |              1 |
+---------+---------+----------------+
```

The preceding examples in this section have used COUNT( ), SUM( ), and AVG( ) for per-group summaries. You can use MIN( ) or MAX( ), too. With a GROUP BY clause, they will tell you the smallest or largest value per group. The following query groups mail table rows by message sender, displaying for each the size of the largest message sent and the date of the most recent message:

```
mysql> SELECT srcuser, MAX(size), MAX(t) FROM mail GROUP BY srcuser;
+---------+-----------+---------------------+
| srcuser | MAX(size) | MAX(t)              |
+---------+-----------+---------------------+
| barb    |     98151 | 2006-05-14 14:42:21 |
| gene    |    998532 | 2006-05-19 22:21:51 |
| phil    |     10294 | 2006-05-17 12:49:23 |
| tricia  |   2394482 | 2006-05-14 17:03:01 |
+---------+-----------+---------------------+
```

You can group by multiple columns and display a maximum for each combination of values in those columns. This query finds the size of the largest message sent between each pair of sender and recipient values listed in the mail table:

```
mysql> SELECT srcuser, dstuser, MAX(size) FROM mail GROUP BY srcuser, dstuser;
+---------+---------+-----------+
| srcuser | dstuser | MAX(size) |
+---------+---------+-----------+
```

```
| barb   | barb   |      98151 |
| barb   | tricia |      58274 |
| gene   | barb   |       2291 |
| gene   | gene   |      23992 |
| gene   | tricia |     998532 |
| phil   | barb   |      10294 |
| phil   | phil   |       1048 |
| phil   | tricia |       5781 |
| tricia | gene   |     194925 |
| tricia | phil   |    2394482 |
+--------+--------+------------+
```

When using aggregate functions to produce per-group summary values, watch out for the following trap, which involves selecting nonsummary table columns not related to the grouping columns. Suppose that you want to know the longest trip per driver in the `driver_log` table. That's produced by this query:

```
mysql> SELECT name, MAX(miles) AS 'longest trip'
    -> FROM driver_log GROUP BY name;
+-------+--------------+
| name  | longest trip |
+-------+--------------+
| Ben   |          152 |
| Henry |          300 |
| Suzi  |          502 |
+-------+--------------+
```

But what if you also want to show the date on which each driver's longest trip occurred? Can you just add `trav_date` to the output column list? Sorry, that won't work:

```
mysql> SELECT name, trav_date, MAX(miles) AS 'longest trip'
    -> FROM driver_log GROUP BY name;
+-------+------------+--------------+
| name  | trav_date  | longest trip |
+-------+------------+--------------+
| Ben   | 2006-08-30 |          152 |
| Henry | 2006-08-29 |          300 |
| Suzi  | 2006-08-29 |          502 |
+-------+------------+--------------+
```

The query does produce a result, but if you compare it to the full table (shown following), you'll see that although the dates for Ben and Henry are correct, the date for Suzi is not:

```
+--------+-------+------------+-------+
| rec_id | name  | trav_date  | miles |
+--------+-------+------------+-------+
|      1 | Ben   | 2006-08-30 |   152 |     ← Ben's longest trip
|      2 | Suzi  | 2006-08-29 |   391 |
|      3 | Henry | 2006-08-29 |   300 |     ← Henry's longest trip
|      4 | Henry | 2006-08-27 |    96 |
|      5 | Ben   | 2006-08-29 |   131 |
|      6 | Henry | 2006-08-26 |   115 |
|      7 | Suzi  | 2006-09-02 |   502 |     ← Suzi's longest trip
|      8 | Henry | 2006-09-01 |   197 |
```

```
|        9 | Ben   | 2006-09-02 |    79 |
|       10 | Henry | 2006-08-30 |   203 |
+----------+-------+------------+-------+
```

So what's going on? Why does the summary statement produce incorrect results? This happens because when you include a GROUP BY clause in a query, the only values that you can select are the grouped columns or summary values calculated from the groups. If you display additional table columns, they're not tied to the grouped columns and the values displayed for them are indeterminate. (For the statement just shown, it appears that MySQL may simply be picking the first date for each driver, regardless of whether it matches the driver's maximum mileage value.)

The general solution to the problem of displaying contents of rows associated with minimum or maximum group values involves a join. The technique is described in Chapter 12. For the problem at hand, the required results are produced as follows:

```
mysql> CREATE TABLE t
    -> SELECT name, MAX(miles) AS miles FROM driver_log GROUP BY name;
mysql> SELECT d.name, d.trav_date, d.miles AS 'longest trip'
    -> FROM driver_log AS d INNER JOIN t USING (name, miles) ORDER BY name;
+-------+------------+--------------+
| name  | trav_date  | longest trip |
+-------+------------+--------------+
| Ben   | 2006-08-30 |          152 |
| Henry | 2006-08-29 |          300 |
| Suzi  | 2006-09-02 |          502 |
+-------+------------+--------------+
```

8.8 Summaries and NULL Values

Problem

You're summarizing a set of values that may include NULL values and you need to know how to interpret the results.

Solution

Understand how aggregate functions handle NULL values.

Discussion

Most aggregate functions ignore NULL values. Suppose that you have a table expt that records experimental results for subjects who are to be given four tests each and that lists the test score as NULL for those tests that have not yet been administered:

```
mysql> SELECT subject, test, score FROM expt ORDER BY subject, test;
+---------+------+-------+
| subject | test | score |
+---------+------+-------+
| Jane    | A    |    47 |
```

```
| Jane    | B |    50 |
| Jane    | C |  NULL |
| Jane    | D |  NULL |
| Marvin  | A |    52 |
| Marvin  | B |    45 |
| Marvin  | C |    53 |
| Marvin  | D |  NULL |
+---------+---+-------+
```

By using a GROUP BY clause to arrange the rows by subject name, the number of tests taken by each subject, as well as the total, average, lowest, and highest scores can be calculated like this:

```
mysql> SELECT subject,
    -> COUNT(score) AS n,
    -> SUM(score) AS total,
    -> AVG(score) AS average,
    -> MIN(score) AS lowest,
    -> MAX(score) AS highest
    -> FROM expt GROUP BY subject;
+---------+---+-------+---------+--------+---------+
| subject | n | total | average | lowest | highest |
+---------+---+-------+---------+--------+---------+
| Jane    | 2 |    97 | 48.5000 |     47 |      50 |
| Marvin  | 3 |   150 | 50.0000 |     45 |      53 |
+---------+---+-------+---------+--------+---------+
```

You can see from the results in the column labeled n (number of tests) that the query counts only five values, even though the table contains eight. Why? Because the values in that column correspond to the number of non-NULL test scores for each subject. The other summary columns display results that are calculated only from the non-NULL scores as well.

It makes a lot of sense for aggregate functions to ignore NULL values. If they followed the usual SQL arithmetic rules, adding NULL to any other value would produce a NULL result. That would make aggregate functions really difficult to use because you'd have to filter out NULL values every time you performed a summary, to avoid getting a NULL result. Ugh. By ignoring NULL values, aggregate functions become a lot more convenient.

However, be aware that even though aggregate functions may ignore NULL values, some of them can still produce NULL as a result. This happens if there's nothing to summarize, which occurs if the set of values is empty or contains only NULL values. The following query is the same as the previous one, with one small difference. It selects only NULL test scores, so there's nothing for the aggregate functions to operate on:

```
mysql> SELECT subject,
    -> COUNT(score) AS n,
    -> SUM(score) AS total,
    -> AVG(score) AS average,
    -> MIN(score) AS lowest,
    -> MAX(score) AS highest
    -> FROM expt WHERE score IS NULL GROUP BY subject;
+---------+---+-------+---------+--------+---------+
```

```
| subject | n | total | average | lowest | highest |
+---------+---+-------+---------+--------+---------+
| Jane    | 0 | NULL  | NULL    | NULL   | NULL    |
| Marvin  | 0 | NULL  | NULL    | NULL   | NULL    |
+---------+---+-------+---------+--------+---------+
```

For COUNT( ), the number of scores per subject is zero and is reported that way. On the other hand, SUM( ), AVG( ), MIN( ), and MAX( ) return NULL when there are no values to summarize. If you don't want these functions to produce NULL in the query output, use IFNULL( ) to map their results appropriately:

```
mysql> SELECT subject,
    -> COUNT(score) AS n,
    -> IFNULL(SUM(score),0) AS total,
    -> IFNULL(AVG(score),0) AS average,
    -> IFNULL(MIN(score),'Unknown') AS lowest,
    -> IFNULL(MAX(score),'Unknown') AS highest
    -> FROM expt WHERE score IS NULL GROUP BY subject;
+---------+---+-------+---------+---------+---------+
| subject | n | total | average | lowest  | highest |
+---------+---+-------+---------+---------+---------+
| Jane    | 0 |     0 | 0.0000  | Unknown | Unknown |
| Marvin  | 0 |     0 | 0.0000  | Unknown | Unknown |
+---------+---+-------+---------+---------+---------+
```

COUNT( ) is somewhat different with regard to NULL values than the other aggregate functions. Like other aggregate functions, COUNT(*expr*) counts only non-NULL values, but COUNT(*) counts rows, regardless of their content. You can see the difference between the forms of COUNT( ) like this:

```
mysql> SELECT COUNT(*), COUNT(score) FROM expt;
+----------+--------------+
| COUNT(*) | COUNT(score) |
+----------+--------------+
|        8 |            5 |
+----------+--------------+
```

This tells us that there are eight rows in the expt table but that only five of them have the score value filled in. The different forms of COUNT( ) can be very useful for counting missing values. Just take the difference:

```
mysql> SELECT COUNT(*) - COUNT(score) AS missing FROM expt;
+---------+
| missing |
+---------+
|       3 |
+---------+
```

Missing and nonmissing counts can be determined for subgroups as well. The following query does so for each subject, providing an easy way to assess the extent to which the experiment has been completed:

```
mysql> SELECT subject,
    -> COUNT(*) AS total,
    -> COUNT(score) AS 'nonmissing',
```

```
    -> COUNT(*) - COUNT(score) AS missing
    -> FROM expt GROUP BY subject;
+---------+-------+-------------+---------+
| subject | total | nonmissing  | missing |
+---------+-------+-------------+---------+
| Jane    |     4 |           2 |       2 |
| Marvin  |     4 |           3 |       1 |
+---------+-------+-------------+---------+
```

8.9 Selecting Only Groups with Certain Characteristics

Problem

You want to calculate group summaries but display the results only for those groups that match certain criteria.

Solution

Use a HAVING clause.

Discussion

You're familiar with the use of WHERE to specify conditions that individual rows must satisfy to be selected by a statement. It's natural, therefore, to use WHERE to write conditions that involve summary values. The only trouble is that it doesn't work. If you want to identify drivers in the driver_log table who drove more than three days, you'd probably first think to write the statement like this:

```
mysql> SELECT COUNT(*), name
    -> FROM driver_log
    -> WHERE COUNT(*) > 3
    -> GROUP BY name;
ERROR 1111 (HY000): Invalid use of group function
```

The problem here is that WHERE specifies the initial constraints that determine which rows to select, but the value of COUNT( ) can be determined only after the rows have been selected. The solution is to put the COUNT( ) expression in a HAVING clause instead. HAVING is analogous to WHERE, but it applies to group characteristics rather than to single rows. That is, HAVING operates on the already-selected-and-grouped set of rows, applying additional constraints based on aggregate function results that aren't known during the initial selection process. The preceding query therefore should be written like this:

```
mysql> SELECT COUNT(*), name
    -> FROM driver_log
    -> GROUP BY name
    -> HAVING COUNT(*) > 3;
+----------+-------+
| COUNT(*) | name  |
+----------+-------+
```

```
|         5 | Henry |
+----------+-------+
```

When you use `HAVING`, you can still include a `WHERE` clause—but only to select rows, not to test summary values.

`HAVING` can refer to aliases, so the previous query can be rewritten like this:

```
mysql> SELECT COUNT(*) AS count, name
    -> FROM driver_log
    -> GROUP BY name
    -> HAVING count > 3;
+-------+-------+
| count | name  |
+-------+-------+
|     5 | Henry |
+-------+-------+
```

8.10 Using Counts to Determine Whether Values Are Unique

Problem

You want to know whether table values are unique.

Solution

Use `HAVING` in conjunction with `COUNT( )`.

Discussion

`DISTINCT` eliminates duplicates but doesn't show which values actually were duplicated in the original data. You can use `HAVING` to find unique values in situations to which `DISTINCT` does not apply. `HAVING` can tell you which values were unique or nonunique.

The following statements show the days on which only one driver was active, and the days on which more than one driver was active. They're based on using `HAVING` and `COUNT( )` to determine which `trav_date` values are unique or nonunique:

```
mysql> SELECT trav_date, COUNT(trav_date)
    -> FROM driver_log
    -> GROUP BY trav_date
    -> HAVING COUNT(trav_date) = 1;
+------------+------------------+
| trav_date  | COUNT(trav_date) |
+------------+------------------+
| 2006-08-26 |                1 |
| 2006-08-27 |                1 |
| 2006-09-01 |                1 |
+------------+------------------+
mysql> SELECT trav_date, COUNT(trav_date)
    -> FROM driver_log
    -> GROUP BY trav_date
```

```
    -> HAVING COUNT(trav_date) > 1;
+------------+------------------+
| trav_date  | COUNT(trav_date) |
+------------+------------------+
| 2006-08-29 |                3 |
| 2006-08-30 |                2 |
| 2006-09-02 |                2 |
+------------+------------------+
```

This technique works for combinations of values, too. For example, to find message sender/recipient pairs between whom only one message was sent, look for combinations that occur only once in the mail table:

```
mysql> SELECT srcuser, dstuser
    -> FROM mail
    -> GROUP BY srcuser, dstuser
    -> HAVING COUNT(*) = 1;
+---------+---------+
| srcuser | dstuser |
+---------+---------+
| barb    | barb    |
| gene    | tricia  |
| phil    | barb    |
| tricia  | gene    |
| tricia  | phil    |
+---------+---------+
```

Note that this query doesn't print the count. The first two examples did so, to show that the counts were being used properly, but you can refer to an aggregate value in a HAVING clause without including it in the output column list.

8.11 Grouping by Expression Results

Problem

You want to group rows into subgroups based on values calculated from an expression.

Solution

Put the expression in the GROUP BY clause.

Discussion

GROUP BY, like ORDER BY, can refer to expressions. This means you can use calculations as the basis for grouping. For example, to find the distribution of the lengths of state names, use those lengths as the grouping characteristic:

```
mysql> SELECT CHAR_LENGTH(name), COUNT(*)
    -> FROM states GROUP BY CHAR_LENGTH(name);
+-------------------+----------+
| CHAR_LENGTH(name) | COUNT(*) |
```

```
+------------------+---------+
|                4 |       3 |
|                5 |       3 |
|                6 |       5 |
|                7 |       8 |
|                8 |      12 |
|                9 |       4 |
|               10 |       4 |
|               11 |       2 |
|               12 |       4 |
|               13 |       3 |
|               14 |       2 |
+------------------+---------+
```

As with ORDER BY, you can write the grouping expression directly in the GROUP BY clause, or use an alias for the expression (if it appears in the output column list), and refer to the alias in the GROUP BY.

You can group by multiple expressions if you like. To find days of the year on which more than one state joined the Union, group by statehood month and day, and then use HAVING and COUNT( ) to find the nonunique combinations:

```
mysql> SELECT
    -> MONTHNAME(statehood) AS month,
    -> DAYOFMONTH(statehood) AS day,
    -> COUNT(*) AS count
    -> FROM states GROUP BY month, day HAVING count > 1;
+----------+------+-------+
| month    | day  | count |
+----------+------+-------+
| February |   14 |     2 |
| June     |    1 |     2 |
| March    |    1 |     2 |
| May      |   29 |     2 |
| November |    2 |     2 |
+----------+------+-------+
```

8.12 Categorizing Noncategorical Data

Problem

You need to summarize a set of values that are not naturally categorical.

Solution

Use an expression to group the values into categories.

Discussion

Recipe 8.11 showed how to group rows by expression results. One important application for doing so is to provide categories for values that are not particularly categorical.

This is useful because GROUP BY works best for columns with repetitive values. For example, you might attempt to perform a population analysis by grouping rows in the states table using values in the pop column. As it happens, that does not work very well due to the high number of distinct values in the column. In fact, they're *all* distinct, as the following query shows:

```
mysql> SELECT COUNT(pop), COUNT(DISTINCT pop) FROM states;
+------------+---------------------+
| COUNT(pop) | COUNT(DISTINCT pop) |
+------------+---------------------+
|         50 |                  50 |
+------------+---------------------+
```

In situations like this, where values do not group nicely into a small number of sets, you can use a transformation that forces them into categories. Begin by determining the range of population values:

```
mysql> SELECT MIN(pop), MAX(pop) FROM states;
+----------+----------+
| MIN(pop) | MAX(pop) |
+----------+----------+
|   506529 | 35893799 |
+----------+----------+
```

You can see from that result that if you divide the pop values by five million, they'll group into six categories—a reasonable number. (The category ranges will be 1 to 5,000,000, 5,000,001 to 10,000,000, and so forth.) To put each population value in the proper category, divide by five million, and use the integer result:

```
mysql> SELECT FLOOR(pop/5000000) AS 'max population (millions)',
    -> COUNT(*) AS 'number of states'
    -> FROM states GROUP BY 'max population (millions)';
+---------------------------+------------------+
| max population (millions) | number of states |
+---------------------------+------------------+
|                         0 |               29 |
|                         1 |               13 |
|                         2 |                4 |
|                         3 |                2 |
|                         4 |                1 |
|                         7 |                1 |
+---------------------------+------------------+
```

Hmm. That's not quite right. The expression groups the population values into a small number of categories, all right, but doesn't report the category values properly. Let's try multiplying the FLOOR( ) results by five:

```
mysql> SELECT FLOOR(pop/5000000)*5 AS 'max population (millions)',
    -> COUNT(*) AS 'number of states'
    -> FROM states GROUP BY 'max population (millions)';
+---------------------------+------------------+
| max population (millions) | number of states |
+---------------------------+------------------+
|                         0 |               29 |
```

```
|                    5 |              13 |
|                   10 |               4 |
|                   15 |               2 |
|                   20 |               1 |
|                   35 |               1 |
+----------------------+-----------------+
```

That still isn't correct. The maximum state population was 35,893,799, which should go into a category for 40 million, not one for 35 million. The problem here is that the category-generating expression groups values toward the lower bound of each category. To group values toward the upper bound instead, use the following technique. For categories of size *n*, you can place a value *x* into the proper category using this expression:

```
FLOOR((x+(n-1))/n)
```

So the final form of our query looks like this:

```
mysql> SELECT FLOOR((pop+4999999)/5000000)*5 AS 'max population (millions)',
    -> COUNT(*) AS 'number of states'
    -> FROM states GROUP BY 'max population (millions)';
+---------------------------+------------------+
| max population (millions) | number of states |
+---------------------------+------------------+
|                         5 |               29 |
|                        10 |               13 |
|                        15 |                4 |
|                        20 |                2 |
|                        25 |                1 |
|                        40 |                1 |
+---------------------------+------------------+
```

The result shows clearly that the majority of U.S. states have a population of five million or less.

This technique works for all kinds of numeric values. For example, you can group `mail` table rows into categories of 100,000 bytes as follows:

```
mysql> SELECT FLOOR((size+99999)/100000) AS 'size (100KB)',
    -> COUNT(*) AS 'number of messages'
    -> FROM mail GROUP BY 'size (100KB)';
+--------------+--------------------+
| size (100KB) | number of messages |
+--------------+--------------------+
|            1 |                 13 |
|            2 |                  1 |
|           10 |                  1 |
|           24 |                  1 |
+--------------+--------------------+
```

In some instances, it may be more appropriate to categorize groups on a logarithmic scale. For example, the state population values can be treated that way as follows:

```
mysql> SELECT FLOOR(LOG10(pop)) AS 'log10(population)',
    -> COUNT(*) AS 'number of states'
    -> FROM states GROUP BY 'log10(population)';
```

```
+-------------------+-------------------+
| log10(population) | number of states |
+-------------------+-------------------+
|                 5 |                7 |
|                 6 |               35 |
|                 7 |                8 |
+-------------------+-------------------+
```

The query shows the number of states that have populations measured in hundreds of thousands, millions, and tens of millions, respectively.

How Repetitive Is a Set of Values?

To assess how much repetition is present in a set of values, use the ratio of COUNT(DISTINCT) and COUNT( ). If all values are unique, both counts will be the same and the ratio will be 1. This is the case for the t values in the mail table and the pop values in the states table:

```
mysql> SELECT COUNT(DISTINCT t) / COUNT(t) FROM mail;
+-----------------------------+
| COUNT(DISTINCT t) / COUNT(t) |
+-----------------------------+
|                      1.0000 |
+-----------------------------+
mysql> SELECT COUNT(DISTINCT pop) / COUNT(pop) FROM states;
+---------------------------------+
| COUNT(DISTINCT pop) / COUNT(pop) |
+---------------------------------+
|                          1.0000 |
+---------------------------------+
```

For a more repetitive set of values, COUNT(DISTINCT) will be less than COUNT( ), and the ratio will be smaller:

```
mysql> SELECT COUNT(DISTINCT name) / COUNT(name) FROM driver_log;
+-----------------------------------+
| COUNT(DISTINCT name) / COUNT(name) |
+-----------------------------------+
|                            0.3000 |
+-----------------------------------+
```

What's the practical use for this ratio? A result close to zero indicates a high degree of repetition, which means the values will group into a small number of categories naturally. A result of 1 or close to it indicates many unique values, with the consequence that GROUP BY won't be very efficient for grouping the values into categories. (That is, there will be a lot of categories, relative to the number of values.) This tells you that to generate a summary, you'll probably find it necessary to impose an artificial categorization on the values, using the techniques described in this recipe.

8.13 Controlling Summary Display Order

Problem

You want to sort the result of a summary statement.

Solution

Use an ORDER BY clause—if GROUP BY doesn't produce the desired sort order.

Discussion

In MySQL, GROUP BY not only groups, it sorts. Thus, there is often no need for an ORDER BY clause in a summary statement. But you can still use ORDER BY if you want a sort order other than the one that GROUP BY produces by default. For example, to determine the number of days driven and total miles for each person in the driver_log table, use this statement:

```
mysql> SELECT name, COUNT(*) AS days, SUM(miles) AS mileage
    -> FROM driver_log GROUP BY name;
+-------+------+---------+
| name  | days | mileage |
+-------+------+---------+
| Ben   |    3 |     362 |
| Henry |    5 |     911 |
| Suzi  |    2 |     893 |
+-------+------+---------+
```

But that sorts by the names. If you want to sort drivers according to who drove the most days or miles, add the appropriate ORDER BY clause:

```
mysql> SELECT name, COUNT(*) AS days, SUM(miles) AS mileage
    -> FROM driver_log GROUP BY name ORDER BY days DESC;
+-------+------+---------+
| name  | days | mileage |
+-------+------+---------+
| Henry |    5 |     911 |
| Ben   |    3 |     362 |
| Suzi  |    2 |     893 |
+-------+------+---------+
mysql> SELECT name, COUNT(*) AS days, SUM(miles) AS mileage
    -> FROM driver_log GROUP BY name ORDER BY mileage DESC;
+-------+------+---------+
| name  | days | mileage |
+-------+------+---------+
| Henry |    5 |     911 |
| Suzi  |    2 |     893 |
| Ben   |    3 |     362 |
+-------+------+---------+
```

The ORDER BY clause in these statements refers to an aggregate value by using an alias. In MySQL 5.0 and up, that is not necessary and you can refer directly to aggregate values in ORDER BY clauses. Before MySQL 5.0, you must alias them and use the alias in the ORDER BY.

Sometimes you can reorder a summary without an ORDER BY clause by choosing an appropriate GROUP BY expression. For example, if you count how many states joined the Union on each day of the week, grouped by day name, the results are sorted in lexical order:

```
mysql> SELECT DAYNAME(statehood), COUNT(*) FROM states
    -> GROUP BY DAYNAME(statehood);
+--------------------+----------+
| DAYNAME(statehood) | COUNT(*) |
+--------------------+----------+
| Friday             |        8 |
| Monday             |        9 |
| Saturday           |       11 |
| Thursday           |        5 |
| Tuesday            |        6 |
| Wednesday          |       11 |
+--------------------+----------+
```

From this you can see that no state entered the Union on a Sunday, but that becomes apparent only after you stare at the query result for a while. The output would be more easily understood were it sorted into day-of-week order. It's possible to do that by adding an explicit ORDER BY to sort on the numeric day-of-week value, but another way to achieve the same result without ORDER BY is to group by DAYOFWEEK( ) rather than by DAYNAME( ):

```
mysql> SELECT DAYNAME(statehood), COUNT(*)
    -> FROM states GROUP BY DAYOFWEEK(statehood);
+--------------------+----------+
| DAYNAME(statehood) | COUNT(*) |
+--------------------+----------+
| Monday             |        9 |
| Tuesday            |        6 |
| Wednesday          |       11 |
| Thursday           |        5 |
| Friday             |        8 |
| Saturday           |       11 |
+--------------------+----------+
```

The implicit ordering done by GROUP BY can add overhead to query processing. If you don't care whether output rows are sorted, add an ORDER BY NULL clause to suppress this sorting and eliminate its overhead:

```
mysql> SELECT name, COUNT(*) AS days, SUM(miles) AS mileage
    -> FROM driver_log GROUP BY name;
+-------+------+---------+
| name  | days | mileage |
+-------+------+---------+
| Ben   |    3 |     362 |
| Henry |    5 |     911 |
| Suzi  |    2 |     893 |
+-------+------+---------+
```

```
mysql> SELECT name, COUNT(*) AS days, SUM(miles) AS mileage
    -> FROM driver_log GROUP BY name ORDER BY NULL;
+-------+------+---------+
| name  | days | mileage |
+-------+------+---------+
| Ben   |    3 |     362 |
| Suzi  |    2 |     893 |
| Henry |    5 |     911 |
+-------+------+---------+
```

The sorting done by GROUP BY is a MySQL extension. To write statements for MySQL that are less likely to need revision when used with other database systems, you may find it beneficial to add an explicit ORDER BY clause in all cases.

8.14 Finding Smallest or Largest Summary Values

Problem

You want to compute per-group summary values but display only the smallest or largest of them.

Solution

Add a LIMIT clause to the statement.

Discussion

MIN( ) and MAX( ) find the values at the endpoints of a range of values, but if you want to know the extremes of a set of summary values, those functions won't work. The arguments to MIN( ) and MAX( ) cannot be other aggregate functions. For example, you can easily find per-driver mileage totals:

```
mysql> SELECT name, SUM(miles)
    -> FROM driver_log
    -> GROUP BY name;
+-------+------------+
| name  | SUM(miles) |
+-------+------------+
| Ben   |        362 |
| Henry |        911 |
| Suzi  |        893 |
+-------+------------+
```

But this doesn't work if you want to select only the row for the driver with the most miles:

```
mysql> SELECT name, SUM(miles)
    -> FROM driver_log
    -> GROUP BY name
    -> HAVING SUM(miles) = MAX(SUM(miles));
ERROR 1111 (HY000): Invalid use of group function
```

Instead, order the rows with the largest SUM( ) values first, and use LIMIT to select the first row:

```
mysql> SELECT name, SUM(miles) AS 'total miles'
    -> FROM driver_log
    -> GROUP BY name
    -> ORDER BY 'total miles' DESC LIMIT 1;
+-------+-------------+
| name  | total miles |
+-------+-------------+
| Henry |         911 |
+-------+-------------+
```

Note that if there is more than one row with the given summary value, a LIMIT 1 query won't tell you that. For example, you might attempt to ascertain the most common initial letter for state names like this:

```
mysql> SELECT LEFT(name,1) AS letter, COUNT(*) AS count FROM states
    -> GROUP BY letter ORDER BY count DESC LIMIT 1;
+--------+-------+
| letter | count |
+--------+-------+
| M      |     8 |
+--------+-------+
```

But eight state names also begin with N. If you need to know all most-frequent values when there may be more than one of them, find the maximum count first, and then select those values with a count that matches the maximum:

```
mysql> SET @max = (SELECT COUNT(*) FROM states
    -> GROUP BY LEFT(name,1) ORDER BY COUNT(*) DESC LIMIT 1);
mysql> SELECT LEFT(name,1) AS letter, COUNT(*) AS count FROM states
    -> GROUP BY letter HAVING count = @max;
+--------+-------+
| letter | count |
+--------+-------+
| M      | 8     |
| N      | 8     |
+--------+-------+
```

Alternatively, put the maximum-count calculation in a subquery and combine the statements into one:

```
mysql> SELECT LEFT(name,1) AS letter, COUNT(*) AS count FROM states
    -> GROUP BY letter HAVING count =
    ->   (SELECT COUNT(*) FROM states
    ->    GROUP BY LEFT(name,1) ORDER BY COUNT(*) DESC LIMIT 1);
+--------+-------+
| letter | count |
+--------+-------+
| M      | 8     |
| N      | 8     |
+--------+-------+
```

8.15 Date-Based Summaries

Problem

You want to produce a summary based on date or time values.

Solution

Use GROUP BY to place temporal values into categories of the appropriate duration. Often this involves using expressions to extract the significant parts of dates or times.

Discussion

To put rows in time order, use an ORDER BY clause to sort a column that has a temporal type. If instead you want to summarize rows based on groupings into time intervals, you need to determine how to categorize each row into the proper interval and use GROUP BY to group them accordingly.

For example, to determine how many drivers were on the road and how many miles were driven each day, group the rows in the `driver_log` table by date:

```
mysql> SELECT trav_date,
    -> COUNT(*) AS 'number of drivers', SUM(miles) As 'miles logged'
    -> FROM driver_log GROUP BY trav_date;
+------------+-------------------+--------------+
| trav_date  | number of drivers | miles logged |
+------------+-------------------+--------------+
| 2006-08-26 |                 1 | 115          |
| 2006-08-27 |                 1 | 96           |
| 2006-08-29 |                 3 | 822          |
| 2006-08-30 |                 2 | 355          |
| 2006-09-01 |                 1 | 197          |
| 2006-09-02 |                 2 | 581          |
+------------+-------------------+--------------+
```

However, this summary will grow lengthier as you add more rows to the table. At some point, the number of distinct dates likely will become so large that the summary fails to be useful, and you'd probably decide to change the category size from daily to weekly or monthly.

When a temporal column contains so many distinct values that it fails to categorize well, it's typical for a summary to group rows using expressions that map the relevant parts of the date or time values onto a smaller set of categories. For example, to produce a time-of-day summary for rows in the `mail` table, do this:[*]

```
mysql> SELECT HOUR(t) AS hour,
    -> COUNT(*) AS 'number of messages',
```

---

[*] Note that the result includes an entry only for hours of the day actually represented in the data. To generate a summary with an entry for every hour, use a join to fill in the "missing" values. See Recipe 12.8.

```
    -> SUM(size) AS 'number of bytes sent'
    -> FROM mail
    -> GROUP BY hour;
+------+--------------------+----------------------+
| hour | number of messages | number of bytes sent |
+------+--------------------+----------------------+
|    7 |                  1 |                 3824 |
|    8 |                  1 |                  978 |
|    9 |                  2 |                 2904 |
|   10 |                  2 |              1056806 |
|   11 |                  1 |                 5781 |
|   12 |                  2 |               195798 |
|   13 |                  1 |                  271 |
|   14 |                  1 |                98151 |
|   15 |                  1 |                 1048 |
|   17 |                  2 |              2398338 |
|   22 |                  1 |                23992 |
|   23 |                  1 |                10294 |
+------+--------------------+----------------------+
```

To produce a day-of-week summary instead, use the DAYOFWEEK( ) function:

```
mysql> SELECT DAYOFWEEK(t) AS weekday,
    -> COUNT(*) AS 'number of messages',
    -> SUM(size) AS 'number of bytes sent'
    -> FROM mail
    -> GROUP BY weekday;
+---------+--------------------+----------------------+
| weekday | number of messages | number of bytes sent |
+---------+--------------------+----------------------+
|       1 |                  1 |                  271 |
|       2 |                  4 |              2500705 |
|       3 |                  4 |              1007190 |
|       4 |                  2 |                10907 |
|       5 |                  1 |                  873 |
|       6 |                  1 |                58274 |
|       7 |                  3 |               219965 |
+---------+--------------------+----------------------+
```

To make the output more meaningful, you might want to use DAYNAME( ) to display weekday names instead. However, because day names sort lexically (for example, "Tuesday" sorts after "Friday"), use DAYNAME( ) only for display purposes. Continue to group based on the numeric day values so that output rows sort that way:

```
mysql> SELECT DAYNAME(t) AS weekday,
    -> COUNT(*) AS 'number of messages',
    -> SUM(size) AS 'number of bytes sent'
    -> FROM mail
    -> GROUP BY DAYOFWEEK(t);
+-----------+--------------------+----------------------+
| weekday   | number of messages | number of bytes sent |
+-----------+--------------------+----------------------+
| Sunday    |                  1 |                  271 |
| Monday    |                  4 |              2500705 |
| Tuesday   |                  4 |              1007190 |
| Wednesday |                  2 |                10907 |
```

```
| Thursday  |                   1 |                873 |
| Friday    |                   1 |              58274 |
| Saturday  |                   3 |             219965 |
+-----------+---------------------+--------------------+
```

A similar technique can be used for summarizing month-of-year categories that are sorted by numeric value but displayed by month name.

Uses for temporal categorizations are numerous:

- DATETIME or TIMESTAMP columns have the potential to contain many unique values. To produce daily summaries, strip off the time of day part to collapse all values occurring within a given day to the same value. Any of the following GROUP BY clauses will do this, although the last one is likely to be slowest:

  ```
  GROUP BY DATE(col_name)
  GROUP BY FROM_DAYS(TO_DAYS(col_name))
  GROUP BY YEAR(col_name), MONTH(col_name), DAYOFMONTH(col_name)
  GROUP BY DATE_FORMAT(col_name,'%Y-%m-%e')
  ```

- To produce monthly or quarterly sales reports, group by MONTH(col_name) or QUARTER(col_name) to place dates into the correct part of the year.

- To summarize web server activity, store your server's logs in MySQL and run statements that collapse the rows into different time categories. Recipe 19.14 discusses how to do this for Apache.

8.16 Working with Per-Group and Overall Summary Values Simultaneously

Problem

You want to produce a report that requires different levels of summary detail. Or you want to compare per-group summary values to an overall summary value.

Solution

Use two statements that retrieve different levels of summary information. Or use a subquery to retrieve one summary value and refer to it in the outer query that refers to other summary values. If it's necessary only to display multiple summary levels, WITH ROLLUP might be sufficient.

Discussion

Sometimes a report involves different levels of summary information. For example, the following report displays the total number of miles per driver from the driver_log table, along with each driver's miles as a percentage of the total miles in the entire table:

```
+-------+--------------+------------------------+
| name  | miles/driver | percent of total miles |
+-------+--------------+------------------------+
| Ben   |          362 |                16.7128 |
| Henry |          911 |                42.0591 |
| Suzi  |          893 |                41.2281 |
+-------+--------------+------------------------+
```

The percentages represent the ratio of each driver's miles to the total miles for all drivers. To perform the percentage calculation, you need a per-group summary to get each driver's miles and also an overall summary to get the total miles. First, run a query to get the overall mileage total:

```
mysql> SELECT @total := SUM(miles) AS 'total miles' FROM driver_log;
+-------------+
| total miles |
+-------------+
|        2166 |
+-------------+
```

Now, calculate the per-group values and use the overall total to compute the percentages:

```
mysql> SELECT name,
    -> SUM(miles) AS 'miles/driver',
    -> (SUM(miles)*100)/@total AS 'percent of total miles'
    -> FROM driver_log GROUP BY name;
+-------+--------------+------------------------+
| name  | miles/driver | percent of total miles |
+-------+--------------+------------------------+
| Ben   |          362 |                16.7128 |
| Henry |          911 |                42.0591 |
| Suzi  |          893 |                41.2281 |
+-------+--------------+------------------------+
```

To combine the two statements into one, use a subquery that computes the total miles:

```
mysql> SELECT name,
    -> SUM(miles) AS 'miles/driver',
    -> (SUM(miles)*100)/(SELECT SUM(miles) FROM driver_log)
    ->   AS 'percent of total miles'
    -> FROM driver_log GROUP BY name;
+-------+--------------+------------------------+
| name  | miles/driver | percent of total miles |
+-------+--------------+------------------------+
| Ben   |          362 |                16.7128 |
| Henry |          911 |                42.0591 |
| Suzi  |          893 |                41.2281 |
+-------+--------------+------------------------+
```

Another type of problem that uses different levels of summary information occurs when you want to compare per-group summary values with the corresponding overall summary value. Suppose that you want to determine which drivers had a lower average miles per day than the group average. Calculate the overall average in a subquery, and then compare each driver's average to the overall average using a HAVING clause:

```
mysql> SELECT name, AVG(miles) AS driver_avg FROM driver_log
    -> GROUP BY name
    -> HAVING driver_avg < (SELECT AVG(miles) FROM driver_log);
+-------+------------+
| name  | driver_avg |
+-------+------------+
| Ben   |   120.6667 |
| Henry |   182.2000 |
+-------+------------+
```

If you just want to display different summary values (and not perform calculations involving one summary level against another), add WITH ROLLUP to the GROUP BY clause:

```
mysql> SELECT name, SUM(miles) AS 'miles/driver'
    -> FROM driver_log GROUP BY name WITH ROLLUP;
+-------+--------------+
| name  | miles/driver |
+-------+--------------+
| Ben   |          362 |
| Henry |          911 |
| Suzi  |          893 |
| NULL  |         2166 |
+-------+--------------+
mysql> SELECT name, AVG(miles) AS driver_avg FROM driver_log
    -> GROUP BY name WITH ROLLUP;
+-------+------------+
| name  | driver_avg |
+-------+------------+
| Ben   |   120.6667 |
| Henry |   182.2000 |
| Suzi  |   446.5000 |
| NULL  |   216.6000 |
+-------+------------+
```

In each case, the output row with NULL in the name column represents the overall sum or average calculated over all drivers.

WITH ROLLUP can present multiple levels of summary, if you group by more than one column. The following statement shows the number of mail messages sent between each pair of users:

```
mysql> SELECT srcuser, dstuser, COUNT(*)
    -> FROM mail GROUP BY srcuser, dstuser;
+---------+---------+----------+
| srcuser | dstuser | COUNT(*) |
+---------+---------+----------+
| barb    | barb    |        1 |
| barb    | tricia  |        2 |
| gene    | barb    |        2 |
| gene    | gene    |        3 |
| gene    | tricia  |        1 |
| phil    | barb    |        1 |
| phil    | phil    |        2 |
| phil    | tricia  |        2 |
| tricia  | gene    |        1 |
```

```
| tricia  | phil   |        1 |
+---------+--------+----------+
```

Adding `WITH ROLLUP` causes the output to include an intermediate count for each `srcuser` value (these are the lines with `NULL` in the `dstuser` column), plus an overall count at the end:

```
mysql> SELECT srcuser, dstuser, COUNT(*)
    -> FROM mail GROUP BY srcuser, dstuser WITH ROLLUP;
+---------+--------+----------+
| srcuser | dstuser | COUNT(*) |
+---------+--------+----------+
| barb    | barb   |        1 |
| barb    | tricia |        2 |
| barb    | NULL   |        3 |
| gene    | barb   |        2 |
| gene    | gene   |        3 |
| gene    | tricia |        1 |
| gene    | NULL   |        6 |
| phil    | barb   |        1 |
| phil    | phil   |        2 |
| phil    | tricia |        2 |
| phil    | NULL   |        5 |
| tricia  | gene   |        1 |
| tricia  | phil   |        1 |
| tricia  | NULL   |        2 |
| NULL    | NULL   |       16 |
+---------+--------+----------+
```

8.17 Generating a Report That Includes a Summary and a List

Problem

You want to create a report that displays a summary, together with the list of rows associated with each summary value.

Solution

Use two statements that retrieve different levels of summary information. Or use a programming language to do some of the work so that you can use a single statement.

Discussion

Suppose that you want to produce a report that looks like this:

```
Name: Ben; days on road: 3; miles driven: 362
  date: 2006-08-29, trip length: 131
  date: 2006-08-30, trip length: 152
  date: 2006-09-02, trip length: 79
Name: Henry; days on road: 5; miles driven: 911
  date: 2006-08-26, trip length: 115
  date: 2006-08-27, trip length: 96
```

```
    date: 2006-08-29, trip length: 300
    date: 2006-08-30, trip length: 203
    date: 2006-09-01, trip length: 197
  Name: Suzi; days on road: 2; miles driven: 893
    date: 2006-08-29, trip length: 391
    date: 2006-09-02, trip length: 502
```

The report shows, for each driver in the `driver_log` table, the following information:

- A summary line showing the driver name, the number of days on the road, and the number of miles driven.

- A list of the dates and mileages for the individual trips from which the summary values are calculated.

This scenario is a variation on the "different levels of summary information" problem discussed in Recipe 8.16. It may not seem like it at first, because one of the types of information is a list rather than a summary. But that's really just a "level zero" summary. This kind of problem appears in many other forms:

- You have a database that lists contributions to candidates in your political party. The party chair requests a printout that shows, for each candidate, the number of contributions and total amount contributed, as well as a list of contributor names and addresses.

- You want to make a handout for a company presentation that summarizes total sales per sales region with a list under each region showing the sales for each state in the region.

Such problems can be solved using a couple of approaches:

- Run separate statements to get the information for each level of detail that you require. (A single query won't produce per-group summary values and a list of each group's individual rows.)

- Fetch the rows that make up the lists and perform the summary calculations yourself to eliminate the summary statement.

Let's use each approach to produce the driver report shown at the beginning of this section. The following implementation (in Python) generates the report using one query to summarize the days and miles per driver, and another to fetch the individual trip rows for each driver:

```python
# select total miles per driver and construct a dictionary that
# maps each driver name to days on the road and miles driven
name_map = { }
cursor = conn.cursor ()
cursor.execute ("""
                SELECT name, COUNT(name), SUM(miles)
                FROM driver_log GROUP BY name
                """)
for (name, days, miles) in cursor.fetchall ():
  name_map[name] = (days, miles)
```

```
# select trips for each driver and print the report, displaying the
# summary entry for each driver prior to the list of trips
cursor.execute ("""
                SELECT name, trav_date, miles
                FROM driver_log ORDER BY name, trav_date
                """)
cur_name = ""
for (name, trav_date, miles) in cursor.fetchall ():
  if cur_name != name:  # new driver; print driver's summary info
    print "Name: %s; days on road: %d; miles driven: %d" \
          % (name, name_map[name][0], name_map[name][1])
    cur_name = name
  print "  date: %s, trip length: %d" % (trav_date, miles)
cursor.close ()
```

An alternate implementation performs summary calculations in the program. By doing this, you can reduce the number of queries required. If you iterate through the trip list and calculate the per-driver day counts and mileage totals yourself, a single query suffices:

```
# get list of trips for the drivers
cursor = conn.cursor ()
cursor.execute ("""
                SELECT name, trav_date, miles FROM driver_log
                ORDER BY name, trav_date
                """)
# fetch rows into data structure because we
# must iterate through them multiple times
rows = cursor.fetchall ()
cursor.close ()

# iterate through rows once to construct a dictionary that
# maps each driver name to days on the road and miles driven
# (the dictionary entries are lists rather than tuples because
# we need mutable values that can be modified in the loop)
name_map = { }
for (name, trav_date, miles) in rows:
  if not name_map.has_key (name): # initialize entry if nonexistent
    name_map[name] = [0, 0]
  name_map[name][0] = name_map[name][0] + 1    # count days
  name_map[name][1] = name_map[name][1] + miles # sum miles

# iterate through rows again to print the report, displaying the
# summary entry for each driver prior to the list of trips
cur_name = ""
for (name, trav_date, miles) in rows:
  if cur_name != name:  # new driver; print driver's summary info
    print "Name: %s; days on road: %d; miles driven: %d" \
          % (name, name_map[name][0], name_map[name][1])
    cur_name = name
  print "  date: %s, trip length: %d" % (trav_date, miles)
```

Should you require more levels of summary information, this type of problem gets more difficult. For example, you might want the report to show driver summaries and trip logs to be preceded by a line that shows the total miles for all drivers:

```
Total miles driven by all drivers combined: 2166

Name: Ben; days on road: 3; miles driven: 362
   date: 2006-08-29, trip length: 131
   date: 2006-08-30, trip length: 152
   date: 2006-09-02, trip length: 79
Name: Henry; days on road: 5; miles driven: 911
   date: 2006-08-26, trip length: 115
   date: 2006-08-27, trip length: 96
   date: 2006-08-29, trip length: 300
   date: 2006-08-30, trip length: 203
   date: 2006-09-01, trip length: 197
Name: Suzi; days on road: 2; miles driven: 893
   date: 2006-08-29, trip length: 391
   date: 2006-09-02, trip length: 502
```

In this case, you need either another query to produce the total mileage, or another calculation in your program that computes the overall total.

## CHAPTER 9

Obtaining and Using Metadata

9.0 Introduction

Most of the SQL statements used so far have been written to work with the data stored in the database. That is, after all, what the database is designed to hold. But sometimes you need more than just data values. You need information that characterizes or describes those values—that is, the statement *metadata*. Metadata information is used most often in relation to processing result sets, but also is available for other aspects of your interaction with MySQL. This chapter describes how to obtain and use the following types of metadata:

Information about statement results

For statements that delete or update rows, you can determine how many rows were changed. For a SELECT statement, you can find out the number of columns in the result set, as well as information about each column in the result set, such as the column name and its display width. Such information often is essential for processing the results. For example, if you're formatting a tabular display, you can determine how wide to make each column and whether to justify values to the left or right.

Information about tables and databases

Information pertaining to the structure of tables and databases is useful for applications that need to enumerate a list of tables in a database or databases hosted on a server (for example, to present a display allowing the user to select one of the available choices). You can also use this information to determine whether tables or databases exist. Another use for table metadata is to determine the legal values for ENUM or SET columns.

Information about the MySQL server

Some APIs provide information about the database server or about the status of your current connection with the server. Knowing the server version can be useful for determining whether it supports a given feature, which helps you build adaptive applications. Information about the connection includes such values as the current user and the default database.

In general, metadata information is closely tied to the implementation of the database system, so it tends to be somewhat database-dependent. This means that if an application uses techniques shown in this chapter, it might need some modification if you port it to other database systems. For example, lists of tables and databases in MySQL are available by issuing SHOW statements. However, SHOW is a MySQL-specific extension to SQL, so even if you're using an API like Perl or Ruby DBI, PEAR DB, DB-API, or JDBC that gives you a database-independent way of issuing statements, the SQL itself is database-specific and will need to be changed to work with other engines.

A more portable source of metadata is the INFORMATION_SCHEMA database, which is available as of MySQL 5.0. This metadata database contains information about databases, tables, columns, character sets, and so forth. INFORMATION_SCHEMA has some advantages over SHOW:

- Other database systems support INFORMATION_SCHEMA, so applications that use it are likely to be more portable than those that use SHOW statements.
- INFORMATION_SCHEMA is used with standard SELECT syntax, so it's more similar to other data-retrieval operations than SHOW statements.

Because of those advantages, recipes in this chapter use INFORMATION_SCHEMA rather than SHOW when possible.

A disadvantage of INFORMATION_SCHEMA is that statements to access it are more verbose than the corresponding SHOW statements. That doesn't matter so much when you're writing programs, but for interactive use, SHOW statements can be more attractive because they require less typing. And if you haven't yet upgraded to MySQL 5.0 or higher, SHOW is your only choice.

The scripts containing the code for the examples in this chapter are found in the *metadata* directory of the `recipes` distribution. (Some of them use utility functions located in the *lib* directory.) To create any tables that you need for trying the examples, use the scripts in the *tables* directory.

As already indicated, recipes developed in this chapter tend to use INFORMATION_SCHEMA rather than SHOW. If you have a version of MySQL older than 5.0, the `recipes` distribution from the first edition of *MySQL Cookbook* might be helpful. That distribution used SHOW statements because INFORMATION_SCHEMA did not exist in MySQL then. Briefly, the SHOW statements that provide information similar to the contents of certain INFORMATION_SCHEMA tables are listed in the following table:

INFORMATION_SCHEMA table	SHOW statement
SCHEMATA	SHOW DATABASES
TABLES	SHOW TABLES
COLUMNS	SHOW COLUMNS

9.1 Obtaining the Number of Rows Affected by a Statement

Problem

You want to know how many rows were changed by an SQL statement.

Solution

Sometimes the row count is the return value of the function that issues the statement. Other times the count is returned by a separate function that you call after issuing the statement.

Discussion

For statements that affect rows (UPDATE, DELETE, INSERT, REPLACE), each API provides a way to determine the number of rows involved. For MySQL, the default meaning of "affected by" is "changed by," not "matched by." That is, rows that are not changed by a statement are not counted, even if they match the conditions specified in the statement. For example, the following UPDATE statement results in an "affected by" value of zero because it does not change any columns from their current values, no matter how many rows the WHERE clause matches:

```
UPDATE limbs SET arms = 0 WHERE arms = 0;
```

The MySQL server allows a client to set a flag when it connects to indicate that it wants rows-matched counts, not rows-changed counts. In this case, the row count for the preceding statement would be equal to the number of rows with an arms value of 0, even though the statement results in no net change to the table. However, not all MySQL APIs expose this flag. The following discussion indicates which APIs enable you to select the type of count you want and which use the rows-matched count by default rather than the rows-changed count.

Perl

In Perl DBI scripts, the row count for statements that modify rows is returned by do( ):

```
my $count = $dbh->do ($stmt);
# report 0 rows if an error occurred
printf "Number of rows affected: %d\n", (defined ($count) ? $count : 0);
```

If you prepare a statement first and then execute it, execute( ) returns the row count:

```
my $sth = $dbh->prepare ($stmt);
my $count = $sth->execute ();
printf "Number of rows affected: %d\n", (defined ($count) ? $count : 0);
```

You can tell MySQL whether to return rows-changed or rows-matched counts by specifying mysql_client_found_rows in the options part of the data source name argument of the connect( ) call when you connect to the MySQL server. Set the option to 0 for rows-changed counts and 1 for rows-matched counts. Here's an example:

```
my %conn_attrs = (PrintError => 0, RaiseError => 1, AutoCommit => 1);
my $dsn = "DBI:mysql:cookbook:localhost;mysql_client_found_rows=1";
my $dbh = DBI->connect ($dsn, "cbuser", "cbpass", \%conn_attrs);
```

`mysql_client_found_rows` changes the row-reporting behavior for the duration of the connection.

Although the default behavior for MySQL itself is to return rows-changed counts, recent versions of the Perl DBI driver for MySQL automatically request rows-matched counts unless you specify otherwise. For applications that depend on a particular behavior, it's best to explicitly set the `mysql_client_found_rows` option in the DSN to the appropriate value.

Ruby

For statements that modify rows, Ruby DBI returns row counts similarly to Perl DBI scripts for the do method. That is, do itself returns the count:

```
count = dbh.do(stmt)
puts "Number of rows affected: #{count}"
```

If you use execute to execute a statement, execute does not return the row count. Instead, use the statement handle rows method to get the count after executing the statement:

```
sth = dbh.execute(stmt)
puts "Number of rows affected: #{sth.rows}"
```

The Ruby DBI driver for MySQL returns rows-changed counts by default, but the driver supports a `mysql_client_found_rows` option that enables you to control whether the server returns rows-changed or rows-matched counts. Its use is analogous to Perl DBI. For example, to request rows-matched counts, do this:

```
dsn = "DBI:Mysql:database=cookbook;host=localhost;mysql_client_found_rows=1"
dbh = DBI.connect(dsn, "cbuser", "cbpass")
```

PHP

In PHP, invoke the connection object's `affectedRows( )` method to find out how many rows a statement changed:

```
$result =& $conn->query ($stmt);
# report 0 rows if the statement failed
$count = (PEAR::isError ($result) ? 0 : $conn->affectedRows ());
print ("Number of rows affected: $count\n");
```

Python

Python's DB-API makes the rows-changed count available as the value of the statement cursor's rowcount attribute:

```
cursor = conn.cursor ()
cursor.execute (stmt)
print "Number of rows affected: %d" % cursor.rowcount
```

To obtain rows-matched counts instead, import the MySQLdb client constants and pass the FOUND_ROWS flag in the client_flag parameter of the connect( ) method:

```
import MySQLdb.constants.CLIENT

conn = MySQLdb.connect (db = "cookbook",
                        host = "localhost",
                        user = "cbuser",
                        passwd = "cbpass",
                        client_flag = MySQLdb.constants.CLIENT.FOUND_ROWS)
```

Java

For statements that modify rows, the MySQL Connector/J JDBC driver provides rows-matched counts rather than rows-changed counts. This is done for conformance with the JDBC specification.

The Java JDBC interface provides row counts two different ways, depending on the method you invoke to execute the statement. If you use executeUpdate( ), the row count is its return value:

```
Statement s = conn.createStatement ();
int count = s.executeUpdate (stmt);
s.close ();
System.out.println ("Number of rows affected: " + count);
```

If you use execute( ), that method returns true or false to indicate whether the statement produces a result set. For statements such as UPDATE or DELETE that return no result set, execute( ) returns false and the row count is available by calling the getUpdateCount( ) method:

```
Statement s = conn.createStatement ();
if (!s.execute (stmt))
{
  // there is no result set, print the row count
  System.out.println ("Number of rows affected: " + s.getUpdateCount ());
}
s.close ();
```

9.2 Obtaining Result Set Metadata

Problem

You already know how to retrieve the rows of a result set (Recipe 2.4). Now you want to know things *about* the result set, such as the column names and data types, or how many rows and columns there are.

Solution

Use the appropriate capabilities provided by your API.

Discussion

For statements such as SELECT that generate a result set, you can get a number of types of metadata. This section discusses the information provided by each API, using programs that show how to display the result set metadata available after issuing a sample statement (SELECT name, foods FROM profile). One of the simplest uses for this information is illustrated by several of the example programs: when you retrieve a row of values from a result set and you want to process them in a loop, the column count stored in the metadata serves as the upper bound on the loop iterator.

Perl

Using the Perl DBI interface, you can obtain result sets two ways. These differ in the scope of result set metadata available to your scripts:

Process the statement using a statement handle

In this case, you invoke prepare( ) to get the statement handle. This handle has an execute( ) method that you invoke to generate the result set, and then you fetch the rows in a loop. With this approach, access to the metadata is available while the result set is active—that is, after the call to execute( ) and until the end of the result set is reached. When the row-fetching method finds that there are no more rows, it invokes finish( ) implicitly, which causes the metadata to become unavailable. (That also happens if you explicitly call finish( ) yourself.) Thus, normally it's best to access the metadata immediately after calling execute( ), making a copy of any values that you'll need to use beyond the end of the fetch loop.

Process the statement using a database handle method that returns the result set in a single operation

With this method, any metadata generated while processing the statement will have been disposed of by the time the method returns, although you can still determine the number of rows and columns from the size of the result set.

When you use the statement handle approach to process a statement, DBI makes result set metadata available after you invoke the handle's execute( ) method. This information is available primarily in the form of references to arrays. For each such type of metadata, the array has one element per column in the result set. Array references are accessed as attributes of the statement handle. For example, $sth->{NAME} points to the column name array, with individual column names available as elements of this array:

```
$name = $sth->{NAME}->[$i];
```

Or you can access the entire array like this:

```
@names = @{$sth->{NAME}};
```

The following table lists the attribute names through which you access array-based metadata and the meaning of values in each array. Names that begin with uppercase are standard DBI attributes and should be available for most database engines. Attribute names that begin with `mysql_` are MySQL-specific and nonportable; the kinds of information they provide might be available in other database systems, but under different attribute names.

Attribute name	Array element meaning
NAME	Column name
NAME_lc	Column name in lowercase
NAME_uc	Column name in uppercase
NULLABLE	0 or empty string = column values cannot be NULL
	1 = column values can be NULL
	2 = unknown
PRECISION	Column width
SCALE	Number of decimal places (for numeric columns)
TYPE	Data type (numeric DBI code)
mysql_is_blob	True if column has a BLOB (or TEXT) type
mysql_is_key	True if column is part of a key
mysql_is_num	True if column has a numeric type
mysql_is_pri_key	True if column is part of a primary key
mysql_max_length	Actual maximum length of column values in result set
mysql_table	Name of table the column is part of
mysql_type	Data type (numeric internal MySQL code)
mysql_type_name	Data type name

Some types of metadata, listed in the following table, are accessible as references to hashes rather than arrays. These hashes have one element per column value. The element key is the column name and its value is the position of the column within the result set. For example:

```
$col_pos = $sth->{NAME_hash}->{col_name};
```

Attribute name	Hash element meaning
NAME_hash	Column name
NAME_hash_lc	Column name in lowercase
NAME_hash_uc	Column name in uppercase

The number of columns in a result set and the number of placeholders in a prepared statement are available as scalar values:

```
$num_cols = $sth->{NUM_OF_FIELDS};
$num_placeholders = $sth->{NUM_OF_PARAMS};
```

Here's some example code that shows how to execute a statement and display result set metadata:

```
my $stmt = "SELECT name, foods FROM profile";
printf "Statement: %s\n", $stmt;
my $sth = $dbh->prepare ($stmt);
$sth->execute();
# metadata information becomes available at this point ...
printf "NUM_OF_FIELDS: %d\n", $sth->{NUM_OF_FIELDS};
print "Note: statement has no result set\n" if $sth->{NUM_OF_FIELDS} == 0;
for my $i (0 .. $sth->{NUM_OF_FIELDS}-1)
{
  printf "--- Column %d (%s) ---\n", $i, $sth->{NAME}->[$i];
  printf "NAME_lc:          %s\n", $sth->{NAME_lc}->[$i];
  printf "NAME_uc:          %s\n", $sth->{NAME_uc}->[$i];
  printf "NULLABLE:         %s\n", $sth->{NULLABLE}->[$i];
  printf "PRECISION:        %s\n", $sth->{PRECISION}->[$i];
  printf "SCALE:            %s\n", $sth->{SCALE}->[$i];
  printf "TYPE:             %s\n", $sth->{TYPE}->[$i];
  printf "mysql_is_blob:    %s\n", $sth->{mysql_is_blob}->[$i];
  printf "mysql_is_key:     %s\n", $sth->{mysql_is_key}->[$i];
  printf "mysql_is_num:     %s\n", $sth->{mysql_is_num}->[$i];
  printf "mysql_is_pri_key: %s\n", $sth->{mysql_is_pri_key}->[$i];
  printf "mysql_max_length: %s\n", $sth->{mysql_max_length}->[$i];
  printf "mysql_table:      %s\n", $sth->{mysql_table}->[$i];
  printf "mysql_type:       %s\n", $sth->{mysql_type}->[$i];
  printf "mysql_type_name:  %s\n", $sth->{mysql_type_name}->[$i];
}
$sth->finish ();  # release result set because we didn't fetch its rows
```

If you use the preceding code to execute the statement SELECT name, foods FROM profile, the output looks like this:

```
Statement: SELECT name, foods FROM profile
NUM_OF_FIELDS: 2
--- Column 0 (name) ---
NAME_lc:          name
NAME_uc:          NAME
NULLABLE:
PRECISION:        20
SCALE:            0
TYPE:             1
mysql_is_blob:
mysql_is_key:
mysql_is_num:     0
mysql_is_pri_key:
mysql_max_length: 7
mysql_table:      profile
mysql_type:       254
mysql_type_name:  char
--- Column 1 (foods) ---
NAME_lc:          foods
NAME_uc:          FOODS
```

```
NULLABLE:         1
PRECISION:        42
SCALE:            0
TYPE:             1
mysql_is_blob:
mysql_is_key:
mysql_is_num:     0
mysql_is_pri_key:
mysql_max_length: 21
mysql_table:      profile
mysql_type:       254
mysql_type_name:  char
```

To get a row count from a result set generated by calling execute( ), you must fetch the rows and count them yourself. The use of $sth->rows( ) to get a count for SELECT statements is explicitly deprecated in the DBI documentation.

You can also obtain a result set by calling one of the DBI methods that uses a database handle rather than a statement handle, such as selectall_arrayref( ) or selectall_hashref( ). These methods provide no access to column metadata. That information already will have been disposed of by the time the method returns, and is unavailable to your scripts. However, you can derive column and row counts by examining the result set itself. The way you do this depends on the kind of data structure a method produces. These structures and the way you use them to obtain result set row and column counts are discussed in Recipe 2.4.

Ruby

Ruby DBI provides result set metadata after you execute a statement with execute, and access to metadata is possible until you invoke the statement handle finish method. The column_names method returns an array of column names (which is empty if there is no result set). If there is a result set, the column_info method returns an array of ColumnInfo objects, one for each column. A ColumnInfo object is similar to a hash and has the elements shown in the following table. Element names that begin with an underscore are MySQL-specific and may not be present for other database engines. (Most of these elements are not present unless you use Ruby DBI 0.1.1 or higher.)

Member name	Member meaning
name	Column name
sql_type	XOPEN type number
type_name	XOPEN type name
precision	Column width
scale	Number of decimal places (for numeric columns)
nullable	True if column allows NULL values
indexed	True if column is indexed
primary	True if column is part of a primary key

Member name	Member meaning
unique	True if column is part of a unique index
mysql_type	Data type (numeric internal MySQL code)
mysql_type_name	Data type name
mysql_length	Column width
mysql_max_length	Actual maximum length of column values in result set
mysql_flags	Data type flags

Here's some example code that shows how to execute a statement and display the result set metadata values for the columns:

```ruby
stmt = "SELECT name, foods FROM profile"
puts "Statement: " + stmt
sth = dbh.execute(stmt)
# metadata information becomes available at this point ...
puts "Number of columns: #{sth.column_names.size}"
puts "Note: statement has no result set" if sth.column_names.size == 0
sth.column_info.each_with_index do |info, i|
  printf "--- Column %d (%s) ---\n", i, info["name"]
  printf "sql_type:         %s\n", info["sql_type"]
  printf "type_name:        %s\n", info["type_name"]
  printf "precision:        %s\n", info["precision"]
  printf "scale:            %s\n", info["scale"]
  printf "nullable:         %s\n", info["nullable"]
  printf "indexed:          %s\n", info["indexed"]
  printf "primary:          %s\n", info["primary"]
  printf "unique:           %s\n", info["unique"]
  printf "mysql_type:       %s\n", info["mysql_type"]
  printf "mysql_type_name:  %s\n", info["mysql_type_name"]
  printf "mysql_length:     %s\n", info["mysql_length"]
  printf "mysql_max_length: %s\n", info["mysql_max_length"]
  printf "mysql_flags:      %s\n", info["mysql_flags"]
end
sth.finish
```

If you use the preceding code to execute the statement SELECT name, foods FROM profile, the output looks like this:

```
Statement: SELECT name, foods FROM profile
Number of columns: 2
--- Column 0 (name) ---
sql_type:         12
type_name:        VARCHAR
precision:        20
scale:            0
nullable:         false
indexed:          false
primary:          false
unique:           false
mysql_type:       254
mysql_type_name:  VARCHAR
```

```
mysql_length:      20
mysql_max_length:  7
mysql_flags:       4097
--- Column 1 (foods) ---
sql_type:          12
type_name:         VARCHAR
precision:         42
scale:             0
nullable:          true
indexed:           false
primary:           false
unique:            false
mysql_type:        254
mysql_type_name:   VARCHAR
mysql_length:      42
mysql_max_length:  21
mysql_flags:       2048
```

To get a row count from a result set generated by calling `execute`, fetch the rows and count them yourself. The `sth.rows` method is not guaranteed to work for result sets.

You can also obtain a result set by calling one of the DBI methods that uses a database handle rather than a statement handle, such as `select_one` or `select_all`. These methods provide no access to column metadata. That information already will have been disposed of by the time the method returns, and is unavailable to your scripts. However, you can derive column and row counts by examining the result set itself.

PHP

In PHP, metadata information for `SELECT` statements is available from PEAR DB after a successful call to `query( )` and remains accessible up to the point at which you free the result set.

To check whether metadata is available, verify that the query result is a result set, and then pass it to the connection object `tableInfo( )` method , which returns a structure containing an array of column information. Each array element contains the members shown in the following table.

Member name	Member meaning
name	Column name
type	Data type name
len	Data length
flags	Data type flags

PEAR DB also makes row and column counts for a result set available via the result's `numRows( )` and `numCols( )` methods.

The following code shows how to access and display result set metadata:

```
$stmt = "SELECT name, foods FROM profile";
print ("Statement: $stmt\n");
$result =& $conn->query ($stmt);
if (PEAR::isError ($result))
  die ("Statement failed\n");
# metadata information becomes available at this point ...
if (is_a ($result, "DB_result"))  # statement generates a result set
{
  $nrows = $result->numRows ();
  $ncols = $result->numCols ();
  $info =& $conn->tableInfo ($result);
}
else                              # statement generates no result set
{
  $nrows = 0;
  $ncols = 0;
}
print ("Number of rows: $nrows\n");
print ("Number of columns: $ncols\n");
if ($ncols == 0)
  print ("Note: statement has no result set\n");
for ($i = 0; $i < $ncols; $i++)
{
  $col_info = $info[$i];
  printf ("--- Column %d (%s) ---\n", $i, $col_info["name"]);
  printf ("type:        %s\n", $col_info["type"]);
  printf ("len:         %s\n", $col_info["len"]);
  printf ("flags:       %s\n", $col_info["flags"]);
}
if ($ncols > 0)   # dispose of result set, if there is one
  $result->free ();
```

The output from the program looks like this:

```
Statement: SELECT name, foods FROM profile
Number of rows: 10
Number of columns: 2
--- Column 0 (name) ---
type:        char
len:         7
flags:       not_null
--- Column 1 (foods) ---
type:        char
len:         21
flags:       set
```

Python

For statements that produce a result set, Python's DB-API makes row and column counts available, as well as a few pieces of information about individual columns.

To get the row count for a result set, access the cursor's rowcount attribute. The column count is not available directly, but after calling fetchone( ) or fetchall( ), you can determine the count as the length of any result set row tuple. It's also possible to determine the column count without fetching any rows by using cursor.description. This is a tuple containing one element per column in the result set, so its length tells you how many columns are in the set. (If the statement generates no result set, such as for UPDATE, the value of `description` is None.) Each element of the `description` tuple is another tuple that represents the metadata for the corresponding column of the result. There are seven metadata values per column; the following code shows how to access them and what they mean:

```
stmt = "SELECT name, foods FROM profile"
print "Statement: ", stmt
cursor = conn.cursor ()
cursor.execute (stmt)
# metadata information becomes available at this point ...
print "Number of rows:", cursor.rowcount
if cursor.description == None:  # no result set
  ncols = 0
else:
  ncols = len (cursor.description)
print "Number of columns:", ncols
if ncols == 0:
  print "Note: statement has no result set"
for i in range (ncols):
  col_info = cursor.description[i]
  # print name, and then other information
  print "--- Column %d (%s) ---" % (i, col_info[0])
  print "Type:          ", col_info[1]
  print "Display size: ", col_info[2]
  print "Internal size:", col_info[3]
  print "Precision:     ", col_info[4]
  print "Scale:         ", col_info[5]
  print "Nullable:      ", col_info[6]
cursor.close
```

The output from the program looks like this:

```
Statement:  SELECT name, foods FROM profile
Number of rows: 10
Number of columns: 2
--- Column 0 (name) ---
Type:         254
Display size:  7
Internal size: 20
Precision:     20
Scale:         0
Nullable:      0
--- Column 1 (foods) ---
Type:         254
Display size:  21
Internal size: 42
Precision:     42
Scale:         0
Nullable:      1
```

Java

JDBC makes result set metadata available through a `ResultSetMetaData` object, which you obtain by calling the `getMetaData( )` method of your `ResultSet` object. The metadata object provides access to several kinds of information. Its `getColumnCount( )` method returns the number of columns in the result set. Other types of metadata, illustrated by the following code, provide information about individual columns and take a column index as their argument. For JDBC, column indexes begin at 1 rather than 0, which differs from the other APIs covered here.

```java
String stmt = "SELECT name, foods FROM profile";
System.out.println ("Statement: " + stmt);
Statement s = conn.createStatement ();
s.executeQuery (stmt);
ResultSet rs = s.getResultSet ();
ResultSetMetaData md = rs.getMetaData ();
// metadata information becomes available at this point ...
int ncols = md.getColumnCount ();
System.out.println ("Number of columns: " + ncols);
if (ncols == 0)
  System.out.println ("Note: statement has no result set");
for (int i = 1; i <= ncols; i++)  // column index values are 1-based
{
  System.out.println ("--- Column " + i
             + " (" + md.getColumnName (i) + ") ---");
  System.out.println ("getColumnDisplaySize: " + md.getColumnDisplaySize (i));
  System.out.println ("getColumnLabel:      " + md.getColumnLabel (i));
  System.out.println ("getColumnType:       " + md.getColumnType (i));
  System.out.println ("getColumnTypeName:   " + md.getColumnTypeName (i));
  System.out.println ("getPrecision:        " + md.getPrecision (i));
  System.out.println ("getScale:            " + md.getScale (i));
  System.out.println ("getTableName:        " + md.getTableName (i));
  System.out.println ("isAutoIncrement:     " + md.isAutoIncrement (i));
  System.out.println ("isNullable:          " + md.isNullable (i));
  System.out.println ("isCaseSensitive:     " + md.isCaseSensitive (i));
  System.out.println ("isSigned:            " + md.isSigned (i));
}
rs.close ();
s.close ();
```

The output from the program looks like this:

```
Statement: SELECT name, foods FROM profile
Number of columns: 2
--- Column 1 (name) ---
getColumnDisplaySize: 20
getColumnLabel:       name
getColumnType:        1
getColumnTypeName:    CHAR
getPrecision:         20
getScale:             0
getTableName:         profile
isAutoIncrement:      false
isNullable:           0
isCaseSensitive:      false
```

```
isSigned:              false
--- Column 2 (foods) ---
getColumnDisplaySize:  42
getColumnLabel:        foods
getColumnType:         1
getColumnTypeName:     CHAR
getPrecision:          42
getScale:              0
getTableName:          profile
isAutoIncrement:       false
isNullable:            1
isCaseSensitive:       false
isSigned:              false
```

The row count of the result set is not available directly; you must fetch the rows and count them.

There are several other JDBC result set metadata calls, but many of them provide no useful information for MySQL. If you want to try them, get a JDBC reference to see what the calls are and modify the program to see what, if anything, they return.

9.3 Determining Whether a Statement Produced a Result Set

Problem

You just executed an SQL statement, but you're not sure whether it produced a result set.

Solution

Check the column count in the metadata. If the count is zero, there is no result set.

Discussion

If you write an application that accepts statement strings from an external source such as a file or a user entering text at the keyboard, you may not necessarily know whether it's a statement such as SELECT that produces a result set or a statement such as UPDATE that does not. That's an important distinction, because you process statements that produce a result set differently from those that do not. Assuming that no error occurred, one way to tell the difference is to check the metadata value that indicates the column count after executing the statement (as shown in Recipe 9.2). A column count of zero indicates that the statement was an INSERT, UPDATE, or some other statement that returns no result set. A nonzero value indicates the presence of a result set, and you can go ahead and fetch the rows. This technique distinguishes SELECT from non-SELECT statements, even for SELECT statements that return an empty result set. (An empty result is different from no result. The former returns no rows, but the column count is still correct; the latter has no columns at all.)

Some APIs provide ways to distinguish statement types other than checking the column count:

- In JDBC, you can issue arbitrary statements using the **execute( )** method, which directly indicates whether there is a result set by returning true or false.
- In PHP, PEAR DB programs should check the result from statement-execution methods to see whether the return value is a **DB_result** object:

```
$result =& $conn->query ($stmt);
if (PEAR::isError ($result))
  die ("Statement failed\n");
if (is_a ($result, "DB_result"))
{
  # statement generates a result set
}
else
{
  # statement generates no result set
}
```

  Do this instead of checking the column count because attempting to invoke numCols( ) on a result that isn't a DB_result object causes an error.
- In Python, the value of **cursor.description** is **None** for statements that produce no result set.

9.4 Using Metadata to Format Query Output

Problem

You want to produce a nicely formatted result set display.

Solution

Let the result set metadata help you. It provides important information about the structure and content of the results.

Discussion

Metadata information is valuable for formatting query results, because it tells you several important things about the columns (such as the names and display widths), even if you don't know what the query was. For example, you can write a general-purpose function that displays a result set in tabular format with no knowledge about what the query might have been. The following Java code shows one way to do this. It takes a result set object and uses it to get the metadata for the result. Then it uses both objects in tandem to retrieve and format the values in the result. The output is similar to that produced by *mysql*: a row of column headers followed by the rows of the result, with columns nicely boxed and lined up vertically. Here's a sample of what the function displays, given the result set generated by the query `SELECT id, name, birth FROM profile`:

```
+----------+--------------------+----------+
|id        |name                |birth     |
+----------+--------------------+----------+
|1         |Fred                |1970-04-13|
|2         |Mort                |1969-09-30|
|3         |Brit                |1957-12-01|
|4         |Carl                |1973-11-02|
|5         |Sean                |1963-07-04|
|6         |Alan                |1965-02-14|
|7         |Mara                |1968-09-17|
|8         |Shepard             |1975-09-02|
|9         |Dick                |1952-08-20|
|10        |Tony                |1960-05-01|
|11        |Juan                |NULL      |
+----------+--------------------+----------+
Number of rows selected: 11
```

The primary problem an application like this must solve is to determine the proper display width of each column. The `getColumnDisplaySize( )` method returns the column width, but we actually need to take into consideration other pieces of information:

- The length of the column name has to be considered (it might be longer than the column width).

- We'll print the word "NULL" for `NULL` values, so if the column can contain `NULL` values, the display width must be at least four.

The following Java function, `displayResultSet( )`, formats a result set, taking the preceding factors into account. It also counts rows as it fetches them to determine the row count, because JDBC doesn't make that value available directly from the metadata.

```java
public static void displayResultSet (ResultSet rs) throws SQLException
{
  ResultSetMetaData md = rs.getMetaData ();
  int ncols = md.getColumnCount ();
  int nrows = 0;
  int[] width = new int[ncols + 1];   // array to store column widths
  StringBuffer b = new StringBuffer (); // buffer to hold bar line

  // calculate column widths
  for (int i = 1; i <= ncols; i++)
  {
    // some drivers return -1 for getColumnDisplaySize();
    // if so, we'll override that with the column name length
    width[i] = md.getColumnDisplaySize (i);
    if (width[i] < md.getColumnName (i).length ())
      width[i] = md.getColumnName (i).length ();
    // isNullable() returns 1/0, not true/false
    if (width[i] < 4 && md.isNullable (i) != 0)
      width[i] = 4;
  }
```

```
    // construct +---+---... line
    b.append ("+");
    for (int i = 1; i <= ncols; i++)
    {
      for (int j = 0; j < width[i]; j++)
        b.append ("-");
      b.append ("+");
    }

    // print bar line, column headers, bar line
    System.out.println (b.toString ());
    System.out.print ("|");
    for (int i = 1; i <= ncols; i++)
    {
      System.out.print (md.getColumnName (i));
      for (int j = md.getColumnName (i).length (); j < width[i]; j++)
        System.out.print (" ");
      System.out.print ("|");
    }
    System.out.println ();
    System.out.println (b.toString ());

    // print contents of result set
    while (rs.next ())
    {
      ++nrows;
      System.out.print ("|");
      for (int i = 1; i <= ncols; i++)
      {
        String s = rs.getString (i);
        if (rs.wasNull ())
          s = "NULL";
        System.out.print (s);
        for (int j = s.length (); j < width[i]; j++)
          System.out.print (" ");
        System.out.print ("|");
      }
      System.out.println ();
    }
    // print bar line, and row count
    System.out.println (b.toString ());
    System.out.println ("Number of rows selected: " + nrows);
  }
```

If you want to be more elaborate, you can also test whether a column contains numeric values, and format it as right-justified if so. In Perl DBI scripts, this is easy to check, because you can access the `mysql_is_num` metadata attribute. For other APIs, it is not so easy unless there is some equivalent "column is numeric" metadata value available. If not, you must look at the data-type indicator to see whether it's one of the several possible numeric types.

Another shortcoming of the `displayResultSet( )` function is that it prints columns using the width of the column as specified in the table definition, not the maximum width of the values actually present in the result set. The latter value is often smaller. You can see this in the sample output that precedes the listing for displayResultSet( ). The id and name columns are 10 and 20 characters wide, even though the widest values are only two and seven characters long, respectively. In Perl, Ruby, PHP, and DB-API, you can get the maximum width of the values present in the result set. To determine these widths in JDBC, you must iterate through the result set and check the column value lengths yourself. This requires a JDBC 2.0 driver that provides scrollable result sets. If you have such a driver (MySQL Connector/J is one), the column-width calculation code in the displayResultSet( ) function can be modified as follows:

```
// calculate column widths
for (int i = 1; i <= ncols; i++)
{
  width[i] = md.getColumnName (i).length ();
  // isNullable() returns 1/0, not true/false
  if (width[i] < 4 && md.isNullable (i) != 0)
    width[i] = 4;
}
// scroll through result set and adjust display widths as necessary
while (rs.next ())
{
  for (int i = 1; i <= ncols; i++)
  {
    byte[] bytes = rs.getBytes (i);
    if (!rs.wasNull ())
    {
      int len = bytes.length;
      if (width[i] < len)
        width[i] = len;
    }
  }
}
rs.beforeFirst ();  // rewind result set before displaying it
```

With that change, the result is a more compact query result display:

```
+--+-------+----------+
|id|name   |birth     |
+--+-------+----------+
|1 |Fred   |1970-04-13|
|2 |Mort   |1969-09-30|
|3 |Brit   |1957-12-01|
|4 |Carl   |1973-11-02|
|5 |Sean   |1963-07-04|
|6 |Alan   |1965-02-14|
|7 |Mara   |1968-09-17|
|8 |Shepard|1975-09-02|
|9 |Dick   |1952-08-20|
|10|Tony   |1960-05-01|
|11|Juan   |NULL      |
+--+-------+----------+
Number of rows selected: 11
```

See Also

The Ruby DBI::Utils::TableFormatter module has an `ascii` method that produces a formatted display much like that described in this section. Use it like this:

```
dbh.execute(stmt) do |sth|
  DBI::Utils::TableFormatter.ascii(sth.column_names, sth.fetch_all)
end
```

9.5 Listing or Checking Existence of Databases or Tables

Problem

You want a list of databases hosted by the MySQL server or a list of tables in a database. Or you want to check whether a particular database or table exists.

Solution

Use `INFORMATION_SCHEMA` to get this information. The `SCHEMATA` table contains a row for each database, and the `TABLES` table contains a row for each table in each database.

Discussion

To retrieve the list of databases hosted by the server, use this statement:

```
SELECT SCHEMA_NAME FROM INFORMATION_SCHEMA.SCHEMATA;
```

Add an `ORDER BY SCHEMA_NAME` clause if you want a sorted result.

To check whether a specific database exists, use a `WHERE` clause with a condition that names the database. If you get a row back, the database exists. If not, it doesn't. The following Ruby method shows how to perform an existence test for a database:

```
def database_exists(dbh, db_name)
  return dbh.select_one("SELECT SCHEMA_NAME
                         FROM INFORMATION_SCHEMA.SCHEMATA
                         WHERE SCHEMA_NAME = ?", db_name) != nil
end
```

To obtain a list of tables in a database, name the database in the `WHERE` clause of a statement that selects from the `TABLES` table:

```
SELECT TABLE_NAME FROM INFORMATION_SCHEMA.TABLES
WHERE TABLE_SCHEMA = 'cookbook';
```

Add an `ORDER BY TABLE_NAME` clause if you want a sorted result.

To obtain a list of tables in the default database, use this statement instead:

```
SELECT TABLE_NAME FROM INFORMATION_SCHEMA.TABLES
WHERE TABLE_SCHEMA = DATABASE();
```

If no database has been selected, `DATABASE( )` returns `NULL`, and no rows match, which is the correct result.

To check whether a specific table exists, use a `WHERE` clause with a condition that names the table. Here's a Ruby method that performs an existence test for a table in a given database:

```
def table_exists(dbh, db_name, tbl_name)
  return dbh.select_one(
              "SELECT TABLE_NAME FROM INFORMATION_SCHEMA.TABLES
              WHERE TABLE_SCHEMA = ? AND TABLE_NAME = ?",
              db_name, tbl_name) != nil
end
```

 The results retrieved from `INFORMATION_SCHEMA` depend on your privileges. You'll see information only for those databases or tables for which you have some privileges. This means that an existence test will return false if the given object exists but you have no privileges for accessing it.

Some APIs provide a database-independent way to get database or table lists. In Perl DBI, the database handle `tables( )` method returns a list of tables in the default database:

```
@tables = $dbh->tables ();
```

The Ruby method is similar:

```
tables = dbh.tables
```

In Java, you can use JDBC methods designed to return lists of databases or tables. For each method, invoke your connection object's `getMetaData( )` method and use the resulting `DatabaseMetaData` object to retrieve the information you want. Here's how to produce a list of databases:

```
// get list of databases
DatabaseMetaData md = conn.getMetaData ();
ResultSet rs = md.getCatalogs ();
while (rs.next ())
  System.out.println (rs.getString (1));  // column 1 = database name
rs.close ();
```

A similar procedure lists the tables in a given database:

```
// get list of tables in database named by dbName; if
// dbName is the empty string, the default database is used
DatabaseMetaData md = conn.getMetaData ();
ResultSet rs = md.getTables (dbName, "", "%", null);
while (rs.next ())
  System.out.println (rs.getString (3));  // column 3 = table name
rs.close ();
```

9.6 Accessing Table Column Definitions

Problem

You want to find out what columns a table has and how they are defined.

Solution

There are several ways to do this. You can obtain column definitions from `INFORMATION_SCHEMA`, from `SHOW` statements, or from *mysqldump*.

Discussion

Information about the structure of tables enables you to answer questions such as "What columns does a table contain and what are their types?" or "What are the legal values for an `ENUM` or `SET` column?" In MySQL, there are several ways to find out about a table's structure:

- Retrieve the information from `INFORMATION_SCHEMA`. The `COLUMNS` table contains the column definitions.
- Use a `SHOW COLUMNS` statement.
- Use the `SHOW CREATE TABLE` statement or the *mysqldump* command-line program to obtain a `CREATE TABLE` statement that displays the table's structure.

The following sections discuss how you can ask MySQL for table information using each of these methods. To try the examples, create the following `item` table that lists item IDs, names, and the colors in which each item is available:

```
CREATE TABLE item
(
  id      INT UNSIGNED NOT NULL AUTO_INCREMENT,
  name    CHAR(20),
  colors  SET('chartreuse','mauve','lime green','puce') DEFAULT 'puce',
  PRIMARY KEY (id)
);
```

Using INFORMATION_SCHEMA to get table structure

To obtain information about the columns in a table by checking `INFORMATION_SCHEMA`, use a statement of the following form:

```
mysql> SELECT * FROM INFORMATION_SCHEMA.COLUMNS
    -> WHERE TABLE_SCHEMA = 'cookbook' AND TABLE_NAME = 'item'\G
*************************** 1. row ***************************
     TABLE_CATALOG: NULL
      TABLE_SCHEMA: cookbook
        TABLE_NAME: item
       COLUMN_NAME: id
  ORDINAL_POSITION: 1
    COLUMN_DEFAULT: NULL
```

```
               IS_NULLABLE: NO
                 DATA_TYPE: int
  CHARACTER_MAXIMUM_LENGTH: NULL
    CHARACTER_OCTET_LENGTH: NULL
         NUMERIC_PRECISION: 10
             NUMERIC_SCALE: 0
         CHARACTER_SET_NAME: NULL
            COLLATION_NAME: NULL
               COLUMN_TYPE: int(10) unsigned
                COLUMN_KEY: PRI
                     EXTRA: auto_increment
                PRIVILEGES: select,insert,update,references
            COLUMN_COMMENT:
*************************** 2. row ***************************
             TABLE_CATALOG: NULL
              TABLE_SCHEMA: cookbook
                TABLE_NAME: item
               COLUMN_NAME: name
           ORDINAL_POSITION: 2
            COLUMN_DEFAULT: NULL
               IS_NULLABLE: YES
                 DATA_TYPE: char
  CHARACTER_MAXIMUM_LENGTH: 20
    CHARACTER_OCTET_LENGTH: 20
         NUMERIC_PRECISION: NULL
             NUMERIC_SCALE: NULL
         CHARACTER_SET_NAME: latin1
            COLLATION_NAME: latin1_swedish_ci
               COLUMN_TYPE: char(20)
                COLUMN_KEY:
                     EXTRA:
                PRIVILEGES: select,insert,update,references
            COLUMN_COMMENT:
*************************** 3. row ***************************
             TABLE_CATALOG: NULL
              TABLE_SCHEMA: cookbook
                TABLE_NAME: item
               COLUMN_NAME: colors
           ORDINAL_POSITION: 3
            COLUMN_DEFAULT: puce
               IS_NULLABLE: YES
                 DATA_TYPE: set
  CHARACTER_MAXIMUM_LENGTH: 32
    CHARACTER_OCTET_LENGTH: 32
         NUMERIC_PRECISION: NULL
             NUMERIC_SCALE: NULL
         CHARACTER_SET_NAME: latin1
            COLLATION_NAME: latin1_swedish_ci
               COLUMN_TYPE: set('chartreuse','mauve','lime green','puce')
                COLUMN_KEY:
                     EXTRA:
                PRIVILEGES: select,insert,update,references
            COLUMN_COMMENT:
```

Here are some of the COLUMNS table values likely to be of most use:

- `COLUMN_NAME` indicates the column name.
- `ORDINAL_POSITION` is the position of the column within the table definition.
- `COLUMN_DEFAULT` is the column's default value.
- `IS_NULLABLE` is YES or NO to indicate whether the column can contain NULL values.
- `DATA_TYPE` and `COLUMN_TYPE` provide data-type information. `DATA_TYPE` is the data-type keyword and `COLUMN_TYPE` contains additional information such as type attributes.
- `CHARACTER_SET_NAME` and `COLLATION_NAME` indicate the character set and collation for string columns. They are NULL for nonstring columns.

To retrieve information only about a single column, add a condition to the WHERE clause that names the appropriate COLUMN_NAME value:

```
mysql> SELECT * FROM INFORMATION_SCHEMA.COLUMNS
    -> WHERE TABLE_SCHEMA = 'cookbook' AND TABLE_NAME = 'item'
    -> AND COLUMN_NAME = 'colors'\G
*************************** 1. row ***************************
           TABLE_CATALOG: NULL
            TABLE_SCHEMA: cookbook
              TABLE_NAME: item
             COLUMN_NAME: colors
        ORDINAL_POSITION: 3
          COLUMN_DEFAULT: puce
             IS_NULLABLE: YES
               DATA_TYPE: set
CHARACTER_MAXIMUM_LENGTH: 32
  CHARACTER_OCTET_LENGTH: 32
       NUMERIC_PRECISION: NULL
           NUMERIC_SCALE: NULL
      CHARACTER_SET_NAME: latin1
          COLLATION_NAME: latin1_swedish_ci
             COLUMN_TYPE: set('chartreuse','mauve','lime green','puce')
              COLUMN_KEY:
                   EXTRA:
              PRIVILEGES: select,insert,update,references
          COLUMN_COMMENT:
```

If you want only certain types of information, replace SELECT * with a list of the values of interest:

```
mysql> SELECT COLUMN_NAME, DATA_TYPE, IS_NULLABLE
    -> FROM INFORMATION_SCHEMA.COLUMNS
    -> WHERE TABLE_SCHEMA = 'cookbook' AND TABLE_NAME = 'item';
+-------------+-----------+-------------+
| COLUMN_NAME | DATA_TYPE | IS_NULLABLE |
+-------------+-----------+-------------+
| id          | int       | NO          |
| name        | char      | YES         |
| colors      | set       | YES         |
+-------------+-----------+-------------+
```

`INFORMATION_SCHEMA` content is easy to use from within programs. Here's a PHP function that illustrates this process. It takes database and table name arguments, selects from `INFORMATION_SCHEMA` to obtain a list of the table's column names, and returns the names as an array. The `ORDER BY ORDINAL_POSITION` clause ensures that the names in the array are returned in table definition order.

```php
function get_column_names ($conn, $db_name, $tbl_name)
{
  $stmt = "SELECT COLUMN_NAME FROM INFORMATION_SCHEMA.COLUMNS
           WHERE TABLE_SCHEMA = ? AND TABLE_NAME = ?
           ORDER BY ORDINAL_POSITION";
  $result =& $conn->query ($stmt, array ($db_name, $tbl_name));
  if (PEAR::isError ($result))
    return (FALSE);
  $names = array();
  while (list ($col_name) = $result->fetchRow ())
    $names[] = $col_name;
  $result->free ();
  return ($names);
}
```

The equivalent routine using Ruby DBI looks like this:

```ruby
def get_column_names(dbh, db_name, tbl_name)
  stmt = "SELECT COLUMN_NAME FROM INFORMATION_SCHEMA.COLUMNS
          WHERE TABLE_SCHEMA = ? AND TABLE_NAME = ?
          ORDER BY ORDINAL_POSITION"
  return dbh.select_all(stmt, db_name, tbl_name).collect { |row| row[0] }
end
```

And in Python, it looks like this:

```python
def get_column_names (conn, db_name, tbl_name):
  stmt = """
          SELECT COLUMN_NAME FROM INFORMATION_SCHEMA.COLUMNS
          WHERE TABLE_SCHEMA = %s AND TABLE_NAME = %s
          ORDER BY ORDINAL_POSITION
         """
  cursor = conn.cursor ()
  cursor.execute (stmt, (db_name, tbl_name))
  names = []
  for row in cursor.fetchall ():
    names.append (row[0])
  cursor.close ()
  return (names)
```

In Perl DBI, this operation is trivial, because `selectcol_arrayref( )` returns the first column of the query result directly:

```perl
sub get_column_names
{
my ($dbh, $db_name, $tbl_name) = @_;

  my $stmt = "SELECT COLUMN_NAME FROM INFORMATION_SCHEMA.COLUMNS
              WHERE TABLE_SCHEMA = ? AND TABLE_NAME = ?
              ORDER BY ORDINAL_POSITION";
```

```
    my $ref = $dbh->selectcol_arrayref ($stmt, undef, $db_name, $tbl_name);
    return defined ($ref) ? @{$ref} : ();
}
```

The routines just shown return an array containing only column names. If you require additional column information, you can write more general routines that return an array of structures, in which each structure contains information about a given column. The *lib* directory of the **recipes** distribution contains some examples. Look for routines named **get_column_info( )** in the library files.

Using SHOW COLUMNS to get table structure

The SHOW COLUMNS statement produces one row of output for each column in the table, with each row providing various pieces of information about the corresponding column.[*] The following example demonstrates the output that SHOW COLUMNS produces for the item table.

```
mysql> SHOW COLUMNS FROM item\G
*************************** 1. row ***************************
  Field: id
   Type: int(10) unsigned
   Null: NO
    Key: PRI
Default: NULL
  Extra: auto_increment
*************************** 2. row ***************************
  Field: name
   Type: char(20)
   Null: YES
    Key:
Default: NULL
  Extra:
*************************** 3. row ***************************
  Field: colors
   Type: set('chartreuse','mauve','lime green','puce')
   Null: YES
    Key:
Default: puce
  Extra:
```

The information displayed by the statement is as follows:

- Field indicates the column's name.
- Type shows the data type.
- Null is YES if the column can contain NULL values, NO otherwise.
- Key provides information about whether the column is indexed.
- Default indicates the default value.
- Extra lists miscellaneous information.

---

[*] SHOW COLUMNS FROM *tbl_name* is equivalent to SHOW FIELDS FROM *tbl_name* or DESCRIBE *tbl_name*.

The format of SHOW COLUMNS changes occasionally, but the fields just described should always be available. SHOW FULL COLUMNS displays additional fields.

SHOW COLUMNS supports a LIKE clause that takes an SQL pattern:

```
SHOW COLUMNS FROM tbl_name LIKE 'pattern';
```

The pattern is interpreted the same way as for the LIKE operator in the WHERE clause of a SELECT statement. (For information about pattern matching, see Recipe 5.10.) With a LIKE clause, SHOW COLUMNS displays information for any column having a name that matches the pattern. If you specify a literal column name, the string matches only that name and SHOW COLUMNS displays information only for that column. However, a trap awaits the unwary here. If your column name contains SQL pattern characters (% or _) and you want to match them literally, you must escape them with a backslash in the pattern string to avoid matching other names as well. The % character isn't used very often in column names, but _ is quite common, so it's possible that you'll run into this issue. Suppose that you have a table that contains the results of carbon dioxide measurements in a column named co_2, and trigonometric cosine and cotangent calculations in columns named cos1, cos2, cot1, and cot2. If you want to get information only for the co_2 column, you can't use this statement:

```
SHOW COLUMNS FROM tbl_name LIKE 'co_2';
```

The _ character means "match any character" in pattern strings, so the statement would return rows for co_2, cos2, and cot2. To match only the co_2 column, write the SHOW command like this:

```
SHOW COLUMNS FROM tbl_name LIKE 'co\_2';
```

Within a program, you can use your API language's pattern matching capabilities to escape SQL pattern characters before putting the column name into a SHOW statement. For example, in Perl, Ruby, and PHP, you can use the following expressions.

Perl:

```
$name =~ s/([%_])/\\$1/g;
```

Ruby:

```
name.gsub!(/([%_])/, '\\\\\1')
```

PHP:

```
$name = ereg_replace ("([%_])", "\\\1", $name);
```

For Python, import the re module, and use its sub( ) method:

```
name = re.sub (r'([%_])', r'\\1', name)
```

For Java, use the java.util.regex package:

```
import java.util.regex.*;

Pattern p = Pattern.compile("([_%])");
```

```
        Matcher m = p.matcher(name);
        name = m.replaceAll ("\\\\$1");
```

If these expressions appear to have too many backslashes, remember that the API language processor itself interprets backslashes and strips off a level before performing the pattern match. To get a literal backslash into the result, it must be doubled in the pattern. PHP has another level on top of that because it strips a set and the pattern processor strips a set.

The need to escape % and _ characters to match a LIKE pattern literally also applies to other forms of the SHOW statement that allow a name pattern in the LIKE clause, such as SHOW TABLES and SHOW DATABASES.

Using CREATE TABLE to get table structure

Another way to obtain table structure information from MySQL is from the CREATE TABLE statement that defines the table. You can get this information using the SHOW CREATE TABLE statement:

```
mysql> SHOW CREATE TABLE item\G
*************************** 1. row ***************************
       Table: item
Create Table: CREATE TABLE `item` (
  `id` int(10) unsigned NOT NULL AUTO_INCREMENT,
  `name` char(20) DEFAULT NULL,
  `colors` set('chartreuse','mauve','lime green','puce') DEFAULT 'puce',
  PRIMARY KEY (`id`)
) ENGINE=MyISAM DEFAULT CHARSET=latin1
```

From the command line, the same information is available from *mysqldump* if you use the --no-data option, which tells *mysqldump* to dump only the structure of the table and not its data:

```
% mysqldump --no-data cookbook item
-- MySQL dump 10.10
--
-- Host: localhost    Database: cookbook
-- -------------------------------------------------------
-- Server version       5.0.27-log

--
-- Table structure for table `item`
--

CREATE TABLE `item` (
  `id` int(10) unsigned NOT NULL auto_increment,
  `name` char(20) default NULL,
  `colors` set('chartreuse','mauve','lime green','puce') default 'puce',
  PRIMARY KEY  (`id`)
) ENGINE=MyISAM DEFAULT CHARSET=latin1;
```

This format is highly informative and easy to read because it shows column information in a format similar to the one you used to create the table in the first place. It also shows the index structure clearly, whereas the other methods do not. However, you'll prob-

---

ably find this method for checking table structure more useful for visual examination than for use within programs. The information isn't provided in regular row-and-column format, so it's more difficult to parse. Also, the format is somewhat subject to change whenever the CREATE TABLE statement is enhanced, which happens from time to time as MySQL's capabilities are extended.

9.7 Getting ENUM and SET Column Information

Problem

You want to know what members an ENUM or SET column has.

Solution

This problem is a subset of getting table structure metadata. Obtain the column definition from the table metadata, and then extract the member list from the definition.

Discussion

It's often useful to know the list of legal values for an ENUM or SET column. Suppose that you want to present a web form containing a pop-up menu that has options corresponding to each legal value of an ENUM column, such as the sizes in which a garment can be ordered, or the available shipping methods for delivering a package. You could hardwire the choices into the script that generates the form, but if you alter the column later (for example, to add a new enumeration value), you introduce a discrepancy between the column and the script that uses it. If instead you look up the legal values using the table metadata, the script always produces a pop-up that contains the proper set of values. A similar approach can be used with SET columns.

To find out what values an ENUM or SET column can have, get the column definition using one of the techniques described in Recipe 9.6 and look at the data type in the definition. For example, if you select from the INFORMATION_SCHEMA COLUMNS table, the COLUMN_TYPE value for the colors column of the item table looks like this:

```
set('chartreuse','mauve','lime green','puce')
```

ENUM columns are similar, except that they say enum rather than set. For either data type, the allowable values can be extracted by stripping off the initial word and the parentheses, splitting at the commas, and removing the enclosing quotes from the individual values. Let's write a get_enumorset_info( ) routine to break out these values from the data-type definition. While we're at it, we can have the routine return the column's type, its default value, and whether values can be NULL. Then the routine can be used by scripts that may need more than just the list of values. Here is a version in Ruby. Its arguments are a database handle, a database name, a table name, and a column name. It returns a hash with entries corresponding to the various aspects of the column definition (or nil if the column does not exist):

```
def get_enumorset_info(dbh, db_name, tbl_name, col_name)
  row = dbh.select_one(
        "SELECT COLUMN_NAME, COLUMN_TYPE, IS_NULLABLE, COLUMN_DEFAULT
         FROM INFORMATION_SCHEMA.COLUMNS
         WHERE TABLE_SCHEMA = ? AND TABLE_NAME = ? AND COLUMN_NAME = ?",
         db_name, tbl_name, col_name)
  return nil if row.nil?
  info = {}
  info["name"] = row[0]
  return nil unless row[1] =~ /^(ENUM|SET)\((.*)\)$/i
  info["type"] = $1
  # split value list on commas, trim quotes from end of each word
  info["values"] = $2.split(",").collect { |val| val.sub(/^'(.*)'$/, "\\1") }
  # determine whether column can contain NULL values
  info["nullable"] = (row[2].upcase == "YES")
  # get default value (nil represents NULL)
  info["default"] = row[3]
  return info
end
```

The routine uses case-insensitive matching when checking the data type and nullable attributes. This guards against future possible lettercase changes in metadata results.

The following example shows one way to access and display each element of the hash returned by get_enumorset_info( ):

```
info = get_enumorset_info(dbh, db_name, tbl_name, col_name)
puts "Information for " + db_name + "." + tbl_name + "." + col_name + ":"
if info.nil?
  puts "No information available (not an ENUM or SET column?)"
else
  puts "Name: " + info["name"]
  puts "Type: " + info["type"]
  puts "Legal values: " + info["values"].join(",")
  puts "Nullable: " + (info["nullable"] ? "yes" : "no")
  puts "Default value: " + (info["default"].nil? ? "NULL" : info["default"])
end
```

That code produces the following output for the item table colors column:

```
Information for cookbook.item.colors:
Name: colors
Type: set
Legal values: chartreuse,mauve,lime green,puce
Nullable: yes
Default value: puce
```

Equivalent routines for other APIs are similar. Such routines are especially handy for generating list elements in web forms. (See Recipes 19.2 and 19.3.)

9.8 Using Table Structure Information in Applications

Problem

It's all well and good to be able to obtain table structure information, but what can you use it for?

Solution

Lots of things are possible: you can display lists of table columns, create web form elements, produce ALTER TABLE statements for modifying ENUM or SET columns, and more.

Discussion

This section describes some uses for the table structure information that MySQL makes available.

Displaying column lists

Probably the simplest use of table information is to present a list of the table's columns. This is common in web-based or GUI applications that allow users to construct statements interactively by selecting a table column from a list and entering a value against which to compare column values. The get_column_names( ) routines shown in Recipe 9.6 can serve as the basis for such list displays.

Interactive record editing

Knowledge of a table's structure can be very useful for interactive record-editing applications. Suppose that you have an application that retrieves a record from the database, displays a form containing the record's content so a user can edit it, and then updates the record in the database after the user modifies the form and submits it. You can use table structure information for validating column values. For example, if a column is an ENUM, you can find out the valid enumeration values and check the value submitted by the user against them to determine whether it's legal. If the column is an integer type, check the submitted value to make sure that it consists entirely of digits, possibly preceded by a + or - sign character. If the column contains dates, look for a legal date format.

But what if the user leaves a field empty? If the field corresponds to, say, a CHAR column in the table, do you set the column value to NULL or to the empty string? This too is a question that can be answered by checking the table's structure. Determine whether the column can contain NULL values. If it can, set the column to NULL; otherwise, set it to the empty string.

Mapping column definitions onto web page elements

Some data types such as ENUM and SET correspond naturally to elements of web forms:

- An ENUM has a fixed set of values from which you choose a single value. This is analogous to a group of radio buttons, a pop-up menu, or a single-pick scrolling list.

- A SET column is similar, except that you can select multiple values; this corresponds to a group of checkboxes or a multiple-pick scrolling list.

By using the table metadata to access the definitions for these types of columns, you can easily determine a column's legal values and map them onto the appropriate form element automatically. This enables you to present users with a list of applicable values from which selections can be made easily without any typing. Recipe 9.7 discussed how to get definitions for these types of columns. The methods developed there are used in Chapter 19, which discusses form generation in more detail.

Adding elements to ENUM or SET column definitions

When you need to modify a column definition, you can use ALTER TABLE. However, it's really a pain to add a new element to an ENUM or SET column definition because you must list not only the new element, but all the existing elements, the default value, and NOT NULL if the column cannot contain NULL values. Suppose that you want to add "hot pink" to the colors column of an item table that has this structure:

```
CREATE TABLE item
(
  id      INT UNSIGNED NOT NULL AUTO_INCREMENT,
  name    CHAR(20),
  colors  SET('chartreuse','mauve','lime green','puce') DEFAULT 'puce',
  PRIMARY KEY (id)
);
```

To change the column definition, use ALTER TABLE as follows:

```
ALTER TABLE item
  MODIFY colors
  SET('chartreuse','mauve','lime green','puce','hot pink')
  DEFAULT 'puce';
```

The ENUM definition doesn't contain many elements, so that statement isn't very difficult to enter manually. However, the more elements a column has, the more difficult and error prone it is to type statements like that. To avoid retyping the existing definition just to add a new element, you have a choice of strategies:

- Write a script that does the work for you. It can examine the table definition and use the column metadata to generate the ALTER TABLE statement.

- Use *mysqldump* to get a CREATE TABLE statement that contains the current column definition, and modify the statement in a text editor to produce the appropriate ALTER TABLE statement that changes the definition.

As an implementation of the first approach, let's develop a Python script *add_element.py* that generates the appropriate ALTER TABLE statement automatically when given database and table names, an ENUM or SET column name, and the new ele-

---

ment value. *add_element.py* will use that information to figure out the correct ALTER TABLE statement and display it:

```
% add_element.py cookbook item colors "hot pink"
ALTER TABLE `cookbook`.`item`
  MODIFY `colors`
  set('chartreuse','mauve','lime green','puce','hot pink')
  DEFAULT 'puce';
```

By having *add_element.py* produce the statement as its output, you have the choice of shoving it into *mysql* for immediate execution or saving the output into a file:

```
% add_element.py cookbook item colors "hot pink" | mysql cookbook
% add_element.py cookbook item colors "hot pink" > stmt.sql
```

The first part of the *add_element.py* script imports the requisite modules and checks the command-line arguments. This is fairly straightforward:

```
#!/usr/bin/python
# add_element.py - produce ALTER TABLE statement to add an element
# to an ENUM or SET column

import sys
import MySQLdb
import Cookbook

if len (sys.argv) != 5:
  print "Usage: add_element.py db_name tbl_name col_name new_element"
  sys.exit (1)
(db_name, tbl_name, col_name, new_elt) = (sys.argv[1:5])
```

After connecting to the MySQL server (code not shown, but is present in the script), the script checks INFORMATION_SCHEMA to retrieve the column definition, whether it allows NULL values, and its default value. The following code does this, checking to make sure that the column really exists in the table:

```
stmt = """
        SELECT COLUMN_TYPE, IS_NULLABLE, COLUMN_DEFAULT
        FROM INFORMATION_SCHEMA.COLUMNS
        WHERE TABLE_SCHEMA = %s AND TABLE_NAME = %s AND COLUMN_NAME = %s
        """
cursor = conn.cursor ()
cursor.execute (stmt, (db_name, tbl_name, col_name))
info = cursor.fetchone ()
cursor.close
if info == None:
  print "Could not retrieve information for table %s.%s, column %s" \
                    % (db_name, tbl_name, col_name)
  sys.exit (1)
```

At this point, if the SELECT statement succeeded, the information produced by it is available as a tuple stored in the info variable. We'll need to use several elements from this tuple. The most important is the COLUMN_TYPE value, which provides the enum(...) or set(...) string containing the column's definition. We can use this string to verify that the column really is an ENUM or SET, and then add the new element to the string just before the closing parenthesis. For the `colors` column, we want to change this:

```
set('chartreuse','mauve','lime green','puce')
```

To this:

```
set('chartreuse','mauve','lime green','puce','hot pink')
```

It's also necessary to check whether column values can be `NULL` and what the default value is so that the program can add the appropriate information to the `ALTER TABLE` statement. The code that does all this is as follows:

```
# get data type string; make sure it begins with ENUM or SET
type = info[0]
if type[0:5].upper() != "ENUM(" and type[0:4].upper() != "SET(":
  print "table %s.%s, column %s is not an ENUM or SET" % \
        (db_name, tbl_name, col_name)
  sys.exit(1)
# insert comma and properly quoted new element just before closing paren
type = type[0:len(type)-1] + "," + conn.literal (new_elt) + ")"

# if column cannot contain NULL values, add "NOT NULL"
if info[1].upper() == "YES":
  nullable = ""
else:
  nullable = "NOT NULL ";

# construct DEFAULT clause (quoting value as necessary)
default = "DEFAULT " + conn.literal (info[2])

print "ALTER TABLE `%s`.`%s`\n  MODIFY `%s`\n  %s\n  %s%s;" \
        % (db_name, tbl_name, col_name, type, nullable, default)
```

That's it. You now have a working `ENUM`- or `SET`-altering program. Still, *add_element.py* is fairly basic and can be improved in various ways:

- Make sure that the element value you're adding to the column isn't already there.
- Modify *add_element.py* to take more than one argument after the column name and add all of them to the column definition at the same time.
- Add an option to indicate that the named element should be deleted rather than added.

Another approach to altering `ENUM` or `SET` columns involves capturing the current definition in a file and editing the file to produce the proper `ALTER TABLE` statement.

1. Run *mysqldump* to get the `CREATE TABLE` statement that contains the column definition:

   ```
   % mysqldump --no-data cookbook item > test.txt
   ```

   The `--no-data` option tells *mysqldump* not to dump the data from the table; it's used here because only the table-creation statement is needed. The resulting file, *test.txt*, should contain this statement:

```
CREATE TABLE `item` (
  `id` int(10) unsigned NOT NULL AUTO_INCREMENT,
  `name` char(20) DEFAULT NULL,
  `colors` set('chartreuse','mauve','lime green','puce') DEFAULT 'puce',
  PRIMARY KEY (`id`)
) ENGINE=MyISAM DEFAULT CHARSET=latin1;
```

2. Edit the *test.txt* file to remove everything but the definition for the colors column:

```
`colors` set('chartreuse','mauve','lime green','puce') DEFAULT 'puce',
```

3. Modify the definition to produce an ALTER TABLE statement that has the new element and a semicolon at the end:

```
ALTER TABLE item MODIFY
`colors` set('chartreuse','mauve','lime green','puce','hot pink')
DEFAULT 'puce';
```

4. Write *test.txt* back out to save it, and then get out of the editor and feed *test.txt* as a batch file to *mysql*:

```
% mysql cookbook < test.txt
```

For simple columns, this procedure is more work than just typing the ALTER TABLE statement manually. However, for ENUM and SET columns with long and ungainly definitions, using an editor to create a *mysql* batch file from *mysqldump* output makes a lot of sense. This technique also is useful when you want to delete or reorder members of an ENUM or SET column, or to add or delete members from the column definition.

Selecting all except certain columns

Sometimes you want to retrieve "almost all" the columns from a table. Suppose that you have an image table that contains a BLOB column named data used for storing images that might be very large, and other columns that characterize the BLOB column, such as its ID, a description, and so forth. It's easy to write a SELECT * statement that retrieves all the columns, but if all you need is the descriptive information about the images and not the images themselves, it's inefficient to drag the BLOB values over the connection along with the other columns. Instead, you want to select everything in the row *except* the data column.

Unfortunately, there is no way to say directly in SQL, "select all columns except this one." You must explicitly name all the columns except data. On the other hand, it's easy to construct that kind of statement by using table structure information. Extract the list of column names, delete the one to be excluded, and then construct a SELECT statement from those columns that remain. The following example shows how to do this in PHP, using the get_column_names( ) function developed earlier in the chapter to obtain the column names for a table:

```
$names = get_column_names ($conn, $db_name, $tbl_name);
$stmt = "";
# construct list of columns to select: all but "data"
foreach ($names as $index => $name)
{
```

```
    if ($name == "data")
      continue;
    if ($stmt != "") # put commas between column names
      $stmt .= ", ";
    $stmt .= "`$name`";
  }
  $stmt = "SELECT $stmt FROM `$db_name`.`$tbl_name`";
```

The equivalent Perl code for constructing the statement is a bit shorter (and correspondingly more cryptic):

```
  my @names = get_column_names ($dbh, $db_name, $tbl_name);
  my $stmt = "SELECT `"
             . join ("`, `", grep (!/^data$/, @names))
             . "` FROM `$db_name`.`$tbl_name`";
```

Whichever language you use, the result is a statement that you can use to select all columns but **data**. It will be more efficient than **SELECT** * because it won't pull the **BLOB** values over the network. Of course, this process does involve an extra round trip to the server to execute the statement that retrieves the column names, so you should consider the context in which you plan to use the **SELECT** statement. If you're going to retrieve only a single row, it might be more efficient simply to select the entire row than to incur the overhead of the extra round trip. But if you're selecting many rows, the reduction in network traffic achieved by skipping the **BLOB** columns will be worth the overhead of the additional query for getting table structure.

9.9 Getting Server Metadata

Problem

You want the MySQL server to tell you about itself.

Solution

Several SQL functions and **SHOW** statements return information about the server.

Discussion

MySQL offers several SQL functions and statements that provide you with information about the server itself and about your current client connection. A few that you may find useful are listed here. To obtain the information provided by any of them, issue the statement, and then process its result set. Both **SHOW** statements allow a **LIKE** '*pattern*' clause for limiting the results only to those rows matching the pattern.

Statement	Information produced by statement
SELECT VERSION( )	Server version string
SELECT DATABASE( )	Default database name (NULL if none)

Statement	Information produced by statement
SELECT USER( )	Current user as given by client when connecting
SELECT CURRENT_USER( )	User used for checking client privileges
SHOW GLOBAL STATUS	Server global status indicators
SHOW VARIABLES	Server configuration variables

A given API might provide alternative ways to access these types of information. For example, JDBC has several database-independent methods for obtaining server metadata. Use your connection object to obtain the database metadata, and then invoke the appropriate methods to get the information in which you're interested. You should consult a JDBC reference for a complete list, but here are a few representative examples:

```
DatabaseMetaData md = conn.getMetaData ();
// can also get this with SELECT VERSION()
System.out.println ("Product version: " + md.getDatabaseProductVersion ());
// this is similar to SELECT USER() but doesn't include the hostname
System.out.println ("Username: " + md.getUserName ());
```

9.10 Writing Applications That Adapt to the MySQL Server Version

Problem

You want to use a given feature that is only available in a particular version of MySQL.

Solution

Ask the server for its version number. If the server is too old to support a given feature, maybe you can fall back to a workaround, if one exists.

Discussion

Each version of MySQL adds features. If you're writing an application that requires certain features, check the server version to determine if they are present; if not, you must perform some sort of workaround (assuming there is one).

To get the server version, issue a SELECT VERSION( ) statement. The result is a string that looks something like 5.0.13-rc or 4.1.10a. In other words, it returns a string consisting of major, minor, and "teeny" version numbers, possibly some letter at the end of the "teeny" version, and possibly some suffix. The version string can be used as is for presentation purposes if you want to produce a status display for the user. However, for comparisons, it's simpler to work with a number—in particular, a five-digit number in *Mmmtt* format, in which *M*, *mm*, *tt* are the major, minor, and teeny version numbers. The conversion can be performed by splitting the string at the periods, stripping off from the third piece the suffix that begins with the first nonnumeric character, and then joining the pieces. For example, `5.0.13-rc.` becomes `50013`, and `4.1.10a` becomes `40110`.

Here's a Perl DBI function that takes a database handle argument and returns a two-element list that contains both the string and numeric forms of the server version. The code assumes that the minor and teeny version parts are less than 100 and thus no more than two digits each. That should be a valid assumption, because the source code for MySQL itself uses the same format.

```perl
sub get_server_version
{
my $dbh = shift;
my ($ver_str, $ver_num);
my ($major, $minor, $teeny);

  # fetch result into scalar string
  $ver_str = $dbh->selectrow_array ("SELECT VERSION()");
  return undef unless defined ($ver_str);
  ($major, $minor, $teeny) = split (/\./, $ver_str);
  $teeny =~ s/\D*$//; # strip any nonnumeric suffix if present
  $ver_num = $major*10000 + $minor*100 + $teeny;
  return ($ver_str, $ver_num);
}
```

To get both forms of the version information at once, call the function like this:

```perl
my ($ver_str, $ver_num) = get_server_version ($dbh);
```

To get just one of the values, call it as follows:

```perl
my $ver_str = (get_server_version ($dbh))[0]; # string form
my $ver_num = (get_server_version ($dbh))[1]; # numeric form
```

The following examples demonstrate how to use the numeric version value to check whether the server supports certain features:

```perl
my $ver_num = (get_server_version ($dbh))[1];
printf "Quoted identifiers: %s\n", ($ver_num >= 32306 ? "yes" : "no");
printf "UNION statement:    %s\n", ($ver_num >= 40000 ? "yes" : "no");
printf "Subqueries:         %s\n", ($ver_num >= 40100 ? "yes" : "no");
printf "Views:              %s\n", ($ver_num >= 50001 ? "yes" : "no");
printf "Strict SQL mode:    %s\n", ($ver_num >= 50002 ? "yes" : "no");
printf "Events:             %s\n", ($ver_num >= 50106 ? "yes" : "no");
```

9.11 Determining the Default Database

Problem

Has any database been selected as the default database? What is its name?

Solution

Use the `DATABASE( )` function.

Discussion

`SELECT DATABASE( )` returns the name of the default database or `NULL` if no database has been selected. The following Ruby code uses the statement to present a status display containing information about the current connection:

```
db = dbh.select_one("SELECT DATABASE()")[0]
puts "Default database: " + (db.nil? ? "(no database selected)" : db)
```

Note that before MySQL 4.1.1, `DATABASE( )` returns an empty string (not `NULL`) if there is no current database.

9.12 Monitoring the MySQL Server

Problem

You want to find out how the server was configured or monitor its state.

Solution

`SHOW VARIABLES` and `SHOW STATUS` are useful for this.

Discussion

The `SHOW VARIABLES` and `SHOW STATUS` statements provide server configuration and performance information:

```
mysql> SHOW VARIABLES;
+----------------------------------+------------------+
| Variable_name                    | Value            |
+----------------------------------+------------------+
| back_log                         | 50               |
| basedir                          | /usr/local/mysql/ |
| bdb_cache_size                   | 8388600          |
| bdb_log_buffer_size              | 0                |
| bdb_home                         |                  |
...
mysql> SHOW /*!50002 GLOBAL */ STATUS;
+---------------------------+----------+
| Variable_name             | Value    |
+---------------------------+----------+
| Aborted_clients           | 319      |
| Aborted_connects          | 22       |
| Bytes_received            | 32085033 |
| Bytes_sent                | 26379272 |
| Connections               | 65684    |
...
```

Both statements allow a LIKE 'pattern' clause that takes an SQL pattern. In that case, only rows for variable names that match the pattern are returned.

The /*!50002 GLOBAL */ comment is present in the SHOW STATUS statement due to a change made in MySQL 5.0.2; before MySQL 5.0.2, status variables were global (server-wide values). In 5.0.2, status variables have global and session (per-connection) values, and SHOW STATUS has been extended to take GLOBAL or SESSION modifiers, with the default being, if neither is given, to display the session values. The comment causes servers from MySQL 5.0.2 and up to display the global values. Servers before 5.0.2 ignore the comment, but display global values because only global values exist in those versions. This idiom is used throughout this chapter.

System and status variable information can be useful for writing administrative applications. For example, the MyISAM key cache hit rate is a measure of how often key requests are satisfied from the cache without reading keys from disk. The following formula calculates the hit rate, where Key_reads and Key_read_requests indicate the number of disk reads and number of requests, respectively:

```
1 - (Key_reads / Key_read_requests)
```

Values close to 1 indicate a high hit rate, which means that the key cache is very efficient. Values close to 0 indicate a low hit rate (possibly a sign that you should increase the value of the key_buffer_size system variable to use a larger cache). It's easy to calculate the hit rate in a program, as the following Ruby code illustrates:

```ruby
# Execute SHOW STATUS to get relevant server status variables, use
# names and values to construct hash of values keyed by names.
stat_hash = {}
stmt = "SHOW /*!50002 GLOBAL */ STATUS LIKE 'Key_read%'"
dbh.select_all(stmt).each do |name, value|
  stat_hash[name] = value
end

key_reads = stat_hash["Key_reads"].to_f
key_reqs = stat_hash["Key_read_requests"].to_f
hit_rate = key_reqs == 0 ? 0 : 1.0 - (key_reads / key_reqs)

puts "        Key_reads: #{key_reads}"
puts "Key_read_requests: #{key_reqs}"
puts "        Hit rate: #{hit_rate}"
```

As another example, you might write a long-running program that probes the server periodically to monitor its activity. A simple application of this type might ask the server to report the number of connections it's received and its uptime, to determine a running display of average connection activity. The statements to obtain this information are:

```
SHOW /*!50002 GLOBAL */ STATUS LIKE 'Connections';
SHOW /*!50002 GLOBAL */ STATUS LIKE 'Uptime';
```

If you want to avoid having to reconnect each time you issue the statements, you can ask the server for its client timeout period and probe it at intervals shorter than that value. You can get the timeout value (in seconds) with this statement:

```
SHOW VARIABLES LIKE 'wait_timeout';
```

The default value is 28800 (8 hours), but it might be configured to a different value on your system.

For system variables, an alternative way to access their values is by referring to them as @@*var_name*. For example:

```
mysql> SELECT @@wait_timeout;
+----------------+
| @@wait_timeout |
+----------------+
| 28800          |
+----------------+
```

This provides the convenience that you can select multiple values in a single row, and you can use the values directly within expressions.

The "MySQL Uncertainty Principle"

Heisenberg's uncertainty principle for measurement of quantum phenomena has a MySQL analog. If you monitor MySQL's status to see how it changes over time, you might notice the curious effect that, for some of the indicators, each time you take a measurement, you change the value you're measuring! For example, you can determine the number of statements the server has received by using the following statement:

```
SHOW /*!50002 GLOBAL */ STATUS LIKE 'Questions'
```

However, that statement is itself a statement, so each time you issue it, you cause the Questions value to change. In effect, your performance assessment instrument contaminates its own measurements, something you might want to take into account.

9.13 Determining Which Storage Engines the Server Supports

Problem

You want to know whether you can create a table using a given storage engine.

Solution

Use the SHOW ENGINES statement to ask the server which storage engines it supports.

Discussion

The SHOW ENGINES statement provides information about which storage engines the server supports. Its output looks like this:

```
mysql> SHOW ENGINES\G
*************************** 1. row ***************************
```

```
 Engine: MyISAM
Support: DEFAULT
Comment: Default engine as of MySQL 3.23 with great performance
*************************** 2. row ***************************
 Engine: MEMORY
Support: YES
Comment: Hash based, stored in memory, useful for temporary tables
*************************** 3. row ***************************
 Engine: InnoDB
Support: YES
Comment: Supports transactions, row-level locking, and foreign keys
*************************** 4. row ***************************
 Engine: BerkeleyDB
Support: NO
Comment: Supports transactions and page-level locking
...
```

The Engine value indicates a storage engine name and the Support value indicates its status. If Support is YES or DEFAULT, the engine is available. If the value is NO or DISABLED, the engine is not available. The following Ruby method uses those rules to determine engine status and return a list of the engines that are available:

```ruby
def get_storage_engines(dbh)
  engines = []
  dbh.select_all("SHOW ENGINES").each do |engine, support|
    engines << engine if ["YES", "DEFAULT"].include?(support.upcase)
  end
  return engines
end
```

## CHAPTER 10

Importing and Exporting Data

10.0 Introduction

Suppose that you have a file named *somedata.csv* that contains 12 columns of data in comma-separated values (CSV) format. From this file you want to extract only columns 2, 11, 5, and 9, and use them to create database rows in a MySQL table that contains `name`, `birth`, `height`, and `weight` columns. You need to make sure that the height and weight are positive integers, and convert the birth dates from *MM/DD/YY* format to *CCYY-MM-DD* format. How can you do this?

In one sense, that problem is very specialized. But in another, it's not at all atypical, because data transfer problems with specific requirements occur frequently when you transfer data into MySQL. It would be nice if datafiles were always nicely formatted and ready to load into MySQL with no preparation, but frequently that is not so. As a result, it's often necessary to preprocess information to put it into a format that MySQL finds acceptable. The reverse also is true; data exported from MySQL may need massaging to be useful for other programs.

Although some data transfer operations are so difficult that they require a great deal of hand checking and reformatting, you can do at least part of the job automatically in most cases. Virtually all transfer problems involve at least some elements of a common set of conversion issues. This chapter discusses what these issues are, how to deal with them by taking advantage of the existing tools at your disposal, and how to write your own tools when necessary. The idea is not to cover all possible import and export situations (an impossible task), but to show some representative techniques and utilities. You can use them as is or adapt them for problems that they don't handle. (There are also commercial conversion tools that may assist you, but my purpose here is to help you do things yourself.)

The first recipes in the chapter cover MySQL's native facilities for importing data (the `LOAD DATA` statement and the *mysqlimport* command-line program), and for exporting data (the `SELECT ... INTO OUTFILE` statement and the *mysqldump* program). For operations that don't require any data validation or reformatting, these facilities often are sufficient. They might even be sufficient for operations that require reformatting because LOAD DATA can perform preprocessing and SELECT can take advantage of functions and expressions for transforming column values into other formats.

For situations where MySQL's native import and export capabilities do not suffice, the chapter moves on to cover techniques for using external supporting utilities and for writing your own. To some extent, you can avoid writing your own tools by using existing programs. For example, *cut* can extract columns from a file, and *sed* and *tr* can be used as postprocessors to convert query output into other formats. But you'll probably eventually reach the point where you decide to write your own programs. When you do, there are two broad sets of issues to consider:

- How to manipulate the *structure* of datafiles. When a file is in a format that isn't suitable for import, you'll need to convert it to a different format. This may involve issues such as changing the column delimiters or line-ending sequences, or removing or rearranging columns in the file.

- How to manipulate the *content* of datafiles. If you don't know whether the values contained in a file are legal, you may want to preprocess it to check or reformat them. Numeric values may need to be verified as lying within a specific range, dates may need to be converted to or from ISO format, and so forth.

Source code for the program fragments and scripts discussed in this chapter is located in the *transfer* directory of the `recipes` distribution, with the exception that some of the utility functions are contained in library files located in the *lib* directory. The code for some of the shorter utilities is shown in full. For the longer ones, the chapter generally discusses only how they work and how to use them, but you have access to the source if you want to investigate in more detail how they're written.

The problems addressed in this chapter involve a lot of text processing and pattern matching. These are particular strengths of Perl, so the program fragments and utilities shown here are written mainly in Perl. Ruby, PHP, Python, and Java provide pattern-matching capabilities, too, so they can of course do many of the same things.

General Import and Export Issues

Incompatible datafile formats and differing rules for interpreting various kinds of values lead to many headaches when transferring data between programs. Nevertheless, certain issues recur frequently. By being aware of them, you'll be able to identify more easily just what you need to do to solve particular import or export problems.

In its most basic form, an input stream is just a set of bytes with no particular meaning. Successful import into MySQL requires being able to recognize which bytes represent structural information and which represent the data values framed by that structure. Because such recognition is key to decomposing the input into appropriate units, the most fundamental import issues are these:

- What is the record separator? Knowing this enables you to partition the input stream into records.

- What is the field delimiter? Knowing this enables you to partition each record into field values. Identifying the data values also might include stripping off quotes from around the values or recognizing escape sequences within them.

The ability to break apart the input into records and fields is important for extracting the data values from it. However, the values may still not be in a form that can be used directly, and you may need to consider other issues:

- Do the order and number of columns match the structure of the database table? Mismatches require columns to be rearranged or skipped.

- Do data values need to be validated or reformatted? If the values are in a format that matches MySQL's expectations, no further processing is necessary. Otherwise, they need to be checked and possibly rewritten.

- How should NULL or empty values be handled? Are they allowed? Can NULL values even be detected? (Some systems export the NULL value as an empty string, making it impossible to distinguish one from the other.)

For export from MySQL, the issues are somewhat the reverse. You can assume that values stored in the database are valid, but they may require reformatting for use by other programs, and it's necessary to add column and record delimiters to form an output stream that has a structure other programs can recognize.

The chapter deals with these issues primarily within the context of performing bulk transfers of entire files, but many of the techniques discussed here can be applied in other situations as well. Consider a web-based application that presents a form for a user to fill in and then processes its contents to create a new row in the database. That is a data import situation. Web APIs generally make form contents available as a set of already parsed discrete values, so the application may not need to deal with record and column delimiters. On the other hand, validation issues remain paramount. You really have no idea what kind of values a user is sending your script, so it's important to check them. Validation is covered in this chapter, and we'll revisit the issue in Recipe 19.6.

File Formats

Data files come in many formats, two of which are used frequently in this chapter:

Tab-delimited format
This is one of the simplest file structures; lines contain values separated by tab characters. A short tab-delimited file might look like this, where the whitespace between column values represents single tab characters:

```
a       b       c
a,b,c   d e     f
```

Comma-separated values (CSV) format
Files written in CSV format vary somewhat, because there is apparently no actual standard describing the format. However, the general idea is that lines consist of

values separated by commas, and values containing internal commas are enclosed within quotes to prevent the commas from being interpreted as value delimiters. It's also common for values containing spaces to be quoted as well. Here is an example, in which each line contains three values:

```
a,b,c
"a,b,c","d e",f
```

It's trickier to process CSV files than tab-delimited files because characters like quotes and commas have a dual meaning: They may represent file structure or be included in the content of data values.

Another important datafile characteristic is the *line-ending sequence*. The most common sequences are carriage return, linefeed, and carriage return/linefeed pair, sometimes referred to here by the abbreviations CR, LF, and CRLF.

Datafiles often begin with a row of column labels. For some import operations, the row of labels is an annoyance because you must discard it to avoid having the labels be loaded into your table as a data row. In other cases, the labels are quite useful:

- For import into existing tables, the labels help you match datafile columns with the table columns if they are not necessarily in the same order.
- The labels can be used for column names when creating a new table automatically or semiautomatically from a datafile. For example, Recipe 10.36 discusses a utility that examines a datafile and guesses the CREATE TABLE statement that should be used to create a table from the file. If a label row is present, the utility uses the labels for column names. Otherwise, it's necessary to make up generic names like c1, c2, and so forth, which isn't very descriptive.

Tab-Delimited, Linefeed-Terminated Format

Although datafiles may be written in many formats, it's unlikely that you'll want to include machinery for reading several different formats within each file-processing utility that you write. I don't want to, either. For that reason, many of the utilities described in this chapter assume for simplicity that their input is in tab-delimited, linefeed-terminated format. (This is also the default format for MySQL's LOAD DATA statement.) By making this assumption, it becomes easier to write programs that read files.

On the other hand, *something* has to be able to read data in other formats. To handle that problem, we'll develop a *cvt_file.pl* script that can read several types of files (Recipe 10.18). The script is based on the Perl Text::CSV_XS module, which despite its name can be used for more than just CSV data. *cvt_file.pl* can convert between many file types, making it possible for other programs that require tab-delimited lines to be used with files not originally written in that format. In other words, you can use *cvt_file.pl* to convert a file to tab-delimited, linefeed-terminated format, and then any program that expects that format can process the file.

Notes on Invoking Shell Commands

This chapter shows a number of programs that you invoke from the command line using a shell like *bash* or *tcsh* under Unix or *cmd.exe* ("the command prompt") under Windows. Many of the example commands for these programs use quotes around option values, and sometimes an option value is itself a quote character. Quoting conventions vary from one shell to another, but the following rules seem to work with most of them (including *cmd.exe* under Windows):

- For an argument that contains spaces, enclose it within double quotes to prevent the shell from interpreting it as multiple separate arguments. The shell will strip off the quotes and then pass the argument to the command intact.

- To include a double quote character in the argument itself, precede it with a backslash.

Some shell commands in this chapter are so long that they're shown as you would enter them using several lines, with a backslash character as the line-continuation character:

```
% prog_name \
    argument1 \
    argument2 ...
```

That works for Unix, but not for Windows, where you'll need to omit the continuation characters and type the entire command on one line:

```
C:\> prog_name argument1 argument2 ...
```

10.1 Importing Data with LOAD DATA and mysqlimport

Problem

You want to load a datafile into a table using MySQL's built-in import capabilities.

Solution

Use the LOAD DATA statement or the *mysqlimport* command-line program.

Discussion

MySQL provides a LOAD DATA statement that acts as a bulk data loader. Here's an example statement that reads a file *mytbl.txt* from your current directory and loads it into the table mytbl in the default database:

```
mysql> LOAD DATA LOCAL INFILE 'mytbl.txt' INTO TABLE mytbl;
```

At some MySQL installations, the LOCAL loading capability may have been disabled for security reasons. If that is true at your site, omit LOCAL from the statement and specify the full pathname to the file. See Recipe 10.2 for more information on local versus non-local data loading.

MySQL also includes a utility program named *mysqlimport* that acts as a wrapper around LOAD DATA so that you can load input files directly from the command line. The *mysqlimport* command that is equivalent to the preceding LOAD DATA statement looks like this, assuming that mytbl is in the cookbook database:

```
% mysqlimport --local cookbook mytbl.txt
```

For *mysqlimport*, as with other MySQL programs, you may need to specify connection parameter options such as --user or --host (Recipe 1.3).

The following list describes LOAD DATA's general characteristics and capabilities; *mysqlimport* shares most of these behaviors. There are some differences that we'll note as we go along, but for the most part you can interpret references to LOAD DATA as references to *mysqlimport* as well.

LOAD DATA provides options to address many of the import issues mentioned in the chapter introduction, such as the line-ending sequence for recognizing how to break input into records, the column value delimiter that allows records to be broken into separate values, the quoting character that may enclose column values, quoting and escaping conventions within values, and NULL value representation:

- By default, LOAD DATA expects the datafile to contain the same number of columns as the table into which you're loading data, and the datafile columns must be present in the same order as in the table. If the file doesn't contain a value for every column or the values aren't in the proper order, you can specify which columns are present and the order in which they appear. If the datafile contains fewer columns than the table, MySQL assigns default values to columns for which no values are present in the datafile.

- LOAD DATA assumes that data values are separated by tab characters and that lines end with linefeeds (newlines). You can specify the data format explicitly if a file doesn't conform to these conventions.

- You can indicate that data values may have quotes around them that should be stripped, and you can specify what the quote character is.

- Several special escape sequences are recognized and converted during input processing. The default escape character is backslash (\), but you can change it if you like. The \N sequence is interpreted to represent a NULL value. The \b, \n, \r, \t, \\, and \0 sequences are interpreted as backspace, linefeed, carriage return, tab, backslash, and ASCII NUL characters. (NUL is a zero-valued byte, which is different from the SQL NULL value.)

- LOAD DATA provides diagnostic information about which input values cause problems. You can display this information by issuing a SHOW WARNINGS statement after the LOAD DATA statement.

The next few sections describe how to import datafiles into MySQL tables using LOAD DATA or *mysqlimport*.

10.2 Specifying the Datafile Location

Problem

You're not sure how to tell LOAD DATA where to look for your datafile, particularly if it's located in another directory.

Solution

It's a matter of knowing the rules that determine where MySQL looks for the file.

Discussion

You can load files that are located on the server host or on the client host from which you issue the LOAD DATA statement. By default, the MySQL server assumes that the datafile is located on the server host. However, that might not be appropriate in all cases:

- If you access the MySQL server from a remote client host and have no means of transferring your file to the server host (such as a login account there), you won't be able to put the file on the server.

- Even if you have a login account on the server host, your MySQL account must be enabled with the FILE privilege, and the file to be loaded must be either world-readable or located in the data directory for the default database. Most MySQL users do not have the FILE privilege (because it enables them to do dangerous things), and you might not want to make the file world readable (for security reasons) or be able to put it in the database directory.

Fortunately, you can load local files that are located on the client host using LOAD DATA LOCAL rather than LOAD DATA. The only permission you need to import a local file is the ability to read the file yourself. One caveat is that the LOCAL keyword might be disabled by default. You may be able to turn it on using the --local-infile option for *mysql*. If that doesn't work, your server has been configured not to allow LOAD DATA LOCAL at all. (Many of the examples in this chapter assume that LOCAL can be used. If that's not true for your system, you'll need to adapt these examples. Omit LOCAL from the statement, make sure that the file is located on the MySQL server host, and specify its pathname using the following rules. For example, specify the full pathname.)

If the LOCAL keyword is not present in the LOAD DATA statement, the MySQL server reads the datafile. It looks for the file on the server host using the following rules:

- An absolute pathname fully specifies the location of the file, beginning from the root of the filesystem. MySQL reads the file from the given location.

- A relative pathname is interpreted two ways, depending on whether it has a single component or multiple components. For a single-component filename such as *mytbl.txt*, MySQL looks for the file in the database directory for the default database. (The statement will fail if you have not selected a default database.) For a multiple-component filename such as *xyz/mytbl.txt*, MySQL looks for the file beginning in the MySQL data directory. That is, it expects to find *mytbl.txt* in a directory named *xyz*.

Database directories are located directly under the server's data directory, so these two statements are equivalent if the default database is cookbook:

```
mysql> LOAD DATA INFILE 'mytbl.txt' INTO TABLE mytbl;
mysql> LOAD DATA INFILE 'cookbook/mytbl.txt' INTO TABLE mytbl;
```

If the LOCAL keyword is specified in the LOAD DATA statement, your client program looks for the file on the client host and sends its contents to the server. The client interprets the pathname the same way your command interpreter does:

- An absolute pathname fully specifies the location of the file, beginning from the root of the filesystem.

- A relative pathname specifies the location of the file relative to your current directory.

If your file is located on the client host, but you forget to indicate that it's local, you'll get an error.

```
mysql> LOAD DATA 'mytbl.txt' INTO TABLE mytbl;
ERROR 1045 (28000): Access denied for user: 'user_name@host_name'
(Using password: YES)
```

That Access denied message can be confusing: if you're able to connect to the server and issue the LOAD DATA statement, it would seem that you've already gained access to MySQL, right? The meaning of the error message is that the MySQL tried to open *mytbl.txt* on the server host and could not access it.

If your MySQL server runs on the host from which you issue the LOAD DATA statement, "remote" and "local" refer to the same host. But the rules just discussed for locating datafiles still apply. Without LOCAL, the server reads the datafile. With LOCAL, the client program reads the file and sends its contents to the server.

mysqlimport uses the same rules for finding files as LOAD DATA. By default, it assumes that the datafile is located on the server host. To indicate that the file is local to the client host, specify the --local (or -L) option on the command line.

LOAD DATA assumes that the table is located in the default database unless you specify the database name explicitly. *mysqlimport* always requires a database argument:

```
% mysqlimport --local cookbook mytbl.txt
```

To use LOAD DATA to load a file into a specific database rather than the default database, qualify the table name with the database name. The following statement does this, indicating that the mytbl table is located in the other_db database:

```
mysql> LOAD DATA LOCAL 'mytbl.txt' INTO TABLE other_db.mytbl;
```

LOAD DATA assumes no relationship between the name of the datafile and the name of the table into which you're loading the file's contents. *mysqlimport* assumes a fixed relationship between the data-file name and the table name. Specifically, it uses the last component of the filename to determine the table name. For example, *mysqlimport* interprets *mytbl*, *mytbl.txt*, *mytbl.dat*, */tmp/mytbl.txt*, */u/paul/data/mytbl.csv*, and *C:\projects\mytbl.txt* all as files containing data for the mytbl table.

Naming Datafiles Under Windows

Windows systems use \ as the pathname separator in filenames. That's a bit of a problem, because MySQL interprets backslash as the escape character in string values. To specify a Windows pathname, use either doubled backslashes or forward slashes instead. These two statements show two ways of referring to the same Windows file:

```
mysql> LOAD DATA LOCAL INFILE 'C:\\projects\\mydata.txt' INTO mytbl;
mysql> LOAD DATA LOCAL INFILE 'C:/projects/mydata.txt' INTO mytbl;
```

If the NO_BACKSLASH_ESCAPES SQL mode is enabled, backslash is not special, and you do not double it:

```
mysql> SET sql_mode = 'NO_BACKSLASH_ESCAPES';
mysql> LOAD DATA LOCAL INFILE 'C:\projects\mydata.txt' INTO mytbl;
```

10.3 Specifying the Structure of the Datafile

Problem

You have a data file that's not in LOAD DATA's default format.

Solution

Use FIELDS and LINES clauses to tell LOAD DATA how to interpret the file.

Discussion

By default, LOAD DATA assumes that datafiles contain lines that are terminated by linefeed (newline) characters and that data values within a line are separated by tab characters. The following statement does not specify anything about the format of the datafile, so MySQL assumes the default format:

```
mysql> LOAD DATA LOCAL INFILE 'mytbl.txt' INTO TABLE mytbl;
```

Two LOAD DATA clauses provide explicit information about the datafile format. A FIELDS clause describes the characteristics of fields within a line, and a LINES clause specifies the line-ending sequence. The following LOAD DATA statement indicates that the input file contains data values separated by colons and lines terminated by carriage returns:

```
mysql> LOAD DATA LOCAL INFILE 'mytbl.txt' INTO TABLE mytbl
    -> FIELDS TERMINATED BY ':'
    -> LINES TERMINATED BY '\r';
```

Each clause follows the table name. If both are present, the FIELDS clause must precede the LINES clause. The line and field termination indicators can contain multiple characters. For example, \r\n indicates that lines are terminated by carriage return/linefeed pairs.

The LINES clause also has a STARTING BY subclause. It specifies the sequence to be stripped from each input record. Like TERMINATED BY, the sequence can have multiple characters. If TERMINATED BY and STARTING BY both are present in the LINES clause, they can appear in any order.

Note that for STARTING BY, everything *up to* the given sequence is stripped from each line. If you specify STARTING BY 'X' and an input line begins with abcX, all four leading characters are stripped.

If you use *mysqlimport*, command options provide the format specifiers. *mysqlimport* commands that correspond to the preceding two LOAD DATA statements look like this:

```
% mysqlimport --local cookbook mytbl.txt
% mysqlimport --local --fields-terminated-by=":" --lines-terminated-by="\r" \
    cookbook mytbl.txt
```

The order in which you specify the options doesn't matter for *mysqlimport*.

You can use hex notation to specify arbitrary format characters for FIELDS and LINES clauses. This can be useful for loading datafiles that use binary format codes. Suppose that a datafile has lines with Ctrl-A between fields and Ctrl-B at the end of lines. The ASCII values for Ctrl-A and Ctrl-B are 1 and 2, so you represent them as 0x01 and 0x02:

```
FIELDS TERMINATED BY 0x01 LINES TERMINATED BY 0x02
```

mysqlimport also understands hex constants for format specifiers. You may find this capability helpful if you don't like remembering how to type escape sequences on the command line or when it's necessary to use quotes around them. Tab is 0x09, linefeed is 0x0a, and carriage return is 0x0d. Here's an example that indicates that the datafile contains tab-delimited lines terminated by CRLF pairs:

```
% mysqlimport --local --lines-terminated-by=0x0d0a \
    --fields-terminated-by=0x09 cookbook mytbl.txt
```

When you import datafiles, don't assume that LOAD DATA (or *mysqlimport*) knows more than it does. It's important always to keep in mind that LOAD DATA knows nothing at all about the format of your datafile. And always make sure that you do know what its format is. If the file has been transferred from one machine to another, its contents may have been changed in subtle ways of which you're not aware.

Some LOAD DATA frustrations occur because people expect MySQL to know things that it cannot possibly know. LOAD DATA makes certain assumptions about the structure of input files, represented as the default settings for the line and field terminators, and for the quote and escape character settings. If your input doesn't match those assumptions, you need to tell MySQL about it.

When in doubt, check the contents of your datafile using a hex dump program or other utility that displays a visible representation of whitespace characters like tab, carriage return, and linefeed. Under Unix, programs such as *od* or *hexdump* can display file contents in a variety of formats. If you don't have these or some comparable utility, the *transfer* directory of the `recipes` distribution contains hex dumpers written in Perl, Ruby, and Python (*hexdump.pl*, *hexdump.rb*, and *hexdump.py*), as well as programs that display printable representations of all characters of a file (*see.pl*, *see.rb*, and *see.py*). You may find them useful for examining files to see what they really contain. In some cases, you may be surprised to discover that a file's contents are different from what you think. This is, in fact, quite likely if the file has been transferred from one machine to another:

- An FTP transfer between machines running different operating systems typically translates line endings to those that are appropriate for the destination machine if the transfer is performed in text mode rather than in binary (image) mode. Suppose that you have tab-delimited linefeed-terminated records in a datafile that load into MySQL on a Unix system just fine using the default LOAD DATA settings. If you copy the file to a Windows machine with FTP using a text transfer mode, the linefeeds might be converted to carriage return/linefeed pairs. On that machine, the file will not load properly with the same LOAD DATA statement if its contents have been changed. Does MySQL have any way of knowing that? No. So it's up to you to tell it, by adding a LINES TERMINATED BY '\r\n' clause to the statement. Transfers between any two systems with dissimilar default line endings can cause these changes.

- Data files pasted into email messages often do not survive intact. Mail software may wrap (break) long lines or convert line-ending sequences. If you must transfer a datafile by email, it's best sent as an attachment.

10.4 Dealing with Quotes and Special Characters

Problem

Your datafile contains quoted values or escaped characters.

Solution

Tell LOAD DATA to be aware of quote and escape characters so that it doesn't load data values into the database uninterpreted.

Discussion

The `FIELDS` clause can specify other format options besides `TERMINATED BY`. By default, `LOAD DATA` assumes that values are unquoted, and it interprets the backslash (\\) as an escape character for special characters. To indicate the value-quoting character explicitly, use `ENCLOSED BY`; MySQL will strip that character from the ends of data values during input processing. To change the default escape character, use `ESCAPED BY`.

The three subclauses of the `FIELDS` clause (`ENCLOSED BY`, `ESCAPED BY`, and `TERMINATED BY`) may be present in any order if you specify more than one of them. For example, these `FIELDS` clauses are equivalent:

```
FIELDS TERMINATED BY ',' ENCLOSED BY '"'
FIELDS ENCLOSED BY '"' TERMINATED BY ','
```

The `TERMINATED BY` sequence can consist of multiple characters. If data values are separated within input lines by something like *@*, you indicate that like this:

```
FIELDS TERMINATED BY '*@*'
```

To disable escape processing entirely, specify an empty escape sequence:

```
FIELDS ESCAPED BY ''
```

When you specify `ENCLOSED BY` to indicate which quote character should be stripped from data values, it's possible to include the quote character literally within data values by doubling it or by preceding it with the escape character. For example, if the quote and escape characters are " and \\, the input value `"a""b\"c"` is interpreted as `a"b"c`.

For *mysqlimport*, the corresponding command options for specifying quote and escape values are `--fields-enclosed-by` and `--fields-escaped-by`. (When using *mysqlimport* options that include quotes or backslashes or other characters that are special to your command interpreter, remember that you may need to quote or escape the quote or escape characters.)

10.5 Importing CSV Files

Problem

You need to load a file that is in CSV format.

Solution

Add the appropriate format-specifier clauses to your `LOAD DATA` statement.

Discussion

Data files in CSV format contain values that are delimited by commas rather than tabs and that may be quoted with double-quote characters. For example, a CSV file *mytbl.txt* containing lines that end with carriage return/linefeed pairs can be loaded into `mytbl` using `LOAD DATA`:

```
mysql> LOAD DATA LOCAL INFILE 'mytbl.txt' INTO TABLE mytbl
    -> FIELDS TERMINATED BY ',' ENCLOSED BY '"'
    -> LINES TERMINATED BY '\r\n';
```

Or like this using *mysqlimport*:

```
% mysqlimport --local --lines-terminated-by="\r\n" \
    --fields-terminated-by="," --fields-enclosed-by="\"" \
    cookbook mytbl.txt
```

10.6 Reading Files from Different Operating Systems

Problem

Different operating systems use different line-ending sequences.

Solution

That's why `LOAD DATA` has a `LINES TERMINATED BY` clause. Use it to your advantage.

Discussion

The line-ending sequence used in a datafile typically is determined by the system from which the file originated. Unix files normally have lines terminated by linefeeds, which you can indicate in a `LOAD DATA` statement like this:

```
LINES TERMINATED BY '\n'
```

However, because \n happens to be the default line terminator for `LOAD DATA`, you don't need to specify a `LINES TERMINATED BY` clause in this case unless you want to indicate explicitly what the line-ending sequence is.

If your system doesn't use the Unix default (linefeed), you need to specify the line terminator explicitly. Files created under Mac OS X or Windows often have lines ending in carriage returns or carriage return/linefeed pairs, respectively. To handle these different kinds of line endings, use the appropriate `LINES TERMINATED BY` clause:

```
LINES TERMINATED BY '\r'
LINES TERMINATED BY '\r\n'
```

For example, to load a Windows file that contains tab-delimited fields and lines ending with CRLF pairs, use this `LOAD DATA` statement:

```
mysql> LOAD DATA LOCAL INFILE 'mytbl.txt' INTO TABLE mytbl
    -> LINES TERMINATED BY '\r\n';
```

The corresponding *mysqlimport* command is:

```
% mysqlimport --local --lines-terminated-by="\r\n" cookbook mytbl.txt
```

10.7 Handling Duplicate Key Values

Problem

Your input contains records that duplicate the values of unique keys in existing table rows.

Solution

Tell LOAD DATA to ignore the new records, or to replace the old ones.

Discussion

By default, an error occurs if you attempt to load a record that duplicates an existing row in the column or columns that form a PRIMARY KEY or UNIQUE index. To control this behavior, specify IGNORE or REPLACE after the filename to tell MySQL to either ignore duplicate rows or to replace old rows with the new ones.

Suppose that you periodically receive meteorological data about current weather conditions from various monitoring stations, and that you store measurements of various types from these stations in a table that looks like this:

```
CREATE TABLE weatherdata
(
  station INT UNSIGNED NOT NULL,
  type    ENUM('precip','temp','cloudiness','humidity','barometer') NOT NULL,
  value   FLOAT,
  PRIMARY KEY (station, type)
);
```

To make sure that you have only one row for each station for each type of measurement, the table includes a primary key on the combination of station ID and measurement type. The table is intended to hold only current conditions, so when new measurements for a given station are loaded into the table, they should kick out the station's previous measurements. To accomplish this, use the REPLACE keyword:

```
mysql> LOAD DATA LOCAL INFILE 'data.txt' REPLACE INTO TABLE weatherdata;
```

mysqlimport has --ignore and --replace options that have the same effect as the IGNORE and REPLACE keywords for LOAD DATA.

10.8 Obtaining Diagnostics About Bad Input Data

Problem

When you issue a LOAD DATA statement, you want to know whether any input values are bad and what's wrong with them.

Solution

Use the information line displayed by LOAD DATA to determine whether there are any problematic input values. If so, use SHOW WARNINGS to find where they are and what the problems are.

Discussion

When a LOAD DATA statement finishes, it returns a line of information that tells you how many errors or data conversion problems occurred. Suppose that you load a file into a table and see the following message when LOAD DATA finishes:

```
Records: 134  Deleted: 0  Skipped: 2  Warnings: 13
```

These values provide some general information about the import operation:

- Records indicates the number of records found in the file.
- Deleted and Skipped are related to treatment of input records that duplicate existing table rows on unique index values. Deleted indicates how many rows were deleted from the table and replaced by input records, and Skipped indicates how many input records were ignored in favor of existing rows.
- Warnings is something of a catchall that indicates the number of problems found while loading data values into columns. Either a value stores into a column properly, or it doesn't. In the latter case, the value ends up in MySQL as something different, and MySQL counts it as a warning. (Storing a string abc into a numeric column results in a stored value of 0, for example.)

What do these values tell you? The Records value normally should match the number of lines in the input file. If it is different from the file's line count, that's a sign that MySQL is interpreting the file as having a format that differs from the format it actually has. In this case, you're likely also to see a high Warnings value, which indicates that many values had to be converted because they didn't match the expected data type. (The solution to this problem often is to specify the proper FIELDS and LINES clauses.)

Assuming that your FIELDS and LINES format specifiers are correct, a nonzero Warnings count indicates the presence of bad input values. You can't tell from the numbers in the LOAD DATA information line which input records had problems or which columns were bad. To get that information, issue a SHOW WARNINGS statement.

Suppose that a table t has this structure:

```
CREATE TABLE t
(
  i INT,
  c CHAR(3),
  d DATE
);
```

And suppose that a datafile *data.txt* looks like this:

```
1              1              1
abc            abc            abc
2010-10-10     2010-10-10     2010-10-10
```

Loading the file into the table causes a number, a string, and a date to be loaded into each of the three columns. Doing so results in a number of data conversions and warnings:

```
mysql> LOAD DATA LOCAL INFILE 'data.txt' INTO TABLE t;
Query OK, 3 rows affected, 5 warnings (0.01 sec)
Records: 3  Deleted: 0  Skipped: 0  Warnings: 5
```

To see the warning messages, use SHOW WARNINGS immediately after the LOAD DATA statement:

```
mysql> SHOW WARNINGS;
+---------+------+------------------------------------------------+
| Level   | Code | Message                                        |
+---------+------+------------------------------------------------+
| Warning | 1265 | Data truncated for column 'd' at row 1         |
| Warning | 1264 | Out of range value for column 'i' at row 2     |
| Warning | 1265 | Data truncated for column 'd' at row 2         |
| Warning | 1265 | Data truncated for column 'i' at row 3         |
| Warning | 1265 | Data truncated for column 'c' at row 3         |
+---------+------+------------------------------------------------+
5 rows in set (0.00 sec)
```

The SHOW WARNINGS output helps you determine which values were converted and why. The resulting table looks like this:

```
mysql> SELECT * FROM t;
+------+------+------------+
| i    | c    | d          |
+------+------+------------+
|    1 | 1    | 0000-00-00 |
|    0 | abc  | 0000-00-00 |
| 2010 | 201  | 2010-10-10 |
+------+------+------------+
```

10.9 Skipping Datafile Lines

Problem

You want LOAD DATA to skip over the first line or lines of your datafile before starting to load records.

Solution

Tell LOAD DATA how many lines to ignore.

Discussion

To skip over the first *n* lines of a datafile, add an `IGNORE` *n* `LINES` clause to the `LOAD DATA` statement. For example, if a tab-delimited file begins with a line consisting of column headers, skip that line like this:

```
mysql> LOAD DATA LOCAL INFILE 'mytbl.txt' INTO TABLE mytbl IGNORE 1 LINES;
```

mysqlimport supports an `--ignore-lines=`*n* option that has the same effect.

`IGNORE` is often useful with files generated by external sources. For example, a program might export data in CSV format with an initial line of column labels. The following statement would be appropriate for skipping the labels in such a file that has carriage return line endings:

```
mysql> LOAD DATA LOCAL INFILE 'mytbl.txt' INTO TABLE mytbl
    -> FIELDS TERMINATED BY ',' ENCLOSED BY '"'
    -> LINES TERMINATED BY '\r'
    -> IGNORE 1 LINES;
```

10.10 Specifying Input Column Order

Problem

The columns in your datafile aren't in the same order as the columns in the table into which you're loading the file.

Solution

Tell `LOAD DATA` how to match the table and the file by indicating which table columns correspond to the datafile columns.

Discussion

`LOAD DATA` assumes that the columns in the datafile have the same order as the columns in the table. If that's not true, specify a list to indicate which table columns the datafile columns should be loaded into. Suppose that your table has columns a, b, and c, but successive columns in the datafile correspond to columns b, c, and a. You can load the file like this:

```
mysql> LOAD DATA LOCAL INFILE 'mytbl.txt' INTO TABLE mytbl (b, c, a);
```

The equivalent *mysqlimport* statement uses the `--columns` option to specify the column list:

```
% mysqlimport --local --columns=b,c,a cookbook mytbl.txt
```

10.11 Preprocessing Input Values Before Inserting Them

Problem

You have values in a datafile that are not in a format that is suitable for loading into a table. For example, values are in the wrong units, or two input fields must be combined and inserted into a single column.

Solution

LOAD DATA has the capability of performing limited preprocessing of input values before inserting them. This enables you to map input data onto more appropriate values before loading them into your table.

Discussion

Recipe 10.10 shows how you can specify a column list for LOAD DATA to indicate how input fields correspond to table columns. The column list also can name user-defined variables, such that for each input record, the input fields are assigned to the variables. You can then perform calculations with those variables before inserting the result into the table. These calculations are specified in a SET clause that names one or more *col_name* = *expr* assignments, separated by commas.

Suppose that you have a datafile that has the following columns, with the first line providing column labels:

```
Date        Time      Name        Weight   State
2006-09-01  12:00:00  Bill Wills  200      Nevada
2006-09-02  09:00:00  Jeff Deft   150      Oklahoma
2006-09-04  03:00:00  Bob Hobbs   225      Utah
2006-09-07  08:00:00  Hank Banks  175      Texas
```

Suppose also that the file must be loaded into a table that has these columns:

```
CREATE TABLE t
(
  dt         DATETIME,
  last_name  CHAR(10),
  first_name CHAR(10),
  weight_kg  FLOAT,
  st_abbrev  CHAR(2)
);
```

There are several mismatches between the datafile fields and the table columns that must be addressed to be able to import the file:

- The file contains separate date and time columns that must be combined into date-and-time values for insertion into the DATETIME column.

- The file contains a name field, which must be split into separate first and last name values for insertion into the first_name and last_name columns.

- The file contains a weight in pounds, which must be converted to kilograms for insertion into the weight_kg column. (The conversion factor is that 1 lb. equals .454 kg.)

- The file contains state names, but the table contains two-letter abbreviations. The name can be mapped to the abbreviation by performing a lookup in the states table.

To handle these conversions, assign each input column to a user-defined variable, and write a SET clause to perform the calculations. (Remember to skip the first line that contains the column labels.)

```
mysql> LOAD DATA LOCAL INFILE 'data.txt' INTO TABLE t
    -> IGNORE 1 LINES
    -> (@date,@time,@name,@weight_lb,@state)
    -> SET dt = CONCAT(@date,' ',@time),
    ->     first_name = SUBSTRING_INDEX(@name,' ',1),
    ->     last_name = SUBSTRING_INDEX(@name,' ',-1),
    ->     weight_kg = @weight_lb * .454,
    ->     st_abbrev = (SELECT abbrev FROM states WHERE name = @state);
```

As a result of this import operation, the table contains these rows:

```
mysql> SELECT * FROM t;
+---------------------+-----------+------------+-----------+-----------+
| dt                  | last_name | first_name | weight_kg | st_abbrev |
+---------------------+-----------+------------+-----------+-----------+
| 2006-09-01 12:00:00 | Wills     | Bill       |      90.8 | NV        |
| 2006-09-02 09:00:00 | Deft      | Jeff       |      68.1 | OK        |
| 2006-09-04 03:00:00 | Hobbs     | Bob        |    102.15 | UT        |
| 2006-09-07 08:00:00 | Banks     | Hank       |     79.45 | TX        |
+---------------------+-----------+------------+-----------+-----------+
```

LOAD DATA can perform data value reformatting, as shown in this section. Other examples showing uses for this capability occur later in the chapter. For example, Recipe 10.33 uses it to perform rewriting of non-ISO dates to ISO format during data import. However, although LOAD DATA can map input values to other values, it cannot outright reject an input record that is found to contain unsuitable values. To do that, you can either preprocess the input file to remove these records or issue a DELETE statement after loading the file.

10.12 Ignoring Datafile Columns

Problem

Your datafile contains columns that should be ignored rather than loaded into the table.

Solution

That's not a problem if the columns are at the ends of the input lines. Otherwise, you can use a column list with LOAD DATA that assigns the columns to be ignored to a dummy user-defined variable.

Discussion

Extra columns that occur at the end of input lines are easy to handle. If a line contains more columns than are in the table, LOAD DATA just ignores them (although it might produce a nonzero warning count).

Skipping columns in the middle of lines is a bit more involved. Suppose that you want to load information from a Unix password file /etc/passwd, which contains lines in the following format:

```
account:password:UID:GID:GECOS:directory:shell
```

Suppose also that you don't want to bother loading the password column. A table to hold the information in the other columns looks like this:

```
CREATE TABLE passwd
(
  account   CHAR(8),  # login name
  uid       INT,      # user ID
  gid       INT,      # group ID
  gecos     CHAR(60), # name, phone, office, etc.
  directory CHAR(60), # home directory
  shell     CHAR(60)  # command interpreter
);
```

To load the file, we need to specify that the column delimiter is a colon, which is easily handled with a FIELDS clause:

```
FIELDS TERMINATED BY ':'
```

However, we must also tell LOAD DATA to skip the second field that contains the password. To do this, add a column list in the statement. The list should include the name of each column to be loaded into the table, and a dummy user-defined variable for any column to be ignored:

```
mysql> LOAD DATA LOCAL INFILE '/etc/passwd' INTO TABLE passwd
    -> FIELDS TERMINATED BY ':'
    -> (account,@dummy,uid,gid,gecos,directory,shell);
```

The corresponding *mysqlimport* command should include a --columns option:

```
% mysqlimport --local \
    --columns="account,@dummy,uid,gid,gecos,directory,shell" \
    --fields-terminated-by=":" cookbook /etc/passwd
```

See Also

Another approach to ignoring columns is to preprocess the input file to remove columns. Recipe 10.19 discusses a utility that can pull out and display data-file columns in any order.

10.13 Exporting Query Results from MySQL

Problem

You want to export the result of a query from MySQL into a file or another program.

Solution

Use the `SELECT ... INTO OUTFILE` statement, or redirect the output of the *mysql* program.

Discussion

MySQL provides a `SELECT ... INTO OUTFILE` statement that exports a query result directly into a file on the server host. If you want to capture the result on the client host instead, another way to export a query is to redirect the output of the *mysql* program. These methods have different strengths and weaknesses, so you should get to know them both and apply whichever one best suits a given situation.

Exporting with the SELECT ... INTO OUTFILE statement

The syntax for this statement combines a regular `SELECT` with `INTO OUTFILE` *filename*. The default output format is the same as for `LOAD DATA`, so the following statement exports the `passwd` table into */tmp/passwd.txt* as a tab-delimited, linefeed-terminated file:

```
mysql> SELECT * FROM passwd INTO OUTFILE '/tmp/passwd.txt';
```

You can change the output format using options similar to those used with `LOAD DATA` that indicate how to quote and delimit columns and records. For example, to export the `passwd` table in CSV format with CRLF-terminated lines, use this statement:

```
mysql> SELECT * FROM passwd INTO OUTFILE '/tmp/passwd.txt'
    -> FIELDS TERMINATED BY ',' ENCLOSED BY '"'
    -> LINES TERMINATED BY '\r\n';
```

`SELECT ... INTO OUTFILE` has the following properties:

- The output file is created directly by the MySQL server, so the filename should indicate where you want the file to be written on the server host. The location for the file is determined using the same rules as for `LOAD DATA` without `LOCAL`, as described in Recipe 10.2. There is no `LOCAL` version of the statement analogous to the `LOCAL` version of `LOAD DATA`.

- You must have the MySQL `FILE` privilege to execute the `SELECT ... INTO` statement.
- The output file must not already exist. (This prevents MySQL from clobbering files that may be important.)
- You should have a login account on the server host or some way to access files on that host. `SELECT ... INTO OUTFILE` will be of no value to you if you cannot retrieve the output file.
- Under Unix, the file is created world readable and is owned by the account used for running the MySQL server. This means that although you'll be able to read the file, you may not be able to delete it.

Using the mysql client to export data

Because `SELECT ... INTO OUTFILE` writes the datafile on the server host, you cannot use it unless your MySQL account has the `FILE` privilege. To export data into a local file, you must use some other strategy. If all you require is tab-delimited output, you can do a "poor-man's export" by executing a `SELECT` statement with the *mysql* program and redirecting the output to a file. That way you can write query results into a file on your local host without the `FILE` privilege. Here's an example that exports the login name and command interpreter columns from the `passwd` table created earlier in this chapter:

```
% mysql -e "SELECT account, shell FROM passwd" --skip-column-names \
    cookbook > shells.txt
```

The `-e` option specifies the statement to execute, and `--skip-column-names` tells MySQL not to write the row of column names that normally precedes statement output (Recipes 1.14 and 1.21).

Note that MySQL writes `NULL` values as the string "NULL". Some sort of postprocessing may be necessary to convert them, depending on what you want to do with the output file.

It's possible to produce output in formats other than tab-delimited by sending the query result into a post-processing filter that converts tabs to something else. For example, to use hash marks as delimiters, convert all tabs to # characters (*TAB* indicates where you type a tab character in the command):

```
% mysql --skip-column-names -e "your statement here" db_name \
    | sed -e "s/TAB/#/g" > output_file
```

You can also use *tr* for this purpose, although the syntax may vary for different implementations of this utility. For Mac OS X or Linux, the command looks like this:

```
% mysql --skip-column-names -e "your statement here" db_name \
    | tr "\t" "#" > output_file
```

The *mysql* commands just shown use `--skip-column-names` to suppress column labels from appearing in the output. Under some circumstances, it may be useful to include the labels. (For example, they might be useful when importing the file later.) If so, omit the `--skip-column-names` option from the command. In this respect, exporting query results with *mysql* is more flexible than `SELECT ... INTO OUTFILE` because the latter cannot produce output that includes column labels.

See Also

Another way to export query results to a file on the client host is to use the *mysql_to_text.pl* utility described in Recipe 10.17. That program has options that enable you to specify the output format explicitly. To export a query result as an Excel spreadsheet, see Recipe 10.38.

10.14 Exporting Tables as Text Files

Problem

You want to export an entire table to a file.

Solution

Use the *mysqldump* program with the `--tab` option.

Discussion

The *mysqldump* program is used to copy or back up tables and databases. It can write table output either as a text datafile or as a set of `INSERT` statements that recreate the rows in the table. The former capability is described here, the latter in Recipes 10.15 and 10.16.

To dump a table as a datafile, you must specify a `--tab` option that indicates the directory on the MySQL server host to which you want the server to write the file. (The directory must already exist; the server won't create it.) For example, to dump the **states** table from the **cookbook** database to a file in the */tmp* directory, use a command like this:

```
% mysqldump --no-create-info --tab=/tmp cookbook states
```

mysqldump creates a datafile using the table name plus a *.txt* suffix, so this command writes a file named */tmp/states.txt*. This form of *mysqldump* is in some respects the command-line equivalent of `SELECT ... INTO OUTFILE`. For example, it writes out a table as a datafile on the server host, and you must have the `FILE` privilege to use it. See Recipe 10.13 for a list of general properties of `SELECT ... INTO OUTFILE`.

If you omit the `--no-create-info` option, *mysqldump* also creates a file */tmp/states.sql* on your local host that contains the `CREATE TABLE` statement for the table. (The latter file will be owned by you, unlike the datafile, which is owned by the server.)

You can name multiple tables after the database name, in which case *mysqldump* writes output files for each of them. If you don't name any tables, *mysqldump* writes output for every table in the database.

mysqldump creates datafiles in tab-delimited, linefeed-terminated format by default. To control the output format, use the `--fields-enclosed-by`, `--fields-terminated-by`, and `--lines-terminated-by` options (that is, the same options that *mysqlimport* understands as format specifiers). For example, to write the `states` table in CSV format with CRLF line endings, use this command:

```
% mysqldump --no-create-info --tab=/tmp \
    --fields-enclosed-by="\"" --fields-terminated-by="," \
    --lines-terminated-by="\r\n" cookbook states
```

A datafile exported this way can be imported using `LOAD DATA` or *mysqlimport*. Be sure to use matching format specifiers when importing if you didn't dump the table using the default format.

10.15 Exporting Table Contents or Definitions in SQL Format

Problem

You want to export tables or databases as SQL statements to make them easier to import later.

Solution

Use the *mysqldump* program without the `--tab` option.

Discussion

As discussed in Recipe 10.14, *mysqldump* causes the MySQL server to write tables as text datafiles on the server host when it's invoked with the `--tab` option. If you omit the `--tab`, the server formats the table rows as the `INSERT` statements and returns them to *mysqldump*, which writes the output on the client host. The output also can include the `CREATE TABLE` statement for each table. This provides a convenient form of output that you can capture in a file and use later to recreate a table or tables. It's common to use such dump files as backups or for copying tables to another MySQL server. This section discusses how to save dump output in a file; Recipe 10.16 shows how to send it directly to another server over the network.

To export a table in SQL format to a file, use a command like this:

```
% mysqldump cookbook states > states.txt
```

That creates an output file *states.txt* that contains both the `CREATE TABLE` statement and a set of `INSERT` statements:

```
-- MySQL dump 10.10
--
-- Host: localhost    Database: cookbook
-- -------------------------------------------------------
-- Server version        5.0.27-log


--
-- Table structure for table `states`
--

CREATE TABLE `states` (
  `name` varchar(30) NOT NULL,
  `abbrev` char(2) NOT NULL,
  `statehood` date default NULL,
  `pop` bigint(20) default NULL,
  PRIMARY KEY  (`abbrev`)
);


--
-- Dumping data for table `states`
--

INSERT INTO `states` VALUES ('Alabama','AL','1819-12-14',4530182);
INSERT INTO `states` VALUES ('Alaska','AK','1959-01-03',655435);
INSERT INTO `states` VALUES ('Arizona','AZ','1912-02-14',5743834);
INSERT INTO `states` VALUES ('Arkansas','AR','1836-06-15',2752629);
INSERT INTO `states` VALUES ('California','CA','1850-09-09',35893799);
INSERT INTO `states` VALUES ('Colorado','CO','1876-08-01',4601403);
...
```

The preceding *mysqldump* output actually was produced by using the
`--skip-extended-insert` option, which causes each row to be written as
a separate `INSERT` statement. If you omit `--skip-extended-insert` (which
is the usual case), *mysqldump* writes multiple-row `INSERT` statements.
Those are more difficult for you and me to read, but more efficient for
the MySQL server to process.

To dump multiple tables, name them all following the database name argument. To
dump an entire database, don't name any tables after the database. This statement
dumps all tables in the cookbook database:

```
% mysqldump cookbook > cookbook.txt
```

If you want to dump all tables in all databases, invoke *mysqldump* like this:

```
% mysqldump --all-databases > dump.txt
```

In that case, the output file also includes CREATE DATABASE and USE *db_name* statements
at appropriate places so that when you read in the file later, each table is created in the
proper database.

Other options are available to control the output format:

`--no-create-info`

Suppress the `CREATE TABLE` statements. Use this option when you want to dump table contents only.

`--no-data`

Suppress the `INSERT` statements. Use this option when you want to dump table definitions only.

`--add-drop-table`

Precede each `CREATE TABLE` statement with a `DROP TABLE` statement. This is useful for generating a file that you can use later to recreate tables from scratch.

`--no-create-db`

Suppress the `CREATE DATABASE` statements that the `--all-databases` option normally produces.

Suppose now that you've used *mysqldump* to create an SQL-format dump file. How do you import the file back into MySQL? One common mistake at this point is to use *mysqlimport*. After all, it's logical to assume that if *mysqldump* exports tables, *mysqlimport* must import them. Right? Sorry, no. That might be logical, but it's not always correct. It's true that if you use the `--tab` option with *mysqldump*, you can import the resulting datafiles with *mysqlimport*. But if you dump an SQL-format file, *mysqlimport* won't process it properly. Use the *mysql* program instead. The way you do this depends on what's in the dump file. If you dumped multiple databases using `--all-databases`, the file will contain the appropriate USE *db_name* statements to select the databases to which each table belongs, and you need no database argument on the command line:

```
% mysql < dump.txt
```

If you dumped tables from a single database, you'll need to tell *mysql* which database to import them into:

```
% mysql db_name < cookbook.txt
```

Note that with this second import command, it's possible to load the tables into a database different from the one from which they came originally. For example, you can use this fact to create copies of a table or tables in a test database to help debug data manipulation statements, without worrying about affecting the original tables.

10.16 Copying Tables or Databases to Another Server

Problem

You want to copy tables or databases from one MySQL server to another.

Solution

Use *mysqldump* and *mysql* together, connected by a pipe.

Discussion

SQL-format output from *mysqldump* can be used to copy tables or databases from one server to another. Suppose that you want to copy the `states` table from the `cookbook` database on the local host to the `cb` database on the host *other-host.example.com*. One way to do this is to dump the output into a file (as described in Recipe 10.15):

```
% mysqldump cookbook states > states.txt
```

Now copy *states.txt* to *other-host.example.com*, and run the following command there to import the table into that MySQL server's `cb` database:

```
% mysql cb < states.txt
```

To accomplish this without using an intermediary file, send the output of *mysqldump* directly over the network to the remote MySQL server. If you can connect to both servers from your local host, use this command:

```
% mysqldump cookbook states | mysql -h other-host.example.com cb
```

The *mysqldump* half of the command connects to the local server and writes the dump output to the pipe. The *mysql* half of the command connects to the remote MySQL server on *other-host.example.com*. It reads the pipe for input and sends each statement to the *other-host.example.com* server.

If you cannot connect directly to the remote server using *mysql* from your local host, send the dump output into a pipe that uses *ssh* to invoke *mysql* remotely on *other-host.example.com*:

```
% mysqldump cookbook states | ssh other-host.example.com mysql cb
```

ssh connects to *other-host.example.com* and launches *mysql* there. It then reads the *mysqldump* output from the pipe and passes it to the remote *mysql* process. *ssh* can be useful when you want to send a dump over the network to a machine that has the MySQL port blocked by a firewall but that enables connections on the SSH port.

To copy multiple tables over the network, name them all following the database argument of the *mysqldump* command. To copy an entire database, don't specify any table names after the database name. *mysqldump* will dump all the tables contained in the database.

If you're thinking about invoking *mysqldump* with the `--all-databases` option to send all your databases to another server, consider that the output will include the tables in the `mysql` database that contains the grant tables. If the remote server has a different user population, you probably don't want to replace that server's grant tables!

10.17 Writing Your Own Export Programs

Problem

MySQL's built-in export capabilities don't suffice.

Solution

Write your own utilities.

Discussion

When existing export software doesn't do what you want, you can write your own programs. This section describes a Perl script, *mysql_to_text.pl*, that executes an arbitrary statement and exports it in the format you specify. It writes output to the client host and can include a row of column labels (two things that `SELECT ... INTO OUTFILE` cannot do). It produces multiple output formats more easily than by using *mysql* with a postprocessor, and it writes to the client host, unlike *mysqldump*, which can write only SQL-format output to the client. You can find *mysql_to_text.pl* in the *transfer* directory of the `recipes` distribution.

mysql_to_text.pl is based on the Text::CSV_XS module, which you'll need to obtain if it's not installed on your system. Once that module has been installed, you can read its documentation like so:

```
% perldoc Text::CSV_XS
```

This module is convenient because it makes conversion of query output to CSV format relatively trivial. All you have to do is provide an array of column values, and the module packages them up into a properly formatted output line. This makes it relatively trivial to convert query output to CSV format. But the real benefit of using the Text::CSV_XS module is that it's configurable; you can tell it what kind of delimiter and quote characters to use. This means that although the module produces CSV format by default, you can configure it to write a variety of output formats. For example, if you set the delimiter to tab and the quote character to `undef`, Text::CSV_XS generates tab-delimited output. We'll take advantage of that flexibility in this section for writing *mysql_to_text.pl*, and later in Recipe 10.18 to write a file-processing utility that converts files from one format to another.

mysql_to_text.pl accepts several command-line options. Some of them are used for specifying MySQL connection parameters (such as `--user`, `--password`, and `--host`). You're already familiar with these, because they're used by the standard MySQL clients like *mysql*. The script also can obtain connection parameters from an option file, if you specify a `[client]` group in the file. *mysql_to_text.pl* also accepts the following options:

--execute=*query*, -e *query*
> Execute *query* and export its output.

`--table=`*tbl_name*, `-t` *tbl_name*

Export the contents of the named table. This is equivalent to using `--execute` to specify a *query* value of `SELECT * FROM` *tbl_name*.

`--labels`

Include an initial row of column labels in the output

`--delim=`*str*

Set the column delimiter to *str*. The option value can consist of one or more characters. The default is to use tabs.

`--quote=`*c*

Set the column value quote character to *c*. The default is to not quote anything.

`--eol=`*str*

Set the end-of-line sequence to *str*. The option value can consist of one or more characters. The default is to use linefeeds.

The defaults for the `--delim`, `--quote`, and `--eol` options correspond to those used by `LOAD DATA` and `SELECT ... INTO OUTFILE`.

The final argument on the command line should be the database name, unless it's implicit in the statement. For example, these two commands are equivalent; each exports the `passwd` table from the `cookbook` database in colon-delimited format:

```
% mysql_to_text.pl --delim=":" --table=passwd cookbook
% mysql_to_text.pl --delim=":" --table=cookbook.passwd
```

To generate CSV output with CRLF line terminators instead, use a command like this:

```
% mysql_to_text.pl --delim="," --quote="\"" --eol="\r\n" \
    --table=cookbook.passwd
```

That's a general description of how you use *mysql_to_text.pl*. Now let's discuss how it works. The initial part of the *mysql_to_text.pl* script declares a few variables, and then processes the command-line arguments, using option-processing techniques developed in Recipe 2.8. As it happens, most of the code in the script is devoted to processing the command-line arguments and getting set up to run the query. Very little of it involves interaction with MySQL.

```perl
#!/usr/bin/perl
# mysql_to_text.pl - export MySQL query output in user-specified text format

# Usage: mysql_to_text.pl [ options ] [db_name] > text_file

use strict;
use warnings;
use DBI;
use Text::CSV_XS;
use Getopt::Long;
$Getopt::Long::ignorecase = 0; # options are case sensitive
$Getopt::Long::bundling = 1;   # allow short options to be bundled

# ... construct usage message variable $usage (not shown) ...
```

```
# Variables for command line options - all undefined initially
# except for options that control output structure, which is set
# to be tab-delimited, linefeed-terminated.
my $help;
my ($host_name, $password, $port_num, $socket_name, $user_name, $db_name);
my ($stmt, $tbl_name);
my $labels;
my $delim = "\t";
my $quote;
my $eol = "\n";

GetOptions (
  # =i means an integer argument is required after the option
  # =s means a string value is required after the option
  "help"          => \$help,         # print help message
  "host|h=s"      => \$host_name,    # server host
  "password|p=s"  => \$password,     # password
  "port|P=i"      => \$port_num,     # port number
  "socket|S=s"    => \$socket_name,  # socket name
  "user|u=s"      => \$user_name,    # username
  "execute|e=s"   => \$stmt,         # statement to execute
  "table|t=s"     => \$tbl_name,     # table to export
  "labels|l"      => \$labels,       # generate row of column labels
  "delim=s"       => \$delim,        # column delimiter
  "quote=s"       => \$quote,        # column quoting character
  "eol=s"         => \$eol           # end-of-line (record) delimiter
) or die "$usage\n";

die  "$usage\n" if defined $help;

$db_name = shift (@ARGV) if @ARGV;

# One of --execute or --table must be specified, but not both
die "You must specify a query or a table name\n\n$usage\n"
  if !defined ($stmt) && !defined ($tbl_name);
die "You cannot specify both a query and a table name\n\n$usage\n"
  if defined ($stmt) && defined ($tbl_name);

# If table name was given, use it to create query that selects entire table
$stmt = "SELECT * FROM $tbl_name" if defined ($tbl_name);

# interpret special chars in the file structure options
$quote = interpret_option ($quote);
$delim = interpret_option ($delim);
$eol = interpret_option ($eol);
```

The interpret_option( ) function (not shown) processes escape and hex sequences for
the --delim, --quote, and --eol options. It interprets \n, \r, \t, and \0 as linefeed,
carriage return, tab, and the ASCII NUL character. It also interprets hex values, which
can be given in 0xnn form (for example, 0x0d indicates a carriage return).

After processing the command-line options, *mysql_to_text.pl* constructs the data
source name (DSN) and connects to the server:

```
my $dsn = "DBI:mysql:";
$dsn .= ";database=$db_name" if $db_name;
$dsn .= ";host=$host_name" if $host_name;
$dsn .= ";port=$port_num" if $port_num;
$dsn .= ";mysql_socket=$socket_name" if $socket_name;
# read [client] group parameters from standard option files
$dsn .= ";mysql_read_default_group=client";

my %conn_attrs = (PrintError => 0, RaiseError => 1, AutoCommit => 1);
my $dbh = DBI->connect ($dsn, $user_name, $password, \%conn_attrs);
```

The database name comes from the command line. Connection parameters can come from the command line or an option file. (Use of MySQL option files is covered in Recipe 2.8.)

After establishing a connection to MySQL, the script is ready to execute the query and produce some output. This is where the Text::CSV_XS module comes into play. First, create a CSV object by calling new( ), which takes an optional hash of options that control how the object handles data lines. The script prepares and executes the query, prints a row of column labels (if the user specified the --labels option), and writes the rows of the result set:

```
my $csv = Text::CSV_XS->new ({
              sep_char => $delim,
              quote_char => $quote,
              escape_char => $quote,
              eol => $eol,
              binary => 1
           });

my $sth = $dbh->prepare ($stmt);
$sth->execute ();
if ($labels)                  # write row of column labels
{
  $csv->combine (@{$sth->{NAME}}) or die "cannot process column labels\n";
  print $csv->string ();
}

my $count = 0;
while (my @val = $sth->fetchrow_array ())
{
  ++$count;
  $csv->combine (@val) or die "cannot process column values, row $count\n";
  print $csv->string ();
}
```

The sep_char and quote_char options in the name( ) call set the column delimiter and quoting character. The escape_char option is set to the same value as quote_char so that instances of the quote character occurring within data values are doubled in the output. The eol option indicates the line-termination sequence. Normally, Text::CSV_XS leaves it to you to print the terminator for output lines. By passing a non-undef eol value to new( ), the module adds that value to every output line automatically. The `binary` option is useful for processing data values that contain binary characters.

The column labels are available in `$sth->{NAME}` after invoking `execute( )`. Each line of output is produced using `combine( )` and `string( )`. The `combine( )` method takes an array of values and converts them to a properly formatted string. `string( )` returns the string so we can print it.

10.18 Converting Datafiles from One Format to Another

Problem

You want to convert a file to a different format to make it easier to work with, or so that another program can understand it.

Solution

Use the *cvt_file.pl* converter script described here.

Discussion

The *mysql_to_text.pl* script discussed in Recipe 10.17 uses MySQL as a data source and produces output in the format you specify via the `--delim`, `--quote`, and `--eol` options. This section describes *cvt_file.pl*, a utility that provides similar formatting options, but for both input and output. It reads data from a file rather than from MySQL, and converts it from one format to another. For example, to read a tab-delimited file *data.txt*, convert it to colon-delimited format, and write the result to *tmp.txt*, invoke *cvt_file.pl* like this:

```
% cvt_file.pl --idelim="\t" --odelim=":" data.txt > tmp.txt
```

The *cvt_file.pl* script has separate options for input and output. Thus, whereas *mysql_to_text.pl* has just a `--delim` option for specifying the column delimiter, *cvt_file.pl* has separate `--idelim` and `--odelim` options to set the input and output line column delimiters. But as a shortcut, `--delim` is also supported; it sets the delimiter for both input and output. The full set of options that *cvt_file.pl* understands is as follows:

`--idelim=str, --odelim=str, --delim=str`
  Set the column delimiter for input, output, or both. The option value can consist of one or more characters.

`--iquote=c, --oquote=c, --quote=c`
  Set the column quote character for input, output, or both.

`--ieol=str, --oeol=str, --eol=str`
  Set the end-of-line sequence for input, output, or both. The option value can consist of one or more characters.

--iformat=*format*, --oformat=*format*, --format=*format*,
> Specify an input format, an output format, or both. This option is shorthand for setting the quote and delimiter values. For example, `--iformat=csv` sets the input quote and delimiter characters to double quote and comma. `--iformat=tab` sets them to "no quotes" and tab.

--ilabels, --olabels, --labels
> Expect an initial line of column labels for input, write an initial line of labels for output, or both. If you request labels for the output but do not read labels from the input, *cvt_file.pl* uses column labels of c1, c2, and so forth.

cvt_file.pl assumes the same default file format as `LOAD DATA` and `SELECT ... INTO OUTFILE`, that is, tab-delimited lines terminated by linefeeds.

cvt_file.pl can be found in the *transfer* directory of the `recipes` distribution. If you expect to use it regularly, you should install it in some directory that's listed in your search path so that you can invoke it from anywhere. Much of the source for the script is similar to *mysql_to_text.pl*, so rather than showing the code and discussing how it works, I'll just give some examples that illustrate how to use it:

- Read a file in CSV format with CRLF line termination, and write tab-delimited output with linefeed termination:

  ```
  % cvt_file.pl --iformat=csv --ieol="\r\n" --oformat=tab --oeol="\n" \
      data.txt > tmp.txt
  ```

- Read and write CSV format, converting CRLF line terminators to carriage returns:

  ```
  % cvt_file.pl --format=csv --ieol="\r\n" --oeol="\r" data.txt > % tmp.txt
  ```

- Produce a tab-delimited file from the colon-delimited */etc/passwd* file:

  ```
  % cvt_file.pl --idelim=":" /etc/passwd > tmp.txt
  ```

- Convert tab-delimited query output from mysql into CSV format:

  ```
  % mysql -e "SELECT * FROM profile" cookbook \
      | cvt_file.pl --oformat=csv > profile.csv
  ```

10.19 Extracting and Rearranging Datafile Columns

Problem

You want to pull out columns from a datafile or rearrange them into a different order.

Solution

Use a utility that can produce columns from a file on demand.

Discussion

cvt_file.pl serves as a tool that converts entire files from one format to another. Another common datafile operation is to manipulate its columns. This is necessary, for example, when importing a file into a program that doesn't understand how to extract or rearrange input columns for itself. To work around this problem, you can rearrange the datafile instead.

Recall that this chapter began with a description of a scenario involving a 12-column CSV file *somedata.csv* from which only columns 2, 11, 5, and 9 were needed. You can convert the file to tab-delimited format like this:

```
% cvt_file.pl --iformat=csv somedata.csv > somedata.txt
```

But then what? If you just want to knock out a short script to extract those specific four columns, that's fairly easy: write a loop that reads input lines and writes only the columns you want in the proper order. But that would be a special-purpose script, useful only within a highly limited context. With just a little more effort, it's possible to write a more general utility *yank_col.pl* that enables you to extract any set of columns. With such a tool, you'd specify the column list on the command line like this:

```
% yank_col.pl --columns=2,11,5,9 somedata.txt > tmp.txt
```

Because the script doesn't use a hardcoded column list, it can be used to pull out an arbitrary set of columns in any order. Columns can be specified as a comma-separated list of column numbers or column ranges. (For example, `--columns=1,10,4-7` means columns 1, 10, 4, 5, 6, and 7.) *yank_col.pl* looks like this:

```perl
#!/usr/bin/perl
# yank_col.pl - extract columns from input

# Example: yank_col.pl --columns=2,11,5,9 filename

# Assumes tab-delimited, linefeed-terminated input lines.

use strict;
use warnings;
use Getopt::Long;
$Getopt::Long::ignorecase = 0; # options are case sensitive

my $prog = "yank_col.pl";
my $usage = <<EOF;
Usage: $prog [options] [data_file]

Options:
--help
    Print this message
--columns=column-list
    Specify columns to extract, as a comma-separated list of column positions
EOF

my $help;
my $columns;
```

```
GetOptions (
  "help"      => \$help,       # print help message
  "columns=s" => \$columns     # specify column list
) or die "$usage\n";

die  "$usage\n" if defined $help;

my @col_list = split (/,/, $columns) if defined ($columns);
@col_list or die "$usage\n";        # nonempty column list is required

# make sure column specifiers are positive integers, and convert from
# 1-based to 0-based values

my @tmp;
for (my $i = 0; $i < @col_list; $i++)
{
  if ($col_list[$i] =~ /^\d+$/)         # single column number
  {
    die "Column specifier $col_list[$i] is not a positive integer\n"
        unless $col_list[$i] > 0;
    push (@tmp, $col_list[$i] - 1);
  }
  elsif ($col_list[$i] =~ /^(\d+)-(\d+)$/)  # column range m-n
  {
    my ($begin, $end) = ($1, $2);
    die "$col_list[$i] is not a valid column specifier\n"
        unless $begin > 0 && $end > 0 && $begin <= $end;
    while ($begin <= $end)
    {
      push (@tmp, $begin - 1);
      ++$begin;
    }
  }
  else
  {
    die "$col_list[$i] is not a valid column specifier\n";
  }
}
@col_list = @tmp;

while (<>)               # read input
{
  chomp;
  my @val = split (/\t/, $_, 10000);  # split, preserving all fields
  # extract desired columns, mapping undef to empty string (can
  # occur if an index exceeds number of columns present in line)
  @val = map { defined ($_) ? $_ : "" } @val[@col_list];
  print join ("\t", @val) . "\n";
}
```

The input processing loop converts each line to an array of values, and then pulls out from the array the values corresponding to the requested columns. To avoid looping through the array, it uses Perl's notation that allows a list of subscripts to be specified all at once to request multiple array elements. For example, if `@col_list` contains the values 2, 6, and 3, these two expressions are equivalent:

```
($val[2] , $val[6], $val[3])
@val[@col_list]
```

What if you want to extract columns from a file that's not in tab-delimited format, or produce output in another format? In that case, combine *yank_col.pl* with the *cvt_file.pl* script discussed in Recipe 10.18. Suppose that you want to pull out all but the password column from the colon-delimited */etc/passwd* file and write the result in CSV format. Use *cvt_file.pl* both to preprocess */etc/passwd* into tab-delimited format for *yank_col.pl* and to postprocess the extracted columns into CSV format:

```
% cvt_file.pl --idelim=":" /etc/passwd \
    | yank_col.pl --columns=1,3-7 \
    | cvt_file.pl --oformat=csv > passwd.csv
```

If you don't want to type all of that as one long command, use temporary files for the intermediate steps:

```
% cvt_file.pl --idelim=":" /etc/passwd > tmp1.txt
% yank_col.pl --columns=1,3-7 tmp1.txt > tmp2.txt
% cvt_file.pl --oformat=csv tmp2.txt > passwd.csv
% rm tmp1.txt tmp2.txt
```

Forcing split( ) to Return Every Field

The Perl `split( )` function is extremely useful, but normally it doesn't return trailing empty fields. This means that if you write only as many fields as `split( )` returns, output lines may not have the same number of fields as input lines. To avoid this problem, pass a third argument to indicate the maximum number of fields to return. This forces `split( )` to return as many fields as are actually present on the line or the number requested, whichever is smaller. If the value of the third argument is large enough, the practical effect is to cause all fields to be returned, empty or not. Scripts shown in this chapter use a field count value of 10,000:

```
# split line at tabs, preserving all fields
my @val = split (/\t/, $_, 10000);
```

In the (unlikely?) event that an input line has more fields than that, it will be truncated. If you think that will be a problem, you can bump up the number even higher.

10.20 Using the SQL Mode to Control Bad Input Data Handling

Problem

By default, MySQL is forgiving about accepting data values that are invalid, out of range, or otherwise unsuitable for the data types of the columns into which you insert

---

them. (The server accepts the values and attempts to coerce them to the closest legal value.) But you want the server to be more restrictive and not accept bad data.

Solution

Set the SQL mode. Several mode values are available to control how strict the server is. Some of these modes apply generally to all input values. Others apply to specific data types such as dates.

Discussion

Normally, MySQL accepts data and coerces it to the data types of your table columns if the input doesn't match. Consider the following table, which has integer, string, and date columns:

```
mysql> CREATE TABLE t (i INT, c CHAR(6), d DATE);
```

Inserting a row with unsuitable data values into the table causes warnings (which you can see with SHOW WARNINGS), but the values are loaded into the table after being coerced to whatever the closest legal value is (or at least to some value that fits the column):

```
mysql> INSERT INTO t (i,c,d) VALUES('-1x','too-long string!','1999-02-31');
mysql> SHOW WARNINGS;
+---------+------+-----------------------------------------+
| Level   | Code | Message                                 |
+---------+------+-----------------------------------------+
| Warning | 1265 | Data truncated for column 'i' at row 1  |
| Warning | 1265 | Data truncated for column 'c' at row 1  |
| Warning | 1265 | Data truncated for column 'd' at row 1  |
+---------+------+-----------------------------------------+
mysql> SELECT * FROM t;
+------+--------+------------+
| i    | c      | d          |
+------+--------+------------+
|   -1 | too-lo | 0000-00-00 |
+------+--------+------------+
```

Prior to MySQL 5.0, the way to prevent these warnings is to check the input data on the client side to make sure that it's legal. This remains a reasonable strategy in certain circumstances (see the sidebar "Server-Side Versus Client-Side Validation" in Recipe 10.21), but MySQL 5.0 and up offers you an alternative: let the server check data values on the server side and reject them with an error if they're invalid. Then you don't have to check them.

To use this strategy, enable restrictions on input data acceptance by setting the sql_mode system variable. You can set the SQL mode to cause the server to be much more restrictive than it is by default. With the proper restrictions in place, data values that would otherwise result in conversions and warnings result in errors instead. Try the preceding INSERT again after enabling "strict" SQL mode:

```
mysql> SET sql_mode = 'STRICT_ALL_TABLES';
mysql> INSERT INTO t (i,c,d) VALUES('-1x','too-long string!','1999-02-31');
ERROR 1265 (01000): Data truncated for column 'i' at row 1
```

Here the statement doesn't even progress to the second and third data values because the first is invalid for an integer column and the server raises an error.

Even without enabling input restrictions, the server as of MySQL 5.0 is a bit more strict about date checking than previous versions. Before 5.0, the server checks only that the month and day parts of date values are in the ranges 1 to 12 and 1 to 31, respectively. This allows a date such as '2005-02-31' to be entered. As of MySQL 5.0, the month must be from 1 to 12 (as before), but the day value must be legal for the given month. This means that '2005-02-31' generates a warning now by default.

Although date checking is somewhat more restrictive as of MySQL 5.0, MySQL still allows dates such as '1999-11-00' or '1999-00-00' that have zero parts, or the "zero" date ('0000-00-00'), and this is true even in strict mode. If you want to restrict these kinds of date values, enable the NO_ZERO_IN_DATE and NO_ZERO_DATE SQL modes to cause warnings, or errors in strict mode. For example, to disallow dates with zero parts or "zero" dates, set the SQL mode like this:

```
mysql> SET sql_mode = 'STRICT_ALL_TABLES,NO_ZERO_IN_DATE,NO_ZERO_DATE';
```

A simpler way to enable these restrictions, and a few more besides, is to enable TRADITIONAL SQL mode. TRADITIONAL mode is actually a constellation of modes, as you can see by setting the sql_mode value and then displaying it:

```
mysql> SET sql_mode = 'TRADITIONAL';
mysql> SELECT @@sql_mode\G
*************************** 1. row ***************************
@@sql_mode: STRICT_TRANS_TABLES,STRICT_ALL_TABLES,NO_ZERO_IN_DATE,
            NO_ZERO_DATE,ERROR_FOR_DIVISION_BY_ZERO,TRADITIONAL,
            NO_AUTO_CREATE_USER
```

You can read more about the various SQL modes in the *MySQL Reference Manual*.

The examples shown set the session value of the sql_mode system variable, so they change the SQL mode only for your current connection. To set the mode globally for all clients, set the global sql_mode value (this requires the SUPER privilege):

```
mysql> SET GLOBAL sql_mode = 'mode_value';
```

10.21 Validating and Transforming Data

Problem

You need to make sure that the data values contained in a file are legal.

Solution

Check them, possibly rewriting them into a more suitable format.

Discussion

Earlier recipes in this chapter show how to work with the structural characteristics of files, by reading lines and breaking them up into separate columns. It's important to be able to do that, but sometimes you need to work with the data content of a file, not just its structure:

- It's often a good idea to validate data values to make sure they're legal for the data types into which you're storing them. For example, you can make sure that values intended for INT, DATE, and ENUM columns are integers, dates in CCYY-MM-DD format, and legal enumeration values, respectively.

- Data values may need reformatting. Rewriting dates from one format to another is especially common; for example, if a program writes dates in MM-DD-YY format to ISO format for import into MySQL. If a program understands only date and time formats and not a combined date-and-time format (such as MySQL uses for the DATETIME and TIMESTAMP data types), you need to split date-and-time values into separate date and time values.

- It may be necessary to recognize special values in the file. It's common to represent NULL with a value that does not otherwise occur in the file, such as -1, Unknown, or N/A. If you don't want those values to be imported literally, you need to recognize and handle them specially.

This is the first of a set of recipes that describe validation and reformatting techniques that are useful in these kinds of situations. Techniques covered here for checking values include pattern matching and validation against information in a database. It's not unusual for certain validation operations to come up over and over, in which case you'll probably find it useful to to construct a library of functions. By packaging validation operations as library routines, it is easier to write utilities based on them, and the utilities make it easier to perform command-line operations on entire files so that you can avoid editing them yourself.

Server-Side Versus Client-Side Validation

As described in Recipe 10.20, you can cause data validation to be done on the server side by setting the SQL mode to be restrictive about accepting bad input data. In this case, the MySQL server raises an error for values that aren't legal for the data types of the columns into which you insert them.

In the next few sections, the focus is validation on the client side rather than on the server side. Client-side validation can be useful when you require more control over validation than simply receiving an error from the server. (For example, if you test values yourself, it's often easier to provide more informative messages about the exact nature of problems with the values.) Also, it might be necessary to couple validation with reformatting to transform complex values so that they are compatible with MySQL data types. You have more flexibility to do this on the client side.

If you want to avoid writing your own library routines, look around to see if someone else has already written suitable routines that you can use. For example, if you check the Perl CPAN (*cpan.perl.org*), you'll find a Data::Validate module hierarchy. The modules there provide library routines that standardize a number of common validation tasks. Data::Validate::MySQL deals specifically with MySQL data types.

Writing an input-processing loop

Many of the validation recipes shown in the new few sections are typical of those that you perform within the context of a program that reads a file and checks individual column values. The general framework for such a file-processing utility can be written like this:

```perl
#!/usr/bin/perl
# loop.pl - Typical input-processing loop

# Assumes tab-delimited, linefeed-terminated input lines.

use strict;
use warnings;

while (<>)                    # read each line
{
  chomp;
  # split line at tabs, preserving all fields
  my @val = split (/\t/, $_, 10000);
  for my $i (0 .. @val - 1) # iterate through columns in line
  {
    # ... test $val[$i] here ...
  }
}
```

The while( ) loop reads each input line and breaks it into fields. Inside the loop, each line is broken into fields. Then the inner for( ) loop iterates through the fields in the line, allowing each to be processed in sequence. If you're not applying a given test uniformly to all the fields, replace the for( ) loop with separate column-specific tests.

This loop assumes tab-delimited, linefeed-terminated input, an assumption that is shared by most of the utilities discussed throughout the rest of this chapter. To use these programs with datafiles in other formats, you may be able to convert the files into tab-delimited format using the *cvt_file.pl* script discussed in Recipe 10.18.

Putting common tests in libraries

For a test that you perform often, it may be useful to package it as a library function. This makes the operation easy to perform and also gives it a name that's likely to make the meaning of the operation clearer than the comparison code itself. For example, the following test performs a pattern match to check that $val consists entirely of digits (optionally preceded by a plus sign), and then makes sure the value is greater than zero:

```perl
$valid = ($val =~ /^\+?\d+$/ && $val > 0);
```

In other words, the test looks for strings that represent positive integers. To make the test easier to use and its intent clearer, you might put it into a function that is used like this:

```
$valid = is_positive_integer ($val);
```

The function itself can be defined as follows:

```
sub is_positive_integer
{
my $s = $_[0];

  return ($s =~ /^\+?\d+$/ && $s > 0);
}
```

Now put the function definition into a library file so that multiple scripts can use it easily. The *Cookbook_Utils.pm* module file in the *lib* directory of the recipes distribution is an example of a library file that contains a number of validation functions. Take a look through it to see which functions may be useful in your own programs (or as a model for writing your own library files). To gain access to this module from within a script, include a use statement like this:

```
use Cookbook_Utils;
```

You must of course install the module file in a directory where Perl will find it. For details on library installation, see Recipe 2.3.

A significant benefit of putting a collection of utility routines into a library file is that you can use it for all kinds of programs. It's rare for a data manipulation problem to be completely unique. If you can pick and choose at least a few validation routines from a library, it's possible to reduce the amount of code you need to write, even for highly specialized programs.

10.22 Using Pattern Matching to Validate Data

Problem

You need to compare a value to a set of values that is difficult to specify literally without writing a really ugly expression.

Solution

Use pattern matching.

Discussion

Pattern matching is a powerful tool for validation because it enables you to test entire classes of values with a single expression. You can also use pattern tests to break up matched values into subparts for further individual testing or in substitution operations to rewrite matched values. For example, you might break a matched date into pieces so that you can verify that the month is in the range from 1 to 12, and the day is within the number of days in the month. You might use a substitution to reorder *MM-DD-YY* or *DD-MM-YY* values into *YY-MM-DD* format.

The next few sections describe how to use patterns to test for several types of values, but first let's take a quick tour of some general pattern-matching principles. The following discussion focuses on Perl's regular expression capabilities. Pattern matching in Ruby, PHP, and Python is similar, although you should consult the relevant documentation for any differences. For Java, use the `java.util.regex` package.

In Perl, the pattern constructor is */pat/*:

```
$it_matched = ($val =~ /pat/);    # pattern match
```

Put an `i` after the */pat/* constructor to make the pattern match case-insensitive:

```
$it_matched = ($val =~ /pat/i);    # case-insensitive match
```

To use a character other than slash, begin the constructor with `m`. This can be useful if the pattern itself contains slashes:

```
$it_matched = ($val =~ m|pat|);    # alternate constructor character
```

To look for a nonmatch, replace the `=~` operator with the `!~` operator:

```
$no_match = ($val !~ /pat/);       # negated pattern match
```

To perform a substitution in `$val` based on a pattern match, use *s/pat/replacement/*. If *pat* occurs within `$val`, it's replaced by *replacement*. To perform a case-insensitive match, put an `i` after the last slash. To perform a global substitution that replaces all instances of *pat* rather than just the first one, add a `g` after the last slash:

```
$val =~ s/pat/replacement/;    # substitution
$val =~ s/pat/replacement/i;   # case-insensitive substitution
$val =~ s/pat/replacement/g;   # global substitution
$val =~ s/pat/replacement/ig;  # case-insensitive and global
```

Here's a list of some of the special pattern elements available in Perl regular expressions:

Pattern	What the pattern matches
^	Beginning of string
$	End of string
.	Any character
\s, \S	Whitespace or nonwhitespace character
\d, \D	Digit or nondigit character
\w, \W	Word (alphanumeric or underscore) or non-word character
[...]	Any character listed between the square brackets
[^...]	Any character not listed between the square brackets
p1|p2|p3	Alternation; matches any of the patterns *p1*, *p2*, or *p3*

Pattern	What the pattern matches
*	Zero or more instances of preceding element
+	One or more instances of preceding element
{n}	n instances of preceding element
{m,n}	m through n instances of preceding element

Many of these pattern elements are the same as those available for MySQL's REGEXP regular expression operator (Recipe 5.11).

To match a literal instance of a character that is special within patterns, such as *, ^, or $, precede it with a backslash. Similarly, to include a character within a character class construction that is special in character classes ([,], or -), precede it with a backslash. To include a literal ^ in a character class, list it somewhere other than as the first character between the brackets.

Many of the validation patterns shown in the following sections are of the form /^pat $/. Beginning and ending a pattern with ^ and $ has the effect of requiring *pat* to match the entire string that you're testing. This is common in data validation contexts, because it's generally desirable to know that a pattern matches an entire input value, not just part of it. (If you want to be sure that a value represents an integer, for example, it doesn't do you any good to know only that it contains an integer somewhere.) This is not a hard-and-fast rule, however, and sometimes it's useful to perform a more relaxed test by omitting the ^ and $ characters as appropriate. For example, if you want to strip leading and trailing whitespace from a value, use one pattern anchored only to the beginning of the string, and another anchored only to the end:

```
$val =~ s/^\s+//;   # trim leading whitespace
$val =~ s/\s+$//;   # trim trailing whitespace
```

That's such a common operation, in fact, that it's a good candidate for being written as a utility function. The *Cookbook_Utils.pm* file contains a function trim_whitespace( ) that performs both substitutions and returns the result:

```
$val = trim_whitespace ($val);
```

To remember subsections of a string that is matched by a pattern, use parentheses around the relevant parts of the pattern. After a successful match, you can refer to the matched substrings using the variables $1, $2, and so forth:

```
if ("abcdef" =~ /^(ab)(.*)$/)
{
  $first_part = $1; # this will be ab
  $the_rest = $2;   # this will be cdef
}
```

To indicate that an element within a pattern is optional, follow it with a ? character. To match values consisting of a sequence of digits, optionally beginning with a minus sign, and optionally ending with a period, use this pattern:

```
/^-?\d+\.?$/
```

You can also use parentheses to group alternations within a pattern. The following pattern matches time values in *hh:mm* format, optionally followed by AM or PM:

```
/^\d{1,2}:\d{2}\s*(AM|PM)?$/i
```

The use of parentheses in that pattern also has the side effect of remembering the optional part in $1. To suppress that side effect, use (?:*pat*) instead:

```
/^\d{1,2}:\d{2}\s*(?:AM|PM)?$/i
```

That's sufficient background in Perl pattern matching to allow construction of useful validation tests for several types of data values. The following sections provide patterns that can be used to test for broad content types, numbers, temporal values, and email addresses or URLs.

The *transfer* directory of the `recipes` distribution contains a *test_pat.pl* script that reads input values, matches them against several patterns, and reports which patterns each value matches. The script is easily extensible, so you can use it as a test harness to try your own patterns.

10.23 Using Patterns to Match Broad Content Types

Problem

You want to classify values into broad categories.

Solution

Use a pattern that is similarly broad.

Discussion

If you need to know whether values are empty or nonempty, or consist only of certain types of characters, the patterns listed in the following table may suffice:

Pattern	Type of value the pattern matches
/^$/	Empty value
/./	Nonempty value
/^\s*$/	Whitespace, possibly empty
/^\s+$/	Nonempty whitespace
/\S/	Nonempty, and not just whitespace
/^\d+$/	Digits only, nonempty
/^[a-z]+$/i	Alphabetic characters only (case-insensitive), nonempty

Pattern	Type of value the pattern matches
/^\w+$/	Alphanumeric or underscore characters only, nonempty

10.24 Using Patterns to Match Numeric Values

Problem

You need to make sure a string looks like a number.

Solution

Use a pattern that matches the type of number you're looking for.

Discussion

Patterns can be used to classify values into several types of numbers.

Pattern	Type of value the pattern matches
/^\d+$/	Unsigned integer
/^-?\d+$/	Negative or unsigned integer
/^[-+]?\d+$/	Signed or unsigned integer
/^[-+]?(\d+(\.\d*)?|\.\d+)$/	Floating-point number

The pattern /^\d+$/ matches unsigned integers by requiring a nonempty value that consists only of digits from the beginning to the end of the value. If you care only that a value begins with an integer, you can match an initial numeric part and extract it. To do this, match just the initial part of the string (omit the $ that requires the pattern to match to the end of the string) and place parentheses around the \d+ part. Then refer to the matched number as $1 after a successful match:

```
if ($val =~ /^(\d+)/)
{
    $val = $1;  # reset value to matched subpart
}
```

You could also add zero to the value, which causes Perl to perform an implicit string-to-number conversion that discards the nonnumeric suffix:

```
if ($val =~ /^\d+/)
{
    $val += 0;
}
```

However, if you run Perl with the -w option or include a use warnings line in your script (which I recommend), this form of conversion generates warnings for values that actually have a nonnumeric part. It will also convert string values like 0013 to the number 13, which may be unacceptable in some contexts.

Some kinds of numeric values have a special format or other unusual constraints. Here are a few examples and how to deal with them:

Zip codes

Zip and Zip+4 codes are postal codes used for mail delivery in the United States. They have values like 12345 or 12345-6789 (that is, five digits, possibly followed by a dash and four more digits). To match one form or the other, or both forms, use the following patterns:

Pattern	Type of value the pattern matches
/^\d{5}$/	Zip code, five digits only
/^\d{5}-\d{4}$/	Zip+4 code
/^\d{5}(-\d{4})?$/	Zip or Zip+4 code

Credit card numbers

Credit card numbers typically consist of digits, but it's common for values to be written with spaces, dashes, or other characters between groups of digits. For example, the following numbers are considered equivalent:

```
0123456789012345
0123 4567 8901 2345
0123-4567-8901-2345
```

To match such values, use this pattern:

```
/^[- \d]+/
```

(Perl allows the \d digit specifier within character classes.) However, that pattern doesn't identify values of the wrong length, and it may be useful to remove extraneous characters. If you require credit card values to contain 16 digits, use a substitution to remove all nondigits, and then check the length of the result:

```
$val =~ s/\D//g;
$valid = (length ($val) == 16);
```

Innings pitched

In baseball, one statistic recorded for pitchers is the number of innings pitched, measured in thirds of innings (corresponding to the number of outs recorded.) These values are numeric, but must satisfy a specific additional constraint: a fractional part is allowed, but if present, must consist of a single digit 0, 1, or 2. That is, legal values are of the form 0, .1, .2, 1, 1.1, 1.2, 2, and so forth. To match an unsigned integer (optionally followed by a decimal point and perhaps a fractional digit of 0, 1, or 2), or a fractional digit with no leading integer, use this pattern:

```
/^(\d+(\.[012]?)?|\.[012])$/
```

The alternatives in the pattern are grouped within parentheses because otherwise the ^ anchors only the first of them to the beginning of the string, and the $ anchors only the second to the end of the string.

10.25 Using Patterns to Match Dates or Times

Problem

You need to make sure a string looks like a date or time.

Solution

Use a pattern that matches the type of temporal value you expect. Be sure to consider issues such as how strict to be about delimiters between subparts and the lengths of the subparts.

Discussion

Dates are a validation headache because they come in so many formats. Pattern tests are extremely useful for weeding out illegal values, but often insufficient for full verification: a date might have a number where you expect a month, but if the number is 13, the date isn't valid. This section introduces some patterns that match a few common date formats. Recipe 10.30 revisits this topic in more detail and discusses how to combine pattern tests with content verification.

To require values to be dates in ISO (*CCYY-MM-DD*) format, use this pattern:

```
/^\d{4}-\d{2}-\d{2}$/
```

The pattern requires the - character as the delimiter between date parts. To allow either - or / as the delimiter, use a character class between the numeric parts (the slashes are escaped with a backslash to prevent them from being interpreted as the end of the pattern constructor):

```
/^\d{4}[-\/]\d{2}[-\/]\d{2}$/
```

Or you can use a different delimiter around the pattern and avoid the backslashes:

```
m|^\d{4}[-/]\d{2}[-/]\d{2}$|
```

To allow any non-digit delimiter (which corresponds to how MySQL operates when it interprets strings as dates), use this pattern:

```
/^\d{4}\D\d{2}\D\d{2}$/
```

If you don't require the full number of digits in each part (to allow leading zeros in values like 03 to be missing, for example), just look for three nonempty digit sequences:

```
/^\d+\D\d+\D\d+$/
```

Of course, that pattern is so general that it will also match other values such as U.S. Social Security numbers (which have the format 012-34-5678). To constrain the sub-part lengths by requiring two to four digits in the year part and one or two digits in the month and day parts, use this pattern:

```
/^\d{2,4}?\D\d{1,2}\D\d{1,2}$/
```

For dates in other formats such as *MM-DD-YY* or *DD-MM-YY*, similar patterns apply, but the subparts are arranged in a different order. This pattern matches both of those formats:

```
/^\d{2}-\d{2}-\d{2}$/
```

If you need to check the values of individual date parts, use parentheses in the pattern and extract the substrings after a successful match. If you're expecting dates to be in ISO format, for example, do something like this:

```
if ($val =~ /^(\d{2,4})\D(\d{1,2})\D(\d{1,2})$/)
{
  ($year, $month, $day) = ($1, $2, $3);
}
```

The library file *lib/Cookbook_Utils.pm* in the `recipes` distribution contains several of these pattern tests, packaged as function calls. If the date doesn't match the pattern, they return `undef`. Otherwise, they return a reference to an array containing the broken-out values for the year, month, and day. This can be useful for performing further checking on the components of the date. For example, `is_iso_date( )` looks for dates that match ISO format. It's defined as follows:

```
sub is_iso_date
{
my $s = $_[0];

  return undef unless $s =~ /^(\d{2,4})\D(\d{1,2})\D(\d{1,2})$/;
  return [ $1, $2, $3 ];  # return year, month, day
}
```

To use the function, do something like this:

```
my $ref = is_iso_date ($val);
if (defined ($ref))
{
  # $val matched ISO format pattern;
  # check its subparts using $ref->[0] through $ref->[2]
}
else
{
  # $val didn't match ISO format pattern
}
```

You'll often find additional processing necessary with dates, because although date-matching patterns help to weed out values that are syntactically malformed, they don't assess whether the individual components contain legal values. To do that, some range checking is necessary. That topic is covered later in Recipe 10.30.

If you're willing to skip subpart testing and just want to rewrite the pieces, you can use a substitution. For example, to rewrite values assumed to be in *MM-DD-YY* format into *YY-MM-DD* format, do this:

```
$val =~ s/^(\d+)\D(\d+)\D(\d+)$/$3-$1-$2/;
```

Time values are somewhat more orderly than dates, usually being written with hours first and seconds last, with two digits per part:

```
/^\d{2}:\d{2}:\d{2}$/
```

To be more lenient, you can allow the hours part to have a single digit, or the seconds part to be missing:

```
/^\d{1,2}:\d{2}(:\d{2})?$/
```

You can mark parts of the time with parentheses if you want to range-check the individual parts, or perhaps to reformat the value to include a seconds part of 00 if it happens to be missing. However, this requires some care with the parentheses and the ? characters in the pattern if the seconds part is optional. You want to allow the entire :\d {2} at the end of the pattern to be optional, but not to save the : character in $3 if the third time section is present. To accomplish that, use (?:*pat*), an alternative grouping notation that doesn't save the matched substring. Within that notation, use parentheses around the digits to save them. Then $3 will be undef if the seconds part is not present, but will contain the seconds digits otherwise:

```
if ($val =~ /^(\d{1,2}):(\d{2})(?::(\d{2}))?$/)
{
  my ($hour, $min, $sec) = ($1, $2, $3);
  $sec = "00" if !defined ($sec); # seconds missing; use 00
  $val = "$hour:$min:$sec";
}
```

To rewrite times from 12-hour format with AM and PM suffixes to 24-hour format, you can do something like this:

```
if ($val =~ /^(\d{1,2}):(\d{2})(?::(\d{2}))?\s*(AM|PM)?$/i)
{
  my ($hour, $min, $sec) = ($1, $2, $3);
  # supply missing seconds
  $sec = "00" unless defined ($sec);
  if ($hour == 12 && (!defined ($4) || uc ($4) eq "AM"))
  {
    $hour = "00"; # 12:xx:xx AM times are 00:xx:xx
  }
  elsif ($hour < 12 && defined ($4) && uc ($4) eq "PM")
  {
    $hour += 12;  # PM times other than 12:xx:xx
  }
  $val = "$hour:$min:$sec";
}
```

The time parts are placed into $1, $2, and $3, with $3 set to undef if the seconds part is missing. The suffix goes into $4 if it's present. If the suffix is AM or missing (undef), the value is interpreted as an AM time. If the suffix is PM, the value is interpreted as a PM time.

See Also

This section is just the beginning of what you can do when processing dates for data-transfer purposes. Date and time testing and conversion can be highly idiosyncratic, and the sheer number of issues to consider is mind-boggling:

- What is the basic date format? Dates come in several common styles, such as ISO (CCYY-MM-DD), U.S. (MM-DD-YY), and British (DD-MM-YY) formats. And these are just some of the more standard formats. Many more are possible. For example, a datafile may contain dates written as June 17, 1959 or as 17 Jun '59.

- Are trailing times allowed on dates or perhaps required? When times are expected, is the full time required or just the hour and minute?

- Do you allow special values like now or today?

- Are date parts required to be delimited by a certain character, such as - or /, or are other delimiters allowed?

- Are date parts required to have a specific number of digits? Or are leading zeros on month and year values allowed to be missing?

- Are months written numerically, or are they represented as month names like January or Jan?

- Are two-digit year values allowed? Should they be converted to have four digits? If so, what is the conversion rule? (What is the transition point within the range 00 to 99 at which values change from one century to another?)

- Should date parts be checked to ensure their validity? Patterns can recognize strings that look like dates or times, but while they're extremely useful for detecting malformed values, they may not be sufficient. A value like 1947-15-99 may match a pattern but isn't a legal date. Pattern testing is thus most useful in conjunction with range checks on the individual parts of the date.

The prevalence of these issues in data-transfer problems means that you'll probably end up writing some of your own validators on occasion to handle very specific date formats. Later sections of this chapter can provide additional assistance. For example, Recipe 10.29 covers conversion of two-digit year values to four-digit form, and Recipe 10.30 discusses how to perform validity checking on components of date or time values.

10.26 Using Patterns to Match Email Addresses or URLs

Problem

You want to determine whether a value looks like an email address or a URL.

Solution

Use a pattern, tuned to the level of strictness you want to enforce.

Discussion

The immediately preceding sections use patterns to identify classes of values such as numbers and dates, which are fairly typical applications for regular expressions. But pattern matching has such widespread applicability that it's impossible to list all the ways you can use it for data validation. To give some idea of a few other types of values that pattern matching can be used for, this section shows a few tests for email addresses and URLs.

To check values that are expected to be email addresses, the pattern should require at least an @ character with nonempty strings on either side:

```
/.@./
```

That's a pretty minimal test. It's difficult to come up with a fully general pattern that covers all the legal values and rejects all the illegal ones,[*] but it's easy to write a pattern that's at least a little more restrictive. For example, in addition to being nonempty, the username and the domain name should consist entirely of characters other than @ characters or spaces:

```
/^[^@ ]+@[^@ ]+$/
```

You may also want to require that the domain name part contain at least two parts separated by a dot:

```
/^[^@ ]+@[^@ .]+\.[^@ .]+/
```

To look for URL values that begin with a protocol specifier of http://, ftp://, or mailto:, use an alternation that matches any of them at the beginning of the string. These values contain slashes, so it's easier to use a different character around the pattern to avoid having to escape the slashes with backslashes:

```
m#^(http://|ftp://|mailto:)#i
```

The alternatives in the pattern are grouped within parentheses because otherwise the ^ will anchor only the first of them to the beginning of the string. The i modifier follows the pattern because protocol specifiers in URLs are not case-sensitive. The pattern is

---

[*] To see how hard it can be to perform pattern matching for email addresses, check Jeffrey E. F. Friedl's *Mastering Regular Expressions* (O'Reilly).

otherwise fairly unrestrictive because it allows anything to follow the protocol specifier. I leave it to you to add further restrictions as necessary.

10.27 Using Table Metadata to Validate Data

Problem

You need to check input values against the legal members of an ENUM or SET column.

Solution

Get the column definition, extract the list of members from it, and check data values against the list.

Discussion

Some forms of validation involve checking input values against information stored in a database. This includes values to be stored in an ENUM or SET column, which can be checked against the valid members stored in the column definition. Database-backed validation also applies when you have values that must match those listed in a lookup table to be considered legal. For example, input records that contain customer IDs can be required to match a row in a customers table, or state abbreviations in addresses can be verified against a table that lists each state. This recipe describes ENUM- and SET-based validation, and Recipe 10.28 discusses how to use lookup tables.

One way to check input values that correspond to the legal values of ENUM or SET columns is to get the list of legal column values into an array using the information in INFORMATION_SCHEMA, and then perform an array membership test. For example, the favorite-color column color from the profile table is an ENUM that is defined as follows:

```
mysql> SELECT COLUMN_TYPE FROM INFORMATION_SCHEMA.COLUMNS
    -> WHERE TABLE_SCHEMA = 'cookbook' AND TABLE_NAME = 'profile'
    -> AND COLUMN_NAME = 'color';
+--------------------------------------------------+
| COLUMN_TYPE                                       |
+--------------------------------------------------+
| enum('blue','red','green','brown','black','white') |
+--------------------------------------------------+
```

If you extract the list of enumeration members from the COLUMN_TYPE value and store them in an array @members, you can perform the membership test like this:

```
$valid = grep (/^$val$/i, @members);
```

The pattern constructor begins and ends with ^ and $ to require $val to match an entire enumeration member (rather than just a substring). It also is followed by an i to specify a case-insensitive comparison because the default collation is latin1_swedish_ci, which is case-insensitive. (If you're working with a column that has a different collation, adjust accordingly.)

In Recipe 9.7, we wrote a function get_enumorset_info( ) that returns ENUM or SET column metadata. This includes the list of members, so it's easy to use that function to write another utility routine, check_enum_value( ), that gets the legal enumeration values and performs the membership test. The routine takes four arguments: a database handle, the table name and column name for the ENUM column, and the value to check. It returns true or false to indicate whether the value is legal:

```perl
sub check_enum_value
{
my ($dbh, $db_name, $tbl_name, $col_name, $val) = @_;

  my $valid = 0;
  my $info = get_enumorset_info ($dbh, $db_name, $tbl_name, $col_name);
  if ($info && uc ($info->{type}) eq "ENUM")
  {
    # use case-insensitive comparison because default collation
    # (latin1_swedish_ci) is case-insensitive (adjust if you use
    # a different collation)
    $valid = grep (/^$val$/i, @{$info->{values}});
  }
  return $valid;
}
```

For single-value testing, such as to validate a value submitted in a web form, that kind of test works well. However, if you're going to be testing a lot of values (like an entire column in a datafile), it's better to read the enumeration values into memory once, and then use them repeatedly to check each of the data values. Furthermore, it's a lot more efficient to perform hash lookups than array lookups (in Perl at least). To do so, retrieve the legal enumeration values and store them as keys of a hash. Then test each input value by checking whether it exists as a hash key. It's a little more effort to construct the hash, which is why check_enum_value( ) doesn't do so. But for bulk validation, the improved lookup speed more than makes up for the hash construction overhead.[†]

Begin by getting the metadata for the column, and then convert the list of legal enumeration members to a hash:

```perl
my $ref = get_enumorset_info ($dbh, $db_name, $tbl_name, $col_name);
my %members;
foreach my $member (@{$ref->{values}})
{
  # convert hash key to consistent lettercase
  $members{lc ($member)} = 1;
}
```

[†] If you want to check for yourself the relative efficiency of array membership tests versus hash lookups, try the *lookup_time.pl* script in the *transfer* directory of the recipes distribution.

The loop makes each enumeration member exist as the key of a hash element. The hash key is what's important here; the value associated with it is irrelevant. (The example shown sets the value to 1, but you could use undef, 0, or any other value.) Note that the code converts the hash keys to lowercase before storing them. This is done because hash key lookups in Perl are case-sensitive. That's fine if the values that you're checking also are case-sensitive, but ENUM columns by default are not. By converting the enumeration values to a given lettercase before storing them in the hash, and then converting the values you want to check similarly, you perform, in effect, a case-insensitive key existence test:

```
$valid = exists ($members{lc ($val)});
```

The preceding example converts enumeration values and input values to lowercase. You could just as well use uppercase—as long as you do so for all values consistently.

Note that the existence test may fail if the input value is the empty string. You'll have to decide how to handle that case on a column-by-column basis. For example, if the column allows NULL values, you might interpret the empty string as equivalent to NULL and thus as being a legal value.

The validation procedure for SET values is similar to that for ENUM values, except that an input value might consist of any number of SET members, separated by commas. For the value to be legal, each element in it must be legal. In addition, because "any number of members" includes "none," the empty string is a legal value for any SET column.

For one-shot testing of individual input values, you can use a utility routine check_set_value( ) that is similar to check_enum_value( ):

```
sub check_set_value
{
my ($dbh, $db_name, $tbl_name, $col_name, $val) = @_;

  my $valid = 0;
  my $info = get_enumorset_info ($dbh, $db_name, $tbl_name, $col_name);
  if ($info && uc ($info->{type}) eq "SET")
  {
    return 1 if $val eq "";    # empty string is legal element
    # use case-insensitive comparison because default collation
    # (latin1_swedish_ci) is case-insensitive (adjust if you use
    # a different collation)
    $valid = 1;    # assume valid until we find out otherwise
    foreach my $v (split (/,/, $val))
    {
      if (!grep (/^$v$/i, @{$info->{values}}))
      {
        $valid = 0; # value contains an invalid element
        last;
      }
    }
  }
}
```

```
    return $valid;
  }
```

For bulk testing, construct a hash from the legal SET members. The procedure is the same as for producing a hash from ENUM elements:

```
my $ref = get_enumorset_info ($dbh, $db_name, $tbl_name, $col_name);
my %members;
foreach my $member (@{$ref->{values}})
{
  # convert hash key to consistent lettercase
  $members{lc ($member)} = 1;
}
```

To validate a given input value against the SET member hash, convert it to the same lettercase as the hash keys, split it at commas to get a list of the individual elements of the value, and then check each one. If any of the elements are invalid, the entire value is invalid:

```
$valid = 1;     # assume valid until we find out otherwise
foreach my $elt (split (/,/, lc ($val)))
{
  if (!exists ($members{$elt}))
  {
    $valid = 0; # value contains an invalid element
    last;
  }
}
```

After the loop terminates, $valid is true if the value is legal for the SET column, and false otherwise. Empty strings are always legal SET values, but this code doesn't perform any special-case test for an empty string. No such test is necessary, because in that case the split( ) operation returns an empty list, the loop never executes, and $valid remains true.

10.28 Using a Lookup Table to Validate Data

Problem

You need to check values to make sure they're listed in a lookup table.

Solution

Issue statements to see whether the values are in the table. However, the way you do this depends on the number of input values and the size of the table.

Discussion

To validate input values against the contents of a lookup table, you can use techniques somewhat similar to those shown in Recipe 10.27 for checking ENUM and SET columns.

However, whereas ENUM and SET columns are limited to a maximum of 65,535 and 64 member values, respectively, a lookup table can have an essentially unlimited number of values. You might not want to read them all into memory.

Validation of input values against the contents of a lookup table can be done several ways, as illustrated in the following discussion. The tests shown in the examples perform comparisons against values exactly as they are stored in the lookup table. To perform case-insensitive comparisons, remember to convert all values to a consistent lettercase.

Issue individual statements

For one-shot operations, you can test a value by checking whether it's listed in the lookup table. The following query returns true (nonzero) a value that is present and false otherwise:

```
$valid = $dbh->selectrow_array (
        "SELECT COUNT(*) FROM $tbl_name WHERE val = ?",
        undef, $val);
```

This kind of test may be suitable for purposes such as checking a value submitted in a web form, but is inefficient for validating large datasets. It has no memory for the results of previous tests for values that have been seen before; consequently, you'll end up issuing a query for every single input value.

Construct a hash from the entire lookup table

If you're going to perform bulk validation of a large set of values, it's more efficient to pull the lookup values into memory, save them in a data structure, and check each input value against the contents of that structure. Using an in-memory lookup avoids the overhead of running a query for each value.

First, run a query to retrieve all the lookup table values and construct a hash from them:

```
my %members;  # hash for lookup values
my $sth = $dbh->prepare ("SELECT val FROM $tbl_name");
$sth->execute ();
while (my ($val) = $sth->fetchrow_array ())
{
  $members{$val} = 1;
}
```

Then check each value by performing a hash key existence test:

```
$valid = exists ($members{$val});
```

This reduces the database traffic to a single query. However, for a large lookup table, that could still be a lot of traffic, and you might not want to hold the entire table in memory.

Performing Lookups with Other Languages

The example shown here for bulk testing of lookup values uses a Perl hash to determine whether a given value is present in a set of values:

```
$valid = exists ($members{$val});
```

Similar data structures exist for other languages. In Ruby, use a hash, and check input values using the has_key? method:

```
valid = members.has_key?(val)
```

In PHP, use an associative array, and perform a key lookup like this:

```
$valid = isset ($members[$val]);
```

In Python, use a dictionary, and check input values using the has_key( ) method:

```
valid = members.has_key (val)
```

For lookups in Java, use a HashMap, and test values with the containsKey( ) method:

```
valid = members.containsKey (val);
```

The *transfer* directory of the **recipes** distribution contains some sample code for lookup operations in each of these languages.

Use a hash as a cache of already-seen lookup values

Another lookup technique is to mix individual statements with a hash that stores lookup value existence information. This approach can be useful if you have a very large lookup table. Begin with an empty hash:

```
my %members;  # hash for lookup values
```

Then, for each value to be tested, check whether it's present in the hash. If not, issue a query to see whether the value is present in the lookup table, and record the result of the query in the hash. The validity of the input value is determined by the value associated with the key, not by the existence of the key:

```
if (!exists ($members{$val})) # haven't seen this value yet
{
  my $count = $dbh->selectrow_array (
                "SELECT COUNT(*) FROM $tbl_name WHERE val = ?",
                undef, $val);
  # store true/false to indicate whether value was found
  $members{$val} = ($count > 0);
}
$valid = $members{$val};
```

For this method, the hash acts as a cache, so that you run a lookup query for any given value only once, no matter how many times it occurs in the input. For datasets that have a reasonable number of repeated values, this approach avoids issuing a separate query for every single test, while requiring an entry in the hash only for each unique value. It thus stands between the other two approaches in terms of the tradeoff between database traffic and program memory requirements for the hash.

Note that the hash is used in a somewhat different manner for this method than for the previous method. Previously, the existence of the input value as a key in the hash determined the validity of the value, and the value associated with the hash key was irrelevant. For the hash-as-cache method, the meaning of key existence in the hash changes from "it's valid" to "it's been tested before." For each key, the value associated with it indicates whether the input value is present in the lookup table. (If you store as keys only those values that are found to be in the lookup table, you'll issue a query for each instance of an invalid value in the input dataset, which is inefficient.)

10.29 Converting Two-Digit Year Values to Four-Digit Form

Problem

You need to convert years in date values from two digits to four digits.

Solution

Let MySQL do this for you, or perform the operation yourself if MySQL's conversion rules aren't appropriate.

Discussion

Two-digit year values are a problem because the century is not explicit in the data values. If you know the range of years spanned by your input, you can add the century without ambiguity. Otherwise, you can only guess. For example, the date 2/10/69 probably would be interpreted by most people in the U.S. as February 10, 1969. But if it represents Mahatma Gandhi's birth date, the year is actually 1869.

One way to convert years to four digits is to let MySQL do it. If you store a date containing a two-digit year, MySQL automatically converts it to four-digit form. MySQL uses a transition point of 1970; it interprets values from 00 to 69 as the years 2000 to 2069, and values from 70 to 99 as the years 1970 to 1999. These rules are appropriate for year values in the range from 1970 to 2069. If your values lie outside this range, you should add the proper century yourself before storing them into MySQL.

To use a different transition point, convert years to four-digit form yourself. Here's a general-purpose routine that converts two-digit years to four digits and allows an arbitrary transition point:

```
sub yy_to_ccyy
{
my ($year, $transition_point) = @_;

  $transition_point = 70 unless defined ($transition_point);
```

```
    $year += ($year >= $transition_point ? 1900 : 2000) if $year < 100;
    return ($year);
}
```

The function uses MySQL's transition point (70) by default. An optional second argument may be given to provide a different transition point. yy_to_ccyy( ) also makes sure the year actually needs converting (is less than 100) before modifying it. That way you can pass year values that do or don't include the century without checking first. Some sample invocations using the default transition point have the following results:

```
$val = yy_to_ccyy (60);        # returns 2060
$val = yy_to_ccyy (1960);      # returns 1960 (no conversion done)
```

But suppose that you want to convert year values as follows, using a transition point of 50:

```
00 .. 49 -> 2000 .. 2049
50 .. 99 -> 1950 .. 1999
```

To do this, pass an explicit transition point argument to yy_to_ccyy( ):

```
$val = yy_to_ccyy (60, 50);    # returns 1960
$val = yy_to_ccyy (1960, 50);  # returns 1960 (no conversion done)
```

The yy_to_ccyy( ) function is one of those included in the *Cookbook_Utils.pm* library file.

10.30 Performing Validity Checking on Date or Time Subparts

Problem

A string passes a pattern test as a date or time, but you want to perform further checking to make sure that it's legal.

Solution

Break up the value into subparts and perform the appropriate range checking on each part.

Discussion

Pattern matching may not be sufficient for checking dates or times. For example, a value like 1947-15-19 might match a date pattern, but it's not actually legal as a date. If you want to perform more rigorous value testing, combine pattern matching with range checking. Break out the year, month, and day values, and then check that they're within the proper ranges. Years should be less than 9999 (MySQL represents dates to an upper limit of 9999-12-31), month values should be in the range from 1 to 12, and days should be in the range from 1 to the number of days in the month. That latter part is the trickiest: it's month-dependent, and for February it's also year-dependent because it changes for leap years.

Suppose that you're checking input dates in ISO format. In Recipe 10.25, we used an `is_iso_date( )` function from the *Cookbook_Utils.pm* library file to perform a pattern match on a date string and break it into component values:

```
my $ref = is_iso_date ($val);
if (defined ($ref))
{
  # $val matched ISO format pattern;
  # check its subparts using $ref->[0] through $ref->[2]
}
else
{
  # $val didn't match ISO format pattern
}
```

`is_iso_date( )` returns undef if the value doesn't satisfy a pattern that matches ISO date format. Otherwise, it returns a reference to an array containing the year, month, and day values.[‡] To perform additional checking on the date parts, pass them to `is_valid_date( )`, another library function:

```
$valid = is_valid_date ($ref->[0], $ref->[1], $ref->[2]);
```

Or, more concisely:

```
$valid = is_valid_date (@{$ref});
```

`is_valid_date( )` checks the parts of a date like this:

```
sub is_valid_date
{
my ($year, $month, $day) = @_;

  # year must be nonnegative, month and day must be positive
  return 0 if $year < 0 || $month < 1 || $day < 1;
  # check maximum limits on individual parts
  return 0 if $year > 9999;
  return 0 if $month > 12;
  return 0 if $day > days_in_month ($year, $month);
  return 1;
}
```

`is_valid_date( )` requires separate year, month, and day values, not a date string. This forces you to break apart candidate values into components before invoking it, but makes it applicable in more contexts. For example, you can use it to check dates like 12 February 2003 by mapping the month to its numeric value before calling `is_valid_date( )`. Were `is_valid_date( )` to take a string argument assumed to be in a specific date format, it would be much less general.

[‡] The *Cookbook_Utils.pm* file also contains is_mmddyy_date( ) and is_ddmmyy_date( ) routines that match dates in U.S. or British format and return undef or a reference to an array of date parts. (The parts returned are always in year, month, day order, not the order in which the parts appear in the input date string.)

`is_valid_date( )` uses a subsidiary function `days_in_month( )` to determine how many days there are in the month represented by the date. `days_in_month( )` requires both the year and the month as arguments, because if the month is 2 (February), the number of days depends on whether the year is a leap year. This means you *must* pass a four-digit year value: two-digit years are ambiguous with respect to the century, which makes proper leap-year testing impossible, as discussed in Recipe 6.17. The `days_in_month( )` and `is_leap_year( )` functions are based on techniques taken straight from that recipe:

```
sub is_leap_year
{
my $year = $_[0];

  return (($year % 4 == 0) && ((($year % 100) != 0) || ($year % 400) == 0));
}

sub days_in_month
{
my ($year, $month) = @_;
my @day_tbl = (31, 28, 31, 30, 31, 30, 31, 31, 30, 31, 30, 31);
my $days = $day_tbl[$month-1];

  # add a day for Feb of leap years
  $days++ if $month == 2 && is_leap_year ($year);
  return ($days);
}
```

To perform validity checking on time values, a similar procedure can be used, although the ranges for the subparts are different: 0 to 23 for the hour, and 0 to 59 for the minute and second. Here is a function `is_24hr_time( )` that checks for values in 24-hour format:

```
sub is_24hr_time
{
my $s = $_[0];

  return undef unless $s =~ /^(\d{1,2})\D(\d{2})\D(\d{2})$/;
  return [ $1, $2, $3 ];  # return hour, minute, second
}
```

The following `is_ampm_time( )` function looks for times in 12-hour format with an optional AM or PM suffix, converting PM times to 24-hour values:

```
sub is_ampm_time
{
my $s = $_[0];

  return undef unless $s =~ /^(\d{1,2})\D(\d{2})\D(\d{2})(?:\s*(AM|PM))?$/i;
  my ($hour, $min, $sec) = ($1, $2, $3);
  if ($hour == 12 && (!defined ($4) || uc ($4) eq "AM"))
  {
    $hour = "00"; # 12:xx:xx AM times are 00:xx:xx
  }
  elsif ($hour < 12 && defined ($4) && uc ($4) eq "PM")
  {
```

```
    $hour += 12;   # PM times other than 12:xx:xx
  }
  return [ $hour, $min, $sec ]; # return hour, minute, second
}
```

Both functions return undef for values that don't match the pattern. Otherwise, they return a reference to a three-element array containing the hour, minute, and second values.

 They don't perform range checks. To do that, pass the array to is_valid_time( ), another utility routine.

10.31 Writing Date-Processing Utilities

Problem

There's a given date-processing operation that you need to perform frequently, so you want to write a utility that does it for you.

Solution

The utilities in this recipe provide some examples that show how to do that.

Discussion

Due to the idiosyncratic nature of dates, you might find it necessary to write date converters from time to time. This section shows some sample converters that serve various purposes:

- *isoize_date.pl* reads a file looking for dates in U.S. format (MM-DD-YY) and converts them to ISO format.

- *cvt_date.pl* converts dates to and from any of ISO, U.S., or British formats. It is more general than *isoize_date.pl*, but requires that you tell it what kind of input to expect and what kind of output to produce.

- *monddccyy_to_iso.pl* looks for dates like Feb. 6, 1788 and converts them to ISO format. It illustrates how to map dates with nonnumeric parts to a format that MySQL will understand.

All three scripts are located in the *transfer* directory of the recipes distribution. They assume datafiles are in tab-delimited, linefeed-terminated format. (Use *cvt_file.pl* first if you need to work with files that have a different format.)

Our first date-processing utility, *isoize_date.pl*, looks for dates in U.S. format and rewrites them into ISO format. You'll recognize that it's modeled after the general input-processing loop shown in Recipe 10.21, with some extra stuff thrown in to perform a specific type of conversion:

```perl
#!/usr/bin/perl
# isoize_date.pl - Read input data, look for values that match
# a date pattern, convert them to ISO format. Also converts
# 2-digit years to 4-digit years, using a transition point of 70.

# By default, this looks for dates in MM-DD-[CC]YY format.

# Assumes tab-delimited, linefeed-terminated input lines.

# Does not check whether dates actually are valid (for example,
# won't complain about 13-49-1928).

use strict;
use warnings;

# transition point at which 2-digit years are assumed to be 19XX
# (below they are treated as 20XX)
my $transition = 70;

while (<>)
{
  chomp;
  my @val = split (/\t/, $_, 10000);  # split, preserving all fields
  for my $i (0 .. @val - 1)
  {
    my $val = $val[$i];
    # look for strings in MM-DD-[CC]YY format
    next unless $val =~ /^(\d{1,2})\D(\d{1,2})\D(\d{2,4})$/;

    my ($month, $day, $year) = ($1, $2, $3);
    # to interpret dates as DD-MM-[CC]YY instead, replace preceding
    # line with the following one:
    #my ($day, $month, $year) = ($1, $2, $3);

    # convert 2-digit years to 4 digits, and then update value in array
    $year += ($year >= $transition ? 1900 : 2000) if $year < 100;
    $val[$i] = sprintf ("%04d-%02d-%02d", $year, $month, $day);
  }
  print join ("\t", @val) . "\n";
}
```

If you feed *isoize_date.pl* an input file that looks like this:

```
Fred     04-13-70
Mort     09-30-69
Brit     12-01-57
Carl     11-02-73
Sean     07-04-63
Alan     02-14-65
Mara     09-17-68
Shepard  09-02-75
Dick     08-20-52
Tony     05-01-60
```

It produces the following output:

```
Fred     1970-04-13
Mort     2069-09-30
Brit     2057-12-01
Carl     1973-11-02
Sean     2063-07-04
Alan     2065-02-14
Mara     2068-09-17
Shepard  1975-09-02
Dick     2052-08-20
Tony     2060-05-01
```

isoize_date.pl serves a specific purpose: it converts only from U.S. to ISO format. It does not perform validity checking on date subparts or allow the transition point for adding the century to be specified. A more general tool would be more useful. The next script, *cvt_date.pl*, extends the capabilities of *isoize_date.pl*; it recognizes input dates in ISO, U.S., or British formats and converts any of them to any other. It also can convert two-digit years to four digits, enables you to specify the conversion transition point, and can warn about bad dates. As such, it can be used to preprocess input for loading into MySQL, or to postprocess data exported from MySQL for use by other programs.

cvt_date.pl understands the following options:

`--iformat=`*format*, `--oformat=`*format*, `--format=`*format*
> Set the date format for input, output, or both. The default *format* value is `iso`; *cvt_date.pl* also recognizes any string beginning with `us` or `br` as indicating U.S. or British date format.

`--add-century`
> Convert two-digit years to four digits.

`--columns=`*column_list*
> Convert dates only in the named columns. By default, *cvt_date.pl* looks for dates in all columns. If this option is given, *column_list* should be a list of one or more column positions or ranges separated by commas. (Ranges can be given as *m-n* to specify columns *m* through *n*.) Positions begin at 1.

`--transition=`*n*
> Specify the transition point for two-digit to four-digit year conversions. The default transition point is 70. This option turns on `--add-century`.

`--warn`
> Warn about bad dates. (Note that this option can produce spurious warnings if the dates have two-digit years and you don't specify `--add-century`, because leap year testing won't always be accurate in that case.)

I won't show the code for *cvt_date.pl* here (most of it is taken up with processing command-line options), but you can examine the source for yourself if you like. As an example of how *cvt_date.pl* works, suppose that you have a file *newdata.txt* with the following contents:

```
name1    01/01/99    38
name2    12/31/00    40
name3    02/28/01    42
name4    01/02/03    44
```

Running the file through *cvt_date.pl* with options indicating that the dates are in U.S. format and that the century should be added produces this result:

```
% cvt_date.pl --iformat=us --add-century newdata.txt
name1    1999-01-01    38
name2    2000-12-31    40
name3    2001-02-28    42
name4    2003-01-02    44
```

To produce dates in British format instead with no year conversion, do this:

```
% cvt_date.pl --iformat=us --oformat=br newdata.txt
name1    01-01-99    38
name2    31-12-00    40
name3    28-02-01    42
name4    02-01-03    44
```

cvt_date.pl has no knowledge of the meaning of each data column, of course. If you have a nondate column with values that match the pattern, it will rewrite that column, too. To deal with that, specify a `--columns` option to limit the columns that *cvt_date.pl* attempts to convert.

isoize_date.pl and *cvt_date.pl* both operate on dates written in all-numeric formats. But dates in datafiles often are written differently, in which case it may be necessary to write a special purpose script to process them. Suppose an input file contains dates in the following format (these represent the dates on which U.S. states were admitted to the Union):

```
Delaware        Dec. 7, 1787
Pennsylvania    Dec 12, 1787
New Jersey      Dec. 18, 1787
Georgia         Jan. 2, 1788
Connecticut     Jan. 9, 1788
Massachusetts   Feb. 6, 1788
Maryland        Apr. 28, 1788
South Carolina  May 23, 1788
New Hampshire   Jun. 21, 1788
Virginia        Jun 25, 1788
...
```

The dates consist of a three-character month abbreviation (possibly followed by a period), the numeric day of the month, a comma, and the numeric year. To import this file into MySQL, you need to convert the dates to ISO format, resulting in a file that looks like this:

```
Delaware        1787-12-07
Pennsylvania    1787-12-12
New Jersey      1787-12-18
Georgia         1788-01-02
Connecticut     1788-01-09
```

```
Massachusetts    1788-02-06
Maryland         1788-04-28
South Carolina   1788-05-23
New Hampshire    1788-06-21
Virginia         1788-06-25
...
```

That's a somewhat specialized kind of transformation, although this general type of problem (converting a particular date format to ISO format) is hardly uncommon. To perform the conversion, identify the dates as those values matching an appropriate pattern, map month names to the corresponding numeric values, and reformat the result. The following script, *monddccyy_to_iso.pl*, illustrates how to do this:

```perl
#!/usr/bin/perl
# monddccyy_to_iso.pl - convert dates from mon[.] dd, ccyy to ISO format

# Assumes tab-delimited, linefeed-terminated input

use strict;
use warnings;

my %map =    # map 3-char month abbreviations to numeric month
(
  "jan" => 1, "feb" => 2, "mar" => 3, "apr" => 4, "may" => 5, "jun" => 6,
  "jul" => 7, "aug" => 8, "sep" => 9, "oct" => 10, "nov" => 11, "dec" => 12
);

while (<>)
{
  chomp;
  my @val = split (/\t/, $_, 10000);    # split, preserving all fields
  for my $i (0 .. @val - 1)
  {
    # reformat the value if it matches the pattern, otherwise assume
    # that it's not a date in the required format and leave it alone
    if ($val[$i] =~ /^([^.]+)\.? (\d+), (\d+)$/)
    {
      # use lowercase month name
      my ($month, $day, $year) = (lc ($1), $2, $3);
      if (exists ($map{$month}))
      {
        $val[$i] = sprintf ("%04d-%02d-%02d",
                  $year, $map{$month}, $day);
      }
      else
      {
        # warn, but don't reformat
        warn "$val[$i]: bad date?\n";
      }
    }
  }
  print join ("\t", @val) . "\n";
}
```

The script only does reformatting, it doesn't validate the dates. To do that, modify the script to use the *Cookbook_Utils.pm* module by adding this statement after the `use warnings` line:

```
use Cookbook_Utils;
```

That gives the script access to the module's `is_valid_date( )` routine. To use it, change this line:

```
if (exists ($map{$month}))
```

To this:

```
if (exists ($map{$month}) && is_valid_date ($year, $map{$month}, $day))
```

10.32 Using Dates with Missing Components

Problem

The dates in your data are incomplete; that is, they have missing subparts.

Solution

MySQL can represent them as ISO-format dates using zero for the missing parts.

Discussion

Some applications use dates that are not complete. For example, you may need to work with input values such as `Mar/2001` that contain only a month and year. In MySQL, it's possible to represent such values as ISO-format dates that have zero in the "missing" parts. (The value `Mar/2001` can be stored as `2001-03-00`.) To convert month/year values to ISO format for import into MySQL, set up a hash to map month names to their numeric values:

```
my %map =    # map 3-char month abbreviations to numeric month
(
  "jan" => 1, "feb" => 2, "mar" => 3, "apr" => 4, "may" => 5, "jun" => 6,
  "jul" => 7, "aug" => 8, "sep" => 9, "oct" => 10, "nov" => 11, "dec" => 12
);
```

Now, convert each input value like this:

```
if ($val =~ /^([a-z]{3})\/(\d{4})$/i)
{
  my ($m, $y) = (lc ($1), $2); # use lowercase month name
  $val = sprintf ("%04d-%02d-00", $y, $map{$m})
}
```

After storing the resulting values into MySQL, you can retrieve them for display in the original month/year format by issuing a `SELECT` statement that rewrites the dates using a `DATE_FORMAT( )` expression:

```
DATE_FORMAT(date_val,'%b/%Y')
```

Applications that use strict SQL mode but require zero parts in dates should be careful not to set the `NO_ZERO_IN_DATE` SQL mode, which causes the server to consider such dates invalid.

10.33 Importing Non-ISO Date Values

Problem

Date values to be imported are not in the ISO (*CCYY-MM-DD*) format that MySQL expects.

Solution

Use an external utility to convert the dates to ISO format before importing the data into MySQL (*cvt_date.pl* is useful here). Or use LOAD DATA's capability for preprocessing input data before it gets loaded into the database.

Discussion

Suppose that you have a table that contains three columns, `name`, `date`, and `value`, where `date` is a `DATE` column requiring values in ISO format (*CCYY-MM-DD*). Suppose also that you're given a datafile *newdata.txt* to be imported into the table, but its contents look like this:

```
name1    01/01/99    38
name2    12/31/00    40
name3    02/28/01    42
name4    01/02/03    44
```

Here the dates are in *MM/DD/YY* format and must be converted to ISO format to be stored as `DATE` values in MySQL. One way to do this is to run the file through the *cvt_date.pl* script shown earlier in the chapter:

```
% cvt_date.pl --iformat=us --add-century newdata.txt > tmp.txt
```

You can then load the *tmp.txt* file into the table. This task also can be accomplished entirely in MySQL with no external utilities by using SQL to perform the reformatting operation. As discussed in Recipe 10.11, LOAD DATA can preprocess input values before inserting them. Applying that capability to the present problem, the date-rewriting LOAD DATA statement looks like this, using the `STR_TO_DATE( )` function (Recipe 6.2) to interpret the input dates:

```
mysql> LOAD DATA LOCAL INFILE 'newdata.txt'
    -> INTO TABLE t (name,@date,value)
    -> SET date = STR_TO_DATE(@date,'%m/%d/%y');
```

With the %y format specifier in STR_TO_DATE( ), MySQL converts the two-digit years to four-digit years automatically, so the original *MM/DD/YY* values end up as ISO values in *CCYY-MM-DD* format. The resulting data after import looks like this:

```
+-------+------------+-------+
| name  | date       | value |
+-------+------------+-------+
| name1 | 1999-01-01 |    38 |
| name2 | 2000-12-31 |    40 |
| name3 | 2001-02-28 |    42 |
| name4 | 2003-01-02 |    44 |
+-------+------------+-------+
```

This procedure assumes that MySQL's automatic conversion of two-digit years to four digits produces the correct century values. This means that the year part of the values must correspond to years in the range from 1970 to 2069. If that's not true, you need to convert the year values some other way. (See Recipe 10.30 for some ideas.)

If the dates are not in a format that STR_TO_DATE( ) can handle, perhaps you can write a stored function to handle them and return ISO date values. In that case, the LOAD DATA statement looks like this, where my_date_interp( ) is the stored function name:

```
mysql> LOAD DATA LOCAL INFILE 'newdata.txt'
    -> INTO TABLE t (name,@date,value)
    -> SET date = my_date_interp(@date);
```

10.34 Exporting Dates Using Non-ISO Formats

Problem

You want to export date values using a format other than the ISO (*CCYY-MM-DD*) format that MySQL uses by default. This might be a requirement when exporting dates from MySQL to applications that don't understand ISO format.

Solution

Use an external utility to rewrite the dates to non-ISO format after exporting the data from MySQL (*cvt_date.pl* is useful here). Or use the DATE_FORMAT( ) function to rewrite the values during the export operation.

Discussion

Suppose that you want to export data from MySQL into an application that doesn't understand ISO-format dates. One way to do this is to export the data into a file, leaving the dates in ISO format. Then run the file through a utility such as *cvt_date.pl* that rewrites the dates into the required format.

Another approach is to export the dates directly in the required format by rewriting them with DATE_FORMAT( ). Suppose that you have the following table:

```
CREATE TABLE datetbl
(
  i   INT,
  c   CHAR(10),
  d   DATE,
  dt  DATETIME,
  ts  TIMESTAMP
);
```

Suppose also that you need to export data from this table, but with the dates in any DATE, DATETIME, or TIMESTAMP columns rewritten in U.S. format (*MM-DD-CCYY*). A SELECT statement that uses the DATE_FORMAT( ) function to rewrite the dates as required looks like this:

```
SELECT
  i,
  c,
  DATE_FORMAT(d, '%m-%d-%Y') AS d,
  DATE_FORMAT(dt, '%m-%d-%Y %T') AS dt,
  DATE_FORMAT(ts, '%m-%d-%Y %T') AS ts
FROM datetbl
```

Thus, if datetbl contains the following rows:

3	abc	2005-12-31	2005-12-31 12:05:03	2005-12-31 12:05:03
4	xyz	2006-01-31	2006-01-31 12:05:03	2006-01-31 12:05:03

The statement generates output that looks like this:

3	abc	12-31-2005	12-31-2005 12:05:03	12-31-2005 12:05:03
4	xyz	01-31-2006	01-31-2006 12:05:03	01-31-2006 12:05:03

10.35 Importing and Exporting NULL Values

Problem

You're not sure how to represent NULL values in a datafile.

Solution

Try to use a value not otherwise present, so that you can distinguish NULL from all other legitimate non-NULL values. When you import the file, look for that value and convert instances of it to NULL.

Discussion

There's no standard for representing NULL values in datafiles, which makes them a bit of a problem for import and export operations. Some of the difficulty arises from the fact that NULL indicates the *absence* of a value, and something that's not there is not easy to represent literally in a datafile. Using an empty column value is the most obvious thing to do, but that's ambiguous for string-valued columns because there is no way to distinguish a NULL represented that way from a true empty string. Empty values can be a problem for other data types as well. For example, if you load an empty value with LOAD DATA into a numeric column, it is stored as 0 rather than as NULL, and thus becomes indistinguishable from a true 0 in the input.

The usual strategy for dealing with this problem is to represent NULL using a value that doesn't otherwise occur in the data. This is how LOAD DATA and *mysqlimport* handle the issue: they understand the value of \N by convention to mean NULL. (\N is interpreted as NULL when it occurs by itself, and not as part of a larger value such as x\N or \Nx.) For example, if you load the following datafile with LOAD DATA, it will treat the instances of \N as NULL:

```
str1    13    1997-10-14
str2    \N    2009-05-07
\N      15    \N
\N      \N    1973-07-14
```

But you might want to interpret values other than \N as signifying NULL, and you might have different conventions in different columns. Consider the following datafile:

```
str1    13 1997-10-14
str2    -1 2009-05-07
Unknown 15
Unknown -1 1973-07-15
```

The first column contains strings, and Unknown signifies NULL. The second column contains integers, and -1 signifies NULL. The third column contains dates, and an empty value signifies NULL. What to do?

To handle situations like this, use LOAD DATA's capability for preprocessing input values: specify a column list that assigns input values to user-defined variables, and use a SET clause that maps the special values to true NULL values. If the datafile is named *has_nulls.txt*, the following LOAD DATA statement properly interprets its contents:

```
mysql> LOAD DATA LOCAL INFILE 'has_nulls.txt'
    -> INTO TABLE t (@c1,@c2,@c3)
    -> SET c1 = IF(@c1='Unknown',NULL,@c1),
    ->     c2 = IF(@c2=-1,NULL,@c2),
    ->     c3 = IF(@c3='',NULL,@c3);
```

The resulting data after import looks like this:

```
+------+------+------------+
| c1   | c2   | c3         |
+------+------+------------+
| str1 |   13 | 1997-10-14 |
| str2 | NULL | 2009-05-07 |
| NULL |   15 | NULL       |
| NULL | NULL | 1973-07-15 |
+------+------+------------+
```

The preceding discussion pertains to interpreting NULL values for import into MySQL, but it's also necessary to think about NULL values when transferring data in the other direction—from MySQL into other programs. Here are some examples:

- SELECT ... INTO OUTFILE writes NULL values as \N. Will another program understand that convention? If not, you need to convert \N to something the program will understand. For example, the SELECT statement can export the column using an expression like this:

      IFNULL(col_name,'Unknown')

- You can use *mysql* in batch mode as an easy way to produce tab-delimited output (Recipe 10.13), but one problem with doing so is that NULL values appear in the output as instances of the word "NULL". If that word occurs nowhere else in the output, you may be able to postprocess it to convert instances of the word to something more appropriate. For example, you can use a one-line *sed* command:

      % sed -e "s/NULL/\\N/g" data.txt > tmp

If the word "NULL" does appear where it represents something other than a NULL value, then it's ambiguous and you should probably export your data differently. For example, your export statement could use IFNULL( ) to map NULL values to something else.

10.36 Guessing Table Structure from a Datafile

Problem

Someone gives you a datafile and says, "Here, put this into MySQL for me." But no table yet exists to hold the data.

Solution

Write the CREATE TABLE statement yourself. Or use a utility that guesses the table structure by examining the contents of the datafile.

Discussion

Sometimes you need to import data into MySQL for which no table has yet been set up. You can create the table yourself, based on any knowledge you might have about the contents of the file. Or you might be able to avoid some of the work by using *guess_table.pl*, a utility located in the *transfer* directory of the recipes distribution. *guess_table.pl* reads the datafile to see what kind of information it contains, and then attempts to produce an appropriate CREATE TABLE statement that matches the contents of the file. This script is necessarily imperfect, because column contents sometimes are ambiguous. (For example, a column containing a small number of distinct strings might be a VARCHAR column or an ENUM.) Still, it's often easier to tweak the CREATE TABLE statement that *guess_table.pl* produces than to write the entire statement from scratch. This utility also has a diagnostic function, although that's not its primary purpose. For example, you might believe a column contains only numbers, but if *guess_table.pl* indicates that it should be created using a VARCHAR type, that tells you the column contains at least one nonnumeric value.

guess_table.pl assumes that its input is in tab-delimited, linefeed-terminated format. It also assumes valid input because any attempt to guess data types based on possibly flawed data is doomed to failure. This means, for example, that if a date column is to be recognized as such, it should be in ISO format. Otherwise, *guess_table.pl* may characterize it as a VARCHAR column. If a datafile doesn't satisfy these assumptions, you may be able to reformat it first using the *cvt_file.pl* and *cvt_date.pl* utilities described in Recipes 10.18 and 10.31.

guess_table.pl understands the following options:

--labels

> Interpret the first input line as a row of column labels, and use them for table column names. If this option is omitted, *guess_table.pl* uses default column names of c1, c2, and so forth.
>
> Note that if the file contains a row of labels, and you neglect to specify this option, the labels will be treated as data values by *guess_table.pl*. The likely result is that the script will characterize *all* columns as VARCHAR columns (even those that otherwise contain only numeric or temporal values), due to the presence of a nonnumeric or nontemporal value in the column.

--lower, --upper

> Force column names in the CREATE TABLE statement to be lowercase or uppercase.

--quote-names, --skip-quote-names

> Quote or do not quote table and column identifiers in the CREATE TABLE statement with ` characters (for example, `mytbl`). This can be useful if an identifier is a reserved word. The default is to quote identifiers.

--report

> Generate a report rather than a CREATE TABLE statement. The script displays the information that it gathers about each column.

--table=*tbl_name*

> Specify the table name to use in the CREATE TABLE statement. The default name is t.

Here's an example of how *guess_table.pl* works. Suppose that a file named *stockdat.csv* is in CSV format and has the following contents:

```
commodity,trade_date,shares,price,change
sugar,12-14-2006,1000000,10.50,-.125
oil,12-14-2006,96000,60.25,.25
wheat,12-14-2006,2500000,8.75,0
gold,12-14-2006,13000,103.25,2.25
```

```
sugar,12-15-2006,970000,10.60,.1
oil,12-15-2006,105000,60.5,.25
wheat,12-15-2006,2370000,8.65,-.1
gold,12-15-2006,11000,101,-2.25
```

The first row indicates the column labels, and the following rows contain data records, one per line. The values in the trade_date column are dates, but they are in *MM-DD-CCYY* format rather than the ISO format that MySQL expects. *cvt_date.pl* can convert these dates to ISO format. However, both *cvt_date.pl* and *guess_table.pl* require input in tab-delimited, linefeed-terminated format. So first let's use *cvt_file.pl* to convert the input to tab-delimited, linefeed-terminated format. Then we can convert the dates with *cvt_date.pl*:

```
% cvt_file.pl --iformat=csv stockdat.csv > tmp1.txt
% cvt_date.pl --iformat=us tmp1.txt > tmp2.txt
```

Then feed the resulting file, *tmp2.txt*, to *guess_table.pl*:

```
% guess_table.pl --labels --table=stocks tmp2.txt > stocks.sql
```

The CREATE TABLE statement that *guess_table.pl* writes to *stocks.sql* looks like this:

```
CREATE TABLE `stocks`
(
  `commodity` VARCHAR(5) NOT NULL,
  `trade_date` DATE NOT NULL,
  `shares` INT UNSIGNED NOT NULL,
  `price` DOUBLE UNSIGNED NOT NULL,
  `change` DOUBLE NOT NULL
);
```

guess_table.pl produces that statement based on deductions such as the following:

- If a column contains only numeric values, it's assumed to be an INT if no values contain a decimal point, and DOUBLE otherwise.

- If a numeric column contains no negative values, the column is likely to be UNSIGNED.

- If a column contains no empty values, *guess_table.pl* assumes that it's probably NOT NULL.

- Columns that cannot be classified as numbers or dates are taken to be VARCHAR columns, with a length equal to the longest value present in the column.

You might want to edit the CREATE TABLE statement that *guess_table.pl* produces, to make modifications such as increasing the size of character fields, changing VARCHAR to CHAR, or adding indexes. Another reason to edit the statement is that if a column has a name that is a reserved word in MySQL, you can rename it.

To create the table, use the statement produced by *guess_table.pl*:

```
% mysql cookbook < stocks.sql
```

Then you can load the datafile into the table (skipping the initial row of labels):

```
mysql> LOAD DATA LOCAL INFILE 'tmp2.txt' INTO TABLE stocks
    -> IGNORE 1 LINES;
```

The resulting data after import looks like this:

```
mysql> SELECT * FROM stocks;
+-----------+------------+---------+--------+--------+
| commodity | trade_date | shares  | price  | change |
+-----------+------------+---------+--------+--------+
| sugar     | 2006-12-14 | 1000000 |   10.5 | -0.125 |
| oil       | 2006-12-14 |   96000 |  60.25 |   0.25 |
| wheat     | 2006-12-14 | 2500000 |   8.75 |      0 |
| gold      | 2006-12-14 |   13000 | 103.25 |   2.25 |
| sugar     | 2006-12-15 |  970000 |   10.6 |    0.1 |
| oil       | 2006-12-15 |  105000 |   60.5 |   0.25 |
| wheat     | 2006-12-15 | 2370000 |   8.65 |   -0.1 |
| gold      | 2006-12-15 |   11000 |    101 |  -2.25 |
+-----------+------------+---------+--------+--------+
```

10.37 Exchanging Data Between MySQL and Microsoft Access

Problem

You want to exchange information between MySQL and Access.

Solution

To use information stored in MySQL, connect to the MySQL server directly from Access. To transfer information from Access to MySQL, use a utility that can perform the transfer directly, or export tables from Access into files and import the files into MySQL.

Discussion

MySQL and Access both understand ODBC, so you can connect to MySQL directly from Access. By making an ODBC connection, Access becomes a frontend through which you use MySQL databases. The *mysql.com* Connector/ODBC area contains a lot of useful information:

http://www.mysql.com/products/connector/odbc/

An excellent description of the procedures for setting up ODBC and for connecting from Access to MySQL over ODBC can be found in W.J. Gilmore's article at the DevShed web site:

http://www.devshed.com/c/a/MySQL/MySQL-and-ODBC/

If your tables currently are in Access and you want to move them into MySQL, you'll need to create tables in MySQL to hold the information and then import the Access data into those tables. Gilmore's article describes how.

You can also choose to export Access tables to files and then import the files into MySQL. This may be necessary, for example, if your MySQL server is on a different machine and doesn't allow connections from your Windows box. If you elect to go this route, some of the issues you need to consider are the file format to use, date format conversion, and how to create the MySQL tables for the data if the tables don't already exist. Several of the scripts described earlier in the chapter (such as *cvt_file.pl*, *cvt_date.pl*, and *guess_table.pl*) can provide assistance in dealing with these issues. The procedure for importing an Access table into MySQL might go something like this:

1. Export the table from Access in some text format, perhaps including the column labels. Should you need to transform the file with other utilities that assume tab-delimited, linefeed-terminated input, it will be most useful to export in that format.

2. If the table contains dates and you did not export them in ISO format, you need to convert them for MySQL. Use *cvt_date.pl* for this.

3. If the MySQL table into which you want to import the Access data does not exist, create it. The *guess_table.pl* utility might be helpful at this point for generating a CREATE TABLE statement.

4. Import the datafile into MySQL with LOAD DATA or *mysqlimport*.

10.38 Exchanging Data Between MySQL and Microsoft Excel

Problem

You want to exchange information between MySQL and Excel.

Solution

Your programming language might provide modules to make this task easier. For example, there are Perl modules that read and write Excel spreadsheet files. You can use them to construct your own data transfer utilities.

Discussion

If you need to transfer Excel files into MySQL, check around for modules that let you do this from your chosen programming language. For example, you can read and write Excel spreadsheets from within Perl scripts by installing a few modules:

- Spreadsheet::ParseExcel::Simple provides an easy-to-use interface for reading Excel spreadsheets.

- Spreadsheet::WriteExcel::Simple enables you to create files in Excel spreadsheet format.

These Excel modules are available from the Perl CPAN. (They're actually frontends to other modules, which you also need to install as prerequisites.) After installing the modules, use these commands to read their documentation:

```
% perldoc Spreadsheet::ParseExcel::Simple
% perldoc Spreadsheet::WriteExcel::Simple
```

These modules make it relatively easy to write a couple of short scripts for converting spreadsheets to and from tab-delimited file format. Combined with techniques for importing and exporting data into and out of MySQL, these scripts can help you move spreadsheet contents to MySQL tables and vice versa. Use them as is, or adapt them to suit your own purposes.

The following script, *from_excel.pl*, reads an Excel spreadsheet and converts it to tab-delimited format:

```perl
#!/usr/bin/perl
# from_excel.pl - read Excel spreadsheet, write tab-delimited,
# linefeed-terminated output to the standard output.

use strict;
use warnings;
use Spreadsheet::ParseExcel::Simple;

@ARGV or die "Usage: $0 excel-file\n";

my $xls = Spreadsheet::ParseExcel::Simple->read ($ARGV[0]);
foreach my $sheet ($xls->sheets ())
{
  while ($sheet->has_data ())
  {
    my @data = $sheet->next_row ();
    print join ("\t", @data) . "\n";
  }
}
```

The *to_excel.pl* script performs the converse operation of reading a tab-delimited file and writing it in Excel format:

```perl
#!/usr/bin/perl
# to_excel.pl - read tab-delimited, linefeed-terminated input, write
# Excel-format output to the standard output.

use strict;
use warnings;
use Spreadsheet::WriteExcel::Simple;

my $ss = Spreadsheet::WriteExcel::Simple->new ();

while (<>)                              # read each row of input
{
  chomp;
  my @data = split (/\t/, $_, 10000); # split, preserving all fields
  $ss->write_row (\@data);            # write row to the spreadsheet
}
```

```
    binmode (STDOUT);
    print $ss->data (); # write the spreadsheet
```

to_excel.pl assumes input in tab-delimited, linefeed-terminated format. Use it in conjunction with *cvt_file.pl* to work with files that are not in that format.

Another Excel-related Perl module, Spreadsheet::WriteExcel::FromDB, reads data from a table using a DBI connection and writes it in Excel format. Here's a short script that exports a MySQL table as an Excel spreadsheet:

```perl
#!/usr/bin/perl
# mysql_to_excel.pl - given a database and table name,
# dump the table to the standard output in Excel format.

use strict;
use warnings;
use DBI;
use Spreadsheet::ParseExcel::Simple;
use Spreadsheet::WriteExcel::FromDB;

# ... process command-line options (not shown) ...

@ARGV == 2 or die "$usage\n";
my $db_name = shift (@ARGV);
my $tbl_name = shift (@ARGV);

# ... connect to database (not shown) ...

my $ss = Spreadsheet::WriteExcel::FromDB->read ($dbh, $tbl_name);
binmode (STDOUT);
print $ss->as_xls ();
```

Each of the three utilities writes to its standard output, which you can redirect to capture the results in a file:

```
% from_excel.pl data.xls > data.txt
% to_excel.pl data.txt > data.xls
% mysql_to_excel.pl cookbook profile > profile.xls
```

10.39 Exporting Query Results as XML

Problem

You want to export the result of a query as an XML document.

Solution

mysql can do that, or you can write your own exporter.

Discussion

You can use *mysql* to produce XML-format output from a query result (Recipe 1.20).

You can also write your own XML-export program. One way to do this is to issue the query and then write it out, adding all the XML markup yourself. But it's easier to install a few Perl modules and let them do the work:

- XML::Generator::DBI issues a query over a DBI connection and passes the result to a suitable output writer.
- XML::Handler::YAWriter provides one such writer.

The following script, *mysql_to_xml.pl*, is somewhat similar to *mysql_to_text.pl* (Recipe 10.17), but doesn't take options for such things as the quote or delimiter characters. They are unneeded for reading XML, because that is done by standard XML parsing routines. The options that *mysql_to_xml.pl* does understand are:

--execute=*query*, -e *query*
    Execute *query*, and export its output.

--table=*tbl_name*, -t *tbl_name*
    Export the contents of the named table. This is equivalent to using --execute to specify a *query* value of SELECT * FROM *tbl_name*.

If necessary, you can also specify standard connection parameter options such as --user or --host. The final argument on the command line should be the database name, unless it's implicit in the query.

Suppose that you want to export the contents of an experimental-data table expt that looks like this:

```
mysql> SELECT * FROM expt;
+---------+------+-------+
| subject | test | score |
+---------+------+-------+
| Jane    | A    |    47 |
| Jane    | B    |    50 |
| Jane    | C    |  NULL |
| Jane    | D    |  NULL |
| Marvin  | A    |    52 |
| Marvin  | B    |    45 |
| Marvin  | C    |    53 |
| Marvin  | D    |  NULL |
+---------+------+-------+
```

To do that, invoke *mysql_to_xml.pl* using either of the following commands:

```
% mysql_to_xml.pl --execute="SELECT * FROM expt" cookbook > expt.xml
% mysql_to_xml.pl --table=cookbook.expt > expt.xml
```

The resulting XML document, *expt.xml*, looks like this:

```
<?xml version="1.0" encoding="UTF-8"?>
<rowset>
```

```
<select query="SELECT * FROM expt">
 <row>
  <subject>Jane</subject>
  <test>A</test>
  <score>47</score>
 </row>
 <row>
  <subject>Jane</subject>
  <test>B</test>
  <score>50</score>
 </row>
 <row>
  <subject>Jane</subject>
  <test>C</test>
 </row>
 <row>
  <subject>Jane</subject>
  <test>D</test>
 </row>
 <row>
  <subject>Marvin</subject>
  <test>A</test>
  <score>52</score>
 </row>
 <row>
  <subject>Marvin</subject>
  <test>B</test>
  <score>45</score>
 </row>
 <row>
  <subject>Marvin</subject>
  <test>C</test>
  <score>53</score>
 </row>
 <row>
  <subject>Marvin</subject>
  <test>D</test>
 </row>
 </select>
</rowset>
```

Each table row is written as a `<row>` element. Within a row, column names and values are used as element names and values, one element per column. Note that NULL values are omitted from the output.

The script produces this output with very little code after it processes the command-line arguments and connects to the MySQL server. The XML-related parts of *mysql_to_xml.pl* are the use statements that pull in the necessary modules and the code to set up and use the XML objects. Given a database handle $dbh and a query string $query, there's not a lot to this process. The code instructs the writer object to send its results to the standard output, and then connects that object to DBI and issues the query:

```perl
#!/usr/bin/perl
# mysql_to_xml.pl - given a database and table name,
# dump the table to the standard output in XML format.

use strict;
use warnings;
use DBI;
use XML::Generator::DBI;
use XML::Handler::YAWriter;

# ... process command-line options (not shown) ...

# ... connect to database (not shown) ...

# create output writer; "-" means "standard output"
my $out = XML::Handler::YAWriter->new (AsFile => "-");
# set up connection between DBI and output writer
my $gen = XML::Generator::DBI->new (
            dbh => $dbh,              # database handle
            Handler => $out,          # output writer
            RootElement => "rowset"   # document root element
          );
# issue query and write XML
$gen->execute ($stmt);

$dbh->disconnect ();
```

Other languages might have library modules to perform similar XML export operations. For example, the Ruby DBI::Utils::XMLFormatter module has a `table` method that easily exports a query result as XML. Here's a simple script that uses it:

```ruby
#!/usr/bin/ruby -w
# xmlformatter.rb - demonstrate DBI::Utils::XMLFormatter.table method

require "Cookbook"

stmt = "SELECT * FROM expt"
# override statement with command line argument if one was given
stmt = ARGV[0] if ARGV.length > 0

begin
  dbh = Cookbook.connect
rescue DBI::DatabaseError => e
  puts "Could not connect to server"
  puts "Error code: #{e.err}"
  puts "Error message: #{e.errstr}"
end

DBI::Utils::XMLFormatter.table(dbh.select_all(stmt))

dbh.disconnect
```

10.40 Importing XML into MySQL

Problem

You want to import an XML document into a MySQL table.

Solution

Set up an XML parser to read the document. Then use the records in the document to construct and execute INSERT statements.

Discussion

Importing an XML document depends on being able to parse the document and extract record contents from it. The way that you do this depends on how the document is written. For example, one format might represent column names and values as attributes of <column> elements:

```
<?xml version="1.0" encoding="UTF-8"?>
<rowset>
  <row>
   <column name="subject" value="Jane" />
   <column name="test" value="A" />
   <column name="score" value="47" />
  </row>
  <row>
   <column name="subject" value="Jane" />
   <column name="test" value="B />
   <column name="score" value="50" />
  </row>
...
</rowset>
```

Another format uses column names as element names and column values as the contents of those elements:

```
<?xml version="1.0" encoding="UTF-8"?>
<rowset>
  <row>
   <subject>Jane</subject>
   <test>A</test>
   <score>47</score>
  </row>
  <row>
   <subject>Jane</subject>
   <test>B</test>
   <score>50</score>
  </row>
...
</rowset>
```

Due to the various structuring possibilities, it's necessary to make some assumptions about the format you expect the XML document to have. For the example here, I'll assume the second format just shown. One way to process this kind of document is to use the XML::XPath module, which enables you to refer to elements within the document using path expressions. For example, the path //row selects all the <row> elements under the document root, and the path * selects all child elements of a given element. You can use these paths with XML::XPath to obtain first a list of all the <row> elements, and then for each row a list of all its columns.

The following script, *xml_to_mysql.pl*, takes three arguments:

```
% xml_to_mysql.pl db_name tbl_name xml_file
```

The filename argument indicates which document to import, and the database and table name arguments indicate which table to import it into. *xml_to_mysql.pl* processes the command-line arguments, connects to MySQL, and then processes the document:

```perl
#!/usr/bin/perl
# xml_to_mysql.pl - read XML file into MySQL

use strict;
use warnings;
use DBI;
use XML::XPath;

# ... process command-line options (not shown) ...

# ... connect to database (not shown) ...

# Open file for reading
my $xp = XML::XPath->new (filename => $file_name);
my $row_list = $xp->find ("//row");      # find set of <row> elements
print "Number of records: " . $row_list->size () . "\n";
foreach my $row ($row_list->get_nodelist ())    # loop through rows
{
  my @name; # array for column names
  my @val;  # array for column values
  my $col_list = $row->find ("*");              # child columns of row
  foreach my $col ($col_list->get_nodelist ())  # loop through columns
  {
    # save column name and value
    push (@name, $col->getName ());
    push (@val, $col->string_value ());
  }
  # construct INSERT statement, and then execute it
  my $stmt = "INSERT INTO $tbl_name ("
        . join (",", @name)
        . ") VALUES ("
        . join (",", ("?") x scalar (@val))
        . ")";
  $dbh->do ($stmt, undef, @val);
}

$dbh->disconnect ();
```

The script creates an `XML::XPath` object, which opens and parses the document. Then the object is queried for the set of `<row>` elements, using the path `//row`. The size of this set indicates how many records the document contains.

To process each row, the script uses the path `*` to ask for all the child elements of the row object. Each child corresponds to a column within the row; using `*` as the path for `get_nodelist()` this way is convenient because you don't need to know in advance which columns to expect. *xml_to_mysql.pl* obtains the name and value from each column and saves them in the `@name` and `@value` arrays. After all the columns have been processed, the arrays are used to construct an `INSERT` statement that names those columns that were found to be present in the row and that includes a placeholder for each data value. (Recipe 2.5 discusses placeholder list construction.) Then the script issues the statement, passing the column values to `do()` to bind them to the placeholders.

In the previous section, we used *mysql_to_xml.pl* to export the contents of the `expt` table as an XML document. *xml_to_mysql.pl* can perform the converse operation of importing the document back into MySQL:

```
% xml_to_mysql.pl cookbook expt expt.xml
```

As it processes the document, the script generates and executes the following set of statements:

```
INSERT INTO expt (subject,test,score) VALUES ('Jane','A','47')
INSERT INTO expt (subject,test,score) VALUES ('Jane','B','50')
INSERT INTO expt (subject,test) VALUES ('Jane','C')
INSERT INTO expt (subject,test) VALUES ('Jane','D')
INSERT INTO expt (subject,test,score) VALUES ('Marvin','A','52')
INSERT INTO expt (subject,test,score) VALUES ('Marvin','B','45')
INSERT INTO expt (subject,test,score) VALUES ('Marvin','C','53')
INSERT INTO expt (subject,test) VALUES ('Marvin','D')
```

Note that these statements do not all insert the same number of columns. MySQL will set the missing columns to their default values.

10.41 Epilogue

Recall the scenario with which this chapter began:

Suppose that you have a file named *somedata.csv* that contains 12 columns of data in comma-separated values (CSV) format. From this file you want to extract only columns 2, 11, 5, and 9, and use them to create database rows in a MySQL table that contains `name`, `birth`, `height`, and `weight` columns. You need to make sure that the height and weight are positive integers, and convert the birth dates from *MM/DD/YY* format to *CCYY-MM-DD* format. How can you do this?

So...how *would* you do that, based on the techniques discussed in this chapter?

Much of the work can be done using the utility programs developed here. You can convert the file to tab-delimited format with *cvt_file.pl*, extract the columns in the desired order with *yank_col.pl*, and rewrite the date column to ISO format with *cvt_date.pl*:

```
% cvt_file.pl --iformat=csv somedata.csv \
    | yank_col.pl --columns=2,11,5,9 \
    | cvt_date.pl --columns=2 --iformat=us --add-century > tmp
```

The resulting file, *tmp*, will have four columns representing the name, birth, height, and weight values, in that order. It needs only to have its height and weight columns checked to make sure they contain positive integers. Using the is_positive_integer( ) library function from the *Cookbook_Utils.pm* module file, that task can be achieved using a short special-purpose script that isn't much more than an input loop:

```
#!/usr/bin/perl
# validate_htwt.pl - height/weight validation example

# Assumes tab-delimited, linefeed-terminated input lines.

# Input columns and the actions to perform on them are as follows:
# 1: name; echo as given
# 2: birth; echo as given
# 3: height; validate as positive integer
# 4: weight; validate as positive integer

use strict;
use warnings;
use Cookbook_Utils;

while (<>)
{
  chomp;
  my ($name, $birth, $height, $weight) = split (/\t/, $_, 4);
  warn "line $.:height $height is not a positive integer\n"
              if !is_positive_integer ($height);
  warn "line $.:weight $weight is not a positive integer\n"
              if !is_positive_integer ($weight);
}
```

The *validate_htwt.pl* script doesn't produce any output (except for warning messages) because it doesn't need to reformat any of the input values. Assuming that *tmp* passes validation with no errors, it can be loaded into MySQL with a simple LOAD DATA statement:

```
mysql> LOAD DATA LOCAL INFILE 'tmp' INTO TABLE tbl_name;
```

## CHAPTER 11

Generating and Using Sequences

11.0 Introduction

A sequence is a set of integers (1, 2, 3, ...) that are generated in order on demand. Sequences are frequently used in databases because many applications require each row in a table to contain a unique value, and sequences provide an easy way to generate them. This chapter describes how to use sequences in MySQL. It covers the following topics:

Using `AUTO_INCREMENT` columns to create sequences
> The `AUTO_INCREMENT` column is MySQL's mechanism for generating a sequence over a set of rows. Each time you create a row in a table that contains an `AUTO_INCREMENT` column, MySQL automatically generates the next value in the sequence as the column's value. This value serves as a unique identifier, making sequences an easy way to create items such as customer ID numbers, shipping package waybill numbers, invoice or purchase order numbers, bug report IDs, ticket numbers, or product serial numbers.

Retrieving sequence values
> For many applications, it's not enough just to create sequence values. It's also necessary to determine the sequence value for a just-inserted row. A web application may need to redisplay to a user the contents of a row created from the contents of a form just submitted by the user. The value may also need to be retrieved so it can be stored in rows of a related table.

Resequencing techniques
> This topic describes how to renumber a sequence that has holes in it due to row deletions, and also discusses reasons to avoid resequencing. Other topics include starting sequences at values other than 1 and adding a sequence column to a table that doesn't have one.

Using an `AUTO_INCREMENT` column to create multiple sequences
> In many cases, the `AUTO_INCREMENT` column in a table is independent of other columns, and its values increment throughout the table in a single monotonic sequence. However, if you create a multiple-column index that contains an

`AUTO_INCREMENT` column, you can use it to generate multiple sequences. For example, if you run a bulletin board that categorizes messages into topics, you can number messages sequentially within each topic by tying an `AUTO_INCREMENT` column to a topic indicator column.

Managing multiple simultaneous `AUTO_INCREMENT` values
Special care is necessary when you need to keep track of multiple sequence values. This can occur when you issue a set of statements that affect a single table or when creating rows in multiple tables that each have an `AUTO_INCREMENT` column. This topic describes what to do in these cases.

Using single-row sequence generators
Sequences also can be used as counters. For example, if you serve banner ads on your web site, you might increment a counter for each impression (that is, for each time you serve an ad). The counts for a given ad form a sequence, but because the count itself is the only value of interest, there is no need to generate a new row to record each impression. MySQL provides a solution for this problem using a mechanism that enables a sequence to be easily generated within a single table row over time. To store multiple counters in the table, add a column that identifies each counter uniquely. The same mechanism also enables creation of sequences that increase by values other than one, by nonuniform values, or even by negative increments.

Numbering query output rows sequentially
This topic suggests ways to generate display-only sequences for the purpose of numbering the rows of output from a query.

The engines for most database systems provide sequence-generation capabilities, although the implementations tend to be engine-dependent. That's true for MySQL as well, so the material in this section is almost completely MySQL-specific, even at the SQL level. In other words, the SQL for generating sequences is itself nonportable, even if you use an API such as DBI or JDBC that provides an abstraction layer. Abstract interfaces may help you process SQL statements portably, but they don't make nonportable SQL portable.

Scripts related to the examples shown in this chapter are located in the *sequences* directory of the `recipes` distribution. For scripts that create the tables used here, look in the *tables* directory.

11.1 Creating a Sequence Column and Generating Sequence Values

Problem

You want to include a sequence column in a table.

Solution

Use an AUTO_INCREMENT column.

Discussion

This section provides the basic background on how AUTO_INCREMENT columns work, beginning with a short example that demonstrates the sequence-generation mechanism. The illustration centers around a bug-collection scenario: your son (eight-year-old Junior) is assigned the task of collecting insects for a class project at school. For each insect, Junior is to record its name ("ant," "bee," and so forth), and its date and location of collection. You have expounded the benefits of MySQL for record-keeping to Junior since his early days, so upon your arrival home from work that day, he immediately announces the necessity of completing this project and then, looking you straight in the eye, declares that it's clearly a task for which MySQL is well-suited. Who are you to argue? So the two of you get to work. Junior already collected some specimens after school while waiting for you to come home and has recorded the following information in his notebook:

Name	Date	Origin
millipede	2006-09-10	driveway
housefly	2006-09-10	kitchen
grasshopper	2006-09-10	front yard
stink bug	2006-09-10	front yard
cabbage butterfly	2006-09-10	garden
ant	2006-09-10	back yard
ant	2006-09-10	back yard
millbug	2006-09-10	under rock

Looking over Junior's notes, you're pleased to see that even at his tender age, he has learned to write dates in ISO format. However, you also notice that he's collected a millipede and a millbug, neither of which actually are insects. You decide to let this pass for the moment; Junior forgot to bring home the written instructions for the project, so at this point it's unclear whether these specimens are acceptable.

As you consider how to create a table to store this information, it's apparent that you need at least name, date, and origin columns corresponding to the types of information that Junior is required to record:

```
CREATE TABLE insect
(
  name    VARCHAR(30) NOT NULL,   # type of insect
  date    DATE NOT NULL,          # date collected
  origin  VARCHAR(30) NOT NULL    # where collected
);
```

However, those columns are not enough to make the table easy to use. Note that the records collected thus far are not unique; both ants were collected at the same time and place. If you put the information into an `insect` table that has the structure just shown, neither ant row can be referred to individually, because there's nothing to distinguish them from one another. Unique IDs would be helpful to make the rows distinct and to provide values that make each row easy to refer to. An `AUTO_INCREMENT` column is good for this purpose, so a better `insect` table has a structure like this:

```
CREATE TABLE insect
(
  id      INT UNSIGNED NOT NULL AUTO_INCREMENT,
  PRIMARY KEY (id),
  name    VARCHAR(30) NOT NULL,    # type of insect
  date    DATE NOT NULL,           # date collected
  origin  VARCHAR(30) NOT NULL     # where collected
);
```

Go ahead and create the `insect` table using this second definition. In Recipe 11.2, we'll discuss the specifics of why the `id` column is declared the way it is.

Now that you have an `AUTO_INCREMENT` column, you want to use it to generate new sequence values. One of the useful properties of an `AUTO_INCREMENT` column is that you don't have to assign its values yourself: MySQL does so for you. There are two ways to generate new `AUTO_INCREMENT` values, demonstrated here using the `id` column of the `insect` table. First, you can explicitly set the `id` column to `NULL`. The following statement inserts the first four of Junior's specimens into the `insect` table this way:

```
mysql> INSERT INTO insect (id,name,date,origin) VALUES
    -> (NULL,'housefly','2006-09-10','kitchen'),
    -> (NULL,'millipede','2006-09-10','driveway'),
    -> (NULL,'grasshopper','2006-09-10','front yard'),
    -> (NULL,'stink bug','2006-09-10','front yard');
```

Second, you can omit the `id` column from the `INSERT` statement entirely. In MySQL, you can create new rows without explicitly specifying values for columns that have a default value. MySQL assigns the default value to each missing column automatically, and the default for an `AUTO_INCREMENT` column happens to be the next sequence number. Thus, you can insert rows into the `insect` table without naming the `id` column at all. This statement adds Junior's other four specimens to the `insect` table that way:

```
mysql> INSERT INTO insect (name,date,origin) VALUES
    -> ('cabbage butterfly','2006-09-10','garden'),
    -> ('ant','2006-09-10','back yard'),
    -> ('ant','2006-09-10','back yard'),
    -> ('millbug','2006-09-10','under rock');
```

Whichever method you use, MySQL determines the next sequence number for each row and assigns it to the `id` column, as you can verify for yourself:

```
mysql> SELECT * FROM insect ORDER BY id;
+----+-------------------+------------+------------+
| id | name              | date       | origin     |
+----+-------------------+------------+------------+
```

```
| 1 | housefly          | 2006-09-10 | kitchen    |
| 2 | millipede         | 2006-09-10 | driveway   |
| 3 | grasshopper       | 2006-09-10 | front yard |
| 4 | stink bug         | 2006-09-10 | front yard |
| 5 | cabbage butterfly | 2006-09-10 | garden     |
| 6 | ant               | 2006-09-10 | back yard  |
| 7 | ant               | 2006-09-10 | back yard  |
| 8 | millbug           | 2006-09-10 | under rock |
+---+-------------------+------------+------------+
```

As Junior collects more specimens, you can add more rows to the table and they'll be assigned the next values in the sequence (9, 10, ...).

The concept underlying AUTO_INCREMENT columns is simple enough in principle: each time you create a new row, MySQL generates the next number in the sequence and assigns it to the row. But there are certain subtleties to know about, as well as differences in how AUTO_INCREMENT sequences are handled for different storage engines. By being aware of these issues, you can use sequences more effectively and avoid surprises. For example, if you explicitly set the id column to a non-NULL value, one of two things happens:

- If the value is already present in the table, an error occurs if the column cannot contain duplicates. For the insect table, the id column is a PRIMARY KEY, so duplicates are not allowed:

  ```
  mysql> INSERT INTO insect (id,name,date,origin) VALUES
      -> (3,'cricket','2006-09-11','basement');
  ERROR 1062 (23000): Duplicate entry '3' for key 1
  ```

- If the value is not present in the table, MySQL inserts the row using that value. In addition, if the value is larger than the current sequence counter, the table's counter is reset to the value plus one. The insect table at this point has sequence values 1 through 8. If you insert a new row with the id column set to 20, that becomes the new maximum value. Subsequent inserts that automatically generate id values will begin at 21. The values 9 through 19 become unused, resulting in a gap in the sequence.

The next recipe looks in more detail at how to define AUTO_INCREMENT columns and how they behave.

11.2 Choosing the Data Type for a Sequence Column

Problem

You want to know more about how to define a sequence column.

Solution

Use the guidelines given here.

Discussion

You should follow certain guidelines when creating an `AUTO_INCREMENT` column. As an illustration, consider how the `id` column in the `insect` table was declared:

```
id INT UNSIGNED NOT NULL AUTO_INCREMENT,
PRIMARY KEY (id)
```

The `AUTO_INCREMENT` keyword informs MySQL that it should generate successive sequence numbers for the column's values, but the other information is important, too:

- `INT` is the column's base data type. You need not necessarily use `INT`, but the column must be one of the integer types: `TINYINT`, `SMALLINT`, `MEDIUMINT`, `INT`, or `BIGINT`. It's important to remember that `AUTO_INCREMENT` is a column attribute that should be applied *only* to integer types.

- The column is declared as `UNSIGNED` to disallow negative values. This is not a requirement for an `AUTO_INCREMENT` column. However, there is no reason to allow negative values because sequences consist only of positive integers (normally beginning at 1). Furthermore, *not* declaring the column to be `UNSIGNED` cuts the range of your sequence in half. For example, `TINYINT` has a range of −128 to 127. Sequences include only positive values, so the range of a `TINYINT` sequence would be 1 to 127. The range of a `TINYINT UNSIGNED` column is 0 to 255, which increases the upper end of the sequence to 255. The maximum sequence value is determined by the specific integer type used, so you should choose a type that is big enough to hold the largest value you'll need. The maximum unsigned value of each integer type is shown in the following table, which you can use to select an appropriate type.

Data type	Maximum unsigned value
TINYINT	255
SMALLINT	65,535
MEDIUMINT	16,777,215
INT	4,294,967,295
BIGINT	18,446,744,073,709,551,615

Sometimes people omit `UNSIGNED` so that they can create rows that contain negative numbers in the sequence column. (Using −1 to signify "has no ID" is an instance of this.) This is a bad idea. MySQL makes no guarantees about how negative numbers will be treated in an `AUTO_INCREMENT` column, so you're playing with fire if you try to use them. For example, if you resequence the column, you'll find that all your negative values get turned into positive sequence numbers.

- `AUTO_INCREMENT` columns cannot contain `NULL` values, so `id` is declared as `NOT NULL`. (It's true that you can specify `NULL` as the column value when you insert a new row, but for an `AUTO_INCREMENT` column, that really means "generate the next sequence

---

value.") MySQL automatically defines `AUTO_INCREMENT` columns as `NOT NULL` if you forget to.

- `AUTO_INCREMENT` columns must be indexed. Normally, because a sequence column exists to provide unique identifiers, you use a `PRIMARY KEY` or `UNIQUE` index to enforce uniqueness. Tables can have only one `PRIMARY KEY`, so if the table already has some other `PRIMARY KEY` column, you can declare an `AUTO_INCREMENT` column to have a `UNIQUE` index instead:

```
id INT UNSIGNED NOT NULL AUTO_INCREMENT,
UNIQUE (id)
```

If the `AUTO_INCREMENT` column is the only column in the `PRIMARY KEY` or `UNIQUE` index, you can declare it as such in the column definition rather than in a separate clause. For example, these definitions are equivalent:

```
id INT UNSIGNED NOT NULL AUTO_INCREMENT,
PRIMARY KEY (id)
```

```
id INT UNSIGNED NOT NULL AUTO_INCREMENT PRIMARY KEY
```

As are these:

```
id INT UNSIGNED NOT NULL AUTO_INCREMENT UNIQUE
```

```
id INT UNSIGNED NOT NULL AUTO_INCREMENT,
UNIQUE (id)
```

Using a separate clause to specify the index helps to emphasize that it's not, strictly speaking, part of the column definition.

When you create a table that contains an `AUTO_INCREMENT` column, it's also important to consider which storage engine to use (MyISAM, InnoDB, and so forth). The engine affects behaviors such as reuse of values that are deleted from the top of the sequence and whether you can set the initial sequence value. In general, MyISAM is the best storage engine for tables that contain `AUTO_INCREMENT` columns because it offers the greatest flexibility for sequence management. This will become apparent in the rest of the chapter.

11.3 The Effect of Row Deletions on Sequence Generation

Problem

You want to know what happens to a sequence when you delete rows from a table that contains an `AUTO_INCREMENT` column.

Solution

It depends on which rows you delete and on the storage engine.

Discussion

We have thus far considered how sequence values in an AUTO_INCREMENT column are generated for circumstances where rows are only added to a table. But it's unrealistic to assume that rows will never be deleted. What happens to the sequence then?

Refer again to Junior's bug-collection project, for which you currently have an insect table that looks like this:

```
mysql> SELECT * FROM insect ORDER BY id;
+----+------------------+------------+------------+
| id | name             | date       | origin     |
+----+------------------+------------+------------+
|  1 | housefly         | 2006-09-10 | kitchen    |
|  2 | millipede        | 2006-09-10 | driveway   |
|  3 | grasshopper      | 2006-09-10 | front yard |
|  4 | stink bug        | 2006-09-10 | front yard |
|  5 | cabbage butterfly| 2006-09-10 | garden     |
|  6 | ant              | 2006-09-10 | back yard  |
|  7 | ant              | 2006-09-10 | back yard  |
|  8 | millbug          | 2006-09-10 | under rock |
+----+------------------+------------+------------+
```

That's about to change because after Junior remembers to bring home the written instructions for the project, you read through them and discover two things that affect the insect table's contents:

- Specimens should include only insects, not other insect-like creatures such as millipedes and millbugs.

- The purpose of the project is to collect as many *different* specimens as possible, not just *as many* specimens as possible. This means that only one ant row is allowed.

These instructions require that a few rows be removed from the insect table—specifically those with id values 2 (millipede), 8 (millbug), and 7 (duplicate ant). Thus, despite Junior's evident disappointment at the reduction in the size of his collection, you instruct him to remove those rows by issuing a DELETE statement:

```
mysql> DELETE FROM insect WHERE id IN (2,8,7);
```

This statement illustrates one reason why it's useful to have unique ID values: they enable you to specify any row unambiguously. The ant rows are identical except for the id value. Without that column in the insect table, it would be more difficult to delete just one of them.

After the unsuitable rows have been removed, the resulting table contents become:

```
mysql> SELECT * FROM insect ORDER BY id;
+----+------------------+------------+------------+
| id | name             | date       | origin     |
+----+------------------+------------+------------+
|  1 | housefly         | 2006-09-10 | kitchen    |
|  3 | grasshopper      | 2006-09-10 | front yard |
```

```
| 4 | stink bug          | 2006-09-10 | front yard |
| 5 | cabbage butterfly  | 2006-09-10 | garden     |
| 6 | ant                | 2006-09-10 | back yard  |
+----+-------------------+-----------+------------+
```

The sequence in the `id` column now has a hole (row 2 is missing) and the values 7 and 8 at the top of the sequence are no longer present. How do these deletions affect future insert operations? What sequence number will the next new row get?

Removing row 2 created a gap in the middle of the sequence. This has no effect on subsequent inserts, because MySQL makes no attempt to fill in holes in a sequence. On the other hand, deleting rows 7 and 8 removes values at the top of the sequence, and the effect of this depends on the storage engine:

- With BDB tables, the next sequence number always is the maximum integer currently present in the column plus one. If you delete rows containing values at the top of the sequence, those values will be reused. (Thus, after deleting rows with values 7 and 8, the next inserted row will be assigned the value 7.)

- For MyISAM or InnoDB tables, values are not reused. The next sequence number is the smallest positive integer that has not previously been used. (For a sequence that stands at 8, the next row gets a value of 9 even if you delete rows 7 and 8 first.) If you require strictly monotonic sequences, you should use one of these storage engines.

If a table uses an engine that differs in value-reuse behavior from the behavior you require, use `ALTER TABLE` to change the table to a more appropriate engine. For example, if you want to change a BDB table to be a MyISAM table (to prevent sequence values from being reused after rows are deleted), do this:

```
ALTER TABLE tbl_name ENGINE = MyISAM;
```

If you don't know what engine a table uses, consult `INFORMATION_SCHEMA` or use `SHOW TABLE STATUS` or `SHOW CREATE TABLE` to find out. For example, the following statement indicates that `insect` is a MyISAM table:

```
mysql> SELECT ENGINE FROM INFORMATION_SCHEMA.TABLES
    -> WHERE TABLE_SCHEMA = 'cookbook' AND TABLE_NAME = 'insect';
+--------+
| ENGINE |
+--------+
| MyISAM |
+--------+
```

 In this chapter, you can assume that if a table's definition has no explicit storage engine, it's a MyISAM table.

If you want to clear out a table and reset the sequence counter, use `TRUNCATE TABLE`:

```
TRUNCATE TABLE tbl_name;
```

11.4 Retrieving Sequence Values

Problem

After creating a row that includes a new sequence number, you want to find out what that number is.

Solution

Issue a `SELECT LAST_INSERT_ID( )` statement. If you're writing a program, your MySQL API may provide a way to get the value directly without issuing a statement.

Discussion

Many applications need to determine the `AUTO_INCREMENT` value of a newly created row. For example, if you get ambitious and write a web-based frontend for entering rows into Junior's `insect` table, you might have the application display each new row nicely formatted in a new page immediately after you hit the Submit button. To do this, you need to know the new `id` value so that you can retrieve the proper row. Another common situation in which the `AUTO_INCREMENT` value is needed occurs when you're using multiple tables: after inserting a row in a master table, typically, you'll need its ID so that you can create rows in other related tables that refer to the master row. (Recipe 11.13 shows how to relate multiple tables using sequence numbers.)

When you generate a new `AUTO_INCREMENT` value, you can get the value from the server by issuing a statement that invokes the `LAST_INSERT_ID( )` function. In addition, many MySQL APIs provide a client-side mechanism for making the value available without issuing another statement. This recipe discusses both methods and provides a comparison of their characteristics.

Using LAST_INSERT_ID( ) to obtain AUTO_INCREMENT values

The obvious (but incorrect) way to determine a new row's `AUTO_INCREMENT` value is based on the fact that when MySQL generates the value, it becomes the largest sequence number in the column. Thus, you might try using the `MAX( )` function to retrieve it:

```
SELECT MAX(id) FROM insect;
```

This is unreliable because it doesn't take into account the multithreaded nature of the MySQL server. The `SELECT` statement does indeed return the maximum `id` value from the table, but it may not be the value that *you* generated. Suppose that you insert a row that generates an `id` value of 9. If another client inserts a row before you issue the `SELECT` statement, `MAX(id)` returns 10, not 9. Methods for solving this problem include grouping the INSERT and SELECT statements as a transaction or locking the table, but MySQL provides a LAST_INSERT_ID( ) function as a simpler way to obtain the proper value. It returns the most recent AUTO_INCREMENT value that you generated during the time you've been connected to the server, regardless of what other clients are doing. For example, you can insert a row into the insect table and then retrieve its id value like this:

```
mysql> INSERT INTO insect (name,date,origin)
    -> VALUES('cricket','2006-09-11','basement');
mysql> SELECT LAST_INSERT_ID();
+------------------+
| LAST_INSERT_ID() |
+------------------+
|                9 |
+------------------+
```

Or you can use the new value to retrieve the entire row, without even knowing what the id is:

```
mysql> INSERT INTO insect (name,date,origin)
    -> VALUES('moth','2006-09-14','windowsill');
mysql> SELECT * FROM insect WHERE id = LAST_INSERT_ID();
+----+------+------------+------------+
| id | name | date       | origin     |
+----+------+------------+------------+
| 10 | moth | 2006-09-14 | windowsill |
+----+------+------------+------------+
```

Can Other Clients Change the Value Returned by LAST_INSERT_ID( )?

You might ask this question if you're concerned about the possibility of getting the wrong value from LAST_INSERT_ID( ) when other clients happen to generate AUTO_INCREMENT values at about the same time you do. There's nothing to worry about. The value returned by LAST_INSERT_ID( ) is maintained by the server on a connection-specific basis. This property is important because it prevents clients from interfering with each other. When you generate an AUTO_INCREMENT value, LAST_INSERT_ID( ) returns that specific value, even when other clients generate new rows in the same table in the meantime. This behavior is by design.

Using API-specific methods to obtain AUTO_INCREMENT values

LAST_INSERT_ID( ) is an SQL function, so you can use it from within any client that understands how to issue SQL statements. On the other hand, you do have to issue a separate statement to get its value. If you're writing your own programs, you may have another choice. Many MySQL interfaces include an API-specific extension that returns the AUTO_INCREMENT value without issuing another statement. Most of our APIs have this capability.

Perl

Use the `mysql_insertid` attribute to obtain the `AUTO_INCREMENT` value generated by a statement. This attribute is accessed through either a database handle or a statement handle, depending on how you issue the statement. The following example references it through the database handle:

```
$dbh->do ("INSERT INTO insect (name,date,origin)
        VALUES('moth','2006-09-14','windowsill')");
my $seq = $dbh->{mysql_insertid};
```

If you're using `prepare( )` and `execute( )`, access `mysql_insertid` as a statement handle attribute:

```
my $sth = $dbh->prepare ("INSERT INTO insect (name,date,origin)
                        VALUES('moth','2006-09-14','windowsill')");
$sth->execute ();
my $seq = $sth->{mysql_insertid};
```

If you find that the value of the `mysql_insertid` attribute is always undefined or zero, you probably have an old version of DBD::mysql that doesn't support it. Try using the `insertid` attribute instead. (`insertid` is available only as a database handle attribute.)

Ruby

The Ruby DBI driver for MySQL exposes the client-side `AUTO_INCREMENT` value using the database handle `func` method that returns driver-specific values:

```
dbh.do("INSERT INTO insect (name,date,origin)
        VALUES('moth','2006-09-14','windowsill')")
seq = dbh.func(:insert_id)
```

PHP

The native PHP interface for MySQL includes a function that returns the most recent `AUTO_INCREMENT` value, but the PEAR DB interface does not. On the other hand, PEAR DB does have its own sequence generation mechanism that you can use instead. See the PEAR documentation for details.

Python

The MySQLdb driver for DB-API provides an `insert_id( )` connection object method for getting the sequence value after you execute a statement that generates an `AUTO_INCREMENT` value:

```
cursor = conn.cursor ()
cursor.execute ("""
                INSERT INTO insect (name,date,origin)
                VALUES('moth','2006-09-14','windowsill')
                """)
seq = conn.insert_id ()
```

Java

The MySQL Connector/J JDBC driver provides a `getLastInsertID( )` method for obtaining `AUTO_INCREMENT` values. It can be used with either `Statement` or `Prepared Statement` objects. This example uses a `Statement`:

```
Statement s = conn.createStatement ();
s.executeUpdate ("INSERT INTO insect (name,date,origin)"
                + " VALUES('moth','2006-09-14','windowsill')");
long seq = ((com.mysql.jdbc.Statement) s).getLastInsertID ();
s.close ();
```

Note that because `getLastInsertID( )` is driver-specific, you access it by casting the `Statement` object to the `com.mysql.jdbc.Statement` type. If you're using a `Prepared Statement` object, cast it to the `com.mysql.jdbc.PreparedStatement` type instead:

```
PreparedStatement s = conn.prepareStatement (
                "INSERT INTO insect (name,date,origin)"
                + " VALUES('moth','2006-09-14','windowsill')");
s.executeUpdate ();
long seq = ((com.mysql.jdbc.PreparedStatement) s).getLastInsertID ();
s.close ();
```

Server-side and client-side sequence value retrieval compared

As mentioned earlier, the value of `LAST_INSERT_ID( )` is maintained on a connection-specific basis on the server side of the MySQL connection. By contrast, the API-specific methods for accessing `AUTO_INCREMENT` values directly are implemented on the client side. Server-side and client-side sequence value retrieval methods have some similarities, but also some differences.

All methods, both server-side and client-side, require that you must access the `AUTO_INCREMENT` value using the same MySQL connection that was used to generate the value in the first place. If you generate an `AUTO_INCREMENT` value, and then disconnect from the server and reconnect before attempting to access the value, you'll get zero. Within a given connection, the persistence of `AUTO_INCREMENT` values can be much longer on the server side of the connection:

- After you issue a statement that generates an `AUTO_INCREMENT` value, the value remains available through `LAST_INSERT_ID( )` even if you issue other statements, as long as none of those statements generate an `AUTO_INCREMENT` value.

- The sequence value available on the client side typically is set for *every* statement, not just those that generate `AUTO_INCREMENT` values. If you issue an `INSERT` statement that generates a new value and then issue some other statement before accessing the client-side sequence value, it probably will have been set to zero. The precise behavior varies among APIs, but if you use the following general guideline, you should be safe: when a statement generates a sequence value that you won't be using immediately, save the value in a variable that you can refer to later. Otherwise, you may find that the sequence value has been wiped out when you do try to access it.

11.5 Renumbering an Existing Sequence

Problem

You have gaps in a sequence column, and you want to resequence it.

Solution

Don't bother. Or at least don't do so without a good reason, of which there are very few.

Discussion

If you insert rows into a table that has an AUTO_INCREMENT column and never delete any of them, values in the column form an unbroken sequence. But if you delete rows, the sequence begins to have holes in it. For example, Junior's insect table currently looks something like this, with gaps in the sequence (assuming that you've inserted the cricket and moth rows shown in the preceding section on retrieving sequence values):

```
mysql> SELECT * FROM insect ORDER BY id;
+----+------------------+------------+-----------+
| id | name             | date       | origin    |
+----+------------------+------------+-----------+
|  1 | housefly         | 2006-09-10 | kitchen   |
|  3 | grasshopper      | 2006-09-10 | front yard |
|  4 | stink bug        | 2006-09-10 | front yard |
|  5 | cabbage butterfly | 2006-09-10 | garden    |
|  6 | ant              | 2006-09-10 | back yard |
|  9 | cricket          | 2006-09-11 | basement  |
| 10 | moth             | 2006-09-14 | windowsill |
+----+------------------+------------+-----------+
```

MySQL won't attempt to eliminate these gaps by filling in the unused values when you insert new rows. People who don't like this behavior tend to resequence AUTO_INCREMENT columns periodically to eliminate the holes. The next few recipes show how to do that. It's also possible to extend the range of an existing sequence, add a sequence column to a table that doesn't currently have one, force deleted values at the top of a sequence to be reused, or specify an initial sequence value when creating or resequencing a table.

Before you decide to resequence an AUTO_INCREMENT column, consider whether you really want or need to do so. It's unnecessary in most cases. In fact, renumbering a sequence sometimes can cause you real problems. For example, you should *not* resequence a column containing values that are referenced by another table. Renumbering the values destroys their correspondence to values in the other table, making it impossible to properly relate rows in the two tables to each other.

Here are reasons that I have seen advanced for resequencing a column:

Aesthetics

Sometimes the desire to renumber a column is for aesthetic reasons. People seem to prefer unbroken sequences to sequences with holes in them. If this is why you want to resequence, there's probably not much I can say to convince you otherwise. Nevertheless, it's not a particularly good reason.

Performance

The impetus for resequencing may stem from the notion that doing so "compacts" a sequence column by removing gaps and enables MySQL to run statements more quickly. This is not true. MySQL doesn't care whether there are holes, and there is no performance gain to be had by renumbering an `AUTO_INCREMENT` column. In fact, resequencing affects performance negatively in the sense that the table remains locked while MySQL performs the operation—which may take a nontrivial amount of time for a large table. Other clients can read from the table while this is happening, but clients that are trying to insert new rows must wait until the operation is complete.

Running out of numbers

The upper limit of a sequence column is determined by the column's data type. If an `AUTO_INCREMENT` sequence is approaching the upper limit of its data type, renumbering packs the sequence and frees up more values at the top. This may be a legitimate reason to resequence a column, but it is still unnecessary in many cases to do so. You may be able to expand the column's range to increase its upper limit without changing the values stored in the column. (See Recipe 11.6.)

If you're determined to resequence a column, despite my advice not to, it's easy to do: drop the column from the table; then put it back. MySQL will renumber the values in the column in unbroken sequence. The following example shows how to renumber the `id` values in the `insect` table using this technique:

```
mysql> ALTER TABLE insect DROP id;
mysql> ALTER TABLE insect
    -> ADD id INT UNSIGNED NOT NULL AUTO_INCREMENT FIRST,
    -> ADD PRIMARY KEY (id);
```

The first `ALTER TABLE` statement gets rid of the `id` column (and as a result also drops the `PRIMARY KEY`, because the column to which it refers is no longer present). The second statement restores the column to the table and establishes it as the `PRIMARY KEY`. (The `FIRST` keyword places the column first in the table, which is where it was originally. Normally, `ADD` puts columns at the end of the table.) When you add an `AUTO_INCREMENT` column to a table, MySQL automatically numbers all the rows consecutively, so the resulting contents of the `insect` table look like this:

```
mysql> SELECT * FROM insect ORDER BY id;
+----+-------------------+------------+------------+
| id | name              | date       | origin     |
+----+-------------------+------------+------------+
|  1 | housefly          | 2006-09-10 | kitchen    |
|  2 | grasshopper       | 2006-09-10 | front yard |
```

```
|  3 | stink bug         | 2006-09-10 | front yard |
|  4 | cabbage butterfly | 2006-09-10 | garden     |
|  5 | ant               | 2006-09-10 | back yard  |
|  6 | cricket           | 2006-09-11 | basement   |
|  7 | moth              | 2006-09-14 | windowsill |
+----+-------------------+------------+------------+
```

One problem with resequencing a column using separate ALTER TABLE statements is that the table will be without that column for the interval between the two operations. This might cause difficulties for other clients that try to access the table during that time. To prevent this from happening, perform both operations with a single ALTER TABLE statement:

```
mysql> ALTER TABLE insect
    -> DROP id,
    -> ADD id INT UNSIGNED NOT NULL AUTO_INCREMENT FIRST;
```

MySQL permits multiple actions to be done with ALTER TABLE (something not true for all database systems). However, notice that this multiple-action statement is not simply a concatenation of the two single-action ALTER TABLE statements. The difference is that it is unnecessary to reestablish the PRIMARY KEY: MySQL doesn't drop it unless the indexed column is missing after all the actions specified in the ALTER TABLE statement have been performed.

11.6 Extending the Range of a Sequence Column

Problem

You want to avoid resequencing a column, but you're running out of room for new sequence numbers.

Solution

Check whether you can make the column UNSIGNED, or change the column to use a larger integer type.

Discussion

Resequencing an AUTO_INCREMENT column changes the contents of potentially every row in the table. It's often possible to avoid this by extending the range of the column, which changes the table's structure rather than its contents:

- If the data type is signed, make it UNSIGNED, and you'll double the range of available values. Suppose that you have an id column that currently is defined like this:

    ```
    id MEDIUMINT NOT NULL AUTO_INCREMENT
    ```

    The upper range of a signed MEDIUMINT column is 8,388,607. This can be increased to 16,777,215 by making the column UNSIGNED with ALTER TABLE:

```
ALTER TABLE tbl_name MODIFY id MEDIUMINT UNSIGNED NOT NULL AUTO_INCREMENT;
```

- If your column is already UNSIGNED and it is not already the largest integer type (BIGINT), converting it to a larger type increases its range. You can use ALTER TABLE for this, too. For example, the id column in the previous example can be converted from MEDIUMINT to BIGINT like so:

```
ALTER TABLE tbl_name MODIFY id BIGINT UNSIGNED NOT NULL AUTO_INCREMENT;
```

Recipe 11.2 includes a table that shows the ranges for each integer data type. You might find it helpful in assessing which type to use.

11.7 Reusing Values at the Top of a Sequence

Problem

You've deleted rows at the top end of your sequence. Can you avoid resequencing the column but still reuse the values that have been deleted?

Solution

Yes, use ALTER TABLE to reset the sequence counter. MySQL will generate new sequence numbers beginning with the value that is one larger than the current maximum in the table.

Discussion

If you have removed rows only from the top of the sequence, those that remain will still be in order with no gaps. (For example, if you have rows numbered 1 to 100 and you remove the rows with numbers 91 to 100, the remaining rows are still in unbroken sequence from 1 to 90.) In this special case, it's unnecessary to renumber the column. Instead, just tell MySQL to resume the sequence beginning with the value one larger that the highest existing sequence number. For BDB tables, that's the default behavior anyway, so the deleted values are reused with no additional action on your part. For MyISAM or InnoDB tables, issue the following statement:

```
ALTER TABLE tbl_name AUTO_INCREMENT = 1;
```

This causes MySQL to reset the sequence counter down as far as it can for creating new rows in the future.

You can use ALTER TABLE to reset the sequence counter if a sequence column contains gaps in the middle, but doing so still will reuse only values deleted from the top of the sequence. It will not eliminate the gaps. Suppose that you have a table with sequence values from 1 to 10 and then delete the rows for values 3, 4, 5, 9, and 10. The maximum remaining value is 8, so if you use ALTER TABLE to reset the sequence counter, the next row will be given a value of 9, not 3. To resequence a table and eliminate the gaps as well, see Recipe 11.5.

11.8 Ensuring That Rows Are Renumbered in a Particular Order

Problem

You resequenced a column, but MySQL didn't number the rows the way you want.

Solution

Select the rows into another table, using an ORDER BY clause to place them in the order you want, and let MySQL number them as it performs the operation. Then the rows will be numbered according to the sort order.

Discussion

When you resequence an AUTO_INCREMENT column, MySQL is free to pick the rows from the table in any order, so it won't necessarily renumber them in the order that you expect. This doesn't matter at all if your only requirement is that each row have a unique identifier. But you might have an application for which it's important that the rows be assigned sequence numbers in a particular order. For example, you may want the sequence to correspond to the order in which rows were created, as indicated by a TIMESTAMP column. To assign numbers in a particular order, use this procedure:

1. Create an empty clone of the table (see Recipe 4.1).
2. Copy rows from the original into the clone using INSERT INTO … SELECT. Copy all columns except the sequence column, using an ORDER BY clause to specify the order in which rows are copied (and thus assigned sequence numbers).
3. Drop the original table and rename the clone to have the original table's name.
4. If the table is a large MyISAM table and has multiple indexes, it will be more efficient to create the new table initially with no indexes except the one on the AUTO_INCREMENT column. Then copy the original table into the new table and add the remaining indexes afterward.

An alternative procedure:

1. Create a new table that contains all the columns of the original table except the AUTO_INCREMENT column.
2. Use INSERT INTO … SELECT to copy the non-AUTO_INCREMENT columns from the original table into the new table.
3. Delete the rows from the original table, and reset the sequence counter to 1 if necessary.

4. Copy rows from the new table back to the original table, using an ORDER BY clause to sort rows into the order in which you want sequence numbers assigned. MyISAM will assign sequence values to the AUTO_INCREMENT column.

11.9 Starting a Sequence at a Particular Value

Problem

Sequences start at 1, but you want to use a different starting value.

Solution

Add an AUTO_INCREMENT clause to your CREATE TABLE statement when you create the table. If the table has already been created, use an ALTER TABLE statement to set the starting value.

Discussion

By default, AUTO_INCREMENT sequences start at one:

```
mysql> CREATE TABLE t
    -> (id INT UNSIGNED NOT NULL AUTO_INCREMENT, PRIMARY KEY (id));
mysql> INSERT INTO t (id) VALUES(NULL);
mysql> INSERT INTO t (id) VALUES(NULL);
mysql> INSERT INTO t (id) VALUES(NULL);
mysql> SELECT id FROM t ORDER BY id;
+----+
| id |
+----+
|  1 |
|  2 |
|  3 |
+----+
```

For MyISAM or InnoDB tables, you can begin the sequence at a specific initial value *n* by including an AUTO_INCREMENT = *n* clause at the end of the CREATE TABLE statement:

```
mysql> CREATE TABLE t
    -> (id INT UNSIGNED NOT NULL AUTO_INCREMENT, PRIMARY KEY (id))
    -> AUTO_INCREMENT = 100;
mysql> INSERT INTO t (id) VALUES(NULL);
mysql> INSERT INTO t (id) VALUES(NULL);
mysql> INSERT INTO t (id) VALUES(NULL);
mysql> SELECT id FROM t ORDER BY id;
+-----+
| id  |
+-----+
| 100 |
| 101 |
| 102 |
+-----+
```

Alternatively, you can create the table and then set the initial sequence value with ALTER TABLE:

```
mysql> CREATE TABLE t
    -> (id INT UNSIGNED NOT NULL AUTO_INCREMENT, PRIMARY KEY (id));
mysql> ALTER TABLE t AUTO_INCREMENT = 100;
mysql> INSERT INTO t (id) VALUES(NULL);
mysql> INSERT INTO t (id) VALUES(NULL);
mysql> INSERT INTO t (id) VALUES(NULL);
mysql> SELECT id FROM t ORDER BY id;
+-----+
| id  |
+-----+
| 100 |
| 101 |
| 102 |
+-----+
```

To start a sequence at *n* for storage engines other than MyISAM or InnoDB, you can use a trick: insert a "fake" row with sequence value *n*-1, and then delete it after inserting one or more "real" rows. The following example illustrates how to start a sequence at 100 for a BDB table:

```
mysql> CREATE TABLE t
    -> (id INT UNSIGNED NOT NULL AUTO_INCREMENT, PRIMARY KEY (id))
    -> ENGINE = BDB;
mysql> INSERT INTO t (id) VALUES(99);
mysql> INSERT INTO t (id) VALUES(NULL);
mysql> INSERT INTO t (id) VALUES(NULL);
mysql> INSERT INTO t (id) VALUES(NULL);
mysql> DELETE FROM t WHERE id = 99;
mysql> SELECT * FROM t ORDER BY id;
+-----+
| id  |
+-----+
| 100 |
| 101 |
| 102 |
+-----+
```

Remember that if you empty a table completely with TRUNCATE TABLE, the sequence may be reset to begin with 1, even for storage engines that normally do not reuse sequence values (Recipe 11.3). In this case, you should reinitialize the sequence value explicitly after clearing the table if you don't want it to begin with 1.

11.10 Sequencing an Unsequenced Table

Problem

You forgot to include a sequence column when you created a table. Is it too late to sequence the table rows?

Solution

No, just add an AUTO_INCREMENT column using ALTER TABLE. MySQL will create the column and number the rows automatically.

Discussion

To add a sequence to a table that doesn't currently contain one, use ALTER TABLE to create an AUTO_INCREMENT column. Suppose that you have a table t that contains name and age columns, but no sequence column:

```
+----------+------+
| name     | age  |
+----------+------+
| boris    |   47 |
| clarence |   62 |
| abner    |   53 |
+----------+------+
```

You can add a sequence column named id to the table as follows:

```
mysql> ALTER TABLE t
    -> ADD id INT NOT NULL AUTO_INCREMENT,
    -> ADD PRIMARY KEY (id);
mysql> SELECT * FROM t ORDER BY id;
+----------+------+----+
| name     | age  | id |
+----------+------+----+
| boris    |   47 |  1 |
| clarence |   62 |  2 |
| abner    |   53 |  3 |
+----------+------+----+
```

MySQL numbers the rows for you automatically. It's not necessary to assign the values yourself. Very handy.

By default, ALTER TABLE adds new columns to the end of the table. To place a column at a specific position, use FIRST or AFTER at the end of the ADD clause. The following ALTER TABLE statements are similar to the one just shown, but place the id column first in the table or after the name column, respectively:

```
ALTER TABLE t
  ADD id INT NOT NULL AUTO_INCREMENT FIRST,
  ADD PRIMARY KEY (id);

ALTER TABLE t
  ADD id INT NOT NULL AUTO_INCREMENT AFTER name,
  ADD PRIMARY KEY (id);
```

For MyISAM or InnoDB tables, you can specify the initial value for a new sequence column by including an AUTO_INCREMENT = n clause in the ALTER TABLE statement:

```
mysql> ALTER TABLE t
    -> ADD id INT NOT NULL AUTO_INCREMENT FIRST,
    -> ADD PRIMARY KEY (id),
```

```
       -> AUTO_INCREMENT = 100;
mysql> SELECT * FROM t ORDER BY id;
+-----+----------+------+
| id  | name     | age  |
+-----+----------+------+
| 100 | boris    |   47 |
| 101 | clarence |   62 |
| 102 | abner    |   53 |
+-----+----------+------+
```

11.11 Using an AUTO_INCREMENT Column to Create Multiple Sequences

Problem

You need to have sequencing behavior that is more complex than a single sequence of values. You need to tie different sequences to the values in other columns of the table.

Solution

Link the AUTO_INCREMENT column to those other columns, making them all part of the same index.

Discussion

When an AUTO_INCREMENT column is the only column in a PRIMARY KEY or UNIQUE index, it generates a single sequence 1, 2, 3, ... in which successive values increase by one each time you add a row, regardless of the contents of the rest of the row. For MyISAM or BDB tables, it's possible to create an index that combines an AUTO_INCREMENT column with other columns to generate multiple sequences within a single table.

Here's how it works: let's say that Junior develops such a passion for bug collecting that he decides to keep it up even after the school project has been completed—except that when freed from the constraints of the teacher's instructions, he's perfectly content to include insect-like bugs such as millipedes, and even to collect multiple instances of any given creature. Junior happily goes outside and collects more specimens over the next few days:

Name	Date	Origin
ant	2006-10-07	kitchen
millipede	2006-10-07	basement
beetle	2006-10-07	basement
ant	2006-10-07	front yard
ant	2006-10-07	front yard

Name	Date	Origin
honeybee	2006-10-08	back yard
cricket	2006-10-08	garage
beetle	2006-10-08	front yard
termite	2006-10-09	kitchen woodwork
cricket	2006-10-10	basement
termite	2006-10-11	bathroom woodwork
honeybee	2006-10-11	garden
cricket	2006-10-11	garden
ant	2006-10-11	garden

After recording this information, he's ready to enter it into the database but wants to number each kind of bug separately (ant 1, ant 2, ..., beetle 1, beetle 2, ..., cricket 1, cricket 2, and so forth). To that end, you look over the data (noting with some alarm Junior's discovery of termites in the house and making a mental note to call the exterminator), and then design a bug table for Junior that looks like this:

```
CREATE TABLE bug
(
    id      INT UNSIGNED NOT NULL AUTO_INCREMENT,
    name    VARCHAR(30) NOT NULL, # type of bug
    date    DATE NOT NULL,        # date collected
    origin  VARCHAR(30) NOT NULL, # where collected
    PRIMARY KEY (name, id)
);
```

This is very similar to the insect table, but has one significant difference: the PRIMARY KEY comprises two columns, not one. As a result, the id column will behave somewhat differently than for the insect table. If the new set of specimens is entered into the bug table in the order in which Junior wrote them down, here's what the resulting table looks like:

```
mysql> SELECT * FROM bug;
+----+-----------+------------+-------------------+
| id | name      | date       | origin            |
+----+-----------+------------+-------------------+
|  1 | ant       | 2006-10-07 | kitchen           |
|  1 | millipede | 2006-10-07 | basement          |
|  1 | beetle    | 2006-10-07 | basement          |
|  2 | ant       | 2006-10-07 | front yard        |
|  3 | ant       | 2006-10-07 | front yard        |
|  1 | honeybee  | 2006-10-08 | back yard         |
|  1 | cricket   | 2006-10-08 | garage            |
|  2 | beetle    | 2006-10-08 | front yard        |
|  1 | termite   | 2006-10-09 | kitchen woodwork  |
|  2 | cricket   | 2006-10-10 | basement          |
|  2 | termite   | 2006-10-11 | bathroom woodwork |
|  2 | honeybee  | 2006-10-11 | garden            |
```

```
|    3 | cricket   | 2006-10-11 | garden             |
|    4 | ant       | 2006-10-11 | garden             |
+------+-----------+------------+--------------------+
```

Looking at the table that way, it appears that the `id` values are being assigned at random —but they're not. Sort the table by `name` and `id`, and it becomes clear how MySQL assigns the values. Specifically, MySQL creates a separate `id` sequence for each distinct `name` value:

```
mysql> SELECT * FROM bug ORDER BY name, id;
+------+-----------+------------+--------------------+
| id   | name      | date       | origin             |
+------+-----------+------------+--------------------+
|    1 | ant       | 2006-10-07 | kitchen            |
|    2 | ant       | 2006-10-07 | front yard         |
|    3 | ant       | 2006-10-07 | front yard         |
|    4 | ant       | 2006-10-11 | garden             |
|    1 | beetle    | 2006-10-07 | basement           |
|    2 | beetle    | 2006-10-08 | front yard         |
|    1 | cricket   | 2006-10-08 | garage             |
|    2 | cricket   | 2006-10-10 | basement           |
|    3 | cricket   | 2006-10-11 | garden             |
|    1 | honeybee  | 2006-10-08 | back yard          |
|    2 | honeybee  | 2006-10-11 | garden             |
|    1 | millipede | 2006-10-07 | basement           |
|    1 | termite   | 2006-10-09 | kitchen woodwork   |
|    2 | termite   | 2006-10-11 | bathroom woodwork  |
+------+-----------+------------+--------------------+
```

When you create a multiple-column `AUTO_INCREMENT` index, note the following points:

- The order in which the `CREATE TABLE` statement defines the indexed columns does not matter. What *is* significant is the order in which the index definition names the columns. The `AUTO_INCREMENT` column must be named last, or the multiple-sequence mechanism will not work.

- A `PRIMARY KEY` cannot contain `NULL` values, but a `UNIQUE` index can. If any of the non-`AUTO_INCREMENT` columns to be indexed might contain `NULL` values, you should create a `UNIQUE` index rather than a `PRIMARY KEY`.

For the `bug` table, the `AUTO_INCREMENT` index has two columns. The same technique can be extended to more than two columns, but the basic concept is the same: for an *n*-column index where the last one is an `AUTO_INCREMENT` column, MySQL generates an independent sequence for each unique combination of values in the non-`AUTO_INCREMENT` columns.

MySQL's mechanism for multiple-column sequences can be easier to use than logically equivalent single-column values. Recall that in Recipe 7.10, we used a `housewares` table that contained rows with three-part product ID values composed of a three-character category abbreviation, a five-digit serial number, and a two-character code indicating country of manufacture:

```
+------------+-------------------+
| id         | description       |
+------------+-------------------+
| DIN40672US | dining table      |
| KIT00372UK | garbage disposal  |
| KIT01729JP | microwave oven    |
| BED00038SG | bedside lamp      |
| BTH00485US | shower stall      |
| BTH00415JP | lavatory          |
+------------+-------------------+
```

The table was used in that chapter to demonstrate how to break apart the `id` values into their constituent parts and sort them separately, using `LEFT( )`, `MID( )`, and `RIGHT( )`. That led to some fairly ugly `ORDER BY` clauses, and an issue that I didn't even bring up in that chapter was the question of just how to generate the serial numbers in the middle of the values.

Sometimes you can replace this kind of multiple-part column with separate columns that are tied together as an `AUTO_INCREMENT` index. For example, another way to manage houseware `id` values like this is to represent them using `category`, `serial`, and `country` columns and tie them together in a `PRIMARY KEY` with the serial number as an `AUTO_INCREMENT` column. This causes serial numbers to increment independently for each combination of category and country. To create the table from scratch, you'd write the `CREATE TABLE` statement like this:

```
CREATE TABLE housewares
(
  category    VARCHAR(3) NOT NULL,
  serial      INT UNSIGNED NOT NULL AUTO_INCREMENT,
  country     VARCHAR(2) NOT NULL,
  description VARCHAR(255),
  PRIMARY KEY (category, country, serial)
);
```

Alternatively, assuming you have the original `housewares` table already created in the form used in the earlier chapter, you can convert it to the new structure "in place" as follows:

```
mysql> ALTER TABLE housewares
    -> ADD category VARCHAR(3) NOT NULL FIRST,
    -> ADD serial INT UNSIGNED NOT NULL AUTO_INCREMENT AFTER category,
    -> ADD country VARCHAR(2) NOT NULL AFTER serial,
    -> ADD PRIMARY KEY (category, country, serial);
mysql> UPDATE housewares SET category = LEFT(id,3);
mysql> UPDATE housewares SET serial = MID(id,4,5);
mysql> UPDATE housewares SET country = RIGHT(id,2);
mysql> ALTER TABLE housewares DROP id;
mysql> SELECT * FROM housewares;
+----------+--------+---------+-------------------+
| category | serial | country | description       |
+----------+--------+---------+-------------------+
| DIN      |  40672 | US      | dining table      |
| KIT      |    372 | UK      | garbage disposal  |
```

```
| KIT       |   1729 | JP      | microwave oven  |
| BED       |     38 | SG      | bedside lamp    |
| BTH       |    485 | US      | shower stall    |
| BTH       |    415 | JP      | lavatory        |
+-----------+--------+---------+-----------------+
```

With the `id` values split into their separate parts, sorting operations become easier to specify because you can refer to individual columns directly rather than by pulling out substrings of the original `id` column. You can also make sorting more efficient by adding additional indexes for the `serial` and `country` columns. But a problem remains: how to display each product ID as a single string rather than as three separate values? Do that with `CONCAT( )`:

```
mysql> SELECT category, serial, country,
    -> CONCAT(category,LPAD(serial,5,'0'),country) AS id
    -> FROM housewares ORDER BY category, country, serial;
+-----------+--------+---------+------------+
| category  | serial | country | id         |
+-----------+--------+---------+------------+
| BED       |     38 | SG      | BED00038SG |
| BTH       |    415 | JP      | BTH00415JP |
| BTH       |    485 | US      | BTH00485US |
| DIN       |  40672 | US      | DIN40672US |
| KIT       |   1729 | JP      | KIT01729JP |
| KIT       |    372 | UK      | KIT00372UK |
+-----------+--------+---------+------------+
```

You can even eliminate the need for `LPAD( )` by declaring `serial` to be a zero-filled column for which values are displayed using five digits:

```
mysql> ALTER TABLE housewares
    -> MODIFY serial INT(5) UNSIGNED ZEROFILL NOT NULL AUTO_INCREMENT;
```

Then MySQL supplies the leading zeros automatically, and the `CONCAT( )` expression becomes simpler:

```
mysql> SELECT category, serial, country,
    -> CONCAT(category,serial,country) AS id
    -> FROM housewares ORDER BY category, country, serial;
+-----------+--------+---------+------------+
| category  | serial | country | id         |
+-----------+--------+---------+------------+
| BED       | 00038  | SG      | BED00038SG |
| BTH       | 00415  | JP      | BTH00415JP |
| BTH       | 00485  | US      | BTH00485US |
| DIN       | 40672  | US      | DIN40672US |
| KIT       | 01729  | JP      | KIT01729JP |
| KIT       | 00372  | UK      | KIT00372UK |
+-----------+--------+---------+------------+
```

This example illustrates an important principle: you might think about values one way (`id` values as single strings), but that doesn't mean you must necessarily represent them in the database that way. If an alternative representation (separate columns) is more efficient or easier to work with, it may well be worth using—even if you must reformat the underlying columns for display purposes to give them the appearance people expect.

If formatting multiple column values into an identifier involves complex calculations or you simply want to hide the details from applications, define a stored function that takes the relevant column values as arguments and returns the identifier. For example:

```
CREATE FUNCTION houseware_id(category VARCHAR(3),
                            serial INT UNSIGNED,
                            country VARCHAR(2))
RETURNS VARCHAR(10) DETERMINISTIC
RETURN CONCAT(category,LPAD(serial,5,'0'),country);
```

Use the function as follows. The result is the same as before, but the caller need not know how the identifiers are constructed:

```
mysql> SELECT category, serial, country,
    -> houseware_id(category,serial,country) AS id
    -> FROM housewares;
+----------+--------+---------+-----------+
| category | serial | country | id        |
+----------+--------+---------+-----------+
| BED      | 38     | SG      | BED00038SG |
| BTH      | 415    | JP      | BTH00415JP |
| BTH      | 485    | US      | BTH00485US |
| DIN      | 40672  | US      | DIN40672US |
| KIT      | 1729   | JP      | KIT01729JP |
| KIT      | 372    | UK      | KIT00372UK |
+----------+--------+---------+-----------+
```

For more information about writing stored functions, see Chapter 16.

11.12 Managing Multiple Simultaneous AUTO_INCREMENT Values

Problem

You're working with two or more tables that contain AUTO_INCREMENT columns, and you're having a hard time keeping track of the sequence values generated for each table.

Solution

Save the values in user-defined variables for later. If you're using statements from within a program, save the sequence values in program variables. Alternatively, you might be able to issue the statements using separate connection or statement objects to keep them from getting mixed up.

Discussion

As described in Recipe 11.4, the LAST_INSERT_ID( ) server-side sequence value indicator function is set each time a statement generates an AUTO_INCREMENT value, whereas client-side sequence indicators may be reset for every statement. What if you issue a statement that generates an AUTO_INCREMENT value, but you don't want to refer to that value until after issuing a second statement that also generates an AUTO_INCREMENT value? In this case, the original value no longer will be accessible, either through LAST_INSERT_ID( ) or as a client-side value. To retain access to it, you should save the value first before issuing the second statement. There are several ways to do this:

- At the SQL level, you can save the value in a user-defined variable after issuing a statement that generates an AUTO_INCREMENT value:

  ```
  INSERT INTO tbl_name (id,...) VALUES(NULL,...);
  SET @saved_id = LAST_INSERT_ID();
  ```

  Then you can issue other statements without regard to their effect on LAST_INSERT_ID( ). To use the original AUTO_INCREMENT value in a subsequent statement, refer to the @saved_id variable.

- At the API level, you can save the AUTO_INCREMENT value in an API language variable. This can be done either by saving the value returned from LAST_INSERT_ID( ) or from any API-specific extension that might be available.

- A third technique can be used from within APIs that enables you to maintain separate client-side AUTO_INCREMENT values. For example, statement handles in Perl have a mysql_insertid attribute, and the attribute value for one handle is unaffected by activity on another. In Java, use separate Statement or PreparedStatement objects.

11.13 Using AUTO_INCREMENT Values to Relate Tables

Problem

You're using sequence values from one table as keys in a second table so that you can relate rows in the two tables to each other. But the associations aren't being set up properly.

Solution

You're probably not inserting rows in the proper order, or you're losing track of the sequence values. Change the insertion order, or save the sequence values so that you can refer to them when you need them.

Discussion

Be careful with `AUTO_INCREMENT` values that are used to generate ID values in a master table if you also store those values in detail table rows for the purpose of linking the detail rows to the proper master table row. This kind of situation is quite common. Suppose that you have an `invoice` table listing invoice information for customer orders, and an `inv_item` table listing the individual items associated with each invoice. Here, `invoice` is the master table and `inv_item` is the detail table. To uniquely identify each order, the `invoice` table could contain an `AUTO_INCREMENT` column `inv_id`. You'd also store the appropriate invoice number in each `inv_item` table row so that you can tell which invoice it goes with. The tables might look something like this:

```
CREATE TABLE invoice
(
  inv_id  INT UNSIGNED NOT NULL AUTO_INCREMENT,
  PRIMARY KEY (inv_id),
  date    DATE NOT NULL
  # ... other columns could go here
  # ... (customer ID, shipping address, etc.)
);
CREATE TABLE inv_item
(
  inv_id    INT UNSIGNED NOT NULL,  # invoice ID (from invoice table)
  INDEX (inv_id),
  qty       INT,                    # quantity
  description VARCHAR(40)           # description
);
```

For these kinds of table relationships, it's typical to insert a row into the master table first (to generate the `AUTO_INCREMENT` value that identifies the row), and then insert the detail rows using `LAST_INSERT_ID( )` to obtain the master row ID. For example, if a customer buys a hammer, three boxes of nails, and (in anticipation of finger-bashing with the hammer) a dozen bandages, the rows pertaining to the order can be inserted into the two tables like so:

```
INSERT INTO invoice (inv_id,date)
  VALUES(NULL,CURDATE());
INSERT INTO inv_item (inv_id,qty,description)
  VALUES(LAST_INSERT_ID(),1,'hammer');
INSERT INTO inv_item (inv_id,qty,description)
  VALUES(LAST_INSERT_ID(),3,'nails, box');
INSERT INTO inv_item (inv_id,qty,description)
  VALUES(LAST_INSERT_ID(),12,'bandage');
```

The first `INSERT` adds a row to the `invoice` master table and generates a new `AUTO_INCREMENT` value for its `inv_id` column. The following `INSERT` statements each add a row to the `inv_item` detail table, using `LAST_INSERT_ID( )` to get the invoice number. This associates the detail rows with the proper master row.

What if you need to process multiple invoices? There's a right way and a wrong way to enter the information. The right way is to insert all the information for the first invoice and then proceed to the next. The wrong way is to add all the master rows into the invoice table and then add all the detail rows to the inv_item table. If you do that, *all* the detail rows in the inv_item table will contain the AUTO_INCREMENT value from the most recently entered invoice row. Thus, all will appear to be part of the same invoice, and rows in the two tables won't have the proper associations.

If the detail table contains its own AUTO_INCREMENT column, you must be even more careful about how you add rows to the tables. Suppose that you want to number the rows in the inv_item table sequentially for each order. The way to do that is to create a multiple-column AUTO_INCREMENT index that generates a separate sequence for the items in each invoice. (Recipe 11.11 discusses this type of index.) Create the inv_item table as follows, using a PRIMARY KEY that combines the inv_id column with an AUTO_INCREMENT column, seq:

```
CREATE TABLE inv_item
(
  inv_id  INT UNSIGNED NOT NULL,  # invoice ID (from invoice table)
  seq     INT UNSIGNED NOT NULL AUTO_INCREMENT,
  PRIMARY KEY (inv_id, seq),
  qty     INT,                    # quantity
  description VARCHAR(40)         # description
);
```

The inv_id column enables each inv_item row to be associated with the proper invoice table row, just as with the original table structure. In addition, the index causes the seq values for the items in each invoice to be numbered sequentially starting at 1. However, now that both tables contain an AUTO_INCREMENT column, you cannot enter information for an invoice the same way as before. To see why it doesn't work, try it:

```
INSERT INTO invoice (inv_id,date)
  VALUES(NULL,CURDATE());
INSERT INTO inv_item (inv_id,qty,description)
  VALUES(LAST_INSERT_ID(),1,'hammer');
INSERT INTO inv_item (inv_id,qty,description)
  VALUES(LAST_INSERT_ID(),3,'nails, box');
INSERT INTO inv_item (inv_id,qty,description)
  VALUES(LAST_INSERT_ID(),12,'bandage');
```

These statements are the same as before, but now behave somewhat differently due to the change in the inv_item table structure. The INSERT into the invoice table works properly. So does the first INSERT into the inv_item table; LAST_INSERT_ID( ) returns the inv_id value from the master row in the invoice table. However, this INSERT also generates its own AUTO_INCREMENT value (for the seq column), which changes the value of LAST_INSERT_ID( ) and causes the master row inv_id value to be "lost." The result is that subsequent inserts into the inv_item store the preceding row's seq value into the inv_id column. This causes the second and following rows to have incorrect inv_id values.

To avoid this difficulty, save the sequence value generated by the insert into the master table and use the saved value for the inserts into the detail table. To save the value, you can use a user-defined variable in SQL or a variable maintained by your program.

Use a user-defined variable

Save the master row `AUTO_INCREMENT` value in a user-defined variable for use when inserting the detail rows:

```
INSERT INTO invoice (inv_id,date)
  VALUES(NULL,CURDATE());
SET @inv_id = LAST_INSERT_ID();
INSERT INTO inv_item (inv_id,qty,description)
  VALUES(@inv_id,1,'hammer');
INSERT INTO inv_item (inv_id,qty,description)
  VALUES(@inv_id,3,'nails, box');
INSERT INTO inv_item (inv_id,qty,description)
  VALUES(@inv_id,12,'bandage');
```

Use an API variable

This method is similar to the previous one, but applies only from within an API. Insert the master row, and then save the `AUTO_INCREMENT` value into an API variable for use when inserting detail rows. For example, in Ruby, you can access the `AUTO_INCREMENT` using the database handle `insert_id` attribute, so the invoice-entry procedure looks something like this:

```
dbh.do("INSERT INTO invoice (inv_id,date) VALUES(NULL,CURDATE())")
inv_id = dbh.func(:insert_id)
sth = dbh.prepare("INSERT INTO inv_item (inv_id,qty,description)
                  VALUES(?,?,?)")
sth.execute(inv_id, 1, "hammer")
sth.execute(inv_id, 3, "nails, box")
sth.execute(inv_id, 12, "bandage")
```

11.14 Using Sequence Generators as Counters

Problem

You're interested only in counting events, so there's no point in creating a table row for each sequence value.

Solution

Use a sequence-generation mechanism that uses just one row per counter.

Discussion

`AUTO_INCREMENT` columns are useful for generating sequences across a set of individual rows. But for some applications, you're interested only in a count of the number of times an event occurs, and there's no value in creating a separate row for each event. Instances include web page or banner ad hit counters, a count of items sold, or the number of votes in a poll. For such applications, you need only a single row to hold the count as it changes over time. MySQL provides a mechanism for this that enables counts to be treated like AUTO_INCREMENT values so that you can not only increment the count, but retrieve the updated value easily.

To count a single type of event, you can use a trivial table with a single row and column. For example, if you're selling copies of a book, you can create a table to record sales for it like this:

```
CREATE TABLE booksales (copies INT UNSIGNED);
```

However, if you're counting sales for multiple book titles, that method won't work so well. You certainly don't want to create a separate single-row counting table per book. Instead, you can count them all within a single table if you include a column that provides a unique identifier for each book. The following table, booksales, does this using a title column for the book title in addition to a copies column that records the number of copies sold:

```
CREATE TABLE booksales
(
  title   VARCHAR(60) NOT NULL,  # book title
  copies  INT UNSIGNED NOT NULL, # number of copies sold
  PRIMARY KEY (title)
);
```

To record sales for a given book, different approaches are possible:

- Initialize a row for the book with a copies value of 0:

  ```
  INSERT INTO booksales (title,copies) VALUES('The Greater Trumps',0);
  ```

  Then increment the copies value for each sale:

  ```
  UPDATE booksales SET copies = copies+1 WHERE title = 'The Greater Trumps';
  ```

  This method requires that you remember to initialize a row for each book or the UPDATE will fail.

- Use INSERT with ON DUPLICATE KEY UPDATE, which initializes the row with a count of 1 for the first sale and increments the count for subsequent sales:

  ```
  INSERT INTO booksales (title,copies)
    VALUES('The Greater Trumps',1)
    ON DUPLICATE KEY UPDATE copies = copies+1;
  ```

  This is simpler because you can use the same statement for initializing and updating the sales count.

To retrieve the sales count (so that you can display a message to the customer such as "you just purchased copy *n* of this book"), issue a SELECT query for the same book title:

```
SELECT copies FROM booksales WHERE title = 'The Greater Trumps';
```

Unfortunately, this is not quite correct. Suppose that between the times when you update and retrieve the count, some other person buys a copy of the book (and thus increments the copies value). Then the SELECT statement won't actually produce the value *you* incremented the sales count to, but rather its most recent value. In other words, other clients can affect the value before you have time to retrieve it. This is similar to the problem discussed earlier that can occur if you try to retrieve the most recent AUTO_INCREMENT value from a column by invoking MAX(*col_name*) rather than LAST_INSERT_ID( ).

There are ways around this (such as by grouping the two statements as a transaction or by locking the table), but MySQL provides a different solution based on LAST_INSERT_ID( ). If you call LAST_INSERT_ID( ) with an expression argument, MySQL treats it like an AUTO_INCREMENT value. To use this feature with the booksales table, modify the count-incrementing statement slightly:

```
INSERT INTO booksales (title,copies)
  VALUES('The Greater Trumps',LAST_INSERT_ID(1))
  ON DUPLICATE KEY UPDATE copies = LAST_INSERT_ID(copies+1);
```

The statement uses the LAST_INSERT_ID(*expr*) construct both to initialize and to increment the count. With an expression argument to LAST_INSERT_ID( ), MySQL treats the expression like an AUTO_INCREMENT value. Then you can invoke LAST_INSERT_ID( ) with no argument to retrieve the value:

```
SELECT LAST_INSERT_ID();
```

By setting and retrieving the copies column this way, you can always get back the value that you set it to, even if some other client has updated it in the meantime. If you're issuing the INSERT statement from within an API that provides a mechanism for fetching the most recent AUTO_INCREMENT value directly, you need not even issue the SELECT query. For example, in Python, you can update a count and get the new value using the insert_id( ) method:

```
cursor = conn.cursor ()
cursor.execute ("""
                INSERT INTO booksales (title,copies)
                VALUES('The Greater Trumps',LAST_INSERT_ID(1))
                ON DUPLICATE KEY UPDATE copies = LAST_INSERT_ID(copies+1)
                """)
count = conn.insert_id ()
```

In Java, the operation looks like this:

```
Statement s = conn.createStatement ();
s.executeUpdate (
    "INSERT INTO booksales (title,copies)"
  + " VALUES('The Greater Trumps',LAST_INSERT_ID(1))"
  + " ON DUPLICATE KEY UPDATE copies = LAST_INSERT_ID(copies+1)");
long count = ((com.mysql.jdbc.Statement) s).getLastInsertID ();
s.close ();
```

The use of LAST_INSERT_ID(*expr*) for sequence generation has certain other properties that differ from true AUTO_INCREMENT sequences:

- AUTO_INCREMENT values increment by one each time, whereas counter values generated by LAST_INSERT_ID(*expr*) can be incremented by whatever value you want. For example, to produce the sequence 10, 20, 30, ..., increment the count by 10 each time. You need not even increment the counter by the same value each time. If you sell a dozen copies of a book rather than a single copy, update its sales count as follows:

```
INSERT INTO booksales (title,copies)
  VALUES('The Greater Trumps',LAST_INSERT_ID(12))
  ON DUPLICATE KEY UPDATE copies = LAST_INSERT_ID(copies+12);
```

- You can start the sequence at any integer, including negative values. It's also possible to produce decreasing sequences by using a negative increment. (For a column that is used to generate a sequence that includes negative values, you should omit UNSIGNED from the column definition.)

- To reset a counter, simply set it to the desired value. Suppose that you want to report to book buyers the sales for the current month, rather than the total sales (for example, to display messages like "you're the *n*th buyer this month"). To clear the counters to zero at the beginning of each month, run this statement:

```
UPDATE booksales SET copies = 0;
```

- One property that's not so desirable is that the value generated by LAST_INSERT_ID(*expr*) is not uniformly available via client-side retrieval methods under all circumstances. You can get it after UPDATE or INSERT statements, but not for SET statements. If you generate a value as follows (in Ruby), the client-side value returned by insert_id will be 0, not 48:

```
dbh.do("SET @x = LAST_INSERT_ID(48)")
seq = dbh.func(:insert_id)
```

To get the value in this case, ask the server for it:

```
seq = dbh.select_one("SELECT LAST_INSERT_ID()")[0]
```

See Also

Recipe 19.12 revisits the single-row sequence-generation mechanism, where it serves as the basis for implementing web page hit counters.

11.15 Generating Repeating Sequences

Problem

You need to create a sequence that contains cycles.

Solution

Generate a sequence, and produce the cyclic elements using the division and modulo operators.

Discussion

Some sequence-generation problems require values that go through cycles. Suppose that you're manufacturing items such as pharmaceutical products or automobile parts, and you must be able to track them by lot number if manufacturing problems are discovered later that require items sold within a particular lot to be recalled. Suppose also that you pack and distribute items 12 units to a box and 6 boxes to a case. In this situation, item identifiers are three-part values: the unit number (with a value from 1 to 12), the box number (with a value from 1 to 6), and a lot number (with a value from 1 to whatever the highest case number happens to be currently).

This item-tracking problem appears to require that you maintain three counters, so you might think about generating the next identifier value using an algorithm like this:

```
retrieve most recently used case, box, and unit numbers
unit = unit + 1      # increment unit number
if (unit > 12)       # need to start a new box?
{
  unit = 1           # go to first unit of next box
  box = box + 1
}
if (box > 6)         # need to start a new case?
{
  box = 1            # go to first box of next case
  case = case + 1
}
store new case, box, and unit numbers
```

You could indeed implement an algorithm that way. However, it's also possible simply to assign each item a sequence number identifier and derive the corresponding case, box, and unit numbers from it. The identifier can come from an AUTO_INCREMENT column or a single-row sequence generator. The formulas for determining the case, box, and unit numbers for any item from its sequence number look like this:

```
unit_num = ((seq - 1) % 12) + 1
box_num = (int ((seq - 1) / 12) % 6) + 1
case_num = int ((seq - 1)/(6 * 12)) + 1
```

The following table illustrates the relationship between some sample sequence numbers and the corresponding case, box, and unit numbers:

seq	case	box	unit
1	1	1	1
12	1	1	12
13	1	2	1
72	1	6	12
73	2	1	1
144	2	6	12

11.16 Numbering Query Output Rows Sequentially

Problem

You want to number the rows of a query result.

Solution

If you're writing your own program, just add the row numbers yourself.

Discussion

A type of sequence that has nothing to do with the contents of your database is to number output rows from a query. When working within an API, you can number the rows by maintaining a counter and displaying its current value with each row's contents. Here is an example in Python, using the `insects` table. It displays a simple numbered list of the distinct values in the `origin` column of the table:

```
cursor = conn.cursor ()
cursor.execute ("SELECT DISTINCT origin FROM insect")
count = 1
for row in cursor.fetchall ():
  print count, row[0]
  count = count + 1
cursor.close ()
```

See Also

The *mysql* program provides no explicit row-numbering facilities, although you can use a user-defined variable to include an extra row number column in a query's output. Another way to produce results that may be suitable for your purposes is to filter *mysql* output through another program that adds row numbers. Recipe 1.27 describes these techniques.

## CHAPTER 12

Using Multiple Tables

12.0 Introduction

For the most part, recipes in earlier chapters have used single tables. But for any application of even moderate complexity, it's likely that you'll need to use multiple tables. Some questions simply cannot be answered using a single table, and the real power of a relational database comes into play when you start to combine the information from multiple sources. There are several reasons to use multiple tables:

- To combine rows from tables to obtain more comprehensive information than can be obtained from individual tables alone
- To hold intermediate results for a multiple-stage operation
- To modify rows in one table based on information from another

A statement that uses multiple tables can be a join between tables, a subquery that nests one `SELECT` within another, or a union that combines the results of multiple `SELECT` statements. Subqueries have already been touched on in earlier chapters to some extent. In this chapter, the primary focus is on joins and unions, although subqueries occur on occasion as well. The following topics are covered here:

Joining tables to find matches or mismatches between rows in different tables
> To solve such problems, you should know which types of joins apply. Inner joins show which rows in one table are matched by rows in another. Outer joins show matching rows, but they can also be used to find which rows in one table are *not* matched by rows in another.

Comparing a table to itself
> Some problems require that you compare a table to itself. This is similar to performing a join between different tables, except that you must use table aliases to disambiguate table references.

Using unions to combine result sets
> For some queries, the required information consists of multiple result sets, either selected from different tables or selected in different ways from the same table. To

produce such a result, use a `UNION` that combines the result sets from multiple `SELECT` statements.

Deleting unmatched rows

> If two related datasets have an imperfect relationship, you can determine which rows are unmatched and remove them if they are unwanted.

Performing joins between tables that are not in the same database

> When you use multiple tables, they might come from the same database or from different databases. On occasion, you may even need to use tables that come from databases hosted by different MySQL servers. For the first two cases, you need to know how to refer to columns from the different tables, which may involve using table aliases or qualifying table names with a database name. In the third case, you can set up a `FEDERATED` table to enable one MySQL server to access a table hosted by another or open a connection to each server and combine the information from them yourself.

The scripts that create the tables used in this chapter can be found in the *tables* directory. For scripts that implement some of the techniques discussed here, look in the *joins* and *unions* directories.

12.1 Finding Rows in One Table That Match Rows in Another

Problem

You need to write a query that uses information from more than one table.

Solution

Use a join—that is, a query that lists multiple tables in its `FROM` clause and tells MySQL how to match information from them.

Discussion

The essential idea behind a *join* is that it combines rows in one table with rows in one or more other tables. Joins enable you to combine information from multiple tables when each table contains only part of the information in which you're interested. Output rows from a join contain more information than rows from either table by itself.

A complete join that produces all possible row combinations is called a *Cartesian product*. For example, joining each row in a 100-row table to each row in a 200-row table produces a result containing 100 × 200, or 20,000 rows. With larger tables, or joins between more than two tables, the result set for a Cartesian product can easily become immense. Because of that, and because you rarely want all the combinations anyway, a join normally includes an `ON` or `USING` clause that specifies how to join rows between tables. (This requires that each table have one or more columns of common information that can be used to link them together logically.) You can also include a WHERE clause that restricts which of the joined rows to select. Each of these clauses narrows the focus of the query.

This recipe introduces basic join syntax and demonstrates how joins help you answer specific types of questions when you are looking for matches between tables. Later recipes show how to identify mismatches between tables (Recipe 12.2) and how to compare a table to itself (Recipe 12.3). The examples assume that you have an art collection and use the following two tables to record your acquisitions. artist lists those painters whose works you want to collect, and painting lists each painting that you've actually purchased:

```
CREATE TABLE artist
(
  a_id  INT UNSIGNED NOT NULL AUTO_INCREMENT, # artist ID
  name  VARCHAR(30) NOT NULL,                 # artist name
  PRIMARY KEY (a_id),
  UNIQUE (name)
);

CREATE TABLE painting
(
  a_id  INT UNSIGNED NOT NULL,                   # artist ID
  p_id  INT UNSIGNED NOT NULL AUTO_INCREMENT,    # painting ID
  title VARCHAR(100) NOT NULL,                   # title of painting
  state VARCHAR(2) NOT NULL,                     # state where purchased
  price INT UNSIGNED,                            # purchase price (dollars)
  INDEX (a_id),
  PRIMARY KEY (p_id)
);
```

You've just begun the collection, so the tables contain only the following rows:

```
mysql> SELECT * FROM artist ORDER BY a_id;
+------+----------+
| a_id | name     |
+------+----------+
|    1 | Da Vinci |
|    2 | Monet    |
|    3 | Van Gogh |
|    4 | Picasso  |
|    5 | Renoir   |
+------+----------+
mysql> SELECT * FROM painting ORDER BY a_id, p_id;
+------+------+-------------------+-------+-------+
| a_id | p_id | title             | state | price |
+------+------+-------------------+-------+-------+
|    1 |    1 | The Last Supper   | IN    |    34 |
|    1 |    2 | The Mona Lisa     | MI    |    87 |
|    3 |    3 | Starry Night      | KY    |    48 |
|    3 |    4 | The Potato Eaters | KY    |    67 |
|    3 |    5 | The Rocks         | IA    |    33 |
|    5 |    6 | Les Deux Soeurs   | NE    |    64 |
+------+------+-------------------+-------+-------+
```

The low values in the `price` column of the `painting` table betray the fact that your collection actually contains only cheap facsimiles, not the originals. Well, that's all right: who can afford the originals?

Each table contains partial information about your collection. For example, the `artist` table doesn't tell you which paintings each artist produced, and the `painting` table lists artist IDs but not their names. To use the information in both tables, you can ask MySQL to show you various combinations of artists and paintings by writing a query that performs a join. A join names two or more tables after the `FROM` keyword. In the output column list, you can name columns from any or all the joined tables, or use expressions that are based on those columns, *tbl_name.** to select all columns from a given table, or * to select all columns from all tables.

The simplest join involves two tables and selects all columns from each. With no restrictions, the join generates output for all combinations of rows (that is, the Cartesian product). The following complete join between the `artist` and `painting` tables shows this:

```
mysql> SELECT * FROM artist, painting;
+------+----------+------+------+--------------------+-------+-------+
| a_id | name     | a_id | p_id | title              | state | price |
+------+----------+------+------+--------------------+-------+-------+
|    1 | Da Vinci |    1 |    1 | The Last Supper    | IN    |    34 |
|    2 | Monet    |    1 |    1 | The Last Supper    | IN    |    34 |
|    3 | Van Gogh |    1 |    1 | The Last Supper    | IN    |    34 |
|    4 | Picasso  |    1 |    1 | The Last Supper    | IN    |    34 |
|    5 | Renoir   |    1 |    1 | The Last Supper    | IN    |    34 |
|    1 | Da Vinci |    1 |    2 | The Mona Lisa      | MI    |    87 |
|    2 | Monet    |    1 |    2 | The Mona Lisa      | MI    |    87 |
|    3 | Van Gogh |    1 |    2 | The Mona Lisa      | MI    |    87 |
|    4 | Picasso  |    1 |    2 | The Mona Lisa      | MI    |    87 |
|    5 | Renoir   |    1 |    2 | The Mona Lisa      | MI    |    87 |
|    1 | Da Vinci |    3 |    3 | Starry Night       | KY    |    48 |
|    2 | Monet    |    3 |    3 | Starry Night       | KY    |    48 |
|    3 | Van Gogh |    3 |    3 | Starry Night       | KY    |    48 |
|    4 | Picasso  |    3 |    3 | Starry Night       | KY    |    48 |
|    5 | Renoir   |    3 |    3 | Starry Night       | KY    |    48 |
|    1 | Da Vinci |    3 |    4 | The Potato Eaters  | KY    |    67 |
|    2 | Monet    |    3 |    4 | The Potato Eaters  | KY    |    67 |
|    3 | Van Gogh |    3 |    4 | The Potato Eaters  | KY    |    67 |
|    4 | Picasso  |    3 |    4 | The Potato Eaters  | KY    |    67 |
|    5 | Renoir   |    3 |    4 | The Potato Eaters  | KY    |    67 |
|    1 | Da Vinci |    3 |    5 | The Rocks          | IA    |    33 |
|    2 | Monet    |    3 |    5 | The Rocks          | IA    |    33 |
|    3 | Van Gogh |    3 |    5 | The Rocks          | IA    |    33 |
|    4 | Picasso  |    3 |    5 | The Rocks          | IA    |    33 |
|    5 | Renoir   |    3 |    5 | The Rocks          | IA    |    33 |
|    1 | Da Vinci |    5 |    6 | Les Deux Soeurs    | NE    |    64 |
|    2 | Monet    |    5 |    6 | Les Deux Soeurs    | NE    |    64 |
|    3 | Van Gogh |    5 |    6 | Les Deux Soeurs    | NE    |    64 |
|    4 | Picasso  |    5 |    6 | Les Deux Soeurs    | NE    |    64 |
|    5 | Renoir   |    5 |    6 | Les Deux Soeurs    | NE    |    64 |
+------+----------+------+------+--------------------+-------+-------+
```

The statement output illustrates why a complete join generally is not useful: it produces a lot of output, and the result is not meaningful. Clearly, you're not maintaining these tables to match every artist with every painting, which is what the preceding statement does. An unrestricted join in this case produces nothing of value.

To answer questions meaningfully, you must combine the two tables in a way that produces only the relevant matches. Doing so is a matter of including appropriate join conditions. For example, to produce a list of paintings together with the artist names, you can associate rows from the two tables using a simple WHERE clause that matches up values in the artist ID column that is common to both tables and that serves as the link between them:

```
mysql> SELECT * FROM artist, painting
    -> WHERE artist.a_id = painting.a_id;
+------+----------+------+------+-------------------+-------+-------+
| a_id | name     | a_id | p_id | title             | state | price |
+------+----------+------+------+-------------------+-------+-------+
|    1 | Da Vinci |    1 |    1 | The Last Supper   | IN    |    34 |
|    1 | Da Vinci |    1 |    2 | The Mona Lisa     | MI    |    87 |
|    3 | Van Gogh |    3 |    3 | Starry Night      | KY    |    48 |
|    3 | Van Gogh |    3 |    4 | The Potato Eaters | KY    |    67 |
|    3 | Van Gogh |    3 |    5 | The Rocks         | IA    |    33 |
|    5 | Renoir   |    5 |    6 | Les Deux Soeurs   | NE    |    64 |
+------+----------+------+------+-------------------+-------+-------+
```

The column names in the WHERE clause include table qualifiers to make it clear which a_id values to compare. The output indicates who painted each painting, and, conversely, which paintings by each artist are in your collection.

Another way to write the same join is to use INNER JOIN rather than the comma operator and indicate the matching conditions with an ON clause:

```
mysql> SELECT * FROM artist INNER JOIN painting
    -> ON artist.a_id = painting.a_id;
+------+----------+------+------+-------------------+-------+-------+
| a_id | name     | a_id | p_id | title             | state | price |
+------+----------+------+------+-------------------+-------+-------+
|    1 | Da Vinci |    1 |    1 | The Last Supper   | IN    |    34 |
|    1 | Da Vinci |    1 |    2 | The Mona Lisa     | MI    |    87 |
|    3 | Van Gogh |    3 |    3 | Starry Night      | KY    |    48 |
|    3 | Van Gogh |    3 |    4 | The Potato Eaters | KY    |    67 |
|    3 | Van Gogh |    3 |    5 | The Rocks         | IA    |    33 |
|    5 | Renoir   |    5 |    6 | Les Deux Soeurs   | NE    |    64 |
+------+----------+------+------+-------------------+-------+-------+
```

In the special case that the matched columns have the same name in both tables and are compared using the = operator, you can use an INNER JOIN with a USING clause instead. This requires no table qualifiers, and each join column is named only once:

```
mysql> SELECT * FROM artist INNER JOIN painting
    -> USING(a_id);
+------+----------+------+-------------------+-------+-------+
| a_id | name     | p_id | title             | state | price |
+------+----------+------+-------------------+-------+-------+
```

```
|     1 | Da Vinci  |    1 | The Last Supper    | IN    |    34 |
|     1 | Da Vinci  |    2 | The Mona Lisa      | MI    |    87 |
|     3 | Van Gogh  |    3 | Starry Night       | KY    |    48 |
|     3 | Van Gogh  |    4 | The Potato Eaters  | KY    |    67 |
|     3 | Van Gogh  |    5 | The Rocks          | IA    |    33 |
|     5 | Renoir    |    6 | Les Deux Soeurs    | NE    |    64 |
+-------+-----------+------+--------------------+-------+-------+
```

Note that when you write a query with a USING clause, SELECT * returns only one instance of each join column (a_id).

Any of ON, USING, or WHERE can include comparisons, so how do you know which join conditions to put in each clause? As a rule of thumb, it's conventional to use ON or USING to specify how to join the tables, and the WHERE clause to restrict which of the joined rows to select. For example, to join tables based on the a_id column, but select only rows for paintings obtained in Kentucky, use an ON (or USING) clause to match the rows in the two tables, and a WHERE clause to test the state column:

```
mysql> SELECT * FROM artist INNER JOIN painting
    -> ON artist.a_id = painting.a_id
    -> WHERE painting.state = 'KY';
+------+-----------+------+------+--------------------+-------+-------+
| a_id | name      | a_id | p_id | title              | state | price |
+------+-----------+------+------+--------------------+-------+-------+
|    3 | Van Gogh  |    3 |    3 | Starry Night       | KY    |    48 |
|    3 | Van Gogh  |    3 |    4 | The Potato Eaters  | KY    |    67 |
+------+-----------+------+------+--------------------+-------+-------+
```

The preceding queries use SELECT * to select all columns. To be more selective about which columns a statement should display, provide a list that names only those columns in which you're interested:

```
mysql> SELECT artist.name, painting.title, painting.state, painting.price
    -> FROM artist INNER JOIN painting
    -> ON artist.a_id = painting.a_id
    -> WHERE painting.state = 'KY';
+-----------+--------------------+-------+-------+
| name      | title              | state | price |
+-----------+--------------------+-------+-------+
| Van Gogh  | Starry Night       | KY    |    48 |
| Van Gogh  | The Potato Eaters  | KY    |    67 |
+-----------+--------------------+-------+-------+
```

You're not limited to two tables when writing joins. Suppose that you prefer to see complete state names rather than abbreviations in the preceding query result. The states table used in earlier chapters maps state abbreviations to names, so you can add it to the previous query to display names:

```
mysql> SELECT artist.name, painting.title, states.name, painting.price
    -> FROM artist INNER JOIN painting INNER JOIN states
    -> ON artist.a_id = painting.a_id AND painting.state = states.abbrev;
+-----------+--------------------+----------+-------+
| name      | title              | name     | price |
+-----------+--------------------+----------+-------+
```

```
| Da Vinci | The Last Supper    | Indiana  | 34 |
| Da Vinci | The Mona Lisa      | Michigan | 87 |
| Van Gogh | Starry Night       | Kentucky | 48 |
| Van Gogh | The Potato Eaters  | Kentucky | 67 |
| Van Gogh | The Rocks          | Iowa     | 33 |
| Renoir   | Les Deux Soeurs    | Nebraska | 64 |
+----------+--------------------+----------+------+
```

Another common use of three-way joins is for enumerating many-to-many relationships. See Recipe 12.5 for an example.

By including appropriate conditions in your joins, you can answer very specific questions, such as the following:

- Which paintings did Van Gogh paint? To answer this question, use the a_id value to find matching rows, add a WHERE clause to restrict output to those rows that contain the artist name, and select the title from those rows:

```
mysql> SELECT painting.title
    -> FROM artist INNER JOIN painting ON artist.a_id = painting.a_id
    -> WHERE artist.name = 'Van Gogh';
+-------------------+
| title             |
+-------------------+
| Starry Night      |
| The Potato Eaters |
| The Rocks         |
+-------------------+
```

- Who painted the *Mona Lisa*? Again you use the a_id column to join the rows, but this time the WHERE clause restricts output to those rows that contain the title, and you select the artist name from those rows:

```
mysql> SELECT artist.name
    -> FROM artist INNER JOIN painting ON artist.a_id = painting.a_id
    -> WHERE painting.title = 'The Mona Lisa';
+----------+
| name     |
+----------+
| Da Vinci |
+----------+
```

- Which artists' paintings did you purchase in Kentucky or Indiana? This is somewhat similar to the previous statement, but it tests a different column (a_id) in the painting table to determine which rows to join with the artist table:

```
mysql> SELECT DISTINCT artist.name
    -> FROM artist INNER JOIN painting ON artist.a_id = painting.a_id
    -> WHERE painting.state IN ('KY','IN');
+----------+
| name     |
+----------+
| Da Vinci |
| Van Gogh |
+----------+
```

The statement also uses `DISTINCT` to display each artist name just once. Try it without `DISTINCT` and you'll see that Van Gogh is listed twice; that's because you obtained two Van Goghs in Kentucky.

- Joins can also be used with aggregate functions to produce summaries. For example, to find out how many paintings you have per artist, use this statement:

```
mysql> SELECT artist.name, COUNT(*) AS 'number of paintings'
    -> FROM artist INNER JOIN painting ON artist.a_id = painting.a_id
    -> GROUP BY artist.name;
+----------+---------------------+
| name     | number of paintings |
+----------+---------------------+
| Da Vinci |                   2 |
| Renoir   |                   1 |
| Van Gogh |                   3 |
+----------+---------------------+
```

A more elaborate statement might also show how much you paid for each artist's paintings, in total and on average:

```
mysql> SELECT artist.name,
    -> COUNT(*) AS 'number of paintings',
    -> SUM(painting.price) AS 'total price',
    -> AVG(painting.price) AS 'average price'
    -> FROM artist INNER JOIN painting ON artist.a_id = painting.a_id
    -> GROUP BY artist.name;
+----------+---------------------+-------------+---------------+
| name     | number of paintings | total price | average price |
+----------+---------------------+-------------+---------------+
| Da Vinci |                   2 |         121 |       60.5000 |
| Renoir   |                   1 |          64 |       64.0000 |
| Van Gogh |                   3 |         148 |       49.3333 |
+----------+---------------------+-------------+---------------+
```

Note that the summary statements produce output only for those artists in the `artist` table for whom you actually have acquired paintings. (For example, Monet is listed in the `artist` table but is not present in the summary because you don't have any of his paintings yet.) If you want the summary to include all artists, even if you have none of their paintings yet, you must use a different kind of join—specifically, an outer join:

- Joins written with the comma operator or `INNER JOIN` are *inner joins*, which means that they produce a result only for values in one table that match values in another table.

- An outer join can produce those matches as well, but also can show you which values in one table are missing from the other. Recipe 12.2 introduces outer joins.

Joins and Indexes

Because a join can easily cause MySQL to process large numbers of row combinations, it's a good idea to make sure that the columns you're comparing are indexed. Otherwise, performance can drop off quickly as table sizes increase. For the `artist` and `painting` tables, joins are made based on the values in the `a_id` column of each table. If you look back at the `CREATE TABLE` statements that were shown for these tables earlier, you'll see that `a_id` is indexed in each table.

The *tbl_name.col_name* notation that qualifies a column name with a table name is always allowable in a join but can be shortened to just *col_name* if the name appears in only one of the joined tables. In that case, MySQL can determine without ambiguity which table the column comes from, and no table name qualifier is necessary. We can't do that for the following join. Both tables have an `a_id` column, so the column reference is ambiguous:

```
mysql> SELECT * FROM artist INNER JOIN painting ON a_id = a_id;
ERROR 1052 (23000): Column 'a_id' in on clause is ambiguous
```

By contrast, the following query is unambiguous. Each instance of `a_id` is qualified with the appropriate table name, only `artist` has a `name` column, and only `painting` has `title` and `state` columns:

```
mysql> SELECT name, title, state FROM artist INNER JOIN painting
    -> ON artist.a_id = painting.a_id;
+----------+------------------+-------+
| name     | title            | state |
+----------+------------------+-------+
| Da Vinci | The Last Supper  | IN    |
| Da Vinci | The Mona Lisa    | MI    |
| Van Gogh | Starry Night     | KY    |
| Van Gogh | The Potato Eaters| KY    |
| Van Gogh | The Rocks        | IA    |
| Renoir   | Les Deux Soeurs  | NE    |
+----------+------------------+-------+
```

To make the meaning of a statement clearer to human readers, it's often useful to qualify column names even when that's not strictly necessary as far as MySQL is concerned. I tend to use qualified names in join examples for that reason.

If you don't want to write complete table names when qualifying column references, give each table a short alias and refer to its columns using the alias. The following two statements are equivalent:

```
SELECT artist.name, painting.title, states.name, painting.price
  FROM artist INNER JOIN painting INNER JOIN states
  ON artist.a_id = painting.a_id AND painting.state = states.abbrev;

SELECT a.name, p.title, s.name, p.price
  FROM artist AS a INNER JOIN painting AS p INNER JOIN states AS s
  ON a.a_id = p.a_id AND p.state = s.abbrev;
```

In AS *alias_name* clauses, the AS is optional.

For complicated statements that select many columns, aliases can save a lot of typing. In addition, aliases are not only convenient but necessary for some types of statements, as will become evident when we get to the topic of self-joins (Recipe 12.3).

12.2 Finding Rows with No Match in Another Table

Problem

You want to find rows in one table that have no match in another. Or you want to produce a list on the basis of a join between tables, and you want the list to include an entry for every row in the first table, even when there are no matches in the second table.

Solution

Use an outer join—a LEFT JOIN or a RIGHT JOIN.

Discussion

Recipe 12.1 focused on inner joins, which are joins that find matches between two tables. However, the answers to some questions require determining which rows do *not* have a match (or, stated another way, which rows have values that are missing from the other table). For example, you might want to know which artists in the **artist** table you don't yet have any paintings by. The same kind of question occurs in other contexts. Some examples:

- You're working in sales. You have a list of potential customers, and another list of people who have placed orders. To focus your efforts on people who are not yet actual customers, you want to find people in the first list who are not in the second.

- You have one list of baseball players, and another list of players who have hit home runs, and you want to know which players in the first list have *not* hit a home run. The answer is determined by finding those players in the first list who are not in the second.

For these types of questions, it's necessary to use an *outer join*. Like an inner join, an outer join can find matches between tables. But unlike an inner join, an outer join can also determine which rows in one table have no match in another. Two types of outer join are LEFT JOIN and RIGHT JOIN.

To see why outer joins are useful, let's consider the problem of determining which artists in the **artist** table are missing from the **painting** table. At present, the tables are small, so it's easy to examine them visually:

```
mysql> SELECT * FROM artist ORDER BY a_id;
+------+----------+
```

```
| a_id | name     |
+------+----------+
|    1 | Da Vinci |
|    2 | Monet    |
|    3 | Van Gogh |
|    4 | Picasso  |
|    5 | Renoir   |
+------+----------+
mysql> SELECT * FROM painting ORDER BY a_id, p_id;
+------+------+-------------------+-------+-------+
| a_id | p_id | title             | state | price |
+------+------+-------------------+-------+-------+
|    1 |    1 | The Last Supper   | IN    |    34 |
|    1 |    2 | The Mona Lisa     | MI    |    87 |
|    3 |    3 | Starry Night      | KY    |    48 |
|    3 |    4 | The Potato Eaters | KY    |    67 |
|    3 |    5 | The Rocks         | IA    |    33 |
|    5 |    6 | Les Deux Soeurs   | NE    |    64 |
+------+------+-------------------+-------+-------+
```

By looking at the tables, you can see that you have no paintings by Monet or Picasso (there are no `painting` rows with an `a_id` value of 2 or 4). But as you acquire more paintings and the tables get larger, it won't be so easy to eyeball them and answer the question by inspection. Can you answer it using SQL? Sure, although first attempts at a solution generally look something like the following statement, which uses a not-equal condition to look for mismatches between the two tables:

```
mysql> SELECT * FROM artist INNER JOIN painting
    -> ON artist.a_id != painting.a_id;
+------+----------+------+------+-------------------+-------+-------+
| a_id | name     | a_id | p_id | title             | state | price |
+------+----------+------+------+-------------------+-------+-------+
|    2 | Monet    |    1 |    1 | The Last Supper   | IN    |    34 |
|    3 | Van Gogh |    1 |    1 | The Last Supper   | IN    |    34 |
|    4 | Picasso  |    1 |    1 | The Last Supper   | IN    |    34 |
|    5 | Renoir   |    1 |    1 | The Last Supper   | IN    |    34 |
|    2 | Monet    |    1 |    2 | The Mona Lisa     | MI    |    87 |
|    3 | Van Gogh |    1 |    2 | The Mona Lisa     | MI    |    87 |
|    4 | Picasso  |    1 |    2 | The Mona Lisa     | MI    |    87 |
|    5 | Renoir   |    1 |    2 | The Mona Lisa     | MI    |    87 |
|    1 | Da Vinci |    3 |    3 | Starry Night      | KY    |    48 |
|    2 | Monet    |    3 |    3 | Starry Night      | KY    |    48 |
|    4 | Picasso  |    3 |    3 | Starry Night      | KY    |    48 |
|    5 | Renoir   |    3 |    3 | Starry Night      | KY    |    48 |
|    1 | Da Vinci |    3 |    4 | The Potato Eaters | KY    |    67 |
|    2 | Monet    |    3 |    4 | The Potato Eaters | KY    |    67 |
|    4 | Picasso  |    3 |    4 | The Potato Eaters | KY    |    67 |
|    5 | Renoir   |    3 |    4 | The Potato Eaters | KY    |    67 |
|    1 | Da Vinci |    3 |    5 | The Rocks         | IA    |    33 |
|    2 | Monet    |    3 |    5 | The Rocks         | IA    |    33 |
|    4 | Picasso  |    3 |    5 | The Rocks         | IA    |    33 |
|    5 | Renoir   |    3 |    5 | The Rocks         | IA    |    33 |
|    1 | Da Vinci |    5 |    6 | Les Deux Soeurs   | NE    |    64 |
|    2 | Monet    |    5 |    6 | Les Deux Soeurs   | NE    |    64 |
|    3 | Van Gogh |    5 |    6 | Les Deux Soeurs   | NE    |    64 |
```

```
|     4 | Picasso   |     5 |     6 | Les Deux Soeurs    | NE    |    64 |
+-------+-----------+-------+-------+--------------------+-------+-------+
```

That output obviously is not correct. (For example, it falsely indicates that each painting was painted by several different artists.) The problem is that the statement produces a list of all combinations of values from the two tables in which the artist ID values aren't the same, whereas what you really need is a list of values in artist that aren't present *at all* in painting. The trouble here is that an inner join can only produce results based on combinations of values that are present in both tables. It can't tell you anything about values that are missing from one of them.

When faced with the problem of finding values in one table that have no match in (or that are missing from) another table, you should get in the habit of thinking, "Aha, that's a LEFT JOIN problem." A LEFT JOIN is one type of outer join: it's similar to an inner join in that it attempts to match rows in the first (left) table with the rows in the second (right) table. But in addition, if a left table row has no match in the right table, a LEFT JOIN still produces a row—one in which all the columns from the right table are set to NULL. This means you can find values that are missing from the right table by looking for NULL. It's easier to understand how this happens by working in stages. Begin with an inner join that displays matching rows:

```
mysql> SELECT * FROM artist INNER JOIN painting
    -> ON artist.a_id = painting.a_id;
+------+-----------+------+------+--------------------+-------+-------+
| a_id | name      | a_id | p_id | title              | state | price |
+------+-----------+------+------+--------------------+-------+-------+
|    1 | Da Vinci  |    1 |    1 | The Last Supper    | IN    |    34 |
|    1 | Da Vinci  |    1 |    2 | The Mona Lisa      | MI    |    87 |
|    3 | Van Gogh  |    3 |    3 | Starry Night       | KY    |    48 |
|    3 | Van Gogh  |    3 |    4 | The Potato Eaters  | KY    |    67 |
|    3 | Van Gogh  |    3 |    5 | The Rocks          | IA    |    33 |
|    5 | Renoir    |    5 |    6 | Les Deux Soeurs    | NE    |    64 |
+------+-----------+------+------+--------------------+-------+-------+
```

In this output, the first a_id column comes from the artist table and the second one comes from the painting table.

Now compare that result with the output you get from a LEFT JOIN. A LEFT JOIN is written much like an INNER JOIN:

```
mysql> SELECT * FROM artist LEFT JOIN painting
    -> ON artist.a_id = painting.a_id;
+------+-----------+------+------+--------------------+-------+-------+
| a_id | name      | a_id | p_id | title              | state | price |
+------+-----------+------+------+--------------------+-------+-------+
|    1 | Da Vinci  |    1 |    1 | The Last Supper    | IN    |    34 |
|    1 | Da Vinci  |    1 |    2 | The Mona Lisa      | MI    |    87 |
|    2 | Monet     | NULL | NULL | NULL               | NULL  |  NULL |
|    3 | Van Gogh  |    3 |    3 | Starry Night       | KY    |    48 |
|    3 | Van Gogh  |    3 |    4 | The Potato Eaters  | KY    |    67 |
|    3 | Van Gogh  |    3 |    5 | The Rocks          | IA    |    33 |
|    4 | Picasso   | NULL | NULL | NULL               | NULL  |  NULL |
+------+-----------+------+------+--------------------+-------+-------+
```

```
| 5 | Renoir   | 5 | 6 | Les Deux Soeurs  | NE | 64 |
+------+----------+------+------+--------------------+-------+-------+
```

The output is similar to that from the inner join, except that the LEFT JOIN also produces at least one output row for every **artist** row, including those that have no **painting** table match. For those output rows, all the columns from **painting** are set to NULL. These are rows that the inner join does not produce.

Next, to restrict the output only to the nonmatched **artist** rows, add a WHERE clause that looks for NULL values in any **painting** column that cannot otherwise contain NULL. This filters out the rows that the inner join produces, leaving those produced only by the outer join:

```
mysql> SELECT * FROM artist LEFT JOIN painting
    -> ON artist.a_id = painting.a_id
    -> WHERE painting.a_id IS NULL;
+------+----------+------+------+-------+-------+-------+
| a_id | name     | a_id | p_id | title | state | price |
+------+----------+------+------+-------+-------+-------+
|    2 | Monet    | NULL | NULL | NULL  | NULL  | NULL  |
|    4 | Picasso  | NULL | NULL | NULL  | NULL  | NULL  |
+------+----------+------+------+-------+-------+-------+
```

Finally, to show only the **artist** table values that are missing from the **painting** table, shorten the output column list to include only columns from the **artist** table. The result is that the LEFT JOIN lists those left-table rows containing a_id values that are not present in the right table:

```
mysql> SELECT artist.* FROM artist LEFT JOIN painting
    -> ON artist.a_id = painting.a_id
    -> WHERE painting.a_id IS NULL;
+------+----------+
| a_id | name     |
+------+----------+
|    2 | Monet    |
|    4 | Picasso  |
+------+----------+
```

A similar kind of operation can be used to report each left-table value along with an indicator as to whether it's present in the right table. To do this, perform a LEFT JOIN that counts the number of times each left-table value occurs in the right table. A count of zero indicates that the value is not present. The following statement lists each artist from the **artist** table and shows whether you have any paintings by the artist:

```
mysql> SELECT artist.name,
    -> IF(COUNT(painting.a_id)>0,'yes','no') AS 'in collection'
    -> FROM artist LEFT JOIN painting ON artist.a_id = painting.a_id
    -> GROUP BY artist.name;
+----------+---------------+
| name     | in collection |
+----------+---------------+
| Da Vinci | yes           |
| Monet    | no            |
| Picasso  | no            |
```

```
| Renoir   | yes            |
| Van Gogh | yes            |
+----------+----------------+
```

A `RIGHT JOIN` is another kind of outer join. It is like `LEFT JOIN` but reverses the roles of the left and right tables. Semantically, `RIGHT JOIN` forces the matching process to produce a row from each table in the right table, even in the absence of a corresponding row in the left table. Syntactically, *tbl1* `LEFT JOIN` *tbl2* is equivalent to *tbl2* `RIGHT JOIN` *tbl1*. This means that you would rewrite the preceding `LEFT JOIN` as follows to convert it to a `RIGHT JOIN` that produces the same results:

```
mysql> SELECT artist.name,
    -> IF(COUNT(painting.a_id)>0,'yes','no') AS 'in collection'
    -> FROM painting RIGHT JOIN artist ON artist.a_id = painting.a_id
    -> GROUP BY artist.name;
+----------+----------------+
| name     | in collection  |
+----------+----------------+
| Da Vinci | yes            |
| Monet    | no             |
| Picasso  | no             |
| Renoir   | yes            |
| Van Gogh | yes            |
+----------+----------------+
```

Elsewhere in this book, I'll generally refer only to `LEFT JOIN` for brevity, but such references apply to `RIGHT JOIN` as well if you reverse the roles of the tables.

Other Ways to Write LEFT JOIN and RIGHT JOIN Queries

As with `INNER JOIN`, if the names of the columns to be matched in an outer join are the same in both tables and you are comparing them with the `=` operator, you can use a `USING` clause rather than `ON`. For example, the following two statements are equivalent:

```
SELECT * FROM t1 LEFT JOIN t2 ON t1.n = t2.n;
SELECT * FROM t1 LEFT JOIN t2 USING (n);
```

As are these:

```
SELECT * FROM t1 RIGHT JOIN t2 ON t1.n = t2.n;
SELECT * FROM t1 RIGHT JOIN t2 USING (n);
```

In the special case that you want to base the comparison on every column that appears in both tables, you can use `NATURAL LEFT JOIN` or `NATURAL RIGHT JOIN` and omit the `ON` or `USING` clause:

```
SELECT * FROM t1 NATURAL LEFT JOIN t2;
SELECT * FROM t1 NATURAL RIGHT JOIN t2;
```

See Also

As shown in this section, `LEFT JOIN` is useful for finding values with no match in another table or for showing whether each value is matched. `LEFT JOIN` may also be used to produce a summary that includes all items in a list, even those for which there's nothing to summarize. This is very common for characterizing the relationship between a master table and a detail table. For example, a LEFT JOIN can produce "total sales per customer" reports that list all customers, even those who haven't bought anything during the summary period. (See Recipe 12.4 for information about master-detail lists.)

You can also use LEFT JOIN to perform consistency checking when you receive two datafiles that are supposed to be related, and you want to determine whether they really are. (That is, you want to check the integrity of their relationship.) Import each file into a MySQL table, and then run a couple of LEFT JOIN statements to determine whether there are unattached rows in one table or the other—that is, rows that have no match in the other table. Recipe 12.13 discusses how to identify (and optionally delete) these unattached rows.

12.3 Comparing a Table to Itself

Problem

You want to compare rows in a table to other rows in the same table. For example, you want to find all paintings in your collection by the artist who painted *The Potato Eaters.* Or you want to know which states listed in the states table joined the Union in the same year as New York. Or you want to know which states did not join the Union in the same year as any other state.

Solution

Problems that require comparing a table to itself involve an operation known as a self-join. It's performed much like other joins, except that you must always use table aliases so that you can refer to the same table different ways within the statement.

Discussion

A special case of joining one table to another occurs when both tables are the same. This is called a *self-join*. Although many people find the idea confusing or strange to think about at first, it's perfectly legal. It's likely that you'll find yourself using self-joins quite often because they are so important.

A tip-off that you need a self-join is when you want to know which pairs of elements in a table satisfy some condition. For example, suppose that your favorite painting is *The Potato Eaters,* and you want to identify all the items in your collection that were done by the artist who painted it. Do so as follows:

1. Identify the row in the painting table that contains the title *The Potato Eaters,* so that you can refer to its a_id value.

2. Use the a_id value to match other rows in the table that have the same a_id value.

3. Display the titles from those matching rows.

The artist ID and painting titles that we begin with look like this:

```
mysql> SELECT a_id, title FROM painting ORDER BY a_id;
+------+-------------------+
| a_id | title             |
+------+-------------------+
|    1 | The Last Supper   |
|    1 | The Mona Lisa     |
|    3 | Starry Night      |
|    3 | The Potato Eaters |
|    3 | The Rocks         |
|    5 | Les Deux Soeurs   |
+------+-------------------+
```

A two-step method for picking out the right titles without a join is to look up the artist's ID with one statement and then use the ID in a second statement to select rows that match it:

```
mysql> SELECT @id := a_id FROM painting WHERE title = 'The Potato Eaters';
+-------------+
| @id := a_id |
+-------------+
|           3 |
+-------------+
mysql> SELECT title FROM painting WHERE a_id = @id;
+-------------------+
| title             |
+-------------------+
| Starry Night      |
| The Potato Eaters |
| The Rocks         |
+-------------------+
```

A different solution that requires only a single statement is to use a self-join. The trick to this lies in figuring out the proper notation to use. First attempts at writing a statement that joins a table to itself often look something like this:

```
mysql> SELECT title
    -> FROM painting INNER JOIN painting
    -> ON a_id = a_id;
    -> WHERE title = 'The Potato Eaters';
ERROR 1066 (42000): Not unique table/alias: 'painting'
```

The problem with that statement is that the column references are ambiguous. MySQL can't tell which instance of the painting table any given column name refers to. The solution is to give at least one instance of the table an alias so that you can distinguish column references by using different table qualifiers. The following statement shows how to do this, using the aliases p1 and p2 to refer to the painting table different ways:

```
mysql> SELECT p2.title
    -> FROM painting AS p1 INNER JOIN painting AS p2
    -> ON p1.a_id = p2.a_id
```

```
    -> WHERE p1.title = 'The Potato Eaters';
+-------------------+
| title             |
+-------------------+
| Starry Night      |
| The Potato Eaters |
| The Rocks         |
+-------------------+
```

The statement output illustrates something typical of self-joins: when you begin with
a reference value in one table instance (*The Potato Eaters*) to find matching rows in a
second table instance (paintings by the same artist), the output includes the reference
value. That makes sense: after all, the reference matches itself. If you want to find only
other paintings by the same artist, explicitly exclude the reference value from the
output:

```
mysql> SELECT p2.title
    -> FROM painting AS p1 INNER JOIN painting AS p2
    -> ON p1.a_id = p2.a_id
    -> WHERE p1.title = 'The Potato Eaters' AND p2.title != 'The Potato Eaters';
+--------------+
| title        |
+--------------+
| Starry Night |
| The Rocks    |
+--------------+
```

A more general way to exclude the reference value without naming it literally is to
specify that you don't want output rows to have the same title as the reference, whatever
that title happens to be:

```
mysql> SELECT p2.title
    -> FROM painting AS p1 INNER JOIN painting AS p2
    -> ON p1.a_id = p2.a_id
    -> WHERE p1.title = 'The Potato Eaters' AND p2.title != p1.title;
+--------------+
| title        |
+--------------+
| Starry Night |
| The Rocks    |
+--------------+
```

The preceding statements use comparisons of ID values to match rows in the two table
instances, but any kind of value can be used. For example, to use the states table to
answer the question "Which states joined the Union in the same year as New York?,"
perform a *temporal pairwise comparison* based on the year part of the dates in the table's
statehood column:

```
mysql> SELECT s2.name, s2.statehood
    -> FROM states AS s1 INNER JOIN states AS s2
    -> ON YEAR(s1.statehood) = YEAR(s2.statehood)
    -> WHERE s1.name = 'New York'
    -> ORDER BY s2.name;
+----------------+------------+
```

```
| name           | statehood  |
+----------------+------------+
| Connecticut    | 1788-01-09 |
| Georgia        | 1788-01-02 |
| Maryland       | 1788-04-28 |
| Massachusetts  | 1788-02-06 |
| New Hampshire  | 1788-06-21 |
| New York       | 1788-07-26 |
| South Carolina | 1788-05-23 |
| Virginia       | 1788-06-25 |
+----------------+------------+
```

Here again, the reference value (New York) appears in the output. If you want to prevent that, add to the ON expression a term that explicitly excludes the reference:

```
mysql> SELECT s2.name, s2.statehood
    -> FROM states AS s1 INNER JOIN states AS s2
    -> ON YEAR(s1.statehood) = YEAR(s2.statehood) AND s1.name != s2.name
    -> WHERE s1.name = 'New York'
    -> ORDER BY s2.name;
+----------------+------------+
| name           | statehood  |
+----------------+------------+
| Connecticut    | 1788-01-09 |
| Georgia        | 1788-01-02 |
| Maryland       | 1788-04-28 |
| Massachusetts  | 1788-02-06 |
| New Hampshire  | 1788-06-21 |
| South Carolina | 1788-05-23 |
| Virginia       | 1788-06-25 |
+----------------+------------+
```

Like the problem of finding other paintings by the painter of *The Potato Eaters*, the statehood problem can be solved by using a user-defined variable and two statements. That will always be true when you're seeking matches for just one particular row in your table. Other problems require finding matches for several rows, in which case the two-statement method will not work. Suppose that you want to find each pair of states that joined the Union in the same year. In this case, the output potentially can include any pair of rows from the states table. There is no fixed reference value, so you cannot store the reference in a variable. A self-join is perfect for this problem:

```
mysql> SELECT YEAR(s1.statehood) AS year,
    -> s1.name AS name1, s1.statehood AS statehood1,
    -> s2.name AS name2, s2.statehood AS statehood2
    -> FROM states AS s1 INNER JOIN states AS s2
    -> ON YEAR(s1.statehood) = YEAR(s2.statehood) AND s1.name != s2.name
    -> ORDER BY year, s1.name, s2.name;
+------+----------------+------------+----------------+------------+
| year | name1          | statehood1 | name2          | statehood2 |
+------+----------------+------------+----------------+------------+
| 1787 | Delaware       | 1787-12-07 | New Jersey     | 1787-12-18 |
| 1787 | Delaware       | 1787-12-07 | Pennsylvania   | 1787-12-12 |
| 1787 | New Jersey     | 1787-12-18 | Delaware       | 1787-12-07 |
| 1787 | New Jersey     | 1787-12-18 | Pennsylvania   | 1787-12-12 |
```

```
| 1787 | Pennsylvania   | 1787-12-12 | Delaware    | 1787-12-07 |
| 1787 | Pennsylvania   | 1787-12-12 | New Jersey  | 1787-12-18 |
...
| 1912 | Arizona        | 1912-02-14 | New Mexico  | 1912-01-06 |
| 1912 | New Mexico     | 1912-01-06 | Arizona     | 1912-02-14 |
| 1959 | Alaska         | 1959-01-03 | Hawaii      | 1959-08-21 |
| 1959 | Hawaii         | 1959-08-21 | Alaska      | 1959-01-03 |
+------+----------------+------------+-------------+------------+
```

The condition in the `ON` clause that requires state pair names not to be identical eliminates the trivially duplicate rows showing that each state joined the Union in the same year as itself. But you'll notice that each remaining pair of states still appears twice. For example, there is one row that lists Delaware and New Jersey, and another that lists New Jersey and Delaware. This is often the case with self-joins: they produce pairs of rows that contain the same values, but for which the values are not in the same order. For techniques that eliminate these "near duplicates" from the query result, see Recipe 14.5.

Some self-join problems are of the "Which values are *not* matched by other rows in the table?" variety. An instance of this is the question "Which states did not join the Union in the same year as any other state?" Finding these states is a "nonmatch" problem, which is the type of problem that typically involves a `LEFT JOIN`. In this case, the solution uses a `LEFT JOIN` of the `states` table to itself:

```
mysql> SELECT s1.name, s1.statehood
    -> FROM states AS s1 LEFT JOIN states AS s2
    -> ON YEAR(s1.statehood) = YEAR(s2.statehood) AND s1.name != s2.name
    -> WHERE s2.name IS NULL
    -> ORDER BY s1.name;
+----------------+------------+
| name           | statehood  |
+----------------+------------+
| Alabama        | 1819-12-14 |
| Arkansas       | 1836-06-15 |
| California     | 1850-09-09 |
| Colorado       | 1876-08-01 |
| Illinois       | 1818-12-03 |
| Indiana        | 1816-12-11 |
| Iowa           | 1846-12-28 |
| Kansas         | 1861-01-29 |
| Kentucky       | 1792-06-01 |
| Louisiana      | 1812-04-30 |
| Maine          | 1820-03-15 |
| Michigan       | 1837-01-26 |
| Minnesota      | 1858-05-11 |
| Mississippi    | 1817-12-10 |
| Missouri       | 1821-08-10 |
| Nebraska       | 1867-03-01 |
| Nevada         | 1864-10-31 |
| North Carolina | 1789-11-21 |
| Ohio           | 1803-03-01 |
| Oklahoma       | 1907-11-16 |
| Oregon         | 1859-02-14 |
```

```
| Rhode Island  | 1790-05-29 |
| Tennessee     | 1796-06-01 |
| Utah          | 1896-01-04 |
| Vermont       | 1791-03-04 |
| West Virginia | 1863-06-20 |
| Wisconsin     | 1848-05-29 |
+---------------+------------+
```

For each row in the states table, the statement selects rows in which the state has a statehood value in the same year, not including that state itself. For rows having no such match, the LEFT JOIN forces the output to contain a row anyway, with all the s2 columns set to NULL. Those rows identify the states with no other state that joined the Union in the same year.

12.4 Producing Master-Detail Lists and Summaries

Problem

Two related tables have a master-detail relationship, and you want to produce a list that shows each master row with its detail rows or a list that produces a summary of the detail rows for each master row.

Solution

This is a one-to-many relationship. The solution to this problem involves a join, but the type of join depends on the question you want answered. To produce a list containing only master rows for which some detail row exists, use an inner join based on the primary key in the master table. To produce a list that includes entries for all master rows, even those that have no detail rows, use an outer join.

Discussion

It's often useful to produce a list from two related tables. For tables that have a master-detail or parent-child relationship, a given row in one table might be matched by several rows in the other. This recipe suggests some questions of this type that you can ask (and answer), using the artist and painting tables from earlier in the chapter.

One form of master-detail question for these tables is, "Which artist painted each painting?" This is a simple inner join that matches each painting row to its corresponding artist row based on the artist ID values:

```
mysql> SELECT artist.name, painting.title
    -> FROM artist INNER JOIN painting ON artist.a_id = painting.a_id
    -> ORDER BY name, title;
+----------+-------------------+
| name     | title             |
+----------+-------------------+
| Da Vinci | The Last Supper   |
| Da Vinci | The Mona Lisa     |
```

```
| Renoir   | Les Deux Soeurs    |
| Van Gogh | Starry Night       |
| Van Gogh | The Potato Eaters  |
| Van Gogh | The Rocks          |
+----------+--------------------+
```

An inner join suffices as long as you want to list only master rows that have detail rows. However, another form of master-detail question you can ask is, "Which paintings did each artist paint?" That question is similar but not quite identical. It will have a different answer if there are artists listed in the `artist` table that are not represented in the `painting` table, and the question requires a different statement to produce the proper answer. In that case, the join output should include rows in one table that have no match in the other. That's a form of "find the nonmatching rows" problem that requires an outer join (Recipe 12.2). Thus, to list each `artist` row, whether there are any `paint ing` rows for it, use a LEFT JOIN:

```
mysql> SELECT artist.name, painting.title
    -> FROM artist LEFT JOIN painting ON artist.a_id = painting.a_id
    -> ORDER BY name, title;
+----------+--------------------+
| name     | title              |
+----------+--------------------+
| Da Vinci | The Last Supper    |
| Da Vinci | The Mona Lisa      |
| Monet    | NULL               |
| Picasso  | NULL               |
| Renoir   | Les Deux Soeurs    |
| Van Gogh | Starry Night       |
| Van Gogh | The Potato Eaters  |
| Van Gogh | The Rocks          |
+----------+--------------------+
```

The rows in the result that have NULL in the `title` column correspond to artists that are listed in the `artist` table for whom you have no paintings.

The same principles apply when producing summaries using master and detail tables. For example, to summarize your art collection by number of paintings per painter, you might ask, "How many paintings are there per artist in the `painting` table?" To find the answer based on artist ID, you can count up the paintings easily with this statement:

```
mysql> SELECT a_id, COUNT(a_id) AS count FROM painting GROUP BY a_id;
+------+-------+
| a_id | count |
+------+-------+
|    1 |     2 |
|    3 |     3 |
|    5 |     1 |
+------+-------+
```

Of course, that output is essentially meaningless unless you have all the artist ID numbers memorized. To display the artists by name rather than ID, join the `painting` table to the `artist` table:

```
mysql> SELECT artist.name AS painter, COUNT(painting.a_id) AS count
    -> FROM artist INNER JOIN painting ON artist.a_id = painting.a_id
    -> GROUP BY artist.name;
+----------+-------+
| painter  | count |
+----------+-------+
| Da Vinci |     2 |
| Renoir   |     1 |
| Van Gogh |     3 |
+----------+-------+
```

On the other hand, you might ask, "How many paintings did each artist paint?" This is the same question as the previous one (and the same statement answers it), as long as every artist in the artist table has at least one corresponding painting table row. But if you have artists in the artist table that are not yet represented by any paintings in your collection, they will not appear in the statement output. To produce a count-per-artist summary that includes even artists with no paintings in the painting table, use a LEFT JOIN:

```
mysql> SELECT artist.name AS painter, COUNT(painting.a_id) AS count
    -> FROM artist LEFT JOIN painting ON artist.a_id = painting.a_id
    -> GROUP BY artist.name;
+----------+-------+
| painter  | count |
+----------+-------+
| Da Vinci |     2 |
| Monet    |     0 |
| Picasso  |     0 |
| Renoir   |     1 |
| Van Gogh |     3 |
+----------+-------+
```

Beware of a subtle error that is easy to make when writing that kind of statement. Suppose that you write the COUNT( ) function slightly differently, like so:

```
mysql> SELECT artist.name AS painter, COUNT(*) AS count
    -> FROM artist LEFT JOIN painting ON artist.a_id = painting.a_id
    -> GROUP BY artist.name;
+----------+-------+
| painter  | count |
+----------+-------+
| Da Vinci |     2 |
| Monet    |     1 |
| Picasso  |     1 |
| Renoir   |     1 |
| Van Gogh |     3 |
+----------+-------+
```

Now every artist appears to have at least one painting. Why the difference? The cause of the problem is that the statement uses COUNT(*) rather than COUNT(painting.a_id). The way LEFT JOIN works for unmatched rows in the left table is that it generates a row with all the columns from the right table set to NULL. In the example, the right table is painting. The statement that uses COUNT(painting.a_id) works correctly, because COUNT (*expr*) counts only non-NULL values. The statement that uses COUNT(*) works incorrectly because it counts *rows*, even those containing NULL that correspond to missing artists.

LEFT JOIN is suitable for other types of summaries as well. To produce additional columns showing the total and average values of the paintings for each artist in the artist table, use this statement:

```
mysql> SELECT artist.name AS painter,
    -> COUNT(painting.a_id) AS 'number of paintings',
    -> SUM(painting.price) AS 'total price',
    -> AVG(painting.price) AS 'average price'
    -> FROM artist LEFT JOIN painting ON artist.a_id = painting.a_id
    -> GROUP BY artist.name;
+----------+---------------------+-------------+---------------+
| painter  | number of paintings | total price | average price |
+----------+---------------------+-------------+---------------+
| Da Vinci |                   2 |         121 |       60.5000 |
| Monet    |                   0 |        NULL |          NULL |
| Picasso  |                   0 |        NULL |          NULL |
| Renoir   |                   1 |          64 |       64.0000 |
| Van Gogh |                   3 |         148 |       49.3333 |
+----------+---------------------+-------------+---------------+
```

Note that COUNT( ) is zero for artists that are not represented, but SUM( ) and AVG( ) are NULL. The latter two functions return NULL when applied to a set of values with no non-NULL values. To display a sum or average value of zero in that case, modify the statement to test the value of SUM( ) or AVG( ) with IFNULL( ):

```
mysql> SELECT artist.name AS painter,
    -> COUNT(painting.a_id) AS 'number of paintings',
    -> IFNULL(SUM(painting.price),0) AS 'total price',
    -> IFNULL(AVG(painting.price),0) AS 'average price'
    -> FROM artist LEFT JOIN painting ON artist.a_id = painting.a_id
    -> GROUP BY artist.name;
+----------+---------------------+-------------+---------------+
| painter  | number of paintings | total price | average price |
+----------+---------------------+-------------+---------------+
| Da Vinci |                   2 |         121 |       60.5000 |
| Monet    |                   0 |           0 |        0.0000 |
| Picasso  |                   0 |           0 |        0.0000 |
| Renoir   |                   1 |          64 |       64.0000 |
| Van Gogh |                   3 |         148 |       49.3333 |
+----------+---------------------+-------------+---------------+
```

12.5 Enumerating a Many-to-Many Relationship

Problem

You want to display a relationship between tables when rows in either table might be matched by multiple rows in the other table.

Solution

This is a many-to-many relationship. It requires a third table for associating your two primary tables and a three-way join to list the correspondences between them.

Discussion

The `artist` and `painting` tables used in earlier sections are related in a one-to-many relationship: a given artist may have produced many paintings, but each painting was created by only one artist. One-to-many relationships are relatively simple and the two tables in the relationship can be joined with a key that is common to both tables.

Even simpler is the one-to-one relationship, which often is used to perform lookups that map one set of values to another. For example, the `states` table contains `name` and `abbrev` columns that list full state names and their corresponding abbreviations:

```
mysql> SELECT name, abbrev FROM states;
+----------------+--------+
| name           | abbrev |
+----------------+--------+
| Alabama        | AL     |
| Alaska         | AK     |
| Arizona        | AZ     |
| Arkansas       | AR     |
...
```

This one-to-one relationship can be used to map state name abbreviations in the `painting` table, which contains a `state` column indicating the state in which each painting was purchased. With no mapping, `painting` entries can be displayed like this:

```
mysql> SELECT title, state FROM painting ORDER BY state;
+-------------------+-------+
| title             | state |
+-------------------+-------+
| The Rocks         | IA    |
| The Last Supper   | IN    |
| Starry Night      | KY    |
| The Potato Eaters | KY    |
| The Mona Lisa     | MI    |
| Les Deux Soeurs   | NE    |
+-------------------+-------+
```

If you want to see the full state names rather than abbreviations, exploit the one-to-one relationship that exists between the two that is enumerated in the `states` table. Join that table to the `painting` table as follows, using the abbreviation values that are common to the two tables:

```
mysql> SELECT painting.title, states.name AS state
    -> FROM painting INNER JOIN states ON painting.state = states.abbrev
    -> ORDER BY state;
+-------------------+----------+
| title             | state    |
+-------------------+----------+
| The Last Supper   | Indiana  |
```

```
| The Rocks         | Iowa     |
| Starry Night      | Kentucky |
| The Potato Eaters | Kentucky |
| The Mona Lisa     | Michigan |
| Les Deux Soeurs   | Nebraska |
+-------------------+----------+
```

A more complex relationship between tables is the many-to-many relationship, which occurs when a row in one table may have many matches in the other, and vice versa. To illustrate such a relationship, this is the point at which database books typically devolve into the "parts and suppliers" problem. (A given part may be available through several suppliers; how can you produce a list showing which parts are available from which suppliers?) However, having seen that example far too many times, I prefer to use a different illustration. So, even though conceptually it's really the same idea, let's use the following scenario: you and a bunch of your friends are avid enthusiasts of euchre, a four-handed card game played with two teams of partners. Each year, you all get together, pair off, and run a friendly tournament. Naturally, to avoid controversy about how different players might remember the results of each tournament, you record the pairings and outcomes in a database. One way to store the results is with a table that is set up as follows, where for each tournament year, you record the team names, win-loss records, players, and player cities of residence:

```
mysql> SELECT * FROM euchre ORDER BY year, wins DESC, player;
+----------+------+------+--------+----------+-------------+
| team     | year | wins | losses | player   | player_city |
+----------+------+------+--------+----------+-------------+
| Kings    | 2005 |   10 |      2 | Ben      | Cork        |
| Kings    | 2005 |   10 |      2 | Billy    | York        |
| Crowns   | 2005 |    7 |      5 | Melvin   | Dublin      |
| Crowns   | 2005 |    7 |      5 | Tony     | Derry       |
| Stars    | 2005 |    4 |      8 | Franklin | Bath        |
| Stars    | 2005 |    4 |      8 | Wallace  | Cardiff     |
| Sceptres | 2005 |    3 |      9 | Maurice  | Leeds       |
| Sceptres | 2005 |    3 |      9 | Nigel    | London      |
| Crowns   | 2006 |    9 |      3 | Ben      | Cork        |
| Crowns   | 2006 |    9 |      3 | Tony     | Derry       |
| Kings    | 2006 |    8 |      4 | Franklin | Bath        |
| Kings    | 2006 |    8 |      4 | Nigel    | London      |
| Stars    | 2006 |    5 |      7 | Maurice  | Leeds       |
| Stars    | 2006 |    5 |      7 | Melvin   | Dublin      |
| Sceptres | 2006 |    2 |     10 | Billy    | York        |
| Sceptres | 2006 |    2 |     10 | Wallace  | Cardiff     |
+----------+------+------+--------+----------+-------------+
```

As shown by the table, each team has multiple players, and each player has participated in multiple teams. The table captures the nature of this many-to-many relationship, but it's also in nonnormal form, because each row unnecessarily stores quite a bit of repetitive information. (Information for each team is recorded multiple times, as is information about each player.) A better way to represent this many-to-many relationship is to use multiple tables:

- Store each team name, year, and record once in a table named euchre_team.

- Store each player name and city of residence once in a table named euchre_player.

- Create a third table, euchre_link, that stores team-player associations and serves as a link, or bridge, between the two primary tables. To minimize the information stored in this table, assign unique IDs to each team and player within their respective tables, and store only those IDs in the euchre_link table.

The resulting team and player tables look like this:

```
mysql> SELECT * FROM euchre_team;
+----+----------+------+------+--------+
| id | name     | year | wins | losses |
+----+----------+------+------+--------+
|  1 | Kings    | 2005 |   10 |      2 |
|  2 | Crowns   | 2005 |    7 |      5 |
|  3 | Stars    | 2005 |    4 |      8 |
|  4 | Sceptres | 2005 |    3 |      9 |
|  5 | Kings    | 2006 |    8 |      4 |
|  6 | Crowns   | 2006 |    9 |      3 |
|  7 | Stars    | 2006 |    5 |      7 |
|  8 | Sceptres | 2006 |    2 |     10 |
+----+----------+------+------+--------+
mysql> SELECT * FROM euchre_player;
+----+----------+--------+
| id | name     | city   |
+----+----------+--------+
|  1 | Ben      | Cork   |
|  2 | Billy    | York   |
|  3 | Tony     | Derry  |
|  4 | Melvin   | Dublin |
|  5 | Franklin | Bath   |
|  6 | Wallace  | Cardiff|
|  7 | Nigel    | London |
|  8 | Maurice  | Leeds  |
+----+----------+--------+
```

The euchre_link table associates teams and players as follows:

```
mysql> SELECT * FROM euchre_link;
+---------+-----------+
| team_id | player_id |
+---------+-----------+
|       1 |         1 |
|       1 |         2 |
|       2 |         3 |
|       2 |         4 |
|       3 |         5 |
|       3 |         6 |
|       4 |         7 |
|       4 |         8 |
|       5 |         5 |
|       5 |         7 |
|       6 |         1 |
```

```
|        6 |         3 |
|        7 |         4 |
|        7 |         8 |
|        8 |         2 |
|        8 |         6 |
+---------+----------+
```

To answer questions about the teams or players using these tables, you need to perform a three-way join, using the link table to relate the two primary tables to each other. Here are some examples:

- List all the pairings that show the teams and who played on them. This statement enumerates all the correspondences between the euchre_team and euchre_player tables and reproduces the information that was originally in the nonnormal euchre table:

```
mysql> SELECT t.name, t.year, t.wins, t.losses, p.name, p.city
    -> FROM euchre_team AS t INNER JOIN euchre_link AS l
    -> INNER JOIN euchre_player AS p
    -> ON t.id = l.team_id AND p.id = l.player_id
    -> ORDER BY t.year, t.wins DESC, p.name;
+----------+------+------+--------+----------+---------+
| name     | year | wins | losses | name     | city    |
+----------+------+------+--------+----------+---------+
| Kings    | 2005 |   10 |      2 | Ben      | Cork    |
| Kings    | 2005 |   10 |      2 | Billy    | York    |
| Crowns   | 2005 |    7 |      5 | Melvin   | Dublin  |
| Crowns   | 2005 |    7 |      5 | Tony     | Derry   |
| Stars    | 2005 |    4 |      8 | Franklin | Bath    |
| Stars    | 2005 |    4 |      8 | Wallace  | Cardiff |
| Sceptres | 2005 |    3 |      9 | Maurice  | Leeds   |
| Sceptres | 2005 |    3 |      9 | Nigel    | London  |
| Crowns   | 2006 |    9 |      3 | Ben      | Cork    |
| Crowns   | 2006 |    9 |      3 | Tony     | Derry   |
| Kings    | 2006 |    8 |      4 | Franklin | Bath    |
| Kings    | 2006 |    8 |      4 | Nigel    | London  |
| Stars    | 2006 |    5 |      7 | Maurice  | Leeds   |
| Stars    | 2006 |    5 |      7 | Melvin   | Dublin  |
| Sceptres | 2006 |    2 |     10 | Billy    | York    |
| Sceptres | 2006 |    2 |     10 | Wallace  | Cardiff |
+----------+------+------+--------+----------+---------+
```

- List the members for a particular team (the 2005 Crowns):

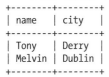

```
mysql> SELECT p.name, p.city
    -> FROM euchre_team AS t INNER JOIN euchre_link AS l
    -> INNER JOIN euchre_player AS p
    -> ON t.id = l.team_id AND p.id = l.player_id
    -> AND t.name = 'Crowns' AND t.year = 2005;
+--------+--------+
| name   | city   |
+--------+--------+
| Tony   | Derry  |
| Melvin | Dublin |
+--------+--------+
```

- List the teams that a given player (Billy) has been a member of:

```
mysql> SELECT t.name, t.year, t.wins, t.losses
    -> FROM euchre_team AS t INNER JOIN euchre_link AS l
    -> INNER JOIN euchre_player AS p
    -> ON t.id = l.team_id AND p.id = l.player_id
    -> WHERE p.name = 'Billy';
+----------+------+------+--------+
| name     | year | wins | losses |
+----------+------+------+--------+
| Kings    | 2005 |   10 |      2 |
| Sceptres | 2006 |    2 |     10 |
+----------+------+------+--------+
```

12.6 Finding Rows Containing Per-Group Minimum or Maximum Values

Problem

You want to find which row within each group of rows in a table contains the maximum or minimum value for a given column. For example, you want to determine the most expensive painting in your collection for each artist.

Solution

Create a temporary table to hold the per-group maximum or minimum values, and then join the temporary table with the original one to pull out the matching row for each group. If you prefer a single-query solution, use a subquery in the FROM clause rather than a temporary table.

Discussion

Many questions involve finding largest or smallest values in a particular table column, but it's also common to want to know what the other values are in the row that contains the value. For example, when you are using the `artist` and `painting` tables, it's possible to answer questions like "What is the most expensive painting in the collection, and who painted it?" One way to do this is to store the highest price in a user-defined variable and then use the variable to identify the row containing the price so that you can retrieve other columns from it:

```
mysql> SET @max_price = (SELECT MAX(price) FROM painting);
mysql> SELECT artist.name, painting.title, painting.price
    -> FROM artist INNER JOIN painting
    -> ON painting.a_id = artist.a_id
    -> WHERE painting.price = @max_price;
+----------+----------------+-------+
| name     | title          | price |
+----------+----------------+-------+
```

```
| Da Vinci | The Mona Lisa |    87 |
+----------+---------------+-------+
```

The same thing can be done by creating a temporary table to hold the maximum price and then joining it with the other tables:

```
mysql> CREATE TABLE tmp SELECT MAX(price) AS max_price FROM painting;
mysql> SELECT artist.name, painting.title, painting.price
    -> FROM artist INNER JOIN painting INNER JOIN tmp
    -> ON painting.a_id = artist.a_id
    -> AND painting.price = tmp.max_price;
+----------+---------------+-------+
| name     | title         | price |
+----------+---------------+-------+
| Da Vinci | The Mona Lisa |    87 |
+----------+---------------+-------+
```

The techniques of using a user-defined variable or a temporary table as just shown were illustrated originally in Recipe 8.5. Their use here is similar except that now we are applying them to multiple tables.

On the face of it, using a temporary table and a join is just a more complicated way of answering the question than with a user-defined variable. Does this technique have any practical value? Yes, it does, because it leads to a more general technique for answering more difficult questions. The previous statements show information only for the single most expensive painting in the entire painting table. What if your question is, "What is the most expensive painting *for each artist*?" You can't use a user-defined variable to answer that question, because the answer requires finding one price per artist, and a variable can hold only a single value at a time. But the technique of using a temporary table works well, because the table can hold multiple rows, and a join can find matches for all of them.

To answer the question, select each artist ID and the corresponding maximum painting price into a temporary table. The table will contain not just the maximum painting price but the maximum within each group, where "group" is defined as "paintings by a given artist." Then use the artist IDs and prices stored in the tmp table to match rows in the painting table, and join the result with the artist table to get the artist names:

```
mysql> CREATE TABLE tmp
    -> SELECT a_id, MAX(price) AS max_price FROM painting GROUP BY a_id;
mysql> SELECT artist.name, painting.title, painting.price
    -> FROM artist INNER JOIN painting INNER JOIN tmp
    -> ON painting.a_id = artist.a_id
    -> AND painting.a_id = tmp.a_id
    -> AND painting.price = tmp.max_price;
+----------+------------------+-------+
| name     | title            | price |
+----------+------------------+-------+
| Da Vinci | The Mona Lisa    |    87 |
| Van Gogh | The Potato Eaters|    67 |
| Renoir   | Les Deux Soeurs  |    64 |
+----------+------------------+-------+
```

To obtain the same result with a single statement, use a subquery in the FROM clause that retrieves the same rows contained in the temporary table:

```
mysql> SELECT artist.name, painting.title, painting.price
    -> FROM artist INNER JOIN painting INNER JOIN
    -> (SELECT a_id, MAX(price) AS max_price FROM painting GROUP BY a_id)
    ->   AS tmp
    -> ON painting.a_id = artist.a_id
    -> AND painting.a_id = tmp.a_id
    -> AND painting.price = tmp.max_price;
+----------+-------------------+-------+
| name     | title             | price |
+----------+-------------------+-------+
| Da Vinci | The Mona Lisa     |    87 |
| Van Gogh | The Potato Eaters |    67 |
| Renoir   | Les Deux Soeurs   |    64 |
+----------+-------------------+-------+
```

Yet another way to answer maximum-per-group questions is to use a LEFT JOIN that joins a table to itself. The following statement identifies the highest-priced painting per artist ID (we are using IS NULL to select all the rows from p1 for which there is *no* row in p2 with a higher price):

```
mysql> SELECT p1.a_id, p1.title, p1.price
    -> FROM painting AS p1 LEFT JOIN painting AS p2
    -> ON p1.a_id = p2.a_id AND p1.price < p2.price
    -> WHERE p2.a_id IS NULL;
+------+-------------------+-------+
| a_id | title             | price |
+------+-------------------+-------+
|    1 | The Mona Lisa     |    87 |
|    3 | The Potato Eaters |    67 |
|    5 | Les Deux Soeurs   |    64 |
+------+-------------------+-------+
```

To display artist names rather than ID values, join the result of the LEFT JOIN to the artist table:

```
mysql> SELECT artist.name, p1.title, p1.price
    -> FROM painting AS p1 LEFT JOIN painting AS p2
    -> ON p1.a_id = p2.a_id AND p1.price < p2.price
    -> INNER JOIN artist ON p1.a_id = artist.a_id
    -> WHERE p2.a_id IS NULL;
+----------+-------------------+-------+
| name     | title             | price |
+----------+-------------------+-------+
| Da Vinci | The Mona Lisa     |    87 |
| Van Gogh | The Potato Eaters |    67 |
| Renoir   | Les Deux Soeurs   |    64 |
+----------+-------------------+-------+
```

The self–LEFT JOIN method is perhaps somewhat less intuitive than using a temporary table or a subquery.

The techniques just shown work for other kinds of values, such as temporal values. Consider the `driver_log` table that lists drivers and trips that they've taken:

```
mysql> SELECT name, trav_date, miles
    -> FROM driver_log
    -> ORDER BY name, trav_date;
+-------+------------+-------+
| name  | trav_date  | miles |
+-------+------------+-------+
| Ben   | 2006-08-29 |   131 |
| Ben   | 2006-08-30 |   152 |
| Ben   | 2006-09-02 |    79 |
| Henry | 2006-08-26 |   115 |
| Henry | 2006-08-27 |    96 |
| Henry | 2006-08-29 |   300 |
| Henry | 2006-08-30 |   203 |
| Henry | 2006-09-01 |   197 |
| Suzi  | 2006-08-29 |   391 |
| Suzi  | 2006-09-02 |   502 |
+-------+------------+-------+
```

One type of maximum-per-group problem for this table is "show the most recent trip for each driver." It can be solved with a temporary table like this:

```
mysql> CREATE TABLE tmp
    -> SELECT name, MAX(trav_date) AS trav_date
    -> FROM driver_log GROUP BY name;
mysql> SELECT driver_log.name, driver_log.trav_date, driver_log.miles
    -> FROM driver_log INNER JOIN tmp
    -> ON driver_log.name = tmp.name AND driver_log.trav_date = tmp.trav_date
    -> ORDER BY driver_log.name;
+-------+------------+-------+
| name  | trav_date  | miles |
+-------+------------+-------+
| Ben   | 2006-09-02 |    79 |
| Henry | 2006-09-01 |   197 |
| Suzi  | 2006-09-02 |   502 |
+-------+------------+-------+
```

You can also use a subquery in the `FROM` clause like this:

```
mysql> SELECT driver_log.name, driver_log.trav_date, driver_log.miles
    -> FROM driver_log INNER JOIN
    -> (SELECT name, MAX(trav_date) AS trav_date
    -> FROM driver_log GROUP BY name) AS tmp
    -> ON driver_log.name = tmp.name AND driver_log.trav_date = tmp.trav_date
    -> ORDER BY driver_log.name;
+-------+------------+-------+
| name  | trav_date  | miles |
+-------+------------+-------+
| Ben   | 2006-09-02 |    79 |
| Henry | 2006-09-01 |   197 |
| Suzi  | 2006-09-02 |   502 |
+-------+------------+-------+
```

Which technique is better: the temporary table or the subquery in the FROM clause? For small tables, there might not be much difference either way. If the temporary table or subquery result is large, a general advantage of the temporary table is that you can index it after creating it and before using it in a join.

See Also

This recipe shows how to answer maximum-per-group questions by selecting summary information into a temporary table and joining that table to the original one or by using a subquery in the FROM clause. These techniques have application in many contexts. One of them is calculation of team standings, where the standings for each group of teams are determined by comparing each team in the group to the team with the best record. Recipe 12.7 discusses how to do this.

12.7 Computing Team Standings

Problem

You want to compute team standings from their win-loss records, including the games-behind (GB) values.

Solution

Determine which team is in first place, and then join that result to the original rows.

Discussion

Standings for sports teams that compete against each other typically are ranked according to who has the best win-loss record, and the teams not in first place are assigned a "games-behind" value indicating how many games out of first place they are. This section shows how to calculate those values. The first example uses a table containing a single set of team records to illustrate the logic of the calculations. The second example uses a table containing several sets of records (that is, the records for all teams in both divisions of a league, for both halves of the season). In this case, it's necessary to use a join to perform the calculations independently for each group of teams.

Consider the following table, standings1, which contains a single set of baseball team records (they represent the final standings for the Northern League in the year 1902):

```
mysql> SELECT team, wins, losses FROM standings1
    -> ORDER BY wins-losses DESC;
+-------------+------+--------+
| team        | wins | losses |
+-------------+------+--------+
| Winnipeg    |   37 |     20 |
| Crookston   |   31 |     25 |
| Fargo       |   30 |     26 |
```

```
| Grand Forks |   28 |     26 |
| Devils Lake |   19 |     31 |
| Cavalier    |   15 |     32 |
+-------------+------+--------+
```

The rows are sorted by the win-loss differential, which is how to place teams in order from first place to last place. But displays of team standings typically include each team's winning percentage and a figure indicating how many games behind the leader all the other teams are. So let's add that information to the output. Calculating the percentage is easy. It's the ratio of wins to total games played and can be determined using this expression:

```
wins / (wins + losses)
```

This expression involves division by zero when a team has not played any games yet. For simplicity, I'll assume a nonzero number of games, but if you want to handle this condition, generalize the expression as follows:

```
IF(wins=0,0,wins/(wins+losses))
```

This expression uses the fact that no division at all is necessary unless the team has won at least one game.

Determining the games-behind value is a little trickier. It's based on the relationship of the win-loss records for two teams, calculated as the average of two values:

- The number of games the second-place team must win to have the same number of wins as the first-place team

- The number of games the first-place team must lose to have the same number of losses as the second-place team

For example, suppose two teams A and B have the following win-loss records:

```
+------+------+--------+
| team | wins | losses |
+------+------+--------+
| A    |   17 |     11 |
| B    |   14 |     12 |
+------+------+--------+
```

Here, team B has to win three more games, and team A has to lose one more game for the teams to be even. The average of three and one is two, thus B is two games behind A. Mathematically, the games-behind calculation for the two teams can be expressed like this:

```
((winsA - winsB) + (lossesB - lossesA)) / 2
```

With a little rearrangement of terms, the expression becomes:

```
((winsA - lossesA) - (winsB - lossesB)) / 2
```

The second expression is equivalent to the first, but it has each factor written as a single team's win-loss differential, rather than as a comparison between teams. This makes it easier to work with, because each factor can be determined independently from a single team record. The first factor represents the first-place team's win-loss differential, so if we calculate that value first, all the other teams GB values can be determined in relation to it.

The first-place team is the one with the largest win-loss differential. To find that value and save it in a variable, use this statement:

```
mysql> SET @wl_diff = (SELECT MAX(wins-losses) FROM standings1);
```

Then use the differential as follows to produce team standings that include winning percentage and GB values:

```
mysql> SELECT team, wins AS W, losses AS L,
    -> wins/(wins+losses) AS PCT,
    -> (@wl_diff - (wins-losses)) / 2 AS GB
    -> FROM standings1
    -> ORDER BY wins-losses DESC, PCT DESC;
+-------------+------+------+--------+---------+
| team        | W    | L    | PCT    | GB      |
+-------------+------+------+--------+---------+
| Winnipeg    | 37   | 20   | 0.6491 | 0.0000  |
| Crookston   | 31   | 25   | 0.5536 | 5.5000  |
| Fargo       | 30   | 26   | 0.5357 | 6.5000  |
| Grand Forks | 28   | 26   | 0.5185 | 7.5000  |
| Devils Lake | 19   | 31   | 0.3800 | 14.5000 |
| Cavalier    | 15   | 32   | 0.3191 | 17.0000 |
+-------------+------+------+--------+---------+
```

There are a couple of minor formatting issues that can be addressed at this point. Typically, standings listings display percentages to three decimal places, and the GB value to one decimal place (with the exception that the GB value for the first-place team is displayed as -). To display *n* decimal places, TRUNCATE(*expr,n*) can be used. To display the GB value for the first-place team appropriately, put the expression that calculates the GB column within a call to IF( ) that maps 0 to a dash:

```
mysql> SELECT team, wins AS W, losses AS L,
    -> TRUNCATE(wins/(wins+losses),3) AS PCT,
    -> IF(@wl_diff = wins-losses,
    ->    '-',TRUNCATE((@wl_diff - (wins-losses))/2,1)) AS GB
    -> FROM standings1
    -> ORDER BY wins-losses DESC, PCT DESC;
+-------------+------+------+-------+------+
| team        | W    | L    | PCT   | GB   |
+-------------+------+------+-------+------+
| Winnipeg    | 37   | 20   | 0.649 | -    |
| Crookston   | 31   | 25   | 0.553 | 5.5  |
| Fargo       | 30   | 26   | 0.535 | 6.5  |
| Grand Forks | 28   | 26   | 0.518 | 7.5  |
| Devils Lake | 19   | 31   | 0.380 | 14.5 |
| Cavalier    | 15   | 32   | 0.319 | 17.0 |
+-------------+------+------+-------+------+
```

These statements order the teams by win-loss differential, using winning percentage as a tie-breaker in case there are teams with the same differential value. It would be simpler just to sort by percentage, of course, but then you wouldn't always get the correct ordering. It's a curious fact that a team with a lower winning percentage can actually be higher in the standings than a team with a higher percentage. (This generally occurs early in the season, when teams may have played highly disparate numbers of games, relatively speaking.) Consider the case in which two teams, A and B, have the following rows:

```
+------+------+--------+
| team | wins | losses |
+------+------+--------+
| A    |    4 |      1 |
| B    |    2 |      0 |
+------+------+--------+
```

Applying the GB and percentage calculations to these team records yields the following result, in which the first-place team actually has a lower winning percentage than the second-place team:

```
+------+------+------+-------+------+
| team | W    | L    | PCT   | GB   |
+------+------+------+-------+------+
| A    |    4 |    1 | 0.800 | -    |
| B    |    2 |    0 | 1.000 | 0.5  |
+------+------+------+-------+------+
```

The standings calculations shown thus far can be done without a join. They involve only a single set of team records, so the first-place team's win-loss differential can be stored in a variable. A more complex situation occurs when a dataset includes several sets of team records. For example, the 1997 Northern League had two divisions (Eastern and Western). In addition, separate standings were maintained for the first and second halves of the season, because season-half winners in each division played each other for the right to compete in the league championship. The following table, standings2, shows what these rows look like, ordered by season half, division, and win-loss differential:

```
mysql> SELECT half, division, team, wins, losses FROM standings2
    -> ORDER BY half, division, wins-losses DESC;
+------+----------+-----------------+------+--------+
| half | division | team            | wins | losses |
+------+----------+-----------------+------+--------+
|    1 | Eastern  | St. Paul        |   24 |     18 |
|    1 | Eastern  | Thunder Bay     |   18 |     24 |
|    1 | Eastern  | Duluth-Superior |   17 |     24 |
|    1 | Eastern  | Madison         |   15 |     27 |
|    1 | Western  | Winnipeg        |   29 |     12 |
|    1 | Western  | Sioux City      |   28 |     14 |
|    1 | Western  | Fargo-Moorhead  |   21 |     21 |
|    1 | Western  | Sioux Falls     |   15 |     27 |
|    2 | Eastern  | Duluth-Superior |   22 |     20 |
|    2 | Eastern  | St. Paul        |   21 |     21 |
|    2 | Eastern  | Madison         |   19 |     23 |
|    2 | Eastern  | Thunder Bay     |   18 |     24 |
|    2 | Western  | Fargo-Moorhead  |   26 |     16 |
```

```
|  2 | Western  | Winnipeg         |  24 |   18 |
|  2 | Western  | Sioux City       |  22 |   20 |
|  2 | Western  | Sioux Falls      |  16 |   26 |
+------+----------+------------------+------+--------+
```

Generating the standings for these rows requires computing the GB values separately for each of the four combinations of season half and division. Begin by calculating the win-loss differential for the first-place team in each group and saving the values into a separate firstplace table:

```
mysql> CREATE TABLE firstplace
    -> SELECT half, division, MAX(wins-losses) AS wl_diff
    -> FROM standings2
    -> GROUP BY half, division;
```

Then join the firstplace table to the original standings, associating each team record with the proper win-loss differential to compute its GB value:

```
mysql> SELECT wl.half, wl.division, wl.team, wl.wins AS W, wl.losses AS L,
    -> TRUNCATE(wl.wins/(wl.wins+wl.losses),3) AS PCT,
    -> IF(fp.wl_diff = wl.wins-wl.losses,
    ->   '-',TRUNCATE((fp.wl_diff - (wl.wins-wl.losses)) / 2,1)) AS GB
    -> FROM standings2 AS wl INNER JOIN firstplace AS fp
    -> ON wl.half = fp.half AND wl.division = fp.division
    -> ORDER BY wl.half, wl.division, wl.wins-wl.losses DESC, PCT DESC;
```

half	division	team	W	L	PCT	GB
1	Eastern	St. Paul	24	18	0.571	-
1	Eastern	Thunder Bay	18	24	0.428	6.0
1	Eastern	Duluth-Superior	17	24	0.414	6.5
1	Eastern	Madison	15	27	0.357	9.0
1	Western	Winnipeg	29	12	0.707	-
1	Western	Sioux City	28	14	0.666	1.5
1	Western	Fargo-Moorhead	21	21	0.500	8.5
1	Western	Sioux Falls	15	27	0.357	14.5
2	Eastern	Duluth-Superior	22	20	0.523	-
2	Eastern	St. Paul	21	21	0.500	1.0
2	Eastern	Madison	19	23	0.452	3.0
2	Eastern	Thunder Bay	18	24	0.428	4.0
2	Western	Fargo-Moorhead	26	16	0.619	-
2	Western	Winnipeg	24	18	0.571	2.0
2	Western	Sioux City	22	20	0.523	4.0
2	Western	Sioux Falls	16	26	0.380	10.0

That output is somewhat difficult to read, however. To make it easier to understand, you'd likely execute the statement from within a program and reformat its results to display each set of team records separately. Here's some Perl code that does that by beginning a new output group each time it encounters a new group of standings. The code assumes that the join statement has just been executed and that its results are available through the statement handle $sth:

```
my ($cur_half, $cur_div) = ("", "");
while (my ($half, $div, $team, $wins, $losses, $pct, $gb)
```

```
            = $sth->fetchrow_array ())
  {
    if ($cur_half ne $half || $cur_div ne $div) # new group of standings?
    {
      # print standings header and remember new half/division values
      print "\n$div Division, season half $half\n";
      printf "%-20s  %3s  %3s  %5s  %s\n", "Team", "W", "L", "PCT", "GB";
      $cur_half = $half;
      $cur_div = $div;
    }
    printf "%-20s  %3d  %3d  %5s  %s\n", $team, $wins, $losses, $pct, $gb;
  }
```

The reformatted output looks like this:

```
Eastern Division, season half 1
Team                 W   L   PCT  GB
St. Paul             24  18  0.571  -
Thunder Bay          18  24  0.428  6.0
Duluth-Superior      17  24  0.414  6.5
Madison              15  27  0.357  9.0

Western Division, season half 1
Team                 W   L   PCT  GB
Winnipeg             29  12  0.707  -
Sioux City           28  14  0.666  1.5
Fargo-Moorhead       21  21  0.500  8.5
Sioux Falls          15  27  0.357  14.5

Eastern Division, season half 2
Team                 W   L   PCT  GB
Duluth-Superior      22  20  0.523  -
St. Paul             21  21  0.500  1.0
Madison              19  23  0.452  3.0
Thunder Bay          18  24  0.428  4.0

Western Division, season half 2
Team                 W   L   PCT  GB
Fargo-Moorhead       26  16  0.619  -
Winnipeg             24  18  0.571  2.0
Sioux City           22  20  0.523  4.0
Sioux Falls          16  26  0.380  10.0
```

This code comes from the script *calc_standings.pl* in the *joins* directory of the recipes distribution. That directory also contains a PHP script, *calc_standings.php*, that produces output in the form of HTML tables, which you might prefer for generating standings in a web environment.

12.8 Using a Join to Fill or Identify Holes in a List

Problem

You want to produce a summary for each of several categories, but some of them are not represented in the data to be summarized. Consequently, the summary has missing categories.

Solution

Create a reference table that lists each category and produce the summary based on a LEFT JOIN between the list and the table containing your data. Then every category in the reference table will appear in the result, even those not present in the data to be summarized.

Discussion

When you run a summary query, normally it produces entries only for the values that are actually present in the data. Let's say you want to produce a time-of-day summary for the rows in the mail table. That table looks like this:

```
mysql> SELECT * FROM mail;
+---------------------+---------+---------+---------+---------+--------+
| t                   | srcuser | srchost | dstuser | dsthost | size   |
+---------------------+---------+---------+---------+---------+--------+
| 2006-05-11 10:15:08 | barb    | saturn  | tricia  | mars    |  58274 |
| 2006-05-12 12:48:13 | tricia  | mars    | gene    | venus   | 194925 |
| 2006-05-12 15:02:49 | phil    | mars    | phil    | saturn  |   1048 |
| 2006-05-13 13:59:18 | barb    | saturn  | tricia  | venus   |    271 |
| 2006-05-14 09:31:37 | gene    | venus   | barb    | mars    |   2291 |
| 2006-05-14 11:52:17 | phil    | mars    | tricia  | saturn  |   5781 |
...
```

To determine how many messages were sent for each hour of the day, use the following statement:

```
mysql> SELECT HOUR(t) AS hour, COUNT(HOUR(t)) AS count
    -> FROM mail GROUP BY hour;
+------+-------+
| hour | count |
+------+-------+
|    7 |     1 |
|    8 |     1 |
|    9 |     2 |
|   10 |     2 |
|   11 |     1 |
|   12 |     2 |
|   13 |     1 |
|   14 |     1 |
|   15 |     1 |
|   17 |     2 |
```

```
|    22 |     1 |
|    23 |     1 |
+------+-------+
```

Here, the summary category is hour of the day. However, the summary is "incomplete" in the sense that it includes entries only for those hours of the day represented in the mail table. To produce a summary that includes all hours of the day, even those during which no messages were sent, create a reference table that lists each category (that is, each hour):

```
mysql> CREATE TABLE ref (h INT);
mysql> INSERT INTO ref (h)
    -> VALUES(0),(1),(2),(3),(4),(5),(6),(7),(8),(9),(10),(11),
    -> (12),(13),(14),(15),(16),(17),(18),(19),(20),(21),(22),(23);
```

Then join the reference table to the mail table using a LEFT JOIN:

```
mysql> SELECT ref.h AS hour, COUNT(mail.t) AS count
    -> FROM ref LEFT JOIN mail ON ref.h = HOUR(mail.t)
    -> GROUP BY hour;
+------+-------+
| hour | count |
+------+-------+
|    0 |     0 |
|    1 |     0 |
|    2 |     0 |
|    3 |     0 |
|    4 |     0 |
|    5 |     0 |
|    6 |     0 |
|    7 |     1 |
|    8 |     1 |
|    9 |     2 |
|   10 |     2 |
|   11 |     1 |
|   12 |     2 |
|   13 |     1 |
|   14 |     1 |
|   15 |     1 |
|   16 |     0 |
|   17 |     2 |
|   18 |     0 |
|   19 |     0 |
|   20 |     0 |
|   21 |     0 |
|   22 |     1 |
|   23 |     1 |
+------+-------+
```

Now the summary includes an entry for every hour of the day because the LEFT JOIN forces the output to include a row for every row in the reference table, regardless of the contents of the mail table.

The example just shown uses the reference table with a LEFT JOIN to fill in holes in the category list. It's also possible to use the reference table to *detect* holes in the dataset—

that is, to determine which categories are not present in the data to be summarized. The following statement shows those hours of the day during which no messages were sent by looking for reference rows for which no `mail` table rows have a matching category value:

```
mysql> SELECT ref.h AS hour
    -> FROM ref LEFT JOIN mail ON ref.h = HOUR(mail.t)
    -> WHERE mail.t IS NULL;
+------+
| hour |
+------+
|    0 |
|    1 |
|    2 |
|    3 |
|    4 |
|    5 |
|    6 |
|   16 |
|   18 |
|   19 |
|   20 |
|   21 |
+------+
```

Reference tables that contain a list of categories are quite useful for summary statements, but creating such tables manually is mind-numbing and error-prone. You might find it preferable to write a script that uses the endpoints of the range of category values to generate the reference table for you. In essence, this type of script acts as an iterator that generates a row for each value in the range. The following Perl script, *make_date_list.pl*, shows an example of this approach. It creates a reference table containing a row for every date in a particular date range. It also indexes the table so that it will be fast in large joins.

```perl
#!/usr/bin/perl
# make_date_list.pl - create a table with an entry for every date in
# a given date range.  The table can be used in a LEFT JOIN when
# producing a summary, to make sure that every date appears in the
# summary, regardless of whether the data to be summarized actually
# contains any values for a given day.

# Usage: make_date_list.pl db_name tbl_name col_name min_date max_date

use strict;
use warnings;
use DBI;

# ... process command-line options (not shown) ...

# Check number of arguments

@ARGV == 5 or die "$usage\n";
my ($db_name, $tbl_name, $col_name, $min_date, $max_date) = @ARGV;
```

```
# ... connect to database (not shown) ...

# Determine the number of days spanned by the date range.

my $days = $dbh->selectrow_array (qq{ SELECT DATEDIFF(?,?) + 1 },
                                  undef, $max_date, $min_date);

print "Minimum date: $min_date\n";
print "Maximum date: $max_date\n";
print "Number of days spanned by range: $days\n";
die "Date range is too small\n" if $days < 1;

# Drop table if it exists, and then recreate it

$dbh->do ("DROP TABLE IF EXISTS $db_name.$tbl_name");
$dbh->do (qq{
        CREATE TABLE $db_name.$tbl_name
        ($col_name DATE NOT NULL, PRIMARY KEY ($col_name))
  });

# Populate table with each date in the date range

my $sth = $dbh->prepare (qq{
        INSERT INTO $db_name.$tbl_name ($col_name) VALUES(? + INTERVAL ? DAY)
  });
foreach my $i (0 .. $days-1)
{
    $sth->execute ($min_date, $i);
}
```

Reference tables generated by *make_date_list.pl* can be used for per-date summaries or
to find dates not represented in the table. Suppose that you want to summarize the
driver_log table to determine how many drivers were on the road each day. The table
has these rows:

```
mysql> SELECT * FROM driver_log ORDER BY rec_id;
+--------+-------+------------+-------+
| rec_id | name  | trav_date  | miles |
+--------+-------+------------+-------+
|      1 | Ben   | 2006-08-30 |   152 |
|      2 | Suzi  | 2006-08-29 |   391 |
|      3 | Henry | 2006-08-29 |   300 |
|      4 | Henry | 2006-08-27 |    96 |
|      5 | Ben   | 2006-08-29 |   131 |
|      6 | Henry | 2006-08-26 |   115 |
|      7 | Suzi  | 2006-09-02 |   502 |
|      8 | Henry | 2006-09-01 |   197 |
|      9 | Ben   | 2006-09-02 |    79 |
|     10 | Henry | 2006-08-30 |   203 |
+--------+-------+------------+-------+
```

A simple summary looks like this:

```
mysql> SELECT trav_date, COUNT(trav_date) AS drivers
    -> FROM driver_log GROUP BY trav_date;
```

```
+------------+---------+
| trav_date  | drivers |
+------------+---------+
| 2006-08-26 |       1 |
| 2006-08-27 |       1 |
| 2006-08-29 |       3 |
| 2006-08-30 |       2 |
| 2006-09-01 |       1 |
| 2006-09-02 |       2 |
+------------+---------+
```

However, that summary does not show dates when no drivers were active. To generate a complete summary that includes the missing dates, use *make_date_list.pl*. From the simple summary just shown, we can tell the minimum and maximum dates, so generate a reference table named `ref` with a date column `d` that spans those dates:

```
% make_date_list.pl cookbook ref d 2006-08-26 2006-09-02
Minimum date: 2006-08-26
Maximum date: 2006-09-02
Number of days spanned by range: 8
```

After creating the reference table, use it in the following statement to generate the complete summary:

```
mysql> SELECT ref.d, COUNT(driver_log.trav_date) AS drivers
    -> FROM ref LEFT JOIN driver_log ON ref.d = driver_log.trav_date
    -> GROUP BY d;
+------------+---------+
| d          | drivers |
+------------+---------+
| 2006-08-26 |       1 |
| 2006-08-27 |       1 |
| 2006-08-28 |       0 |
| 2006-08-29 |       3 |
| 2006-08-30 |       2 |
| 2006-08-31 |       0 |
| 2006-09-01 |       1 |
| 2006-09-02 |       2 |
+------------+---------+
```

This second summary includes additional rows that show those dates when no drivers were active. To list only those no-driver dates, use this statement:

```
mysql> SELECT ref.d
    -> FROM ref LEFT JOIN driver_log ON ref.d = driver_log.trav_date
    -> WHERE driver_log.trav_date IS NULL
    -> ORDER BY d;
+------------+
| d          |
+------------+
| 2006-08-28 |
| 2006-08-31 |
+------------+
```

12.9 Calculating Successive-Row Differences

Problem

You have a table containing successive cumulative values in its rows, and you want to compute the differences between pairs of successive rows.

Solution

Use a self-join that matches up pairs of adjacent rows and calculates the differences between members of each pair.

Discussion

Self-joins are useful when you have a set of absolute (or cumulative) values that you want to convert to relative values representing the differences between successive pairs of rows. For example, if you take an automobile trip and write down the total miles traveled at each stopping point, you can compute the difference between successive points to determine the distance from one stop to the next. Here is such a table that shows the stops for a trip from San Antonio, Texas to Madison, Wisconsin. Each row shows the total miles driven as of each stop:

```
mysql> SELECT seq, city, miles FROM trip_log ORDER BY seq;
+-----+------------------+-------+
| seq | city             | miles |
+-----+------------------+-------+
|   1 | San Antonio, TX  |     0 |
|   2 | Dallas, TX       |   263 |
|   3 | Benton, AR       |   566 |
|   4 | Memphis, TN      |   745 |
|   5 | Portageville, MO |   878 |
|   6 | Champaign, IL    |  1164 |
|   7 | Madison, WI      |  1412 |
+-----+------------------+-------+
```

A self-join can convert these cumulative values to successive differences that represent the distances from each city to the next. The following statement shows how to use the sequence numbers in the rows to match pairs of successive rows and compute the differences between each pair of mileage values:

```
mysql> SELECT t1.seq AS seq1, t2.seq AS seq2,
    -> t1.city AS city1, t2.city AS city2,
    -> t1.miles AS miles1, t2.miles AS miles2,
    -> t2.miles-t1.miles AS dist
    -> FROM trip_log AS t1 INNER JOIN trip_log AS t2
    -> ON t1.seq+1 = t2.seq
    -> ORDER BY t1.seq;
+------+------+------------------+------------------+--------+--------+------+
| seq1 | seq2 | city1            | city2            | miles1 | miles2 | dist |
+------+------+------------------+------------------+--------+--------+------+
|    1 |    2 | San Antonio, TX  | Dallas, TX       |      0 |    263 |  263 |
```

```
|     2 |    3 | Dallas, TX         | Benton, AR         |     263 |     566 |  303 |
|     3 |    4 | Benton, AR         | Memphis, TN        |     566 |     745 |  179 |
|     4 |    5 | Memphis, TN        | Portageville, MO   |     745 |     878 |  133 |
|     5 |    6 | Portageville, MO   | Champaign, IL      |     878 |    1164 |  286 |
|     6 |    7 | Champaign, IL      | Madison, WI        |    1164 |    1412 |  248 |
+-------+------+--------------------+--------------------+---------+---------+------+
```

The presence of the seq column in the trip_log table is important for calculating successive difference values. It's needed for establishing which row precedes another and matching each row *n* with row *n*+1. The implication is that a table should include a sequence column that has no gaps if you want to perform relative-difference calculations from absolute or cumulative values. If the table contains a sequence column but there are gaps, renumber it. If the table contains no such column, add one. Recipes 11.5 and 11.10 describe how to perform these operations.

A somewhat more complex situation occurs when you compute successive differences for more than one column and use the results in a calculation. The following table, player_stats, shows some cumulative numbers for a baseball player at the end of each month of his season. ab indicates the total at-bats, and h the total hits the player has had as of a given date. (The first row indicates the starting point of the player's season, which is why the ab and h values are zero.)

```
mysql> SELECT id, date, ab, h, TRUNCATE(IFNULL(h/ab,0),3) AS ba
    -> FROM player_stats ORDER BY id;
+----+------------+-----+----+-------+
| id | date       | ab  | h  | ba    |
+----+------------+-----+----+-------+
|  1 | 2006-04-30 |   0 |  0 | 0.000 |
|  2 | 2006-05-31 |  38 | 13 | 0.342 |
|  3 | 2006-06-30 | 109 | 31 | 0.284 |
|  4 | 2006-07-31 | 196 | 49 | 0.250 |
|  5 | 2006-08-31 | 304 | 98 | 0.322 |
+----+------------+-----+----+-------+
```

The last column of the query result also shows the player's batting average as of each date. This column is not stored in the table but is easily computed as the ratio of hits to at-bats. The result provides a general idea of how the player's hitting performance changed over the course of the season, but it doesn't give a very informative picture of how the player did during each individual month. To determine that, it's necessary to calculate relative differences between pairs of rows. This is easily done with a self-join that matches each row *n* with row *n*+1 to calculate differences between pairs of at-bats and hits values. These differences enable computation of batting average during each month:

```
mysql> SELECT
    -> t1.id AS id1, t2.id AS id2,
    -> t2.date,
    -> t1.ab AS ab1, t2.ab AS ab2,
    -> t1.h AS h1, t2.h AS h2,
    -> t2.ab-t1.ab AS abdiff,
    -> t2.h-t1.h AS hdiff,
```

```
   ->  TRUNCATE(IFNULL((t2.h-t1.h)/(t2.ab-t1.ab),0),3) AS ba
   ->  FROM player_stats AS t1 INNER JOIN player_stats AS t2
   ->  ON t1.id+1 = t2.id
   ->  ORDER BY t1.id;
+-----+-----+------------+-----+-----+----+----+--------+-------+-------+
| id1 | id2 | date       | ab1 | ab2 | h1 | h2 | abdiff | hdiff | ba    |
+-----+-----+------------+-----+-----+----+----+--------+-------+-------+
|   1 |   2 | 2006-05-31 |   0 |  38 |  0 | 13 |     38 |    13 | 0.342 |
|   2 |   3 | 2006-06-30 |  38 | 109 | 13 | 31 |     71 |    18 | 0.253 |
|   3 |   4 | 2006-07-31 | 109 | 196 | 31 | 49 |     87 |    18 | 0.206 |
|   4 |   5 | 2006-08-31 | 196 | 304 | 49 | 98 |    108 |    49 | 0.453 |
+-----+-----+------------+-----+-----+----+----+--------+-------+-------+
```

These results show much more clearly than the original table that the player started off well but had a slump in the middle of the season, particularly in July. They also indicate just how strong his performance was in August.

12.10 Finding Cumulative Sums and Running Averages

Problem

You have a set of observations measured over time and want to compute the cumulative sum of the observations at each measurement point. Or you want to compute a running average at each point.

Solution

Use a self-join to produce the sets of successive observations at each measurement point, and then apply aggregate functions to each set of values to compute its sum or average.

Discussion

Recipe 12.9 illustrates how a self-join can produce relative values from absolute values. A self-join can do the opposite as well, producing cumulative values at each successive stage of a set of observations. The following table shows a set of rainfall measurements taken over a series of days. The values in each row show the observation date and the amount of precipitation in inches:

```
mysql> SELECT date, precip FROM rainfall ORDER BY date;
+------------+--------+
| date       | precip |
+------------+--------+
| 2006-06-01 |   1.50 |
| 2006-06-02 |   0.00 |
| 2006-06-03 |   0.50 |
| 2006-06-04 |   0.00 |
| 2006-06-05 |   1.00 |
+------------+--------+
```

To calculate cumulative rainfall for a given day, add that day's precipitation value with the values for all the previous days. For example, determine the cumulative rainfall as of 2006-06-03 like this:

```
mysql> SELECT SUM(precip) FROM rainfall WHERE date <= '2006-06-03';
+-------------+
| SUM(precip) |
+-------------+
|        2.00 |
+-------------+
```

If you want the cumulative figures for all days that are represented in the table, it would be tedious to compute the value for each of them separately. A self-join can do this for all days with a single statement. Use one instance of the `rainfall` table as a reference, and determine for the date in each row the sum of the `precip` values in all rows occurring up through that date in another instance of the table. The following statement shows the daily and cumulative precipitation for each day:

```
mysql> SELECT t1.date, t1.precip AS 'daily precip',
    -> SUM(t2.precip) AS 'cum. precip'
    -> FROM rainfall AS t1 INNER JOIN rainfall AS t2
    -> ON t1.date >= t2.date
    -> GROUP BY t1.date;
+------------+--------------+-------------+
| date       | daily precip | cum. precip |
+------------+--------------+-------------+
| 2006-06-01 |         1.50 |        1.50 |
| 2006-06-02 |         0.00 |        1.50 |
| 2006-06-03 |         0.50 |        2.00 |
| 2006-06-04 |         0.00 |        2.00 |
| 2006-06-05 |         1.00 |        3.00 |
+------------+--------------+-------------+
```

The self-join can be extended to display the number of days elapsed at each date, as well as the running averages for amount of precipitation each day:

```
mysql> SELECT t1.date, t1.precip AS 'daily precip',
    -> SUM(t2.precip) AS 'cum. precip',
    -> COUNT(t2.precip) AS 'days elapsed',
    -> AVG(t2.precip) AS 'avg. precip'
    -> FROM rainfall AS t1 INNER JOIN rainfall AS t2
    -> ON t1.date >= t2.date
    -> GROUP BY t1.date;
+------------+--------------+-------------+--------------+-------------+
| date       | daily precip | cum. precip | days elapsed | avg. precip |
+------------+--------------+-------------+--------------+-------------+
| 2006-06-01 |         1.50 |        1.50 |            1 |    1.500000 |
| 2006-06-02 |         0.00 |        1.50 |            2 |    0.750000 |
| 2006-06-03 |         0.50 |        2.00 |            3 |    0.666667 |
| 2006-06-04 |         0.00 |        2.00 |            4 |    0.500000 |
| 2006-06-05 |         1.00 |        3.00 |            5 |    0.600000 |
+------------+--------------+-------------+--------------+-------------+
```

In the preceding statement, the number of days elapsed and the precipitation running averages can be computed easily using COUNT( ) and AVG( ) because there are no missing days in the table. If missing days are allowed, the calculation becomes more complicated, because the number of days elapsed for each calculation no longer will be the same as the number of rows. You can see this by deleting the rows for the days that had no precipitation to produce a couple of "holes" in the table:

```
mysql> DELETE FROM rainfall WHERE precip = 0;
mysql> SELECT date, precip FROM rainfall ORDER BY date;
+------------+--------+
| date       | precip |
+------------+--------+
| 2006-06-01 |   1.50 |
| 2006-06-03 |   0.50 |
| 2006-06-05 |   1.00 |
+------------+--------+
```

Deleting those rows doesn't change the cumulative sum or running average for the dates that remain, but it does change how they must be calculated. If you try the self-join again, it yields incorrect results for the days-elapsed and average precipitation columns:

```
mysql> SELECT t1.date, t1.precip AS 'daily precip',
    -> SUM(t2.precip) AS 'cum. precip',
    -> COUNT(t2.precip) AS 'days elapsed',
    -> AVG(t2.precip) AS 'avg. precip'
    -> FROM rainfall AS t1 INNER JOIN rainfall AS t2
    -> ON t1.date >= t2.date
    -> GROUP BY t1.date;
+------------+--------------+-------------+--------------+-------------+
| date       | daily precip | cum. precip | days elapsed | avg. precip |
+------------+--------------+-------------+--------------+-------------+
| 2006-06-01 |         1.50 |        1.50 |            1 |    1.500000 |
| 2006-06-03 |         0.50 |        2.00 |            2 |    1.000000 |
| 2006-06-05 |         1.00 |        3.00 |            3 |    1.000000 |
+------------+--------------+-------------+--------------+-------------+
```

To fix the problem, it's necessary to determine the number of days elapsed a different way. Take the minimum and maximum date involved in each sum and calculate a days-elapsed value from them using the following expression:

```
DATEDIFF(MAX(t2.date),MIN(t2.date)) + 1
```

That value must be used for the days-elapsed column and for computing the running averages. The resulting statement is as follows:

```
mysql> SELECT t1.date, t1.precip AS 'daily precip',
    -> SUM(t2.precip) AS 'cum. precip',
    -> DATEDIFF(MAX(t2.date),MIN(t2.date)) + 1 AS 'days elapsed',
    -> SUM(t2.precip) / (DATEDIFF(MAX(t2.date),MIN(t2.date)) + 1)
    -> AS 'avg. precip'
    -> FROM rainfall AS t1 INNER JOIN rainfall AS t2
    -> ON t1.date >= t2.date
    -> GROUP BY t1.date;
+------------+--------------+-------------+--------------+-------------+
| date       | daily precip | cum. precip | days elapsed | avg. precip |
```

```
+------------+------------+------------+------------+------------+
| 2006-06-01 |       1.50 |       1.50 |          1 |   1.500000 |
| 2006-06-03 |       0.50 |       2.00 |          3 |   0.666667 |
| 2006-06-05 |       1.00 |       3.00 |          5 |   0.600000 |
+------------+------------+------------+------------+------------+
```

As this example illustrates, calculation of cumulative values from relative values requires only a column that enables rows to be placed into the proper order. (For the rainfall table, that's the date column.) Values in the column need not be sequential, or even numeric. This differs from calculations that produce difference values from cumulative values (Recipe 12.9), which require that a table have a column that contains an unbroken sequence.

The running averages in the rainfall examples are based on dividing cumulative precipitation sums by number of days elapsed as of each day. When the table has no gaps, the number of days is the same as the number of values summed, making it easy to find successive averages. When rows are missing, the calculations become more complex. What this demonstrates is that it's necessary to consider the nature of your data and calculate averages appropriately. The next example is conceptually similar to the previous ones in that it calculates cumulative sums and running averages, but it performs the computations yet another way.

The following table shows a marathon runner's performance at each stage of a 26-kilometer run. The values in each row show the length of each stage in kilometers and how long the runner took to complete the stage. In other words, the values pertain to intervals within the marathon and thus are relative to the whole:

```
mysql> SELECT stage, km, t FROM marathon ORDER BY stage;
+-------+----+----------+
| stage | km | t        |
+-------+----+----------+
|     1 |  5 | 00:15:00 |
|     2 |  7 | 00:19:30 |
|     3 |  9 | 00:29:20 |
|     4 |  5 | 00:17:50 |
+-------+----+----------+
```

To calculate cumulative distance in kilometers at each stage, use a self-join that looks like this:

```
mysql> SELECT t1.stage, t1.km, SUM(t2.km) AS 'cum. km'
    -> FROM marathon AS t1 INNER JOIN marathon AS t2
    -> ON t1.stage >= t2.stage
    -> GROUP BY t1.stage;
+-------+----+---------+
| stage | km | cum. km |
+-------+----+---------+
|     1 |  5 |       5 |
|     2 |  7 |      12 |
|     3 |  9 |      21 |
|     4 |  5 |      26 |
+-------+----+---------+
```

Cumulative distances are easy to compute because they can be summed directly. The calculation for accumulating time values is a little more involved. It's necessary to convert times to seconds, total the resulting values, and convert the sum back to a time value. To compute the runner's average speed at the end of each stage, take the ratio of cumulative distance over cumulative time. Putting all this together yields the following statement:

```
mysql> SELECT t1.stage, t1.km, t1.t,
    -> SUM(t2.km) AS 'cum. km',
    -> SEC_TO_TIME(SUM(TIME_TO_SEC(t2.t))) AS 'cum. t',
    -> SUM(t2.km)/(SUM(TIME_TO_SEC(t2.t))/(60*60)) AS 'avg. km/hour'
    -> FROM marathon AS t1 INNER JOIN marathon AS t2
    -> ON t1.stage >= t2.stage
    -> GROUP BY t1.stage;
+-------+----+----------+---------+----------+--------------+
| stage | km | t        | cum. km | cum. t   | avg. km/hour |
+-------+----+----------+---------+----------+--------------+
|     1 |  5 | 00:15:00 |       5 | 00:15:00 |      20.0000 |
|     2 |  7 | 00:19:30 |      12 | 00:34:30 |      20.8696 |
|     3 |  9 | 00:29:20 |      21 | 01:03:50 |      19.7389 |
|     4 |  5 | 00:17:50 |      26 | 01:21:40 |      19.1020 |
+-------+----+----------+---------+----------+--------------+
```

We can see from this that the runner's average pace increased a little during the second stage of the race, but then (presumably as a result of fatigue) decreased thereafter.

12.11 Using a Join to Control Query Output Order

Problem

You want to sort a statement's output using a characteristic of the output that cannot be specified using ORDER BY. For example, you want to sort a set of rows by subgroups, putting first those groups with the most rows and last those groups with the fewest rows. But "number of rows in each group" is not a property of individual rows, so you can't use it for sorting.

Solution

Derive the ordering information and store it in an auxiliary table. Then join the original table to the auxiliary table, using the auxiliary table to control the sort order.

Discussion

Most of the time when you sort a query result, you use an ORDER BY clause that names which column or columns to use for sorting. But sometimes the values you want to sort by aren't present in the rows to be sorted. This is the case when you want to use group characteristics to order the rows. The following example uses the rows in the driver_log table to illustrate this. The table contains these rows:

```
mysql> SELECT * FROM driver_log ORDER BY rec_id;
+--------+-------+------------+-------+
| rec_id | name  | trav_date  | miles |
+--------+-------+------------+-------+
|      1 | Ben   | 2006-08-30 |   152 |
|      2 | Suzi  | 2006-08-29 |   391 |
|      3 | Henry | 2006-08-29 |   300 |
|      4 | Henry | 2006-08-27 |    96 |
|      5 | Ben   | 2006-08-29 |   131 |
|      6 | Henry | 2006-08-26 |   115 |
|      7 | Suzi  | 2006-09-02 |   502 |
|      8 | Henry | 2006-09-01 |   197 |
|      9 | Ben   | 2006-09-02 |    79 |
|     10 | Henry | 2006-08-30 |   203 |
+--------+-------+------------+-------+
```

The preceding statement sorts the rows using the ID column, which is present in the rows. But what if you want to display a list and sort it on the basis of a summary value not present in the rows? That's a little trickier. Suppose that you want to show each driver's rows by date, but place those drivers who drive the most miles first. You can't do this with a summary query, because then you wouldn't get back the individual driver rows. But you can't do it without a summary query, either, because the summary values are required for sorting. The way out of the dilemma is to create another table containing the summary value per driver and then join it to the original table. That way you can produce the individual rows and also sort them by the summary values.

To summarize the driver totals into another table, do this:

```
mysql> CREATE TABLE tmp
    -> SELECT name, SUM(miles) AS driver_miles FROM driver_log GROUP BY name;
```

This produces the values we need to put the names in the proper total-miles order:

```
mysql> SELECT * FROM tmp ORDER BY driver_miles DESC;
+-------+--------------+
| name  | driver_miles |
+-------+--------------+
| Henry |          911 |
| Suzi  |          893 |
| Ben   |          362 |
+-------+--------------+
```

Then use the name values to join the summary table to the driver_log table, and use the driver_miles values to sort the result. The following statement shows the mileage totals in the result. That's only to clarify how the values are being sorted. It's not actually necessary to display them; they're needed only for the ORDER BY clause.

```
mysql> SELECT tmp.driver_miles, driver_log.*
    -> FROM driver_log INNER JOIN tmp
    -> ON driver_log.name = tmp.name
    -> ORDER BY tmp.driver_miles DESC, driver_log.trav_date;
+--------------+--------+-------+------------+-------+
| driver_miles | rec_id | name  | trav_date  | miles |
+--------------+--------+-------+------------+-------+
```

```
|       911 |      6 | Henry | 2006-08-26 |   115 |
|       911 |      4 | Henry | 2006-08-27 |    96 |
|       911 |      3 | Henry | 2006-08-29 |   300 |
|       911 |     10 | Henry | 2006-08-30 |   203 |
|       911 |      8 | Henry | 2006-09-01 |   197 |
|       893 |      2 | Suzi  | 2006-08-29 |   391 |
|       893 |      7 | Suzi  | 2006-09-02 |   502 |
|       362 |      5 | Ben   | 2006-08-29 |   131 |
|       362 |      1 | Ben   | 2006-08-30 |   152 |
|       362 |      9 | Ben   | 2006-09-02 |    79 |
+-----------+--------+-------+------------+-------+
```

To avoid using the temporary table, select the same rows using a subquery in the
FROM clause:

```
mysql> SELECT tmp.driver_miles, driver_log.*
    -> FROM driver_log INNER JOIN
    -> (SELECT name, SUM(miles) AS driver_miles
    -> FROM driver_log GROUP BY name) AS tmp
    -> ON driver_log.name = tmp.name
    -> ORDER BY tmp.driver_miles DESC, driver_log.trav_date;
+--------------+--------+-------+------------+-------+
| driver_miles | rec_id | name  | trav_date  | miles |
+--------------+--------+-------+------------+-------+
|          911 |      6 | Henry | 2006-08-26 |   115 |
|          911 |      4 | Henry | 2006-08-27 |    96 |
|          911 |      3 | Henry | 2006-08-29 |   300 |
|          911 |     10 | Henry | 2006-08-30 |   203 |
|          911 |      8 | Henry | 2006-09-01 |   197 |
|          893 |      2 | Suzi  | 2006-08-29 |   391 |
|          893 |      7 | Suzi  | 2006-09-02 |   502 |
|          362 |      5 | Ben   | 2006-08-29 |   131 |
|          362 |      1 | Ben   | 2006-08-30 |   152 |
|          362 |      9 | Ben   | 2006-09-02 |    79 |
+--------------+--------+-------+------------+-------+
```

12.12 Combining Several Result Sets in a Single Query

Problem

You want to select rows from several tables, or several sets of rows from a single table
—all as a single result set.

Solution

Use a UNION operation to combine multiple SELECT results into one.

Discussion

A join is useful for combining columns from different tables side by side. It's not so
useful when you want a result set that includes a set of rows from several tables, or

multiple sets of rows from the same table. These are instances of the type of operation for which a UNION is useful. A UNION enables you to run several SELECT statements and combine their results. That is, rather than running multiple queries and receiving multiple result sets, you receive a single result set.

Suppose that you have two tables that list prospective and actual customers, and a third that lists vendors from whom you purchase supplies, and you want to create a single mailing list by merging names and addresses from all three tables. UNION provides a way to do this. Assume that the three tables have the following contents:

```
mysql> SELECT * FROM prospect;
+---------+-------+------------------------+
| fname   | lname | addr                   |
+---------+-------+------------------------+
| Peter   | Jones | 482 Rush St., Apt. 402 |
| Bernice | Smith | 916 Maple Dr.          |
+---------+-------+------------------------+
mysql> SELECT * FROM customer;
+-----------+------------+---------------------+
| last_name | first_name | address             |
+-----------+------------+---------------------+
| Peterson  | Grace      | 16055 Seminole Ave. |
| Smith     | Bernice    | 916 Maple Dr.       |
| Brown     | Walter     | 8602 1st St.        |
+-----------+------------+---------------------+
mysql> SELECT * FROM vendor;
+------------------+---------------------+
| company          | street              |
+------------------+---------------------+
| ReddyParts, Inc. | 38 Industrial Blvd. |
| Parts-to-go, Ltd.| 213B Commerce Park. |
+------------------+---------------------+
```

The tables have columns that are similar but not identical. prospect and customer use different names for the first name and last name columns, and the vendor table includes only a single name column. None of that matters for UNION; all you need to do is make sure to select the same number of columns from each table, and in the same order. The following statement illustrates how to select names and addresses from the three tables all at once:

```
mysql> SELECT fname, lname, addr FROM prospect
    -> UNION
    -> SELECT first_name, last_name, address FROM customer
    -> UNION
    -> SELECT company, '', street FROM vendor;
+------------------+----------+------------------------+
| fname            | lname    | addr                   |
+------------------+----------+------------------------+
| Peter            | Jones    | 482 Rush St., Apt. 402 |
| Bernice          | Smith    | 916 Maple Dr.          |
| Grace            | Peterson | 16055 Seminole Ave.    |
| Walter           | Brown    | 8602 1st St.           |
| ReddyParts, Inc. |          | 38 Industrial Blvd.    |
```

```
| Parts-to-go, Ltd. |              | 213B Commerce Park.  |
+-------------------+----------+----------------------+
```

The column names in the result set are taken from the names of the columns retrieved by the first SELECT statement. Notice that, by default, a UNION eliminates duplicates; Bernice Smith appears in both the prospect and customer tables, but only once in the final result. If you want to select all rows, including duplicates, follow each UNION keyword with ALL:

```
mysql> SELECT fname, lname, addr FROM prospect
    -> UNION ALL
    -> SELECT first_name, last_name, address FROM customer
    -> UNION ALL
    -> SELECT company, '', street FROM vendor;
+-------------------+----------+----------------------+
| fname             | lname    | addr                 |
+-------------------+----------+----------------------+
| Peter             | Jones    | 482 Rush St., Apt. 402 |
| Bernice           | Smith    | 916 Maple Dr.        |
| Grace             | Peterson | 16055 Seminole Ave.  |
| Bernice           | Smith    | 916 Maple Dr.        |
| Walter            | Brown    | 8602 1st St.         |
| ReddyParts, Inc.  |          | 38 Industrial Blvd.  |
| Parts-to-go, Ltd. |          | 213B Commerce Park.  |
+-------------------+----------+----------------------+
```

Because it's necessary to select the same number of columns from each table, the SELECT for the vendor table (which has just one name column) retrieves a dummy (empty) last name column. Another way to select the same number of columns is to combine the first and last name columns from the prospect and customer tables into a single column:

```
mysql> SELECT CONCAT(lname,', ',fname) AS name, addr FROM prospect
    -> UNION
    -> SELECT CONCAT(last_name,', ',first_name), address FROM customer
    -> UNION
    -> SELECT company, street FROM vendor;
+-------------------+----------------------+
| name              | addr                 |
+-------------------+----------------------+
| Jones, Peter      | 482 Rush St., Apt. 402 |
| Smith, Bernice    | 916 Maple Dr.        |
| Peterson, Grace   | 16055 Seminole Ave.  |
| Brown, Walter     | 8602 1st St.         |
| ReddyParts, Inc.  | 38 Industrial Blvd.  |
| Parts-to-go, Ltd. | 213B Commerce Park.  |
+-------------------+----------------------+
```

To sort the result set, place each SELECT statement within parentheses and add an ORDER BY clause after the final one. Any columns specified by name in the ORDER BY should refer to the column names used in the first SELECT, because those are the names used for the columns in the result set. For example, to sort by name, do this:

```
mysql> (SELECT CONCAT(lname,', ',fname) AS name, addr FROM prospect)
    -> UNION
    -> (SELECT CONCAT(last_name,', ',first_name), address FROM customer)
    -> UNION
    -> (SELECT company, street FROM vendor)
    -> ORDER BY name;
+-------------------+------------------------+
| name              | addr                   |
+-------------------+------------------------+
| Brown, Walter     | 8602 1st St.           |
| Jones, Peter      | 482 Rush St., Apt. 402 |
| Parts-to-go, Ltd. | 213B Commerce Park.     |
| Peterson, Grace   | 16055 Seminole Ave.    |
| ReddyParts, Inc.  | 38 Industrial Blvd.    |
| Smith, Bernice    | 916 Maple Dr.          |
+-------------------+------------------------+
```

It's possible to ensure that the results from each SELECT appear consecutively, although you must generate an extra column to use for sorting. Enclose each SELECT within parentheses, add a sort-value column to each one, and place an ORDER BY at the end that sorts using that column:

```
mysql> (SELECT 1 AS sortval, CONCAT(lname,', ',fname) AS name, addr
    -> FROM prospect)
    -> UNION
    -> (SELECT 2 AS sortval, CONCAT(last_name,', ',first_name) AS name, address
    -> FROM customer)
    -> UNION
    -> (SELECT 3 AS sortval, company, street FROM vendor)
    -> ORDER BY sortval;
+---------+-------------------+------------------------+
| sortval | name              | addr                   |
+---------+-------------------+------------------------+
|       1 | Jones, Peter      | 482 Rush St., Apt. 402 |
|       1 | Smith, Bernice    | 916 Maple Dr.          |
|       2 | Peterson, Grace   | 16055 Seminole Ave.    |
|       2 | Smith, Bernice    | 916 Maple Dr.          |
|       2 | Brown, Walter     | 8602 1st St.           |
|       3 | ReddyParts, Inc.  | 38 Industrial Blvd.    |
|       3 | Parts-to-go, Ltd. | 213B Commerce Park.    |
+---------+-------------------+------------------------+
```

If you also want the rows within each SELECT sorted, include a secondary sort column in the ORDER BY clause. The following query sorts by name within each SELECT:

```
mysql> (SELECT 1 AS sortval, CONCAT(lname,', ',fname) AS name, addr
    -> FROM prospect)
    -> UNION
    -> (SELECT 2 AS sortval, CONCAT(last_name,', ',first_name) AS name, address
    -> FROM customer)
    -> UNION
    -> (SELECT 3 AS sortval, company, street FROM vendor)
    -> ORDER BY sortval, name;
+---------+-------------------+------------------------+
| sortval | name              | addr                   |
```

```
+---------+-------------------+------------------------+
|       1 | Jones, Peter      | 482 Rush St., Apt. 402 |
|       1 | Smith, Bernice    | 916 Maple Dr.          |
|       2 | Brown, Walter     | 8602 1st St.           |
|       2 | Peterson, Grace   | 16055 Seminole Ave.    |
|       2 | Smith, Bernice    | 916 Maple Dr.          |
|       3 | Parts-to-go, Ltd. | 213B Commerce Park.    |
|       3 | ReddyParts, Inc.  | 38 Industrial Blvd.    |
+---------+-------------------+------------------------+
```

Similar syntax can be used for LIMIT as well. That is, you can limit the result set as a whole with a trailing LIMIT clause, or for individual SELECT statements. Typically, LIMIT is combined with ORDER BY. Suppose that you want to select a lucky prizewinner for some kind of promotional giveaway. To select a single winner at random from the combined results of the three tables, do this:

```
mysql> (SELECT CONCAT(lname,', ',fname) AS name, addr FROM prospect)
    -> UNION
    -> (SELECT CONCAT(last_name,', ',first_name), address FROM customer)
    -> UNION
    -> (SELECT company, street FROM vendor)
    -> ORDER BY RAND() LIMIT 1;
+-----------------+---------------------+
| name            | addr                |
+-----------------+---------------------+
| Peterson, Grace | 16055 Seminole Ave. |
+-----------------+---------------------+
```

To select a single winner from each table and combine the results, do this instead:

```
mysql> (SELECT CONCAT(lname,', ',fname) AS name, addr
    -> FROM prospect ORDER BY RAND() LIMIT 1)
    -> UNION
    -> (SELECT CONCAT(last_name,', ',first_name), address
    -> FROM customer ORDER BY RAND() LIMIT 1)
    -> UNION
    -> (SELECT company, street
    -> FROM vendor ORDER BY RAND() LIMIT 1);
+-----------------+---------------------+
| name            | addr                |
+-----------------+---------------------+
| Smith, Bernice  | 916 Maple Dr.       |
| ReddyParts, Inc.| 38 Industrial Blvd. |
+-----------------+---------------------+
```

If that result surprises you ("Why didn't it pick three rows?"), remember that Bernice is listed in two tables and that UNION eliminates duplicates. If the first and second SELECT statements each happen to pick Bernice, one instance will be eliminated and the final result will have only two rows. (If there are no duplicates among the three tables, the statement will always return three rows.) You could of course assure three rows in all cases by using UNION ALL.

12.13 Identifying and Removing Mismatched or Unattached Rows

Problem

You have two datasets that are related, but possibly imperfectly so. You want to determine whether there are records in either dataset that are "unattached" (not matched by any record in the other dataset), and perhaps remove them if so. This might occur, for example, when you receive data from an external source and must check it to verify its integrity.

Solution

Use a LEFT JOIN to identify unmatched values in each table. If there are any and you want to get rid of them, use a multiple-table DELETE statement. It's also possible to identify or remove nonmatching rows by using NOT IN subqueries.

Discussion

Inner joins are useful for identifying relationships, and outer joins are useful for identifying the *lack* of relationship. This property of outer joins is valuable when you have datasets that are supposed to be related but for which the relationship might be imperfect.

Mismatches between datasets can occur if you receive two datafiles from an external source that are supposed to be related but for which the integrity of the relationship actually is imperfect. It can also occur as an anticipated consequence of a deliberate action. Suppose that an online discussion board uses a parent table that lists discussion topics and a child table that rows the articles posted for each topic. If you purge the child table of old article rows, that may result in any given topic row in the parent table no longer having any children. If so, the lack of recent postings for the topic indicates that it is probably dead and that the parent row in the topic table can be deleted, too. In such a situation, you delete a set of child rows with the explicit recognition that the operation may strand parent rows and cause them to become eligible for being deleted as well.

However you arrive at the point where related tables have unmatched rows, you can analyze and modify them using SQL statements. Specifically, restoring their relationship is a matter of identifying the unattached rows and then deleting them:

- To identify unattached rows, use a LEFT JOIN, because this is a "find unmatched rows" problem. (See Recipe 12.2 for information about LEFT JOIN.)
- To delete rows that are unmatched, use a multiple-table DELETE statement that specifies which rows to remove using a similar LEFT JOIN.

The presence of unmatched data is useful to know about because you can alert whoever gave you the data. This may be a signal of a flaw in the data collection method that must be corrected. For example, with sales data, a missing region might mean that some regional manager didn't report in and that the omission was overlooked.

The following example shows how to identify and remove mismatched rows using two datasets that describe sales regions and volume of sales per region. One dataset contains the ID and location of each sales region:

```
mysql> SELECT * FROM sales_region ORDER BY region_id;
+-----------+------------------------+
| region_id | name                   |
+-----------+------------------------+
|         1 | London, United Kingdom |
|         2 | Madrid, Spain          |
|         3 | Berlin, Germany        |
|         4 | Athens, Greece         |
+-----------+------------------------+
```

The other dataset contains sales volume figures. Each row contains the amount of sales for a given quarter of a year and indicates the sales region to which the row applies:

```
mysql> SELECT * FROM sales_volume ORDER BY region_id, year, quarter;
+-----------+------+---------+--------+
| region_id | year | quarter | volume |
+-----------+------+---------+--------+
|         1 | 2006 |       1 | 100400 |
|         1 | 2006 |       2 | 120000 |
|         3 | 2006 |       1 | 280000 |
|         3 | 2006 |       2 | 250000 |
|         5 | 2006 |       1 |  18000 |
|         5 | 2006 |       2 |  32000 |
+-----------+------+---------+--------+
```

A little visual inspection reveals that neither table is fully matched by the other. Sales regions 2 and 4 are not represented in the sales volume table, and the sales volume table contains rows for region 5, which is not in the sales region table. But we don't want to check the tables by inspection. We want to find unmatched rows by using SQL statements that do the work for us.

Mismatch identification is a matter of using outer joins. For example, to find sales regions for which there are no sales volume rows, use the following LEFT JOIN:

```
mysql> SELECT sales_region.region_id AS 'unmatched region row IDs'
    -> FROM sales_region LEFT JOIN sales_volume
    ->   ON sales_region.region_id = sales_volume.region_id
    -> WHERE sales_volume.region_id IS NULL;
+--------------------------+
| unmatched region row IDs |
+--------------------------+
|                        2 |
|                        4 |
+--------------------------+
```

Conversely, to find sales volume rows that are not associated with any known region, reverse the roles of the two tables:

```
mysql> SELECT sales_volume.region_id AS 'unmatched volume row IDs'
    -> FROM sales_volume LEFT JOIN sales_region
    ->   ON sales_volume.region_id = sales_region.region_id
    -> WHERE sales_region.region_id IS NULL;
+--------------------------+
| unmatched volume row IDs |
+--------------------------+
|                        5 |
|                        5 |
+--------------------------+
```

In this case, an ID appears more than once in the list if there are multiple volume rows for a missing region. To see each unmatched ID only once, use SELECT DISTINCT:

```
mysql> SELECT DISTINCT sales_volume.region_id AS 'unmatched volume row IDs'
    -> FROM sales_volume LEFT JOIN sales_region
    ->   ON sales_volume.region_id = sales_region.region_id
    -> WHERE sales_region.region_id IS NULL
+--------------------------+
| unmatched volume row IDs |
+--------------------------+
|                        5 |
+--------------------------+
```

To get rid of unmatched rows, you can use their IDs in a multiple-table DELETE statement. To construct the proper multiple-table DELETE statement for removing unmatched rows from a table, just take the SELECT statement that you use to identify those rows, and replace the stuff leading up to the FROM keyword with DELETE *tbl_name*. For example, the SELECT that identifies childless parents looks like this:

```
SELECT sales_region.region_id AS 'unmatched region row IDs'
FROM sales_region LEFT JOIN sales_volume
  ON sales_region.region_id = sales_volume.region_id
WHERE sales_volume.region_id IS NULL;
```

The corresponding DELETE looks like this:

```
DELETE sales_region
FROM sales_region LEFT JOIN sales_volume
  ON sales_region.region_id = sales_volume.region_id
WHERE sales_volume.region_id IS NULL;
```

Conversely, the statement to identify parentless children is as follows:

```
SELECT sales_volume.region_id AS 'unmatched volume row IDs'
FROM sales_volume LEFT JOIN sales_region
  ON sales_volume.region_id = sales_region.region_id
WHERE sales_region.region_id IS NULL;
```

And the corresponding DELETE statement removes them:

```
DELETE sales_volume
FROM sales_volume LEFT JOIN sales_region
```

```
      ON sales_volume.region_id = sales_region.region_id
  WHERE sales_region.region_id IS NULL;
```

You can also identify or delete mismatched rows by using NOT IN subqueries. The statements to display or remove sales_region rows that match no sales_volume rows look like this:

```
SELECT region_id AS 'unmatched region row IDs'
FROM sales_region
WHERE region_id NOT IN (SELECT region_id FROM sales_volume);

DELETE FROM sales_region
WHERE region_id NOT IN (SELECT region_id FROM sales_volume);
```

The statements to identify or delete mismatched sales_volume rows are similar but have the roles of the tables reversed:

```
SELECT region_id AS 'unmatched volume row IDs'
FROM sales_volume
WHERE region_id NOT IN (SELECT region_id FROM sales_region);

DELETE FROM sales_volume
WHERE region_id NOT IN (SELECT region_id FROM sales_region);
```

Using Foreign Keys to Enforce Referential Integrity

One feature a database system offers to help you maintain consistency between tables is the ability to define foreign key relationships. This means you can specify explicitly in the table definition that a primary key in a parent table (such as the region_id column of the sales_region table) is a parent to a key in another table (the region_id column in the sales_volume table). By defining the ID column in the child table as a foreign key to the ID column in the parent, the database system can enforce certain constraints against illegal operations. For example, it can prevent you from creating a child row with an ID that is not present in the parent or from deleting parent rows without also deleting the corresponding child rows first. A foreign key implementation may also offer cascaded delete and update: if you delete or update a parent row, the database engine cascades the effect of the delete or update to any child tables and automatically deletes or updates the child rows for you. The InnoDB storage engine in MySQL supports foreign keys and cascaded deletes and updates.

12.14 Performing a Join Between Tables in Different Databases

Problem

You want to use tables in a join, but they're not located in the same database.

Solution

Use database name qualifiers to tell MySQL where to find the tables.

Discussion

Sometimes it's necessary to perform a join on two tables that are located in different databases. To do this, qualify table and column names sufficiently so that MySQL knows what you're referring to. Thus far, we have used the artist and painting tables with the implicit understanding that both are in the cookbook database, which means that we can simply refer to the tables without specifying any database name when cookbook is the default database. For example, the following statement uses the two tables to associate artists with their paintings:

```
SELECT artist.name, painting.title
  FROM artist INNER JOIN painting
  ON artist.a_id = painting.a_id;
```

But suppose instead that artist is in the db1 database and painting is in the db2 database. To indicate this, qualify each table name with a prefix that specifies which database it's in. The fully qualified form of the join looks like this:

```
SELECT db1.artist.name, db2.painting.title
  FROM db1.artist INNER JOIN db2.painting
  ON db1.artist.a_id = db2.painting.a_id;
```

If there is no default database, or it is neither db1 nor db2, it's necessary to use this fully qualified form. If the default database is either db1 or db2, you can dispense with the corresponding qualifiers. For example, if the default database is db1, you can omit the db1 qualifiers:

```
SELECT artist.name, db2.painting.title
  FROM artist INNER JOIN db2.painting
  ON artist.a_id = db2.painting.a_id;
```

Conversely, if the default database is db2, no db2 qualifiers are necessary:

```
SELECT db1.artist.name, painting.title
  FROM db1.artist INNER JOIN painting
  ON db1.artist.a_id = painting.a_id;
```

12.15 Using Different MySQL Servers Simultaneously

Problem

You want to execute a statement that uses tables located in databases that are hosted by different MySQL servers.

Solution

Set up a FEDERATED table, which enables one MySQL server to access a table hosted by another MySQL server. Other approaches are to open separate connections to each server and combine the information from the two tables yourself, or to copy one of the tables from one server to the other so that you can work with both tables using a single server.

Discussion

Throughout this chapter, we have assumed that all the tables involved in a multiple-table operation are managed by a single MySQL server. If this assumption is invalid, the tables become more difficult to work with because a connection to a MySQL server enables you to directly access only tables hosted by that server. However, MySQL supports a FEDERATED storage engine that enables you to remotely access tables that are hosted by another MySQL server. For a FEDERATED table, the local MySQL server takes on the role of a client that connects to another MySQL server so that it can access the remote table on your behalf and make its contents appear to be local.

Here is an example that illustrates the problem, using the artist and painting tables. Suppose that you want to find the names of paintings by Da Vinci. This requires determining the ID for Da Vinci in the artist table and matching it to rows in the painting table. If both tables are located within the same database, you can identify the paintings by using the following statement to perform a join between the tables:

```
mysql> SELECT painting.title
    -> FROM artist INNER JOIN painting
    -> ON artist.a_id = painting.a_id
    -> WHERE artist.name = 'Da Vinci';
+-----------------+
| title           |
+-----------------+
| The Last Supper |
| The Mona Lisa   |
+-----------------+
```

Now suppose that the painting table is not available on the MySQL server to which we normally connect but is located remotely on another MySQL server. We can access the remote table as though it is local by creating a FEDERATED table that is defined to have the same structure as the remote table. The CREATE TABLE statement for the FEDERATED table must include table options to specify the FEDERATED storage engine and a connection string that tells our server how to connect to the remote server and locate the table. Recipe 12.1 shows the original structure of the painting table. To set up a corresponding FEDERATED table, define it like this:

```
CREATE TABLE fed_painting
(
  a_id  INT UNSIGNED NOT NULL,                # artist ID
  p_id  INT UNSIGNED NOT NULL AUTO_INCREMENT, # painting ID
  title VARCHAR(100) NOT NULL,                # title of painting
  state VARCHAR(2) NOT NULL,                  # state where purchased
  price INT UNSIGNED,                         # purchase price (dollars)
  INDEX (a_id),
  PRIMARY KEY (p_id)
)
```

```
ENGINE = FEDERATED
CONNECTION = 'mysql://cbuser:cbpass@remote.example.com/cookbook/painting';
```

The CONNECTION string used here has the following format:

```
mysql://user_name:pass_val@host_name/db_name/tbl_name
```

In other words, the remote server host is remote.example.com, the MySQL username and password are cbuser and cbpass, and the table is named painting in the cookbook database. Adjust the parameters in the connection string as necessary for your network. After creating the FEDERATED table, you can use it to access the remote table as though it were local. For example, to perform the join described earlier in this section, write it as shown here:

```
mysql> SELECT fed_painting.title
    -> FROM artist INNER JOIN fed_painting
    -> ON artist.a_id = fed_painting.a_id
    -> WHERE artist.name = 'Da Vinci';
+-----------------+
| title           |
+-----------------+
| The Last Supper |
| The Mona Lisa   |
+-----------------+
```

Currently, FEDERATED tables can be used to access only other MySQL servers, not servers for other database engines.

 In MySQL 5.0 binary distributions, the FEDERATED storage engine is not enabled unless you use a MySQL-Max server. In MySQL 5.1, FEDERATED is enabled by default in binary distributions. If you compile MySQL from source (for either version), use the --with-federated-stor age-engine configuration option to enable FEDERATED support.

Another approach to joining tables that are hosted by different servers is to write a program that simulates a join:

1. Open a separate connection to each database server.
2. Run a loop that fetches artist IDs and names from the server that manages the artist table.
3. Each time through the loop, use the current artist ID to construct a statement that looks for painting table rows that match the artist ID value. Send the statement to the server that manages the painting table. As you retrieve painting titles, display them along with the current artist name.

This technique enables simulation of a join between tables located on any two servers. Incidentally, it also can be used when you need to work with tables that are hosted by different types of database engines. (For example, you can simulate a join between a MySQL table and a PostgreSQL table this way.)

A third approach is to copy one of the tables from one server to the other. Then you can work with both tables using the same server, which enables you to perform a proper join between them. See Recipe 10.16 for information on copying tables between servers.

12.16 Referring to Join Output Column Names in Programs

Problem

You need to process the result of a join from within a program, but the column names in the result set aren't unique.

Solution

Revise the query using column aliases so that each column has a unique name, or refer to the columns by position.

Discussion

Joins typically retrieve columns from related tables, so it's not unusual for columns selected from different tables to have the same names. Consider the following join that shows the items in your art collection (originally seen in Recipe 12.1). For each painting, it displays artist name, painting title, the state in which you acquired the item, and how much it cost:

```
mysql> SELECT artist.name, painting.title, states.name, painting.price
    -> FROM artist INNER JOIN painting INNER JOIN states
    -> ON artist.a_id = painting.a_id AND painting.state = states.abbrev;
+----------+-------------------+----------+-------+
| name     | title             | name     | price |
+----------+-------------------+----------+-------+
| Da Vinci | The Last Supper   | Indiana  |    34 |
| Da Vinci | The Mona Lisa     | Michigan |    87 |
| Van Gogh | Starry Night      | Kentucky |    48 |
| Van Gogh | The Potato Eaters | Kentucky |    67 |
| Van Gogh | The Rocks         | Iowa     |    33 |
| Renoir   | Les Deux Soeurs   | Nebraska |    64 |
+----------+-------------------+----------+-------+
```

The statement is written using table qualifiers for each output column. Nevertheless, the column names in the output are not distinct because MySQL doesn't include table names in the column headings. If you're processing the result of the join from within one of your own programs and fetching rows into a data structure that references column values by name, nonunique column names can cause some values to become inaccessible. The following Perl script fragment illustrates the difficulty:

```
$stmt = qq{
  SELECT artist.name, painting.title, states.name, painting.price
  FROM artist INNER JOIN painting INNER JOIN states
  ON artist.a_id = painting.a_id AND painting.state = states.abbrev
```

```
};
$sth = $dbh->prepare ($stmt);
$sth->execute ();
# Determine the number of columns in result set rows two ways:
# - Check the NUM_OF_FIELDS statement handle attribute
# - Fetch a row into a hash and see how many keys the hash contains
$count1 = $sth->{NUM_OF_FIELDS};
$ref = $sth->fetchrow_hashref ();
$count2 = keys (%{$ref});
print "The statement is: $stmt\n";
print "According to NUM_OF_FIELDS, the result set has $count1 columns\n";
print "The column names are: " . join sort (",", @{$sth->{NAME}})) . "\n";
print "According to the row hash size, the result set has $count2 columns\n";
print "The column names are: " . join sort (",", @{$sth->{NAME}})) . "\n";
```

The script issues the statement and then determines the number of columns in the result, first by checking the NUM_OF_FIELDS attribute and then by fetching a row into a hash and counting the number of hash keys. Executing this script results in the following output:

```
According to NUM_OF_FIELDS, the result set has 4 columns
The column names are: name,name,title,price
According to the row hash size, the result set has 3 columns
The column names are: name,price,title
```

There is a problem here: the column counts don't match. The second count is 3 (not 4) because the nonunique column names cause multiple column values to be mapped onto the same hash element. As a result of these hash-key collisions, some of the values are lost. To solve this problem, make the column names unique by supplying aliases. For example, the statement can be rewritten like this:

```
SELECT
  artist.name AS painter, painting.title,
  states.name AS state, painting.price
FROM artist INNER JOIN painting INNER JOIN states
  ON artist.a_id = painting.a_id AND painting.state = states.abbrev
```

If you make that change and rerun the script, its output becomes:

```
According to NUM_OF_FIELDS, the result set has 4 columns
The column names are: painter,price,state,title
According to the row hash size, the result set has 4 columns
The column names are: painter,price,state,title
```

Now the two column counts are the same, which indicates that no values are lost when fetching into a hash.

Another way to address the problem that requires no column renaming is to fetch the row into something other than a hash. For example, you can fetch the row into an array and refer to the columns by ordinal position within the array:

```
while (my @val = $sth->fetchrow_array ())
{
  print "painter: $val[0], title: $val[1], "
```

```
        . "state: $val[2], price: $val[3]\n";
    }
```

The name-clash problem just described might have different solutions in other languages. For example, the problem doesn't occur in quite the same way in Python scripts that use the MySQLdb module. Suppose that you retrieve a row using a dictionary, Python's analog to a Perl hash (Recipe 2.4). In this case, MySQLdb notices clashing column names and places them in the dictionary using a key consisting of the table name and column name. Thus, for the following statement, the dictionary keys would be name, title, states.name, and price:

```
SELECT artist.name, painting.title, states.name, painting.price
FROM artist INNER JOIN painting INNER JOIN states
  ON artist.a_id = painting.a_id AND painting.state = states.abbrev
```

That means column values won't get lost. Unfortunately, it's still necessary to be aware of nonunique names. If you try to refer to column values using just the column names, you won't get the results you expect for those names that are reported with a leading table name. This problem does not occur if you use aliases to make each column name unique because the dictionary entries will have the names that you assign.

## CHAPTER 13

Statistical Techniques

13.0 Introduction

This chapter covers several topics that relate to basic statistical techniques. For the most part, these recipes build on those described in earlier chapters, such as the summary techniques discussed in Chapter 8. The examples here thus show additional ways to apply the material from those chapters. Broadly speaking, the topics discussed in this chapter include:

- Techniques for data characterization, such as calculating descriptive statistics, generating frequency distributions, counting missing values, and calculating least-squares regressions or correlation coefficients

- Randomization methods, such as how to generate random numbers and apply them to randomizing of a set of rows or to selecting individual items randomly from the rows

- Rank assignments

Statistics covers such a large and diverse array of topics that this chapter necessarily only scratches the surface and simply illustrates a few of the potential areas in which MySQL may be applied to statistical analysis. Note that some statistical measures can be defined in different ways (for example, do you calculate standard deviation based on n degrees of freedom, or $n–1$?). For that reason, if the definition I use for a given term doesn't match the one you prefer, you'll need to adapt the queries or algorithms shown here to some extent.

You can find scripts related to the examples discussed here in the *stats* directory of the `recipes` distribution, and scripts for creating some of the example tables in the *tables* directory.

13.1 Calculating Descriptive Statistics

Problem

You want to characterize a dataset by computing general descriptive or summary statistics.

Solution

Many common descriptive statistics, such as mean and standard deviation, can be obtained by applying aggregate functions to your data. Others, such as median or mode, can be calculated based on counting queries.

Discussion

Suppose that you have a table `testscore` containing observations representing subject ID, age, sex, and test score:

```
mysql> SELECT subject, age, sex, score FROM testscore ORDER BY subject;
+---------+-----+-----+-------+
| subject | age | sex | score |
+---------+-----+-----+-------+
|       1 |   5 | M   |     5 |
|       2 |   5 | M   |     4 |
|       3 |   5 | F   |     6 |
|       4 |   5 | F   |     7 |
|       5 |   6 | M   |     8 |
|       6 |   6 | M   |     9 |
|       7 |   6 | F   |     4 |
|       8 |   6 | F   |     6 |
|       9 |   7 | M   |     8 |
|      10 |   7 | M   |     6 |
|      11 |   7 | F   |     9 |
|      12 |   7 | F   |     7 |
|      13 |   8 | M   |     9 |
|      14 |   8 | M   |     6 |
|      15 |   8 | F   |     7 |
|      16 |   8 | F   |    10 |
|      17 |   9 | M   |     9 |
|      18 |   9 | M   |     7 |
|      19 |   9 | F   |    10 |
|      20 |   9 | F   |     9 |
+---------+-----+-----+-------+
```

A good first step in analyzing a set of observations is to generate some descriptive statistics that summarize their general characteristics as a whole. Common statistical values of this kind include:

- The number of observations, their sum, and their range (minimum and maximum)
- Measures of central tendency, such as mean, median, and mode
- Measures of variation, such as standard deviation and variance

Aside from the median and mode, all of these can be calculated easily by invoking aggregate functions:

```
mysql> SELECT COUNT(score) AS n,
    -> SUM(score) AS sum,
    -> MIN(score) AS minimum,
    -> MAX(score) AS maximum,
    -> AVG(score) AS mean,
    -> STDDEV_SAMP(score) AS 'std. dev.',
    -> VAR_SAMP(score) AS 'variance'
    -> FROM testscore;
+----+------+---------+---------+--------+-----------+----------+
| n  | sum  | minimum | maximum | mean   | std. dev. | variance |
+----+------+---------+---------+--------+-----------+----------+
| 20 | 146  |       4 |      10 | 7.3000 |    1.8382 |   3.3789 |
+----+------+---------+---------+--------+-----------+----------+
```

The STDDEV_SAMP() and VAR_SAMP() functions produce sample measures rather than population measures. That is, for a set of n values, they produce a result that is based on $n-1$ degrees of freedom. If you want the population measures, which are based on n degrees of freedom, use the STDDEV_POP() and VAR_POP() functions instead. STDDEV() and VARIANCE() are synonyms for STDDEV_POP() and VAR_POP().

Standard deviation can be used to identify outliers—values that are uncharacteristically far from the mean. For example, to select values that lie more than three standard deviations from the mean, you can do something like this:

```
SELECT @mean := AVG(score), @std := STDDEV_SAMP(score) FROM testscore;
SELECT score FROM testscore WHERE ABS(score-@mean) > @std * 3;
```

MySQL has no built-in function for computing the mode or median of a set of values, but you can compute them yourself. The mode is the value that occurs most frequently. To determine what it is, count each value and see which one is most common:

```
mysql> SELECT score, COUNT(score) AS frequency
    -> FROM testscore GROUP BY score ORDER BY frequency DESC;
+-------+-----------+
| score | frequency |
+-------+-----------+
|     9 |         5 |
|     6 |         4 |
|     7 |         4 |
|     4 |         2 |
|     8 |         2 |
|    10 |         2 |
|     5 |         1 |
+-------+-----------+
```

In this case, 9 is the modal score value.

The median of a set of ordered values can be calculated like this:[*]

- If the number of values is odd, the median is the middle value.
- If the number of values is even, the median is the average of the two middle values.

Based on that definition, use the following procedure to determine the median of a set of observations stored in the database:

1. Issue a query to count the number of observations. From the count, you can determine whether the median calculation requires one or two values, and what their indexes are within the ordered set of observations.

2. Issue a query that includes an ORDER BY clause to sort the observations and a LIMIT clause to pull out the middle value or values.

3. If there is a single middle value, it is the median. Otherwise, take the average of the middle values.

For example, if a table t contains a score column with 37 values (an odd number), you need to select a single value to get the median, using a statement like this:

```
SELECT score FROM t ORDER BY score LIMIT 18,1
```

If the column contains 38 values (an even number), the statement becomes:

```
SELECT score FROM t ORDER BY score LIMIT 18,2
```

Then you can select the values returned by the statement and compute the median from their average.

The following Perl function implements a median calculation. It takes a database handle and the names of the database, table, and column that contain the set of observations. Then it generates the statement that retrieves the relevant values and returns their average:

```
sub median
{
my ($dbh, $db_name, $tbl_name, $col_name) = @_;
my ($count, $limit);

  $count = $dbh->selectrow_array ("SELECT COUNT($col_name)
                                   FROM $db_name.$tbl_name");
  return undef unless $count > 0;
  if ($count % 2 == 1)  # odd number of values; select middle value
  {
    $limit = sprintf ("LIMIT %d,1", ($count-1)/2);
  }
  else            # even number of values; select middle two values
  {
    $limit = sprintf ("LIMIT %d,2", $count/2 - 1);
  }
```

---

[*] Note that the definition of median given here isn't fully general; it doesn't address what to do if the middle values in the dataset are duplicated.

```
my $sth = $dbh->prepare ("SELECT $col_name
                          FROM $db_name.$tbl_name
                          ORDER BY $col_name $limit");
$sth->execute ();
my ($n, $sum) = (0, 0);
while (my $ref = $sth->fetchrow_arrayref ())
{
  ++$n;
  $sum += $ref->[0];
}
return ($sum / $n);
}
```

The preceding technique works for a set of values stored in the database. If you happen to have already fetched an ordered set of values into an array @val, you can compute the median like this instead:

```
if (@val == 0)        # if array is empty, median is undefined
{
  $median = undef;
}
elsif (@val % 2 == 1)   # if array size is odd, median is middle number
{
  $median = $val[(@val-1)/2];
}
else                  # array size is even; median is average
{                     # of two middle numbers
  $median = ($val[@val/2 - 1] + $val[@val/2]) / 2;
}
```

The code works for arrays that have an initial subscript of 0; for languages that use 1-based array indexes, adjust the algorithm accordingly.

13.2 Per-Group Descriptive Statistics

Problem

You want to produce descriptive statistics for each subgroup of a set of observations.

Solution

Use aggregate functions, but employ a GROUP BY clause to arrange observations into the appropriate groups.

Discussion

Recipe 13.1 shows how to compute descriptive statistics for the entire set of scores in the testscore table. To be more specific, you can use GROUP BY to divide the observations into groups and calculate statistics for each of them. For example, the subjects in the `testscore` table are listed by age and sex, so it's possible to calculate similar statistics by age or sex (or both) by application of appropriate GROUP BY clauses.

Here's how to calculate by age:

```
mysql> SELECT age, COUNT(score) AS n,
    -> SUM(score) AS sum,
    -> MIN(score) AS minimum,
    -> MAX(score) AS maximum,
    -> AVG(score) AS mean,
    -> STDDEV_SAMP(score) AS 'std. dev.',
    -> VAR_SAMP(score) AS 'variance'
    -> FROM testscore
    -> GROUP BY age;
+-----+---+------+---------+---------+--------+-----------+----------+
| age | n | sum  | minimum | maximum | mean   | std. dev. | variance |
+-----+---+------+---------+---------+--------+-----------+----------+
|   5 | 4 |   22 |       4 |       7 | 5.5000 |    1.2910 |   1.6667 |
|   6 | 4 |   27 |       4 |       9 | 6.7500 |    2.2174 |   4.9167 |
|   7 | 4 |   30 |       6 |       9 | 7.5000 |    1.2910 |   1.6667 |
|   8 | 4 |   32 |       6 |      10 | 8.0000 |    1.8257 |   3.3333 |
|   9 | 4 |   35 |       7 |      10 | 8.7500 |    1.2583 |   1.5833 |
+-----+---+------+---------+---------+--------+-----------+----------+
```

By sex:

```
mysql> SELECT sex, COUNT(score) AS n,
    -> SUM(score) AS sum,
    -> MIN(score) AS minimum,
    -> MAX(score) AS maximum,
    -> AVG(score) AS mean,
    -> STDDEV_SAMP(score) AS 'std. dev.',
    -> VAR_SAMP(score) AS 'variance'
    -> FROM testscore
    -> GROUP BY sex;
+-----+----+------+---------+---------+--------+-----------+----------+
| sex | n  | sum  | minimum | maximum | mean   | std. dev. | variance |
+-----+----+------+---------+---------+--------+-----------+----------+
| M   | 10 |   71 |       4 |       9 | 7.1000 |    1.7920 |   3.2111 |
| F   | 10 |   75 |       4 |      10 | 7.5000 |    1.9579 |   3.8333 |
+-----+----+------+---------+---------+--------+-----------+----------+
```

By age and sex:

```
mysql> SELECT age, sex, COUNT(score) AS n,
    -> SUM(score) AS sum,
    -> MIN(score) AS minimum,
    -> MAX(score) AS maximum,
    -> AVG(score) AS mean,
    -> STDDEV_SAMP(score) AS 'std. dev.',
    -> VAR_SAMP(score) AS 'variance'
    -> FROM testscore
    -> GROUP BY age, sex;
+-----+-----+---+------+---------+---------+--------+-----------+----------+
| age | sex | n | sum  | minimum | maximum | mean   | std. dev. | variance |
+-----+-----+---+------+---------+---------+--------+-----------+----------+
|   5 | M   | 2 |    9 |       4 |       5 | 4.5000 |    0.7071 |   0.5000 |
```

5	F	2	13	6	7	6.5000	0.7071	0.5000
6	M	2	17	8	9	8.5000	0.7071	0.5000
6	F	2	10	4	6	5.0000	1.4142	2.0000
7	M	2	14	6	8	7.0000	1.4142	2.0000
7	F	2	16	7	9	8.0000	1.4142	2.0000
8	M	2	15	6	9	7.5000	2.1213	4.5000
8	F	2	17	7	10	8.5000	2.1213	4.5000
9	M	2	16	7	9	8.0000	1.4142	2.0000
9	F	2	19	9	10	9.5000	0.7071	0.5000
+-----+----+---+------+---------+--------+----------+---------+

13.3 Generating Frequency Distributions

Problem

You want to know the frequency of occurrence for each value in a table.

Solution

Derive a frequency distribution that summarizes the contents of your dataset.

Discussion

A common application for per-group summary techniques is to generate a breakdown of the number of times each value occurs. This is called a *frequency distribution*. For the testscore table, the frequency distribution looks like this:

```
mysql> SELECT score, COUNT(score) AS occurrence
    -> FROM testscore GROUP BY score;
+-------+------------+
| score | occurrence |
+-------+------------+
|     4 |          2 |
|     5 |          1 |
|     6 |          4 |
|     7 |          4 |
|     8 |          2 |
|     9 |          5 |
|    10 |          2 |
+-------+------------+
```

If you express the results in terms of percentages rather than as counts, you produce a relative frequency distribution. To break down a set of observations and show each count as a percentage of the total, use one query to get the total number of observations and another to calculate the percentages for each group:

```
mysql> SELECT @n := COUNT(score) FROM testscore;
mysql> SELECT score, (COUNT(score)*100)/@n AS percent
    -> FROM testscore GROUP BY score;
+-------+---------+
| score | percent |
+-------+---------+
```

```
|    4 |      10 |
|    5 |       5 |
|    6 |      20 |
|    7 |      20 |
|    8 |      10 |
|    9 |      25 |
|   10 |      10 |
+-------+---------+
```

The distributions just shown summarize the number of values for individual scores. However, if the dataset contains a large number of distinct values and you want a distribution that shows only a small number of categories, you may want to lump values into categories and produce a count for each category. "Lumping" techniques are discussed in Recipe 8.12.

One typical use of frequency distributions is to export the results for use in a graphing program. In the absence of such a program, you can use MySQL itself to generate a simple ASCII chart as a visual representation of the distribution. For example, to display an ASCII bar chart of the test score counts, convert the counts to strings of * characters:

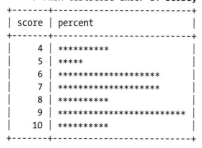

```
mysql> SELECT score, REPEAT('*',COUNT(score)) AS occurrences
    -> FROM testscore GROUP BY score;
+-------+-------------+
| score | occurrences |
+-------+-------------+
|     4 | **          |
|     5 | *           |
|     6 | ****        |
|     7 | ****        |
|     8 | **          |
|     9 | *****       |
|    10 | **          |
+-------+-------------+
```

To chart the relative frequency distribution instead, use the percentage values:

```
mysql> SELECT @n := COUNT(score) FROM testscore;
mysql> SELECT score, REPEAT('*',(COUNT(score)*100)/@n) AS percent
    -> FROM testscore GROUP BY score;
+-------+---------------------------+
| score | percent                   |
+-------+---------------------------+
|     4 | *********                 |
|     5 | *****                     |
|     6 | ******************        |
|     7 | ******************        |
|     8 | *********                 |
|     9 | ************************  |
|    10 | *********                 |
+-------+---------------------------+
```

The ASCII chart method is fairly crude, obviously, but it's a quick way to get a picture of the distribution of observations, and it requires no other tools.

If you generate a frequency distribution for a range of categories where some of the categories are not represented in your observations, the missing categories will not appear in the output. To force each category to be displayed, use a reference table and a LEFT JOIN (a technique discussed in Recipe 12.8). For the testscore table, the possible scores range from 0 to 10, so a reference table should contain each of those values:

```
mysql> CREATE TABLE ref (score INT);
mysql> INSERT INTO ref (score)
    -> VALUES(0),(1),(2),(3),(4),(5),(6),(7),(8),(9),(10);
```

Then join the reference table to the test scores to generate the frequency distribution:

```
mysql> SELECT ref.score, COUNT(testscore.score) AS occurrences
    -> FROM ref LEFT JOIN testscore ON ref.score = testscore.score
    -> GROUP BY ref.score;
+-------+-------------+
| score | occurrences |
+-------+-------------+
|     0 |           0 |
|     1 |           0 |
|     2 |           0 |
|     3 |           0 |
|     4 |           2 |
|     5 |           1 |
|     6 |           4 |
|     7 |           4 |
|     8 |           2 |
|     9 |           5 |
|    10 |           2 |
+-------+-------------+
```

This distribution includes rows for scores 0 through 3, none of which appear in the frequency distribution shown earlier.

The same principle applies to relative frequency distributions:

```
mysql> SELECT @n := COUNT(score) FROM testscore;
mysql> SELECT ref.score, (COUNT(testscore.score)*100)/@n AS percent
    -> FROM ref LEFT JOIN testscore ON ref.score = testscore.score
    -> GROUP BY ref.score;
+-------+---------+
| score | percent |
+-------+---------+
|     0 |       0 |
|     1 |       0 |
|     2 |       0 |
|     3 |       0 |
|     4 |      10 |
|     5 |       5 |
|     6 |      20 |
|     7 |      20 |
|     8 |      10 |
|     9 |      25 |
|    10 |      10 |
+-------+---------+
```

13.4 Counting Missing Values

Problem

A set of observations is incomplete. You want to find out how much so.

Solution

Count the number of NULL values in the set.

Discussion

Values can be missing from a set of observations for any number of reasons: a test may not yet have been administered, something may have gone wrong during the test that requires invalidating the observation, and so forth. You can represent such observations in a dataset as NULL values to signify that they're missing or otherwise invalid, and then use summary statements to characterize the completeness of the dataset.

If a table t contains values to be summarized along a single dimension, a simple summary will do to characterize the missing values. Suppose that t looks like this:

```
mysql> SELECT subject, score FROM t ORDER BY subject;
+---------+-------+
| subject | score |
+---------+-------+
|       1 |    38 |
|       2 |  NULL |
|       3 |    47 |
|       4 |  NULL |
|       5 |    37 |
|       6 |    45 |
|       7 |    54 |
|       8 |  NULL |
|       9 |    40 |
|      10 |    49 |
+---------+-------+
```

COUNT(*) counts the total number of rows, and COUNT(score) counts only the number of nonmissing scores. The difference between the two values is the number of missing scores, and that difference in relation to the total provides the percentage of missing scores. These calculations are expressed as follows:

```
mysql> SELECT COUNT(*) AS 'n (total)',
    -> COUNT(score) AS 'n (nonmissing)',
    -> COUNT(*) - COUNT(score) AS 'n (missing)',
    -> ((COUNT(*) - COUNT(score)) * 100) / COUNT(*) AS '% missing'
    -> FROM t;
+-----------+----------------+-------------+-----------+
| n (total) | n (nonmissing) | n (missing) | % missing |
+-----------+----------------+-------------+-----------+
|        10 |              7 |           3 |     30.00 |
+-----------+----------------+-------------+-----------+
```

As an alternative to counting NULL values as the difference between counts, you can count them directly using SUM(ISNULL(score)). The ISNULL( ) function returns 1 if its argument is NULL, zero otherwise:

```
mysql> SELECT COUNT(*) AS 'n (total)',
    -> COUNT(score) AS 'n (nonmissing)',
    -> SUM(ISNULL(score)) AS 'n (missing)',
    -> (SUM(ISNULL(score)) * 100) / COUNT(*) AS '% missing'
    -> FROM t;
+-----------+----------------+-------------+-----------+
| n (total) | n (nonmissing) | n (missing) | % missing |
+-----------+----------------+-------------+-----------+
|        10 |              7 |           3 |     30.00 |
+-----------+----------------+-------------+-----------+
```

If values are arranged in groups, occurrences of NULL values can be assessed on a per-group basis. Suppose that t contains scores for subjects that are distributed among conditions for two factors A and B, each of which has two levels:

```
mysql> SELECT subject, A, B, score FROM t ORDER BY subject;
+---------+------+------+-------+
| subject | A    | B    | score |
+---------+------+------+-------+
|       1 |    1 |    1 |    18 |
|       2 |    1 |    1 |  NULL |
|       3 |    1 |    1 |    23 |
|       4 |    1 |    1 |    24 |
|       5 |    1 |    2 |    17 |
|       6 |    1 |    2 |    23 |
|       7 |    1 |    2 |    29 |
|       8 |    1 |    2 |    32 |
|       9 |    2 |    1 |    17 |
|      10 |    2 |    1 |  NULL |
|      11 |    2 |    1 |  NULL |
|      12 |    2 |    1 |    25 |
|      13 |    2 |    2 |  NULL |
|      14 |    2 |    2 |    33 |
|      15 |    2 |    2 |    34 |
|      16 |    2 |    2 |    37 |
+---------+------+------+-------+
```

In this case, the query uses a GROUP BY clause to produce a summary for each combination of conditions:

```
mysql> SELECT A, B, COUNT(*) AS 'n (total)',
    -> COUNT(score) AS 'n (nonmissing)',
    -> COUNT(*) - COUNT(score) AS 'n (missing)',
    -> ((COUNT(*) - COUNT(score)) * 100) / COUNT(*) AS '% missing'
    -> FROM t
    -> GROUP BY A, B;
+------+------+-----------+----------------+-------------+-----------+
| A    | B    | n (total) | n (nonmissing) | n (missing) | % missing |
+------+------+-----------+----------------+-------------+-----------+
|    1 |    1 |         4 |              3 |           1 |     25.00 |
|    1 |    2 |         4 |              4 |           0 |      0.00 |
```

```
|    2 |    1 |          4 |                2 |             2 |   50.00 |
|    2 |    2 |          4 |                3 |             1 |   25.00 |
+------+------+------------+------------------+-------------+----------+
```

13.5 Calculating Linear Regressions or Correlation Coefficients

Problem

You want to calculate the least-squares regression line for two variables or the correlation coefficient that expresses the strength of the relationship between them.

Solution

Apply summary functions to calculate the necessary terms.

Discussion

When the data values for two variables X and Y are stored in a database, the least-squares regression for them can be calculated easily using aggregate functions. The same is true for the correlation coefficient. The two calculations are actually fairly similar, and many terms for performing the computations are common to the two procedures.

Suppose that you want to calculate a least-squares regression using the age and test score values for the observations in the **testscore** table:

```
mysql> SELECT age, score FROM testscore;
+-----+-------+
| age | score |
+-----+-------+
|   5 |     5 |
|   5 |     4 |
|   5 |     6 |
|   5 |     7 |
|   6 |     8 |
|   6 |     9 |
|   6 |     4 |
|   6 |     6 |
|   7 |     8 |
|   7 |     6 |
|   7 |     9 |
|   7 |     7 |
|   8 |     9 |
|   8 |     6 |
|   8 |     7 |
|   8 |    10 |
|   9 |     9 |
|   9 |     7 |
|   9 |    10 |
|   9 |     9 |
+-----+-------+
```

The following equation expresses the regression line, where a and b are the intercept and slope of the line:

$$Y = bX + a$$

Letting age be X and score be Y, begin by computing the terms needed for the regression equation. These include the number of observations; the means, sums, and sums of squares for each variable; and the sum of the products of each variable:[†]

```
mysql> SELECT
    -> @n := COUNT(score) AS N,
    -> @meanX := AVG(age) AS 'X mean',
    -> @sumX := SUM(age) AS 'X sum',
    -> @sumXX := SUM(age*age) AS 'X sum of squares',
    -> @meanY := AVG(score) AS 'Y mean',
    -> @sumY := SUM(score) AS 'Y sum',
    -> @sumYY := SUM(score*score) AS 'Y sum of squares',
    -> @sumXY := SUM(age*score) AS 'X*Y sum'
    -> FROM testscore\G
*************************** 1. row ***************************
               N: 20
          X mean: 7.000000000
           X sum: 140
X sum of squares: 1020
          Y mean: 7.300000000
           Y sum: 146
Y sum of squares: 1130
         X*Y sum: 1053
```

From those terms, calculate the regression slope and intercept as follows:

```
mysql> SELECT
    -> @b := (@n*@sumXY - @sumX*@sumY) / (@n*@sumXX - @sumX*@sumX)
    -> AS slope;
+-------------+
| slope       |
+-------------+
| 0.775000000 |
+-------------+
mysql> SELECT @a := (@meanY - @b*@meanX) AS intercept;
+----------------------+
| intercept            |
+----------------------+
| 1.875000000000000000 |
+----------------------+
```

The regression equation then is:

```
mysql> SELECT CONCAT('Y = ',@b,'X + ',@a) AS 'least-squares regression';
+----------------------------------------+
| least-squares regression               |
+----------------------------------------+
| Y = 0.775000000X + 1.875000000000000000 |
+----------------------------------------+
```

[†] You can see where these terms come from by consulting any standard statistics text.

To compute the correlation coefficient, many of the same terms are used:

```
mysql> SELECT
    -> (@n*@sumXY - @sumX*@sumY)
    -> / SQRT((@n*@sumXX - @sumX*@sumX) * (@n*@sumYY - @sumY*@sumY))
    -> AS correlation;
+------------------+
| correlation      |
+------------------+
| 0.61173620442199 |
+------------------+
```

13.6 Generating Random Numbers

Problem

You need a source of random numbers.

Solution

Invoke MySQL's RAND( ) function.

Discussion

MySQL has a RAND( ) function that produces random numbers between 0 and 1:

```
mysql> SELECT RAND(), RAND(), RAND();
+------------------+-------------------+------------------+
| RAND()           | RAND()            | RAND()           |
+------------------+-------------------+------------------+
| 0.18768198246852 | 0.0052350517411111 | 0.46312934203365 |
+------------------+-------------------+------------------+
```

When invoked with an integer argument, RAND( ) uses that value to seed the random number generator. You can use this feature to produce a repeatable series of numbers for a column of a query result. The following example shows that RAND( ) without an argument produces a different column of values per query, whereas RAND(*N*) produces a repeatable column:

```
mysql> SELECT i, RAND(), RAND(10), RAND(20) FROM t;
+------+------------------+------------------+------------------+
| i    | RAND()           | RAND(10)         | RAND(20)         |
+------+------------------+------------------+------------------+
|    1 | 0.60170396939079 | 0.65705152196535 | 0.15888261251047 |
|    2 | 0.10435410784963 | 0.12820613023658 | 0.63553050033332 |
|    3 | 0.71665866180943 | 0.66987611602049 | 0.70100469486881 |
|    4 | 0.27023101623192 | 0.96476222012636 | 0.59843200407776 |
+------+------------------+------------------+------------------+
mysql> SELECT i, RAND(), RAND(10), RAND(20) FROM t;
+------+------------------+------------------+------------------+
| i    | RAND()           | RAND(10)         | RAND(20)         |
+------+------------------+------------------+------------------+
```

```
|    1 | 0.55794027034001 | 0.65705152196535 | 0.15888261251047 |
|    2 | 0.22995210460383 | 0.12820613023658 | 0.63553050033332 |
|    3 | 0.47593974273274 | 0.66987611602049 | 0.70100469486881 |
|    4 | 0.68984243058585 | 0.96476222012636 | 0.59843200407776 |
+------+------------------+------------------+------------------+
```

If you want to seed RAND( ) randomly, pick a seed value based on a source of entropy. Possible sources are the current timestamp or connection identifier, alone or perhaps in combination:

```
RAND(UNIX_TIMESTAMP())
RAND(CONNECTION_ID())
RAND(UNIX_TIMESTAMP()+CONNECTION_ID())
```

How Random Is RAND( )?

Does the RAND( ) function generate evenly distributed numbers? Check it out for yourself with the following Python script, *rand_test.py*, from the *stats* directory of the recipes distribution. It uses RAND( ) to generate random numbers and constructs a frequency distribution from them, using .1-sized categories. This provides a means of assessing how evenly distributed the values are:

```
#!/usr/bin/python
# rand_test.pl - create a frequency distribution of RAND() values.
# This provides a test of the randomness of RAND().

# Method: Draw random numbers in the range from 0 to 1.0,
# and count how many of them occur in .1-sized intervals

import MySQLdb
import Cookbook

npicks = 1000   # number of times to pick a number
bucket = [0] * 10 # buckets for counting picks in each interval

conn = Cookbook.connect ()
cursor = conn.cursor ()

for i in range (0, npicks):
  cursor.execute ("SELECT RAND()")
  (val,) = cursor.fetchone ()
  slot = int (val * 10)
  if slot > 9:
    slot = 9     # put 1.0 in last slot
  bucket[slot] = bucket[slot] + 1

cursor.close ()
conn.close ()

# Print the resulting frequency distribution

for slot in range (0, 9):
  print "%2d  %d" % (slot+1, bucket[slot])
```

The *stats* directory also contains equivalent scripts in other languages.

However, it's probably better to use other seed value sources if you have them. For example, if your system has a */dev/random* or */dev/urandom* device, you can read the device and use it to generate a value for seeding RAND( ).

13.7 Randomizing a Set of Rows

Problem

You want to randomize a set of rows or values.

Solution

Use ORDER BY RAND( ).

Discussion

MySQL's RAND( ) function can be used to randomize the order in which a query returns its rows. Somewhat paradoxically, this randomization is achieved by adding an ORDER BY clause to the query. The technique is roughly equivalent to a spreadsheet randomization method. Suppose that you have a set of values in a spreadsheet that looks like this:

```
Patrick
Penelope
Pertinax
Polly
```

To place these in random order, first add another column that contains randomly chosen numbers:

```
Patrick      .73
Penelope     .37
Pertinax     .16
Polly        .48
```

Then sort the rows according to the values of the random numbers:

```
Pertinax     .16
Penelope     .37
Polly        .48
Patrick      .73
```

At this point, the original values have been placed in random order, because the effect of sorting the random numbers is to randomize the values associated with them. To re-randomize the values, choose another set of random numbers, and sort the rows again.

In MySQL, you can achieve a similar effect by associating a set of random numbers with a query result and sorting the result by those numbers. To do this, add an ORDER BY RAND( ) clause:

```
mysql> SELECT name FROM t ORDER BY RAND();
+----------+
| name     |
+----------+
| Pertinax |
| Penelope |
| Patrick  |
| Polly    |
+----------+
mysql> SELECT name FROM t ORDER BY RAND();
+----------+
| name     |
+----------+
| Patrick  |
| Pertinax |
| Penelope |
| Polly    |
+----------+
```

Applications for randomizing a set of rows include any scenario that uses selection without replacement (choosing each item from a set of items until there are no more items left). Some examples of this are:

- Determining the starting order for participants in an event. List the participants in a table, and select them in random order.

- Assigning starting lanes or gates to participants in a race. List the lanes in a table, and select a random lane order.

- Choosing the order in which to present a set of quiz questions.

- Shuffling a deck of cards. Represent each card by a row in a table, and shuffle the deck by selecting the rows in random order. Deal them one by one until the deck is exhausted.

To use the last example as an illustration, let's implement a card deck-shuffling algorithm. Shuffling and dealing cards is randomization plus selection without replacement: each card is dealt once before any is dealt twice; when the deck is used up, it is reshuffled to rerandomize it for a new dealing order. Within a program, this task can be performed with MySQL using a table deck that has 52 rows, assuming a set of cards with each combination of 13 face values and 4 suits:

1. Select the entire table, and store it into an array.

2. Each time a card is needed, take the next element from the array.

3. When the array is exhausted, all the cards have been dealt. "Reshuffle" the table to generate a new card order.

Setting up the deck table is a tedious task if you insert the 52 card records by writing all the INSERT statements manually. The deck contents can be generated more easily in combinatorial fashion within a program by generating each pairing of face value with suit. Here's some PHP code that creates a deck table with face and suit columns, and then populates the table using nested loops to generate the pairings for the INSERT statements:

```
$result =& $conn->query ("
            CREATE TABLE deck
            (
              face  ENUM('A', 'K', 'Q', 'J', '10', '9', '8',
                         '7', '6', '5', '4', '3', '2') NOT NULL,
              suit  ENUM('hearts', 'diamonds', 'clubs', 'spades') NOT NULL
            )");
if (PEAR::isError ($result))
  die ("Cannot issue CREATE TABLE statement\n");

$face_array = array ("A", "K", "Q", "J", "10", "9", "8",
                     "7", "6", "5", "4", "3", "2");
$suit_array = array ("hearts", "diamonds", "clubs", "spades");

# insert a "card" into the deck for each combination of suit and face

$stmt =& $conn->prepare ("INSERT INTO deck (face,suit) VALUES(?,?)");
if (PEAR::isError ($stmt))
  die ("Cannot insert card into deck\n");
foreach ($face_array as $index => $face)
{
  foreach ($suit_array as $index2 => $suit)
  {
    $result =& $conn->execute ($stmt, array ($face, $suit));
    if (PEAR::isError ($result))
      die ("Cannot insert card into deck\n");
  }
}
```

Shuffling the cards is a matter of issuing this statement:

```
SELECT face, suit FROM deck ORDER BY RAND();
```

To do that and store the results in an array within a script, write a shuffle_deck( ) function that issues the query and returns the resulting values in an array (again shown in PHP):

```
function shuffle_deck ($conn)
{
  $result =& $conn->query ("SELECT face, suit FROM deck ORDER BY RAND()");
  if (PEAR::isError ($result))
    die ("Cannot retrieve cards from deck\n");
  $card = array ();
  while ($obj =& $result->fetchRow (DB_FETCHMODE_OBJECT))
    $card[] = $obj;   # add card record to end of $card array
  $result->free ();
  return ($card);
}
```

Deal the cards by keeping a counter that ranges from 0 to 51 to indicate which card to select. When the counter reaches 52, the deck is exhausted and should be shuffled again.

13.8 Selecting Random Items from a Set of Rows

Problem

You want to pick an item or items randomly from a set of values.

Solution

Randomize the values, and then pick the first one (or the first few, if you need more than one).

Discussion

When a set of items is stored in MySQL, you can choose one at random as follows:

1. Select the items in the set in random order, using `ORDER BY RAND( )` as described in Recipe 13.7.
2. Add `LIMIT 1` to the query to pick the first item.

For example, a simple simulation of tossing a die can be performed by creating a `die` table containing rows with values from 1 to 6 corresponding to the six faces of a die cube, and then picking rows from it at random:

```
mysql> SELECT n FROM die ORDER BY RAND() LIMIT 1;
+------+
| n    |
+------+
|    6 |
+------+
mysql> SELECT n FROM die ORDER BY RAND() LIMIT 1;
+------+
| n    |
+------+
|    4 |
+------+
mysql> SELECT n FROM die ORDER BY RAND() LIMIT 1;
+------+
| n    |
+------+
|    5 |
+------+
mysql> SELECT n FROM die ORDER BY RAND() LIMIT 1;
+------+
| n    |
+------+
|    4 |
+------+
```

As you repeat this operation, you pick a random sequence of items from the set. This is a form of selection with replacement: an item is chosen from a pool of items and then returned to the pool for the next pick. Because items are replaced, it's possible to pick the same item multiple times when making successive choices this way. Other examples of selection with replacement include:

- Selecting a banner ad to display on a web page
- Picking a row for a "quote of the day" application
- "Pick a card, any card" magic tricks that begin with a full deck of cards each time

If you want to pick more than one item, change the LIMIT argument. For example, to draw five winning entries at random from a table named drawing that contains contest entries, use RAND( ) in combination with LIMIT:

```
SELECT * FROM drawing ORDER BY RAND() LIMIT 5;
```

A special case occurs when you're picking a single row from a table that you know contains a column with values in the range from 1 to *n* in unbroken sequence. Under these circumstances, it's possible to avoid performing an ORDER BY operation on the entire table by picking a random number in that range and selecting the matching row:

```
SET @id = FLOOR(RAND()*n)+1;
SELECT ... FROM tbl_name WHERE id = @id;
```

This will be much quicker than ORDER BY RAND( ) LIMIT 1 as the table size increases.

13.9 Assigning Ranks

Problem

You want to assign ranks to a set of values.

Solution

Decide on a ranking method, and then put the values in the desired order and apply the method to them.

Discussion

Some kinds of statistical tests require assignment of ranks. This section describes three ranking methods and shows how each can be implemented by using user-defined variables. The examples assume that a table t contains the following scores, which are to be ranked with the values in descending order:

```
mysql> SELECT score FROM t ORDER BY score DESC;
+-------+
| score |
+-------+
|     5 |
|     4 |
|     4 |
|     3 |
|     2 |
```

```
|     2 |
|     2 |
|     1 |
+-------+
```

One type of ranking simply assigns each value its row number within the ordered set of values. To produce such rankings, keep track of the row number and use it for the current rank:

```
mysql> SET @rownum := 0;
mysql> SELECT @rownum := @rownum + 1 AS rank, score
    -> FROM t ORDER BY score DESC;
+------+-------+
| rank | score |
+------+-------+
|    1 |     5 |
|    2 |     4 |
|    3 |     4 |
|    4 |     3 |
|    5 |     2 |
|    6 |     2 |
|    7 |     2 |
|    8 |     1 |
+------+-------+
```

That kind of ranking doesn't take into account the possibility of ties (instances of values that are the same). A second ranking method does so by advancing the rank only when values change:

```
mysql> SET @rank = 0, @prev_val = NULL;
mysql> SELECT @rank := IF(@prev_val=score,@rank,@rank+1) AS rank,
    -> @prev_val := score AS score
    -> FROM t ORDER BY score DESC;
+------+-------+
| rank | score |
+------+-------+
|    1 |     5 |
|    2 |     4 |
|    2 |     4 |
|    3 |     3 |
|    4 |     2 |
|    4 |     2 |
|    4 |     2 |
|    5 |     1 |
+------+-------+
```

A third ranking method is something of a combination of the other two methods. It ranks values by row number, except when ties occur. In that case, the tied values each get a rank equal to the row number of the first of the values. To implement this method, keep track of the row number and the previous value, advancing the rank to the current row number when the value changes:

```
mysql> SET @rownum = 0, @rank = 0, @prev_val = NULL;
mysql> SELECT @rownum := @rownum + 1 AS row,
    -> @rank := IF(@prev_val!=score,@rownum,@rank) AS rank,
```

```
       -> @prev_val := score AS score
       -> FROM t ORDER BY score DESC;
+------+------+-------+
| row  | rank | score |
+------+------+-------+
|    1 |    1 |     5 |
|    2 |    2 |     4 |
|    3 |    2 |     4 |
|    4 |    4 |     3 |
|    5 |    5 |     2 |
|    6 |    5 |     2 |
|    7 |    5 |     2 |
|    8 |    8 |     1 |
+------+------+-------+
```

Ranks are easy to assign within a program as well. For example, the following Ruby fragment ranks the scores in t using the third ranking method:

```
dbh.execute("SELECT score FROM t ORDER BY score DESC") do |sth|
  rownum = 0
  rank = 0
  prev_score = nil
  puts "Row\tRank\tScore\n"
  sth.fetch do |row|
    score = row[0]
    rownum += 1
    rank = rownum if rownum == 1 || prev_score != score
    prev_score = score
    puts "#{rownum}\t#{rank}\t#{score}"
  end
end
```

The third type of ranking is commonly used outside the realm of statistical methods. Recall that in Recipe 3.16, we used a table al_winner that contained the American League pitchers who won 15 or more games during the 2001 baseball season:

```
mysql> SELECT name, wins FROM al_winner ORDER BY wins DESC, name;
+----------------+------+
| name           | wins |
+----------------+------+
| Mulder, Mark   |   21 |
| Clemens, Roger |   20 |
| Moyer, Jamie   |   20 |
| Garcia, Freddy |   18 |
| Hudson, Tim    |   18 |
| Abbott, Paul   |   17 |
| Mays, Joe      |   17 |
| Mussina, Mike  |   17 |
| Sabathia, C.C. |   17 |
| Zito, Barry    |   17 |
| Buehrle, Mark  |   16 |
| Milton, Eric   |   15 |
| Pettitte, Andy |   15 |
| Radke, Brad    |   15 |
| Sele, Aaron    |   15 |
+----------------+------+
```

These pitchers can be assigned ranks using the third method as follows:

```
mysql> SET @rownum = 0, @rank = 0, @prev_val = NULL;
mysql> SELECT @rownum := @rownum + 1 AS row,
    -> @rank := IF(@prev_val!=wins,@rownum,@rank) AS rank,
    -> name,
    -> @prev_val := wins AS wins
    -> FROM al_winner ORDER BY wins DESC;
+------+------+----------------+------+
| row  | rank | name           | wins |
+------+------+----------------+------+
|    1 |    1 | Mulder, Mark   |   21 |
|    2 |    2 | Clemens, Roger |   20 |
|    3 |    2 | Moyer, Jamie   |   20 |
|    4 |    4 | Garcia, Freddy |   18 |
|    5 |    4 | Hudson, Tim    |   18 |
|    6 |    6 | Zito, Barry    |   17 |
|    7 |    6 | Sabathia, C.C. |   17 |
|    8 |    6 | Mussina, Mike  |   17 |
|    9 |    6 | Mays, Joe      |   17 |
|   10 |    6 | Abbott, Paul   |   17 |
|   11 |   11 | Buehrle, Mark  |   16 |
|   12 |   12 | Milton, Eric   |   15 |
|   13 |   12 | Pettitte, Andy |   15 |
|   14 |   12 | Radke, Brad    |   15 |
|   15 |   12 | Sele, Aaron    |   15 |
+------+------+----------------+------+
```

## CHAPTER 14

Handling Duplicates

14.0 Introduction

Tables or result sets sometimes contain duplicate rows. In some cases this is acceptable. For example, if you conduct a web poll that records date and client IP number along with the votes, duplicate rows may be allowable, because it's possible for large numbers of votes to appear to originate from the same IP number for an Internet service that routes traffic from its customers through a single proxy host. In other cases, duplicates will be unacceptable, and you'll want to take steps to avoid them. Operations related to handling of duplicate rows include the following:

- Preventing duplicates from being created within a table in the first place. If each row in a table is intended to represent a single entity (such as a person, an item in a catalog, or a specific observation in an experiment), the occurrence of duplicates presents significant difficulties in using it that way. Duplicates make it impossible to refer to every row in the table unambiguously, so it's best to make sure duplicates never occur.

- Counting the number of duplicates to determine if they are present and to what extent.

- Identifying duplicated values (or the rows containing them) so you can see what they are and where they occur.

- Eliminating duplicates to ensure that each row is unique. This may involve removing rows from a table to leave only unique rows. Or it may involve selecting a result set in such a way that no duplicates appear in the output. For example, to display a list of the states in which you have customers, you probably wouldn't want a long list of state names from all customer records. A list showing each state name only once suffices and is easier to understand.

Several tools are at your disposal for dealing with duplicate rows. Choose them according to the objective that you're trying to achieve:

- Creating a table to include a primary key or unique index prevents duplicates from being added to the table. MySQL uses the index as a constraint to enforce the requirement that each row in the table contains a unique key in the indexed column or columns.

- In conjunction with a unique index, the INSERT IGNORE and REPLACE statements enable you to handle insertion of duplicate rows gracefully without generating errors. For bulk-loading operations, the same options are available in the form of the IGNORE or REPLACE modifiers for the LOAD DATA statement.

- If you need to determine whether a table contains duplicates, use GROUP BY to categorize rows into groups, and COUNT( ) to see how many rows are in each group. These techniques are described in Chapter 8, in the context of producing summaries, but they're useful for duplicate counting and identification as well. A counting summary is essentially an operation that groups values into categories to determine how frequently each one occurs.

- SELECT DISTINCT is useful for removing duplicate rows from a result set (see Recipe 3.8 for more information). For an existing table that already contains duplicates, adding a unique index can remove them. If you determine that there are *n* identical rows in a table, you can use DELETE ... LIMIT to eliminate *n*–1 instances from that specific set of rows.

Scripts related to the examples shown in this chapter are located in the *dups* directory of the recipes distribution. For scripts that create the tables used here, look in the *tables* directory.

14.1 Preventing Duplicates from Occurring in a Table

Problem

You want to prevent a table from ever containing duplicates.

Solution

Use a PRIMARY KEY or a UNIQUE index.

Discussion

To make sure that rows in a table are unique, some column or combination of columns must be required to contain unique values in each row. When this requirement is satisfied, you can refer to any row in the table unambiguously by using its unique identifier. To make sure a table has this characteristic, include a PRIMARY KEY or UNIQUE index in the table structure when you create the table. The following table contains no such index, so it would allow duplicate rows:

```
CREATE TABLE person
(
  last_name   CHAR(20),
  first_name  CHAR(20),
```

```
  address     CHAR(40)
);
```

To prevent multiple rows with the same first and last name values from being created in this table, add a `PRIMARY KEY` to its definition. When you do this, the indexed columns must be `NOT NULL`, because a `PRIMARY KEY` does not allow `NULL` values:

```
CREATE TABLE person
(
  last_name   CHAR(20) NOT NULL,
  first_name  CHAR(20) NOT NULL,
  address     CHAR(40),
  PRIMARY KEY (last_name, first_name)
);
```

The presence of a unique index in a table normally causes an error to occur if you insert a row into the table that duplicates an existing row in the column or columns that define the index. Recipe 14.2 discusses how to handle such errors or modify MySQL's duplicate-handling behavior.

Another way to enforce uniqueness is to add a `UNIQUE` index rather than a `PRIMARY KEY` to a table. The two types of indexes are similar, with the exception that a `UNIQUE` index can be created on columns that allow `NULL` values. For the `person` table, it's likely that you'd require both the first and last names to be filled in. If so, you still declare the columns as `NOT NULL`, and the following table definition is effectively equivalent to the preceding one:

```
CREATE TABLE person
(
  last_name   CHAR(20) NOT NULL,
  first_name  CHAR(20) NOT NULL,
  address     CHAR(40),
  UNIQUE (last_name, first_name)
);
```

If a `UNIQUE` index does happen to allow `NULL` values, `NULL` is special because it is the one value that can occur multiple times. The rationale for this is that it is not possible to know whether one unknown value is the same as another, so multiple unknown values are allowed. (An exception to this is that BDB tables allow at most one `NULL` value in a column that has a `UNIQUE` index.)

It may of course be that you'd want the `person` table to reflect the real world, for which people do sometimes have the same name. In this case, you cannot set up a unique index based on the name columns, because duplicate names must be allowed. Instead, each person must be assigned some sort of unique identifier, which becomes the value that distinguishes one row from another. In MySQL, it's common to accomplish this by using an `AUTO_INCREMENT` column:

```
CREATE TABLE person
(
  id          INT UNSIGNED NOT NULL AUTO_INCREMENT,
  last_name   CHAR(20),
```

```
  first_name  CHAR(20),
  address     CHAR(40),
  PRIMARY KEY (id)
);
```

In this case, when you create a row with an `id` value of `NULL`, MySQL assigns that column a unique ID automatically. Another possibility is to assign identifiers externally and use those IDs as unique keys. For example, citizens in a given country might have unique taxpayer ID numbers. If so, those numbers can serve as the basis for a unique index:

```
CREATE TABLE person
(
  tax_id      INT UNSIGNED NOT NULL,
  last_name   CHAR(20),
  first_name  CHAR(20),
  address     CHAR(40),
  PRIMARY KEY (tax_id)
);
```

See Also

If an existing table already contains duplicate rows that you want to remove, see Recipe 14.4. Chapter 11 further discusses `AUTO_INCREMENT` columns.

14.2 Dealing with Duplicates When Loading Rows into a Table

Problem

You've created a table with a unique index to prevent duplicate values in the indexed column or columns. But this results in an error if you attempt to insert a duplicate row, and you want to avoid having to deal with such errors.

Solution

One approach is to just ignore the error. Another is to use an `INSERT IGNORE`, `REPLACE`, or `INSERT ... ON DUPLICATE KEY UPDATE` statement, each of which modifies MySQL's duplicate-handling behavior. For bulk-loading operations, `LOAD DATA` has modifiers that enable you to specify how to handle duplicates.

Discussion

By default, MySQL generates an error when you insert a row that duplicates an existing unique key value. Suppose that the `person` table has the following structure, with a unique index on the `last_name` and `first_name` columns:

```
CREATE TABLE person
(
  last_name   CHAR(20) NOT NULL,
  first_name  CHAR(20) NOT NULL,
```

```
    address      CHAR(40),
    PRIMARY KEY (last_name, first_name)
);
```

An attempt to insert a row with duplicate values in the indexed columns results in an error:

```
mysql> INSERT INTO person (last_name, first_name)
    -> VALUES('X1','Y1');
Query OK, 1 row affected (0.00 sec)
mysql> INSERT INTO person (last_name, first_name)
    -> VALUES('X1','Y1');
ERROR 1062 (23000): Duplicate entry 'X1-Y1' for key 1
```

If you're issuing the statements from the *mysql* program interactively, you can simply say, "Okay, that didn't work," ignore the error, and continue. But if you write a program to insert the rows, an error may terminate the program. One way to avoid this is to modify the program's error-handling behavior to trap the error and then ignore it. See Recipe 2.2 for information about error-handling techniques.

If you want to prevent the error from occurring in the first place, you might consider using a two-query method to solve the duplicate-row problem:

- Issue a SELECT to see whether the row is already present.
- Issue an INSERT if the row is not present.

But that doesn't really work: another client might insert the same row after the SELECT and before the INSERT, in which case the error would still occur for your INSERT. To make sure that doesn't happen, you could use a transaction or lock the tables, but then you've gone from two statements to four. MySQL provides three single-query solutions to the problem of handling duplicate rows. Choose from among them according to the duplicate-handling behavior you want to affect:

- Use INSERT IGNORE rather than INSERT if you want to keep the original row when a duplicate occurs. If the row doesn't duplicate an existing row, MySQL inserts it as usual. If the row is a duplicate, the IGNORE keyword tells MySQL to discard it silently without generating an error:

```
mysql> INSERT IGNORE INTO person (last_name, first_name)
    -> VALUES('X2','Y2');
Query OK, 1 row affected (0.00 sec)
mysql> INSERT IGNORE INTO person (last_name, first_name)
    -> VALUES('X2','Y2');
Query OK, 0 rows affected (0.00 sec)
```

The row count value indicates whether the row was inserted or ignored. From within a program, you can obtain this value by checking the rows-affected function provided by your API (see Recipes 2.4 and 9.1).

- Use REPLACE rather than INSERT if you want to replace the original row with the new one when a duplicate occurs. If the row is new, it's inserted just as with INSERT. If it's a duplicate, the new row replaces the old one:

```
mysql> REPLACE INTO person (last_name, first_name)
    -> VALUES('X3','Y3');
Query OK, 1 row affected (0.00 sec)
mysql> REPLACE INTO person (last_name, first_name)
    -> VALUES('X3','Y3');
Query OK, 2 rows affected (0.00 sec)
```

The rows-affected value in the second case is 2 because the original row is deleted and the new row is inserted in its place.

- Use INSERT … ON DUPLICATE KEY UPDATE if you want to modify columns of an existing row when a duplicate occurs. If the row is new, it's inserted. If it's a duplicate, the ON DUPLICATE KEY UPDATE clause indicates how to modify the existing row in the table. In other words, this statement can initialize or update a row as necessary. The rows-affected count indicates what happened: 1 for an insert, 2 for an update.

INSERT IGNORE is more efficient than REPLACE because it doesn't actually insert duplicates. Thus, it's most applicable when you just want to make sure a copy of a given row is present in a table. REPLACE, on the other hand, is often more appropriate for tables in which other nonkey columns need to be replaced. INSERT … ON DUPLICATE KEY UPDATE is appropriate when you must insert a record if it doesn't exist, but just update some of its columns if the new record is a duplicate in the indexed columns.

Suppose that you're maintaining a table named passtbl for a web application that contains email addresses and password hash values, and that is keyed by email address:

```
CREATE TABLE passtbl
(
  email    VARCHAR(60) NOT NULL,
  password VARBINARY(60) NOT NULL,
  PRIMARY KEY (email)
);
```

How do you create new rows for new users, but change passwords of existing rows for existing users? A typical algorithm for handling row maintenance might look like this:

1. Issue a SELECT to see whether a row already exists with a given email value.

2. If no such row exists, add a new one with INSERT.

3. If the row does exist, update it with UPDATE.

These steps must be performed within a transaction or with the tables locked to prevent other users from changing the tables while you're using them. In MySQL, you can use REPLACE to simplify both cases to the same single-statement operation:

```
REPLACE INTO passtbl (email,password) VALUES(address,hash_value);
```

If no row with the given email address exists, MySQL creates a new one. If a row does exist, MySQL replaces it; in effect, this updates the password column of the row associated with the address.

INSERT IGNORE and REPLACE are useful when you know exactly what values should be stored in the table when you attempt to insert a row. That's not always the case. For example, you might want to insert a row if it doesn't exist, but update only certain parts of it otherwise. This commonly occurs when you use a table for counting. Suppose that you're recording votes for candidates in polls, using the following table:

```
CREATE TABLE poll_vote
(
  poll_id      INT UNSIGNED NOT NULL AUTO_INCREMENT,
  candidate_id INT UNSIGNED,
  vote_count   INT UNSIGNED,
  PRIMARY KEY (poll_id, candidate_id)
);
```

The primary key is the combination of poll and candidate number. The table should be used like this:

- The first time a vote is received for a given poll candidate, a new row should be inserted with a vote count of 1.

- For all subsequent votes for that poll candidate, the vote count of the existing record should be incremented.

Neither INSERT IGNORE nor REPLACE are appropriate here because for all votes except the first, you don't know what the vote count should be. INSERT ... ON DUPLICATE KEY UPDATE works better here. The following example shows how it works, beginning with an empty table:

```
mysql> SELECT * FROM poll_vote;
Empty set (0.01 sec)
mysql> INSERT INTO poll_vote (poll_id,candidate_id,vote_count) VALUES(14,2,1)
    -> ON DUPLICATE KEY UPDATE vote_count = vote_count + 1;
Query OK, 1 row affected (0.01 sec)
mysql> SELECT * FROM poll_vote;
+---------+--------------+------------+
| poll_id | candidate_id | vote_count |
+---------+--------------+------------+
| 14      | 2            | 1          |
+---------+--------------+------------+
1 row in set (0.01 sec)
mysql> INSERT INTO poll_vote (poll_id,candidate_id,vote_count) VALUES(14,2,1)
    -> ON DUPLICATE KEY UPDATE vote_count = vote_count + 1;
Query OK, 2 rows affected (0.00 sec)
mysql> SELECT * FROM poll_vote;
+---------+--------------+------------+
| poll_id | candidate_id | vote_count |
+---------+--------------+------------+
| 14      | 2            | 2          |
+---------+--------------+------------+
1 row in set (0.00 sec)
```

For the first INSERT, no row for the candidate exists, so the row is inserted. For the second INSERT, the row already exists, so MySQL just updates the vote count. With INSERT ... ON DUPLICATE KEY UPDATE, there is no need to check whether the row exists because MySQL does that for you. The row count indicates what action the INSERT statement performs: 1 for a new row and 2 for an update to an existing row.

The techniques just described have the benefit of eliminating overhead that might otherwise be required for a transaction. But this benefit comes at the price of portability because they all involve MySQL-specific syntax. If portability is a high priority, you might prefer to stick with a transactional approach.

See Also

For bulk record-loading operations in which you use the LOAD DATA statement to load a set of rows from a file into a table, duplicate-row handling can be controlled using the statement's IGNORE and REPLACE modifiers. These produce behavior analogous to that of the INSERT IGNORE and REPLACE statements. See Recipe 10.7 for more information.

The use of INSERT ... ON DUPLICATE KEY UPDATE for initializing and updating counts is further demonstrated in Recipes 11.14 and 19.12.

14.3 Counting and Identifying Duplicates

Problem

You want to determine whether a table contains duplicates, and to what extent they occur. Or you want to see the rows that contain the duplicated values.

Solution

Use a counting summary that looks for and displays duplicated values. To see the rows in which the duplicated values occur, join the summary to the original table to display the matching rows.

Discussion

Suppose that your web site includes a sign-up page that enables visitors to add themselves to your mailing list to receive periodic product catalog mailings. But you forgot to include a unique index in the table when you created it, and now you suspect that some people are signed up multiple times. Perhaps they forgot they were already on the list, or perhaps people added friends to the list who were already signed up. Either way, the result of having duplicate rows is that you mail out duplicate catalogs. This is an additional expense to you, and it annoys the recipients. This section discusses how to find out if duplicates are present in a table, how prevalent they are, and how to display the duplicated rows. (For tables that do contain duplicates, Recipe 14.4 describes how to eliminate them.)

To determine whether duplicates occur in a table, use a counting summary (a topic covered in Chapter 8). Summary techniques can be applied to identifying and counting duplicates by grouping rows with GROUP BY and counting the rows in each group using `COUNT( )`. For the examples here, assume that catalog recipients are listed in a table named `catalog_list` that has the following contents:

```
mysql> SELECT * FROM catalog_list;
+-----------+-------------+-------------------------+
| last_name | first_name  | street                  |
+-----------+-------------+-------------------------+
| Isaacson  | Jim         | 515 Fordam St., Apt. 917 |
| Baxter    | Wallace     | 57 3rd Ave.             |
| McTavish  | Taylor      | 432 River Run           |
| Pinter    | Marlene     | 9 Sunset Trail          |
| BAXTER    | WALLACE     | 57 3rd Ave.             |
| Brown     | Bartholomew | 432 River Run           |
| Pinter    | Marlene     | 9 Sunset Trail          |
| Baxter    | Wallace     | 57 3rd Ave., Apt 102    |
+-----------+-------------+-------------------------+
```

Suppose that you want to define "duplicate" using the `last_name` and `first_name` columns. That is, recipients with the same name are assumed to be the same person. The following statements are typical of those used to characterize the table and to assess the existence and extent of duplicate values:

- The total number of rows in the table:

```
mysql> SELECT COUNT(*) AS rows FROM catalog_list;
+------+
| rows |
+------+
|    8 |
+------+
```

- The number of distinct names:

```
mysql> SELECT COUNT(DISTINCT last_name, first_name) AS 'distinct names'
    -> FROM catalog_list;
+----------------+
| distinct names |
+----------------+
|              5 |
+----------------+
```

- The number of rows containing duplicated names:

```
mysql> SELECT COUNT(*) - COUNT(DISTINCT last_name, first_name)
    ->   AS 'duplicate names'
    -> FROM catalog_list;
+-----------------+
| duplicate names |
+-----------------+
|               3 |
+-----------------+
```

- The fraction of the rows that contain unique or nonunique names:

```
mysql> SELECT COUNT(DISTINCT last_name, first_name) / COUNT(*)
    ->   AS 'unique',
    -> 1 - (COUNT(DISTINCT last_name, first_name) / COUNT(*))
```

```
->    AS 'nonunique'
-> FROM catalog_list;
+--------+------------+
| unique | nonunique  |
+--------+------------+
| 0.6250 |    0.3750  |
+--------+------------+
```

These statements help you characterize the extent of duplicates, but they don't show you which values are duplicated. To see the duplicated names in the `catalog_list` table, use a summary statement that displays the nonunique values along with the counts:

```
mysql> SELECT COUNT(*) AS repetitions, last_name, first_name
    -> FROM catalog_list
    -> GROUP BY last_name, first_name
    -> HAVING repetitions > 1;
+-------------+-----------+------------+
| repetitions | last_name | first_name |
+-------------+-----------+------------+
|           3 | Baxter    | Wallace    |
|           2 | Pinter    | Marlene    |
+-------------+-----------+------------+
```

The statement includes a `HAVING` clause that restricts the output to include only those names that occur more than once. (If you omit the clause, the summary lists unique names as well, which is useless when you're interested only in duplicates.) In general, to identify sets of values that are duplicated, do the following:

1. Determine which columns contain the values that may be duplicated.
2. List those columns in the column selection list, along with `COUNT(*)`.
3. List the columns in the `GROUP BY` clause as well.
4. Add a `HAVING` clause that eliminates unique values by requiring group counts to be greater than one.

Queries constructed that way have the following form:

```
SELECT COUNT(*), column_list
FROM tbl_name
GROUP BY column_list
HAVING COUNT(*) > 1
```

It's easy to generate duplicate-finding queries like that within a program, given database and table names and a nonempty set of column names. For example, here is a Perl function `make_dup_count_query( )` that generates the proper query for finding and counting duplicated values in the specified columns:

```
sub make_dup_count_query
{
my ($db_name, $tbl_name, @col_name) = @_;

    return (
        "SELECT COUNT(*)," . join (",", @col_name)
      . "\nFROM $db_name.$tbl_name"
```

```
        . "\nGROUP BY " . join (",", @col_name)
        . "\nHAVING COUNT(*) > 1"
    );
}
```

make_dup_count_query( ) returns the query as a string. If you invoke it like this:

```
$str = make_dup_count_query ("cookbook", "catalog_list",
                             "last_name", "first_name");
```

the resulting value of $str is:

```
SELECT COUNT(*),last_name,first_name
FROM cookbook.catalog_list
GROUP BY last_name,first_name
HAVING COUNT(*) > 1
```

What you do with the query string is up to you. You can execute it from within the script that creates it, pass it to another program, or write it to a file for execution later. The *dups* directory of the recipes distribution contains a script named *dup_count.pl* that you can use to try the function (as well as some translations into other languages). Recipe 14.4 discusses use of the make_dup_count_query( ) function to implement a duplicate-removal technique.

Summary techniques are useful for assessing the existence of duplicates, how often they occur, and displaying which values are duplicated. But if duplicates are determined using only a subset of a table's columns, a summary in itself cannot display the entire content of the rows that contain the duplicate values. (For example, the summaries shown thus far display counts of duplicated names in the catalog_list table or the names themselves, but don't show the addresses associated with those names.) To see the original rows containing the duplicate names, join the summary information to the table from which it's generated. The following example shows how to do this to display the catalog_list rows that contain duplicated names. The summary is written to a temporary table, which then is joined to the catalog_list table to produce the rows that match those names:

```
mysql> CREATE TABLE tmp
    -> SELECT COUNT(*) AS count, last_name, first_name FROM catalog_list
    -> GROUP BY last_name, first_name HAVING count > 1;
mysql> SELECT catalog_list.*
    -> FROM tmp INNER JOIN catalog_list USING(last_name, first_name)
    -> ORDER BY last_name, first_name;
+-----------+------------+----------------------+
| last_name | first_name | street               |
+-----------+------------+----------------------+
| Baxter    | Wallace    | 57 3rd Ave.          |
| BAXTER    | WALLACE    | 57 3rd Ave.          |
| Baxter    | Wallace    | 57 3rd Ave., Apt 102 |
| Pinter    | Marlene    | 9 Sunset Trail       |
| Pinter    | Marlene    | 9 Sunset Trail       |
+-----------+------------+----------------------+
```

Duplicate Identification and String Case Sensitivity

For strings that have a case-insensitive collation, values that differ only in lettercase are considered the same for comparison purposes. To treat them as distinct values, compare them using a case-sensitive or binary collation. Recipe 5.9 shows how to do this.

14.4 Eliminating Duplicates from a Table

Problem

You want to remove duplicate rows from a table so that it contains only unique rows.

Solution

Select the unique rows from the table into a second table that you use to replace the original one. Or add a unique index to the table using ALTER TABLE, which will remove duplicates as it builds the index. Or use DELETE ... LIMIT *n* to remove all but one instance of a specific set of duplicate rows.

Discussion

Recipe 14.1 discusses how to prevent duplicates from being added to a table by creating it with a unique index. However, if you forget to include a unique index when you create a table, you may discover later that it contains duplicates and that it's necessary to apply some sort of duplicate-removal technique. The catalog_list table used earlier is an example of this, because it contains several instances in which the same person is listed multiple times:

```
mysql> SELECT * FROM catalog_list ORDER BY last_name, first_name;
+-----------+-------------+-------------------------+
| last_name | first_name  | street                  |
+-----------+-------------+-------------------------+
| Baxter    | Wallace     | 57 3rd Ave.             |
| BAXTER    | WALLACE     | 57 3rd Ave.             |
| Baxter    | Wallace     | 57 3rd Ave., Apt 102    |
| Brown     | Bartholomew | 432 River Run           |
| Isaacson  | Jim         | 515 Fordam St., Apt. 917|
| McTavish  | Taylor      | 432 River Run           |
| Pinter    | Marlene     | 9 Sunset Trail          |
| Pinter    | Marlene     | 9 Sunset Trail          |
+-----------+-------------+-------------------------+
```

The table contains redundant entries and it would be a good idea to remove them, to eliminate duplicate mailings and reduce postage costs. To do this, you have several options:

- Select the table's unique rows into another table, and then use that table to replace the original one. The result is to remove the table's duplicates. This works when "duplicate" means "the entire row is the same as another."

- Add a unique index to the table using ALTER TABLE. This operation turns duplicate rows into unique rows, where "duplicate" means "the index values are the same."

- You can remove duplicates for a specific set of duplicate rows by using DELETE ... LIMIT *n* to remove all but one row.

This recipe discusses each of these duplicate-removal method. When you consider which of them to choose under various circumstances, the applicability of a given method to a specific problem is often determined by several factors:

- Does the method require the table to have a unique index?

- If the columns in which duplicate values occur may contain NULL, will the method remove duplicate NULL values?

- Does the method prevent duplicates from occurring in the future?

Removing duplicates using table replacement

If a row is considered to duplicate another only if the entire row is the same, one way to eliminate duplicates from a table is to select its unique rows into a new table that has the same structure, and then replace the original table with the new one. To perform table replacement, use the following procedure:

1. Create a new table that has the same structure as the original one. CREATE TABLE ... LIKE is useful for this (see Recipe 4.1):

    ```
    mysql> CREATE TABLE tmp LIKE catalog_list;
    ```

2. Use INSERT INTO ... SELECT DISTINCT to select the unique rows from the original table into the new one:

    ```
    mysql> INSERT INTO tmp SELECT DISTINCT * FROM catalog_list;
    ```

    Select rows from the tmp table to verify that the new table contains no duplicates:

    ```
    mysql> SELECT * FROM tmp ORDER BY last_name, first_name;
    +-----------+-------------+-------------------------+
    | last_name | first_name  | street                  |
    +-----------+-------------+-------------------------+
    | Baxter    | Wallace     | 57 3rd Ave.             |
    | Baxter    | Wallace     | 57 3rd Ave., Apt 102    |
    | Brown     | Bartholomew | 432 River Run           |
    | Isaacson  | Jim         | 515 Fordam St., Apt. 917 |
    | McTavish  | Taylor      | 432 River Run           |
    | Pinter    | Marlene     | 9 Sunset Trail          |
    +-----------+-------------+-------------------------+
    ```

3. After creating the new tmp table that contains unique rows, use it to replace the original catalog_list table:

```
mysql> DROP TABLE catalog_list;
mysql> RENAME TABLE tmp TO catalog_list;
```

The effective result of this procedure is that catalog_list no longer contains duplicates.

This table-replacement method works in the absence of an index (although it might be slow for large tables). For tables that contain duplicate NULL values, it removes those duplicates. It does not prevent the occurrence of duplicates in the future.

This method requires rows to be completely identical for rows to be considered duplicates. Thus, it treats as distinct those rows for Wallace Baxter that have slightly different street values.

If duplicates are defined only with respect to a subset of the columns in the table, create a new table that has a unique index for those columns, select rows into it using INSERT IGNORE, and then replace the original table with the new one:

```
mysql> CREATE TABLE tmp LIKE catalog_list;
mysql> ALTER TABLE tmp ADD PRIMARY KEY (last_name, first_name);
mysql> INSERT IGNORE INTO tmp SELECT * FROM catalog_list;
mysql> SELECT * FROM tmp ORDER BY last_name, first_name;
+-----------+-------------+-------------------------+
| last_name | first_name  | street                  |
+-----------+-------------+-------------------------+
| Baxter    | Wallace     | 57 3rd Ave.             |
| Brown     | Bartholomew | 432 River Run           |
| Isaacson  | Jim         | 515 Fordam St., Apt. 917 |
| McTavish  | Taylor      | 432 River Run           |
| Pinter    | Marlene     | 9 Sunset Trail          |
+-----------+-------------+-------------------------+
mysql> DROP TABLE catalog_list;
mysql> RENAME TABLE tmp TO catalog_list;
```

The unique index prevents rows with duplicate key values from being inserted into tmp, and IGNORE tells MySQL not to stop with an error if a duplicate is found. One shortcoming of this method is that if the indexed columns can contain NULL values, you must use a UNIQUE index rather than a PRIMARY KEY, in which case the index will not remove duplicate NULL keys. (UNIQUE indexes allow multiple NULL values.) This method does prevent occurrence of duplicates in the future.

Removing duplicates by adding an index

To remove duplicates from a table "in place," add a unique index to the table with ALTER TABLE, using the IGNORE keyword to tell it to discard rows with duplicate key values during the index construction process. The original catalog_list table looks like this without an index:

```
mysql> SELECT * FROM catalog_list ORDER BY last_name, first_name;
+-----------+-------------+-------------------------+
| last_name | first_name  | street                  |
+-----------+-------------+-------------------------+
| Baxter    | Wallace     | 57 3rd Ave.             |
| BAXTER    | WALLACE     | 57 3rd Ave.             |
```

```
| Baxter    | Wallace     | 57 3rd Ave., Apt 102     |
| Brown     | Bartholomew | 432 River Run            |
| Isaacson  | Jim         | 515 Fordam St., Apt. 917 |
| McTavish  | Taylor      | 432 River Run            |
| Pinter    | Marlene     | 9 Sunset Trail           |
| Pinter    | Marlene     | 9 Sunset Trail           |
+-----------+-------------+--------------------------+
```

Add a unique index, and then check what effect doing so has on the table contents:

```
mysql> ALTER IGNORE TABLE catalog_list
    -> ADD PRIMARY KEY (last_name, first_name);
mysql> SELECT * FROM catalog_list ORDER BY last_name, first_name;
+-----------+-------------+--------------------------+
| last_name | first_name  | street                   |
+-----------+-------------+--------------------------+
| Baxter    | Wallace     | 57 3rd Ave.              |
| Brown     | Bartholomew | 432 River Run            |
| Isaacson  | Jim         | 515 Fordam St., Apt. 917 |
| McTavish  | Taylor      | 432 River Run            |
| Pinter    | Marlene     | 9 Sunset Trail           |
+-----------+-------------+--------------------------+
```

If the indexed columns can contain NULL, you must use a UNIQUE index rather than a PRIMARY KEY. In that case, the index will not remove duplicate NULL key values. In addition to removing existing duplicates, the method prevents the occurrence of duplicates in the future.

Removing duplicates of a particular row

You can use LIMIT to restrict the effect of a DELETE statement to a subset of the rows that it otherwise would delete. This makes the statement applicable to removing duplicate rows. Suppose that you have a table t with the following contents:

```
+-------+
| color |
+-------+
| blue  |
| green |
| blue  |
| blue  |
| red   |
| green |
| red   |
+-------+
```

The table lists blue three times, and green and red twice each. To remove the extra instances of each color, do this:

```
mysql> DELETE FROM t WHERE color = 'blue' LIMIT 2;
mysql> DELETE FROM t WHERE color = 'green' LIMIT 1;
mysql> DELETE FROM t WHERE color = 'red' LIMIT 1;
mysql> SELECT * FROM t;
+-------+
| color |
```

```
+-------+
| blue  |
| green |
| red   |
+-------+
```

This technique works in the absence of a unique index, and it eliminates duplicate NULL values. It's handy if you want to remove duplicates only for a specific set of rows within a table. However, if there are many different sets of duplicates that you want to remove, this is not a procedure you'd want to carry out by hand. The process can be automated by using the techniques discussed earlier in Recipe 14.3 for determining which values are duplicated. There, we wrote a make_dup_count_query( ) function to generate the statement needed to count the number of duplicate values in a given set of columns in a table. The result of that statement can be used to generate a set of DELETE ... LIMIT *n* statements that remove duplicate rows and leave only unique rows. The *dups* directory of the recipes distribution contains code that shows how to generate these statements.

In general, using DELETE ... LIMIT *n* is likely to be slower than removing duplicates by using a second table or by adding a unique index. Those methods keep the data on the server side and let the server do all the work. DELETE ... LIMIT *n* involves a lot of client-server interaction because it uses a SELECT statement to retrieve information about duplicates, followed by several DELETE statements to remove instances of duplicated rows. Also, this technique does not prevent duplicates from occurring in the future.

14.5 Eliminating Duplicates from a Self-Join Result

Problem

Self-joins often produce rows that are "near" duplicates—that is, rows that contain the same values but in different orders. Because of this, SELECT DISTINCT will not eliminate the duplicates.

Solution

Select column values in a specific order within rows to make rows with duplicate sets of values identical. Then you can use SELECT DISTINCT to remove duplicates. Alternatively, retrieve rows in such a way that near-duplicates are not even selected.

Discussion

Self-joins can produce rows that are duplicates in the sense that they contain the same values, yet are not identical. Consider the following statement (originally seen in Recipe 12.3), which uses a self-join to find all pairs of states that joined the Union in the same year:

```
mysql> SELECT YEAR(s1.statehood) AS year,
    -> s1.name AS name1, s1.statehood AS statehood1,
    -> s2.name AS name2, s2.statehood AS statehood2
    -> FROM states AS s1 INNER JOIN states AS s2
    -> ON YEAR(s1.statehood) = YEAR(s2.statehood) AND s1.name != s2.name
    -> ORDER BY year, s1.name, s2.name;
+------+--------------+------------+--------------+------------+
| year | name1        | statehood1 | name2        | statehood2 |
+------+--------------+------------+--------------+------------+
| 1787 | Delaware     | 1787-12-07 | New Jersey   | 1787-12-18 |
| 1787 | Delaware     | 1787-12-07 | Pennsylvania | 1787-12-12 |
| 1787 | New Jersey   | 1787-12-18 | Delaware     | 1787-12-07 |
| 1787 | New Jersey   | 1787-12-18 | Pennsylvania | 1787-12-12 |
| 1787 | Pennsylvania | 1787-12-12 | Delaware     | 1787-12-07 |
| 1787 | Pennsylvania | 1787-12-12 | New Jersey   | 1787-12-18 |
...
| 1912 | Arizona      | 1912-02-14 | New Mexico   | 1912-01-06 |
| 1912 | New Mexico   | 1912-01-06 | Arizona      | 1912-02-14 |
| 1959 | Alaska       | 1959-01-03 | Hawaii       | 1959-08-21 |
| 1959 | Hawaii       | 1959-08-21 | Alaska       | 1959-01-03 |
+------+--------------+------------+--------------+------------+
```

The condition in the ON clause that requires state pair names not to be identical eliminates the trivially duplicate rows showing that each state joined the Union in the same
year as itself. But each remaining pair of states still appears twice. For example, there
is one row that lists Delaware and New Jersey, and another that lists New Jersey and
Delaware. Each such pair of rows may be considered as effective duplicates because
they contain the same values. However, because the values are not listed in the same
order within the rows, they are not identical and you can't get rid of the duplicates by
adding DISTINCT to the statement.

One way to solve this problem is to make sure that state names are always listed in a
specific order within a row. This can be done by selecting the names with a pair of
expressions that place the lesser value first in the output column list:

```
IF(val1<val2,val1,val2) AS lesser_value,
IF(val1<val2,val2,val1) AS greater_value
```

Applying this technique to the state-pairs query yields the following result, in which
the expressions display state names in lexical order within each row:

```
mysql> SELECT YEAR(s1.statehood) AS year,
    -> IF(s1.name<s2.name,s1.name,s2.name) AS name1,
    -> IF(s1.name<s2.name,s1.statehood,s2.statehood) AS statehood1,
    -> IF(s1.name<s2.name,s2.name,s1.name) AS name2,
    -> IF(s1.name<s2.name,s2.statehood,s1.statehood) AS statehood2
    -> FROM states AS s1 INNER JOIN states AS s2
    -> ON YEAR(s1.statehood) = YEAR(s2.statehood) AND s1.name != s2.name
    -> ORDER BY year, name1, name2;
+------+------------+------------+------------+------------+
| year | name1      | statehood1 | name2      | statehood2 |
+------+------------+------------+------------+------------+
| 1787 | Delaware   | 1787-12-07 | New Jersey | 1787-12-18 |
| 1787 | Delaware   | 1787-12-07 | New Jersey | 1787-12-18 |
```

```
| 1787 | Delaware    | 1787-12-07 | Pennsylvania | 1787-12-12 |
| 1787 | Delaware    | 1787-12-07 | Pennsylvania | 1787-12-12 |
| 1787 | New Jersey  | 1787-12-18 | Pennsylvania | 1787-12-12 |
| 1787 | New Jersey  | 1787-12-18 | Pennsylvania | 1787-12-12 |
...
| 1912 | Arizona     | 1912-02-14 | New Mexico   | 1912-01-06 |
| 1912 | Arizona     | 1912-02-14 | New Mexico   | 1912-01-06 |
| 1959 | Alaska      | 1959-01-03 | Hawaii       | 1959-08-21 |
| 1959 | Alaska      | 1959-01-03 | Hawaii       | 1959-08-21 |
+------+-------------+------------+--------------+------------+
```

Duplicate rows are still present in the output, but now duplicate pairs are identical and you can eliminate the extra copies by adding DISTINCT to the statement:

```
mysql> SELECT DISTINCT YEAR(s1.statehood) AS year,
    -> IF(s1.name<s2.name,s1.name,s2.name) AS name1,
    -> IF(s1.name<s2.name,s1.statehood,s2.statehood) AS statehood1,
    -> IF(s1.name<s2.name,s2.name,s1.name) AS name2,
    -> IF(s1.name<s2.name,s2.statehood,s1.statehood) AS statehood2
    -> FROM states AS s1 INNER JOIN states AS s2
    -> ON YEAR(s1.statehood) = YEAR(s2.statehood) AND s1.name != s2.name
    -> ORDER BY year, name1, name2;
+------+-------------+------------+--------------+------------+
| year | name1       | statehood1 | name2        | statehood2 |
+------+-------------+------------+--------------+------------+
| 1787 | Delaware    | 1787-12-07 | New Jersey   | 1787-12-18 |
| 1787 | Delaware    | 1787-12-07 | Pennsylvania | 1787-12-12 |
| 1787 | New Jersey  | 1787-12-18 | Pennsylvania | 1787-12-12 |
...
| 1912 | Arizona     | 1912-02-14 | New Mexico   | 1912-01-06 |
| 1959 | Alaska      | 1959-01-03 | Hawaii       | 1959-08-21 |
+------+-------------+------------+--------------+------------+
```

An alternative approach to removing nonidentical duplicates relies not so much on detecting and eliminating them as on selecting rows in such a way that only one row from each pair ever appears in the query result. This makes it unnecessary to reorder values within output rows or to use DISTINCT. For the state-pairs query, selecting only those rows in which the first state name is lexically less than the second automatically eliminates rows whose names appear in the other order:[*]

---

[*] The same constraint also eliminates those rows in which the state names are identical.

```
mysql> SELECT YEAR(s1.statehood) AS year,
    -> IF(s1.name<s2.name,s1.name,s2.name) AS name1,
    -> IF(s1.name<s2.name,s1.statehood,s2.statehood) AS statehood1,
    -> IF(s1.name<s2.name,s2.name,s1.name) AS name2,
    -> IF(s1.name<s2.name,s2.statehood,s1.statehood) AS statehood2
    -> FROM states AS s1 INNER JOIN states AS s2
    -> ON YEAR(s1.statehood) = YEAR(s2.statehood) AND s1.name < s2.name
    -> ORDER BY year, name1, name2;
+------+----------------+------------+----------------+------------+
| year | name1          | statehood1 | name2          | statehood2 |
+------+----------------+------------+----------------+------------+
| 1787 | Delaware       | 1787-12-07 | New Jersey     | 1787-12-18 |
| 1787 | Delaware       | 1787-12-07 | Pennsylvania   | 1787-12-12 |
| 1787 | New Jersey     | 1787-12-18 | Pennsylvania   | 1787-12-12 |
...
| 1912 | Arizona        | 1912-02-14 | New Mexico     | 1912-01-06 |
| 1959 | Alaska         | 1959-01-03 | Hawaii         | 1959-08-21 |
+------+----------------+------------+----------------+------------+
```

## CHAPTER 15

Performing Transactions

15.0 Introduction

The MySQL server can handle multiple clients at the same time because it is multi-threaded. To deal with contention among clients, the server performs any necessary locking so that two clients cannot modify the same data at once. However, as the server executes SQL statements, it's very possible that successive statements received from a given client will be interleaved with statements from other clients. If a client issues multiple statements that are dependent on each other, the fact that other clients may be updating tables in between those statements can cause difficulties. Statement failures can be problematic, too, if a multiple-statement operation does not run to completion. Suppose that you have a `flight` table containing information about airline flight schedules and you want to update the row for Flight 578 by choosing a pilot from among those available. You might do so using three statements as follows:

```
SELECT @p_val := pilot_id FROM pilot WHERE available = 'yes' LIMIT 1;
UPDATE pilot SET available = 'no' WHERE pilot_id = @p_val;
UPDATE flight SET pilot_id = @p_val WHERE flight_id = 578;
```

The first statement chooses one of the available pilots, the second marks the pilot as unavailable, and the third assigns the pilot to the flight. That's straightforward enough in practice, but in principle there are a couple of significant difficulties with the process:

Concurrency issues

> If two clients want to schedule pilots, it's possible that both of them would run the initial SELECT query and retrieve the same pilot ID number before either of them has a chance to set the pilot's status to unavailable. If that happens, the same pilot would be scheduled for two flights at once.

Integrity issues

> All three statements must execute successfully as a unit. For example, if the SELECT and the first UPDATE run successfully, but the second UPDATE fails, the pilot's status is set to unavailable without the pilot being assigned a flight. The database will be left in an inconsistent state.

To prevent concurrency and integrity problems in these types of situations, transactions are helpful. A transaction groups a set of statements and guarantees the following properties:

- No other client can update the data used in the transaction while the transaction is in progress; it's as though you have the server all to yourself. For example, other clients cannot modify the pilot or flight records while you're booking a pilot for a flight. By preventing other clients from interfering with the operations you're performing, transactions solve concurrency problems arising from the multiple-client nature of the MySQL server. In effect, transactions serialize access to a shared resource across multiple-statement operations.

- Statements in a transaction are grouped and are committed (take effect) as a unit, but only if they all succeed. If an error occurs, any actions that occurred prior to the error are rolled back, leaving the relevant tables unaffected as though none of the statements had been issued at all. This keeps the database from becoming inconsistent. For example, if an update to the `flights` table fails, rollback causes the change to the `pilots` table to be undone, leaving the pilot still available. Rollback frees you from having to figure out how to undo a partially completed operation yourself.

This chapter shows the syntax for the SQL statements that begin and end transactions. It also describes how to implement transactional operations from within programs, using error detection to determine whether to commit or roll back. The final recipe discusses some workarounds that you can use to simulate transactions in applications that use nontransactional storage engines. Sometimes it's sufficient to lock your tables across multiple statements using LOCK TABLE and UNLOCK TABLE. This prevents other clients from interfering, although there is no rollback if any of the statements fail. Another alternative may be to rewrite statements so that they don't require transactions.

Scripts related to the examples shown here are located in the *transactions* directory of the `recipes` distribution.

15.1 Choosing a Transactional Storage Engine

Problem

You want to use transactions.

Solution

Check your MySQL server to determine which transactional storage engines it supports.

Discussion

MySQL supports several storage engines, but not all of them support transactions. To use transactions, you must use a transaction-safe storage engine. Currently, the transactional engines include InnoDB, NDB, and BDB, and others may become available. To see which of them your MySQL server supports, check the output from the SHOW ENGINES statement:

```
mysql> SHOW ENGINES\G
*************************** 1. row ***************************
 Engine: MyISAM
Support: DEFAULT
Comment: Default engine as of MySQL 3.23 with great performance
*************************** 2. row ***************************
 Engine: MEMORY
Support: YES
Comment: Hash based, stored in memory, useful for temporary tables
*************************** 3. row ***************************
 Engine: InnoDB
Support: YES
Comment: Supports transactions, row-level locking, and foreign keys
*************************** 4. row ***************************
 Engine: BerkeleyDB
Support: YES
Comment: Supports transactions and page-level locking
...
```

The output shown is for MySQL 5.0. The transactional engines can be determined from the Comment values; those that actually are available have YES or DEFAULT as the Support value. In MySQL 5.1, SHOW ENGINES output includes a Transaction column that indicates explicitly which engines support transactions.

After determining which transactional storage engines are available, you can create a table that uses a given engine by adding an ENGINE = *tbl_engine* clause to your CREATE TABLE statement:

```
CREATE TABLE t1 (i INT) ENGINE = InnoDB;
CREATE TABLE t2 (i INT) ENGINE = BDB;
```

If you have an existing application that uses nontransactional tables, but you need to modify it to perform transactions, you can alter the tables to use a transactional storage engine. For example, MyISAM tables are nontransactional and trying to use them for transactions will yield incorrect results because they do not support rollback. In this case, you can use ALTER TABLE to convert the tables to a transactional type. Suppose that t is a MyISAM table. To make it an InnoDB table, do this:

```
ALTER TABLE t ENGINE = InnoDB;
```

One thing to consider before altering a table is that changing it to use a transactional storage engine may affect its behavior in other ways. For example, the MyISAM engine provides more flexible handling of AUTO_INCREMENT columns than do other storage engines. If you rely on MyISAM-only sequence features, changing the storage engine will cause problems. See Chapter 11 for more information.

15.2 Performing Transactions Using SQL

Problem

You need to issue a set of statements that must succeed or fail as a unit—that is, you need to perform a transaction.

Solution

Manipulate MySQL's auto-commit mode to enable multiple-statement transactions, and then commit or roll back the statements depending on whether they succeed or fail.

Discussion

This recipe describes the SQL statements that control transactional behavior in MySQL. The immediately following recipes discuss how to perform transactions from within programs. Some APIs require that you implement transactions by issuing the SQL statements discussed in this recipe; others provide a special mechanism that enables transaction management without writing SQL directly. However, even in the latter case, the API mechanism will map program operations onto transactional SQL statements, so reading this recipe will give you a better understanding of what the API is doing on your behalf.

MySQL normally operates in auto-commit mode, which commits the effect of each statement immediately as soon as it executes. (In effect, each statement is its own transaction.) To perform a transaction, you must disable auto-commit mode, issue the statements that make up the transaction, and then either commit or roll back your changes. In MySQL, you can do this two ways:

- Issue a START TRANSACTION (or BEGIN) statement to suspend auto-commit mode, and then issue the statements that make up the transaction. If the statements succeed, record their effect in the database and terminate the transaction by issuing a COMMIT statement:

```
mysql> CREATE TABLE t (i INT) ENGINE = InnoDB;
mysql> START TRANSACTION;
mysql> INSERT INTO t (i) VALUES(1);
mysql> INSERT INTO t (i) VALUES(2);
mysql> COMMIT;
mysql> SELECT * FROM t;
+------+
| i    |
+------+
```

```
|    1 |
|    2 |
+------+
```

If an error occurs, don't use COMMIT. Instead, cancel the transaction by issuing a ROLLBACK statement. In the following example, t remains empty after the transaction because the effects of the INSERT statements are rolled back:

```
mysql> CREATE TABLE t (i INT) ENGINE = InnoDB;
mysql> START TRANSACTION;
mysql> INSERT INTO t (i) VALUES(1);
mysql> INSERT INTO t (x) VALUES(2);
ERROR 1054 (42S22): Unknown column 'x' in 'field list'
mysql> ROLLBACK;
mysql> SELECT * FROM t;
Empty set (0.00 sec)
```

- Another way to group statements is to turn off auto-commit mode explicitly by setting the autocommit session variable to 0. After that, each statement you issue becomes part of the current transaction. To end the transaction and begin the next one, issue a COMMIT or ROLLBACK statement:

```
mysql> CREATE TABLE t (i INT) ENGINE = InnoDB;
mysql> SET autocommit = 0;
mysql> INSERT INTO t (i) VALUES(1);
mysql> INSERT INTO t (i) VALUES(2);
mysql> COMMIT;
mysql> SELECT * FROM t;
+------+
| i    |
+------+
|    1 |
|    2 |
+------+
```

To turn auto-commit mode back on, use this statement:

```
mysql> SET autocommit = 1;
```

Not Everything Can Be Undone

Transactions have their limits, because not all statements can be part of a transaction. For example, if you issue a DROP DATABASE statement, don't expect to restore the database by executing a ROLLBACK.

15.3 Performing Transactions from Within Programs

Problem

You're writing a program that needs to implement transactional operations.

Solution

Use the transaction abstraction provided by your language API, if it has such a thing. If it doesn't, use the API's usual statement execution mechanism to issue the transactional SQL statements directly using the usual API database calls.

Discussion

When you issue statements interactively with the *mysql* program (as in the examples shown in the previous recipe), you can see by inspection whether statements succeed or fail and determine on that basis whether to commit or roll back. From within a non-interactive SQL script stored in a file, that doesn't work so well. You cannot commit or roll back conditionally according to statement success or failure, because MySQL includes no IF/THEN/ELSE construct for controlling the flow of the script. (There is an IF( ) function, but that's not the same thing.) For this reason, it's most common to perform transactional processing from within a program, because you can use your API language to detect errors and take appropriate action. This recipe discusses some general background on how to do this. The next recipes provide language-specific details for the MySQL APIs for Perl, Ruby, PHP, Python, and Java.

Every MySQL API supports transactions, even if only in the sense that you can explicitly issue transaction-related SQL statements such as START TRANSACTION and COMMIT. However, some APIs also provide a transaction abstraction that enables you to control transactional behavior without working directly with SQL. This approach hides the details and provides better portability to other database engines that have different underlying transaction SQL syntax. An API abstraction is available for each of the languages that we use in this book.

The next few recipes each implement the same example to illustrate how to perform program-based transactions. They use a table t containing the following initial rows that show how much money two people have:

```
+------+------+
| name | amt  |
+------+------+
| Eve  |   10 |
| Ida  |    0 |
+------+------+
```

The sample transaction is a simple financial transfer that uses two UPDATE statements to give six dollars of Eve's money to Ida:

```
UPDATE money SET amt = amt - 6 WHERE name = 'Eve';
UPDATE money SET amt = amt + 6 WHERE name = 'Ida';
```

The intended result is that the table should look like this:

```
+------+------+
| name | amt  |
+------+------+
| Eve  |    4 |
```

```
| Ida  |    6 |
+------+------+
```

It's necessary to execute both statements within a transaction to ensure that both of them take effect at once. Without a transaction, Eve's money disappears without being credited to Ida if the second statement fails. By using a transaction, the table will be left unchanged if statement failure occurs.

The sample programs for each language are located in the *transactions* directory of the `recipes` distribution. If you compare them, you'll see that they all employ a similar framework for performing transactional processing:

- The statements of the transaction are grouped within a control structure, along with a commit operation.
- If the status of the control structure indicates that it did not execute successfully to completion, the transaction is rolled back.

That logic can be expressed as follows, where `block` represents the control structure used to group statements:

```
block:
  statement 1
  statement 2
  ...
  statement n
  commit
if the block failed:
  roll back
```

If the statements in the block succeed, you reach the end of the block and commit them. Otherwise, occurrence of an error raises an exception that triggers execution of the error-handling code where you roll back the transaction.

The benefit of structuring your code as just described is that it minimizes the number of tests needed to determine whether to roll back. The alternative—checking the result of each statement within the transaction and rolling back on individual statement errors—quickly turns your code into an unreadable mess.

A subtle point to be aware of when rolling back within languages that raise exceptions is that it may be possible for the rollback itself to fail, causing another exception to be raised. If you don't deal with that, your program itself may terminate. To handle this, issue the rollback within another block that has an empty exception handler. The sample programs do this as necessary.

Those sample programs that disable auto-commit mode explicitly when performing a transaction take care to enable auto-commit afterward. In applications that perform all database processing in transactional fashion, it's unnecessary to do this. Just disable auto-commit mode once after you connect to the database server, and leave it off.

Checking How API Transaction Abstractions Map onto SQL Statements

For APIs that provide a transaction abstraction, you can see how the interface maps onto the underlying SQL statements: enable the general query log for your MySQL server and then watch the logfile to see what statements the API executes when you run a transactional program. (See the *MySQL Reference Manual* for instructions on enabling the log.)

15.4 Using Transactions in Perl Programs

Problem

You want to perform a transaction in a Perl DBI script.

Solution

Use the standard DBI transaction support mechanism.

Discussion

The Perl DBI transaction mechanism is based on explicit manipulation of auto-commit mode:

1. Turn on the `RaiseError` attribute if it's not enabled and disable `PrintError` if it's on. You want errors to raise exceptions without printing anything, and leaving `PrintError` enabled can interfere with failure detection in some cases.

2. Disable the `AutoCommit` attribute so that a commit will be done only when you say so.

3. Execute the statements that make up the transaction within an `eval` block so that errors raise an exception and terminate the block. The last thing in the block should be a call to `commit( )`, which commits the transaction if all its statements completed successfully.

4. After the `eval` executes, check the `$@` variable. If `$@` contains the empty string, the transaction succeeded. Otherwise, the `eval` will have failed due to the occurrence of some error and `$@` will contain an error message. Invoke `rollback( )` to cancel the transaction. If you want to display an error message, print `$@` before calling `rollback( )`.

The following code shows how to follow those steps to perform our sample transaction:

```
# set error-handling and auto-commit attributes correctly
$dbh->{RaiseError} = 1; # raise exception if an error occurs
$dbh->{PrintError} = 0; # don't print an error message
$dbh->{AutoCommit} = 0; # disable auto-commit
```

```
eval
{
  # move some money from one person to the other
  $dbh->do ("UPDATE money SET amt = amt - 6 WHERE name = 'Eve'");
  $dbh->do ("UPDATE money SET amt = amt + 6 WHERE name = 'Ida'");
  # all statements succeeded; commit transaction
  $dbh->commit ();
};

if ($@) # an error occurred
{
  print "Transaction failed, rolling back. Error was:\n$@\n";
  # roll back within eval to prevent rollback
  # failure from terminating the script
  eval { $dbh->rollback (); };
}
```

The code shown does not save the current values of the error-handling and auto-commit attributes before executing the transaction or restore them afterward. If you save and restore them, your transaction-handling code becomes more general because it does not affect other parts of your program that might use different attribute values, but more lines of code are required. To make transaction processing easier (while avoiding repetition of the extra code if you execute multiple transactions), create a couple of convenience functions to handle the processing that occurs before and after the eval:

```
sub transaction_init
{
my $dbh = shift;
my $attr_ref = {};  # create hash in which to save attributes

  $attr_ref->{RaiseError} = $dbh->{RaiseError};
  $attr_ref->{PrintError} = $dbh->{PrintError};
  $attr_ref->{AutoCommit} = $dbh->{AutoCommit};
  $dbh->{RaiseError} = 1; # raise exception if an error occurs
  $dbh->{PrintError} = 0; # don't print an error message
  $dbh->{AutoCommit} = 0; # disable auto-commit
  return ($attr_ref);   # return attributes to caller
}

sub transaction_finish
{
my ($dbh, $attr_ref, $error) = @_;

  if ($error) # an error occurred
  {
    print "Transaction failed, rolling back. Error was:\n$error\n";
    # roll back within eval to prevent rollback
    # failure from terminating the script
    eval { $dbh->rollback (); };
  }
  # restore error-handling and auto-commit attributes
  $dbh->{AutoCommit} = $attr_ref->{AutoCommit};
  $dbh->{PrintError} = $attr_ref->{PrintError};
```

```
        $dbh->{RaiseError} = $attr_ref->{RaiseError};
    }
```

By using those two functions, our sample transaction can be simplified considerably:

```
$ref = transaction_init ($dbh);
eval
{
    # move some money from one person to the other
    $dbh->do ("UPDATE money SET amt = amt - 6 WHERE name = 'Eve'");
    $dbh->do ("UPDATE money SET amt = amt + 6 WHERE name = 'Ida'");
    # all statements succeeded; commit transaction
    $dbh->commit ();
};
transaction_finish ($dbh, $ref, $@);
```

In Perl DBI, an alternative to manipulating the AutoCommit attribute manually is to begin a transaction by invoking begin_work( ). This method disables AutoCommit and causes it to be enabled again automatically when you invoke commit( ) or rollback( ) later.

15.5 Using Transactions in Ruby Programs

Problem

You want to perform a transaction in a Ruby DBI script.

Solution

Use the standard DBI transaction support mechanism. Actually, Ruby provides two mechanisms.

Discussion

The Ruby DBI module provides a couple of ways to perform transactions, although both of them rely on manipulation of auto-commit mode. One approach uses a begin/rescue block, and you invoke the commit and rollback methods explicitly:

```
begin
  dbh['AutoCommit'] = false
  dbh.do("UPDATE money SET amt = amt - 6 WHERE name = 'Eve'")
  dbh.do("UPDATE money SET amt = amt + 6 WHERE name = 'Ida'")
  dbh.commit
  dbh['AutoCommit'] = true
rescue DBI::DatabaseError => e
  puts "Transaction failed"
  puts "#{e.err}: #{e.errstr}"
  begin           # empty exception handler in case rollback fails
    dbh.rollback
    dbh['AutoCommit'] = true
  rescue
  end
end
```

Ruby also supports a `transaction` method, which is associated with a code block and which commits or rolls back automatically depending on whether the code block succeeds or fails:

```
begin
  dbh['AutoCommit'] = false
  dbh.transaction do |dbh|
    dbh.do("UPDATE money SET amt = amt - 6 WHERE name = 'Eve'")
    dbh.do("UPDATE money SET amt = amt + 6 WHERE name = 'Ida'")
  end
  dbh['AutoCommit'] = true
rescue DBI::DatabaseError => e
  puts "Transaction failed"
  puts "#{e.err}: #{e.errstr}"
  dbh['AutoCommit'] = true
end
```

With the `transaction` method, there is no need to invoke `commit` or `rollback` explicitly yourself. `transaction` does raise an exception if it rolls back, so the example still uses a `begin/rescue` block for error detection.

15.6 Using Transactions in PHP Programs

Problem

You want to perform a transaction in a PHP script.

Solution

Use the standard PEAR DB transaction support mechanism.

Discussion

The PEAR DB module supports a transaction abstraction that can be used to perform transactions. Use the `autoCommit( )` method to disable auto-commit mode. Then, after issuing your statements, invoke either `commit( )` or `rollback( )` to commit or roll back the transaction.

The following code uses exceptions to signal transaction failure, which means that PHP 5 is required. (Earlier versions of PHP do not support exceptions.) The PEAR DB transaction-handling methods do not raise exceptions themselves when they fail, so the example program uses status checking within the `try` block to determine when to raise its own exception:

```
try
{
  $result =& $conn->autoCommit (FALSE);
  if (PEAR::isError ($result))
    throw new Exception ($result->getMessage ());
  $result =& $conn->query (
```

```
                     "UPDATE money SET amt = amt - 6 WHERE name = 'Eve'");
    if (PEAR::isError ($result))
      throw new Exception ($result->getMessage ());
    $result =& $conn->query (
                     "UPDATE money SET amt = amt + 6 WHERE name = 'Ida'");
    if (PEAR::isError ($result))
      throw new Exception ($result->getMessage ());
    $result =& $conn->commit ();
    if (PEAR::isError ($result))
      throw new Exception ($result->getMessage ());
    $result =& $conn->autoCommit (TRUE);
    if (PEAR::isError ($result))
      throw new Exception ($result->getMessage ());
  }
  catch (Exception $e)
  {
    print ("Transaction failed: " . $e->getMessage () . ".\n");
    # empty exception handler in case rollback fails
    try
    {
      $conn->rollback ();
      $conn->autoCommit (TRUE);
    }
    catch (Exception $e2) { }
  }
```

15.7 Using Transactions in Python Programs

Problem

You want to perform a transaction in a DB-API script.

Solution

Use the standard DB-API transaction support mechanism.

Discussion

The Python DB-API abstraction provides transaction processing control through connection object methods. The DB-API specification indicates that database connections
should begin with auto-commit mode disabled. Therefore, when you open a connection to the database server, MySQLdb disables auto-commit mode, which implicitly
begins a transaction. End each transaction with either commit( ) or rollback( ). The
commit( ) call occurs within a try statement, and the rollback( ) occurs within the
except clause to cancel the transaction if an error occurs:

```
    try:
      cursor = conn.cursor ()
      # move some money from one person to the other
      cursor.execute ("UPDATE money SET amt = amt - 6 WHERE name = 'Eve'")
      cursor.execute ("UPDATE money SET amt = amt + 6 WHERE name = 'Ida'")
```

```
    cursor.close ()
    conn.commit()
except MySQLdb.Error, e:
    print "Transaction failed, rolling back. Error was:"
    print e.args
    try:  # empty exception handler in case rollback fails
      conn.rollback ()
    except:
      pass
```

15.8 Using Transactions in Java Programs

Problem

You want to perform a transaction in a JDBC application.

Solution

Use the standard JDBC transaction support mechanism.

Discussion

To perform transactions in Java, use your `Connection` object to turn off auto-commit mode. Then, after issuing your statements, use the object's `commit( )` method to commit the transaction or `rollback( )` to cancel it. Typically, you execute the statements for the transaction in a `try` block, with `commit( )` at the end of the block. To handle failures, invoke `rollback( )` in the corresponding exception handler:

```
try
{
  conn.setAutoCommit (false);
  Statement s = conn.createStatement ();
  // move some money from one person to the other
  s.executeUpdate ("UPDATE money SET amt = amt - 6 WHERE name = 'Eve'");
  s.executeUpdate ("UPDATE money SET amt = amt + 6 WHERE name = 'Ida'");
  s.close ();
  conn.commit ();
  conn.setAutoCommit (true);
}
catch (SQLException e)
{
  System.err.println ("Transaction failed, rolling back.");
  Cookbook.printErrorMessage (e);
  // empty exception handler in case rollback fails
  try
  {
    conn.rollback ();
    conn.setAutoCommit (true);
  }
```

```
    catch (Exception e2) { }
}
```

15.9 Using Alternatives to Transactions

Problem

You need to perform transactional processing, but your application uses a nontran-sactional storage engine.

Solution

Some transaction-like operations are amenable to workarounds such as explicit table locking. In certain cases, you might not actually even need a transaction; by rewriting your statements, you can entirely eliminate the need for a transaction.

Discussion

Transactions are valuable, but sometimes they cannot or need not be used:

- Your application may use a storage engine that does not support transactions. For example, if you use MyISAM tables, you cannot use transactions because the MyISAM storage engine is nontransactional. Each update to a MyISAM table takes effect immediately without a commit and cannot be rolled back. In this case, you have no choice but to use some kind of workaround for transactions. One strategy that can be helpful in some situations is to use explicit table locking to prevent concurrency problems.

- Applications sometimes use transactions when they're not really necessary. You may be able to eliminate the need for a transaction by rewriting statements. This might even result in a faster application.

Grouping statements using locks

If you're using a nontransactional storage engine but you need to execute a group of statements without interference by other clients, you can do so by using LOCK TABLE and UNLOCK TABLE:[*]

1. Use LOCK TABLE to obtain locks for all the tables you intend to use. (Acquire write locks for tables you need to modify, and read locks for the others.) This prevents other clients from modifying the tables while you're using them.
2. Issue the statements that must be executed as a group.
3. Release the locks with UNLOCK TABLE. Other clients will regain access to the tables.

---

[*] LOCK TABLES and UNLOCK TABLES are synonyms for LOCK TABLE and UNLOCK TABLE.

Locks obtained with `LOCK TABLE` remain in effect until you release them and thus can apply over the course of multiple statements. This gives you the same concurrency benefits as transactions. However, there is no rollback if errors occur, so table locking is not appropriate for all applications. For example, you might try performing an operation that transfers funds from Eve to Ida as follows:

```
LOCK TABLE money WRITE;
UPDATE money SET amt = amt - 6 WHERE name = 'Eve';
UPDATE money SET amt = amt + 6 WHERE name = 'Ida';
UNLOCK TABLE;
```

Unfortunately, if the second update fails, the effect of the first update is not rolled back. Despite this caveat, there are certain types of situations where table locking may be sufficient for your purposes:

- A set of statements consisting only of `SELECT` queries. If you want to run several `SELECT` statements and prevent other clients from modifying the tables while you're querying them, locking will do that. For example, if you need to run several summary queries on a set of tables, your summaries may appear to be based on different sets of data if other clients are allowed to change rows in between your summary queries. This will make the summaries inconsistent. To prevent that from happening, lock the tables while you're using them.

- Locking also can be useful for a set of statements in which only the *last* statement is an update. In this case, the earlier statements don't make any changes and there is nothing that needs to be rolled back should the update fail.

Rewriting statements to avoid transactions

Sometimes applications use transactions unnecessarily. Suppose that you have a table `meeting` that records meeting and convention information (including the number of tickets left for each event), and that you're writing a Ruby application containing a `get_ticket( )` method that dispenses tickets. One way to implement the function is to check the ticket count, decrement it if it's positive, and return a status indicating whether a ticket was available. To prevent multiple clients from attempting to grab the last ticket at the same time, issue the statements within a transaction:

```
def get_ticket(dbh, meeting_id)
  count = 0
  begin
    dbh['AutoCommit'] = false
    # check the current ticket count
    row = dbh.select_one("SELECT tix_left FROM meeting
                          WHERE meeting_id = ?",
                        meeting_id)
    count = row[0]
    # if there are tickets left, decrement the count
    if count > 0
      dbh.do("UPDATE meeting SET tix_left = tix_left-1
             WHERE meeting_id = ?",
           meeting_id)
```

```
    end
    dbh.commit
    dbh['AutoCommit'] = true
  rescue DBI::DatabaseError => e
    count = 0        # if an error occurred, no tix available
    begin            # empty exception handler in case rollback fails
      dbh.rollback
      dbh['AutoCommit'] = true
    rescue
    end
  end

  return count > 0
end
```

The method dispenses tickets properly, but involves a certain amount of unnecessary work. It's possible to do the same thing without using a transaction at all, if auto-commit mode is enabled. Decrement the ticket count only if the count is greater than zero, and then check whether the statement affected a row:

```
def get_ticket(dbh, meeting_id)
  count = dbh.do("UPDATE meeting SET tix_left = tix_left-1
                  WHERE meeting_id = ? AND tix_left > 0",
                 meeting_id)
  return count > 0
end
```

In MySQL, the row count returned by an UPDATE statement indicates the number of rows changed. This means that if there are no tickets left for an event, the UPDATE won't change the row and the count will be zero. This makes it easy to determine whether a ticket is available using a single statement rather than with the multiple statements required by the transactional approach. The lesson here is that although transactions are important and have their place, you may be able to avoid them and end up with a faster application as a result. The single-statement solution is an example of what the *MySQL Reference Manual* refers to as an "atomic operation." The manual discusses these as an efficient alternative to transactions.

## CHAPTER 16

Using Stored Routines, Triggers, and Events

16.0 Introduction

This chapter discusses the following kinds of database objects:

Stored routines (functions and procedures)
> A stored function performs a calculation and returns a value that can be used in expressions just like a built-in function such as `RAND( )`, `NOW( )`, or `LEFT( )`. A stored procedure performs calculations for which no return value is needed. Procedures are not used in expressions, they are invoked with the `CALL` statement. A procedure might be executed to update rows in a table or produce a result set that is sent to the client program. One reason for using a stored routine is that it encapsulates the code for performing a calculation. This enables you to perform the calculation easily by invoking the routine rather than by repeating all its code each time.

Triggers
> A trigger is an object that is defined to activate when a table is modified. Triggers are available for `INSERT`, `UPDATE`, and `DELETE` statements. For example, you can check values before they are inserted into a table, or specify that any row deleted from a table should be logged to another table that serves as a journal of data changes. Triggers are useful for automating these actions so that you don't need to remember to do them yourself each time you modify a table.

Events
> An event is an object that executes SQL statements at a scheduled time or times. You can think of an event as something like a Unix *cron* job, but that runs within MySQL. For example, events can help you perform administrative tasks such as deleting old table records periodically or creating nightly summaries.

Stored routines and triggers are supported as of MySQL 5.0. Event support begins with MySQL 5.1.

These different kinds of objects have in common the property that they are user-defined but stored on the server side for later execution. This differs from sending an SQL statement from the client to the server for immediate execution. Each of these objects also has the property that it is defined in terms of other SQL statements to be executed when the object is invoked. The object has a body that is a single SQL statement, but that statement can use compound-statement syntax (a BEGIN … END block) that contains multiple statements. This means that the body can range from very simple to extremely complex. The following stored procedure is a trivial routine that does nothing but set a user-defined variable and for which the body consists of a single SET statement:

```
CREATE PROCEDURE get_time()
SET @current_time = CURTIME();
```

For more complex operations, a compound statement is necessary:

```
CREATE PROCEDURE part_of_day()
BEGIN
  CALL get_time();
  IF @current_time < '12:00:00' THEN
    SET @day_part = 'morning';
  ELSEIF @current_time = '12:00:00' THEN
    SET @day_part = 'noon';
  ELSE
    SET @day_part = 'afternoon or night';
  END IF;
END;
```

Here, the BEGIN … END block contains multiple statements, but is itself considered to constitute a single statement. Compound statements enable you to declare local variables and to use conditional logic and looping constructs. Note also that one stored procedure can invoke another: part_of_day( ) calls get_time( ). These capabilities provide you with considerably more flexibility for algorithmic expression than you have when you write inline expressions in noncompound statements such as SELECT or UPDATE.

The statements within a compound statement must each be terminated by a ; character. That requirement causes a problem if you use the *mysql* client to define an object that uses compound statements because *mysql* itself interprets ; to determine statement boundaries. The solution to this problem is to redefine *mysql*'s statement delimiter while you're defining a compound-statement object. Recipe 16.1 covers how to do this; make sure that you read that recipe before proceeding to those that follow it.

Due to space limitations, this chapter illustrates by example but does not otherwise go into much detail about the extensive syntax for stored routines, triggers, and events. For complete syntax descriptions, see the *MySQL Reference Manual*.

The scripts for the examples shown in this chapter can be found in the *routines*, *triggers*, and *events* directories of the recipes distribution. Scripts to create some of the tables are in the *tables* directory.

In addition to the stored routines shown in this chapter, others can be found elsewhere in this book. See, for example, Recipes 5.7, 6.2, and 11.11.

Privileges for Stored Routines, Triggers, and Events

When you create a stored routine, the following privilege requirements must be satisfied or you will have problems:

- To create a stored routine, you must have the CREATE ROUTINE privilege.
- If binary logging is enabled for your MySQL server (which is common practice), there are some additional requirements for creating stored functions (but not stored procedures). These requirements are necessary to ensure that if you use the binary log for replication or for restoring backups, function invocations cause the same effect when reexecuted as they do when originally executed:
  - You must have the SUPER privilege, and you must declare either that the function is deterministic or does not modify data by using one of the DETERMINISTIC, NO SQL, or READS SQL DATA characteristics. (It's possible to create functions that are not deterministic or that modify data, but they might not be safe for replication or for use in backups.)
  - Alternatively, if you enable the log_bin_trust_function_creators system variable, the server waives both of the preceding requirements.

To create a trigger in MySQL 5.0, you must have the SUPER privilege. In MySQL 5.1, you must have the TRIGGER privilege for the table associated with the trigger.

To create events, you must have the EVENT privilege for the database in which the events are created.

16.1 Creating Compound-Statement Objects

Problem

You want to define a stored routine, a trigger, or an event, but its body contains instances of the ; statement terminator. This is the same terminator that *mysql* uses by default, so *mysql* misinterprets the definition and produces an error.

Solution

Redefine the *mysql* statement terminator with the delimiter command.

Discussion

Each stored routine, trigger, or event is an object with a body that must be a single SQL statement. However, these objects often perform complex operations that require several statements. To handle this, you write the statements within a BEGIN ... END block that forms a compound statement. That is, the block is itself a single statement but can contain multiple statements, each terminated by a ; character. The BEGIN ... END block can contain statements such as SELECT or INSERT, but compound statements also allow for conditional statements such as IF or CASE, looping constructs such as WHILE or REPEAT, or other BEGIN ... END blocks.

Compound-statement syntax provides you with a lot of flexibility, but if you define compound-statement objects within *mysql*, you'll quickly run into a small problem: statements within a compound statement each must be terminated by a ; character, but *mysql* itself interprets ; to figure out where each statement ends so that it can send them one at a time to the server to be executed. Consequently, *mysql* stops reading the compound statement when it sees the first ; character, which is too early. The solution to this problem is to tell *mysql* to recognize a different statement delimiter. Then *mysql* will ignore the ; character within the object body. You terminate the object itself with the new delimiter, which *mysql* recognizes and then sends the entire object definition to the server. You can restore the *mysql* delimiter to its original value after defining the compound-statement object.

Suppose that you want to define a stored function that calculates and returns the average size in bytes of mail messages listed in the mail table. The function can be defined with a body part consisting of a single SQL statement like this:

```
CREATE FUNCTION avg_mail_size()
RETURNS FLOAT READS SQL DATA
RETURN (SELECT AVG(size) FROM mail);
```

The RETURNS FLOAT clause indicates the type of the function's return value, and READS SQL DATA indicates that the function reads but does not modify data. The body of the function follows those clauses and consists of the single RETURN statement that executes a subquery and returns the value that it produces to the caller. (Every stored function must have at least one RETURN statement.)

In *mysql*, you can enter that statement as shown and there is no problem. The definition requires just the single terminator at the end and none internally, so no ambiguity arises. But suppose instead that you want to define the function to take an argument naming a user that is interpreted as follows:

- If the argument is NULL, the function returns the average size for all messages (as before).

- If the argument is non-NULL, the function returns the average size for messages sent by that user.

To accomplish this, the routine needs a more complex body that uses a BEGIN ... END block:

```
CREATE FUNCTION avg_mail_size(user VARCHAR(8))
RETURNS FLOAT READS SQL DATA
BEGIN
  IF user IS NULL THEN
```

```
      # return average message size over all users
      RETURN (SELECT AVG(size) FROM mail);
   ELSE
      # return average message size for given user
      RETURN (SELECT AVG(size) FROM mail WHERE srcuser = user);
   END IF;
END;
```

If you try to define the function within *mysql* by entering that definition as is, *mysql* will improperly interpret the first semicolon in the function body as ending the definition. To handle this, use the `delimiter` command to change the *mysql* delimiter to something else temporarily. The following example shows how to do this and then restore the delimiter to its default value:

```
mysql> delimiter $$
mysql> CREATE FUNCTION avg_mail_size (user VARCHAR(8))
    -> RETURNS FLOAT READS SQL DATA
    -> BEGIN
    ->   IF user IS NULL THEN
    ->     # return average message size over all users
    ->     RETURN (SELECT AVG(size) FROM mail);
    ->   ELSE
    ->     # return average message size for given user
    ->     RETURN (SELECT AVG(size) FROM mail WHERE srcuser = user);
    ->   END IF;
    -> END;
    -> $$
Query OK, 0 rows affected (0.02 sec)
mysql> delimiter ;
```

After defining the stored function, you can invoke it the same way as built-in functions:

```
mysql> SELECT avg_mail_size(NULL), avg_mail_size('barb');
+---------------------+-----------------------+
| avg_mail_size(NULL) | avg_mail_size('barb') |
+---------------------+-----------------------+
|        237386.5625  |                 52232 |
+---------------------+-----------------------+
```

The same principles apply to defining other objects that use compound statements (stored procedures, triggers, and events).

16.2 Using a Stored Function to Encapsulate a Calculation

Problem

A particular calculation to produce a value must be performed frequently by different applications, but you don't want to write out the expression for it each time it's needed. Or a calculation is difficult to perform inline within an expression because it requires conditional or looping logic.

Solution

Use a stored function to hide all the ugly details of the calculation and make it easy to perform.

Discussion

Stored functions enable you to simplify your applications because you can write out the code that produces a calculation result once in the function definition, and then simply invoke the function whenever you need to perform the calculation. Stored functions also enable you to use more complex algorithmic constructs than are available when you write a calculation inline within an expression. This section shows an example that illustrates how stored functions can be useful in these ways. Granted, the example is not actually *that* complex, but you can apply the same principles used here to write functions that are much more elaborate.

Different states in the U.S. charge different rates for sales tax. If you sell goods to people from different states and must charge tax using the rate appropriate for customer state of residence, tax computation is something you'll need to do for every sale. You can handle this with a table that lists the sales tax rate for each state, and a stored function that calculates amount of tax given the amount of a sale and a state.

To set up the table, use the *sales_tax_rate.sql* script in the *tables* directory of the recipes distribution. The sales_tax_rate table has two columns: state (a two-letter abbreviation), and tax_rate (a DECIMAL value rather than a FLOAT, to preserve accuracy).

The stored function, sales_tax( ) can be defined as follows:

```
CREATE FUNCTION sales_tax(state_param CHAR(2), amount_param DECIMAL(10,2))
RETURNS DECIMAL(10,2) READS SQL DATA
BEGIN
  DECLARE rate_var DECIMAL(3,2);
  DECLARE CONTINUE HANDLER FOR SQLSTATE '02000' SET rate_var = 0;
  SELECT tax_rate INTO rate_var
    FROM sales_tax_rate WHERE state = state_param;
  RETURN amount_param * rate_var;
END;
```

The function looks up the tax rate for the given state, and returns the tax as the product of the sale amount and the tax rate.

Suppose that the tax rates for Vermont and New York are 1 and 9 percent, respectively. Try the function to see whether the tax is computed correctly for a sales amount of $100:

```
mysql> SELECT sales_tax('VT',100.00), sales_tax('NY',100.00);
+------------------------+------------------------+
| sales_tax('VT',100.00) | sales_tax('NY',100.00) |
+------------------------+------------------------+
|                   1.00 |                   6.00 |
+------------------------+------------------------+
```

For a location not listed in the tax rate table, the function should fail to determine a rate and compute a tax of zero:

```
mysql> SELECT sales_tax('ZZ',100.00);
+------------------------+
| sales_tax('ZZ',100.00) |
+------------------------+
|                   0.00 |
+------------------------+
```

Obviously, if you take sales from locations not listed in the table, the function cannot determine the rate for those locations. In this case, the function assumes a tax rate is 0 percent. This is done by means of a `CONTINUE` handler, which kicks in if a No Data condition (SQLSTATE value `02000`) occurs. That is, if there is no row for the given `state_param` value, the `SELECT` statement fails to find a sales tax rate. In that case, the `CONTINUE` handler sets the rate to 0 and continues execution with the next statement after the `SELECT`. (This handler is an example of the kind of logic that you can use in a stored routine that is not available in inline expressions.)

16.3 Using a Stored Procedure to "Return" Multiple Values

Problem

You want to perform an operation that produces two or more values, but a stored function can return only a single value.

Solution

Use a stored procedure that has `OUT` or `INOUT` parameters, and pass user-defined variables for those parameters when you invoke the procedure. A procedure does not "return" a value the way a function does, but it can assign values to those parameters, which will be the values of the variables when the procedure returns.

Discussion

Unlike stored function parameters, which are input values only, a stored procedure parameter can be any of three types:

- An `IN` parameter is for input only. This is the default parameter type if you specify no type.
- An `INOUT` parameter is used to pass a value in, and it can also be used to pass a value back out.
- An `OUT` parameter is used to pass a value out.

This means that if you need to produce multiple values from an operation, you can use `INOUT` or `OUT` parameters. The following example illustrates this, using an `IN` parameter for input, and passing back three values via `OUT` parameters.

Recipe 16.1 showed an avg_mail_size( ) function that returns the average mail message size for a given sender. The function returns a single value. If you want additional information, such as the number of messages and total message size, a function will not work. You could write three separate functions, but it's also possible to use a single procedure that retrieves multiple values about a given mail sender. The following procedure, mail_sender_stats( ), runs a query on the mail table to retrieve mail-sending statistics about a given username, which is the input value. The procedure determines how many messages that user sent, and the total and average size of the messages in bytes, which it returns through three OUT parameters:

```
CREATE PROCEDURE mail_sender_stats(IN user VARCHAR(8),
                                   OUT messages INT,
                                   OUT total_size FLOAT,
                                   OUT avg_size FLOAT)
BEGIN
  # Use IFNULL() to return 0 for SUM() and AVG() in case there are
  # no rows for the user (those functions return NULL in that case).
  SELECT COUNT(*), IFNULL(SUM(size),0), IFNULL(AVG(size),0)
  INTO messages, total_size, avg_size
  FROM mail WHERE srcuser = user;
END;
```

To use the procedure, pass a string containing the username, and three user-defined variables to receive the OUT values. After the procedure returns, check the variable values:

```
mysql> CALL mail_sender_stats('barb',@messages,@total_size,@avg_size);
mysql> SELECT @messages, @total_size, @avg_size;
+-----------+------------+-----------+
| @messages | @total_size | @avg_size |
+-----------+------------+-----------+
| 3         | 156696      | 52232     |
+-----------+------------+-----------+
```

16.4 Using a Trigger to Define Dynamic Default Column Values

Problem

A column in a table needs to be initialized to a nonconstant value, but MySQL allows only constant default values.

Solution

Use a BEFORE INSERT trigger. This enables you to initialize a column to the value of an arbitrary expression. In other words, the trigger performs dynamic column initialization by calculating the default value.

Discussion

Other than TIMESTAMP columns, which can be initialized to the current date and time, the default value for a column in MySQL must be a constant value. You cannot define a column with a DEFAULT clause that refers to a function call (or other arbitrary expression), and you cannot define one column in terms of the value assigned to another column. That means each of these column definitions is illegal:

```
d       DATE DEFAULT NOW()
i       INT DEFAULT (... some subquery ...)
hashval CHAR(32) DEFAULT MD5(blob_col)
```

However, you can work around this limitation by setting up a suitable trigger, which enables you to initialize a column however you want. In effect, the trigger enables you to define dynamic (or calculated) default column values.

The appropriate type of trigger for this is BEFORE INSERT, because that enables you to set column values before they are inserted into the table. (An AFTER INSERT trigger can examine column values for a new row, but by the time the trigger activates, it's too late to change the values.)

Suppose that you want to use a table for storing large data values such as PDF or XML documents, images, or sounds, but you also want to be able to look them up quickly later. A TEXT or BLOB data type might be suitable for storing the values, but is not very suitable for finding them. (Comparisons in a lookup operation will be slow for large values.) To work around this problem, use the following strategy:

1. Compute some kind of hash value for each data value and store it in the table along with the data.
2. To look up the row containing a particular data value, compute the hash value for the value and search the table for that hash value. For best performance, make sure that the hash column is indexed.

To implement this strategy, a BEFORE INSERT trigger is helpful because you can have the trigger compute the hash value to be stored in the table for new data values. (If you might change the data value later, you should also set up a BEFORE UPDATE trigger to recompute the hash value.)

The following example assumes that you want to store documents in a table, along with the document author and title. In addition, the table contains a column for storing the hash value computed from the document contents. To generate hash values, the example uses the MD5() function, which returns a 32-byte string of hexadecimal characters. That's actually still somewhat long to use for a comparison value. Nevertheless, it's a lot shorter than full-column comparisons based on contents of very long documents.

First, create a table to hold the document information and the hash values calculated from the document contents. The following table uses a MEDIUMBLOB column to allow storage of documents up to 16 MB in size:

```
CREATE TABLE doc_table
(
  author   VARCHAR(100) NOT NULL,
  title    VARCHAR(100) NOT NULL,
  document MEDIUMBLOB NOT NULL,
  doc_hash CHAR(32) NOT NULL,
  PRIMARY KEY (doc_hash)
);
```

Next, to handle inserts, create a `BEFORE INSERT` trigger that uses the document to be inserted to calculate the hash value and causes that value to be stored in the table:

```
CREATE TRIGGER bi_doc_table BEFORE INSERT ON doc_table
FOR EACH ROW SET NEW.doc_hash = MD5(NEW.document);
```

This trigger is simple and its body contains only a single SQL statement. For a trigger body that needs to execute multiple statements, use `BEGIN ... END` compound-statement syntax. In that case, if you use *mysql* to create the event, you'll need to change the statement delimiter while you're defining the trigger, as discussed in Recipe 16.1.

Within the trigger, `NEW.col_name` refers to the new value to be inserted into the given column. By assigning a value to `NEW.col_name` within the trigger, you cause the column to have that value in the new row.

Finally, insert a row and check whether the trigger correctly initializes the hash value for the document:

```
mysql> INSERT INTO doc_table (author,title,document)
    -> VALUES('Mr. Famous Writer','My Life as a Writer',
    ->        'This is the document');
mysql> SELECT * FROM doc_table\G;
*************************** 1. row ***************************
  author: Mr. Famous Writer
   title: My Life as a Writer
document: This is the document
doc_hash: 5282317909724f9f1e65318be129539c
mysql> SELECT MD5('This is the document');
+--------------------------------+
| MD5('This is the document')    |
+--------------------------------+
| 5282317909724f9f1e65318be129539c |
+--------------------------------+
```

The first `SELECT` shows that the `doc_hash` column was initialized even though the `INSERT` provided no value for it. The second `SELECT` shows that the hash value stored in the row by the trigger is correct.

The example thus far demonstrates how a trigger enables you to initialize a row column in a way that goes beyond what is possible with the `DEFAULT` clause in the column's definition. The same idea applies to updates, and it's a good idea to apply it in the present scenario: when initialization of a column is a function of the value in another column (as is the case for `doc_hash`), it is dependent on that column. Therefore, you should also update it whenever the column on which it depends is updated. For example, if you update a value in the document column, you should also update the corresponding doc_hash value. This too can be handled by a trigger. Create a BEFORE UPDATE trigger that does the same thing as the INSERT trigger:

```
CREATE TRIGGER bu_doc_table BEFORE UPDATE ON doc_table
FOR EACH ROW SET NEW.doc_hash = MD5(NEW.document);
```

Test the UPDATE trigger by updating the document value and checking whether the hash value is updated properly:

```
mysql> UPDATE doc_table SET document = 'A new document'
    -> WHERE document = 'This is the document';
mysql> SELECT * FROM doc_table\G;
*************************** 1. row ***************************
  author: Mr. Famous Writer
   title: My Life as a Writer
document: A new document
doc_hash: 21c03f63d2f01b598665d4d960f3a4f2
mysql> SELECT MD5('A new document');
+----------------------------------+
| MD5('A new document')            |
+----------------------------------+
| 21c03f63d2f01b598665d4d960f3a4f2 |
+----------------------------------+
```

16.5 Simulating TIMESTAMP Properties for Other Date and Time Types

Problem

The TIMESTAMP data type provides auto-initialization and auto-update properties. You would like to use these properties for other temporal data types, but the other types allow only constant values for initialization, and they don't auto-update.

Solution

Use an INSERT trigger to provide the appropriate current date or time value at record creation time. Use an UPDATE trigger to update the column to the current date or time when the row is changed.

Discussion

Recipe 6.5 describes the special initialization and update properties of the TIMESTAMP data type that enable you to record row creation and modification times automatically. These properties are not available for other temporal types, although there are reasons you might like them to be. For example, if you use separate DATE and TIME columns to store record-modification times, you can index the DATE column to enable efficient date-based lookups. (With TIMESTAMP, you cannot index just the date part of the column.)

One way to simulate TIMESTAMP properties for other temporal data types is to use the following strategy:

- When you create a row, initialize a DATE column to the current date and a TIME column to the current time.
- When you update a row, set the DATE and TIME columns to the new date and time.

However, this strategy requires all applications that use the table to implement the same strategy, and it fails if even one application neglects to do so. To place the burden of remembering to set the columns properly on the MySQL server and not on application writers, use triggers for the table. This is, in fact, a particular application of the general strategy discussed in Recipe 16.4 that uses triggers to provide calculated values for initializing (or updating) row columns.

The following example shows how to use triggers to simulate TIMESTAMP properties for each of the DATE, TIME, and DATETIME data types. Begin by creating the following table, which has a nontemporal column for storing data and columns for the DATE, TIME, and DATETIME temporal types:

```
CREATE TABLE ts_emulate
(
  data CHAR(10),
  d    DATE,
  t    TIME,
  dt   DATETIME
);
```

The intent here is that applications will insert or update values in the **data** column, and MySQL should set the temporal columns appropriately to reflect the time at which modifications occur. To accomplish this, set up triggers that use the current date and time to initialize the temporal columns for new rows, and to update them when existing rows are changed. A BEFORE INSERT trigger handles new row creation by invoking the CURDATE( ), CURTIME( ), and NOW( ) functions to get the current date, time, and date-and-time values and using those values to set the temporal columns:

```
CREATE TRIGGER bi_ts_emulate BEFORE INSERT ON ts_emulate
FOR EACH ROW SET NEW.d = CURDATE(), NEW.t = CURTIME(), NEW.dt = NOW();
```

A BEFORE UPDATE trigger handles updates to the temporal columns when the **data** column changes value. An IF statement is required here to emulate the TIMESTAMP property that an update occurs only if the values in the row actually change from their current values:

```
CREATE TRIGGER bu_ts_emulate BEFORE UPDATE ON ts_emulate
FOR EACH ROW
BEGIN
  # update temporal columns only if the nontemporal column changes
  IF NEW.data <> OLD.data THEN
    SET NEW.d = CURDATE(), NEW.t = CURTIME(), NEW.dt = NOW();
  END IF;
END;
```

To test the INSERT trigger, create a couple of rows, but supply a value only for the data column. Then verify that MySQL provides the proper default values for the temporal columns:

```
mysql> INSERT INTO ts_emulate (data) VALUES('cat');
mysql> INSERT INTO ts_emulate (data) VALUES('dog');
mysql> SELECT * FROM ts_emulate;
+------+------------+----------+---------------------+
| data | d          | t        | dt                  |
+------+------------+----------+---------------------+
| cat  | 2006-06-23 | 13:29:44 | 2006-06-23 13:29:44 |
| dog  | 2006-06-23 | 13:29:49 | 2006-06-23 13:29:49 |
+------+------------+----------+---------------------+
```

Change the data value of one row to verify that the BEFORE UPDATE trigger updates the temporal columns of the changed row:

```
mysql> UPDATE ts_emulate SET data = 'axolotl' WHERE data = 'cat';
mysql> SELECT * FROM ts_emulate;
+---------+------------+----------+---------------------+
| data    | d          | t        | dt                  |
+---------+------------+----------+---------------------+
| axolotl | 2006-06-23 | 13:30:12 | 2006-06-23 13:30:12 |
| dog     | 2006-06-23 | 13:29:49 | 2006-06-23 13:29:49 |
+---------+------------+----------+---------------------+
```

Issue another UPDATE, but this time use one that does not change any data column values. In this case, the BEFORE UPDATE trigger should notice that no value change occurred and leave the temporal columns unchanged:

```
mysql> UPDATE ts_emulate SET data = data;
mysql> SELECT * FROM ts_emulate;
+---------+------------+----------+---------------------+
| data    | d          | t        | dt                  |
+---------+------------+----------+---------------------+
| axolotl | 2006-06-23 | 13:30:12 | 2006-06-23 13:30:12 |
| dog     | 2006-06-23 | 13:29:49 | 2006-06-23 13:29:49 |
+---------+------------+----------+---------------------+
```

The preceding example shows how to simulate the auto-initialization and auto-update properties offered by TIMESTAMP columns. If you want only one of those properties and not the other, create only one trigger and omit the other.

16.6 Using a Trigger to Log Changes to a Table

Problem

You have a table that maintains current values of items that you track (such as auctions being bid on), but you'd also like to maintain a journal (or history) of changes to the table.

Solution

Use triggers to "catch" table changes and write them to a separate log table.

Discussion

Suppose that you conduct online auctions, and that you maintain information about each currently active auction in a table that looks like this:

```
CREATE TABLE auction
(
  id   INT UNSIGNED NOT NULL AUTO_INCREMENT,
  ts   TIMESTAMP,
  item VARCHAR(30) NOT NULL,
  bid  DECIMAL(10,2) NOT NULL,
  PRIMARY KEY (id)
);
```

The auction table contains information about the currently active auctions (items being bid on and the current bid for each auction). When an auction begins, you enter a row into the table. Its bid column gets updated for each new bid on the item. When the auction ends, the bid value is the final price and the row is removed from the table. As the auction proceeds, the ts column is updated to reflect the time of the most recent bid.

If you also want to maintain a journal that shows all changes to auctions as they progress from creation to removal, you can modify the auction table to allow multiple records per item and add a status column to show what kind of action each row represents. Or you could leave the auction table unchanged and set up another table that serves to record a history of changes to the auctions. This second strategy can be implemented with triggers.

To maintain a history of how each auction progresses, use an auction_log table with the following columns:

```
CREATE TABLE auction_log
(
  action ENUM('create','update','delete'),
  id     INT UNSIGNED NOT NULL,
  ts     TIMESTAMP,
  item   VARCHAR(30) NOT NULL,
  bid    DECIMAL(10,2) NOT NULL,
  INDEX (id)
);
```

The auction_log table differs from the auction table in two ways:

- It contains an action column to indicate for each row what kind of change was made.

- The `id` column has a nonunique index (rather than a primary key, which requires unique values). This allows multiple rows per `id` value because a given auction can generate many rows in the log table.

To ensure that changes to the `auction` table are logged to the `auction_log` table, create a set of triggers. The triggers should write information to the `auction_log` table as follows:

- For inserts, log a row-creation operation showing the values in the new row.
- For updates, log a row-update operation showing the new values in the updated row.
- For deletes, log a row-removal operation showing the values in the deleted row.

For this application, `AFTER` triggers are used, because they will activate only after successful changes to the `auction` table. (`BEFORE` triggers might activate even if the row-change operation fails for some reason.) The trigger definitions look like this:

```
CREATE TRIGGER ai_auction AFTER INSERT ON auction
FOR EACH ROW
BEGIN
  INSERT INTO auction_log (action,id,ts,item,bid)
  VALUES('create',NEW.id,NOW(),NEW.item,NEW.bid);
END;

CREATE TRIGGER au_auction AFTER UPDATE ON auction
FOR EACH ROW
BEGIN
  INSERT INTO auction_log (action,id,ts,item,bid)
  VALUES('update',NEW.id,NOW(),NEW.item,NEW.bid);
END;

CREATE TRIGGER ad_auction AFTER DELETE ON auction
FOR EACH ROW
BEGIN
  INSERT INTO auction_log (action,id,ts,item,bid)
  VALUES('delete',OLD.id,OLD.ts,OLD.item,OLD.bid);
END;
```

The `INSERT` and `UPDATE` triggers use `NEW.col_name` to access the new values being stored in rows. The `DELETE` trigger uses `OLD.col_name` to access the existing values from the deleted row. The `INSERT` and `UPDATE` triggers use `NOW()` to get the row-modification times; the `ts` column is initialized automatically to the current date and time, but `NEW.ts` will not contain that value.

Suppose that an auction is created with an initial bid of five dollars:

```
mysql> INSERT INTO auction (item,bid) VALUES('chintz pillows',5.00);
mysql> SELECT LAST_INSERT_ID();
+------------------+
| LAST_INSERT_ID() |
+------------------+
```

```
|             792 |
+-----------------+
```

The SELECT statement fetches the auction ID value to use for subsequent actions on the
auction. Then the item receives three more bids before the auction ends and is removed:

```
mysql> UPDATE auction SET bid = 7.50 WHERE id = 792;
... time passes ...
mysql> UPDATE auction SET bid = 9.00 WHERE id = 792;
... time passes ...
mysql> UPDATE auction SET bid = 10.00 WHERE id = 792;
... time passes ...
mysql> DELETE FROM auction WHERE id = 792;
```

At this point, no trace of the auction remains in the auction table, but if you query the
auction_log table, you can obtain a complete history of what occurred:

```
mysql> SELECT * FROM auction_log WHERE id = 792 ORDER BY ts;
+--------+-----+---------------------+----------------+-------+
| action | id  | ts                  | item           | bid   |
+--------+-----+---------------------+----------------+-------+
| create | 792 | 2006-06-22 21:24:14 | chintz pillows |  5.00 |
| update | 792 | 2006-06-22 21:27:37 | chintz pillows |  7.50 |
| update | 792 | 2006-06-22 21:39:46 | chintz pillows |  9.00 |
| update | 792 | 2006-06-22 21:55:11 | chintz pillows | 10.00 |
| delete | 792 | 2006-06-22 22:01:54 | chintz pillows | 10.00 |
+--------+-----+---------------------+----------------+-------+
```

With the strategy just outlined, the auction table remains relatively small, but we can
always find information about auction histories as necessary by looking in the
auction_log table.

16.7 Using Events to Schedule Database Actions

Problem

You want to set up a database operation that runs periodically without user
intervention.

Solution

Create an event that executes according to a schedule.

Discussion

As of MySQL 5.1, one of the capabilities available to you is an event scheduler that
enables you to set up database operations that run at times that you define. This section
describes what you must do to use events, beginning with a simple event that writes a
row to a table at regular intervals. Why bother creating such an event? One reason is
that the rows serve as a log of continuous server operation, similar to the MARK line that

some Unix `syslogd` servers write to the system log periodically so that you know they're alive.

Begin with a table to hold the mark records. It contains a `TIMESTAMP` column (which MySQL will initialize automatically) and a column to store a message:

```
mysql> CREATE TABLE mark_log (ts TIMESTAMP, message VARCHAR(100));
```

Our logging event will write a string to a new row. To set it up, use a `CREATE EVENT` statement:

```
mysql> CREATE EVENT mark_insert
    -> ON SCHEDULE EVERY 5 MINUTE
    -> DO INSERT INTO mark_log (message) VALUES('-- MARK --');
```

The `mark_insert` event causes the message `'-- MARK --'` to be logged to the `mark_log` table every five minutes. Use a different interval for more or less frequent logging.

This event is simple and its body contains only a single SQL statement. For an event body that needs to execute multiple statements, use `BEGIN ... END` compound-statement syntax. In that case, if you use *mysql* to create the event, you need to change the statement delimiter while you're defining the event, as discussed in Recipe 16.1.

At this point, you should wait a few minutes and then select the contents of the `mark_log` table to verify that new rows are being written on schedule. However, if this is the first event that you've set up, you might find that the table remains empty no matter how long you wait:

```
mysql> SELECT * FROM mark_log;
Empty set (0.00 sec)
```

If that's the case, very likely the event scheduler isn't running (which is its default state until you enable it). Check the scheduler status by examining the value of the `event_scheduler` system variable:

```
mysql> SHOW VARIABLES LIKE 'event_scheduler';
+-----------------+-------+
| Variable_name   | Value |
+-----------------+-------+
| event_scheduler | 0     |
+-----------------+-------+
```

To enable the scheduler interactively if it is not running, execute the following statement (which requires the `SUPER` privilege):

```
mysql> SET GLOBAL event_scheduler = 1;
```

That statement enables the scheduler, but only until the server shuts down. To make sure that the scheduler runs each time the server starts, set the system variable to 1 in your *my.cnf* option file:

```
[mysqld]
event_scheduler=1
```

When the event scheduler is enabled, the `mark_insert` event eventually will create many rows in the table. There are several ways that you can affect event execution to prevent the table from growing forever:

- Drop the event:

    ```
    mysql> DROP EVENT mark_insert;
    ```

    This is the simplest way to stop an event from occurring. But if you want it to resume later, you must re-create it.

- Suspend execution for the event:

    ```
    mysql> ALTER EVENT mark_insert DISABLE;
    ```

    Disabling an event leaves it in place but causes it not to run until you reactivate it:

    ```
    mysql> ALTER EVENT mark_insert ENABLE;
    ```

- Let the event continue to run, but set up another event that "expires" old `mark_log` rows. This second event need not run so frequently (perhaps once a day). Its body should contain a `DELETE` statement that removes rows older than a given threshold. The following definition creates an event that deletes rows that are more than two days old:

    ```
    mysql> CREATE EVENT mark_expire
        -> ON SCHEDULE EVERY 1 DAY
        -> DO DELETE FROM mark_log WHERE ts < NOW() - INTERVAL 2 DAY;
    ```

    If you adopt this strategy, you have cooperating events, such that one event adds rows to the `mark_log` table and the other removes them. They act together to maintain a log that contains recent records but does not become too large.

To check on event activity, look in the server's error log, where it records information about which events it executes and when.

## CHAPTER 17

Introduction to MySQL on the Web

17.0 Introduction

This chapter and the next few discuss some of the ways that MySQL can help you build a better web site. One significant benefit is that MySQL enables you to create a more interactive site because it becomes easier to provide dynamic content rather than static content. Static content exists as pages in the web server's document tree that are served exactly as is. Visitors can access only the documents that you place in the tree, and changes occur only when you add, modify, or delete those documents. By contrast, dynamic content is created on demand. Rather than opening a file and serving its contents directly to the client, the web server executes a script that generates the page and sends the resulting output. For example, a script can process a keyword request and return a page that lists items in a catalog that match the keyword. Each time a keyword is submitted, the script produces a result appropriate for the request. And that's just for starters; web scripts have access to the power of the programming language in which they're written, so the actions that they perform to generate pages can be quite extensive. For example, web scripts are important for form processing, and a single script may be responsible for generating a form and sending it to the user, processing the contents of the form when the user submits it later, and storing the contents in a database. By operating this way, web scripts interact with users of your web site and tailor the information provided according to what those users want to see.

This chapter covers the introductory aspects of writing scripts that use MySQL in a web environment. Some of the material is not MySQL-related, but is necessary to establish the initial groundwork for using your database from within the context of web programming. The topics covered here include:

- How web scripting differs from writing static HTML documents or scripts intended to be executed from the command line.

- Prerequisites for running web scripts. In particular, you must have a web server installed and it must be set up to recognize your scripts as programs to be executed, rather than as static files to be served literally over the network.

- How to use each of our API languages to write a short web script that queries the MySQL server for information and displays the results in a web page.

- How to properly encode output. HTML consists of text to be displayed interspersed with special markup constructs. However, if the text contains special characters, you must encode them to avoid generating malformed web pages. Each API provides a mechanism for doing this.

The following chapters go into more detail on topics such as how to display query results in various formats (paragraphs, lists, tables, and so forth), working with images, form processing, and tracking a user across the course of several page requests as part of a single user session.

This book uses the Apache web server for Perl, Ruby, PHP, and Python scripts. It uses the Tomcat server for Java scripts written using JSP notation. Apache and Tomcat are available from the Apache Group:

http://httpd.apache.org
http://tomcat.apache.org

Because Apache installations are fairly prevalent, I'm going to assume that it is already installed on your system and that you just need to configure it. Recipe 17.2 discusses how to configure Apache for Perl, Ruby, PHP, and Python, and how to write a short web script in each language. Recipe 17.3 discusses JSP script writing using Tomcat. Tomcat is less widely deployed than Apache, so some additional installation information is provided in Appendix C. You can use servers other than Apache and Tomcat if you like, but you'll need to adapt the instructions given here.

The scripts for the examples in this chapter can be found in the `recipes` distribution under the directories named for the servers used to run them. For Perl, Ruby, PHP, and Python examples, look under the *apache* directory. For Java (JSP) examples, look under the *tomcat* directory.

I assume here that you have some basic familiarity with HTML. For Tomcat, it's also helpful to know something about XML, because Tomcat's configuration files are written as XML documents, and JSP pages contain elements written using XML syntax. If you don't know any XML, see the quick summary in the sidebar "XML and XHTML in a Nutshell." In general, the web scripts in this book produce output that is valid not only as HTML, but as XHTML, the transitional format between HTML and XML. (This is another reason to become familiar with XML.) For example, XHTML requires closing tags, so paragraphs are written with a closing `</p>` tag following the paragraph body. The use of this output style will be obvious for scripts written using languages like PHP in which the HTML tags are included literally in the script. For interfaces that generate HTML for you, conformance to XHTML is a matter of whether the module itself produces XHTML. For example, the Perl CGI.pm module does generate XHTML, but the Ruby `cgi` module does not.

XML and XHTML in a Nutshell

XML is similar in some ways to HTML, and because more people know HTML, it's perhaps easiest to characterize XML in terms of how it differs from HTML:

- In HTML, lettercase of tag and attribute names does not matter. In XML, the names are case-sensitive.
- In HTML, tag attributes can be specified with a quoted or unquoted value, or sometimes with no value at all. In XML, every tag attribute must have a value, and the value must be quoted.
- Every opening tag in XML must have a corresponding closing tag. This is true even if there is no body, although a shortcut tag form can be used in that case. For example, in HTML, you can write `<br>`, but XML requires a closing tag. You could write this as `<br></br>`, but the element has no body, so a shortcut form `<br/>` can be used that combines the opening and closing tags. However, when writing XML that will be translated into HTML, it's safer to write the tag as `<br />` with a space preceding the slash. The space helps older browsers to not think the tag name is `br/` and thus ignore it as an unrecognized element.

XHTML is a transitional format used for the migration of the Web away from HTML and toward XML. It's less strict than XML, but more strict than HTML. For example, XHTML tag and attribute names must be lowercase and attributes must have a double-quoted value.

In HTML you might write a radio button element like this:

```
<INPUT TYPE=RADIO NAME="my button" VALUE=3 CHECKED>
```

In XHTML, the tag name must be lowercase, the attribute values must be quoted, the `checked` attribute must be given a value, and there must be a closing tag:

```
<input type="radio" name="my button" value="3" checked="checked"></input>
```

The element has no body in this case, so the single-tag shortcut form can be used:

```
<input type="radio" name="my button" value="3" checked="checked" />
```

For additional information about HTML, XHTML, or XML, see Appendix D.

17.1 Basic Principles of Web Page Generation

Problem

You want to produce a web page from a script rather than by writing it manually.

Solution

Write a program that generates the page when it executes. This gives you more control over what is sent to the client than when you write a static page, although it may also require that you provide more parts of the response. For example, it may be necessary to write the headers that precede the page body.

Discussion

HTML is a markup language—that's what the "ML" stands for. HTML consists of a mix of plain text to be displayed and special markup indicators or constructs that control how the plain text is displayed. Here is a very simple HTML page that specifies a title in the page header, and a body with a white background containing a single paragraph:

```
<html>
<head>
<title>Web Page Title</title>
</head>
<body bgcolor="white">
<p>Web page body.</p>
</body>
</html>
```

It's possible to write a script that produces that same page, but doing so differs in some ways from writing a static page. For one thing, you're writing in two languages at once. (The script is written in your programming language, and the script itself writes HTML.) Another difference is that you may have to produce more of the response that is sent to the client. When a web server sends a static page to a client, it actually sends a set of one or more header lines first that provide additional information about the page. For example, an HTML document is preceded by a `Content-Type:` header that lets the client know what kind of information to expect, and a blank line that separates any headers from the page body:

```
Content-Type: text/html

<html>
<head>
<title>Web Page Title</title>
</head>
<body bgcolor="white">
<p>Web page body.</p>
</body>
</html>
```

For static HTML pages, the web server produces header information automatically. When you write a web script, you may need to provide the header information yourself. Some APIs (such as PHP) may send a content-type header automatically, but enable you to override the default type. For example, if your script sends a JPEG image to the client instead of an HTML page, you should have the script change the content type from `text/html` to `image/jpeg`.

Writing web scripts also differs from writing command-line scripts, both for input and for output. On the input side, the information given to a web script is provided by the web server rather than by command-line arguments or by input that you type in. This means your scripts do not obtain data using input statements. Instead, the web server puts information into the execution environment of the script, which then extracts that information from its environment and acts on it.

On the output side, command-line scripts typically produce plain-text output, whereas web scripts produce HTML, images, or whatever other type of content you need to send to the client. Output produced in a web environment usually must be highly structured to ensure that it can be understood by the receiving client program.

Any programming language enables you to generate output by means of print statements, but some languages also offer special assistance for producing web pages. This support typically is provided by means of special modules:

- For Perl scripts, a popular module is CGI.pm. It provides features for generating HTML markup, form processing, and more.

- In Ruby, the `cgi` module provides capabilities similar to CGI.pm.

- PHP scripts are written as a mix of HTML and embedded PHP code. That is, you write HTML literally into the script, and then drop into "program mode" whenever you need to generate output by executing code. PHP replaces the code by its output in the resulting page that is sent to the client.

- Python includes `cgi` and `urllib` modules that help perform web programming tasks.

- For Java, we'll write scripts according to the JSP specification, which allows scripting directives and code to be embedded into web pages. This is similar to the way that PHP works.

Other page-generating packages are available besides those used in this book—some of which can have a marked effect on the way you use a language. For example, Mason, embPerl, ePerl, and AxKit enable you to treat Perl as an embedded language, somewhat like the way that PHP works. Similarly, the *mod_snake* Apache module enables Python code to be embedded into HTML templates.

Another approach to dynamic page generation separates page design and script writing. A web page is designed as a template that contains simple markers to indicate where to substitute values that can vary per request, and a script obtains the data to be displayed. With this approach, the script fetches the data as one phase of page generation. The script then invokes a template engine as another phase of page generation that places the data into the template and generates the final page as output. This decouples page design from script writing. Recipe 18.10 explores this approach to page generation further, using the Ruby PageTemplate and PHP Smarty template packages.

Before you can run any scripts in a web environment, your web server must be set up properly. Information about doing this for Apache and Tomcat is provided in Recipes 17.2 and 17.3, but conceptually, a web server typically runs a script in one of two ways. First, the web server can use an external program to execute the script. For example, it can invoke an instance of the Python interpreter to run a Python script. Second, if the server has been enabled with the appropriate language processing ability, it can execute the script itself. Using an external program to run scripts requires no special capability on the part of the web server, but is slower because it involves starting up a separate process, as well as some additional overhead for writing request information to the script and reading the results from it. If you embed a language processor into the web server, it can execute scripts directly, resulting in much better performance.

Like most web servers, Apache can run external scripts. It also supports the concept of extensions (modules) that become part of the Apache process itself (either by being compiled in or dynamically loaded at runtime). One common use of this feature is to embed language processors into the server to accelerate script execution. Perl, Ruby, PHP, and Python scripts can be executed either way. Like command-line scripts, externally executed web scripts are written as executable files that begin with a #! line specifying the pathname of the appropriate language interpreter. Apache uses the pathname to determine which interpreter runs the script. Alternatively, you can extend Apache using modules such as *mod_perl* for Perl, *mod_ruby* for Ruby, *mod_php* for PHP, and *mod_python* or *mod_snake* for Python. This gives Apache the ability to directly execute scripts written in those languages.

For Java JSP scripts, the scripts are compiled into Java servlets and run inside a process known as a *servlet container*. This is similar to the embedded-interpreter approach in the sense that the scripts are run by a server process that manages them, rather than by starting up an external process for each script. The first time a client requests a given JSP page, the container compiles the page into a servlet in the form of executable Java byte code, and then loads it and runs it. The container caches the byte code so that the script can run directly with no compilation phase for subsequent requests. If you modify the script, the container notices this when the next request arrives, recompiles the script into a new servlet, and reloads it. The JSP approach provides a significant advantage over writing servlets directly, because you don't have to compile code yourself or handle servlet loading and unloading. Tomcat can handle the responsibilities of both the servlet container and the web server that communicates with the container.

If you run multiple servers on the same host, they must listen for requests on different port numbers. In a typical configuration, Apache listens on the default HTTP port (80) and Tomcat listens on another port such as 8080. The examples here use a server hostname of *localhost* to represent URLs for scripts processed using Apache and Tomcat. The examples use a different port (8080) for Tomcat scripts. Typical forms for URLs that you'll see in this book are as follows:

```
http://localhost/cgi-bin/my_perl_script.pl
http://localhost/cgi-bin/my_ruby_script.rb
http://localhost/cgi-bin/my_python_script.py
http://localhost/mcb/my_php_script.php
http://localhost:8080/mcb/my_jsp_script.jsp
```

Change the hostname and port number as necessary for pages served by your own servers.

17.2 Using Apache to Run Web Scripts

Problem

You want to run Perl, Ruby, PHP, or Python programs in a web environment.

Solution

Execute them using the Apache server.

Discussion

This recipe describes how to configure Apache for running Perl, Ruby, PHP, and Python scripts. It also illustrates how to write web-based scripts in each language.

There are typically several directories under the Apache root directory. Here I'll assume that directory to be *usr/local/apache*, although it may be different on your system. For example, on Windows, you might find Apache under *C:\Program Files*. The directories under the Apache root include *bin* (which contains *httpd*—that is, Apache itself—and other Apache-related executable programs), *conf* (for configuration files, notably *httpd.conf*, the primary file used by Apache), *htdocs* (the root of the document tree), and *logs* (for logfiles). The layout might differ on your system. For example, you might find the configuration files in *etc/httpd* and the logs under *var/log/httpd*. Modify the following instructions accordingly.

To configure Apache for script execution, edit the *httpd.conf* file in the *conf* directory. Typically, executable scripts are identified either by location or by filename suffix. A location can be either language-neutral or language-specific.

Apache configurations often have a *cgi-bin* directory under the Apache root directory in which you can install scripts that should run as external programs. It's configured using a `ScriptAlias` directive:

```
ScriptAlias /cgi-bin/ /usr/local/apache/cgi-bin/
```

The second argument is the actual location of the script directory in your filesystem, and the first is the pathname in URLs that corresponds to that directory. Thus, the directive just shown associates scripts located in *usr/local/apache/cgi-bin* with URLs that have *cgi-bin* following the hostname. For example, if you install the Ruby script *myscript.rb* in the directory *usr/local/apache/cgi-bin* on the host *localhost*, you'd request it with this URL:

```
http://localhost/cgi-bin/myscript.rb
```

When configured this way, the *cgi-bin* directory can contain scripts written in any language. Because of this, the directory is language-neutral, so Apache needs to be able to figure out which language processor to use to execute each script that is installed there. To provide this information, the first line of the script should begin with #! followed by the pathname to the program that executes the script. For example, a script that begins with the following line will be run by Perl:

```
#!/usr/bin/perl
```

Under Unix, you must also make the script executable (use *chmod* +x), or it won't run properly. The #! line just shown is appropriate for a system that has Perl installed as */usr/bin/perl*. If your Perl interpreter is installed somewhere else, modify the line accordingly. If you're on a Windows machine with Perl installed as *C:\Perl\bin\perl.exe*, the #! line should look like this:

```
#!C:\Perl\bin\perl
```

For Windows, another option that is simpler is to set up a filename extension association between script names that end with a *.pl* suffix and the Perl interpreter. Then the script can begin like this:

```
#!perl
```

Directories used only for scripts generally are placed outside of your Apache document tree. As an alternative to using specific directories for scripts, you can identify scripts by filename extension, so that files with a particular suffix become associated with a specific language processor. In this case, you can place them anywhere in the document tree. This is the most common way to use PHP. For example, if you have Apache configured with PHP support built in using the *mod_php* module, you can tell it that scripts having names ending with *.php* should be interpreted as PHP scripts. To do so, add this line to *httpd.conf*:

```
AddType application/x-httpd-php .php
```

You may also have to add (or uncomment) a `LoadModule` directive for *php*.

With PHP enabled, you can install a PHP script *myscript.php* under *htdocs* (the Apache document root directory). The URL for invoking the script becomes:

```
http://localhost/myscript.php
```

If PHP runs as an external standalone program, you'll need to tell Apache where to find it. For example, if you're running Windows and you have PHP installed as *C:\Php\php.exe*, put the following lines in *httpd.conf* (note the use of forward slashes in the pathnames rather than backslashes):

```
ScriptAlias /php/ "C:/Php/"
AddType application/x-httpd-php .php
Action application/x-httpd-php /php/php.exe
```

For purposes of showing URLs in examples, I'm going to assume that Perl, Ruby, and Python scripts are in your *cgi-bin* directory, and that PHP scripts are in the *mcb* directory

---

of your document tree, identified by the *.php* extension. That means the URLs for scripts in these languages will look like this:

```
http://localhost/cgi-bin/myscript.pl
http://localhost/cgi-bin/myscript.rb
http://localhost/cgi-bin/myscript.py
http://localhost/mcb/myscript.php
```

If you plan to use a similar setup, make sure that you have a *cgi-bin* directory that Apache knows about, and an *mcb* directory under your Apache document root. Then, to deploy Perl, Ruby, or Python web scripts, install them in the *cgi-bin* directory. To deploy PHP scripts, install them in the *mcb* directory.

Some of the scripts use modules or library files that are specific to this book. If you have these files installed in a library directory that your language processors search by default, they should be found automatically. Otherwise, you'll need to indicate where the files are located. An easy way to do this is by using `SetEnv` directives in your *httpd.conf* file to set environment variables that can be seen by your scripts when Apache invokes them. (Use of the `SetEnv` directive requires that the *mod_env* Apache module be enabled.) For example, if you install library files in */usr/local/lib/mcb*, the following directives enable Perl, Ruby, and Python scripts to find them:

```
SetEnv PERL5LIB /usr/local/lib/mcb
SetEnv RUBYLIB /usr/local/lib/mcb
SetEnv PYTHONPATH /usr/local/lib/mcb
```

For PHP, add */usr/local/lib/mcb* to the value of `include_path` in your *php.ini* configuration file.

For background information on library-related environment variables and the *php.ini* file, see Recipe 2.3.

After Apache has been configured to support script execution, restart it. Then you can begin to write scripts that generate web pages. The remainder of this section describes how to do so for Perl, Ruby, PHP, and Python. The examples for each language connect to the MySQL server, run a simple query, and display the results in a web page. The scripts shown here indicate whether there are any additional modules or libraries that web scripts typically need to include. (Later on, I'll generally assume that the proper modules have been included and will show only script fragments.)

Before we proceed further, I should mention a couple of debugging tips:

- If you request a web script and get an error page in response, have a look at the Apache error log, which is a useful source of diagnostic information when you're trying to figure out why a script doesn't work. A common name for this log is *error_log* in the *logs* directory. If you don't find any such file, check *httpd.conf* for an `ErrorLog` directive to see where Apache logs its errors.

- Sometimes it's helpful to directly examine the output that a web script generates. You can do this by invoking the script from the command line. You'll see the HTML produced by the script, as well as any error messages that it might print. Some web modules expect to see a parameter string, and might even prompt you for one when you invoke the script at the command line. When this is the case, you might be able to supply the parameters as an argument on the command line to avoid the prompt. For example, the Ruby `cgi` module expects to see parameters, and will prompt you for them if they are missing:

```
% myscript.rb
(offline mode: enter name=value pairs on standard input)
```

At the prompt, enter the parameter values and then enter Ctrl-D (EOF). To avoid the prompt, supply the parameters on the command line:

```
% myscript.rb "param1=val1;param2=val2;param3=val3"
```

To specify "no parameters" explicitly, provide an empty argument:

```
% myscript.rb ""
```

Web Security Note

Under Unix, scripts are associated with particular user and group IDs when they execute. Scripts that you execute from the command line run with your own user and group IDs, and have the filesystem privileges associated with your account. Scripts executed by a web server don't run with your user and group ID, nor will they have your privileges. Instead, they run under the user and group ID of the account the web server has been set to run as, and with that account's privileges. (To determine what account this is, look for `User` and `Group` directives in the *httpd.conf* configuration file.) This means that if you expect web scripts to read and write files, those files must be accessible to the account used to run the web server. For example, if your server runs under the `nobody` account and you want a script to be able to store uploaded image files into a directory called *uploads* in the document tree, you must make that directory readable and writable by the `nobody` user.

Another implication is that if other people can write scripts to be executed by your web server, those scripts too will run as `nobody` and they can read and write the same files as your own scripts. That is, files used by your scripts cannot be considered private only to your scripts. A solution to this problem is to use the Apache suEXEC mechanism. (If you are using an ISP for web hosting, you might find that suEXEC is already enabled.)

Perl

The following listing shows our first web-based Perl script, *show_tables.pl*. It produces an appropriate `Content-Type:` header, a blank line to separate the header from the page content, and the initial part of the page. Then it retrieves and displays a list of tables in the `cookbook` database. The table list is followed by the trailing HTML tags that close the page:

```perl
#!/usr/bin/perl
# show_tables.pl - Display names of tables in cookbook database
# by generating HTML directly
```

```perl
use strict;
use warnings;
use Cookbook;

# Print header, blank line, and initial part of page

print <<EOF;
Content-Type: text/html

<html>
<head>
<title>Tables in cookbook Database</title>
</head>
<body bgcolor="white">

<p>Tables in cookbook database:</p>
EOF

# Connect to database, display table list, disconnect

my $dbh = Cookbook::connect ();
my $stmt = "SELECT TABLE_NAME FROM INFORMATION_SCHEMA.TABLES
            WHERE TABLE_SCHEMA = 'cookbook' ORDER BY TABLE_NAME";
my $sth = $dbh->prepare ($stmt);
$sth->execute ();
while (my @row = $sth->fetchrow_array ())
{
  print "$row[0]<br />\n";
}
$dbh->disconnect ();

# Print page trailer

print <<EOF;
</body>
</html>
EOF
```

To try the script, install it in your *cgi-bin* directory and request it from your browser as follows:

```
http://localhost/cgi-bin/show_tables.pl
```

show_tables.pl generates the Content-Type: header explicitly and it produces HTML elements by including literal tags in print statements. Another approach to web page generation is to use the CGI.pm module, which makes it easy to write web scripts without writing literal HTML tags. CGI.pm provides an object-oriented interface and a function call interface, so you can use it to write web pages in either of two styles. Here's a script, *show_tables_oo.pl*, that uses the CGI.pm object-oriented interface to produce the same report as *show_tables.pl*:

```perl
#!/usr/bin/perl
# show_tables_oo.pl - Display names of tables in cookbook database
# using the CGI.pm object-oriented interface
```

```
use strict;
use warnings;
use CGI;
use Cookbook;

# Create CGI object for accessing CGI.pm methods

my $cgi = new CGI;

# Print header, blank line, and initial part of page

print $cgi->header ();
print $cgi->start_html (-title => "Tables in cookbook Database",
                        -bgcolor => "white");

print $cgi->p ("Tables in cookbook database:");

# Connect to database, display table list, disconnect

my $dbh = Cookbook::connect ();
my $stmt = "SELECT TABLE_NAME FROM INFORMATION_SCHEMA.TABLES
            WHERE TABLE_SCHEMA = 'cookbook' ORDER BY TABLE_NAME";
my $sth = $dbh->prepare ($stmt);
$sth->execute ();
while (my @row = $sth->fetchrow_array ())
{
  print $row[0], $cgi->br ();
}
$dbh->disconnect ();

# Print page trailer

print $cgi->end_html ();
```

The script includes the CGI.pm module with a use CGI statement, and then creates a CGI object, $cgi, through which it invokes the various HTML-generation calls. header( ) generates the Content-Type: header and start_html( ) produces the initial page tags up through the opening <body> tag. After generating the first part of the page, *show_tables_oo.pl* retrieves and displays information from the server. Each table name is followed by a <br /> tag, produced by invoking the br( ) method. end_html( ) produces the closing </body> and </html> tags. When you install the script in your *cgi-bin* directory and invoke it from a browser, you can see that it generates the same type of page as *show_tables.pl*.

CGI.pm calls often take multiple parameters, many of which are optional. To enable you to specify just those parameters you need, CGI.pm understands *-name => value* notation in parameter lists. For example, in the start_html( ) call, the title parameter sets the page title and bgcolor sets the background color. The *-name => value* notation also allows parameters to be specified in any order, so these two statements are equivalent:

```
print $cgi->start_html (-title => "My Page Title", -bgcolor => "white");
print $cgi->start_html (-bgcolor => "white", -title => "My Page Title");
```

To use the CGI.pm function call interface rather than the object-oriented interface, you must write scripts a little differently. The use line that references CGI.pm should import the method names into your script's namespace so that you can invoke them directly as functions without having to create a CGI object. For example, to import the most commonly used methods, the script should include this statement:

```
use CGI qw(:standard);
```

The following script, *show_tables_fc.pl*, is the function call equivalent of the *show_tables_oo.pl* script just shown. It uses the same CGI.pm calls, but invokes them as standalone functions rather than through a $cgi object:

```
#!/usr/bin/perl
# show_tables_fc.pl - Display names of tables in cookbook database
# using the CGI.pm function-call interface

use strict;
use warnings;
use CGI qw(:standard);  # import standard method names into script namespace
use Cookbook;

# Print header, blank line, and initial part of page

print header ();
print start_html (-title => "Tables in cookbook Database",
                  -bgcolor => "white");

print p ("Tables in cookbook database:");

# Connect to database, display table list, disconnect

my $dbh = Cookbook::connect ();
my $stmt = "SELECT TABLE_NAME FROM INFORMATION_SCHEMA.TABLES
            WHERE TABLE_SCHEMA = 'cookbook' ORDER BY TABLE_NAME";
my $sth = $dbh->prepare ($stmt);
$sth->execute ();
while (my @row = $sth->fetchrow_array ())
{
  print $row[0], br ();
}
$dbh->disconnect ();

# Print page trailer

print end_html ();
```

Install the *show_tables_fc.pl* script in your *cgi-bin* directory and request it from your browser to verify that it produces the same output as *show_tables_oo.pl*.

This book uses the CGI.pm function call interface for Perl-based web scripts from this point on. You can get more information about CGI.pm at the command line by using the following commands to read the installed documentation:

```
% perldoc CGI
% perldoc CGI::Carp
```

Appendix D lists other sources of information for this module, both online and in print form.

Ruby

The Ruby `cgi` module provides an interface to HTML-generating methods. To use it, create a `CGI` object and invoke its methods to produce HTML page elements. Methods are named after the HTML elements to which they correspond. Their invocation syntax follows these principles:

- If an element should have attributes, pass them as arguments to the method.
- If the element has body content, specify the content in a code block associated with the method call.

For example, the following method call produces a `<P>` element that includes an `align` attribute and content of "This is a sentence":

```
cgi.p("align" => "left") { "This is a sentence" }
```

The output looks like this:

```
<P align="left">This is a sentence.</P>
```

To display generated HTML content, pass it in a code block to the `cgi.out` method. The following Ruby script, *show_tables.rb*, retrieves a list of tables in the **cookbook** database and displays them in an HTML document:

```
#!/usr/bin/ruby -w
# show_tables.rb - Display names of tables in cookbook database

require "cgi"
require "Cookbook"

# Connect to database, display table list, disconnect

dbh = Cookbook.connect
stmt = "SELECT TABLE_NAME FROM INFORMATION_SCHEMA.TABLES
        WHERE TABLE_SCHEMA = 'cookbook' ORDER BY TABLE_NAME"
rows = dbh.select_all(stmt)
dbh.disconnect

cgi = CGI.new("html4")

cgi.out {
  cgi.html {
    cgi.head {
      cgi.title { "Tables in cookbook Database" }
```

```
        } +
    cgi.body("bgcolor" => "white") {
      cgi.p { "Tables in cookbook Database:" } +
      rows.collect { |row| row[0] + cgi.br }.join
    }
  }
}
```

The collect method iterates through the row array containing the table names and produces a new array containing each name with a <br> appended to it. The join method concatenates the strings in the resulting array.

The script includes no explicit code for producing the Content-Type: header because cgi.out generates one.

Install the script in your *cgi-bin* directory and request it from your browser as follows:

```
http://localhost/cgi-bin/show_tables.rb
```

If you invoke Ruby web scripts from the command line so that you examine the generated HTML, you'll see that the HTML is all on one line and is difficult to read. To make the output easier to understand, process it through the CGI.pretty utility method, which adds line breaks and indentation. Suppose that your page output call looks like this:

```
cgi.out {
  page content here
}
```

To change the call to use CGI.pretty, write it like this:

```
cgi.out {
  CGI.pretty(page content here)
}
```

PHP

PHP doesn't provide much in the way of tag shortcuts, which is surprising given that language's web orientation. On the other hand, because PHP is an embedded language, you can simply write your HTML literally in your script without using print statements. Here's a *show_tables.php* script that shifts back and forth between HTML mode and PHP mode:

```
<?php
# show_tables.php - Display names of tables in cookbook database

require_once "Cookbook.php";

?>

<html>
<head>
<title>Tables in cookbook Database</title>
</head>
```

```
<body bgcolor="white">

<p>Tables in cookbook database:</p>

<?php

# Connect to database, display table list, disconnect
$conn =& Cookbook::connect ();
$stmt = "SELECT TABLE_NAME FROM INFORMATION_SCHEMA.TABLES
        WHERE TABLE_SCHEMA = 'cookbook' ORDER BY TABLE_NAME";
$result =& $conn->query ($stmt);
while (list ($tbl_name) = $result->fetchRow ())
  print ($tbl_name . "<br />\n");
$result->free ();
$conn->disconnect ();

?>

</body>
</html>
```

To try the script, put it in the *mcb* directory of your web server's document tree and request it from your browser as follows:

```
http://localhost/mcb/show_tables.php
```

The PHP script includes no code to produce the Content-Type: header because PHP produces one automatically. (If you want to override this behavior and produce your own headers, consult the header( ) function section in the PHP manual.)

Except for the break tags, *show_tables.php* includes HTML content by writing it outside of the <?php and ?> tags so that the PHP interpreter simply writes it without interpretation. Here's a different version of the script that produces all the HTML using **print** statements:

```
<?php
# show_tables_print.php - Display names of tables in cookbook database
# using print() to generate all HTML

require_once "Cookbook.php";

print ("<html>\n");
print ("<head>\n");
print ("<title>Tables in cookbook Database</title>\n");
print ("</head>\n");
print ("<body bgcolor=\"white\">\n");
print ("<p>Tables in cookbook database:</p>\n");

# Connect to database, display table list, disconnect
$conn =& Cookbook::connect ();
$stmt = "SELECT TABLE_NAME FROM INFORMATION_SCHEMA.TABLES
        WHERE TABLE_SCHEMA = 'cookbook' ORDER BY TABLE_NAME";
$result =& $conn->query ($stmt);
while (list ($tbl_name) = $result->fetchRow ())
  print ($tbl_name . "<br />\n");
```

```
$result->free ();
$conn->disconnect ();

print ("</body>\n");
print ("</html>\n");
?>
```

Sometimes it makes sense to use one approach, sometimes the other—and sometimes both within the same script. If a section of HTML doesn't refer to any variable or expression values, it can be clearer to write it in HTML mode. Otherwise it may be clearer to write it using **print** or **echo** statements, to avoid switching between HTML and PHP modes frequently.

Python

A standard installation of Python includes **cgi** and **urllib** modules that are useful for web programming. However, we don't actually need them yet, because the only web-related activity of our first Python web script is to generate some simple HTML. Here's a Python version of the MySQL table-display script:

```python
#!/usr/bin/python
# show_tables.py - Display names of tables in cookbook database

import MySQLdb
import Cookbook

# Print header, blank line, and initial part of page

print """Content-Type: text/html

<html>
<head>
<title>Tables in cookbook Database</title>
</head>
<body bgcolor="white">

<p>Tables in cookbook database:</p>
"""

# Connect to database, display table list, disconnect

conn = Cookbook.connect ()
cursor = conn.cursor ()
stmt = """
    SELECT TABLE_NAME FROM INFORMATION_SCHEMA.TABLES
    WHERE TABLE_SCHEMA = 'cookbook' ORDER BY TABLE_NAME
    """
cursor.execute (stmt)
for (tbl_name, ) in cursor.fetchall ():
  print tbl_name + "<br />"
cursor.close ()
conn.close ()

# Print page trailer
```

```
print """
</body>
</html>
"""
```

Put the script in Apache's *cgi-bin* directory and request it from your browser like this:

```
http://localhost/cgi-bin/show_tables.py
```

17.3 Using Tomcat to Run Web Scripts

Problem

You want to run Java-based programs in a web environment.

Solution

Write programs using JSP notation and execute them using a servlet container such as Tomcat.

Discussion

As described in Recipe 17.2, Apache can be used to run Perl, Ruby, PHP, and Python scripts. For Java, a different approach is needed because Apache doesn't serve JSP pages. Instead, we'll use Tomcat, a server designed for processing Java in a web environment. Apache and Tomcat are very different servers, but there is a familial relationship—like Apache, Tomcat is a development effort of the Apache Software Foundation.

This recipe provides an overview of JSP programming with Tomcat, but makes several assumptions:

- You have some familiarity with the concepts underlying JavaServer Pages, such as what a servlet container is, what an application context is, and what the basic JSP scripting elements are.
- The Tomcat server has been installed so that you can execute JSP pages, and you know how to start and stop it.
- You are familiar with the Tomcat *webapps* directory and how a Tomcat application is structured. In particular, you understand the purpose of the *WEB-INF* directory and the *web.xml* file.
- You know what a tag library is and how to use one.

I recognize that this is a lot to assume. If you're unfamiliar with JSP or need instructions for installing Tomcat, Appendix C provides the necessary background information.

Once you have Tomcat in place, you should install the following components so that you can work through the JSP examples in this book:

- The `mcb` sample application located in the *tomcat* directory of the `recipes` distribution.
- A MySQL JDBC driver. You might already have one installed for use with the scripts in earlier chapters, but Tomcat needs a copy, too. This book uses MySQL Connector/J.
- The JSP Standard Tag Library (JSTL), which contains tags for performing database activities, conditional testing, and iterative operations within JSP pages.

This section discusses how to install these components, provides a brief overview of some of the JSTL tags, and describes how to write the JSP equivalent of the MySQL table-display script that was implemented in Recipe 17.2 using Perl, Ruby, PHP, and Python.

Installing the mcb application

Web applications for Tomcat typically are packaged as files WAR (web archive) files and installed under its *webapps* directory, which is roughly analogous to Apache's *htdocs* document root directory. The `recipes` distribution includes a sample application named `mcb` that you can use for trying the JSP examples described here. Look in the distribution's *tomcat* directory, where you will find a file named *mcb.war*. Copy that file to Tomcat's *webapps* directory.

Here's an example installation procedure for Unix, assuming that the `recipes` distribution and Tomcat are located at */u/paul/recipes* and */usr/local/jakarta-tomcat*. Adjust the pathnames as necessary for your own system. The command to install *mcb.war* looks like this:

```
% cp /u/paul/recipes/tomcat/mcb.war /usr/local/jakarta-tomcat/webapps
```

For Windows, if the relevant directories are *C:\recipes* and *C:\jakarta-tomcat*, use this command:

```
C:\> copy C:\recipes\tomcat\mcb.war C:\jakarta-tomcat\webapps
```

After copying the *mcb.war* file to the *webapps* directory, restart Tomcat. As distributed, Tomcat is configured by default to look for WAR files under *webapps* when it starts up and automatically unpack any that have not already been unpacked. This means that restarting Tomcat after copying *mcb.war* to the *webapps* directory should be enough to unpack the `mcb` application. When Tomcat finishes its startup sequence, look under *webapps* and you should see a new *mcb* directory under which are all the files contained in *mcb.war*. (If Tomcat doesn't unpack *mcb.war* automatically, see the sidebar "Unpacking a WAR File Manually.") If you like, have a look around in the *mcb* directory at this point. It should contain several files that clients can request using a browser. There should also be a *WEB-INF* subdirectory, which is used for information that is private—that is, available for use by scripts in the *mcb* directory, but not directly accessible by clients.

Next, verify that Tomcat can serve pages from the mcb application context by requesting some of them from your browser. The following URLs request in turn a static HTML page, a servlet, and a simple JSP page:

```
http://localhost:8080/mcb/test.html
http://localhost:8080/mcb/servlet/SimpleServlet
http://localhost:8080/mcb/simple.jsp
```

Adjust the hostname and port number in the URLs appropriately for your installation.

Unpacking a WAR File Manually

WAR files are actually ZIP-format archives that can be unpacked using *jar*, *WinZip*, or any other tool that understands ZIP files. However, when unpacking a WAR file manually, you'll need to create its top-level directory first. The following sequence of steps shows one way to do this, using the *jar* utility to unpack a WAR file named *mcb.war* that is assumed to be located in Tomcat's *webapps* directory. For Unix, change location to the *webapps* directory, and then issue the following commands:

```
% mkdir mcb
% cd mcb
% jar xf ../mcb.war
```

For Windows, the commands are only slightly different:

```
C:\> mkdir mcb
C:\> cd mcb
C:\> jar xf ..\mcb.war
```

Unpacking the WAR file in the *webapps* directory creates a new application context, so you'll need to restart Tomcat before it notices the new application.

Installing the JDBC driver

The JSP pages in the mcb application need a JDBC driver for connecting to the cookbook database. The following instructions describe how to install the MySQL Connector/J driver; the installation procedure for other drivers should be similar.

To install MySQL Connector/J for use by Tomcat applications, place a copy of it in Tomcat's directory tree. Assuming that the driver is packaged as a JAR file (as is the case for MySQL Connector/J), there are three likely places under the Tomcat root directory where you can install it, depending on how visible you want the driver to be:

- To make the driver available only to the mcb application, place it in the *mcb/ WEB-INF/lib* directory under Tomcat's *webapps* directory.
- To make the driver available to all Tomcat applications but not to Tomcat itself, place it in the *shared/lib* directory under the Tomcat root.
- To make the driver available both to applications and to Tomcat, place it in the *common/lib* directory under the Tomcat root.

I recommend installing a copy of the driver in the *common/lib* directory. That gives it the most global visibility (it will be accessible both by Tomcat and by applications), and you'll need to install it only once. If you enable the driver only for the mcb application by placing a copy in *mcb/WEB-INF/lib*, but then develop other applications that use MySQL, you'll need to either copy the driver into those applications or move it to a more global location.

Making the driver more globally accessible also is useful if you think it likely that at some point you'll elect to use JDBC-based session management or realm authentication. Those activities are handled by Tomcat itself above the application level, so Tomcat needs access to the driver to carry them out.

Here's an example installation procedure for Unix, assuming that the MySQL Connector/J driver and Tomcat are located at */tmp/mysql-connector-java-bin.jar* and */usr/local/jakarta-tomcat*. Adjust the pathnames as necessary for your own system. The command to install the driver looks like this:

```
% cp /tmp/mysql-connector-java-bin.jar /usr/local/jakarta-tomcat/common/lib
```

For Windows, if the components are installed at *C:\mysql-connector-java-bin.jar* and *C:\jakarta-tomcat*, use this command:

```
C:\> copy C:\mysql-connector-java-bin.jar C:\jakarta-tomcat\common\lib
```

After installing the driver, restart Tomcat and then request the following mcb application page to verify that Tomcat can find the JDBC driver properly:

```
http://localhost:8080/mcb/jdbc_test.jsp
```

You might need to edit *jdbc_test.jsp* first to change the connection parameters.

Installing the JSTL distribution

Most of the scripts that are part of the mcb sample application use JSTL, so it's necessary to install it or those scripts won't work. To install a tag library into an application context, copy the library's files into the proper locations under the application's *WEB-INF* directory. Generally, this means installing at least one JAR file and a tag library descriptor (TLD) file, and adding some tag library information to the application's *web.xml* file. JSTL actually consists of several tag sets, so there are there are several JAR files and TLD files. The following instructions describe how to install JSTL for use with the mcb application:

1. Make sure that the *mcb.war* file has been unpacked to create the mcb application directory hierarchy under the Tomcat *webapps* directory. (Refer back to the section called "Installing the mcb application".) This is necessary because the JSTL files must be installed under the *mcb/WEB-INF* directory, which will not exist until *mcb.war* has been unpacked.

2. Get the JSTL distribution from the Jakarta Project web site. Go to the Jakarta Taglibs project page, which is accessible at *http://jakarta.apache.org/taglibs/*.

Follow the Standard Taglib link to get to the JSTL information page; the latter has a Downloads section from which you can get the binary JSTL distribution. Be sure to get version 1.1.2 or higher.

3. Unpack the JSTL distribution into some convenient location, preferably outside of the Tomcat hierarchy. The commands to do this are similar to those used to unpack Tomcat itself (see the section "Installing a Tomcat Distribution" in Appendix C). For example, to unpack a ZIP-format distribution, use the following command, adjusting the filename as necessary:

```
% jar xf jakarta-taglibs-standard.zip
```

4. Unpacking the distribution creates a directory containing several files. Copy the JAR files (*jstl.jar*, *standard.jar*, and so forth) to the *mcb/WEB-INF/lib* directory. These files contain the class libraries that implement the JSTL tag actions. Copy the tag library descriptor files (*c.tld*, *sql.tld*, and so forth) to the *mcb/WEB-INF* directory. These files define the interface for the actions implemented by the classes in the JAR files.

5. The *mcb/WEB-INF* directory contains a file named *web.xml* that is the web application deployment descriptor file (a fancy name for "configuration file"). Modify *web.xml* to add `<taglib>` entries for each of the JSTL TLD files. The entries look something like this:

```
<taglib>
  <taglib-uri>http://java.sun.com/jsp/jstl/core</taglib-uri>
  <taglib-location>/WEB-INF/c.tld</taglib-location>
</taglib>
<taglib>
  <taglib-uri>http://java.sun.com/jsp/jstl/sql</taglib-uri>
  <taglib-location>/WEB-INF/sql.tld</taglib-location>
</taglib>
```

Each `<taglib>` entry contains a `<taglib-uri>` element that specifies the symbolic name by which mcb JSP pages refer to the corresponding TLD file, and a `<taglib-location>` element that indicates the location of the TLD file under the mcb application directory. (You'll find that *web.xml* as distributed already contains these entries. However, you should take a look at them to make sure they match the filenames of the TLD files that you just installed in the previous step.)

6. The *mcb/WEB-INF* directory also contains a file named *jstl-mcb-setup.inc*. This file is not part of JSTL itself, but it contains a JSTL `<sql:setDataSource>` tag that is used by many of the mcb JSP pages to set up a data source for connecting to the cookbook database. The file looks like this:

```
<sql:setDataSource
  var="conn"
  driver="com.mysql.jdbc.Driver"
  url="jdbc:mysql://localhost/cookbook"
  user="cbuser"
  password="cbpass"
/>
```

Edit the `driver`, `url`, `user`, and `password` tag attributes as necessary to change the connection parameters to those that you use for accessing the `cookbook` database. Do not change the `var` attribute.

7. The JSTL distribution also includes WAR files containing documentation and examples (*standard-doc.war* and *standard-examples.war*). If you want to install these, copy them into Tomcat's *webapps* directory. (I recommend that you install the documentation so that you can access it locally from your own server. It's useful to install the examples as well, because they provide helpful demonstrations showing how to use JSTL tags in JSP pages.)

8. Restart Tomcat so that it notices the changes you've just made to the `mcb` application and so that it unpacks the WAR files containing the JSTL documentation and examples. If Tomcat doesn't unpack WAR files for you automatically, refer back to the sidebar "Unpacking a WAR File Manually."

After installing JSTL and restarting Tomcat, request the following `mcb` application page to verify that Tomcat can find the JSTL tags properly:

```
http://localhost:8080/mcb/jstl_test.jsp
```

Writing JSP pages with JSTL

This section discusses the syntax for some of the JSTL tags used most frequently by `mcb` JSP pages. The descriptions are very brief, and many of these tags have additional attributes that allow them to be used in ways other than those shown here. For more information, consult the JSTL specification (see Appendix D).

A JSP page that uses JSTL must include ain `taglib` directive for each tag set that the page uses. Examples in this book use the core and database tags, identified by the following `taglib` directives:

```
<%@ taglib uri="http://java.sun.com/jsp/jstl/core" prefix="c" %>
<%@ taglib uri="http://java.sun.com/jsp/jstl/sql" prefix="sql" %>
```

The `uri` values should match the symbolic values that are listed in the *web.xml* `<taglib>` entries (see the previous section the section called "Installing the JSTL distribution"). The `prefix` values indicate the initial string used in tag names to identify tags as part of a given tag library.

JSTL tags are written in XML format, using a special syntax for tag attributes to include expressions. Within tag attributes, text is interpreted literally unless enclosed within `${...}`, in which case it is interpreted as an expression to be evaluated. The following sections summarize some of the commonly used core and database tags.

The JSTL core tag set. The following tags are part of the JSTL core tag set:

`<c:out>`
    This tag evaluates its `value` attribute and is replaced by the result. One common use for this tag is to provide content for the output page. The following tag produces the value 3:

```
<c:out value="${1+2}"/>
```

`<c:set>`

This tag assigns a value to a variable. For example, to assign a string to a variable named `title` and then use the variable later in the `<title>` element of the output page, do this:

```
<c:set var="title" value="JSTL Example Page"/>

<html>
<head>
<title><c:out value="${title}"/></title>
</head>
...
```

This example illustrates a principle that is generally true for JSTL tags: to specify a variable into which a value is to be stored, name it without using `${...}` notation. To refer to that variable's value later, use it within `${...}` so that it is interpreted as an expression to be evaluated.

`<c:if>`

This tag evaluates the conditional test given in its `test` attribute. If the test result is true, the tag body is evaluated and becomes the tag's output; if the result is false, the body is ignored:

```
<c:if test="${1 != 0}">
1 is not equal to 0
</c:if>
```

The comparison operators are `==`, `!=`, `<`, `>`, `<=`, and `>=`. The alternative operators `eq`, `ne`, `lt`, `gt`, `le`, and `ge` make it easier to avoid using special HTML characters in expressions. Arithmetic operators are `+`, `-`, `*`, `/` (or `div`), and `%` (or `mod`). Logical operators are `&&` (or `and`), `||` (or `or`), and `!` (or `not`). The special `empty` operator is true if a value is empty or `null`:

```
<c:set var="x" value=""/>
<c:if test="${empty x}">
x is empty
</c:if>
<c:set var="y" value="hello"/>
<c:if test="${!empty y}">
y is not empty
</c:if>
```

The `<c:if>` tag does not provide any "else" clause. To perform if/then/else testing, use the `<c:choose>` tag.

`<c:choose>`

This is another conditional tag, but it allows multiple conditions to be tested. Include a `<c:when>` tag for each condition that you want to test explicitly, and a `<c:otherwise>` tag if there is a "default" case:

```
<c:choose>
  <c:when test="${count == 0}">
    Please choose an item
  </c:when>
  <c:when test="${count gt 1}">
    Please choose only one item
  </c:when>
  <c:otherwise>
    Thank you for choosing exactly one item
  </c:otherwise>
</c:choose>
```

`<c:forEach>`

This tag acts as an iterator, enabling you to loop over a set of values. The following example uses a `<c:forEach>` tag to loop through a set of rows in the result set from a query (represented here by the `rs` variable):

```
<c:forEach items="${rs.rows}" var="row">
  id = <c:out value="${row.id}"/>,
  name = <c:out value="${row.name}"/>
  <br />
</c:forEach>
```

Each iteration of the loop assigns the current row to the variable `row`. Assuming that the query result includes columns named `id` and `name`, their values are accessible as `row.id` and `row.name`.

The JSTL database tag set. The JSTL database tags enable you to issue SQL statements and access their results:

`<sql:setDataSource>`

This tag sets up connection parameters to be used when JSTL contacts the database server. For example, to specify parameters for using the MySQL Connector/J driver to access the **cookbook** database, the tag looks like this:

```
<sql:setDataSource
  var="conn"
  driver="com.mysql.jdbc.Driver"
  url="jdbc:mysql://localhost/cookbook"
  user="cbuser"
  password="cbpass"
/>
```

The `driver`, `url`, `user`, and `password` attributes specify the connection parameters, and the `var` attribute names the variable to associate with the connection. By convention, mcb JSP pages in this book use the variable **conn**, so tags occurring later in the page that require a data source can refer to the connection using the expression `${conn}`.

To avoid listing connection parameters repeatedly in JSP pages that use MySQL, you can put the `<sql:setDataSource>` tag in a file and include the file from each page that needs a database connection. For the **recipes** distribution, this include file is *WEB-INF/jstl-mcb-setup.inc.* JSP pages can access the file as follows to set up the database connection:

```
<%@ include file="/WEB-INF/jstl-mcb-setup.inc" %>
```

To change the connection parameters used by the `mcb` pages, edit *jstl-mcb-setup.inc.*

`<sql:update>`

To issue a statement such as `UPDATE`, `DELETE`, or `INSERT` that doesn't return rows, use a `<sql:update>` tag. A `dataSource` tag attribute indicates the data source, the rows-affected count resulting from the statement is returned in the variable named by the `var` attribute, and the statement itself should be specified in the tag body:

```
<sql:update dataSource="${conn}" var="count">
  DELETE FROM profile WHERE id > 100
</sql:update>
Number of rows deleted: <c:out value="${count}"/>
```

`<sql:query>`

To process statements that return a result set, use `<sql:query>`. As with `<sql:update>`, the `dataSource` attribute indicates the data source, and the text of the statement is given in the tag body. The `<sql:query>` tag also takes a `var` attribute that names a variable to associate with the result set so that you can access the rows of the result:

```
<sql:query dataSource="${conn}" var="rs">
  SELECT id, name FROM profile ORDER BY id
</sql:query>
```

By convention, the `mcb` JSP pages use `rs` as the name of the result set variable. Strategies for accessing the contents of a result set are outlined shortly.

`<sql:param>`

You can write data values literally into a statement string, but JSTL also allows the use of placeholders, which is helpful for values that contain characters that are special in SQL statements. Use a `?` character for each placeholder in the statement string, and provide values to be bound to the placeholders using `<sql:param>` tags in the body of the statement-issuing tag. A data value can be specified either in the body of an `<sql:param>` tag or in its `value` attribute:

```
<sql:update dataSource="${conn}" var="count">
  DELETE FROM profile WHERE id > ?
  <sql:param>100</sql:param>
</sql:update>

<sql:query dataSource="${conn}" var="rs">
  SELECT id, name FROM profile WHERE cats = ? AND color = ?
  <sql:param value="1"/>
  <sql:param value="green"/>
</sql:query>
```

The contents of a result set returned by `<sql:query>` are accessible several ways. Assuming that you have associated a variable named `rs` with the result set, you can access row *i* of the result either as `rs.rows[i]` or as `rs.rowsByIndex[i]`, where row numbers begin at 0. The first form produces a row with columns that can be accessed by name. The second form produces a row with columns that can be accessed by column number (beginning with 0). For example, if a result set has columns named `id` and `name`, you can access the values for the third row by using column names like this:

```
<c:out value="${rs.rows[2].id}"/>
<c:out value="${rs.rows[2].name}"/>
```

To use column numbers instead, do this:

```
<c:out value="${rs.rowsByIndex[2][0]}"/>
<c:out value="${rs.rowsByIndex[2][1]}"/>
```

You can also use `<c:forEach>` as an iterator to loop through the rows in a result set. To access column values by name, iterate using `rs.rows`:

```
<c:forEach items="${rs.rows}" var="row">
  id = <c:out value="${row.id}"/>,
  name = <c:out value="${row.name}"/>
  <br />
</c:forEach>
```

To access column values by number, iterate using `rs.rowsByIndex`:

```
<c:forEach items="${rs.rowsByIndex}" var="row">
  id = <c:out value="${row[0]}"/>,
  name = <c:out value="${row[1]}"/>
  <br />
</c:forEach>
```

The number of rows in the result set is available as `rs.rowCount`:

```
Number of rows selected: <c:out value="${rs.rowCount}"/>
```

Names of the columns in the result set are available using `rs.columnNames`:

```
<c:forEach items="${rs.columnNames}" var="name">
  <c:out value="${name}"/>
  <br />
</c:forEach>
```

Writing a MySQL script using JSP and JSTL

Recipe 17.2 shows how to write Perl, Ruby, PHP, and Python versions of a script to display the names of the tables in the `cookbook` database. With the JSTL tags, we can write a corresponding JSP page that provides that information as follows:

```
<%-- show_tables.jsp - Display names of tables in cookbook database --%>

<%@ taglib uri="http://java.sun.com/jsp/jstl/core" prefix="c" %>
<%@ taglib uri="http://java.sun.com/jsp/jstl/sql" prefix="sql" %>
<%@ include file="/WEB-INF/jstl-mcb-setup.inc" %>
```

```
<html>
<head>
<title>Tables in cookbook Database</title>
</head>
<body bgcolor="white">

<p>Tables in cookbook database:</p>

<sql:query dataSource="${conn}" var="rs">
  SELECT TABLE_NAME FROM INFORMATION_SCHEMA.TABLES
  WHERE TABLE_SCHEMA = 'cookbook' ORDER BY TABLE_NAME
</sql:query>

<c:forEach items="${rs.rowsByIndex}" var="row">
  <c:out value="${row[0]}"/><br />
</c:forEach>

</body>
</html>
```

The `taglib` directives identify which tag libraries the script needs, and the `include` directive pulls in the code that sets up a data source for accessing the `cookbook` database. The rest of the script generates the page content.

Assuming that you've installed the *mcb.war* file in your Tomcat server's *webapps* directory as described earlier, you should find the *show_tables.jsp* script in the *mcb* subdirectory. Request it from your browser as follows:

```
http://localhost:8080/mcb/show_tables.jsp
```

The JSP script does not produce any `Content-Type:` header explicitly. The JSP engine produces a default header with a content type of `text/html` automatically.

17.4 Encoding Special Characters in Web Output

Problem

Certain characters are special in web pages and must be encoded if you want to display them literally. Because database content often contains instances of these characters, scripts that include query results in web pages should encode those results to prevent browsers from misinterpreting the information.

Solution

Use the methods that are provided by your API for performing HTML-encoding and URL-encoding.

Discussion

HTML is a markup language: it uses certain characters as markers that have a special meaning. To include literal instances of these characters in a page, you must encode them so that they are not interpreted as having their special meanings. For example, < should be encoded as < to keep a browser from interpreting it as the beginning of a tag. Furthermore, there are actually two kinds of encoding, depending on the context in which you use a character. One encoding is appropriate for HTML text, another is used for text that is part of a URL in a hyperlink.

The MySQL table-display scripts shown in Recipes 17.2 and 17.3 are simple demonstrations of how to produce web pages using programs. But with one exception, the scripts have a common failing: they take no care to properly encode special characters that occur in the information retrieved from the MySQL server. (The exception is the JSP version of the script. The <c:out> tag used there handles encoding automatically, as we'll discuss shortly.)

As it happens, I deliberately chose information to display that is unlikely to contain any special characters; the scripts should work properly even in the absence of any encoding. However, in the general case, it's unsafe to assume that a query result will contain no special characters, so you must be prepared to encode it for display in a web page. Neglecting to do this often results in scripts that generate pages containing malformed HTML that displays incorrectly.

This recipe describes how to handle special characters, beginning with some general principles, and then discusses how each API implements encoding support. The API-specific examples show how to process information drawn from a database table, but they can be adapted to any content you include in a web page, no matter its source.

General encoding principles

One form of encoding applies to characters that are used in writing HTML constructs; another applies to text that is included in URLs. It's important to understand this distinction so that you don't encode text inappropriately.

 Encoding text for inclusion in a web page is an entirely different issue from encoding special characters in data values for inclusion in an SQL statement. Recipe 2.5 discusses the latter issue.

Encoding characters that are special in HTML. HTML markup uses < and > characters to begin and end tags, & to begin special entity names (such as   to signify a nonbreaking space), and " to quote attribute values in tags (such as <p align="left">). Consequently, to display literal instances of these characters, you should encode them as HTML entities so that browsers or other clients understand your intent. To do this, convert the special characters <, >, &, and " to the corresponding HTML entity designators shown in the following table.

Special character	HTML entity
<	&lt;
>	&gt;
&	&amp;
"	&quot;

Suppose that you want to display the following string literally in a web page:

```
Paragraphs begin and end with <p> & </p> tags.
```

If you send this text to the client browser exactly as shown, the browser will misinterpret it: the `<p>` and `</p>` tags will be taken as paragraph markers and the `&` may be taken as the beginning of an HTML entity designator. To display the string the way you intend, encode the special characters as the `&lt;`, `&gt;`, and `&amp;` entities:

```
Paragraphs begin and end with &lt;p&gt; &amp; &lt;/p&gt; tags.
```

The principle of encoding text this way is also useful within tags. For example, HTML tag attribute values usually are enclosed within double quotes, so it's important to perform HTML-encoding on attribute values. Suppose that you want to include a text-input box in a form, and you want to provide an initial value of `Rich "Goose" Gossage` to be displayed in the box. You cannot write that value literally in the tag like this:

```
<input type="text" name="player_name" value="Rich "Goose" Gossage" />
```

The problem here is that the double-quoted `value` attribute includes internal double quotes, which makes the `<input>` tag malformed. The proper way to write it is to encode the double quotes:

```
<input type="text" name="player_name" value="Rich &quot;Goose&quot; Gossage" />
```

When a browser receives this text, it decodes the `&quot;` entities back to " characters and interprets the `value` attribute value properly.

Encoding characters that are special in URLs. URLs for hyperlinks that occur within HTML pages have their own syntax and their own encoding. This encoding applies to attributes within several tags:

```
<a href="URL">
<img src="URL">
<form action="URL">
<frame src="URL">
```

Many characters have special meaning within URLs, such as :, /, ?, =, &, and ;. The following URL contains some of these characters:

```
http://localhost/myscript.php?id=428&name=Gandalf
```

Here the : and / characters segment the URL into components, the ? character indicates that parameters are present, and the & character separates the parameters, each of which is specified as a *name=value* pair. (The ; character is not present in the URL just shown, but commonly is used instead of & to separate parameters.) If you want to include any of these characters literally within a URL, you must encode them to prevent the browser from interpreting them with their usual special meaning. Other characters such as spaces require special treatment as well. Spaces are not allowed within a URL, so if you want to reference a page named *my home page.html* on the local host, the URL in the following hyperlink won't work:

```
<a href="http://localhost/my home page.html">My Home Page</a>
```

URL-encoding for special and reserved characters is performed by converting each such character to % followed by two hexadecimal digits representing the character's ASCII code. For example, the ASCII value of the space character is 32 decimal, or 20 hexadecimal, so you'd write the preceding hyperlink like this:

```
<a href="http://localhost/my%20home%20page.html">My Home Page</a>
```

Sometimes you'll see spaces encoded as + in URLs. That is legal, too.

Use the appropriate encoding method for the context. Be sure to encode information properly for the context in which you're using it. Suppose that you want to create a hyperlink to trigger a search for items matching a search term, and you want the term itself to appear as the link label that is displayed in the page. In this case, the term appears as a parameter in the URL, and also as HTML text between the <a> and </a> tags. If the search term is "cats & dogs", the unencoded hyperlink construct looks like this:

```
<a href="/cgi-bin/myscript?term=cats & dogs">cats & dogs</a>
```

That is incorrect because & is special in both contexts and the spaces are special in the URL. The link should be written like this instead:

```
<a href="/cgi-bin/myscript?term=cats%20%26%20dogs">cats &amp; dogs</a>
```

Here, & is HTML-encoded as & for the link label, and is URL-encoded as %26 for the URL, which also includes spaces encoded as %20.

Granted, it's a pain to encode text before writing it to a web page, and sometimes you know enough about a value that you can skip the encoding. (See the sidebar, "Do You Always Need to Encode Web Page Output?") But encoding is the safe thing to do most of the time. Fortunately, most APIs provide functions to do the work for you. This means you need not know every character that is special in a given context. You just need to know which kind of encoding to perform, so that you can call the appropriate function to produce the intended result.

Do You Always Need to Encode Web Page Output?

If you *know* a value is legal in a particular context within a web page, you need not encode it. For example, if you obtain a value from an integer-valued column in a database table that cannot be NULL, it must necessarily be an integer. No HTML- or URL-encoding is needed to include the value in a web page, because digits are not special in HTML text or within URLs. On the other hand, suppose that you solicit an integer value using a field in a web form. You might be expecting the user to provide an integer,

---

but the user might be confused and enter an illegal value. You could handle this by displaying an error page that shows the value and explains that it's not an integer. But if the value contains special characters and you don't encode it, the page won't display the value properly, possibly further confusing the user.

Encoding special characters using web APIs

The following encoding examples show how to pull values out of MySQL and perform both HTML-encoding and URL-encoding on them to generate hyperlinks. Each example reads a table named `phrase` that contains short phrases and then uses its contents to construct hyperlinks that point to a (hypothetical) script that searches for instances of the phrases in some other table. The table contains the following rows:

```
mysql> SELECT phrase_val FROM phrase ORDER BY phrase_val;
+--------------------------+
| phrase_val               |
+--------------------------+
| are we "there" yet?      |
| cats & dogs              |
| rhinoceros               |
| the whole > sum of parts |
+--------------------------+
```

The goal here is to generate a list of hyperlinks using each phrase both as the hyperlink label (which requires HTML-encoding) and in the URL as a parameter to the search script (which requires URL-encoding). The resulting links look something like this:

```
<a href="/cgi-bin/mysearch.pl?phrase=are%20we%20%22there%22%20yet%3F">
are we &quot;there&quot; yet?</a>
<a href="/cgi-bin/mysearch.pl?phrase=cats%20%26%20dogs">
cats &amp; dogs</a>
<a href="/cgi-bin/mysearch.pl?phrase=rhinoceros">
rhinoceros</a>
<a href="/cgi-bin/mysearch.pl?phrase=the%20whole%20%3E%20sum%20of%20parts">
the whole &gt; sum of parts</a>
```

The initial part of the `href` attribute value will vary per API. Also, the links produced by some APIs will look slightly different because they encode spaces as + rather than as %20.

Perl. The Perl CGI.pm module provides two methods, `escapeHTML( )` and `escape( )`, that handle HTML-encoding and URL-encoding. There are three ways to use these methods to encode a string `$str`:

- Invoke `escapeHTML( )` and `escape( )` as CGI class methods using a `CGI::` prefix:

    ```
    use CGI;
    printf "%s\n%s\n", CGI::escape ($str), CGI::escapeHTML ($str);
    ```

- Create a `CGI` object and invoke `escapeHTML( )` and `escape( )` as object methods:

```
use CGI;
my $cgi = new CGI;
printf "%s\n%s\n", $cgi->escape ($str), $cgi->escapeHTML ($str);
```

- Import the names explicitly into your script's namespace. In this case, neither a CGI object nor the CGI:: prefix is necessary and you can invoke the methods as standalone functions. The following example imports the two method names in addition to the set of standard names:

```
use CGI qw(:standard escape escapeHTML);
printf "%s\n%s\n", escape ($str), escapeHTML ($str);
```

I prefer the last alternative because it is consistent with the CGI.pm function call interface that you use for other imported method names. Just remember to include the encoding method names in the use CGI statement for any Perl script that requires them, or you'll get "undefined subroutine" errors when the script executes.

The following code reads the contents of the phrase table and produces hyperlinks from them using escapeHTML( ) and escape( ):

```
my $stmt = "SELECT phrase_val FROM phrase ORDER BY phrase_val";
my $sth = $dbh->prepare ($stmt);
$sth->execute ();
while (my ($phrase) = $sth->fetchrow_array ())
{
  # URL-encode the phrase value for use in the URL
  my $url = "/cgi-bin/mysearch.pl?phrase=" . escape ($phrase);
  # HTML-encode the phrase value for use in the link label
  my $label = escapeHTML ($phrase);
  print a ({-href => $url}, $label), br (), "\n";
}
```

Ruby.   The Ruby cgi module contains two methods, CGI.escapeHTML( ) and CGI.escape( ), that perform HTML-encoding and URL-encoding. However, both methods raise an exception unless the argument is a string. One way to deal with this is to apply the to_s method to any argument that might not be a string, to force it to string form and convert nil to the empty string. For example:

```
stmt = "SELECT phrase_val FROM phrase ORDER BY phrase_val"
dbh.execute(stmt) do |sth|
  sth.fetch do |row|
    # make sure that the value is a string
    phrase = row[0].to_s
    # URL-encode the phrase value for use in the URL
    url = "/cgi-bin/mysearch.rb?phrase=" + CGI.escape(phrase)
    # HTML-encode the phrase value for use in the link label
    label = CGI.escapeHTML(phrase)
    page << cgi.a("href" => url) { label } + cgi.br + "\n"
  end
end
```

page is used here as a variable that "accumulates" page content and that eventually you pass to cgi.out to display the page.

PHP. In PHP, the `htmlspecialchars( )` and `urlencode( )` functions perform HTML-encoding and URL-encoding. Use them as follows:

```
$stmt = "SELECT phrase_val FROM phrase ORDER BY phrase_val";
$result =& $conn->query ($stmt);
if (!PEAR::isError ($result))
{
  while (list ($phrase) = $result->fetchRow ())
  {
    # URL-encode the phrase value for use in the URL
    $url = "/mcb/mysearch.php?phrase=" . urlencode ($phrase);
    # HTML-encode the phrase value for use in the link label
    $label = htmlspecialchars ($phrase);
    printf ("<a href=\"%s\">%s</a><br />\n", $url, $label);
  }
  $result->free ();
}
```

Python. In Python, the `cgi` and `urllib` modules contain the relevant encoding methods. `cgi.escape( )` and `urllib.quote( )` perform HTML-encoding and URL-encoding. However, both methods raise an exception unless the argument is a string. One way to deal with this is to apply the `str( )` method to any argument that might not be a string, to force it to string form and convert None to the string "None". (If you want None to convert to the empty string, you need to test for it explicitly.) For example:

```
import cgi
import urllib

stmt = "SELECT phrase_val FROM phrase ORDER BY phrase_val"
cursor = conn.cursor ()
cursor.execute (stmt)
for (phrase,) in cursor.fetchall ():
  # make sure that the value is a string
  phrase = str (phrase)
  # URL-encode the phrase value for use in the URL
  url = "/cgi-bin/mysearch.py?phrase=" + urllib.quote (phrase)
  # HTML-encode the phrase value for use in the link label
  label = cgi.escape (phrase, 1)
  print "<a href=\"%s\">%s</a><br />" % (url, label)
cursor.close ()
```

The first argument to `cgi.escape( )` is the string to be HTML-encoded. By default, this function converts <, >, and & characters to their corresponding HTML entities. To tell `cgi.escape( )` to also convert double quotes to the " entity, pass a second argument of 1, as shown in the example. This is especially important if you're encoding values to be placed into a double-quoted tag attribute.

Java. The `<c:out>` JSTL tag automatically performs HTML-encoding for JSP pages. (Strictly speaking, it performs XML-encoding, but the set of characters affected is <, >, &, ", and ', which includes all those needed for HTML-encoding.) By using `<c:out>` to display text in a web page, you need not even think about converting special characters to HTML entities. If for some reason you want to suppress encoding, invoke `<c:out>` with an encodeXML attribute value of `false`:

```
<c:out value="value to display" encodeXML="false"/>
```

To URL-encode parameters for inclusion in a URL, use the `<c:url>` tag. Specify the URL string in the tag's `value` attribute, and include any parameter values and names in `<c:param>` tags in the body of the `<c:url>` tag. A parameter value can be given either in the `value` attribute of a `<c:param>` tag or in its body. Here's an example that shows both uses:

```
<c:url var="urlStr" value="myscript.jsp">
  <c:param name="id" value ="47"/>
  <c:param name="color">sky blue</c:param>
</c:url>
```

This will URL-encode the values of the `id` and `color` parameters and add them to the end of the URL. The result is placed in an object named `urlStr`, which you can display as follows:

```
<c:out value="${urlStr}"/>
```

 The `<c:url>` tag does not encode special characters such as spaces in the string supplied in its `value` attribute. You must encode them yourself, so it's probably best to avoid creating pages with spaces in their names, to avoid the likelihood that you'll need to refer to them.

To display entries from the `phrase` table, use the `<c:out>` and `<c:url>` tags as follows:

```
<sql:query dataSource="${conn}" var="rs">
  SELECT phrase_val FROM phrase ORDER BY phrase_val
</sql:query>

<c:forEach items="${rs.rows}" var="row">
  <%-- URL-encode the phrase value for use in the URL --%>
  <c:url var="urlStr" value="/mcb/mysearch.jsp">
    <c:param name="phrase" value ="${row.phrase_val}"/>
  </c:url>
  <a href="<c:out value="${urlStr}"/>">
    <%-- HTML-encode the phrase value for use in the link label --%>
    <c:out value="${row.phrase_val}"/>
  </a>
  <br />
</c:forEach>
```

## CHAPTER 18

Incorporating Query Results into Web Pages

18.0 Introduction

When you store information in your database, you can easily retrieve it for use on the Web in a variety of ways. Query results can be displayed as unstructured paragraphs or as structured elements such as lists or tables; you can display static text or create hyperlinks. Query metadata can be useful when formatting query results, too, such as when generating an HTML table that displays a result set and uses its metadata to get the column headings for the table. These tasks combine statement processing with web scripting, and are primarily a matter of properly encoding any special characters in the results (like & or <) and adding the appropriate HTML tags for the types of elements you want to produce.

This chapter shows how to generate several types of web output from query results:

- Paragraphs
- Lists
- Tables
- Hyperlinks
- Navigation indexes (single- and multiple-page)

The chapter also covers techniques for inserting binary data into your database and for retrieving and transferring that kind of information to clients. (It's easiest and most common to work with text for creating web pages from database content, but you can also use MySQL to help service requests for binary data such as images, sounds, or PDF files.) You can also serve query results for download rather than for display in a page. Finally, the chapter discusses the use of template packages for generating web pages.

The recipes here build on the techniques shown in Chapter 17 for generating web pages from scripts and for encoding output for display. See that chapter if you need background in these topics.

Scripts to create the tables used in this chapter are located in the *tables* directory of the recipes distribution. The scripts for the examples can be found under the directories named for the servers used to run them. For Perl, Ruby, PHP, and Python examples, look under the *apache* directory. Utility routines used by the example scripts are found in files located in the *lib* directory. (See Recipe 17.2 for information on configuring Apache so that scripts can be run by it and find their library files.) For Java (JSP) examples, look under the *tomcat* directory; you should already have installed these in the process of setting up the mcb application context (Recipe 17.3).

Note that although the scripts in this chapter are intended to be invoked from your browser after they have been installed, many of them (JSP pages excepted) can also be invoked from the command line if you want to see the raw HTML they produce (Recipe 17.2).

Not all languages are represented in every section of this chapter. If a particular section has no example for a language in which you're interested, check the recipes distribution. It might contain the implementation you want, even if it's not shown here.

18.1 Displaying Query Results as Paragraph Text

Problem

You want to display a query result as free text.

Solution

Display it within paragraph tags.

Discussion

Paragraphs are useful for displaying free text with no particular structure. In this case all you need to do is retrieve the text to be displayed, encode it to convert special characters to the corresponding HTML entities, and wrap each paragraph within <p> and </p> tags. The following examples show how to produce paragraphs for a status display that includes the current date and time, the server version, the client username, and the default database name (if any). These values are available from the following query:

```
mysql> SELECT NOW(), VERSION(), USER(), DATABASE();
+---------------------+------------+------------------+------------+
| NOW()               | VERSION()  | USER()           | DATABASE() |
+---------------------+------------+------------------+------------+
| 2006-10-17 15:47:33 | 5.0.27-log | cbuser@localhost | cookbook   |
+---------------------+------------+------------------+------------+
```

In Perl, the CGI.pm module provides a p( ) function that adds paragraph tags around the string you pass to it. p( ) does not HTML-encode its argument, so you should take care of that by calling escapeHTML( ):

```
($now, $version, $user, $db) =
  $dbh->selectrow_array ("SELECT NOW(), VERSION(), USER(), DATABASE()");
$db = "NONE" unless defined ($db);
print p (escapeHTML ("Local time on the MySQL server is $now."));
print p (escapeHTML ("The server version is $version."));
print p (escapeHTML ("The current user is $user."));
print p (escapeHTML ("The default database is $db."));
```

In Ruby, use the cgi module escapeHTML method to encode the paragraph text, and then pass it to the p method to produce the paragraph tags:

```
(now, version, user, db) =
  dbh.select_one("SELECT NOW(), VERSION(), USER(), DATABASE()")
db = "NONE" if db.nil?
cgi = CGI.new("html4")
cgi.out {
  cgi.p { CGI.escapeHTML("Local time on the MySQL server is #{now}.") } +
  cgi.p { CGI.escapeHTML("The server version is #{version}.") } +
  cgi.p { CGI.escapeHTML("The current user is #{user}.") } +
  cgi.p { CGI.escapeHTML("The default database is #{db}.") }
}
```

In PHP, put <p> and </p> tags around the encoded paragraph text:

```
$result =& $conn->query ("SELECT NOW(), VERSION(), USER(), DATABASE()");
if (!PEAR::isError ($result))
{
  list ($now, $version, $user, $db) = $result->fetchRow ();
  $result->free ();
  if (!isset ($db))
    $db = "NONE";
  $para = "Local time on the MySQL server is $now.";
  print ("<p>" . htmlspecialchars ($para) . "</p>\n");
  $para = "The server version is $version.";
  print ("<p>" . htmlspecialchars ($para) . "</p>\n");
  $para = "The current user is $user.";
  print ("<p>" . htmlspecialchars ($para) . "</p>\n");
  $para = "The default database is $db.";
  print ("<p>" . htmlspecialchars ($para) . "</p>\n");
}
```

Or, after fetching the query result, you can print the paragraph by beginning in HTML mode and switching between modes:

```
<p>Local time on the MySQL server is
<?php print (htmlspecialchars ($now)); ?>.</p>
<p>The server version is
<?php print (htmlspecialchars ($version)); ?>.</p>
<p>The current user is
<?php print (htmlspecialchars ($user)); ?>.</p>
<p>The default database is
<?php print (htmlspecialchars ($db)); ?>.</p>
```

To display paragraphs in Python, do something like this:

```
cursor = conn.cursor ()
cursor.execute ("SELECT NOW(), VERSION(), USER(), DATABASE()")
(now, version, user, db) = cursor.fetchone ()
cursor.close ()
if db is None:  # check database name
  db = "NONE"
para = ("Local time on the MySQL server is %s.") % now
print "<p>" + cgi.escape (para, 1) + "</p>"
para = ("The server version is %s.") % version
print "<p>" + cgi.escape (para, 1) + "</p>"
para = ("The current user is %s.") % user
print "<p>" + cgi.escape (para, 1) + "</p>"
para = ("The default database is %s.") % db
print "<p>" + cgi.escape (para, 1) + "</p>"
```

In JSP, the paragraph display can be produced as follows, using **rowsByIndex** to access
the result set row's columns by numeric index and **<c:out>** to encode and print the text:

```
<sql:query dataSource="${conn}" var="rs">
  SELECT NOW(), VERSION(), USER(), DATABASE()
</sql:query>
<c:set var="row" value="${rs.rowsByIndex[0]}"/>
<c:set var="db" value="${row[3]}"/>
<c:if test="${empty db}">
  <c:set var="db" value="NONE"/>
</c:if>

<p>Local time on the server is <c:out value="${row[0]}"/>.</p>
<p>The server version is <c:out value="${row[1]}"/>.</p>
<p>The current user is <c:out value="${row[2]}"/>.</p>
<p>The default database is <c:out value="${db}"/>.</p>
```

See Also

Recipe 18.10 discusses how to generate paragraphs using templates.

18.2 Displaying Query Results as Lists

Problem

A query result contains a set of items that should be displayed as a structured list.

Solution

There are several types of HTML lists. Write the list items within tags that are appropriate for the type of list you want to produce.

Discussion

More structured than paragraphs and less structured than tables, lists provide a useful way to display a set of individual items. HTML provides several styles of lists, such as ordered lists, unordered lists, and definition lists. You may also want to nest lists, which requires list-within-list formatting.

Lists generally consist of opening and closing tags that enclose a set of items, each of which is delimited by its own tags. List items correspond naturally to rows returned from a query, so generating an HTML list structure from within a program is a matter of encoding your query result, enclosing each row within the proper item tags, and adding the opening and closing list tags.

Two approaches to list generation are common. To print the tags as you process the result set, do this:

1. Print the list opening tag.
2. Fetch and print each result set row as a list item, including the item tags.
3. Print the list closing tag.

Alternatively, you can process the list in memory:

1. Store the list items in an array.
2. Pass the array to a list generation function that adds the appropriate tags.
3. Print the result.

The examples that follow demonstrate both approaches.

Ordered lists

An ordered list consists of items that have a particular sequence. Browsers typically display ordered lists as a set of numbered items:

```
1. First item
2. Second item
3. Third item
```

You need not specify the item numbers, because browsers add them automatically. The HTML for an ordered list is enclosed within `<ol>` and `</ol>` tags, and contains items that are enclosed within `<li>` and `</li>` tags:

```
<ol>
  <li>First item</li>
  <li>Second item</li>
  <li>Third item</li>
</ol>
```

Suppose that you have an `ingredient` table that contains numbered ingredients for a cooking recipe:

```
+----+--------------------------------+
| id | item                           |
```

```
+----+-------------------------------+
|  1 | 3 cups flour                  |
|  2 | 1/2 cup raw ("unrefined") sugar |
|  3 | 3 eggs                        |
|  4 | pinch (< 1/16 teaspoon) salt  |
+----+-------------------------------+
```

The table contains an `id` column, but you need only fetch the text values in the proper order to display them as an ordered list, because a browser adds item numbers itself. The items contain the special characters " and <, so you should HTML-encode them before adding the tags that convert the items to an HTML list. The result looks like this:

```
<ol>
  <li>3 cups flour</li>
  <li>1/2 cup raw (&quot;unrefined&quot;) sugar</li>
  <li>3 eggs</li>
  <li>pinch (&lt; 1/16 teaspoon) salt</li>
</ol>
```

One way to create such list from a script is by printing the HTML as you fetch the rows of the result set. Here's how you might do so in a JSP page using the JSTL tags:

```
<sql:query dataSource="${conn}" var="rs">
  SELECT item FROM ingredient ORDER BY id
</sql:query>
<ol>
<c:forEach items="${rs.rows}" var="row">
  <li><c:out value="${row.item}"/></li>
</c:forEach>
</ol>
```

In PHP, the same operation can be performed like this:

```
$stmt = "SELECT item FROM ingredient ORDER BY id";
$result =& $conn->query ($stmt);
if (PEAR::isError ($result))
  die (htmlspecialchars ($result->getMessage ()));
print ("<ol>\n");
while (list ($item) = $result->fetchRow ())
  print ("<li>" . htmlspecialchars ($item) . "</li>\n");
$result->free ();
print ("</ol>\n");
```

It's not necessary to add newlines after the closing tags as this example does; web browsers don't care if they're present or not. I like to add them because the HTML produced by a script is easier to examine directly if it's not all on a single line, which simplifies debugging.

The preceding examples use an approach to HTML generation that interleaves row fetching and output generation. It's also possible to separate (or *decouple*) the two operations: retrieve the data first, and then write the output. Queries tend to vary from list to list, but generating the list itself often is fairly stereotypical. If you put the list-generation code into a utility function, you can reuse it for different queries. The two issues that the function must handle are HTML-encoding the items (if they aren't already encoded) and adding the proper HTML tags. For example, a function named `make_ordered_list( )` can be written as follows in PHP. It takes the list items as an array argument and returns the list as a string:

```php
function make_ordered_list ($items, $encode = TRUE)
{
  $str = "<ol>\n";
  foreach ($items as $k => $v)
  {
    if ($encode)
      $v = htmlspecialchars ($v);
    $str .= "<li>$v</li>\n";
  }
  $str .= "</ol>\n";
  return ($str);
}
```

After writing the utility function, you can fetch the data first and then print the HTML like so:

```php
# fetch items for list
$stmt = "SELECT item FROM ingredient ORDER BY id";
$result =& $conn->query ($stmt);
if (PEAR::isError ($result))
  die (htmlspecialchars ($result->getMessage ()));
$items = array ();
while (list ($item) = $result->fetchRow ())
  $items[] = $item;
$result->free ();

# generate HTML list
print (make_ordered_list ($items));
```

In Python, the utility function can be defined like this:

```python
def make_ordered_list (items, encode = True):
  list = "<ol>\n"
  for item in items:
    if item is None:  # handle possibility of NULL item
      item = ""
    # make sure item is a string, and then encode if necessary
    item = str (item)
    if encode:
      item = cgi.escape (item, 1)
    list = list + "<li>" + item + "</li>\n"
  list = list + "</ol>\n"
  return list
```

And used like this:

```python
# fetch items for list
stmt = "SELECT item FROM ingredient ORDER BY id"
cursor = conn.cursor ()
cursor.execute (stmt)
items = []
```

```
for (item,) in cursor.fetchall ():
  items.append (item)
cursor.close ()

# generate HTML list
print make_ordered_list (items)
```

The second argument to make_ordered_list( ) indicates whether it should perform
HTML-encoding of the list items. The easiest thing is to let the function handle this for
you (which is why the default is true). However, if you're creating a list from items that
themselves include HTML tags, you wouldn't want the function to encode the special
characters in those tags. For example, if you're creating a list of hyperlinks, each list
item will contain <a> tags. To prevent these from being converted to <a>, pass
make_ordered_list( ) a second argument that evaluates to false.

If your API provides functions to generate HTML structures, you need not write them
yourself, of course. That's the case for the Perl CGI.pm and Ruby cgi modules. For
example, in Perl, generate each item by invoking its li( ) function to add the opening
and closing item tags, save up the items in an array, and pass the array to ol( ) to add
the opening and closing list tags:

```
my $stmt = "SELECT item FROM ingredient ORDER BY id";
my $sth = $dbh->prepare ($stmt);
$sth->execute ();
my @items = ();
while (my $ref = $sth->fetchrow_arrayref ())
{
  # handle possibility of NULL (undef) item
  my $item = (defined ($ref->[0]) ? escapeHTML ($ref->[0]) : "");
  push (@items, li ($item));
}
print ol (@items);
```

The reason for converting NULL values (represented by undef) to the empty string is to
avoid having Perl generate uninitialized-value warnings when run with warnings enabled. (The ingredient table doesn't actually contain any NULL values, but the technique
is useful for dealing with tables that might.)

The previous example intertwines row fetching and HTML generation. To use a more
decoupled approach that separates fetching the items from printing the HTML, first
retrieve the items into an array. Then pass the array by reference to li( ) and the result
to ol( ):

```
# fetch items for list
my $stmt = "SELECT item FROM ingredient ORDER BY id";
my $item_ref = $dbh->selectcol_arrayref ($stmt);

# generate HTML list, handling possibility of NULL (undef) items
$item_ref = [ map { defined ($_) ? escapeHTML ($_) : "" } @{$item_ref} ];
print ol (li ($item_ref));
```

Note two things about the li( ) function:

- It doesn't perform any HTML-encoding; you must do that yourself.
- It can handle a single value or an array of values. However, if you pass an array, you should pass it by reference. When you do that, `li( )`, adds `<li>` and `</li>` tags to each array element, and then concatenates them and returns the resulting string. If you pass the array itself rather than a reference, `li( )` concatenates the items first, and then adds a single set of tags around the result, which is usually not what you want. This behavior is shared by several other CGI.pm functions that can operate on single or multiple values. For example, the table data `td( )` function adds a single set of `<td>` and `</td>` tags if you pass it a scalar or list. If you pass a list reference, it adds the tags to each item in the list.

Should You Intertwine or Decouple Row Fetching and HTML Generation?

If you want to write a script in a hurry, you can probably get it running most quickly by writing code that prints HTML from query rows as you fetch them. There are, however, certain advantages to separating data retrieval from output production. The most obvious ones are that by using a utility function to generate the HTML, you have to write the function only once, and you can share it among scripts. But there are other benefits as well:

- Functions that generate HTML structures can be used with data obtained from other sources, not just from a database.
- The decoupled approach takes advantage of the fact that you need not generate output directly. You can construct a page element in memory, and then print it when you're ready. This is particularly useful for building pages that consist of several components, because it gives you more latitude to create the components in the order that's most convenient. (On the other hand, if you're retrieving very large result sets, this approach can entail considerable memory use.)
- Decoupling row fetching and output generation gives you more flexibility in the types of output you produce. If you decide to generate an unordered list rather than an ordered list, just call a different output function; the data collection phase need not change. This is true even if you decide to use a different output format (XML or WML rather than HTML, for example). In this case, you still need only a different output function; data collection remains unchanged.
- By prefetching the list items, you can make adaptive decisions about what type of list to create. Although we are not yet to the point of discussing web forms, they make heavy use of their own kinds of lists. In that context, having items in hand before generating an HTML structure from them can be useful if you want to choose the list type based on the size of the list. For example, you can display a set of radio buttons if the number of items is small, or a pop-up menu or scrolling list if the number is large.

The Ruby equivalent of the previous example looks like this:

```
# fetch items for list
stmt = "SELECT item FROM ingredient ORDER BY id"
```

```
items = dbh.select_all(stmt)

list = ""
items.each do |item|
  list << cgi.li { CGI.escapeHTML(item.to_s) }
end
list = cgi.ol { list }
```

Unordered lists

An unordered list is like an ordered list except that browsers display all the items with the same marker character, such as a bullet:

- First item
- Second item
- Third item

"Unordered" refers to the fact that the marker character provides no sequence information. You can of course display the items in any order you choose. The HTML tags for an unordered list are the same as for an ordered list except that the opening and closing tags are <ul> and </ul> rather than <ol> and </ol>:

```
<ul>
  <li>First item</li>
  <li>Second item</li>
  <li>Third item</li>
</ul>
```

For APIs where you print the tags directly, use the same procedure as for ordered lists, but print <ul> and </ul> instead of <ol> and </ol>. Here is an example in JSP:

```
<sql:query dataSource="${conn}" var="rs">
  SELECT item FROM ingredient ORDER BY id
</sql:query>
<ul>
<c:forEach items="${rs.rows}" var="row">
  <li><c:out value="${row.item}"/></li>
</c:forEach>
</ul>
```

In Perl, create an unordered list by using the CGI.pm ul( ) function rather than ol( ):

```
# fetch items for list
my $stmt = "SELECT item FROM ingredient ORDER BY id";
my $item_ref = $dbh->selectcol_arrayref ($stmt);

# generate HTML list, handling possibility of NULL (undef) items
$item_ref = [ map { defined ($_) ? escapeHTML ($_) : "" } @{$item_ref} ];
print ul (li ($item_ref));
```

If you're writing your own utility function for unordered lists, it's easily derived from a function that generates ordered lists. For example, it's simple to adapt make_ordered_list( ) to create make_unordered_list( ), because they differ only in the opening and closing list tags used.

Definition lists

A definition list consists of two-part items, each including a term and a definition. "Term" and "definition" have loose meanings, because you can display any kind of information you want. For example, the following `doremi` table associates the name of each note in a musical scale with a mnemonic phrase for remembering it, but the mnemonics aren't exactly what you'd call definitions:

```
+----+------+---------------------------+
| id | note | mnemonic                  |
+----+------+---------------------------+
|  1 | do   | A deer, a female deer     |
|  2 | re   | A drop of golden sun      |
|  3 | mi   | A name I call myself      |
|  4 | fa   | A long, long way to run   |
|  5 | so   | A needle pulling thread   |
|  6 | la   | A note to follow so       |
|  7 | ti   | A drink with jam and bread |
+----+------+---------------------------+
```

Nevertheless, the `note` and `mnemonic` columns can be displayed as a definition list:

```
do
    A deer, a female deer
re
    A drop of golden sun
mi
    A name I call myself
fa
    A long, long way to run
so
    A needle pulling thread
la
    A note to follow so
ti
    I drink with jam and bread
```

The HTML for a definition list begins and ends with `<dl>` and `</dl>` tags. Each item has a term enclosed within `<dt>` and `</dt>` tags and a definition enclosed within `<dd>` and `</dd>` tags:

```
<dl>
  <dt>do</dt> <dd>A deer, a female deer</dd>
  <dt>re</dt> <dd>A drop of golden sun</dd>
  <dt>mi</dt> <dd>A name I call myself</dd>
  <dt>fa</dt> <dd>A long, long way to run</dd>
  <dt>so</dt> <dd>A needle pulling thread</dd>
  <dt>la</dt> <dd>A note to follow so</dd>
  <dt>ti</dt> <dd>A drink with jam and bread</dd>
</dl>
```

In a JSP page, you can generate the definition list like this:

```
<sql:query dataSource="${conn}" var="rs">
  SELECT note, mnemonic FROM doremi ORDER BY note
</sql:query>
```

```
<dl>
<c:forEach items="${rs.rows}" var="row">
  <dt><c:out value="${row.note}"/></dt>
  <dd><c:out value="${row.mnemonic}"/></dd>
</c:forEach>
</dl>
```

In PHP, create the list like this:

```
$stmt = "SELECT note, mnemonic FROM doremi ORDER BY id";
$result =& $conn->query ($stmt);
if (PEAR::isError ($result))
  die (htmlspecialchars ($result->getMessage ()));
print ("<dl>\n");
while (list ($note, $mnemonic) = $result->fetchRow ())
{
  print ("<dt>" . htmlspecialchars ($note) . "</dt>\n");
  print ("<dd>" . htmlspecialchars ($mnemonic) . "</dd>\n");
}
$result->free ();
print ("</dl>\n");
```

Or fetch the data and then pass it to a utility function that takes arrays of terms and definitions and returns the list as a string:

```
# fetch items for list
$stmt = "SELECT note, mnemonic FROM doremi ORDER BY id";
$result =& $conn->query ($stmt);
if (PEAR::isError ($result))
  die (htmlspecialchars ($result->getMessage ()));
$terms = array ();
$defs = array ();
while (list ($note, $mnemonic) = $result->fetchRow ())
{
  $terms[] = $note;
  $defs[] = $mnemonic;
}
$result->free ();

# generate HTML list
print (make_definition_list ($terms, $defs));
```

The make_definition_list( ) function can be written like this:

```
function make_definition_list ($terms, $definitions, $encode = TRUE)
{
  $str = "<dl>\n";
  $n = count ($terms);
  for ($i = 0; $i < $n; $i++)
  {
    $term = $terms[$i];
    $definition = $definitions[$i];
    if ($encode)
    {
      $term = htmlspecialchars ($term);
      $definition = htmlspecialchars ($definition);
    }
```

```
    $str .= "<dt>$term</dt>\n<dd>$definition</dd>\n";
  }
  $str .= "</dl>\n";
  return ($str);
}
```

In Ruby, use the `dt` and `dd` methods to create the list item content, and then pass it to the `dl` method to add the outermost list tags:

```
stmt = "SELECT note, mnemonic FROM doremi ORDER BY id"
list = ""
dbh.execute(stmt) do |sth|
  sth.fetch do |row|
    list << cgi.dt { CGI.escapeHTML(row["note"].to_s) }
    list << cgi.dd { CGI.escapeHTML(row["mnemonic"].to_s) }
  end
end
list = cgi.dl { list }
```

Here is another example (in Perl). Each term is a database name, and the corresponding definition indicates how many tables are in the database. The numbers are obtained from INFORMATION_SCHEMA using a query that counts the number of tables in each database. You can create the terms and definitions by invoking `dt( )` and `dd( )`, save them in an array, and pass the array to `dl( )`:

```
# count number of tables per database
my $sth = $dbh->prepare ("SELECT TABLE_SCHEMA, COUNT(TABLE_NAME)
                          FROM INFORMATION_SCHEMA.TABLES
                          GROUP BY TABLE_SCHEMA");
$sth->execute ();
my @items = ();
while (my ($db_name, $tbl_count) = $sth->fetchrow_array ())
{
  push (@items, dt (escapeHTML ($db_name)));
  push (@items, dd (escapeHTML ($tbl_count . " tables")));
}
print dl (@items);
```

The counts indicate the number of tables accessible to the MySQL account that the script uses when it connects to the MySQL server. If there are databases or tables that are not accessible, you cannot get information about them and they are not included in the counts.

Unmarked lists

A type of list not normally discussed as such is a list with no markings at all. This is simply a set of items, each on a separate line. An unmarked list is very easy to produce: fetch each item and add a break tag after it. Here's an example in JSP:

```
<c:forEach items="${rs.rows}" var="row">
  <c:out value="${row.item}"/><br />
</c:forEach>
```

If you already have the items in an array, just iterate through it. For example, in Ruby, if you have a set of items in an array named `items`, generate the list like this:

```
list = items.collect { |item| CGI.escapeHTML(item.to_s) + cgi.br }.join
```

Nested lists

Some applications display information that is most easily understood when presented as a list of lists. The following example displays state names as a definition list, grouped by the initial letter of the names. For each item in the list, the term is the initial letter, and the definition is an unordered list of the state names beginning with that letter:

A
- Alabama
- Alaska
- Arizona
- Arkansas

C
- California
- Colorado
- Connecticut

D
- Delaware

...

One way to produce such a list (in Perl) is as follows:

```
# get list of initial letters
my $ltr_ref = $dbh->selectcol_arrayref (
                "SELECT DISTINCT UPPER(LEFT(name,1)) AS letter
                 FROM states ORDER BY letter");
my @items = ();
# get list of states for each letter
foreach my $ltr (@{$ltr_ref})
{
  my $item_ref = $dbh->selectcol_arrayref (
                "SELECT name FROM states WHERE LEFT(name,1) = ?
                 ORDER BY name", undef, $ltr);
  $item_ref = [ map { escapeHTML ($_) } @{$item_ref} ];
  # convert list of states to unordered list
  my $item_list = ul (li ($item_ref));
  # for each definition list item, the initial letter is
  # the term, and the list of states is the definition
  push (@items, dt ($ltr));
  push (@items, dd ($item_list));
}
print dl (@items);
```

The preceding example uses one query to get the list of distinct letters, and another for each letter to find the states associated with each letter. You could also retrieve all the information using a single query, and then march through the result set and begin a new list item each time you reach a new letter:

```
my $sth = $dbh->prepare ("SELECT name FROM states ORDER BY name");
$sth->execute ();
```

```
  my @items = ();
  my @names = ();
  my $cur_ltr = "";
  while (my ($name) = $sth->fetchrow_array ())
  {
    my $ltr = uc (substr ($name, 0, 1));  # initial letter of name
    if ($cur_ltr ne $ltr)         # beginning a new letter?
    {
      if (@names)     # any stored-up names from previous letter?
      {
        # for each definition list item, the initial letter is
        # the term, and the list of states is the definition
        push (@items, dt ($cur_ltr));
        push (@items, dd (ul (li (\@names))));
      }
      @names = ();
      $cur_ltr = $ltr;
    }
    push (@names, escapeHTML ($name));
  }
  if (@names)              # any remaining names from final letter?
  {
    push (@items, dt ($cur_ltr));
    push (@items, dd (ul (li (\@names))));
  }
  print dl (@items);
```

A third approach uses a single query but separates the data-collection and HTML-generation phases:

```
  # collect state names and associate each with the proper
  # initial-letter list
  my $sth = $dbh->prepare ("SELECT name FROM states ORDER BY name");
  $sth->execute ();
  my %ltr = ();
  while (my ($name) = $sth->fetchrow_array ())
  {
    my $ltr = uc (substr ($name, 0, 1));  # initial letter of name
    # initialize letter list to empty array if this is
    # first state for it, and then add state to array
    $ltr{$ltr} = [] unless exists ($ltr{$ltr});
    push (@{$ltr{$ltr}}, $name);
  }

  # now generate the output lists
  my @items = ();
  foreach my $ltr (sort (keys (%ltr)))
  {
    # encode list of state names for this letter, generate unordered list
    my $ul_str = ul (li ([ map { escapeHTML ($_) } @{$ltr{$ltr}} ]));
    push (@items, dt ($ltr), dd ($ul_str));
  }
  print dl (@items);
```

See Also

Recipe 18.10 discusses how to generate lists using templates.

18.3 Displaying Query Results as Tables

Problem

You want to display a query result as an HTML table.

Solution

Use each row of the result as a table row. If you want an initial row of column labels, supply your own or perhaps use the query metadata to obtain the names of the columns in the query result.

Discussion

HTML tables are useful for presenting highly structured output. One reason they're popular for displaying the results of queries is that they consist of rows and columns, so there's a natural conceptual correspondence between HTML tables and database tables or query results. In addition, you can obtain column headers for the table by accessing the query metadata. The basic structure of an HTML table is as follows:

- The table begins and ends with `<table>` and `</table>` tags and encloses a set of rows.

- Each row begins and ends with `<tr>` and `</tr>` tags and encloses a set of cells.

- Tags for data cells are `<td>` and `</td>`. Tags for header cells are `<th>` and `</th>`. (Typically, browsers display header cells using boldface or other emphasis.)

- Tags may include attributes. For example, to put a border around each cell, add a `border="1"` attribute to the `<table>` tag. To right-justify a table cell, add an `align="right"` attribute to the `<td>` tag.

Note that you should always supply the closing tag for each table element. This is a good idea in general for any HTML element, but especially so for tables. If you omit closing tags, the resulting browser behavior is unpredictable.

Suppose that you want to display the contents of your CD collection:

```
mysql> SELECT year, artist, title FROM cd ORDER BY artist, year;
+------+----------------+------------------+
| year | artist         | title            |
+------+----------------+------------------+
| 1999 | Adrian Snell   | City of Peace    |
| 1999 | Charlie Peacock | Kingdom Come    |
| 2004 | Dave Bainbridge | Veil of Gossamer |
| 1990 | Iona           | Iona             |
| 2001 | Iona           | Open Sky         |
```

```
| 1998 | jaci velasquez  | jaci velasquez    |
| 1989 | Richard Souther | Cross Currents    |
| 1987 | The 77s         | The 77s           |
| 1982 | Undercover      | Undercover        |
+------+-----------------+-------------------+
```

To display this query result as a bordered HTML table, you need to produce output that looks something like this:

```
<table border="1">
  <tr>
    <th>Year</th>
    <th>Artist</th>
    <th>Title</th>
  </tr>
  <tr>
    <td>1999</td>
    <td>Adrian Snell</td>
    <td>City of Peace</td>
  </tr>
  <tr>
    <td>1999</td>
    <td>Charlie Peacock</td>
    <td>Kingdom Come</td>
  </tr>
  ... other rows here ...
  <tr>
    <td>1982</td>
    <td>Undercover</td>
    <td>Undercover</td>
  </tr>
</table>
```

To convert the results of a query to an HTML table, wrap each value from a given result set row in cell tags, each row in row tags, and the entire set of rows in table tags. A JSP page might produce an HTML table from the cd table query like this:

```
<table border="1">
  <tr>
    <th>Year</th>
    <th>Artist</th>
    <th>Title</th>
  </tr>
<sql:query dataSource="${conn}" var="rs">
  SELECT year, artist, title FROM cd ORDER BY artist, year
</sql:query>
<c:forEach items="${rs.rows}" var="row">
  <tr>
    <td><c:out value="${row.year}"/></td>
    <td><c:out value="${row.artist}"/></td>
    <td><c:out value="${row.title}"/></td>
  </tr>
</c:forEach>

</table>
```

In Perl scripts, the CGI.pm functions table( ), tr( ), td( ), and th( ) produce the table, row, data cell, and header cell elements. However, the tr( ) function that generates a table row should be invoked as Tr( ) to avoid a conflict with the built-in Perl tr function that transliterates characters.* Thus, to display the contents of the cd table as an HTML table, do this:

```
my $sth = $dbh->prepare ("SELECT year, artist, title
                          FROM cd ORDER BY artist, year");
$sth->execute ();
my @rows = ();
push (@rows, Tr (th ("Year"), th ("Artist"), th ("Title")));
while (my ($year, $artist, $title) = $sth->fetchrow_array ())
{
  push (@rows, Tr (
              td (escapeHTML ($year)),
              td (escapeHTML ($artist)),
              td (escapeHTML ($title))
          ));
}
print table ({-border => "1"}, @rows);
```

Sometimes a table can be easier to make sense of if you display the rows in alternating colors, particularly if the table cells don't include borders. To do this, add a bgcolor attribute to each <th> and <td> tag, and alternate the color value for each row. An easy way to do this is by using a variable that toggles between two values. In the following example, the $bgcolor variable alternates between the values silver and white:

```
my $sth = $dbh->prepare ("SELECT year, artist, title
                          FROM cd ORDER BY artist, year");
$sth->execute ();
my $bgcolor = "silver";   # row-color variable
my @rows = ();
push (@rows, Tr (
            th ({-bgcolor => $bgcolor}, "Year"),
            th ({-bgcolor => $bgcolor}, "Artist"),
            th ({-bgcolor => $bgcolor}, "Title")
        ));
while (my ($year, $artist, $title) = $sth->fetchrow_array ())
{
  # toggle the row-color variable
  $bgcolor = ($bgcolor eq "silver" ? "white" : "silver");
  push (@rows, Tr (
              td ({-bgcolor => $bgcolor}, escapeHTML ($year)),
              td ({-bgcolor => $bgcolor}, escapeHTML ($artist)),
              td ({-bgcolor => $bgcolor}, escapeHTML ($title))
          ));
}
print table ({-border => "1"}, @rows);
```

---

* If you use the CGI.pm object-oriented interface, there is no ambiguity. In that case, you invoke the tr( ) method through a CGI object and it is unnecessary to invoke it as Tr( ):

```
$cgi->tr ( ... );
```

The preceding table-generation examples hardwire the column headings into the code, as well as knowledge about the number of columns. With a little effort, you can write a more general function that takes a database handle and an arbitrary statement, then executes the statement, and then returns its result as an HTML table. The function can get the column labels from the statement metadata automatically. To produce labels that differ from the table column names, specify column aliases in the statement:

```
my $tbl_str = make_table_from_query (
                $dbh,
                "SELECT
                    year AS Year, artist AS Artist, title AS Title
                 FROM cd
                 ORDER BY artist, year"
            );
print $tbl_str;
```

Any kind of statement that returns a result set can be passed to this function. You could, for example, use it to construct an HTML table from the result of a CHECK TABLE statement, which returns a result set that indicates the outcome of the check operation.

```
print p("Result of CHECK TABLE operation:");
my $tbl_str = make_table_from_query ($dbh, "CHECK TABLE profile");
print $tbl_str;
```

What does the make_table_from_query( ) function look like? Here's an implementation in Perl:

```
sub make_table_from_query
{
# db handle, query string, parameters to be bound to placeholders (if any)
my ($dbh, $stmt, @param) = @_;

  my $sth = $dbh->prepare ($stmt);
  $sth->execute (@param);
  my @rows = ();
  # use column names for cells in the header row
  push (@rows, Tr (th ([ map { escapeHTML ($_) } @{$sth->{NAME}} ])));
  # fetch each data row
  while (my $row_ref = $sth->fetchrow_arrayref ())
  {
    # encode cell values, avoiding warnings for undefined
    # values and using   for empty cells
    my @val = map {
                defined ($_) && $_ !~ /^\s*$/ ? escapeHTML ($_) : " "
              } @{$row_ref};
    my $row_str;
    for (my $i = 0; $i < @val; $i++)
    {
      # right-justify numeric columns
      if ($sth->{mysql_is_num}->[$i])
      {
        $row_str .= td ({-align => "right"}, $val[$i]);
      }
      else
      {
```

```
        $row_str .= td ($val[$i]);
      }
    }
    push (@rows, Tr ($row_str));
  }
  return (table ({-border => "1"}, @rows));
}
```

`make_table_from_query( )` does some extra work to right-justify numeric columns so that the values line up better. It also enables you to pass values to be bound to place-holders in the statement. Just specify them after the statement string:

```
my $tbl_str = make_table_from_query (
              $dbh,
              "SELECT
                 year AS Year, artist AS Artist, title AS Title
               FROM cd
               WHERE year < ?
               ORDER BY artist, year",
              1990
            );
print $tbl_str;
```

The   Trick for Empty Table Cells

A display problem sometimes occurs for HTML tables that include borders around cells: when a table cell is empty or contains only whitespace, many browsers do not show a border around the cell. This makes the table look irregular. To avoid this problem, the `make_table_from_query( )` function puts a nonbreaking space (` `) into cells that would otherwise be empty, so that borders for them display properly.

One thing to watch out for with program-generated tables is that browsers cannot render a table in a window until they've seen the entire thing. If you have a very large result set, it may take a very long time to display. Strategies for dealing with this problem include partitioning your data across multiple tables within a single page (so that the browser can display each table as it receives it), or across multiple pages. If you use multiple tables on a page, you should probably include some width attribute information in your header and data cell tags. Otherwise, each table will be sized to the actual widths of the values in its columns. If these differ across tables, your page will have a vertically ragged appearance.

See Also

Recipe 18.10 discusses how to generate tables using templates.

To display a table in such a way that the user can click on any column heading to sort the table's contents by that column, see Recipe 19.11.

18.4 Displaying Query Results as Hyperlinks

Problem

You want to use database content to generate clickable hyperlinks.

Solution

Add the proper tags to the content to generate anchor elements.

Discussion

The examples in the preceding sections generate static text, but database content also is useful for creating hyperlinks. If you store web-site URLs or email addresses in a table, you can easily convert them to active links in web pages. All you need to do is encode the information properly and add the appropriate HTML tags.

Suppose that you have a table that contains company names and web sites, such as the following `book_vendor` table that lists booksellers and publishers:

```
mysql> SELECT * FROM book_vendor ORDER BY name;
+----------------+------------------+
| name           | website          |
+----------------+------------------+
| Amazon.com     | www.amazon.com   |
| Barnes & Noble | www.bn.com       |
| Bookpool       | www.bookpool.com |
| O'Reilly Media | www.oreilly.com  |
+----------------+------------------+
```

This table has content that readily lends itself to the creation of hyperlinked text. To produce a hyperlink from a row, add the `http://` protocol designator to the `website` value, use the result as the `href` attribute for an `<a>` anchor tag, and use the `name` value in the body of the tag to serve as the link label. For example, the row for Barnes & Noble can be written like this:

```
<a href="http://www.bn.com">Barnes &amp; Noble</a>
```

JSP code to produce a bulleted (unordered) list of hyperlinks from the table contents looks like this:

```
<sql:query dataSource="${conn}" var="rs">
  SELECT name, website FROM book_vendor ORDER BY name
</sql:query>

<ul>
<c:forEach items="${rs.rows}" var="row">
  <li>
    <a href="http://<c:out value="${row.website}"/>">
      <c:out value="${row.name}"/></a>
  </li>
```

```
</c:forEach>
</ul>
```

When displayed in a web page, each vendor name in the list becomes an active link that may be selected to visit the vendor's web site. In Python, the equivalent operation looks like this:

```
stmt = "SELECT name, website FROM book_vendor ORDER BY name"
cursor = conn.cursor ()
cursor.execute (stmt)
items = []
for (name, website) in cursor.fetchall ():
  items.append ("<a href=\"http://%s\">%s</a>" \
        % (urllib.quote (website), cgi.escape (name, 1)))
cursor.close ()

# print items, but don't encode them; they're already encoded
print make_unordered_list (items, False)
```

CGI.pm-based Perl scripts produce hyperlinks by invoking the a( ) function as follows:

```
a ({-href => "url-value"}, "link label")
```

The function can be used to produce the vendor link list like this:

```
my $stmt = "SELECT name, website FROM book_vendor ORDER BY name";
my $sth = $dbh->prepare ($stmt);
$sth->execute ();
my @items = ();
while (my ($name, $website) = $sth->fetchrow_array ())
{
  push (@items, a ({-href => "http://$website"}, escapeHTML ($name)));
}
print ul (li (\@items));
```

Ruby scripts use the cgi module a method to produce hyperlinks:

```
stmt = "SELECT name, website FROM book_vendor ORDER BY name"
list = ""
dbh.execute(stmt) do |sth|
  sth.fetch do |row|
    list << cgi.li {
            cgi.a("href" => "http://#{row[1]}") {
              CGI.escapeHTML(row[0].to_s)
            }
          }
  end
end
list = cgi.ul { list }
```

Generating links using email addresses is another common web programming task. Assume that you have a table newsstaff that lists the department, name, and (if known) email address for the news anchors and reporters employed by a television station, WRRR:

```
mysql> SELECT * FROM newsstaff;
+-----------------+---------------+------------------------+
```

```
| department       | name           | email                    |
+------------------+----------------+--------------------------+
| Sports           | Mike Byerson   | mbyerson@wrrr-news.com   |
| Sports           | Becky Winthrop | bwinthrop@wrrr-news.com  |
| Weather          | Bill Hagburg   | bhagburg@wrrr-news.com   |
| Local News       | Frieda Stevens | NULL                     |
| Local Government | Rex Conex      | rconex@wrrr-news.com     |
| Current Events   | Xavier Ng      | xng@wrrr-news.com        |
| Consumer News    | Trish White    | twhite@wrrr-news.com     |
+------------------+----------------+--------------------------+
```

From this you want to produce an online directory containing email links to all personnel, so that site visitors can easily send mail to any staff member. For example, a row for a sports reporter named Mike Byerson with an email address of mbyerson@wrrr-news.com will become an entry in the listing that looks like this:

```
Sports: <a href="mailto:mbyerson@wrrr-news.com">Mike Byerson</a>
```

It's easy to use the table's contents to produce such a directory. First, let's put the code to generate an email link into a helper function, because it's the kind of operation that's likely to be useful in several scripts. In Perl, the function might look like this:

```perl
sub make_email_link
{
my ($name, $addr) = @_;

  $name = escapeHTML ($name);
  # return name as static text if address is undef or empty
  return $name if !defined ($addr) || $addr eq "";
  # return a hyperlink otherwise
  return a ({-href => "mailto:$addr"}, $name);
}
```

The function handles instances where the person has no email address by returning just the name as static text. To use the function, write a loop that pulls out names and addresses and displays each email link preceded by the staff member's department:

```perl
my $stmt = "SELECT department, name, email FROM newsstaff
            ORDER BY department, name";
my $sth = $dbh->prepare ($stmt);
$sth->execute ();
my @items = ();
while (my ($dept, $name, $email) = $sth->fetchrow_array ())
{
  push (@items,
        escapeHTML ($dept) . ": " . make_email_link ($name, $email));
}
print ul (li (\@items));
```

Equivalent email link generator functions for Ruby, PHP, and Python look like this:

```ruby
def make_email_link(name, addr = nil)
  name = CGI.escapeHTML(name.to_s)
  # return name as static text if address is nil or empty
  return name if addr.nil? or addr == ""
  # return a hyperlink otherwise
```

```
    return "<a href=\"mailto:#{addr}\">#{name}</a>"
  end

  function make_email_link ($name, $addr = NULL)
  {
    $name = htmlspecialchars ($name);
    # return name as static text if address is NULL or empty
    if ($addr === NULL || $addr == "")
      return ($name);
    # return a hyperlink otherwise
    return (sprintf ("<a href=\"mailto:%s\">%s</a>", $addr, $name));
  }

  def make_email_link (name, addr = None):
    name = cgi.escape (name, 1)
    # return name as static text if address is None or empty
    if addr is None or addr == "":
      return name
    # return a hyperlink otherwise
    return "<a href=\"mailto:%s\">%s</a>" % (addr, name)
```

For a JSP page, you can produce the newsstaff listing as follows:

```
<sql:query dataSource="${conn}" var="rs">
  SELECT department, name, email
  FROM newsstaff
  ORDER BY department, name
</sql:query>

<ul>
<c:forEach items="${rs.rows}" var="row">
  <li>
    <c:out value="${row.department}"/>:
    <c:set var="name" value="${row.name}"/>
    <c:set var="email" value="${row.email}"/>
    <c:choose>
      <%-- null or empty value test --%>
      <c:when test="${empty email}">
        <c:out value="${name}"/>
      </c:when>
      <c:otherwise>
        <a href="mailto:<c:out value="${email}"/>">
          <c:out value="${name}"/></a>
      </c:otherwise>
    </c:choose>
  </li>
</c:forEach>
</ul>
```

18.5 Creating a Navigation Index from Database Content

Problem

A list of items in a web page is long. You want to make it easier for users to move around in the page.

Solution

Create a navigation index containing links to different sections of the list.

Discussion

It's easy to display lists in web pages (Recipe 18.2). But if a list contains a lot of items, the page containing it may become quite long. In such cases, it's often useful to break up the list into sections and provide a navigation index, in the form of hyperlinks that enable users to reach sections of the list quickly without scrolling the page manually. For example, if you retrieve rows from a table and display them grouped into sections, you can include an index that lets the user jump directly to any section. The same idea can be applied to multiple-page displays as well, by providing a navigation index in each page so that users can reach any other page easily.

This recipe provides two examples to illustrate these techniques, both of which are based on the `kjv` table that was introduced in Recipe 5.15. The examples implement two kinds of display, using the verses from the book of Esther stored in the `kjv` table:

- A single-page display that lists all verses in all chapters of Esther. The list is broken into 10 sections (one per chapter), with a navigation index that has links pointing to the beginning of each section.

- A multiple-page display consisting of pages that each show the verses from a single chapter of Esther, and a main page that instructs the user to choose a chapter. Each of these pages also displays a list of chapters as hyperlinks to the pages that display the corresponding chapter verses. These links enable any page to be reached easily from any other.

Creating a single-page navigation index

This example displays all verses in Esther in a single page, with verses grouped into sections by chapter. To display the page so that each section contains a navigation marker, place an `<a name>` anchor element before each chapter's verses:

```
<a name="1">Chapter 1</a>
  ... list of verses in chapter 1...
<a name="2">Chapter 2</a>
  ... list of verses in chapter 2...
<a name="3">Chapter 3</a>
  ... list of verses in chapter 3...
...
```

That generates a list that includes a set of markers named 1, 2, 3, and so forth. To construct the navigation index, build a set of hyperlinks, each of which points to one of the name markers:

```
<a href="#1">Chapter 1</a>
<a href="#2">Chapter 2</a>
<a href="#3">Chapter 3</a>
...
```

The # in each href attribute signifies that the link points to a location within the same page. For example, href="#3" points to the anchor with the name="3" attribute.

To implement this kind of navigation index, you can use a couple of approaches:

- Retrieve the verse rows into memory and determine from them which entries are needed in the navigation index. Then print both the index and verse list.
- Figure out all the applicable anchors in advance and construct the index first. The list of chapter numbers can be determined by this statement:

```
SELECT DISTINCT cnum FROM kjv WHERE bname = 'Esther' ORDER BY cnum;
```

You can use the query result to build the navigation index, and then fetch the verses for the chapters later to create the page sections that the index entries point to.

Here's a script, *esther1.pl*, that uses the first approach. It's an adaptation of one of the nested-list examples shown in Recipe 18.2.

```perl
#!/usr/bin/perl
# esther1.pl - display book of Esther in a single page,
# with navigation index

use strict;
use warnings;
use CGI qw(:standard escape escapeHTML);
use Cookbook;

my $title = "The Book of Esther";

my $page = header ()
         . start_html (-title => $title, -bgcolor => "white")
         . h3 ($title);

my $dbh = Cookbook::connect ();

# Retrieve verses from the book of Esther and associate each one with the
# list of verses for the chapter it belongs to.

my $sth = $dbh->prepare ("SELECT cnum, vnum, vtext FROM kjv
                          WHERE bname = 'Esther'
                          ORDER BY cnum, vnum");
$sth->execute ();
my %verses = ();
while (my ($cnum, $vnum, $vtext) = $sth->fetchrow_array ())
{
```

```
    # Initialize chapter's verse list to empty array if this is
    # first verse for it, and then add verse number/text to array.
    $verses{$cnum} = [] unless exists ($verses{$cnum});
    push (@{$verses{$cnum}}, p (escapeHTML ("$vnum. $vtext")));
  }

  # Determine all chapter numbers and use them to construct a navigation
  # index.  These are links of the form <a href="#num>Chapter num</a>, where
  # num is a chapter number a'#' signifies a within-page link.  No URL- or
  # HTML-encoding is done here (the text that is displayed here doesn't need
  # it).  Make sure to sort chapter numbers numerically (use { a <=> b }).
  # Separate links by nonbreaking spaces.

  my $nav_index;
  foreach my $cnum (sort { $a <=> $b } keys (%verses))
  {
    $nav_index .= " " if $nav_index;
    $nav_index .= a ({-href => "#$cnum"}, "Chapter $cnum");
  }

  # Now display list of verses for each chapter.  Precede each section by
  # a label that shows the chapter number and a copy of the navigation index.

  foreach my $cnum (sort { $a <=> $b } keys (%verses))
  {
    # add an <a name> anchor for this section of the state display
    $page .= p (a ({-name => $cnum}, font ({-size => "+2"}, "Chapter $cnum"))
          . br ()
          . $nav_index);
    $page .= join ("", @{$verses{$cnum}});  # add array of verses for chapter
  }

  $dbh->disconnect ();

  $page .= end_html ();

  print $page;
```

Creating a multiple-page navigation index

This example shows a Perl script, *esther2.pl*, that is capable of generating any of several pages, all based on the verses in the book of Esther stored in the kjv table. The initial page displays a list of the chapters in the book, along with instructions to select a chapter. Each chapter in the list is a hyperlink that reinvokes the script to display the list of verses in the corresponding chapter. Because the script is responsible for generating multiple pages, it must be able to determine which page to display each time it runs. To make that possible, the script examines its own URL for a chapter parameter that indicates the number of the chapter to display. If no chapter parameter is present, or its value is not an integer, the script displays its initial page.

The URL to request the initial page looks like this:

```
http://localhost/cgi-bin/esther2.pl
```

The links to individual chapter pages have the following form, where *cnum* is a chapter number:

```
http://localhost/cgi-bin/esther2.pl?chapter=cnum
```

esther2.pl uses the CGI.pm param( ) function to obtain the **chapter** parameter value like so:

```
my $cnum = param ("chapter");
if (!defined ($cnum) || $cnum !~ /^\d+$/)
{
  # No chapter number was present or it was malformed
}
else
{
  # A chapter number was present
}
```

If no **chapter** parameter is present in the URL, $cnum will be undef. Otherwise, $cnum is set to the parameter value, which we check to make sure that it's an integer. (That covers the case where a garbage value may have been specified by someone trying to crash the script.)

Here is the entire *esther2.pl* script:

```
#!/usr/bin/perl
# esther2.pl - display book of Esther over multiple pages, one page per
# chapter, with navigation index

use strict;
use warnings;
use CGI qw(:standard escape escapeHTML);
use Cookbook;

# Construct navigation index as a list of links to the pages for each
# chapter in the the book of Esther.  Labels are of the form "Chapter
# n"; the chapter numbers are incorporated into the links as chapter=num
# parameters

# $dbh is the database handle, $cnum is the number of the chapter for
# which information is currently being displayed.  The label in the
# chapter list corresponding to this number is displayed as static
# text; the others are displayed as hyperlinks to the other chapter
# pages.  Pass 0 to make all entries hyperlinks (no valid chapter has
# a number 0).

# No encoding is done because the chapter numbers are digits and don't
# need it.

sub get_chapter_list
{
my ($dbh, $cnum) = @_;

  my $nav_index;
  my $ref = $dbh->selectcol_arrayref (
                    "SELECT DISTINCT cnum FROM kjv
```

```
                    WHERE bname = 'Esther' ORDER BY cnum"
            );
  foreach my $cur_cnum (@{$ref})
  {
    my $link = url () . "?chapter=$cur_cnum";
    my $label = "Chapter $cur_cnum";
    $nav_index .= br () if $nav_index;      # separate entries by <br>
    # use static bold text if entry is for current chapter,
    # use a hyperlink otherwise
    $nav_index .= ($cur_cnum == $cnum
                    ? strong ($label)
                    : a ({-href => $link}, $label));
  }
  return ($nav_index);
}

# Get the list of verses for a given chapter.  If there are none, the
# chapter number was invalid, but handle that case sensibly.

sub get_verses
{
my ($dbh, $cnum) = @_;

  my $ref = $dbh->selectall_arrayref (
                    "SELECT vnum, vtext FROM kjv
                     WHERE bname = 'Esther' AND cnum = ?",
                    undef, $cnum);
  my $verses = "";
  foreach my $row_ref (@{$ref})
  {
    $verses .= p (escapeHTML ("$row_ref->[0]. $row_ref->[1]"));
  }
  return ($verses eq ""      # no verses?
          ? p ("No verses in chapter $cnum were found.")
          : p ("Chapter $cnum:") . $verses);
}

# ----------------------------------------------------------------------

my $title = "The Book of Esther";

my $page = header () . start_html (-title => $title, -bgcolor => "white");

my ($left_panel, $right_panel);

my $dbh = Cookbook::connect ();

my $cnum = param ("chapter");
if (!defined ($cnum) || $cnum !~ /^\d+$/)
{
  # Missing or malformed chapter; display main page with a left panel
  # that lists all chapters as hyperlinks and a right panel that provides
  # instructions.
  $left_panel = get_chapter_list ($dbh, 0);
  $right_panel = p (strong ($title))
```

```
                       . p ("Select a chapter from the list at left.");
        }
        else
        {
          # Chapter number was given; display a left panel that lists chapters
          # chapters as hyperlinks (except for current chapter as bold text)
          # and a right panel that lists the current chapter's verses.
          $left_panel = get_chapter_list ($dbh, $cnum);
          $right_panel = p (strong ($title))
                         . get_verses ($dbh, $cnum);
        }

        $dbh->disconnect ();

        # Arrange the page as a one-row, three-cell table (middle cell is a spacer)

        $page .= table (Tr (
                        td ({-valign => "top", -width => "15%"}, $left_panel),
                        td ({-valign => "top", -width => "5%"}, " "),
                        td ({-valign => "top", -width => "80%"}, $right_panel)
                       ));

        $page .= end_html ();

        print $page;
```

See Also

esther2.pl examines its execution environment using the `param( )` function. Recipe 19.5 further discusses web script parameter processing.

Recipe 19.10 discusses another navigation problem: how to split display of a result set across multiple pages and create previous-page and next-page links.

18.6 Storing Images or Other Binary Data

Problem

You want to store images in MySQL.

Solution

That's not difficult, provided that you follow the proper precautions for encoding the image data.

Discussion

Web sites are not limited to displaying text. They can also serve various forms of binary data such as images, music files, PDF documents, and so forth. Images are a common kind of binary data, and because image storage is a natural application for a database, a very common question is "How do I store images in MySQL?" Many people will answer this question by saying, "Don't do it!" and some of the reasons are discussed in the sidebar "Should You Store Images in Your Database?" Because it's important to know how to work with binary data, this section does show how to store images in MySQL. Nevertheless, in recognition that that may not always be the best thing to do, the section also shows how to store images in the filesystem.

Although the discussion here is phrased in terms of working with images, the principles apply to any kind of binary data, such as PDF files or compressed text. In fact, they apply to any kind of data at all, including text. People tend to think of images as special somehow, but they're not.

One reason that image storage confuses people more often than does storing other types of information like text strings or numbers is that it's difficult to type in an image value manually. For example, you can easily use *mysql* to enter an INSERT statement to store a number like `3.48` or a string like `Je voudrais une bicyclette rouge`, but images contain binary data and it's not easy to refer to them by value. So you need to do something else. Your options are:

- Use the `LOAD_FILE( )` function.
- Write a program that reads in the image file and constructs the proper INSERT statement for you.

Should You Store Images in Your Database?

Deciding where to store images is a matter of trade-offs. There are advantages and disadvantages regardless of whether you store images in the database or in the filesystem:

- Storing images in a database table bloats the table. With a lot of images, you're more likely to approach any limits your operating system places on table size. On the other hand, if you store images in the filesystem, directory lookups may become slow. To avoid this, you may be able to implement some kind of hierarchical storage or use a filesystem that has good lookup performance for large directories (such as the Reiser filesystem that is available on Linux).
- Using a database centralizes storage for images that are used across multiple web servers on different hosts. Images stored in the filesystem must be stored locally on the web server host. In a multiple-host situation, that means you must replicate the set of images to the filesystem of each host. If you store the images in MySQL, only one copy of the images is required because each web server can get the images from the same database server.
- When images are stored in the filesystem, they constitute in essence a foreign key. Image manipulation requires two operations: one in the database and one in the filesystem. This in turn means that if you require transactional behavior, it's more difficult to implement—not only do you have two operations, but they take place in different domains. Storing images in the database is simpler because adding,

updating, or removing an image requires only a single row operation. It becomes unnecessary to make sure the image table and the filesystem remain in synchrony.

• It can be faster to serve images over the Web from the filesystem than from the database, because the web server itself opens the file, reads it, and writes it to the client. Images stored in the database must be read and written twice. First, the MySQL server reads the image from the database and writes it to your web script. Then the script reads the image and writes it to the client.

• Images stored in the filesystem can be referred to directly in web pages by means of `<img>` tag links that point to the image files. Images stored in MySQL must be served by a script that retrieves an image and sends it to the client. However, even if images are stored in the filesystem and accessible to the web server, you might still want to serve them through a script. This would be appropriate if you need to account for the number of times you serve each image (such as for banner ad displays where you charge customers by the number of ad impressions) or if you want to select an image at request time (such as when you pick an ad at random).

• If you store images in the database, you need to use a data type such as a `BLOB`. This is a variable length type, so the table itself will have variable-length rows. For the MyISAM storage engine, operations on fixed-length rows are often quicker, so you may gain some table lookup speed by storing images in the filesystem and using fixed-length types for the columns in the image table.

Storing images with LOAD_FILE( )

The `LOAD_FILE( )` function takes an argument indicating a file to be read and stored in the database. For example, an image stored in */tmp/myimage.png* might be loaded into a table like this:

```
INSERT INTO mytbl (image_data) VALUES(LOAD_FILE('/tmp/myimage.png'));
```

To load images into MySQL with `LOAD_FILE( )`, certain requirements must be satisfied:

• The image file must be located on the MySQL server host.
• The file must be readable by the server.
• You must have the `FILE` privilege.

These constraints mean that `LOAD_FILE( )` is available only to some MySQL users.

Storing images using a script

If `LOAD_FILE( )` is not an option, or you don't want to use it, you can write a short program to load your images. The program should either read the contents of an image file and create a row that contains the image data, or create a row that indicates where in the filesystem the image file is located. If you elect to store the image in MySQL, include the image data in the row-creation statement the same way as any other kind of data. That is, you either use a placeholder and bind the data value to it, or else encode the data and put it directly into the statement string.

The script shown in this recipe, *store_image.pl*, runs from the command line and stores an image file for later use. The script takes no side in the debate over whether to store images in the database or the filesystem. Instead, it demonstrates how to implement *both* approaches! Of course, this requires twice the storage space. To adapt this script for your own use, you'll want to retain only the parts that are appropriate for whichever storage method you want to implement. The necessary modifications are discussed at the end of this section.

The *store_image.pl* script uses an `image` table that includes columns for the image ID, name, and MIME type, and a column in which to store the image data:

```
CREATE TABLE image
(
  id    INT UNSIGNED NOT NULL AUTO_INCREMENT, # image ID number
  name  VARCHAR(30) NOT NULL,                 # image name
  type  VARCHAR(20) NOT NULL,                 # image MIME type
  data  MEDIUMBLOB NOT NULL,                  # image data
  PRIMARY KEY (id),                           # id and name are unique
  UNIQUE (name)
);
```

The `name` column indicates the name of the image file in the directory where images are stored in the filesystem. The `data` column is a `MEDIUMBLOB`, which is good for images smaller than 16 MB. If you need larger images, use a `LONGBLOB` column.

It is possible to use the `name` column to store full pathnames to images in the database, but if you put them all under the same directory, you can store names that are relative to that directory, and `name` values will take less space. That's what *store_image.pl* does. It needs to know the pathname of the image storage directory, which is what its `$image_dir` variable is for. You should check this variable's value and modify it as necessary before running the script. The default value reflects where I like to store images, but you'll need to change it according to your own preferences. Make sure to create the directory if it doesn't exist before you run the script, and set its access permissions so that the web server can read and write files there. You'll also need to check and possibly change the image directory pathname in the *display_image.pl* script discussed later in this chapter.

 The image storage directory should be outside the web server document tree. Otherwise, a user who knows or can guess the location may be able to upload executable code and cause it to run by requesting it with a web browser.

store_image.pl looks like this:

```
#!/usr/bin/perl
# store_image.pl - read an image file, store in the image table and
# in the filesystem.  (Normally, you'd store images only in one
# place or another; this script demonstrates how to do both.)
```

```perl
use strict;
use warnings;
use Fcntl;      # for O_RDONLY, O_WRONLY, O_CREAT
use FileHandle;
use Cookbook;

# Default image storage directory and pathname separator
# (CHANGE THESE AS NECESSARY)
# The location should NOT be within the web server document tree
my $image_dir = "/usr/local/lib/mcb/images";
my $path_sep = "/";

# Reset directory and pathname separator for Windows/DOS
if ($^O =~ /^MSWin/i || $^O =~ /^dos/)
{
  $image_dir = "C:\\mcb\\images";
  $path_sep = "\\";
}

-d $image_dir or die "$0: image directory ($image_dir)\ndoes not exist\n";

# Print help message if script was not invoked properly

(@ARGV == 2 || @ARGV == 3) or die <<USAGE_MESSAGE;
Usage: $0 image_file mime_type [image_name]

image_file = name of the image file to store
mime_time = the image MIME type (e.g., image/jpeg or image/png)
image_name = alternate name to give the image

image_name is optional; if not specified, the default is the
image file basename.
USAGE_MESSAGE

my $file_name = shift (@ARGV);  # image filename
my $mime_type = shift (@ARGV);  # image MIME type
my $image_name = shift (@ARGV); # image name (optional)

# if image name was not specified, use filename basename
# (allow either / or \ as separator)
($image_name = $file_name) =~ s|.*[/\\]|| unless defined $image_name;

my $fh = new FileHandle;
my ($size, $data);

sysopen ($fh, $file_name, O_RDONLY)
  or die "Cannot read $file_name: $!\n";
binmode ($fh);      # helpful for binary data
$size = (stat ($fh))[7];
sysread ($fh, $data, $size) == $size
  or die "Failed to read entire file $file_name: $!\n";
$fh->close ();

# Save image file in filesystem under $image_dir.  (Overwrite file
# if an old version exists.)
```

```
my $image_path = $image_dir . $path_sep . $image_name;

sysopen ($fh, $image_path, O_WRONLY|O_CREAT)
  or die "Cannot open $image_path: $!\n";
binmode ($fh);      # helpful for binary data
syswrite ($fh, $data, $size) == $size
  or die "Failed to write entire image file $image_path: $!\n";
$fh->close ();

# Save image in database table.  (Use REPLACE to kick out any old image
# that has the same name.)

my $dbh = Cookbook::connect ();
$dbh->do ("REPLACE INTO image (name,type,data) VALUES(?,?,?)",
          undef,
          $image_name, $mime_type, $data);
$dbh->disconnect ();
```

If you invoke the script with no arguments, it displays a short help message. Otherwise, it requires two arguments that specify the name of the image file and the MIME type of the image. By default, the file's basename (final component) is also used as the name of the image stored in the database and in the image directory. To use a different name, provide it using an optional third argument.

The script is fairly straightforward. It performs the following actions:

1. Check that the proper number of arguments was given and initialize some variables from them.

2. Make sure the image directory exists. If it does not, the script cannot continue.

3. Open and read the contents of the image file.

4. Store the image as a file in the image directory.

5. Store a row containing identifying information and the image data in the image table.

store_image.pl uses REPLACE rather than INSERT so that you can replace an old image with a new version having the same name simply by loading the new one. The statement specifies no id column value; id is an AUTO_INCREMENT column, so MySQL assigns it a unique sequence number automatically. Note that if you replace an image by loading a new one with the same name as an existing image, the REPLACE statement will generate a new id value. If you want to keep the old value, you should use INSERT ... ON DUPLICATE KEY UPDATE instead (Recipe 11.14). This will insert the row if the name doesn't already exist, or update the image value if it does.

The REPLACE statement that stores the image information into MySQL is relatively mundane:

```
$dbh->do ("REPLACE INTO image (name,type,data) VALUES(?,?,?)",
          undef,
          $image_name, $mime_type, $data);
```

If you examine that statement looking for some special technique for handling binary data, you'll be disappointed, because the $data variable that contains the image isn't treated as special in any way. The statement refers to all column values uniformly using ? placeholder characters and the values are passed at the end of the do( ) call. Another way to accomplish the same result is to perform escape processing on the column values explicitly and then insert them directly into the statement string:

```
$image_name = $dbh->quote ($image_name);
$mime_type = $dbh->quote ($mime_type);
$data = $dbh->quote ($data);
$dbh->do ("REPLACE INTO image (name,type,data)
          VALUES($image_name,$mime_type,$data)");
```

Many people think image-handling is a lot more troublesome than it really is. If you properly handle image data in a statement by using placeholders or by encoding it, you'll have no problems. If you don't, you'll get errors. It's as simple as that. This is *no* different from how you should handle other kinds of data, even text. After all, if you insert into a statement a piece of text that contains quotes or other special characters without escaping them, the statement will blow up in your face. So the need for placeholders or encoding is not some special thing that's necessary only for images— it's necessary for all data. Say it with me: "I will always use placeholders or encode my column values. Always. Always, always, *always.*" (Having said that, I feel obliged to point out that if you know enough about a given value—for example, if you're absolutely certain that it's an integer—there are times you can get away with breaking this rule. Nevertheless, it's never wrong to follow the rule.)

To try the script, change location into the *apache/images* directory of the **recipes** distribution. That directory contains the *store_image.pl* script, and some sample images are in its *flags* subdirectory (they're pictures of national flags for several countries). To store one of these images, run the script like this under Unix:

```
% ./store_image.pl flags/iceland.jpg image/jpeg
```

Or like this under Windows:

```
C:\> store_image.pl flags\iceland.jpg image/jpeg
```

store_image.pl takes care of image storage, and the next section discusses how to retrieve images to serve them over the Web. What about deleting images? I'll leave it to you to write a utility to remove images that you no longer want. If you are storing images in the filesystem, remember to delete both the database row *and* the image file that the row points to.

store_image.pl stores each image both in the database and in the filesystem for illustrative purposes, but of course that makes it inefficient. Earlier, I mentioned that if you use this script as a basis for your own applications, you should modify it to store images only in one place—either in the database or in the filesystem—not in both places. The modifications are as follows:

- To adapt the script to store images only in MySQL, there is no need to create an image directory, and you can delete the code that checks for that directory's existence and that writes image files there.
- To adapt the script for storage only in the filesystem, drop the `data` column from the `image` table, and modify the `REPLACE` statement so it doesn't refer to that column.

These modifications also apply to the *display_image.pl* image processing script shown in Recipe 18.7.

See Also

Recipe 18.7 shows how to retrieve images for display over the Web. Recipe 19.8 discusses how to upload images from a web page for storage into MySQL.

18.7 Retrieving Images or Other Binary Data

Problem

You can store images or other binary data values in your database, using the techniques discussed in Recipe 18.6. But how do you get them back out?

Solution

You need nothing more than a `SELECT` statement. Of course, what you *do* with the information after you retrieve it might be a little more involved.

Discussion

As described in Recipe 18.6, it's difficult to issue a statement manually that stores a literal image value into a database, so normally you use `LOAD_FILE()` or write a script that encodes the image data for insertion. However, there is no problem at all entering a statement that retrieves an image:

```
SELECT * FROM image WHERE id = 1;
```

But binary information tends not to show up well on text-display devices, so you probably don't want to do this interactively from the *mysql* program unless you want your terminal window to turn into a horrible mess of gibberish, or possibly even to lock up. It's more common to use the information for display in a web page. Or you might send it to the client for downloading, although that is more common for nonimage binary data such as PDF files. (Recipe 18.9 discusses downloading.)

To display an image in a web page, include an `<img>` tag in the page that tells the client's web browser where to get the image. If you've stored images as files in a directory that the web server has access to, you can refer to an image directly. For example, if the image file *iceland.jpg* is located in the */usr/local/lib/mcb/images* directory, you can reference it like this:

```
<img src="/usr/local/lib/mcb/images/iceland.jpg" />
```

If you use this approach, make sure that each image filename has an extension (such as *.gif* or *.png*) that enables the web server to determine what kind of Content-Type: header to generate when it sends the file to the client.

If the images are stored in a database table instead, or in a directory that is not accessible to the web server, the <img> tag can refer to a script that knows how to fetch images and send them to clients. To do this, the script should respond by sending a Content-Type: header that indicates the image format, a Content-Length: header that indicates the number of bytes of image data, a blank line, and finally the image itself as the body of the response.

The following script, *display_image.pl*, demonstrates how to serve images over the Web. It requires a name parameter that indicates which image to display, and allows an optional location parameter that specifies whether to retrieve the image from the image table or from the filesystem. The default is to retrieve image data from the image table. For example, the following URLs display an image from the database and from the filesystem, respectively:

```
http://localhost/cgi-bin/display_image.pl?name=iceland.jpg
http://localhost/cgi-bin/display_image.pl?name=iceland.jpg;location=fs
```

The script looks like this:

```perl
#!/usr/bin/perl
# display_image.pl - display image over the Web

use strict;
use warnings;
use CGI qw(:standard escapeHTML);
use FileHandle;
use Cookbook;

sub error
{
my $msg = escapeHTML ($_[0]);

  print header (), start_html ("Error"), p ($msg), end_html ();
  exit (0);
}

# -----------------------------------------------------------------------

# Default image storage directory and pathname separator
# (CHANGE THESE AS NECESSARY)
my $image_dir = "/usr/local/lib/mcb/images";
# The location should NOT be within the web server document tree
my $path_sep = "/";

# Reset directory and pathname separator for Windows/DOS
```

```perl
if ($^O =~ /^MSWin/i || $^O =~ /^dos/)
{
  $image_dir = "C:\\mcb\\images";
  $path_sep = "\\";
}

my $name = param ("name");
my $location = param ("location");

# make sure image name was specified
defined ($name) or error ("image name is missing");
# use default of "db" if the location is not specified or is
# not "db" or "fs"
(defined ($location) && $location eq "fs") or $location = "db";

my $dbh = Cookbook::connect ();

my ($type, $data);

# If location is "db", get image data and MIME type from image table.
# If location is "fs", get MIME type from image table and read the image
# data from the filesystem.

if ($location eq "db")
{
  ($type, $data) = $dbh->selectrow_array (
                        "SELECT type, data FROM image WHERE name = ?",
                        undef,
                        $name)
       or error ("Cannot find image with name $name");
}
else
{
  $type = $dbh->selectrow_array (
                        "SELECT type FROM image WHERE name = ?",
                        undef,
                        $name)
       or error ("Cannot find image with name $name");
  my $fh = new FileHandle;
  my $image_path = $image_dir . $path_sep . $name;
  open ($fh, $image_path)
    or error ("Cannot read $image_path: $!");
  binmode ($fh);     # helpful for binary data
  my $size = (stat ($fh))[7];
  read ($fh, $data, $size) == $size
    or error ("Failed to read entire file $image_path: $!");
  $fh->close ();
}

$dbh->disconnect ();

# Send image to client, preceded by Content-Type: and Content-Length:
# headers.
```

```
print header (-type => $type, -Content_Length => length ($data));
print $data;
```

18.8 Serving Banner Ads

Problem

You want to display banner ads by choosing images on the fly from a set of images.

Solution

Use a script that selects a random row from an image table and sends the image to the client.

Discussion

The *display_image.pl* script shown in Recipe 18.7 assumes that the URL contains a parameter that names the image to be sent to the client. Another application might determine which image to display for itself. One popular image-related use for web programming is to serve banner advertisements for display in web pages. A simple way to do this is by means of a script that picks an image at random each time it is invoked. The following Python script, *banner.py*, shows how to do this, where the "ads" are the flag images in the image table:

```
#!/usr/bin/python
# banner.py - serve randomly chosen banner ad from image table
# (sends no response if no image can be found)

import MySQLdb
import Cookbook

conn = Cookbook.connect ()

stmt = "SELECT type, data FROM image ORDER BY RAND() LIMIT 1"
cursor = conn.cursor ()
cursor.execute (stmt)
row = cursor.fetchone ()
cursor.close ()
if row is not None:
  (type, data) = row
  # Send image to client, preceded by Content-Type: and
  # Content-Length: headers.  The Expires:, Cache-Control:, and
  # Pragma: headers help keep browsers from caching the image
  # and reusing it for successive requests for this script.
  print "Content-Type: %s" % type
  print "Content-Length: %s" % len (data)
  print "Expires: Sat, 01 Jan 2000 00:00:00 GMT"
  print "Cache-Control: no-cache"
  print "Pragma: no-cache"
  print ""
```

```
    print data

  conn.close ()
```

banner.py sends a few headers in addition to the usual `Content-Type:` and `Content-Length:` headers. The extra headers help keep browsers from caching the image. `Expires:` specifies a date in the past to tell the browser that the image is out of date. The `Cache-Control:` and `Pragma:` headers tell the browser not to cache the image. The script sends both headers because some browsers understand one, and some the other.

Why suppress caching? Because if you don't, the browser will send a request for *banner.py* only the first time it sees it in a link. On subsequent requests for the script, the browser will reuse the image, which rather defeats the intent of having each such link resolve to a randomly chosen image.

Install the *banner.py* script in your *cgi-bin* directory. Then, to place a banner in a web page, use an `<img>` tag that invokes the script. For example, if the script is installed as */cgi-bin/banner.py*, the following page references it to include an image below the introductory paragraph:

```
<!-- bannertest1.html - page with single link to banner-ad script -->
<html>
<head>
<title>Banner Ad Test Page 1</title>
</head>
<body bgcolor="white">

<p>You should see an image below this paragraph.</p>

<img src="/cgi-bin/banner.py" />

</body>
</html>
```

If you request this page, it should display an image, and you should see a succession of randomly chosen images each time you reload the page. (I am assuming here that you have loaded several images into the `image` table by now using the *store_image.pl* script discussed in Recipe 18.6. Otherwise you won't see any images at all!) If you modify *banner.py* not to send the cache-related headers, you likely will see the same image each time you reload the page.

The cache-control headers suppress caching for links to *banner.py* that occur over the course of successive page requests. Another complication occurs if multiple links to the script occur within the *same* page. The following page illustrates what happens:

```
<!-- bannertest2.html - page with multiple links to banner-ad script -->
<html>
<head>
<title>Banner Ad Test Page 2</title>
</head>
<body bgcolor="white">
```

```
<p>You should see two images below this paragraph,
and they probably will be the same.</p>

<img src="/cgi-bin/banner.py" />
<img src="/cgi-bin/banner.py" />

<p>You should see two images below this paragraph,
and they probably will be different.</p>

<img src="/cgi-bin/banner.py?image1" />
<img src="/cgi-bin/banner.py?image2" />

</body>
</html>
```

The first pair of links to *banner.py* are identical. What you'll probably find when you
request this page is that your browser will notice that fact, send only a single request
to the web server, and use the image that is returned where both links appear in the
page. As a result, the first pair of images displayed in the page will be identical. The
second pair of links to *banner.py* show how to solve this problem. The links include
some extra fluff at the end of the URLs that make them look different. *banner.py* doesn't
use that information at all, but making the links look different fools the browser into
sending two image requests. The result is that the second pair of images will differ from
each other—unless *banner.py* happens to randomly select the same image both times,
of course.

18.9 Serving Query Results for Download

Problem

You want to send database information to a browser for downloading rather than for
display.

Solution

Unfortunately, there's no good way to force a download. A browser will process information sent to it according to the `Content-Type:` header value, and if it has a handler
for that value, it will treat the information accordingly. However, you may be able to
trick the browser by using a "generic" content type for which it's unlikely to have a
handler.

Discussion

Earlier sections of this chapter discuss how to incorporate the results of database queries
into web pages, to display them as paragraphs, lists, tables, or images. But what if you
want to produce a query result that the user can download to a file instead? It's not
difficult to generate the response itself: send a `Content-Type:` header preceding the in-

formation, such as `text/plain` for plain text, `image/jpeg` for a JPEG image, or `application/pdf` or `application/msexcel` for a PDF or Excel document. Then send a blank line and the content of the query result. The problem is that there's no way to force the browser to download the information. If it knows what to do with the response based on the content type, it will try to handle the information as it sees fit. If it knows how to display text or images, it will. If it thinks it's supposed to give a PDF or Excel document to a PDF viewer or to Excel, it will. Most browsers enable the user to select a download explicitly (for example, by right-clicking or Ctrl-clicking on a link), but that's a client-side mechanism. You have no access to it on the server end.

About the only thing you can do is try to fool the browser by faking the content type. The most generic type is `application/octet-stream`. Most users are unlikely to have any content handler specified for it, so if you send a response using that type, it's likely to trigger a download by the browser. The disadvantage of this, of course, is that the response contains a false indicator about the type of information it contains. You can try to alleviate this problem by suggesting a default filename for the browser to use when it saves the file. If the filename has a suffix indicative of the file type, such as *.txt*, *.jpg*, *.pdf*, or *.xls*, that may help the client (or the operating system on the client host) determine how to process the file. To suggest a name, include a `Content-Disposition:` header in the response that looks like this:

```
Content-disposition: attachment; filename="suggested_name"
```

The following PHP script, *download.php*, demonstrates one way to produce downloadable content. When first invoked, it presents a page containing a link that can be selected to initiate the download. The link points back to *download.php* but includes a `download` parameter. When you select the link, it reinvokes the script, which sees the parameter and responds by issuing a query, retrieving a result set, and sending it to the browser for downloading. The `Content-Type:` and `Content-Disposition:` headers in the response are set by invoking the `header( )` function. (This must be done before the script produces any other output, or `header( )` will have no effect.)

```php
<?php
# download.php - retrieve result set and send it to user as a download
# rather than for display in a web page

require_once "Cookbook.php";
require_once "Cookbook_Webutils.php";

$title = "Result Set Downloading Example";

# If no download parameter is present, display instruction page

if (!get_param_val ("download"))
{
  # construct self-referential URL that includes download parameter
  $url = get_self_path () . "?download=1";
?>

<html>
```

```
<head>
<title><?php print ($title); ?></title>
</head>
<body bgcolor="white">

<p>
Select the following link to commence downloading:
<a href="<?php print ($url); ?>">download</a>
</p>

</body>
</html>

<?php
  exit ();
} # end of "if"

# The download parameter was present; retrieve a result set and send
# it to the client as a tab-delimited, newline-terminated document.
# Use a content type of application/octet-stream in an attempt to
# trigger a download response by the browser, and suggest a default
# filename of "result.txt".

$conn =& Cookbook::connect ();
if (PEAR::isError ($conn))
  die ("Cannot connect to server: "
       . htmlspecialchars ($conn->getMessage ()));

$stmt = "SELECT * FROM profile";
$result =& $conn->query ($stmt);
if (PEAR::isError ($result))
  die ("Cannot execute query: "
       . htmlspecialchars ($result->getMessage ()));

header ("Content-Type: application/octet-stream");
header ("Content-Disposition: attachment; filename=\"result.txt\"");

while ($row =& $result->fetchRow ())
  print (join ("\t", $row) . "\n");
$result->free ();

$conn->disconnect ();

?>
```

download.php uses a couple of functions that we haven't covered yet:

- `get_self_path( )` returns the script's own pathname. This is used to construct a URL that points back to the script and that includes a `download` parameter.

- `get_param_val( )` determines whether that parameter is present.

These functions are included in the *Cookbook_Webutils.php* file and are discussed further in Recipes 19.1 and 19.5.

Another way to produce downloadable content is to generate the query result, write it to a file on the server side, compress it, and send the result to the browser. The browser likely will run some kind of uncompress utility to recover the original file.

18.10 Using a Template System to Generate Web Pages

Problem

Your scripts mix the code for retrieving information from your database with the code for generating HTML. You want to decouple these activities so that they can be performed separately.

Solution

Use a template system that enables you to design the general layout of the page but plug in specific data on a request-specific basis. Then you can obtain the data separately and pass it to the template system for output generation.

Discussion

In this chapter, we've been using an approach that retrieves data for a web page and generates the HTML for the page all in the same script. That has the advantage of simplicity, but there are disadvantages as well, and there are alternatives.

The primary disadvantage of mixing everything together is that there is little functional decoupling (separation of function) between the logic involved in obtaining the data needed for the page (the business or application logic) and the logic that formats the data for display (the presentation logic).

An alternative approach to web page generation is to use some kind of template system that enables functional decomposition of phases of the page-generation process. A template system does this by separating business logic from the presentation logic. If you're partial to the Model-View-Controller (MVC) architecture, templates help you implement MVC logic by taking care of the View part.

There are many template packages to choose from, as a few minutes searching the Internet quickly reveals. Here, we'll briefly explore two (PageTemplate for Ruby and Smarty for PHP), each of which uses the following approach:

1. The web server invokes a script in response to a client request for a web page.

2. The script determines what must be displayed and retrieves any data necessary to make that happen.

3. The script calls the template engine, passing a page template to it along with the data to insert into the template.

4. The template engine looks for special markers in the template that indicate where to insert data values, replaces them with the appropriate values, and produces the result as its output. The output is the web page that is sent to the client as the response to the client's request.

Typically, template engines are used in web contexts to produce HTML, but depending on your requirements, you could produce other formats such as plain text or XML.

A template system provides the benefits of functional decoupling in the following way:

- A programmer can change the implementation of how to obtain the information to be displayed without caring about what it will look like when displayed. For example, if you want to change database systems, you can do that in the application logic without requiring changes to any templates (the presentation logic).

- A page designer can change the way information is displayed by changing the templates, without knowing anything about how to obtain the information. It could come from a file, a database, or whatever. The designer simply assumes that the information is available and doesn't care where it comes from. In particular, the designer doesn't need to know how to write programs.

That last sentence might be considered subject to debate. Although it's true that page designers do not, for the most part, need to know a programming language, it's also true that templates are embedded with special markers that indicate where to substitute data values. Depending on the complexity of the data to be displayed and the markup syntax of the template package, the markup can range from very simple to looking like a program itself! Nevertheless, it's easier to understand template markers than a general-purpose programming language.

In this section, we'll revisit some of the topics that were addressed earlier in the chapter: Generating paragraphs (Recipe 18.1), lists (Recipe 18.2), and tables (Recipe 18.3). But here we'll consider how to create these structures in web pages by designing page templates for PageTemplate and Smarty. Before doing so, the discussion begins for each template package with a short tutorial that shows how to use markup for the following concepts:

Value substitution
    How to indicate where to substitute values into a template. A given value can be substituted as is, or it can be subjected to HTML-encoding or URL-encoding first.

Conditional testing
    How to select or ignore part of a template based on the result of a test.

Iteration (looping)
    How to process part of a template repeatedly, once per element of a data structure such as an array or hash. This is useful for generating lists and tables.

Appendix A indicates where to get PageTemplate and Smarty. I assume in the remainder of this recipe that you have already installed them. The example templates and scripts discussed here can be found under the *apache* directory of the `recipes` distribution, in the *pagetemplate* and *smarty* subdirectories.

The examples use *.tmpl* as the extension for template files, but there is no requirement for either template package that you use that particular extension. (For example, Smarty applications often use *.tpl*.)

Using page template for web page generation in Ruby

A PageTemplate web application consists of an HTML template file for the output page, and a Ruby script that gathers the data needed by the template and calls the template engine to process the template. In PageTemplate, the markup indicators are [% and %]. The content between the markers tells PageTemplate what action to perform.

Value substitution. To indicate where a value goes in a PageTemplate template file, use a [%var *var_name*%] directive:

```
[%var myvar%]
```

PageTemplate replaces the directive with the value of the *var_name* variable. By default, the value is substituted as is. To perform HTML-encoding or URL-encoding of the value, add the appropriate preprocessor name to the directive:

```
[%var myvar :escapeHTML%]
[%var myvar :escapeURI%]
```

`:escapeHTML` has the same effect as invoking `CGI.escapeHTML( )` to make sure that special characters such as `<` or `&` are converted to the corresponding `&lt;` and `&amp;` entities. `:escapeURI` has the same effect as `CGI.escape( )`.

Any value referred to by a [%var%] directive must be a string, or able to produce a string if the `to_s` method is applied to it.

Conditional testing. A conditional test begins with an [%if *var_name*%] directive, ends with [%endif%], and optionally contains an [%else%] directive:

```
[%if myvar%]
  myvar is true
[%else%]
  myvar is false
[%endif%]
```

If `myvar` evaluates to true, PageTemplate processes the content following the [%if%] directive. Otherwise, it processes the content following [%else%]. For a simple conditional with no "else" part, omit the [%else%] part.

Iteration. The [%in *var_name*%] construct provides iteration over the members of the list named by the given variable. The template content between the [%in%] and [%endin%] directives is processed once per member. If the list members are hashes, you can refer to the hash elements by name. Suppose that `mylist` is an array consisting of items, each of which is a hash with this structure:

```
{ "first_name" => value, "last_name" => value }
```

The hash members are `first_name` and `last_name`, so an iterator can process the list and refer to its item members as follows:

```
[%in mylist%]
  Name: [%var first_name%] [%var last_name%]
[%endin%]
```

If the list is a simple indexed list, its elements don't have names. In that case, you can provide a name in the [%in%] directive by which to refer to the elements:

```
[%in mylist: myitem%]
  Item: [%var myitem%]
[%endin%]
```

The following template file, *pt_demo.tmpl*, demonstrates the concepts just discussed:

```
<!-- pt_demo.tmpl -->
<html>
<head>
<title>PageTemplate Demonstration</title>
</head>
<body>

<p>Value substitution:</p>
<p>
  My name is [%var character_name%],
  and I am [%var character_role%].
</p>

<p>Value substitution with encoding:</p>
<p>
  HTML-encoding: [%var str_to_encode :escapeHTML%];
  URL-encoding: [%var str_to_encode :escapeURI%]
</p>

<p>Conditional testing:</p>
<p>
  [%if id%]
    You requested information for item number [%var id%].
  [%else%]
    You didn't choose any item!
  [%endif%]
</p>

<p>Iteration:</p>
<p>
  Colors of the rainbow:
  [%in colors: color%]
    [%var color%]
  [%endin%]
</p>
</body>
</html>
```

We also need a script to go with the template. The basic skeleton of a Ruby script that uses PageTemplate looks like this:

```
#!/usr/bin/ruby -w

# Access required modules
require "PageTemplate"
require "cgi"

...obtain data to be displayed in the output page...

# Create template object
pt = PageTemplate.new

# Load template file
pt.load("template_file_name")

# Assign values to template variables
pt["var_name1"] = value1
pt["var_name2"] = value2
...

# Generate output (cgi.out adds headers)
cgi = CGI.new("html4")
cgi.out { pt.output }
```

The script begins by including the required Ruby library files: PageTemplate to generate the page, and cgi because its out method provides an easy way to send the page to the client complete with any required headers.

The next steps are to create a template object, load the template file, and associate values with the variables named in the template. The filename should be an absolute variable or a pathname relative to the script's current working directory at the point when the template object is created. The syntax for assigning a value to a template variable is similar to hash-value assignment:

```
pt["var_name"] = value
```

Finally, the script generates output. This is done with the template object's output method. As shown, the script prints output from the template using the cgi object's out method, which takes care of adding the page headers.

We can adapt that skeleton to write a *pt_demo.rb* script that accompanies the *pt_demo.tmpl* template file:

```
#!/usr/bin/ruby -w
# pt_demo.rb - PageTemplate demonstration script

require "PageTemplate"
require "cgi"

pt = PageTemplate.new
pt.load("pt_demo.tmpl")
pt["character_name"] = "Peregrine Pickle"
pt["character_role"] = "a young country gentleman"
pt["str_to_encode"] = "encoded text: (<>&'\" =;)"
pt["id"] = 47846
```

```
pt["colors"] = ["red","orange","yellow","green","blue","indigo","violet"]

cgi = CGI.new("html4")
cgi.out { pt.output }
```

To try the application, copy the *pt_demo.rb* and *pt_demo.tmpl* files to your Ruby web script directory and then request the script with your web browser. For example, if you copy the files to your usual *cgi-bin* directory, use this URL to request the script:

```
http://localhost/cgi-bin/pt_demo.rb
```

You might prefer to install the *.tmpl* file somewhere other than the *cgi-bin* directory because it isn't an executable file. If you do that, adjust the pathname in the `pt.load` call.

The preceding tutorial is sufficient background for developing templates to produce paragraphs, lists, and tables that display information retrieved from MySQL.

Paragraph generation. Our first PageTemplate-based MySQL application requires only the production of simple paragraphs. The application is patterned after the discussion in Recipe 18.1. The scripts developed there connect to the MySQL server, issue a query to retrieve some information, and write out a few paragraphs to report the query result: the current time, the server version, the MySQL username, and the current database. For an equivalent PageTemplate application, we need a template file and a Ruby script, here named *pt_paragraphs.tmpl* and *pt_paragraphs.rb*.

Begin by designing the page template. For this application, the template is quite simple. It requires only simple value substitution, not conditionals or iterators. Use the [%var *var_name%*] construct to make a template for a page containing simple paragraphs:

```
<!-- pt_paragraphs.tmpl -->
<html>
<head>
<title>[%var title :escapeHTML%]</title>
</head>
<body bgcolor="white">

<p>Local time on the MySQL server is [%var now :escapeHTML%].</p>
<p>The server version is [%var version :escapeHTML%].</p>
<p>The current user is [%var user :escapeHTML%].</p>
<p>The default database is [%var db :escapeHTML%].</p>

</body>
</html>
```

The *pt_paragraphs.tmpl* template uses `:escapeHTML` in the [%var%] directives based on the assumption that we don't necessarily have much knowledge about whether the data values contain special characters. That completes the page design.

Next, write the Ruby script that retrieves the data and invokes the template engine. The directives embedded within the template indicate that the accompanying script will need to provide values for template variables named `title`, `now`, `version`, `user`, and `db`:

```
#!/usr/bin/ruby -w
# pt_paragraphs.rb - generate HTML paragraphs

require "PageTemplate"
require "cgi"
require "Cookbook"

title = "Query Output Display - Paragraphs"

dbh = Cookbook.connect

# Retrieve data required for template
(now, version, user, db) =
  dbh.select_one("SELECT NOW(), VERSION(), USER(), DATABASE()")
db = "NONE" if db.nil?

dbh.disconnect

pt = PageTemplate.new
pt.load("pt_paragraphs.tmpl")
pt["title"] = title
pt["now"] = now
pt["version"] = version
pt["user"] = user
pt["db"] = db

cgi = CGI.new("html4")
cgi.out { pt.output }
```

This script is a lot like the *pt_demo.rb* script discussed earlier. The main differences are that it uses the Cookbook module (for its connect method) and it obtains the data required for the page template by connecting to MySQL and issuing queries.

List generation. Lists contain repeating elements, so they are produced with the Page-Template [%in%] directive that iterates through a list. The following template generates an ordered list, an unordered list, and a definition list:

```
<!-- pt_lists.tmpl -->
<html>
<head>
<title>[%var title :escapeHTML%]</title>
</head>
<body bgcolor="white">

<p>Ordered list:</p>

<ol>
[%in list: item %]
  <li>[%var item :escapeHTML%]</li>
[%endin%]
</ol>

<p>Unordered list:</p>

<ul>
```

```
[%in list: item %]
  <li>[%var item :escapeHTML%]</li>
[%endin%]
</ul>

<p>Definition list:</p>

<dl>
[%in defn_list%]
  <dt>[%var note :escapeHTML%]</dt>
  <dd>[%var mnemonic :escapeHTML%]</dd>
[%endin%]
</dl>

</body>
</html>
```

The first two lists differ only in the surrounding tags (<ol> versus <ul>), and they use the same data for the list items. The values come from a simple array, so we provide another argument to the [%in%] directive that associates a name (item) with values in the list and gives us a way to refer to them.

For the definition list, each item requires both a term and a definition. We'll assume that the script can provide a list of structured values that have members named note and mnemonic.

The script that retrieves the list data from MySQL and processes the template looks like this:

```
#!/usr/bin/ruby -w
# pt_lists.rb - generate HTML lists

require "PageTemplate"
require "cgi"
require "Cookbook"

title = "Query Output Display - Lists"

dbh = Cookbook.connect

# Fetch items for ordered, unordered lists
# (create an array of "scalar" values; the list actually consists of
# DBI::Row objects, but for single-column rows, applying the to_s
# method to each object results in the column value)

stmt = "SELECT item FROM ingredient ORDER BY id"
list = dbh.select_all(stmt)

# Fetch terms and definitions for a definition list
# (create a list of hash values, one hash per row)

defn_list = []
stmt = "SELECT note, mnemonic FROM doremi ORDER BY id"
dbh.execute(stmt) do |sth|
  sth.fetch_hash do |row|
```

```
      defn_list << row
    end
  end

  dbh.disconnect

  pt = PageTemplate.new
  pt.load("pt_lists.tmpl")
  pt["title"] = title
  pt["list"] = list
  pt["defn_list"] = defn_list

  cgi = CGI.new("html4")
  cgi.out { pt.output }
```

Recall that for the definition list, the template expects that the list items are structured values containing `note` and `mnemonic` members. The script should satisfy this requirement by creating an array of hashes, in which each hash is of this form:

```
  { "note" => val1, "mnemonic" => val2 }
```

This is easily accomplished by selecting the `note` and `mnemonic` columns from the table that contains the data, and using the `fetch_hash` function to retrieve the rows as hashes.

Table generation. Designing a template for an HTML table is similar to designing one for a list because they both have repeating elements and thus use iterators. For a table, the repeating element is the row (using the `<tr>` element). Within each row, you write the values for the cells using `<td>` elements. The natural data structure for this is an array of hashes, where each hash has elements keyed by the column names.

The example shown here displays the contents of the `cd` table, which has three columns: `year`, `artist`, and `title`. Assuming that we use a template variable named `rows` to hold the table contents, the following template generates the table. Actually, the template generates the table *twice* (once with all rows the same color, and once with alternating row colors):

```
  <!-- pt_tables.tmpl -->
  <html>
  <head>
  <title>[%var title :escapeHTML%]</title>
  </head>
  <body bgcolor="white">

  <p>HTML table:</p>

  <table border="1">
  <tr>
    <th>Year</th>
    <th>Artist</th>
    <th>Title</th>
  </tr>
  [%in rows%]
    <tr>
      <td>[%var year :escapeHTML%]</td>
```

```
      <td>[%var artist :escapeHTML%]</td>
      <td>[%var title :escapeHTML%]</td>
    </tr>
[%endin%]
</table>

<p>HTML table with rows in alternating colors:</p>

<table border="1">
<tr>
  <th bgcolor="silver">Year</th>
  <th bgcolor="silver">Artist</th>
  <th bgcolor="silver">Title</th>
</tr>
[%in rows%]
  [%if __ODD__ %]
  <tr bgcolor="white">
  [%else%]
  <tr bgcolor="silver">
  [%endif%]
    <td>[%var year :escapeHTML%]</td>
    <td>[%var artist :escapeHTML%]</td>
    <td>[%var title :escapeHTML%]</td>
  </tr>
[%endin%]
</table>

</body>
</html>
```

The first table template generates a "plain" table. The second template generates a table that has alternating row colors. Switching between colors is easy to do by using a conditional directive that tests the value of the built-in __ODD__ variable that is true for every odd-numbered row.

To fetch the table data and process the template, use this script:

```
#!/usr/bin/ruby -w
# pt_tables.rb - generate HTML tables

require "PageTemplate"
require "cgi"
require "Cookbook"

title = "Query Output Display - Tables"

dbh = Cookbook.connect

# Fetch table rows
# (create a list of hash values, one hash per row)

rows = []
stmt = "SELECT year, artist, title FROM cd ORDER BY artist, year"
dbh.execute(stmt) do |sth|
  sth.fetch_hash do |row|
```

```
      rows << row
    end
  end

  dbh.disconnect

  pt = PageTemplate.new
  pt.load("pt_tables.tmpl")
  pt["title"] = title
  pt["rows"] = rows

  cgi = CGI.new("html4")
  cgi.out { pt.output }
```

Using Smarty for web page generation in PHP

A Smarty web application consists of an HTML template file for the output page, and a PHP script that gathers the data needed by the template and calls the template engine to process the template. In Smarty templates, the markup indicators are { and }, which surround the commands that tell Smarty what actions you want taken.

Value substitution. To indicate where to substitute a value in a Smarty template, use {$*var_name*} notation. The substitution uses the value with no preprocessing. If you want to HTML-encode or URL-encode the value, add a modifier. The following three lines substitute a value without modification, with HTML-encoding, and with URL-encoding, respectively:

```
{$myvar}
{$myvar|escape}
{$myvar|escape:"url"}
```

Conditional testing. A conditional test begins with {if *expr*}, ends with {/if}, and optionally contains one or more {elseif *expr*} clauses and an {else} clause. Each *expr* can be a variable or a more complex expression (unlike PageTemplate, which allows only a variable name). Here is a simple if-then-else test:

```
{if $myvar}
  myvar is true
{else}
  myvar is false
{/if}
```

Iteration. Smarty has multiple iterator constructs. The {foreach} command names the variable containing the list of values to iterate over and indicates the name by which the body of the loop will refer to each value. The following construct specifies $mylist as the name of the list and uses myitem for the list item name:

```
{foreach from=$mylist item=myitem}
  {$myitem}
{/foreach}
```

The {section} command names the variable containing the list of values and the name to use for subscripting the list variable within the loop:

```
{section loop=$mylist name=myitem}
  {$mylist[myitem]}
{/section}
```

Note that the syntax for referring to list items is different for `{section}` than for
`{foreach}`. The `$mylist[myitem]` syntax shown is useful for iterating through a list of
scalar values. If you need to iterate through structured values such as associative arrays,
refer to structure members as `$mylist[myitem].`*member_name*. The list and table applications discussed later illustrate this syntax further.

The following template file, *sm_demo.tmpl*, demonstrates the preceding concepts:

```
<!-- sm_demo.tmpl -->
<html>
<head>
<title>Smarty Demonstration</title>
</head>
<body>

<p>Value substitution:</p>
<p>
  My name is {$character_name},
  and I am {$character_role}.
</p>

<p>Value substitution with encoding:</p>
<p>
  HTML-encoding: {$str_to_encode|escape};
  URL-encoding: {$str_to_encode|escape:"url"}
</p>

<p>Conditional testing:</p>
<p>
  {if $id}
    You requested information for item number {$id}.
  {else}
    You didn't choose any item!
  {/if}
</p>

<p>Iteration:</p>
<p>
  Colors of the rainbow (using foreach):
  {foreach from=$colors item=color}
    {$color}
  {/foreach}
</p>
<p>
  Colors of the rainbow (using section):
  {section loop=$colors name=color}
    {$colors[color]}
  {/section}
</p>
</body>
</html>
```

We also need a script to accompany the template. An outline for a PHP script that uses Smarty looks like this:

```php
<?php
require_once "Smarty.class.php";

...obtain data to be displayed in the output page...

# Create template object
$smarty = new Smarty ();

# Assign values to template variables
$smarty->assign ("var_name1", value1);
$smarty->assign ("var_name2", value2);
...

# Process the template to produce output
$smarty->display("template_file_name");
?>
```

The *Smarty.class.php* file gives you access to Smarty's capabilities. As mentioned earlier, I assume that you have Smarty installed already. To make it easy for your PHP scripts to access the *Smarty.class.php* file without having to specify its full pathname, you should add the directory where that file is located to the value of the `include_path` configuration variable in your *php.ini* file. For example, if *Smarty.class.php* is installed in */usr/local/lib/php/smarty*, add that directory to the value of `include_path`.

The rest of the skeleton shows the essential steps for using Smarty: create a new Smarty template object, specify values for template variables with `assign( )`, and then pass the template filename to the `display( )` object to generate the output.

The skeleton is easily adapted to produce the following script, *sm_demo.php*, to go along with the *sm_demo.tmpl* template:

```php
<?php
# sm_demo.php - Smarty demonstration script

require_once "Smarty.class.php";

$smarty = new Smarty ();

$smarty->assign ("character_name", "Peregrine Pickle");
$smarty->assign ("character_role", "a young country gentleman");
$smarty->assign ("str_to_encode", "encoded text: (<>&'\" =;)");
$smarty->assign ("id", 47846);
$colors = array ("red","orange","yellow","green","blue","indigo","violet");
$smarty->assign ("colors", $colors);

$smarty->display ("sm_demo.tmpl");
?>
```

We now have a simple Smarty application (the template file and the PHP script that uses it), but a bit of additional setup is required before we can deploy the application. Smarty uses a set of directories to do its work, so you'll need to create them first. By default, Smarty assumes that these directories are located in the same directory where the PHP script is installed. The following instructions assume that this directory is *mcb* under your Apache document root (the same PHP directory that has been used throughout this chapter).

Change location to the *mcb* directory and create these four directories:

```
% mkdir cache
% mkdir configs
% mkdir templates
% mkdir templates_c
```

The directories you just created must be readable by the web server, and two of them must also be writable. To do this on Unix, set the group permissions appropriately, and then change their group to be that used by the web server. Set the group permissions with these commands:

```
% chmod g+rx cache configs templates templates_c
% chmod g+w cache templates_c
```

Next, determine the correct group name to use for the directories. To do this, look in the Apache *httpd.conf* file for a `Group` line, which might look like this:

```
Group www
```

That line indicates that Apache runs using the `www` group ID. Other common values are `nobody` or `apache`. Use the group name in the following command, which should be executed as `root`:

```
# chgrp www cache configs templates templates_c
```

That completes the Smarty directory setup. You can deploy the Smarty demonstration application by copying *sm_demo.php* to the *mcb* directory and *sm_demo.tmpl* to the *mcb/templates* directory. Then request the script with your web browser:

```
http://localhost/mcb/sm_demo.php
```

For each of the following applications, follow the same principle that the PHP script goes in the *mcb* directory and the Smarty template goes in *mcb/templates*.

If you want to keep your application subdirectories outside of your document tree, create them somewhere other than in the *mcb* directory. In this case, you need to let your PHP scripts know where they are by setting several members of your Smarty object after you create it. For example, if you create the Smarty directories under */usr/local/lib/mcb/smarty*, you modify your scripts to tell Smarty about their location as follows:

```
$smarty = new Smarty ();
$smarty->cache_dir = "/usr/local/lib/mcb/smarty/cache";
$smarty->config_dir = "/usr/local/lib/mcb/smarty/configs";
$smarty->template_dir = "/usr/local/lib/mcb/smarty/templates";
$smarty->compile_dir = "/usr/local/lib/mcb/smarty/templates_c";
```

Paragraph generation. The Smarty equivalent to the PageTemplate file shown earlier for generating paragraphs is as follows:

```
<!-- sm_paragraphs.tmpl -->
<html>
<head>
<title>{$title|escape}</title>
</head>
<body bgcolor="white">

<p>Local time on the MySQL server is {$now|escape}.</p>
<p>The server version is {$version|escape}.</p>
<p>The current user is {$user|escape}.</p>
<p>The default database is {$db|escape}.</p>

</body>
</html>
```

The template uses nothing more than {$*var_name*} value substitution, plus the escape modifier to tell Smarty to perform HTML-escaping on the values.

To retrieve the data referred to in the template and then invoke Smarty, use this script:

```
<?php
# sm_paragraphs.php - generate HTML paragraphs

require_once "Smarty.class.php";
require_once "Cookbook.php";

$title = "Query Output Display - Paragraphs";

$conn =& Cookbook::connect ();
if (PEAR::isError ($conn))
  die ("Cannot connect to server: "
       . htmlspecialchars ($conn->getMessage ()));

$result =& $conn->query ("SELECT NOW(), VERSION(), USER(), DATABASE()");
if (PEAR::isError ($result))
  die (htmlspecialchars ($result->getMessage ()));
list ($now, $version, $user, $db) = $result->fetchRow ();
$result->free ();
if (!isset ($db))
  $db = "NONE";

$conn->disconnect ();

$smarty = new Smarty ();
$smarty->assign ("title", $title);
$smarty->assign ("now", $now);
$smarty->assign ("version", $version);
$smarty->assign ("user", $user);
$smarty->assign ("db", $db);
$smarty->display ("sm_paragraphs.tmpl");

?>
```

List generation. The following template generates three lists. The first two are ordered and unordered lists that use the same set of scalar item values. The third list is a definition list that requires two values per iteration through a set of items:

```
<!-- sm_lists.tmpl -->
<html>
<head>
<title>{$title|escape}</title>
</head>
<body bgcolor="white">

<p>Ordered list:</p>

<ol>
{foreach from=$list item=cur_item}
  <li>{$cur_item|escape}</li>
{/foreach}
</ol>

<p>Unordered list:</p>

<ul>
{foreach from=$list item=cur_item}
  <li>{$cur_item|escape}</li>
{/foreach}
</ul>

<p>Definition list:</p>

<dl>
{section loop=$defn_list name=cur_item}
  <dt>{$defn_list[cur_item].note|escape}</dt>
  <dd>{$defn_list[cur_item].mnemonic|escape}</dd>
{/section}
</dl>

</body>
</html>
```

The definition list uses the {section} command and the $*list*[*item*].*member* notation mentioned earlier for referring to members of structured values.

The script that processes the template needs to fetch the values for the ordered and unordered lists as an array of scalar values. For the definition list, the script should create an array of associative arrays that have members named note and mnemonic:

```
<?php
# sm_lists.php - generate HTML lists

require_once "Smarty.class.php";
require_once "Cookbook.php";

$title = "Query Output Display - Lists";

$conn =& Cookbook::connect ();
```

```
if (PEAR::isError ($conn))
  die ("Cannot connect to server: "
      . htmlspecialchars ($conn->getMessage ()));

# Fetch items for ordered, unordered lists
# (create an array of scalar values)

$stmt = "SELECT item FROM ingredient ORDER BY id";
$result =& $conn->query ($stmt);
if (PEAR::isError ($result))
  die (htmlspecialchars ($result->getMessage ()));
$list = array ();
while (list ($item) = $result->fetchRow ())
  $list[] = $item;
$result->free ();

# Fetch terms and definitions for a definition list
# (create an array of associative arrays)

$stmt = "SELECT note, mnemonic FROM doremi ORDER BY id";
$defn_list =& $conn->getAll ($stmt, array (), DB_FETCHMODE_ASSOC);
if (PEAR::isError ($defn_list))
  die (htmlspecialchars ($result->getMessage ()));

$conn->disconnect ();

$smarty = new Smarty ();
$smarty->assign ("title", $title);
$smarty->assign ("list", $list);
$smarty->assign ("defn_list", $defn_list);
$smarty->display ("sm_lists.tmpl");

?>
```

The script uses getAll( ) to fetch the values for the definition list. This is a connection object method that executes a query and retrieves the result set in a single call. By setting the fetch mode to DB_FETCHMODE_ASSOC, you get an array of associative arrays, each of which has members named note and mnemonic—perfect for creating an HTML definition list in Smarty.

Table generation. To generate an HTML table, we need an iterator for looping through the list of rows to produce a <tr> element per row. As with the definition list in the previous application, this is easily done by using a {section} command and referring to the values for cells within the row by using $list[item].member syntax. The following script uses that syntax to generate two tables (one "plain" table, and one that has alternating row colors):

```
<!-- sm_tables.tmpl -->
<html>
<head>
<title>{$title|escape}</title>
</head>
<body bgcolor="white">
```

```
<p>HTML table:</p>

<table border="1">
<tr>
  <th>Year</th>
  <th>Artist</th>
  <th>Title</th>
</tr>
{section loop=$rows name=row}
  <tr>
    <td>{$rows[row].year|escape}</td>
    <td>{$rows[row].artist|escape}</td>
    <td>{$rows[row].title|escape}</td>
  </tr>
{/section}
</table>

<p>HTML table with rows in alternating colors:</p>

<table border="1">
<tr>
  <th bgcolor="silver">Year</th>
  <th bgcolor="silver">Artist</th>
  <th bgcolor="silver">Title</th>
</tr>
{section loop=$rows name=row}
  <tr bgcolor="{cycle values="white,silver"}">
    <td>{$rows[row].year|escape}</td>
    <td>{$rows[row].artist|escape}</td>
    <td>{$rows[row].title|escape}</td>
  </tr>
{/section}
</table>

</body>
</html>
```

To produce alternating row colors for the second table, the template uses a {cycle}
command, which alternately selects white and silver for successive iterations through
the row list. {cycle} provides a nice convenience here for a task that you would otherwise handle using a conditional and the $smarty.section.*list*.iteration value that
returns the current iteration number (beginning with 1):

```
{if $smarty.section.row.iteration % 2 == 1}
<tr bgcolor="white">
{else}
<tr bgcolor="silver">
{/if}
```

The following script fetches the table rows and processes the template:

```
<?php
# smtables.php - generate HTML tables

require_once "Smarty.class.php";
```

```php
require_once "Cookbook.php";

$title = "Query Output Display - Tables";

$conn =& Cookbook::connect ();
if (PEAR::isError ($conn))
  die ("Cannot connect to server: "
       . htmlspecialchars ($conn->getMessage ()));

# Fetch items for table

$stmt = "SELECT year, artist, title FROM cd ORDER BY artist, year";
$rows =& $conn->getAll ($stmt, array (), DB_FETCHMODE_ASSOC);
if (PEAR::isError ($rows))
  die (htmlspecialchars ($result->getMessage ()));

$conn->disconnect ();

$smarty = new Smarty ();
$smarty->assign ("title", $title);
$smarty->assign ("rows", $rows);
$smarty->display ("sm_tables.tmpl");

?>
```

## CHAPTER 19

Processing Web Input with MySQL

19.0 Introduction

The previous chapter describes how to retrieve information from MySQL and display it in web pages using various types of HTML constructs such as tables or hyperlinks. That's a use of MySQL to send information in one direction (from web server to user), but web-based database programming is also useful for collecting information sent in the other direction (from user to web server), such as the contents of a submitted form. For example, if you're processing a survey form, you might store the information for later use. If the form contains search keywords, you'd use them as the basis for a query that searches the database for information the user wants to see.

MySQL comes into these activities in a fairly obvious way, as the repository for storing information or as the source from which search results are drawn. But before you can process input from a form, you have to create the form and send it to the user. MySQL can help with this, too, because it's often possible to use information stored in your database to generate form elements such as radio buttons, checkboxes, pop-up menus, or scrolling lists:

- You can select a set of items from a table that lists countries, states, or provinces and convert them into a pop-up menu in a form that collects address information.

- You can use the list of legal values for an ENUM column that contains allowable salutations (Mr., Mrs., and so forth) to generate a set of radio buttons.

- You can use lists of available colors, sizes, or styles stored in an inventory database to construct fields for a clothing ordering form.

- If you have an application that enables the user to pick a database or table, you can query the MySQL server for a list of databases or tables and use the resulting names to create a list element.

By using database content to generate form elements, you lessen the amount of explicit knowledge your programs must have about table structure and content, and you enable them to determine what they need automatically. A script that uses database content to figure out for itself how to generate form elements will also adaptively handle changes to the database. To add a new country, create a new row in the table that stores the list of countries. To add a new salutation, change the definition of the ENUM column. In each case, you change the set of items in a form element by updating the database, not by modifying the script; the script adapts to the change automatically, without additional programming.

The first part of this chapter covers the following topics relating to web input processing:

Generating forms and form elements
One way to use database content for form construction is by selecting a list of items from a table and using them to create the options in a list element. But metadata can be used as well. There is a natural correspondence between ENUM columns and single-pick form elements like radio button sets or pop-up menus. In both cases, only one from a set of possible values may be chosen. There is a similar correspondence between SET columns and multiple-pick elements like checkbox groups; any or all of the possible values may be chosen. To construct metadata-based form elements, obtain the column description from the table metadata stored in INFORMATION_SCHEMA, extract the set of legal ENUM or SET values, and use them for the items in the form element.

Initializing forms using database contents
In addition to using the database to create structural elements of forms, you can also use it to initialize forms. For example, to enable a user to modify an existing record, retrieve it from the database and load it into a form's fields before sending the form to the user for editing.

Processing input gathered over the Web
This includes input not only from form fields, but also the contents of uploaded files, or parameters that are present in URLs. Regardless of how you obtain the information, you'll face a common set of issues in dealing with it: extracting and decoding the information, performing constraint or validity checking on it, and re-encoding the information for statement construction to avoid generating malformed statements or storing information inaccurately.

The second part of the chapter illustrates several ways to apply the techniques developed in the first part. These include applications that show how to use MySQL to present a web-based search interface, create paged displays that contain next-page and previous-page links, implement per-page hit counting and logging, and perform Apache logging to a database.

Scripts to create the tables used in this chapter are located in the *tables* directory of the recipes distribution. The scripts for the examples can be found under the directories named for the servers used to run them. For Perl, Ruby, PHP, and Python examples, look under the *apache* directory. Utility routines used by the example scripts are found in files located in the *lib* directory. (See Recipe 17.2 for information on configuring Apache so that scripts can be run by it and find their library files.) For Java (JSP) examples, look under the *tomcat* directory; you should already have installed these examples in the process of setting up the mcb application context (Recipe 17.3).

Note that although the scripts in this chapter are intended to be invoked from your browser after they have been installed, many of them (JSP pages excepted) can also be invoked from the command line if you want to see the raw HTML they produce. (See Recipe 17.2.)

To provide a concrete context for discussion, many of the form-processing examples in this chapter are based on the following scenario. In the lucrative field of "construct-a-cow" business endeavors, you run an operation that manufactures build-to-order ceramic bovine figurines, and you want to design an online ordering application that lets customers make selections for several aspects of the product. For each order, it's necessary to collect several types of information:

Cow color
> The particular list of colors available at any particular time changes occasionally, so for flexibility, the values can be stored in a database table. To change the set of colors that customers can choose from, just update the table.

Cow size
> There is a fixed set of sizes that doesn't change often (small, medium, large), so the values can be represented as elements of an ENUM column.

The all-important cow accessory items
> These include a bell, horns, a sporty-looking tail ribbon, and a nose ring. Accessories can be represented in a SET column, because a customer may want to select more than one of them. In addition, you know from past experience that most customers order horns and a cow bell, so it's reasonable to use those for the column's default value.

Customer name and address (street, city, state)
> The possible state names are already stored in the states table, so we can use them as the basis for the corresponding form element.

Given the preceding discussion, a cow_order table can be designed like this:

```
CREATE TABLE cow_order
(
  id          INT UNSIGNED NOT NULL AUTO_INCREMENT,
  # cow color, figurine size, and accessory items
  color       VARCHAR(20),
  size        ENUM('small','medium','large') DEFAULT 'medium',
  accessories SET('cow bell','horns','nose ring','tail ribbon')
              DEFAULT 'cow bell,horns',
  # customer name, street, city, and state (abbreviation)
  cust_name   VARCHAR(40),
  cust_street VARCHAR(40),
  cust_city   VARCHAR(40),
  cust_state  CHAR(2),
  PRIMARY KEY (id)
);
```

The `id` column provides a unique identifier for each row. It's a good idea to have such a value, and in fact will be necessary when we get to Recipe 19.4, which shows how to use web forms to edit existing rows. For that type of activity, you must be able to tell which row to update, which is difficult to do without a unique row identifier.

The list of available colors is maintained in a separate table, `cow_color`:

```
CREATE TABLE cow_color (color CHAR(20));
```

For purposes of illustration, assume that the `cow_color` table contains the following rows:

An application can use the tables just described to generate list elements in an order entry form, making it unnecessary for the application to have a lot of specialized built-in knowledge about the available options. The next several recipes describe how to do this, and how to process the input that you obtain when a user submits a form.

19.1 Writing Scripts That Generate Web Forms

Problem

You want to write a script that gathers input from a user.

Solution

Create a form from within your script and send it to the user. The script can arrange to have itself invoked again to process the form's contents when the user fills it in and submits it.

Discussion

Web forms are a convenient way to enable your visitors to submit information such as a set of search keywords, a completed survey result, or a response to a questionnaire. Forms are also beneficial for you as a developer because they provide a structured way to associate data values with names by which to refer to them.

A form begins and ends with `<form>` and `</form>` tags. Between those tags, you can place other HTML constructs, including special elements that become input fields in the page that the browser displays. The `<form>` tag that begins a form should include two attributes, `action` and `method`. The `action` attribute tells the browser what to do with the form when the user submits it. This will be the URL of the script that should be invoked to process the form's contents. The `method` attribute indicates to the browser what kind of HTTP request it should use to submit the form. The value will be either `get` or `post`, depending on the type of request you want the form submission to generate. Recipe 19.5 discusses the difference between these two request methods; for now, we'll always use `post`.

Most of the form-based web scripts shown in this chapter share some common behaviors:

- When first invoked, the script generates a form and sends it to the user to be filled in.

- The `action` attribute of the form points back to the same script, so that when the user completes the form and submits it, the web server invokes the script again to process the form's contents.

- The script determines whether it's being invoked by a user for the first time or whether it should process a submitted form by checking its execution environment to see what input parameters are present. For the initial invocation, the environment will contain none of the parameters named in the form.

This approach isn't the only one you can adopt, of course. One alternative is to place a form in a static HTML page and have it point to the script that processes the form. Another is to have one script generate the form and a second script process it.

If a form-creating script wants to have itself invoked again when the user submits the form, it should determine what its own pathname within the web server tree is and use that value for the `action` attribute of the opening `<form>` tag. For example, if a script is installed as */cgi-bin/myscript* in your web tree, you could write the `<form>` tag like this:

```
<form action="/cgi-bin/myscript" method="post">
```

However, each of our language APIs provides a way for a script to obtain its own pathname. That means no script needs to have its pathname hardwired into it, which gives you greater latitude to install the script where you want.

Perl

In Perl scripts, the CGI.pm module provides three methods that are useful for creating `<form>` elements and constructing the `action` attribute. `start_form( )` and `end_form( )` generate the opening and closing form tags, and `url( )` returns the script's own pathname. Using these methods, a script generates a form like this:

```
print start_form (-action => url (), -method => "post");
# ... generate form elements here ...
print end_form ();
```

`start_form( )` supplies a default request method of `post`, so you can omit the `method` argument if you're constructing `post` forms.

Ruby

In Ruby scripts, create a `cgi` object, and use its `form` method to generate a form. The method arguments provide the `<form>` tag attributes, and the block following the method call provides the form content. To get the script pathname, use the `SCRIPT_NAME` member of the `ENV` hash:

```
cgi.out {
  cgi.form("action" => ENV["SCRIPT_NAME"], "method" => "post") {
    # ... generate form elements here ...
  }
}
```

The `form` method supplies a default request method of `post`, so you can omit the `method` argument if you're constructing `post` forms.

The script pathname is also available from the `cgi.script_name` method.

PHP

In PHP, a script's pathname can be obtained from the `PHP_SELF` member of the `$HTTP_SERVER_VARS` array or the `$_SERVER` array. Unfortunately, checking multiple sources of information is a lot of fooling around just to get the script pathname in a way that works reliably for different versions and configurations of PHP, so a utility routine to get the path is useful. The following function, `get_self_path( )`, shows how to use `$_SERVER` if it's available and fall back to `$HTTP_SERVER_VARS` otherwise. The function thus prefers the most recently introduced language features, but still works for scripts running under older versions of PHP:

```
function get_self_path ()
{
global $HTTP_SERVER_VARS;

  $val = NULL;
  if (isset ($_SERVER["PHP_SELF"]))
    $val = $_SERVER["PHP_SELF"];
  else if (isset ($HTTP_SERVER_VARS["PHP_SELF"]))
    $val = $HTTP_SERVER_VARS["PHP_SELF"];
  return ($val);
}
```

`$HTTP_SERVER_VARS` is a global variable, but must be declared as such explicitly using the `global` keyword if used in a nonglobal scope (such as within a function). `$_SERVER` is a "superglobal" array and is accessible in any scope without being declared as global.

The `get_self_path( )` function is part of the *Cookbook_Webutils.php* library file located in the *lib* directory of the `recipes` distribution. If you install that file in a directory that PHP searches when looking for include files, a script can obtain its own pathname and use it to generate a form as follows:

```
include "Cookbook_Webutils.php";

$self_path = get_self_path ();
print ("<form action=\"$self_path\" method=\"post\">\n");
# ... generate form elements here ...
print ("</form>\n");
```

Python

Python scripts can get the script pathname by importing the os module and accessing the SCRIPT_NAME member of the os.environ object:

```
import os

print "<form action=\"" + os.environ["SCRIPT_NAME"] + "\" method=\"post\">"
# ... generate form elements here ...
print "</form>"
```

Java

In JSP pages, the request path is available through the implicit request object that the JSP processor makes available. Use that object's getRequestURI( ) method as follows:

```
<form action="<%= request.getRequestURI () %>" method="post">
<%-- ... generate form elements here ... --%>
</form>
```

See Also

The examples shown in this section have an empty body between the opening and closing form tags. For a form to be useful, you'll need to create body elements that correspond to the types of information that you want to obtain from users. It's possible to hardwire these elements into a script, but Recipes 19.2 and 19.3 describe how MySQL can help you create the elements on the fly based on information stored in your database.

19.2 Creating Single-Pick Form Elements from Database Content

Problem

A form needs to present a field that offers several options but enables the user to select only one of them.

Solution

Use a single-pick list element. These include radio button sets, pop-up menus, and scrolling lists.

Discussion

Single-pick form elements enable you to present multiple choices from which a single option can be selected. Our construct-a-cow scenario involves several sets of single-pick choices:

- The list of colors in the `cow_color` table. These can be obtained with the following statement:

```
mysql> SELECT color FROM cow_color ORDER BY color;
+---------------+
| color         |
+---------------+
| Black         |
| Black & White |
| Brown         |
| Cream         |
| Red           |
| Red & White   |
| See-Through   |
+---------------+
```

Note that some of the colors contain a & character, which is special in HTML. This means they will need HTML-encoding when placed into list elements. (We'll perform encoding for all the list elements in the form as a matter of course, but those values illustrate why it's a good idea to get in that habit.)

- The list of legal figurine sizes in the `size` column of the `cow_order` table. The column is represented as an ENUM, so the possible values and the default value can be obtained from INFORMATION_SCHEMA:

```
mysql> SELECT COLUMN_TYPE, COLUMN_DEFAULT
    -> FROM INFORMATION_SCHEMA.COLUMNS
    -> WHERE TABLE_SCHEMA='cookbook' AND TABLE_NAME='cow_order'
    -> AND COLUMN_NAME='size';
+--------------------------------+----------------+
| COLUMN_TYPE                    | COLUMN_DEFAULT |
+--------------------------------+----------------+
| enum('small','medium','large') | medium         |
+--------------------------------+----------------+
```

- The list of state names and abbreviations. These are available from the `states` table:

```
mysql> SELECT abbrev, name FROM states ORDER BY name;
+--------+----------------+
| abbrev | name           |
+--------+----------------+
| AL     | Alabama        |
| AK     | Alaska         |
| AZ     | Arizona        |
| AR     | Arkansas       |
| CA     | California     |
| CO     | Colorado       |
| CT     | Connecticut    |
...
```

The number of choices varies for each of the lists just described. As shown, there are 3 figurine sizes, 7 colors, and 50 states. The differing numbers of choices lead to different decisions about how to represent the lists in a form:

- The figurine size values are best represented as a set of radio buttons or a pop-up menu; a scrolling list is unnecessary because the number of choices is small.

- The set of colors can reasonably be displayed using any of the single-pick element types; it's small enough that a set of radio buttons wouldn't take a lot of space, but large enough that you may want to enable scrolling—particularly if you make additional colors available.

- The list of states is likely to have more items than you'd want to present as a set of radio buttons, so it's most suitable for presentation as a pop-up menu or scrolling list.

The following discussion describes the HTML syntax for these types of elements and then shows how to generate them from within scripts:

Radio buttons

A group of radio buttons consists of `<input>` elements of type `radio`, all with the same `name` attribute. Each element also includes a `value` attribute. A label to display can be given after the `<input>` tag. To mark an item as the default initial selection, add a `checked` attribute. The following radio button group displays the possible cow figurine sizes, using `checked` to mark `medium` as the initially selected value:

```
<input type="radio" name="size" value="small" />small
<input type="radio" name="size" value="medium" checked="checked" />medium
<input type="radio" name="size" value="large" />large
```

Pop-up menus

A pop-up menu is a list that begins and ends with `<select>` and `</select>` tags, with each item in the menu enclosed within `<option>` and `</option>` tags. Each `<option>` element has a `value` attribute, and its body provides a label to be displayed. To indicate a default selection, add a `selected` attribute to the appropriate `<option>` item. If no item is so marked, the first item becomes the default, as is the case for the following pop-up menu:

```
<select name="color">
<option value="Black">Black</option>
<option value="Black &amp; White">Black &amp; White</option>
<option value="Brown">Brown</option>
<option value="Cream">Cream</option>
<option value="Red">Red</option>
<option value="Red &amp; White">Red &amp; White</option>
<option value="See-Through">See-Through</option>
</select>
```

Scrolling lists

A scrolling list is displayed as a set of items in a box. The list may contain more items than are visible in the box, in which case the browser displays a scrollbar that the user can use to bring the other items into view. The HTML syntax for scrolling lists is similar to that for pop-up menus, except that the opening `<select>` tag includes a `size` attribute indicating how many rows of the list should be visible in the box. By default, a scrolling list is a single-pick element; Recipe 19.3 discusses how to allow multiple picks.

The following single-pick scrolling list includes an item for each U.S. state, of which six will be visible at a time:

```
<select name="state" size="6">
<option value="AL">Alabama</option>
<option value="AK">Alaska</option>
<option value="AZ">Arizona</option>
<option value="AR">Arkansas</option>
<option value="CA">California</option>
...
<option value="WV">West Virginia</option>
<option value="WI">Wisconsin</option>
<option value="WY">Wyoming</option>
</select>
```

Radio button sets, pop-up menus, and scrolling lists have several things in common:

A name for the element
> When the user submits the form, the browser associates this name with whatever value the user selected.

A set of values, one for each item in the list
> These determine which values are available to be selected.

A set of labels, one for each item
> These determine what the user sees when the form is displayed.

An optional default value
> This determines which item in the list is selected initially when the browser displays the list.

To produce a list element for a form using database content, issue a statement that selects the appropriate values and labels, encode any special characters they contain, and add the HTML tags that are appropriate for the kind of list you want to display. Should you desire to indicate a default selection, add a `checked` or `selected` attribute to the proper item in the list.

Let's consider how to produce form elements for the color and state lists first. Both of these are produced by fetching a set of column values from a table. Then we'll construct the figurine size list, which takes its values from a column's definition rather than its contents.

In JSP, you can display a set of radio buttons for the colors using JSTL tags as follows. The color names are used as both the values and the labels, so you print them twice:

```
<sql:query dataSource="${conn}" var="rs">
  SELECT color FROM cow_color ORDER BY color
```

```
    </sql:query>

    <c:forEach items="${rs.rows}" var="row">
      <input type="radio" name="color"
        value="<c:out value="${row.color}"/>"
      /><c:out value="${row.color}"/><br />
    </c:forEach>
```

`<c:out>` performs HTML entity encoding, so the & character that is present in some of the color values is converted to `&amp;` automatically and does not cause display problems in the resulting web page.

To display a pop-up menu instead, the retrieval statement is the same, but the row-fetching loop is different:

```
    <sql:query dataSource="${conn}" var="rs">
      SELECT color FROM cow_color ORDER BY color
    </sql:query>

    <select name="color">
    <c:forEach items="${rs.rows}" var="row">
      <option value="<c:out value="${row.color}"/>">
      <c:out value="${row.color}"/></option>
    </c:forEach>
    </select>
```

The pop-up menu can be changed easily to a scrolling list. All you need to do is add a `size` attribute to the opening `<select>` tag. For example, to make three colors visible at a time, generate the list like this:

```
    <sql:query dataSource="${conn}" var="rs">
      SELECT color FROM cow_color ORDER BY color
    </sql:query>

    <select name="color" size="3">
    <c:forEach items="${rs.rows}" var="row">
      <option value="<c:out value="${row.color}"/>">
      <c:out value="${row.color}"/></option>
    </c:forEach>
    </select>
```

Generating a list element for the set of states is similar, except that the labels are not the same as the values. To make the labels more meaningful to customers, display the full state names. But the value that is returned when the form is submitted should be an abbreviation, because that is what gets stored in the `cow_order` table. To produce a list that way, select both the abbreviations and the full names, and then insert them into the proper parts of each list item. For example, to create a pop-up menu, do this:

```
    <sql:query dataSource="${conn}" var="rs">
      SELECT abbrev, name FROM states ORDER BY name
    </sql:query>

    <select name="state">
    <c:forEach items="${rs.rows}" var="row">
      <option value="<c:out value="${row.abbrev}"/>">
```

```
    <c:out value="${row.name}"/></option>
  </c:forEach>
  </select>
```

The preceding JSP examples use an approach that prints each list item individually. List element generation in CGI.pm-based Perl scripts proceeds on a different basis: extract the information from the database first, and then pass it all to a function that returns a string representing the form element. The functions that generate single-pick elements are `radio_group( )`, `popup_menu( )`, and `scrolling_list( )`. These have several arguments in common:

`name`
> What you want to call the element.

`values`
> The values for the items in the list. This should be a reference to an array.

`labels`
> The labels to associate with each value. This argument is optional; if it's missing, CGI.pm uses the values as the labels. Otherwise, the `labels` argument should be a reference to a hash that associates each value with its corresponding label. For example, to produce a list element for cow colors, the values and labels are the same, so no `labels` argument is necessary. However, to produce a state list, `labels` should be a reference to a hash that maps each state abbreviation to its full name.

`default`
> The initially selected item in the element. This argument is optional. For a radio button set, CGI.pm automatically selects the first button by default if this argument is missing. To defeat that behavior, provide a default value that is not present in the `values` list. (This value cannot be `undef` or the empty string.)

Some of the functions take additional arguments. For `radio_group( )`, you can supply a `linebreak` argument to specify that the buttons should be displayed vertically rather than horizontally. `scrolling_list( )` takes a `size` argument indicating how many items should be visible at a time. (The CGI.pm documentation describes additional arguments that are not used here at all. For example, there are arguments for laying out radio buttons in tabular form, but we're not going to be that fancy.)

To construct a form element using the colors in the `cow_color` table, begin by retrieving them into an array:

```
my $color_ref = $dbh->selectcol_arrayref (
                    "SELECT color FROM cow_color ORDER BY color");
```

`selectcol_arrayref( )` returns a reference to the array, which is the kind of value needed for the `values` argument of the CGI.pm functions that create list elements. To create a group of radio buttons, a pop-up menu, or a single-pick scrolling list, invoke the functions as follows:

```
print radio_group (-name => "color",
                   -values => $color_ref,
                   -linebreak => 1);    # display buttons vertically

print popup_menu (-name => "color",
                  -values => $color_ref);

print scrolling_list (-name => "color",
                      -values => $color_ref,
                      -size => 3);        # display 3 items at a time
```

The values and the labels for the color list are the same, so no `labels` argument need be given; CGI.pm will use the values as labels by default. Note that we haven't HTML-encoded the colors here, even though some of them contain an & character. CGI.pm functions for generating form elements automatically perform HTML-encoding, unlike its functions for creating nonform elements.

To produce a list of states for which the values are abbreviations and the labels are full names, we do need a `labels` argument. It should be a reference to a hash that maps each value to the corresponding label. Construct the value list and label hash as follows:

```
my @state_values;
my %state_labels;
my $sth = $dbh->prepare ("SELECT abbrev, name
                         FROM states ORDER BY name");
$sth->execute ();
while (my ($abbrev, $name) = $sth->fetchrow_array ())
{
  push (@state_values, $abbrev);  # save each value in an array
  $state_labels{$abbrev} = $name; # map each value to its label
}
```

Pass the resulting list and hash by reference to `popup_menu( )` or `scrolling_list( )`, depending on which kind of list element you want to produce:

```
print popup_menu (-name => "state",
                  -values => \@state_values,
                  -labels => \%state_labels);

print scrolling_list (-name => "state",
                      -values => \@state_values,
                      -labels => \%state_labels,
                      -size => 6);        # display 6 items at a time
```

The Ruby `cgi` module also has methods for generating radio buttons, pop-up menus, and scrolling lists. You can examine the *form_element.rb* script to see how to use them. However, I am not going to discuss them here because I find them awkward to use, particularly when it's necessary to ensure that values are properly escaped or that certain group members are selected by default.

If you're using an API that doesn't provide a ready-made set of functions for producing form elements (or those functions are inconvenient to use), you may elect either to print HTML as you fetch list items from MySQL, or write utility routines that generate the form elements for you. The following discussion considers how to implement both approaches, using PHP and Python.

In PHP, the list of values from the cow_color table can be presented in a pop-up menu as follows using a fetch-and-print loop like this:

```
print ("<select name=\"color\">\n");
$stmt = "SELECT color FROM cow_color ORDER BY color";
$result =& $conn->query ($stmt);
if (!PEAR::isError ($result))
{
  while (list ($color) = $result->fetchRow ())
  {
    $color = htmlspecialchars ($color);
    print ("<option value=\"$color\">$color</option>\n");
  }
  $result->free ();
}
print ("</select>\n");
```

Python code to do the same is similar:

```
stmt = "SELECT color FROM cow_color ORDER BY color"
cursor = conn.cursor ()
cursor.execute (stmt)
print "<select name=\"color\">"
for (color, ) in cursor.fetchall ():
  color = cgi.escape (color, 1)
  print "<option value=\"%s\">%s</option>" % (color, color)
cursor.close ()
print "</select>"
```

The state list requires different values and labels, so the code is slightly more complex. In PHP, it looks like this:

```
print ("<select name=\"state\">\n");
$stmt = "SELECT abbrev, name FROM states ORDER BY name";
$result =& $conn->query ($stmt);
if (!PEAR::isError ($result))
{
  while ($row =& $result->fetchRow ())
  {
    $abbrev = htmlspecialchars ($row[0]);
    $name = htmlspecialchars ($row[1]);
    print ("<option value=\"$abbrev\">$name</option>\n");
  }
  $result->free ();
}
print ("</select>\n");
```

And in Python, like this:

```
stmt = "SELECT abbrev, name FROM states ORDER BY name"
cursor = conn.cursor ()
cursor.execute (stmt)
print "<select name=\"state\">"
for (abbrev, name) in cursor.fetchall ():
```

```
        abbrev = cgi.escape (abbrev, 1)
        name = cgi.escape (name, 1)
        print "<option value=\"%s\">%s</option>" % (abbrev, name)
    cursor.close ()
    print "</select>"
```

Radio buttons and scrolling lists can be produced in similar fashion. But rather than doing so, let's use a different approach and construct a set of functions that generate form elements, given the proper information. The functions return a string representing the appropriate kind of form element. They're invoked as follows:

```
make_radio_group (name, values, labels, default, vertical)
make_popup_menu (name, values, labels, default)
make_scrolling_list (name, values, labels, default, size, multiple)
```

These functions have several arguments in common:

name
>   The name of the form element.

values
>   An array or list of values for the items in the element.

labels
>   Another array that provides the corresponding element label to display for each value. The two arrays must be the same size. (If you want to use the values as the labels, just pass the same array to the function twice.)

default
>   The initial value of the form element. This should be a scalar value, except for make_scrolling_list( ). We'll write that function to handle either single-pick or multiple-pick lists (and use it for the latter purpose in Recipe 19.3), so its default value is allowed to be either a scalar or an array. If there is no default, pass a value that isn't contained in the values array; typically, an empty string will do.

Some of the functions also have additional arguments that apply only to particular element types:

vertical
>   This applies to radio button groups. If true, it indicates that the items should be stacked vertically rather than horizontally.

size, multiple
>   These arguments apply to scrolling lists. size indicates how many items in the list are visible, and multiple should be true if the list allows multiple selections.

The implementation of some of these list-generating functions is discussed here, but you can find the code for all of them in the *lib* directory of the **recipes** distribution. All of them act like CGI.pm for form element functions in the sense that they automatically perform HTML-encoding of argument values that are incorporated into the list. (The Ruby version of the library file includes utility methods for generating these elements, too, even though the cgi module has methods for creating them; I think the utility methods are easier to use than the cgi methods.)

In PHP, the make_radio_group( ) function for creating a set of radio buttons is written like this:

```
function make_radio_group ($name, $values, $labels, $default, $vertical)
{
  $str = "";
  for ($i = 0; $i < count ($values); $i++)
  {
    # select the item if it corresponds to the default value
    $checked = ($values[$i] == $default ? " checked=\"checked\"" : "");
    $str .= sprintf (
              "<input type=\"radio\" name=\"%s\" value=\"%s\"%s />%s",
              htmlspecialchars ($name),
              htmlspecialchars ($values[$i]),
              $checked,
              htmlspecialchars ($labels[$i]));
    if ($vertical)
      $str .= "<br />"; # display items vertically
    $str .= "\n";
  }
  return ($str);
}
```

The function constructs the form element as a string, which it returns. To use make_radio_group( ) to present cow colors, invoke it after fetching the items from the cow_color table, as follows:

```
$values = array ();
$stmt = "SELECT color FROM cow_color ORDER BY color";
$result =& $conn->query ($stmt);
if (!PEAR::isError ($result))
{
  while ($row =& $result->fetchRow ())
    $values[] = $row[0];
  $result->free ();
}
print (make_radio_group ("color", $values, $values, "", TRUE));
```

The $values array is passed to make_radio_group( ) twice because it's used both for the values and the labels.

If you want to present a pop-up menu, use the following function instead:

```
function make_popup_menu ($name, $values, $labels, $default)
{
  $str = "";
  for ($i = 0; $i < count ($values); $i++)
  {
    # select the item if it corresponds to the default value
    $checked = ($values[$i] == $default ? " selected=\"selected\"" : "");
    $str .= sprintf (
              "<option value=\"%s\"%s>%s</option>\n",
              htmlspecialchars ($values[$i]),
```

```
            $checked,
            htmlspecialchars ($labels[$i]));
  }
  $str = sprintf (
          "<select name=\"%s\">\n%s</select>\n",
          htmlspecialchars ($name),
          $str);
  return ($str);
}
```

make_popup_menu( ) has no $vertical parameter, but otherwise you invoke it the same
way as make_radio_group( ):

```
print (make_popup_menu ("color", $values, $values, ""));
```

The make_scrolling_list( ) function is similar to make_popup_menu( ), so I won't show
its implementation here. To invoke it to produce a single-pick list, pass the same arguments as for make_popup_menu( ), but indicate how many rows should be visible at
once, and add a multiple argument of FALSE:

```
print (make_scrolling_list ("color", $values, $values, "", 3, FALSE));
```

The state list uses labels that are different from the values. Fetch the labels and values
like this:

```
$values = array ();
$labels = array ();
$stmt = "SELECT abbrev, name FROM states ORDER BY name";
$result =& $conn->query ($stmt);
if (!PEAR::isError ($result))
{
  while ($row =& $result->fetchRow ())
  {
    $values[] = $row[0];
    $labels[] = $row[1];
  }
  $result->free ();
}
```

Then use the values and labels to generate the type of list you want:

```
print (make_popup_menu ("state", $values, $labels, ""));
```

```
print (make_scrolling_list ("state", $values, $labels, "", 6, FALSE));
```

Ruby and Python implementations of the utility functions are similar to the PHP versions. For example, the Python version of make_popup_menu( ) looks like this:

```
def make_popup_menu (name, values, labels, default):
  result_str = ""
  # make sure name and default are strings
  name = str (name)
  default = str (default)
  for i in range (len (values)):
    # make sure value and label are strings
    value = str (values[i])
    label = str (labels[i])
```

```
      # select the item if it corresponds to the default value
      if value == default:
        checked = " selected=\"selected\""
      else:
        checked = ""
      result_str = result_str + \
            "<option value=\"%s\"%s>%s</option>\n" \
             % (cgi.escape (value, 1),
                checked,
                cgi.escape (label, 1))

    result_str = "<select name=\"%s\">\n%s</select>\n" \
          % (cgi.escape (name, 1), result_str)
    return result_str
```

To present the cow colors in a form, fetch them like this:

```
values = []
stmt = "SELECT color FROM cow_color ORDER BY color"
cursor = conn.cursor ()
cursor.execute (stmt)
for (color, ) in cursor.fetchall ():
  values.append (color)
cursor.close ()
```

Then convert the list to a form element using one of the following calls:

```
print make_radio_group ("color", values, values, "", True)

print make_popup_menu ("color", values, values, "")

print make_scrolling_list ("color", values, values, "", 3, False)
```

To present the state list, fetch the names and abbreviations:

```
values = []
labels = []
stmt = "SELECT abbrev, name FROM states ORDER BY name"
cursor = conn.cursor ()
cursor.execute (stmt)
for (abbrev, name) in cursor.fetchall ():
  values.append (abbrev)
  labels.append (name)
cursor.close ()
```

Then pass them to the appropriate function:

```
print make_popup_menu ("state", values, labels, "")

print make_scrolling_list ("state", values, labels, "", 6, False)
```

Something the Ruby and Python utility methods in the *lib* directory do that their PHP counterparts do not is explicitly convert to string form all argument values that get incorporated into the list. This is necessary because the Ruby `CGI.escapeHTML( )` and Python `cgi.escape( )` methods raise an exception if you try to use them to HTML-encode nonstring values.

We have thus far considered how to fetch rows from the `cow_color` and `states` tables and convert them to form elements. Another element that needs to be part of the form for the online cow-ordering application is the field for specifying cow figurine size. The legal values for this field come from the definition of the `size` column in the `cow_order` table. That column is an ENUM, so getting the legal values for the corresponding form element is a matter of getting the column definition and parsing it apart. In other words, we need to use the column metadata rather than the column data.

As it happens, a lot of the work involved in this task has already been done in Recipe 9.7, which develops utility routines to get ENUM or SET column metadata. In Perl, for example, invoke the `get_enumorset_info( )` function as follows to get the `size` column metadata:

```
my $size_info = get_enumorset_info ($dbh, "cookbook", "cow_order", "size");
```

The resulting `$size_info` value is a reference to a hash that has several members, two of which are relevant to our purposes here:

```
$size_info->{values}
$size_info->{default}
```

The `values` member is a reference to a list of the legal enumeration values, and `default` is the column's default value. This information is in a format that can be converted directly to a form element such as a group of radio buttons or a pop-up menu as follows:

```
print radio_group (-name => "size",
                    -values => $size_info->{values},
                    -default => $size_info->{default},
                    -linebreak => 1);   # display buttons vertically

print popup_menu (-name => "size",
                  -values => $size_info->{values},
                  -default => $size_info->{default});
```

The default value is `medium`, so that's the value that will be selected initially when the browser displays the form.

The equivalent Ruby metadata-fetching method returns a hash. Use it as follows to generate form elements from the `size` column metadata:

```
size_info = get_enumorset_info(dbh, "cookbook", "cow_order", "size")

form << make_radio_group("size",
                         size_info["values"],
                         size_info["values"],
                         size_info["default"],
                         true)    # display items vertically

form << make_popup_menu("size",
                        size_info["values"],
                        size_info["values"],
                        size_info["default"])
```

The metadata function for PHP returns an associative array, which is used in similar fashion:

```
$size_info = get_enumorset_info ($conn, "cookbook", "cow_order", "size");

print (make_radio_group ("size",
                         $size_info["values"],
                         $size_info["values"],
                         $size_info["default"],
                         TRUE));   # display items vertically

print (make_popup_menu ("size",
                        $size_info["values"],
                        $size_info["values"],
                        $size_info["default"]));
```

The Python version of the metadata function returns a dictionary:

```
size_info = get_enumorset_info (conn, "cookbook", "cow_order", "size")

print make_radio_group ("size",
                        size_info["values"],
                        size_info["values"],
                        size_info["default"],
                        True)   # display items vertically

print make_popup_menu ("size",
                       size_info["values"],
                       size_info["values"],
                       size_info["default"])
```

When you use ENUM values like this to create list elements, the values are displayed in the order they are listed in the column definition. The size column definition lists the values in the proper display order (small, medium, large), but for columns for which you want a different order, sort the values appropriately.

To demonstrate how to process column metadata to generate form elements in JSP pages, I'm going to use a function embedded into the page. A better approach would be to write a custom action in a tag library that maps onto a class that returns the information, but custom tag writing is beyond the scope of this book. The examples take the following approach instead:

1. Use JSTL tags to query INFORMATION_SCHEMA for the ENUM column definition, and then move the definition into page context.

2. Invoke a function that extracts the definition from page context, parses it into an array of individual enumeration values, and moves the array back into page context.

3. Access the array using a JSTL iterator that displays each of its values as a list item. For each value, compare it to the column's default value and mark it as the initially selected item if it's the same.

The function that extracts legal values from an ENUM or SET column definition is named getEnumOrSetValues( ). Place it into a JSP page like this:

```
<%@ page import="java.util.*" %>
<%@ page import="java.util.regex.*" %>

<%!
// declare a class method for busting up ENUM/SET values.
// typeDefAttr - the name of the page context attribute that contains
// the columm type definition
// valListAttr - the name of the page context attribute to stuff the
// column value list into

void getEnumOrSetValues (PageContext ctx,
                         String typeDefAttr,
                         String valListAttr)
{
  String typeDef = ctx.getAttribute (typeDefAttr).toString ();
  List values = new ArrayList ();

  // column must be an ENUM or SET
  Pattern pc = Pattern.compile ("(enum|set)\\((.*)\\)",
                                Pattern.CASE_INSENSITIVE);
  Matcher m = pc.matcher (typeDef);
  // matches() fails unless it matches entire string
  if (m.matches ())
  {
    // split value list on commas, trim quotes from end of each word
    String[] v = m.group (2).split (",");
    for (int i = 0; i < v.length; i++)
      values.add (v[i].substring (1, v[i].length() - 1));
  }
  ctx.setAttribute (valListAttr, values);
}

%>
```

The function takes three arguments:

ctx

The page context object.

typeDefAttr

The name of the page attribute that contains the column definition. This is the function "input."

valListAttr

The name of the page attribute into which to place the resulting array of legal column values. This is the function "output."

To generate a list element from the size column, begin by fetching the column metadata. Extract the column value list into a JSTL variable named values and the default value into a variable named default as follows:

```
<sql:query dataSource="${conn}" var="rs">
  SELECT COLUMN_TYPE, COLUMN_DEFAULT
  FROM INFORMATION_SCHEMA.COLUMNS
  WHERE TABLE_SCHEMA = 'cookbook' AND TABLE_NAME = 'cow_order'
  AND COLUMN_NAME = 'size'
</sql:query>
<c:set var="typeDef" scope="page" value="${rs.rowsByIndex[0][0]}"/>
<% getEnumOrSetValues (pageContext, "typeDef", "values"); %>
<c:set var="default" scope="page" value="${rs.rowsByIndex[0][1]}"/>
```

Then use the value list and default value to construct a form element. For example, produce a set of radio buttons like this:

```
<c:forEach items="${values}" var="val">
  <input type="radio" name="size"
    value="<c:out value="${val}"/>"
    <c:if test="${val == default}">checked="checked"</c:if>
  /><c:out value="${val}"/><br />
</c:forEach>
```

or a pop-up menu like this:

```
<select name="size">
<c:forEach items="${values}" var="val">
  <option
    value="<c:out value="${val}"/>"
    <c:if test="${val == default}">selected="selected"</c:if>
  >
  <c:out value="${val}"/></option>
</c:forEach>
</select>
```

Don't Forget to HTML-Encode All List Content in Forms

The Ruby, PHP, and Python utility routines described in this recipe for generating list elements perform HTML-encoding of attribute values for the HTML tags that make up the list, such as the `name` and `value` attributes. They also encode the labels. I've noticed that many published accounts of list generation do not do this, or they encode the labels but not the values. That is a mistake. If either the label or the value contains a special character like & or <, the browser may misinterpret them, and your application will misbehave. It's also important to make sure that your encoding function turns double quotes into " entities (or ", which is equivalent), because tag attributes are so often enclosed within double quotes. Failing to convert a double quote to the entity name in an attribute value results in a double quote within a double-quoted string, which is malformed.

If you're using the Perl CGI.pm module or the JSTL tags to produce HTML for form elements, encoding is taken care of for you. CGI.pm's form-related functions automatically perform encoding. Similarly, using the JSTL `<c:out>` tag to write attribute values from JSP pages will produce properly encoded values.

The list-generating methods discussed here are not tied to any particular database table, so they can be used to create form elements for all kinds of data, not just those shown for the cow-ordering scenario. For example, to enable a user to pick a table name in a database administration application, you can generate a scrolling list that contains an item for each table in the database. A CGI.pm-based script might do so like this:

```
my $stmt = "SELECT TABLE_NAME FROM INFORMATION_SCHEMA.TABLES
            WHERE TABLE_SCHEMA = 'cookbook' ORDER BY TABLE_NAME";
my $table_ref = $dbh->selectcol_arrayref ($stmt);
print scrolling_list (-name => "table",
                      -values => $table_ref,
                      -size => 10);      # display 10 items at a time
```

Query results need not necessarily even be related to database tables. For example, if you want to present a list with an entry for each of the last seven days from within a JSP page, you can calculate the dates using this statement:

```
<sql:query dataSource="${conn}" var="rs">
  SELECT
    CURDATE() - INTERVAL 6 DAY,
    CURDATE() - INTERVAL 5 DAY,
    CURDATE() - INTERVAL 4 DAY,
    CURDATE() - INTERVAL 3 DAY,
    CURDATE() - INTERVAL 2 DAY,
    CURDATE() - INTERVAL 1 DAY,
    CURDATE()
</sql:query>
```

Then use the dates to generate a list element:

```
<c:set var="dateList" value="${rs.rowsByIndex[0]}"/>
<c:forEach items="${dateList}" var="date">
  <input type="radio" name="date"
    value="<c:out value="${date}"/>"
  /><c:out value="${date}"/><br />
</c:forEach>
```

Of course, if your programming language makes it reasonably easy to perform date calculations, it is more efficient to generate the list of dates on the client side without sending a statement to the MySQL server.

19.3 Creating Multiple-Pick Form Elements from Database Content

Problem

A form needs to present a field that offers several options and enables the user to select any number of them.

Solution

Use a multiple-pick list element, such as a set of checkboxes or a scrolling list.

Discussion

Multiple-pick form elements enable you to present multiple choices, any number of which can be selected, or possibly even none of them. For our example scenario in which customers order cow figurines online, the multiple-pick element is represented by the set of accessory items that are available. The `accessory` column in the `cow_order` table is represented as a `SET`, so the allowable and default values can be obtained with the following statement:

```
mysql> SELECT COLUMN_TYPE, COLUMN_DEFAULT FROM INFORMATION_SCHEMA.COLUMNS
    -> WHERE TABLE_SCHEMA='cookbook' AND TABLE_NAME='cow_order'
    -> AND COLUMN_NAME='accessories';
+-----------------------------------------------+----------------+
| COLUMN_TYPE                                    | COLUMN_DEFAULT |
+-----------------------------------------------+----------------+
| set('cow bell','horns','nose ring','tail ribbon') | cow bell,horns |
+-----------------------------------------------+----------------+
```

The values listed in the definition can reasonably be represented as either a set of checkboxes or as a multiple-pick scrolling list. Either way, the cow bell and horns items should be selected initially, because each is present in the column's default value. The following discussion shows the HTML syntax for these elements, and then describes how to generate them from within scripts.

 The material in this section relies heavily on Recipe 19.2, which discusses radio buttons, pop-up menus, and single-pick scrolling lists. I assume that you've already read that section.

Checkboxes

A group of checkboxes is similar to a group of radio buttons in that it consists of `<input>` elements that all have the same `name` attribute. However, the `type` attribute is `checkbox` rather than `radio`, and you can specify `checked` for as many items in the group as you want to be selected by default. If no items are marked as `checked`, none are selected initially. The following checkbox set shows the cow accessory items with the first two items selected by default:

```
<input type="checkbox" name="accessories" value="cow bell"
  checked="checked" />cow bell
<input type="checkbox" name="accessories" value="horns"
  checked="checked" />horns
<input type="checkbox" name="accessories" value="nose ring" />nose ring
<input type="checkbox" name="accessories" value="tail ribbon" />tail ribbon
```

Scrolling lists

A multiple-pick scrolling list has most syntax in common with its single-pick counterpart. The differences are that you include a `multiple` attribute in the opening `<select>` tag, and default value selection is different. For a single-pick list, you can add `selected` to at most one item, and the first item is selected by default in the absence of an explicit `selected` attribute. For a multiple-pick list, you can add a `selected` attribute to as many of the items as you like, and no items are selected by default in the absence of `selected` attributes.

If the set of cow accessories is represented as a multiple-pick scrolling list with `cow bell` and `horns` selected initially, it looks like this:

```
<select name="accessories" size="3" multiple="multiple">
<option value="cow bell" selected="selected">cow bell</option>
<option value="horns" selected="selected">horns</option>
<option value="nose ring">nose ring</option>
<option value="tail ribbon">tail ribbon</option>
</select>
```

In CGI.pm-based Perl scripts, you create checkbox sets or scrolling lists by invoking `checkbox_group( )` or `scrolling_list( )`. These functions take `name`, `values`, `labels`, and `default` arguments, just like their single-pick cousins. But because multiple items can be selected initially, CGI.pm allows the `default` argument to be specified as either a scalar value or a reference to an array of values. (It also accepts the argument name `defaults` as a synonym for `default`.)

To get the list of legal values for a `SET` column, we can do the same thing as in Recipe 19.2 for `ENUM` columns—that is, call a utility routine that returns the column metadata:

```
my $acc_info = get_enumorset_info ($dbh, "cookbook", "cow_order", "accessories");
```

However, the default value for a `SET` column is not in a form that is directly usable for form element generation. MySQL represents `SET` default values as a list of zero or more items, separated by commas; for example, the default for the `accessories` column is `cow bell,horns`. That doesn't match the list-of-values format that the CGI.pm functions expect, so it's necessary to split the default value at the commas to obtain an array. The following expression shows how to do so, taking into account the possibility that the default column value might be `undef` (`NULL`):

```
my @acc_def = (defined ($acc_info->{default})
                ? split (/,/, $acc_info->{default})
                : () );
```

After splitting the default value, pass the resulting array by reference to whichever of the list-generating functions you want to use:

```
print checkbox_group (-name => "accessories",
                      -values => $acc_info->{values},
                      -default => \@acc_def,
                      -linebreak => 1);   # display buttons vertically

print scrolling_list (-name => "accessories",
                      -values => $acc_info->{values},
                      -default => \@acc_def,
                      -size => 3,          # display 3 items at a time
                      -multiple => 1);     # create multiple-pick list
```

When you use SET values like this to create list elements, the values are displayed in the order they are listed in the column definition. That may not correspond to the order in which you want them to appear; if not, sort the values appropriately.

For Ruby, PHP, and Python, we can create utility functions to generate multiple-pick items. They'll have the following invocation syntax:

```
make_checkbox_group (name, values, labels, default, vertical)
make_scrolling_list (name, values, labels, default, size, multiple)
```

The name, values, and labels arguments to these functions are similar to those of the single-pick utility routines described in Recipe 19.2. make_checkbox_group( ) takes a vertical argument to indicate whether the items should be stacked vertically rather than horizontally. make_scrolling_list( ) has already been described in Recipe 19.2 for producing single-pick lists. To use it here, the multiple argument should be true to produce a multiple-pick list. For both functions, the default argument can be an array of multiple values if several items should be selected initially.

make_checkbox_group( ) looks like this (shown here in Ruby; the PHP and Python versions are similar):

```ruby
def make_checkbox_group(name, values, labels, default, vertical)
  # make sure default is an array (converts a scalar to an array)
  default = [ default ].flatten
  str = ""
  for i in 0...values.length do
    # select the item if it corresponds to one of the default values
    checked = (default.include?(values[i]) ? " checked=\"checked\"" : "")
    str << sprintf(
              "<input type=\"checkbox\" name=\"%s\" value=\"%s\"%s />%s",
              CGI.escapeHTML(name.to_s),
              CGI.escapeHTML(values[i].to_s),
              checked,
              CGI.escapeHTML(labels[i].to_s))
    str << "<br />" if vertical   # display items vertically
    str << "\n"
  end
  return str
end
```

To fetch the cow accessory information and present it using checkboxes, do this:

```ruby
acc_info = get_enumorset_info(dbh, "cookbook", "cow_order", "accessories")
if acc_info["default"].nil?
  acc_def = []
else
  acc_def = acc_info["default"].split(",")
end

form << make_checkbox_group("accessories",
                            acc_info["values"],
                            acc_info["values"],
                            acc_def,
                            true)       # display items vertically
```

To display a scrolling list instead, invoke make_scrolling_list( ):

```
form << make_scrolling_list("accessories",
                            acc_info["values"],
                            acc_info["values"],
                            acc_def,
                            3,          # display 3 items at a time
                            true)       # create multiple-pick list
```

In PHP, fetch the accessory information, and then present checkboxes or a scrolling list as follows:

```
$acc_info = get_enumorset_info ($conn, "cookbook", "cow_order", "accessories");
$acc_def = explode (",", $acc_info["default"]);

print (make_checkbox_group ("accessories[]",
                            $acc_info["values"],
                            $acc_info["values"],
                            $acc_def,
                            TRUE));   # display items vertically

print (make_scrolling_list ("accessories[]",
                            $acc_info["values"],
                            $acc_info["values"],
                            $acc_def,
                            3,        # display 3 items at a time
                            TRUE));   # create multiple-pick list
```

Note that the field name in the PHP examples is specified as accessories[] rather than as accessories. In PHP, you must add [] to the name if you want to allow a field to have multiple values. If you omit the [], the user will be able to select multiple items while filling in the form, but PHP will return only one of them to your script. This issue comes up again when we discuss how to process the contents of submitted forms in Recipe 19.5.

In Python, to fetch the cow accessory information and present it using checkboxes or a scrolling list, do this:

```
acc_info = get_enumorset_info (conn, "cookbook", "cow_order", "accessories")
if acc_info["default"] == None:
  acc_def = ""
else:
  acc_def = acc_info["default"].split (",")

print make_checkbox_group ("accessories",
                            acc_info["values"],
                            acc_info["values"],
                            acc_def,
                            True)   # display items vertically

print make_scrolling_list ("accessories",
                            acc_info["values"],
                            acc_info["values"],
                            acc_def,
```

```
            3,      # display 3 items at a time
            True)   # create multiple-pick list
```

In JSP pages, the `getEnumOrSetValues()` function used earlier to get the value list for the `size` column (an `ENUM`) can also be used for the `accessory` column (a `SET`). The column definition and default value can be obtained from `INFORMATION_SCHEMA`. Query the `COLUMNS` table, parse the type definition into a list of values named `values`, and put the default value in `defList` like this:

```
<sql:query dataSource="${conn}" var="rs">
  SELECT COLUMN_TYPE, COLUMN_DEFAULT
  FROM INFORMATION_SCHEMA.COLUMNS
  WHERE TABLE_SCHEMA = 'cookbook'
  AND TABLE_NAME = 'cow_order'
  AND COLUMN_NAME = 'accessories'
</sql:query>
<c:set var="typeDef" scope="page" value="${rs.rowsByIndex[0][0]}"/>
<% getEnumOrSetValues (pageContext, "typeDef", "values"); %>
<c:set var="defList" scope="page" value="${rs.rowsByIndex[0][1]}"/>
```

For a `SET` column, the `defList` value might contain multiple values, separated by commas. It needs no special treatment; the JSTL `<c:forEach>` tag can iterate over such a string, so initialize the default values for a checkbox set as follows:

```
<c:forEach items="${values}" var="val">
  <input type="checkbox" name="accessories"
    value="<c:out value="${val}"/>"
    <c:forEach items="${defList}" var="default">
      <c:if test="${val == default}">checked="checked"</c:if>
    </c:forEach>
  /><c:out value="${val}"/><br />
</c:forEach>
```

For a multiple-pick scrolling list, do this:

```
<select name="accessories" size="3" multiple="multiple">
<c:forEach items="${values}" var="val">
  <option
    value="<c:out value="${val}"/>"
    <c:forEach items="${defList}" var="default">
      <c:if test="${val == default}">selected="selected"</c:if>
    </c:forEach>
  >
  <c:out value="${val}"/></option>
</c:forEach>
</select>
```

19.4 Loading a Database Record into a Form

Problem

You want to display a form but initialize it using the contents of a database record. This enables you to present a record-editing form.

Solution

Generate the form as you usually would, but populate it with database content. That is, instead of setting the form element defaults to their usual values, set them to the values of columns in the database record.

Discussion

The examples in earlier recipes that show how to generate form fields have either supplied no default value or have used the default value as specified in an ENUM or SET column definition as the field default. That's most appropriate for presenting a "blank" form that you expect the user to fill in. However, for applications that present a web-based interface for record editing, it's more likely that you'd want to fill in the form using the content of an existing record for the initial values. This section discusses how to do that.

The examples shown here illustrate how to generate an editing form for rows from the cow_order table. Normally, you would allow the user to specify which record to edit. For simplicity, assume the use of the record that has an id value of 1, with the following contents:

```
mysql> SELECT * FROM cow_order WHERE id = 1\G
*************************** 1. row ***************************
         id: 1
      color: Black & White
       size: large
 accessories: cow bell,nose ring
  cust_name: Farmer Brown
cust_street: 123 Elm St.
  cust_city: Katy
 cust_state: TX
```

To generate a form with contents that correspond to a database record, use the column values for the element defaults as follows:

- For <input> elements such as radio buttons or checkboxes, add a checked attribute to each list item that matches the column value.

- For <select> elements such as pop-up menus or scrolling lists, add a selected attribute to each list item that matches the column value.

- For text fields represented as <input> elements of type text, set the value attribute to the corresponding column value. For example, a 60-character field for cust_name can be presented initialized to Farmer Brown like this:

    ```
    <input type="text" name="cust_name" value="Farmer Brown" size="60" />
    ```

To present a <textarea> element instead, set the body to the column value. To create a field 40 columns wide and 3 rows high, write it like this:

```
<textarea name="cust_name" cols="40" rows="3">
Farmer Brown
</textarea>
```

- In a record-editing situation, it's a good idea to include a unique value in the form so that you can tell which record the form contents represent when the user submits it. Use a hidden field to do this. Its value is not displayed to the user, but the browser returns it with the rest of the field values. Our sample record has an `id` column with a value of `1`, so the hidden field looks like this:

```
<input type="hidden" name="id" value="1" />
```

The following examples show how to produce a form with `id` represented as a hidden field, `color` as a pop-up menu, `size` as a set of radio buttons, and `accessories` as a set of checkboxes. The customer information values are represented as text input boxes, except that `cust_state` is a single-pick scrolling list. You could make other choices, of course, such as to present the sizes as a pop-up menu rather than as radio buttons.

The `recipes` distribution scripts for the examples in this section are named *cow_edit.pl*, *cow_edit.jsp*, and so forth.

The following procedure outlines how to load the sample `cow_table` record into an editing form for a CGI.pm-based Perl script:

1. Retrieve the column values for the record that you want to load into the form:

```
my $id = 1;      # select record number 1
my ($color, $size, $accessories,
    $cust_name, $cust_street, $cust_city, $cust_state) =
        $dbh->selectrow_array (
                "SELECT
                    color, size, accessories,
                    cust_name, cust_street, cust_city, cust_state
                 FROM cow_order WHERE id = ?",
                undef, $id);
```

2. Begin the form:

```
print start_form (-action => url ());
```

3. Generate the hidden field containing the `id` value that uniquely identifies the `cow_order` record:

```
print hidden (-name => "id", -value => $id, -override => 1);
```

The `override` argument forces CGI.pm to use the value specified in the `value` argument as the hidden field value. If `override` is not true, CGI.pm normally tries to use values present in the script execution environment to initialize form fields, even if you provide values in the field-generating calls. (CGI.pm does this to make it easier to redisplay a form with the values the user just submitted. For example, if you find that a form has been filled in incorrectly, you can redisplay it and ask the user to correct any problems. To make sure that a form element contains the value you specify, it's necessary to override this behavior.)

4. Create the fields that describe the cow figurine specifications. These fields are generated the same way as described in Recipes 19.2 and 19.3, except that the default values come from the contents of record 1. The code here presents color as a popup menu, size as a set of radio buttons, and accessories as a set of checkboxes. Note that it splits the accessories value at commas to produce an array of values, because the column value might name several accessory items:

```perl
my $color_ref = $dbh->selectcol_arrayref (
                    "SELECT color FROM cow_color ORDER BY color");

print br (), "Cow color:", br ();
print popup_menu (-name => "color",
                    -values => $color_ref,
                    -default => $color,
                    -override => 1);

my $size_info = get_enumorset_info ($dbh, "cookbook",
                                "cow_order", "size");

print br (), "Cow figurine size:", br ();
print radio_group (-name => "size",
                    -values => $size_info->{values},
                    -default => $size,
                    -override => 1,
                    -linebreak => 1);

my $acc_info = get_enumorset_info ($dbh, "cookbook",
                                "cow_order", "accessories");
my @acc_val = (defined ($accessories)
                    ? split (/,/, $accessories)
                    : () );

print br (), "Cow accessory items:", br ();
print checkbox_group (-name => "accessories",
                        -values => $acc_info->{values},
                        -default => \@acc_val,
                        -override => 1,
                        -linebreak => 1);
```

5. Create the customer information fields. These are represented as text input fields, except the state, which is shown here as a single-pick scrolling list:

```perl
print br (), "Customer name:", br ();
print textfield (-name => "cust_name",
                    -value => $cust_name,
                    -override => 1,
                    -size => 60);

print br (), "Customer street address:", br ();
print textfield (-name => "cust_street",
                    -value => $cust_street,
                    -override => 1,
                    -size => 60);

print br (), "Customer city:", br ();
```

```
print textfield (-name => "cust_city",
                 -value => $cust_city,
                 -override => 1,
                 -size => 60);

my @state_values;
my %state_labels;
my $sth = $dbh->prepare ("SELECT abbrev, name
                          FROM states ORDER BY name");
$sth->execute ();
while (my ($abbrev, $name) = $sth->fetchrow_array ())
{
  push (@state_values, $abbrev);  # save each value in an array
  $state_labels{$abbrev} = $name; # map each value to its label
}

print br (), "Customer state:", br ();
print scrolling_list (-name => "cust_state",
                      -values => \@state_values,
                      -labels => \%state_labels,
                      -default => $cust_state,
                      -override => 1,
                      -size => 6);      # display 6 items at a time
```

6. Create a form submission button and terminate the form:

```
print br (),
      submit (-name => "choice", -value => "Submit Form"),
      end_form ();
```

The same general procedure applies to other APIs. For example, in a JSP page, you can fetch the record to be edited and extract its contents into scalar variables like this:

```
<c:set var="id" value="1"/>
<sql:query dataSource="${conn}" var="rs">
  SELECT
    id, color, size, accessories,
    cust_name, cust_street, cust_city, cust_state
  FROM cow_order WHERE id = ?
  <sql:param value="${id}"/>
</sql:query>

<c:set var="row" value="${rs.rows[0]}"/>
<c:set var="id" value="${row.id}"/>
<c:set var="color" value="${row.color}"/>
<c:set var="size" value="${row.size}"/>
<c:set var="accessories" value="${row.accessories}"/>
<c:set var="cust_name" value="${row.cust_name}"/>
<c:set var="cust_street" value="${row.cust_street}"/>
<c:set var="cust_city" value="${row.cust_city}"/>
<c:set var="cust_state" value="${row.cust_state}"/>
```

Then use the values to initialize the various form elements, such as:

- The hidden field for the ID value:

```
<input type="hidden" name="id" value="<c:out value="${id}"/>"/>
```

- The color pop-up menu:

```
<sql:query dataSource="${conn}" var="rs">
  SELECT color FROM cow_color ORDER BY color
</sql:query>
<br />Cow color:<br />
<select name="color">
<c:forEach items="${rs.rows}" var="row">
  <option
    value="<c:out value="${row.color}"/>"
    <c:if test="${row.color == color}">selected="selected"</c:if>
  ><c:out value="${row.color}"/></option>
</c:forEach>
</select>
```

- The cust_name text field:

```
<br />Customer name:<br />
<input type="text" name="cust_name"
  value="<c:out value="${cust_name}"/>"
  size="60" />
```

For Ruby, PHP, or Python, create the form using the utility functions developed in Recipes 19.2 and 19.3. See the *cow_edit.rb*, *cow_edit.php*, and *cow_edit.py* scripts for details.

19.5 Collecting Web Input

Problem

You want to extract the input parameters that were submitted as part of a form or specified at the end of a URL.

Solution

Use the capabilities of your API that provide a means of accessing the names and values of the input parameters in the execution environment of a web script.

Discussion

Earlier recipes in this chapter discussed how to retrieve information from MySQL and use it to generate various forms of output, such as static text, lists, hyperlinks, or form elements. In this recipe, we discuss the opposite problem—how to collect input from the Web. Applications for such input are many. For example, you can use the techniques shown here to extract the contents of a form submitted by a user. You might interpret the information as a set of search keywords, and then run a query against a product catalog to show the matching items to a customer. In this case, you use the Web to collect information from which you can determine the client's interests. From that you construct an appropriate search statement and display the results. If a form represents a survey, a mailing list sign-up sheet, or a poll, you might just store the values, using the data to create a new database record (or perhaps to update an existing record).

A script that receives input over the Web and uses it to interact with MySQL generally processes the information in a series of stages:

1. Extract the input from the execution environment. When a request arrives that contains input parameters, the web server places the input into the environment of the script that handles the request, and the script queries its environment to obtain the parameters. It may be necessary to decode special characters in the parameters to recover the actual values submitted by the client, if the extraction mechanism provided by your API doesn't do it for you. (For example, you might need to convert %20 to space.)

2. Validate the input to make sure that it's legal. You cannot trust users to send legal values, so it's a good idea to check input parameters to make sure they look reasonable. For example, if you expect a user to enter a number into a field, you should check the value to be sure that it's really numeric. If a form contains a pop-up menu that was constructed using the allowable values of an ENUM column, you might expect the value that you actually get back to be one of these values. But there's no way to be sure except to check. Remember, you don't even know that there is a real user on the other end of the network connection. It might be a malicious script roving your web site, trying to hack into your site by exploiting weaknesses in your form-processing code.

   If you don't check your input, you run the risk of entering garbage into your database or corrupting existing content. It is true that you can prevent entry of values that are invalid for the data types in your table columns by enabling strict SQL mode. However, there might be additional semantic constraints on what your application considers legal, in which case it is still useful to check values in your script before attempting to enter them. Also, by checking in your script, you may be able to present more meaningful error messages to users about problems in the input than the messages returned by the MySQL server when it detects bad data. For these reasons, it might be best to consider strict SQL mode a valuable additional level of protection, but one that is not necessarily sufficient in itself. That is, you can combine strict mode on the server side with client-side validation. See Recipe 10.20 for additional information about setting the SQL mode for strict input value checking.

3. Construct a statement based on the input. Typically, input parameters are used to add a record to a database, or to retrieve information from the database for display to the client. Either way, you use the input to construct a statement and send it to the MySQL server. Statement construction based on user input should be done with care, using proper escaping to avoid creating malformed or dangerous SQL statements. Use of placeholders is a good idea here.

The rest of this recipe explores the first of these three stages of input processing. Recipes 19.6 and 19.7 cover the second and third stages. The first stage (pulling input from the execution environment) has little to do with MySQL, but is covered here because it's how you obtain the information that is used in the later stages.

Input obtained over the Web can be received in several ways, two of which are most common:

- As part of a `get` request, in which case input parameters are appended to the end of the URL. For example, the following URL invokes a PHP script named *price_quote.php* and specifies `item` and `quantity` parameters with values `D-0214` and `60`:

      http://localhost/mcb/price_quote.php?item=D-0214&quantity=60

  Such requests commonly are received when a user selects a hyperlink or submits a form that specifies `method="get"` in the `<form>` tag. A parameter list in a URL begins with `?` and consists of *name=value* pairs separated by `;` or `&` characters. (It's also possible to place information in the middle of a URL, but this book doesn't cover that.)

- As part of a `post` request, such as a form submission that specifies `method="post"` in the `<form>` tag. The contents of a form for a `post` request are sent as input parameters in the body of the request, rather than at the end of the URL.

You may also have occasion to process other types of input, such as uploaded files. Those are sent using `post` requests, but as part of a special kind of form element. Recipe 19.8 discusses file uploading.

When you gather input for a web script, you should consider how the input was sent. (Some APIs distinguish between input sent via `get` and `post`; others do not.) However, after you have pulled out the information that was sent, the request method doesn't matter. The validation and statement construction stages do not need to know whether parameters were sent using `get` or `post`.

The `recipes` distribution includes some scripts in the *apache/params* directory (*tomcat/mcb* for JSP) that process input parameters. Each script enables you to submit `get` or `post` requests, and shows how to extract and display the parameter values thus submitted. Examine these scripts to see how the parameter extraction methods for the various APIs are used. Utility routines invoked by the scripts can be found in the library modules in the *lib* directory of the distribution.

Web input extraction conventions

To obtain input parameters passed to a script, you should familiarize yourself with your API's conventions so that you know what it does for you, and what you must do yourself. For example, you should know the answers to these questions:

- How do you determine which parameters are available?

- How do you pull a parameter value from the environment?
- Are values thus obtained the actual values submitted by the client, or do you need to decode them further?
- How are multiple-valued parameters handled (for example, when several items in a checkbox group are selected)?
- For parameters submitted in a URL, which separator character does the API expect between parameters? This may be & for some APIs and ; for others. ; is preferable as a parameter separator because it's not special in HTML like & is, but many browsers or other user agents separate parameters using &. If you construct a URL within a script that includes parameters at the end, be sure to use a parameter-separator character that the receiving script will understand.

Perl. The Perl CGI.pm module makes input parameters available to scripts through the param( ) function. param( ) provides access to input submitted via either get or post, which simplifies your task as the script writer. You don't need to know which method a form used for submitting parameters. You don't need to perform any decoding, either; param( ) handles that as well.

To obtain a list of names of all available parameters, call param( ) with no arguments:

```
@param_names = param ();
```

To obtain the value of a specific parameter, pass its name to param( ). In scalar context, param( ) returns the parameter value if it is single-valued, the first value if it is multiple-valued, or undef if the parameter is not available. In array context, param( ) returns a list containing all the parameter's values, or an empty list if the parameter is not available:

```
$id = param ("id");
@options = param ("options");
```

A parameter with a given name might not be available if the form field with that name was left blank, or if there isn't any field with that name. Note too that a parameter value may be defined but empty. For good measure, you may want to check both possibilities. For example, to check for an age parameter and assign a default value of unknown if the parameter is missing or empty, you can do this:

```
$age = param ("age");
$age = "unknown" if !defined ($age) || $age eq "";
```

CGI.pm understands both ; and & as URL parameter separator characters.

Ruby. For Ruby scripts that use the cgi module, web script parameters are available through the same cgi object that you create for generating HTML elements. Its param method returns a hash of parameter names and values, so you can access this hash or get the parameter names as follows:

```
params = cgi.params
param_names = cgi.params.keys
```

The value of a particular parameter is accessible either through the hash of parameter names and values or directly through the `cgi` object:

```
id = cgi.params["id"]
id = cgi["id"]
```

The two access methods differ slightly. The `params` method returns each parameter value as an array. The array contains multiple entries if the parameter has multiple values, and is empty if the parameter is not present. The `cgi` object returns a single string. If the parameter has multiple values, only the first is returned. If the parameter is not present, the value is the empty string. For either access method, use the `has_key?` method to test whether a parameter is present.

The following listing shows how to get the parameter names and loop through each parameter to print its name and value, printing multiple-valued parameters as a comma-separated list:

```
params = cgi.params
param_names = cgi.params.keys
param_names.sort!
page << cgi.p { "Parameter names:" + param_names.join(", ") }

list = ""
param_names.each do |name|
  val = params[name]
  list << cgi.li {
            "type=#{val.class}, name=#{name}, value=" +
            CGI.escapeHTML(val.join(", "))
          }
end
page << cgi.ul { list }
```

The `cgi` module understands both `;` and `&` as URL parameter separator characters.

PHP. Input parameters can be available to PHP in several ways, depending on your configuration settings:

- If the `track_vars` variable is on, parameters are available in the `$HTTP_GET_VARS` and `$HTTP_POST_VARS` arrays. For example, if a form contains a field named `id`, the value will be available as `$HTTP_GET_VARS["id"]` or `$HTTP_POST_VARS["id"]`, depending on whether the form was submitted via GET or POST. If you access `$HTTP_GET_VARS` and `$HTTP_POST_VARS` in a nonglobal scope, such as within a function, you must declare them using the `global` keyword to make them accessible.

- As of PHP 4.1, parameters also are available in the `$_GET` and `$_POST` arrays if `track_vars` is on. These are analogous to `$HTTP_GET_VARS` and `$HTTP_POST_VARS` except that they are "superglobal" arrays that are automatically available in any scope. (For example, it is unnecessary to declare `$_GET` and `$_POST` with `global` inside of functions.) The `$_GET` and `$_POST` arrays are the preferred means of accessing input parameters.

- If the `register_globals` variable is on, parameters are assigned to global variables of the same name. In this case, the value of a field named `id` will be available as the variable `$id`, regardless of whether the request was sent via GET or POST. This is dangerous, for reasons described shortly.

The `track_vars` and `register_globals` settings can be compiled into PHP or configured in the PHP *php.ini* file. `track_vars` is always enabled as of PHP 4.0.3, so I'll assume that this is true for your PHP installation.

`register_globals` makes it convenient to access input parameters through global variables, but the PHP developers recommend that it be disabled for security reasons. Suppose that you write a script that requires the user to supply a password, which is represented by the `$password` variable. In the script, you might check the password like this:

```
if (check_password ($password))
  $password_is_ok = 1;
```

The intent here is that if the password matches, the script sets `$password_is_ok` to `1`. Otherwise `$password_is_ok` is left unset (which compares false in Boolean expressions). But suppose that someone invokes your script as follows:

```
http://your.host.com/chkpass.php?password_is_ok=1
```

If `register_globals` is enabled, PHP sees that the `password_is_ok` parameter is set to `1` and sets the corresponding `$password_is_ok` variable to `1`. The result is that when your script executes, `$password_is_ok` is `1` no matter what password was given, or even if *no* password was given! The problem with `register_globals` is that it enables outside users to supply default values for global variables in your scripts. The best solution is to disable `register_globals`, in which case you need to check the global arrays for input parameter values. If you cannot disable `register_globals`, take care not to assume that PHP variables have no value initially. Unless you're expecting a global variable to be set from an input parameter, it's best to initialize it explicitly to a known value. The password-checking code should be written as follows to make sure that only `$password` (and not `$password_is_ok`) can be set from an input parameter. That way, `$password_is_ok` is assigned a value by the script itself whatever the result of the test:

```
$password_is_ok = 0;
if (check_password ($password))
  $password_is_ok = 1;
```

The PHP scripts in this book do not rely on the `register_globals` setting. Instead, they obtain input through the global parameter arrays.

Another complicating factor when retrieving input parameters in PHP is that they may need some decoding, depending on the value of the `magic_quotes_gpc` configuration variable. If magic quotes are enabled, any quote, backslash, and NUL characters in input parameter values accessed by your scripts will be escaped with backslashes. I suppose that this is intended to save you a step by allowing you to extract values and use them directly in SQL statement strings. However, that's only useful if you plan to use web input in a statement with no preprocessing or validity checking, which is dangerous. You should check your input first, in which case it's necessary to strip out the slashes, anyway. This means that having magic quotes turned on isn't really very useful.

Given the various sources through which input parameters may be available, and the fact that they may or may not contain extra backslashes, extracting input in PHP scripts can be an interesting problem. If you have control of your server and can set the values of the various configuration settings, you can of course write your scripts based on those settings. But if you do not control your server or are writing scripts that need to run on several machines, you may not know in advance what the settings are. Fortunately, with a bit of effort it's possible to write reasonably general-purpose parameter extraction code that works correctly with very few assumptions about your PHP operating environment. The following utility function, `get_param_val( )`, takes a parameter name as its argument and returns the corresponding parameter value. If the parameter is not available, the function returns an unset value. (`get_param_val( )` uses a helper function, `strip_slash_helper( )`, which is discussed shortly.)

```
function get_param_val ($name)
{
global $HTTP_GET_VARS, $HTTP_POST_VARS;

  $val = NULL;
  if (isset ($_GET[$name]))
    $val = $_GET[$name];
  else if (isset ($_POST[$name]))
    $val = $_POST[$name];
  else if (isset ($HTTP_GET_VARS[$name]))
    $val = $HTTP_GET_VARS[$name];
  else if (isset ($HTTP_POST_VARS[$name]))
    $val = $HTTP_POST_VARS[$name];
  if (isset ($val) && get_magic_quotes_gpc ())
    $val = strip_slash_helper ($val);
  return ($val);
}
```

To use this function to obtain the value of a single-valued parameter named `id`, call it like this:

```
$id = get_param_val ("id");
```

You can test `$id` to determine whether the `id` parameter was present in the input:

```
if (isset ($id))
  ... id parameter is present ...
else
  ... id parameter is not present ...
```

For a form field that might have multiple values (such as a checkbox group or a multiple-pick scrolling list), you should represent it in the form using a name that ends in []. For example, a list element constructed from the SET column `accessories` in the `cow_order` table has one item for each allowable set value. To make sure PHP treats the element value as an array, name the field `accessories[]`, not `accessories`. (See Recipe 19.3 for an example.) When the form is submitted, PHP places the array of values in a parameter named without the [ ]. To access it, do this:

```
$accessories = get_param_val ("accessories");
```

The value of the $accessories variable will be an array, whether the parameter has multiple values, a single value, or even no values. The determining factor is not whether the parameter actually *has* multiple values, but whether you named the corresponding field in the form using [ ] notation.

The get_param_val() function checks the $_GET, $_POST, $HTTP_GET_VARS, and $HTTP_POST_VARS arrays for parameter values. Thus, it works correctly regardless of whether the request was made by GET or POST, or whether register_globals is enabled. The only thing that the function assumes is that track_vars is enabled.

get_param_val() also works correctly regardless of whether magic quoting is enabled. It uses a helper function strip_slash_helper() that performs backslash stripping from parameter values if necessary:

```
function strip_slash_helper ($val)
{
  if (!is_array ($val))
    $val = stripslashes ($val);
  else
  {
    foreach ($val as $k => $v)
      $val[$k] = strip_slash_helper ($v);
  }
  return ($val);
}
```

strip_slash_helper() checks whether a value is a scalar or an array and processes it accordingly. The reason it uses a recursive algorithm for array values is that in PHP it's possible to create nested arrays from input parameters.

To make it easy to obtain a list of all parameter names, use another utility function:

```
function get_param_names ()
{
global $HTTP_GET_VARS, $HTTP_POST_VARS;

  # construct an array in which each element has a parameter name as
  # both key and value.  (Using names as keys eliminates duplicates.)
  $keys = array ();
  if (isset ($_GET))
  {
    foreach ($_GET as $k => $v)
      $keys[$k] = $k;
  }
  else if (isset ($HTTP_GET_VARS))
  {
    foreach ($HTTP_GET_VARS as $k => $v)
      $keys[$k] = $k;
  }
```

```
    if (isset ($_POST))
    {
      foreach ($_POST as $k => $v)
        $keys[$k] = $k;
    }
    else if (isset ($HTTP_POST_VARS))
    {
      foreach ($HTTP_POST_VARS as $k => $v)
        $keys[$k] = $k;
    }
    return ($keys);
}
```

get_param_names( ) returns a list of parameter names present in the HTTP variable arrays, with duplicate names removed if there is overlap between the arrays. The return value is an array with its keys and values both set to the parameter names. This way you can use either the keys or the values as the list of names. The following example prints the names, using the values:

```
$param_names = get_param_names ();
foreach ($param_names as $k => $v)
    print (htmlspecialchars ($v) . "<br />\n");
```

To construct URLs that point to PHP scripts and that have parameters at the end, you should separate the parameters by & characters. To use a different character (such as ;), change the separator by means of the arg_separator configuration variable in the PHP initialization file.

Python. The Python cgi module provides access to the input parameters that are present in the script environment. Import that module, and then create a FieldStorage object:

```
import cgi

params = cgi.FieldStorage ()
```

The FieldStorage object contains information for parameters submitted via either GET or POST requests, so you need not know which method was used to send the request. The object also contains an element for each parameter present in the environment. Its key( ) method returns a list of available parameter names:

```
param_names = params.keys ()
```

If a given parameter, name, is single-valued, the value associated with it is a scalar that you can access as follows:

```
val = params[name].value
```

If the parameter is multiple-valued, params[name] is a list of MiniFieldStorage objects that have name and value attributes. Each of these has the same name (it will be equal to name) and one of the parameter's values. To create a list containing all the values for such a parameter, do this:

```
val = []
for item in params[name]:
  val.append (item.value)
```

You can distinguish single-valued from multiple-valued parameters by checking the type. The following listing shows how to get the parameter names and loop through each parameter to print its name and value, printing multiple-valued parameters as a comma-separated list. This code requires that you import the **types** module in addition to the **cgi** module.

```
params = cgi.FieldStorage ()
param_names = params.keys ()
param_names.sort ()
print "<p>Parameter names:", param_names, "</p>"
items = []
for name in param_names:
  if type (params[name]) is not types.ListType:  # it's a scalar
    ptype = "scalar"
    val = params[name].value
  else:                                          # it's a list
    ptype = "list"
    val = []
    for item in params[name]:   # iterate through MiniFieldStorage
      val.append (item.value)   # items to get item values
    val = ",".join (val)        # convert to string for printing
  items.append ("type=" + ptype + ", name=" + name + ", value=" + val)
print make_unordered_list (items)
```

Python raises an exception if you try to access a parameter that is not present in the **FieldStorage** object. To avoid this, use **has_key( )** to find out if the parameter exists:

```
if params.has_key (name):
  print "parameter " + name + " exists"
else:
  print "parameter " + name + " does not exist"
```

Single-valued parameters have attributes other than **value**. For example, a parameter representing an uploaded file has additional attributes you can use to get the file's contents. Recipe 19.8 discusses this further.

The **cgi** module expects URL parameters to be separated by **&** characters. If you generate a hyperlink to a Python script based on the **cgi** module and the URL includes parameters, don't separate them by **;** characters.

Java. Within JSP pages, the implicit **request** object provides access to the request parameters through the following methods:

getParameterNames( )

> Returns an enumeration of **String** objects, one for each parameter name present in the request.

getParameterValues(String name)

> Returns an array of **String** objects, one for each value associated with the parameter, or **null** if the parameter does not exist.

```
getParameterValue(String name)
```
Returns the first value associated with the parameter, or `null` if the parameter does not exist.

The following example shows one way to use these methods to display request parameters:

```
<%@ page import="java.util.*" %>

<ul>
<%
  Enumeration e = request.getParameterNames ();
  while (e.hasMoreElements ())
  {
    String name = (String) e.nextElement ();
    // use array in case parameter is multiple-valued
    String[] val = request.getParameterValues (name);
    out.println ("<li> name: " + name + "; values:");
    for (int i = 0; i < val.length; i++)
      out.println (val[i]);
    out.println ("</li>");
  }
%>
</ul>
```

Request parameters are also available within JSTL tags, using the special variables `param` and `paramValues`. `param[name]` returns the first value for a given parameter and thus is most suited for single-valued parameters:

```
color value:
<c:out value="${param['color']}"/>
```

`paramValues[name]` returns an array of values for the parameter, so it's useful for parameters that can have multiple values:

```
accessory values:
<c:forEach items="${paramValues['accessories']}" var="val">
  <c:out value="${val}"/>
</c:forEach>
```

If a parameter name is legal as an object property name, you can also access the parameter using dot notation:

```
color value:
<c:out value="${param.color}"/>
accessory values:
<c:forEach items="${paramValues.accessories}" var="val">
  <c:out value="${val}"/>
</c:forEach>
```

To produce a list of parameter objects with **key** and **value** attributes, iterate over the `paramValues` variable:

```
<ul>
  <c:forEach items="${paramValues}" var="p">
    <li>
```

```
        name:
        <c:out value="${p.key}"/>;
        values:
        <c:forEach items="${p.value}" var="val">
          <c:out value="${val}"/>
        </c:forEach>
      </li>
    </c:forEach>
  </ul>
```

To construct URLs that point to JSP pages and that have parameters at the end, you should separate the parameters by & characters.

19.6 Validating Web Input

Problem

After extracting the parameters supplied to a script, you want to check them to be sure they're valid.

Solution

Web input processing is one form of data import, so after you've extracted the input parameters, you can validate them using the techniques discussed in Chapter 10.

Discussion

One phase of web form processing is to extract the input that comes back when the user submits the form. It's also possible to receive input in the form of parameters at the end of a URL. Either way, if you're going to store the input in your database, it's a good idea to check it to be sure that it's valid.

When clients send input to you over the Web, you don't really know what they're sending. If you present a form for users to fill out, most of the time they'll probably be nice and enter the kinds of values you expect. But a malicious user can save the form to a file, modify the file to allow form options you don't intend, reload the file into a browser window, and submit the modified form. Your form-processing script won't know the difference. If you write it only to process the kinds of values that well-intentioned users will submit, the script may misbehave or crash when presented with unexpected input—or perhaps even do bad things to your database. (Recipe 19.7 discusses what kinds of bad things can happen.) For this reason, it's prudent to perform some validity checking on web input before using it to construct SQL statements.

Preliminary checking is a good idea even for nonmalicious users. If you require a field to be filled in and the user forgets to provide a value, you'll need to remind the user to supply one. This might involve a simple "Is the parameter present?" check, or it might be more involved. Typical validation operations include the following:

- Checking content format, such as making sure a value looks like an integer or a date. This may involve some reformatting for acceptability to MySQL (for example, changing a date from *MM/DD/YY* to ISO format).

- Determining whether a value is a member of a legal set of values. Perhaps the value must be listed in the definition for an `ENUM` or `SET` column, or must be present in a lookup table.

- Filtering out extraneous characters such as spaces or dashes from telephone numbers or credit card numbers.

Some of these operations have little to do with MySQL, except in the sense that you want values to be appropriate for the types of the columns in which you'll store them or against which you'll match them. For example, if you're going to store a value in an `INT` column, you can make sure that it's an integer first, using a test like this (shown here using Perl):

```
$val =~ /^\d+$/
    or die "Hey! '" . escapeHTML ($val) . "' is not an integer!\n";
```

For other types of validation, MySQL is intimately involved. If a field value is to be stored into an `ENUM` column, you can make sure the value is one of the legal enumeration values by checking the column definition in `INFORMATION_SCHEMA`.

Having described some of the kinds of web input validation you might want to carry out, I won't further discuss them here. These and other forms of validation testing are described in Chapter 10. That chapter is oriented largely toward bulk input validation, but the techniques discussed there apply to web programming as well because processing form input or URL parameters is in essence a data import operation.

19.7 Storing Web Input in a Database

Problem

Input obtained over the Web cannot be trusted and should not be entered into a database without taking the proper precautions.

Solution

Sanitize data values by using placeholders or a quoting function so that SQL statements you construct are valid and not subject to SQL injection attacks. Also, enabling strict SQL mode causes the MySQL server to reject values that are invalid for column data types.

Discussion

After you've extracted input parameter values in a web script and checked them to make sure they're valid, you're ready to use them to construct an SQL statement. This is actually the easy part of input processing, although it's necessary to take the proper precautions to avoid making a mistake that you'll regret. First, let's consider what can go wrong, and then see how to prevent problems.

Suppose that you have a search form that contains a keyword field and acts as a frontend to a simple search engine. When a user submits a keyword, you intend to use it to find matching rows in a table by constructing a statement like this:

```
SELECT * FROM mytbl WHERE keyword = 'keyword_val'
```

Here, `keyword_val` represents the value entered by the user. If the value is something like `eggplant`, the resulting statement is:

```
SELECT * FROM mytbl WHERE keyword = 'eggplant'
```

The statement returns all eggplant-matching rows, presumably generating a small result set. But suppose that the user is tricky and tries to subvert your script by entering the following value:

```
eggplant' OR 'x'='x
```

In this case, the statement becomes:

```
SELECT * FROM mytbl WHERE keyword = 'eggplant' OR 'x'='x'
```

That statement matches every row in the table! If the table is quite large, the input effectively becomes a form of denial-of-service attack, because it causes your system to divert resources away from legitimate requests into doing useless work. This type of attack is known as *SQL injection* because the user is injecting executable SQL code into your statement where you expect to receive only a nonexecutable data value. Likely results of SQL injection attacks include the following:

- Extra load on the MySQL server
- Out-of-memory problems in your script as it tries to digest the result set received from MySQL
- Extra network bandwidth consumption as the script sends the results to the client

If your script generates a DELETE or UPDATE statement, the consequences of this kind of subversion can be much worse. Your script might issue a statement that empties a table completely or changes all of its rows, when you intended to allow it to affect only a single row.

The implication of the preceding discussion is that providing a web interface to your database opens you up to certain forms of security vulnerabilities. However, you can prevent these problems by means of a simple precaution that you should already be following: don't put data values literally into statement strings. Use placeholders or an encoding function instead. For example, in Perl you can handle an input parameter by using a placeholder:

```
$sth = $dbh->prepare ("SELECT * FROM mytbl WHERE keyword = ?");
$sth->execute (param ("keyword"));
# ... fetch result set ...
```

Or by using `quote( )`:

```
$keyword = $dbh->quote (param ("keyword"));
$sth = $dbh->prepare ("SELECT * FROM mytbl WHERE keyword = $keyword");
$sth->execute ();
# ... fetch result set ...
```

Either way, if the user enters the subversive value, the statement becomes harmless:

```
SELECT * FROM mytbl WHERE keyword = 'eggplant\' OR \'x\'=\'x'
```

As a result, the statement matches no rows rather than all rows—definitely a more suitable response to someone who's trying to break your script.

Placeholder and quoting techniques for Ruby, PHP, Python, and Java are similar, and have been discussed in Recipe 2.5. For JSP pages written using the JSTL tag library, you can quote input parameter values using placeholders and the `<sql:param>` tag (Recipe 17.3). For example, to use the value of a form parameter named `keyword` in a `SELECT` statement, do this:

```
<sql:query dataSource="${conn}" var="rs">
  SELECT * FROM mytbl WHERE keyword = ?
  <sql:param value="${param['keyword']}"/>
</sql:query>
```

One issue not covered by placeholder techniques involves a question of interpretation: If a form field is optional, what should you store in the database if the user leaves the field empty? Perhaps the value represents an empty string—or perhaps it should be interpreted as `NULL`. One way to resolve this question is to consult the column metadata. If the column can contain `NULL` values, interpret an empty field as `NULL`. Otherwise, take an empty field to mean an empty string.

Placeholders and encoding functions apply only to SQL data values. One issue not addressed by them is how to handle web input used for other kinds of statement elements such as the names of databases, tables, and columns. If you intend to include such values into a statement, you must insert them literally, which means you should check them first. For example, if you construct a statement such as the following, you should verify that `$tbl_name` contains a reasonable value:

```
SELECT * FROM $tbl_name;
```

But what does "reasonable" mean? If you don't have tables containing strange characters in their names, it may be sufficient to make sure that `$tbl_name` contains only alphanumeric characters or underscores. An alternative is to issue a statement that determines whether the table actually exists. (You can check `INFORMATION_SCHEMA` or use `SHOW TABLES`.) This is more foolproof, at the cost of an additional statement.

A better option is to use an identifier-quoting routine, if you have one. This approach requires no extra statement because it renders any string safe for use in a statement. If the identifier does not exist, the statement simply fails as it should. Recipe 2.6 discusses this option further.

For additional protection in your web scripts, combine client-side checking of input values with strict server-side checking. You can set the server SQL mode to be restrictive about accepting input values so that it rejects values that don't match your table column data types. For discussion of the SQL mode and input value checking, see Recipe 10.20.

You Should Try to Break Your Scripts

The discussion in this recipe has been phrased in terms of guarding against other users from attacking your scripts. But it's not a bad idea to put yourself in the place of an attacker and adopt the mindset, "How can I break this application?" That is, consider whether there is some input you can submit to it that the application won't handle, and that will cause it to generate a malformed statement. If you can cause an application to misbehave, so can other people, either deliberately or accidentally. Be wary of bad input, and write your applications accordingly. It's better to be prepared than to just hope.

See Also

Several other recipes in this chapter illustrate how to incorporate web input into statements. Recipe 19.8 shows how to upload files and load them into MySQL. Recipe 19.9 demonstrates a simple search application using input as search keywords. Recipes 19.10 and 19.11 process parameters submitted via URLs.

19.8 Processing File Uploads

Problem

You want to allow files to be uploaded to your web server and stored in your database.

Solution

Present the user with a web form that includes a file field. When the user submits the form, extract the file and store it.

Discussion

One special kind of web input is an uploaded file. A file is sent as part of a post request, but it's handled differently from other post parameters, because a file is represented by several pieces of information such as its contents, its MIME type, its original filename on the client, and its name in temporary storage on the web server host.

To handle file uploads, you must send a special kind of form to the user; this is true no matter what API you use to create the form. When the user submits the form, the operations that check for and process an uploaded file are API-specific.

To create a form that enables files to be uploaded, the opening `<form>` tag should specify the `post` method and must also include an `enctype` (encoding type) attribute with a value of `multipart/form-data`:

```
<form method="post" enctype="multipart/form-data" action="script_name">
```

If the form is submitted using the `application/x-www-form-urlencoded` encoding type, file uploads will not work properly.

To include a file upload field in the form, use an `<input>` element of type `file`. For example, to present a 60-character file field named `upload_file`, the element looks like this:

```
<input type="file" name="upload_file" size="60" />
```

The browser displays this field as a text input box into which the user can enter the name manually. It also presents a Browse button that enables the user to select the file via a standard file-browsing system dialog. When the user chooses a file and submits the form, the browser encodes the file contents for inclusion into the resulting `post` request. At that point, the web server receives the request and invokes your script to process it. The specifics vary for particular APIs, but file uploads generally work like this:

- The file will already have been uploaded and stored in a temporary directory by the time your upload-handling script begins executing. All your script has to do is read it. The temporary file is available to your script either as an open file descriptor or the temporary filename, or perhaps both. The size of the file can be obtained through the file descriptor. The API may also make available other information about the file, such as its MIME type. (But note that some browsers may not send a MIME value.)

- The web server automatically deletes uploaded files when your script terminates. If you want a file's contents to persist beyond the end of your script's execution, the script must save the file to a more permanent location, such as in a database or somewhere else in the filesystem. If you save the file in the filesystem, the directory where you store it must be accessible to the web server. (But don't put it under the document root or any user home directories, or a remote attacker would effectively be able to install scripts and HTML files on your web server.)

- The API might enable you to control the location of the temporary file directory or the maximum size of uploaded files. Changing the directory to one that is accessible only to your web server may improve security a bit against local exploits by other users with login accounts on the server host.

This recipe discusses how to create forms that include a file upload field. It also demonstrates how to handle uploads using a Perl script, *post_image.pl*. The script is somewhat similar to the *store_image.pl* script for loading images from the command line (Recipe 18.6). *post_image.pl* differs in that it enables you to store images over the Web by uploading them, and it stores images only in MySQL, whereas *store_image.pl* stores them in both MySQL and the filesystem.

This recipe also discusses how to obtain file upload information using PHP and Python. It does not repeat the entire image-posting scenario shown for Perl, but the **recipes** distribution contains equivalent implementations of *post_image.pl* for the other languages.

Uploads in Perl

You can specify multipart encoding for a form several ways using the CGI.pm module. The following statements are equivalent:

```
print start_form (-action => url (), -enctype => "multipart/form-data");

print start_form (-action => url (), -enctype => MULTIPART ());

print start_multipart_form (-action => url ());
```

The first statement specifies the encoding type literally. The second uses the CGI.pm **MULTIPART( )** function, which is easier than trying to remember the literal encoding value. The third statement is easiest of all, because **start_multipart_form( )** supplies the **enctype** parameter automatically. (Like **start_form( )**, **start_multipart_form( )** uses a default request method of **post**, so you need not include a **method** argument.)

Here's a simple form that includes a text field that enables the user to assign a name to an image, a file field so that the user can select the image file, and a Submit button:

```
print start_multipart_form (-action => url ()),
      "Image name:", br (),
      textfield (-name =>"image_name", -size => 60),
      br (), "Image file:", br (),
      filefield (-name =>"upload_file", -size => 60),
      br (), br (),
      submit (-name => "choice", -value => "Submit"),
      end_form ();
```

When the user submits an uploaded file, begin processing it by extracting the parameter value for the file field:

```
$file = param ("upload_file");
```

The value for a file upload parameter is special in CGI.pm because you can use it two ways. You can treat it as an open file handle to read the file's contents or pass it to **uploadInfo( )** to obtain a reference to a hash that provides information about the file such as its MIME type. The following listing shows how *post_image.pl* presents the form and processes a submitted form. When first invoked, *post_image.pl* generates a form with an upload field. For the initial invocation, no file will have been uploaded, so the script does nothing else. If the user submitted an image file, the script gets the image name, reads the file contents, determines its MIME type, and stores a new row in the image table. For illustrative purposes, *post_image.pl* also displays all the information that the uploadInfo( ) function makes available about the uploaded file.

```perl
#!/usr/bin/perl
# post_image.pl - allow user to upload image files via post requests

use strict;
use warnings;
use CGI qw(:standard escapeHTML);
use Cookbook;

print header (), start_html (-title => "Post Image", -bgcolor => "white");

# Use multipart encoding because the form contains a file upload field

print start_multipart_form (-action => url ()),
      "Image name:", br (),
      textfield (-name =>"image_name", -size => 60),
      br (), "Image file:", br (),
      filefield (-name =>"upload_file", -size => 60),
      br (), br (),
      submit (-name => "choice", -value => "Submit"),
      end_form ();

# Get a handle to the image file and the name to assign to the image

my $image_file = param ("upload_file");
my $image_name = param ("image_name");

# Must have either no parameters (in which case that script was just
# invoked for the first time) or both parameters (in which case the form
# was filled in).  If only one was filled in, the user did not fill in the
# form completely.

my $param_count = 0;
++$param_count if defined ($image_file) && $image_file ne "";
++$param_count if defined ($image_name) && $image_name ne "";

if ($param_count == 0)      # initial invocation
{
  print p ("No file was uploaded.");
}
elsif ($param_count == 1)   # incomplete form
{
  print p ("Please fill in BOTH fields and resubmit the form.");
}
else             # a file was uploaded
{
my ($size, $data);

  # If an image file was uploaded, print some information about it,
  # then save it in the database.

  # Get reference to hash containing information about file
  # and display the information in "key=x, value=y" format
```

```
my $info_ref = uploadInfo ($image_file);
print p ("Information about uploaded file:");
foreach my $key (sort (keys (%{$info_ref})))
{
  printf p ("key="
            . escapeHTML ($key)
            . ", value="
            . escapeHTML ($info_ref->{$key}));
}
$size = (stat ($image_file))[7]; # get file size from file handle
print p ("File size: " . $size);

binmode ($image_file);  # helpful for binary data
if (sysread ($image_file, $data, $size) != $size)
{
  print p ("File contents could not be read.");
}
else
{
  print p ("File contents were read without error.");

  # Get MIME type, use generic default if not present

  my $mime_type = $info_ref->{'Content-Type'};
  $mime_type = "application/octet-stream" unless defined ($mime_type);

  # Save image in database table.  (Use REPLACE to kick out any
  # old image that has the same name.)

  my $dbh = Cookbook::connect ();
  $dbh->do ("REPLACE INTO image (name,type,data) VALUES(?,?,?)",
            undef,
            $image_name, $mime_type, $data);
  $dbh->disconnect ();
}
}

print end_html ();
```

Uploads in PHP

To write an upload form in PHP, include a file field. If you like, you can also include a
hidden field preceding the file field that has a name of MAX_FILE_SIZE and a value of the
largest file size that you're willing to accept:

```
<form method="post" enctype="multipart/form-data"
  action="<?php print (get_self_path ()); ?>">
<input type="hidden" name="MAX_FILE_SIZE" value="4000000" />
Image name:<br />
<input type="text" name="image_name" size="60" />
<br />
Image file:<br />
<input type="file" name="upload_file" size="60" />
<br /><br />
```

```
<input type="submit" name="choice" value="Submit" />
</form>
```

Be aware that MAX_FILE_SIZE is advisory only, because it can be subverted easily. To specify a value that cannot be exceeded, use the upload_max_filesize configuration variable in the *php.ini* PHP configuration file. There is also a file_uploads variable that controls whether file uploads are allowed at all.

When the user submits the form, file upload information may be obtained as follows:

- As of PHP 4.1, file upload information from post requests is placed in an array, $_FILES, that has one entry for each uploaded file. Each entry is itself an array with four elements. For example, if a form has a file field named upload_file and the user submits a file, information about it is available in the following variables:

  ```
  $_FILES["upload_file]["name"]
  $_FILES["upload_file]["tmp_name"]
  $_FILES["upload_file]["size"]
  $_FILES["upload_file]["type"]
  ```

  These variables represent the original filename on the client host, the temporary filename on the server host, the file size in bytes, and the file MIME type. Be careful here, because there may be an entry for an upload field even if the user submitted no file. In this case, the tmp_name value will be the empty string or the string none.

- Earlier PHP 4 releases have file upload information in an array, $HTTP_POST_FILES, that has entries that are structured like those in $_FILES. For a file field named upload_file, information about it is available in the following variables:

  ```
  $HTTP_POST_FILES["upload_file]["name"]
  $HTTP_POST_FILES["upload_file]["tmp_name"]
  $HTTP_POST_FILES["upload_file]["size"]
  $HTTP_POST_FILES["upload_file]["type"]
  ```

$_FILES is a superglobal array (global in any scope). $HTTP_POST_FILES must be declared with the global keyword if used in a nonglobal scope, such as within a function.

To avoid fooling around figuring out which array contains file upload information, it makes sense to write a utility routine that does all the work. The following function, get_upload_info( ), takes an argument corresponding to the name of a file upload field. Then it examines the $_FILES and $HTTP_POST_FILES arrays as necessary and returns an associative array of information about the file, or a NULL value if the information is not available. For a successful call, the array element keys are "tmp_name", "name", "size", and "type".

```
function get_upload_info ($name)
{
global $HTTP_POST_FILES, $HTTP_POST_VARS;

# Look for information in PHP 4.1 $_FILES array first.
# Check the tmp_name member to make sure there is a file. (The entry
# in $_FILES might be present even if no file was uploaded.)
if (isset ($_FILES))
```

```
{
  if (isset ($_FILES[$name])
      && $_FILES[$name]["tmp_name"] != ""
      && $_FILES[$name]["tmp_name"] != "none")
    return ($_FILES[$name]);
}
# Look for information in PHP 4 $HTTP_POST_FILES array next.
else if (isset ($HTTP_POST_FILES))
{
  if (isset ($HTTP_POST_FILES[$name])
      && $HTTP_POST_FILES[$name]["tmp_name"] != ""
      && $HTTP_POST_FILES[$name]["tmp_name"] != "none")
    return ($HTTP_POST_FILES[$name]);
}
return (NULL);
}
```

See the *post_image.php* script for details about how to use this function to get image information and store it in MySQL.

The `upload_tmp_dir` PHP configuration variable controls where uploaded files are saved. This is */tmp* by default on many systems, but you may want to override it to reconfigure PHP to use a different directory that's owned by the web server user ID and thus more private.

Uploads in Python

A simple upload form in Python can be written like this:

```
print """
<form method="post" enctype="multipart/form-data" action="%s">
Image name:<br />
<input type="text" name="image_name", size="60" />
<br />
Image file:<br />
<input type="file" name="upload_file", size="60" />
<br /><br />
<input type="submit" name="choice" value="Submit" />
</form>
""" % (os.environ["SCRIPT_NAME"])
```

When the user submits the form, its contents can be obtained using the `FieldStorage( )` method of the `cgi` module (Recipe 19.5). The resulting object contains an element for each input parameter. For a file upload field, you get this information as follows:

```
form = cgi.FieldStorage ()
if form.has_key ("upload_file") and form["upload_file"].filename != "":
  image_file = form["upload_file"]
else:
  image_file = None
```

According to most of the documentation that I have read, the `file` attribute of an object that corresponds to a file field should be true if a file has been uploaded. Unfortunately, the `file` attribute seems to be true even when the user submits the form but leaves the file field blank. It may even be the case that the `type` attribute is set when no file actually was uploaded (for example, to `application/octet-stream`). In my experience, a more reliable way to determine whether a file really was uploaded is to test the `filename` attribute:

```
form = cgi.FieldStorage ()
if form.has_key ("upload_file") and form["upload_file"].filename:
  print "<p>A file was uploaded</p>"
else:
  print "<p>A file was not uploaded</p>"
```

Assuming that a file was uploaded, access the parameter's `value` attribute to read the file and obtain its contents:

```
data = form["upload_file"].value
```

See the *post_image.py* script for details about how to use this function to get image information and store it in MySQL.

19.9 Performing Searches and Presenting the Results

Problem

You want to implement a web-based search interface.

Solution

Present a form containing fields that enable the user to supply search parameters such as keywords. Use the keywords to construct a database query, and then display the query results.

Discussion

A script that implements a web-based search interface provides a convenience for people who visit your web site because they don't have to know any SQL to find information in your database. Instead, visitors supply keywords that describe what they're interested in and your script figures out the appropriate statements to run on their behalf. A common paradigm for this activity involves a form containing one or more fields for entering search parameters. The user fills in the form, submits it, and receives back a new page containing the records that match the parameters.

As the writer of such a script, you must handle these operations:

1. Generate the form and send it to the users.

2. Interpret the submitted form and construct an SQL statement based on its contents. This includes proper use of placeholders or quoting to prevent bad input from crashing or subverting your script.

3. Execute the statement and display its result. This can be simple if the result set is small, or more complex if it is large. In the latter case, you may want to present the matching records using a paged display—that is, a display consisting of multiple pages, each of which shows a subset of the entire statement result. Multiple-page displays have the benefit of not overwhelming the user with huge amounts of information all at once. Recipe 19.10 discusses how to implement them.

This recipe demonstrates a script that implements a minimal search interface: a form with one keyword field, from which a statement is constructed that returns at most one record. The script performs a two-way search through the contents of the **states** table. That is, if the user enters a state name, it looks up the corresponding abbreviation. Conversely, if the user enters an abbreviation, it looks up the name. The script, *search_state.pl*, looks like this:

```perl
#!/usr/bin/perl
# search_state.pl - simple "search for state" application

# Present a form with an input field and a submit button.  User enters
# a state abbreviation or a state name into the field and submits the
# form.  Script finds the abbreviation and displays the full name, or
# finds the name and displays the abbreviation.

use strict;
use warnings;
use CGI qw(:standard escapeHTML);
use Cookbook;

my $title = "State Name or Abbreviation Lookup";

print header (), start_html (-title => $title, -bgcolor => "white");

# Extract keyword parameter.  If it's present and nonempty,
# attempt to perform a lookup.

my $keyword = param ("keyword");

if (defined ($keyword) && $keyword !~ /^\s*$/)
{
  my $dbh = Cookbook::connect ();
  my $found = 0;
  my $s;

  # first try looking for keyword as a state abbreviation;
  # if that fails, try looking for it as a name
  $s = $dbh->selectrow_array ("SELECT name FROM states WHERE abbrev = ?",
                              undef, $keyword);
  if ($s)
  {
    ++$found;
```

```
    print p ("You entered the abbreviation: " . escapeHTML ($keyword));
    print p ("The corresponding state name is : " . escapeHTML ($s));
  }
  $s = $dbh->selectrow_array ("SELECT abbrev FROM states WHERE name = ?",
                             undef, $keyword);
  if ($s)
  {
    ++$found;
    print p ("You entered the state name: " . escapeHTML ($keyword));
    print p ("The corresponding abbreviation is : " . escapeHTML ($s));
  }
  if (!$found)
  {
    print p ("You entered the keyword: " . escapeHTML ($keyword));
    print p ("No match was found.");
  }

  $dbh->disconnect ();
}

print p (qq{
Enter a state name into the form and select Search, and I will show you
the corresponding abbreviation.
Or enter an abbreviation and I will show you the full name.
});

print start_form (-action => url ()),
      "State: ",
      textfield (-name => "keyword", -size => 20),
      br (),
      submit (-name => "choice", -value => "Search"),
      end_form ();

print end_html ();
```

The script first checks to see whether a keyword parameter is present. If so, it runs the statements that look for a match to the parameter value in the states table and displays the results. Then it presents the form so that the user can enter a new search.

When you try the script, you'll notice that the value of the keyword field carries over from one invocation to the next. That's due to CGI.pm's behavior of initializing form fields with values from the script environment. If you don't like this behavior, defeat it and make the field come up blank each time by supplying an empty value explicitly and an override parameter in the textfield( ) call:

```
print textfield (-name => "keyword",
                 -value => "",
                 -override => 1,
                 -size => 20);
```

Alternatively, clear the parameter's value in the environment before generating the field:

```
param (-name => "keyword", -value => "");
print textfield (-name => "keyword", -size => 20);
```

19.10 Generating Previous-Page and Next-Page Links

Problem

A statement matches so many rows that displaying them all in a single web page produces an unwieldy result.

Solution

Split the statement output across several pages and include links that enable the user to navigate among pages.

Discussion

If a statement matches a large number of rows, showing them all in a single web page can result in a display that's difficult to navigate. For such cases, it can be more convenient for the user if you split the result among multiple pages. Such a paged display avoids overwhelming the user with too much information, but is more difficult to implement than a single-page display.

A paged display typically is used in a search context to present rows that match the search parameters supplied by the user. To simplify things, the examples in this recipe don't have any search interface. Instead, they implement a paged display that presents 10 rows at a time from the result of a fixed statement:

```
SELECT name, abbrev, statehood, pop FROM states ORDER BY name;
```

MySQL makes it easy to select just a portion of a result set: add a LIMIT clause that indicates which rows you want. The two-argument form of LIMIT takes values indicating how many rows to skip at the beginning of the result set, and how many to select. The statement to select a section of the states table thus becomes:

```
SELECT name, abbrev, statehood, pop FROM states ORDER BY name
LIMIT skip,select;
```

One issue, then, is to determine the proper values of *skip* and *select* for any given page. Another is to generate the links that point to other pages or the statement result. This second issue presents you with a choice: which paging style should you use for the links?

- One style of paged display presents only "previous page" and "next page" links. To do this, you need to know whether any rows precede or follow those you're displaying in the current page.

- Another paging style displays a link for each available page. This enables the user to jump directly to any page, not just the previous or next page. To present this kind of navigation, you have to know the total number of rows in the result set and the number of rows per page, so that you can determine how many pages there are.

Paged displays with previous-page and next-page links

The following script, *state_pager1.pl*, presents rows from the **states** table in a paged display that includes navigation links only to the previous and next pages. For a given page, you can determine which links are needed as follows:

- A "previous page" link is needed if there are rows in the result set preceding those shown in the current page. If the current page starts at row one, there are no such rows.

- A "next page" link is needed if there are rows in the result set following those shown in the current page. You can determine this by issuing a **SELECT COUNT(*)** statement to see how many rows the statement matches in total. Another method is to select one more row than you need. For example, if you're displaying 10 rows at a time, try to select 11 rows. If you get 11, there is a next page. If you get 10 or less, there isn't. *state_pager1.pl* uses the latter approach.

To determine its current position in the result set and how many rows to display, *state_pager1.pl* looks for **start** and **per_page** input parameters. When you first invoke the script, these parameters won't be present, so they're initialized to 1 and 10, respectively. Thereafter, the script generates "previous page" and "next page" links to itself that include the proper parameter values in the URLs for selecting the previous or next sections of the result set.

```perl
#!/usr/bin/perl
# state_pager1.pl - paged display of states, with prev-page/next-page links

use strict;
use warnings;
use CGI qw(:standard escape escapeHTML);
use Cookbook;

my $title = "Paged U.S. State List";

my $page = header ()
        . start_html (-title => $title, -bgcolor => "white")
        . h3 ($title);

my $dbh = Cookbook::connect ();

# Collect parameters that determine where we are in the display and
# verify that they are integers.
# Default to beginning of result set, 10 records/page if parameters
# are missing/malformed.

my $start = param ("start");
$start = 1
  if !defined ($start) || $start !~ /^\d+$/ || $start < 1;
```

```
my $per_page = param ("per_page");
$per_page = 10
  if !defined ($per_page) || $per_page !~ /^\d+$/ || $per_page < 1;;

# If start > 1, then we'll need a live "previous page" link.
# To determine whether there is a next page, try to select one more
# record than we need.  If we get that many, display only the first
# $per_page records, but add a live "next page" link.

# Select the records in the current page of the result set, and
# attempt to get an extra record.  (If we get the extra one, we
# won't display it, but its presence tells us there is a next
# page.)

my $stmt = sprintf ("SELECT name, abbrev, statehood, pop
                    FROM states
                    ORDER BY name LIMIT %d,%d",
                    $start - 1,        # number of records to skip
                    $per_page + 1);    # number of records to select

my $tbl_ref = $dbh->selectall_arrayref ($stmt);

$dbh->disconnect ();

# Display results as HTML table
my @rows;
push (@rows, Tr (th (["Name", "Abbreviation", "Statehood", "Population"])));
for (my $i = 0; $i < $per_page && $i < @{$tbl_ref}; $i++)
{
  # get data values in row $i
  my @cells = @{$tbl_ref->[$i]};  # get data values in row $i
  # map values to HTML-encoded values, or to   if null/empty
  @cells = map {
             defined ($_) && $_ ne "" ? escapeHTML ($_) : " "
           } @cells;
  # add cells to table
  push (@rows, Tr (td (\@cells)));
}

$page .= table ({-border => 1}, @rows) . br ();

# If we're not at the beginning of the query result, present a live
# link to the previous page.  Otherwise, present static text.

if ($start > 1)        # live link
{
  my $url = sprintf ("%s?start=%d;per_page=%d",
                     url (),
                     $start - $per_page,
                     $per_page);
  $page .= "[" . a ({-href => $url}, "previous page") . "] ";
}
else                    # static text
{
  $page .= "[previous page]";
```

```
}

# If we got the extra record, present a live link to the next page.
# Otherwise, present static text.

if (@{$tbl_ref} > $per_page)   # live link
{
  my $url = sprintf ("%s?start=%d;per_page=%d",
                     url (),
                     $start + $per_page,
                     $per_page);
  $page .= "[" . a ({-href => $url}, "next page") . "]";
}
else                           # static text
{
  $page .= "[next page]";
}

$page .= end_html ();

print $page;
```

Paged displays with links to each page

The next script, *state_pager2.pl*, is much like *state_pager1.pl*, but presents a paged display that includes navigation links to each page of the query result. To do this, it's necessary to know how many rows there are in all. *state_pager2.pl* determines this by running a **SELECT COUNT(*)** statement. Because the script then knows the total row count, it need not select an extra row when fetching the section of the result to be displayed.

Omitting the parts of *state_pager2.pl* that are the same as *state_pager1.pl*, the middle part that retrieves rows and generates links is implemented as follows:

```
# Determine total number of records

my $total_recs = $dbh->selectrow_array ("SELECT COUNT(*) FROM states");

# Select the records in the current page of the result set

my $stmt = sprintf ("SELECT name, abbrev, statehood, pop
                     FROM states
                     ORDER BY name LIMIT %d,%d",
                     $start - 1,      # number of records to skip
                     $per_page);      # number of records to select

my $tbl_ref = $dbh->selectall_arrayref ($stmt);

$dbh->disconnect ();

# Display results as HTML table
my @rows;
push (@rows, Tr (th (["Name", "Abbreviation", "Statehood", "Population"])));
for (my $i = 0; $i < @{$tbl_ref}; $i++)
{
  # get data values in row $i
```

```
my @cells = @{$tbl_ref->[$i]};   # get data values in row $i
# map values to HTML-encoded values, or to   if null/empty
@cells = map {
            defined ($_) && $_ ne "" ? escapeHTML ($_) : " "
        } @cells;
# add cells to table
push (@rows, Tr (td (\@cells)));
}

$page .= table ({-border => 1}, @rows) . br ();

# Generate links to all pages of the result set.  All links are
# live, except the one to the current page, which is displayed as
# static text.  Link label format is "[m to n]" where m and n are
# the numbers of the first and last records displayed on the page.

for (my $first = 1; $first <= $total_recs; $first += $per_page)
{
  my $last = $first + $per_page - 1;
  $last = $total_recs if $last > $total_recs;
  my $label = "$first to $last";
  my $link;

  if ($first != $start) # live link
  {
    my $url = sprintf ("%s?start=%d;per_page=%d",
                        url (),
                        $first,
                        $per_page);
    $link = a ({-href => $url}, $label);
  }
  else                    # static text
  {
    $link = $label;
  }
  $page .= "[$link] ";
}
```

19.11 Generating "Click to Sort" Table Headings

Problem

You want to display a query result in a web page as a table that enables the user to select which column to sort the table rows by.

Solution

Make each column heading a hyperlink that redisplays the table, sorted by the corresponding column.

Discussion

When a web script runs, it can determine what action to take by examining its environment to find out what parameters are present and what their values are. In many cases these parameters come from a user, but there's no reason a script cannot add parameters to URLs itself. This is one way a given invocation of a script can send information to the next invocation. The effect is that the script communicates with itself by means of URLs that it generates to cause specific actions. An application of this technique is for showing the result of a query such that a user can select which column of the result to use for sorting the display. This is done by making the column headers active links that redisplay the table, sorted by the selected column.

The examples here use the `mail` table, which has the following contents:

```
mysql> SELECT * FROM mail;
+---------------------+---------+---------+---------+---------+---------+
| t                   | srcuser | srchost | dstuser | dsthost | size    |
+---------------------+---------+---------+---------+---------+---------+
| 2006-05-11 10:15:08 | barb    | saturn  | tricia  | mars    |   58274 |
| 2006-05-12 12:48:13 | tricia  | mars    | gene    | venus   |  194925 |
| 2006-05-12 15:02:49 | phil    | mars    | phil    | saturn  |    1048 |
| 2006-05-13 13:59:18 | barb    | saturn  | tricia  | venus   |     271 |
| 2006-05-14 09:31:37 | gene    | venus   | barb    | mars    |    2291 |
| 2006-05-14 11:52:17 | phil    | mars    | tricia  | saturn  |    5781 |
| 2006-05-14 14:42:21 | barb    | venus   | barb    | venus   |   98151 |
| 2006-05-14 17:03:01 | tricia  | saturn  | phil    | venus   | 2394482 |
| 2006-05-15 07:17:48 | gene    | mars    | gene    | saturn  |    3824 |
| 2006-05-15 08:50:57 | phil    | venus   | phil    | venus   |     978 |
| 2006-05-15 10:25:52 | gene    | mars    | tricia  | saturn  |  998532 |
| 2006-05-15 17:35:31 | gene    | saturn  | gene    | mars    |    3856 |
| 2006-05-16 09:00:28 | gene    | venus   | barb    | mars    |     613 |
| 2006-05-16 23:04:19 | phil    | venus   | barb    | venus   |   10294 |
| 2006-05-17 12:49:23 | phil    | mars    | tricia  | saturn  |     873 |
| 2006-05-19 22:21:51 | gene    | saturn  | gene    | venus   |   23992 |
+---------------------+---------+---------+---------+---------+---------+
```

To retrieve the table and display its contents as an HTML table, you can use the techniques discussed in Recipe 18.3. Here we'll use those same concepts but modify them to produce "click to sort" table column headings.

A "plain" HTML table includes a row of column headers consisting only of the column names:

```
<tr>
  <th>t</th>
  <th>srcuser</th>
  <th>srchost</th>
  <th>dstuser</th>
  <th>dsthost</th>
  <th>size</th>
</tr>
```

To make the headings active links that reinvoke the script to produce a display sorted by a given column name, we need to produce a header row that looks like this:

```
<tr>
  <th><a href="script_name?sort=t">t</a></th>
  <th><a href="script_name?sort=srcuser">srcuser</a></th>
  <th><a href="script_name?sort=srchost">srchost</a></th>
  <th><a href="script_name?sort=dstuser">dstuser</a></th>
  <th><a href="script_name?sort=dsthost">dsthost</a></th>
  <th><a href="script_name?sort=size">size</a></th>
</tr>
```

To generate such headings, the script needs to know the names of the columns in the table, as well as its own URL. Recipes 9.6 and 19.1 show how to obtain this information using statement metadata and information in the script's environment. For example, in PHP, a script can generate the header row for the columns in a given statement as follows, where `tableInfo( )` returns an array containing metadata for a query result. `$info[i]` contains information about column *i* and `$info[i]["name"]` contains the column's name.

```
$self_path = get_self_path ();
print ("<tr>\n");
$info =& $conn->tableInfo ($result, NULL);
if (PEAR::isError ($info))
  die (htmlspecialchars ($result->getMessage ()));
for ($i = 0; $i < $result->numCols (); $i++)
{
  $col_name = $info[$i]["name"];
  printf ("<th><a href=\"%s?sort=%s\">%s</a></th>\n",
          $self_path,
          urlencode ($col_name),
          htmlspecialchars ($col_name));
}
print ("</tr>\n");
```

The following script, *clicksort.php*, implements this kind of table display. It checks its environment for a **sort** parameter that indicates which column to use for sorting. The script then uses the parameter to construct a statement of the following form:

```
SELECT * FROM $tbl_name ORDER BY $sort_col LIMIT 50
```

There is a small bootstrapping problem for this kind of script. The first time you invoke it, there is no sort column name in the environment, so the script doesn't know which column to sort by initially. What should you do? There are a couple possibilities:

- You can retrieve the results unsorted.
- You can hardwire one of the column names into the script as the default.
- You can look up the column names from `INFORMATION_SCHEMA` and use one of them (such as the first) as the default. To look up the name on the fly, use this statement:

```
SELECT COLUMN_NAME FROM INFORMATION_SCHEMA.COLUMNS
WHERE TABLE_SCHEMA = "cookbook" AND TABLE_NAME = "mail"
AND ORDINAL_POSITION = 1;
```

The following script looks up the name from INFORMATION_SCHEMA. It also uses a LIMIT clause when retrieving results as a precaution that prevents the script from dumping huge amounts of output if the table is large.

```php
<?php
# clicksort.php - display query result as HTML table with "click to sort"
# column headings

# Rows from the database table are displayed as an HTML table.
# Column headings are presented as hyperlinks that reinvoke the
# script to redisplay the table sorted by the corresponding column.
# The display is limited to 50 rows in case the table is large.

require_once "Cookbook.php";
require_once "Cookbook_Webutils.php";

$title = "Table Display with Click-To-Sort Column Headings";

?>

<html>
<head>
<title><?php print ($title); ?></title>
</head>
<body bgcolor="white">

<?php
# ----------------------------------------------------------------------

# names for database and table and default sort column; change as desired
$db_name = "cookbook";
$tbl_name = "mail";

$conn =& Cookbook::connect ();
if (PEAR::isError ($conn))
  die ("Cannot connect to server: "
       . htmlspecialchars ($conn->getMessage ()));

print ("<p>" . htmlspecialchars ("Table: $db_name.$tbl_name") . "</p>\n");
print ("<p>Click on a column name to sort by that column.</p>\n");

# Get the name of the column to sort by: If missing, use the first column.

$sort_col = get_param_val ("sort");
if (!isset ($sort_col))
{
  $stmt = "SELECT COLUMN_NAME FROM INFORMATION_SCHEMA.COLUMNS
           WHERE TABLE_SCHEMA = ? AND TABLE_NAME = ?
           AND ORDINAL_POSITION = 1";
  $result =& $conn->query ($stmt, array ($db_name, $tbl_name));
  if (PEAR::isError ($result))
    die (htmlspecialchars ($result->getMessage ()));
  if (!(list ($sort_col) = $result->fetchRow ()))
    die (htmlspecialchars ($result->getMessage ()));
  $result->free ();
```

```
}

# Construct query to select records from the table, sorting by the
# named column.  (The column name comes from the environment, so quote
# it to avoid an SQL injection attack.)
# Limit output to 50 rows to avoid dumping entire contents of large tables.

$stmt = "SELECT * FROM $db_name.$tbl_name";
$stmt .= " ORDER BY " . $conn->quoteIdentifier ($sort_col);
$stmt .= " LIMIT 50";

$result =& $conn->query ($stmt);
if (PEAR::isError ($result))
  die (htmlspecialchars ($result->getMessage ()));

# Display query results as HTML table.  Use query metadata to get column
# names, and display names in first row of table as hyperlinks that cause
# the table to be redisplayed, sorted by the corresponding table column.

print ("<table border=\"1\">\n");
$self_path = get_self_path ();
print ("<tr>\n");
$info =& $conn->tableInfo ($result, NULL);
if (PEAR::isError ($info))
  die (htmlspecialchars ($result->getMessage ()));
for ($i = 0; $i < $result->numCols (); $i++)
{
  $col_name = $info[$i]["name"];
  printf ("<th><a href=\"%s?sort=%s\">%s</a></th>\n",
          $self_path,
          urlencode ($col_name),
          htmlspecialchars ($col_name));
}
print ("</tr>\n");
while ($row =& $result->fetchRow ())
{
  print ("<tr>\n");
  for ($i = 0; $i < $result->numCols (); $i++)
  {
    # encode values, using   for empty cells
    $val = $row[$i];
    if (isset ($val) && $val != "")
      $val = htmlspecialchars ($val);
    else
      $val = " ";
    printf ("<td>%s</td>\n", $val);
  }
  print ("</tr>\n");
}
$result->free ();
print ("</table>\n");

$conn->disconnect ();

?>
```

```
</body>
</html>
```

The `$sort_col` value comes from the **sort** parameter of the environment, so it should be considered dangerous: An attacker might submit a URL with a **sort** parameter designed to attempt an SQL injection attack. To prevent this, `$sort_col` should be quoted when you construct the **SELECT** statement that retrieves rows from the displayed table. You cannot use a placeholder to quote the value because that technique applies to data values. (`$sort_col` is used as an identifier, not a data value.) However, some MySQL APIs, PEAR DB among them, provide an identifier-quoting function. *clicksort.php* uses **quoteIdentifier( )** to make the `$sort_col` value safe for inclusion in the SQL statement.

Another approach to validating the column name is to check the **COLUMNS** table of **INFORMATION_SCHEMA**. If the sort column is not listed there, it is invalid. The *clicksort.php* script shown here does not do that. However, the **recipes** distribution contains a Perl counterpart script, *clicksort.pl*, that does perform this kind of check. Have a look at it if you want more information.

The cells in the rows following the header row contain the data values from the database table, displayed as static text. Empty cells are displayed using ` ` so that they display with the same border as nonempty cells (see Recipe 18.3).

19.12 Web Page Access Counting

Problem

You want to count the number of times a page has been accessed.

Solution

Implement a hit counter, keyed to the page you want to count. This can be used to display a counter in the page. The same technique can be used to record other types of information as well, such as the number of times each of a set of banner ads has been served.

Discussion

This recipe discusses access counting, using hit counters for the examples. Counters that display the number of times a web page has been accessed are not such a big thing as they used to be, presumably because page authors now realize that most visitors don't really care how popular a page is. Still, the general concept has application in several contexts. For example, if you're displaying banner ads in your pages (Recipe 18.8), you may be charging vendors by the number of times you serve their ads. To do so, you need to count the number of accesses for each one. You can adapt the technique shown in this section for such purposes.

There are several methods for writing a page that displays a count of the number of times it has been accessed. The most basic is to maintain the count in a file. When the page is requested, open the file, read the count, increment it, and write the new count back to the file and display it in the page. This has the advantage of being easy to implement and the disadvantage that it requires a counter file for each page that includes a hit count. It also doesn't work properly if two clients access the page at the same time, unless you implement some kind of locking protocol in the file access procedure. It's possible to reduce counter file litter by keeping multiple counts in a single file, but that makes it more difficult to access particular values within the file, and it doesn't solve the simultaneous-access problem. In fact, it makes it worse, because a multiple-counter file has a higher likelihood of being accessed by multiple clients simultaneously than does a single-counter file. So you end up implementing storage and retrieval methods for processing the file contents, and locking protocols to keep multiple processes from interfering with each other. Hmm... those sound suspiciously like the problems that a database management system such as MySQL already takes care of! Keeping the counts in the database centralizes them into a single table, SQL provides the storage and retrieval interface, and the locking problem goes away because MySQL serializes access to the table so that clients can't interfere with each other. Furthermore, depending on how you manage the counters, you might be able to update the counter and retrieve the new sequence value using a single statement.

I'll assume that you want to log hits for more than one page. To do that, create a table that has one row for each page to be counted. This means that it's necessary to have a unique identifier for each page, so that counters for different pages don't get mixed up. You could assign identifiers somehow, but it's easier just to use the page's path within your web tree. Web programming languages typically make this path easy to obtain; in fact, we've already discussed how to do so in Recipe 19.1. On that basis, you can create a `hitcount` table as follows:

```
CREATE TABLE hitcount
(
  path  VARCHAR(255)
        CHARACTER SET latin1 COLLATE latin1_general_cs NOT NULL,
  hits  BIGINT UNSIGNED NOT NULL,
  PRIMARY KEY (path)
);
```

This table definition involves some assumptions:

- The `path` column that stores page pathnames has a character set of `latin1` and a case-sensitive collation of `latin1_general_cs`. Use of a case-sensitive collation is appropriate for a web platform where pathnames are case-sensitive, such as most versions of Unix. For Windows or for HFS+ filesystems under Mac OS X, filenames are not case-sensitive, so you would choose a collation that is not case-sensitive, such as `latin1_swedish_ci`. If your filesystem is set up to use pathnames in a different character set, you should change the character set and collation.

- The `path` column has a maximum length of 255 characters, which limits you to page paths no longer than that.

- The `path` column is indexed as a `PRIMARY KEY` to require unique values. Either a `PRIMARY KEY` or `UNIQUE` index is required because we will implement the hit-counting algorithm using an `INSERT` statement with an `ON DUPLICATE KEY UPDATE` clause to insert a row if none exists for the page or update the row if it does exist. (Recipe 11.14 provides background that further explains `ON DUPLICATE KEY UPDATE`.)

- The table is set up to count page hits for a single document tree, such as when your web server is used to serve pages for a single domain. If you institute a hit count mechanism on a host that serves multiple virtual domains, you may want to add a column for the domain name. This value is available in the `SERVER_NAME` value that Apache puts into your script's environment. In this case, the `hitcount` table index should include both the hostname and the page path.

The general logic involved in hit counter maintenance is to increment the `hits` column of the row for a page, and then retrieve the updated counter value:

```
UPDATE hitcount SET hits = hits + 1 WHERE path = 'page path';
SELECT hits FROM hitcount WHERE path = 'page path';
```

Unfortunately, if you use that approach, you may often not get the correct value. If several clients request the same page simultaneously, several `UPDATE` statements may be issued in close temporal proximity. The following `SELECT` statements then wouldn't necessarily get the corresponding `hits` value. This can be avoided by using a transaction or by locking the `hitcount` table, but that slows down hit counting. MySQL provides a solution that enables each client to retrieve its own count, no matter how many updates happen at the same time:

```
UPDATE hitcount SET hits = LAST_INSERT_ID(hits+1) WHERE path = 'page path';
SELECT LAST_INSERT_ID();
```

The basis for updating the count here is `LAST_INSERT_ID(expr)`, which is discussed in Recipe 11.14. The `UPDATE` statement finds the relevant row and increments its counter value. The use of `LAST_INSERT_ID(hits+1)` rather than just `hits+1` tells MySQL to treat the value as though it were an `AUTO_INCREMENT` value. This allows it to be retrieved in the second statement using `LAST_INSERT_ID( )`. The `LAST_INSERT_ID( )` function returns a connection-specific value, so you always get back the value corresponding to the `UPDATE` issued on the same connection. In addition, the `SELECT` statement doesn't need to query a table, so it's very fast.

However, there's still a problem here. What if the page isn't listed in the `hitcount` table? In that case, the `UPDATE` statement finds no row to modify and you get a counter value of zero. You could deal with this problem by requiring that any page that includes a hit counter must be registered in the `hitcount` table before the page goes online. An easier approach is to use MySQL's `INSERT ... ON DUPLICATE KEY UPDATE` syntax, which inserts a row with a count of 1 if it does not exist, and updates its counter if it does exist:

```
INSERT INTO hitcount (path,hits) VALUES('some path',LAST_INSERT_ID(1))
ON DUPLICATE KEY UPDATE hits = LAST_INSERT_ID(hits+1);
```

The counter value then can be retrieved as the value of the LAST_INSERT_ID( ) function:

```
SELECT LAST_INSERT_ID();
```

The first time you request a count for a page, the statement inserts a row because the page won't be listed in the table yet. The statement creates a new counter and returns a value of one. For each request thereafter, the statement updates the existing row for the page with the new count. That way, web page designers can include counters in pages with no advance preparation required to initialize the hitcount table with a row for the page.

A further efficiency can be gained by eliminating the SELECT statement altogether, which is possible if your API provides a means for direct retrieval of the most recent sequence number. For example, in Perl, you can update the count and get the new value with only one SQL statement like this:

```
$dbh->do ("INSERT INTO hitcount (path,hits) VALUES(?,LAST_INSERT_ID(1))
        ON DUPLICATE KEY UPDATE hits = LAST_INSERT_ID(hits+1)",
        undef, $page_path);
$count = $dbh->{mysql_insertid};
```

To make the counter mechanism easier to use, put the code in a utility function that takes a page path as an argument and returns the count. In Perl, a hit-counting function might look like this, in which the arguments are a database handle and the page path:

```
sub get_hit_count
{
my ($dbh, $page_path) = @_;
my $count;

  $dbh->do ("INSERT INTO hitcount (path,hits) VALUES(?,LAST_INSERT_ID(1))
          ON DUPLICATE KEY UPDATE hits = LAST_INSERT_ID(hits+1)",
          undef, $page_path);
  $count = $dbh->{mysql_insertid};
  return $count
}
```

The CGI.pm script_name( ) function returns the local part of the URL, so you use get_hit_count( ) like this:

```
my $count = get_hit_count ($dbh, script_name ());
print p ("This page has been accessed $count times.");
```

The counter-update mechanism involves a single SQL statement, so it is unnecessary to use transactions or explicit table locking to prevent race conditions that might result if multiple clients simultaneously request a page.

A Ruby version of the hit counter looks like this:

```
def get_hit_count(dbh, page_path)
  dbh.do("INSERT INTO hitcount (path,hits) VALUES(?,LAST_INSERT_ID(1))
        ON DUPLICATE KEY UPDATE hits = LAST_INSERT_ID(hits+1)",
```

```
        page_path)
    return dbh.func(:insert_id)
  end
```

Use the counter method as follows:

```
self_path = ENV["SCRIPT_NAME"]
count = get_hit_count(dbh, self_path)
page << cgi.p { "This page has been accessed " + count.to_s + " times." }
```

In Python, the counting function looks like this:

```
def get_hit_count (conn, page_path):
  cursor = conn.cursor ()
  cursor.execute ("""
          INSERT INTO hitcount (path,hits) VALUES(%s,LAST_INSERT_ID(1))
          ON DUPLICATE KEY UPDATE hits = LAST_INSERT_ID(hits+1)
          """, (page_path,))
  cursor.close ()
  return (conn.insert_id ())
```

Use the function as follows:

```
self_path = os.environ["SCRIPT_NAME"]
count = get_hit_count (conn, self_path)
print "<p>This page has been accessed %d times.</p>" % count
```

The recipes distribution includes demonstration hit counter scripts for Perl, Ruby, PHP, and Python under the *apache/hits* directory. A JSP version is under the *tomcat/ mcb* directory. Install any of these in your web tree, invoke it from your browser a few times, and watch the count increase. First, you'll need to create the hitcount table, as well as the hitlog table described in Recipe 19.13. (The hit-counting scripts show a count and also a log of the most recent hits. Recipe 19.13 discusses the logging mechanism.) Both tables can be created using the *hits.sql* script provided in the *tables* directory.

19.13 Web Page Access Logging

Problem

You want to know more about a page than just the number of times it's been accessed, such as the time of access and the host from which the request originated.

Solution

Maintain a hit log rather than a simple counter.

Discussion

The hitcount table used in Recipe 19.12 records only the access count for each page registered in it. If you want to record other information about page access, use a different approach. Suppose that you want to track the client host and time of access for each request. In this case, you need to log a row for each page access rather than just a count. But you can still maintain the counts by using a multiple-column index that combines the page path and an AUTO_INCREMENT sequence column:

```
CREATE TABLE hitlog
(
  path  VARCHAR(255)
          CHARACTER SET latin1 COLLATE latin1_general_cs NOT NULL,
  hits  BIGINT UNSIGNED NOT NULL AUTO_INCREMENT,
  t     TIMESTAMP,
  host  VARCHAR(255),
  INDEX (path,hits)
) ENGINE = MyISAM;
```

See Recipe 19.12 for notes on choosing the character set and collation for the path column.

To insert new rows into the hitlog table, use this statement:

```
INSERT INTO hitlog (path, host) VALUES(path_val,host_val);
```

For example, in a JSP page, hits can be logged like this:

```
<c:set var="host"><%= request.getRemoteHost () %></c:set>
<c:if test="${empty host}">
  <c:set var="host"><%= request.getRemoteAddr () %></c:set>
</c:if>
<c:if test="${empty host}">
  <c:set var="host">UNKNOWN</c:set>
</c:if>

<sql:update dataSource="${conn}">
  INSERT INTO hitlog (path, host) VALUES(?,?)
  <sql:param><%= request.getRequestURI () %></sql:param>
  <sql:param value="${host}"/>
</sql:update>
```

The hitlog table has the following useful properties:

- Access times are recorded automatically in the TIMESTAMP column t when you insert new rows.

- By linking the path column to an AUTO_INCREMENT column hits, the counter values for a given page path increment automatically whenever you insert a new row for that path. The counters are maintained separately for each distinct path value. This counting mechanism requires that you use the MyISAM (or BDB) storage engine, which is why the table definition includes an explicit ENGINE = MyISAM clause. (For more information on how multiple-column sequences work, see Recipe 11.11.)

- There's no need to check whether the counter for a page already exists, because you insert a new row each time you record a hit for a page, not just for the first hit.

- To determine the current counter value for each page, select the row for each distinct path value that has the largest hits value:

```
SELECT path, MAX(hits) FROM hitlog GROUP BY path;
```

To determine the counter for a given page, use this statement:

```
SELECT MAX(hits) FROM hitlog WHERE path = 'path_name';
```

19.14 Using MySQL for Apache Logging

Problem

You don't want to use MySQL to log accesses for just a few pages, as shown in Recipe 19.13. You want to log all page accesses, and you don't want to have to put logging code in each page explicitly.

Solution

Tell Apache to log page accesses to a MySQL table.

Discussion

The uses for MySQL in a web context aren't limited just to page generation and processing. You can use it to help you run the web server itself. For example, most Apache servers are set up to log a record of page requests to a file. But it's also possible to send log records to a program instead, from which you can write the records wherever you like—such as to a database. With log records in a database rather than a flat file, the log becomes more highly structured and you can apply SQL analysis techniques to it. Logfile analysis tools may be written to provide some flexibility, but often this is a matter of deciding which summaries to display and which to suppress. It's more difficult to tell a tool to display information it wasn't built to provide. With log entries in a table, you gain additional flexibility. Want to see a particular report? Write the SQL statements that produce it. To display the report in a specific format, issue the statements from within an API and take advantage of your language's output production capabilities.

By handling log entry generation and storage using separate processes, you gain some additional flexibility. Some of the possibilities are to send logs from multiple web servers to the same MySQL server, or to send different logs generated by a given web server to different MySQL servers.

This recipe shows how to set up web request logging from Apache into MySQL and demonstrates some summary queries you may find useful.

Setting up database logging

Apache logging is controlled by directives in the *httpd.conf* configuration file. For example, a typical logging setup uses `LogFormat` and `CustomLog` directives that look like this:

```
LogFormat "%h %l %u %t \"%r\" %>s %b" common
CustomLog /usr/local/apache/logs/access_log common
```

The `LogFormat` line defines a format for log records and gives it the nickname `common`. The `CustomLog` directive indicates that lines should be written in that format to the *access_log* file in Apache's *logs* directory. To set up logging to MySQL instead, use the following procedure:[*]

1. Decide what values you want to record and set up a table that contains the appropriate columns.

2. Write a program to read log lines from Apache and write them into the database.

3. Set up a `LogFormat` line that defines how to write log lines in the format the program expects, and a `CustomLog` directive that tells Apache to write to the program rather than to a file.

Suppose that you want to record the date and time of each request, the host that issued the request, the request method and URL pathname, the status code, the number of bytes transferred, the referring page, and the user agent (typically a browser or spider name). A table that includes columns for these values can be created as follows:

```
CREATE TABLE httpdlog
(
  dt      DATETIME NOT NULL,            # request date
  host    VARCHAR(255) NOT NULL,        # client host
  method  VARCHAR(4) NOT NULL,          # request method (GET, PUT, etc.)
  url     VARCHAR(255)                  # URL path
            CHARACTER SET latin1 COLLATE latin1_general_cs NOT NULL,
  status  INT NOT NULL,                 # request status
  size    INT,                          # number of bytes transferred
  referer VARCHAR(255),                 # referring page
  agent   VARCHAR(255)                  # user agent
);
```

Most of the string columns use `VARCHAR` and are not case-sensitive. The exception, `url`, is declared with a case-sensitive collation as is appropriate for a server running on a system with case-sensitive filenames. See Recipe 19.12 for notes on choosing the character set and collation for the `path` column.

The `httpdlog` table definition shown here doesn't include any indexes. If you plan to run summary queries, you should add appropriate indexes to the table. Otherwise, the summaries will slow down dramatically as the table becomes large. The choice of which columns to index will be based on the types of statements you intend to run to analyze the table contents. For example, statements to analyze the distribution of client host values will benefit from an index on the `host` column.

Next, you need a program to process log lines produced by Apache and insert them into the `httpdlog` table. The following script, *httpdlog.pl*, opens a connection to the

---

[*] If you're using logging directives such as `TransferLog` rather than `LogFormat` and `CustomLog`, you'll need to adapt the instructions in this section.

MySQL server, and then loops to read input lines. It parses each line into column values and inserts the result into the database. When Apache exits, it closes the pipe to the logging program. That causes *httpdlog.pl* to see end of file on its input, terminate the loop, disconnect from MySQL, and exit.

```perl
#!/usr/bin/perl
# httpdlog.pl - Log Apache requests to httpdlog table

# path to directory containing Cookbook.pm (CHANGE AS NECESSARY)
use lib qw(/usr/local/lib/mcb);
use strict;
use warnings;
use Cookbook;

my $dbh = Cookbook::connect ();
my $sth = $dbh->prepare (qq{
                INSERT DELAYED INTO httpdlog
                  (dt,host,method,url,status,size,referer,agent)
                  VALUES (?,?,?,?,?,?,?,?)
                });

while (<>)  # loop reading input
{
  chomp;
  my ($dt, $host, $method, $url, $status, $size, $refer, $agent)
                        = split (/\t/, $_);
  # map "-" to NULL for some columns
  $size = undef if $size eq "-";
  $agent = undef if $agent eq "-";
  $sth->execute ($dt, $host, $method, $url,
                $status, $size, $refer, $agent);
}

$dbh->disconnect ();
```

Install the *httpdlog.pl* script where you want Apache to look for it. On my system, the Apache root directory is */usr/local/apache*, so */usr/local/apache/bin* is a reasonable installation directory. The path to this directory will be needed shortly for constructing the `CustomLog` directive that instructs Apache to log to the script.

The purpose of including the `use lib` line is so that Perl can find the *Cookbook.pm* module. This line will be necessary if the environment of scripts invoked by Apache for logging does not enable Perl to find the module. Change the path as necessary for your system.

The script uses `INSERT DELAYED` rather than `INSERT`. The advantage of using `DELAYED` is that the MySQL server buffers the row in memory and then later inserts a batch of rows at a time, which is more efficient. This also enables the client to continue immediately rather than having to wait if the table is busy. The disadvantage is that if the MySQL server crashes, any rows buffered in memory at the time are lost. I figure that this is not very likely, and that the loss of a few log records is not a serious problem. If you disagree, just remove `DELAYED` from the statement.

httpdlog.pl assumes that input lines contain `httpdlog` column values delimited by tabs (to make it easy to break apart input lines), so Apache must write log entries in a matching format. The `LogFormat` field specifiers to produce the appropriate values are shown in the following table.

Specifier	Meaning
`%{%Y-%m-%d %H:%M:%S}t`	The date and time of the request, in MySQL's DATETIME format
`%h`	The host from which the request originated
`%m`	The request method (get, post, and so forth)
`%U`	The URL path
`%>s`	The status code
`%b`	The number of bytes transferred
`%{Referer}i`	The referring page
`%{User-Agent}i`	The user agent

To define a logging format named `mysql` that produces these values with tabs in between, add the following `LogFormat` directive to your *httpd.conf* file:

```
LogFormat \
"%{%Y-%m-%d %H:%M:%S}t\t%h\t%m\t%U\t%>s\t%b\t%{Referer}i\t%{User-Agent}i" \
mysql
```

Most of the pieces are in place now. We have a log table, a program that writes to it, and a `mysql` format for producing log entries. All that remains is to tell Apache to write the entries to the *httpdlog.pl* script. However, until you know that the output format really is correct and that the program can process log entries properly, it's premature to tell Apache to log directly to the program. To make testing and debugging a bit easier, have Apache log `mysql`-format entries to a file instead. That way, you can look at the file to check the output format, and you can use it as input to *httpdlog.pl* to verify that the program works correctly. To instruct Apache to log lines in `mysql` format to the file *test_log* in Apache's log directory, use this `CustomLog` directive:

```
CustomLog /usr/local/apache/logs/test_log mysql
```

Then restart Apache to enable the new logging directives. After your web server receives a few requests, take a look at the *test_log* file. Verify that the contents are as you expect, and then feed the file to *httpdlog.pl*:

```
% /usr/local/apache/bin/httpdlog.pl test_log
```

After *httpdlog.pl* finishes, take a look at the `httpdlog` table to make sure that it looks correct. Once you're satisfied, tell Apache to send log entries directly to *httpdlog.pl* by modifying the `CustomLog` directive as follows:

```
CustomLog "|/usr/local/apache/bin/httpdlog.pl" mysql
```

The | character at the beginning of the pathname tells Apache that *httpdlog.pl* is a program, not a file. Restart Apache and new entries should appear in the `httpdlog` table as visitors request pages from your site.

Nothing you have done to this point changes any logging you may have been doing originally. For example, if you were logging to an *access_log* file before, you still are now. Thus, Apache will be sending entries both to the original logfile and to MySQL. If that's what you want, fine. Apache doesn't care if you log to multiple destinations. But you'll use more disk space if you do. To disable file logging, comment out your original `CustomLog` directive by placing a # character in front of it, and then restart Apache.

Analyzing the logfile

Now that you have Apache logging into the database, what can you do with the information? That depends on what you want to know. Here are some examples that show the kinds of questions you can use MySQL to answer easily:

- How many rows are in the request log?

  ```
  SELECT COUNT(*) FROM httpdlog;
  ```
- How many different client hosts have sent requests?

  ```
  SELECT COUNT(DISTINCT host) FROM httpdlog;
  ```
- How many different pages have clients requested?

  ```
  SELECT COUNT(DISTINCT url) FROM httpdlog;
  ```
- What are the 10 most popular pages?

  ```
  SELECT url, COUNT(*) AS count FROM httpdlog
  GROUP BY url ORDER BY count DESC LIMIT 10;
  ```
- How many requests have been received for those *favicon.ico* files that certain browsers like to check for?

  ```
  SELECT COUNT(*) FROM httpdlog WHERE url LIKE '%/favicon.ico%';
  ```
- What is the range of dates spanned by the log?

  ```
  SELECT MIN(dt), MAX(dt) FROM httpdlog;
  ```
- How many requests have been received each day?

  ```
  SELECT DATE(dt) AS day, COUNT(*) FROM httpdlog GROUP BY day;
  ```

Answering this question requires stripping off the time-of-day part from the `dt` values so that requests received on a given date can be grouped. The statement does this using the `DATE()` function to convert `DATETIME` values to `DATE` values. However, if you intend to run a lot of statements that use just the date part of the `dt` values, it would be more efficient to create the `httpdlog` table with separate `DATE` and `TIME` columns, change the `LogFormat` directive to produce the date and time as separate output values, and modify *httpdlog.pl* accordingly. Then you can operate on the request dates directly without stripping off the time, and you can index the date column for even better performance.

- What is the hour-of-the-day request histogram?

```
SELECT HOUR(dt) AS hour, COUNT(*) FROM httpdlog GROUP BY hour;
```

- What is the average number of requests received each day?

```
SELECT COUNT(*)/(DATEDIFF(MAX(dt), MIN(dt)) + 1)
FROM httpdlog;
```

The numerator is the total number of requests in the table. The denominator is the number of days spanned by the records.

- What is the longest URL recorded in the table?

```
SELECT MAX(LENGTH(url)) FROM httpdlog;
```

If the url column is defined as VARCHAR(255) and this statement produces a value of 255, it's likely that some URL values were too long to fit in the column and were truncated at the end. To avoid this, change the column definition to allow more characters. For example, to allow up to 5,000 characters, modify the url column as follows:

```
ALTER TABLE httpdlog
  MODIFY url VARCHAR(5000)
  CHARACTER SET latin1 COLLATE latin1_general_cs NOT NULL;
```

- What is the total number of bytes served and the average bytes per request?

```
SELECT
  COUNT(size) AS requests,
  SUM(size) AS bytes,
  AVG(size) AS 'bytes/request'
FROM httpdlog;
```

The statement uses COUNT(size) rather than COUNT(*) to count only those requests with a non-NULL size value. If a client requests a page twice, the server may respond to the second request by sending a header indicating that the page hasn't changed rather than by sending content. In this case, the log entry for the request will have NULL in the size column.

- How much traffic has there been for each kind of file (based on filename extension such as .html, .jpg, or .php)?

```
SELECT
  SUBSTRING_INDEX(SUBSTRING_INDEX(url,'?',1),'.',-1) AS extension,
  COUNT(size) AS requests,
  SUM(size) AS bytes,
  AVG(size) AS 'bytes/request'
FROM httpdlog
WHERE url LIKE '%.%'
GROUP BY extension;
```

The WHERE clause selects only `url` values that have a period in them, to eliminate pathnames that refer to files that have no extension. To extract the extension values for the output column list, the inner `SUBSTRING_INDEX( )` call strips off any parameter string at the right end of the URL and leaves the rest. (This turns a value like `/cgi-bin/script.pl?id=43` into `/cgi-bin/script.pl`. If the value has no parameter part, `SUBSTRING_INDEX( )` returns the entire string.) The outer `SUBSTRING_INDEX( )` call strips everything up to and including the rightmost period from the result, leaving only the extension.

Other logging issues

The preceding discussion shows a simple method for hooking Apache to MySQL, which involves writing a short script that communicates with MySQL and then telling Apache to write to the script rather than to a file. This works well if you log all requests to a single file, but certainly won't be appropriate for every possible configuration that Apache is capable of. For example, if you have virtual servers defined in your *httpd.conf* file, you might have separate `CustomLog` directives defined for each of them. To log them all to MySQL, you can change each directive to write to *httpdlog.pl*, but then you'll have a separate logging process running for each virtual server. That brings up two issues:

- How do you associate log records with the proper virtual server? One solution is to create a separate log table for each server and modify *httpdlog.pl* to take an argument that indicates which table to use. Another is to use a table that has a `vhost` column, an Apache log format that includes the `%v` virtual host format specifier, and a logging script that uses the `vhost` value when it generates `INSERT` statements. The *apache/httpdlog* directory of the `recipes` distribution contains information about doing this.

- Do you really want a lot of *httpdlog.pl* processes running? If you have many virtual servers, you may want to consider using a logging module that installs directly into Apache. Some of these can multiplex logging for multiple virtual hosts through a single connection to the database server, reducing resource consumption for logging activity.

Logging to a database rather than to a file enables you to bring the full power of MySQL to bear on log analysis, but it doesn't eliminate the need to think about space management. Web servers can generate a lot of activity, and log records use space regardless of whether you write them to a file or to a database. One way to save space is to expire records now and then. For example, to remove log records that are more than a year old, run the following statement periodically:

```
DELETE FROM httpdlog WHERE dt < NOW() - INTERVAL 1 YEAR;
```

If you have MySQL 5.1 or higher, you can set up an event that runs the `DELETE` statement on a scheduled basis (Recipe 16.7).

With respect to disk space consumed by web logging activity, be aware that if you have query logging enabled for the MySQL server, each request will be written to the `httpdlog` table and also to the query logfile. Thus, you may find disk space disappearing more quickly than you expect, so it's a good idea to have some kind of logfile rotation or expiration set up for the MySQL server.

## CHAPTER 20

Using MySQL-Based Web Session Management

20.0 Introduction

Many web applications interact with users over a series of requests and, as a result, need to remember information from one request to the next. A set of related requests is called a *session*. Sessions are useful for activities such as performing login operations and associating a logged-in user with subsequent requests, managing a multiple-stage online ordering process, gathering input from a user in stages (possibly tailoring the questions asked to the user's earlier responses), and remembering user preferences from visit to visit. Unfortunately, HTTP is a stateless protocol, which means that web servers treat each request independently of any other—unless you take steps to ensure otherwise.

This chapter shows how to make information persist across multiple requests, which will help you develop applications for which one request retains memory of previous ones. The techniques shown here are general enough that you should be able to adapt them to a variety of state-maintaining web applications.

Session Management Issues

Some session management methods rely on information stored on the client. One way to implement client-side storage is to use cookies, which are implemented as information that is transmitted back and forth in special request and response headers. When a session begins, the application generates and sends the client a cookie containing the initial information to be stored. The client returns the cookie to the server with each subsequent request to identify itself and to enable the application to associate the requests as belonging to the same client session. At each stage of the session, the application uses the data in the cookie to determine the state (or status) of the client. To modify the session state, the application sends the client a new cookie containing updated information to replace the old cookie. This mechanism allows data to persist across requests while still affording the application the opportunity to update the information as necessary. Cookies are easy to use, but have some disadvantages. For example, it's possible for the client to modify cookie contents, possibly tricking the application into misbehaving. Other client-side session storage techniques suffer the same drawback.

The alternative to client-side storage is to maintain the state of a multiple-request session on the server side. With this approach, information about what the client is doing is stored somewhere on the server, such as in a file, in shared memory, or in a database. The only information maintained on the client side is a unique identifier that the server generates and sends to the client when the session begins. The client sends this value to the server with each subsequent request so that the server can associate the client with the appropriate session. Common techniques for tracking the session ID are to store it in a cookie or to encode it in request URLs. (The latter is useful for clients that have cookies disabled.) The server can get the ID as the cookie value or by extracting it from the URL.

Server-side session storage is more secure than storing information on the client because the application maintains control over the contents of the session. The only value present on the client side is the session ID, so the client can't modify session data unless the application permits it. It's still possible for a client to tinker with the ID and send back a different one, but if IDs are unique and selected from a very large pool of possible values, it's extremely unlikely that a malicious client will be able to guess the ID of another valid session. If you are concerned about other clients stealing valid session IDs by network snooping, you should set up a secure connection (for example, by using SSL). But that is beyond the scope of this book.

Server-side methods for managing sessions commonly store session contents in persistent storage such as a file or a database. Database-backed storage has different characteristics from file-based storage, such as that you eliminate the filesystem clutter that results from having many session files, and you can use the same MySQL server to handle session traffic for multiple web servers. If this appeals to you, the techniques shown in the chapter will help you integrate MySQL-based session management into your applications. The chapter shows how to implement server-side database-backed session management for several of our API languages:

- For Perl, the Apache::Session module includes most of the capabilities that you need for managing sessions. It can store session information in files or in any of several database systems, including MySQL, PostgreSQL, and Oracle.

- The Ruby CGI::Session class provides a session-handling capability that uses temporary files by default. However, the implementation allows other storage managers to be used. One such is the mysql-session package that enables session storage via MySQL.

- PHP includes native session support. The implementation uses temporary files by default, but is sufficiently flexible that applications can supply their own handler routines for session storage. This makes it possible to plug in a storage module that writes information to MySQL.

- For Java-based web applications running under the Tomcat web server, Tomcat provides session support at the server level. All you need to do is modify the server configuration to use MySQL for session storage. Application programs need do nothing to take advantage of this capability, so there are no changes at the application level.

Session support for different APIs can use very different approaches. For Perl, the language itself provides no session support, so a script must include a module such as Apache::Session explicitly if it wants to implement a session. Ruby is similar. In PHP, the session manager is built in. Scripts can use it with no special preparation, but only as long as they want to use the default storage method, which is to save session information in files. To use an alternative method (such as storing sessions in MySQL), an application must provide its own routines for the session manager to use. Still another approach is used for Java applications running under Tomcat, because Tomcat itself manages many of the details associated with session management, including where to store session data. Individual applications need not know or care where this information is stored.

Python is not discussed in this chapter. I have not found a standalone Python session management module that I felt was suitable for discussion here, and I didn't want to write one from scratch. If you're writing Python applications that require session support, you might want to look into a toolkit such as Zope, WebWare, or Albatross.

Despite the differing implementations, session management typically involves a common set of tasks:

- Determine whether the client provided a session ID. If not, it's necessary to generate a unique session ID and send it to the client. Some session managers figure out how to transmit the session ID between the server and the client automatically. PHP does this, as does Tomcat for Java programs. The Perl Apache::Session module leaves it up to the application developer to manage ID transmission.

- Store values into the session for use by later requests and retrieve values placed into the session by earlier requests. This involves performing whatever actions are necessary that involve session data: incrementing a counter, validating a login request, updating a shopping cart, and so forth.

- Terminate the session when it's no longer needed. Some session managers make provision for expiring sessions automatically after a certain period of inactivity. Sessions may also be ended explicitly, if the request indicates that the session should terminate (such as when the client selects a logout action). In response, the session manager destroys the session record. It might also be necessary to tell the client to release information. If the client sends the session identifier by means of a cookie, the application should instruct the client to discard the cookie. Otherwise, the client may continue to submit it after its usefulness has ended. Another approach to session "termination" is to delete all information from the session record. In effect, this causes the session to restart with the client's next request because none of the previous session information is available.

Session managers impose little constraint on what applications can store in session records. Sessions usually can accommodate relatively arbitrary data, such as scalars, arrays, or objects. To make it easy to store and retrieve session data, session managers typically serialize session information by converting it to a coded scalar string value before storing it and unserialize it after retrieval. The conversion to and from serialized strings generally is not something you must deal with when providing storage routines. It's necessary only to make sure the storage manager has a large enough repository in which to store the serialized strings. For backing store implemented using MySQL, this means you use one of the BLOB data types. Our session managers use MEDIUMBLOB, which is large enough to hold session records up to 16 MB. (When assessing storage needs, remember that stored data is serialized, which takes more space than raw data.)

The rest of the chapter shows a session-based script for each API. Each script performs two tasks. It maintains a counter value that indicates how many requests have been received during the current session, and records a timestamp for each request. In this way, the scripts illustrate how to store and retrieve a scalar value (the counter) and a nonscalar value (the timestamp array). They require very little user interaction. You just reload the page to issue the next request, which results in extremely simple code.

Session-based applications often include some way for the user to log out explicitly and terminate the session. The example scripts implement a form of "logout," but it is based on an implicit mechanism: sessions are given a limit of 10 requests. As you reinvoke a script, it checks the counter to see whether the limit has been reached and destroys the session data if so. The effect is that the session values will not be present on the next request, so the script starts a new session.

The example session scripts for Perl, Ruby, and PHP can be found under the *apache* directory of the recipes distribution; the PHP session module is located in the *lib* directory; and the JSP examples are under the *tomcat* directory. The SQL scripts for creating the session storage tables are located in the *tables* directory. As used here, the session tables are created in the cookbook database and accessed through the same MySQL account as that used elsewhere in this book. If you don't want to mix session management activities with those pertaining to the other cookbook tables, consider setting up a separate database and MySQL account to be used only for session data. This is true particularly for Tomcat, where session management takes place above the application level. You might not want the Tomcat server storing information in "your" database; if not, give the server its own database.

20.1 Using MySQL-Based Sessions in Perl Applications

Problem

You want to use session storage for Perl scripts.

Solution

The Apache::Session module provides a convenient way to use several different storage types, including one based on MySQL.

Discussion

Apache::Session is an easy-to-use Perl module for maintaining state information across multiple web requests. Despite the name, this module is not dependent on Apache and can be used in nonweb contexts—for example, to maintain persistent state across multiple invocations of a command-line script. On the other hand, Apache::Session doesn't handle any of the issues associated with tracking the session ID (sending it to the client in response to the initial request and extracting it from subsequent requests). The example application shown here uses cookies to pass the session ID, on the assumption that the client has cookies enabled.

Installing Apache::Session

If you don't have Apache::Session, you can get it from CPAN (visit *http:// cpan.perl.org*). Installation is straightforward, although Apache::Session does require several other modules that you may need to get first. (When you install it, Apache::Session should tell you which required modules you need if any are missing. If you install it using a *cpan install* Apache::Session command, that should install it and take care of the dependencies.) After you have everything installed, create a table in which to store session records. The specification for the table comes from the MySQL storage handler documentation, which you can read using this command:

```
% perldoc Apache::Session::Store::MySQL
```

The table can be placed in any database you like (we'll use cookbook). By default, the table is named sessions, but recent versions of Apache::Session enable you to specify the table name. We'll use a table named perl_session that has the following structure:

```
CREATE TABLE perl_session
(
  id        CHAR(32) NOT NULL,  # session identifier
  a_session MEDIUMBLOB,         # session data
  PRIMARY KEY (id)
);
```

The id column holds session identifiers, which are 32-character MD5 values generated by Apache::Session. The a_session column holds session data in the form of serialized strings. Apache::Session uses the Storable module to serialize and unserialize session data. (The Apache::Session::Store::MySQL documentation indicates that `a_session` is a `TEXT` column, but any `BLOB` or `TEXT` data type large enough to hold the anticipated session records should work.)

The Apache::Session interface

To use the `perl_session` table in a script, access the MySQL-related session module:

```
use Apache::Session::MySQL;
```

Apache::Session represents session information using a hash. It uses Perl's `tie` mechanism to map hash operations onto the storage and retrieval methods used by the underlying storage manager. Thus, to open a session, you should declare a hash variable and pass it to `tie`. The other arguments to `tie` are the name of the session module, the session ID, and information about the database to use. There are two ways to specify the database connection. One method is to pass a reference to a hash that contains connection parameters (and the session table name if you do not use the default name):

```
my %session;
tie %session,
  "Apache::Session::MySQL",
  $sess_id,
  {
    DataSource => "DBI:mysql:host=localhost;database=cookbook",
    UserName => "cbuser",
    Password => "cbpass",
    LockDataSource => "DBI:mysql:host=localhost;database=cookbook",
    LockUserName => "cbuser",
    LockPassword => "cbpass",
    TableName => "perl_session"
  };
```

In this case, Apache::Session uses the parameters to open its own connection to MySQL, which it closes when you close or destroy the session.

The other method is to pass the handle for an already open database connection (represented here by `$dbh`):

```
my %session;
tie %session,
  "Apache::Session::MySQL",
  $sess_id,
  {
    Handle => $dbh,
    LockHandle => $dbh,
    TableName => "perl_session"
  };
```

If you pass a handle to an open connection as just shown, Apache::Session leaves it open when you close or destroy the session, on the assumption that you're using the handle for other purposes elsewhere in the script. You should close the connection yourself when you're done with it.

The $sess_id argument to tie represents the session identifier. Its value should be either undef to begin a new session, or a valid ID corresponding to an existing session record. In the latter case, the value should match that of the id column in some existing perl_session table row.

After the session has been opened, you can access its contents. For example, after opening a new session, you'll want to determine what its identifier is so that you can send it to the client. That value can be obtained like this:

```
$sess_id = $session{_session_id};
```

Session hash element names that begin with an underscore (such as _session_id) are reserved by Apache::Session for internal use. Other than that, you can use names of your own choosing for storing session values.

To save a scalar value in the session, store it by value. To access a scalar, read the value directly. For example, you might maintain a scalar counter value as follows, where the counter is initialized if the session is new, and then incremented and retrieved for display:

```
$session{count} = 0 if !exists ($session{count}); # initialize counter
++$session{count};                                 # increment counter
print "counter value: $session{count}\n";          # print value
```

To save a nonscalar value such as an array or a hash into the session record, store a reference to it:

```
$session{my_array} = \@my_array;
$session{my_hash} = \%my_hash;
```

In this case, changes made to @my_array or %my_hash before you close the session will be reflected in the session contents. To save an independent copy of an array or hash in the session that will not change when you modify the original, create a reference to the copy like this:

```
$session{my_array} = [ @my_array ];
$session{my_hash} = { %my_hash };
```

To retrieve a nonscalar value, dereference the reference stored in the session:

```
@my_array = @{$session{my_array}};
%my_hash = %{$session{my_hash}};
```

To close a session when you're done with it, pass it to untie:

```
untie (%session);
```

When you close a session, Apache::Session saves it to the perl_session table if you've made changes to it. This also makes the session values inaccessible, so don't close the session until you're done accessing it.

Apache::Session notices changes to "top-level" session record values, but might not detect a change to a member of a value stored by reference (such as an array element). If this is a problem, you can force Apache::Session to save a session when you close it by assigning any top-level session element a value. The session ID is always present in the session hash, so the following idiom provides a convenient way to force session saving:

```
$session{_session_id} = $session{_session_id};
```

An open session can be terminated rather than closed. Doing so removes the corresponding row from the `perl_session` table, so that it can no longer be used:

```
tied (%session)->delete ();
```

A sample application

The following script, *sess_track.pl*, is a short but complete implementation of an application that uses a session. It uses Apache::Session to keep track of the number of requests in the session and the time of each request, updating and displaying the information each time it is invoked. *sess_track.pl* uses a cookie named `PERLSESSID` to pass the session ID. This is done by means of the CGI.pm cookie management interface.[*]

```
#!/usr/bin/perl
# sess_track.pl - session request counting/timestamping demonstration

use strict;
use warnings;
use CGI qw(:standard);
use Cookbook;
use Apache::Session::MySQL;

my $title = "Perl Session Tracker";

my $dbh = Cookbook::connect ();        # connection to MySQL
my $sess_id = cookie ("PERLSESSID");   # session ID (undef if new session)
my %session;                           # session hash
my $cookie;                            # cookie to send to client

# open the session

tie %session, "Apache::Session::MySQL", $sess_id,
            {
              Handle => $dbh,
              LockHandle => $dbh,
              TableName => "perl_session"
            };
if (!defined ($sess_id))            # this is a new session
```

---

[*] For information about CGI.pm cookie support, use the following command and read the section describing the `cookie( )` function:

```
% perldoc CGI
```

```
{
  # get new session ID, initialize session data, create cookie for client
  $sess_id = $session{_session_id};
  $session{count} = 0;            # initialize counter
  $session{timestamp} = [ ];      # initialize timestamp array
  $cookie = cookie (-name => "PERLSESSID", -value => $sess_id);
}

# increment counter and add current timestamp to timestamp array

++$session{count};
push (@{$session{timestamp}}, scalar (localtime (time ())));

# construct content of page body

my $page_body =
    p ("This session has been active for $session{count} requests.")
  . p ("The requests occurred at these times:")
  . ul (li ($session{timestamp}));

if ($session{count} < 10) # close (and save) session
{
  untie (%session);
}
else                      # destroy session after 10 invocations
{
  tied (%session)->delete ();
  # reset cookie to tell browser to discard session cookie
  $cookie = cookie (-name => "PERLSESSID",
                    -value => $sess_id,
                    -expires => "-1d");   # "expire yesterday"
}

$dbh->disconnect ();

# generate the output page; include cookie in headers if it's defined

print
  header (-cookie => $cookie)
         . start_html (-title => $title, -bgcolor => "white")
         . $page_body
         . end_html ();
```

Try the script by installing it in your *cgi-bin* directory and requesting it from your browser. To reinvoke it, use your browser's Reload function.

sess_track.pl opens the session and increments the counter prior to generating any page output. This is necessary because the client must be sent a cookie containing the session name and identifier if the session is new. Any cookie sent must be part of the response headers, so the page body cannot be printed until after the headers are sent.

The script also generates the part of the page body that uses session data but saves it in a variable rather than writing it immediately. The reason for this is that, should the session need to be terminated, the script resets the cookie to be one that tells the browser to discard the session it has. This must be determined prior to sending the headers or any page content.

Session expiration

The Apache::Session module requires only the `id` and `a_session` columns in the `perl_session` table, and makes no provision for timing out or expiring sessions. On the other hand, the module doesn't restrict you from adding other columns, so you could include a `TIMESTAMP` column in the table to record the time of each session's last update. For example, you can add a `TIMESTAMP` column `t` to the `perl_session` table using `ALTER TABLE`:

```
ALTER TABLE perl_session ADD t TIMESTAMP NOT NULL, ADD INDEX (t);
```

Then you'd be able to expire sessions by running a statement periodically to sweep the table and remove old records. The following statement uses an expiration time of four hours:

```
DELETE FROM perl_session WHERE t < NOW() - INTERVAL 4 HOUR;
```

The `ALTER TABLE` statement indexes `t` to make the `DELETE` operation faster.

20.2 Using MySQL-Based Storage in Ruby Applications

Problem

You want to use session storage for Ruby scripts.

Solution

Use the `CGI::Session` class interface. By default, it uses temporary files for backing store, but you can configure it to use MySQL instead.

Discussion

The `CGI::Session` class manages session storage. It identifies sessions by means of cookies, which it adds transparently to the responses sent to the client. `CGI::Session` allows you to supply a storage-management class to be used in place of the default manager that uses temporary files. We'll use the `mysql-session` package, which is based on the Ruby DBI interface and stores session records using MySQL. `mysql-session` is available from the Ruby Application Archive. See Appendix A for information about obtaining and installing it.

To use `mysql-session` in a script, you need to access these modules:

```
require "cgi"
require "cgi/session"
require "mysqlstore"
```

To create a session, first create a `CGI` object . Then invoke `CGI::Session.new`, which takes several arguments. The first is a `CGI` object associated with the script. (This object must exist before you can open the session.) Other arguments provide information about the session itself. Those following are relevant no matter which storage manager you use:

`session_key`
> The session key that the session manager uses as the name of the cookie to be sent to the client. The default key value is `_session_key`; we will use `RUBYSESSID`.

`new_session`
> This argument should be true to force a new session to be created, or false to use an existing session, which is assumed to have already been created during a previous request. It's also possible to create a session if it does not exist and use the current session if it does. To enable that behavior, omit the `new_session` argument (which is what the example script in this recipe does).

`database_manager`
> The name of the class that provides storage management for session records. If this argument is omitted, the session manager uses temporary files.

To use the `mysql-session` package as the storage manager, the `database_manager` argument should be `CGI::Session::MySQLStore`. In that case, `mysql-session` enables several other arguments for the `CGI::Session.new` method. You can pass in arguments that instruct the session manager to establish its own connection to MySQL, or you can open your own connection and pass its database handle to the session manager.

The following discussion shows both approaches, but either way, we'll need a table for storing session records. For `mysql-session`, create a table named `ruby_session` with the following structure:

```
CREATE TABLE ruby_session
(
  session_id    VARCHAR(255) NOT NULL,
  session_value MEDIUMBLOB NOT NULL,
  update_time   DATETIME NOT NULL,
  PRIMARY KEY (session_id)
);
```

Now we return to session creation. To have the session manager open its own connection to MySQL, create the session like this:

```
cgi = CGI.new("html4")
sess_id = cgi.cookies["RUBYSESSID"]
session = CGI::Session.new(
              cgi,
              "session_key" => "RUBYSESSID",
              "database_manager" => CGI::Session::MySQLStore,
              "db.host" => "127.0.0.1",
              "db.user" => "cbuser",
              "db.pass" => "cbpass",
              "db.name" => "cookbook",
```

```
                "db.table" => "ruby_session",
                "db.hold_conn" => 1
            )
```

The db.*xxx* parameters used in that code tell mysql-session how to connect to the server, as well as the database and table to use for session records:

db.host

  The host where the MySQL server is running.

db.user, db.pass

  The username and password of the MySQL account to use.

db.name, db.table

  The database and table name for the session table.

db.hold_conn

  By default, mysql-session opens and closes a connection each time it needs to send a statement to the MySQL server. If you supply the db.hold_conn parameter with a value of 1, mysql-session opens the connection only once and holds it open until the session ends.

Another way to create a session is to open your own database connection first and pass the database handle as a parameter:

```
cgi = CGI.new("html4")
sess_id = cgi.cookies["RUBYSESSID"]
session = CGI::Session.new(
                cgi,
                "session_key" => "RUBYSESSID",
                "database_manager" => CGI::Session::MySQLStore,
                "db.dbh" => dbh,
                "db.name" => "cookbook",
                "db.table" => "ruby_session"
            )
```

In this case, the db.host, db.user, db.pass, and db.hold_conn parameters are not used. In addition, you are responsible for closing the connection after the session is no longer needed.

Whichever way you create the session, its ID is available while it is open as the session.session_id attribute.

To close the session, invoke the close method of the session object. If you want to destroy the session instead, invoke its delete method.

The session manager stores data using key/value pairs, using strings for the values. It does not know the types of the values that you store. I find the following strategy useful for dealing with type-conversion issues:

1. After opening the session, extract values from the session and convert them from "generic" string form to properly typed values.

2. Work with the typed values until it is time to close the session.

3. Convert the typed values to string form, store them in the session, and close it.

The following script uses the `CGI::Session` session manager to track the number of requests in a session and the time of each request. After 10 requests, the script deletes the session to cause a new session to begin for the next request:

```ruby
#!/usr/bin/ruby -w
# sess_track.rb - session request counting/timestamping demonstration

require "Cookbook"
require "cgi"
require "cgi/session"
require "mysqlstore"

title = "Ruby Session Tracker";

dbh = Cookbook::connect

cgi = CGI.new("html4")
session = CGI::Session.new(
                cgi,
                "session_key" => "RUBYSESSID",
                "database_manager" => CGI::Session::MySQLStore,
                "db.dbh" => dbh,
                "db.name" => "cookbook",
                "db.table" => "ruby_session"
            )

# extract string values from session

count = session["count"]
timestamp = session["timestamp"]

# convert variables to proper types

count = (count.nil? ? 0 : count.to_i)
timestamp = "" if timestamp.nil?
timestamp = timestamp.split(",")

# increment counter and add current timestamp to timestamp array

count = count + 1
timestamp << Time.now().strftime("%Y-%m-%d %H:%M:%S")

# construct content of page body

page = ""

page << cgi.p {"This session has been active for #{count} requests."}
page << cgi.p {"The requests occurred at these times:"}
list = ""
timestamp.each do |t|
  list << cgi.li { t.to_s }
end
page << cgi.ul { list }
```

```
if count < 10
  # convert session variables to strings, store them back
  # into the session, and close (and save) the session
  session["count"] = count.to_s
  session["timestamp"] = timestamp.join(",")
  session.close()
else
  # destroy session after 10 invocations
  session.delete()
end

dbh.disconnect

# generate the output page

cgi.out {
  cgi.html {
    cgi.head { cgi.title { title } } +
    cgi.body("bgcolor" => "white") { page }
  }
}
```

CGI::Session makes no provision for expiring sessions, but you can discard old session records using the technique discussed in Recipe 20.1. If you do this, you should index the update_time column to make DELETE statements faster:

```
ALTER TABLE ruby_session ADD INDEX (update_time);
```

20.3 Using MySQL-Based Storage with the PHP Session Manager

Problem

You want to use session storage for PHP scripts.

Solution

PHP includes session management. By default, it uses temporary files for backing store, but you can configure it to use MySQL instead.

Discussion

This section shows how to use the PHP native session manager and how to extend it by implementing a storage module that saves session data in MySQL. If your PHP configuration has the track_vars configuration variable enabled, session variables are available as elements of the $HTTP_SESSION_VARS global array or the $_SESSION super-global array. track_vars is always enabled as of PHP 4.0.3, so I'll assume that this is true for your PHP installation. If the register_globals configuration variable is enabled as well, session variables also exist in your script as global variables of the same names. However, this is less secure, so this variable is assumed *not* to be enabled here. (Recipe 19.5 discusses PHP's global and superglobal arrays and the security implications of `register_globals`.)

The PHP session management interface

PHP's session management capabilities are based on a small set of functions, all of which are documented in the PHP manual. The following list describes those likely to be most useful for day-to-day session programming:

`session_start ( )`
> Opens a session and extracts any variables previously stored in it, making them available in the script's global namespace. For example, a session variable named x becomes available as `$_SESSION["x"]` or `$HTTP_SESSION_VARS["x"]`. This function *must* be called first before using the relevant session variable array.

`session_register (var_name)`
> Registers a variable in the session by setting up an association between the session record and a variable in your script. For example, to register `$count`, do this:
>
> ```
> session_register ("count");
> ```
>
> If you make any changes to the variable while the session remains open, the new value is saved to the session record when the session is closed.
>
> However, I mention this function only to point out that *we will not use it.* `session_register( )` is effective only if `register_globals` is enabled, which is a security risk. To avoid reliance on `register_globals`, we will get session variables from either the `$_SESSION` array or the `$HTTP_SESSION_VARS` array.

`session_unregister (var_name)`
> Unregisters a session variable so that it is not saved to the session record. Unlike `session_register( )`, this function is not dependent on the `register_globals` setting.

`session_write_close ( )`
> Writes the session data and closes the session. The PHP documentation indicates that normally you need not call this function because PHP saves an open session automatically when your script ends. However, it appears that in PHP 5, that might not always be true when you provide your own session handler. To be safe, call this function to save your changes.

`session_destroy ( )`
> Removes the session and any data associated with it.

`session_name ($name)`
> The PHP session manager determines which session to use by means of the session identifier. It looks for the identifier by checking the following sources: a global variable named `$PHPSESSID`; a cookie, get, or post variable named `PHPSESSID`; or a

URL parameter of the form PHPSESSID=*value*. (If none of these are found, the session manager generates a new identifier and begins a new session.) The default identifier name is PHPSESSID, but you can change it. To make a global (site-wide) change, edit the session.name configuration variable in *php.ini*. To make the change for an individual script, call session_name($name) before starting the session, where $name represents the session name to use. To determine the current session identifier name, call session_name( ) with no argument.

Specifying a user-defined storage module

The PHP session management interface just described makes no reference to any kind of backing store. That is, the description specifies nothing about how session information actually gets saved. By default, PHP uses temporary files to store session data, but the session interface is extensible so that other storage modules can be defined. To override the default storage method and store session data in MySQL, you must do several things:

1. Set up a table to hold session records and write the routines that implement the storage module. This is done once, prior to writing any scripts that use the new module.

2. Tell PHP that you're supplying a user-defined storage manager. You can do this globally in *php.ini* (in which case you make the change once), or within individual scripts (in which case it's necessary to declare your intent in each script).

3. Register the storage module routines within each script that wants to use the module.

Creating the session table.   Any MySQL-based storage module needs a database table in which to store session information. Create a table named php_session that includes the following columns:

```
CREATE TABLE php_session
(
  id    CHAR(32) NOT NULL,
  data  MEDIUMBLOB,
  t     TIMESTAMP NOT NULL,
  PRIMARY KEY (id),
  INDEX (t)
);
```

You'll recognize the structure of this table as quite similar to the perl_session table used in Recipe 20.1 for the Apache::Session Perl module. The id column holds session identifiers, which are unique 32-character strings (they look suspiciously like Apache::Session identifiers, which is not surprising, given that PHP uses MD5 values, just like the Perl module). The data column holds session information. PHP serializes session data into a string before storing it, so php_session needs only a large generic string column to hold the resulting serialized value. The t column is a TIMESTAMP that MySQL updates automatically whenever a session record is updated. This column is

---

not required, but it's useful for implementing a garbage collection policy based on each session's last update time.

A small set of statements suffices to manage the contents of the php_session table as we have defined it:

- To retrieve a session's data, issue a simple SELECT based on the session identifier:

```
SELECT data FROM php_session WHERE id = 'sess_id';
```

- To write session data, a REPLACE serves to update an existing row (or to create a new one if no such row exists):

```
REPLACE INTO php_session (id,data) VALUES('sess_id','sess_data');
```

  REPLACE also updates the timestamp in the row when creating or updating a row, which is important for garbage collection.

  Some storage manager implementations use a combination of INSERT and a fallback to UPDATE if the INSERT fails because a row with the given session ID already exists (or an UPDATE with a fallback to INSERT if the UPDATE fails because a row with the ID does *not* exist). In MySQL, a dual-statement approach is unnecessary; REPLACE performs the required task with a single statement.

- To destroy a session, delete the corresponding row:

```
DELETE FROM php_session WHERE id = 'sess_id';
```

- Garbage collection is performed by removing old rows. The following statement deletes rows that have a timestamp value more than *sess_life* seconds old:

```
DELETE FROM php_session WHERE t < NOW() - INTERVAL sess_life SECOND;
```

  The PHP session manager supplies the value of *sess_life* when it invokes the garbage collection routine. (The table definition for php_session indexes t to make DELETE statements faster.)

These statements form the basis of the routines that make up our MySQL-backed storage module. The primary function of the module is to open and close MySQL connections and to issue the proper statements at the appropriate times.

Writing the storage management routines. User-defined session storage modules have a specific interface, implemented as a set of handler routines that you register with PHP's session manager by calling session_set_save_handler( ). The format of the function is as follows, where each argument is a handler routine name specified as a string:

```
session_set_save_handler (
    "mysql_sess_open",      # function to open a session
    "mysql_sess_close",     # function to close a session
    "mysql_sess_read",      # function to read session data
    "mysql_sess_write",     # function to write session data
    "mysql_sess_destroy",   # function to destroy a session
    "mysql_sess_gc"         # function to garbage-collect old sessions
);
```

The order of the handler routines must be as shown, but you can name them as you like. They need not necessarily be named mysql_sess_open( ), mysql_sess_close( ), and so forth. The routines should be written according to the following specifications:

mysql_sess_open ($save_path, $sess_name)
> Performs whatever actions are necessary to begin a session. $save_path is the name of the location where sessions should be stored; this is useful for file storage only. $sess_name indicates the name of the session identifier (for example, PHPSESSID). For a MySQL-based storage manager, both arguments can be ignored. The function should return TRUE or FALSE to indicate whether the session was opened successfully.

mysql_sess_close ( )
> Closes the session, returning TRUE for success or FALSE for failure.

mysql_sess_read ($sess_id)
> Retrieves the data associated with the session identifier and returns it as a string. If there is no such session, the function should return an empty string. If an error occurs, it should return FALSE.

mysql_sess_write ($sess_id, $sess_data)
> Saves the data associated with the session identifier, returning TRUE for success or FALSE for failure. PHP itself takes care of serializing and unserializing the session contents, so the read and write functions need deal only with serialized strings.

mysql_sess_destroy ($sess_id)
> Destroys the session and any data associated with it, returning TRUE for success or FALSE for failure. For MySQL-based storage, destroying a session amounts to deleting the row from the php_session table that is associated with the session ID.

mysql_sess_gc ($gc_maxlife)
> Performs garbage collection to remove old sessions. This function is invoked on a probabilistic basis. When PHP receives a request for a page that uses sessions, it calls the garbage collector with a probability defined by the session.gc_probability configuration variable in *php.ini*. For example, if the probability value is 1 (that is, 1%), PHP calls the collector approximately once every hundred requests. If the value is 100, it calls the collector for every request—which probably would result in more processing overhead than you'd want.
>
> The argument to gc( ) is the maximum session lifetime in seconds. Sessions older than that should be considered subject to removal. The function should return TRUE for success or FALSE for failure.

To register the handler routines, call session_set_save_handler( ), which should be done in conjunction with informing PHP that you'll be using a user-defined storage module. The default storage management method is defined by the session.save_handler configuration variable. You can change the method globally by modifying the *php.ini* initialization file, or within individual scripts:

- To change the storage method globally, edit *php.ini*. The default configuration setting specifies the use of file-based session storage management:

```
session.save_handler = files;
```

Modify this to indicate that sessions will be handled by a user-level mechanism:

```
session.save_handler = user;
```

If you're using PHP as an Apache module, you need to restart Apache after modifying *php.ini* so that PHP notices the changes.

The problem with making a global change is that every PHP script that uses sessions will be expected to provide its own storage management routines. This may have unintended side effects for other script writers if they are unaware of the change. For example, other developers that use the web server may want to continue using file-based sessions.

- The alternative to making a global change is to specify a different storage method by calling ini_set( ) on a per-script basis:

```
ini_set ("session.save_handler", "user");
```

ini_set( ) is less intrusive than a global configuration change. The storage manager we'll develop here uses ini_set( ) so that database-backed session storage is triggered only for those scripts that request it.

To make it easy to access an alternative session storage module, it's useful to create a library file, *Cookbook_Session.php*. The only thing a script need do to use the library file is to include it prior to starting the session. The outline of the file looks like this:

```php
<?php
# Cookbook_Session.php - MySQL-based session storage module

require_once "Cookbook.php";

# Define the handler routines

function mysql_sess_open ($save_path, $sess_name) ...
function mysql_sess_close () ...
function mysql_sess_read ($sess_id) ...
function mysql_sess_write ($sess_id, $sess_data) ...
function mysql_sess_destroy ($sess_id) ...
function mysql_sess_gc ($gc_maxlife) ...

# Initialize the connection identifier, select user-defined
# session handling and register the handler routines

$mysql_sess_conn = FALSE;
ini_set ("session.save_handler", "user");
session_set_save_handler (
        "mysql_sess_open",
        "mysql_sess_close",
        "mysql_sess_read",
        "mysql_sess_write",
```

```
          "mysql_sess_destroy",
          "mysql_sess_gc"
       );
?>
```

The library file includes *Cookbook.php* so that it can access the connection routine for opening a connection to the cookbook database. Then it defines the handler routines (we'll get to the details of these functions shortly). Finally, it initializes the connection identifier, tells PHP to get ready to use a user-defined session storage manager, and registers the handler functions. Thus, a PHP script that wants to store sessions in MySQL performs all the necessary setup simply by including the *Cookbook_Session.php* file:

```
require_once "Cookbook_Session.php";
```

 The interface provided by the *Cookbook_Session.php* library file exposes a global database connection identifier variable ($mysql_sess_conn) as well as a set of handler routines named mysql_sess_open( ), mysql_sess_close( ), and so forth. Scripts that use the library should avoid using these global names for other purposes.

Now let's see how to implement each handler routine:

Opening a session

PHP passes two arguments to this function: the save path and the session name. The save path is used for file-based storage, and we don't need to know the session name, so both arguments are irrelevant for our purposes and can be ignored. The function therefore need do nothing but open a connection to MySQL:

```
function mysql_sess_open ($save_path, $sess_name)
{
global $mysql_sess_conn;

  # open connection to MySQL if it's not already open
  if (!$mysql_sess_conn)
  {
    # Do NOT use =& operator here!
    $mysql_sess_conn = Cookbook::connect ();
    if (PEAR::isError ($mysql_sess_conn))
    {
      $mysql_sess_conn = FALSE;
      return (FALSE);
    }
  }
  return (TRUE);
}
```

mysql_session_open( ) uses = rather than =& to assign the result of the connection call, to ensure that the connection handler value doesn't disappear when the function returns.

Closing a session

The close handler checks whether a connection to MySQL is open and closes it if so:

```
function mysql_sess_close ()
{
global $mysql_sess_conn;

  if ($mysql_sess_conn)      # close connection if it's open
  {
    $mysql_sess_conn->disconnect ();
    $mysql_sess_conn = FALSE;
  }
  return (TRUE);
}
```

Reading session data

The `mysql_sess_read( )` function uses the session ID to look up the data for the corresponding session record and returns it. It returns the empty string if no such record exists. If an error occurs, it returns **FALSE**:

```
function mysql_sess_read ($sess_id)
{
global $mysql_sess_conn;

  $stmt = "SELECT data FROM php_session WHERE id = ?";
  $result =& $mysql_sess_conn->query ($stmt, array ($sess_id));
  if (!PEAR::isError ($result))
  {
    list ($data) = $result->fetchRow ();
    $result->free ();
    if (isset ($data))
      return ($data);
    return ("");
  }
  return (FALSE);
}
```

Writing session data

`mysql_sess_write( )` creates a new record if there is none for the session yet, or replaces the existing record if there is one:

```
function mysql_sess_write ($sess_id, $sess_data)
{
global $mysql_sess_conn;

  $stmt = "REPLACE php_session (id, data) VALUES(?,?)";
  $result =& $mysql_sess_conn->query ($stmt, array ($sess_id, $sess_data));
  return (!PEAR::isError ($result));
}
```

Destroying a session

When a session is no longer needed, `mysql_sess_destroy( )` removes the corresponding record:

```
function mysql_sess_destroy ($sess_id)
{
global $mysql_sess_conn;

  $stmt = "DELETE FROM php_session WHERE id = ?";
  $result =& $mysql_sess_conn->query ($stmt, array ($sess_id));
  return (!PEAR::isError ($result));
}
```

Performing garbage collection

The TIMESTAMP column t in each session record indicates when the session was last updated. mysql_sess_gc( ) uses this value to implement garbage collection. The argument $sess_maxlife specifies how old sessions can be (in seconds). Older sessions are considered expired and candidates for removal, which is easily done by deleting session records having a timestamp that differs from the current time by more than the allowed lifetime:

```
function mysql_sess_gc ($sess_maxlife)
{
global $mysql_sess_conn;

  $stmt = "DELETE FROM php_session WHERE t < NOW() - INTERVAL ? SECOND";
  $result =& $mysql_sess_conn->query ($stmt, array ($sess_maxlife));
  return (TRUE);  # ignore errors
}
```

Using the storage module.   Install the *Cookbook_Session.php* file in a public library directory accessible to your scripts. (On my system, I put PHP library files in */usr/local/lib/ mcb* and modify *php.ini* so that the include_path variable names that directory. See Recipe 2.3.) To try the storage module, install the following example script, *sess_track.php*, in your web tree and invoke it a few times to see how the information display changes:

```
<?php
# sess_track.php - session request counting/timestamping demonstration

require_once "Cookbook_Session.php";
# needed for make_unordered_list(), get_session_val(), set_session_val()
require_once "Cookbook_Webutils.php";

$title = "PHP Session Tracker";

# Open session and extract session values

session_start ();
$count = get_session_val ("count");
$timestamp = get_session_val ("timestamp");

# If the session is new, initialize the variables

if (!isset ($count))
  $count = 0;
if (!isset ($timestamp))
```

```
  $timestamp = array ();

# Increment counter, add current timestamp to timestamp array

++$count;
$timestamp[] = date ("Y-m-d H:i:s T");

if ($count < 10)  # save modified values into session variable array
{
  set_session_val ("count", $count);
  set_session_val ("timestamp", $timestamp);
}
else               # destroy session variables after 10 invocations
{
  session_unregister ("count");
  session_unregister ("timestamp");
}
session_write_close (); # save session changes

# Produce the output page

?>
<html>
<head>
<title><?php print ($title); ?></title>
</head>
<body bgcolor="white">

<?php

print ("<p>This session has been active for $count requests.</p>\n");
print ("<p>The requests occurred at these times:</p>\n");
print make_unordered_list ($timestamp);

?>

</body>
</html>
```

The script includes the *Cookbook_Session.php* library file to enable the MySQL-based storage module, and then uses the PHP session manager interface in typical fashion. First, it opens the session and attempts to extract the session variables. For the first request, the session variables will not be set and must be initialized. This is determined by the isset( ) tests. The scalar variable $count starts out at zero, and the nonscalar variable $timestamp starts out as an empty array. For successive requests, the session variables will have the values assigned to them by the previous request.

Next, the script increments the counter, adds the current timestamp to the end of the timestamp array, and produces an output page that displays the count and the access times. If the session limit of 10 invocations has been reached, the script unregisters the session variables, which causes $count and $timestamp not to be saved to the session record. The effect is that the session restarts on the next request.

Finally, *sess_track.php* calls `session_write_close( )` to write out the changes to session data.

The output page is produced only after updating the session record because PHP might determine that a cookie containing the session ID needs to be sent to the client. That determination must be made before generating the page body because cookies are sent in the headers.

As mentioned earlier, we assume that `register_globals` is not enabled. Thus, we cannot use the PHP `session_register( )` function to register session variables and it is necessary to access session variables another way. The two possibilities are to use the `$HTTP_SESSION_VARS` global array or (as of PHP 4.1) the `$_SESSION` superglobal array. For example, after calling `session_start( )`, a session variable named `count` will be available as `$HTTP_SESSION_VARS["count"]` or `$_SESSION["count"]`.

It's possible to adopt an approach that uses the PHP session variable arrays but still enables you to work with simple variable names to manipulate session variables:

1. Don't use `session_register( )`. Instead, copy session variables directly from a global session variable array into the `$count` and `$timestamp` variables.

2. After you're done using your session variables, copy them back into the session variable array before writing the session.

However, it's messy to determine which global array to use for session variable storage because that may depend on your version of PHP. Instead of making this determination each time you want to access a session variable, it's easier to write a couple of utility functions that do the work. That is the purpose of the `get_session_val( )` and `set_session_val( )` functions used in the script. They access session variables for the counter value and timestamp array and store modified values back into the session:

```
function get_session_val ($name)
{
global $HTTP_SESSION_VARS;

  $val = NULL;
  if (isset ($_SESSION[$name]))
    $val = $_SESSION[$name];
  else if (isset ($HTTP_SESSION_VARS[$name]))
    $val = $HTTP_SESSION_VARS[$name];
  return ($val);
}

function set_session_val ($name, $val)
{
global $HTTP_SESSION_VARS;

  if (isset ($_SESSION))
    $_SESSION[$name] = $val;
  $HTTP_SESSION_VARS[$name] = $val;
}
```

These routines can be found in the *Cookbook_Webutils.php* library file, along with the routines that get other kinds of web script parameter values (see Recipe 19.5). They are in *Cookbook_Webutils.php* rather than in *Cookbook_Session.php* so that you can call them even if you elect not to use the MySQL-based session storage that *Cookbook_Session.php* implements.

20.4 Using MySQL for Session-Backing Store with Tomcat

Problem

You want to use session storage for Java-based scripts.

Solution

Tomcat handles session management for you. By default, it uses temporary files for backing store, but you can configure it to use MySQL instead by supplying the appropriate JDBC parameters in Tomcat's *server.xml* configuration file.

Discussion

The Perl, Ruby, and PHP session mechanisms described earlier in this chapter require applications to indicate explicitly that they want to use MySQL-based session storage. For Perl and Ruby, a script must state that it wants to use the appropriate session module. For PHP, the session manager is built into the language, but each application that wants to use a MySQL storage module must register it.

For Java applications that run under Tomcat, a different framework applies. Tomcat itself manages sessions, so if you want to store session information in MySQL, you do so by reconfiguring Tomcat, not your applications. In other words, web-based Java programs are relieved of some of the messy session-related details that must be handled at the application level in other languages. For example, session IDs are handled by the Tomcat server rather than at the application level. If cookies are enabled, Tomcat uses them. Otherwise, it uses URL rewriting to encode the session ID in the URL. Application developers need not care which method is used because the ID is available to them the same way regardless of how it's transmitted.

To illustrate the independence of applications from the session management method used by Tomcat, this section shows a simple JSP application that uses a session. Then it shows how to reconfigure Tomcat to store session information in MySQL rather than in the default session store—without requiring any changes at all to the application. First, though, it's necessary to describe the session interface.

The Servlet and JSP Session Interface

Tomcat uses the standard session interface described in the Java Servlet Specification. This interface can be used both by servlets and by JSP pages. Within a servlet, you gain access to the session by importing the `javax.servlet.http.HttpSession` class and in-voking the `getSession( )` method of your `HttpRequest` object:

```
import javax.servlet.http.*;
HttpSession session = request.getSession ();
```

In JSP pages, session support is enabled by default, so it's as though those statements have already been issued by the time the page begins executing. That is, the session is available implicitly through a `session` variable that's already been set up for you.

The complete session interface is defined in the `HttpSession` section of the Java Servlet Specification (see Appendix D). Some representative methods of session objects are listed here:

`isNew ( )`
> Returns true or false to indicate whether the session has just begun with the current request.

`getAttribute (String attrName)`
> Session contents consist of attributes, which are objects that are bound to names. To access a session attribute, specify its name. The `getAttribute( )` method returns the `Object` bound to the given name, or `null` if there is no object with that name.

`setAttribute (String attrName, Object obj)`
> Adds the object to the session and binds it to the given name.

`removeAttribute (String attrName)`
> Removes the attribute with the given name from the session.

`invalidate ( )`
> Invalidates the session and any data associated with it. The next request from the client will begin a new session.

A sample JSP session application

The following example shows a JSP page, *sess_track.jsp*, that maintains a session request counter and a log of the request times. To illustrate the session-related operations more explicitly, this page consists primarily of embedded Java code that uses the `HttpSession` session interface directly:

```
<%--
  sess_track.jsp - session request counting/timestamping demonstration
--%>

<%@ page import="java.util.*" %>
<%
  // get session variables, initializing them if not present

  int count;
  Object obj = session.getAttribute ("count");
  if (obj == null)
    count = 0;
  else
```

```
      count = Integer.parseInt (obj.toString ());

    ArrayList timestamp = (ArrayList) session.getAttribute ("timestamp");
    if (timestamp == null)
      timestamp = new ArrayList ();

    // increment counter, add current timestamp to timestamp array

    count = count + 1;
    timestamp.add (new Date ());

    if (count < 10)   // save updated values in session object
    {
      session.setAttribute ("count", String.valueOf (count));
      session.setAttribute ("timestamp", timestamp);
    }
    else              // restart session after 10 requests
    {
      session.removeAttribute ("count");
      session.removeAttribute ("timestamp");
    }
%>

<html>
<head>
<title>JSP Session Tracker</title>
</head>
<body bgcolor="white">

<p>This session has been active for <%= count %> requests.</p>

<p>The requests occurred at these times:</p>
<ul>
<%
  for (int i = 0; i < timestamp.size (); i++)
    out.println ("<li>" + timestamp.get (i) + "</li>");
%>
</ul>

</body>
</html>
```

Invoke *sess_track.jsp* a few times from your browser to see how the display changes.

The `session.setAttribute( )` method used in *sess_track.jsp* places information into the session so that it can be found by later invocations of the script. But session attributes also can be shared with other scripts. To see this, make a copy of *sess_track.jsp* and invoke the copy from your browser. You'll see that it accesses the same session information as *sess_track.jsp* (scripts in the same application context access the same information).

Some of the session-related operations shown in *sess_track.jsp* can be done using tags from JSTL, which provides a `sessionScope` variable for getting at the implicit JSP session object:

```
<%--
  sess_track2.jsp - session request counting/timestamping demonstration
--%>

<%@ page import="java.util.*" %>
<%@ taglib uri="http://java.sun.com/jsp/jstl/core" prefix="c" %>

<c:if test="${empty sessionScope.count}">
  <c:set var="count" scope="session" value="0"/>
</c:if>
<c:set var="count" scope="session" value="${sessionScope.count+1}"/>

<%
  ArrayList timestamp = (ArrayList) session.getAttribute ("timestamp");
  if (timestamp == null)
    timestamp = new ArrayList ();
  // add current timestamp to timestamp array, store result in session
  timestamp.add (new Date ());
  session.setAttribute ("timestamp", timestamp);
%>

<html>
<head>
<title>JSP Session Tracker</title>
</head>
<body bgcolor="white">

<p>This session has been active for
<c:out value="${sessionScope.count}"/>
requests.</p>

<p>The requests occurred at these times:</p>
<ul>
<c:forEach items="${sessionScope.timestamp}" var="t">
  <li><c:out value="${t}"/></li>
</c:forEach>
</ul>

<%-- has session limit of 10 requests been reached? --%>

<c:if test="${sessionScope.count ge 10}">
  <c:remove var="count" scope="session"/>
  <c:remove var="timestamp" scope="session"/>
</c:if>

</body>
</html>
```

Telling Tomcat to save session records in MySQL

The Tomcat documentation pertaining to session management can be found at:

> http://tomcat.apache.org/tomcat-5.0-doc/config/manager.html

Tomcat has its own default session storage mechanism (temporary files). To override the default and save sessions in MySQL via JDBC instead, use the following procedure:

1. Create a table to hold session records.
2. Make sure that Tomcat has access to the proper JDBC driver.
3. Modify Tomcat's *server.xml* configuration file to specify use of a persistent session manager for the relevant application context or contexts.

None of these steps involve modifying the sample session application in any way, which is a reflection of how Tomcat implements session support above the application level.

Creating the Tomcat session table. Tomcat stores several types of information into the session table:

- The session ID. By default, IDs are 32-character MD5 values.
- The application name.
- The session data. This is a serialized string.
- Whether the session is valid, as a single byte.
- The maximum inactivity time allowed, as a 32-bit integer measured in seconds.
- The last access time, as a 64-bit integer.

These specifications are satisfied by the following table, which you should create before proceeding to the next section:

```
CREATE TABLE tomcat_session
(
  id             VARCHAR(32) NOT NULL,
  app            VARCHAR(255),
  data           MEDIUMBLOB,
  valid_session  CHAR(1) NOT NULL,
  max_inactive   INT NOT NULL,
  last_access    BIGINT NOT NULL,
  PRIMARY KEY (id),
  INDEX (app)
);
```

Placing the JDBC driver where Tomcat can find it. Because Tomcat itself manages sessions, it must be able to access the JDBC driver used to store sessions in a database. It's common to store drivers in the *lib* directory of the Tomcat tree so that all applications have access to them. But for a driver to be accessible to Tomcat as well, it should go in the *common/lib* directory. (Thus, if you have the MySQL Connector/J driver installed in *lib*, move it to *common/lib*.) After a restart, Tomcat will be able to use it. For more information about using MySQL Connector/J with Tomcat, see Recipe 17.3.

Modifying the Tomcat configuration file. To tell Tomcat to use the `tomcat_session` table, it's necessary to modify the *server.xml* file in Tomcat's *conf* directory. Do this by placing a `<Manager>` element in the body of the `<Context>` element of each application context that should use MySQL-based session storage. (If a context has no such element, create one.) For the `mcb` application context, the `<Context>` element can be created like this:

```
<Context path="/mcb" docBase="mcb" debug="0" reloadable="true">
  <Manager
```

```
      className="org.apache.catalina.session.PersistentManager"
      debug="0"
      saveOnRestart="true"
      minIdleSwap="900"
      maxIdleSwap="1200"
      maxIdleBackup="600">
      <Store
        className="org.apache.catalina.session.JDBCStore"
        driverName="com.mysql.jdbc.Driver"
        connectionURL=
          "jdbc:mysql://localhost/cookbook?user=cbuser&amp;password=cbpass"
        sessionTable="tomcat_session"
        sessionIdCol="id"
        sessionAppCol="app"
        sessionDataCol="data"
        sessionValidCol="valid_session"
        sessionMaxInactiveCol="max_inactive"
        sessionLastAccessedCol="last_access"
      />
    </Manager>
  </Context>
```

The `<Manager>` element attributes specify general session-related options. Within the `<Manager>` element body, the `<Store>` element attributes provide the specifics pertaining to the JDBC driver. The following discussion focuses on the attributes shown in the example, but there are others that you can use. See the Tomcat session-management documentation for more information.

The `<Manager>` attributes shown in the example have the following meanings:

className
:   Indicates the Java class that implements persistent session storage. It must be `org.apache.catalina.session.PersistentManager`.

debug
:   Indicates the logging detail level. A value of zero disables debug output; higher numbers generate more output.

saveOnRestart
:   Enables application sessions to survive server restarts. It should be **true** if you want Tomcat to save current sessions when it shuts down (and reload them when it starts up).

maxIdleBackup
:   Indicates the number of seconds before inactive sessions are eligible for being saved to MySQL. A value of **-1** means "never."

minIdleSwap
:   Indicates how many seconds a session can be idle before becoming eligible to be swapped (saved to MySQL and passivated out of server memory). A value of **-1** means "never."

maxIdleSwap

Indicates how many seconds a session can be idle before it should be swapped. A value of -1 means "never." If this feature is enabled, the value should be greater than minIdleSwap and maxIdleBackup.

Within the body of the `<Manager>` element, the `<Store>` element indicates how to connect to the database server, which database and table to use for storing session records, and the names of the columns in the table:

className

The name of a class that implements the `org.apache.catalina.Store` interface. For JDBC-based storage managers, the value of this attribute must be `org.apache.catalina.session.JDBCStore`.

driverName

The class name for the JDBC driver. For the MySQL Connector/J driver, the attribute value should be `com.mysql.jdbc.Driver`.

connectionURL

Indicates how to connect to the database server. The following URL connects to the MySQL server on the local host, using a database, username, and password of cookbook, cbuser, and cbpass, respectively:

```
jdbc:mysql://localhost/cookbook?user=cbuser&password=cbpass
```

However, *server.xml* entries are written in XML, so the & character that separates the user and password connection parameters must be written as the & entity, like so:

```
jdbc:mysql://localhost/cookbook?user=cbuser&amp;password=cbpass
```

When Tomcat reads the *server.xml* file, the XML parser converts & back to &, which is what gets passed to the JDBC driver.

sessionTable

Names the table in which to store session records. For our example, this is the tomcat_session table described earlier. (The database that contains the table is given in the connectionURL value.)

The remaining `<Store>` attributes in the example indicate the column names in the session table. These attributes are sessionIdCol, sessionAppCol, sessionDataCol, sessionValidCol, sessionMaxInactiveCol, and sessionLastAccessedCol, which correspond in the obvious way to the columns contained in the tomcat_session table.

After you modify the *server.xml* file, restart Tomcat. Then invoke the *sess_track.jsp* or *sess_track2.jsp* scripts a few times to initiate a session. Each should behave the same way as before you reconfigured Tomcat. After a period of inactivity equal to the `<Manager>` element maxIdleBackup attribute value, you should see a session record appear in the tomcat_session table. If you watch the MySQL query log, you should also see sessions being saved to MySQL when you shut down Tomcat.

Changing *server.xml* is a global change, somewhat similar to changing `session.save_handler` in PHP's *php.ini* file. However, unlike PHP, in which modifying the global initialization file affects other developers on the same host in such a way that they may have to change their session-based scripts, modifying Tomcat's configuration to use JDBC-based backing store for session management is completely invisible to servlets and JSP pages. Thus, you can make the change without worrying that other developers who use the same Tomcat server will accuse you of acting toward them with malice aforethought.

Session expiration in Tomcat

Session persistence is 60 minutes by default. To provide an explicit duration for a session manager, add a `maxInactiveInterval` to the appropriate `<Manager>` element in the server's *conf/server.xml* file. To provide a duration that is specific to a particular application context, add a `<session-config>` element to the context's *WEB-INF/web.xml* file. For example, to use a value of 30 minutes, specify it like this:

```
<session-config>
  <session-timeout>30</session-timeout>
</session-config>
```

If you modify either *server.xml* or *web.xml*, restart Tomcat.

Session tracking in Tomcat

Although your JSP pages need do nothing to have Tomcat set up sessions or to use JDBC for session storage, they may need to take a small step to make sure that sessions move from request to request properly. This is necessary if you generate pages that contain hyperlinks to other pages that participate in the same session.

Tomcat automatically generates a session identifier and tracks the session using cookies if it receives a cookie from the client that contains the session ID. If the client has cookies disabled, Tomcat tracks the session by rewriting URLs to include the session ID. You need not determine which method Tomcat is using, but you should take care to ensure proper propagation of the session ID in case it is being passed by URL rewriting. This means that if you create a page that includes a link to another page that is part of the session, you should not just list the path to the page like this:

```
To go to the next page,
<a href="nextpage.jsp">click here</a>.
```

This link doesn't contain the session ID. If Tomcat happens to be tracking the session using URL rewriting, you'll lose the ID when the user selects the link. Instead, pass the link to `encodeURL()` to enable Tomcat to add the session ID to the URL as necessary:

```
To go to the next page,
<a href="<%= response.encodeURL ("nextpage.jsp") %>">click here</a>.
```

If Tomcat is tracking the session with cookies, `encodeURL()` returns the URL unchanged. However, if Tomcat is tracking the session by means of URL rewriting, `encodeURL( )` adds the session ID to the page path automatically, so that it looks something like this:

```
mypage.jsp;jsessionid=xxxxxxxxxxxxxxx
```

You should generate URLs using `encodeURL( )` like this for links in any tag that takes the user to a page in the current session. This includes `<a>`, `<form>`, and `<frame>` tags, and possibly even `<img>` tags, if for some reason those tags invoke a script that generates images on a session-specific basis.

It's probably best to develop the habit of using `encodeURL( )` as a matter of routine when writing URLs for session-based applications. Even if you think everyone who uses the application will have cookies enabled, your assumption may prove incorrect some day.

The `java.net.URLEncoder.encode( )` method has a name similar to `encodeURL( )`, but it's different. It converts special characters to %xx notation to make them safe for use in URLs.

Obtaining MySQL Software

Most of the table definitions and programs discussed in this book are available online so that you can avoid typing them in yourself. To run the examples, you'll also need access to MySQL, of course, as well as the appropriate MySQL-specific interfaces for the programming languages that you want to use. This appendix describes what software you need and where to get it.

Obtaining Sample Source Code and Data

The examples in this book are based on source code and sample data from two distributions named `recipes` and `mcb-kjv` that are available at the *MySQL Cookbook* companion web site (see Preface). Visit the site at this address:

> *http://www.kitebird.com/mysql-cookbook/*

The `recipes` distribution is the primary source of examples. It's available as a compressed *tar* file (*recipes.tar.gz*) or as a ZIP file (*recipes.zip*). Either distribution format when unpacked creates a directory named *recipes*.

The `recipes` distribution contains programs as shown in the book, but in many cases also includes implementations in additional languages. For example, a script shown in the book using Python may be available in the `recipes` distribution in Perl, Ruby, PHP, or Java as well. This may save you some translation effort should you want to convert a program as shown in the book to a different language.

The Kitebird site provides access to the `mcb-kjv` distribution, which contains the text of the King James Version of the Bible, formatted suitably for loading into MySQL. It's used in Chapter 5, as the source of a reasonably large body of text for examples that demonstrate FULLTEXT searches, and occasionally elsewhere in the book. This distribution is provided separately from the `recipes` distribution due to its size. It's available as a compressed *tar* file (*mcb-kjv.tar.gz*) or as a ZIP file (*mcb-kjv.zip*). Either distribution format when unpacked creates a directory named *mcb-kjv*.

The `mcb-kjv` distribution was derived from KJV text originally obtained from the Unbound Bible site (*http://www.unboundbible.org*). I have restructured that text to be more usable for the examples in this book. The `mcb-kjv` distribution includes notes that describe the modifications that I made.

Obtaining MySQL and Related Software

If you're going to access a MySQL server run by somebody else, you need only the MySQL client software on your own machine. To run your own server, you'll need a full MySQL distribution.

To write your own MySQL-based programs, you'll need to communicate with the server through a language-specific API. The Perl, Ruby, PHP, and Python interfaces rely on the MySQL C API client library to handle the low-level client-server protocol. For Perl, Ruby, and Python, you must install the C client library and header files first. PHP includes the MySQL client support files, but must be compiled with MySQL support enabled or you won't be able to use it. The Java JDBC driver for MySQL implements the client-server protocol itself, so it does not require the MySQL C client library.

You may not need to install the client software yourself—it might already have been built and installed for you by others. This is a common situation if you have an account with an Internet Service Provider (ISP) for computing services such as a web server that is already enabled to provide access to MySQL. Under such circumstances, the MySQL libraries and header files will already have been installed by the ISP staff.

MySQL

Visit the following site to obtain a MySQL distribution:

> *http://dev.mysql.com/*

MySQL distributions include installation instructions, and the MySQL Reference Manual also provides extensive installation information. The manual is available online at the MySQL site and in printed form from MySQL Press.

If you need to install the MySQL C client library and header files, they're available if you install MySQL from a source distribution, or if you install MySQL using a binary (precompiled) distribution other than an RPM binary distribution. Under Linux, you have the option of installing MySQL using RPM files, but be aware that the client library and header files are not installed unless you install the development RPM. (There are separate RPM files for the server, the standard client programs, and the development libraries and header files.) If you don't install the development RPM, you'll join the many Linux users who've asked, "I installed MySQL, but I cannot find the libraries or header files; where are they?"

Perl Support

General Perl information is available at:

http://www.perl.org/

Perl software can be obtained from the Comprehensive Perl Archive Network (CPAN):

http://cpan.perl.org/

To write MySQL-based Perl programs, you'll need the DBI module and the MySQL-specific DBD module, DBD::mysql.

To install these modules under Unix, it may be easiest to let Perl itself help you. For example, to install DBI and DBD::mysql, run the following commands (you'll probably need to do this as `root`):

```
# perl -MCPAN -e shell
cpan> install DBI
cpan> install DBD::mysql
```

If the last command complains about failed tests, use `force install DBD::mysql` instead. Under ActiveState Perl for Windows, you can use the *ppm* utility:

```
C:\> ppm
ppm> install DBI
ppm> install DBD-mysql
```

You can use the CPAN shell or *ppm* to install other Perl modules mentioned in this book as well.

Ruby Support

To obtain Ruby itself, visit:

http://www.ruby-lang.org/

The Ruby DBI module is available at RubyForge:

http://rubyforge.org/projects/ruby-dbi/

You'll need at least version 0.1.1 of Ruby DBI to be able to use all the features described in this book, such as option file support and SQLSTATE support.

The Ruby DBI driver for MySQL requires the `mysql-ruby` module, available from the Ruby Application Archive:

http://raa.ruby-lang.org/project/mysql-ruby/

The PageTemplate package used in Chapter 18 can be obtained from RubyForge:

http://rubyforge.org/projects/pagetemplate/

If you plan to use session support as described in Chapter 20, you'll need the `mysql-session` package, available from the Ruby Application Archive:

http://raa.ruby-lang.org/project/mysql-session/

For `mysql-session`, obtain the package, unpack it, and install its *mysqlstore.rb* and *sqlthrow.rb* files in some directory that your Ruby interpreter searches when looking for library files.

PHP Support

PHP software distributions and installation instructions are available here:

http://www.php.net/

PHP source distributions include the MySQL client library, so you need not obtain it separately. However, you'll need to enable MySQL support explicitly when you configure the distribution. If you use a binary distribution, be sure that it includes MySQL support.

PHP includes a *pear* command-line utility that you can run to install various PEAR modules. Run it without arguments for a help message. To install the PEAR DB module for database access support, use this command:

```
# pear install DB
```

The Smarty template package used in Chapter 18, can be obtained from the Smarty site:

http://smarty.php.net/

Python Support

Python software distributions and installation instructions are available here:

http://www.python.org/

MySQLdb, the DB-API driver module that provides MySQL support, is available at SourceForge:

http://sourceforge.net/projects/mysql-python/

Java Support

You'll need a Java compiler to build and run Java programs. The *javac* and *jikes* compilers are two possible choices. On many systems, you'll find these installed already. Otherwise, you can get a compiler as part of the Java Software Development Kit (SDK). If no SDK is installed on your system, versions are available for Solaris, Linux, and Windows at Sun's Java site:

http://java.sun.com/j2se/

Several Java drivers are available that provide MySQL connectivity for the JDBC interface. This book assumes the use of MySQL Connector/J, which is available here:

http://dev.mysql.com/downloads/

Web Servers

In the web programming chapters, this book uses Apache for Perl, Ruby, PHP, and Python scripts, and Tomcat for JavaServer Pages scripts. Apache and Tomcat both are available from the Apache Software Group; visit the following sites:

http://httpd.apache.org/
http://tomcat.apache.org/

The Apache Jakarta Project site provides access to the Jakarta implementation of the JSP Standard Tag Library that is used in this book for writing JSP pages:

http://jakarta.apache.org/taglibs/

For information about configuring Apache and Tomcat to run MySQL-based scripts, see Recipes 17.2 and 17.3.

Executing Programs from the Command Line

As you work through this book, you'll run many examples using the *mysql* client program, and there are lots of programs in the `recipes` distribution for you to try as you read. And of course one purpose of the book is to enable you to write your own MySQL-based programs. Consequently, you'll often need to execute programs at the command line—that is, at the prompt of your shell or command interpreter. For best use of this book, you should be able to run *mysql* easily (by entering just its name), and you should be able to execute programs from the `recipes` distribution or that you write yourself. To accomplish those goals, it's important that your `PATH` environment variable be set correctly, and that you know how to make programs executable. This appendix shows how to do those things; if you already know how, you can skip it.

Setting Environment Variables

An environment variable has a value that can be accessed by programs that you run. By setting environment variables, you modify your operating environment. One such variable is `PATH`, which is used by your command interpreter to determine which directories to search when it looks for programs such as *mysql* that you tell it to execute. If your `PATH` is set correctly, you can invoke programs easily no matter what your current directory is. If `PATH` is not set correctly, your command interpreter will not find them. For example, if the `PATH` value does not include the directory where *mysql* is installed, a "command not found" error may occur if you attempt to run *mysql* by entering its name. You must run it either by specifying its full pathname, or by changing location into the directory where it is installed. Both strategies are unpleasant, and more so with repetition. It's much better to set your `PATH` value to name the directories containing the programs you want to use.

Other environment variables are important in other contexts. For example, if you run Perl or Ruby scripts that use module files that you've installed, you may need to set the `PERL5LIB` or `RUBYLIB` variable to tell Perl or Ruby where to find those modules. For Java, the `JAVA_HOME` variable should be set to indicate the location of your Java installation, and `CLASSPATH` should be set to the list of libraries and class files that your Java programs need.

The following discussion describes how to set environment variables. The examples demonstrate how to make it easier to run MySQL programs by modifying your `PATH` setting to add the directory where MySQL programs are installed. However, the discussion applies to other environment variables as well because the variable-setting syntax is the same.

Here are some general principles to keep in mind regarding environment variables:

- It's possible to set an environment variable from the command line, but the variable will retain its value only until you exit the command interpreter. To cause the setting to take effect permanently, set it in the appropriate shell startup file on Unix or by using the Environment Variables interface on Windows (this can be found on the System Control Panel under Advanced). The change takes effect for subsequent invocations of your command interpreter (for example, your next login on Unix, or the next console window that you open on Windows).

- Some variables (`PATH` among them) have a value that lists the pathnames for one or more directories. Under Unix, it's conventional to separate the pathnames using the colon character (:). Under Windows, pathnames can contain colons, so the separator is the semicolon character (;).

- You can check your current environment variable settings by executing an *env* or *printenv* command on Unix, or a *set* command in a console window on Windows.

Setting the PATH Variable on Unix

Your choice of command interpreter determines the syntax for setting environment variables. In addition, for settings that you put in a startup file, the file to use is interpreter-specific. The following table shows typical startup files for commonly used Unix command interpreters. If you've never looked through your command interpreter's startup files, it's a good idea to do so to familiarize yourself with their contents.

Command interpreter	Possible startup files
sh, bash, ksh	.profile, .bash_profile, .bash_login, .bashrc
csh, tcsh	.login, .cshrc, .tcshrc

The examples assume that MySQL programs are installed in the */usr/local/mysql/bin* directory and that you want to add that directory to your existing `PATH` value. That is, the examples assume that there is already a `PATH` setting in one of your startup files. If you have no `PATH` setting currently, add the appropriate line or lines to one of the files.

- For a shell in the Bourne shell family (*sh*, *bash*, *ksh*), look in your startup files for a line that sets and exports the `PATH` variable:

```
export PATH=/bin:/usr/bin:/usr/local/bin
```

Change the setting to add the appropriate directory:

```
export PATH=/usr/local/mysql/bin:/bin:/usr/bin:/usr/local/bin
```

The assignment and the export might be on separate lines:

```
PATH=/bin:/usr/bin:/usr/local/bin
export PATH
```

Change the setting to this:

```
PATH=/usr/local/mysql/bin:/bin:/usr/bin:/usr/local/bin
export PATH
```

- For a shell in the C shell family (*csh*, *tcsh*), look in your startup files for a *setenv PATH* command:

```
setenv PATH /bin:/usr/bin:/usr/local/bin
```

Change the setting to add the appropriate directory:

```
setenv PATH /usr/local/mysql/bin:/bin:/usr/bin:/usr/local/bin
```

It's also possible that your path will be set with a *set path* command, which uses different syntax:

```
set path = (/usr/local/mysql/bin /bin /usr/bin /usr/local/bin)
```

path is not an environment variable, but for C shells, setting path also sets PATH and vice versa.

Adjust the instructions for the pathname actually used on your system.

Setting the PATH Variable on Windows

To set environment variables on Windows, click the Start Menu, right-click My Computer → Properties → Advanced → Environment Variables. You should see a window that enables you to define environment variables or change the values of existing variables. For example, your PATH variable might have a value like this:

```
C:\WINDOWS;C:\WINDOWS\COMMAND
```

To make it easier to run MySQL programs such as *mysql*, change the value to include the directory where those programs are installed. Adding a directory of *C:\Program Files\MySQL\MySQL Server 5.0\bin* results in a PATH setting that should look like this:

```
C:\Program Files\MySQL\MySQL Server 5.0\bin;C:\WINDOWS;C:\WINDOWS\COMMAND
```

Executing Programs

This section describes how to execute programs from the command line. You can use this information to run programs that you obtain from the recipes distribution or that you write yourself. The first set of instructions applies to scripts written in Perl, Ruby, PHP, or Python. A second set of instructions applies to Java programs.

The example programs can be found in the *progdemo* directory of the `recipes` distribution.

Executing Perl, Ruby, PHP, or Python Scripts

The following discussion shows how to execute scripts, using Perl for the examples. However, the principles are similar for Ruby, PHP, and Python scripts.

Begin with an example script named *perldemo.pl* that consists of a simple print statement:

```
print "I am a Perl program.\n";
```

A script-execution method that works on any platform is to invoke the *perl* program and tell it the name of the script to run:

```
% perl perldemo.pl
I am a Perl program.
```

For a script written in another language, invoke the *ruby*, *php*, or *python* program.

It's also possible to set up a script so that it is directly executable. The procedure is different for Unix and Windows. Both procedures are described here.

On Unix, to make a script directly executable, include a line at the top of the file that begins with #! and that specifies the pathname of the program that should execute the script. Here is a script named *perldemo2.pl* with a #! line that names the *perl* program (if *perl* has a different location on your system, you'll need to change the pathname):

```
#!/usr/bin/perl
print "I am a Perl program.\n";
```

Next, enable the executable access mode with *chmod +x*:

```
% chmod +x perldemo2.pl
```

At this point, the script can be run the same way as its earlier counterpart (that is, you can use *perl perldemo2.pl*), but now you should also be able to execute it by entering just its name. However, assuming that the script is located in your current directory, your shell might not find it. The shell searches for programs in the directories named in your PATH environment variable, but for security reasons, the search path for Unix shells often is deliberately set not to include the current directory (.). In that case, include a leading path of ./ to explicitly indicate the script's location:

```
% ./perldemo2.pl
I am a Perl program.
```

If you install the script by copying it to a directory that is named in your PATH setting, the leading path is unnecessary when you invoke the script.

On Windows, the procedure for making scripts executable is somewhat different. *chmod* is not used. Instead, programs are treated as executable based on their filename extensions (such as *.exe* or *.bat*). Windows allows you to set up filename associations such that a program can be associated with filenames that end with a particular suffix. This means that you can set up associations so that Perl, Ruby, PHP, or Python are used to execute files with names that end in *.pl*, *.rb*, *.php*, or *.py*, respectively. (In fact, the installer for a given language might even create the association for you.) Then you can invoke a script with a given extension directly from the command line without naming its language interpreter:

```
C:\> perldemo.pl
I am a Perl program.
```

No leading path is needed to invoke a script that is located in the current directory because the Windows command interpreter includes that directory in its search path by default.

Keep the preceding principles in mind when you run scripts from within a directory of the recipes distribution. For example, if you are currently located in the *metadata* directory of the distribution and you want to execute the *get_server_version.rb* Ruby script, you can do so with either of these commands on Unix:

```
% ruby get_server_version.rb
% ./get_server_version.rb
```

On Windows, you can use either of these commands:

```
C:\> ruby get_server_version.rb
C:\> get_server_version.rb
```

Compiling and Executing Java Programs

Java programming requires a software development kit (SDK). If a Java SDK is not already installed on your system, obtain one and install it. For Solaris, Linux, and Windows, Java SDKs are available at *java.sun.com*. For Mac OS X, current versions come with an SDK; for earlier versions that do not, *javac* and other support needed for building Java applications is included in the Developer Tools distribution available at *connect.apple.com*.

After verifying that a Java SDK is installed, set the JAVA_HOME environment variable if it is not already set. Its value should be the pathname of the directory where the SDK is installed. If the SDK installation directory is */usr/local/java/jdk* on Unix or *C:\jdk* on Windows, set JAVA_HOME as follows:

- For a shell in the Bourne shell family (*sh*, *bash*, *ksh*):

  ```
  export JAVA_HOME=/usr/local/java/jdk
  ```

  If you are using the original Bourne shell, sh, you may need to split this into two commands:

```
JAVA_HOME=/usr/local/java/jdk
export JAVA_HOME
```

- For a shell in the C shell family (*csh*, *tcsh*):

```
setenv JAVA_HOME=/usr/local/java/jdk
```

- For Windows, get to the Environment Variables window as described earlier in "Setting Environment Variables," and set JAVA_HOME to this value:

```
C:\jdk
```

Adjust the instructions for the pathname actually used on your system.

With a Java SDK in place and JAVA_HOME set, you should be able to compile and run Java programs. Here is a sample program:

```
public class JavaDemo
{
  public static void main (String[] args)
  {
    System.out.println ("I am a Java program.");
  }
}
```

The **class** statement indicates the program's name, which in this case is JavaDemo. The name of the file containing the program should match this name and include a *.java* extension, so the filename for the program is *JavaDemo.java*. Compile the program using *javac*:

```
% javac JavaDemo.java
```

If you prefer a different Java compiler, just substitute its name. For example, if you'd rather use Jikes, compile the file like this instead:

```
% jikes JavaDemo.java
```

The Java compiler generates compiled byte code to produce a class file named *JavaDemo.class*. Use the *java* program to run the class file (specified without the *.class* extension):

```
% java JavaDemo
I am a Java program.
```

To compile and run MySQL-based programs written in Java, you'll need the MySQL Connector/J JDBC driver (Recipe 2.1). If Java cannot find the driver, you'll need to set your CLASSPATH environment variable. Its value should include at least your current directory (.) and the pathname of the MySQL Connector/J driver. If the driver has a pathname of */usr/local/lib/java/lib/mysql-connector-java-bin.jar* (Unix) or *C:\Java\lib\mysql-connector-java-bin.jar* (Windows), set CLASSPATH as follows:

- For a shell in the Bourne shell family (*sh*, *bash*, *ksh*):

```
export CLASSPATH=.:/usr/local/lib/java/lib/mysql-connector-java-bin.jar
```

- For a shell in the C shell family (*csh*, *tcsh*):

```
setenv CLASSPATH .:/usr/local/lib/java/lib/mysql-connector-java-bin.jar
```

- For Windows, get to the Environment Variables window as described earlier in "Setting Environment Variables," and set CLASSPATH to this value:

```
.;C:\Java\lib\mysql-connector-java-bin.jar
```

Adjust the instructions for the pathname actually used on your system. You might also need to add other class directories or libraries to your CLASSPATH setting. The specifics depend on how your system is set up.

JSP and Tomcat Primer

This appendix describes some essential concepts of JavaServer Pages (JSP) programming, which is used earlier in this book beginning with Chapter 17. The necessary background is fairly extensive, which is why the material is presented here in a separate appendix rather than breaking up the flow of that chapter. The topics discussed here are:

- A brief overview of servlet and JSP technologies
- Setting up the Tomcat server
- Tomcat's directory structure
- The layout of web applications
- Elements of JSP pages

For pointers to additional information about JSP pages, servlets, or Tomcat, see Appendix D.

Servlet and JavaServer Pages Overview

Java servlet technology is a means by which to execute Java programs efficiently in a web environment. The Java Servlet Specification defines the conventions of this environment, which may be summarized briefly as follows:

- Servlets run inside a servlet container, which itself either runs inside a web server or communicates with one. Servlet containers are also known as *servlet engines*.
- The servlet container receives requests from the web server and executes the appropriate servlet to process the request. The container then receives the response from the servlet and gives it to the web server, which in turn returns it to the client. A servlet container thus provides the connection between servlets and the web server under which they run. The container acts as the servlet runtime environment, with responsibilities that include determining the mapping between client

requests and the servlets that handle them, as well as loading, executing, and unloading servlets as necessary.

- Servlets communicate with their container according to established conventions. Each servlet is expected to implement methods with well-known names to be called in response to various kinds of requests. For example, GET and POST requests are routed to methods named `doGet( )` and `doPost( )`.

- Servlets that can be run by a container are arranged into logical groupings called "contexts." (Contexts might correspond, for example, to subdirectories of the document tree that is managed by the container.) Contexts also can include resources other than servlets, such as HTML pages, images, or configuration files.

- A context provides the basis for a "web application," which the Java Servlet Specification defines as follows:

  > A Web application is a collection of servlets, HTML pages, classes, and other resources that make up a complete application on a Web server.

  In other words, an application is a group of related servlets that work together, without interference from other unrelated servlets. Servlets within a given application context can share information with each other, but servlets in different contexts cannot. For example, a gateway or login servlet might establish a user's credentials, which then are placed into the context environment to be shared with other servlets within the same context as proof that the user has logged in properly. Should those servlets find the proper credentials not to be present in the environment when they execute, they can redirect to the gateway servlet automatically to require the user to log in. Servlets in another context cannot gain access to these credentials. Contexts thus provide a measure of security by preventing one application from invading another. They also can insulate applications from the effects of another application crashing; the container can keep the noncrashed applications running while it restarts the one that failed.

- Sharing of information between servlets may take place at several scope levels, which enables them to work together within the scope of a single request or across multiple requests.

The following listing shows what a simple servlet looks like. It's a Java program that implements a `SimpleServlet` class. The class has a `doGet( )` method to be invoked by the servlet container when it receives a `get` request for the servlet. It also has a `doPost( )` method to handle the possibility that a `post` request may be received instead; it's simply a wrapper that invokes `doGet( )`. `SimpleServlet` produces a short HTML page that includes some static text that is the same each time the servlet runs, and two dynamic elements (the current date and client IP address) that vary over time and for each client:

```java
import java.io.*;
import java.util.*;
import javax.servlet.*;
import javax.servlet.http.*;
```

```java
public class SimpleServlet extends HttpServlet
{
  public void doGet (HttpServletRequest request,
                     HttpServletResponse response)
    throws IOException, ServletException
  {
    PrintWriter out = response.getWriter ();

    response.setContentType ("text/html");
    out.println ("<html>");
    out.println ("<head>");
    out.println ("<title>Simple Servlet</title>");
    out.println ("</head>");
    out.println ("<body bgcolor=\"white\">");
    out.println ("<p>Hello.</p>");
    out.println ("<p>The current date is "
            + new Date ()
            + ".</p>");
    out.println ("<p>Your IP address is "
            + request.getRemoteAddr ()
            + ".</p>");
    out.println ("</body>");
    out.println ("</html>");
  }

  public void doPost (HttpServletRequest request,
                      HttpServletResponse response)
    throws IOException, ServletException
  {
    doGet (request, response);
  }
}
```

As you will no doubt observe, this "simple" servlet really isn't so simple! It requires a fair amount of machinery to import the requisite classes and to establish the **doGet( )** and **doPost( )** methods that provide the standard interface to the servlet container. Compare the servlet to the following PHP script, which does the same thing in a much more concise fashion:

```php
<html>
<head>
<title>Simple PHP Page</title>
</head>
<body bgcolor="white">

<p>Hello.</p>
<p>The current date is <?php print (date ("D M d H:i:s T Y")); ?>.</p>
<p>Your IP address is <?php print ($_SERVER["REMOTE_ADDR"]); ?>.</p>

</body>
</html>
```

The contrast between the Java servlet and the PHP script illustrates one of the problems with writing servlets—the amount of repetitious overhead:

- A certain minimal set of classes must be imported into each servlet.
- The framework for setting up the servlet class and the doGet( ) or doPost( ) methods is fairly stereotypical, often varying among servlets only in the servlet class name.
- Each fragment of HTML is produced with an output statement.

The first two points can be addressed by using a prototype file that you copy when beginning a new servlet. The third point (wrapping each line of HTML within a print statement) is not so easily addressed and is possibly the single most tedious aspect of servlet writing. It also leads to another issue: A servlet's code may be easy enough to read as Java, but it's sometimes difficult to discern the structure of the HTML that the code generates. The problem is that you're really trying to write in two languages at once (that is, you're writing Java that writes HTML), which isn't really optimal for either language.

JSP Pages: An Alternative to Servlets

One of the reasons for the invention of JavaServer Pages was to relieve the burden involved in creating web pages with a lot of print statements. JSP uses a notational approach that is similar to PHP: Write the HTML literally and embed the code to be executed within special markers. The following listing shows a JSP page that is equivalent to the SimpleServlet servlet, but looks much more like the corresponding PHP script:

```
<html>
<head>
<title>Simple JSP Page</title>
</head>
<body bgcolor="white">

<p>Hello.</p>
<p>The current date is <%= new java.util.Date () %>.</p>
<p>Your IP address is <%= request.getRemoteAddr () %>.</p>

</body>
</html>
```

The JSP page is more concise than the servlet in several ways:

- The standard set of classes required to run a servlet need not be imported. This is done automatically.
- The HTML is written more naturally, without using print statements.
- No class definition is required, nor any doGet( ) or doPost( ) methods.
- The response and out objects need not be declared, because they're set up for you and ready to use as implicit objects. In fact, the JSP page just shown doesn't refer to out explicitly at all, because its output-producing constructs write to out automatically.
- The default content type is text/html; there's no need to specify it explicitly.

- The script includes literal Java by placing it within special markers. The page just shown uses <%= and %>, which mean "evaluate the expression and display its result." There are other markers as well, each of which has a specific purpose. (For a brief summary, see "Elements of JSP Pages" later in this appendix.)

When a servlet container receives a request for a JSP page, it treats the page as a template containing literal text plus executable code embedded within special markers. The container produces an output page from the template to send to the client. Literal text from the template is left unmodified, the executable code is replaced by any output that it generates, and the combined result is returned to the client as the response to the request. That's the conceptual view of JSP processing, at least. When a container processes a JSP request, this is what really happens:

1. The container translates the JSP page into a servlet—that is, into an equivalent Java program. Instances of template text are converted to print statements that output the text literally. Instances of code are placed into the program so that they execute with the intended effect. This is all placed within a wrapper that provides a unique class name and that includes `import` statements to pull in the standard set of classes necessary for the servlet to run properly in a web environment.
2. The container compiles the servlet to produce an executable class file.
3. The container executes the class file to generate an output page, which is returned to the client as the response to the request.
4. The container also caches the executable class so that when the next request for the JSP page arrives, the container can execute the class directly and skip the translation and compilation phases. If the container notices that a JSP page has been modified the next time it is requested, it discards the cached class and recompiles the modified page into a new executable class.

Notationally, JSP pages provide a more natural way to write web pages than do servlets. Operationally, the JSP engine provides the benefits of automatic compilation after the page is installed in the document tree or modified thereafter. When you write a servlet, any changes require recompiling the servlet, unloading the old one, and loading the new one. That can lead to an emphasis on messing with the servlet itself rather than a focus on the servlet's purpose. JSP reverses the emphasis so that you think more about what the page does than about the mechanics of getting it compiled and loaded properly.

The differences between servlets and JSP pages do not imply any necessity of choosing to use only one or the other. Application contexts in a servlet container can include both, and because JSP pages are converted into servlets anyway, they can all intercommunicate.

JSP is similar enough to certain other technologies that it can provide a migration path away from them. For example, the JSP approach is much like that used in Microsoft's Active Server Pages (ASP). However, JSP is vendor- and platform-neutral, whereas ASP is proprietary. JSP thus provides an attractive alternative technology for anyone looking to move away from ASP.

Custom Actions and Tag Libraries

A servlet looks a lot like a Java program, because that's what it is. The JSP approach encourages a cleaner separation of HTML (presentation) and code, because you need not generate HTML from within Java print statements. On the other hand, JSP doesn't *require* separation of HTML and code, so it's still possible to end up with lots of embedded Java in a page if you're not careful.

One way to avoid inclusion of literal Java in JSP pages is to use another JSP feature known as *custom actions*. These take the form of special tags that look a lot like HTML tags (because they are written as XML elements). Custom actions enable tags to be defined that perform tasks on behalf of the page in which they occur. For example, a `<sql:query>` tag might communicate with a database server to issue a query. Custom actions typically come in groups, which are known as *tag libraries* and are designed as follows:

- The actions performed by the tags are implemented by a set of classes. These are just regular Java classes, except that they are written according to a set of interface conventions that enable the servlet container to communicate with them in a standard way. (The conventions define how tag attributes and body content are passed to tag handler classes, for example.) Typically, the set of classes is packaged into a JAR file.

- The library includes a tag library descriptor (TLD) file that specifies how each tag maps onto the corresponding class. This enables the JSP processor to determine which class to invoke for each custom tag that appears in a JSP page. The TLD file also indicates how each tag behaves, such as whether it has any required attributes. This information is used at page translation time to determine whether a JSP page uses the tags in the library correctly. For example, if a tag requires a particular attribute and the tag is used in a page without it, the JSP processor can detect that problem and issue an appropriate error message.

Tag libraries make it easier to write entire pages using tag notation rather than switching between tags and Java code. The notation is JSP-like, not Java-like, but the effect of placing a custom tag in a JSP page is like making a method call. This is because a tag reference in a JSP page maps onto a method invocation in the servlet that the page is translated into.

To illustrate the difference between the embedded-Java and tag library approaches, compare two JSP scripts that set up a connection to a MySQL server and display a list of tables in the cookbook database. The first one does so using Java embedded within the page:

```
<%@ page import="java.sql.*" %>
```

```
<html>
<head>
<title>Tables in cookbook Database</title>
</head>
<body bgcolor="white">

<p>Tables in cookbook database:</p>

<%
  Connection conn = null;
  String url = "jdbc:mysql://localhost/cookbook";
  String user = "cbuser";
  String password = "cbpass";

  Class.forName ("com.mysql.jdbc.Driver").newInstance ();
  conn = DriverManager.getConnection (url, user, password);

  Statement s = conn.createStatement ();
  s.executeQuery ("SELECT TABLE_NAME FROM INFORMATION_SCHEMA.TABLES"
                  + " WHERE TABLE_SCHEMA = 'cookbook'"
                  + " ORDER BY TABLE_NAME");
  ResultSet rs = s.getResultSet ();
  while (rs.next ())
    out.println (rs.getString (1) + "<br />");
  rs.close ();
  s.close ();
  conn.close ();
%>

</body>
</html>
```

The same thing can be done by using a tag library, such as the JSP Standard Tag Library (JSTL). JSTL consists of several tag sets grouped by function. Using its core and database tags, the preceding JSP page can be converted as follows to avoid entirely the use of literal Java:

```
<%@ taglib uri="http://java.sun.com/jsp/jstl/core" prefix="c" %>
<%@ taglib uri="http://java.sun.com/jsp/jstl/sql" prefix="sql" %>

<html>
<head>
<title>Tables in cookbook Database</title>
</head>
<body bgcolor="white">

<p>Tables in cookbook database:</p>

<sql:setDataSource
  var="conn"
  driver="com.mysql.jdbc.Driver"
  url="jdbc:mysql://localhost/cookbook"
  user="cbuser"
  password="cbpass"
/>
```

```
<sql:query dataSource="${conn}" var="rs">
  SELECT TABLE_NAME FROM INFORMATION_SCHEMA.TABLES
  WHERE TABLE_SCHEMA = 'cookbook'
  ORDER BY TABLE_NAME
</sql:query>
<c:forEach items="${rs.rowsByIndex}" var="row">
  <c:out value="${row[0]}"/><br />
</c:forEach>

</body>
</html>
```

The `taglib` directives identify the TLD files that the page uses and indicate that actions from the corresponding tag sets will be identified by prefixes of `c` and `sql`. (In effect, a prefix sets up a namespace for a set of tags.) The `<sql:dataSource>` tag sets up the parameters for connecting to the MySQL server, `<sql:query>` issues a query, `<c:forEach>` loops through the result, and `<c:out>` adds each table name in the result to the output page. (I'm glossing over details, of course. For more information about the JSTL tags, see Recipe 17.3.)

If it's likely that you'd connect to the database server the same way from most JSP pages in your application context, a further simplification can be achieved by moving the `<sql:dataSource>` tag to an include file. If you name the file *jstl-mcb-setup.inc* and place it in the application's *WEB-INF* directory, any page within the application context can set up the connection to the MySQL server by accessing the file with an `include` directive. (By convention, application contexts use their *WEB-INF* directory for private context-specific information. See the section "Web Application Structure.") Modifying the preceding page to use the include file results in a script that looks like this:

```
<%@ taglib uri="http://java.sun.com/jsp/jstl/core" prefix="c" %>
<%@ taglib uri="http://java.sun.com/jsp/jstl/sql" prefix="sql" %>
<%@ include file="/WEB-INF/jstl-mcb-setup.inc" %>

<html>
<head>
<title>Tables in cookbook Database</title>
</head>
<body bgcolor="white">

<p>Tables in cookbook database:</p>

<sql:query dataSource="${conn}" var="rs">
  SELECT TABLE_NAME FROM INFORMATION_SCHEMA.TABLES
  WHERE TABLE_SCHEMA = 'cookbook'
  ORDER BY TABLE_NAME
</sql:query>
<c:forEach items="${rs.rowsByIndex}" var="row">
  <c:out value="${row[0]}"/><br />
</c:forEach>

</body>
</html>
```

You're still *using* Java when you use a tag library, because tag actions map onto Java class invocations. But the notation follows XML conventions, so it's less like writing program code and more like writing HTML page elements. If your organization produces web content using a "separation of powers" workflow, custom actions enable elements of the page that are produced dynamically to be packaged in a way that is easier for designers and other non-programmers to deal with. They don't have to develop or work directly with the classes that implement tag actions; that's left to the programmers who write the classes that correspond to the tags.

Setting Up a Tomcat Server

The preceding discussion provides a brief introduction to servlets and JSP pages, but says nothing about how you actually use a server to run them. This section describes how to install Tomcat, a JSP-aware web server. Tomcat, like Apache, is a development effort of the Apache Software Foundation.

As described earlier, servlets execute inside a container, which is an engine that communicates with or plugs into a web server to handle requests for pages that are produced by executing servlets. Some servlet containers can operate in standalone fashion, such that they function both as container and web server. That is how Tomcat works. By installing it, you get a fully functioning server with servlet-processing capabilities. In fact, Tomcat is a reference implementation for both the servlet and JSP specifications, so it also acts as a JSP engine, providing JSP-to-servlet translation services. The servlet container part is named Catalina, and the JSP processor is named Jasper.

It's possible to use the container part of Tomcat in conjunction with other web servers. For example, you can set up a cooperative arrangement between Apache and Tomcat under which Apache acts as a front end that passes servlet and JSP requests through to Tomcat and handles other requests itself. You can find information about setting up Apache and Tomcat to work together this way on the Tomcat web site.

To run a Tomcat server, you need three things:

A Java Software Development Kit (SDK)
> This is required because Tomcat needs to compile Java servlets as part of its operation. You most likely already have an SDK installed if you've been compiling Java programs while reading earlier chapters. If you don't have an SDK, see Appendix B for information on obtaining and installing one.

Tomcat itself
> Tomcat is available from *http://tomcat.apache.org*. A fair amount of Tomcat documentation is available there, too. In particular, if you're a newcomer to Tomcat, I recommend that you read the Introduction and the Application Developer's Guide.

Some knowledge of XML
> Tomcat configuration files are written as XML documents, and many scripting elements within JSP pages follow XML syntax rules. If you're new to XML, the "XML and XHTML in a Nutshell" sidebar in Recipe 17.0 describes some of its characteristics in comparison to HTML.

Installing a Tomcat Distribution

Currently, Tomcat is available in several versions (such as 4.1, 5.0, and 5.5). This section describes Tomcat 5.0. The instructions should also work for Tomcat 5.5, although you might need to upgrade your version of Java (Tomcat 5.5 requires JS2E 5.0).

To install Tomcat, get a binary distribution from *tomcat.apache.org*. (I assume that you don't intend to build it from source, which is more difficult.) Tomcat distributions are available in several file formats, distinguished by filename extensions that have the following meanings:

.tar.gz
> A compressed *tar* file, usually used for Unix installs

.zip
> A ZIP archive, applicable to either Unix or Windows

.exe
> An executable installer, used on Windows only

If you're using Linux, the vendor of your Linux distribution might make Tomcat available on the distribution media or via an online APT or RPM repository. This method is not covered here in any depth. See your Linux distribution documentation or contact your vendor for details.

For a distribution packaged as a *tar* or ZIP file, you should place it in the directory under which you want to install Tomcat, and then run the installation command in that directory to unpack the distribution there. The Windows *.exe* installer prompts you to indicate where to install Tomcat, so it too can be run from any directory. The following commands are representative of those needed to install each distribution type. (Change the version numbers in the filenames to reflect the actual Tomcat distribution that you're using.)

To install Tomcat from a compressed *tar* files, unpack it like this:

```
% tar zxf jakarta-tomcat-5.0.28.tar.gz
```

If you have trouble unpacking a Tomcat *tar* file distribution under Mac OS X, use *gnutar* rather than *tar*. On older versions of Mac OS X, *tar* has some problems with long filenames that *gnutar* does not. (In current versions, both programs are the same.) It may also be necessary to use a GNU-compatible version of *tar* under Solaris.

If your version of *tar* doesn't understand the z option, do this instead:

```
% gunzip -c jakarta-tomcat-5.0.28.tar.gz | tar xf -
```

If you use a ZIP archive, you can unpack it with the *jar* utility or any other program that understands ZIP format (such as the Windows *WinZip* application). For example, to use *jar*, do this:

```
% jar xf jakarta-tomcat-5.0.28.zip
```

The Windows *.exe* distribution is directly executable. Launch it, and then indicate where you want to place Tomcat when the installer prompts for a location. If you use this installer, be sure that you already have a Java SDK installed first; the installer puts some files into the SDK hierarchy, an operation that fails if the SDK isn't present. For versions of Windows that have service management (such as Windows NT, 2000, or XP), the *.exe* installer gives you the option of installing Tomcat as a service so that it starts automatically at system boot time.

Most of the installation methods create a directory and unpack Tomcat under it. The top-level directory of the resulting hierarchy is the Tomcat root directory. I'll assume here that the Tomcat root is */usr/local/jakarta-tomcat* under Unix. Under Windows, I'll assume *C:\jakarta-tomcat*. (The actual directory name likely will have a version number at the end.) The Tomcat root contains various text files containing information that is useful in the event that you have general or platform-specific problems. It also contains a number of directories. If you want to explore these now, see the section "Tomcat's Directory Structure." Otherwise, proceed to the next section, "Starting and Stopping Tomcat," to find out how to run Tomcat.

Starting and Stopping Tomcat

Tomcat can be controlled manually, and also set to run automatically when your system starts up. It's good to become familiar with the Tomcat startup and shutdown commands that apply to your platform, because you'll probably find yourself needing to stop and restart Tomcat fairly often—at least while you're setting it up initially. For example, if you modify Tomcat's configuration files or install a new application, you must restart Tomcat to get it to notice the changes.

Before running Tomcat, you'll need to set a couple of environment variables. Make sure JAVA_HOME is set to the pathname of your SDK so that Tomcat can find it. You might also need to set CATALINA_HOME to the pathname of the Tomcat root directory.

To start and stop Tomcat manually under Unix, change location into the *bin* directory under the Tomcat root. I find that it's useful to make the shell scripts in that directory executable (this is a one-time operation):

```
% chmod +x *.sh
```

You can control Tomcat with the following two shell scripts:

```
% ./startup.sh
% ./shutdown.sh
```

To run Tomcat automatically at system boot time, look for a startup script such as */etc/rc.local* or */etc/rc.d/rc.local* (the pathname depends on your operating system) and add a few lines to it:

```
export JAVA_HOME=/usr/local/java/jdk
export CATALINA_HOME=/usr/local/jakarta-tomcat
$CATALINA_HOME/bin/startup.sh &
```

These commands will run Tomcat as `root`, however. To run it under a different user account, change the last command to invoke Tomcat with *su* instead and specify the username:

```
su -c $CATALINA_HOME/bin/startup.sh user_name &
```

If you use *su* to specify a username, make sure that Tomcat's directory tree is accessible to that user or you will have file permission problems when Tomcat tries to access files. One way to do this is to run the following command as `root` in the Tomcat root directory:

```
# chown -R user_name .
```

Linux users who install Tomcat from vendor-supplied package files may find that the installation creates a script named *tomcat* (or perhaps something like *tomcat4* or *tomcat5*) in the */etc/rc.d/init.d* directory that can be used manually or for automatic startup. To use the script manually, change location into that directory and use these commands:

```
% ./tomcat start
% ./tomcat stop
```

For automatic startup, you must activate the script by running the following command as `root`:

```
# chkconfig --add tomcat
```

Linux package installation also might create a user account with a login name such as `tomcat` or `tomcat5` that is intended to be used for running Tomcat.

For Windows users, the distribution includes a pair of batch files in the *bin* directory for controlling Tomcat manually:

```
C:\> startup.bat
C:\> shutdown.bat
```

If you elected to install Tomcat as a service for versions of Windows that have service management, such as Windows NT, 2000, or XP, you should control Tomcat using the services console. You can use this to start or stop Tomcat, or to set Tomcat to run automatically when Windows starts. (The service name is `Apache Tomcat`.)

To try Tomcat, start it using whatever instructions are applicable to your platform. Then request the default page using your browser. The URL will look something like this:

```
http://localhost:8080/
```

Adjust your hostname and port number appropriately. For example, Tomcat normally runs on port 8080 by default, but if you install from package files under Linux, Tomcat may use a port number of 8180. If your browser receives the page correctly, you should see the Tomcat logo and links to examples and documentation. It's useful at this point to follow the examples link and try a few of the JSP pages there, to see whether they compile and execute properly.

If you find that, despite setting the JAVA_HOME variable, Tomcat can't find your Java compiler, try setting your PATH environment variable to explicitly include the directory containing the compiler. Normally, this is the *bin* directory under your SDK installation. You probably already have PATH set to something already. If so, you'll want to add the *bin* directory to the current PATH setting. (See Appendix B for information about setting your PATH value.)

Tomcat's Directory Structure

For writing JSP pages, it's not strictly necessary to be familiar with the hierarchy of Tomcat's directory layout. But it certainly doesn't hurt, so change location into the Tomcat root directory and have a look around. You'll find a number of standard directories, which are described in the following discussion, grouped by function. Note that your installation layout may not be exactly as described here. Some distribution formats omit a few of the directories, and the *logs* and *work* directories might not be created until you've started Tomcat for the first time.

Application Directories

From the point of view of an application developer, the *webapps* directory is the most important part of Tomcat's directory hierarchy. Each application context has its own directory, which is placed within the *webapps* directory under the Tomcat root.

Tomcat processes client requests by mapping them onto locations under the *webapps* directory. For a request that begins with the name of a directory located under *webapps*, Tomcat looks for the appropriate page within that directory. For example, Tomcat serves the following two requests using the *index.html* and *test.jsp* pages in the *mcb* directory:

```
http://localhost:8080/mcb/index.html
http://localhost:8080/mcb/test.jsp
```

For requests that don't begin with the name of a *webapps* subdirectory, Tomcat serves them from a special subdirectory named *ROOT*, which provides the default application context.* For the following request, Tomcat serves the *index.html* page from the *ROOT* directory:

---

* The *webapps/ROOT* directory is distinct from the Tomcat root directory, which is the top-level directory of the Tomcat tree.

```
http://localhost:8080/index.html
```

Applications typically are packaged as web archive (WAR) files and Tomcat by default looks for WAR files that need to be unpacked when it starts up. Thus, to install an application, you generally copy its WAR file to the *webapps* directory, restart Tomcat, and let Tomcat unpack it. The layout of individual application directories is described later in the section "Web Application Structure."

A web application is a group of related servlets that work together, without interference from other unrelated servlets. Essentially what this means for Tomcat is that an application is everything under a subdirectory of the *webapps* directory. Because contexts are kept separate by servlet containers like Tomcat, one practical implication of this structure is that scripts in one application directory can't mess with anything in another application directory.

Configuration and Control Directories

Two directories contain configuration and control files. The *bin* directory contains control scripts for Tomcat startup and shutdown, and *conf* contains Tomcat's configuration files, which are written as XML documents. Tomcat reads its configuration files only at startup time. If you modify any of them, you must restart Tomcat for your changes to take effect.

The most important configuration file is *server.xml*, which controls Tomcat's overall behavior. Another file, *web.xml*, provides application configuration defaults. This file is used in conjunction with any *web.xml* file an application may have of its own. The *tomcat-users.xml* file defines credentials for users that have access to protected server functions, such as the Manager application that enables you to control applications from your browser. (See "Restarting Applications Without Restarting Tomcat," later) This file can be superseded by other user information storage mechanisms. For example, you can store Tomcat user records in MySQL instead. For instructions, look in the *tomcat* directory of the `recipes` distribution.

Class Directories

Several Tomcat directories are used for class files and libraries. They differ in function according to whether you want to make classes visible to applications, to Tomcat, or to both:

shared

> This directory has two subdirectories, *classes* and *lib*, for class files and libraries that are visible to applications but not to Tomcat.

common

> This directory has two subdirectories, *classes* and *lib*, for class files and libraries that should be visible both to applications and to Tomcat.

server

> This directory has two subdirectories, *classes* and *lib*, for class files and libraries that are visible to Tomcat but not to applications.

Operational Directories

If they weren't set up as part of the Tomcat installation process, Tomcat creates two additional directories that serve operational purposes when you start it for the first time. Tomcat writes log files to the *log* directory and uses a *work* directory for temporary files.

The files in the *logs* directory can be useful for diagnosing problems. For example, if Tomcat has a problem starting properly, the reason usually will have been written into one of the logfiles.

When Tomcat translates a JSP page into a servlet and compiles it into an executable class file, it stores the resulting *.java* and *.class* files under the *work* directory. (When you first begin working with JSP pages, you may find it instructive to have a look under the *work* directory to compare your original JSP pages with the corresponding servlets that Tomcat produces.)

Restarting Applications Without Restarting Tomcat

If you modify a JSP page, Tomcat recompiles it automatically when the page is next requested. But if the page uses a JAR or class file under the application's *WEB-INF* directory and you update one of them, Tomcat normally won't notice the change until you restart it.

One way to avoid restarts for an application is to provide a `<Context>` element for the application in Tomcat's *server.xml* file that specifies a `reloadable` attribute of `true`. That will cause Tomcat to look for changes not only in JSP pages that are requested directly, but also for changes in classes and libraries under the *WEB-INF* directory that the pages use. For example, to write such a `<Context>` element for an application named `mcb`, you could add a line like this to Tomcat's *server.xml* file:

```
<Context path="/mcb" docBase="mcb" debug="0" reloadable="true"/>
```

The `<Context>` element attributes tell Tomcat four things:

path
> Indicates the URL that maps to pages from the application context. The value is the part of the URL that follows the hostname and port number.

docBase
> Indicates where the application context directory is located, relative to the *webapps* directory in the Tomcat tree.

debug

> Sets the context debugging level. A value of zero disables debug output; higher numbers generate more output.

reloadable

> Specifies Tomcat recompilation behavior when a client requests a JSP page located in the application context. By default, Tomcat recompiles a page only after noticing a modification to the page itself. Setting `reloadable` to `true` tells Tomcat to also check any classes or libraries stored under the application's *WEB-INF* directory that the page uses.

After modifying *server.xml* to add the `<Context>` element, restart Tomcat to make the change take effect.

Having Tomcat check for class and library changes can be extremely useful during application development to avoid repeated restarts. However, as you might expect, automatic class checking adds a lot of processing overhead and incurs a significant performance penalty. It's better used on development systems than on production systems.

Another way to get Tomcat to recognize application changes without restarting the entire server is to use the Manager application. This enables you to reload applications on request from a browser, without the overhead caused by enabling the `reloadable` attribute. The Manager application is invoked using the path */manager* at the end of the URL by which you access your Tomcat server. The URL also includes the command that you want to execute. For example, the following request shows which contexts are running:

```
http://localhost:8080/manager/list
```

To shut down and reload the `mcb` application without restarting Tomcat, use a URL like this:

```
http://localhost:8080/manager/reload?path=/mcb
```

For more information on using the Manager application and what its allowable commands are, see the Manager App HOW-TO:

http://tomcat.apache.org/tomcat-5.0-doc/manager-howto.html

This document may also be available locally by following the documentation link on your Tomcat server's home page. Note particularly the part that describes how to set up a Tomcat user with the `manager` role, because you'll need to provide a name and password to gain access to the Manager application. By default, user records are defined in Tomcat's *tomcat-users.xml* configuration file. The *tomcat* directory of the `recipes` distribution contains information on storing Tomcat user records in MySQL instead.

Web Application Structure

Each web application corresponds to a single servlet context and exists as a collection of resources. Some of these resources are visible to clients, whereas others are not. For example, an application's JSP pages may be available to clients, but the configuration, property, or class files that are used by the JSP pages can be hidden. The location of components within the application hierarchy determines whether clients can see them. This enables you to make resources public or private depending on where you put them.

Java Servlet Specification 2.4 defines the standard for web application layout. This helps application developers by providing conventions that indicate where to put what, along with rules that define which parts of the application the container will make available to clients and which parts are hidden.

Each web application corresponds to a single servlet context. In Tomcat, these are represented by directories under the *webapps* directory that serves as the "parent" of all web applications. Within an application directory, you'll find a *WEB-INF* subdirectory, and usually other files such as HTML pages, JSP pages, or image files. The files that are located in the application's top-level directory are public and may be requested by clients. The *WEB-INF* directory has special significance. Its mere presence signifies to Tomcat that its parent directory actually represents an application. *WEB-INF* is thus the only required component of a web application; it must exist, even if it's empty. If *WEB-INF* is nonempty, it typically contains application-specific configuration files, classes, and possibly other information. Three of its most common primary components are:

```
WEB-INF/web.xml
WEB-INF/classes
WEB-INF/lib
```

web.xml is the web application deployment descriptor file. It gives the container a standard way to discover how to handle the resources that make up the application. The deployment descriptor is often used for purposes such as defining the behavior of JSP pages and servlets, setting up access control for protected information, specifying error pages to be used when problems occur, and defining where to find tag libraries.

The *classes* and *lib* directories under *WEB-INF* hold class files and libraries, and sometimes other information. Individual class files go under *classes*, using a directory structure that corresponds to the class hierarchy. (For example, a class file *MyClass.class* that implements a class named `com.kitebird.jsp.MyClass` would be stored in the directory *classes/com/kitebird/jsp*.) Class libraries packaged as JAR files go in the *lib* directory instead. Tomcat looks in the *classes* and *lib* directories automatically when processing requests for pages from the application. This enables your pages to use application-specific information with a minimum of fuss.

The *WEB-INF* directory is private. Its contents are available to the application's servlets and JSP pages but cannot be accessed directly through a browser, so you can place information there that should not be displayed to clients. For example, you can store a properties file under *WEB-INF* that contains connection parameters for a database server. Or if you have an application that allows image files to be uploaded by one page and downloaded later by another page, putting the images into a directory under *WEB-INF* makes them private. Because Tomcat will not serve the contents of *WEB-INF* directly, your JSP pages can implement an access control policy that determines who can perform image operations. (A simple policy might require clients to specify a name and password before being allowed to upload images.) The *WEB-INF* directory is also beneficial in that it gives you a known location for private files that is fixed with respect to the application's root directory, no matter what machine you deploy the application on.

Clients that attempt to circumvent the private nature of the *WEB-INF* directory by issuing requests containing names such as *Web-Inf* in the path will find that its name is interpreted in case-sensitive fashion, even on systems with filenames that are not case-sensitive, such as Windows or HFS+ filesystems under Mac OS X. On such systems, you should take care not to create the *WEB-INF* directory with a name like *Web-Inf*, *web-inf*, and so forth. The operating system itself may not consider the name any different from *WEB-INF*, but Tomcat will. The result is that none of the resources in the directory will be available to your JSP pages. Under Windows, it may be necessary to create a *WEB-INF* directory from the prompt in a console window. (Windows Explorer may not respect the lettercase you use when creating or renaming a directory, just as it does not necessarily display directory names the same way the *DIR* command does from the command line in a console window.)

The preceding discussion describes web application layout in terms of a directory hierarchy, because that's the easiest way to explain it. However, an application need not necessarily exist that way. A web application typically is packaged as a WAR file, using the standard layout for components prescribed by the servlet specification. But some containers can run an application directly from its WAR file without unpacking it. Furthermore, a container that does unpack WAR files is free to do so into any filesystem structure it wishes.

Tomcat uses the simplest approach, which is to store an application in the filesystem using a directory structure that is the same as the directory tree from which the file was originally created. You can see this correspondence by comparing the structure of a WAR file to the directory hierarchy that Tomcat creates by unpacking it. For example, the WAR file for an application someapp can be examined using the this command:

```
% jar tf someapp.war
```

The list of pathnames displayed by the command corresponds to the layout of the *someapp* directory created by Tomcat when it unpacks the file under the *webapps* directory. To verify this, recursively list the contents of the *someapp* directory using one of these commands:

```
% ls -R someapp          (Unix)
C:\> dir /s someapp      (Windows)
```

If you were to set up a context manually for an application named myapp, the steps would be something like those shown in the following procedure. (If you want to see what the resulting application hierarchy should be, have a look at the *tomcat/myapp* directory of the recipes distribution.)

1. Change location into the *webapps* subdirectory of the Tomcat directory tree.

2. Create a directory in the *webapps* directory with the same name as the application (*myapp*), then change location into that directory.

3. In the *myapp* directory, create a directory named *WEB-INF*. The presence of this directory signals to Tomcat that *myapp* is an application context, so it must exist. Then restart Tomcat so it notices the new application.

4. Create a short test page named *page1.html* in the *myapp* directory that you can request from a browser to make sure that Tomcat is serving pages for the application. This is just a plain HTML file, to avoid complications that might arise from use of embedded Java, tag libraries, and so forth:

```
<html>
<head>
<title>Test Page</title>
</head>
<body bgcolor="white">
<p>
This is a test.
</p>
</body>
</html>
```

To request the page, use a URL like this, adjusting it appropriately for your own server hostname and port number:

```
http://localhost:8080/myapp/page1.html
```

5. To try a simple JSP page, make a copy of *page1.html* named *page2.jsp*. That creates a valid JSP page (even though it contains no executable code), so you should be able to request it and see output identical to that produced by *page1.html*:

```
http://localhost:8080/myapp/page2.jsp
```

6. Copy *page2.jsp* to *page3.jsp* and modify the latter to contain some embedded Java code by adding a couple of lines that print the current date and client IP number:

```
<html>
<head>
<title>Test Page</title>
</head>
<body bgcolor="white">
<p>
This is a test.
The current date is <%= new java.util.Date() %>.
Your IP number is <%= request.getRemoteAddr () %>.
</p>
```

```
        </body>
      </html>
```

The `Date( )` method returns the current date, and `getRemoteAddr( )` returns the client IP number from the object associated with the client request. After making the changes, request *page3.jsp* from your browser and the output should include the current date and the IP number of the host from which you requested the page.

At this point, you have a simple application context that consists of three pages (one of which contains executable code) and an empty *WEB-INF* directory. For most applications, *WEB-INF* will contain a *web.xml* file that serves as the web application deployment descriptor file to tell Tomcat how the application is configured. If you look through *web.xml* files in other applications that you install under Tomcat, you'll find that they can be rather complex, but a minimal deployment descriptor file looks like this:

```
<?xml version="1.0" encoding="ISO-8859-1"?>

<web-app xmlns="http://java.sun.com/xml/ns/j2ee"
  xmlns:xsi="http://www.w3.org/2001/XMLSchema-instance"
  xsi:schemaLocation="http://java.sun.com/xml/ns/j2ee
  http://java.sun.com/xml/ns/j2ee/web-app_2_4.xsd"
  version="2.4">

</web-app>
```

Adding information to the *web.xml* file is a matter of placing new elements between the `<web-app>` and `</web-app>` tags. As a simple illustration, you can add a `<welcome-file-list>` element to specify a list of files that Tomcat should look for when clients send a request URL that ends with *myapp* and no specific page. Whichever file Tomcat finds first becomes the default page that is sent to the client. For example, to specify that Tomcat should consider *page3.jsp* and *index.html* to be valid default pages, create a *web.xml* file in the *WEB-INF* directory that looks like this:

```
<?xml version="1.0" encoding="ISO-8859-1"?>

<web-app xmlns="http://java.sun.com/xml/ns/j2ee"
  xmlns:xsi="http://www.w3.org/2001/XMLSchema-instance"
  xsi:schemaLocation="http://java.sun.com/xml/ns/j2ee
  http://java.sun.com/xml/ns/j2ee/web-app_2_4.xsd"
  version="2.4">

  <welcome-file-list>
    <welcome-file>page3.jsp</welcome-file>
    <welcome-file>index.html</welcome-file>
  </welcome-file-list>

</web-app>
```

Restart Tomcat so it reads the new application configuration information, and then issue a request that specifies no explicit page:

```
http://localhost:8080/myapp/
```

The *myapp* directory contains a page named *page3.jsp*, which is listed as one of the default pages in the *web.xml* file, so Tomcat should execute *page3.jsp* and send the result to your browser.

Elements of JSP Pages

An earlier section of this appendix described some general characteristics of JSP pages. This section discusses in more detail the kinds of constructs you can use.

JSP pages are templates that contain static parts and dynamic parts:

- Literal text in a JSP page that is not enclosed within special markers is static; it's sent to the client without change. The JSP examples in this book produce HTML pages, so the static parts of JSP scripts are written in HTML. But you can also write pages that produce other forms of output, such as plain text, XML, or WML.

- The nonstatic (dynamic) parts of JSP pages consist of code to be evaluated. You distinguish code from static text by enclosing it within special markers. Some markers indicate page-processing directives or scriptlets. A directive gives the JSP engine information about how to process the page, whereas a scriptlet is a mini-program that is evaluated and replaced by whatever output it produces. Other markers take the form of tags written as XML elements; they are associated with classes that act as tag handlers to perform the desired actions.

The following sections discuss the various types of dynamic elements that JSP pages can contain.

Scripting Elements

Several sets of scripting markers allow you to embed Java code or comments in a JSP page:

`<% ... %>`
> The `<%` and `%>` markers indicate a scriptlet—that is, embedded Java code. The following scriptlet invokes `print( )` to write a value to the output page:
>
> ```
> <% out.print (1+2); %>
> ```

`<%= ... %>`
> These markers indicate an expression to be evaluated. The result is added to the output page, which makes it easy to display values with no explicit print statement. For example, these two constructs both display the value 3, but the second is easier to write:
>
> ```
> <% out.print (1+2); %>
> <%= 1+2 %>
> ```

`<%! ... %>`
> The `<%!` and `%>` markers allow class variables and methods to be declared.

```
<%-- ... --%>
```
Text within these markers is treated as a comment and ignored. JSP comments disappear entirely and do not appear in the output that is returned to the client. If you're writing a JSP page that produces HTML and you want the comment to appear in the final output page, use an HTML comment instead:

```
<%-- this comment will not be part of the final output page --%>
<!-- this comment will be part of the final output page -->
```

When a JSP page is translated into a servlet, all scripting elements effectively become part of the same servlet. This means that a variable declared in one element can be used by other elements later in the page. It also means that if you declare a given variable in two elements, the resulting servlet is illegal and an error will occur.

The `<% ... %>` and `<%! ... %>` markers both can be used to declare variables, but differ in their effect. A variable declared within `<% ... %>` is an object (or instance) variable; it is initialized each time that the page is requested. A variable declared within `<%! ... %>` is a class variable, initialized only at the beginning the life of the page. Consider the following JSP page, *counter.jsp*, which declares `counter1` as an object variable and `counter2` as a class variable:

```
<%-- counter.jsp - demonstrate object and class variable counters --%>

<% int counter1 = 0; %>     <%-- object variable --%>
<%! int counter2 = 0; %>    <%-- class variable --%>
<% counter1 = counter1 + 1; %>
<% counter2 = counter2 + 1; %>
<p>Counter 1 is <%= counter1 %></p>
<p>Counter 2 is <%= counter2 %></p>
```

If you install the page and request it several times, the value of `counter1` will be 1 for every request. The value of `counter2` increments across successive requests (even if different clients request the page), until Tomcat is restarted.

In addition to variables that you declare yourself, JSP pages have access to a number of objects that are declared for you implicitly. These are discussed in the later section, "Implicit JSP Objects."

JSP Directives

The `<%@ and %>` markers indicate a JSP directive that provides the JSP processor with information about the kind of output the page produces, the classes or tag libraries it requires, and so forth.

```
<%@ page ... %>
```
page directives provide several kinds of information, which are indicated by one or more *attribute="value"* pairs following the page keyword. The following directive specifies that the page scripting language is Java and that it produces an output page with a content type of `text/html`:

```
<%@ page language="java" contentType="text/html" %>
```

This particular directive need not actually be specified at all, because `java` and `text/html` are the default values for their respective attributes.

If a JSP page produces non-HTML output, be sure to override the default content type. For example, if a page produces plain text, use this directive:

```
<%@ page contentType="text/plain" %>
```

An `import` attribute causes Java classes to be imported. In a regular Java program, you would do this using an `import` statement. In a JSP page, use a `page` directive instead:

```
<%@ page import="java.util.Date" %>
<p>The date is <%= new Date () %>.</p>
```

If you refer to a particular class only once, it may be more convenient to omit the directive and just refer to the class by its full name when you use it:

```
<p>The date is <%= new java.util.Date () %>.</p>
```

<%@ include ... %>

The `include` directive inserts the contents of a file into the page translation process. That is, the directive is replaced by the contents of the included file, which is then translated itself. The following directive causes inclusion of a file named *my-setup-stuff.inc* from the application's *WEB-INF* directory:

```
<%@ include file="/WEB-INF/my-setup-stuff.inc" %>
```

A leading `/` indicates a filename relative to the application directory (a context-relative path). No leading `/` means the file is relative to the location of the page containing the `include` directive.

Include files allow content (either static or dynamic) to be shared easily among a set of JSP pages. For example, you can use them to provide standard headers or footers for a set of JSP pages, or to execute code for common operations such as setting up a connection to a database server.

<%@ taglib ... %>

A `taglib` directive indicates that the page uses custom actions from a given tag library. The directive includes attributes that tell the JSP engine how to locate the TLD file for the library and also the name you'll use in the rest of the page to signify tags from the library. For example, a page that uses the core and database-access tags from JSTL might include the following `taglib` directives:

```
<%@ taglib uri="http://java.sun.com/jsp/jstl/core" prefix="c" %>
<%@ taglib uri="http://java.sun.com/jsp/jstl/sql" prefix="sql" %>
```

The `uri` (Uniform Resource Identifier) attribute uniquely identifies the tag library so that the JSP engine can find its TLD file. The TLD defines the behavior (the interface) of the actions so that the JSP processor can make sure the page uses the library's tags correctly. A common convention for constructing unique `uri` values is to use a string that includes the host from which the tag library originates. That makes the `uri` value look like a URL, but it's just an identifier; it doesn't mean that the JSP engine actually goes to that host to fetch the descriptor file. The rules for interpreting the `uri` value are described in the later section "Using a Tag Library."

The `prefix` attribute indicates how tags from the library will be invoked. The directives just shown indicate that core and database tags will have the forms `<c:xxx>` and `<sql:xxx>`. For example, you can use the `out` tag from the core library as follows to display a value:

```
<c:out value="Hello, world."/>
```

Or you might issue a query with the database `query` tag like this:

```
<sql:query dataSource="${conn}" var="result">
  SELECT id, name FROM profile ORDER BY id
</sql:query>
```

Action Elements

Action element tags can refer to standard (predefined) JSP actions, or to custom actions in a tag library. Tag names include a prefix and a specific action:

- Tag names with a `jsp` prefix indicate predefined action elements. For example, `<jsp:forward>` forwards the current request to another page. This action is available to any page run under a standard JSP processor.

- Custom actions are implemented by tag libraries. The prefix of the tag name must match the `prefix` attribute of a `taglib` directive that appears earlier in the page, so that the JSP processor can determine which library the tag is part of. To use custom tags, the library must be installed first. See "Using a Tag Library," next.

Actions are written as XML elements within a JSP page, and their syntax follows normal XML rules. An element with a body is written with separate opening and closing tags:

```
<c:if test="${x == 0}">
  x is zero
</c:if>
```

If the tag has no body, the opening and closing tags can be combined:

```
<jsp:forward page="some_other_page.jsp"/>
```

Using a Tag Library

Suppose that you have a tag library consisting of a JAR file *mytags.jar* and a tag library descriptor file *mytags.tld*. To make the library available to the JSP pages in a given application, both files must be installed. Typically, you put the JAR file in the application's *WEB-INF/lib* directory and the TLD file in the *WEB-INF* directory.

A JSP page that uses the tag library must include an appropriate `taglib` directive before using any of the actions that the library provides:

```
<%@ taglib uri="tld-location" prefix="taglib-identifier" %>
```

The **prefix** attribute tells Tomcat how you'll refer to tags from the library in the rest of the JSP page. If you use a **prefix** value of **mytags**, you can refer to tags later in the page like this:

```
<mytags:sometag attr1="attribute value 1" attr2="attribute value 2">
tag body
</mytags:sometag>
```

The **prefix** value is a name of your own choosing, but you must use it consistently throughout the page, and you cannot use the same value for two different tag libraries.

The **uri** attribute tells the JSP processor how to find the tag library's TLD file. The value can be either direct or indirect:

- You can specify the **uri** value directly as the pathname to the TLD file, which typically will be installed in the *WEB-INF* directory:

  ```
  <%@ taglib uri="/WEB-INF/mytags.tld" prefix="mytags" %>
  ```

  A leading / indicates a filename relative to the application directory (a context-relative path). No leading / means the file is relative to the location of the page containing the **taglib** directive.

  If an application uses lots of tag libraries, a common convention for keeping TLD files from cluttering up the *WEB-INF* directory is to put them in a *tld* subdirectory of the *WEB-INF* directory. In that case, the **uri** value would be written like this instead:

  ```
  <%@ taglib uri="/WEB-INF/tld/mytags.tld" prefix="mytags" %>
  ```

  The disadvantage of specifying a TLD file pathname directly is that if a new version of the tag library is released and the TLD file has a different name, you'll need to modify the **taglib** directive in every JSP page that refers to the file.

- Another way to specify the location of the TLD file is by using the pathname to the tag library JAR file:

  ```
  <%@ taglib uri="/WEB-INF/lib/mytags.jar" prefix="mytags" %>
  ```

  The JSP processor can find the TLD file this way, provided a copy of it is included in the JAR file as *META-INF/taglib.tld*. However, this method suffers the same problem as specifying the TLD filename directly—if a new version of the library comes out with a different JAR file pathname, you must update **taglib** directives in individual JSP pages. It also doesn't work for containers that can't find TLD files in JAR files. (Older versions of Tomcat have this problem, for example.)

- A third way to specify the location of the TLD file is to do so indirectly. Assign a symbolic name to the library and add a **<taglib>** entry to the application's *web.xml* file that maps the symbolic name to the pathname of the TLD file. Then refer to the symbolic name in your JSP pages. Suppose that you define the symbolic name for the **mytags** tag library as:

```
http://terrific-tags.com/mytags
```

The `<taglib>` entry in *web.xml* should list the symbolic name and provide the path to the corresponding TLD file. If the file is installed in the *WEB-INF* directory, write the entry like this:

```
<taglib>
  <taglib-uri>http://terrific-tags.com/mytags</taglib-uri>
  <taglib-location>/WEB-INF/mytags.tld</taglib-location>
</taglib>
```

If the file is installed in *WEB-INF/tld* instead, write the entry like this:

```
<taglib>
  <taglib-uri>http://terrific-tags.com/mytags</taglib-uri>
  <taglib-location>/WEB-INF/tld/mytags.tld</taglib-location>
</taglib>
```

Either way, you refer to the tag library in JSP pages using the symbolic name, like this:

```
<%@ taglib uri="http://terrific-tags.com/mytags" prefix="mytags" %>
```

Using a symbolic TLD name involves a level of indirection, but has a significant advantage in that it provides a more stable means by which to refer to the tag library in JSP pages. You specify the actual location of the TLD file only in *web.xml*, rather than in individual JSP pages. If a new version of the tag library comes out and the TLD file has a different name, just change the `<taglib-location>` value in *web.xml* and restart Tomcat to enable your JSP pages to use the new library. There's no need to change any of the JSP pages that use the tags.

Implicit JSP Objects

When a servlet runs, the servlet container passes it two arguments representing the request and the response, but you must declare other objects yourself. For example, you can use the **response** argument to obtain an output-writing object like this:

```
PrintWriter out = response.getWriter ();
```

A convenience that JSP provides in comparison to servlet writing is a set of implicit objects—that is, standard objects that are provided as part of the JSP execution environment. You can refer to any of these objects without explicitly declaring them. Thus, in a JSP page, the **out** object can be treated as having already been set up and made available for use. Some of the more useful implicit objects are:

pageContext
 An object that provides the environment for the page.

request
 An object that contains information about the request received from the client, such as the parameters submitted in a form.

---

response

> The response being constructed for transmission to the client. You can use it to specify response headers, for example.

out

> The output object. Writing to this object via methods such as `print( )` or `println( )` adds text to the response page.

session

> Tomcat provides access to a session that can be used to carry information from request to request. This enables you to write applications that interact with the user in what seems to be a cohesive series of events. Sessions are described more fully in Chapter 20.

application

> This object provides access to information that is shared on an application-wide basis.

Levels of Scope in JSP Pages

JSP pages have access to several scope levels, which can be used to store information that varies in how widely available it is. The scope levels are:

Page scope

> Information that is available only to the current JSP page.

Request scope

> Information that is available to any of the JSP pages or servlets that are servicing the current client request. It's possible for one page to invoke another during request processing; placing information in request scope enables such pages to communicate with each other.

Session scope

> Information that is available to any page servicing a request that is part of a given session. Session scope can span multiple requests from a given client.

Application scope

> Information that is available to any page that is part of the application context. Application scope can span multiple requests, sessions, or clients.

One context knows nothing about other contexts, but pages served from within the same context can share information with each other by registering attributes (objects) in one of the scopes that are higher than page scope.

To move information into or out of a given scope, use the `setAttribute( )` or `getAttribute( )` methods of the implicit object corresponding to that scope (`pageContext`, `request`, `session`, or `application`). For example, to place a string value `tomcat.example.com` into request scope as an attribute named `myhost`, use the `request` object:

```
request.setAttribute ("myhost", "tomcat.example.com");
```

setAttribute( ) stores the value as an `Object`. To retrieve the value later, fetch it by name using getAttribute( ) and then coerce it back to string form:

```
Object obj;
String host;
obj = request.getAttribute ("myhost");
host = obj.toString ();
```

When used with the pageContext object, setAttribute( ) and getAttribute( ) default to page context. Alternatively, they can be invoked with an additional parameter of `PAGE_SCOPE`, `REQUEST_SCOPE`, `SESSION_SCOPE`, or `APPLICATION_SCOPE` to specify a scope level explicitly. The following statements have the same effect as those just shown:

```
pageContext.setAttribute ("myhost", "tomcat.example.com",
                          pageContext.REQUEST_SCOPE);
obj = pageContext.getAttribute ("myhost", pageContext.REQUEST_SCOPE);
host = obj.toString ();
```

References

This appendix lists some references that you should find helpful if you want more information about topics discussed in this book.

MySQL Resources

The primary MySQL web site is *http://www.mysql.com/*.

Bibliography

AB, MySQL. *MySQL Administrator's Guide and Language Reference*. Indianapolis: MySQL Press, 2006. 0-672-32870-4.

This is the printed form of the MySQL Reference Manual that is available online at the MySQL web site, *http://dev.mysql.com/doc/*.

DuBois, Paul. *MySQL*. Indianapolis: Sams Developers Library, 2005. 0-672-32673-6.

This book provides general information about MySQL use and administration. It also covers MySQL programming, with chapters on the C, Perl, and PHP APIs.

Perl Resources

The primary MySQL web site is *http://www.mysql.com/*.

Additional DBI and CGI.pm documentation is available from the command line:

```
% perldoc DBI
% perldoc DBI::FAQ
% perldoc DBD::mysql
% perldoc CGI.pm
```

Or online:

> *http://dbi.perl.org/*
> *http://search.cpan.org/dist/CGI.pm/*

Bibliography

Wall, Larry, Tom Christiansen, and Jon Orwant. *Programming Perl*. Sebastopol, CA: O'Reilly Media, 2000. 0-596-00027-8.

Christiansen, Tom, and Nathan Torkington. *Perl Cookbook*. Sebastopol, CA: O'Reilly Media, 2003. 0-596-00313-7.

Descartes, Alligator, and Tim Bunce. *Programming the Perl DBI*. Sebastopol, CA: O'Reilly Media, 2000. 1-565-92699-4.

Book-length coverage of DBI; one of the authors (Bunce) is its primary architect.

Stein, Lincoln. *Official Guide to Programming with CGI.pm*. New York: Wiley Computer Publishing, 1998. 0-471-24744-8.

Lincoln Stein is the author of CGI.pm; his book is the standard reference work on the module.

DuBois, Paul. *MySQL and Perl for the Web*. Indianapolis: New Riders, 2001. 0-735-71054-6.

This book uses CGI.pm extensively in combination with the DBI module to show how to integrate MySQL into web-based applications.

Ruby Resources

The primary Ruby web site is *http://www.ruby-lang.org/*, where you can download Ruby distributions and find links to documentation.

Bibliography

Thomas, Dave, Chad Fowler, and Andy Hunt. *Programming Ruby: The Pragmatic Programmer's Guide*. Pragmatic Press, 2004. 0-974-51405-5.

Carlson, Lucas, and Leonard Richardson. *Ruby Cookbook*. Sebastopol, CA: O'Reilly Media, 2006. 0-596-52369-6.

PHP Resources

The primary PHP web site is *http://www.php.net/*, which provides access to PHP distributions and documentation. The site for PEAR, the PHP Extension and Add-on Repository, is *http://pear.php.net/*; PEAR includes the DB database abstraction module.

Bibliography

Sklar, David. *Learning PHP 5*. Sebastopol, CA: O'Reilly Media, 2004. 0-596-00560-1.

Sklar, David, and Adam Trachtenberg. *PHP Cookbook*. Sebastopol, CA: O'Reilly Media, 2002. 0-596-10101-5.

Python Resources

The primary Python web site is *http://www.python.org/*, which provides access to Python distributions and documentation.

General documentation for the DB-API database access interface is available at *http://www.python.org/topics/database/*. Documentation for MySQLdb, the MySQL-specific DB-API driver, is at *http://sourceforge.net/projects/mysql-python/*.

The Vaults of Parnassus serves as a general repository for Python source code: *http://www.vex.net/~x/parnassus/*.

Bibliography

Beazley, David M.. *Python Essential Reference*. Indianapolis: Sams, 2006. 0-672-32862-3.

Martelli, Alex, Anna Ravenscroft, and David Ascher. *Python Cookbook*. Sebastopol, CA: O'Reilly Media, 2005. 0-596-00797-3.

Java Resources

The primary Java web site is *http://java.sun.com/*. Sun's Java site provides access to documentation (including the specifications) for JDBC, servlets, JSP, and the JSP Standard Tag Library:

- JDBC general information: *http://java.sun.com/javase/technologies/database.jsp*
- JDBC documentation: *http://java.sun.com/j2se/1.5.0/docs/guide/jdbc/*
- Java servlets: *http://java.sun.com/products/servlet/*
- JavaServer Pages: *http://java.sun.com/products/jsp/*
- JSP Standard Tag Library: *http://java.sun.com/products/jsp/jstl/*

Bibliography

Reese, George. *Database Programming with JDBC and Java*. Sebastopol, CA: O'Reilly Media, 2000. 1-565-92616-1.

Bergsten, Hans. *JavaServer Pages*. Sebastopol, CA: O'Reilly Media, 2003. 0-596-00563-6.

Bayern, Shawn. *JSTL in Action*. Greenwich, CT: Manning Publications, 2002. 1-930-11052-9.

Other Resources

These resources provide information about other topics covered in this book.

Bibliography

Musciano, Chuck, and Bill Kennedy. *HTML & XHTML: The Definitive Guide*. Sebastopol, CA: O'Reilly Media, 2006. 0-596-52732-2.

Friedl, Jeffrey E. F.. *Mastering Regular Expressions*. Sebastopol, CA: O'Reilly Media, 2006. 0-596-52812-4.

Index

Symbols

!= (not equal to), identifying NULL values, 144

!~ operator (Perl), 436

" (quotes)
API quoting functions, 105
handling, 101
identifiers, inserting into statements, 112
LOAD DATA statement and, 405
string literals and, 180

(hash), writing to option files, 10

#!, writing shell scripts and, 39

$ (dollar sign), matching patterns, 194, 446
Perl, 436

$# shell variables, 41

$: ($LOAD_PATH) variable (Ruby), 78

$@ variable (Perl), 67
transactions and, 634

$HTTP_POST_FILES array (PHP), 813

$HTTP_SERVER_VARS PHP variable, 766

$HTTP_SESSION_VARS PHP variable, 854

$LOAD_PATH variable ($:) (Ruby), 78

$_GET PHP variable, 797

$_HTTP_GET_VARS PHP variable, 797

$_POST PHP variable, 797

$_SERVER PHP variable, 766

$_SESSION PHP variable, 854

${ ... } JSTL notation, 684

% (percent sign), as a format specifier, 110

%% format sequence, 219

& (ampersand), in HTML entities, 689

( ) (parentheses), matching patterns, 197, 438

* (asterisk)

COUNT( ) function, summarizing with, 315
FULLTEXT searches and, 211
pattern matching, 194
Perl pattern matches and, 437
SELECT statements, using in, 133

+ (plus sign), matching patterns, 194
Perl, 437

- (dash), matching dates and, 441

--fields-terminated-by option, 418

--no-create-db option, 420

--no-create-info option, 417

--pager option, 23

--tee option
creating scripts from previous statements, 33

-> prompt, 14

-B (batch) option, 26

-L (local) option, 402

-w (warnings) option
Perl, 439

. (dot), matching patterns, 194
Perl, 436

./ command, 39

.bat files, 42

/ (forward slash)
Java, connecting to databases, 62
writing pathname in option files, 10

/.../.../ substitution Perl pattern matches, 436

/./ (nonempty value) pattern match, 438

/^$/ (empty value) pattern match, 438

"0E0" value, 88

: (colon)
PERL5LIB library files, installing, 74

; (semicolon)

We'd like to hear your suggestions for improving our indexes. Send email to *index@oreilly.com*.

compound-statement objects and, 645
files, reading statements from, 18
PERL5LIB library files, installing, 74
terminating statements, 13, 21
    APIs and, 87
writing to option files, 10
< (less than)
    output, sending to files/programs, 25
    reading statements from other programs, 20
    redirecting input, 18
<% ... %> JSP scripting markers, 909
<%! ... %> JSP scripting markers, 909
<%-- ... --%> JSP scripting markers, 910
<%= ... %> JSP scripting markers, 909
<%@ ... %> JSP scripting markers, 910
<< (here document), 40
<=> comparison operator, 143
<? ... ?> (PHP tags), 57, 79, 676
<c:out> JSTL tag, 896
<c:when> JSTL tag, 684
<sql:query> JSTL database tag, 896
<taglib-location> element, 682
<ul> unordered list HTML tag, 706
= (equal sign)
    identifying NULL values, 144
=& operator (PHP), 58
== (equal to), 116
=== (triple equal operator), 116
=~ operator (Perl), 436
> (greater than)
    output, sending to files/programs, 25
    redirecting input, 18
? (question mark), as a placeholder, 103, 108
@ (at sign)
    matching email addresses, 445
    user-defined variables and, 34
@INC array (Perl), 77
[ ] (square brackets)
    pattern matching, 194
    Perl pattern elements, 436
    writing groupname values, 124
[% ... %] markup indicators (PageTemplate), 743
[^...] Perl pattern element, 436
\ (backslashes)
    handling for data-safe insertion, 101
    LOAD DATA, escape characters and, 400

SHOW COLUMNS statement, escaping
    SQL pattern characters, 379
string literals and, 181
writing pathnames in option files, 10
\. command, 19
\0 (ASCII NUL), 181
\c sequence, 14
\G command, 30
\n (newline)
    different operating systems, reading files
        from, 407
    LOAD DATA statement and, 403
\n statement, 23
\P (pager) statement, 23
\S (nonwhitespace) Perl pattern element, 436
\W (non-word) Perl pattern element, 436
^ (caret), matching patterns, 194, 446
    Perl, 436
` (backticks), quoting identifiers, 112
{ } (curly brackets)
    markup indicators in Smarty templates, 751
    matching patterns, 194
{m,n} Perl pattern element, 437
{n} Perl pattern element, 437
| (pipe)
    alternation, pattern matching, 194
    copying tables/databases to different
        servers, 420
    output, sending to files/programs, 24
    reading statements from other programs, 20

A

-A (skip-auto-rehash) option, 17
<a> HTML anchor tag, 717
a( ) function (Perl), 718
absolute values in rows, 559, 561
abstractions, 634
Access (Microsoft), 469
access counting, 827–831
access denied message, 6
access logging, 831
access privileges, setting library files, 75
accounts, 4
action elements (JSP), 912
--add-databases option, 421
--add-drop-table option, 420
affectedRows( ) method (PHP), 95, 356

AFTER INSERT trigger, 651
AGAINST( ) function, 205
aggregate functions, 314
    handling NULL values, 330
aliases (column), 138, 140
align attribute (<td> HTML tag), 712
ALTER TABLE statement, 136, 383, 489
    eliminating duplicates from tables, 618–
        622
    ENUM/SET columns definitions, adding
        elements, 384
    resequencing columns, 495
    reusing values at top of sequence, 497
    storage engines, checking or changing, 167
    transactional storage engines and, 629
ambiguous column names, 525
ambiguous table names, 576
ampersand (&), in HTML entities, 689
ANSI_QUOTES SQL mode, 112
    string literals and, 179
Apache web server, 662, 667–678
    logging, 833–840
Apache::Session module (Perl), 842, 845–850
API (application programming interface), 45,
        48–50
    library files, installing, 74
    result set metadata, obtaining, 358–367
    special characters and, 692
    special characters and NULL values, 101–
        111
    statements, sending, 87
    transactions and, 630
application object (JSP), 915
application programming interface (see API)
application scope (JSP), 915
arbitrary column delimiters in output, 26–27
@ARGV array, 120
ARGV array (Ruby), 122
arrays
    query( ) method and, 108
    rows, fetching, 89
ASCII NUL (\0), 181
assigning ranks, 602–605
asterisk (*)
    COUNT( ) function, summarizing with,
        315
    FULLTEXT searches and, 211
    pattern matching, 194
    Perl pattern matches and, 437

SELECT statements, using in, 133
at sign (@)
    matching email addresses, 445
    user-defined variables and, 34
attributes (HTML/XML/XHTML), 663
auto-commit mode, 631
    Perl DBI transaction, 634
auto-completion, 16
AutoCommit attribute (Perl), 53, 634
autoCommit( ) method (PHP), 637
AUTO_INCREMENT values, 481, 498
    creating multiple sequences, 502–507
    data types, choosing for, 486
    generating columns/values and, 483–485
    managing multiple simultaneous values,
        507
    relating tables with, 508–511
    resequencing columns, 494–496
    retrieving sequence values and, 490
    row deletions, effects of, 487–490
    sequence generators as counters, 511
    stating sequences at particular values, 499
    unsequenced tables, 501
AUTO__INCREMENT values
    extending ranges of sequence columns, 496
auxiliary tables, 565
average set of values, 319
AVG( ) function, 539, 563
    IFNULL( ) function and, 332
    subgroups, dividing into, 328
    summarizing with, 319
AxKit, 665

B

\b (backspace), 181
-B (batch) option
    shell scripts and, 39
%b format sequence, 218
backslashes (\)
    handling for data-safe insertion, 101
    LOAD DATA, escape characters and, 400
    SHOW COLUMNS statement, escaping
        SQL pattern characters, 379
    string literals and, 181
    writing pathnames in option files, 10
backspace (\b), 181
backspace key, editing statements, 16
backticks (`), quoting identifiers, 112
banner ads, 736–738

down arrow key, editing statements, 16
DriverManager.getConnection( ) method
    (Java), 62
driverName attribute (JDBL Store element),
    871
DROP DATABASE statement, 631
DROP TABLE statement, creating temporary
    tables and, 165
DSN (data source name), 52
<dt> definition term HTML tag, 707
dt( ) function (Perl), 709
duplicates, 607–624
    counting/identifying, 614–618
    self-join results and, 622–624
    tables, preventing, 608–610

E

-e (execute) option, 21
    shell scripts and, 39
-E (vertical) option, 31
%e format sequence, 218
email addresses, using patterns to match, 445
embPerl, 665
encapsulation, 72
ENCLOSED BY subclauses, 406
end_form( ) method (Perl), 765
end_html( ) CCI.pm module (Perl), 672
ENGINE clause, 167
entities (HTML), 689
ENUM values, 86, 178, 449
    column information, getting, 381–382
    sorting, 309–312
    table metadata, using to validate data, 446
environment variables, 72
    Apache, 669
    CATALINA_HOME, 899
    CLASSPATH, 63, 74, 886
    JAVA_HOME, 885, 899
    PAGER, 23
    PATH, 881, 901
    PERL5LIB, 74, 669
    PYTHONPATH, 74, 669
    RUBYLIB, 74, 669
    setting, 881
    Tomcat, 899
ePerl, 665
equal sign (=)
    identifying NULL values, 144
equal to (==), 116

equality, comparing stings for, 188
err DBI::DatabaseError method (Ruby), 68
error log (Apache), 669
errors, checking for, 45, 64–70, 87
Esc, canceling statements (Windows), 15
escape sequences, 181
escape( ) method (Perl), 692
ESCAPED BY subclauses, 406
escapeHTML method (Ruby), 699
escapeHTML( ) method (Perl), 692, 699
eval blocks (Perl), 67
    transactions and, 634
EVENT privilege, 645
events, 643
Excel (Microsoft), exchanging data with, 470
execute method (Ruby), 94
--execute option, 21
execute( ) method
    Java, 100, 111
        determining whether a statement
            produced a result set, 368
    Perl
        obtaining the number of rows affected by
            statements, 355
        result set metadata, obtaining, 358
        retrieving sequence values, 492
        sending statements, 89
    PHP, 108
    Python, 96, 109
execute( ) method (Perl)
    placeholders and, 105
executeQuery( ) method (Java), 98, 111
executeUpdate( ) method (Java), 98, 111, 357
executing programs, 881
EXIT statement
    starting and stopping mysql, 8
EXPLAIN statement, 87
export issues, 396
export programs, writing, 422–426
expression results, grouping by, 335
extension-hiding, disabling, 8
extensions (modules), 666

F

%f (floating-point) format specifier, 110
failures (statement), 627
FEDERATED tables, 576
fetch method (Ruby), 93
fetchall method (Python), 364

getSQLState( ) method (Java), 70
getString( ) method (Java), 99, 139
getUpdateCount( ) method (Java), 357
getUserInfo( ) method (PHP), 68
get_column_info( ) method (Perl), 378
get_column_names( ) function (PHP), 387
GLOBAL modifiers, 392
GNU Readline library, 16
gnutar files, 898
go statement (see \g)
GRANT statement
    CREATE DATABASE statement and, 4
    setting up user accounts, 3
graphical user interface (GUI), 22
    table information and, 383
greater than (see >)
grep program, 40, 195
GROUP BY clause, 273, 335, 348
    date-based summaries and, 344
    descriptive statistics and, 587
    duplicates, counting and identifying, 614
    summaries and NULL values, 331
groupname values, 124
GUI (graphical user interface), 22
    table information and, 383

H

-h (hostname) option, 3, 7
    option files and, 9
-H (HTML) option, 27
%H format sequence, 219
handle methods, 358
handles (Perl), 53
hash (#)
    writing to option files, 10
hashes (Perl), using connect( ) method, 53
HAVING clause, 333, 347, 616
    unique values, determining with, 334
header( ) CGI.pm module (Perl), 672
    downloads, handling, 739
here document (<<), 40
hex notation, 180
    mysqlimport and, 404
hexdump program, 405
hh:mm:ss time format, 215
hidden values, sorting, 280
history files, 33
hit counters, 827
holes in lists, filling, 554–558

--host option, 7, 400
    option files and, 9
hostname (-h) (see -h (hostname))
hostnames, 3
    parameters from the command line, getting, 119
    sorting in domain order, 300–302
hosts
    user accounts, setting up, 3
HOUR( ) function, 227, 239
htdocs directory, 668
HTML, 662, 663–667
    definition lists, 707–709
    encoding, 782
    JSP markup and, 894
    nested lists, 710–712
    ordered lists, 701–705
    PHP code and, 56
    placeholders and, 103
    producing with output, 27
    query results, displaying
        lists, 700–712
        paragraph text, 698–700
    special characters, encoding for, 688–695
    tables, displaying query results, 712–716
    unmarked lists, 709
    unordered lists, 706
--html option, 28
htmlspecialchars( ) method (PHP), 694
HTTP, 841
httpd, 667
httpd.conf file, 667
$HTTP_SESSION_VARS array, 855
hyperlinks
    encoding characters for, 690
    query results, displaying, 717–719

I

i (case-insensitive) flag for Perl pattern
        constructors, 436
%i format sequence, 219
IDENTIFIED BY statement, 3
identifiers, 112–113
IDs (sessions), 842
IF( ) function, 144, 307, 317, 550
IFNULL( ) function, 145, 332, 539
IGNORE keyword, 408
--ignore option, 408
IGNORE statement, 608

obtaining the number of rows affected by statements, 355–357

query output and, 368–372

result set, obtaining, 357–367

server, getting, 388

storage engines, determining, 393

table column definition, accessing, 374–381

table structure information, using in applications, 383–388

table, using to validate data, 446–449

writing applications that adapt to MySQL server versions, 389–390

Microsoft Access, 469

Microsoft Excel, 470

Microsoft Windows (see Windows)

MID( ) function, 200, 227

  fixed-length substrings, sorting by, 293

  variable-length substrings, sorting by, 296

MIN( ) function, 153, 314

  case-sensitivity for, 325

  finding smallest/largest values, 342

  finding values associated with, 323–325

  IFNULL( ) function and, 332

  subgroups, dividing into, 328

  summarizing with, 318

minIdleSwap attribute (JDBC Manager element), 870

minor version numbers, 389

MINUTE( ) function, 226, 227, 239

mixed-order sorting, 277

MM-DD-YY format, 442

MM/DD/YY format, 395

MOD( ) function, 290

Model-View-Controller (MVC), 741

modularization, 72

modules (see library files)

modules (Perl), 76

mod_snake Apache module (Python), 665

MONTH( ) function, 226, 227

MONTHNAME( ) function, 227

multibyte characters, 172

multiple table, 517–581

multiple-column sorts, 277

multiple-page navigation indexes, 723

multiple-pick forms, 783–788

multiple-request sessions, 842

multiple-statement transactions, 630

MVC (Mode-View-Controller), 741

.my.cnf file, 8

my.ini file, 8

my.ini, my.cnf files, 124

MyISAM tables, 315, 489

MySQL C client library, 876

mysql program, 1

  copying tables/databases to different servers, 420

  duplicates, removing, 611

  getting parameters from command line, 119

  stopping and starting, 6–8

  transactions and, 632

  user accounts, setting up, 3

  when not found by command interpreter, 12

mysql prompt

  issuing statements, 13

MySQL Query Browser, 2

MySQL Reference Manual, 876

MySQL Uncertainty Principle, 393

mysql-session package (Ruby), 842

mysql.default_host configuration variables, 59

mysql.default_password configuration variable, 59

mysql.default_port configuration variable, 59

mysql.default_socket configuration variable, 59

mysql.default_user configuration variable, 59

mysql> prompt (see mysql program)

mysqladmin, 7

  getting parameters from command line, 119

  option files and, 9

mysqld server, 1

MySQLdb database driver module, 59, 82, 97

  retrieving sequence values, 492

  special characters and, 109

mysqldump, 7, 395

  adding elements to ENUM/SET column definitions, 384

  copying tables/databases to different servers, 420

  exporting tables as SQL formatted text, 418

  exporting tables as text files, 417

  option files and, 9

  reading statements from other programs, 21

pipe (|)
  alternation, pattern matching, 194
  copying tables/databases to different
      servers, 420
  output, sending to files/programs, 24
  reading statements from other programs,
      20
placeholders, 102–105, 806
  Perl DBI scripts and, 105
  Ruby DBI and, 108
plus sign (+), matching patterns, 194
  Perl, 437
.pm extension (Perl modules), 76
point-and-click interface, 2
pop-up menus (HTML), 769
popup_menu( ) function (JSP), 772
POSIX character classes, 196
POST requests, 796, 890
PostgreSQL, 49
ppm utility, 877
PRECISION attribute, 359
precision Ruby member name, 361
prefix values (Tomcat), 683
prepare( ) method
    Perl, 89, 105
        result set metadata, obtaining, 358
    PHP, 108
prepare( ) method (Perl), 492
prepareStatement( ) method (Java), 111
previous-page links, generating, 818–822
PRIMARY KEY index, 408, 502
    preventing duplicates in tables, 608–610
primary Ruby member name, 361
PrintError attribute (Perl), 65, 634
printErrorMessage( ) method (Java), 82
privileges for stored routines, 645
Process ID (PID) values, 169
protocol designator, 62
--protocol=tcp option, 8
Python, 45
    command-line arguments, 122
    connecting, selecting and disconnecting to
        database, 59
    error checking, 69
    executing scripts, 884
    forms, generating, 767, 774
    generating unique table names, 169
    hyperlinks, displaying from query results,
        718

library files, 80–82
NULL values and, 116
obtaining the number of rows affected by
    statements, 356
option files and, 127
paragraphs, encoding query results with,
    700
result set metadata, obtaining, 364
retrieving sequence values, 492
special characters and NULL values,
    handling, 109
SQL pattern characters, escaping, 379
statements, sending and retrieving, 96
transactions, 638
uploads, 814
web scripts, 665
PYTHONPATH environment variable, 74, 81,
    669

Q

qualifier
    column name, 525
    table name, 576
Query Browser, 2
query logs, debugging, 64
query results
    downloads, serving for, 738–741
    exporting, 415–417
    hyperlinks, displaying, 717–720
    lists (HTML), displaying, 700–712
    metadata, using to format, 368–372
    paragraph text, displaying, 698–700
    saving in tables, 162–165
    tables (HTML), displaying, 712–716
    web pages, incorporating, 697–758
query results, sorting, 273–312
query( ) method (PHP), 68, 95, 108
question mark (?), as a placeholder, 103, 108
QUIT statement, starting and stopping mysql,
    6, 7
quote( ) method
    Perl, 107
    Ruby, 108
quotes (")
    API quoting functions, 105
    handling, 101
    identifiers, inserting into statements, 112
    LOAD DATA statement and, 405
    string literals and, 180

quoteSmart( ) method (PEAR DB), 109
quote_identifier( ) method (Perl), 112

R

\r (carriage return), 181
%r format sequence, 218
radio buttons (HTML), 769
radio_group( ) function (JSP), 772
RaiseError attribute (Perl), 65, 88
    transactions, using, 634
RAND( ) function, 596, 602
    rows, randomizing sets, 598
random numbers, 596–597
raw protocol, 48
re module (Python), 379
READS SQL DATA characteristic, 645
read_mysql_option_file( ) function (PHP),
    126
recipes distribution, xxii
record separators, 396
record-editing applications, 383
reference tables, 554
references (Perl), 53
REGEXP operator, 194, 199, 437
register_globals PHP variable, 798, 854
regular expressions, 26, 191, 194–198
Reiser filesystem, 727
relative ordering, comparing strings for, 188
relative pathnames, 402
reloadable <Context> attribute, 904
--replace option, 408
REPLACE statement, 408, 608, 610
request object (JSP), 914
request parameters, 803
request scope (JSP), 915
require keyword (PHP), 57
response object (JSP), 915
result set metadata, 357–367
    determining whether a statement produces,
        367
result sets
    combining in single queries, 567–571
    identifying NULL values in, 113
    sorting, 146
ResultSet object (Java), 366
RETURN statement, 646
RETURNS FLOAT clause, 646
right arrow key, editing statements, 16
RIGHT( ) function, 193, 198, 200

fixed-length substrings, sorting by, 293
    variable-length substrings, sorting by, 296
rollback method (Ruby), 636
ROLLBACK statement, 631
rollback( ) method
    Java, 639
    Perl, 634
    PHP, 637
    Python, 638
root password, 3
rowcount method (Python), 97
rows
    deletions of sequence generation, 487–490
    duplicates, 142, 408, 607–624
        loading in tables, dealing with, 610–614
    fetch method (Ruby), 93
    fetching with Perl, 89
    finding in one table, matching another,
        518–526
    many-to-many relationships, 541
    middle of result set, selecting, 153
    mismatched or unattached, identifying,
        572–575
    obtaining the number of affected by
        statements, 355
    per-group minimum/maximum, finding,
        544–548
    random items, selecting, 601
    randomizing sets of, 598–600
    renumbering in a particular order, 498
    selecting from beginning or end of result set,
        151–153
    specifying which to select, 134
    successive differences, calculation, 559–
        561
    tracking modification times with
        TIMESTAMP, 223–226
Ruby, 45
    cgi module and, 674
    CGI.escapeHTML( ) method, 693
    CGI.escape( ) method, 693
    command-line arguments and, 121
    connecting, selecting and disconnecting to
        databases, 54–56
    definition list, generating, 709
    ENUM and SET column information,
        getting, 381
    error checking, 68
    executing scripts, 884

About the Author

Paul DuBois was one of the first contributors to the online *MySQL Reference Manual*, a renowned documentation project that supported MySQL administrators and database developers in the first few years of MySQL's existence in the late 1990s. Paul went on to write several books on MySQL, including the first edition of *MySQL Cookbook*.

Colophon

Our look is the result of reader comments, our own experimentation, and feedback from distribution channels. Distinctive covers complement our distinctive approach to technical topics, breathing personality and life into potentially dry subjects.

The animal on the cover of *MySQL Cookbook*, Second Edition, is a green anole. These common lizards can be found in the southeastern United States, the Caribbean, and South America. Green anoles dwell in moist, shady environments, such as trees and shrubs. They subsist on small insects such as crickets, roaches, moths, grubs, and spiders.

Green anoles are slight in build, with narrow heads and long, slender tails that can be twice as long as their bodies. The special padding on their feet enables them to climb, cling, and run on any surface. They range from six to eight inches long. Though, as their name implies, green anoles are usually bright green, their color can change to match their surroundings, varying among gray-brown, brown, and green. Male anoles have pink dewlaps that they extend when courting or protecting their territory.

The cover image is a 19th-century engraving from the Dover Pictorial Archive. The cover font is Adobe ITC Garamond. The text font is Linotype Birka; the heading font is Adobe Myriad Condensed; and the code font is LucasFont's TheSans Mono Condensed.

Better than e-books

Buy *MySQL Cookbook*, 2n Edition, and access
the digital edition FREE on Safari for 45 days.

Go to www.oreilly.com/go/safarienabled
and type in coupon code QOTVHXA

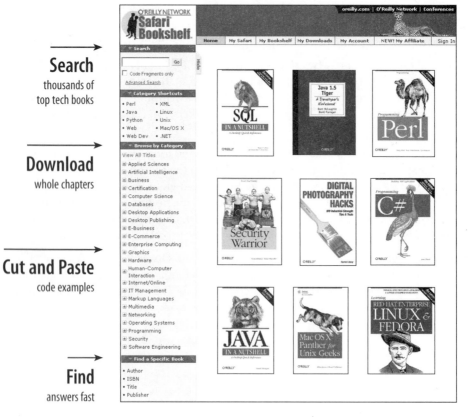

Search
thousands of
top tech books

Download
whole chapters

Cut and Paste
code examples

Find
answers fast

Search Safari! The premier electronic reference
library for programmers and IT professionals.

 Addison Wesley

 Sun microsystems

 ALPHA

 Java

 Microsoft Press

 Peachpit Press

Adobe Press

O'REILLY

SAMS

 New Riders

que

Cisco Press

 macromedia PRESS

 PRENTICE HALL PTR